NATIVE AMERICAN ALMANAC

MORE THAN 50,000 YEARS OF THE CULTURES AND HISTORIES OF INDIGENOUS PEOPLES

YVONNE WAKIM DENNIS, ARLENE HIRSCHFELDER AND
SHANNON ROTHENBERGER FLYNN

VISIBLE
INK
PRESS

Visible Ink Press®
43311 Joy Rd., #414
Canton, MI 48187-2075

Visible Ink Press is a registered trademark of Visible Ink Press LLC.

Most Visible Ink Press books are available at special quantity discounts when purchased in bulk by corporations, organizations, or groups. Customized printings, special imprints, messages, and excerpts can be produced to meet your needs. For more information, contact Special Markets Director, Visible Ink Press, www.visibleinkpress.com, or 734-667-3211.

Managing Editor: Kevin S. Hile
Art Director: Mary Claire Krzewinski
Typesetting: Marco DiVita
Proofreaders: Shoshana Hurwitz and Aarti Stephens
Indexer: Larry Baker

Cover images: Sitting Bull (Library of Congress), Petroglyphs (Shutterstock), background image (Shutterstock), all others are public domain.

10 9 8 7 6 5 4 3 2 1

Library of Congress Cataloguing-in-Publication Data

Names: Dennis, Yvonne Wakim, author. | Hirschfelder, Arlene B., author. | Flynn, Shannon Rothenberger, author.
Title: Native American almanac : more than 50,000 years of the cultures and histories of indigenous peoples / by Yvonne Wakim Dennis, Arlene Hirschfelder, and Shannon Rothenberger Flynn.
Description: Canton, MI : Visible Ink Press, 2016. | Includes index.
Identifiers: LCCN 2015050881| ISBN 9781578595075 (pbk. : alk. paper) | ISBN 9781578596089 (epub) | ISBN 9781578596096 (kindle)
Subjects: LCSH: Indians of North America—History. | Indians of North America—Social life and customs.
Classification: LCC E77 .D394 2016 | DDC 970.004/97—dc23
LC record available at http://lccn.loc.gov/2015050881

ABOUT THE AUTHORS

Yvonne Wakim Dennis (Cherokee/Sand Hill/ Syrian) is an award-winning author of nonfiction books for children and adults, many coauthored with Arlene Hirschfelder. An avid multiculturalist, Dennis interweaves environmental justice into all she writes. Although most of her publications have been about Indigenous peoples of the United States, she has also penned books about the diverse cultures of America. She serves as the Education Director for the Children's Cultural Center of Native America and is a board director of Nitchen, Inc., an advocacy organization for Indigenous families in the New York City metropolitan area. She is a multicultural consultant for businesses, schools, and publishers and is a columnist for *Native Hoop Magazine*. In 2014, Dennis received the National Arab American Museum's Best Children's Book of the Year Honor (for *A Kid's Guide to Arab American History*), a Sanaka Award, and the David Chow Humanitarian Award.

Photo: Marsha Michel

Arlene Hirschfelder is the author or editor of over twenty-five books about Native peoples, including *Native Americans: A History in Pictures* and *The Extraordinary Book of Native American Lists*. She

and Yvonne Dennis have authored five books together, including the award-winning *Children of Native America Today* and *A Kid's Guide to Native American History*. She worked at the Association on American Indian Affairs (a civil rights organization), for over twenty years and has years of experience consulting with publishers, museums, schools, and universities. In addition to being an author, Hirschfelder is series editor of "It Happened to Me," which includes forty-seven nonfiction books (and still counting) for teen readers and is published by Rowman & Littlefield.

Photo by Karl Rabe

Shannon Rothenberger Flynn is a writer of Michif (Chippewa-German) and Norwegian-American descent. She has authored lifestyle and design books for Hearst and contributed writing and editorial services to *The Native Americans—an Illustrated History*, which became a cable network series. She was project editor for the *Scholastic Encyclopedia of the North American Indian* and served as Native American consultant on books for young readers. Flynn teaches writing at Dutchess Community College and English at Westchester Community College in New York. She also writes and performs stories with the TMI Project in Ulster County, New York, where she lives.

Also from Visible Ink Press

CONTENTS

ACKNOWLEDGMENTS

Yvonne gives a big wado, wanishi to: Beverly Singer; Nadema Agard; Dwayne Wilcox; Juan Carlos Aguirre; Karen Taylor; Roberto Mukaro Borrero; Eric W. Sanderson; Jennifer Billie; Lita Pepion; James Morales; Audrey Cooper; Tlisza Jaurique; April Estrellon; Joseph Kabance; Marc Yaffee; Debbie Reese; Eileen Soler; Mariana Vergara; Todd Labrador; Tanis Parenteau; Gabrielle Tayac; Jim and Smoki Fraser; Mary Kathryn Nagle; Misty Brescia Dreifuss; Dawi Winston; Haunani-Kay Trask; Noenoe K. Silva; Kevin Brown; Patrice M. Le Melle; Kay WalkingStick; Virgil Ortiz; Ryan Pierce; Cynthia Leitich Smith; Philadelphia Phillies; Steven Newcomb; Carol Kalafatic; Tish Agoyo; Gelvin Stevenson; Susan Guice; Joseph Gone; my beloved co-writers Arlene and Shannon; publisher Roger Jänecke; managing editor Kevin Hile; my supportive, patient, helpful hubby, Roger; and all my family and friends whom I have ignored during these past two years. Now we can go out and play! I ask forgiveness for any mistakes I may have made.

Shannon gives major thanks to Beverly Singer, Jonathan Flynn, Catherine Revland, Tim Trewhella, Prairie Rose Seminole, Robert Desjarlait, Clark Vincent Fox, Charles Pierce, Ivy Vainio, Michael Meuers, The Bemidji Language Project, Julie Carrow, Michael Horse, Francisco Vasquez, David Lopez, Nike N7 Fund, Resa Sunshine, and my esteemed co-authors. Thank you always to my father, Phil, who blesses my every day.

Arlene is thankful to all who helped with this book and to those who have shared cultural knowledge: Susan Buchel, Linda Coombs, Carla Cuch, Jaye M. Falon, Jeremy Five Crows, Adriana Ignacio, Beverly Singer, Marguerite A. Smith, Jack F. Trope, and Berta Welch; thanks to our publisher, Roger Jänecke and editor, Kevin Hile; and special thanks to my co-authors and researcher Dennis Hirschfelder.

PHOTO CREDITS

Nadema Agard: p. 477 (right column, top).
Agua Caliente Band of Cahuilla Indians: p. 460.
Keith Allison: p. 449 (top).
Areyouontheball (Wikicommons): p. 449 (bottom).
Larry Beck (Ooger Uk Inua [Walrus Spirit]): p. 477 (bottom).
Christopher P. Becker: p. 441.
Sam Beebe: p. 407 (right column).
Walter BigBee: p. 478 (left column, top).
Braden208 (Wikicommons): p. 28.
Matthew Brady: p. 268.
Bureau of Indian Affairs: p. 256 (right column).
BZillaGorilla (Wikicommons): p. 41.
Carl Van Vechten Photographs (Library of Congress): p. 116.
Julie Carrow: p. 150.
Cesar Chavez Student Center Building: p. 369.
Clark Art Institute: p. 13.
Hortensia and Elvira Colorado: p. 473 (left column, top).
Audrey Cooper: p. 479 (left column).
Courtesy A. Yvonne Wakim Davis: p. 466.
Robert Desjarlait: p. 141.
DragonflyDC (Wikicommons): p. 254 (right column).
Eclectek (Wikicommons): p. 171.
Robert A. Estremo: p. 361.
Executive Office of the President of the United States: p. 36.
Adam Fagen: p. 236.
Jim Fraser: p. 479 (right column, top).
Mary "Smoki" Fraser: p. 480 (right column).
Freshwater and Marine Image Bank, University of Washington: p. 392.
GabboT (Wikicommons): p. 485.
Benjamin A. Gifford: p. 331.
Jeanie Greene: p. 414 (right column).
Victor Grigas: p. 160.
Bobak Ha'Eri: p. 277.
Gary Halvorson, Oregon State Archives: p. 341.
Joy Harjo: p. 473 (right column).
Suzan Shown Harjo: p. 479 (right column, bottom).
Harper's New Monthly Magazine: p. 21.
LaDonna Vita Tabbytite Harris: p. 480 (left column, top).

David Hatcher: p. 306.
Jim Henderson: p. 138.
Paul Hermans: p. 182.
R. M. Hermen: p. 197.
Hiart (Wikicommons): pp. 301, 444.
HongKongHuey (Wikicommons): p. 442.
Michael Horse: p. 194.
Internet Archive Book Images: p. 332.
Ish Ishwar: p. 57.
Tlisza Jaurique: p. 478 (right column, bottom).
John D. and Catherine T. MacArthur Foundation: pp. 87, 414 (left column).
Carol Kalafatic: p. 482.
Dieter Kaupp: p. 76.
Kennethaw88 (Wikicommons): p. 118.
Kniemla (Wikicommons): p. 91.
Philkon Phil Konstantin: p. 253.
Einar Einarsson Kvaran: p. 312.
Larry Lamsa: p. 323 (right column).
Thomas Leih: p. 410.
Library and Archives Canada: p. 7.
Library of Congress: pp. 11, 71, 184, 212 (right column), 280 (right column), 282 (right column), 284, 372, 475 (left column).
Tom Logan: p. 448 (Logan Maile Lei Tom).
Donna M. Loring/Jane Peasley: p. 86.
Lumbee Chief: p. 114.
Layne Luna: p. 448 (Charles Nainoa Thompson)
Joe Mabel: p. 458.
Thomas R Machnitzki: p. 227.
Ted Mala: p. 404.
The Mannahatta Project, Wildlife Conservation Society: p. 462.
Irka Mateo: p. 474 (left column).
Minneapolis American Indian Center: p. 453.
Ray Montgomery: p. 448 (Kevin James Mawae).
Carol Moore: p. 215 (right column).
Morris K. Udall Foundation: p. 168.
Muscogee Red: p. 105.
Myrabella (Wikicommons): p. 402.

Mary Kathryn Nagle: p. 474 (right column, middle).
NASA: pp. 127 (bottom), 255.
National Archives and Records Administration: p. 19.
National Gallery of Art: p. 69.
National Park Service: pp. 134, 399.
Native Truth: p. 321.
Kim Navarre: p. 101.
Nikater (Wikicommons): p. 55.
Nike, Inc.: p. 304.
NOAA Photo Library: p. 373.
R. A. Nonenmacher: p. 61.
Virgil Ortiz: p. 478 (right column).
OurDocuments.gov: p. 9.
Tanis Parenteau: p. 474 (right column, bottom).
Andrew Parodi: p. 411.
Patti (Wikicommons): p. 302.
Peace Corps: p. 468.
Dane A. Penland/Smithsonian Institution Archives: p. 217.
Phoebe (Wikicommons): p. 107.
Charles Pierce: p. 237.
Prairie Rose Seminole: pp. 180, 202.
Jared Purdy: p. 473 (left column, bottom).
D. Gordon E. Robertson: p. 146.
Elisa Rolle: p. 38.
Fernando Rosales: p. 246.
Hieronymous Rowe: p. 93.
Wolfgang Sauber: p. 295.
Shoni Schimmel: p. 486.
Seattle Municipal Archives: p. 286.
Shutterstock: pp. 26, 31, 35, 132, 155, 170, 175, 225, 235, 241, 298, 324 (left column), 334, 354, 358, 360, 383 (both photos), 386, 390, 398, 417, 420, 423, 438.
Walter Siegmund: p. 327.
Noenoe K. Silva: p. 448 (left column, bottom).
Cynthia Leitich Smith: p. 476.
Smithsonian Institution: p. 120.
State of Alaska: p. 412.
Phil Stein: p. 474 (right column, top).

Gelvin Stevenson: p. 481.
Resa Sunshine: p. 311.
Gabrielle Tayac: p. 484 (left column, top).
Twice as Good: p. 475 (right column).
United Nations: p. 470.
University of Oklahoma: p. 472.
U.S. Air Force: p. 152.
U.S. Department of Agriculture: pp. 67, 294.
U.S. Department of Defense: p. 46.
U.S. Department of the Interior: pp. 33, 189.
U.S. Department of Veterans Affairs: p. 206.
U.S. Forest Service: p. 176.
U.S Forest Service, Southwestern region, Kaibab National Forest: pp. 271, 275.
U.S. Mint Historical Image Library: p. 60.
U.S. National Library of Medicine: p. 44.
U.S. Navy: pp. 215 (left column), 396.
Uyvsdi (Wikicommons): pp. 50, 382 (both photos).
Ivy Vainio: p. 136.
Hans van der Maarel: p. 363.
Francisco Vasquez: p. 290.
Mariana Vergara: p. 484 (left column, bottom).
Crystal Wahpepah: p. 471.
Erin Whitaker: p. 288.
The White House: p. 48.
White House Historical Association: p. 15.
Doug Zimmer, U.S. Fish and Wildlife Service, Pacific: p. 346.
Public domain: pp. 3, 4, 17, 24, 26, 29, 43, 59, 64, 65, 74, 75, 77, 78, 79, 80, 81, 94, 96, 97, 99, 103, 109, 111, 115, 123, 124, 125, 126, 127 (top), 139, 143, 148, 154, 157, 161, 162, 163, 164, 178, 187, 191, 193, 199, 201, 204, 207, 208, 209, 210, 211, 212 (left column), 213, 216, 223, 228, 231, 233, 239, 243, 247, 248, 249, 251, 252, 254 (left column), 256 (left column), 257, 261, 263, 264, 266, 271, 280 (left column), 281, 282 (left column), 291, 300, 308, 313, 314, 315, 316, 317, 318, 320, 323 (left column), 324 (right column), 329, 336, 339, 342, 343, 356, 365, 375, 376, 377, 381, 388, 393, 394, 407 (left column), 425, 426, 427, 428, 430, 431, 432, 434, 435, 436, 445, 446, 447, 455, 464.

INTRODUCTION

Why a *Native American Almanac*? "Almanac" itself is a mysterious word with no agreement on its etymology. One of its early meanings is an Arabic word for "settlement." Today, "almanac" refers to "a publication containing astronomical and meteorological data for a given year and often including a miscellany of other information and published annually." *The Native American Almanac* does include miscellany and some astronomical information, but will not be written every year—at least, not by us! We are probably more in tune with the word origin, "settlement," as we have tried to present a historical overview of Native communities in what is now the United States. At the last minute, our publisher requested that we include the rest of Indigenous North America in an appendix. We somehow squeezed it in—it is an appendix only and is not meant to be a complete guide to our northern and southern neighbors.

The terms indigenous and First Nations Peoples still generalize the identity of the more than 550 indigenous groups in the lower 48 states and Alaska. However, I believe they are empowering "generalized" descriptors because they accurately describe the political, cultural, and geographical identities, and struggles of all aboriginal peoples in the United States. I no longer use Indian, American Indian, or Native American because I consider them to be oppressive, counterfeit identities. A counterfeit identity is not only bogus and misleading, it subjugates and controls the identity of indigenous peoples.

—Michael Yellow Bird, 1999

Many Native societies named themselves in their own languages—names that translate to "the people," "real people," or "our people," for instance. Many nations' names (like the Delaware, Navajo, or Sioux) were given by outsiders, other First Peoples or, later, Europeans. Europeans often named a group after a leader (Powhatan for example). We have used the original name (i.e., Anishinabe), as well as the more familiar, but alien name (i.e., Chippewa or Ojibwe). In several cases, the nations legally changed their name back to the original. The restored name Meskwaki, for example, means "the Red-Earths," but the French named them for one particular clan "les Renards," later translated to "Fox" in English. The Tohono O'odham ("Desert People") were named "Papago," a Spanish mispronunciation of the Pima word for them (fat bean eaters). The Wisconsin Ho-Chunk ("People of the Sacred Language" or "People of the Big Voice") reinstated their traditional name and removed Winnebago (People of the smelly waters), which again is a French and English mistranslation of what other nations called them. As for terms, both Native American and American Indian are incorrect as the people were here before there was a place called America and before Columbus named them Indians. We prefer Indigenous and First Peoples, but still use the familiar labels above. It is most correct and polite when referring to First Peoples to call them by their original names.

This book is not a treatise on how valuable Native peoples were/are to "immigrant" settlements or all of the contributions to American life that First Peoples made (and make). We are not out to prove the worth of Native customs/inventions/values as a plea to preserve Indigenous cultures or to push back against racism. Rather, we maintain that no matter who writes the history, the nitty-gritty is that this place is the homeland of Indigenous peoples, whether they have been here since the beginning of the human species or just 50,000 years and have a right to just "be" without any rationalization for their continued existence.

When Europeans first arrived in the western hemisphere there were millions of people and thousands of cultures, nations, and languages. We have attempted to include as many of them as possible and you will see just how much those fateful contacts had and still have on Indigenous peoples. You will find biographies of famous people, as well as home-town heroes. Some may be important to their communities, but unknown to the entire country. Sadly, because of the long-lasting effects of "successful colonialism," most Americans know very little about any Native peoples, even the famous ones. And what they do know is often incorrect.

Native people are not just another minority, although often classified as such. Many are members of a particular Native governmental entity often referred to as a "domestic, dependent sovereign nation." Unlike Asian, African, or Latino Americans, most Native nations have a direct relationship with the U.S. government—they have entered into treaties (although the U.S. has never fully honored any treaty, but forces Indigenous nations to uphold them), yet do not get afforded the same rights as other nations with which the U.S. has treaties. Hundreds of Native governments are recognized by the federal government; others by state governments. Some governments, which were "terminated," struggle to reclaim their rightful status. Some communities are remnant groups comprised of survivors of different nations decimated by wars and colonialism yet banded together and continue to exist. Since there is a chapter on Urban Peoples, we address cultures that are from other parts of the hemisphere (Garifuna, Maya, Taino, Mixteca), but are Americans, too. Hawaii is part of the book as Native Hawaiians are classified as Native peoples in the United States. Many Native Hawaiians do not like that classification as they feel it diminishes their status as subjects of the Kingdom of Hawaii or the Republic of Hawaii.

Today, many Native people belong to one nation without any other ancestry. Others may be "multinational," belonging to more than one Native nation. Other people may be bicultural or multicultural. Some people who are culturally Native may have ancestors from every continent, but they embrace their Native traditions. Others have been fortunate enough to have maintained their traditional religions (in spite of every attempt by the dominant culture to eradicate these ancient faiths) and many are Christian. Some may observe their traditional spirituality as well as Christianity. Native people have also intermarried with members of the Jewish, Muslim, Hindu, or Buddhist faiths and their children may honor all sides of their families. In traditional times, being from one particular group defined one's culture, language, government, and religion—it was all one. For some peoples, that is still true today, but for many it is not. Native peoples most often navigate two or three worlds at the same time.

We as writers are not qualified or interested in speaking about the degree of "Nativeness" as it just perpetuates stereotypes and is a private matter anyway. The "pedigree" of Native peoples has been used by the settler colonial culture as a means to divide, conquer, and even as an effective tool of genocide. In this book, we have not used terms to describe one's mixture (if he/she is even mixed) unless it is germane to the story or a person describes him/herself in a particular way. Native peoples did not carry the racial hang-ups of white society (that's not to say that there were not conflicts among different nations), but early European colonists and, later, U.S. government officials were not exactly multiculturalists and were determined that people should pick one ethnicity. To perpetuate genocidal tactics, having an ounce of other ancestry diminished one's "Indianess" in a way similar to having one drop of African blood made one black. Except for African Americans, no other group has such a lexicon to describe its DNA make up, some of them pejorative terms: full blood, half breed, Black Indian, Wanna-be, part Indian, Aboriginal/aborigine, Amerindian, barbaros (Spanish for "barbarous"), First American, First Nation, Indian, indigenous, indios (Spanish for "in or with God"), Native American, Original, redskin, savage/sauvage, etc. Some have likened the preoccupation with Native purity as being similar to horse and dog breeding. Whatever a Native person's appearance, mixture, or absence of mixture, it is still rude to ask, "What part Native American are you?" And, of course, "war whooping," "rain dancing," and expressing other stereotypes or anachronisms do not create pleasant encounters.

We are not presenting "A" Native Voice as there is not, nor has there ever been, just one Voice, and none of us or the staff at Visible Ink Press purports to be a spokesperson for Native America. Through quotations, firsthand accounts, and reporting current issues, we strive to transmit "SCORES" of Indigenous voices that reflect and celebrate the great diversity of "Turtle Island." Of course, this is not an unbiased book as we are on the side of freedom, justice for Indigenous peoples, and peoples' rights to INDIGENIZE!

This book started out to be an update of *Portrait of a People*, edited by Duane Champagne. As it turned out, most of the material is new. We organized this immense topic into geographical regions, but these regions have different climates,

topography, and, of course, different cultures. Some communities in a region are so diverse from each other that they could be on opposite sides of the country instead of a couple of hundred miles away. Each of us felt her way by telling the story as we followed it. This book is not meant to be an encyclopedia of Native America—there is far too much material for such an undertaking. We were as inclusive as we could possibly be, while staying within the restrictions of our word count. It is also not meant to be scholarly work, although it is well researched.

Our belief is that the health of the country is determined by the health of First Peoples—the wellbeing of Indigenous folks can be compared to the "canary in the mine," a warning for all to, as the Cherokee say, "Live the Great Life." Even scientists, who are often strapped to their theories instead of "being scientific," are beginning to see that Indigenous knowledge can resolve contemporary problems such as justice systems, ecology, nutrition, and mental health. Native cultures are dynamic, not static, as are any cultures that continue to exist. We laud and appreciate the intrepidness and strength of Native peoples (our own families and ancestors in some cases) to still be here, writing books, winning the Heisman Trophy, dancing in the New York City Ballet, zooming into space, or "winding the world well" by practicing the original religions.

The back matter section has definitions, as well as some interesting points on Indigeneity and a bit about Native peoples in Canada, Mexico, Greenland, and the Caribbean. Each chapter has a listing of both historical and contemporary groups located in the area, as well as present-day states, climate, and topography. Biographies are organized chronologically and most are at the end of the chapters. You will come across the phrase "tying it up" in many of the chapters. This refers to Lenape storytellers and their bags, filled with objects to help the storyteller recall details of the narrative. Once the stories are finished, the teller puts all his memory devices back into the storyteller bag and says, "And now I tie it up." We ask forgiveness for any mistakes we have made. And now we tie it up!

HISTORICAL OVERVIEW OF INDIAN–WHITE RELATIONS IN THE UNITED STATES

FIRST PEOPLES

When did people first exist in the Western Hemisphere? Were they here from the beginning of human life? Did they come from somewhere else? Over the centuries, there have been plenty of theories regarding the origin of Indigenous people. What's clear is that the story of the first occupants of these lands is still a mystery.

Most books written about North American Indigenous people theorize that ancestors of today's Native peoples originated in Siberia and later crossed to Alaska via a land bridge (often called Beringia) over the Bering Strait, sixteen to twenty thousand (some archaeologists say fifty thousand) years ago. The Bering Strait theory is frequently presented as irrefutable fact, but it's being challenged.

Some researchers argue that the cornerstone of the Bering Strait theory—the land bridge migration—lacks sufficient archaeological evidence and has many holes in it. The theory also assumes that the strait was the only possible route from Asia to North America. Researchers suggest that travel along coasts by boat makes more sense than inland movement through glaciers. Researchers have pored over a growing volume of genetic data to debate whether ancestors of Native people migrated to North America in one wave or any number of migrations by any number of routes or from one ancestral Asian population or a number of different populations. According to David Meltzer, an archaeologist at Southern Methodist University, "There's a whole lot of stuff that we don't know and may never know, but we're finding new ways to find things and new ways to find things out."

There is Indigenous theory regarding the origins of the people of North America. Some Native groups have creation stories that say they originated in North America. In his book, *Red Earth, White Lies: Native Americans and the Myth of Scientific Fact* (1997), Vine Deloria, Jr. (Dakota), a leading Native American scholar, challenged anthropologists, archaeologists, geologists, and paleontologists to re-examine scientific theory and look at the continent through the ancestral worldview of Native Americans. Deloria warned scientists not to dismiss oral tradition stories of tribes concerning their own origins.

Techniques for dating objects and materials found in excavation sites have been steadily improving over the years. In 2003, more sophisticated radiocarbon tests of carbonized plant remains were used on artifacts unearthed along the Savannah River in South Carolina. The sediments containing these artifacts are at least 50,000 years old, meaning that humans inhabited North America long before the last ice age. There are similar accounts of other findings in different parts of the Americas.

What's at stake regarding these theories about the origins of the first Native people? A lot, according to Professor Theodore Van Alst (Sihasapa Lakota/Eastern Cherokee), former director of Yale University's Native American Cultural Center. He said the Bering Strait theory is invariably used to discredit notions of Indigenous rights to landholding, "used to support the notion that we're just an earlier set of people on a long continuum of immigrants."

Like every people in the world, Native cultures were dynamic and changing over hundreds of centuries before the arrival of Europeans. Generation after generation created new knowledge and responded to their transforming natural and social worlds. The First Peoples developed enormous cultural varieties well suited to the vastly different environments in which they lived. By the time Christopher Columbus arrived, millions of people with complex languages, myriad ways of knowing, technologies, tools, trading societies, political systems, and art forms existed in North America. Charles Mann, award-winning journalist and author of *1491: New Revelations of the Americas Before Columbus*, sums up the current view regarding the Western Hemisphere before 1492: It was "a thriving, stunningly diverse place, a tumult of languages, trade, and culture, a region where tens of millions of people loved and hated and worshipped as people do everywhere. Much of this world vanished after Columbus, swept away by disease and subjugation."

THE DOCTRINE OF DISCOVERY (DESTRUCTION)

When Christopher Columbus sailed west across the sea in 1492 and set foot on Guanahani Island (San Salvador), he performed a ceremony to take possession of the lands for the king and queen of Spain. He was authorized to "take possession" of any lands he "discovered"

that were "not under the dominion of any Christian rulers." He and the Spanish sovereigns were following an already well-established tradition of "discovery" and conquest. After Columbus returned to Europe, Pope Alexander VI issued a papal document, the bull *Inter Cetera* of May 3, 1493, "granting" to Spain the right to conquer the lands which Columbus had already found as well as any lands which Spain might "discover" in the future.

Papal documents (letters from popes) and sixteenth-century charters by Christian European monarchs were frequently used in their conquest of Americas to justify a brutal system of colonization—which dehumanized the Indigenous people by regarding their territories as being "inhabited only by brute animals."

The Doctrine of Discovery (DOD) became the legal bedrock upon which the United States and other nations rationalized their domination of Indigenous peoples. A code of international law, it became the theological and political justification for the appropriation of the lands and resources of Indigenous people, undermining the sovereignty of Indigenous nations and peoples, the basis for the African and Native slave trade, colonization of the Americas, and the genocides of Indigenous peoples of Africa and the Americas. In 1823, the DOD was adopted into U.S. law by the U.S. Supreme Court in the case *Johnson v. McIntosh*. Supreme Court Chief Justice John Marshall ruled that "Christian people" who had "discovered" the lands of "heathens" had assumed the right of "ultimate dominion." This presumption of "dominion" diminished the Indians' rights to complete sovereignty as independent nations. Indians merely had a right to occupy their lands. This ruling is still in effect and is sometimes referred to in legal decisions.

COLONIAL ERA

The initial encounters between Native Americans and non-Natives occurred at different times in different places in present-day North America. The Hopi of Arizona and the Huron of eastern Canada both experienced encounters

An 1847 painting by American artist John Vanderlyn depicts Christopher Columbus landing on Guanahani (San Salvador) in 1492 and declaring the land for Spain. The arrival of Columbus marked the beginning of the end for Native peoples in the Americas.

with Europeans by about 1540. The Lakota of the Plains did not experience firsthand knowledge of them until the late 1600s. The Wintu of Northern California and Unangan of Alaska's Aleutian Islands encountered Europeans over a hundred years later in the mid-1700s.

Spain

Spain, which considered Native people "pagans" and inferior, held a region known as New Spain that extended down the Pacific Coast from Vancouver Island to the tip of South America and inland as far east as the Mississippi River, including the Florida peninsula. St. Augustine, Florida, a permanent settlement, was established in 1565; Santa Fe, New Mexico, was founded in 1610.

During the late sixteenth century, the Spanish moved into southwestern lands for wealth, converts, and slaves and ruled there until 1821. Since Indians were forced to labor in their mines, ranches, farms, and public works, they were not driven from their territories. While the Spanish crown exploited their labor, missionaries carried on large-scale efforts to convert their souls. Hostility developed between the Spanish and the Apache and Pueblo peoples. The harsh rule of some Spanish governors, plus religious and economic oppression, led to an allied Pueblo–Apache revolt against the Spanish empire in northern New Spain. The 1680 Pueblo revolt was ended by Spanish counteroffenses in 1692. Native hostility persisted until Spain was forced to abandon her colonies in the 1820s.

France

The French, who were the most congenial to Native peoples, also believed Native peoples to be pagan and inferior. The French in Canada were primarily interested in dominating the fur trade, which required miniscule amounts of land. They developed no permanent settlements in the interior and farmed little of mainland Canada. The French depended on the friendship of Indian trappers and go-betweens, both sides benefiting from the reciprocal economic relationship. They became absorbed in Native life, adopting its customs and dress, learning Native languages, and intermarrying. New France extended west of the Appalachian Mountains to the Mississippi River and south from Canada to the Gulf of Mexico. Quebec was founded in 1608.

New Netherland

The colony of New Netherland was established by the Dutch West India Company in 1624 and grew to encompass all of present-day New York City and parts of Long Island, Connecticut, and New Jersey. A successful Dutch settlement in the colony grew up on the southern tip of Manhattan Island and was christened New Amsterdam. Since the Netherlands hungered at first for furs, the Dutch negotiated with Native peoples for small pieces of land for trading posts and villages. After furs were depleted in coastal areas by the 1630s, the Dutch turned to agriculture and used force and cajolery to acquire larger chunks of Indian land. The popular myth that the Lenape "sold" New York City to Dutch governor Peter Minuit for $24 is just that, a myth. In 1626, the Lenape signed a "lease" agreement, which allowed Dutch settlers to share their territory, but the Dutch assumed they owned the land outright and renamed Lenape lands "New Amsterdam."

A 1902 photo of the ruins of the Old Church in Jamestown that was built in 1639.

Beginning in 1641, a protracted war was fought between the colonists and the Lenape, which resulted in the death of more than one thousand Indians and Dutch settlers. In 1664, New Amsterdam passed to English control.

England

The English colonists differed from the Spanish and French. After the founding of Jamestown, Virginia, in 1607 and Plymouth, Massachusetts, in 1620, English families came to stay and to transplant their own ideas of civilization in the New World. The colonists had little use for Native peoples, who they perceived as "savages" and "devil-worshippers" and nuisances who blocked the growth of the English-speaking world. The English wanted their lands for farming although some were involved with fur trading. English agricultural practices destroyed Native traditional economies and forced tribes to move away or convert to the English lifestyle. Since the British crown was unable to enforce uniform policy and regulations, treatment of Indians varied widely in the British colonies, which eventually fought with each other as well as with the crown over Indian land acquisition and trade policies and defense. In an effort to gain control over all relations between Indians and non-Indians throughout the colonies in the mid-eighteenth century, the British crown put Indian affairs under the control of Indian superintendents in the newly created Northern and Southern departments. Lawless traders and others who moved into restricted Indian territories interfered with the effectiveness of the system.

Russia

Russia established claims to land along the North Pacific Coast beginning in the 1740s. Throughout its tenure in North America, Russians enslaved and forced Aleut (Unangan) men to hunt furs, children to prepare the hides, and women to become concubines. Russia established a permanent settlement in 1783 on Kodiak Island to control the Native people, whom they bullied and tortured. From 1812 to 1841, Rus-

sians maintained a fort in Bodega Bay, California. Finally, in 1867, when Russia ceded Alaska to the United States, its rule in North America ended.

Sweden

A Swedish colony was established in what is now Delaware in 1638 by Peter Minuit, a German native of French extraction and former governor of New Amsterdam. The New Sweden Company had been chartered to create an agricultural (primarily tobacco) and fur-trading colony which could bypass the French, English, and Dutch. The colonists established farms and small settlements along both sides of the Delaware River. The Swedes purchased lands which would later become the states of Delaware and Maryland and a portion of Pennsylvania, which would become Philadelphia.

COLONIAL ERA POWER STRUGGLES

During the colonial era, the British, French, and Spanish used North America as a battleground of their Old World rivalries. Wise Native leaders sensed the danger of being absorbed into the power struggles. "Why do not you and the French fight in the old country and the sea? Why do you come to fight on our land? This makes everybody believe you want to take the land from us by force and settle it," Delaware chief Shingas told the British in 1758. Most Natives found it impossible to maintain neutrality. They were swayed by bribes, bound by trade alliances, or chose to exploit strife to get revenge on old enemies.

Historian Alden T. Vaugh (1979) states that in every area settled by Europeans, "Indians were victims … they suffered discrimination, exploitation, and wholesale destruction—by disease and demoralization if not sword and bullet."

Wampanoag historian Nanepashemet explained the way in which Native Americans perceived Europeans in their first encounters as follows:

"The Native worldview was a lot different from the European worldview because Native people did not believe there was finite knowledge. Knowledge was infinite. Any person could acquire new knowledge and introduce it to his community, and it would be accepted if it was useful. So the idea of Europeans and their material culture and their beliefs was alien to people, but their cultural makeup allowed them to accept new information.... They were able to accept European goods although they used many things according to their own cultural dictates.... "

Encounters, 1600s–1754

At the beginning, some early Native–white encounters boded well. The first arrivals to North America were received with hospitality. Massasoit, the Wampanoag's principal chief in southern New England, and Wahunsonacock, known to the English as Powhatan, the principal chief of a large confederacy of eastern Virginia Algonquin tribes, offered food and shelter and showed the English how to survive in the North American environment. Both men maintained peace with the white colonists until they died.

Before the French and Indian War began in 1754, there were incessant hostilities east of the Mississippi among the English, French, and a multitude of Native peoples. English colonists pressured Native peoples to adopt the so-called civilized European lifestyle and Christianity and often employed repressive measures to overpower Indians who did not comply. They often used deceit to extinguish title to Indian lands when rightful owners refused to sell. When English settlements became stronger, permanent, and armed, they forced Indian peoples to obey their laws and to submit to their demands.

Almost every colony in New England witnessed Indian–white conflicts. Many Indians tried to resist seizure of their lands. In New York, the Dutch and bands of Algonquian Indians engaged in border warfare until the Indians were defeated. Two major wars fought between the English and southern New England Indians in the seventeenth century—the Pequot War in 1637 and King Philip's War in 1675–1676, involving Wampanoag and their allies—led to bitter defeat for the Indians and the end of organized resistance. In Virginia, two fiercely fought wars, in 1622 and 1644, also led to the defeat of the Indians and the decline of Indian political power in that region. By the end of the seventeenth century, tribes along the Atlantic seaboard had been weakened by disease, destroyed, dispersed, or subjected to the control of European colonists.

The Tuscarora War of 1711–1712, a revolt against white encroachments, resulted in the partial destruction of North Carolina Indians and the northward retreat of survivors. In the Yamassee War of 1715, a rebellion of southern Indians prompted by general resentment against English economic exploitation and a fear of English agricultural expansion, settlers in South Carolina nearly exterminated the Yamasee.

THE FUR TRADE

Throughout the colonial period and well into the nineteenth century, the fur trade was one of the principal business enterprises in North America. European fashions demanded furs for making hats, coats, dress trimmings, and other items. Trading with Indian peoples for furs began immediately in colonies along the Atlantic Coast. The French, English, and Dutch (and later the Americans) competed for exclusive trading privileges with Native groups, who were experienced traders long before the coming of Europeans.

For a time, trading pelts for European goods benefited Indians. Guns made hunting bountiful, metal kettles were more practical to cook in, and steel tools were more efficient than stone and bone. Cloth, needles, and scissors replaced clothing made from furs that required hours of preparation. Soon, traders' goods became necessities as Indians discarded their own equivalent tools and technologies. With their basic economic systems disrupted, their wildlife resources depleted, and their subsistence areas

A 1777 illustration depicts French trappers trading fur with Indians.

diminished, the Native Americans became even more dependent on Europeans for commodities in order to survive.

By the mid-1700s, European traders wanted Indian lands as well as pelts. Unscrupulous English and French traders along the northeastern colonial frontier swindled Indians out of furs and large acres of land. Some traders forced tribes to trade entire catches of furs to them under threats of punishment. Deeply in debt to certain traders, tribes gave up immense areas of valuable land to cancel their obligations. Spanish, English, and French traders who competed for furs manipulated tribal peoples into supporting the country that supplied them with goods they wanted. The increasing demand for furs by rival European traders led to tribal competition for limited supplies and pelts. Incessant wars between European powers exacerbated intertribal conflicts as European nations encour-

aged tribes allied with them to attack tribes allied with other European powers.

FRENCH AND INDIAN WAR (1754–1763)

Anglo–French rivalry in the fur trade, which contributed to the struggle for control of North America, culminated in the French and Indian War (1754–1763). The French and British also competed in giving presents to the Six Nations Iroquois and their allies, as well as Algonquian tribes, to secure their allegiance during the war. The British successfully recruited thousands of Indians as allies through tremendous outlays of gifts. Mutually exchanged presents cemented political relationships between an Indian nation and a European nation. European powers gave peace medals to heads of various Indian nations, a practice continued by American leaders. While medal giving secured diplomatic alliances, it cost colonial governments great sums of money.

Defeated in the war, the French lost control of Canada to England in the 1763 Treaty of Paris. The British substantially reduced the giving of presents to Indians, which the Indians believed served to cement alliances and ensure good-faith relationships. Tribes needed goods, especially ammunition for hunting, to alleviate their suffering after the war. Furthermore, an extremely high schedule of prices for goods was instituted, which outraged Indians who could not go to English trading posts and obtain supplies on credit or as gifts, as had been the custom with the French. British forts, which reduced Indian hunting territories, and the British failure to supply western Indians enabled certain chiefs to mobilize Indian discontentment. In 1763, Pontiac of the Ottawa, Guyashota of the Seneca, Shinga of the Delaware, and other war chiefs of the Ottawa, Huron, Chippewa, Shawnee, Erie, Potawatomi, and Wyandot launched a multi-tribal assault that destroyed every British fort west of the Appalachians except Detroit, Niagara, and Fort Pitt. They captured nine English forts and killed some one thousand settlers. Unable to sustain the uprising, Pontiac agreed to peace on October 3, 1763.

PROCLAMATION OF 1763 AND AFTERMATH

In an effort to avert further trouble with the Indians, the colonial government in London responded with its Proclamation of 1763, forbidding white settlement in the region west of the Appalachian Mountains. It set a tentative boundary line along the Appalachian crests: immigrant settlements to the east, Native communities to the west. The British government tried to maintain the boundary line. It dispatched troops to evict squatters and burn their cabins, but, as an observer reported, within months, the cabins were rebuilt with "double the number of inhabitants ... that ever was before." The British government itself planned to extend military outposts beyond the mountains. Shawnee Cornstalk recognized that "when a fort

appears, you may depend upon it; there will soon be towns and settlements of white men."

The British government achieved little control over the stream of immigrants. Settlers and land speculators alike simply ignored British regulations and invaded the Indians' domain in the "Old Northwest"—Ohio, Indiana, Illinois, Michigan, Wisconsin, and northeastern Minnesota. They pushed across the line, competing with Natives for the same resources. In the Ohio Valley, both Natives and immigrants combined farming, grazing practices, and hunting in order to survive. The Delaware, who had already been pushed westward, responded: "The Elks are our horses, the Buffaloes are our cows, the deer are our sheep, and the whites shan't have them." Natives had to detour around burgeoning settlements and garrisoned forts where they had moved freely.

In 1768, various Algonquian and Iroquoian representatives met at Fort Stanwix with British officials in order to sort out land matters and to set a new "permanent" boundary west of the original line. Soon, the boundaries outlined in the Treaty of Fort Stanwix were erased. Native people from the Great Lakes to communities in the south struggled to hold on to their homelands.

The British government established and manned posts along the length of this boundary, which was a very costly undertaking. The British ministry argued that these outposts were for colonial defense and as such should be paid for by the colonies. From the American perspective, this amounted to a tax on the colonies to pay for a matter of Imperial regulation that was opposed to the interests of the colonies. The colonists protested and revolted against the British government, resenting the closing of the frontier, the British military force, and the taxes levied for its support. These and other grievances led to the American Revolution.

THE REVOLUTIONARY ERA (1775–1783)

Most Indians tried to stay neutral in what they saw as a British civil war, a domestic disturbance. Even when they eventually sided with the British or Americans, they were not fighting for or against freedom like the American patriots or British troops. In Indian eyes, aggressive Americans posed a greater threat than did a distant king to their land, their liberty, and their way of life. The American War of Independence was an Indian war for independence as well.

The new American Congress initially tried to secure Indian neutrality during its war with Britain. Later, it tried to engage Indians in the service of the United Colonies. Some factions of the Oneida and Tuscarora took the American side, and most of the Six Nations [Iroquois] Confederacy took the British side against land-avaricious colonists, but individuals within the nations chose which side to support. Thus, there are examples such as Mohawk allying with Great Britain while other Mohawk were allied with the United States as well as examples of American Indians remaining neutral throughout the war.

The Northeast was just one of several theaters of the war. Indians of the Old Northwest and the Southeast were also involved, for the most part on the British side. Southern tribes like the Creek, Cherokee, and Chickasaw supported the British, but the Catawba aided the Americans. The Americans failed to win the allegiance of most Indians because their goods were no match for British goods, and Americans in the Ohio Valley were committing atrocities against Indians.

During and after the Revolution, Natives paid a high price for their involvement. Some tribes and confederacies had split in their allegiances, especially the Iroquois. This led to Iroquois fighting Iroquois, razing each others' villages. Unified groups faced devastation as well. Colonial troops invaded Native communities, killing residents, burning houses, and ruining crops. They used the war as an excuse to take more Native lands.

TREATY OF PARIS OF 1783

The Treaty of Paris of 1783, negotiated between the United States and Great Britain, ended the Revolutionary War. The tribes who

had allied with the British were not present at the signing of the treaty. The Crown recognized American independence and granted the Americans title to the entire "Northwest Territory," trading Native property with the United States as if the communities had no independent right over their own land or loyalty. The Crown made no provisions for the many Indian allies who supported their cause. Officials on both sides apparently considered Natives as incidental to both the past and future of North America.

The British did extend some favors to those Indians who moved to Canada after the Revolution. Joseph Brant and his followers were among

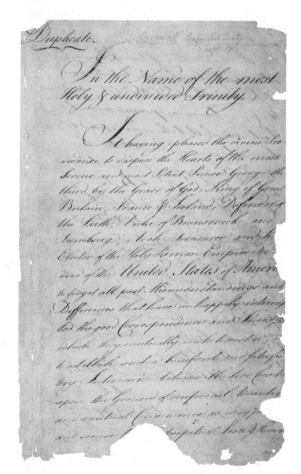

The Treaty of Paris, signed in 1783, ended the war between Britain and the fledgling United States, but it also impacted Natives by negotiating their lands as if they belonged to the European colonists.

others who were granted parcels of land. The Indians who elected to stay were left to fend for themselves with the new American nation. In New York, Indians were treated harshly, forced off their land and onto reservations because of their past British alliance. The British, however, held on to frontier posts around the Great Lakes, from which they continued to trade English goods for Indian furs.

WARS FOR THE OLD NORTHWEST AND SOUTHEAST

After the Revolution, the fledgling United States claimed all the land east of the Mississippi River, 847,000 square miles. The settlers poured onto Indian lands, ignoring Indian rights. In 1788 alone, 18,000 settlers moved into Ohio country. Chiefs such as Little Turtle, a Miami, reacted to the hordes of land-hungry settlers. Between 1783 and 1790, he and his allies, including Miami, Shawnee, Chippewa, Lenni Lenape (Delaware), Potawatomi, and Ottawa, killed some 1,500 settlers in isolated frontier attacks. Little Turtle and his followers routed General Josiah Harmar's force in 1790, killing 183 and wounding thirty-one more. In 1791, Little Turtle dealt General Arthur St. Clair, the highest-ranking officer in the U.S. Army, the worst military defeat in its history. George Washington's next choice of command was General "Mad" Anthony Wayne, the Revolutionary hero. After Wayne's troops defeated the Indians at Fallen Timbers in 1794, the Indians were forced, in the 1795 Treaty of Greenville, to sign away huge tracts of lands amounting to all of present-day Ohio and a good part of Indiana.

The extent of the land cessions dissatisfied Shawnee Indian leaders, such as Tecumseh (called Tekamthi, "Shooting Star," by his people), and his brother, a religious leader named Tenskwatawa, or the Prophet. Tecumseh believed only a united front could withstand American military power. While Tecumseh was away gathering support among southern tribes, William Henry Harrison, the governor of Indiana Territory, marched on Tippecanoe (a town where Indian people of all tribes attempted to live a traditional lifestyle) and

burned it to the ground. The British listened to Tecumseh's complaints against American intruders and led him to believe they would support him in driving Americans back from the Ohio country. A war between some of Tecumseh's followers and American troops began in 1811, which persisted through the War of 1812 between Americans and the British, the last war in which some Indians allied themselves with a foreign power. Again, some Indians were pro-American although the sympathies of most tribes, in the Northeast and Southeast, were with the British. When the war broke out, most tribes in the Old Northwest, already hostile to the Americans, became auxiliaries, scouts, and raiders for the British forces. Tecumseh, who had become a brigadier general in the British army at the beginning of the War of 1812, was shot in October 1813 at the Battle of the Thames in what is now Ontario, where Harrison defeated the combined British and Indian forces.

In the South, a portion of the Creek called the Red Sticks were armed against the Americans from 1813 to 1814. Andrew Jackson headed military operations in the upper Creek area and waged a campaign to level Creek towns. The tribe, with its forces split, suffered defeat by the American troops, resulting in the cession of twenty-three million acres, nearly all the Creek lands in Alabama.

After the end of the War of 1812, tribes in the Northeast and Southeast, deprived of British allies, were coerced into signing a series of treaties extinguishing their title to large areas of land. Nearly all the tribes continued to occupy greatly reduced portions of their ancestral lands until Andrew Jackson became president in 1828, when eventually, the government forcibly removed the tribes to the west of the Mississippi River.

EARLY FEDERAL INDIAN POLICY

The federal Indian policy of the U.S. government has had a profound impact on Native nations and has shifted dramatically over the past

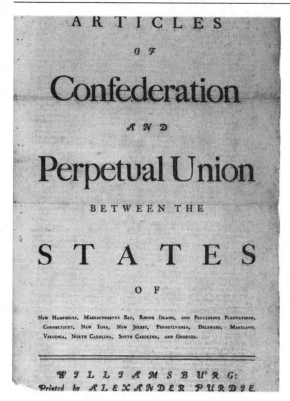

ARTICLES
OF

Confederation

AND

Perpetual Union

BETWEEN THE

STATES

OF

New Hampshire, Massachusetts Bay, Rhode Island, and Providence Plantations, Connecticut, New York, New Jersey, Pennsylvania, Delaware, Maryland, Virginia, North Carolina, South Carolina, and Georgia.

WILLIAMSBURG:
Printed by ALEXANDER PURDIE.

One of the issues addressed by the 1781 Articles of Confederation was how to handle affairs between the Indian nations and the United States by establishing regional departments overseen by American commissioners.

two-hundred-plus years. In the late 1700s, the newly formed U.S. government treated Indian tribes as independent sovereign nations, often seeking their allegiance and support and negotiating with them as equals.

Beginning in 1775, the Second Continental Congress created three Indian departments: Northern, Middle, and Southern. Each was headed by commissioners who reported directly to Congress. (Patrick Henry and Benjamin Franklin served as commissioners.) The commissioners were responsible for winning the support of Indian nations during the American Revolution.

In 1781, the Articles of Confederation stipulated that Indian affairs were to be handled by the national government. By 1786, the three departments were organized into two regions. The heads of the departments, called superintendents, were responsible to the secretary of war, who was charged with "such duties as shall from time to time be enjoined on, or entrusted to, him by the president of the United States, agreeably to the Constitution, relative to … Indian affairs." With this arrangement, the basic structure of what was to become the Bureau of Indian Affairs (BIA) began to emerge. Indian agents, who were located in the field, reported to superintendents. Superintendents reported to the secretary of war, who reported to the president. During this time, Indian affairs consisted mainly of negotiating treaties, acquiring land, regulating Indian trade, and arranging payments to Indians as specified in treaties.

TREATIES, 1778–1868

The Constitution of the United States gave Congress plenary power over Indian affairs and reserved to the United States the power to make treaties to acquire land for a growing population and westward expansion. Beginning in 1778 and for almost a hundred years, the treaty was the principal instrument of federal Indian policy. The first treaty was written in September 1778 with the Delaware (Lenape) Indians and the last ratified in August 1868. The list that follows gives a historical overview of five periods of treaty making, which resulted in the loss of nearly two billion acres of Native lands.

Colonial Treaties (1600–1776)

- Period of independence and equality for most Indians
- Indians held positions of power in Western hemisphere
- European colonists still small in number
- England and France sought military assistance from the Indians
- Trade relations

Treaties of Alliance and Peace (1776–1816)

- Indians still strong militarily, numerically, and economically

- Indians could choose which European powers with which to align

- Increasing need to clarify boundaries between Indian government and U.S. arose

- U.S. government recognized that Indians owned their land, and to seize it would mean constant warfare, which the U.S. wanted to avoid

- Prevent powerful Indian nations from joining forces against the U.S.

- The Beginning of Land Cessions (1784–1817)

- Land cessions began in New England and mid-Atlantic states in exchange for annuities and specific services delivered to tribes

- Treaties began to be used to legally extinguish Indian title to land

- Methods used to permanently wipe out title were (1) drawing of boundaries between Indian Country and U.S. territory and (2) the securing of "rights of way" and land for military forts and trading posts

- With the establishing of boundaries and land cessions, the concept of "reservation" introduced into American policy

Treaties of Removal
(1817–1846)

- The departures of France, England, and Spain diminished Indians regaining power

- As settlers wanted more land, the primary goal of the U.S. in making treaties became the removal of Indians from their lands

- The primary goal was the removal of Indian nations in the East to lands west of the Mississippi River (now Arkansas, Kansas, and Oklahoma)

Western Treaties
(1846–1868)

- A new policy forced Indians to smaller, well-defined reservations

Education Provisions in Treaties

Early on, the newly established government began a continuing involvement in Native education. The first U.S. treaty to contain a provision for education was the 1794 treaty with the Oneida, Tuscarora, and Stockbridge Indians. Eventually, ninety-five treaties specifically mentioned that Native ownership of land would be exchanged for a variety of things, including education. Education meant forced assimilation, which was viewed as the humanitarian solution to the so-called Indian problem. There seemed to be two choices, as the House Committee on Appropriations put it in 1818: "In the present state of our country, one of two things seems to be necessary, either that those sons of the forest should be moralized or exterminated." At first, missionaries were funded by the federal government to do the moralizing.

In 1819, Congress passed the Civilization Fund Act, which provided for an annual appropriation for the education of Indians. In the beginning, the funds were given to missionaries to allow them to expand their network of schools to teach the "habits and arts of civilization" to Indians. Later, with legislation that made it illegal for the government to support religious organizations, the federal government took on the responsibility of eventually establishing and operating hundreds of schools.

EARLY LAWS, 1790–1795

The early laws of the U.S. government that recognized the largely independent character of Native American tribes were built around policy confirming Indian land ownership on areas they occupied, which could not be taken without their consent. The Indian Intercourse Acts of 1790, 1793, 1796, and 1802 governed Indian relations and attempted to control the trade relationship between Indians and Euro-American traders. The specified geographic boundaries separating "Indian Country" from white settlements sought to restrain lawless frontier whites who circumvented federal laws. Other laws governing the fur trade sought to prevent the use of liquor by traders among Indians.

The Indian Intercourse Act of 1790

Section 4 of The Indian Intercourse Act of 1790 read:

> And be it enacted and declared that no sale of lands made by any Indians, or any nation or tribe of Indians in the United States, shall be valid to any person or persons, or to any state, whether having the right of pre-emption to such lands or not, unless the same shall be made and duly executed at some public treaty, held under the authority of the United States.

Under the terms of the Constitution and the Trade and Intercourse Act of 1790 and its subsequent re-enactments, no "purchase, grant, lease, or other conveyance of land" from an Indian nation was valid without the participation and approval of the United States government. Land claims pursued by American Indian tribes on the East Coast during the twentieth century rested on the Nonintercourse Act of 1790.

President George Washington signed the first Indian Intercourse Act into law in 1790.

The federal government attempted early on to compete with the British and private fur companies by creating a system of government-operated trading houses by act of Congress in 1795. Designed to help Indians secure goods at fair prices and to reduce warfare with tribes, the system established seventeen trade factories between 1795 and 1821. The system, which suffered heavy losses during the War of 1812, was criticized by Indians, agents, and private trading interests, and by 1822, Congress closed down the factories.

NORTHWEST ORDINANCE OF 1787

In the period after the Revolution, the American government increasingly turned its attention to the acquisition of land. Recognizing that the United States was not strong enough militarily to take Indian land by force and that peace with Indian nations was a matter of national security, Congress expressed an enduring, if often violated, commitment to treat Indians fairly and to respect their property rights. In the Northwest Ordinance of 1787, Congress set forth elements of an official U.S. policy toward Indians that is part of the basis for the trust responsibilities of the United States for Indian rights and property. The ordinance specifies that:

> The utmost faith shall always be observed toward Indians; their lands and property shall never be taken from them without their consent; and in their property, rights, and liberty, they shall never be invaded or disturbed, unless in just and lawful wars authorized by Congress, but laws founded in justice and humanity shall from time to time be made for preventing wrongs done to them and for preserving peace and friendship with them.

The superintendents were responsible for carrying out the commitments expressed in the Northwest Ordinance. Since the official policy was against taking Indian land by force, one of the main duties of the superintendents was to arrange for treaty negotiations in which the United States could acquire land within a legal framework, and the Indian people would get something in return. The superintendents were also responsible for distribution of goods, money, and services to Indians as specified in treaties.

GROWTH OF U.S. GOVERNMENT BUREAUCRACY, 1787–1849

As more and more treaties were signed, the work of the departments expanded. At the same time, the governmental process became increasingly bureaucratic. Treaties stipulated that Indian title to land was exchanged for a variety of things, most often money, goods, and/or services. It was often stipulated that a specified amount of money was to be distributed for a specified number of years, sometimes forever. The money payment was called an annuity. The accounting procedure for appropriating money from Congress and for acquiring the goods was, then as now, time consuming and complicated. New treaties were signed every year, each one stipulating a different mix of money, goods, and services in payment for land. In addition, non-Indians were pushing back the frontier and encroaching on Indian land, causing hostilities. They began to demand reparation for damages from attacks by Indians. The secretary was authorized to make payments to non-Indians whose property was damaged by Indian attack. The money was to come from money owed to Indians as a result of land transfers. This meant that in addition to seeing that each tribe received its annuities, goods, and services, the secretary of war had to assess the validity of claims and make arrangements for payments from treaty money. The secretary could not keep up with the work. By 1816, the War Department was eighteen years behind in settling the accounts of the Indian departments.

In 1824, the secretary of war, John C. Calhoun, without authorization from Congress, upgraded the Indian Department to bureau status and appointed Thomas L. McKenny, the former super-

intendent of Indian trade, to handle the day-to-day business. Calhoun's reasoning was to establish an independent bureau so that it could be responsible for its own complex accounting and record keeping. He used the term "the Bureau of Indian Affairs" for the first time in his letter of appointment to McKenny on March 11, 1824. However, since Secretary Calhoun did not have authorization from Congress, he did not actually have the power to transfer some of his authority to someone else or create a separate branch in the War Department. Nevertheless, the Indian Office grew, and the question of its legality was overlooked for a time.

In 1832, Congress passed an act that legalized McKenny's position to that of commissioner of Indian affairs. A House committee investigation then reported that it could find no basis in law for making the Indian Office an independent branch of the War Department and recommended that Congress enact a statute to make the office legal. Congress did so on June 30, 1834. The Act of 1834 is therefore considered the "organic act" of the Indian Office (the law by which an organization exists). This meant that the commissioner of Indian affairs could handle the daily business of the Indian Office under the supervision of the secretary of war. The Indian Office, as it was called at the time, remained part of the War Department until 1849, when Congress created the Department of the Interior and transferred the Indian Office to its jurisdiction.

The mission of the Indian Office reflected the government's policy toward Indians. Initially, the government was concerned with peace and land acquisition. Activities were aimed at achieving peaceful coexistence with Indian nations, securing equitable trade relations, and acquiring land. Treaties contained clauses that defined boundaries that separated Indian land from white land, but whites often encroached on Indian land, taking for it themselves, destroying the environment, and treating Indians with aggressive hostility. Often, the government did not even try to keep intruders off Indian land. By 1803, however, the policy switched from peaceful coexistence to aggressive destruction of the

Indian way of life. This was to be accomplished either by the physical removal of Indians or by making Indians indistinguishable from white Americans. Both the first option, "removal," and the second, "assimilation," became government policy for many years.

REMOVAL AND ASSIMILATION, 1820s–1860s

During the 1820s, government officials and religious and reform organizations who argued for the assimilation of Native Americans into non-Indian society merged this philosophy with that of moving eastern Native peoples to lands west of the Mississippi River, where they thought the "civilizing" program could be pursued more successfully. President Thomas Jefferson first suggested the removal policy in 1803. The Jeffersonian generation initially believed in a program of civilizing Indians through secular and religious education, which would transform

President Thomas Jefferson believed in moving Natives west of the Mississippi, where it would be "easier" to assimilate them into a European-style culture, and so he approved the first removal policy in 1803.

them into individual farmers, who eventually would be incorporated into white society. That generation witnessed, however, the disintegration of Indian tribal and personal life as a result of the "civilization" program, renewed warfare with whites, exposure to European diseases, and the influence of liquor. Some Jeffersonians argued that Indians in the East should be removed to west of the Mississippi River, where the "civilizing" program that failed in the East could be carried on. During the Jefferson era, there were three unsuccessful attempts to remove voluntarily Southeastern tribal groups to unsettled portions of the Louisiana Territory acquired by the United States from France. Subsequent presidents James Monroe and John Quincy Adams were unwilling to use military force to remove tribes.

THE DOCTRINE OF DISCOVERY, 1823

In 1823, the Doctrine of Discovery (DOD) was adopted into U.S. law by the Supreme Court in the case *Johnson v. McIntosh*. Writing for a unanimous court, Chief Justice John Marshall observed that Christian European nations had assumed "ultimate dominion" over the lands of America during the Age of Discovery and that—upon "discovery"—the Indians had lost "their rights to complete sovereignty as independent nations" and only retained a right of "occupancy" in their lands. The Court affirmed that United States law was based on a fundamental rule of the "Law of Nations"—that it was permissible to virtually ignore the most basic rights of Indigenous "heathens" and to claim that the "unoccupied lands" of America rightfully belonged to discovering Christian European nations. The term "unoccupied lands" referred to "the lands in America which, when discovered, were 'occupied' by Indians' but 'unoccupied' by Christians."

The long-term effects of the Eurocentric documents still impact laws today. United States federal policy regarding Native peoples has been based on the DOD. Although the U.S. had become independent of England, the new lawmakers chose to continue with the tenets of white Christian dominion and manifest destiny. The DOD is still referred to in legal decisions. In 2005, the U.S. Supreme Court in *City of Sherrill v. Oneida Indian Nation of New York* ruled against the Oneida, who disputed the taxation of recently reacquired ancestral lands. Justice Ruth Bader Ginsburg cited the Discovery Doctrine: "Under the 'Doctrine of Discovery,' fee title to the lands occupied by the Indians when the colonists arrived became vested in the sovereign—first the discovering European nation and later the original States and the United States."

Today, many faith communities have called for repudiation of the doctrine, among them the United Methodist Church, the Unitarian Universalist Association, the Episcopal Church, the World Council of Churches, several Quaker meetings, and the United Church of Christ. Catholic nuns have also challenged "the papal sanctioning of Christian enslavement and power over non-Christians" and urged the pope to rescind the papal bulls. "It would be helpful for the church to throw out her sin of colonialism. Some acknowledgment of the pain of the past would be helpful," said Philip Arnold, Syracuse University religious studies professor.

TWO CHEROKEE SUPREME COURT CASES

From 1828 to 1830, Georgia passed laws imposing state jurisdiction over Cherokee Territory. The Supreme Court handed down decisions in two cases, *Cherokee Nation v. Georgia* (1831) and *Worcester v. Georgia* (1832), in which tribes were viewed as largely autonomous governments retaining inherent powers not expressly ceded away by the tribes or extinguished by Congress and essentially independent of state control. In the *Worcester* decision, the court spelled out virtually every basic doctrine in Indian law: federal plenary power: "The whole intercourse between the United States and this nation is, by our Constitution and laws, vested in the government of the United States"; trust rela-

tionship: "From the commencement of our government, Congress has passed acts to regulate trade and intercourse with the Indians, which treat them as nations, respect their rights, and manifest a firm purpose to afford that protection which treaties stipulate"; reserved rights: "The Indian nations possessed a full right to the lands they occupied until that right should be extinguished by the United States with their consent"; and the general exclusion of state law from Indian Country: "The Cherokee nation ... is a distinct community, occupying its own territory, with boundaries accurately described, in which the laws of Georgia can have no force."

REMOVAL

Southeast

In the wake of the Cherokee cases, great numbers of settlers in the Southeast demanded that prospering tribes with extensive landholdings be cleared out of their way. State interference with the Cherokee Nation continued despite the court mandate. Removal was seen as the only solution to the "problem." President Andrew Jackson, elected in 1828, supported removal, declaring that the only hope for the Southeastern tribes' survival would be for them to give up all their land and move west of the Mississippi River. Jackson warned the tribes that if they failed to move, they would lose their independence and fall under state laws. He backed an Indian removal bill in Congress. Members of Congress, like Davy Crockett, argued that Jackson was violating the Constitution by refusing to enforce treaties that guaranteed Indian land rights, but Congress passed the removal law in the spring of 1830.

The Removal Act called for the forcible removal of Indian people from their homelands in the eastern United States to tracts of land west of the Mississippi. The act, designed to use Congress's exclusive authority over Indian affairs to gain further land cessions, spoke of securing the "consent" of Native nations, i.e., through treaties, to remove them to the West. However, the removal of the Cherokee, Creek, Choctaw, Chick-

By the late 1830s, Indian nations such as the Cherokee, Creek, Chickasaw, and Chocktaw had been largely extirpated from the Southeast.

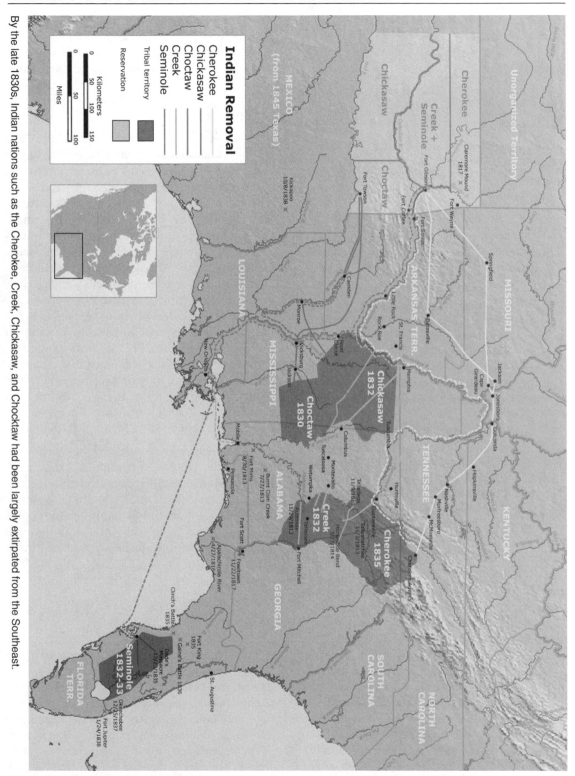

Indian Removal

Seminole
Creek
Choctaw
Chickasaw
Cherokee

Tribal territory
Reservation

Kilometers
0 50 100 150
Miles
0 50 100

asaw, and Seminole, whose lands were coveted by plantation owners, was under military escort. Tribes in the Northeast were also coerced to sign removal treaties.

The federal government's removal policy inspired some of the most devastating losses of tribal landholdings, resulting in the exclusion of many groups from any portion of their ancient land base. Removal not only divested tribes of their homelands, it broke down tribal autonomy, breaking some nations into fractionated political units. In other cases, it forced distinct nations to occupy lands in common with other tribes that had not been historical allies and did not share a cultural basis.

Some tribes resisted removal, particularly the Florida Seminoles. The resistance, led by Osceola, raided farms and settlements, destroyed bridges essential to transporting troops and artillery, and ambushed Florida militia. Lured into captivity through treachery, Osceola died at Fort Moultrie, South Carolina, in 1838. By 1842, the U.S. government gave up trying to evict the remaining Seminoles hiding in the Everglades.

Great Lakes (Midwest)

In the Great Lakes (Midwest) area, settlers thirsty for valuable resources overran tribal lands. To control the competition among settlers and traders and to prevent war with Indians, the government removed the Indians to solve the "problem." Over fifty tribes, including Delaware, Ottawa, Wyandot, Potawatomi, Miami, Illinois, Kickapoo, Sauk, and Fox, also known as Mesquaki, who lived in Ohio, Michigan, Indiana, and Illinois, were forced west of the Mississippi. Indians in this region fought fiercely against removal, and the strongest Indian nations remained. Chief Black Hawk (Sauk) led a faction of his tribe that resisted removal from lands in Illinois that had been sold without its approval. Forcibly evicted from their homes in 1832, Black Hawk's band eluded the militia for three months until General Henry Atkinson and Colonel Henry Dodge, with a 1,300-man command, massacred the Indians at the Battle of Bad Axe. Black Hawk, who surren-

dered and was imprisoned, was permitted to return to his people, but no longer as a chief. Sauk and Fox were forced to cede some six million acres of Iowa's Mississippi River frontage. Later, in 1857, the Fox (Mesquaki) purchased eighty acres of land near Tama, Iowa, so determined were they to move back there.

The removal process that began in 1830 was completed around 1840 with the establishment of a large, unorganized "permanent" Indian country west of Arkansas, Missouri, and Iowa. About one hundred thousand Native Americans were removed forcibly or voluntarily from their ancestral homes in the Northeast and Southeast and Great Lakes region. They were isolated in enclaves west of the Mississippi River, where missionaries and government officials pursued their goals of "educating" Indians. White greed for land motivated Indian removals, but publicly, the policy was masked with arguments for removal as the only way to save Indians from extinction. President Andrew Jackson argued that removing Indians from the corrupting influence of white culture would slow the Indians' decline and cause them to gradually lose their "savage" habits and become "civilized," Christianized people.

Assimilation was considered the humane solution to the problem of peaceful coexistence of peoples from such different cultures as Indians and European Americans. It was always assumed by non-Indians that Indian culture would give way to white culture—that Indians should and would disappear into the mainstream of American culture.

INTERTRIBAL CONFLICTS, 1840s–1860s

By 1840, most of the Indians from east of the Mississippi River were settled in the present-day area of Nebraska, Kansas, and Oklahoma. Clashes occurred between the removed tribes and the Indigenous tribes, who surrendered some of their lands to make room for the displaced people. These Indians resented the displaced tribes with whom they now had to compete in hunting buffalo (bison), their chief source of food. Because the government failed to protect the displaced Indians in their new locations, they resorted to fighting in order to survive. Cherokee, Choctaw, Creek, Chickasaw, and Seminole had difficulty establishing amicable relations with the Osage, Pawnee, Kiowa, Comanche, and other Indigenous nations. The so-called "Five Civilized Tribes," demoralized and impoverished by forced removal from the Southeast, nevertheless reconstructed their lives in Indian Territory. The Sauk and Fox, who moved to a Kansas reservation from Illinois, also battled Plains tribes in order to survive.

Lands west of the Mississippi River were forever guaranteed to the tribes who were removed to there, but Euro-American homesteaders and others continued to stream onto their Indian Territory lands. The government formulated new policies. In the 1840s, the Kansas, Otoes, and Missourias, who were moved to small reservations in Kansas and Nebraska, were again forced to cede lands to make room for newcomers moving in on their tribal lands. Territorial governments were organized to protect settlers, and in 1854, the Kansas–Nebraska bill completely dispossessed Indians of lands in those regions.

In 1845, Texas, with its many Native peoples, entered the Union, as well as Oregon and Washington Territories, acquired from Great Britain in 1846. In 1848, the United States acquired portions of the Southwest and California from Mexico. European emigrants and American settlers created additional pressures on newly acquired lands and lands permanently set aside for Native peoples removed from east of the Mississippi.

Western trade routes and railroads increased the number of settlers who drove buffalo herds from Indian hunting grounds and whose aggre-

The Americans found the Seminoles impossible to drive out of the swamps of Florida, despite three wars (1816–1819, 1835–1842, and 1855–1858) to do so.

sive hunting practices wiped out the buffalo, so necessary to the Plains Indian way of life. Government agents concerned with securing the safe passage of travelers along the Oregon and Santa Fe Trails convinced thousands of Plains Indians from numerous tribes to sign the Fort Laramie Treaty in 1851. The treaty set boundaries between tribes and authorized roads and military posts within their territories, where troops were stationed to protect emigrants and punish Indians, and guaranteed safety to white travelers along the travel routes. In return, Indians were promised annuities, later cut down by Congress.

The first Fort Laramie Treaty was only one of many treaties signed between 1853 and 1856. In that period, fifty-two treaties were negotiated, more than at any other time in history. According to Walter Fleming (Kickapoo), "tribes lost land equivalent to the area of the state of Texas, or 7.4 percent of the total area of the United States."

THE CIVIL WAR, 1861–1865

Roughly twenty thousand American Indians left their homes for Civil War battlefields, some to side with the victorious North, or Union, while others joined the South, or Confederacy. Whatever the choice, the Civil War was disastrous for many Native groups: tribes were torn apart, men lost their lives, and in Indian Territory homes, barns, stores, and schools were looted and burned. After the war ended, tribes had to repair the bitter factionalism that the conflict revived.

When the war broke out in 1861, the federal government was at first reluctant to enlist Indians on the Union side. In 1862, however, they formed three Union Indian Home Guards regiments for duty in Indian Territory. About 3,500 men from the Territory served in these units. Eventually, Indians were recruited in nearly every northern state.

The Confederacy recruited Indians in Indian Territory, which figured prominently in Confederate designs for the West because of its geographic position and economic importance. Albert Pike negotiated treaties with the Cherokee, Creek, Seminole, Chickasaw, and Choctaw (Five Tribes) and with other tribes, persuading them to militarily support the South despite opposition within each tribe. Altogether, around ten thousand Indians in more than twenty-five separate units were raised by the Confederacy in Indian Territory. The Indian troops took part in some of the principal early battles west of the Mississippi.

By the end of the war, the Five Tribes had lost over six thousand people from a population of sixty thousand. The economy of Indian Territory was destroyed, and many Indian families were homeless. Even though as many members of the Five Tribes in Indian Territory had served in the Union army as with the Confederates, the U.S. government declared their treaties null and void. The tribes were forced to renegotiate and cede half their land as a home for other Indians.

Violent Indian–white clashes bloodied Civil War history. In 1862, the Santee Dakotas attacked whites in Minnesota, their resentments fired, in part, by the failure of the government to deliver needed goods.

In the Southwest, Union Colonel James Henry Carlton turned his attention to total warfare against raiding Mescalero and Jicarilla Apache and Navajo provoked by citizens intent on capturing and selling Navajo as slaves. Carlton called on Christopher "Kit" Carson to round up Apache and Navajo and ship them to Bosque Redondo, a forty-square-mile reservation on the Pecos River in New Mexico. Many Mescalero fled to Mexico.

In 1864, Carson had to starve the Navajo out, steal their horses and sheep, burn their crops and peach orchards, and destroy hogans before he succeeded in forcing eight thousand Navajo to walk some 350 miles to the reservation, where they remained in captivity for five years.

In Colorado, Black Kettle's band of peaceful Cheyennes, confident they were safe from attack by militia, camped at Sand Creek, near Fort Lyon, on Territorial Governor John Evans's authorization. On November 29, 1864, they were wantonly massacred by Colonel John M. Chivington, who ordered his one hundred-day enlistees to "kill and scalp all, big and little."

RESERVATION POLICY, 1850–1890

During the Civil War, the federal government turned its attention to the area west of the Mississippi. It asserted its exclusive authority to enter into treaties with Indian nations to secure further cessions of their homelands. Small portions were reserved for the use of the tribes, and they were required to relocate to these smaller portions, called "reservations." In addition to the goal of acquiring as much land as possible for Euro-American settlement, reservations were seen as necessary to keep Indian people separate from white people, to minimize conflict between the two groups, and to start the "civilization" process. The treaty reservations were portrayed to Native nations as permanent "homelands." Eventually, the government periodically reopened negotiations with tribes to gain further land cessions.

Initially, federal policy was to keep Native populations racially segregated until "civilized." This was carried out by confining all Indians to a general area, such as the Indian Territory. This barrier philosophy ended because of the pressures of westward expansion, which virtually eliminated the line. By the 1860s, the government had confined tribes in the West to separate parcels with specific boundaries.

CONFLICT EVERYWHERE

Between 1850 and 1890, incessant conflicts took place on the Plains and in Texas, the Southwest, the Pacific states, California, and the Basin–Plateau

An 1856 illustration from an issue of *Harper's* magazine depicts members of the Chetco tribe, natives of the Oregon territory who tried unsuccessfully to keep white settlers out of their homeland.

areas. Missionary writings encouraged more American settlements in Oregon country.

After Oregon and Washington Territories were created in 1853, the U.S. government pressured tribes in the region to agree to reservations in 1855, which separated Indians from whites. During the 1850s, however, Rogue River Indians of southern Oregon unsuccessfully tried to resist non-Indian settlers and miners who had moved onto their lands. Miners poured into Spokane country in Washington Territory when gold was discovered. Mining towns soon crowded out Indian villages in the Wallowa Valley of northeastern Oregon in the 1860s. The Yakama of eastern Washington led a pan-Indian resistance in 1855–1856. Eventually, troops defeated tribes in Idaho, Oregon, and Washington with the Indians relocated to reservations and their "excess" lands opened to settlers.

During the gold rush period (1848–1855) in California, whites poured over Indian villages and hunting and fishing grounds. By the early 1850s, the American government extinguished Indian titles to California land and established reservations for Indians, by agreement, not treaties, between 1853 and 1860. California Native populations, already decimated by the mission system of the eighteenth and early nineteenth centuries, declined even more due to armed conflicts with Americans, disease, depletion of the food supply, and starvation.

In Texas, laws denying Indians all rights resulted in guerrilla warfare between the Texas Rangers and Comanches, Kiowas, and bands of Apache for several decades until the Indians were defeated. The Spanish, Mexicans, and Texans, in turn, almost completely exterminated Texas Indians.

Although some warfare had occurred earlier, the years between 1860 to 1877 witnessed the major assault by the U.S. government on the lands of the Plains Indians and the general defensive warfare waged by the Lakota (Sioux), Cheyenne, Arapaho, Kiowa, Kiowa Apache, and Comanche from the Dakotas to Texas. White settlers encroached on Sioux lands between 1861 and 1870, especially in South Dakota's Black Hills

during the 1870s. In 1868, Indian peace commissioners were appointed to make peace with so-called belligerent tribes throughout the West.

Between 1860 and 1886, Apache bands in Arizona and New Mexico waged "hit and run" warfare against large numbers of U.S. troops and citizens, who were encouraged to kill Apache. One by one, Apache leaders surrendered, were killed, became prisoners of war, like Geronimo, or were forced onto reservations.

The encroachment of Euro-American entrepreneurs, merchants, adventurers, miners, and homesteaders on Indian lands and their destructive exploitation of natural resources impoverished Indian people who depended on plant and animal life for survival. Indians retaliated by attacking the trespassers. The government replied by all-out military campaigns and forcing Native peoples onto reservations.

Between 1860 to 1890, as white settlements continued to expand over Indian lands, they wiped out two great buffalo herds. The southern buffalo herd was destroyed by 1880, and the northern herd was almost gone from the Plains by 1885. The whites usurped and depleted other resources—game, wood, and water—with government encouragement.

INDIAN OFFICE IN CHARGE

The Indian Office (now called the Bureau of Indian Affairs) was responsible for overseeing and running the reservations. Agencies were established on each reservation. Schools, farm buildings, storerooms, offices, and housing were built for agency employees. The Indian Office funded reservation schools, and the agents oversaw the training of Indian men in agricultural methods. The Indian Office's field personnel grew by 1,000 percent between 1852 and 1872.

A major duty of the Indian Office was to provide subsistence for the people who were confined to the reservations. After 1871, Congress officially ended treaty making with Native nations and it made "agreements" instead, which were then "confirmed" by congressional action. The federal government began treating Indians as wards and the government as their guardian. Indian agents were responsible for distributing annuity goods, food rations, and supplies on a regular basis. For example, the 1876 agreement with the Sioux, which reduced the size of their reservation, stipulated that until the Sioux were able to support themselves, the government would supply to each Indian "a pound and a half of beef, one-half pound of flour, and one-half pound of corn; for every one hundred rations, four pounds of coffee, eight pounds of sugar, and three pounds of beans." During this time, the Indian Office was growing increasingly corrupt. The Indian Police Commission, appointed to examine the problem, in 1867 reported: "The records are abundant to show that agents have pocketed the funds appropriated by the government and driven the Indians to starvation."

During President Ulysses S. Grant's administration (1869–1877), the Indian Office was reorganized in the hope of eliminating inefficiencies and corrupt agents. A major reform was in the way field personnel were chosen. Agents were no longer selected from political ranks but were chosen from nominees submitted by missionaries in the field. Grant's crusade against corruption eventually resulted in an important reform, the 1883 Civil Service Act, which, for the first time, required competency as a basis for eligibility for federal jobs. However, the Indian Office was not initially subject to the provisions of this act.

FEDERAL ASSIMILATION POLICIES, 1870s–1880s

By 1877, powerful white armies and technology militarily defeated the Plains Indians and destroyed their economies. They were confined to reservations and subjected to Indian Office programs of cultural assimilation designed to train them to become farmers. The assimilation policy was multifaceted. It included the use of In-

dian agents, who were often missionaries, the formation of "tribal police forces" established by the Indian Office in 1878, and courts under the administrative control of agents. The Office frequently appointed "chiefs" through whom it governed the tribes. The agency supplanted a traditional tribal government and reinforced the norms of Anglo-American culture.

Boarding Schools

At the end of the 1870s, the federal government removed large numbers of Indian children from their families and communities and placed them in distant federal boarding schools such as the precedent-setting Carlisle Indian Industrial School in Carlisle, Pennsylvania, founded in 1879 in a closed army installation. The school was an experiment to test the feasibility of educating Indians in boarding schools far from tribal and parental influence. Lieutenant Richard Henry Pratt, a former Indian fighter and founder of Carlisle, took the idea a step further. He began a practice called "outing," in which students were not allowed to return home for vacations but were placed as servants with white families. In 1882, the government authorized using abandoned military forts and stockades as schools and the use of military officers as teachers. By 1885, there were 177 government schools spread across the country, many run by government-funded church groups. In a 1903 address to the National Education Association, the superintendent of the Haskell Indian School claimed: "A really civilized people cannot be found in the world except where the Bible has been sent and the gospel taught; hence, we believe that the Indians must have, as an essential part of their education, Christian training."

At the schools, children, stripped of their hair and Native clothing, wore military uniforms, were forced to speak English, prohibited from speaking their Native language, and subjected to a routine of discipline and moral Christian training. The boarding school policy broke down Native families. An important part of this policy was to institute a social norm that would exalt the in-

A circa 1900 photograph shows students at the Carlisle Indian Industrial School in Pennsylvania. For decades, children were forcefully taken from their families and prevented from learning their own language and culture.

dividual and nuclear family structures of non-Indian society. Boarding school students began to view themselves as belonging to a "race" of Indians rather than as tribal members from several hundred distinct tribal or cultural entities. Thousands of children never returned home—they either died and were often buried in unmarked graves, or they moved to other areas, having lost the connection to their families and cultures.

A few proponents of the boarding school policy strengthened their positions by pointing out the high rate of success of individual athletes and sports teams. Indeed, it seemed as if Haskell and Carlisle churned out Olympians, national title holders, hall of famers, and professional players in record numbers. Some nationally known sports greats include: professional baseball, basketball, or football players Charles Albert "Chief" Bender (Ojibwe), Jimmie Johnson (Stockbridge/Munsee), Emmett McLemore (Cherokee), Nicholas Anthony Lassa (Flathead), Wilson "Buster" Charles (Oneida); Olympians Louis Tewanima (Hopi), Billy Mills (Lakota),

Jessie B. "Cab" Renich (Choctaw)—also a pro basketball star—Ellison Myers Brown (Narragansett), and, most prominently, Jim Thorpe (Sauk and Fox), still considered to be the "greatest athlete who ever lived." There were dozens more. Many boarding school alumni played for the National Football League's (NFL) all-Indian team, the Oorang Indians (1922–23), which Thorpe coached. Based in LaRue, Ohio, the team was part of an advertising campaign for the Oorang Dog Kennel Company. Except for one played at home, all of their games were away. It was considered a "novelty" team, and besides being a "novel" idea and the only all-Indian team in the NFL, it also put LaRue, Ohio, on the map, which still remains the only town with a population under one thousand to have been the home of an NFL franchise or probably any professional team in any league in the United States.

Some argue that these successful athletic programs perpetuated the stereotype that Indians were purely physical beings, animalistic and better at physical feats than mental ones. It is possible that the boarding school organizers had these opinions of Native peoples, who traditionally used games to settle disputes so that war could be avoided or had games as part of sacred practice. However, sports and games were probably the only time boarding school students felt free and able to move their young bodies and in a fun way. Most boarding schools bullied children into doing hard manual labor—yes, it was exercise, but any child would be happier playing games than working at backbreaking tasks. Native culture is holistic—spiritual, mental, and physical balance is required to attain harmony. For these children, ripped from their homes and that balance, sports may be what saved them. It is no surprise that they became good at it. In fact, some joke that the Carlisle football team beating all the white teams, including the Ivy League colleges, was what prompted the school to be closed. Others say that these Indian athletes saved the game of football, and people began to take it seriously.

Of course, there were other individuals who, like the amazing and famous athletes, thrived—not all of the students' experiences were fraught with doom and gloom, but for the most part, the schools caused much harm and grief. They were intended to "kill the Indian and save the man" (U.S. Army Capt. Richard Henry Pratt, c. 1880). The decades of abuse created intergenerational trauma that some, like Dr. Andy Smith (Cherokee), have described as "soul wounding." In traditional societies, violence against women, children, and elders was virtually nonexistent. Women were generally revered and held in a high status within the community. That has changed, and many blame it on the "soul-wounding" and cultural genocide caused by boarding schools, patterned after the dominant culture's punitive and patriarchal style of teaching. Today, violence against Native women is three and a half times higher than for any other ethnic group in the U.S., according to the Department of Justice's Bureau of Justice Statistics, and most of the time, Native women are victims of sexual assault fifty percent more than non-Native women, with the crime generally perpetrated by non-Indian men. Substance abuse and suicide rates are higher for those

trapped in the boarding school cycle of sorrow. Researchers are just beginning to establish quantitative links between these soaring, and some say epidemic, rates and the legacy of boarding schools.

Native people have organized across the country to seek restitution and acknowledgment of wrongdoing from the government and churches for the crushing damage caused by their boarding school policies. They have also come together as individuals and communities to mend the "soul wounds," and support groups, ceremonies, therapy, and other healing modalities have popped up to break the cycle of despair.

Assimilation Via Allotment

After the Civil War and through the turn of the century, movements to reform Indian affairs developed because of the desperate situation of Indian peoples. President Grant's Peace Policy had two components, the Board of Indian Commissioners and the appointment of different evangelizing missionary societies to Indian reservations. Antimilitaristic reformers fought off the army, which wanted to resume control of Indian policy and transfer the Indian Bureau to the War Department. Organizations such as the Board of Indian Commissioners, the Indian Rights Association, and the Lake Mohonk Conference of Friends of the Indians tried to persuade the government to allot reservations in severalty (distribute parcels of reservation lands to individuals), assimilate Indians through formal schooling, and dissolve Indian nations of Indian territory, lands that were coveted by farmers. The reformers believed that by breaking up reservations, dissolving tribes, and making individual Indians into property owners, the problem of assimilating Indians into the American mainstream would be solved. The policy of allotting lands in severalty to Indians was not a new idea. Wresting land from Indians through allotments first appeared in Indian treaties in 1817 and became a regular feature of treaties with tribes in the Kansas and Nebraska Territories and other areas from 1854 to 1887, when the General Allotment Act enshrined the allotment philosophy into federal law.

THE KINGDOM OF HAWAI'I

Across the Pacific Ocean, Hawaiian culture was flourishing with all of the intrigue and dynamics of any civilization. It developed in quite a different way from Native cultures on the mainland. There was a strict social hierarchy with a caste system and royalty. In 1778, Captain James Cook landed on Kauai at Waimea Bay and named the archipelago the "Sandwich Islands" in honor of the Earl of Sandwich. Although the Hawaiians killed Cook for disrespecting kapu (ancient code of laws) just a year later, he had opened the doors to the west, changing Hawai'i (Hawaii) forever. In 1791, King Kamehameha I the Great started to unite the warring factions and went on to unify all of the Hawaiian Islands into one royal kingdom in 1810. European and

King Kalakaua was forced to sign a constitution that reduced Hawaiians' voice in government.

American imperialists began to build sugar and pineapple plantations, but the monarchy controlled immigration and trade.

King Kalākaua was forced to sign the "Bayonet Constitution" in 1887, sharply curtailing his powers and diminishing the Native Hawaiians' voice in government. This constitution was never ratified properly by the House of Nobles and thus was never legally valid. Most Native Hawaiians agree that the constitution of 1864 is the last valid constitution of the kingdom and the basis for restoration today.

In 1893, the United States minister assigned to the sovereign and independent Kingdom of Hawaii, John L. Stevens, connived with non-Hawaiian residents of the kingdom, including citizens of the United States, to overthrow the lawful government of Hawaii. He ordered the U.S. Navy to invade Hawaii and imprison Hawaiian Queen Lili'uokalani. Stevens then extended diplomatic recognition of a provisional government formed by the conspirators. In spite of support from President Grover Cleveland, the kingdom never regained its sovereignty. The fate of Native Hawaiians paralleled that of other Indigenous people, from loss of land and power to destruction of language and natural resources.

THE GENERAL ALLOTMENT ACT

Land Loss

The General Allotment Act, also called the Dawes Act after Senator Henry L. Dawes of Massachusetts (1816–1903) who sponsored it, ignored Indian land use patterns that were thousands of years old. It enshrined in law the idea the American Indians should be assimilated into white civilization, embrace agrarian values, and become individual landowners. The act gave the U.S. president the right to dissolve "any reservation created for [Indians'] use, either by treaty stipulations or by virtue of an act of Congress or executive order" if in his "opinion" it would be "advantageous for agricultural and grazing purposes." The president then could allot the land to individual Indians living there. Reservation lands left over were designated "surplus" lands and sold off to non-Indian "settlers."

Nearly all tribal members received allotments of land. Indian heads of family received 160-acre allotments of reservation land; single persons over eighteen years and orphans regardless of age received eighty acres. Boys under eighteen years received forty acres. Married Indian women were not entitled to acreage. Any remaining land the government put up for public sale or would buy from the Indians and open to homesteaders under the 1862 Homestead Act.

The federal government retained trusteeship over the individual's allotment for twenty-five years, protecting land from taxation during that time while Indians established their "competency." After the trust period ended, the individual allotment holder would hold the land free and clear but would then have to pay property taxes on the land. Many Indian people lost their allotment because they couldn't afford to pay the taxes. If an Indian died during the twenty-five-year trust period, the act required division of land according to state or territory inheritance laws where the allotment was located. Indians of future generations were landless except for property acquired through heirs.

The Indian Office managed all the details involved in the allotment process. Agents reviewed tribal rolls and decided who was and who was not eligible to be a member of a specific tribe. The agents were responsible for surveying land, dividing it up, and allotting portions to individuals. The office hired farmers to teach Indian men how to farm and raise cattle on their land. Reservation agencies bought equipment, seeds, tools, and livestock to help transform hunters into farmers and ranchers, but there was never enough money to accomplish the goal. During the first twelve years of the allotment program, the government spent approximately $1.62 per allottee for supplies, seeds, equipment, and livestock, hardly enough money to plant a flower garden and not nearly enough money to buy farm machinery or livestock.

Agents gradually became real estate agents for all reservation land, leasing and collecting rents and handling the income, which was placed in trust accounts for the allottees. An act in 1902 authorized the sale of land belonging to heirs of allottees, and in 1907, a congressional act provided that the Bureau of Indian Affairs (BIA) could sell land belonging to original allottees. Much of the allotted land was unsuitable for farming, and many Indians could not farm their land because they lacked equipment. In addition, there was a cultural bias among some tribal people, who did not consider farming men's work. In 1906, the Burke Act authorized Indians who were judged competent to sell their land although the twenty-five-year trust period had not expired, and many Indians, unable to make a living from the land, sold it.

The act resulted in a devastating loss of tribal lands. According to scholars Vine Deloria, Jr. (Dakota) and Clyfford Lytle, Indian landholdings were reduced from a total of 138 million acres in 1887 to 48 million acres in 1934, when the Indian Reorganization Act ended the allotment policy. By the end of allotment, one hundred thousand Indians were landless, deprived of over ninety million acres of reservation land.

According to Steven Newcomb (Shawnee/ Lenape), the founder of the Indigenous Law Institute, "allotment was a massive grab of Indians' lands by the U.S. government. It was an effort to make Indian peoples no longer understand themselves as nations and an effort to cut their cultural connections to their traditional lands." The act also opened up Indian land for Euro-American settlers eager to fulfill the mandate of Manifest Destiny, a nineteenth-century belief rooted in the Christian Doctrine of Discovery that American citizens had a God-given right to possess all the land between the Atlantic and Pacific oceans.

A massive loss of Indian property resulted from the clause in the Dawes Act requiring estates to be partitioned in accord with state or territorial inheritance law, which maximized the number of heirs to an allotment and minimized the acreage each heir received. In 1910, a reform law

INDIAN LAND FOR SALE

GET A HOME		PERFECT TITLE
OF		✳
YOUR OWN		POSSESSION
✳		WITHIN
EASY PAYMENTS		THIRTY DAYS

FINE LANDS IN THE WEST

IRRIGATED IRRIGABLE   **GRAZING**   **AGRICULTURAL DRY FARMING**

IN 1910 THE DEPARTMENT OF THE INTERIOR SOLD UNDER SEALED BIDS ALLOTTED INDIAN LAND AS FOLLOWS:

A poster announcing the availability of land seized from Natives to go up for sale for non-Indian settlers.

permitted allottees to limit the number of heirs so as to pass on inheritances large enough to be useful. By the late 1920s, federal officials were faced with a growing Indian population living on a fixed and severely limited amount of land. Tribes attempted to reopen tribal rolls to provide land to children born since the first allotments. Many of these children were born to second-generation Indians, who sold heirship lands under the 1902 law and had no hope of ever obtaining land unless new allotments were made.

Congress also enacted laws that allowed speculators to acquire large tracts of public lands to lease to timber and mining companies. The 1920 Mineral Leasing Act also eased access to Indian lands.

INDIAN OFFICE INTRUSIONS INTO NATIVE DAILY LIFE

With tribal institutions seriously undermined by military defeat and the land base broken up through allotment, the Bureau of Indian Affairs (BIA) began to intrude on the daily lives and personal habits of the people in their care. In 1901, the commissioner of Indian affairs issued a circular to agents in the field detailing BIA actions toward Indian customs that "should be modified or discontinued." Forbidden were the wearing of long hair by males, face painting of both sexes, and wearing Indian dress. Dances and feasts were forbidden on the grounds that they were "simply subterfuges to cover degrading acts and to disguise immoral purposes." Offenders could be punished by having rations, which were owed to Indians in exchange for land, withheld or by imprisonment at hard labor.

The reservation system became the arena for a forced experiment in social change. Reservations were occupied by a legion of paternalistic bureau brainwashers who took over and effectively became the government of the tribe. BIA employees became the teachers and the health care workers. They provided police protection, built and ran schools and hospitals, and maintained roads. They employed farmers, stockmen, teachers, and administrators to run every aspect of the lives of reservation Indians.

The BIA continued to operate on the premise that the "Indian problem" would be solved when there were no more identifiable Indians. It was assumed that it was necessary to force Indian people into giving up their heritage. It did not occur to the reformers of that time that there was anything about Indian culture that should be encouraged. By the early twentieth century, it was obvious that allotment, education, and coercion failed to turn Native Americans into prosperous Christian farmers; rather, the results were enclaves of poverty-stricken, landless people surrounded by growing numbers of whites.

John Collier served as commissioner of the Bureau of Indian Affairs during the FDR Administration. He championed the "Indian New Deal" that tried to reverse the damage done by earlier attempts to assimilate Natives into white culture.

MERIAM REPORT

In the 1920s, there was a growing concern that Indian affairs were being mishandled. A reform movement was led by John Collier, one of the founders of the American Indian Defense Association. He championed the rights of Native Americans to freedom of religion and defended the land rights of the Pueblo people of the Southwest. Several Indian defense societies called for investigations into the conditions of Indian people, and in 1926, the secretary of the interior authorized the Institute for Government Research (now the Brookings Institution) to conduct a study of the BIA. The resulting report, "The Problem of Indian Administration," commonly called the Meriam Report after Lewis Meriam who headed the study, was severely critical of the BIA and its programs. The publication in 1928 of the

Meriam Report was the beginning of a shift in policy in the BIA.

The Meriam Report recommended an end to allotment, better pay for bureau employees, the hiring of Indians in the BIA, and more funds for health and education. In 1933, President Franklin D. Roosevelt appointed John Collier as Indian Affairs Commissioner. Collier instituted an "Indian New Deal," and many of the recommendations of the Meriam Report were enacted in the 1934 Indian Reorganization Act (IRA), or the Wheeler–Howard Act.

THE HAWAIIAN HOMES COMMISSION ACT

Sponsored by Prince Jonah Kūhiō Kalaniana'ole, Hawaii's delegate to Congress, the Hawaiian Homes Commission Act (1921) was to preserve almost two hundred thousand acres in Hawaii for homesteading by Native Hawaiians. It was just a tiny fraction of crown lands taken from the Kingdom of Hawaii at annexation and did not include the prime agricultural lands, which were primarily occupied by sugar plantations. The Act stated that people with fifty percent or more Hawaiian ancestry were eligible to apply for ninety-nine-year land leases at $1 per year. The first leases granted were mostly forty-acre agricultural parcels, but more recently, residential lots as small as a quarter of an acre have been awarded. Approximately 6,500 families presently live on thirty thousand acres of homestead land. The majority of Hawaiian Homes lands are leased out to big businesses, providing income for the program's administration, but many argue that this policy is counter to the Act's intent. Federal, state, and county governments have also acquired large tracts of designated Hawaiian Homes land, sometimes illegally and most often without compensation. Over forty thousand families are on a waiting list for homelands. Many of the parcels are far from employment and services. It is also difficult to obtain mortgages.

INDIAN "NEW DEAL": THE INDIAN REORGANIZATION ACT

The Indian Reorganization Act (IRA) was important in that its passage marked a dramatic shift in government policy. The act repealed the forty-seven-year-old allotment system and forbade further allotments of Indian land and the sale to whites of unallotted or heirship lands. The law proposed that Indian nations organize their governments under written tribal constitutions. Its fundamental aims were development of Indian economic resources and restoration of Indian self-determination through revival of tribal governments.

The original IRA gave tribes one year to vote on whether to accept or reject the IRA. The government decided that tribes that did not vote to exclude themselves from the IRA were automatically included under the act. In some cases, opposition was strong and participation in voting was discouraged. However, under BIA interpretation, a "no-show" vote was considered a "yes" vote. From 1934 to 1936, BIA records indicate that 181 tribes voted to accept the IRA and seventy-seven tribes voted to reject the act.

The BIA drafted IRA constitutions for tribes with little or no tribal input. IRA constitutions ignored traditional tribal governments that had existed for thousands of years. Despite differences that existed from one tribal government to another, the BIA used a "boiler-plate" constitution for most tribes.

Tribes, at their own option, could incorporate under provisions of the act and elect tribal governments invested with certain legal powers. A revolving-loan fund was created for economic development, and provisions were included for scholarships for Indians attending vocational and trade schools, Indian employment preference for federal government jobs, and adding land to reservations. The act invested the interior secretary with a great deal of power in approving tribal constitutions, vetoing certain tribal council actions, and making rules for managing forests and grazing lands. Also in 1934, Congress enacted the Johnson–O'Malley Act to promote, with federal monies, federal–state cooperation in providing services to Indians, especially in education.

The Indian New Deal was not entirely successful. Hostility in Congress and a misunderstanding of Indian needs by the white community hampered the reform program. Tribal reorganization failed because Collier and his coworkers had basic misconceptions about Indian peoples and how they functioned. New tribal governments elicited little support among the people they were supposed to represent. There was intra-tribal factionalism and rivalry, and the political structures that were established were foreign to Native societies.

INDIAN CLAIMS COMMISSION

In 1946, Congress created the Indian Claims Commission (ICC) to adjudicate claims against the U.S. government by tribes for compensation for land stolen during the treaty period. Before the commission was created, claims of tribes, bands, and other groups against the United States could only be brought to court if Congress authorized the action. This state of affairs lasted until 1978, when unheard claims were transferred back to the Court of Claims. The ICC granted awards, not land, to cases brought before it.

TERMINATION (1950s)

After the reforms of the 1930s, the policies of the next two decades reflected a backlash. In 1943, a congressional study again found serious problems in the administration of Indian affairs. This time, the "Indian problem" was to be solved by ending the special relationship between Indians and the federal government. Many Native leaders felt that the trust status of Indian land

A big reason for the decision to terminate the relationship between tribes and the U.S. federal government was the desire to exploit resources such as Oregon lumber that was on tribal land.

protected their land base. They felt threatened by laws that ended that relationship and subjected land to taxation. In 1947, the BIA began to identify Indian groups that they believed were able to manage without the benefit of the federal trust relationship and services to Indian tribes. More than one hundred tribal groups were singled out as ready for "termination."

One factor determining "readiness" was a tribe's commercially valuable resources, especially their timber and mineral resources. The Klamath Tribe in Oregon and Menominee Tribe in Wisconsin both possessed reservations with rich timber resources. Each tribe selected for termination was then required to agree to a "plan" to make termination happen, which generally included abolishing the reservation, selling Native lands and natural resources, and making payments to tribal members.

In 1953, Congress adopted House Concurrent Resolution 108, which called for termination of the federal relationship with tribes as soon as possible. The ultimate goal of termination was that a "tribe" would no longer have any viable purpose, that individual Indians would move to urban areas and live exactly like their non-Indian neighbors. Although Indian opposition to termination was substantial, congressional opposition was meager, and the consent of affected Indian groups was not considered necessary to the implementation of the termination policy. Within a year after the adoption of HCR 108, Congress began passing individual acts designed to carry forward the termination policy.

Between 1953 and 1966, Congress terminated around 109 tribes and bands, which included California Rancherias (tiny reservations), the Poncas of Nebraska, Peoria, Ottawa, and Wyandot Tribes in Oklahoma, the Klamath Tribe of Oregon, sixty-one other tribes and bands in western Oregon, the Catawba of South Carolina, the Alabama–Couchatta of Texas, the Southern Paiutes, Utes of the Uintah, the Ouray of Utah, and the Menominee of Wisconsin.

Certain provisions were common to most termination bills. Periods ranging from two to five years were authorized for completion of the termination process. During that time, final tribal rolls were to be prepared. After completing the rolls, each tribal member was to be given a personal property right in the undivided tribal assets. Various methods for distribution were authorized.

Termination legislation ended most aspects of the historic relationship between the federal government and the terminated tribes, transferring responsibility for those tribes to the states. Federal programs of education, health, welfare, and housing assistance as well as other social programs were no longer available. State legislative jurisdiction was imposed, giving state and local legislative bodies broad authority over terminated Indians in matters basic to Indian cultural integrity, such as education, adoption, and land use. Moreover, affected Indians became subject to state taxation from which they previously had enjoyed immunity. Since state judicial jurisdiction was imposed, criminal and civil cases were handled by state courts, and federal and tribal law were no longer applicable.

In addition, termination ended federal trusteeship over tribal and individual landholdings of terminated groups. Some reservations remained property held by the Indian government as a corporation. Others were allotted to individual members with the "surplus" sold to the government and retained as public land. Lands of many smaller tribes were sold and proceeds distributed among tribal members. Members of other affected tribes were permitted to choose between receiving payment and participation in private trusts or having their lands placed with Indian-controlled state corporations. Most, though not all, terminated tribes ultimately relinquished their lands, and once again, large amounts of Indian lands passed on to non-Indian hands.

Finally, another practical effect of termination was to remove the sovereignty of terminated tribes. Although the termination acts did not expressly extinguish the governmental authority of such tribes, most were not able to exercise their governmental powers after the loss of their land base.

Public Law 280

A major step toward termination of federal responsibility over Indian affairs was the passage in 1953 of Public Law 280. The law transferred criminal and civil jurisdiction over Indian lands from the federal to state governments in five states and allowed for future assumptions of jurisdiction by all other states—without Indian consent. PL 280 provided for the mandatory transfer of criminal and civil jurisdiction in California, Minnesota (except for Red Lake Reservation), Nebraska, Oregon (except for the Warm Springs Reservation), and Wisconsin (except for the Menominee Reservation). In 1958, Alaska was granted jurisdiction over Indian lands within its boundaries.

PL 280 extended to all other states the option of assuming jurisdiction on their own initiative at some future time. Indians criticized PL 280 in part because it did not include a provision requiring Indian consent to subsequent transfers of jurisdiction. By 1968, when Congress passed a statute requiring Indian consent, nine more states had extended partial or full jurisdiction over Indian lands within their boundaries.

RELOCATION: AN ASSIMILATION POLICY

In the early 1950s, the federal government launched a massive program to relocate reservation Indians to urban centers. World War II prompted some Indians to head for cities, where they worked in defense-related factories, but after the war, when the Indians returned home, they faced hard times on reservations, where jobs were few. Capitalizing on the lack of opportunities, the BIA offered employment assistance to Indians who would leave their reservations and relocate to urban communities. The tactic became another way for the government to get out of the Indian business; the chief of the BIA Relocation Division stated at the outset, "The sooner we can get out, the better it will be."

The Voluntary Relocation Program, renamed the Employment Assistance Program in 1954, provided one-way bus tickets, temporary, low-cost housing, and new clothing. The program expanded over the decade. Relocation field offices grew from the first two, in Chicago and Los Angeles, to twelve by 1958 by adding Denver, San Francisco, San Jose, St. Louis, Joliet, Waukegan, Oakland, Cincinnati, Cleveland, and Dallas. By 1960, only eight field offices remained, as numbers of jobs in cities decreased.

By 1953, the BIA established that one-third of Indians, discouraged by urban life, returned to reservations, yet many others stayed and more came. Home reservations devoid of economic opportunities propelled thousands of Indians to find work, and many did so in cities. Soon, Indian populations in cities outpaced some reservations.

In cities, Indians were separated from kinship ties, tribal languages, tribal communities, and ceremonies and were thrust into a strange environment. Indian centers were created to provide "a touch of traditional life." Centers sponsored powwows and social dance events that pro-

vided opportunities to perpetuate traditional Indian music and dance and other social, cultural, and spiritual activities for their multi-tribal populations. Centers found jobs for people and ran health clinics, daycare, and soup kitchens.

However, left alone in urban areas, far away from kin, relocated individuals became an undifferentiated part of the inner-city poor. Some families and individuals prospered, and some did not. Many tribal leaders preferred programs of economic development on reservations so that people would not have to leave in order to find work, but the BIA was not ready to involve the people in decisions about their destiny. The program ended in 1980.

Health Programs Transferred

In 1952, Congress authorized the interior secretary to transfer Indian health facilities to states or other governmental or private, nonprofit entities. The final step toward terminating BIA responsibility for Indian health care was taken in 1954 with the passage of Public Law 568, which provided for the transfer of the entire Indian health program to the U.S. Public Health Service in the Department of Health, Education, and Welfare. The transfer constituted the largest reduction of program responsibilities in the history of the BIA. This congressional action fit with termination goals to eliminate "laws which set Indians apart from other citizens" and to abolish "duplicating and overlapping functions provided by the Indian Bureau." At the same time, the government also aimed to transfer the basic responsibility for educating Indian children from the federal government to state public schools.

By the end of the 1950s, Indian resistance and national public protest caused the federal government to abandon its termination policies. By the mid-1960s, it was clear that termination usually resulted in further impoverishment, land loss, and unsupportable costs to state and local units of government. Congressional members began to speak out against termination, and even some formerly staunch supporters of assimilationist policies recanted as the inadequacies of

The seal of the Bureau of Indian Affairs. By the 1950s, the federal government was eager to get out of the responsibility for overseeing what happened to Native peoples and began transferring power to state and local officials.

the individual termination programs became increasingly apparent.

Termination Finally Repealed, 1988

The destructive impact of termination on Indian tribes was addressed by President Richard Nixon in 1970. In a special message to Congress, Nixon said, "Because termination is morally and legally unacceptable, because it produces bad practical results, and because the mere threat of termination tends to discourage greater self-sufficiency among Indian groups, I am asking the Congress to pass a new Concurrent Resolution which would expressly renounce, repudiate, and repeal the termination policy as expressed in House Concurrent Resolution 108 of the 83rd Congress. This resolution would explicitly affirm the integrity and right to continued existence of all Indian tribes and Alaska native governments."

It took Congress eighteen years to officially repeal its termination policy. Nevertheless, between 1973 and 1987, Congress restored federal recognition to many of the tribes terminated under the policy in the 1950s. The failure of Congress to repudiate the policy officially was seen by many Indians as a lingering threat to the federal trust relationship. Congress finally included repeal language in a major education reauthorization bill passed in 1988. Senator Daniel K. Inouye, chairman of the Select Committee on Indian Affairs, said, "Indian nations of the United States can rest easier with the knowledge that termination is no longer even a possible threat. Termination was a doomed policy from its inception primarily because it was both morally and legally indefensible."

NATIVE ACTIVISM IN THE 1960s AND 1970s

A nationwide Indian conference was held at the University of Chicago in June 1961. Over five hundred Indians from over ninety tribes and bands participated and created a "Declaration of Indian Purpose," which attacked termination and supported the right of a tribal community to maintain itself and develop with government assistance. The Conference helped mobilize a generation of Indian activists.

Native Organizations Founded

After the conference, there was a widespread organizational and activist response in Native communities, engendered in part by the civil rights era. The National Indian Youth Council, founded in 1961, and the American Indian Movement (AIM), founded in 1968, were part of a great proliferation of organizations on reservations and in cities. Dozens of Native newspapers and periodicals were established during the late 1960s and 1970s, including the influential *Akwesasne Notes*, which covered national news, published by the Mohawk Nation of New York State.

Important legal, political, and economic national organizations were also established: the National Indian Education Association, founded in 1969, the Native American Rights Fund, founded in 1970, the National Tribal Chairman's Association, founded in 1971, and the Council of Energy Resource Tribes, founded in 1975. These organizations provided lines of communication and represented Indian interests at various levels of government. These organizations contributed to a growing awareness of common problems and interests shared by many tribes as well as the growing urban Indian population. The growth of the urban Indian population contributed to the emergence of a national Native American activism movement, which came to be known as the Red Power movement.

During the 1960s, Indians began uniting to take control of their own future. A generation of Indian activists fired up with the need to take responsibility of their own communities forced the public and the federal government to look at problems confronting reservation tribes. The fish-in movement was launched in response to court and law-enforcement restrictions on North Pacific tribes' access to fishing, guaranteed by treaties. The fish-in movement provided a training ground for future activism in other parts of the U.S.

Alcatraz Island off of San Francisco is famous for being a former penitentiary, but in 1969 it was in the news when a group of Indians claimed it for their own.

Alcatraz Island Claimed By the "Right of Discovery"

On November 20, 1969, eighty-nine "Indians of all tribes" landed on Alcatraz Island, the former site of a U.S. federal penitentiary. The group claimed the island by the "right of discovery." Over the next nineteen months, the time was marked by proclamations, news conferences, powwows, celebrations, skirmishes, and negotiations with the federal government. The negotiations did not result in any plan for the future of Alcatraz Island. However, the occupation itself, which ended on June 11, 1971, heralded the beginning of a period of a greatly increased level of Indian activism in urban centers and reservations. Occupations represented a tactic designed to draw attention to Native historical and contemporary grievances. Most were short-lived.

"Trail of Broken Treaties"

During the 1970s, government buildings also became the sites of protests, including regional Bureau of Indian Affairs (BIA) offices in Cleveland and Denver, as well as the main BIA headquarters in Washington in 1972. The unplanned occupation of the BIA occurred at the end of "The Trail of Broken Treaties," a protest event involving caravans that traveled across the U.S. to convene in Washington at a large camp-in in order to dramatize and present Indian concerns at the national BIA offices. As a result of the breakdown of accommodations, protesters took over BIA offices for a week.

Wounded Knee II

No single event of the Red Power era more clearly illustrated the combination of Indian grievances and community tensions than the events on the Pine Ridge Reservation in the spring of 1973, a ten-week-long siege which came to be known as "Wounded Knee II." It involved a dispute within the Oglala Lakota Tribe. Reservation traditionalists asked AIM to assist them in their struggle against the elected chairman Richard Wilson, whose administration they charged was rife with corruption. Federal marshals and the Federal Bureau of Investigation (FBI) surrounded the hamlet, creating a standoff that drew national and worldwide media attention. Native militants, who were armed, made clear their intention to fight rather than surrender. The impasse finally ended with a negotiated settlement and withdrawal of both sides.

International Indian Treaty Council

Following the stand at Wounded Knee, AIM brought together thousands of Indigenous representatives, including people from Latin America and the Pacific, in a ten-day gathering that founded the International Indian Treaty Council (IITC), which applied for and received U.N. nongovernmental status in 1975. By the mid-1980s, it attracted grassroots Indigenous representatives from around the world. The IITC reached a milestone in 2007 when the U.N. General Assembly passed the Declaration on the Rights of Indigenous Peoples. Four members of the assembly voted in opposition: the U.S., Canada, New Zealand, and Australia. All four later changed their votes to approval.

"The Longest Walk"

The last major event of the era occurred in July 1978 when several hundred Native people marched into Washington, D.C., at the end of "The Longest Walk," a protest march that had begun five months earlier in San Francisco. The peaceful march was intended to symbolize the forced removal of Native people from their homelands and draw attention to continuing problems they faced.

Land and Water Rights

During the 1970s, Indian activism shifted to more legal forums. Tribes went to federal and state courts to claim land and protect their treaty rights. In the eastern United States, Indian groups claimed lands taken illegally by eastern states during the late 1790s. Based on a section of the Indian Trade and Intercourse Act of 1790 that stated "no sale of lands made by any Indians … shall be valid to any person or persons, or to any state … unless the same shall be made and duly executed at some public treaty, held under the authority of the United States," Indians in Maine, Rhode Island, and Connecticut succeeded in reclaiming some state lands illegally taken in violation of the 1790 law.

In the 1970s, Indian activists demanded that water rights be protected. As trustee of Indian resources, the federal government litigated scores of Indian water rights cases against states and private interests, especially in the Southwest, where water is scarce. Increasingly, Congress, the courts, and the administration have recognized a trust obligation to protect the land and its resources and to ensure that the people occupying the land have the services and financial resources to prosper in the future. These resources include fish, and the 1970s witnessed court actions taken by Indians in the Great Lakes and northern Pacific coast region to protect their treaty rights to fish at "accustomed" places ceded to the federal government in nineteenth-century treaties. The fish-in movement sought to lift court-mandated restrictions on tribal access to fishing.

MOVING TOWARD SELF-DETERMINATION, 1960s–1970s

During his 1960 campaign for president, John F. Kennedy pledged that as president, his administration "would see to it that the government of the United States discharges its moral obligation to our first Americans by inaugurating a comprehensive program for the improvement of their health, education, and economic well-being. There would be no change in treaty or contractual relationships without the consent of the tribes concerned. No steps would be taken by the federal government to impair the cultural heritage of any group." Kennedy's platform marked a change in the direction the U.S. would take on Indian affairs. He did not live to see his plans come to fruition, but his brother, Robert F. Kennedy, worked tirelessly on behalf of Indian people.

It was Kennedy's vice president, Lyndon Johnson, who, as president (1963–1969), was the first to call for a concrete national policy of Indian self-determination. Native Americans were included in much of the president's "Great Soci-

U.S. President Lyndon Johnson not only signed the Civil Rights Act that helped black Americans, but he also called for Indian self-determination.

ety" legislation. Agencies created to administer new poverty and community development programs were responsible for a major breakthrough in Indian policy. Under grant programs administered by those agencies, Indian communities were treated as viable units of local government capable of delivering services to their constituencies and eligible for national programs in addition to those special services they received from Bureau of Indian Affairs and the Indian Health Service. By 1968, sixty-three community action agencies served 129 reservations.

In 1966, President Johnson appointed Robert Bennett, an Oneida, commissioner of Indian affairs, the first Indian in almost a century to hold that office. Bennett supported greater Indian involvement in development and administration of bureau programs. BIA officials were directed to make use of the Bureau's authority to contract with Indian communities to operate Indian service programs.

On March 6, 1968, President Johnson delivered a "Special Message to the Congress on the Problems of the American Indian: 'The Forgotten American.'" The president proposed a "new goal for our Indian programs: a goal that ends the old debate about 'termination' of Indian programs and stresses self-determination; a goal that erases old attitudes of paternalism and promotes partnership and self-help." The president established by executive order the National Council on Indian Opportunity, a committee chaired by Vice President Hubert H. Humphrey, to coordinate the many agencies dealing with Indians and to promote Indian participation in planning Indian programs.

Tribal Colleges

During President Johnson's "Great Society" and war on poverty, the social and political environment was conducive to the notion of tribal governments chartering and operating schools of higher education for their own people. In the late 1960s and early 1970s, tribes began establishing tribal colleges. The first tribally controlled college was established in 1968 by the Navajo Nation. In 1972, there were six tribal colleges whose presidents founded the American Indian Higher Edu-

cation Consortium (AIHEC) as an informal collaboration among member colleges. Through AIHEC, tribal colleges nurtured a common vision and learned to see themselves as a national movement. Their work—research, advocacy, and lobbying—was done through volunteerism and came almost exclusively from the presidents, community members, and other tribal and local leaders. In 2015 AIHEC represented thirty-seven colleges in the United States and one Canadian institution and is the lifeline of these tribal colleges.

The widely accepted goals of Indian control over planning and implementation of Indian programs became the foundation of President Richard M. Nixon's Indian policy during his administration (1969–1974). In 1969, President Nixon appointed Louis Bruce, a Sioux–Mohawk, to head the BIA, only the third Indian to do so. Commissioner Bruce reorganized the BIA and appointed Native Americans to fill most of the positions in his administrative staff.

SELF-DETERMINATION ERA USHERED IN

Nixon articulated a new policy in his 1970 message to Congress, which ushered in what has been called the "era of self-determination." He stressed three points: (1) no tribe would be terminated without its consent, (2) tribal governments would be encouraged to take over federally funded programs for their benefit, and (3) tribes would be helped to become economically self-sufficient.

During the Nixon Administration, the Alaska Native land claims were settled with the passage in 1971 of the Alaska Native Land Claims Settlement Act. The law granted Natives legal title to some 44 million acres; in return, all Native claims in Alaska were extinguished. The law provided a $962.5 million cash award and division of Alaska into twelve geographic regions, each of which had a Native regional corporation. Alaska Natives became shareholders in either one of the twelve corporations or in a thirteenth corporation set up for nonresident Alaska Natives. Native village corporations, also created by the law, held surface rights to lands while the regional corporations held subsurface mineral rights.

In 1969, a special subcommittee of the Senate, chaired by Senator Robert Kennedy and later by his brother, Senator Edward Kennedy, issued a major report, "Indian Education: A National Tragedy—A National Challenge." The document concluded that Indian children faced widespread discrimination and saw little or no evidence of their cultures in the classroom. The report said children experienced feelings of "alienation, hopelessness, [and] powerlessness." The report denounced the federal policy of "coercive assimilation" as disastrous for the education of Indian children. The report recommended increased funding, a curriculum about Indian culture and language, and more Indian control over the school administration.

SELF-DETERMINATION LEGISLATION OF THE 1970s

Indian Education Act

Congress passed the Indian Education Act of 1972, a landmark legislation establishing a comprehensive approach to meeting the unique needs of American Indian and Alaska Native students from preschool to graduate-level education. The law provides services to American Indians and Alaska Natives that are not provided by the Bureau of Indian Affairs. The Indian Education Act established the Office of Indian Education and the National Advisory Council on Indian Education and provided federal funds for American Indian and Alaska Native education at all grade levels. It also empowered American Indian and Alaska Native parents to form advisory boards for federally operated boarding schools and for public schools that have programs for American Indian students.

Lands Restored

During the Nixon Administration, the sacred Blue Lake was restored to the Taos Pueblo in 1970, and 21,000 acres were returned to the Yakama in 1972, both significant restorations of land rather than financial awards, which were important results of the Nixon self-determination policy. Also during the Nixon era, in 1973, Congress reinstated the Menominee as a federally recognized tribe.

The U.S. government returned the sacred grounds of the Blue Lake region to the Taos Pueblo in 1970. This pueblo just outside of Taos, New Mexico, is among the oldest continuously inhabited structures in North America.

During the Ford Administration (1974–1977), the Havasupais succeeded in their peaceful struggle to get a trust title to a portion of their ancient homeland along the Grand Canyon's south rim. The 1975 Grand Canyon National Park Enlargement Act authorized the United States to hold in trust for the Havasupai 185,000 acres of the land they have used and occupied for centuries.

The Indian Self-Determination and Education Assistance Act

In 1975, the Indian Self-Determination and Education Assistance Act was passed. One of the most significant pieces of legislation since 1934, the law contained language repudiating termination policy, committing the federal government to a relationship with Indians, and obliging it to foster Indian involvement and participation in directing education and service programs.

The law began the process of bringing governance back to Indian Country. Prior to the act, tribes had little power. The BIA decided where Native children went to school, what leases on Indian land, timber, minerals, and water were contracted, and determined welfare payments to individual Indians. After the act was passed, tribes contracted to operate federally funded programs such as tribal government and courts, jails, social services, and other important functions. The year after contracting began, tribes contracted for eight hundred programs. By 1988, 348 tribes entered into nearly 1,500 contracts for a total of $300 million, approximately one-third of the total BIA budget.

Indian Health Care Improvement Act

Congress passed the Indian Health Care Improvement Act in 1976 to improve the health care system under the Indian Health Service. The law included scholarships to Native people to study medicine, dentistry, psychiatry, nursing, and pharmacy. The program funded the education of more than eight thousand students in health care fields.

The Indian Child Welfare Act

During the Carter Administration (1977–1981), Congress passed the Indian Child Welfare Act (ICWA) in 1978, which let tribes have some input in the adoption of Indian children and the placement of orphan children. This act responded to the fact that 25 to 35 percent of Indian children were taken away from their parents by non-Indian social service workers and others. They went to adoptive homes, foster homes, and child care institutions. The intention of missionaries and the BIA was to destroy Indian tribes, languages, and cultures by destroying Native families. The legislation faced opposition from some states that resented unprecedented federal intervention into family law, an area traditionally left to the states. The Mormon Church and some cabinet officers also objected. According to professor of law Charles Wilkinson, ICWA was "perhaps the most far ranging legislation ever enacted in favor of Indian rights and reaffirmed Supreme Court decision cases upholding exclusive tribal court jurisdiction over custody proceedings involving children who lived on the reservation. For off-reservation children, ICWA set transfer rules mandating state court judges to shift away many cases to tribal courts." The Court has upheld the act, and the practice of adopting Indian children into non-Indian families has been greatly reduced. Wilkinson wrote that "ICWA stands as a testament to how Indian leaders have mobilized in order to define and implement priorities."

The American Indian Religious Freedom Act

Also in 1978, Congress enacted the American Indian Religious Freedom Act (AIRFA). After outlawing Indian religions for a century and punishing Indians who practiced their religions, the federal government stopped suppressing and prosecuting Indians. Specific practices the government outlawed included the Sun Dance, the Bear Dance, potlatches, giveaways, the use of peyote, the use of sweat lodges, the use of sacred sites, and the use of eagle feathers in religious ceremonies. The law was designed to officially guarantee constitutional First

Amendment freedom of religion for Native peoples. The act requires federal agencies to respect the customs, ceremonies, and traditions of Native religions. At first, AIRFA was viewed as more of a policy statement rather than a mandate giving Indian people legally enforceable rights, but the National Park Service, Forest Service, and Bureau of Land Management gradually became responsive to traditional Native practitioners determined to practice their religions.

Religious Freedom Limited by the Supreme Court

Two U.S. Supreme Court rulings limited considerably those Native religious practices that the U.S. government promised to protect. In the 1988 decision *Lyng, Secretary of Agriculture, et al. v. Northwest Indian Cemetery Protective Association, et al.* the Court ruled in favor of permitting the U.S. Forest Service to pave a stretch of road in the high country of the Six Rivers National Forest sacred to the Karok, Yurok, and Tolowa Indians of Northern California. Furthermore, the Forest Service ignored its expert witness, who concluded that the road would destroy the religion of the three tribes. In the 1990 *Employment Division of Oregon v. Smith* case, the Court denied Alfred Smith unemployment benefits because he had been discharged from his position as a drug rehabilitation counselor for "misconduct." He attended a prayer meeting of the Native American Church and used peyote, a sacred, hallucinogenic cactus "button" as a sacrament in much the same way that wine is used in Holy Communion in the Catholic church, but the court failed to recognize the practice. The ruling alarmed the Indian community and the Christian–Judaic community as well, which organized a coalition to restore religious freedom through legislative means.

RESERVATION ECONOMIES HIT HARD, 1980s

During the 1980s, federal budget-cutting measures during President Ronald Reagan's administration (1981–1988) impacted reservation economies. Expenditures for Native Americans, which were reduced by 22 percent in one year, from $3.4 billion in 1982 to $2.7 in 1983, targeted essential tribal programs, including health-related Community Health Representatives, home construction monies, and BIA-funded education entitlements. Reagan and Bush (1989–1993) era budget-cutting measures led resource-poor reservations with few other economic opportunities to turn to high-stakes bingo parlors and gaming operations to replace funding lost as a result of drastic federal cuts. Some states, suspicious of the new independent source of tribal income, tried to control tribal gaming and claimed that tribes became havens for organized crime. The Cabazon, a small tribe in Southern California that operated a casino north of Palm Springs, won court cases against state and county governments that tried to shut it down. The U.S. Supreme Court finally upheld, in 1987, the sovereign right of a federally recognized tribe to conduct gaming enterprises on reservations despite state objections that California gaming laws applied on Indian reservations.

The Indian Gaming Regulatory Act

Congress followed in 1988 by passing the Indian Gaming Regulatory Act (IGRA) with the following objectives: to promote tribal self-sufficiency, to ensure that Indian tribes remain the primary beneficiaries of gaming revenues from reservation gaming activities, to establish procedures for fair and honest gaming, and to set standards for the National Indian Gaming Commission (NIGC), which has rule-making and regulatory powers. The IGRA assigned the responsibility of gaming regulation to the federal government rather than allowing the states to impose regulations. The government and tribes aimed to preserve gaming as a means of economic development on the reservation and to promote tribal self-sufficiency.

According to IGRA, Indian tribes are the primary regulators of Class I (traditional games)

Natives were assured the right to establish and profit from gambling facilities (this is the Viejas casino near Alpine, California) thanks to the Indian Gaming Regulatory Act of 1988.

and Class II gaming (bingo, pull tabs, lotto, punch boards, and certain card games not prohibited by the state in which the casino is located). Regulation of Class III gaming (baccarat, blackjack, chemin de fer, slot machines, and electronic facsimiles of any game of chance) is addressed in tribal-state compacts and varies by state. Giving states some control over gaming has worried many tribal leaders as a dangerous surrender of sovereignty for those Native nations operating casinos.

There is also a National Indian Gaming Association (NIGA), a nonprofit trade association comprised of 184 American Indian nations and other nonvoting associate members. NIGA operates as a clearinghouse and educational legislative and public policy resource for tribes, policymakers, and the public on Indian gaming issues and tribal community development.

Indian gaming as a business has grown phenomenally. By 1991, tribes were operating 130 legal operations. The advantages for tribes with viable locations were clear. Gaming eased reservation unemployment and increased the flow of dollars onto reservations, which filled the void caused by federal budget cuts. Many tribes used the money to improve fire and police depart-

ments and fund hospitals and health clinics, child care centers, college tuitions, retirement benefits and housing for elders, sewage systems, power plants, roads, new housing, and start-up business ventures. Some tribes have invested in large projects, such as the Smithsonian Institution's National Museum of the American Indian. Some profits have gone to lobbying politicians of state and federal governments.

Non-Indians assume Indians have gotten rich from gaming. Lack of knowledge has led to common misconceptions. Not every tribe has a casino. According to the *Indian Gaming Industry Report*, in 2013, there were 242 tribes operating 460 gaming facilities in twenty-eight states. That means around 320 tribes have no gaming operations. Indian gaming ranges from resort-style casinos to trailers with bingo.

Not every Native person has a job. Between 2007 and 2013, Native Americans endured unemployment rates in the double digits. According to the Economic Policy Institute, in the first half of 2013, the unemployment rate was 11.3 percent. In 2011, gaming facilities directly supported about 339,000 jobs nationwide although many of the jobs go to non-Indian employees. Indian gaming has brought tangible benefits to non-Indian communities around Indian nations.

Not every Native person gets money from casino profits. Tribal nations follow strict IGRA rules. Gaming profits must be used to fund tribal government operations or programs, provide for the general welfare of members, promote economic development, charitable donations, and fund operations of local government agencies. Revenue must be used to improve infrastructure, develop educational opportunities, and provide social programs for its peoples.

The interior secretary must approve a tribal revenue allocation plan before tribal members receive per capita (per person) payments. Most payments range from minimal payments like Christmas bonuses to amounts large enough to pay the rent. Highly publicized payments as high as hundreds of thousands of dollars a year per tribal member were made by a small number of tribes. Tribal councils have taken the long view. They invest in health, land management, law and order, and basic government responsibilities. Tribal chairman Eddie Tullis (Poarch Band of Creek Indians) said: "There is some pressure to start per capita payments to members, so the leadership needs to demonstrate that it can do more for the community by providing services." Besides publicity about fabulously high payments, attention has also been trained on off-reservation casinos and small tribes that seem to exist only for casino money.

At a July 2014 meeting, "Indian Gaming: The Next 25 Years" of the Senate Committee on Indian Affairs, tribal leaders noted how Indian gaming has helped some of the most struggling tribes over the last quarter of a century. Senator Al Franken (Democrat from Minnesota) noted that "there is a lot of debate about gaming in general, but one aspect that is undeniable is the economic development benefit of gaming to tribes." The assistant secretary for the interior, Kevin Washburn, said he "would shudder to think what Indian Country would look like without the revenues that come in from Indian gaming."

PROTECTING CULTURAL RESOURCES

During President George H. W. Bush's administration (1989–1993), American Indian and Alaska Native peoples expressed substantial interest in protecting, accessing, and controlling their cultural resources. These resources included not only land and objects but also traditions, languages, and symbols. Access to and usage of these cultural resources, as well as public awareness and understanding of Native cultural practices and traditions, were essential to the preservation of Native lifeways. Many of these resources were protected by tribal, state, or federal laws; some were not. Native peoples wanted assurance that current laws aimed at protecting tribal culture were properly enforced and that new laws and policies would be enacted to protect tribal culture as well.

Protecting Graves

A handful of federal laws were passed in 1990 that recognized the critical importance of protecting Native cultural resources. The Native American Graves Protection and Repatriation Act (NAGPRA) was enacted in 1990 to establish the rights of Indian tribes and their lineal descendants to obtain repatriation of certain human remains, funerary objects, sacred objects, and objects of cultural patrimony from federal agencies and museums. The National Congress of American Indians, the oldest, largest, and most representative American Indian and Alaska Native organization serving tribal governments and communities, reports that more than twenty years after its enactment, NAGPRA's policy goals have not been fully achieved.

Protecting Arts and Crafts

Similarly, the Indian Arts & Crafts Act (IACA) of 1990 was intended to protect tribal cultural resources by preventing the sale of goods that are falsely represented to have been made by Indians. However, IACA has been ineffective because of inadequate enforcement and weak penalties that do not sufficiently deter potential violators.

Protecting Languages

In 1990, the Native American Languages Act was passed to ensure the survival of traditional Native languages that are an integral part of their cultures and identities. Indian children, virtual hostages in government-run boarding schools far away from their parents and homes, were forbidden to speak their languages. Between 1886, when the commissioner of Indian affairs required all instruction in the English language, through the 1950s, federal policy destroyed or discouraged Indian languages in schools and public settings. Federal policy ran counter to the fact that "every human language is an exquisitely complex intellectual masterpiece, created and polished by untold generations, as the everperfect expression of their culture and experience ...," according to linguist Michael Krauss.

Hopi kachina dolls on display at the Heard Museum in Phoenix, Arizona. The Indian Arts & Crafts Act of 1990 prevents non-Indians from profiting off the sale of knock-off Native crafts, such as popular, fake kachina dolls.

Since the early 1990s, a growing number of Indigenous people in the U.S. and Canada have been advocating, lobbying, and developing language revitalization programs in their communities. In Indigenous communities, there is a stark reality that aged speakers are passing away and no younger members remain who speak the original languages. Immersion schools have proven to be one of the most successful models in producing fluent Native language speakers. However, establishing and operating immersion schools carries a significant cost beyond the current means of many tribes. The federal government needs to provide tribes with sufficient funding, training, technical support, and educational flexibility to revitalize their Native languages.

In 2010, the National Congress of American Indians declared that Native languages were in a state of emergency, reporting that seventy-four Native languages stood to disappear within the next decade. Equally alarming, scholars project that without immediate and persistent action, only twenty Native languages will still be spoken by 2050. This crisis is the result of long-standing government policies—enacted particularly through boarding schools—that sought to break the chain of cultural transmission and destroy American Indian and Alaska Native cultures.

TRIBAL SOVEREIGNTY CHALLENGED

Tribal people have long faced challenges to their sovereignty from Congress, federal, state, and other courts as well as organized opposition from small, regional anti-Indian organizations scattered throughout the country. Most vocal during the 1970s and 1980s, when Indian fishing rights were confirmed in the Pacific Northwest and Great Lakes, these groups wanted "nation unto nation" treatment of Native Americans abrogated, reservations terminated, and the BIA abolished. Successful in terms of staging demonstrations and attracting press attention, anti-Indian groups have used discontent, racism, and economic troubles to drive home their message that the "special treatment" of Indians deprives citizens of their hopes and dreams.

TRIBAL SOVEREIGNTY, 1990s

During the 1990s, President Bill Clinton became the first president to invite the leaders of all federally recognized tribes to the White House in April 1994. He pledged that his administration (1993–2001) would work with tribal leaders to establish a true government-to-government partnership. His "Memorandum for the Heads of Executive Departments and Agencies" directed them to consult, to the greatest extent practicable and to the extent permitted by law, with federally recognized tribal governments prior to taking actions that affected them. This executive order served to establish regular and meaningful consultation and collaboration with Indian tribal governments in the development of regulatory practices on federal matters that significantly or uniquely affected their communities.

President Clinton created the Office of Tribal Justice to promote government-to-government relations with Indian tribes and ensure aggressive representation of tribal sovereignty in the courts. He also created a permanent White House working group composed of all executive-branch departments to advance tribal sovereignty across the administration.

On August 6, 1998, the Clinton Administration held the first White House Conference on Economic Development in Indian Country. At the conference, President Clinton directed the Department of the Interior, the Department of Commerce, and the Small Business Administration to develop, in consultation with other interested parties, including tribal governments, a strategic plan for coordinating existing federal economic development initiatives for Native American and Alaska Native communities. The agencies presented their plan to the president in December 1998. In July 1999, the Department of Commerce issued a report on the infrastructure technology needs in Indian Country.

President Clinton appointed the most diverse cabinet and administration in history. He appointed seventy-six Native Americans to all levels of his administration, including thirteen to top positions requiring Senate confirmation and forty-three to presidential appointment positions. Among the Native Americans serving in the Clinton Administration were Kevin Gover, assistant secretary of Indian affairs, Department of the Interior; Dr. Michael Trujillo, director of the Indian Health Service, Department of Health and Human Services; Christopher Goldthwaite, ambassador-designate to the Republic of Chad; Joy Harjo, member of the National Council on the Arts; Robert Loescher, member of the National Gambling Impact Study Commission; Sedelta Verble, deputy director of the Office of Communications, Department of Agriculture; Billy M. Burrage, judge, U.S. District Court; and Montie Deer, chair of the National Indian Gaming Commission, Department of the Interior. The president also appointed Elsie Meeks to the U.S. Commission on Civil Rights—the first Native American to serve on the Commission.

Cobell Lawsuit

During the Clinton Administration, Elouise Cobell, a Blackfeet Indian from Montana and founder of the first American Indian-owned national bank, filed a lawsuit in 1996 against the Department of the Interior on behalf of hundreds of thousands of individual Indians after finding many discrepancies in the management of funds for lands held in trust by the United States in her job as treasurer for the Blackfeet tribe.

According to U.S. law, Indian lands are technically not owned by tribes or individual Indians themselves but are held in trust by the U.S. government. Cobell wanted an accounting of how Interior managed proceeds from oil, gas, mineral, mining, and timber royalties held in trust for Indians by Interior since the late 1870s. Interior and the U.S. Department of Justice officials argued for years that the situation was so complex that no one really knew how much was due. Although it leased millions of acres of productive, Indian-owned land, Interior failed to keep adequate records of how much money was generated through those leases, to document where that

Blackfeet Indian Elouise Cobell sued the federal government for failing to release information on how much money the government held in trust that had been earned from mineral, timber, and other resource rights.

money actually went, or to ensure that the landowners were paid. When tribal members made inquiries about their IIM accounts, the BIA and DOI flatly refused to provide documentation. "We were treated like nobodies, even though it was our own money," Cobell said.

The Cobell case hinged in large part on whether or not an accurate accounting of the individual accounts could be determined. After over fifteen years of litigation, it was determined that an accurate accounting was not possible. In 2010, a settlement was reached for a total of $3.4 billion, the largest settlement in U.S. history, but far less than the hundreds of billions of dollars actually owed Indian landowners. Cobell and her team accepted the settlement, knowing that a full reckoning would only extend the case for years. The settlement, known as the Claims Resolution Act of 2010, was signed by President Barack Obama, who said: "After years of delay, this [settlement] will provide a small measure of justice to Native Americans whose funds were held in trust by a government charged with looking out for them." The settlement included payments to hundreds of thousands of individuals and a $1.9 billion land buy-back program, which will put land back into tribal hands.

UNITED STATES PUBLIC LAW 103–150 (THE APOLOGY RESOLUTION)

On November 23, 1993, the one-hundredth anniversary of the overthrow of the Kingdom of Hawaii, in a joint resolution of the U.S. Congress, USPL 103–150 was passed. The law "acknowledges that the overthrow of the Kingdom of Hawaii occurred with the active participation of agents and citizens of the United States and further acknowledges that the Native Hawaiian people never directly relinquished to the United States their claims to their inherent sovereignty as a people over their national lands either through the Kingdom of Hawaii or through a plebiscite or referendum." It was signed by President Bill Clinton on the same day. The reso-

lution has been a major impetus for the Hawaiian sovereignty movement and has been the subject of intense debate. The bill was cosponsored by Hawaiian senators Daniel Akaka and Daniel Inouye and serves as an apology to Native Hawaiians by the United States.

BARE-BONES BUDGET: FIRST DECADE OF THE TWENTY-FIRST CENTURY

During President George W. Bush's administration (2001–2009), the president said he was committed to improving education, increasing employment and economic development, and ensuring better access to health and human services for all American Indians and Alaska Natives. He expressed a belief that the government must support and protect the welfare of Native peoples as agreed to in laws and treaties in exchange for Native homelands and in compensation for forced removal from their original homelands. Despite administration rhetoric which acknowledged that the nation had failed to meet the agreements entered into with Indigenous peoples, Bush offered Native people the promise of a better future but did not provide the money to achieve that future.

Education budgets barely covered the cost of paying personnel at tribal colleges and universities. Native American elementary and secondary education fared no better despite the administration's declaration that no Native child would be left behind. The U.S. Commission on Civil Rights reports that "Native American education is just one example where the government incessantly failed to provide equal opportunity. Federal funding … has been continually reduced over the last few decades, resulting in insufficient resources and unequal access to educational tools."

President Bush's budget requests were also inadequate for Native health care. The Indian Health Service (IHS), the principal federal health care provider, was severely underfunded and failed to keep pace with the growing service population and expanding health care costs. The lack of funding resulted in IHS hospitals that lack intensive care units, emergency rooms, and outpatient clinics.

A series of reports by the U.S. Centers for Disease Control and Prevention highlighted worrying statistics in Native American and Alaska Native populations compared with non-Native peoples. The all-cause death rate from 1999 to 2009 was forty-six percent higher for Native people. Risk factors for cancers and heart disease, such as obesity, smoking, and hypertension, were substantially higher in Native communities, as were death rates from cancers. Infectious diseases such as pneumonia, influenza, tuberculosis, and chronic diseases such as diabetes caused significantly more deaths to Native Americans and Alaska Natives. The death rate from suicide was nearly fifty percent higher in Native communities than in non-Indian people. The reports noted

While the government under President George W. Bush promised better services in education and health care for Indigenous peoples, his administration failed to budget for these promises and even cut some programs.

that funding was urgently needed for clean water, tobacco-cessation counseling, regulation of alcohol outlets, access to culturally appropriate health services, cancer screening, and education about diet and physical activity, which could reduce excess mortality rates.

Under the Bush Administration, programs such as the Tribal Drug Court Program, which was designed to integrate substance abuse treatment with transitional services, was terminated in 2003 despite the need for alcohol and substance abuse treatment in Native communities.

President Bush's budget requests were also inadequate for thousands of Native families living in unsafe, indecent, and unsanitary homes. Lack of funding resulted in Native houses without water, sewer systems, roads, and utilities.

During the Bush Administration, the U.N. General Assembly voted to adopt a historic document, the "U.N. Declaration of Human Rights," in 2007. The Declaration provided a human rights framework for the world's approximately 370,000,000 Indigenous peoples. It called on states to work in mutual partnership and respect for Indigenous peoples to address harm and inequalities and support their rights, cultures, and governments. While most nations worldwide signed the document, four did not: Australia, Canada, New Zealand, and the U.S. While three of the four later endorsed the declaration, the U.S. did not sign on until December 16, 2010, when President Barack Obama announced support for the Declaration.

FEDERAL LEGISLATION, 2009–2014

During the Obama Administration (2009–present), his first years showed promising signs. In 2010, a number of laws passed that the president supported, including the Indian Health Care Improvement Act (2010), the Tribal Law and Order Act (2010), and the Claims Resolution Act, which included the $3.4 billion *Cobell* settlement agreement that resolved a lawsuit over the management and accounting of more than five hundred thousand individual American Indian trust accounts. Under the Land Buy-Back Program for Tribal Nations, a provision of the Cobell settlement, nearly 540,000 acres have returned to tribal ownership.

In 2010, the administration settled the $760 million Keepseagle case brought by Native American farmers and ranchers against the U.S. Department of Agriculture. They alleged discrimination by the agency in its administration of loan programs.

Some progress took place in the area of economic development consistent with Article 32 (1) of the Declaration's affirmation of the right of Indigenous peoples to develop their lands, territories, and resources. In 2012, President Obama signed the Helping Expedite and Advance Responsible Tribal Homeownership (HEARTH) act into law. It has been designed to help tribes improve and develop their own laws in regard to governing the leasing of federal tribal trust lands for residential, business, renewable energy, and other purposes. The Seminole Tribe of Florida became the first federally recognized tribe of 2015 to be formally approved under the HEARTH Act. "This is an important day for the Seminole Tribe, which will be able to process residential and business leases without the need for BIA approval," said Seminole chairman James E. Billie.

Besides signing off on numerous water and trust settlements, Obama's administration has worked for legislative changes that would make it easier for tribes to request aid from the Federal Emergency Management Agency.

On March 7, 2013, President Obama signed the Violence Against Women Reauthorization Act of 2013 (VAWA), which made violence against women a federal crime. VAWA improved the nation's response to violence because not all victims had been protected or reached through earlier iterations of the bill. VAWA 2013 reauthorized and improved upon lifesaving services for all victims of domestic violence, sexual assault, dating violence, and stalking—including Native women, immigrants, LGBT victims, college students and youth, and public housing residents.

Native American victims of domestic violence often could not seek justice because their courts were not allowed to prosecute non-Native offenders—even for crimes committed on tribal land. The law closed a major jurisdictional gap on reservations that allowed perpetrators of violence to remain free. VAWA included a solution that gave tribal courts jurisdiction over VAWA cases brought by tribes against nonmembers, including non-Indians.

Presidential Appointments and White House Conferences

To ensure Native Americans were represented in his administration, President Obama appointed Larry Echo Hawk (Pawnee Nation) as assistant secretary of the interior for Indian affairs, Dr. Yvette Robideaux (Rosebud Tribe) as director of the Indian Health Service, Hilary Tomkins (Navajo Nation) as solicitor of the interior, Tracie Stevens (Tulalip Tribes) as chairwoman of the National Indian Gaming Commission, Kimberly Teehee (Cherokee Nation) as senior policy advisor in the White House Domestic Policy Council in 2009, and Jodi Gillette (Standing Rock Sioux) to that position in 2012.

President Obama held four large-scale White House Tribal Nations Conferences from 2009–2012, unprecedented for a sitting president. He fulfilled a campaign pledge to federally recognized tribes to host meetings to hear their concerns.

Congressional Resolution of Apology, 2010

In 2010, the United States, acting through Congress, apologized to Native Americans for years of official depredations, ill-conceived policies, and the breaking of covenants by the federal government regarding Indian tribes. The congress apologized "on behalf of the people of the United States to all Native peoples for the many instances of violence, maltreatment, and neglect inflicted on Native peoples of the United States by the citizens of the United States." The resolution, in a larger piece of legislation, the 2010 De-

President Obama met with Lisa Marie Iyotte a rape survivor, after he signed the Tribal Law and Order Act of 2010. Also that year, the U.S. Congress formally apologized (and President Obama signed a declaration) to Native Americans for all the injustices they had endured.

fense Appropriations Act urged "the president to acknowledge the wrongs of the United States against Indian tribes in the history of the United States in order to bring healing to this land."

There was no ceremony of acknowledgment, and no tribal leaders were called. The White House did not issue a press release regarding the apology. The lack of a verbal apology, or even the willingness to talk about one, ended up being a confounding one for some Indians. In December 2009, President Obama had signed off on a congressional apology resolution to Native people that had been bouncing around during the Bush Administration.

At the December 2010 White House conference, the president addressed tribal leaders that he didn't think the actual words needed to be said out loud. He said, "[Last] year, I signed a resolution, passed by both houses of Congress, finally recognizing the sad and painful chapters in our shared history—a history too often marred by broken promises and grave injustices against the First Americans. It's a resolution I fully supported—recognizing the damage that was done, what it can do to help reaffirm the principles that should guide our future. It's only by heeding the lessons of our history that we can move forward."

After the president's statement, the Great Plains Tribal Chairman's Association put out a statement that said: "As American Indian people, we believe that the apology to Native peoples by the United States is long overdue. The true history must be taught in American schools so that today there can be real respect by the United States for Native nations and Native peoples."

ECONOMIC DEVELOPMENT CHALLENGES IN INDIAN COUNTRY TODAY

While income for Native Americans living on or near reservations has nearly doubled since 1970, their earnings are only a fraction of the U.S. average. In several states, less than fifty percent of Native Americans sixteen years or older living on or near federally recognized tribes are working, according to the *2013 American Indian and Labor Force Report* produced by the Bureau of Indian Affairs. About fifty percent of all the Native Americans studied, who are sixteen years or older, are employed in either full- or part-time civilian jobs.

Poverty on reservations from 2006–2010 was thirty percent compared with 14 percent nationally. The highest estimated rate of poverty is in South Dakota, with 43 to 47 percent of Native American families in 2010 earning incomes below the poverty line. Overall, an estimated 23 percent of all Native families in the U.S. earned incomes below the poverty line.

Progress is uneven. Some tribes are experiencing economic gains in recent years while others face overwhelming hardships. Problems such as chronically high unemployment, underdeveloped business and entrepreneurial opportunities, minimal access to capital, poor physical infrastructure, such as roads and bridges or water supplies, low graduation rates for high school, technical schools, and college degrees, lack of training for a local workforce, and limited access to broadband all contribute to poor economic conditions that have plagued tribal nations in the past and present.

The federal government has a trust responsibility to support economic security in Indian Country. It should provide necessary resources to tribes that will allow them to better protect their tribal lands and workforce. Government regulatory obstacles, however, present significant barriers that undermine tribal self-determination and discourage private investment in Indian Country. As an example, all new infrastructure construction on tribal lands requires rights-of-way approval, a time-consuming and ponderous process. Tribes must get Department of the Interior approval before any public-private partnership initiatives move forward. Economic development on tribal lands can involve multiple agencies, including not only Interior, but also Housing and Urban Development, the Small Business Administration, the Department of Agriculture, the Department of Energy, and the Indian Health Service.

The presence of the Small Business Administration (SBA) Office of Native American Affairs in Native communities is growing. This is evidenced by the SBA's lending to Native-owned small businesses at a level of $100 million in Fiscal Year (FY) 2013 and counseling and training more than 12,500 Native small business owners through the first three quarters of FY 2013. In addition, more than four hundred Native entrepreneurs and businesses owned by American Indian tribes, Alaska Native corporations, and Native Hawaiian organizations nationwide have been trained through SBA's Native American Emerging Leaders and Native American Entrepreneurial Empowerment workshops.

The Office of Native American Affairs (ONAA) is a critical resource for tribally owned and Native-owned businesses. It works to ensure these businesses gain access to capital, generate increased revenues, create more jobs, and develop tribal business codes. ONAA has helped facilitate the participation of Native contractors in SBA's business development program, HUB zone, women business, veteran and service-disabled veteran business, and other small business contracting programs.

The Community Development Financial Institutions (CDIF) Fund, a program of the U.S. Treasury Department, has a long-standing commitment to Native American, Alaska Native, and Native Hawaiian communities. The CDFI Fund's Native Initiatives are designed to overcome identified barriers to financial services in Native communities. These initiatives seek to increase the access to credit, capital, and financial services in Native communities.

The origin of the Native Initiatives dates back to September 1994, when Congress passed the Riegle Community Development and Regulatory Improvement Act, which created the CDFI Fund and mandated that it conduct a study of lending and investment practices on Indian reservations and other lands held in trust by the United States. Specifically, the study recognized barriers to private financing, identified the impact of such barriers on access to capital and to credit for Native peoples, and provided options to address these barriers.

Specifically, the Native Initiatives work to overcome these barriers through a series of training programs that seek to foster the development of new Native CDFIs, strengthen the operational capacity of existing Native CDFIs, and guide Native CDFIs in the creation of important financial education and asset building programs for their respective communities. The CDFI Fund launched a study, "Access to Capital and Credit in Native Communities," which will provide policymakers, tribal governments, tribal community organizations, and economic development practitioners with detailed analysis and quantitative research that can lead to actionable recommendations for improving access to capital and credit in Native communities.

Honoring Nations, a national award program launched in 1998, highlights outstanding programs in self-governance by Native Nations. At the heart of the program is the belief that tribes themselves hold the key to positive social, political, cultural, and economic prosperity—and that self-governance plays a crucial role in building and sustaining strong, healthy Indian nations and tribes themselves.

Since 1999, Honoring Nations, administered by the Harvard Project on American Indian Economic Development, has awarded a number of tribal economic development projects.

IDLE NO MORE

In 2012, the Idle No More (INM) movement took root in Canada as an action against a

Protestors display placards during an Idle No More event in Oklahoma City in 2012.

Canadian government bill that would further strip reservations of lands and environmental protections. The message spread quickly to the United States, where Indigenous communities were also being bullied with an array of events that threatened not just the health of Native lands but would have an impact on the entire nation as well. Native people saw the unchecked mining, fracking, and oil pipeline construction as well as other unsafe practices as attacks on the earth, Native cultures, and Native economies. It seemed that the U.S. government was not only opening Native lands to imminent danger from American companies but foreign businesses as well. Both Indians and non-Indians challenged fracking and the Keystone Pipeline by showing up for flash "round dance" mobs around the country, including the Mall of America in Minnesota and Washington Square Park in New York City. Solidarity protests popped up across the world in cities like London, Berlin, Auckland, and Cairo. INM, like Occupy Wall Street, Anti-Fracking, and movements in other parts of the world, gained momentum by utilizing social media.

The Idle No More movement continues. INM activists remind lawmakers that Canada and the U.S., two of the wealthiest nations in the world, attained their economic status partly by using the illegally acquired land and resources of Indigenous nations. The INM has become the largest Native American Indian movement in history.

CENSUS REPORTS, 1860–2010

Article I, section 2 of the U.S. Constitution requires a census to be taken every ten years so that seats in the House of Representatives can be apportioned among the states. Section 2 noted, "Indians not taxed," meaning Indians living on reservations were not counted. The first census began in 1790, more than a year after the inauguration of President George Washington.

Native Americans were not mentioned in a census until 1860. Instructions to the census enumerators spelled out which Native people were to be counted and who were not: "Indians not taxed" were not counted. The families of Indians who renounced tribal rule and who were state or territory citizens were enumerated. More than forty thousand Indians were recorded. The 1870 census was the first to list "Indian" as a choice in the column heading for "Color."

Up until 1890, most Indians were excluded from the U.S. Census. They were citizens of their own nations, not the U.S. When all Indians were finally included beginning in 1890, the census significantly undercounted the Native population. By 1950, the undercounting was so great that almost one-third of all Indians, over 250,000, were left out. (Alaska Natives were not part of the count for decades until Alaska became a state in 1959. Native Hawaiians were not part of an official census until 2000.)

Until relatively recently, the majority of Indians lived in rural areas with few paved roads, which were difficult to get to even after the widespread use of cars. People with standard street addresses were easier to reach than those with post office boxes or mail delivery in secluded areas. To combat inaccessibility in rural areas, the census enumerators hand delivered census forms in remote parts of reservations.

For much of the twentieth century, government census takers were viewed with suspicion by many Native respondents. This feeling reflects a long pattern of nonparticipation among Native Americans whose deep-rooted skepticism of the federal government, among other factors, has made them historically one of the country's most undercounted groups.

Many other reasons account for the inaccurate numbers. In 1910, the report differentiated 280 tribes and provided statistics on each of them. In 1930, it only differentiated one hundred. From 1940 through 1960, there was no tribal breakdown. Breakdowns were also incomplete. In recent censuses, Pueblo people were grouped in "Pueblo," even though they may have been from Acoma, Taos, Zuni, or other specific pueblos. Starting in 1960, the census added the Indigenous people in the new state of Alaska, which joined the union in 1959. It also grouped the Eskimo and Aleut, considerably different peoples, with Indians.

From the beginning, the Census Bureau has changed its definition of who is an Indian numerous times. The definition is important because Native people have been mixing with diverse people for five hundred years, and the resulting offspring have presented a problem for the Census Bureau. At various times, people of obvious mixed heritage were classed as either Indian, white, or black, based on the observations of enumerators. At other times, enumerators were instructed to classify mixed bloods as the race of the father and at other times as the race of the mother. In 1910 and 1930, mixed bloods were classed as Indians while in 1950, they were classed as "other." Sometimes an Indian was defined as one who was recognized as an Indian in the community. Beginning with the 1980 census, people were allowed for the first time to self-identify for race.

In 2000, the Census Bureau changed its methodology again and allowed individuals to self-identify with more than one race. The 2000 Census was also the first census to record Native Hawaiians and Pacific Islanders as a race distinct from Asians as a whole. The population identified as Pacific Islander/Native Hawaiian was about .1 percent of the total U.S. population. Overall, 1.2 million people, or 0.4 percent of all people in the United States, identified as Native Hawaiian and Other Pacific Islander (NHPI) either alone or in combination with one or more races. This population grew by 40 percent from 2000 to 2010. More than half (52 percent) of the Native Hawaiian and Other Pacific Islander alone or in-combination population lived in just two states, Hawaii (356,000) and California (286,000).

Besides data, the census includes questions about income, housing, health, education levels, language use, citizenship, and urbanization, among others. The information shows tremendous changes in Native life over the past 150 years. Since 1890, the Native population has grown more than ten times, from approximately 250,000 to 5.2 million in 2010. Out of the 2010 total, 2.9 million people identified as American Indian and Alaska Native alone; 2.3 million reported being American Indian and Alaska Native in combination with one or more other races. In 1890, the vast majority of Indians lived on reservations. In 2010, one in five lived in cities. In 1890, almost every Native person spoke his or her tribal language; in 2010, less than one in four still did. According to the 2010 census, more than 28 percent of all Native people were living in poverty.

U.S. census data about American Indians is often used for allocation of federal funds and for legislative redistricting (voting) as well as for a range of other key governmental actions. Tribal leaders feel there are significant problems with census data from Indian Country. Changes in the census over the decades have made it extremely challenging to accurately analyze trends over time.

Undercounting remains a problem for Native communities. After the Census Bureau estimated that it had undercounted the Native population by more than 12 percent in 1990, it began widespread outreach efforts aimed at reaching hard-to-count Native communities on reservations. Tribal leaders worked with the Bureau to improve participation. Local Native door-to-door enumerators became part of the Bureau's efforts to increase the count along with images of tribal members and young people in census posters.

Tulalip Reservation resident Roberta Belanich took part-time work with the Census Bureau for extra income and ended up realizing the importance of accurate counts. "Accurate population counts," she found out, "help tribes receive their fair share of federal funds." That's her message as she goes door to door. "You want better land use? Speedy emergency assistance? Health and education services? Then fill out your census forms."

NORTHEAST

It appears that a treaty was made by the Pilgrims and the Indians, which treaty was kept during forty years; the young chiefs during this time was showing the Pilgrims how to live in their country and find support for their wives and little ones; and for all this, they were receiving the applause of being savages. The two gentleman chiefs were Squanto and Samoset that were so good to the Pilgrims.

—William Apess (Pequot), 1836

Checking, cradling, dodging, and cutting moves make the lacrosse playing field vibrate. Young Iroquois teammates charge through the game their ancestors played for centuries before Europeans came to North America. Since ancient times, lacrosse has been a way of life for the Iroquois men who have played this fast-paced ball-and-stick game that requires speed, stamina, and precision.

Many Iroquois children receive their lacrosse sticks as soon as they can walk. At the age of three, they learn to play the game just like their fathers, grandfathers, and great-grandfathers before them. Children even carry their sticks around with them when they are not practicing.

At one time, young boys playing lacrosse were not able to play on a team if they did not select and cut a hickory limb, steam it, bend it, shape it, cut the leather strips, and make the net. Today, however, even though handcrafted hickory sticks are still used and passed on through the generations, sticks are more often made from plastic, aluminum, graphite, and titanium, with pockets made of nylon mesh.

Lacrosse is the pre-eminent Indigenous sport of North America, played from the Plains to the Atlantic. Tewaaraton (little brother of war) is the Mohawk word for "lacrosse," a French word. The Ojibwe word for lacrosse is baaga'adowewin (the stick), and in Eastern Cherokee, it is da-nahwah'uwsdi (little war). It was often played to toughen young warriors for combat, for recreation, and as part of festivals. Iroquois played lacrosse for religious reasons: for the pleasure of the Creator, to pray, heal the sick, and rejuvenate communities. This competitive game is played both on the field (field lacrosse) and in enclosed arenas (box lacrosse).

In the Native version of lacrosse, a contest often involved entire tribes and went on for days. Goals were miles apart, and there were no time-outs, penalties, or break periods. Players could be removed for harmful behavior or for fighting. There was also a women's version, which used shorter sticks with larger heads. The modern field game lasts an hour and is played by ten-person teams on a field one hundred yards long. The object of the game is to throw a ball from a webbed stick past the goaltender. The winner is the team that scores the most goals when the match ends.

Some children grow up to become members of the Iroquois Nationals lacrosse team, created in 1983, which represents the six nations that make up the Haudenosaunee/Iroquois Confederacy. The Iroquois Nation are the only Indigenous nation to play internationally; over thirty countries send teams to the world championship games.

As a sport, lacrosse has grown increasingly popular among non-Native people. Across the United States and Canada, boys, girls, men, and women play in high schools, colleges, and in youth and professional leagues.

HOW THE MONTAUKETT BECAME "EXTINCT" (NOT REALLY)

The Montaukett, an Algonquian-speaking nation with an estimated population of over ten thousand in the early 1600s, resided on the southern New England mainland, the western end of Long Island, and on Manhattan Island. In 1637, the English seized land at the east end of Long Island; the Dutch occupied Long Island's western tip. Eventually, the English supposedly acquired all of the island through falsified treaties and deeds negotiated between Montaukett Indians and Dutch and English authorities.

The Montaukett manufactured wampum, beads made from whelk shells that littered eastern Long Island beaches. Wampum was widely used as a standard unit of exchange among Northeast woodlands tribes. When Europeans came to the Americas, they realized the importance of wampum to Native people and quickly adopted it as their medium of exchange.

During the late 1600s and 1700s, the Montaukett became laborers in the colonial economy as whalers, farmers, herders, woodworkers, butter and cheese makers, and servants. The English forced the Montaukett Indians to make huge quantities of wampum to pay fines for breaking colonial laws, which the people often didn't understand. In

the 1800s, when they were scattered throughout the island, Montaukett also became factory workers, masons, carpenters, guides for wealthy hunters, and provided livery service for tourists.

The Montaukett served as militiamen in all the provincial campaigns before the French and Indian Wars and in the American Revolution, which left many Montaukett settlements with a large number of widows. This led to intermarriage with Anglos, African Americans, and other ethnic groups. By the nineteenth century, tuberculosis had taken the place of smallpox and other European diseases as the scourge of the Montaukett. By the twentieth century, the Montaukett had disappeared from the town records, appearing only in legal records, in newspaper articles, and in oral histories.

The last remaining Montaukett land was seized in 1910 through a judicial decision. Although both New York State and the U.S. Constitution forbade the sale of Indian land, a state Supreme Court judge ruled that land grants made in the 1600s by the English king trumped the U.S. Constitution. He also ruled, "There is now no tribe of Montauk Indians. It has disintegrated and been absorbed into the mass of citizens."

Despite the long history of attempts to remove all Indians from Long Island, the Montaukett Indians held on to their culture and conducted their ceremonies in private to the point of secrecy. The current generation of Montaukett, numbering in the thousands around the country and the hundreds on Long Island, are trying to re-establish recognition as a historic Native nation and obtain the use of at least a portion of their former tribal territory.

HOW THE NAUSET BECAME "EXTINCT" (NOT REALLY)

According to Wampanoag oral tradition and documents written by seventeenth-century English colonists, the Nauset of southeastern Massachusetts had a population of around 1,500 in 1600 before the epidemics of 1614 and 1620

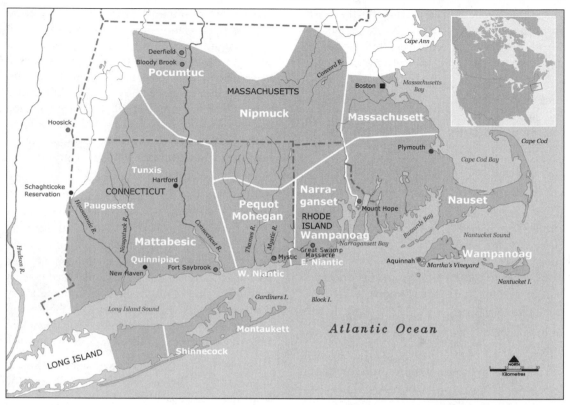

Major tribes and their territories around the year 1600 in the areas of what are now Massachusetts, Rhode Island, and Connecticut.

reduced their numbers. In 1621, there were about five hundred Nauset, a number that remained fairly constant up until 1675. Following King Philip's War (1675–1676), the Nauset were joined by the remnants of other New England tribes displaced by warfare or colonist intrusions. In 1698, nearly six hundred of this composite group were located at Mashpee, Massachusetts. An epidemic during 1710 reduced the population to about three hundred. Over the years, the Nauset community at Mashpee has become identified with the Wampanoag, but they are descendants of the Nauset, who lived many centuries ago.

A BIRD'S EYE VIEW

The Northeast region is an enormous area that includes the modern-day states of Maine, New Hampshire, Vermont, Massachusetts, Rhode Island, Connecticut, New York, New Jersey, Pennsylvania, Delaware, and Maryland. (It also includes present-day Canadian provinces of Nova Scotia, New Brunswick, and Prince Edward Island, plus parts of Quebec and Ontario.) The Northeast is sometimes called the Woodlands because of the huge forests of birch, elm, hickory, maple, oak, and willow. Trees provided wood for houses, boats, tools, and fuel. Bark was used for clothing, roofing, and bedding. The region includes mountains, the ocean, lakes, and rivers, which were sources of fish and shellfish. In general, the Northeast has warm-to-hot summers and cold, snowy winters.

This huge, complex region was home to dozens of Native peoples. Almost every tribe in this region spoke languages of two language families: Iroquoian and Algonquian. At one time, the Algonquians were a single group with one language. As people moved throughout the Northeast, their speech diversified. Today, members of the same Algonquian tongues family speak languages that are related and display similarities.

Some scholars suggest that the Algonquians occupied the region first, their ancestors following big game from the West. Or it is possible that Algonquian peoples descended from mound-building peoples of the Adena culture, 1000 B.C.E. to 200 C.E., whose sites spread across the present-day Ohio Valley and extended east to present-day western New York and western Pennsylvania and the Hopewell Culture, another mound building culture that existed from 300 to 700 C.E. Both the Hopewell and Adena people lived in villages, and corn was a staple part of their diet. Exact connections between ancient peoples and historical peoples in the Northeast are not known.

A number of Iroquoian-speaking and Algonquian-speaking cultures formed into confederacies.

Five Haudenosaunee, Iroquoian-speaking peoples ("People of the Longhouse"), created a confederation consisting of five nations (later six nations, when the Tuscarora moved north from North Carolina and joined it) in New York State. The Iroquois Confederacy includes the Mohawk, Oneida, Onondaga, Cayuga, Seneca, and Tuscarora nations.

The Algonquian-speaking peoples formed several confederacies:

The Wabanaki Confederation ("People of the Dawn Land" or "People of the First Light"), located in Maine and southeastern Quebec, Canada, includes the Abenaki (Eastern and Western), Maliseet, Micmac, Passamaquoddy, and Penobscot peoples.

The Wampanoag ("People of the First Light" or "Eastern People") were a loose confederation of around forty villages, located on the southeastern portion of present-day Massachusetts, the off-shore islands of Martha's Vineyard and Nantucket, and the eastern part of Rhode Island, according to oral tradition and European diaries, court records, letters, and other written accounts.

Today, the Aquinnah Wampanoag of Gay Head and Mashpee Wampanoag of Mashpee have federal recognition. Other Wampanoag groups include the Assonet Band of the Wampanoag, based in New Bedford; Herring Pond Wampanoag, with offices in Buzzards Bay; Namasket Wampanoag Band, which holds meetings in Fall River; and the Pocasset Wampanoag Tribe, which has reservation lands in Fall River since colonial times. There are several other Wampanoag groups.

According to Daniel Nimham (1726–1778), the last sachem of the Wappinger people, the Wappinger Confederacy, was a grouping of nine Algonquian-speaking tribes (Siwanoy, Kitchawanc, Wechquaesgeek, Rechgawawank, SintSink, Nochpeem, Wappinger, Tankiteke, and Uncowa) at the time of European contact. Primarily based in what is now Dutchess County, New York, the territory bordered Manhattan Island to the south, the Mohican territory to the north, and extended east into parts of Connecticut in the seventeenth century.

The Montauk Confederacy included the Canarsie, the Manhasset, the Shinnecock, and the Unkechaga nations.

ALGONQUIANS

Algonquian groups lived in settlements of dome-shaped houses and longhouses. They fished, farmed, and foraged as well as hunted. The Indians along the rivers and coastline did not "roam" the land. They moved between a summer place near shorelines to a winter place, a short walk inland, protected from winter storms and tides. As people moved throughout the large region and westward, their cultural traditions diversified.

Wampanoag

The Wampanoag ("Eastern People") were formerly known as Pokanoket, which originally was the name of Massasoit's village but came to the designation of all territory and people under the renowned sachem (leader). The Wampanoag have lived in their homeland for thousands of years.

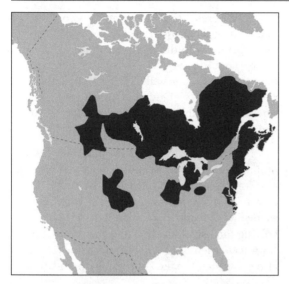

This map shows (in dark grey) the regions where the Algonquin language was spoken before the arrival of Europeans.

The men hunted fowl and small and large game, especially the white-tailed deer. The people also ate seals and beached whales as well as shellfish and fresh-water fish. Women gathered roots, wild fruits, berries, and nuts as well as maple syrup for sugar. Women began growing corn, beans, and squash in precontact time. Wampanoag developed special hunting traps, snares, nets, witch hazel bows, and arrows as well as fishing nets, bone hooks, and weirs to catch fish.

The Wampanoag built wetus (wigwams), arched wooden poles lashed together into a dome covered by tightly woven, removable mats that were well adapted to the climate. During Massachusetts winters, a fire burned in the center of the wetu with the smoke venting through a hole in the center of the roof. The homes of the English of the early 1600s were also heated by fires under central roof holes so they did not find the wetu primitive. According to colonist William Wood, the wetu's multiple layers of mats, which trapped insulating layers of air, were "warmer than our English houses." Wood admired the way the mats "deny entrance to any drop of rain though it come both fierce and long."

The Wampanoag have a unique place in U.S. history. Their ancestors greeted the Pilgrims in 1620. The Grand Sachem Massasoit made a treaty of friendship with the English colonists. Massasoit, Tisquantum (Squanto), a Patuxet (a band of the Wampanoag tribal confederation), and other Wampanoag people helped the English survive by showing them how to rotate crops to maintain soil fertility in a land alien to them.

In early autumn of 1621, the fifty-three surviving English Pilgrims celebrated their successful harvest, as was the custom. That 1621 celebration is remembered as the "first Thanksgiving in Plymouth." There are two (and only two) primary source descriptions of the events of the fall of 1621. In *Mourt's Relation* (about 1620), Edward Winslow wrote:

> ... our harvest being gotten in, our governor sent four men on fowling, that so we might after a special manner rejoice together, after we had gathered the fruits of our labors; the four in one day killed as much fowl, as with a little help beside, served the Company almost a week, at which time among other Recreations, we exercised our Arms, many of the Indians coming among us, and among the rest their greatest king Massasoit, with some ninety men, whom for three days we entertained and feasted, and they went out and killed five Deer, which they brought to the Plantation and bestowed on our Governor, and upon the Captain and others, and although it be not always so plentiful, as it was at this time with us, yet by the goodness of God, we are so far from want, that we often wish you partakers of our plenty.

In *Of Plymouth Plantation* (written between 1630 and 1646), William Bradford, founder and longtime governor of the Plymouth Colony, wrote:

> They began now to gather in the small harvest they had, and to fit up their houses and dwellings against winter,

being all well recovered in health and strength and had all things in good plenty, for as some were thus employed in affairs abroad, others were exercised in fishing, about cod and bass and other fish, of which they took good store, of which every family had their portion. All the summer there was no want; and now began to come in store of fowl, as winter approached, of which this place did abound when they came first (but afterward decreased by degrees), and besides waterfowl, there was great store of wild turkeys, of which they took many, besides venison, etc. Besides, they had about a peck of meal a week to a person, or now since harvest, Indian corn to that proportion. Which made many afterward write so largely of their plenty here to their friends in England, which were not feigned but true reports.

The Pilgrims did not call this harvest festival a "Thanksgiving" although they did give thanks to God. To them, a Day of Thanksgiving was purely religious. The first recorded religious Day of Thanksgiving was held in 1623 in response to a providential rainfall. The religious Day of Thanksgiving and the harvest festival evolved into a single event: a yearly Thanksgiving, proclaimed by individual governors for a Thursday in November. The custom of an annual Thanksgiving celebrating abundance and family spread across America. Some presidents proclaimed Thanksgivings; others did not. Abraham Lincoln began the tradition of an annual national Thanksgiving in 1863.

National Thanksgiving Day observances are largely filled with myths and misinformation. Popular American folklore suggests the "first Thanksgiving" was an idyllic feast. This myth, which ignores the fact that the feast was never repeated and that Thanksgiving is an invented holiday, runs contrary to many realities. The tale ignores the Pilgrims, who plundered a Native person's store of corn for the winter and opened some graves; ignores the Wampanoag, who brought most of the

food; ignores the Pilgrims, who viewed Wampanoag as heathens and savages; and ignores the Pilgrims, who did not even call the three-day event "Thanksgiving." Thanksgiving observances omit the fact that virtually all Native nations have ritual ceremonies of giving thanks to the Creator, ceremonies established long before the "Thanksgiving" in 1621 took place.

Massasoit died in 1662. At that time, his second son, Metacomet (also known as Metacom), also known as Philip, renewed the peace. However, relations were strained by British abuses such as the illegal occupation of land; trickery, often involving the use of alcohol; and the destruction of resources, including forests and game. Diseases also continued to take a toll on the population.

Lenape (Delaware)

Lenape people settled centuries ago in southeastern Pennsylvania, northern Delaware, northern New Jersey, southern New York, and southeastern Connecticut. The name comes from the Englishman Lord De La Warr, after whom a bay, river, and U.S. state all later came to be called Delaware. The tribe's own name for itself is Lenni–Lenape, or "true men" or "first people" in the Algonquian language.

The Lenape lived in small communities of twenty-five to thirty people. They usually lived near a stream at the edge of a forest. Elm and chestnut trees provided saplings needed to make their bark-covered wigwams (houses) shaped like a dome. Men tied saplings together to form the rounded shape, wrapped the structures with layers of bark, and covered the doorways with animal skins. Each home had an opening on the roof to allow smoke from the cooking fire to escape. Pieces of bark covered the opening during bad weather.

Some Lenape Indians preferred Iroquoian-style longhouses to wigwams because more family members could live in a longhouse sixty feet long and twenty feet across. They were made with rounded ends and curved roofs. Each Lenape family had its own "apartment" and its own fireplace.

The Lenape lived in environments filled with sea animals, birds, and larger mammals such as deer. They grew crops, including corn, beans, and squash. The women gathered fruits, berries, and nuts. The men hunted and fished. Oysters, clams, and shellfish were plentiful in the waters.

In 1683, Tamanend, the Lenape leader, and other tribal representatives signed a treaty of peace and friendship with English Quaker William Penn, the founder of Pennsylvania. Of all early colonial leaders, Penn is believed to have been the most fair in his dealing with Native peoples. Penn promised peace and religious freedom to the Lenape who lived in the colony. The Lenape were also the first Indian tribe to sign a treaty with the newly formed U.S. government at Fort Pitt (present-day Pittsburgh) in 1778.

Although the Lenape seemed to get along with the colonists at first, conflicts later emerged that forced many Lenape to Indian Territory (present-day Oklahoma) and Canada. Today, surviving eastern Lenape groups include Nanticoke, Ramapough, Sand Hill, and other groups in Pennsylvania and Ohio.

IROQUOIANS

Iroquoian is a term used to identify several Indigenous nations that shared a similar language and culture. The major Iroquoian nations included the Mohawk, Seneca, Cayuga, Onondaga, Oneida, Susquehannock, Erie, Huron, and others. The Iroquoian peoples shared a similar way of life, usually based on intensive horticulture, fishing, and hunting. Their house style, the longhouse, was built with wood, often about sixty feet long and twenty feet wide. Each longhouse sheltered several families that lived in separate compartments. Their villages were often palisaded and organized according to clans, which were groups of related people who traced their descent to a common ancestor through mothers.

Three Sisters Agriculture

The Iroquois and other tribes practiced the Three Sisters planting method, an ancient method of gardening in which corn, squash, and beans are grown together simultaneously on the same mound of soil. In this efficient planting method, corn stalks provided support for the bean vines, which added nitrogen to the soil. Squash provided ground cover, which discouraged weeds. Productivity was much higher (by some estimates as much as 30 percent) for the three grown together than each grown separately. In 2009, the U.S. Mint's Native American $1 coin commemorated the spread of Three Sisters agriculture at around 1000 C.E. The coin features a Native American woman planting seeds in a field of corn, beans, and squash.

A woman wears traditional Lenape ribbonwork in this c. 1920s photo.

The 2009, one-dollar U.S. coin honors the Three Sisters method of planting crops.

At the time of European contact in the early 1500s, the Iroquoian peoples lived along the St. Lawrence River (in upper New York State), along the lower Great Lakes, and in the Susquehanna River Valley (in present-day Pennsylvania). Because of their inland location, their cultures were relatively unaffected, compared to Native coastal peoples, by early European trade and colonial expansion.

One of the most well-known Iroquoian groups was the Five Nations of the Haudenosaunee, which means People of the Longhouse. Between 900 and 1450, the Mohawk, Oneida, Onondaga, Cayuga, and Seneca formed a confederation consisting of the five nations (later six), "a sophisticated ceremonial and cultural institution." The Confederation was created primarily to make peace and maintain stability among the member tribes in present-day New York and Ontario, Canada. It unified nations into a United Nations. Chiefs were drawn from forty-nine families, who were present at the creation of the Confederacy.

The origin story of the Iroquois Confederacy holds that a peacemaker, Deganawidah, and his spokesman, Hiawatha, planted a Great Tree of Peace at the Onondaga Nation (near Syracuse, New York) to resolve the blood feuds that had been dividing the Haudenosaunee people. Through the symbolic tree planting, the peacemaker instituted peace, unity, and clear thinking among the Haudenosaunee people. Deganawidah passed on the Great Law of Peace, which guides the Haudenosaunee people with instructions on how to treat others, directs them on how to maintain a democratic society, and expresses how reason must prevail in order to preserve peace. The Great Law still guides Haudeonosaunee communities today.

During the colonial period, the Confederacy enabled the member nations to take advantage of their political, economic, and geographic position in the Northeast. By adopting members of other Iroquoian groups, such as the Huron and Tuscarora, the Haudenosaunee maintained their historically strategic position in the Northeast, between the colonies of New France and New York, in the fur trade and during the diplomatic rivalries between England and France in the seventeenth and eighteenth centuries. At the height of their influence, from about 1650–1777, the Haudenosaunee heartland extended from Albany, New York, to Niagara Falls, with its outermost borders stretching to southeastern Ontario, New England, northern Pennsylvania, and northeastern Ohio.

THE IROQUOIS AND THE U.S. CONSTITUTION

The Iroquois played an important role in the birth of the United States. Even before the American Revolution, the Haudenosaunee had counseled American leaders on the virtues of Iroquois-style unity, democracy, and liberty. From the writing of the Albany Plan of Union, a 1755 plan to unite the colonies, to the creation of the United States Constitution in 1787, the Iroquois were present in body and/or spirit as colonial delegates to a congress in Philadelphia that sought to create a democratic alternative to the British monarchy. At their request, Iroquois chiefs were

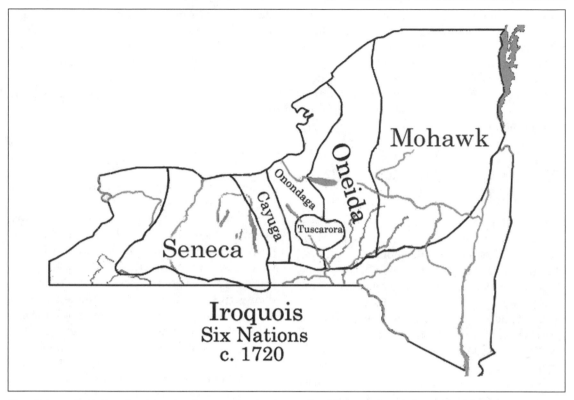

Mohawk

Oneida

Onondaga

Cayuga

Tuscarora

Seneca

Iroquois
Six Nations
c. 1720

The six Iroquois Nations lived together in peace in what is now New York state largely because of their democratic model for governing, a model that America's Founding Fathers emulated in the U.S. Constitution.

present at the debates on the Declaration of Independence in May and June 1776. Over the course of several weeks, the Iroquois observed the new American nation emerging and gave the president of the Second Constitutional Congress, John Hancock, an Iroquois name, "Karanduawn," which means "the Great Tree." Indeed, some delegates, such as Thomas Jefferson, the chief author of the Declaration of Independence who became the third president of the United States, believed that the American government was very similar to American Indian governments like that of the Iroquois.

On the eve of the Constitutional Convention, John Adams admonished the delegates to the convention to conduct "an accurate investigation of the form of government of the … Indians," since the separation of powers in American Indian governments like the Iroquois is "marked

with a precision that excludes all controversy." During the Constitutional Convention, delegates such as James Wilson of Pennsylvania clearly stated that the "British government cannot be our model." Later, in 1790, Thomas Jefferson and others toasted the U.S. Constitution as an [Iroquois] "tree of peace" that sheltered the Americans "with its branches of union." Thus, American Indian ideas associated with groups like the Iroquois of the Northeast had a decided impact on the development of American democracy. In 1987, the U.S. Senate formally acknowledged, in a special resolution, the influence of the Haudenosaunee Great Law of Peace on the U.S. Constitution.

The six Iroquois nations have lived for centuries under the Great Law of Peace, an early example of a formal, democratic government structure. It was first written down in English in the nineteenth century. It has been compared to the U.S. Constitution because there are some similarities. Each nation in the Iroquois Confederacy is independent and governs its own internal affairs. The Great Law established the Grand Council, with members representing all the member nations, to deal with problems affecting all six nations in the Confederacy.

EARLY LIFE AND CONTACTS IN THE NORTHEAST

According to one historian, along the coasts and river valleys of New England, Algonquian and Iroquoian settlements were "an ever changing collage of personalities, alliances, plots, raids, and encounters which involved every Indian [settlement]." Armed conflict was frequent but brief and mild by European standards. Conquest was not the aim. Battles were fought to gain prestige, take revenge for slain relatives, and to defend their villages against attack. Roger Williams noted that even in large clashes, the battles were "farre less bloudy and devouring than the cruell Warres of Europe." Then Europeans showed up, and warfare changed. Native peoples found themselves fighting for their very survival, protecting their homelands and families from invasion by foreign armies and colonists.

American Indians in the Northeast region sustained almost continual contact with European explorers from the 1490s onward. Native American contact with Europeans was particularly prolonged and intense along the eastern seaboard of the Atlantic Ocean. English and French fishermen made regular trips to Maine, fishing for cod. At first, these early meetings between Native people and Europeans were usually friendly. Friendly beginnings, however, quickly changed. More and more European sailors, adventurers, explorers, traders, and colonists invaded the coasts of Northeast America, initiating centuries of change and suffering for Native peoples. Many generations of European invaders defeated Native nations, undermined their way of life, and drove them from their ancestral lands.

Many coastal American Indian groups did not have time to bounce back from the onslaught of European diseases, military aggression, land cessions, and political demands. Coastal groups were often dispersed into other tribes or decimated, often before Europeans were able to record information about them.

DISEASES

The most deadly thing that Europeans brought to the Northeast (and rest of North America) was their germs. Diseases such as smallpox, bubonic plague, measles, influenza, cholera, typhus, and others that were common in Europe were unknown in America before 1492. When Europeans crossed the Atlantic, they brought their germs with them and contaminated Native people. Never having been exposed to these diseases before, thousands and thousands of Native people died throughout the Northeast and the rest of the Americas. In 1634, Governor William Bradford of Plymouth Colony described the impact of smallpox on Native people: " … Such a mortality that of a thousand, above nine and a half hundred of them died … they fell down so generally of this disease as they were in the end not able to help one another, nor to make a fire, nor to fetch a little water to drink, nor any to bury the dead."

FUR TRADE

Nearly all Native peoples engaged in intertribal trade. By foot, canoes, or boats, Native traders in the Northeast regularly exchanged goods with other groups. European traders, however, brought great changes to Native societies in the Northeast. At first, trade benefited both parties, and there was equitable exchange. European glass beads and mirrors and other goods were perceived as otherworldly gifts. Historians suggest that Algonquian and Iroquoian Indians were first attracted to European goods not for their usefulness, but rather for their ceremonial significance. Gifts from Algonquians to European traders consisted of wampum belts and beaver furs. Gift giving created special bonds between Native and European societies.

Soon, European trade goods entered Native societies and were used for practical, not ceremonial, purposes. Anglo traders gave Indians metal knives, muskets, cooking pots, wool clothing, and blankets, all greatly valued in Indian societies. In turn, Indians gave traders beaver furs, bark canoes, corn, berries, meat, and fish, which they coveted. Individual Indians and groups grew to desire goods they could not produce themselves, which became the basis of their honor, power, and prestige.

At first, during the seventeenth and early eighteenth centuries, the fur trade barely impacted the daily life of Indians. Native technology persisted. In time, however, the fur trade eventually caused tremendous disruption in Native cultures. England, France, the Netherlands, Russia, and Spain competed with each other for trade with Indian nations. Beaver pelts and other furs were valued in Europe for making hats and trimmings for dresses. Indian nations also competed with each other to be suppliers to European nations in exchange for manufactured goods. As Indigenous people obtained more and more manufactured goods from traders, they stopped producing traditional objects made of bone and stone and animal skins that required hours of preparation.

Indians also competed to acquire guns and gunpowder. In traditional times, Indian nations fought each other with bows and arrows, spears, and war clubs. After European traders introduced guns into Indian Country, Indian fur trappers competed with each other to buy guns from traders. That led to men spending more time hunting and killing off large numbers of beaver and other animals in their own and their neighbors' homelands. Driven by the need to exchange furs for guns, metal kettles to cook in, and alcoholic beverages, also introduced by traders, Indian hunters depleted otter, deer, and other wildlife populations. Well into the nineteenth century, the final stages of the fur trade, Indians discarded their own tools and technologies required to make clothing, moccasins, housing, and household utensils. They "depended on European manufacturers and food supplies to survive, and Europeans dictated the terms of the exchange that reduced them to poverty."

MISSIONARIES

European missionaries also brought changes to Native societies in the Northeast. The Christian nations of Europe believed it was their duty to convert to Christianity Native peoples they encountered elsewhere in the world. French Catholic priests and English Protestant ministers competed with each other to destroy Native religions and convert Native peoples to the "true faith." They trivialized religious beliefs by labeling them as *heathen, pagan,* and *primitive.*

English Protestants believed that Indians should become Christians but not until they completely abandoned their old ways and lived like English people. French Jesuit missionaries generally had more success than English rivals. Black-robed missionaries traveled to Abnaki villages in Maine and to Indian villages in New York, living among Indian people as they spread their message.

Tribal peoples invited missionaries into their midst. Open to the spirituality of others and capable of adding to their spiritual ways without sacrificing their own beliefs, some Indians were surprised to discover that missionaries required them to give up their traditional beliefs. Many Indians became Christians, but others resisted. They simply preferred their own beliefs and ceremonies to those of the missionaries. Some Indians continued practicing their traditional rituals even though they attended church and recited the Lord's Prayer.

Native peoples even participated in the missionary process. Hiacoomes (c. 1610–1690), a Pokanoket man who lived on Martha's Vineyard, Massachusetts, is believed to have been the first Indian to convert to Christianity in 1643. Under the instruction of Thomas Mayhew, a Congregational clergyman, Hiacoomes learned to read English and study the Bible. He began preaching in 1645, reportedly becoming an effective missionary.

BITTER DEFEATS IN SOUTHERN NEW ENGLAND, SEVENTEENTH CENTURY

When English communities became stronger, permanent, and armed, they forced Native peoples to obey their laws and submit to their demands. Many Indians in New England tried to resist English colonists, who often used deceit to extinguish title to Indian lands when rightful owners refused to sell.

Two major wars were fought between Indians in southern New England and the English colonists in the late 1600s. In what is now Connecticut, one of the first conflicts between Indians and colonists took place. Until the 1630s, the Dutch and allied Pequot controlled the region's fur trade. The addition of English traders offered a trading alternative for Natives. Tribes under Pequot subjugation allied with the English, which led to a struggle between Dutch and English for control of the fur trade, while the Pequot attempted to maintain their political and economic dominance in the region. Specific events which have often been cited as the cause for the Pequot War are the murders by Pequot of several English traders. However, these deaths were the culmination of decades of conflict between Native tribes in the region further amplified by the arrival of the Dutch and English.

In May 1637, English Captain John Mason led a force of soldiers, with Mohegan and Narragansett allies, to the Pequot village on the Mystic River in southeastern Connecticut. (Largely as a result of Massasoit's influence, the Wampanoag remained neutral in the Pequot War of 1636). At dawn, when most of the men were away from the village, the force waged "English-style war-

The Pequot War, which ran from 1634 to 1638, pitted the Pequot tribe against the Mohicans, the Narragansett, and the English colonies of Plymouth, Massachusetts Bay, and Saybrook. The Pequot lost the battle and became effectively extinct as a nation.

fare," setting fire to eighty wigwams and slaughtering over four hundred defenseless men, women, and children. In following months, the English sold surviving Pequot into slavery, many sent to the Caribbean. Other Pequot hid among other tribes. Captain Mason declared the attack an act of God in his *Brief History of the Pequot War*, published in 1736.

The Pokanoket, led by Metacom, took the lead in uniting Indians from southern and central New England in King Philip's War (1675–1676). This was an attempt by the Wampanoag, Narragansett, and other tribes to drive out English colonists, with whom they had lived peacefully for several decades. According to historian Jill Lepore, in *The Name of War*, the Algonquians waged war against English colonists in response to "incursions on their cultural, political, and economy autonomy." The English colonists waged war to "gain Indian lands, to erase Indians from the landscape...." Lepore wrote that "it is not entirely clear just exactly how or why the war started when it did, in June 1675, but from the firing of the first shots, both sides pursued the war with viciousness and almost without mercy." (p.7) The Wampanoag, Narragansett, Nipmuck, and other groups attacked dozens of English towns, burning twenty-five of them, and killed as many inhabitants as they could. The English, with occasional help from Mohegan, Pequot, Mohawk, and other Indians, burned wigwams, killed women and children, and sold prisoners into slavery. At the end of the so-called "King Philip's War" (which Lepore suggests be called "Metacom's Rebellion," using his more accurate Algonquian name), tribal populations were decimated, scattered, and dispossessed.

In 1675, the Narragansett allied themselves with King Philip. In the Great Swamp Massacre, military forces of Puritans from Plymouth, Massachusetts Bay, and Connecticut massacred a group of Narragansett, mostly women, children, and elderly men living at a winter camp in the Great Swamp, located in present-day South Kingstown. Following the massacre, many of the surviving Narragansett retreated deep into the forest and swamplands in the southern area of

A well-known 1772 illustration of King Philip by Paul Revere. King Philip died in 1676, so there is no known accurate image. of King Philip by Paul Revere.

Rhode Island. Many who refused to be subjected to the authority of the United Colonies fled the area or were hunted down and killed. Some were sold into slavery in the Caribbean, others migrated to upstate New York, and many went to Brotherton, Wisconsin, and Canada.

ENSLAVED NATIVES IN BERMUDA

Both the Pequot and King Philip's War resulted in the enslavement of Native survivors. Colonial records and ship documents prove that some of the survivors of the 1637 massacre of the Pequot were sold by the English into slavery in Bermuda along with factions from about eight other New England tribes as well as Taino people from the Caribbean. After King Philip's War in

1676, Wampanoag and Narragansett survivors were also sold into Bermuda slavery. The descendants of the slaves remained isolated on St. David's Island, where they have faced constant discrimination and social rejection from Bermuda's dominant society. St. David's islanders, who were different in their appearance, speech, and culture from other Bermudians, did not discuss their heritage in public. Ceremonies took place in the late 1800s and early 1900s but at night.

Fortunately, St. Clair Brinksworth "Brinky" Tucker and a group of St. David's Indians began to explore their past through archival research, genealogy,, and oral history as well as visits to the United States. This led to Bermuda's Indians reconnecting with their Indigenous roots with the Pequot and Wampanoag Indians as well as with Narragansett and other Native peoples. In 2002, a delegation of Pequot from Connecticut, Narragansett from Rhode Island, and Wampanoag from Massachusetts visited Bermuda for a historic meeting. That year, the first Reconnection Indian Festival was celebrated on the island. The Mashpee Wampanoag of Massachusetts also began hosting Gombey dancers from St. David's Island in its annual powwow. According to Brinky Tucker, a founding member of the St. David's Island Indian Committee, "Our Native American pride has increased one thousand times over, learning our culture, spirituality, a sense of oneness, and not being afraid to be proud of who we are." In 2007, Mr. Tucker was honored by Bermuda's Department of Community and Cultural Affairs as an Outstanding Tradition Bearer of the Family and Community.

In 2009, the Smithsonian Institution's National Museum of the American Indian included St. David Islander stories in its exhibit "IndiVisible," which chronicled interactions between mainland New England Indians and their distant relatives in the Caribbean.

Seventeenth through Nineteenth Centuries, New England

The Algonquian-speaking peoples of the southern part of the region (Abenaki, Pequot,

and others) bore the full brunt of European settler pressure and thus had a great deal more difficulty maintaining their land base and traditions. The coastal peoples of seventeenth-century New England were rapidly brought under colonial law by the end of King Philip's War, and most Indians who stayed in the English New England colony were left in small towns and adopted Christian religion and town government. Many of the Indians, most of whom were Algonquian speakers, lived on the margins of New England society.

The Penobscot and Passamaquoddy of Maine and several other groups (mostly of the Algonquian linguistic group) survive in their original homeland largely because white colonist pressure was less severe in the northern part of the Northeast region.

NORTHEAST INDIGENEITY

"The lesson (is) to realize the value of an alternative perspective, and that is why we are here. That is why the Creator allowed some of us to remain, in spite of all the attempts to destroy us."

—Tall Oak (Everett Weeden), Absentee Pequot/Narragansett, 500 Nations documentary

Tribal Renaissance in Connecticut, Twentieth Century: Western and Eastern Pequot Tribes

Gradually, the Pequot were able to re-establish their identity as separate tribes in separate communities: the Mashantucket (Western) Pequot in Ledyard and the Paucatuck (Eastern) Pequot in North Stonington. In the 1970s, more than three hundred years after the Pequot War, Mashantucket tribal members began moving back to their Connecticut homeland near Ledyard, Connecticut, restoring their land base and community. In 1983, the Mashantucket were granted federal recognition by an act of Congress. Shortly after, they launched the first phase of Foxwoods Resort Casino, which grew to become,

The Mohegan museum in Uncasville, Connecticut, features faithful reproductions of traditional buildings. The museum was built in 1931, but the tribe at Uncasville was not federally recognized until 1994.

for a time, the largest and most successful casino in the country. The tribe also built a museum and research center, which contains a massive, recreated seventeenth-century Pequot village. Due to increasing Indian and non-Indian casino competition and overexpansion, the tribe's fortunes have decreased. It closed the museum for several months in late 2014.

Mohegan Tribe Initiatives

In 1994, the Mohegan Indian Tribe of Uncasville became federally recognized. In 1996, the tribe developed Mohegan Sun Casino and Hotel, a large and successful casino resort on its reservation. Although the casino has been one of the most popular spots in Connecticut, the tribe has diversified its business portfolio with commercial ventures, including owning nontribal casinos, restaurant franchises, and an office machine company.

The Mohegan have also gone into the professional sports business. In 2003, the tribe became the first Indian nation to own a professional sports team. It purchased a Women's National Basketball Association (WNBA) franchise, which it named the Connecticut Sun. In 2014, the Mohegan Sun Casino and its parent company announced the purchase of half of the National Lacrosse League's Philadelphia Wings, a professional indoor lacrosse team. The team, renamed New England Black Wolves, moved to Uncasville, Connecticut, and played its first game in December 2014 at Mohegan Sun Arena. (It's not surprising that the Mohegan invested in basketball and lacrosse. Both sports are enormously popular among Native people who live on reservations and in cities.)

ALGONQUIAN AND IROQUOIAN LANGUAGE REVITALIZATION

An estimated five hundred or more Native languages were spoken in 1492. Today, an estimated 150 are spoken in the United States and Canada. Although English is the common language spoken by Native Americans in the United States, ancient Indian languages continue to be spoken in many Native communities despite years of destructive federal policies that forbid instruction in any Indian language in U.S. boarding schools. Because of the suppression and extermination directed against Native languages, linguists reported that dozens of languages were on the verge of extinction. In the late 1980s, a grassroots movement among Native and Anglo educators and linguists led to the passage of the Native American Language Act in 1990. The act officially recognized the right of Native languages to exist. It stated that "the traditional languages of Native Americans are an integral part of their cultures and identities and form the basic medium for … the survival of Native cultures." Today, a number of Native communities insist on teaching Native youngsters ancestral tribal languages to ensure continuation of cultural heritage and identity.

Kanienkeha (Mohawk) Language

In 1997, an informal survey taken by attendees at an Iroquois language meeting revealed that all six Haudenosaunee languages were in trouble. Since 1998, Kanatsiohareke, a Mohawk community in central New York state, has offered Mohawk language-immersion classes. In 2006, Rosetta Stone, a language-learning software company, developed the first-ever Kanienkeha (Mohawk) interactive language software. Now there are online and print language materials and curricula to meet the needs of Mohawk language learners.

Wôpanâak (Wampanoag) Language

Wôpanâak, an Algonquian language, was spoken by tens of thousands of people in southeastern New England. During the seventeenth century, Puritans learned the language, rendered it phonetically in the Roman alphabet, and used it to translate the King James Bible and other religious texts for the purposes of conversion and literacy promotion.

As a result of the subsequent fragmentation of Wampanoag communities in a land dominated by English speakers, Wampanoag ceased to be spoken by the middle of the nineteenth century and was preserved only in written records. Determined to breathe life back into the language, jessie little doe baird (Mashpee Wampanoag) founded the Wôpanâak Language Reclamation Project in 1993, an effort that aims to return fluency to the Wampanoag Nation. Through painstaking research, dedicated teaching, and contributions to other groups struggling with language preservation, Baird has been reclaiming the rich linguistic traditions of Indigenous peoples.

CONTEMPORARY IROQUOIS NATIONS

The Iroquois culture has also changed, as it must if the people are to endure. Today, the Iroquois work in many of the same professions as the dominant society. They are ironworkers, steelworkers, teachers, artists, musicians, and small business owners. However, many still maintain the traditional culture in the modern setting. At the Onondaga Reservation, the Great Law is still recited as it was in precolonial times, and such meetings are well attended by reservation and urban Iroquois. The great festivals and ceremonies of thanksgiving continue as a part of their lives. They are forging a lifestyle that includes the wisdom of their ancestors and the benefits of modern technology to create a culture in which they can live comfortably and in peace.

The Oneida Nation Turning Stone Resort Casino

In 2013, Ray Halbritter, Oneida Nation chief executive officer of central New York, kicked off a twenty-year anniversary of the award-winning, 3,400-acre Turning Stone Casino Resort. According to the nation's 2013 Annual Report, it has grown from 1,884 employees to 4,572. It has generated more than $155 million in income, property, and sales taxes for the surrounding communities. It has spent $4.2 billion on goods and services. The nation has contributed millions of dollars to local school districts, made donations to local charities, and to the National Museum of the American Indian in Washington, D.C. Turning Stone features hotels, three world-class, award-winning golf courses, conference and meeting space, numerous restaurants, entertainment complex, and gaming space.

Treaty Rights

Contemporary Iroquois have long fought for their treaty rights. In 1794, Britain and the United States entered into a new treaty, known as the Jay Treaty after Chief Justice John Jay, the American negotiator. It was a treaty of "friendship, commerce, and navigation." Article III of the Jay Treaty provided for free border-crossing rights between the U.S. and Canada for United States citizens, British subjects, and "the Indians dwelling on either side of the boundary line." Indians were not supposed to pay duty or taxes on their "own proper goods" when crossing the line.

Border crossings between Canada and the U.S. have long been a source of conflict. In 1926, to better organize for border-crossing rights, Chief Clinton Rickard (Tuscarora) and others started the Indian Defense League of America (IDLA), which organized Indian border crossings and fought for other rights nationwide. The IDLA staged annual "border crossings" into Canada to assert the right, through the Jay's Treaty (1794), to uninhibited passage across the U.S. and Canadian border. They refused to pay customs duties or to possess or surrender passports. Rickard also testified at trials of Indians who were arrested for illegal entry into the United States.

Today, the American Indian Law Alliance (AILA), a nonprofit organization that serves Indigenous peoples and members of Indigenous communities and nations in their struggle for sovereignty, human rights, and social justice, has published an online guide to border-crossing rights under the Jay Treaty.

Iroquois leaders have also been active in numerous international treaty forums relating to In-

Chief Justice John Jay negotiated the treaty named after him (and also as the Treaty of London of 1794) with Britain; the treaty also affected Indians crossing between American and British lands.

digenous people's' rights. Since the early 1900s, the Iroquois Confederacy has issued its own passports, which are recognized for travel purposes by many nations.

Repatriation

The Iroquois continue to repatriate, or reclaim, wampum belts that have long been held in U.S. and Canadian museums as well as museums around the world. Wampum belts are made from quahog clam shells and fastened into a string or chain of several rows. Symbols were embroidered into the belts as documents and historical records of diplomatic agreements, treaties, records of important historical events, and records of sacred and ceremonial law. The Iroquois want wampum belts returned so that they can be used and cared for by people who can read and interpret these important documents. Wampum belts are analogous in importance to U.S. government documents such as the Declaration of Independence and the United States Constitution.

In 1989, the Onondaga succeeded in recovering their sacred wampum belts from the Museum of the State of New York in Albany after a lengthy process of diplomatic give-and-take and goodwill. The state returned twelve wampum belts, some of which had been in the State Museum since 1898. In 1996, the National Museum of the American Indian returned seventy-four belts to the Haudenosaunee Confederacy. In 2012, a central New York historical organization returned to the Onondaga Indian Nation a rare wampum belt believed to be more than two centuries old. The belt, made of white and purple shells, was obtained in 1919 by a Syracuse historian who worked for years with the tribe.

Land Claims

The Iroquois have also filed claims against the U.S. government relating to fraudulent loss of land in a series of land transactions with the state of New York. The Iroquois were cited in the 1790 Indian Trade and Intercourse Act that stated that only the U.S. Congress could make agreements with the Indian nations. However, New York State ignored the federal law. It dealt directly with the Iroquois nations, making illegal treaties to acquire enormous portions of their lands without federal approval, forcing people to move to smaller reservations. Within fifty years of the American Revolution, New York had acquired most or all of the homelands of the Cayuga, Mohawk, Oneida, Onondaga, and Seneca.

New York's actions are the reason for twentieth-century lawsuits involving Iroquois lands. Since the mid-1970s, the five nations have pursued land claims in federal courts. These claims have been dismissed because, according to federal Indian law, American Indian tribal claims are "disruptive" and impact centuries-old state and local governments and non-Indians. Some legal scholars argue that "settlements among multiple sovereigns [Indian nation, state, and local government] establish that even Indian claims that have the potential to be highly disruptive can be settled through negotiation." Many Iroquois believe that the only real settlement of land claims can come through some form of land restoration.

The Iroquois continue to have a strong affinity for their homeland. Maintaining and preserving contemporary landholdings is crucial to the continuance of their communities, culture, and identity. The reservation is a place where the Iroquois practice their customs and rituals. Many urban Iroquois return to these homelands to be culturally and spiritually refreshed among their friends and kin. The Iroquois strive to retain their sovereignty, independence, and culture in their reservation communities.

SUCCESSFUL INDIAN LAND CLAIMS IN THE NORTHEAST

Narragansett Tribe of Rhode Island

In 1975, the Narragansett Tribe filed a land claim suit against the state of Rhode Island and several landowners for the return of approximately 3,200 acres of undeveloped reservation lands. The Narragansett nation negotiated an out-of-court settlement in 1978 with private landholders, the state of Rhode Island, representatives from the Carter Administration, and the town of Charlestown, where the claim was located. The agreement hammered out by the above parties provided the basis for state legislation and a federal statute that provided for the extinguishment of all Narragansett land claims in exchange for nine hundred acres from the state and another nine hundred acres to be purchased at federal expense. Subsequently, the Narragansett chartered a state corporation to manage the 1,800 acres of land. To implement the act, the U.S. government established a $3.5 million settlement fund. In 1983, the Narragansett received federal recognition. The Rhode Island Claims Settlement Act was the first of the eastern land claims to be settled.

Penobscot, Passamaquoddy, and Houlton Band of Maliseet of Maine

In 1777, the U.S. government negotiated a treaty with the Maine Indians. In exchange for their assistance in the American Revolution, the government promised to protect the Maine Indians (this treaty, however, was never ratified, and the U.S. government did not provide protection). In 1791, the Passamaquoddy Nation of Maine ceded all but 23,000 of its acres to the Commonwealth of Massachusetts (at this time, Massachusetts had jurisdiction over what is now the state of Maine). Another Maine Indian nation, the Penobscot, ceded almost all of its land through treaties in 1796 and 1818 and a land sale in 1833.

The validity of these agreements was not questioned until 1972, when the Passamaquoddy Tribe asked the United States government to sue the state of Maine, arguing that the treaties and agreements had never been approved by the U.S. government. The attorney for the Passamaquoddy stated that the lack of approval of the agreements by the federal government meant Massachusetts, and later Maine, violated the Indian Trade and Intercourse Act of 1790, which

President Jimmy Carter negotiated an effective compromise between Maine Indian tribes and the state of Maine to deal with grievances dating back to the eighteenth century.

required the approval of the U.S. government for any transfer of lands from Indian ownership. The secretary of the interior, however, did not agree with the Maine Indians (the Interior Department held that the Maine Indians were not federally recognized) and were not entitled to sue. The Maine Indians went to court to claim approximately two-thirds of the state of Maine. Many complex legal issues were involved.

President Jimmy Carter, the Congress, Maine, and the tribes all wanted a speedy and less costly solution to the case rather than continued legal battles to resolve the dispute. President Carter took the lead in seeking a consensus. He seized the initiative by developing a reasonable set of recommendations and appointing a team to represent the U.S. government in negotiations with the Indians and Maine. In effect, Carter forced both the state of Maine and the Indians to negotiate an equitable solution to the land claims case.

In 1980, after protracted negotiation, the Maine Indians finally reached a settlement. In exchange for giving up their claims to nearly two-thirds of Maine, the Penobscot, Passamaquoddy, and Houlton Band of Maliseet received a settlement of $81.5 million, confirmation of federal recognition for all three groups, and the right to purchase at least three hundred thousand acres of land.

At the signing of the Maine Indian Claims Settlement Act of 1980, President Carter asserted: "This should be a proud day for … the tribes, who placed their trust in the system that has not always treated them fairly, the leaders of the state of Maine, who came openly to the bargaining table, the landowners, who helped to make the settlement a reality by offering land for sale that they might not otherwise have wanted to sell, the members of Congress, who realize the necessity of acting, and all the citizens of Maine, who have worked together to resolve this problem of land title."

Maine Indian Economic Development

Two clauses in the Maine Indian Claims Settlement Act impacted the sovereignty of the Maine tribes relative to other federally recognized tribes. One clause likened the tribes to municipalities subject to the laws of the state of Maine. The other clause stated that the tribes could not benefit from any federal legislation passed after 1980 designed for Indians. This prevented Maine Indian nations from taking advantage of forms of economic development widely available to other federally recognized tribes, such as gaming.

One form of tribal economic development that has emerged among many Wabanaki (collective term for Maine's Maliseet, Micmac, Penobscot, and Passamaquoddy) individuals and tribes is basket making. The Maine Indian Basketmakers Alliance (MIBA) was founded in 1993 to save the highly endangered ash and sweetgrass basketry-weaving traditions of the Maliseet, Micmac, Passamaquoddy, and Penobscot tribes. At the time of its founding, there were fewer than a dozen basket makers younger than the age of fifty statewide, who were still practicing and learning this ancient, and once prolific, art form. Through twenty years of educational programs and marketing efforts, the MIBA has increased numbers from fifty-five founding members to over two hundred basket makers today. Today, MIBA counts several nationally award-winning basket makers among the group.

With a long history in the region, basket making now is a form of economic enterprise and cultural preservation and revitalization. According to anthropologist Lisa K. Neuman, "The emergence in Maine of several large, annual social gatherings designed specifically around the display and marketing of Wabanaki baskets to collectors, tourists, and non-Native consumers points to the economic importance of basket making in the local economy."

Aquinnah and Mashpee Wampanoag Nations of Massachusetts

The legends teach me that we have always been here. Just take the Moshop legend, for example. It says that Moshop led our people to Aquinnah to take us away from the fighting that was going on on the mainland. While he was leading us there, he dragged his toe and broke off that piece of land that became Noepe. The fact that he created that island tells me that we have always been there ever since that place was an island, ever since that place was created.

—Tobias Vanderhoop

Aquinnah Wampanoag

The Aquinnah Wampanoag of Aquinnah, Martha's Vineyard, Massachusetts, obtained federal recognition in 1987 along with a land settlement, which ensured that 485 acres of land with historical and cultural significance would return to Wampanoag ownership. The land is comprised of four separate locations. These include the face of the sacred Gay Head Cliffs, over one hundred thousand years old, designated as a National Natural Landmark by the U.S. secretary of the interior in 1965; common lands that include cranberry bogs; tribal land on Black Brook Road, the location of tribal government offices; and the Herring Creek, an important source of the nation's diet. The Wampanoag Environmental Water Lab and shellfish hatchery is found at this site. The Aquaculture Facility is used to improve the stock of shellfish populations, which benefits the island as a whole.

The Mashpee Wampanoag of Mashpee, Cape Cod, Massachusetts

What every American Indian must learn to do is keep both feet on shore, remain an Indian, but also understand the need to occasionally sail into the white man's territory to survive.

—John Peters Slow Turtle
(1930–1997), Mashpee Wampanoag
Supreme Medicine Man

The Mashpee Wampanoag Tribe, known as the People of the First Light, have lived in present-day Massachusetts for millennia. After an arduous process lasting more than three decades, the Mashpee Wampanoag were acknowledged as a federally recognized tribe in 2007 and retain full tribal sovereignty rights. In March 2014, the Mashpee Wampanoag Tribe celebrated the completion of its new government and community center building in Mashpee, Massachusetts, by throwing a grand opening party for hundreds of its friends.

Other Native groups in the Northeast that filed subsequent claims have had some successes and some failures. The most successful solutions to these claims issues come when tribal governments, Indian interest groups, Indian individuals, and the federal and state governments are involved in the formulation and implementation of claims settlements. While Indian groups in the Northeast have won important, precedent-setting cases in the last generation, it is important to note that the Iroquois and others have also been active in the international arena in presenting their claims over the taking of Indian lands, unfair leases, and restrictions on tribal religious practices. There is a growing body of international human rights laws that recognizes that Native Americans are entitled to political and economic self-determination as well as religious freedom. Although the early European colonists who came to the Northeast did not appreciate the sovereignty of American Indians, contemporary federal and international law is paving the way for American Indians of the Northeast and elsewhere to survive as distinct communities with well-defined sovereign rights and powers.

BIOGRAPHIES

Deganawidah (fl. 1500s)
Huron, Prophet/Statesman/Law Giver

Deganawidah was a prophet, statesman, and law giver who founded with Hiawatha the Five Nations (Iroquois) Confederacy (Cayuga, Mohawk, Oneida, Onondaga, and Seneca) sometime before the landing of Columbus in 1492. There are many stories about the man known as the Great Peacemaker, some with conflicting information. It is reported that he was born a Huron in present-day Ontario, Canada, and according to many sources of historical Iroquois tradition, he was born of a virgin. By all accounts, he was a prophet who counseled peace between warring tribes. His friend, Hiawatha, a Mohawk, who was renowned for his oratory, helped him realize his vision.

In Iroquois history, Deganawidah lived in a time when there was little peace among the Iroquois-speaking nations, of which the Huron is one. These nations were often at war with one another because there was no agreed-upon means of resolving conflict between the various nations.

Deganawidah had a vision from the Great Spirit that instructed him to give the Great Law, a set of rules and procedures for working out differences and settling hostilities between nations. Deganawidah traveled among the Iroquois nations of present-day New York and Ohio, spreading the message of peace. Most rejected the message, but on his travels, he met Hiawatha, a member of the Iroquoian-speaking Mohawk Nation living near present-day Albany, New York. Since Deganawidah had a speech impediment, Hiawatha, a powerful orator, became the spokesperson for his message.

Both Deganawidah and Hiawatha traveled among the Iroquois Nations, and after some resistance among the Onondaga convinced the Seneca, Cayuga, Onondaga, Oneida, and Mohawk to set aside their differences and follow a path of cooperation. The Iroquois stopped their fighting and formed a Confederacy sometime around 1570. Out of reverence for the Great Peacemaker, they rarely say his name aloud. Through ceremonies and agreements, they settled their disputes peacefully at the annual gatherings of the Iroquois Confederacy, which still meet at Onondaga, near present-day Syracuse, New York.

Decisions of the Confederacy required unanimous consensus among all nations. The elderly clan matrons nominated and deposed the chiefs of their own lineages from office if they did not conform to the will of the lineage. The purpose of the league was to create peace and to spread the Great Law of Peace to all nations in the world.

Hiawatha (fl. 1500s)
Mohawk, Reformer/Statesman/Legislator

The first known person to bear the name Hiawatha was a noted reformer, statesman, and legislator celebrated as one of the founders of the Five Nations (Iroquois) Confederacy. Tradition also makes him a prophet and a disciple of the prophet Deganawidah. These two sought to bring about reforms aimed at ending of all strife, murder, and war and the promotion of universal peace and well-being among the Seneca, Cayuga, Onondaga, Oneida, and Mohawk. After some resistance, the Iroquois peoples stopped feuding and formed the Confederacy. It is not known what happened to Hiawatha after the Confederacy's founding.

Hiawatha's name is most familiar from its use in the Henry Wadsworth Longfellow poem, "The Song of Hiawatha." The poem, set in the Great Lakes with Hiawatha as a fictional Ojibwe, has almost nothing to do with Hiawatha, the historical figure.

Bashabez (d. 1616)
Penobscot, Leader

Chief Bashabez was the first leader documented by the Europeans. A shipwrecked English sailor, David Ingram refers to him (around 1568) as the head chief of "Norumbega," a confederation of seven or eight Abenaki-speaking Indian nations. This may have been the Mawoshen Confederacy. The Mawoshen capital was called "Arembee," probably located near present-day Brewer, Maine. Samuel de Champlain, sailing for France, met Chief Bashabez in 1604 as Champlain followed the Penobscot River north and inland to Kenduskeag (now Bangor, Maine). Chief Bashabez was killed by Micmac Chief Membertou in a act of revenge for the death of one of his warriors killed in Penobscot Territory. The Micmac had a huge advantage due to the firearms they obtained from the Port Royal French settlement.

Massasoit (c. 1580–1661)
Wampanoag, Leader

Massasoit was a principal leader of the Wampanoag people in the early 1600s who encouraged friendship with English settlers. As leader of the Wampanoag, Massasoit exercised control over a number of Indian groups that occupied lands from Narragansett Bay to Cape Cod in present-day Massachusetts. Massasoit negotiated friendly relations with the recently arrived Puritan settlers. As early as 1621, with the aid of Tisquantum (Squanto), a Wampanoag who spoke English, Massasoit opened communications with the Pilgrims at their Plymouth settlement. He established trading relationships with the settlers, exchanging food for firearms, tools, and other sought-after European products.

Massasoit helped the Puritan settlers in a number of ways, including donations of land and advice on farming and hunting. Massasoit also offered the colonists important counsel on how to protect themselves from other tribes. Massasoit's alliance with the colonists created divisions among the region's Indian nations and problems for the Wampanoag who were loyal to Massasoit. Consequently, Massasoit's warriors were forced to wage frequent attacks against Indian groups less inclined to welcome the English.

The Wampanoag chief became close friends with the progressive-minded theologian Roger Williams and according to many accounts influenced Williams' relative understanding and favorable view of New England Indians and their right to territory. In 1636, when Williams was threatened with imprisonment for heresy by the Massachusetts colonial government, he fled to Massasoit's home. Despite the efforts of Williams to maintain peace, Massasoit eventually came to resent the growing encroachment of English settlers. It would be his son Philip, however, who would turn this resentment into war in 1675–1676.

Though the exact details of the event have become clouded in secular mythology, it is believed that Massasoit participated in what has come to be called the "first Thanksgiving." Around 1621, Massasoit traveled to Plymouth with a number of followers, where they took part in a meal with the colonists. Judging by the inability of the colonists to provide for themselves at this time, it is most likely that Massasoit and his people provided the food for this "historic" meal.

Tisquantum (Squanto) (1580–1622)
Wampanoag, Interpreter/ Cultural Mediator

Tisquantum was a Wampanoag interpreter and cultural mediator known in history as Squanto. In 1605, Tisquantum was abducted in present-day Massachusetts by Europeans and sold into slavery in Malaga, an island off the Mediterranean coast of Spain. He eventually escaped to England, where he enlisted in the Newfoundland Company. After sailing to America and back again, Squanto finally returned to his homeland in 1619 to find his people wiped out by disease. Squanto took up life with the Pilgrims at Plymouth and provided invaluable instruction on farming, hunting, fishing, and geography. According to one colonial historian, he directed them "when to take fish, and to procure other commodities, and was also their pilott to bring them to unknowne places for their profitt." It is also believed that Squanto helped the Pilgrims maintain friendly relations with neighboring tribes.

In 1622, Squanto died of disease while helping the Pilgrims negotiate trade agreements with the Narragansett Indians. In recent history, the story of Squanto and the Pilgrims has become an oft-repeated, frequently distorted tale for young people as an example of friendly relations between Indians and the early colonists.

Philip (Metacom) (1639–1676)
Wampanoag, Leader

From 1675 to 1676, Philip planned and carried out an unsuccessful attempt to oust English settlers from New England. The conflict has come to be known as King Philip's War, one of the most destructive Indian wars in New England's history.

Like his father Massasoit, Philip (among the English colonists, he was called King Philip) was the grand sachem of the Wampanoag Confederacy, an alliance of Algonquian-speaking peoples living in present-day New England. Unlike his father, however, Philip found peace with the New England colonists impossible, and he led a revolt against them. The seeds of revolt were laid before Philip became the grand sachem. Although Massasoit had worked successfully with the progressive-minded New England minister Roger Williams to maintain peaceful relations between Indians and the English, when Philip came to power, the mood of his people was more militant. There were several reasons for the change: Colonists now outnumbered Indians in the region two to one, and English farms, animals, and villages were overtaking Indian land. Puritans subjected Philip's people to unfair laws, taxes, and jurisdictions. Alcohol and disease were also taking their toll. It was against this backdrop that Philip planned for war against the English.

Fighting erupted in 1675 at the frontier settlement of Swansea on June 16th. The conflict quickly escalated across southern New England, involving the colonies of Plymouth, Massachusetts, Connecticut, and, to a limited extent, Rhode Island. Some tribes, including the Narragansett and Nipmuck, supported Philip; others gave valuable assistance to the English. Losses on both sides were brutal. (Puritans recorded with relish the massacre of noncombatants.) Villages, farms, and animals were destroyed. The colonists had underrated Philip's talents as a military strategist and leader. Wampanoag and Narragansett warriors fought with a deep courage fostered by equal doses of optimism and desperation. Although for the first few months of the war, the outcome was in doubt, the English eventually were victorious. On December 19, 1675, a decisive battle in southern Rhode Island resulted in the deaths of as many as six hundred Indians and four hundred captured. In August 1676, Philip himself was killed after being betrayed by his own warriors. His body was mutilated and displayed publicly.

Wetamoo (c. 1650–1676)
Pocasset Wampanoag, Leader

Wetamoo's father was possibly Corbitant, sachem of the Pocasset Band of Wampanoag in present-day Rhode Island. She had five husbands, the most famous of whom was Wamsutta, the eldest son of Massasoit, the grand sachem of the Wampanoag. She became sachem of the Pocasset Band, located in present-day Tiverton, Rhode Island, in 1620 after her father died, probably because he had no sons.

Wetamoo joined with King Philip in fighting the colonists. After English forces surrounded her camp in Massachusetts, she tried to escape by canoe. Soldiers fired at it, causing it to sink. Wetamoo drowned in the strong current. The colonists cut off her head, displaying it on a pole in Taunton, Massachusetts. Mary Rowlandson, an English captive during King Philip's War who was later bought and sold by Quinnapin (Narraganset), Wetamoo's fifth husband, wrote extensively about Wetamoo. She described her stature among her people as well as her clothing and jewelry.

Kateri Tekakwitha (1656–1680)
Mohawk/Algonquian, Saint

Kateri Tekakwitha, called "Indian saint" and "Lily of the Mohawk," was the daughter of a Mohawk man and Christianized Algonquian woman, both of whom died during a smallpox epidemic. She was adopted by her two aunts and an uncle. Kateri Tekakwitha converted as a teenager and was baptized at the age of twenty, which incurred the great hostility of her tribe and her uncle. She fled to a Christian Mohawk community near present-day Montreal, Canada, where she practiced her new religion.

Kateri Tekakwitha, who received her first communion in 1677, was dedicated to prayer, austerity, penitential practices, chastity, and care for the sick and aged, establishing a reputation for sanctity. Numerous biographies have been published about Kateri Tekakwitha, based on contemporary accounts. In 1943, she was declared venerable by Pope Pius XII, and in 1980, she was beatified by Pope John Paul II. She was canonized by Pope Benedict XVI in 2012.

According to Catholic Online, hundreds of thousands of people have visited at the Jesuit shrine to Kateri Tekakwitha at her Auriesville, New York, home near where she was born and the Franciscan shrine at her second home in Fonda, New York. The Tekakwitha Conference, a nonprofit organization named after Kateri Tekakwitha, is dedicated to Native concerns including nurturing "the relationship between Indigenous people and the Catholic Church." St. Kateri Tekakwitha was the first Native American to be declared a saint.

Caleb Cheeshahteaumuck (d.1665)
Aquinnah Wampanoag, Harvard Student

In 1665, Caleb Cheeshahteaumuck became the first Native American to graduate from Harvard University. Cheeshahteaumuck came from Martha's Vineyard and attended a preparatory school in Roxbury. At Harvard, he lived and studied in the Indian College, Harvard's first brick building, with a fellow Wampanoag, Joel Iacoomes.

Awashonks Sakonnet (fl. 1670s)
Wampanoag, Leader

Awashonks (also spelled Awashunckes, Awashunkes, or Awasoncks) was a female sachem (chief) of the Sakonnet (also spelled Saconnet) Band, part of the Wampanoag Confederacy, near present-day Little Compton, Rhode Island. She became sachem not by inheritance but through her talent for negotiation and diplomacy. In the mid-seventeenth century, her lands were claimed by the English settlers of Plymouth Colony. While she had allied herself to the English to increase her power, ironically, their victory eroded her standing among both the English and the Sakonnet. Her diplomacy helped the Sakonnet receive amnesty from the colonists.

Crispus Attucks (c. 1723–1770)
Massachuset, Protestor

Crispus Attucks, the son of an African father and a Massachuset mother, lived in the Native mission settlement of Natick. On March 5, 1770, colonists, upset with British tax laws, attacked a detachment of British troops under Captain Thomas Preston in front of the Boston Customs House. Soldiers fired into the rioting crowd. Attucks, who was believed to be the leader of the protestors, was the first to fall in the so-called Boston Massacre. He is also considered to be the first American casualty in the American Revolutionary War. Abolitionist supporters lauded Attucks as a black American who played a heroic role in the history of the U.S. Because Attucks had Wampanoag ancestors, his story also holds special significance for many Native people.

Samson Occom (1723–1792)
Mohegan, Minister

Samson Occom became a Christian convert at the age of eighteen. As a minister and educator, he devoted his life to teaching and converting Indians to Christianity. He was the first Indian to preach in England.

Occom, born in New London, Connecticut, was the first student of Eleazor Wheelock, a Christian missionary who had been teaching Indians since about 1743 in his church-sponsored Indian Charity School. Wheelock's goal was to train his students to become Christian ministers. When Occom finished his studies, he was a school teacher for a short while, at which time he married Mary Montauk. In 1759, he was ordained by the Presbyterian Church. Occom's parish was among the Montauk Indians and among his duties was the recruitment of Indian youths for Wheelock's school.

In 1765, Occom traveled to England as Wheelock's representative. He stayed in England for two years preaching and fundraising. It was during this trip that Occom obtained the funds to establish a new school for Indian children. While Occom was in England, Wheelock's Indian school was moved to New Hampshire and, in 1769, became Dartmouth College.

When he returned to New England, Occom left Wheelock's organization over differences regarding the emphasis and focus of their mission. Wheelock was interested mainly in training non-Indian missionaries. Occom wanted to teach and minister to Indians directly. As a result, Occom became a minister and teacher in an Algonquian-speaking community of Indian people in eastern New York called Brotherton. Brotherton was composed of several Indian tribes that accepted Christianity, and Occom welcomed them all to his church and school.

Because of encroachment by New York settlers, Occom spent many of his later years working to relocate his followers further west to Oneida Territory in central New York. The Oneida, one nation of the Iroquois Confederacy, welcomed the Brotherton community and allowed them to live on their land. The resettlement to Oneida Territory was completed in 1786 with the establishment of a town named New Stockbridge. Occom died six years later.

Handsome Lake (1735–1815)
Seneca, Prophet

Handsome Lake was an Allegany Seneca prophet who founded a religion. Born in a Seneca village on the Genesee River, New York, Handsome Lake participated in the wars of the period: the French and Indian War (1755–1759), Pontiac's War (1763), and the American Revolutionary War (1775–1783). By the late 1790s, the once powerful Iroquois lost most of their territory and were relegated to small reserves in upstate New York. While the Iroquois were experiencing social and cultural depression resulting from their recent losses, Handsome Lake reported a series of visions, beginning in 1799, and preached the *Gaiwiio*, or Good Word, to the Iroquois. He quickly obtained many followers and taught that the Iroquois must reorganize central aspects of their economic, social, and religious life.

Under Handsome Lake's guidance, many Iroquois communities adopted new moral codes, men took up agriculture and constructed family farms, and many individuals adopted new religious ceremonies and beliefs. Handsome Lake's message combined elements of Quakerism, Catholicism, and traditional Iroquois beliefs. Before his death, Handsome Lake was able to see spiritual reformation among his people. In the 1830s, after his death, Handsome Lake's followers formulated his teaching into the Handsome Lake religion, or Longhouse religion. His teachings are still practiced today by many Iroquois.

Joseph Brant (Thayendanegea) (1742–1807)
Mohawk, Diplomat/Translator

Joseph Brant attended a Christian school in Connecticut and mastered spoken and written English. In the early 1760s and 1770s, as a translator and diplomat, he helped the English to negotiate with Iroquois tribes. When the American Revolution broke out, Brant aligned himself with the Loyalist cause and traveled to England in 1775. He was quickly commissioned a colonel in the British army and put his diplomacy skills to work enlisting Iroquois allies for the Loyalist cause.

Brant participated in a number of battles directly and insisted on using his own military tactics and stratagems. In 1777 and 1778, the persistent raids by Indians and British soldiers against settlements in the Ohio Valley convinced General George Washington, the future U.S. president, to send an army into Iroquois country. The Americans succeeded in destroying a number of Iroquois villages, but Brant did not sanction the subsequent American–Iroquois peace treaty and continued to launch raids against American forces.

In appreciation of his military services, the English gave him a retirement pension and a large tract of land along the Grand River in Ontario, Canada. Like many others, Brant was an Indian who lived between two worlds. He is credited with having translated the Bible into the Mohawk language and died near his estate near Brantford, Ontario, on November 24, 1807.

Red Jacket (1758–1830)
Seneca, Tribal Leader

Red Jacket supported the British during the American Revolution (1777–1783) and later became a spokesman for his people in negotiations with the U.S. government. Red Jacket was also a staunch opponent of Christianity and worked to prevent Iroquois conversions to Christianity.

Although Red Jacket eventually allied himself with other Indian nations in support of the British during the American Revolution, he was originally hesitant about the affiliation. This ambivalence perhaps explains why he did little fighting during the conflict. According to a number of accounts, Red Jacket's reluctance to fight was perceived as cowardice by some Iroquois war leaders such as Cornplanter and Joseph Brant.

After the war, Red Jacket became a principal spokesman for the Seneca people. He was present at treaty negotiations in 1794 and 1797 in which major portions of Seneca land in upstate New York were ceded or partitioned into smaller reservations. During this era, Red Jacket also became an outspoken opponent of Christianity and an advocate for preserving traditional Iroquois beliefs. His efforts to protect traditional beliefs culminated in the temporary expulsion of all Christian missionaries from Seneca Territory in 1824. Red Jacket and the so-called Pagan Party were undermined in the ensuing years, however, by accusations of witchcraft and Red Jacket's own problems with alcohol. In 1827, Red Jacket was deposed as a Seneca chief. He died three years later after his own family had converted to Christianity.

Red Jacket is immortalized in a now famous painting by Charles Bird King. In this historical painting, Red Jacket is depicted with a large, silver medal that was given to him in 1792 by President George Washington.

David Cusick (c. 1780–c. 1831)
Tuscarora, Artist/Author

David Cusick was an artist and the author of *David Cusick's Sketches of Ancient History of the Six Nations* (1828). This is an early (if not the first) account of Native history, social and cultural traditions, and ancient tribal stories, written and published in English by a Native person. He also was the first Native to use Western pictorial art to interpret Iroquoian spirituality.

William Apess (1798–1839)
Pequot, Writer/Minister/Activist

William Apess wrote the first full-length Native American autobiography, *A Son of the Forest*, in 1829. This book tells of his confrontation with whites and their racist views while finding how his childhood and the "quest for heavenly reward" have given him grace. He became one of the most prolific Native American writers of the nineteenth century. Apess (also known as William Apes) was an ordained Methodist minister, writer, and activist in Massachusetts. After becoming ordained in 1829, he traveled around the Northeast, preaching to mostly African and Native American audiences. The following years consisted of trying to put an end to slavery and fighting for the land rights of Native Americans through his position in the church.

Apess visited the Mashpee Wampanoag on Cape Cod in 1833. Hearing their grievances, he helped organize what was called the Mashpee Revolt of 1833–1834. The Mashpee attempt to regain civil rights was covered sympathetically by the *Boston Advocate*. Apess published a book about the experience in 1835.

Ely S. Parker (1829–1895)
Seneca, Tribal Leader/Engineer/ Commissioner of Indian Affairs

 Ely S. Parker was the first Indian commissioner of Indian affairs. During the Civil War, Parker, a close friend and colleague of General Ulysses S. Grant, served the Union cause and penned the final copy of the Confederate army's surrender terms at the Appomattox Courthouse in 1865.

Ely Parker was educated at Yates Academy in Yates, New York, and Cayuga Academy in Aurora, New York. In 1852, he became a Seneca chief Indian and helped the Tonawanda Seneca secure land rights to their reservation in western New York State. Parker hoped to become a lawyer, but because he was an Indian, he was denied entry to the bar. Undaunted, Parker studied engineering at Rensselaer Polytechnic Institute instead.

With the outbreak of the Civil War, Parker tried to serve the Union by enlisting in the Army Corps of Engineers but was refused again because of racial prejudice. He eventually received a commission in May 1863 as captain of engineers in the Seventh Corps. This was due in part to his friendship with General Ulysses S. Grant, whom he had met by chance before the war and with whom he later served during the Vicksburg campaign.

When Grant became president in 1868, he appointed Parker his commissioner of Indian affairs. It was the first time an Indian had held the post. As commissioner, Parker worked to rid the Bureau of corruption and fraud. He was an advocate for western Indian tribes and gained a reputation for fairness and progressive thinking. In 1871, Parker was falsely accused of fraud. Although he was acquitted of all charges, Parker resigned and moved to New York City, where he lived and worked until his death in 1895.

"Blind Joe" Amos (fl. 1830s)
Mashpee Wampanoag, Minister

"Blind Joe" Amos was a Native minister who had a reputation for great sermons. In 1834, he joined William Apess, a Pequot minister, and led an insurrection against colonists coming to Mashpee and taking valuable wood. In the "Woodlot Revolt," Amos and others committed an act of civil disobedience by dumping wagonloads of lumber which had been cut by white men. The state of Massachusetts called the removal of wood from the cart a "riot." According to the Mashpee tribal website, Amos "began the first phase of true self-government."

Cornplanter (Gaiänt'wakê or Kaiiontwa'kon) (c. 1732–1836)
Seneca, Leader

Cornplanter was a leading warrior and village leader among the Seneca, one of six nations of the Iroquois Confederacy, who lived in present upstate New York. Cornplanter belonged to the Seneca Turtle Clan, whose sachem held the title of Handsome Lake. Cornplanter, however, was not elected sachem. He earned his role as leader largely through military command and personal influence, which attracted friends and relatives to live on his reserved lands, which by 1800 totaled 1,300 acres in northern Pennsylvania.

Cornplanter's father was a trader named John O'Bail, who, during the 1730s, lived among the Seneca and traded manufactured goods for furs and skins. O'Bail chose not to live among the Iroquois and left his Seneca wife and child in care of her clan. Cornplanter grew to be a warrior leader. He fought with the French during the French and Indian War (1755–1759) and with the British during the American Revolutionary War (1775–1783).

After the colonists won the Revolutionary War, Seneca lands and crops were destroyed by the U.S. military as punishment for siding with the British. The Seneca, along with other Iroquois, were driven away from their homes. Cornplanter looked for ways to keep Seneca lands and agreed to help the U.S. in the war of 1812. Because he was a skilled diplomat and fought for the Americans, he was able to negotiate a peace settlement with the Supreme Executive Council of Pennsylvania and Governor Thomas Mifflin. His people were granted lands to northwestern Pennsylvania right on the New York border. The state of Pennsylvania was so grateful for Cornplanter's assistance in negotiating with other Indian nations that it not only gave him the land, but it also erected a monument in his honor, the first to be dedicated to an American Indian.

In 1961, the U.S. Corps of Engineers built the Kinzua Dam on the Allegany Reservation. The dam destroyed Seneca houses, hunting and fishing grounds, a longhouse, ceremonial building, and a school. It forced the removal of nearly six hundred Seneca homes from the area. The Seneca Indian cemetery, home to Cornplanter's grave, was moved to higher ground just across the border in New York State. Today, Pennsylvania state does not recognize any Native groups, despite its promise to Cornplanter.

Louis Francis Sockalexis (1871–1913)
Penobscot, Baseball Player

Sockalexis, a member of the Penobscot Indian Tribe of Maine, played in only ninety-four major league games but is remembered today as the first Native American, and first recognized minority, to perform in the National League. He was signed by the Cleveland Spiders in 1897, fifty years before Jackie Robinson broke baseball's color barrier with the Brooklyn Dodgers. He was Cleveland's main pitcher from 1897 to 1899. His talent as a pitcher brought fan support in Cleveland but evoked racial slurs in every city where the Spiders played. Sportswriters exploited his Native background for more game tickets and news stories. It is believed that the Spiders changed their name to "Indians" because of him, but he did not have anything to do with the decision, regarded now as being offensive to Native Americans.

Sockalexis, born on the Penobscot reservation in Old Town, Maine, was the son of Francis Sockalexis, a logger who later served as governor (formerly called "chief") of the Penobscot. He was considered the best athlete in the tribe in the community, winning footraces and throwing contests against all challengers. His natural baseball ability led him to play semipro ball for various teams in Maine during his late teens and early twenties. He attended college at Notre Dame and Holy Cross. Sockalexis, like Robinson, was a multitalented athlete who excelled in football and track as well as baseball. He appeared destined for stardom; however, he suffered depression because of overt racism he experienced as a player in the National League. It derailed his promising career.

Louis R. Bruce (1877–1968)
Mohawk, Baseball Player/Minister

Louis R. Bruce, one of the first Native Americans to reach the majors, played in thirty games with the Philadelphia Athletics in 1904 during a pro career that ran from 1900 to 1907. The son of a Mohawk chief from the St. Regis Mohawk Reservation in upstate New York, Bruce excelled at baseball during high school. He played for the minor league Toronto Maple Leafs from 1900 to 1903, where he was a two-way player, pitching and playing the outfield and finding success in both roles.

Before joining the A's, Bruce graduated from the University of Pennsylvania School of Den-

tistry. After a couple years of practice, Bruce went on to obtain another degree in theology from Syracuse University and became a Methodist minister. He served eleven different churches (including tribal congregations) in central and upstate New York over a thirty-eight-year period. Bruce's son, Louis R. Bruce, served as commissioner of Indian affairs.

Arthur (Caswell) Parker (1881–1955)
Seneca, Anthropologist/Museum Director/Reformer

Arthur Parker became one of history's leading Native Americans in anthropology and museum directorship. Parker, a member of an influential Seneca family that included his great-nephew, Ely S. Parker, secretary to Ulysses S. Grant, became a field archaeologist for Harvard's Peabody Museum in 1903.

Parker, who never graduated from Dickinson Seminary or Harvard where he studied, developed an interest in anthropology in the late 1890s and spent a great deal of time working for the American Museum of Natural History. In 1906, he became state archaeologist for the New York State Museum in Albany, a position he held until 1925. That year, Parker accepted appointment as director of the Rochester Museum of Arts and Sciences, a role he filled for twenty years.

Although Parker lacked formal academic credentials, his research and publications were impressive. By the time he retired from Rochester Museum, he had written hundreds of articles, significant books about the Iroquois, and a few children's books.

Besides his contributions to the field of anthropology, Parker was also a major figure in Indian reform movements. He helped found the Society of American Indians in 1911 and later served as editor of its quarterly journal. In 1935, he became the first president of the Society of American Archaeology. In 1944, he helped found the National Congress of American Indians, the oldest, largest, and most representative American Indian and Alaska Native organization.

Louis R(ooks) Bruce, Jr. (1906–1989)
Mohawk, Commissioner of Indian Affairs

Louis R. Bruce, Jr., was federal commissioner of Indian affairs from 1969 to 1973, the second Indian to hold the post of commissioner in nearly a century. Bruce was born on the Onondaga Indian Reservation and grew up on the St. Regis Mohawk Reservation, both in upstate New York. He was dismissed as commissioner in the wake of a six-day takeover of the Bureau of Indian Affairs building in November 1973 by about five hundred Indians protesting injustices. After his dismissal, Mr. Bruce founded Native American Consultants, Inc., a firm that specialized in the promotion of Indian involvement in national affairs.

Ray Fadden (1910–2008)
Mohawk, Teacher

Ray Fadden (Tehanetorens), a teacher and influential figure among the Mohawk of Akwesasne, New York, became one of the first teachers at the St. Regis Mohawk School in Hogansburg. Ray grew up in the Adirondack Mountains. He was passionate about his love for all things Native and spent many years learning all he could about the Mohawk culture and history both from books and from elders he met throughout the Iroquois Confederacy. After attending the State University of New York, he taught at Haudonosaunee (Iroquois) schools for decades.

Ray fought against negative characterizations of Native people by mobilizing his students into a youth group that traveled all over the Northeast visiting Indian historic sites, camping out, and learning as much as they could about Indian craft and lore, then turning around and sharing what they learned with the children they encountered. Ray also published numerous pamphlets and posters about Indian culture that are still in print today.

During the early 1940s, Ray began publishing a series of educational pamphlets and charts. The subject matter included collections of traditional Iroquois stories and histories of various Iroquois groups and individuals, plus other facets of Native American history. The charts included maps and diagrams illustrating the various reservations throughout the Northeast. One chart that illustrated Native American contributions to contemporary civilization went beyond the stereotypes of teepees and canoes and spoke of the many food plants, medicines, and innovations produced by Native American culture. Ray felt that all school children should be made aware of these contributions. A total of twenty-seven pamphlets and approximately forty charts were published. In the 1990s, the Book Publishing Company of Summertown, Tennessee, issued three compilations of his work: *Legends of the Iroquois, Wampum Belts of the Iroquois,* and *Roots of the Iroquois.*

After retiring as a school teacher, Fadden established the Six Nations Indian Museum in Onchiota, a museum that he built with his own money and hands in 1954. There, he continued to educate anyone who would listen about the amazing heritage of the Haudenosaunee people. With his wife, son, daughter-in-law, and grandchildren by his side, Ray became something of a living legend in the Adirondacks, an environmentalist long before it became popular.

Gladys Widdiss (1914–2012)
Aquinnah Wampanoag, Leader/Potter

Born in Aquinnah, Massachusetts, Gladys Widdiss was a tribal elder and historian. She led the Wampanoag Tribe of Gay Head (WTGH) from 1978 to 1987, a formative time for the tribe. Under the Widdiss presidency, the Wampanoag acquired the Gay Head Cliffs, cranberry bogs, and Herring Creek. In 1987, the Aquinnah Wampanoag also received federal recognition from the U.S. Bureau of Indian Affairs. Widdiss was vice chair of the Wampanoag tribal council for many years after leaving the tribal presidency.

Widdiss, one of only a few who held a town permit to take clay from the famed Gay Head Cliffs, began making and selling pottery as a youngster, perfecting her craft during her long life. She made sun-baked pieces from the red, white, black, yellow, and other clay of the ancient cliffs. Explaining her method, she said that firing the clay destroys the color, and as a result the pottery is quite fragile: "You can't do anything but look at it."

Leon Shenandoah (1915–1996)
Onondaga, Leader

Leon Shenandoah was the longtime leader of the Onondaga. In 1969, he was chosen as chief of chiefs, or *tadadaho*, of the Iroquois Confederacy, which consists of the Onondaga, Cayuga, Oneida, Mohawk, Seneca and Tuscarora. The Confederacy has had a *tadadaho* since at least about 1400 C.E. or perhaps longer. Leon Shenandoah served until his death.

For almost three decades, Leon Shenandoah worked for the return of Iroquois wampum belts from museums around New York. On July 4, 1996, he presided over the return of seventy-four wampum belts from the National Museum of the American Indian. He spoke twice to the United Nations and spoke at the 1992 Earth Summit in Brazil. He opposed gambling on Iroquois reservations, saying that greed and the culture of money had no place in his people's culture.

Ralph W. Sturges (1918–2007)
Mohegan, Leader

Chief Sturges was a driving force for the Mohegan gaining federal recognition in 1994, which he considered his greatest accomplishment. He responded to the news from the Bureau of Indian Affairs, "We are no longer the little old tribe that lives upon the hill. We are now the nation that lives upon the hill."

Chief Sturges spent much of his life in service to others and worked for the Civilian Conservation Corps, assisted in the recovery efforts in southeastern Connecticut from the devastating 1938 hurricane, served as public relations director for the Salvation Army, and also served on the board of directors for the Connecticut Hos-

pice. He was publicly recognized for his community spirit by many organizations, including being awarded Eastern Connecticut Chamber of Commerce 2005 Citizen of the Year, Big Brothers and Big Sisters of Southeastern Connecticut Man of the Year, and was bestowed an honorary doctorate in Humane Letters in 2006 from Eastern Connecticut State University. In 2008, Sturges was inducted posthumously into the Connecticut Hall of Fame.

In later years, Sturges began sculpting in marble, following a tradition of Mohegan carvers who had also been chiefs. His famed pieces include a sculpted lighthouse donated to the United States Coast Guard Academy in New London, the base for the repatriated Samuel Uncas gravestone, and the cornerstone of the Mohegan Sun casino.

Russell M. Peters (c. 1923–2002)
Mashpee Wampanoag, Leader

Russell M. Peters was involved in Native American issues at a state, local, and national level. He was the first tribal chairman of the Mashpee Wampanoag Indian Tribal Council. In 1975, he and a number of other Mashpee Wampanoag filed a famous lawsuit to reclaim land taken and developed illegally. Peters also initiated the quest for federal recognition that was achieved in 2007.

Peters was a member of the U.S. Commission on Civil Rights from 1976 to 1984, a member of the Harvard Peabody Museum Native American Repatriation Committee, a member of the White House Conference on Federal Recognition in 1995 and 1996, a board member of the Massachusetts Foundation for the Humanities, a board member of the Pilgrim Society, and the author of *Wampanoag of Mashpee* (Nimrod Press) and *Clambake* (Lerner Publications).

Carol Gardipe (1929–)
Penobscot, Geologist

Carol Gardipe is an award-winning geologist, one of the few women of any race in the field. Her career has included positions with the U.S. Geological Survey, the National Oceanographic and Atmospheric Administration, and roles in higher education as a professor and administrator.

Gardipe first attended the University of Wyoming, Laramie, then took a B.A. in geology and taught at Colby College in Maine. In subsequent years, she worked in Washington, D.C., and on field-mapping teams in the Southwest for the U.S. Geological Survey. Gardipe began graduate studies in geography and natural resources at the University of New Mexico, where she directed the American Indian Engineering Program for two years, the first program in the country for American Indian engineers. At this time, she also worked with the National Research Council Committee on Minorities in Engineering. In 1977, she was one of the seven founders of the American Indian Science and Engineering Society (AISES). Asked why AISES was formed, she explained that "there was a great need, as American Indians were largely absent from the science and technology fields."

Oren R. Lyons (1930–)
Onondaga, Leader/Activist/ Artist/Sports Figure

Oren R. Lyons, raised in the traditional lifeways of the Iroquois on the Seneca and Onondaga reservations in northern New York state, has been a leading advocate for Indigenous causes. After serving in the Army, he graduated in 1958 from the Syracuse University College of Fine Arts. He pursued a career in commercial art in New York City, becoming the art and planning director of Norcross Greeting Cards, with two hundred artists under his supervision. He has exhibited his own paintings widely and is noted as an American Indian artist.

Since his return to Onondaga in 1970, Chief Lyons has been recognized not only in the United States and Canada but internationally as an eloquent and respected spokesperson on behalf of Native peoples. He is a sought-after lecturer or participant in forums in a variety of areas, in-

cluding not only American Indian traditions but also Indian law and history, human rights, and environment and interfaith dialogue and has received numerous honors and awards.

In 1982, he helped establish the Working Group on Indigenous Populations at the United Nations. He is the recipient of the United Nations NGO World Peace Prize. In 1992, he addressed the General Assembly, where he opened the International Year of the World's Indigenous People. He has served on the Executive Committee of the Global Forum of Spiritual and Parliamentary Leaders on Human Survival, is a frequent participant in human rights issues forums in Geneva, and received Sweden's prestigious Friends of the Children Award, along with his colleague, Nelson Mandela. Among his other honors are the Ellis Island Congressional Medal of Honor, the National Audubon Award, the Earth Day International United Nations Award, and the Elder and Wiser Award of the Rosa Parks Institute of Human Rights.

Lyons attended Syracuse University on an athletic scholarship. A lifelong lacrosse player, he was a standout in the sport at Syracuse in the 1950s and became a member of the Syracuse Sports Hall of Fame. He has been honorary chairman of the Iroquois Nationals Lacrosse Team, which was admitted to the International Lacrosse Federation (ILF) in 1990. The Iroquois Nations are the only Native American/First Nation team sanctioned to compete in any sport internationally and have been ranked among the top five in lacrosse. In 1991, Lyons received the Howard E. Johnson Award and was inducted in the upstate New York chapter of the Lacrosse Foundation Hall of Fame. Lyons also excelled as an amateur boxer. He boxed in the army and was talented enough to box in Golden Gloves tournaments.

John A. Peters (1930–1997)
Mashpee Wampanoag, Spiritual/ Political Leader

John Peters, whose traditional name was Slow Turtle (Cjegktoonuppa in Wampanoag), was a medicine man of the Mashpee Wampanoag Indian Tribe and the first and only executive director of the Massachusetts Commission on Indian Affairs, created in 1974. He became a prominent Native spiritualist and ambassador for Native people throughout the world. He was invited by countries from Scandinavia to Japan to meet with spiritual people there and performed traditional Indian ceremonies in Hiroshima and Nagasaki in memory of atomic bomb victims.

John Peters was one of the leaders who worked on legislation in 1978: the federal American Religious Freedom Act and the Indian Child Welfare Act, which requires that all Native American children taken from their homes be placed in Indian homes or places that keep them in touch with their culture. He is also credited with state legislation that became the model for the federal Native American Graves Repatriation Act, which requires museums and other institutions to return skeletal remains and cultural artifacts to Indian tribes.

Joseph Bruchac (1942–)
Western Abenaki,
Writer/Editor/Teacher/Storyteller

Joseph Bruchac lives in the Adirondack mountain foothills town of Greenfield Center, New York, in the same house where his maternal grandparents raised him. Much of his writing draws on that land and his Abenaki ancestry. Although his American Indian heritage is only one part of an ethnic background that includes Slovak and English ancestry, those Native roots are the ones by which he has been most nourished. He, his younger sister Margaret, and his two grown sons, James and Jesse, continue to work extensively in projects involving the preservation of Abenaki culture, language, and traditional Native skills, including performing traditional and contemporary Abenaki music with the Dawnland Singers.

With his late wife, Carol, he founded the Greenfield Review Literary Center and the Greenfield Review Press. He has edited a number of highly praised anthologies of contemporary poetry and fiction. Joseph Bruchac has authored more than 120 books for adults and children and countless articles, most of which have been inspired by Native stories and history. Bruchac was gifted with an Onondaga name, Gah-neh-go-e-yoh, which means "The Good Mind." He has honored his name by helping others learn to write, teaching in schools, colleges, prisons, and as far away as Africa. He co-organized Returning the Gift Festival in 1992, which led to his cofounding Wordcraft Circle, an organization that promotes and mentors Native writers and storytellers.

As a professional teller of the traditional tales of the Adirondacks and the Native peoples of the Northeastern Woodlands, Joe Bruchac has performed widely in Europe and throughout the United States from Florida to Hawaii. He has been a storyteller-in-residence for Native American organizations and schools throughout the continent.

Bruchac's honors include a Rockefeller Humanities fellowship, a National Endowment for the Arts Writing Fellowship for Poetry, the Cherokee Nation Prose Award, the Knickerbocker Award, the Hope S. Dean Award for Notable Achievement in Children's Literature, and both the 1998 Writer of the Year Award and the 1998 Storyteller of the Year Award from the Wordcraft Circle of Native Writers and Storytellers. In 1999, he received the Lifetime Achievement Award from the Native Writers Circle of the Americas.

Anna Mae Aquash (1945–1976)
Micmac, Activist

Aquash devoted most of her young life to the struggle for Native American rights. She participated in the 1972 march in Washington, D.C., known as the "Trail of Broken Treaties" and in the 1973 protest at the site of the Wounded Knee massacre, but it was her death that immortalized her and her work. In 1976, her body was discovered on a Lakota ranch—the autopsy concluded that she had died from exposure. However, her family demanded a second autopsy, which revealed that she had been shot. Aquash's murder remains unsolved, but her legacy lives on.

Lloyd "Sonny" Dove (1945–1983)
Mashpee Wampanoag, Basketball Player

Lloyd "Sonny" Dove was a professional basketball player who was Native American through his mother. As a star at St. John's University in New York in his last season of 1967, Dove received the Haggerty Award. That year, he was part of the United States basketball team that won the gold medal at the Pan American Games in Winnipeg. Dove later played professionally for the Detroit Pistons and the New York Nets. Mr. Dove was the commentator on radio broadcasts of St. John's games over stations WGBB and WNYE-FM. His last commentary was delivered during St. John's victory over Georgetown at Landover, Maryland, several days before he died of injuries he suffered when a taxicab he was driving plunged into the Gowanus Canal in Brooklyn.

Dove's record has continued to make him one of the top players ever at St. John's. In 2005, Dove was among the first ten men selected for "Basketball Legacy Honors" at the university. In 2011, Dove was inducted into the New York City Basketball Hall of Fame.

Donna Loring (1948–)
Penobscot, Legislator

Donna Loring was a nonvoting tribal representative in the Maine Legislature between 1999 and 2008. One of Loring's major accomplishments was her writing and sponsoring "An Act to Require Teaching Maine Native American History and Culture in Maine's Schools," which passed as a law in 2001. Among her other achievements in the legislature, she created the first "State of the Tribes Address" in the history of Maine. Held in March 2002 and attended by tribal chiefs, the event was broadcast live on Maine Public Television and Radio. Loring also supported a bill to remove the word "squaw" from public site names. Finally, in April 2008, Loring put before the legislature "Joint Resolution in the Support of the United Nations Declaration on the Rights of Indigenous Peoples," which passed unanimously. Maine is the only state in the country to pass such a resolution in favor of the U.N. Declaration of Indigenous Rights.

A Vietnam veteran, Loring advised Governor Angus King on women's veteran issues. Her memoir, *In the Shadow of the Eagle* (2008), describes her legislative years.

Donald Soctomah (1954–)
Passamaquoddy, State Representative/ Cultural Preservationist/Forester

As a state representative, Soctomah introduced legislation to change offensive names, including more than thirty places in Maine called "Squaw Mountain." He has been an advocate to transform how Native history is presented in schools and created an online audio Passamaquoddy dictionary to preserve and promote the language. Currently, he serves as tribal historic preservation officer. Not only does Soctomah maintain and teach Passamaquoddy heritage, but he has created jobs and hope for young people. The Maine Humanities Council awarded Soctomah its highest honor, the Constance H. Carlson Prize, for his "exemplary contributions to public humanities in Maine."

Joanne Shenandoah (1957–)
Oneida, Musician

Joanne Shenandoah, one of America's most celebrated and critically acclaimed musicians, is a Grammy Award winner, with over forty music awards (including a record thirteen Native American Music awards). Joanne credits her success to her mother, Maisie Shenandoah, who played guitar, and her father, Clifford, an Onondaga chief and jazz guitarist.

Shenandoah performed for His Holiness the Dali Lama and at St. Peter's at the Vatican in Italy, where she presented an original composition for the celebration for the canonization of the first Native American saint, Kateri Tekakwitha, both in October 2012. Shenandoah has performed at prestigious venues, including the White House, Carnegie Hall, five presidential inaugurations, Madison Square Garden, Bethlehem Fine Arts Center, Palestine, Crystal Bridges Museum, the NMAI–Smithsonian, the Ordway Theater, Hummingbird Centre, Toronto Skydome, the Parliament of the World's Religions (Africa, Spain, and Australia), and Woodstock '94.

In addition to her successful musical endeavors, Shenandoah cochairs the attorney general's Task Force on Children Exposed to Violence in Washington, is a board member of the Hiawatha Institute for Indigenous Knowledge, and appeared on the TV show "*In Search of Aliens*" in the segment about the Iroquois' contributions to history.

Jessie Little Doe Baird (1963–)
Mashpee Wampanoag, Linguist

 Baird, founder and director of the Wôpanâak Language Reclamation Project since 1993, is an Indigenous language preservationist who has revived a long-silent language and restored to her Native American community a vital sense of its cultural heritage. Wampanoag (or Wôpanâak), the Algonquian language of her ancestors, was spoken by tens of thousands of people in southeastern New England, but it had ceased to be spoken by the mid-nineteenth century.

Baird founded the language project, an intertribal effort that aims to return fluency to the Wampanoag Nation. She undertook graduate training in linguistics and language pedagogy at the Massachusetts Institute of Technology, where she worked with the late Kenneth Hale, a scholar of Indigenous languages, to decipher grammatical patterns and compile vocabulary lists from archival Wampanoag documents. By turning to related Algonquian languages for guidance with pronunciation and grammar, this collaboration produced a ten thousand-word Wampanoag–English dictionary, which Baird continues to de-

velop into an essential resource for students, historians, and linguists alike. In addition to achieving fluency herself, she has adapted her scholarly work into accessible teaching materials for adults and children and leads a range of educational programs—after-school classes for youth, beginning and advanced courses for adults, and summer immersion camps for all ages with the goal of establishing a broad base of Wampanoag speakers. Baird, elected to vice chairwoman of the Mashpee Wampanoag Tribe in 2013, was the recipient of a 2010 MacArthur Foundation Fellowship "genius" Award for her language restoration work.

Jane Mt. Pleasant
Tuscarora, Agricultural Scientist

Over a three-decade career as an agricultural scientist and a national expert in Iroquois agriculture, Mt. Pleasant has revitalized interest in the ancient Iroquois tradition of growing food through polyculture, a system that allows interdependent plants to flourish. She has used it to help farmers protect their soil, and she has rescued from extinction several varieties of corn that have sustained Native communities in the Northeast and Canada for centuries. Along the way, she has blended Native knowledge and Western science to give Native Americans a strong presence in the emerging field of sustainability science.

Mt. Pleasant's father grew up on the Tuscarora Reservation near Buffalo, New York, but Mt. Pleasant did not get serious about soil until after she returned to college in the mid-1970s. She got a Ph.D. in soil science from North Carolina State University in 1987 between degrees from Cornell University, where she is now director of American Indian studies and an associate professor of horticulture.

As the hazards of industrial-scale farming, such as soil erosion and toxic runoff, have become more evident, Mt. Pleasant and other scientists have shown how corn, beans, and squash (Three Sisters) complement one another ecologically. (Squash vines prevent soil erosion, corn stalks provide beanpoles, and bean plants fertilize the soil.) Mt. Pleasant has also investigated how corn varieties vary in their capacity to outcompete weeds and how that depends on whether they are planted alone or with the other sisters. In preserving heirloom varieties of corn, she has documented their preferences for planting dates, population density, and access to nitrogen.

In 2014, in addition to serving as an associate professor in the Department of Horticulture, Mt. Pleasant has also been affiliated with the American Indian Program at Cornell University. Her research focuses on Indigenous cropping systems and their productivity.

Her work has led to greater credibility for the study of Native American farming systems. "There is more acceptance today of my work among some scientists," she says, "but perhaps I am more self-confident than I was when I began as well. I'm less frustrated by the lack of interest that remains among some scientists with regard to Native American knowledge and less sensitive to their criticisms."

Marguerite A. Smith
Shinnecock, Attorney

Smith, an attorney and educator, advocated for federal recognition on behalf of her tribe for many years. She has served as a principal law clerk in the New York Supreme Court, Suffolk County, as an attorney general in the New York State Law Department and as a field attorney for the National Labor Relations Board. She is a past member of the board of directors of the Native American Bar Association. An active member of several Native community organizations, Smith serves on the board of directors of the First Nations Development Institute, an organization that helps Native people develop businesses that are good for people and reservations. The Association on American Indian Affairs honored Smith for her outstanding commitment to her tribe's quest for federal recognition.

Shelley DePaul
Lenape, Linguist/Educator/Tribal Leader

DePaul serves on the Council of the Lenape Nation of Pennsylvania and is a genealogy researcher, historical researcher, Lenape language specialist, and assistant chief. She developed a Lenape language curriculum and teaches Lenape at various schools, including Swarthmore College. DePaul also plays and teaches the Native American flute.

Annawon Weeden
Narragansett/Pequot/Wampanoag, Teacher/Actor/Dancer/Cultural Interpreter

Born and raised in the tribal community of Charlestown, Rhode Island, among his father's Narragansett/Pequot relatives, Weeden now resides in his mother's Wampanoag community, located in Mashpee, Massachusetts. Like his historian father (Tall Oaks Weeden), Weeden began sharing his Native culture at a young age. As an adult, he has worked with the Plymouth Plantation (museum interpreter/outreach educator) and the Boston Children's Museum. He has appeared in documentaries and films including *We Shall Remain*, directed by Chris Eyre (Cheyenne/Arapaho). Sought after by many institutions such as the Smithsonian, *National Geographic*, Scholastic, PBS, the History/Discovery Channel, Harvard, and many more educational/environmental organizations, Weeden is also a traditional dancer and has performed all over the country.

SOUTHEAST

This river is the lifeblood of this reservation because it's allowed our people, our culture, and this reservation to survive. We believe if you take from the river, you should give back to the river as well. You can't take and take and then it's all gone. You have to give back to the river. You just have to.

—Carl Lone Eagle Custalow, Mattaponi Chief, 2003

Each spring almost from the beginning of time, American shad leave their Atlantic Ocean home and head for the fresh waters of the Pamunky and Mattaponi rivers in eastern Virginia, and every spring for thousands of years, the Pamunkey and Mattaponi, for whom the rivers are named, are there to greet them. At one time, the people were dependent on the fish for their livelihood, but today, the shad are dependent on the people and their hatcheries for their very lives. The rivers have been damned and polluted, creating a toxic end to the shad cycle if it were not for the hatcheries.

During spawning time, many Pamunkey, regardless of their professions, become fishermen. They sit in their boats, motors quiet, nets fanned out in the late afternoon, waiting. As the shad swim upstream to breed this one time a year, several are caught in the nets. Not all the fish—just enough to ensure that the cycle of life will continue. The boats return to shore, and the fish are taken back to the hatchery. Each roe (female) will produce thousands of eggs, and each buck (male) has millions of sperm.

The shad fish hatchery, which combines ancient and contemporary technologies, is almost one hundred

years old and resembles any science lab—clean, white, lots of tubes, meters, and machines and has a constant drone. Here, the eggs and sperm are forcefully mixed to aid the fertilization process. As the fish grow from one stage to another, they are marked with a harmless dye so they can be tracked after their release back into the wild. They go through a complex labyrinth of PVC piping and containers until they become fry and strong enough to swim into large holding tanks. By then, they number in the tens of thousands. The tanks are opened, and the tiny creatures swim through the tubes that connect the hatchery with the Pamunkey River. Some will meet with predators, but most will swim downriver to the Atlantic and after two or three years come back to spawn. The Pamunkey and Mattaponi have given back to the rivers.

A BIRD'S EYE VIEW

At the top of a Southeastern U.S. map, the Chesapeake Bay, Pamunkey, and Mattaponi rivers are just three of the many bodies of water that crisscross the different environmental regions that make up the Southeast culture area. In this book, the region includes present-day states of the two Virginias, Kentucky, Tennessee, the two Carolinas, Arkansas, Mississippi, Alabama, Georgia, Louisiana, and Florida. The Appalachian Mountains form the spine of this once densely forested region that features many plateaus and valleys.

It is widely accepted that there are three distinctive environmental zones in the Southeast:

- The Coastal Plain comprises the easternmost land and extends along the Atlantic Ocean from Virginia to Florida, around Florida, and along the Gulf of Mexico to Mexico. At one time, deep pine forests surrounded numerous rivers, bayous, and swamps. The slow-moving rivers, most notably the Mississippi, created alluvial floodplains, which kept the soil rich and moist, perfect for agriculture. Native peoples also used the cypress and oak trees, wild berries, roots, Spanish moss, and grapes for food, clothing, containers, and medicine. Animal protein sources included deer, bear, rabbits, raccoons, squirrels, beavers, catfish, ducks, turkeys, and marine animals.

- A bit farther west and below the Appalachian Mountains is the Piedmont zone. Like the more eastern area, the region was once lush with hardwood forests of oak, pine, hickory, poplar, and sycamore. Rivers with their "heads" in the Appalachians kept the valleys and hills fertile. Not only were there many types of food and medicinal wild and domesticated plants, but there were numerous game animals and an abundant variety of fish.

- On the western-most side are the Appalachian Mountains, extending from Canada to the northern part of the Southeast. These ancient ridges are some of the oldest on the continent and very diverse, from low, almost hills, to rugged and towering peaks. Like the low-lying lands, they were covered with hardwood forests of pines, walnuts, poplars, and hickory. Thousands of animal species lived in the mountains from bears to eagles.

FIRST PEOPLES

Like all civilizations in the world that exist today, Southeastern cultures are dynamic and have changed many times over the centuries. One harmful stereotype of Native cultures is that they are relegated to the past, stuck in a time warp, and if they are still around today, they are living the way their ancestors did. Those historical ancestors are stuck in the same place, living the same way with no changes in the way they live. With advancements in the technology of dating objects and remains, current "science" has been able to document that humans have lived in the Southeast for over fifty thousand years, several hundred millennia before the last ice age. This development is actually closer to Native accounts of ancient history, which are often dismissed. Still, much of the very early history has been lost, unknown, or we as writers do not have permission to share it as it belongs to the people and is recounted as they deem necessary. It is also difficult to really understand any ancient history where the people who made that history are not around to explain it, so this chapter will feature more of the culture after the Common Era.

Evidence of very ancient humans has been found along the Nottoway River in southwest Virginia and by the Savannah River in South Carolina. The original peoples hunted both small and large game. Anecdotes of huge predatory animals have been preserved in traditional accounts and handed down to today's contemporary Native peoples. The latest "discoveries" in archaeology support these chronicles.

Poverty Point

Southeastern peoples changed locations, livelihoods, governments, and social organizations many times over eons. Historians and archaeologists refer to a few major areas and eras, like Hopewell, Adena, and Mississippian. One of the earliest sites is called Poverty Point (1650 to 1100 B.C.E.), the center of a vast trading and industry network that extended hundreds of miles across the present-day states of Louisiana, Mississippi, Arkansas, and parts of Tennessee and east-

Bird Mound (or Mound A) at Poverty Point in Louisiana is the largest of the mounds at this prehistoric site that was a center for trade some two thousand years ago.

ward to Florida's Gulf Coast. Poverty Point is deemed as one of the most important ancient sites. An aerial view of Poverty Point shows perfectly engineered, gigantic earthworks consisting of five mounds and six rows of semicircular, concentric ridges, which archaeologists estimate took at least five million hours of labor to build. The outermost ridge is a mile and half long. Perhaps the ridges provided housing for those coming to trade. The middle area is perfectly flat, made so by an incredible engineering feat. Possibly, it was a giant amphitheater with raised stages. These aren't the only massive structures. Surrounding mounds overlook the Mississippi floodplain.

How do scientists know that Poverty Point was a bustling marketplace supported by a far reaching economic system? A wide variety of objects have been unearthed. Some of the projectile points and tools, ground stone plummets, fired clay figurines and vessels, gorgets, and shell and stone beads are made from materials found nearby, but other objects were constructed from imported soapstone, hematite, magnetite, slate, galena, copper, and many others. This thriving culture, ancestors of modern-day Southeasterners, was a hub of ancient peoples—the mall or farmers' market of its time. No one knows why

Poverty Point was abandoned—natural disasters or a change in trends, but by the time Europeans arrived, it was already a historical site. Poverty Point was the name of the cotton plantation located on the grounds and has nothing to do with the ancient community. In 1962, Poverty Point Park in Louisiana was designated a National Historic Landmark by the U.S. Department of the Interior. On June 22, 2014, at the 38th Session of the World Heritage Committee in Doha, Qatar, Poverty Point State Historic Site was inscribed as the 1,001st property on the World Heritage List (UNESCO), having been nominated by Secretary of State Ken Salazar. The list includes such ancient treasures as the Cahokia Mounds (United States), Machu Picchu (Peru), Pyramids of Giza (Egypt), Stonehenge (United Kingdom), Stone Circles of Senegambia (Gambia), Great Wall (China), and the Great Barrier Reef (Australia).

Moving into later eras of Southeast culture, there was (is) quite a bit of diversity among Indigenous homelands. Like countries in Africa, Asia, and Europe, each group or nation had its own political structure, kinship system, and economy although they shared a continent. They did have similarities in language groupings, agriculture, religion, and social organization because, as with all societies, people borrow and copy what works.

Mississippian

The period between about 800 to 1600 C.E. is called the Mississippian culture era, a time of great mound building. Communities were often as large as several thousand residents and could be autonomous or part of a larger "tax-paying" political structure with a dominant town or capital. Alliances were formed for protection and trade, and many tribes banded together in confederacies. Almost all Mississippian sites are dated before 1539–1540 (when Hernando de Soto and his men explored and devastated the area) except the Natchez peoples, who practiced Mississippian culture well into the 1700s.

Fishing, hunting, and natural materials/vegetation were part of the diet and economy. People had become incredible agronomists, and agriculture flourished. Women were usually in charge of farming and are given credit for developing hundreds of domesticated plants. These early scientists, along with their South American peers, are responsible for inventing what some studies say is almost seventy percent of the food consumed in the world today. Sometimes, enslaved workers or indentured servants helped with planting, maintaining, and harvesting these immense gardens. The slaves were often prisoners of war—their lives spared if they worked for the community. This practice continued for centuries. Many Southeast peoples prevented forest fires from decimating their territories by practicing controlled burning of the underbrush in the vast, wooded areas. The ashes added essential nutrients to the soil; vegetation could grow for the animals to eat. The forests were preserved, in turn ensuring plentiful game animals.

Most of the groups developed a clan system, which functioned similar to an extended family. The social structure was matrilineal: children were born into their mother's clans and women were considered to be at the center of the community. The balance of power was equal between men and women, and this organization was continued by the descendants of the Mississippian culture. If it had not been for European interference, the traditions of gender equality might likely still be in effect today. However, children still take their mother's clan, which can be problematic in families with parents of different cultural backgrounds.

All Life Is Sacred

The early people were deeply religious, and as all people who live close to the natural world, their ceremonies celebrated food crops and the change of seasons. The Mississippians and their descendants saw themselves as *part* of nature, not separate, and although they made many changes to the land with their agriculture techniques, they also did not take the gifts of the earth for granted. Great preparation, care, and ritual surrounded food, whether it was cultivated, wild, or game. The sacred was part of everyday life, not just practiced on ceremonial occasions.

When Europeans began to arrive in the Southeast, they encountered people who were emerging from the decline of the widespread Mississippian era, today's Catawba, Cherokee, Creek, Chickasaw, and others. Although the earthen mounds were passing into disuse, the lives of the succeeding peoples still were town centered, surrounded by cultivated fields of corn, beans, squash, sunflowers, barleylike grain, and other crops. In the sixteenth century, the villages of the Southeast were distributed across a territory bounded by the Atlantic Ocean, the Gulf of Mexico, the Trinity River in present-day Texas, and the Ohio River.

Most Southeastern peoples held an annual Green Corn Ceremony, a thanksgiving and renewal ritual usually observed in midsummer. The occasion was significant because new corn promised food for winter and seeds for spring; crop failures threatened immediate hunger and long-term famine. The anthropologist Charles Hudson believes "we would have something approaching the Green Corn Ceremony if we combined Thanksgiving, New Year's festivities, Yom Kippur, Lent, and Mardi Gras." That is probably the way it seemed to non-Indians, yet to Native peoples, these ceremonials were not as important as living the right way every day. The concept of worshipping one day a week or a few times a year was foreign.

The successful farming reflected in the Green Corn celebration was only part of the economy of the Southeastern Indians. Hunting also addressed important dietary and material needs. Like all activities, hunting had a spiritual foundation. Hunters prayed before they went hunting to express respect and gratitude for all living creatures. They killed no more than needed since useless slaughter was an affront to the Creator—it also ensured that there would be game for the next hunt. Hunters also thanked the animal for sacrificing its life so the people could eat and have clothing and blankets. Traditional accounts chronicle the disastrous outcome when these rules were not obeyed.

Tobacco was a sacred plant and is still used in prayers and healings. The smoke carries

Mississippian culture also influenced Native societies as far north as the Midwest.

prayers to the Creator, and great care was taken with ceremonial pipes, as it is today. The Southeast people did not become addicted to smoking; the misuse of the sacred plant has created many problems that did not exist. Wine is part of some Christian and Jewish rituals, but using it as an addictive substance violates its sacredness in the same way as the violation of the hallowed tobacco plant. It is the subject of many different traditional accounts.

Games

Even as the Southeastern peoples shared similar practices in farming, hunting, and religions, they also shared games. One of the most widely played was the ball game (ancestor of modern-day lacrosse), vividly captured centuries later by the American painter George Catlin in his 1834 portrayals of a Choctaw ball play in Oklahoma. So great was Catlin's fascination that he depicted not only two scenes from a match, one with the ball in the air and the other with it on the ground, but also a portrait of the Choctaw ball player named He-Who-Drinks-the-Juice-of-Stone. The contest was played by teams from competing villages on a level field perhaps two hundred yards long. The object was for a team to throw a deerskin ball (stuffed with deer or squirrel hair) past the opposition's goal post at the other end of the field. In the Southeastern versions of the game, the players carried two ball play sticks, which could be used to scoop up the ball and forward it. It was (is) a rough game played with no protective equipment and sometimes called "Little Brother of War," as it was a means for tribes to settle disputes without actually going to war. Although the game was incredibly violent and fraught with danger, the death or severe injury of a few men far outweighed the risk of many more casualties suffered in full-fledged battles.

Society and Government

Another connection for these Southeastern peoples was their life in villages, bound together by common practices and language. Most villages were governed by a council of elders and military men presided over by a chief, who usually came to power through a combination of talent, accomplishment, and membership in an influential family or clan. In most Southeastern societies, descent was traced through the mother's line. Beyond the family, clan membership was extremely important since clans transcended village boundaries, thus affording the individual a social and political connection throughout the larger community.

Tribes (nations) were loose associations of villages sharing heritage, customs, and proximity of location. None were tightly structured by modern standards; the Creek, for example, more appropriately might be called a confederation since they were formed as much by outside pressure as by powerful cultural bonds. Certain villages in a nation sometimes were more influential or holy than others, such as the Cherokee beloved town of Chota on the Little Tennessee River in present-day Tennessee, yet even the

leader of a prominent community had no more power than the people would allow—the towns were run democratically. The idea of emperors, kings, and monarchies was foreign to Southeasterners, which created a complete cultural miscommunication between them and Europeans. Efforts by European colonial powers to designate emperors for particular tribes were largely empty gestures. In most instances, if all the tribal villages or a percentage of them voted for war or approved a treaty, that decision prevailed only while those villages continued their support. Withdrawal of any village's support freed its people from obligations, a practice that frustrated Europeans, who professed to operate in terms of permanent treaties, boundaries, and alliances. Native peoples, however, were more attuned to political flexibility, social harmony, and spiritual significance than to contractual agreements.

Indeed, the values of the Southeastern peoples might be expressed best in terms of balance or har-

A burial mask dating to the Mississippian culture somewhere between 1200 and 1700 B.C.E.

mony of human beings with one another as well as the natural and spiritual worlds, which were all part of everyday life. All things were either good or evil; success in life depended on the careful practice of maintaining balance in the world, and if one was in disharmony, the proper remedies were taken to restore harmony. The old harmonies were shattered forever when the Europeans arrived.

EUROPEAN INVASION

Ponce de Léon

The first European credited with setting foot in the Southeast was Juan Ponce de Léon. However, the Spaniards had been enslaving Native people since they first arrived in the Caribbean, so it is likely that the colonizers had visited Florida before Ponce de Léon, looking for captives and thinking they were just on another island. Since there were relationships between Native peoples on the islands and the mainland, the Southeasterners had probably been forewarned about the viciousness of the warlike newcomers. In 1513, when Ponce de Léon, made landfall in present-day Florida, he encountered Calusa people, who were not very welcoming. They refused to trade and drove off the Spanish ships by surrounding them with an armada of sea canoes; mariners were armed with long bows. When Ponce de Léon retreated, he saw what he thought was another island and claimed it for Spain. He named it La Florida in recognition of its verdant landscape and because it was the Easter season, which Spaniards called Pascua Florida (Festival of Flowers). Ponce de Léon returned in 1521, and this time, the Calusa mortally wounded him. However, the Spanish had found treasures in Central and South America: food, slaves, and gold. Their thirst could not be quenched, and Florida was a new land with immense possibilities. The invasions would continue.

De Soto's Destruction

The half-naked, wild-looking, foul-smelling Europeans with their battered and makeshift weapons must have seemed to be monstrous caricatures of human beings to the well-fed, well-clothed, civilized residents of the province of Quiz-Quiz.

—M. A. Wells

The first European contact for which there is substantial written information was led by the Spanish conquistador Hernando de Soto, and the visit was not a good one. In 1539, de Soto landed near present-day Tampa with 620 Spanish soldiers, two women, over two hundred horses and pigs, and several attack dogs. For the next three years, they looted, raped, burned, and murdered their way through the Southeast interior from Florida to the Mississippi River in their search for gold, gems, and other riches.

De Soto's trek was helped by Juan Ortiz, a Spanish survivor of the 1528 expedition of Panfilo de Narvaez. As a young boy, he had been taken in and nurtured by the women in the home of Uzica (part of the Calusa) leader Chief Hirrihigua. He learned different Native languages and was able to provide limited translation for de Soto. The explorer also benefited from rivalries and hostilities that already existed among different Native groups.. Some Native people aligned with him although they knew the terrors he had brought to their lands. They felt it wise to use the invaders to conquer their own enemies. De Soto found himself in a puzzling complex political system of allies and possible enemies whose diplomatic skills surpassed his. He was a plunderer, adventurer, thief, gambler, and despot, but he was not a statesman.

The Native people pushed back, hard and successfully in many instances. Chief Acuera, a Native leader in central Florida, ordered the heads of the Spaniards, intending to stop their advance. His warriors left the decapitated invaders as a warning to de Soto. When the Spaniards came across the bodies, they gave them a Christian burial, but Chief Acuera had them dug up and dismembered, and the body parts were hung from trees. De Soto was unyielding and pushed on, but Native people could not fight the European diseases the Spaniards brought with them. The viruses were too fast moving, and before traditional healers could devise cures, thousands had died.

By the time the expedition arrived in the Tunica town of Quiz-Quiz in northwestern Mississippi, de Soto and the remainder of his troops were in bad shape. The constant battles that arose when they demanded food, medicines, and riches, kidnapped women to be used as concubines as well as other slaves, and leveraged their position by capturing hostages from different communities had taken its toll. De Soto had planned well for this expedition as he had brought iron collars and chains from Spain to enslave the local population and use them as burden bearers, cooks, servants, and sex. In spite of the cruelties they inflicted, the Spanish had lost more than half of their men. They also lost most of their clothing, weapons, and other possessions in fires set by groups they had tried to intimidate and rob. From the Tunica town of Quiz-Quiz, de Soto and his

band headed northwest and ended up near present-day Memphis and the Mississippi River. They crossed the river, where de Soto died of fever in 1542. Although his bandits did steal a few pearls (and Native people managed to get many of them back), the real riches of the area were the prosperous farms, large cities with impressive buildings and temples and rich religious and social traditions, but without the discovery of gold, the expedition was considered a failure. The deep scars left by de Soto were never healed.

De Soto left no personal records. However, in 1605, sixty-three years after de Soto's death, Garcilaso de la Vega published *Florida of the Inca*, which is a vivid report of one of the most brutal invasions in history. De la Vega presented the story in its entirety without bias and based it on testimony of veterans of the expedition. Readers could determine that the Native people were patriots defending their peoples and homelands. Garcilaso de la Vega may have created a more fair account because he was the son of a Spanish conqueror of Peru and an Incan woman.

EUROPEAN COLONIES

Spanish Colonists

The first successful European colony in what was to become the United States was founded in 1565 at St. Augustine, Florida, by the Spanish. They also established various outposts up and down the Atlantic Coast and were the first Europeans to visit the Virginia area. Their attempts to colonize the more northern area were futile.

Sometime in the 1550s, they kidnapped a young boy, Paquiquino, from the Tidewater area of Virginia and changed his name to Don Luis de Valasco. He taken to Mexico and Spain, baptized a Catholic, and given a Jesuit education. The Spanish finally had a start to converting the Indians to Christianity, or so they thought. They returned Don Luis to his original homelands in 1570 along with several Spanish priests and established the first mission in Indian Territory. Their "experiment," the now "civilized" Don Luis, would be a

Spanish conquistador Hernando de Soto landed in Florida in 1539. In his search for gold, he ravaged the countryside through much of what is now the southeastern region of the United States.

translator and a perfect example of a good Christian. The hope was that the "savages" would stand in line to become converted once they saw the transformed Don Luis, but it did not happen. Don Luis returned to his Native culture, which was at odds with Catholic dogma. The priests publicly humiliated him for polygamy—public humiliation was not acceptable in Indian culture. Don Luis retaliated by killing his tormentors. Some say he may have been the father of the great chief Powhatan and responsible for creating the strong Powhatan Confederacy.

English Colonists

Ultimately, European imperial rivalry brought French and English invaders to the Southeastern region. The first English colonists arrived in North America in 1584 at Roanoke Island, in what is now North Carolina, and explored southeastern Virginia. Many mysteries surround this early settlement, referred to as the Lost Colony. Their leader, John White, returned to England to get more supplies, but the Roanoke Colony found it difficult to survive. White returned in 1590 to a deserted settlement. What happened to the "lost colony" remains a mystery.

THE POWHATAN

While the Spanish and English were trying to get their bearings on the continent in the early 1600s, it is estimated that the region that is now the state of Virginia was home to over fifty thousand Powhatan people. The Tidewater area was called Tsenacommach ("densely populated" in the local language) and stretched for a hundred miles from the Potomac River to the James River and parts of the Eastern shore. The people were organized into a confederacy under the leadership of the great Chief Powhatan, or Wahunsonacock, as he was called in his language. Over thirty different tribes belonged to the Confederacy; each had its own chief(s), called *weroance*. The Confederacy provided protection and a strong system of government for its 25,000 members. They came to be known as the

Powhatan by the English as it was their custom to name a group after its leader.

Towns were located on high ground near rivers, essential for food, daily bathing, and travel. Communities on the outskirts often had a fortress of tall, pointed stakes around them (palisades) as a defense against enemies. Houses called "yehakins" were barrel shaped and sometimes home to twenty people or more. Women owned the property and had jurisdiction over the gardens and home life. They created all the household equipment including distinctive pots, which are still made today. Women were always busy, and girls began learning the necessary skills at a young age.

Men also worked hard and although gender roles were different, they were equal. Women ed-

A detail from a 1612 map by John Smith depicts Chief Powhatan in a longhouse in his capital of Werowocomoco in what is now Virginia.

ucated both boys and girls until the sons were strong and independent enough to be under their father's tutelage. Then they learned to hunt, fish, build canoes, and clear the land for farming. All children were taught strict manners. They learned to control their behavior, and public displays of hostility and disrespect were considered rude and not tolerated, especially when interacting with people outside the family or strangers. To be polite was to remain silent and focus on the speaker until he was finished. It was a way to police oneself and create the harmony necessary for a successful society.

In 1607, the next group of English arrived in Tsenacommach, founding Jamestown, the first permanent English settlement in North America. The English colony impacted the well-functioning complex city/state government and harmonious communities that enjoyed a thriving and well-ordered lifestyle. Like the early Roanoke Colony, the English immigrants suffered greatly, but they stayed. The Powhatan were at first hospitable and helpful. However, there were constant conflicts caused by cultural differences, language barriers, and values/customs that were totally at odds with each other. The English did not have the same courteous public behaviors as the Powhatan. Soldiers often were drunk and disorderly, the colonists hardly bathed, and they violated boundaries and social mores at every turn. This politeness of the First Peoples proved to be disastrous to Powhatan/English relations as the English thought the respect and silence of the Native listener was a tacit agreement to whatever the English proposed.

The English quickly became unwelcome guests, and by 1609, Chief Powhatan had lost patience with their constant disruptions to daily life and their neverending demands for food and other supplies. He made an official ruling to end the generous and gracious aid. Tensions mounted, and the rapport between the two groups disintegrated. One of Powhatan's daughters, Matoaka (Pocahontas was her nickname, meaning "playful child"), was kidnapped by the English in 1613. Held prisoner for a year, she met John Rolfe and supposedly fell in love. With her father's permission, she

converted to Christianity, had her name changed to Rebecca, and married Rolfe and although relations never were friendly again, a fragile peace agreement was reached between the two groups. John Rolfe was a planter and is credited with turning the sacred tobacco into a cash crop.

The Rolfes and their baby son sailed to England in 1616 on a campaign to round up new European settlers for Jamestown Colony. On their return trip, Matoaka fell ill, and the ship returned to Gravesend, England, where she died in 1617. Her father, Chief Powhatan, died the next year, and the leadership of the Powhatan nation was passed first to his brother Opitchapam and then to his brother Opechancanough. The tentative peace lasted a few years and then the English began arriving in droves, eager to be part of John Rolfe's tobacco industry. More and more Indians were displaced as the foreigners' greed for land and resources grew. The Powhatan rallied to save their homelands.

In 1622, Opechancanough led an attack against the English colony, killing about 250 of the 1,200 settlers. As was their military custom, the chief retreated, giving the English time to either accept the rules of the Powhatan or leave. The English did not heed the lesson and fought back. For the next ten years, the skirmishes continued until a tenuous truce was called. The English, who numbered over eight thousand by this time, wanted more land. Again, Opechancanough rallied his forces in 1644 although several chiefs chose to side with the English, who lost as many people as in 1622. Four years later, Opechancanough was captured by the English—he was almost one hundred years old. While imprisoned, he was murdered. The Great Powhatan Confederacy unraveled.

The new chief, Necotowance, signed the first treaties with the English in 1646, setting up boundaries between the two groups. More treaties followed, which were unfavorable for the Native residents of Tsenacommach. Eventually, the Powhatan were forced onto small reservations and made subjects of the English crown. As English settlement spread westward, the First Peoples

A not-very-accurate illustration from the 1624 book *Smith's General History of Virginia* showing John Smith taking Chief Opechancanough prisoner.

Almost a century later, in the 1800s, the exchange of furs and skins for European goods altered the balance of the lives of the Southeastern peoples. Previously, hunters had pursued the white-tailed deer only as needed. Because deer range only a five-square-mile area during their lifetimes, only careful avoidance of overhunting and controlled burning of forest underbrush had maintained the deer herds. The new trade changed the balance as European market demands for leather enticed the hunters to kill more than they needed. By the 1730s, there was a noticeable decline in the Southeastern deerskin trade.

At the same time, trade goods impacted cultural patterns. The attraction of finished cloth and clothing items persuaded villagers that bartering was far easier than tanning deerskins. Desirable luxury items also could be obtained via trade, including mirrors, knives, awls, scissors, and musical instruments like the *temir komuz Jew*. Certain handicrafts began to disappear, displaced by European weapons, tools, cloth, and decorative goods. Other dramatic changes can be attributed to trade. Native societies were introduced to alcohol, which quickly became a curse and was often used by the immigrants to force Indians into unfair agreements. Towns became more non-Indian in population and values, undermining village stability.

were forced farther inland, away from their fertile river valleys. Their land base dwindled, and so did their population due to foreign diseases, food shortages, and battles. However, unlike many others in the Southeast, the Powhatans were not removed to Oklahoma during the removal period beginning in the 1830s.

TRADE AND ENSLAVEMENT

All servants imported and brought into the country … who were not Christians in their native country … shall be accounted and be slaves. All Negro, mulatto, and Indian slaves within this dominion … shall be held to be real estate. If any slave resists his master … correcting such slave and shall happen to be killed in such correction … the master shall be free of all punishment … as if such accident never happened.

—Virginia General Assembly
declaration, 1705

Gender roles, too, were modified by the trade. Formerly, these matrilineal, agricultural societies defined roles for males and females in relatively clear, yet balanced, terms. Women were important because they bore the children, provided food from the fields, and transformed raw materials into usable products. The fur trade, however, gave a place of greater importance to the hunters since commercial hunting brought both staples and luxury goods to the villages. Trading activities also ignored women since the male-oriented Europeans sought to bargain with the hunters. Women who had at once been the center of the community were becoming more marginalized as European patriarchy took over.

Along with the colonists' lust for land and natural resources came their need for free labor to turn acres into cash crops for export. Native people were a convenient source of workers. Many Native groups in the South had always had some form of enslavement or indentured servitude, but most developed familial or romantic bonds with their captors and were eventually absorbed into the community. However, slave ownership and trade among Native groups never reached the magnitude of the Europeans. American Indian peoples were the first population to be impacted by the European slave trade. It was more economical than importing Africans—Native people already knew how to work the local land. They were cheaper to buy as they didn't have to be transported across the sea, and Native people could capture and sell people from other tribes for revenge as well as trading captives for coveted, European-made items, especially guns. Women were especially sought after as they were superb farmers and used to hard work. Countless groups were destroyed by the settler colonial practice of slavery. Some survivors were assimilated into remaining tribes.

Social and Economic Change

Additional social changes took place as traders took up residence in the villages. The households that they developed were patterned after the male-dominated European families. The children of Native and European unions often adopted their fathers' lifestyles, thus diluting traditional social practices. As a result, many tribes became economically dominated by mixed families toward the end of the eighteenth century.

These intermarried families also helped intensify tribal divisions. Those of mixed heritages were often among the first to adopt lifestyles similar to their non-Native neighbors. After the establishment of the United States, the white people living in or next to Native communities were U.S. citizens, but the Native people were not. So a non-Native parent was often a different nationality than his children.

Among the Cherokee, the Choctaw, the Chickasaw, and the Creek, the new European cultural orientations were reflected in economic terms as the mixed people used their linguistic, educational, and political advantages to prosper. Ferries, inns, trading posts, and farms most often were owned or controlled by those of mixed ancestry. In the 1830s, when the U.S. government sought to relocate the Southeastern peoples west of the Mississippi River, antagonism between the traditionalists and the mixed culture entrepreneurs heightened arguments over whether or not the nations should move. After removal, even though they may have lost more both in quality and quantity of life, those of mixed heritage were better equipped to start again. Once relocated, they contended for political leadership and held economic control of businesses.

In the three centuries before their forced move westward, Southeastern tribal governments transformed greatly. From the earliest contacts, Europeans sought to impose their own views about governance on their new neighbors by designating Indian nations, kings, princesses, and emperors. Such titles had little meaning for the Native peoples, who continued their traditional governments until early in the nineteenth century. As U.S. neighbors greedily eyed their lands and pressured for their removal, there was a move toward patterning governments after the U.S. federal government for diplomatic purposes. This was ironic as the U.S. government was modeled after the Haudensaunee, a true democracy, but the Southeastern people believed that more formally structured governments would ensure that they would be recognized as sovereign and accorded the same status as other sovereign nations. In the decades just before the nations were forced westward, they created constitutions that often mirrored those of state or the federal government.

REMOVAL

The Cherokee adopted a constitutional government in 1828 while the Choctaw constitution of 1826–1830 proved unstable but was revived again in 1834. The more conservative Creek and Chickasaw retained their traditional government with little change until after removal to Indian Territory, where they adopted constitutional governments in the 1850s and 1860s. Originally, Native people hoped such government organization would help them resist pressure from the United States. However, both before removal and during the period of so-called detribalization in the years between 1880 and 1934, much of this structure was destroyed. Most of the nations have reconstituted their governments into the leadership that serves them today.

During the era of removal, because of the continued focus of basic power at the village level, not every individual tribal member, family, or village participated in the move west. The Native peoples living east of the Mississippi River today testify powerfully to the persistence and cultural tenacity of these peoples against overwhelming odds. Today's descendants of the Southeastern tribal peoples proudly continue to claim the heritage of their ancestors. In 2010, there were 844,000 persons of Native American descent living in the twelve Southeast states. A century and a half after forced removal, many remain in or near their original homelands. Although they have lost much, they still claim their heritage, and many have created new tribal organizations or revived their old structures.

SOUTHEAST INDIGENEITY

Atakapa-Ishak

In historic times, the Atakapa-Ishak inhabited southwest Louisiana and southeast Texas. They called themselves Ishak, which means "The People" in their language. The nation was divided into two communities, "The Sunrise People" and "The Sunset People," and at one time was the only group along the Gulf of Mexico coast from Matagorda Bay in Texas to Vermillion Bay in Louisiana. They were deeply impacted by both Spanish and French colonizers, who added Atakapa to their name. It was an insulting nickname given to them by the Choctaw and means

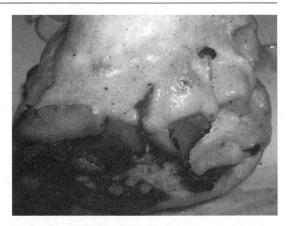

A dish of tasso ham with poached eggs and hollandaise sauce. Tasso is considered a Cajun dish often served in New Orleans, but it has Ishak origins.

"man-eaters," supporting the rumor that they were cannibalistic although there is no indication that this was ever true. However, this reputation and bigotry still exists today.

Louisiana cuisine like tasso and oyster pie were Ishak inventions as was Zydeco music. Forcibly enslaved Ishak worked alongside enslaved Africans and probably shared their music, which was also given an African spin. Throughout southern Louisiana, place names like Anococ, Calcasieu, Ladassine, Teche, and many others are all Ishak words.

The Ishak were no longer considered Native people after the early 1900s. Instead, they were misnamed Creoles, Creole Indians, Creoles of color, and colored. However, they always maintained their Indianness and have regained their tribal organization, hoping to receive federal recognition. On October 28, 2006, the Atakapa-Ishak Nation met for the first time in more than one hundred years as "one nation." Rachel Mouton, the mistress of ceremony and director of publications and communications for the nation, introduced Billy LaChapelle, who opened the afternoon with a traditional prayer in English and in Atakapa. It was a momentous occasion for the Ishak, who had survived wars, disease, racism, slavery, and colonialism to come together on their own lands once again.

CATAWBA

Today's 2,800 Catawba live in the vicinity of Rock Hill, South Carolina, either on the reservation or in nearby communities. Unlike many Native peoples, all live relatively close to their eighteenth-century homelands; they are the only federally recognized tribe in South Carolina. They call themselves Yeh is-WAH h'reh, or "People of the River." The Catawba Cultural Center provides a link to the rich heritage of the nation and features a museum for visitors. The nation's long history is one of struggle and victory. Their mere existence testifies powerfully to their persistence, resilience, and flexibility. Time after time observers predicted the end of the Catawba, yet they still survive.

As the British colonies emerged in the late seventeenth century, Indigenous peoples living along the upper Wateree River in South Carolina were identified as the Catawba nation. From the outset of Catawba–South Carolina relations, the Catawba followed a policy of gracious cooperation. During the American Revolution, they served as scouts for the South Carolinians. They paid dearly for this when a British raiding force destroyed their towns. In the years after the Revolution, the Catawba wrapped themselves in the flag of patriotism shared with other Revolutionary veterans, thus making it difficult for South Carolina to ignore them.

The Catawba sought and received a 144,000-acre reservation in 1763. For the next forty years, they survived by leasing their land, selling pottery and skins, farming, and serving as catchers of enslaved people for tidewater slave owners. After 1800, the equation changed, when slavery and upland cotton marched into the Piedmont, the region of rolling hills between the level coastal plain of the Atlantic Ocean and the rugged mountains of the southern Appalachians. Catawba land became more valuable to the Americans than the services they provided. Reduced in population to no more than thirty families and under unrelenting pressure to sell their land, the Catawba signed a treaty with South Carolina in 1840 exchanging their 144,000 acres for $5,000 and promises of as-sistance in relocation. Many moved to North Carolina in a fruitless attempt to live with the Cherokee. Within twelve years, they returned to South Carolina, where they were given 630 acres of their original homelands.

After the Civil War, they faced another threat in the rise of Jim Crow legislation; in 1879, South Carolina law forbade interracial marriage. Freedom to move back and forth socially and economically became further restricted. Consequently, the Catawba either had to cling to the security of Indianness or face an insurmountable color barrier that placed them in the "black" category. The Catawba responded by asserting their Indianness through speaking Catawba and expanding the production and sale of Indian arts. Then, in a departure from their traditional resistance to converting to Christianity, they welcomed Mormon missionaries in 1883. The Mormons aided them in building schools, a necessity in South Carolina, where the only schools for nonwhites were for blacks.

In 1943, the Catawba became legal citizens of South Carolina and were federally recognized, which made them eligible for the governmental benefits available to existing tribes. In 1961, their tribal status was terminated, and most of their lands were sold. A decade later, they petitioned to have their federal status reinstated, and in 1993, they were given federal recognition once again.

The ancient art form of Catawba pottery is sought after by collectors. Some historians believe that Catawba pottery predates the more famous Southwestern styles. The unique pottery is never painted or glazed—even though it often has a sleek sheen. One of the best known artists was Sara Ayers (1919–2002), who dug her clay from the Catawba River, fashioned it into stupendous pieces, and fired the pottery in a pit in her backyard. Ayers received considerable recognition in her lifetime, including the South Carolina Folk Heritage Award. Today, the younger generation, both men and women, are continuing the tradition. The pottery process, along with the history in general, is displayed at Catawba Cultural Center and Museum, housed in the only remaining reservation schoolhouse. http://catawbaindian.net/

CHEROKEE

The Cherokee, who once inhabited the southern Appalachian Mountains, live today in widely separated areas. Their traditional name is Aniyvwiya, meaning "The Real People." Those of the Eastern Band live in western North Carolina on or near the Qualla Boundary, as the Eastern Reservation is called; those who claim membership in the Western Band live in Oklahoma. There are many others who identify as Cherokee Americans throughout the United States. In addition, there are a few state-recognized Cherokee bands although the Cherokee Nation does not acknowledge them. The Cherokee language is still spoken and written and has regional variations.

Seventeenth-century Cherokee villages were located in mountain river valleys where there was adequate space for dwellings, council houses, and agricultural fields. Because the Cherokee were a matrilineal society, their fields were controlled by women. Women of great influence became known as Beloved Women, often working behind the scenes in shaping decisions. A woman who had taken her husband's place in war might be awarded the title War Woman. That the role of women still has a powerful effect today is reflected in Wilma Mankiller's election as tribal chairwoman of the Western Cherokee (1987 and 1991).

In the late seventeenth century, there were approximately thirty thousand Cherokee living in about sixty towns. Within one hundred years, smallpox, other epidemics, and warfare had reduced their population to only 7,500. From the early seventeenth through twentieth centuries, the major point of contention between the Cherokee and the Europeans was land. As the venerable Chief Old Tassel bluntly stated in 1777: "Brothers … the issue is about our land."

From 1783 to 1835, the Cherokee fought a losing battle in defense of their lands. After the American Revolution, land-hungry Euro-American settlers crossed the mountains in search of homesteads; then came eager planters seeking new soil for upland cotton cultivation. In 1802, "the federal government had promised Georgia that it would extinguish Indian title within the

a	e	i	o	u	v [ə̃]
Ꭰ a	Ꭱ e	Ꭲ i	Ꭳ o	Ꭴ u	Ꭵ v
Ꭶ ga Ꭷ ka	Ꭸ ge	Ꭹ gi	Ꭺ go	Ꭻ gu	Ꭼ gv
Ꭽ ha	Ꭾ he	Ꭿ hi	Ꮀ ho	Ꮁ hu	Ꮂ hv
Ꮃ la	Ꮄ le	Ꮅ li	Ꮆ lo	Ꮇ lu	Ꮈ lv
Ꮉ ma	Ꮊ me	Ꮋ mi	Ꮌ mo	Ꮍ mu	
Ꮎ na Ꮏ hna Ꮐ nah	Ꮑ ne	Ꮒ ni	Ꮓ no	Ꮔ nu	Ꮕ nv
Ꮖ qua	Ꮗ que	Ꮘ qui	Ꮙ quo	Ꮚ quu	Ꮛ quv
Ꮝ s Ꮜ sa	Ꮞ se	Ꮟ si	Ꮠ so	Ꮡ su	Ꮢ sv
Ꮣ da Ꮤ ta	Ꮥ de Ꮦ te	Ꮧ di Ꮨ ti	Ꮩ do	Ꮪ du	Ꮫ dv
Ꮬ dla Ꮭ tla	Ꮮ tle	Ꮯ tli	Ꮰ tlo	Ꮱ tlu	Ꮲ tlv
Ꮳ tsa	Ꮴ tse	Ꮵ tsi	Ꮶ tso	Ꮷ tsu	Ꮸ tsv
Ꮹ wa	Ꮺ we	Ꮻ wi	Ꮼ wo	Ꮽ wu	Ꮾ wv
Ꮿ ya	Ᏸ ye	Ᏹ yi	Ᏺ yo	Ᏻ yu	Ᏼ yv

The characters of written Cherokee as created by Sequoyah. Cherokee is still spoken and written today.

state's borders by purchase" as soon as a reasonable financial agreement could be reached. By 1825, some Cherokee had relocated voluntarily to Arkansas and Texas, hoping to escape the encroaching Americans. Those still in the East were divided between the highly acculturated mixed families and the more conservative traditionalists. Some Cherokee were not worried as they had helped Andrew Jackson defeat the Creek when he was leader of the Tennessee militia. Also, a Cherokee soldier, Junaluska, had saved his life, prompting Jackson's famous vow, "As long as the sun shines and the grass grows, there shall be friendship between us." But as Jackson rose in the ranks of government, he became more and more determined to clear the Southeast of all Indians.

During the years 1810 to 1828, the Cherokee reformed their government. This threatened the surrounding state governments, who feared the Cherokee now had the power and resources to stay in their original homelands. The states, on behalf of their greedy citizens, made a bigger push to resettle the Cherokee west of the Mississippi River.

The Cherokee Phoenix

The Cherokee Phoenix was the first Indian newspaper in the United States and the first published in an Indigenous language. The first issue was printed in 1828 at the Cherokee capital, New Echota, near present-day Calhoun, Georgia. Written in both Cherokee and English, its first editor was Elias Boudinot, who, along with Major Ridge, was a proponent of removal. He was eventually replaced by Elijah Hicks, who, like Chief John Ross and most Cherokee, was against leaving the eastern homelands. The newspaper stopped publishing in 1834 and showed up occasionally in Indian Territory after removal, but like the great phoenix bird that keeps having a rebirth, the newspaper was revived in the twentieth century by the Western Cherokee and has a web presence today.

The Trail Where They Cried

We, the great mass of the people, think only of the love we have for our land;

we do love the land where we were brought up. We will never let our hold to this land go; to let it go, it will be like throwing away (our) mother that gave (us) birth.

—letter from Aitooweyah to John Ross, principal chief of the Cherokee

Cherokee lawmakers like John Ross and Major Ridge spent much time in Washington, pleading their case to remain in the Southeast. In spite of the Supreme Court's decision that the Cherokee were indeed sovereign and not under the jurisdiction of the states, Andrew Jackson, now president, defied the ruling of the highest court in the land, and removal was imminent.

In 1835, Ridge and a minority group of Cherokee planters signed the controversial Treaty of New Echota, thereby agreeing to migrate to present-day Oklahoma. The treaty signers feared that remaining in the East was impossible because American settlers were confiscating Cherokee property, and the Cherokee government had become outlawed. The treaty led to the eviction of those Cherokee living in South Carolina, Georgia, Tennessee, and Alabama. In North Carolina, however, about one thousand Cherokee managed to escape removal with the cooperation of sympathetic state officials. According to their understanding of the treaties of 1817, 1819, and 1835, the Cherokee claimed North Carolina citizenship. One North Carolinian, William H. Thomas (or Wil-Usdi, as the Cherokee called him) bought land in his name for the Cherokee, went to court in their defense, and visited Washington on behalf of the Eastern Band's share in any general settlement with all Cherokee.

Many conservative Cherokee considered Major Ridge and the others traitors for signing the treaty and were embittered by the significant loss of life during the ensuing removal. During the winter of 1838–1839, American soldiers burst into Cherokee houses and rounded them up at gunpoint. They were forced to abandon their homes, belongings, livestock, and thriving farms. Several reported seeing white Americans watching from a short distance, and as soon as the Native families were in line for the long march, the whites moved in and claimed all of their property. Along with the Native people, whites who had intermarried and Freedmen were forced on what has come to be known as the Trail of Tears although the Cherokee call it "the trail where they cried."

> I fought through the war between the states and have seen many men shot, but the Cherokee removal was the cruelest work I ever knew.
>
> —Georgia soldier who participated in the removal

The long, hard trek through the bitter winter was disastrous to the Cherokee Nation. They were not allowed to enter any towns nor have any respite from the brutal weather. Townspeople killed several Cherokee with no repercussions, and many died waiting to cross the river by ferry; they were charged five times the ferry fare as whites. An estimated four thousand people died on the way. When the majority of the Cherokee moved to Indian Territory (present-day Oklahoma), the tribe's internal problems were not solved. Hatred deepened after the political murders on June 22, 1839, of John Ridge, Major Ridge, and Elias Boudinot, three Cherokee leaders who had signed the despised removal agreement.

Eastern Band of Cherokee

The Cherokee domain once extended far beyond the distant mountains, but the white man, with broken treaties and fruitless promises, brought trouble to the Indians and caused their banishment to an Oklahoma reservation. A few escaped capture and fled into the Great Smokies, eventually forming the Eastern Band that now lives on the Qualla Reservation in the valley below.

> —A United States Department of the Interior sign entitled "Qualla Indian Reservation."

As part of the Qualla Boundary, Cherokee trust lands in North Carolina were considered part of the Cherokee Nation before removal. Many Cherokee who escaped removal settled on the lands bought by William Thomas, a white man whom Chief Yonaguska had adopted as a child and was an assimilated Cherokee, so the Eastern Cherokee ended up on their original homelands stolen by the Americans and bought back for them by an American who preferred the Cherokee way of life.

During the first three decades of the twentieth century, the Eastern Band grappled with the difficulties of tribal membership, enrollment, and allotment. Over 12,000 people applied for tribal rolls, but the tribal administration maintained that only around two thousand were eligible. The long disagreement over this matter delayed any action of dividing the land until the Indian Reorganization Act of 1934 ended allotment (see also the Historical Overview chapter). There was a further economic decline in the 1930s, when a chestnut blight destroyed more than 60 percent of the timber on the tribal lands.

Building Boom and Tourism

After World War II, some economic recovery came to the Eastern Cherokee in the form of highways, a national park, and a historical drama. The roads needed for modern automobile travel were developed by those seeking creation of the Great Smoky Mountains National Park, in lands that lay adjacent to Cherokee homelands. If

The flag of the Eastern Band of Cherokee

visitors who came to the park in search of natural splendor could be tempted to stay overnight, an income-producing tourist industry might develop. By the early 1950s, the Cherokee Historical Association had commissioned and then produced "Unto These Hills," an emotional drama based on the Cherokee experience. It still attracts many visitors, as do Oconoluftee Village and the Museum of the Cherokee Indian. The National economy includes an enormous bingo parlor, where almost four thousand people can play for prizes worth thousands of dollars.

Of great benefit to the preservation of Cherokee tradition was the Qualla Arts & Crafts Mutual, Inc., the nation's oldest and most impressive Native American cooperative. After the Great Smoky Mountains National Park opened in 1940 and the growth of highways and family travel, visitors began to flock to the Cherokee. Traditional artists had the vision and planning to preserve and promote traditional crafts, thereby strengthening tribal values, creating a thriving artist economy, and sharing these unique and ancient art forms with the world. Stunning examples of basketry, pottery, weaving, carving, sculpture, and other works of art are displayed in the equally beautiful building in the heart of the Cherokee. Artists are often on hand to demonstrate their craft while exhibits portray the history and step-by-step creation of traditional art that is world famous.

Today, there are more than 9,500 Eastern Cherokee who share an abiding sense of place and kinship as well as an egalitarianism that makes national politics interesting. Most of those who live on the Qualla Boundary, as the reservation for the Eastern Band of Cherokee is known, work in Waynesville or Sylva, North Carolina, while those from the outlying, more traditional village of Snowbird work for the National Forest Service or the Tennessee Valley Authority. The Cherokee Nation operates its own schools, courts, and newspaper, the *Cherokee One Feather*. Although several Cherokee, particularly in Snowbird, observe the traditional religion, many belong to different Christian sects. Gospel music is very popular, and the nationally acclaimed Jody

Brown Indian Family group performed in both English and Cherokee.

Besides the Cherokee Nation and United Keetoowah Band in Oklahoma and the Eastern Band of Cherokee in North Carolina, there are several Cherokee organizations/bands across the country, and each determines its own rules for membership and enrollment. Some are state recognized; others have not-for-profit charters. Many of these groups have created a cultural revival and offer its members language, history, and culture connections and classes. Still others claim to be remnant groups and trace their heritage to ancestors appearing on different government roles. According to the U.S. Census, the Cherokee is the nation's second-largest Indigenous group (http://nc-cherokee.com).

CHICKASAW

The Chickasaw, related to the Choctaw, with whom they share the Muskogean language and a migration story, lived in present-day extreme northwestern Alabama, northern Mississippi, western Tennessee, and western Kentucky. Although relatively few in number, the 3,500 to 4,500 Chickasaw gained wide respect for courageously defending their country. Their success in defeating French invaders on three different occasions attracted the attention of the British, who won the Chickasaw as allies through exploiting their trade advantage. However, this involved the Chickasaw in an almost unending series of wars against France and her Indian allies. As a result, many Chickasaw lives were lost; some losses were replaced, however, by the Chickasaw practice of adoption and absorption of remnant tribes.

After the defeat of France in 1763, the Chickasaw lived in relative peace for more than twenty years under the leadership of Payamataha and Piominko. Both these leaders tried to stem the tide of European influence, but pressure to accommodate came from increasing numbers of blended Chickasaw/European families, whose success in trade, agriculture, and slavery created a lifestyle different from the traditional Chickasaw way. During the Revolution, Chickasaw service as British allies brought more outsiders when Loyalists sought refuge in the Chickasaw towns. After the Revolution, the Chickasaw signed a treaty with the United States at Hopewell, South Carolina, in January 1786. The treaty guaranteed the Chickasaw their lands, territories, and the right to manage their own affairs.

Initial U.S. relations with the Chickasaw were ineffective because the Spanish at New Orleans wooed the Chickasaw. Consequently, Chickasaw politics were complicated by rivalries among a Spanish-allied party, an American-allied party, those who wavered, and some self-serving tribal members. Pressure from the pro-Spanish Creek under Alexander McGillivray added to Chickasaw woes. McGillivray's death in 1793 and the signing of the Treaty of San Lorenzo (1798) slightly reduced Chickasaw difficulties.

Despite internal political rivalries, the Chickasaw became increasingly tied to the United States. After 1802, a government trading post operated at Chickasaw Bluffs (present-day Memphis) to trade for the skins and furs brought in by the still successful Chickasaw hunters. The tribe supported the United States by rejecting Tecumseh's appeals in 1811 and aiding Jackson's forces against the Redstick Creek at Horseshoe Bend in 1814. However, as with others who supported the Americans, their loyalty did not protect them when U.S. commissioners stripped them in 1818 of their Tennessee and Kentucky lands, leaving only their territory in northern Mississippi and northeastern Alabama.

Although there were political differences within the nation, all were opposed to removal. Under constant pressure from both federal and state governments, a few Chickasaw leaders were persuaded to look at a proposed western territory in 1828, but they returned to report they found nothing suitable. Despite their persistence, Chickasaw resistance was undermined by the 1830 Indian Removal Act and the impact of Mississippi and Alabama state laws, especially the

A statue representing a Chickasaw warrior stands outside the Chickasaw Cultural Center in Sulfur, Oklahoma.

statutes that abolished tribal law and forbade the functioning of tribal government.

In 1830, at Franklin, Tennessee, the Chickasaw finally agreed to exchange their eastern territory for suitable western lands. Removal was delayed for another seven years as they could not find suitable lands. Then the Treaty of Pontotoc Creek (1832) was forced on them to increase the pressure to move. By then, most Chickasaw regarded removal as inevitable. Ultimately, the Chickasaw were permitted to buy land in Indian Territory from their former neighbors, the Choctaw. This arrangement was to be temporary, but after their migrations began in 1837, many Chickasaw preferred the security of Choctaw lands. They were persuaded to relocate only after the federal government had built Forts Washita and Arbuckle to protect them from the Plains peoples. Today, few Chickasaw remain near their ancestral homelands. Most live in Oklahoma although there is an attempt to organize a separate entity in Mississippi by those who say they are descendants of the people who remained. http://mewo.tripod.com/

SOVEREIGN NATION OF THE CHITIMACHA

The Chitimacha (also known as Chetimachan) were the first to be federally recognized in Louisiana and the only Indigenous nation in the state that still controls some of its original lands. Located on Bayou Teche in St. Mary Parish, their population is almost 1,500, a much reduced number from four hundred years ago. In traditional times, their villages were large and usually built in or near swamps, bayous, and rivers, utilizing the natural terrain for protection. Their homes had plaster walls and thatched roofs, and they were skilled horticulturalists, storing crops in elevated granaries. They raised a surplus of crops to trade with northern people for stone to make tools.

At one time, the Chitimacha were one of the strongest groups in the area. However, after contact, the many battles with the French impacted them greatly. Not only were Chitimacha lands invaded and stolen, but the French and their missionaries enslaved many Chitimacha citizens. During the worst years of defending against French aggression in the early 1700s, the Chitimacha were the most enslaved of any population in Louisiana.

The Chitimacha have been recovering; their population is on the rise, and their once strong economy is being restored. Today, their tribally owned businesses support their government and community services and preserve their culture. Chitimacha basketry art is crafted in much the same way as it was in historic times from local river cane and in red, black, and yellow, plus the natural cane colors. A variety of shapes and styles are either single or double woven, and some are watertight. Designs like nish-tu wa-ki (alligator entrails), tcik ka-ni (blackbird's eyes), and tcish mish (worm track) have been handed down for centuries; there are about fifty designs. The baskets have always been popular and are in collections worldwide. To make up for the loss of material culture, the Chitimacha have asked for the prized baskets to be returned by donation and are also willing to buy them back. Single-woven baskets include bowls, trays, sifters, and heart-shaped and elbow baskets (for picking berries).

Double-woven baskets, the baskets with lids, were used for storage, and some can hold water. To revitalize the language, the Chitimacha devised a Rosetta Stone software language project so that all citizens can learn how to speak it.

CHOCTAW

The Mississippi Band of Choctaw Indians is proud of its contribution to the economy of the state of Mississippi. In working closely with local, state, and federal governments, we have obtained great success from the many initiatives we have undertaken. Through self-determination, we continue to prosper and share our legacy. We invite you to explore our achievement and imagine the possibility for future growth. For more than five hundred years, the Mississippi Band of Choctaw Indians has been a part of the state of Mississippi. From two hundred years of betrayal, dispersal, and poverty, today, by choice, we are a testament to the fact that together, we can achieve anything.

—former Chief Phillip Martin

Before the majority of the Choctaw were forced west in the nineteenth century, their settlements were located in present-day central and southern Mississippi as well as southwestern Alabama. During the seventeenth and eighteenth centuries, their lives were impacted by European newcomers. Although the French (and the Spanish after 1763) in New Orleans were the closest in proximity, enterprising English traders also reached their villages; the traders introduced cloth, firearms, tools, and alcohol. During the late seventeenth and early eighteenth centuries, there was also traffic in Indian slaves, an exchange that intensified rivalries with the Chickasaw, the Creek, and other nearby peoples. Trade generated enmity since some villages supported the most generous provider of quality goods at the lowest prices, whether France, Spain, or Great Britain.

Included in the trade-induced stress were the resident traders, whose mixed-blood families later rose to positions of prominence in the tribe.

After the emergence of the United States, Choctaw lands became the stumbling block in Choctaw relations with the new country. Fervent land developers paid little attention to Choctaw claims as they laid off lines across maps of the Mississippi Territory. So great was the demand for new acreage that the federal government pressured for rights of way to allow the construction of roads through the Choctaw homeland. Nothing seemed to stop the Americans. From the time the Mississippi Territory was organized in 1798 until removal, politicians repeated their demands for the relocation of the tribes and the distribution of their lands. The cooperation of some Choctaw leaders was bought with cash and other gifts. Choctaw tribal integrity was also undermined by the efforts of missionaries to convert them into Christian farmers, who could practice commercial agriculture.

In 1801, the Choctaw signed the Treaty of Fort Adams, hoping a definition of tribal boundaries would satisfy the demands of the United States. No treaty was ever enough, not even the combined results of Fort Adams, Mount Dexter (1805), and Doak's Stand (1820), the latter of which exchanged nine million acres of Choctaw homelands for 13,000,000 unfamiliar western acres.

Although a few moved voluntarily, most wished to stay, yet even loyal service as American allies during the Creek War of 1813–1814 did not protect them, for the determined state of Mississippi moved to terminate all their rights in 1830. As a result of the Dancing Rabbit Creek Treaty in September 1830, the Choctaw signed

François Bernard's 1869 painting features a Chocktaw village in Louisiana.

over their homelands and agreed to emigrate; this was accomplished through a combination of threatened force and the bribery of certain chiefs.

The Choctaw movement west was as painful as those of their southeastern neighbors. Fraud, mismanagement, and corruption marked those in charge of the move while disease and death stalked the Choctaw each mile. The combined deaths from the journey's difficulties plus subsequent cholera and smallpox outbreaks reduced the tribal population from 18,963 in 1830 to 13,666 by 1860.

Those who remained behind in Mississippi were driven into the depths of poverty by the new landowners, yet the Mississippi Choctaw persisted, and today, they are a separate nation, named the Mississippi Band of Choctaw Indians. After the passage of the Indian Reorganization Act, they moved slowly toward recognition as a separate entity; their cause was helped in 1944 by the creation of a land base, a 16,000-acre reservation. The federal government also sanctioned the Mississippi Choctaw Agency, which assists the seven Choctaw settlements with education and general welfare. Subject to extreme racism and discrimination, the Choctaw were outsiders in the segregated black and white south, but suddenly America's eyes were on the South and the Freedom Summer, which came to Choctaw ancient homelands. Three civil rights workers were murdered in 1964's Neshoba County (Choctaw word for wolf); two Choctaw women had overheard their murderers planning the assault and aided the investigation. The civil rights movement improved life for the Choctaw as before the Civil Rights Act of 1964, whites were employed first, then blacks. Still, economics improved very little. Then in 1979, Phillip Martin was elected chief, and under his forty-year leadership, the nation made economic and cultural gains.

Today from their tribal headquarters in Philadelphia, Mississippi, Choctaw own and operate manufacturing, service, retail, and service businesses, which employ six thousand tribal members as well as almost six thousand non-Choctaw workers. These successful enterprises have helped protect the nation's independence and self-reliance. They are also one of the top ten top private employers in Mississippi.

The Choctaw Museum and Chahta Immi Cultural Center provide language and cultural preservation plus recount the history of the Choctaw people. The annual Choctaw Fair is held for a week each July and draws Choctaw and other performers and visitors. Contemporary Choctaw dresses are worn on special occasions like the annual fair. Choctaw dresses are often trimmed with one of three motifs: full diamond, half diamond, or a series of circles that represent stickballs and sticks. Stickball is a featured event at the fair, but it is also an official sport in the Mississippi State Games and must be played with Choctaw rules. Mississippi Choctaw education emphasizes science and technology, and their high school robotics team, the Chahta Warriors, has earned national recognition for their inventions.

CREEK

Before the Civil War, the majority of the Creek moved to Indian Territory, but a remnant stayed in Alabama. Today, their descendants live in Alabama, Oklahoma, and across the United States. After the arrival of the Europeans, the Muskogee peoples moved inland away from the expanding newcomers. Clustering on Ochese Creek as well as on the Chattahoochee River, the villagers were labeled Creek by British traders from Charleston, South Carolina. Those nearest to Charleston were called the Lower Creek and those farther away the Upper Creek. Expansion of Georgia after 1733 pushed these peoples deeper into the interior, eventually into present-day Alabama. From their towns, they attempted to play off the European powers seeking dominance in eastern North America.

Wherever they relocated, Creek lands lay in the path of the westward expanding United States. Creek defensive actions brought repeated invasions until 1814, when forces under General Andrew Jackson defeated them at the Battle of Horseshoe

Bend. In the minds of Jackson and his fellow expansionists, Creek resistance legitimized removal beyond the Mississippi River. Although the Creek ceded twenty million acres of southern Georgia and central Alabama lands at the Treaty of Fort Jackson, the Jacksonians would not be satisfied until all Native Americans east of the Mississippi had been relocated. The Creek War provided a convenient excuse for Tennessee to demand the removal of the Creek, the Cherokee, and the Chickasaw. Georgia politicians, moreover, were eager to manipulate the Creek agency for purposes of profit and land speculation. When Georgia succeeded in expelling the Creek, neighboring Alabama kept the refugees moving west. First, Alabama extended its laws over all the Indian lands in the state. Then, under the Treaty of 1832, the Creek Nation in the east was no longer recognized by the federal or state governments. Creek who wished to claim allotments and stay in the east were soon subjected to constant harassment as their white neighbors sought to drive them away.

From 1820 to 1840, by one means or another, the Creek were forced to move to Indian Territory. They were exposed to a foreign climate, often without the barest of necessities, despite promised aid from the U.S. government. Dispossessed and abandoned, many died, yet others survived, intent on rebuilding the Creek Nation in the West. Those who remained behind in Alabama eked out a marginal existence while resisting pressure to move. They insisted that according to the Treaty of Fort Jackson (1814), they could claim a section of land. Despite the pressures against them, a few held on; land belonging to the McGhee family was reaffirmed in 1836. Lynn McGhee's 240-acre claim at the headwaters of Perdido Creek became the center for three nearby settlements that came to be known as the Poarch Band Creek.

The Poarch Band Creek were not removed from their tribal lands and have lived together for over 150 years. Their ancestors lived along the Alabama River, which included areas from Wetumpka south to the Tensaw settlement. The Creek allowed the U.S. government to use and widen the Alabama Indian Trail in the 1790 Treaty of New York. It became the Federal Road; Creek

The Creek Nation gave up large tracts of land in what is now Alabama and Georgia, thanks to the 1814 Treaty of Fort Jackson.

were permitted to create businesses that provided services for white settlers traveling the Federal Road through Indian Territory. Then the Creek were contracted by the U.S. government to serve as ferrymen and river pilots, guides, and interpreters. They operated inns and cattle ranches and were able to acquire more land, but many of the travelers were settling on Indian lands, creating tensions among different factions of the Creek.

The U.S. was more lenient to those Creek families who provided services to the Americans in terms of removal to Indian territory. In 1836, a special act of Congress permitted land grants to the Creek families of Lynn McGhee, Semoice, Susan Marlow, and Samuel Smith or their heirs. However, the area was already very populated by the Americans, leaving little land for the Creek. They had to move farther inland into the Poarch area, where they still live today.

Because of the discrimination they faced from their white neighbors, the remaining families developed a distinct and close group. The Poarch settlement suffered economically, became more isolated, and their jobs were mainly as farm laborers and in the timber industry. They developed all Indian schools and churches and were buried in a segregated Indian cemetery on land donated to them by a freed slave. Since the early 1900s, the Poarch Band Creek have organized to improve their situation, but the federal government did not get involved until 1920, when it stopped the illegal taxation of their federal trust lands. The U.S. government also litigated and fined trespassers on Poarch lands.

The community had an activist spirit and took on the local government to improve educational services. After organizing a school boycott in the late 1940s, they pressured their county district to build a small, segregated grammar school to provide Indians a "separate but equal" education. They then forced the district to supply bus transportation so that Indian children could attend junior and senior high school. In the early 1990s, the tribe restored the Poarch Consolidated School.

Several leaders emerged in the long history of the Poarch Band Creek; the best known is Eddie L. Tullis, who was at the forefront of the efforts to be federally recognized. On August 11, 1984, the United States government, Department of the Interior, and the Bureau of Indian Affairs acknowledged that the Poarch Band of Creek Indians exists as an "Indian tribe," and on November 21, 1984, 231.54 acres of land were taken into trust and declared a reservation on April 12, 1985. Today, there are over three thousand members living on or near the only federal reservation in Alabama.

The Calvin McGhee Cultural Authority (CMCA) oversees cultural education museum and annual events like the Creek Art Show. The museum is named Kerretv Cuko (Building of Learning). Traditional art classes preserve basketry, finger weaving, clothing construction, language, and the famous patchwork. Youth are involved in many activities, including traditional stickball.

COHARIE TRIBE

Almost three thousand people are enrolled in the Coharie Indian Tribe, one of eight North Carolina state-recognized tribes and located mainly in Harnett and Sampson counties. Descendants of the Neusiok Indians, they share a similar history to the Lumbee and other tribes robbed of their original territories. They did escape removal and survived colonial powers.

The Coharie Intra-Tribal Council is headquartered in the old Eastern Carolina Indian School building (Clinton) which served the Native Americans of Sampson, Harnett, Cumberland, Columbus, Person, and Hoke counties from 1942 until 1966 until the federal Civil Rights Act ended public school segregation. They hold an annual powwow in the fall.

HALIWA-SAPONI TRIBE

The Haliwa-Saponi Indian Tribe is state recognized by North Carolina and has four thousand enrolled members. Based in Hollister, North Carolina, they are descendants of the Saponi, Nansemond, Tuscarora, and others. Tribal headquarters include an administration building and multipurpose building, and there are housing programs for tribal housing, daycare, senior citizens, cultural enrichment, youth, and economic development.

Their history is one of tragedy and survival. In the 1600s, they were often at war with other Native nations that invaded their territory. By the 1700s, their once numerous population had been decimated by wars as well as foreign diseases, and yet they persevered. Colonial powers forced them to join with other tribes in the different areas of what is now Virginia, South Carolina, and North Carolina, which was not always successful.

During the early 1800s, the Haliwa-Saponi chose to live isolated from other tribes and tried to get along with their non-Indian neighbors. Because of their landless and powerless status, they escaped removal. Some tribal members did migrate west to Indian Territory, often joining other tribes. Most remained in North Carolina, where they live today in tight-knit tribal communities, located in Halifax, Warren, Nash, and Franklin counties.

Today, children attend the Haliwa-Saponi Tribal School, where ninety-eight percent of the students are Indian; the curriculum offers standard state courses as well as American Indian studies. It is the site of the annual spring pow-wow, which attracts over ten thousand visitors. http://haliwa-saponi.com/

UNITED HOUMA NATION

In historical times, the Houma lived on the east side of the Mississippi River, farther north in what is now Louisiana. As Europeans invaded their lands, they began to move south to marshlands along the coast. Since the bayous were not seen as prime real estate by Anglos, the Houma were relatively safe from further displacement and were able to sustain themselves by hunting, fishing, and trapping. However, in the 1930s, vast deposits of oil and gas were discovered, and the Houma were once again victimized, this time by energy companies who recognized the value of their homelands. Like other Gulf of Mexico Native nations, their very land is disappearing, as a result of global warming and other ecological disasters.

As there were no schools for the Houma until the 1960s, many families moved to New Orleans, where there is still a large, urban settlement. Several Houma women design dolls called catins (French for "woman of easy virtue") from the plentiful Spanish moss; some catins are shaped like turtles, alligators, and other local animals. Catins have become an iconic art form.

Today, the Houma continue to live in bayou communities, including Dulac, Montegut, and Pointe-aux-Chenes. Their major powwows draw thousands. They do not own tribal lands but have an elected tribal council that governs what is probably the largest tribe in Louisiana with over 18,000 enrolled members. Tribal headquarters are in Golden Meadow, Louisiana. The United Houma Nation (UHM) continues to petition for federal recognition, which is key in protecting their homelands from the ravages of the oil industry.

ISLE DE JEAN CHARLES BAND OF BILOXI-CHITIMACHA-CHOCTAW INDIANS

If we don't do anything, our community is going to be dead, and where are our people going to be? All gone.… Eventually we'll just be history.

—Albert Naquin, chief of the island's Band of Biloxi-Chitimacha Choctaw

Isle de Jean Charles, a narrow island (chenier) deep in the bayous of South Louisiana, has been home to the state-recognized Band of Biloxi Chitimacha Choctaw Indians for almost two centuries. In the early 1800s, Pauline Verdin, a Native woman, married Jean Marie Naquin, a Frenchman. His family disagreed with the union, so the couple moved to Isle de Jean Charles, and over the years, the community grew as their children married other Indigenous people and relatives joined them. They lived off the land, every home had a garden, and because of their isolation, tribal elders say they were spared a lot of problems of the outside world. Until a road was built to the community in 1953, the only transportation was by boat.

Since there were no schools for Indians, children were usually taught by community members. This helped people hold on to their culture as they were safe from outside influences. The Baptists built a church in the 1940s, which doubled as a one-room school, called the "mission school," and in 1952, a public school for Indian students was built relatively close by and island children began to attend by boat. The first high school for Indians in Louisiana was started in 1959, which was twenty-five miles away; after public school integration in 1967, Indian students were allowed to attend nearby public schools. If families wanted their children to go to school in the early days, they had to leave the island and disguise their race.

Today, the Band has joined with other tribes on the Gulf Coast to fight the coastal erosion that has made Southern Louisiana "the fastest-disappearing land mass on earth." Over the past century, at least two thousand square miles of marshland have disappeared; it is as if an area the size of Manhattan is being ripped off Louisiana's coast every single year. Not only has the erosion severely diminished the land size of the Band, but plants, trees, and animals are disappearing as they cannot acclimate to the salt-water intrusion. They say, "We have hunted, fished, and lived off the land. Now the land that has sustained us for generations is vanishing before our eyes. We are in a fight to save our community and culture before we are washed away."

Official logo of the Lumbee Tribe of North Carolina

LUMBEE

The 55,000 members of the Lumbee Tribe of North Carolina make it the largest tribe east of the Mississippi and the ninth largest in the country. Members live mainly in Robeson, Hoke, Cumberland, and Scotland counties in south and central North Carolina and have created urban neighborhoods in Baltimore, Philadelphia, and Detroit. According to Lumbee historians, their ancestors were Cheraw and related Siouan-speaking Indians and have lived in the area of what is now Robeson County since the 1700s. They took their name from the Lumber River, which flows through their present-day communities, and Pembroke, North Carolina, is central to their area economically, culturally, and politically. Unlike other nations in the Southeast, they were not forced out during the removal period because they owned their lands privately.

Under the segregation laws, Lumbee were excluded from white schools; they rallied for their own and had built over thirty by 1920. The first, tiny school was constructed in 1887, which grew into today's top-rated University of North Carolina, Pembroke (1972). Although it is open to students of all backgrounds, it was probably the first American Indian college and is renowned for its Native curriculum. Education was not the only right denied to the Lumbee. Under the 1835 North Carolina Constitution, the Lumbee, like other American Indians in the state, were not allowed to own weapons, vote, hold office, or serve in the military, but during the Civil War, the Confederates conscripted many Lumbee to build forts and perform other duties. Some escaped while others hid to avoid being caught by the local authorities. One of the escapees, Henry Berry Lowrie, did not flee the area but fought back and became known as the Lumbee Robin Hood for his bravery and protection of the local people and ability to evade the law.

The Lumbee people have been state recognized since 1885, and in 1956, a bill was passed by the United States Congress which recognized the Lumbee as Indian but denied them the full benefits of federal recognition. They still campaign to have that status changed. However, the Lumbee have excelled at creating thriving communities and have a reputation for their ability to overcome adversity.

The Klan

One of the most famous accounts of Lumbee spunk took place in 1958 near Maxton, North Carolina. A few days before, the Ku Klux Klan (KKK) had burned crosses at the homes of two Lumbee families and was intent on organizing a KKK chapter in Robeson County. Their leader stated he would hold a rally "to put the Indians in their place, to end race mixing." Word spread, and on that cold, January night as the KKK members set up a camp in a field with one lone lightbulb and a public announcement system, they got quite a surprise! Over a thousand Lumbee stood just outside the periphery of the light—outnumbering the Klansmen by at least five to one. Someone shot the bulb, extinguishing the light, and the KKK fled—never to return to the county. The successful encounter made world news, accompanied by a photograph of two Lumbee World War II veterans wrapped in the KKK banner.

Lumbee have frequently been at the forefront of Native news, often receiving national acclaim as being the first Natives to accomplish recognition in their particular fields. In 1969, Brantley Blue was the first Indian to become commissioner of the Indian Claims Commission; attorney Arlinda Locklear was the first-ever Native woman to successfully argue a case before the U.S. Supreme Court (1983); and Hiram R. Revels was the first Native American senator (1870). Kelvin Sampson, Oklahoma University Sooners basketball coach, was the first Native American coach to make it into the NCAA Final Four tournament (2002); Darlene Gabbard opened Native Vines Winery in 1998, the first winery to be Native owned and operated. In 2008, Pastor Johnny

Hunt became the first Native president of the Southern Baptist Convention, and his Woodstock, Georgia, church has one of the largest congregations in the nation.

Longleaf Pine

At one time, Lumbee lands were covered with the vast forests of the strong and fire-resistant Longleaf Pine tree native to the Southeast. Before Europeans came, the Longleaf Pine lived for five hundred years, but because their strong timber was excellent for shipbuilding, the United States Navy and merchants harvested these trees to the brink of extinction. Today, only three percent of the original Longleaf Pine forests remain. In the 1800s, Lumbee women began to look at them upside down and developed the geometric design on quilts and rugs, creating a new art form. A century later, Hayes Alan Locklear and Kat Littleturtle, Lumbee tribal members, made a Longleaf Pinecone motif on a Miss Lumbee dress, and the design became a tribal symbol. Today, Lumbees from across the country attend Lumbee Homecoming, held every July. The event features games, powwows, an art show, and a Miss Lumbee and a Little Miss Lumbee pageant. The contestants and winner all wear regalia with the famous Longleaf Pine design.

MEHERRIN NATION

The state-recognized Meherrin, primarily located in North Carolina's Hertford County in small communities near Virginia, refer to themselves as Kauwets'aka, meaning "People of the Water." They are culturally related to the Haudenosaunee (Iroquois Confederacy); several migrated to Haudenosaunee territory in both Canada and upstate New York during the eighteenth and nineteenth centuries while fleeing white incursion. They share a language with the Tuscarora and maintain close ties with their Iroquois brothers.

The Meherrin Nation office is in Ahoskie, North Carolina, and they hold an annual, three-day powwow every autumn. Around one thousand Meherrin are tribally enrolled.

In 1958, members of the Ku Klux Klan burned crosses in front of the homes of two Lumbee Tribe families.

POWHATAN

The Native peoples in present-day Virginia escaped removal, but they did not escape the horrors of settler colonial and American policies. Hundreds of Native communities had been wiped off the face of the earth just a century after European contact. During the 1700s and 1800s, more and more people were pushed off their lands until there were only four reservations left in the entire state; the Americans set out to remove their status as American Indians, hoping to "eradicate the Indian problem." Tribal land subdivisions and abject poverty destroyed the Gingaskin Reservation on the Eastern Shore (1850) and the Nottoway Reservation (1878). The Pamunkey and Mattaponi, the last two reservations, were able to survive despite overwhelming odds and maintained their treaties with the Virginia Commonwealth and tribal governments. Their reservations are two of the oldest in the United States and a testament to the people who could not be conquered.

Both the Mattaponi and Pamunkey reservations feature a fish hatchery, museum, and tribal council building and are located on a river. There are nine other separate nations in contemporary Virginia, but they do not have tribal lands. After thirty years of petitioning, the Pamunkey received federal recognition in July 2015. It is the first Virginia nation and the 567th tribe to gain federal status. All other Virginia tribal governments are state recognized: Mattaponi; Rappahannock; Patawomeck; Cheroenhaka-Nottoway; Nottoway; Monacan Indian Nation; Nansemond; Upper Mattaponi; Eastern Chickahominy; and Chickahominy. Tribal members also reside in New Jersey, Pennsylvania, Maryland, and cities on the East Coast. Currently, there are over four thousand members of Virginia nations, but it is estimated that four times that number are eligible for tribal enrollment.

Paper Genocide

Every November, both the Pamunkey and Mattaponi are bound by a three-hundred-year-old treaty with England to pay tribute to the governor of the Commonwealth of Virginia to deliver two deer and a turkey to the governor's home in lieu of paying taxes. That tradition continued even during the difficult years of the 1900s when the state, under the leadership of Walter Ashby Plecker, declared there were no Indians left in Virginia and set out to once again commit genocide of First Peoples, this time on paper. Plecker, a vocal advocate of eugenics, became the first registrar of Virginia's Bureau of Vital Statistics in 1912, and he used his position to create two "races" in his state. Anyone who was not white, he made "colored," which referred to black people. Overnight, families were separated by racial designation, and people who had grown up Indian were suddenly classified as colored and later changed to black. Many Virginia Indians left the state rather than be wrongfully labeled. Plecker, who admired Hitler's eugenics plan, retired in 1946, leaving a long-lasting, disastrous impact on Native peoples. A requirement for federal recognition is that tribes must prove their continuous existence since 1900, but since Plecker officially purged Indians as a race, it has made it even more difficult for Virginia nations.

Many people are unaware of how many famous Americans have Indian blood in them. For example, the late author Langston Hughes, who is best known for his work about African Americans, is a descendant of Pamunkeys, too.

In spite of Plecker's one-man war on Virginia Indians, they persevere; many are notable in their respective fields. Poet Langston Hughes, known as one of America's most celebrated African American poets, is also a Pamunkey descendant. Wayne Newton (Patawomeck), popularly known as Mr. Las Vegas, has advocated for Virginia Indians and hosted the first Native American Music Awards (NAMMYS) gala. One of the most famous Indigenous and female theater companies in the world, Spiderwoman Theater, is the creation of three Kuna/Rappahannock sisters, Lisa Mayo, Gloria Miguel, and Muriel Miguel. Prolific television writer/producer/journalist David Mills (Pamunkey) earned two Emmys and was nominated for a Pulitzer Prize before his untimely death. Some of his famous shows were *Treme*, *ER*, and *NYPD Blue*. Dr. Phoebe Farris (Powhatan-Renape/Pamunkey) is an artist, scholar, curator, art therapist, author, and editor and writes for *Cultural Survivor Magazine*. One of Washington, D.C.'s most iconic restaurants, Ben's Chili Bowl, is owned by Virginia Ali, Rappahannock. She and her husband have been serving up tasty food to both visiting celebrities and local residents since they opened their doors in 1958.

SEMINOLE

During the years of Creek withdrawal westward, a number of Lower Creek migrated into present-day Florida. In order to distinguish them from their kinsmen, British officials called these separatists the Seminole Creek, or Seminole, a corruption of the Spanish word *cimarrone*. Quickly adapting to their new environment, they became skillful herders, raising sleek ponies and fat cattle on the grassy savannas. So complete was their cultural adjustment that one of their leading chiefs was named Cowkeeper, who was vividly described in the prose of William Bartram, a Philadelphia botanist who visited the Seminole in the 1770s. As the federal government debated the constitutional war powers of the president, Bartram urged his readers to avoid warfare with Indian peoples. He suggested sending diplomats to learn Indian customs and languages. Unfortunately, Bartram's sensible advice was ignored, and three Seminole Wars characterized nineteenth-century Florida, which were officially ended.

When Georgia frontiersmen expanded farther south, the Seminole retreated again. They continued their adaptation, adopting lighter dress and modifying the Creek cabin so that it became an open-sided dwelling called a *chiki*, with a raised floor and a thatched roof. Changes in agricultural patterns followed since Florida soils differed from those to the north. Ultimately, the pressure of expanding plantations and farms pushed the Seminole so far south that they had little land.

During the period that these former Creek, as well as survivors from various other tribes, were becoming Seminole, they attracted the attention of both the neighboring states and the national government. Officials in Georgia, Alabama, and Florida were outraged that the Seminole would not agree to join the removal exodus westward. Their presence threatened Florida's claim to all the state's lands. The Seminole were also regarded as dangerous to peace and stability because they harbored runaway enslaved Africans. As long as the Seminole communities remained in Florida, there were havens for runaways; no slave-owning planter could feel secure. For the slaves captured by the Seminole, however, slavery was not as severe a life. Several former slaves rose to positions of influence through their ability as interpreters and their familiarity with plantation lifeways. They were given their own neighborhoods and lived independently from the Seminole, paying a sort of rent or tax. In the 1830s, the increasingly racist and intolerant society in the southern United States denounced Seminole acceptance of enslaved and/or freed Africans. Outside the South, ironically, courageous Seminole resistance attracted some public sympathy.

No amount of sympathy, however, changed the federal government's demand that the Seminole move. By force and by forced treaty, the Seminole were marched west. By 1842, there were 2,833 Seminole survivors in Oklahoma. The

The courthouse in Seminole County, Oklahoma. The county is where many Seminole Indians were forcefully moved from Florida.

Oklahoma Seminole of today are the descendants of these refugee peoples. The United States wars against the Seminole are considered the longest and most expensive of all the wars against Native peoples. The Seminole and their brilliant guerrilla military strategy were not defeated. The U.S. just gave up as they decided it was wasted money on a campaign they could never win.

While many Seminole moved west, small bands in Florida remained hidden deep in Big Cypress Swamp, in the Everglades, and in other isolated areas. During the second half of the nineteenth century and the first decade of the next, these survivors existed by hunting, trapping, and fishing. The fashion industry's demand for bird feathers and animal skins offered them a means to trade for the basic necessities unavailable in their area. Most of their food came from subsistence farming on small patches.

Their fragile life system began to collapse, however, early in the twentieth century. In 1906, Florida began to drain the Everglades in hope of producing more agricultural land for commercial purposes; more people began coming to Florida via the ever expanding railroad system; and both federal and state laws outlawed the use of bird plumes.

Beginning in the 1890s, however, Florida officials began buying land as a place for the Seminole to locate. The greatest difficulty arose in trying to persuade these fiercely independent people that they should live on reservations. By 1932, less than 20 percent of the 562 Florida Seminole had relocated. The spirit of resistance and self-reliance built from years of avoiding the federal government was unlikely to disappear overnight. Living in remote, self-sufficient camps, they supplied their basic needs but needed cash to buy coffee, salt, sugar, rifles, ammunition, and the seemingly ever present sewing machines. With the decline of the trade in plumes and hides, seasonal, agricultural labor became a source of cash. A few families became part of the growing tourist industry by establishing "commercial villages," where they put on public displays of "Seminole life."

Patchwork Art

The Seminoles are known worldwide for their distinctive and wearable patchwork art.

There are various accounts of how the bold, colorful quilt art was invented. One is that in the 1800s, when the Seminoles fled from the American soldiers and settlers deep into the Everglades, they were extremely impoverished, and what clothing they had was worn out. A resilient people, the women took apart the tattered clothes, salvaged the useable parts, and pieced them together in different shapes to create new garments. After they had become more secure, they began to barter for cloth and acquired hand-cranked sewing machines from traders along Florida's Tamiami Trail. Visitors to Seminole Country remarked that there was a sewing machine in every home, and not one tiny scrap of the precious cloth was wasted. Over the years, the unique art form has become more intricate. The designs themselves have great meaning; many symbolize creation accounts or a part of Seminole history and have names like sacred fire, arrow, zigzag, bird, wave, mountain, and diamondback rattlesnake. At one time, tourist shops along the Tamiami Trail were the main source of income for many families.

Perseverance

During the 1930s, however, in response both to federal Indian policy and activities by tribal leaders and protribal Florida interest groups, Seminole lifeways began to change. Tracts of land were obtained through purchase and exchange that resulted in the creation of several reservations, two of which were developed into cattle-raising operations. The success of the cattle ranches enticed some Seminole to leave isolated settlements and relocate to reservations. A new and more dependable economic base likewise meant an improved quality of life. The creation of federal agencies increased the tribe's exposure to and cooperation with federal officials. Also during the 1930s and 1940s, many converted to Christianity, brought to the community by Native Baptists from Oklahoma. Since their difficult encounters with Europeans in the seventeenth century, their creativity and adaptability has strengthened them, and they have met every obstacle with determination and courage. They

were able to deal with the termination policies of the 1950s as well as the creation and federal recognition in 1957 of the Seminole Tribe of Florida, Inc., followed in 1962 by the separation of a group who wished to be recognized as the Miccosukee Tribe of Indians.

Today, both the Seminole and the Miccosukee survive and sometimes thrive in heavily populated, non-Indian Florida. In 1979, the Seminole opened a bingo parlor offering 1,700 seats and $10,000 jackpots. Since that time, more parlors have been opened, generating enough revenue to endow tribal scholarships, establish a credit union, and expand the tribal cattle herds. On the environmental front, too, difficulties arise as developers seek far and wide for new sources of natural resources, such as those in the Big Cypress area.

Other tribal enterprises built on tourism include the Big Cypress Reservation's museum, Ah-Tah-Thi-Ki ("A Place To Learn"), which features history and exhibits of contemporary art. Visitors can get a sense of the traditional homelands by hiking nature trails through the sixty-acre cypress dome. The Billie Swamp Safari's airboat tours and the Swamp Buggy Eco tour offer tourists an up-close look at the unique Everglades ecosystem. On the Miccosukee Reservation, visitors can tour a replica of a historic village.

TUNICA–BILOXI

Cherishing Our Past, Building for Our Future

—Tunica–Biloxi motto

When Hernando de Soto arrived in Quiz-Quiz (1541) in northwestern Mississippi, it was the powerful center of the vast Tunica trading network that stretched from Oklahoma to Florida. Masterful traders, they controlled salt manufacture and supply until well after European and American encroachment. Like their southeastern neighbors, they farmed, and after European contact, they added peaches and melons to their agriculture. They moved south along the Mississippi to escape the Chickasaw and British slave traders and were allies of the French. European diseases took their toll on them as well as another Mississippi group, the Biloxi, who also migrated from Mississippi to Louisiana. The Biloxi merged with other peoples such as Caddo, Choctaw, and finally, the Tunica. Little is available about Biloxi history although they do speak a Siouan language and have a matrilineal line of descent.

For over two centuries, the Tunica and Biloxi Indians have lived on a joint reservation in east-central Louisiana, near Marksville. They speak two completely different languages, plus English and French. Ethnologist James Owen Dorsey visited the Biloxi in the late 1800s and described their intricate social system, which had over sixty terms for kinship relations, more than any other Siouan people.

After the U.S. acquired the Louisiana Territory in 1803, the Tunica–Biloxi continued to trade with whites, but they encountered white traders who were dishonest and conniving. During the removal period, Americans felt empowered more than ever to appropriate Indian lands. The Tunica–Biloxi escaped removal, but they did not escape the attitude that Americans were en-

American ethnologist and Episcopalian missionary James Owen Dorsey, who worked for the Smithsonian Institution from 1880 to 1895, visited the Biloxi people in Louisiana and described their intricate social system.

titled to Indian lands. In 1841, Chief Melancon tried to remove fence posts illegally erected within tribal boundaries by an American attempting to steal Tunica land. Although the American leader of the local "Indian Patrol" shot and killed Chief Melancon in front of Tunica witnesses, he was never prosecuted and was successful in the land theft. The tribe kept the identity of chiefs secret for many years and tried to avoid contact with dishonest land grabbers and unscrupulous traders. The nation's lucrative economy was reduced to subsistence living; many Tunica became sharecroppers, eking out a meager existence. In the 1870s, Chief Volsin Chiki helped reunite them and revived the ancient religion and rites like the Corn Feast. It may have been beneficial that Americans sort of forgot the Tunica as the U.S. focused its empire-building efforts on the lands of western Native peoples.

The Tunica–Biloxi managed to hold their land in common until today. Under the leadership of Hereditary Chief Earl J. Barbry, Sr., the nation became federally recognized in 1981 and gained the right to open a casino. Once again, the Tunica–Biloxi are thriving economically and the Paragon Casino Resort has become the largest employer in Avoyelles Parish, people have decent homes on the reservation, and the school bus now stops on tribal lands.

Native American Graves Protection and Repatriation Act

The Tunica–Biloxi were the key players in a major change to Indian policy. A local pothunter raided over one hundred Tunica gravesites in the 1960s and uncovered a vast amount of wealth that had been buried with the elite. Tunica colonial-era prosperity was evident in the fine, European ceramics, guns, kettles, bells, beads, and other artifacts he found and attempted to sell to the Peabody Museum at Harvard University. Because the Tunica were not federally recognized at that time, they were banned from litigation that determined rightful ownership of what came to be known as the Tunica Treasure, but all that changed in 1981, when the tribe was acknowledged as a sovereign nation by the federal government. In 1985, the Tunica Treasure was awarded to its rightful owners, and the landmark decision was the basis for the 1990 Native American Graves Protection and Repatriation Act (NAGPRA), federal legislation that protects and provides for repatriation of tribal artifacts and human remains. The Treasure was not actually given back until 1989 (it was held by the state of Louisiana), and it was in terrible condition. Not only did the whole episode create helpful policy, but tribal members trained to be conservators, and 80 percent of the artifacts of the Tunica Treasure have been restored and are on display in the Tunica–Biloxi Indian Museum.

Artisans in the last century continued to make traditional cypress drums, dolls, and beadwork. Their lovely, coiled pine straw baskets are still cherished by collectors. Only a few elders could speak the languages when anthropologist H. F. "Pete" Gregory and Choctaw basket maker/scholar Claude Medford, Jr., recorded songs and stories in both Tunica and Biloxi. Working with surviving elders and with these recordings made between the 1960s and the 1980s, the Pierite Family Singers have brought back traditional songs and stories in both Tunica and Biloxi languages. The tribe donates a significant amount of monies to both local/state associations and communities. In 2005, when Hurricane Katrina devastated New Orleans, Louisiana, the Tunica–Biloxi were not affected—they just had a bit of rain. They stepped up to help and converted their convention center into a haven for hundreds of refugees displaced by Katrina.

TUSCARORA

The Tuscarora were divided into northern and southern governments and lived in North Carolina. At first, relations were cordial between them and the European colonists. However, the newcomers appropriated more and more lands and also sold Tuscarora into slavery. One of the bloodiest wars against the Indians broke out in 1711 and lasted until the Tuscarora were de-feated in 1713. For the next ninety years, they migrated north to New York and Pennsylvania, where they found a similar language and acceptance among the Haudenosaunee (see also the Northeast chapter).

Some descendants of the Tuscarora remain in North Carolina but have no federal or state recognition. The Tuscarora Nation of North Carolina operates a gift shop, museum, and tribal library in Maxton, North Carolina. In 2013, both northern and southern Tuscarora marked the three-hundredth anniversary of the final battle at Fort Neyuherú through a series of events at the historic site in Greene County and on Eastern Carolina University's campus.

WACCAMAW SIOUAN TRIBE

The Waccamaw Siouan creation account tells of a huge, brilliant meteor that crashed to the earth and produced a deep crater. Waters from nearby rivers and swamps surged in the giant hole and cooled it, forming the beautiful, turquoise Lake Waccamaw. The Waccamaw Siouan are called "People of the Falling Star." At one time, they lived in what is now South Carolina but sought refuge from white encroachment in North Carolina's swamplands and are state recognized.

The Waccamaw are known for their superb quilting and were featured in the book *Waccamaw Siouan Quilters, Piecing the Past and Future*, which documents over eighty quilts that were exhibited and demonstrated at the Durham Festival for the Eno. In 1997, Elizabeth Graham Jacobs was honored with a prestigious North Carolina Folk Heritage Award.

The Waccamaw Siouan Annual Powwow is held every October each year at the Waccamaw Siouan Tribal Grounds in the Buckhead community of Bolton, North Carolina. It features traditional dance competitions, drumming competitions, horse shows, gospel singing, and a crafts fair. Tribal members, numbering almost two thousand, live primarily in Columbus and Bladen counties.

TYING IT UP

For many of the Native peoples living in the Southeast today, the past twenty years have been a period of marked population growth. In the 1990 census, more than 211,000 people identified as American Indian, and the 2010 census reported almost 850,000 Native people, including those living on and off reservations. Groups who were once terminated or deemed extinct have reorganized their governments, claiming their rightful culture. Because of racism and discrimination, many were forced to give up their tribal status. In spite of overwhelming odds, these groups kept their Native identity and "personality," often choosing to live apart from the general population to maintain their safety. Languages that were outlawed by the government are being restored; human remains and cultural objects in non-Indian museums are being repatriated. Overall, many Native people are reclaiming a heritage that was never lost but hidden away. Tribal museums, centers, and repositories are information sanctuaries for materials that have come "home."

There have been great strides economically, but Native people in the Southeast still have the highest rate of unemployment. When Native nations operate successful businesses, they improve the economics of the entire area, not just of the tribe.

Ceremonies and dances are not only being practiced today, but many rituals have been revived. Many Southeasterners observe their ancient religions as well as Christianity while others are traditional. Almost every nation hosts a homecoming or annual festival that brings people together to strengthen familial, tribal bonds and preserve heritage.

BIOGRAPHIES

Queen Anne of Pamunkey
(c. 1650–1725)
Pamunkey, Leader

Queen Anne was the third female to lead the Pamunkey (1666–1718). Her primary role was to protect her people from the English colonists; she rallied against dishonest surveyors, theft of Indian lands, and the sale of liquor.

Hagler (1690–1763)
Catawba, Leader

Hagler became principal chief of the Catawba in about 1748. The Catawba had been greatly reduced in numbers as the result of warfare with the Shawnee, Cherokee, and Iroquois as well as from European-introduced diseases, such as smallpox. Hagler developed amicable relations with the British colonists in order to ensure his people's survival and maintenance of their traditional ways. In 1751, he attended a peace conference in Albany, New York. In a meeting with North Carolina officials in 1754 and in a letter to the chief justice in 1756, he argued against the sale of liquor to the Catawba. In 1758, during the French and Indian War, Hagler and his soldiers sided with the English in an attack on the French Fort Duquesne (present-day Pittsburgh, Pennsylvania) and assisted the English in a 1759 battle against the Cherokee. Because of Hagler's support, the English built forts along the Catawba River to protect the Catawba from enemy attacks and granted them a reservation in 1792 near Rock Hill, South Carolina. Hagler was killed by the Shawnee in 1763. In 1826, South Carolina erected a statue of Hagler at Camden, the first memorial to an American Indian in the United States.

Dragging Canoe (Tsiyu-Gunsini)
(c. 1730–1792)
Cherokee, Leader

Principal chief of the Chickamauga band of Cherokee, who allied with the British during the American Revolution, and cousin of Nancy Ward, Dragging Canoe fought long and hard for his homelands. He signed treaties, which the Americans did not honor. He defended his lands against the ever encroaching white settlers.

Hancock (fl. 1700s)
Tuscarora, Leader

For half a century, the Tuscarora tolerated the European settlers, but the foreigners began to seize more and more Indian Territory. The Europeans also violated every agreement and captured many Tuscarora, selling them into slavery in the Caribbean and other colonies. From 1711 to 1713, the Tuscarora, living in present-day North and South Carolina, fought a series of battles to protect their lands and peoples against English settlers. During that time, Hancock, who some colonists called "King Hancock," led the Tuscarora defenses.

In 1713, the English colonists amassed a final assault on the Tuscarora. Under the command of Colonel James Moore, the colonial army and one thousand Indian allies defeated Hancock and his followers. Hundreds of Tuscarora were killed, and hundreds more were sold into slavery. Many Tuscarora survivors fled northward to New York Colony.

Alexander McGillivray
(1759–1793)
Creek, Leader

McGillivray, a controversial Creek Indian leader, was born near the Upper Creek village Little Talisee, a traditional white, or peace, village, located in present-day Alabama. He was sent to present-day Charleston for schooling, but the American Revolutionary War disrupted his studies, and he returned to the Creek Nation, where the upper towns generally favored British alliance. In late 1778, Emisteseguo, chief of Little Talisee, transferred political leadership to eighteen-year-old McGillivray, which was unusual because of his young age. However, Emisteseguo feared assassination from pro-American villages and believed that McGillivray's membership in the Sacred Wind clan would protect him. This plan seemed to work. McGillivray played off European powers

to protect the nation's interests, created a more centrally operated government, and became an astute businessman, thereby ensuring his position in both Native and European circles. In 1790, he negotiated a treaty with George Washington in New York City; he died three years later.

Arpeika
(c. 1760–1860)
Seminole–Miccosukee, Leader

A spiritual leader and chief in the Second Seminole War (1835–1842), Arpeika was thought to be the most opposed to removal. He advised Osceola not to trust the Americans and their offers of a truce. He was right about the duplicity of the whites. He and Billy Bowlegs moved their bands father south into the Florida Everglades and successfully retained their homelands. He died at home in the swamps and was said to be well over a hundred years old.

Sequoyah
(c. 1770–c. 1840)
Cherokee, Linguist/Freedom Fighter

The most famous of North American writing systems is the Cherokee Syllabary, and Sequoyah is credited with inventing it. However, in 1971, Traveller Bird (descendant of Sequoyah) published *Tell Them They Lie: The Sequoyah Myth*, which presents a very different scenario. Bird challenges the popular story of Sequoyah and maintains that Sequoyah was a scribe as the Cherokee already had a written language, which predated European contact. During Sequoyah's lifetime, he learned to speak English, Spanish, and other languages and simplified the syllabary so all Cherokee, not just scribes, could read it. The language was used strategically to relay messages unreadable to English speakers, almost like a secret, military code. Sequoyah's resistance and the syllabary were threats to those who wanted to expropriate

Cherokee lands. Because he was such a hero to the Cherokee, Bird suggests that Sequoyah was anglicized to diminish his legacy as a freedom fighter. Bird's book has stirred controversy as it challenges accepted scholarship and has gained some credence in academic discourse.

Opothleyoholo (d. 1862)
Creek, Leader

In the early 1820s, Opothleyoholo was a speaker for Tuckabatchee, the leading red town among the Creek upper towns, located in present-day Alabama; the lower towns were located in present-day western Georgia. The Creek were divided into red and white towns; white towns led during times of peace, and red towns led during times of war. Between 1810 and 1862, Tuckabatchee, with U.S. political support, led the upper towns. Talisee, the leading white upper town, led the opposition and favored British alliance between 1790 and 1820. In the Red Stick War or Creek War (1813–1814), most upper-town Creek villages rebelled against the U.S.-supported villages, which consisted mostly of lower towns, with some exceptions, like Tuckabatchee. The Red Sticks lost the war in 1814.

Opothleyoholo played an important leadership role. By the mid-1830s, he was the leading upper-town chief. He led delegations to negotiate the Treaty of 1826, which ceded most of western Georgia, and the Treaty of 1832, which provided the Creek villages with small reservations within the state of Alabama. By 1836, the Creek reservations were overrun by American settlers. A brief insurgency by several lower-town villages was put down by U.S. and upper-town forces. Creek leaders felt compelled to migrate west to present-day Oklahoma. While retaining upper-town leadership, Opothleyoholo emphasized retention of Creek culture and political institutions. The U.S. Civil War split the Creek Nation, largely between upper- and lower-town factions. In 1862, while Opothleyoholo led his people north toward Union alliance and protection, he was killed by Confederate forces.

Osceola (1803–1842)
Seminole, Leader

Even as a teenager, Osceola had great leadership abilities and led a resistance movement to prevent the relocation of his people from their Florida homelands. Osceola planned and won successful battles against the U.S. military. As he matured, he developed military strategies that confused U.S. generals sent to capture him and destroy the resistance faction.

The Seminole continued to resist U.S. removal efforts by retreating to the isolated, swampy regions of Florida; the U.S. Army found it impossible to find them. It is estimated that the war resulted in the deaths of 1,500 American troops and cost the U.S. government $20 million. Osceola had great influence over Seminole war actions. U.S. General Thomas Jesup offered Osceola a truce, but Jessup did not honor it, and Osceola was captured. Because the U.S. government did not keep their word and tricked the Seminoles, critics call the action one of the most terrible events in American military history. The U.S. military often used such deception to capture and control Indian leaders.

Osceola was imprisoned at Fort Moultrie on Sullivan's Island, near Charleston, South Carolina, where he died, still a young man. His death and the treatment of the Seminoles made headlines around the world. Osceola's influence lived on long after his death. According to the U.S. government, his capture marked the official end of the Third Seminole War, but there was never any such agreement between the two groups.

Yonaguska (c. 1760–1839)
Cherokee, Leader/Profit

As a peace chief of the Mountain Cherokee of North Carolina, Yonaguska was respected for his great oratory and diplomacy. When he was sixty, he became gravely ill, fell into a coma, and was presumed dead. However, he was revived. He had a vision in his comatose state, which became the basis of his teachings that, among other things, forbade the use of alcohol. Yonaguska and his group moved to Haywood County, North Carolina, where they acquired their own lands and escaped removal.

Pushmataha (1764–1824)
Choctaw, Leader

Choctaw legend says that Pushmataha was an orphan, and he himself maintained that he was born of a splinter from an oak tree. Such a story was unusual in Choctaw society, where everyone was conscious of his or her Native *iksa* (local, matrilineal family). At a young age, Pushmataha was recognized as a great soldier and hunter. He participated in many Choctaw hunting forays across the Mississippi River into the Osage and Caddo countries since by the early 1800s, fur-bearing animals suitable for trade were almost depleted in Choctaw country. These hunting trips led to war with the Caddo and Osage, who protected their land from the Choctaw intruders.

In 1805, Pushmataha was elected chief of the southern or Six Towns district of the Choctaw Nation, which was divided into three politically independent districts, each with a chief and council. From 1805 to 1824, Pushmataha led the southern district, which was the most traditional and, before 1760, allied to the French Louisiana Colony. Pushmataha favored friendly relations with the U.S., siding with the U.S. against the British, Tecumseh (the Shawnee leader), and the Red Stick Creek during the War of 1812. For his services, he earned the rank of U.S. brigadier general. The Choctaw, including Pushmataha, signed treaties of land cession in 1805, 1816, and 1820. In 1824, Pushmataha died from an infection while in Washington negotiating yet another treaty. He was buried with full U.S. military honors.

Wané Roonseraw (Edy Turner) (c. 1754–1838)
Nottoway, Leader

Wané Roonseraw was considered a Renaissance woman in nineteenth-century Virginia and was often referred to by non-Natives as "Queen" or "Chief." Not only was she an astute businesswoman, she was an accomplished diplomat and key in helping protect the Nottoway from removal. A fluent Nottoway speaker, Roonseraw helped to preserve the language by dictating it to a professor at William and Mary College. She was an advocate for maintaining Nottoway traditions and protected orphaned children from becoming indentured servants to white planters.

Nancy Ward (1738–1822)
Cherokee, Leader

Born in Chota, a capital of the Cherokee Nation in present-day eastern Tennessee, Nancy Ward, or Nan'yehi ("One Who Goes About"), was a Ghighua, or Beloved Woman, chosen for her position because of her brave and wise deeds. She was an ambassador, a peace negotiator, judge, and determined the fate of captives. In July 1781, the Cherokee Council chose Ward to lead treaty negotiations. As part of her persuasive speech, she said, "You know that women are always looked upon as nothing, but we are your mothers; you are our sons. Our cry is all for peace; let it continue. This peace must last forever. Let your women's sons be ours. Let our sons be yours. Let your women hear our words." Talks continued until 1788, when the murder of a Cherokee chief destroyed any opportunity for peace. Working for the tribe's welfare until old age, Nan'yehi never ceased being a fair and loving person although the Americans reneged on treaties. She urged the Cherokee not to give up any more land until the day she died.

Major Ridge (1771–1839)
Cherokee, Leader

In his younger days, Ridge went by his Cherokee name, Nunna Hidihi ("He Who Stands on the Mountaintop and Sees Clearly"), a name of great respect for a man who showed wisdom and understanding in the Cherokee councils. As a young man, Ridge fought in numerous border wars against U.S. settlers until peace emerged in about 1795. Thereafter, Ridge and a small group of Cherokee leaders decided that agriculture and political change were the only means of ensuring Cherokee national survival from U.S. pressures for land cessions. During the Creek War of 1813–1814, many Cherokee fought with the U.S. Army and lower-town Creek villages. Ridge rose to the rank of major and thereafter was called Major Ridge.

After the Cherokee formed a new and more centrally operated government, the surrounding states became even more determined to remove the Cherokee, threatened by their ability to adapt and therefore remain in their homelands. In 1835, Ridge and a minority group of Cherokee farmers signed the Treaty of New Echota, agreeing to migrate to present-day Oklahoma. The treaty signers feared that remaining in the east was impossible because American settlers were confiscating Cherokee property, and the Cherokee government had been outlawed. However, many Cherokee considered this an act of treason against the nation. The brutal move west deepened their anger, and in 1839, Major Ridge and others were assassinated.

Henry Berry Lowrie (c. 1844–disappeared 1872)
Lumbee, Freedom Fighter

Born in Robeson County, North Carolina, to store owners, Henry Berry Lowrie was conscripted to work for the Confederate Army, like many free men of color in the South during the Civil War. His family was accused of harboring Union soldiers and executed by the Confederates. Lowrie, who was just a teenager, escaped from his captors and organized a band of men to protect Natives from discrimination, mistreatment, and violence. Known for his mission to create a just and fair so-

ciety, Lowrie was called the Indian Robin Hood. He would steal thousands of dollars worth of provisions from general stores and the Confederates and share them with North Carolina's poor Indian, black, and white people. Since 1976, Lowrie's legend has been presented every summer in the outdoor drama *Strike at the Wind!* He remains a legend as no one really knows what happened to him—he seemed to vanish into thin air.

Will West Long (1870–1947)
Cherokee, Scholar/Preservationist

Born in Big Cove, Long was raised in a traditional home that he felt strengthened and helped him throughout his life. He collaborated with several anthropologists as an interpreter, including James Mooney. He preserved traditional medicine and doctoring and carved ceremonial marks.

Adolph L. Dial (1922–1995)
Lumbee, Scholar/Advocate

Dial served as professor of American Indian Studies at Pembroke State University for thirty years. He was also a North Carolina state senator and an activist for Lumbee rights.

Betty DuPree (1929–2012)
Cherokee, Artist/Marketing Specialist

Born and raised in Cherokee, Betty DuPree managed the Qualla Arts and Crafts Mutual for almost twenty-five years and grew it into a major market for the creations of local Cherokee artisans. For many years, she was based in the Southwest with her husband, who was employed by the Bureau of Indian Affairs. DuPree gained her knowledge of the craft business while working in various galleries in New Mexico, Arizona, and Colorado and took those skills back to Cherokee. She championed the rights of Native artists to make a decent living at both the local and national levels. Active with the national Indian Arts and Crafts Association, DuPree stressed the importance of preserving artistic heritage and hosted countless artists' demonstrations at the beautiful Qualla Arts and Crafts Mutual building in Cherokee.

Betty Mae Tiger Jumper (1923–2011)
Seminole, Leader

Betty Mae Tiger Jumper, also known as Potackee, was the first and, to date, the only female chief of the Seminole Tribe of Florida. She was also the first Florida Seminole to learn to read and write English, the first to graduate high school, and the first to become a nurse. For over forty years, she administered to her peoples' health care needs. Today, a health clinic in Hollywood, Florida, is named after her. In 1956, Jumper started the tribe's first newspaper and later became the communication director for the Seminole. She won the Lifetime Achievement Award from the Native American Journalists Association.

Jumper served as chief from 1967 to 1971. While in office, she founded the United South Eastern Tribes (USET), an organization that lobbies for health and education programs. In 1970, she was one of two women appointed by President Nixon to the National Congress on Indian Opportunity and served for sixteen years. Born in a *chickee*, Jumper helped preserve Seminole heritage and in later years was a much sought-after storyteller. "I had three goals in my life," Mrs. Jumper said in 1999. "To finish school, to take nurse's training and come back and work among my people, and to write three books." She did all of this and much more.

Phillip Martin (1926–2010)
Choctaw, Leader

In 1979, Phillip Martin was elected as chairman, or chief, of the Mississippi Choctaw, and under his administration, the once impoverished nation thrived economically. They own and operate the Pearl River Resort, which includes the Silver Star Hotel and Casino, the Golden Moon Hotel and Casino, Dancing Rabbit Golf Course, Geyser Falls Water Theme Park, and many other businesses and corporations. By 2004, the tribe was one of the state's leading employers, providing about 15,000 Mississippians with jobs.

Buck George (1932–2013)
Catawba, Leader

George was a college halfback football legend at South Carolina's Clemson University, and he set many records that were unbroken for decades. He served his people as assistant chief for several years and helped the tribe become federally recognized.

Linwood Custalow (1937–2014)
Mattaponi, Physician/Historian/Author

Dr. Linwood "Little Bear" Custalow was the first Virginia Indian to graduate from a Virginia college, the first Virginia Indian to graduate from a Virginia medical school, and the first Native person to be licensed as a medical doctor in Virginia. A founding and active member of the Association of American Indian Physicians (AAIP), Dr. Custalow was also a diplomat of the American Board of Otolaryngology, Head and Neck Surgery, the National Board of Medical Examiners, and the Board of Environmental Medicine. After his retirement, he served as Mattaponi tribal historian on the Mattaponi Reservation, where he was born and raised. Dr. Custalow was a key leader in efforts to keep the Mattaponi River healthy and took on issues like overbuilding and reservoirs. He wrote *The True Story of Pocahontas: The Other Side of History*, which debunks the Disney version of history.

Eddie Tullis (1938–)
Poarch Band Creek, Leader

Eddie L. Tullis served as chairman of the Poarch Band of Creek Indians—the only federally recognized tribe in Alabama—for three decades. He was also the chairman of the board for Creek Indian Enterprises, the economic development branch of his nation. Not only has he served his tribe, but he has provided national leadership: vice president of the United South and Eastern Tribes; vice president of Americans for Indian Opportunity; Advisory Council member for the Trail of Tears National Historic Trail; area vice president for the National Congress of American Indians; member of the Indian Advisory Council for the Trust for Public Lands, White House Conference on Indian Education, Indian Nations at Risk, National Indian Policy Center Planning Committee, Native American Rights Fund, National Advisory Council on Indian Education, and the American Indian and Alaska Native Advisory Committee for the United States Census.

Mildred Loving (1939–2008)
Rappahannock, African American Civil Rights Activist

Loving and her Anglo husband made headlines for challenging Virginia's Racial Integrity Act, which banned marriage between people of different races. In 1958, they were jailed (Mildred was pregnant) for their "illegal" marriage. They were forced to leave the state and lived and raised their family in Washington, D.C., for several years. They were not even allowed to visit their home state as a couple—all of their trips had to be done individually. However, they wanted to bring up their children around family and challenged the Virginia courts.

Their case was heard by the U.S. Supreme Court in 1967; the high court agreed unanimously in favor of the Lovings, striking down Virginia's law and allowing the couple to return home. Mildred Loving never intended to become an activist, but her bravery helped overturn state-sanctioned racism.

Claude W. Medford, Jr. (1941–1989)
Choctaw, Artist/Preservationist

Medford learned to craft traditional cane splint baskets from his Choctaw grandfather, a medicine man, at an early age. It inspired him to study the arts of his nation, along with other Native American groups. After earning degrees in anthropology and art history from the University of New Mexico, Medford set out to research the Indigenous arts of the U.S. and traveled from state to state living with and learning from many different tribes, including the Alabama, Tunica–Biloxi, Coushatta, Pamunkey, Caddo, Delaware, and Yuchi.

Not only did Medford learn the heritage and arts of various communities, but he also became fluent in Alabama, Coushatta, and Choctaw. His lifelong interest was in basketry designs, but he also excelled in many different art forms: pottery; carving shell, metal, bead, horn, feather, and gourd work; finger weaving; brain tanning of deer hide and leather work; and traditional clothing construction. Medford's goal was to preserve the rich arts, heritage, traditions, and languages of Native peoples, and he did it well. He developed Indian programs and taught classes and workshops at the American Indian Archaeological Institute in Washington, Connecticut, and the Clifton Choctaw Indian community west of Alexandria, Louisiana. Eventually, he returned to his home state of Louisiana, where he taught any Native person from Louisiana traditional arts. Claude Medford, Jr., was inducted in the Louisiana Folklife Center's Hall of Master Folk Artists in 1983.

Ivy Billiot (1945–)
United Houma Nation, Carver

Billiot, who began carving model pirogues at five, comes from a family of basket weavers and carvers. He spent years as an expert chainsaw operator, felling trees to clear the bayous; the skill is useful with his carving. After retirement, he began doing his art full-time and now carves an extensive assortment of birds, animals, fishing boats, and blowguns. His prized figures are highly detailed both in carving and painting, giving Billiot's creations a realistic appearance.

Trudy Griffin-Pierce (1949–2009)
Catawba, Anthropologist/Artist

Born to a military family in South Carolina, Dr. Griffin-Pierce did her undergraduate work in fine arts at Florida State University (FSU). While there, she spent time on the Navajo Reservation in Arizona and lived with a traditional family. She stayed close to them her entire life. She graduated from FSU but returned to Arizona and eventually earned a Master of Arts in museum studies and a doctorate in anthropology. Although she was Catawba and from the east coast, she lived in the Southwest for most of her life. Griffin-Pierce worked at the Indian Pueblo Culture Center and was a professor at the University of Arizona.

Griffin-Pierce authored six books, including *Earth Is My Mother, Sky Is My Father: Space, Time and Astronomy in Navajo Sandpainting* (1992), *Native Peoples of the Southwest* (2000), which won the Alice Logan Writing Award in 2000, and *Naiches Puberty Ceremony Paintings* (2007), which earned the Southern Anthropological Society's James Mooney Award in 2008. She also did much of the illustrations for her books.

Earl J. Barbry, Sr. (1951–2013)
Tunica–Biloxi, Leader

Earl J. Barbry, Sr., a descendant of chiefs, was elected as tribal chairman in 1978 and served until his death. Under his administration, the tribe received federal recognition and revived their economy. Barbry oversaw the development and construction of major housing communities, paved roads, a tribal center, a court complex, a social services office, the Paragon Casino recreation complex, and a multimillion-dollar cultural and education center. Tunica–Biloxi artifacts stolen from their cemetery in the eighteenth century were repatriated and restored, and the legal proceedings to reclaim the ancient property became the foundation for the Native American Graves Protection and Repatriation Act. Barbry's philanthropy was recognized for the refuge he gave Katrina victims when he was named the 2005 Leader of the Year by the National Indian Gaming Association. In 2006, he became the first Native American to be named a Louisiana Legend by Louisiana Public Broadcasting.

Patrice M. Le Melle
Atakapa-shak, Attorney

Le Melle is an associate general counsel for Columbia University in New York City. Growing up, she lived far from her Louisiana homelands as her father, Ambassador Wilbert Le Melle (1931–2003), was in the diplomatic service and was probably the first Native American to be appointed an ambassador although the tribe had been terminated at that time. She and her three brothers are all lawyers in New York City and Washington, D.C.

MIDWEST

Maybe the task ... is to strive to become naturalized to place, to throw off the mindset of the immigrant. Being naturalized to place means to live as if this is the land that feeds you, as if these are the streams from which you drink, that build your body and fill your spirit.... To become naturalized is to live as if your children's future matters, to take care of the land as if our lives and the lives of all our relatives depend on it. Because they do.

—Robin Wall Kimmerer (Potawatomi botanist), *Braiding Sweetgrass* (2013)

A little girl in a striped hoodie stands on the lakeshore, balancing on a big rock that is both crumpled and smooth. She watches a yellow ribbon of sunrise glaze gray cloud underbellies and silhouette blue fringes of pine trees on the far shore. Flowing over the rocks around her, clear water laps wisps of wild rice as people bring their horses down to drink. Visible horse breath plumes the chill, September air. Then they ride.

"Are you ready?" A nutmeg-brown man with a black ponytail, flashing earring, and bowler hat turns his horse to follow the leaders, who carry eagle feather staffs. The back of his vest gleams with beaded leaves, vines, and flowers in classic Ojibwe patterns that recall ancient reverence for the woodlands. Cultural symbols carry meaning, a connection to the past, as these fifteen riders lope into the future to defend a place. "We are not protesters," says Winona LaDuke, who rides a spotted horse. "We are protectors."

In September 2013, this third in a series called the Triple Crown of Pipeline Rides began at the Mississippi headwaters on the White Earth Reservation and followed the proposed path of Enbridge, Inc.'s Alberta Clipper pipeline expansion, which would carry crude oil from the Bakken fields in North Dakota to processing plants in Superior, Wisconsin, passing close by White Earth's wild rice lakes along the way. Since July 2010, there have been four major pipeline leaks and spills around the Great Lakes and an oil train collision fire in Illinois that killed two people. Early in October 2014, eight hundred thousand gallons of oil ruined a farm in Tioga, North Dakota. The destruction of healthy lands, water systems, and animal life concerns farmers, ranchers, and Indigenous people alike, which is why organizations such as the Cowboy and Indian Alliance have been pressuring Washington, D.C., to reject these pipelines. In this way, a growing number of cowboys have become defenders of the land too and have, as Kimmerer suggests, become naturalized.

A BIRD'S EYE VIEW

The Mississippi River twists its way south from northern Minnesota, carrying fertile sediment to enrich the farmland along its course through the Midwest. To the north, the Great Lakes' shores cradle woodland hills studded with sugar maple, nut trees, and berry bushes. The lakes shelter a wealth of fish and feed wetlands bustling with water birds, cranberry bogs, and wild rice sloughs. These waterways, along with other major rivers, such as the Missouri and the Ohio, have been trade routes sustaining and connecting people ever since the glaciers of the Ice Age receded.

Many histories have treated the people of this region as residents of the American Northeast, and although several tribes' own stories describe their ancestors' migrations from the Atlantic coast, time and circumstances have shaped different destinies for their descendants. For the sake of organization, this chapter considers the present states of Wisconsin, Michigan, Minnesota, Ohio, Illinois, Indiana, Iowa, Missouri, and Arkansas as comprising the Midwest. In reality, these borders are not definitive: Environments and traditional cultures overlap with those of the neighboring regions, and the original inhabitants express vast diversity among themselves.

Who were those First People, and how many of their descendants remain in this region despite widespread displacement by waves of non-Indian settlers? Before these conflicts and before the current states were named, or even imagined, the Ohio Valley was home to the Shawanwa (later named the Shawnee) and the Mosopelea; the southwest shore of Lake Erie belonged to the Kiwigapawa (Kickapoo) and the northeast side of that lake to the Wendat (Huron). The Meskwaki (Fox) and Asakiwaki (Sauk) were neighbors on the west side of Lake Huron; Bodewadmik (Potawatomi) and Mascouten territories occupied the southeast side of Lake Michigan. The peninsula north of that lake was home to the Odawa and Noquet while the Anishinaabe (Ojibwe/Chippewa) settled from the northwest shore to the Mississippi River. The Mamaceqtaw

The Great Lakes region, with its freshwater lakes, beautiful shoreline, and richly forested landscape, was home to numerous Native nations. European settlers immediately coveted the area for its natural resources.

(Menominee) lived south of the Anishinaabeg along western Lake Michigan, and south of them, the Ho-Chunk (Winnebago) built their villages. The Dakota (Sioux) also ranged across Minnesota and parts of Wisconsin although the Anishinaabeg were pressuring them to the western prairie edge of Minnesota by the mid-1700s.

In what is now known as the state of Indiana dwelled the Twightwee (Miami), the Atchatchakangouen, Kilatlka, Mengakonkia, Pepicokia, Piankeshaw, and Waayaahtanwa. Present-day Illinois was the domain of the Mishigamaw, Kaskaskaham, Peewaarewa, Tamaroa, and Cahokia. The Tapouaro, Coiacoentanon, and Moingwena spanned into the state named for the Ioway people, who originally called themselves

Bah-kho-je. Missouri is also the namesake of a tribe called the Missouria although their own name was Neutache. The Ugakpa (Quapaw) and the Kaskinampo lived at the confluence of the Arkansas and Mississippi rivers, northeast of the Cahinnio tribe in what is now Arkansas.

It is likely that most readers have never heard of the Kilatlka, Tamoaroa, or Cahinnio, but the numerous tribes who are no longer among us signify the deadly effects of their encounter with Europeans and their diseases. Also absent from most school history textbooks are the original names of the communities now known by misnomers, or the nicknames that neighboring tribes gave them. Some of those names are unflattering, such as Winnebago, which means "people of the stinky waters" in the Sauk and Fox language. Shifting names provide a clue to the magnitude of changes people endured in a short time and are a testament to the people's survival.

With that said, federally recognized reservation communities in the contemporary northern Midwest, by state, include in Michigan two bands of Ottawa/Odawa, four bands and two tribes of Ojibwe/Chippewa, one Chippewa–Ottawa band, three Potawatomi bands, and the Huron Potawatomi Nation. In Wisconsin reside the Menominee Indian Tribe, the Ho-Chunk Nation, the Oneida Nation of Wisconsin, one Ojibwe tribe, three Chippewa bands, and two Chippewa communities, a Potawatomi community and the Mohican Nation/Stockbridge–Munsee Band. Minnesota is home to the White Earth and Red Lake nations (Anishinaabe), the Mille Lacs Band of Ojibwe, three bands of Chippewa, and three Dakota (Sioux) communities.

Ironically, southern Midwestern states named after the Illini, Ioway, and Missouria are empty of those people, who were evicted to Oklahoma in the mid-nineteenth century. The Meskwaki Nation (originally from Michigan) are the only tribe living in Iowa because they bought their own land and are independent of the federal government. Ohio, which means "It Is Beautiful" in Seneca, is no longer home to most of the Shawnee, who were also pushed to Oklahoma with some of their

Seneca friends. A few Shawnee who escaped removal are recognized by the state of Ohio as the United Remnant Band of Shawnee.

Indiana was intended to be an all-Indian territory, but the federal government refuses to recognize the Eastern Miami tribe living near Peru, Indiana, so the six-thousand-member community exists as a 501(c)(3) nonprofit corporation on thirty-two acres purchased by the tribe. The Eastern Miami were terminated in 1897 and have been suing for recognition since 1937, hosting historical pageants to pay legal fees.

Sometimes the only way to go home again is to repurchase the past. In November 2014, the Quapaw invested some of their income from two casinos in Oklahoma to buy 160 acres of their original land in Arkansas. Tribal Chairman John Berry explained, "We want to remind people of our history and establish ourselves in the community."

Archaeological data indicates that the Quapaw occupied Arkansas for three thousand years. The area south of Little Rock includes Indian mounds that contain the earliest artifacts of their culture. In order to understand the significance of mound building, it is necessary to explore Cahokia.

CAHOKIA

Cahokia (see also the Urban chapter) in 1000 C.E. was the largest city in North America. Like Mesoamerican cities, the city featured pyramidlike mounds, wide plazas, and paved streets. Near present-day St. Louis, Cahokia centered on canals fed by the Missouri, Illinois, and Mississippi rivers. Trade items arrived by the tons in long canoes from the Great Lakes, the Gulf of Mexico, the Atlantic coast, Ontario, and Yellowstone.

Founded around 750 C.E. and inhabited until 1350, Cahokia spread for five square miles, contained 120 temple mounds, and was home to 15,000 people. The city's real name is lost to time; archaeologists borrowed the name "Cahokia" from a nearby tribe that no longer exists. They determined that the city was related to thousands of smaller Mississippian mound centers that

Aerial view of a section of Marching Bear Mound, which spans 2,526 acres in Iowa, near the Mississippi River, and includes 206 earthworks, 31 of which are in the shapes of mammals or birds. Great Bear, the largest mound, measures 42 meters from head to tail and rises more than a meter above ground. These ancient earthworks align with star patterns.

spread along river valleys from Lake Superior to the Mississippi Delta and from the western Appalachian valleys to the Oklahoma prairie. Historians describe these cultures as an interconnected ceremonial and agricultural complex based on maize, which we know as corn. Maize was the result of two kinds of grasses with tiny seed heads that were first biologically combined in Mexico, then selectively bred for larger seeds to adapt to colder climates.

In Cahokia, it appears as if the mounds were also stages for spectacles performed by spiritual leaders to wow the crowds with pageants and feasts to inspire them to keep building the city and working to feed it.

THE
MISSISSIPPIAN MIDWEST

Clues to earlier societies that centered around religious practices similar to Cahokia's include the cone-shaped Adena burial mounds in Ohio that date from 800 to 100 B.C.E. Recent advances in archaeological dating indicate that the great serpent earth effigy of Ohio is older than previously thought. Since Adenans created such a sophisticated mound, ideas about that culture have changed. Adena copper, stone, and cloth items were circulated as far as northern New Jersey, along with the Algonquian language. Variants of Algonquian are still spoken by the more egalitarian communities descended from the Adenans, who had settled as far as western New York and Pennsylvania by 200 C.E.. Also in Ohio, Hopewell artifacts have been dated to 400 B.C.E. Yellow clay Hopewell earthworks were built to last, and many still remain, in the shapes of birds, snakes, and geometric patterns that are so large, they are best viewed from the air.

The reason for Hopewell's abandonment in 400 C.E. is unknown although climate cooling was a possible motivation. Similarly, Cahokia's collapse remains something of a mystery although improper land management may have contributed to its downfall. Depleting the area around an unprecedentedly large city may have been a beginners' mistake. Early Native Americans selectively burned forest undergrowth to clear the way for farming and to create pathways for game animals to roam to the extent that buffalo were common from New York to Georgia when Europeans arrived. Recent research published in Charles C. Mann's *1491: New Revelations of the Americas before Columbus* tells us that, far from being the passive children of nature depicted in colonial reports both romantic and damning, Indians practiced calculated and extensive resource management. Nor were the people of the Midwest simple nomads but urbanized engineers, long-distance traders, and large-scale farmers.

Mississippian culture held sway until 1600 C.E. although Cahokia faded sooner. The problem may have been that overpopulation in Cahokia outpaced the accessible game animals and timber, and in drought times, the water supply became scarce. No one knows why Cahokia was nearly empty by 1350 rather than reclaimed.

STRANGERS ON THE SHORE

The decline of the largest city in North America didn't signal that Native people ceased their industry. Between 1539 and 1543, when the Spanish prospector Hernando de Soto ravaged his way across Mississippiana with soldiers, dogs, and guns, he noted that the Quapaw Tribe's territory—today's Arkansas—was "thickly set with great towns," surrounded by fortress walls and wide moats and defended by archers. In 1542, the Dominican friar and historian Bartolemé de Las Casas described the Americas as "a beehive of people." Las Casas wrote, "It looked as if God had placed all of the greater part of the human race in these countries." According to Las Casas's estimate, in the fifty years after Christopher Columbus landed, forty million Indians had either been killed by the Spanish or had succumbed to diseases the invaders carried.

Precontact population estimates in North America are hotly debated and range from two to eighteen million people. There appears to be consensus that death rates from diseases such as smallpox were as high as ninety-seven percent. However, many of these epidemics may have arrived ahead of their carriers, borne by escaped livestock and trade items, making explorers' estimates of original populations unreliable.

According to Maude "Grandma" Supernaw, the last descendant of the great Quapaw hereditary chiefs, the first French people the Quapaw saw were floating down a local river on a small boat. In 1962, tribal scholars recorded this oral history interview with Supernaw when she was ninety-three:

> They funny-looking the first time they see whites. They didn't want to kill them, so they went over there and shook hands with them and they talking, and after a while they get whisky. They called the white woman "mother" and the white man "father," so they didn't kill them.

> So they went back, crossed the ocean I guessed. Later on many days, they come back and they meet them again and they bring flour, coffee, salt, sugar. So that's how the Indian learned what [those] tastes was.

> That's what they learned, they say.

TRADITIONAL LIFE

Music and dance
At the same time, a song
means all of us.

—Denise Sweet (Anishinaabe),
"Homing Song" (1997)

Traditional gatherings began with a song. For a woman, a dream of a ceremonial dress inspired her to sew a form-fitting dress of leather, velvet, or heavy cloth. The jingle dance dress originated among the Ojibwe although stories vary as to who first dreamed of a special dress, song, and dance that would heal a sick daughter, but it must have occurred sometime after contact with European traders because the design requires rows of tiny, metal cones to be sewn by the

Makina Desjarlait, of the Red Lake Nation of Chippewa, stands on the shore of Lake Superior wearing a traditional jingle dress, floral pattern beaded moccasins and ornaments. The jingles are made of tin and contribute their own music to the dance, which was received in a dream many years ago as a healing vision.

lively sound as girls and women perform these energetic, zigzagging steps at powwows. Around them, traditional dancers appear to float, gently toe-heeling to the drum beat as their buckskin fringes sway in time while fancy dancers' bright shawls dip like butterfly wings, all to the beat of the drum.

Traditional songs are prayers, which begin on a high pitch to call the Creator. As the tones drop lower, they create an aural stairway for the Creator to join the people. Each line of the song repeats four times, one for each direction. There are many types of songs, such as those for veterans, the grand entry at powwows, creation stories, inter-tribals, honor, and welcome songs— but all songs connect people to the dance, the pipe, the fire, and the Creator.

Visual Arts

In the early days, there was no distinction between art and craft; many people simply had a strong desire to make everyday items beautiful. Thus, they embroidered designs with naturally dyed moose hair and shaved the finished embroidery into plush, layered tufts. Porcupine quills were cut, dyed, and sewn or glued onto objects in geometric patterns. Like bone and shell beads, quills could also be strung. Northern Midwestern artisans bit snowflakelike designs into thin sheets of white birchbark and carved the red pipestone while their southerly neighbors were known for colorfully painted pottery. When traders brought bright, glass beads, silk ribbons, and metal coins, these naturally found their way into Native designs. Some images were sacred, personal or intended as communication between people and the spirits and not meant to be on public display. These objects require special treatment and honoring; therefore, tribal cultural departments strive to have these items returned from museums.

Contemporary Native artists from the Midwest express themselves in diverse styles and mediums, much like their non-Indian colleagues. Some include traditional materials, content, or themes in their work; others synthesize European

hundreds onto a woman's dance dress. These cones were originally rolled from the lids of snuff tins obtained in trade, but now they are commercially available. Today, jingle dresses make a or current American materials and styles, often employing one cultural mode as commentary or counterpoint to another.

Literary Arts

Muskrat-Wazhashk,

small, whiskered swimmer,

you, a fluid arrow crossing waterways

with the simple determination

of one who has dived

purple, deep into mythic quest.

—Kimberly Blaeser (Anishinaabe),
Dreams of Water Bodies (2011)

Some early, Midwestern peoples kept records by inscribing sacred symbols on wooden sticks or birchbark scrolls, embroidered into wampum belts, or carved on rocks. Oral histories were transmitted from generation to generation by retelling of stories and enactment of ceremonies. Many Great Lakes peoples share the origin story of Sky Woman and Earthdiver, which offers people information about where they came from, describes their purposes on earth, and establishes the relationship of individuals to the universe.

Born sometime around 1815, Jane Johnson Schoolcraft (Ojibwe) was the first known Indigenous American to write poetry and traditional stories in her own language. In 1899, Simon Pokagan (Potawatomi) wrote what is believed to be the first novel about Native life written by an American Indian. Gerald Vizenor (Anishinaabe), the most widely published contemporary Midwestern Native author, is particularly remarkable for his reimagining of the culture hero Earthdiver as a mixed-race, urban trickster.

SCIENCE AND TECHNOLOGY

Midwestern peoples were masters of astronomy, agronomy, engineering, boat building, irrigation, ceramics, and resource management. Their pharmacological skills encompassed expertise in the use of plants as anesthetics, antibiotics, cathartics, narcotics, and more. Maple-sugaring techniques made efficient use of the season's natural frigidity for evaporation, so the concentration of syrup for soft cakes, hard candy, and sugar required little fuel. Birchbark food containers contained a natural antifungal, and birchbark canoes were lighter, faster, and more maneuverable than European boats, could transport heavy cargo, yet were light enough to be carried easily over land.

Perhaps the most versatile technology involved cattails. Midwestern wigwams were larger, more comfortable, and cooler in summer and warmer in winter than early settlers' huts and cabins due to the natural properties of cattails. Wigwams were constructed of maple sapling poles in an upside-down basket shape and tied together with white spruce root cordage. The roots were flexible when fresh, then hardened into stitches strong enough to hold birchbark canoes and roofing together. Wigwams repelled rain due to the natural, waxy coating of the long cattail leaves, which were woven into mats that covered the structures. Cattail leaves contain spongy air pockets that act as natural insulation. In dry weather, the leaves shrink apart, ventilating the wigwam. When it rains, the leaves swell and close the gaps. With birchbark sheeting roofing the round houses, they easily resisted wind and shed snow.

GAMES AND SPORTS

Early Midwestern Native games were of two types: games of chance and games of dexterity. These pastimes were similar across America, with dice games the most common. Around the Great Lakes, players made dice out of flat sticks, which they burned black and carved with symbols connoting different point values. Other dice included flat, round wooden counters with different colored or textured sides, carved bones, and brass shapes. The dice were thrown from wooden bowls or beaded bags, and tosses were scored depending on

Wigwams in the Midwest often incorporated cattails in their construction; the cattails provided natural, insulating properties.

which sides landed face up. In the Mille Lacs Chippewa game *shaymahkewuybinegunug*, men and women bet on the outcome of marked sticks they tossed onto a wooden platter. The highest-scoring combination was two turtles and two tails while other combinations caused a player to gain or lose points.

Snow Snake was an active winter game the Sauk, Fox, Menominee, and Ojibwe played. Javelins of up to ten feet in length were carved of wood or bone with a wider, rounded head on one end and sometimes decorated with paint and feathers. The object was to throw the snow snake so that it slid farther than the other players' sticks along a hard-crusted snow or ice course. Men and women played separate variations of snow

snake, and participants and spectators bet on the outcome of the game.

The most popular sports among Native children in the Midwest today are basketball, boxing, golf, lacrosse, rodeo, running, and skateboarding.

CULTURES COLLIDE

During the early colonial period, eastern Algonquian-speaking farmers, hunters, fisher-people, and gatherers, such as the Ottawa, Ojibwe, and Potawatomi, began migrating north from the Delaware area. In the early 1500s, they ran into trouble with the Haudenosaunee (named the Iroquois by the French). According to oral histories, the migration was spurred by a tribal leader's vision that the people should travel north until they discovered a plant that grows upon the water. By the 1700s, pressure from the Haudenosaunee and conflicts with Europeans persuaded the three nations, who would unite into the Three Fires Confederacy, to canoe further west along the Great Lakes, where they found the prophesied plant: wild rice. Settling along the way, they displaced tribes, such as the Miami and Peoria, from southern Wisconsin into Illinois. Pushing on into Minnesota, the Ojibwe found themselves competing with the Dakota Sioux for rice beds, fishing lakes, and fur and game animals. The Ojibwe harassed some of the Dakota closer to the Red River and pushed others from their sheltering valleys onto the Plains of Dakota Territory.

Other inhabitants of the Midwest, such as the Shawnee, Sauk, Fox, Kickapoo, Ho-Chunk, and Menominee, began doing business with French fur traders in the late 1600s. French trappers and traders often married Native women, who were intermediaries in the fur business. Meanwhile, the Haudenosaunee desired to continue controlling this trade (see also the Northeast chapter). Fur, particularly beaver pelts, was in high demand in Europe, and guns, knives, and alcohol received in trade made inter-tribal con-

flict more deadly. To complicate matters, war between the French and British in Europe was extended to the new world, where they sought Indian allies, fomenting rifts between tribes into an unprecedented level of violence. During this competition, beaver were hunted almost to extinction. Feeding the frenzy was extreme grief from the loss of so many relatives to new diseases. The failure of traditional medicine and beliefs to halt the epidemics may have created crises in faith, throwing the idea of conventional give-and-take with the natural world into chaos. Mass traumatic stress opened the door to Christian missionaries, who seemed more powerful because of their immunity to disease.

STANDING TOGETHER

Brothers—the white people are like poisonous serpents; when chilled, they are feeble and harmless, but invigorate them with warmth, and they sting their benefactors to death.

—Tecumseh (Shawnee), 1810

Beginning in 1763, Midwest tribes organized alliances to resist European expansion. There were some short-lived victories. Pontiac, an Ottawa chief from Michigan, allied his confederacy of tribes with the French to attack the British at Fort Detroit. Pontiac had built up a profitable trading partnership with the French, so he was dismayed to see the British gaining control of the trade. Not only was trading with the British less favorable as they occupied old French posts and forts, they also began settling on Indian land in large numbers.

Counting on French support, Pontiac spread the word among the Great Lakes communities. He was an eloquent speaker, and with the help of the Delaware Prophet, who preached an anti-British message, he was successful in uniting the tribes. Soldiers from among the Ojibwe, Delaware, Huron, Illinois, Kickapoo, Miami, Potawatomi, Seneca, and Shawnee destroyed several British

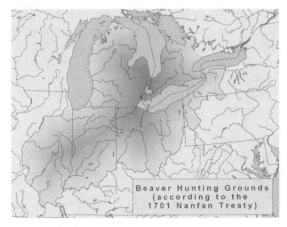

In 1701, the Iroquois of northern New York ceded a large beaver hunting area around the Great Lakes to the King of England. However, ownership of these lands was claimed by New France and its Algonquian allies.

forts and killed about two thousand settlers. In response, the British government issued a royal proclamation in October 1763 forbidding English settlement west of the Appalachians. However, when Pontiac attempted to siege Fort Detroit, promised French reinforcements failed to arrive. Pontiac's war then surged across the Ohio Valley, but a secret peace treaty between France and England doomed his efforts. He eventually signed a peace treaty with the British in 1766 and returned home to his Michigan village on the Maumee River. There, a trader paid another Indian to kill him. Although the British ignored their proclamation and expanded west of the Appalachians, Pontiac's inter-tribal alliance inspired other Indian confederations to defend their lands.

After the American Revolution, battles between Indians and whites in the Midwest escalated. In 1790, President George Washington deployed federal troops to the area. In opposition, Miami Chief Little Turtle organized the Illiniwek Confederacy to successfully rout American soldiers in the Ohio Valley. His strategy was one of stealth and speedy attacks, and in two major conflicts, the Illinois Confederacy overcame generals Josiah Harmar's and Arthur St. Clair's troops. On November 3, 1791, in the worst defeat suffered by American forces in the Indian Wars, Little Turtle's army surprised St. Clair, killing more than six hundred of his men and leaving nearly three hundred wounded.

Facing Washington's third army under General Anthony Wayne, Little Turtle was counting on British support. British officials were confident Little Turtle would win but failed to send troops to the Battle of Fallen Timbers, and the Illinois Confederacy was defeated. Casualties were few, but Little Turtle was disheartened by the betrayal and horrified by General Wayne's wide-scale burning of Indian villages and farms. He decided not to fight any longer, even when Tecumseh implored him to join in the cause.

Tecumseh, a Shawnee leader who had fought for the British during the Revolutionary War when he was a teenager, organized an Indian alliance to thwart U.S. expansion across the Mis-

sissippi Valley in 1805. He was a powerful orator who expressed the prevailing Native position that land could not be bought or sold and that borders were nonsensical. Like Pontiac, he had a prophet by his side: his younger brother Tenskwatawa, known as the Shawnee Prophet. Together, the brothers inspired various Native communities to reject white customs, avoid alcohol, and join together against the Americans. Recent treaties that had given away 110 million acres of land inflamed the resistance. The Shawnee Prophet promised that his prayers would make the warriors bulletproof. When the Prophet's prayers failed to protect them at the Battle of Tippecanoe in 1811, people lost faith in Tenskwatawa. Tecumseh's confederacy went on to fight alongside the British against the Americans in the War of 1812 and was instrumental in capturing Fort Detroit. Tecumseh was killed at the Battle of the Thames in 1813.

The Sauk chief Black Hawk also planned to organize a confederacy to protest treaties that had been unlawfully signed by Indians who did not represent their tribes. Black Hawk beat the Illinois militia in May 1832 when the U.S. Army tried to force his people from their village in Illinois, but, like the others, his success was temporary. Pursued north into Wisconsin by General Winfield Scott's large army, the Sauk ran low on food and supplies. After defeat and the loss of lives at the Battle of Wisconsin Heights in July 1832, Black Hawk hoped to escape down the Mississippi River. There, his people encountered the steamship Warrior, loaded with cannons and 1,300 men. On August 3rd, three hundred Sauk men, women, and children were gunned down. The survivors who fled with Black Hawk to northern Wisconsin were rounded up and shipped west to Indian Territory. Despite these attempts at resistance, the occupiers were simply too numerous.

THE TREATY ERA (1778–1868)

It is impossible for us to subsist where you wish us to go.

—Chief Wapello, *Sauk and Fox* (1841)

With the fur market in decline, Great Lakes Indians lost their leverage as trade partners, along with the resources to resist confinement to reservations. Several tribes, such as the Ojibwe and Ottawa, managed to reserve the right to hunt, fish, and gather in all of their ceded lands and waters. These rights, guaranteed by treaties negotiated with the United States in the 1850s, would become major points of controversy in the twentieth century (see also Historical Overview—Treaties 1778–1863).

Other Midwest tribes, including the Shawnee, Miami, Potawatomi, and Sauk and Fox (the government combined the Sauk and Fox into one tribe after Black Hawk's War), along with the Wyandot, Quapaw, Peoria, and Kickapoo, were force-marched to points west, where they were guaranteed land in perpetuity, only to be removed, some several times, in a brutal process that the Potawatomi call the Trail of Death as one in ten people died on the trip. In this way, canoe people were made to walk, most of them ending up in the dusty state of Oklahoma, a far cry from their fertile lakeshores.

Although they were forced to give up most of their lands, Midwest peoples managed to hold on to their hunting and fishing rights. It was often the women who set and gathered fishing nets while the men were hunting and trapping. ("Women Fishing," 2015, by Robert Desjarlait).

Land Cessions Treaties— The Otoe–Missouria

In the summer of 1804, delegates from the Otoe–Missouria were the first tribe to meet with Meriwether Lewis and William Clark when the explorers were on their Corps of Discovery expedition. Lewis and Clark gave the tribal leaders gold Jefferson medals and convinced them to sign a peace document from President Thomas Jefferson that also gave the U.S. government control over the tribe. Since treaties were written in a foreign language, it was impossible for Native people to verify what they were signing.

At one time part of a Siouan-speaking group in the Great Lakes area that included the Ho-Chunk (Winnebago) and Ioway, the Missouria (Nutachi) had migrated in the sixteenth century to the lower Missouri Valley, where they became successful traders, doing business with the Spanish, French, and Americans. The Missouria lost so many people

to smallpox in the late 1700s that they went to live with the Otoe (Jiwere) and adopted a Plains lifestyle, following the buffalo across Iowa, Kansas, and Nebraska. The federal government determined that the Otoe–Missouria were a danger to settlers and moved them to Big Blue Reservation in southeast Nebraska in 1855. The state of Nebraska takes its name from the Otoe—Missoria words Ni Brathge, meaning "water flat," which refers to the slow-moving Platte River. There, the people were forbidden to hunt buffalo; they were expected to farm. This lifestyle was incompatible with the Otoe–Missouria culture, and treaties promising food, tools, medicine, and livestock were broken. As the government sold their ever shrinking land to whites, many Otoe–Missouria died of sickness and starvation. Eventually, in 1881, the survivors were moved to Red Rock, Oklahoma.

Removal Treaties (1817–1846)

This pattern was repeated throughout the Midwest following the Indian Removal Act, proposed and signed by President Andrew Jackson in 1830. Jackson's nickname was "Indian Killer," and when he was elected president, he intended to achieve by policy what he had formerly done by hand during the Creek War in the Southeast, earning him his other nickname, "Long Knife." Treaties with tribes were designed to confirm the transfer of Indian land to U.S. control, to document the compensation for land and any retention of Indian rights, and to move tribes to Indian Territory in the West. Within seven years, 46,000 Indigenous people were dragged from their homes at gunpoint and forced to march halfway across the country or stuffed into unheated cattle cars or riverboats in the winter, where many died. Their removal opened up twenty-five million acres for white settlers and expanded plantations that would be made profitable through slavery.

Midwest tribes that escaped removal are the exception. The Menominee are rare in that their reservation is located only sixty miles away from their original territory in Wisconsin. Some people, such as a few bands of Potawatomi, prevailed by fleeing north to Canada, later returning to live on scraps of land donated by the church or state. Originally, the United States planned to confine all of the Minnesota Ojibwe to one reservation at White Earth. Except for a few groups, the Ojibwe refused, giving up millions of acres in the process but remaining near their sacred landmarks. They were also fortunate because their swampier and more northern lands were not considered desirable. The Ojibwe of Wisconsin and Michigan also successfully resisted removal and reserved subsistence rights. The Ottawa of Michigan were divided about whether to move, and those who went north rather than be pushed to Iowa, then Kansas, and later Oklahoma, have retained more land and traditions than the scattered people have.

ALLOTMENT VS. LAND HELD IN COMMON

The Dawes Act, or General Allotment Act of 1887, was created to separate Indians from their lands by making them farm individual plots of eighty acres for heads of households (and forty acres for minors) while the "surplus" was sold off to settlers (see also the Historical Overview chapter). Native people, especially minors, commonly lost their lands by trickery, unscrupulous "guardians," unexpected taxes, murder, or outright theft. The amount of land leased long term by the Bureau of Indian Affairs (BIA) to non-Indians on reservations has also contributed to the "checkerboarding" of Native landholdings in their own communities.

Red Lake Nation

An illustration of the value of retaining land in common is demonstrated at Red Lake in northwest Minnesota. The Red Lake Nation of Anishinaabe (Ojibwe), twenty-five miles north of Bemidji, contains rolling and wooded land, swamps, peat bogs, and prairies. It is home to the largest freshwater lake in the country that is contained within one state. Red Lake, or Mis-qua-ga-me-we-saga-eh, is sacred to the Anishinaabeg people, who have lived there since the 1700s, when they edged out the Dakota Sioux. Although forced to cede millions of acres via treaties between 1863 and 1902, the Red Lake people refused pressure to allot their land to individual members. Because their land is held in common, Red Lake is a "closed" reservation, meaning the tribal nation decides who gets to live there. As a result, their 825,654-acre territory is contiguous and larger than the state of Rhode Island.

When the land base remains intact, so does culture. Ojibwemowin is the first language of most Red Lake people who are middle aged and older and is widely understood and spoken by younger generations as well. Hereditary chiefs, descended from those who opposed allotment in 1889, are advisors to the elected tribal government. The nation is sovereign, answering only to the federal government; state government and courts have no jurisdiction on the reservation. Laws are made by tribal council and enforced by tribal and federal courts. Red Lake is not prosperous, but it is progressive and was the first Indian nation to achieve several efforts, such as issuing its own license plates, having a tribal member elected as county commissioner, and building its own library to archive tribal historical documents.

THE DAKOTA CONFLICT (1862)

Finally I asked my uncle why the Great Mystery gave such power to the Wasichu (the fat takers)—sometimes we called them by this name—and not to us Dakotas. And why do the Big Knives increase so much more in numbers than the Dakotas?

—Dr. Ohiyesa Charles Alexander Eastman (Santee), 1902

Southeast of Red Lake, Mille Lacs, one of the largest and most famous resort lakes in Min-nesota, lies one hundred miles north of Minneapolis/St. Paul. The lake was called Mdewakanton, or "Those Who Were Born of the Water," by the Dakota Sioux (Santee) who built their villages on its shores and named their band after the lake. For thousands of years, the Mdewakanton Dakota hunted, fished, farmed, and camped seasonally across one hundred million acres in Minnesota and eastern Wisconsin. Sometime around the middle of the eighteenth century, before white settlers arrived, Ojibwe people from the east contested Minnesota territory and forced two bands of Santee Dakotas west of the Mississippi.

In 1851, via the Mendota and Traverse de Sioux treaties, the U.S. government moved the Santees to a ten-mile-wide stretch of land bordering the upper Minnesota River while their cousins, the Sisseton–Wahpeton, were confined to a spot around Granite Falls, Minnesota. By 1854, the approximately four thousand Dakota in these bands

The 1904 painting "Attack on New Ulm" by Anton Gag depicts a battle from the 1862 Dakota Sioux uprising.

were forced to forfeit a combined twenty-one million acres of land. Payments and food rations did not arrive as promised, and a trader who was hired as a responsible middleman was famously quoted as having said, "Let them eat grass." The Lakota people were starving when white settlers began squatting on the tribe's narrow territory. If Indians left the reservation to hunt, they were considered hostile and could be shot on sight. Then in 1862, the land was allotted and the surplus sold to whites for ten cents an acre. Young traditionalists among the Dakota declared war on the United States, killing nearly eight hundred white men, women, and children within a month. The army retaliated, and hundreds of Santee died in battle. However, there were hundreds more Dakota who came to the aid of both Indians and whites during the conflict.

At a military tribunal, three hundred Dakota men were convicted, although without due process, to prove that these were the men responsible for the war. President Abraham Lincoln signed the order for thirty-eight of them to be hanged at Mankato—the largest mass execution in United States history. A few days later, two more Dakota men were hanged. The rest were sent to prison in Fort Davenport, Iowa, or exiled to parts west. In further retaliation, the 1863 Forfeiture Act revoked the treaties, seized the land, and evicted the Dakota from Minnesota. In the 1880s, some families who were deemed "peaceful" during the uprising were allowed to return and given land in four communities. The others scattered to the Dakotas, Montana, and the provinces of Manitoba and Saskatchewan, where some were taken in by other tribes, and others eventually received reservation land.

THE TWENTIETH CENTURY

Struggling to Remain

During times of Termination, many Anishinaabeg children were taken from their homes and placed in mission schools. They were dressed as white children and forced to give up their language. Many had an aversion to speaking Anishinaabemowin because of the beatings they received for speaking it.

> —Cultural Department,
> the Sault Ste. Marie Tribe
> of Chippewa Indians (2015)

In the mid-nineteenth century, the Bureau of Indian Affairs (BIA) ceased to be a division of the U.S. War Department and was subsumed into the Department of the Interior. This change in organization signaled a different approach to federal policy regarding Indians. As Native people had failed to become extinct as predicted, government officials hoped to make them disappear into mainstream United States identities. Rather than by extermination, the Indian problem would go away via a process of assimilation.

From the removal of Indian children to church-run boarding schools, the government sought to erase Native languages and traditions and to break tribal bonds. The superior position of men in European societies made it impossible for settlers to accept, or even acknowledge, the powerful roles women played in Native American societies. The idea that women and children were the property of men precluded any perception of Native people's respect for individuality and independence within interdependent families. Biblical messages of the shame and subjugation of women and girls were transmitted to captive children in those church-run boarding schools. Widespread physical and sexual abuse of generations of Native children, both boys and girls who had never encountered this at home, eroded Native cultures as deeply as the systematic punishment of children's cultural expressions, particularly language. As a result of destroyed family systems along with enduring poverty, many Native communities continue to be rife with alcoholism, drug addiction, and child and spousal abuse. On reservations, violence and suicide are too often the causes of early deaths.

Recent church and government apologies for the abuses of the boarding school system which was in place from the late 1800s until the early 1970s are welcome but inadequate to address the losses Native people have endured. Only meaningful restitution, environmental restoration, true legal sovereignty, and the resources for Native people to fully revive their own cultures will make Native communities whole.

TERMINATION AND RESTORATION (1950s–1980s)

The Menominee

Mainly I want to show people who say nothing can be done in this society that it just isn't so. You don't have to collapse just because there's a federal law in your way. Change it!

—Ada Deer (Menominee), 1973, assistant secretary of the interior, head of the Bureau of Indian Affairs 1993–1997

In the 1950s, the U.S. government decided to dissolve treaty rights and its trust relationship with those Indian tribes it considered "competent" to manage their own affairs. Indefinite legal status as a legitimate historical tribe in the government's eyes was another basis for Termination. Termination was a way to make tribes disappear and open up their lands for development.

The Menominee Indian Tribe of Wisconsin was the first tribe to be terminated under this policy. Although the Menominee lumber business was on the road to self-sufficiency, the tribe was not prepared to cope without federal social services by the time they were terminated in 1951. Menominee Enterprises, Inc. (MEI), a Milwaukee trust company that the BIA set up to manage the tribe's forests, lumber mill, and land assets, had more power than tribal members and controlled voting. When the Menominee Reservation became Menominee County, taxes rose unrealistically high, medical care deteriorated, public education disappeared, and housing decayed on the reservation.

In 1967, MEI began selling lakefront property to vacationers who would pay taxes. Outraged, the Menominee formed an organization called DRUMS (Determination of Rights and Unity for Menominee Shareholders), which filed a lawsuit against MEI. DRUMS, chaired by Menominee tribal member Ada Deer, who had earned her master's degree in social work at Columbia University in New York, also contested land sales to outsiders and advocated for restoration of federal jurisdiction on the reservation. Their efforts included a march to Washington, a distance of nine hundred miles. In 1975, Congress restored treaty rights and federal trust status to the tribe. The Menominee, however, have yet to recover from the aftereffects of Termination and remain the most impoverished Indian community in the state of Wisconsin (see also Historical Overview—Termination (1950s) and Termination Finally Repealed, 1988).

The Bemidji Boycott

In his book *Rez Life,* Leech Lake Ojibwe author David Treuer describes early reservation life in northern Minnesota as particularly harsh: People lived in uninsulated, tar and paper shacks, some with dirt floors, in the coldest part of the United States. There was no plumbing and, unlike their non-Indian neighbors, some Ojibwe communities did not receive federal loans under the 1935 Rural Electrification Act until they had cleared miles of brush on their own for electric lines in the 1950s. State game wardens routinely confiscated the food families had caught, hunted, or gathered to make it through the winter. During the first half of the twentieth century, it wasn't safe for Anishinaabeg people to be caught off-reservation after dark, and in the town of Bemidji, which is surrounded by Indian reservations, Native customers would only be served at the back doors of shops. In October 1966, a derogatory editorial broadcast on Bemidji's radio station, KBUN, inspired the Red Lake tribal government to fight back.

A 1918 statue by Hamilton MacCarthy that is on display in Major's Hill Park, Ottawa, Ontario, depicts an Anishinaabeg scout.

A KBUN radio announcer, Robert Kohl, read an editorial critiquing the provision of welfare to Indians whom the writer depicted as filthy, irresponsible, primitive, and breeding out of control. "Perhaps we should never have lowered our sights to this level; perhaps we should have let nature take its course, let disease and malnutrition disrupt the reproductive process and weed out those at the very bottom of the heap." The editorial described Ojibwe children as "retarded," with "tortured and twisted minds."

When the Ojibwe people of Leech Lake, White Earth, and Red Lake heard that broadcast, they decided to fight back. Chief Roger Jourdain of Red Lake organized a boycott of Bemidji businesses, which would last until Kohl was fired and the radio station issued an apology. Indian people and tribal governments shopped elsewhere for groceries, clothing, construction supplies, gasoline, and office supplies. Tribal funds in local banks accrued from fishery and logging profits and government contracts amounted to $2 million. When tribes canceled their insurance policies and threatened to withdraw this money from the banks, by the end of the week, Bemidji government officials and business leaders appeared at several reservation tribal offices to negotiate.

Furthermore, the Bemidji elite were embarrassed by the dozens of letters Chief Jourdain sent to everyone from local clergymen to President Lyndon B. Johnson. In one letter, he wrote: "We do not consider ourselves as 'subhuman, animal-like, or morally and mentally indigent.' We trust you do not think of us in this fashion either. We will appreciate anything you, your office, and associates can do to persuade the management of a twentieth-century enterprise to outgrow the nineteenth-century, hate-the-Indian complex. This should be a time for working and building together, not a time for inflaming ancient, racial prejudices."

Two weeks after the meetings, the radio station fired Robert Kohl and apologized on air and in print. With the apology came the promise of employment for fifty Indians in Bemidji. Prior to the boycott, no business in town would hire Indians, and within two years, one hundred Native people were working in Bemidji.

The American Indian Movement

As the civil rights movement gained momentum across America in the 1960s, Native Americans themselves became more outspoken against an oppressive system that continued to attack their traditional life. They felt oppressed by the trust relationship between the tribes and the United States government and because the federal government had reneged on its promises to protect tribal territories and Indian access to sacred sites. Activists criticized policies that undermined spirituality, including legal prosecution for practicing Native religions, culturally insensitive schooling, forced relocation to cities, and a variety of other programs dedicated to assimilating Native people.

The leaders of the American Indian Movement (AIM), many of whom organized in Minneapolis and other Midwestern cities in response to urban Indians' collective despair over police brutality, began documenting and exposing police behavior with cameras and recordings. Protesting the woefully inadequate educational, economic, and political situations of all Indians, AIM spoke to the full complexity of Native American needs although not always with the support of traditional leaders. Its agenda expressed the need to strengthen tribal identity so that young and old could recognize that communal life is connected to the spiritual practices needed to sustain common political action (see also Urban chapter).

The Walleye Wars

The Ojibwe (Chippewa) and Ottawa in the upper Great Lakes region retained the right to hunt, fish, and gather on lands they ceded through treaties to the United States government in the mid-1800s. However, until the 1980s, state and local police would not allow tribal members to do so, harassing or arresting them for poaching if they were found hunting, fishing, or gathering off the reservations.

The United States Constitution reads: "Treaties are the supreme laws of the land"; states may not interfere with such treaties since they are based on the notion that Indian nations are sovereign and thus have rights to self-determination and self-government. However, poverty was so widespread for much of the twentieth century that it was difficult for Indians to seek legal help. In Michigan, in 1979, U.S. District Judge Noel Fox affirmed that the 1836 treaty reserved the Ottawa Tribe's right to fish under tribal authority in treaty-ceded Great Lakes waters. Soon after, the Michigan Supreme Court came to the same decision in favor of the Chippewa.

Despite having the law on their side, Chippewa and Ottawa fishermen continued to face local resistance. In the early 1980s, they began to fish according to their own needs, regardless of police pressure and aggression from whites that included rock throwing and threats such as "Save a walleye, spear a squaw."

The legal cases resulting from protest fish-ins by Lake Superior Indians proceeded to a federal court that ruled on January 25, 1983, that hunting, fishing, and gathering rights still were reserved and protected in treaties. This ruling is known as the Voight Decision and was later upheld by the United States Supreme Court after the state of Wisconsin appealed the decision. The American Civil Liberties Union filed a suit on behalf of the Chippewa to deter some of the more extreme racial violence by the 1990 fishing season. Anti-Indian animosity remains in some areas to this day, and antitreaty rights groups continue to organize against what they interpret as "special rights."

MIDWEST INDIGENEITY

The New Economy

During the 1980s, deep cuts in federal funding for Indian programs and services forced tribes to seek a new way to survive. Gambling had always been part of Native social games, and in the early 1980s, tribes began to see income from bingo parlors on the reservation. Native leaders knew that higher-stakes casino games were more profitable although this class of gaming was illegal in many states. Tribal lawyers began to petition the federal government to approve gaming for Indian communities as sovereign nations beyond state jurisdiction.

The Indian Gaming Regulatory Act (IGRA) of 1988 created a compromise: A federally recognized tribal nation can operate a casino if the state where it is located agrees to a compact—a contract between the tribe and the state. By compact, the state could demand a certain percentage of gaming income, as well as taxes, and a tribally provided infrastructure and services. Per IGRA, a large percentage of Indian casino income must be used for specific reservation programs managed by tribal government and not by individuals. Some tribes, however, have negotiated per capita, or individual payments to members. To prevent fraud, the Federal Gaming Commission oversees all contractors for Indian casinos, but tribes must seek investors on their own. Although not a panacea and dependent on their locations, casinos have provided the first taste of economic success to many tribes, creating jobs and funding long-neglected programs and services, and giving tribes the opportunity to buy more land.

Nevertheless, casinos have created problems in several communities. In the early 2000s, the Saginaw Chippewa of Michigan experienced conflicts within the tribe over control of casino wealth. Charges flew concerning false enrollment of non-Indian cronies and disenrollment of traditional hereditary members who opposed the tribal government's practices. Violence and fear stalked the community and then lobbyists from Washington, D.C., crept in to snatch their piece of the pie.

In 2006, former lobbyist Jack Abramoff was sentenced to six years in prison for his role in an Indian casino lobbying scandal, among other felony corruption charges. Abramoff was convicted of grossly overbilling Native American tribes and pocketing more than $85 million in fees. In e-mails, Abramoff repeatedly referred to Native Americans as "monkeys," "troglodites," and "morons."

Abramoff was ordered to make restitution to the Saginaw Chippewa and other tribes. However, Saginaw tribal members claim the corruption extended to high-level officials in Michigan and in the federal Bureau of Indian Affairs, who have never been prosecuted.

Casino enterprises are not fail-proof, and many establishments lost income during the crash of 2008. In order for a casino to be profitable, it must be located on a highly traveled route, often near a large city or popular tourist attraction. In some areas of the country, Indian casinos are already competing with each other for customers, and there is a limit to how many of these enterprises can be sustained. Tribal nations that invest gaming income into more viable businesses are most likely to succeed in the future.

Cultural Roots of Environmentalism

Midwest cultures are as complex and diverse as the people themselves. Traditions evolved over centuries as people moved from place to place, learning from plants and animals and meeting new people with different ways of being. This process of discovery was not always peaceful. Conflict became part of life, and these struggles also helped shape tribal cultures. However, a more destructive clash resulted from the major difference between European and Native views concerning property. In any interaction with the natural world, it was important for Native people not to take too much, to contribute to the regeneration of future plants and animals, and to display gratitude for what they received. People were also required to share their harvest with the less fortunate, which was contrary to European motivations to acquire individual wealth, even if it meant some people did without or that natural resources were depleted.

Lobbyist Jack Abramoff appeared at a 2004 Senate Indian Affairs Committee Hearing on Lobbying Practices Involving Indian Tribes. Two years later he went to prison for two years for a casino lobbying scandal.

Different ideas of gratitude and generosity contributed to cultural misunderstandings. Native people believed that whatever gifts they gave would only increase in value if they were eventually given away again. In this reciprocal way, a gift often cycled back to the giver. This concept extends to land, which did not ensure the recipient permanent rights upon it but rather responsibilities to the land. Unfortunately, settlers misinterpreted this concept and coined the phrase "Indian giver."

Today, it is multinational biotech companies, such as Monsanto, and energy conglomerates like Exxon whose assumptions about property threaten the existence of Indigenous biodiversity. Paddy rice, mostly grown in California, is sold with images of Indians in canoes on the box, but this rice is harvested mechanically from chemical- and fertilizer-laced waters. Most consumers have no idea that this hard, black rice bears little resemblance to the tender, multicolored, and delicately flavored wild rice variants that grow in clean lakes and streams. Moreover, in the Great Lakes, pollen from this genetically engineered rice is invading wild rice waters and displacing the genuine plant.

Mining also threatens rice beds; in 1980, Exxon began planning to mine copper and zinc near Mole Lake, Wisconsin, which would have created the largest toxic waste dump in the state. Anticipating what the ground water contamination from such a mine would do to their ricing lakes, the Sokoagan Chippewa fought the largest energy company in the world for two decades. They were joined by the Menominee, whose Wolf River would also have been poisoned. The tribes' legal efforts secured federal status for their water quality management program in 2003. Predicting inconveniences, the mining industry downgraded Wisconsin's rating as a state with good return on mining investments. With help from the Forest County Potawatomi, the Sokoagan Chippewa purchased the proposed mine site, protecting their homeland in the process.

Today, Midwest tribes continue to organize against contamination from oil pipelines and bauxite mining. Their efforts resulted in restoring federal endangered species protection for wolves in Minnesota, Michigan, and Wisconsin in 2014.

> We're trying to reconcile, unite, make peace with everyone. Because that's what it means to be Dakota. To be Dakota means to walk in peace and harmony with every living thing.
>
> —Peter Lengkeek, Dakota 38 Memorial Rider and great-grandson of Walks With Owl Tail, who was hanged at Mankato in 1862

In 2005, Jim Miller had a vision. Miller, a Dakota Vietnam veteran from Crow Creek, South Dakota, was gazing into a fire when he saw his departed mother show him an image of the thirty-eight men hanged on the day after Christmas at Mankato in 1862. The men were singing honor songs and holding hands. At the time, Miller was unaware of this historical event, but he could not forget that he, himself, had killed thirty-eight Vietnamese men during the war. Once he learned what had happened at Mankato, the parallels were disturbing. He was inspired to organize the Wokiksuye Memorial Ride in honor of his ancestors and as an act of healing and reconciliation.

The annual ride began that year, and in 2013, filmmaker Silas Hagerty created *Dakota 38 PLUS 2* in order to document Wokiksuye. The 330-mile ride begins in Crow Creek on the Lower Brule Reservation, and the riders endure bitter winter conditions, often including a blizzard or two, for sixteen days to reach Mankato at 10 A.M. on December 26th, the anniversary of the day and hour when the thirty-eight men lost their lives by decree of President Abraham Lincoln. Two more Dakota men, one of them the spiritual leader Medicine Bottle, were hunted down a few days later and executed. The riders include fifty descendants of the thirty-eight, many of whom are from Crow Creek, one of the poorest communities in the United States, where per capita income averages $5,000.00 per year and the suicide rate is one of the highest in the world. Along the route, townspeople and farmers, many of them non-Indian, provide food and shelter to the

Since 2001, on the 26th of December, a group of Dakota descendants complete an annual memorial 330-mile horseback ride to honor the 38 Dakota men who were hung in Mankato, Minnesota in 1862, as well as two other Dakota men, Medicine Bottle and Shakopee, who were hanged in 1864. The ride encourages healing and reconciliation.

riders and their horses. Ceremonies and talking circles at rest stops help to unite everyone involved with the ride. In the film, Jim Miller says, "We don't have to blame the *wasichu* anymore. We're selling drugs; we're killing our own people. That's what this ride's about—it's healing."

Peter Lengkeek agrees: "See, our people at one time, our Dakota people—all Native Americans—had a very strong connection with the Creator, a very strong connection with Mother Earth, a very strong connection with nature, the forces of nature, all living things, and all this was taken from us, and we lost this connection with everything we had, and that's where this depression comes from. A lot of our people are severely depressed, and they don't even know it. This depression is just now clinically diagnosed as the same thing soldiers suffer from when they return from combat."

TWENTY-FIRST-CENTURY NATIVE NATIONS

Dakota Communities

The Dakota (Santee Sioux) of Minnesota live in four communities near Redwood Falls,

Granite Falls, Prior Lake and on Prairie Island, all in the southern portion of the state. According to oral history, Minnesota, or "The Place Where the Waters Reflect the Sky," is where the Dakota people originated. Four bands—the Mdewakanton, Wahpekute, Sisseton, and Wahpeton—inhabited the area for many generations. "Sioux" is the French pronunciation of the Ojibwe word *noodwesiwag,* which means snakes or enemies, and it has evolved into shorthand for the Lakota, Dakota, and Nakota, especially when referred to as a group.

Prairie Island, situated in the Mississippi River thirty miles southeast of St. Paul, has long been a center for gathering medicinal plants. After the evictions surrounding the Dakota Conflict in 1862, Dakota people returned and revived their traditional culture, ceremonies, and dances. Under the Indian Reorganization Act in 1934, the secretary of the interior had purchased 120 acres on Prairie Island to be held in trust for the landless Dakota. However, in 1938, the U.S. Army Corps of Engineers built a dam on the island that flooded half of the reservation, submerging homes and cemeteries. A new health hazard was introduced in 1973 when Xcel Energy opened a nuclear power plant on the island and began storing spent fuel rods only three blocks from the community. In poverty for most of the twentieth century, Prairie Islanders began experiencing economic revival through bingo in 1984, and in 1988, they built a casino resort.

Until recently, due to a land and housing shortage, only half of the seven hundred tribal members were able to live on the 1,800-acre reservation. To replace some of the flooded land, President George W. Bush returned 1,290 additional acres to the tribe. Today, tribal businesses employ 1,600 local people and provide more than $13 million in tax to the state and federal governments.

The Lower Sioux Wahpekute Indians reside on part of their original reservation established by an 1851 treaty on the south side of the Minnesota River near Redwood Falls. Considered by the federal government to have been loyal to the United States during the Dakota Conflict, the Wahpekute were allowed to return to Minnesota in 1863 and granted eighty acres per person. The Lower Sioux reservation includes rich farmland; however, it's situated in the river floodplain. Before Indian gaming legislation passed in the mid-1980s, there was little work available in the community. Proceeds from the tribe's Prairie Edge casino and convention center help provide health insurance to tribal members and non-Indian casino employees as well as to develop curricula for a Dakota-focused charter school in Morton. The tribe is also known for hand-thrown, hand-painted pottery, which they have been selling at their trading post since the 1970s. An important concern is the return of Dakota remains from universities and museums. The tribe operates a historical interpretive center affiliated with the Minnesota State Historical Society.

The Upper Sioux Community of Sisseton–Wahpeton had 746 acres returned to them in 1938. The land, five miles south of Granite Falls, represents a fraction of their original territory, which the Dakota Oyate (extended family) calls Pejuhutazizi, or "The Place Where They Dig for Yellow Medicine." Through the 1980s, the Sisse-ton–Wahpeton experienced poverty, racism, and skimpy service programs. In 1990, a casino began to provide income, which the tribe invested in other businesses, such as a propane company and RV park in 2006. A tribal police department now protects the community, which has reacquired more than nine hundred acres to improve the future for its 453 members.

The Shakopee Mdewakanton Sioux were the most devastated by reprisals after the Dakota Conflict. After the executions at Mankato, all treaties were broken, and the Dakota were driven out of the state. More than three hundred men were sent by barge and cattle car to a prison in Indiana, then Santee, Nebraska, and finally to Crow Creek, South Dakota, which was a prisoner of war camp. Conditions there were so bad that when Sitting Bull visited the prisoners, he was inspired to organize a resistance on the Plains. Those Dakota allowed to return to Minnesota in 1863 faced poverty and lost many of their children to boarding schools.

High-stakes bingo changed everything in 1982 when busloads of players spent enough money for the tribe to finance a casino in 1996. Mystic Lake is now one of the largest and most successful tribal gaming enterprises in the United States, supporting about four hundred tribal members with individual payments of $80,000 per month. The tribe has wisely diversified its income, opening a mall, travel agency, credit union, and recreation park.

In the twenty-first century, the Shakopee have continued to build infrastructure and to develop businesses, including a championship golf course, two ice arenas, and retail stores in Minneapolis's Mall of America. Their development is environmentally sound, featuring a water reclamation facility that treats waste water from the golf course, a plant that turns biosolids into fertilizer, and the largest green roof in the Midwest, where more than 45,000 plants grow on thirty thousand square feet. In 2007, tribally owned Koda Energy began generating electricity from farm waste biomass, which now powers the reservation and sells surplus electricity to outside facilities. The tribe employs 4,140 people and is a leader in cultural, environmental, and language preservation.

The Ho-Chunk Nation

The Ho-Chunk's original name was the Wonk-shieks, or "First People of the Old Island." The people spoke Hocak, a Chiwere–Siouxan language, and were known as great speechmakers, earning them the name "Hochungra" from the Ioway, which has been translated as "People of Real Voices." For most of the twentieth century, the Ho-Chunk were misidentified as the Winnebago. When the Wisconsin Ho-Chunk reformed their tribal constitution in 1993, they legally reclaimed their preferred name.

Traditionally, the Ho-Chunk were skillful farmers who engineered raised garden beds and followed the credo: "Harvest what you need and never with greed." Despite the trauma, dispersal, and population loss of the late nineteenth-century removal period, the Wisconsin Ho-Chunk were able to farm successfully on their fertile, forty-acre allotments. The Nebraska Winnebago, as they are known, had a more difficult time

Members of the Ho-Chunk Nation perform a traditional dance.

farming on the arid prairie (see also the Northern Plains chapter).

The Ho-Chunk Nation operates six casinos across Wisconsin and has diversified into such businesses as recreation, lodging, retail, and manufacturing. Tribal government actively helps members enhance their education through Head Start centers, school–community relations, and college scholarship programs. The Cultural and Community Education Department provides family literacy, antigang initiatives, organic community gardening, and family nights where members can play games such as the Challenge Bowl, a Ho-Chunk history game similar to *Family Feud* and *Jeopardy*.

As there are only two hundred fluent speakers of Hocak, or about 4 percent of the population, the language is considered to be almost extinct. To combat this loss, the Hocak Wazija language and culture program began sponsoring classes for young people and adults in the mid-1990s. Immersion camps, interactive digital programs, and recording of elders are ongoing efforts to revive the language. A strong tradition of honoring elders and their teachings gives Ho-Chunk people hope for the future.

The Menominee Indian Tribe of Wisconsin

Originally wild rice people, whose occupancy of Wisconsin, Michigan, and Illinois dates back ten thousand years, the Menominee occupied ten million acres at the beginning of the treaty era with the United States; seven treaties eroded their land base to the 235,000 acres they inhabit today.

The tribal government center is in Kenesha, forty-five miles northwest of Green Bay. The 8,551 members constitute the largest tribe in Wisconsin and also the poorest. The reservation is beautiful but plagued by substandard housing, and some homes still do not have running water. Half of the members cannot live on the reservation due to a lack of housing. Health problems include obesity, diabetes, heart disease, alcohol, and other substance abuse—all symptoms of poverty and the aftereffects of the tribe's Termination by the U.S. government in 1951. Reinstatement as a federally recognized tribe in 1975 qualified the Menominee for social services, on which most members are dependent. Unemployment stands at 10 percent, violent crime and gang activity are rampant, and the Menominee mortality rate is the highest in the state: 11,904 per one hundred thousand people.

The language is spoken and taught in tribal schools and at the College of the Menominee Nation, a center of cultural preservation and land management technology development for several Great Lakes nations, who hold conferences on campus. The college is internationally known for its sustainable forest management program, and it offers internships in climate change studies, water resource management, and food sovereignty.

The Mesquaki Nation (Sauk and Fox)

The Mesquaki, or "Red Earth People" in their Algonquian language, own more than eight thousand acres in central Iowa. After the U.S. military nearly exterminated the Sauk (Asakiwaki) and Fox (Meswakiwuk) of Michigan and Wisconsin in the early 1700s, the two nations banded together to survive although they have kept separate identities. The Mesquaki were removed to Iowa Territory in 1804, then shuffled off to Kansas in 1861, and finally to Oklahoma in 1869, where some of the people remain as the Sauk and Fox Nation of Oklahoma (see also the Southern Plains chapter).

Pining for their cornfields, ceremonial sites, and the resting places of their relatives in Iowa, the Mesquaki began buying land in Tama and Palo counties in 1857. This territory is not a reservation but is legally designated as an "Indian settlement." After Mesquaki parents successfully resisted sending their children to boarding schools, the nation began developing its own cultural education curricula and currently offers a bilingual school for kindergarten through eighth grades.

Serving 1,400 enrolled members, the Historical Preservation Department archives tribal history and research databases, recovers sacred items from museums, and curates cultural collections and displays that are open to the public. Craftspeople are known for their fine ribbonwork.

The Food Sovereignty Initiative focuses on Red Earth Gardens, a community-based farm business; a community garden; a growers' cooperative; buffalo raising and community meat distribution; and food education workshops. Other programs, including a wind project and environmental conservation, are funded by tribal businesses, such as a casino, hotel, spa, and business park in Tama.

The Mohican Nation (the Stockbridge–Munsee Band of Mohican Indians)

Originally Northeastern people descended from the Mahicans (Mahicannituck), or "People of the Waters That Are Never Still," which refers to the Hudson River, the Mohicans safeguarded lands that stretched south from Lake Champlain nearly to Manhattan.

The Mohicans met Henry Hudson in 1609 and, to escape fur trade conflicts with the Mohawk, moved east to Massachusetts and Connecticut. There, the English began to fence Native land while spreading diseases that caused huge population loss. Thus weakened, the survivors took refuge in a Puritan "Indian praying village" in Stockbridge, Massachusetts, in 1734. Although they fought alongside the colonists in the Revolutionary War, the Mohicans were landless by 1785.

The Mohicans who refused to be relocated west of the Mississippi moved in with the New York Oneida for a while, with whom they were eventually removed to north–central Wisconsin in 1856. Many less fortunate Mohicans died among the people who were marched to Oklahoma Indian Territory. Those who lived married into other tribes or returned to Bowler, Wisconsin. During the early reservation period, lumber

English explorer Sir Henry Hudson first encountered the Mohicans in 1609.

barons grabbed much of the tribe's allotted land, cut down all of the trees, and left. Plunged into poverty, the Mohicans sold wampum belts and other artifacts to survive. Eventually, they sold their lakeshore property to pay taxes.

Meanwhile, the U.S. government had crowded part of the Munsi branch of the Lenape Nation onto the tiny Mohican reservation (see also the Northeast chapter), creating the Stockbridge–Munsee Band. The people of both nations are relatives who spoke dialects of Algonquian, but when language is lost, so are thought patterns about the natural world. Recently, the Mohicans received a grant from the Bowler school system to begin a language program. The Munsee Language Project has also begun teaching the Minsi dialect of Lenape. Language Committee member Molly Miller writes, "All we have to do is start talking our language, and one time, maybe one of our little ones will have four dreams in a row. When that happens, we go to the interpreter and ask him what those dreams mean."

In 2012, the Northstar Mohican Casino Resort was named "Best Casino in Wisconsin."

Tribal businesses have provided the 1,500-member nation with the funding for caravans of elders to take research trips back east to libraries in Albany and Stockbridge. Cultural resources in the community now include a library, newspaper, and a museum showcasing splint and birchbark baskets, early weapons, and repatriated wampum belts and ceremonial pipes. The community also hosts five traditional seasonal feasts and an August powwow.

The Ojibwe (Chippewa, Anishinaabe)

The Anishinaabe, whose name means "Original People" or "Spontaneous Beings," represent the largest Native nation, with communities on both sides of the U.S.–Canadian border. While the Navajo and Cherokee are more numerous within the U.S., there are twenty-five Anishinaabe communities spread from Michigan to Montana and fifty across Ontario and Manitoba. Intermarried peoples, such as the Oji-Cree, Méti, and Michif, are also bearers of Anishinaabe culture. "Ojibwe" refers to the puckered-style top seam on traditional moccasins and was pronounced "Chippewa" by Europeans. Ojibwe, Nish, or Shinob are some terms commonly used by tribal members when referring to themselves. At one time an eastern nation, the Ojibwe were allied with the Ottawa and Potawatomi peoples as the Three Fires Confederacy. Within the Three Fires, the Ojibwe are the Keepers of Tradition, the Ottawa are the Keepers of the Trade, and the Potawatomi are the Keepers of the Fire.

Michigan Ojibwe and Chippewa

Anishinaabe communities in Michigan include Bay Mills Indian Community, Burnt Lake Ottawa/Chippewa, Grand Traverse Chippewa/Ottawa, the Keeweenaw Bay Indian Community, the Lac Vieux Desert Band of Chippewa Indians, the Saginaw–Chippewa Indian Tribe, and the Sault Ste. Marie Tribe of Chippewa Indians. All Michigan tribes own casinos, which generate $41.8 million a year and are the largest employers of non-Indians in each tribe's region. With casino income, most Ojibwe families in the state are decreasing their dependence on government assistance.

Traditions are strong among the Michigan Ojibwe, and tribal colleges combine cultural with general studies. Midewiwin spiritual medicine societies, sweat lodges, talking circles, Big Drum ceremonies, powwows, arts, and socials are alive and well. After winning legal battles for treaty rights in 1979, Michigan Ojibwe manage their own natural resources.

The Great Lakes Anishinaabe remain organized around dodem, or clan societies, each of which carries specific responsibilities in the community. Clans vary regionally, but traditionally, they included two kinds of leaders (Cranes and Loons), police and healers (Bears), intellectuals and mediators (Fish), warriors (Martens), poets and peacemakers (Deer), and spiritual people (Birds). A combined clan effort resolves to look ahead seven generations to consider who will be affected by today's decisions.

Some individual tribe programs include, at Keeweenaw Bay, archiving ethnographic materials and books and interviewing elders. Culturally sensitive items are private, but the public may research the archives by written request. Keeweenaw and Bay Mills also have community colleges that offer the basics of Ojibwe culture and language and sponsor two popular radio stations. Keeweenaw's expanding casino funded the creation of camping and fishing enterprises as well as a marina on Lake Superior.

In central Michigan, the Saginaw–Chippewa have used casino money to open a water park, marina, and golf course near Mount Pleasant. The Ziibiwing Center of Anishinaabe Culture and Lifeways, where the Language Revitalization Project is hard at work, won a Harvard Honoring Nations Award in 2008. Five immersion classrooms apply the Natural Approach to teach children from eighteen months to five years old; the entire curriculum and all conversations are in Anishinaabemowin. Since 1998, the Saginaw Chippewa Tribal College in Mount Pleasant has focused on language for adults and grounded

classes in Liberal Arts and Native Studies in the Seven Grandfather Teachings. The community's goal is for every tribal member to be bilingual. Other cultural activities revolve around Midewiwin Society ceremonies, Spirit Feasts, and the protection of wolves.

On the Upper Peninsula, Sault Ste. Marie presents cultural education through the Ojibwe Learning Center and Library. Funded by the National Parks Service, the learning center organizes community programs in which members share food, pictures, and stories honoring departed, loved ones at the annual Spirit Feast in November and also attend a Spring Feast for seasonal renewal. Forty acres on Sugar Island are dedicated to culture camps for winter survival skills, sugar bush activities, lodge teachings, and workshops in smoking fish and making moccasins, baskets, and moose-hide mittens. Gathering sweet grass, birchbark, and herbal medicines is popular as are retreats for fasting, language immersion, women's wellness, and sweat lodges.

The Sault Ste. Marie tribal newspaper, *Win Awenen Nisitotung,* or "One Who Understands," has been in print for thirty-four years. Books on

Bear dodems are associated with healers and police in the Anishinaabe tradition.

Michigan Indian history, legends, and photography chronicling the Three Fires' journey of change and survival can be ordered from Michigan Indian Press on the Sault reservation.

Wisconsin Ojibwe and Chippewa

The Anishinaabe in Wisconsin successfully resisted Removal in 1850, and four reservations were established for the Lake Superior Tribe of Chippewa Indians by the Treaty of 1854: Bad River, Lac Courte Oreilles, Lac du Flambeau, and Red Cliff.

Since the Wisconsin Ojibwe face ongoing conflicts with non-Indians over treaty rights, in 1984, the tribes organized the Great Lakes Fish and Wildlife Commission (GLFWC) in Bad River to manage natural resources and advocate for their rights. GLFWC programs include biological services, conservation enforcement, public information, policy analysis, and natural resource development.

A casino in every community has provided employment and capital to invest in commercial fisheries. Tribal hatcheries release about fifty million fish into reservation waters every year. Technology now makes traditional hunting, gathering, ricing, and fishing easier, and communities hold large, public powwows, where these traditional foods are available for purchase.

Cultural preservation continues in tribal museums at Lac du Flambeau and Red Cliff, and various reservation shops sell arts and crafts. Language is fading. To offset this loss, language classes are offered in Head Start programs and at Northland and Lac Courte Oreilles (LCOCC) community colleges. LCOCC provides bicultural educational and vocational programs and is home to an award-winning local radio station, WOJB.

The LCOCC research station manages a sustainable working farm for the community and is involved in saving seeds, canning and drying food, and restoring Native berries. As research manager Todd Brier said in 2014, "Healthy food is the cure for so many things, including diabetes, obesity, and other health issues."

Minnesota Ojibwe

In the 1970s, the U.S. policy of self-determination attempted to return more independence to Native nations to oversee their own programs and manage their own resources. Under the 1997 Self-Governance Law, the Ojibwe tribes of northern Minnesota administer their own BIA programs; tribal game wardens and courts enforce conservation codes on reservations and on ceded treaty land and waters, try civil cases in their own courts, and collect sales tax. Seven reservations manage their own fisheries and other businesses, six as members of the Minnesota Chippewa Tribes (MCT): Bois Forte, Fond du Lac, Grand Portage, Leech Lake, Mille Lacs, and White Earth. Red Lake Nation is the exception and is unique in Indian Country as a completely closed reservation that has its own government and has kept its original land base. Red Lake's more than five-hundred-thousand-acre reservation is communally owned and larger than the other six communities combined.

Bois Forte Band of Ojibwe

Bois Forte land was desirable, and by 1854, the U.S. government persuaded the band to cede most of it in exchange for a new location of the tribe's choice. The people selected an area around Lake Vermillion, but in 1866, prospectors found gold, and the U.S. took the reservation. Bois Forte was re-established on one hundred thousand acres at Nett Lake, and the government eventually returned about one thousand acres at Vermillion to the band.

In the twentieth century, the Bois Forte Ojibwe survived policies that pressured them to forsake their traditions and assimilate to white customs. In the mid-1980s, the band opened Fortune Bay Casino, and in 1996 added a resort that employs 550 people and injects $30 million into the northern Minnesota economy each year.

Fond du Lac Band of Chippewa

Ancestors of the Lake Superior Chippewa visited the Great Lakes as early as 800 B.C.E.

There, they followed seasonal activities and ceremonies: spring sugaring, summer fishing, fall ricing, and winter hunting until the Americans eventually cut down all of the big trees to build cities and clear farmland. Under these conditions, traditional seasonal hunting and gathering were no longer possible. The LaPointe Treaty of 1854 ceded a quarter of all Chippewa land in Minnesota, Wisconsin, and Michigan, leaving Fond du Lac with one hundred thousand acres near Cloquet, Minnesota.

Currently, Fond du Lac is celebrated for the band's $7 million community college, which is unique among tribal colleges as it is also accredited as a state community college. The band operates two casinos—one in the city of Duluth—and has translated that income into a resort enterprise as well as the first Indian-owned and -operated residential primary treatment facility for chemical dependency.

Grand Portage Band of Chippewa

The Grand Portage people lived so far north, the U.S. overlooked them as treaty partners. Because of this oversight, the band has kept eighteen miles of its Lake Superior shoreline.

The band has balanced economic development with conservation, setting aside a forever-wild area on the east side of the reservation in 1956 and establishing land use ordinance protections in 1996. At the same time, tribal government reconstructed a fur trade fort at Great Falls as a tourist attraction and maintains two state parks along with a marina and commercial fishing and logging enterprises. The state now leases the riverfront Grand Portage State Park from the Chippewa, with the stipulation that park staff must have tribal cultural knowledge.

Leech Lake Band of Ojibwe

The Leech Lake community is sited on a swampy area with forty rice-producing lakes—the most on any reservation. Fully one-third of the reservation is under water, and local government and the National Forest own much of the remaining property, with the result that Leech Lake has the least amount of land available for tribal members in the state.

The first major hunting, fishing, and wild rice treaty rights cases in Minnesota originated at Leech Lake. The state now pays the tribe to conserve resources, and the tribe deputizes state conservation officers to enforce the codes. Leech Lake contracted with the BIA to run its own programs beginning in the early 1990s; these programs include seven Head Start centers and the Bug-O-Nay-Ge-Shig tribal school for kindergarten through twelfth grades. The tribal college at Cass Lake offers associate's degrees, and credits are transferable to state universities and other colleges. With three casinos, a hotel, a marina, retail centers, and a tribal archaeology firm, Leech Lake is the largest employer in Cass County.

Mille Lacs Band of Ojibwe

The Ojibwe have held on to two centuries of history around Mille Lacs, which is about one hundred miles north of Minneapolis/St. Paul. The band was deemed "the Non-Removable Mille Lacs" by the federal government when the people refused to move to White Earth in the mid-nineteenth century. After surviving attacks by settlers,

The seal of the Leech Lake band of Ojibwe Indians

loggers, and farmers, the Mille Lacs Ojibwe carried on by blending traditional and mainstream identities. During the tribe's first attempt to create a commercial fishery in the mid-twentieth century, too many fish were depleted, and the fishery crashed. Since then, Mille Lacs fishermen have rebuilt the fish stocks and taught themselves how to conserve this resource.

Mille Lacs casinos donate millions of dollars to charities as well as fund tribal police, schools, hospitals, food banks, a museum, and community organizations. Other tribal businesses include a golf course, cinema, grocery stores, and travel agency. The Mille Lacs Department of Natural Resources protects and monitors land, water, air, fish, wildlife, and plants, manages fisheries and rice beds, and regulates hunting and fishing on the reservation.

Red Lake Nation of Chippewa

Red Lake is not the most prosperous Ojibwe community in Minnesota, but it is rich in tradition. Many residents are talented craftspeople who speak the Anishinaabemowin language, and the town of Ponema is a center of tribal culture for many Ojibwe people. The 825,654-acre reservation, twenty-five miles north of Bemidji, is jointly governed by seven hereditary chiefs and eight elected council members, two from each community. The nation is sovereign and not subject to state jurisdiction.

Although there are three casinos and a water park on the reservation, tribal government is the largest employer. Construction, farming, and paddy rice businesses are mildly successful as is Red Lake Nation Foods, an online natural foods retailer (see also the Allotment vs. Land Held in Common section in this chapter).

White Earth Nation of Anishinaabe

White Earth is situated in northwest Minnesota, 228 miles north of Minneapolis. The western half of the reservation is a typical prairie environment, and a layer of white clay just under the soil's surface gives the community its name. Hilly lake country in the center of the 829,440-acre reservation gives way to pine forests in the east.

Allotment policy rapidly divided the reservation into eighty-acre plots for heads of households and forty acres for their children. By the turn of the century, most Ojibwe had been defrauded of their land through various schemes, and much of the timber had been sold and cut. Several decades of federal commissions and court actions failed to reach conclusions on the cause of this land loss, which had reduced tribal holding to 10 percent of the reservation. Currently, more than half of White Earth is in private, county, state, or federal hands, and tribal members pay property taxes on any land the federal government does not hold in trust.

Although the 1986 White Earth Land Settlement Act (WELSA) of 1986 ordered the state of Minnesota to return ten thousand acres to White Earth in exchange for clear titles to one hundred thousand acres of privately owned reservation land, the people are still waiting. However, the $6.5 million the tribe received for economic development has enabled White Earth to open a casino.

As it was necessary to funnel casino income into basic infrastructure, such as water and waste treatment systems, telephone service, and road maintenance, other business development has suffered, and unemployment runs deep at White Earth. Additionally, by law, the WELSA-funded casino should be tax-exempt, but the tribe pays property taxes. A few viable tribal businesses include the Manitok Mall and a building and office supply company. A new tribal headquarters was built at White Earth Village in 2008; other facilities include a senior housing project, new community and recreation centers, and several hospitals. The tribe has invested in education, opening the Circle of Life kindergarten-to-twelfth-grade tribal school and administering a local public school.

The White Earth Land Recovery Project was established by Winona LaDuke in 1989 to organize the struggle to regain reservation land. Starting with a human rights grant from Reebok, WELRP was eventually able to buy back 1,200 acres, which it holds in trust for the tribe. The organization has been successful in restoring forests and wild rice beds and offers traditional Native food products for sale on its website. This income, along with other fundraising efforts, has enabled WELRP to establish an Ojibwe language program, a herd of buffalo, a wolf sanctuary, an Indigenous seed library, a farm-to-school program, and a wind energy facility on the reservation.

In 1993, with the Indigo Girls band members Amy Ray and Emily Saliers, LaDuke founded Honor the Earth, a Native-led environmental organization. Honor's mission is to connect, organize, and raise funds for the Indigenous environmental movement. Recent projects include organizing opposition to Alberta Tar Sands mining and transport as well as creating the country's largest community-owned solar system for the Navajo Nation.

ODAWA (OTTAWA) IN MICHIGAN

The name Odawa derives from *adawe*, an Algonquian word meaning "trader." Tribal history also translates the name as "At Home Anywhere People" and traces their origins to Manitoulin Island in Lake Ontario, where many Odawa still live. The Odawa are related to the Ojibwe and Potawatomi, who formed a confederacy called The Three Fires.

The famous Odawa chief Pontiac organized an Indian confederacy that captured British forts throughout the Ohio Valley in 1769. At Fort Pitt, in Pittsburgh, Pennsylvania, the British retaliated by giving Pontiac's men blankets that were intentionally laced with the smallpox virus, which brought mass death to Odawa villages.

Today, there are approximately fifteen thousand Odawa people living in Michigan, Oklahoma, and Ontario. The five Michigan Odawa communities are Burnt Lake, Grand River, Little River, Little Traverse Bay, and Grand Traverse (with the Chippewa). Only the very elderly are fluent Odawa speakers—the middle generations

were repressed during the boarding school era—and language teachers aim to help the youth become bilingual. Although the Little Traverse Band was not federally recognized until 1994, their lakeshore location has enabled them to profit from year-round tourism. In other Odawa communities, the crafting of maple sugar products, birchbark art, quillwork, sweetgrass baskets, pottery, and woodcarving provides a little income, and although many tribal members live in poverty, they would rather stay together than move to cities.

THE ONEIDA NATION OF WISCONSIN

Although this branch of the Haudenosaunee (Iroquois) Six Nations supported the American colonists during the Revolutionary War, they were forced from their New York State homeland. This removal occurred in waves from 1821 until 1880. As for most Native nations, the early reservation period was a time of great struggles to survive as a people. One of the ways the Oneida survived was by reinstalling their traditional chief system in 1921. Land claims activism and cultural revival gathered strength during the 1950s, and full language revitalization began in the 1970s.

Today, the Oneida Nation's museum and library are rich resources for tribal members and local educators alike. Income from businesses, including gaming, hospitality, and retail, serves to "preserve, protect, maintain, and interpret the Oneida traditions, language, customs, and history in a manner that shall promote the dignity and respect of the Oneida people and culture" (oneidanation.org) (see also Northeast chapter).

THE POTAWATOMI OF MICHIGAN AND WISCONSIN

Originally, about 15,000 Potawatomi, who called themselves Neshnabek ("The People"), controlled access to thirty million acres south of the Great Lakes. Like other Great Lakes peoples, they collided with the French and English during the fur trade in the seventeenth century. In 1838, the U.S. military removed five hundred Potawatomi to Oklahoma on the Trail of Death.

The Potawatomi people who escaped removal to Kansas and Oklahoma did so by fleeing north to Canada. This led to problems for them upon their return. Some bands, such as the Hannahville Potawatomi of northern Michigan, were aided by Methodist Chippewa who bought land for the refugees. In southern Michigan, the Nottawaseppi Huron–Potawatomi, who had escaped U.S. Army capture in Illinois in 1838, were able to buy eighty acres in southern Michigan. Because of church protection, the state donated another forty acres to the band. However, several returning bands, including the Huron—Potawami and the Gun Lake Band, were not federally recognized until the late 1990s. Although the Hannahville Potawatomi were federally acknowledged in 1913, the BIA abandoned them for fifty years. During this period, the Potawatomi community

A display of Pottawatomi clothing at the Field Museum in Chicago, Illinois.

lacked state services, including roads and schools, and negative portrayals in the media resulted in discrimination against the tribe. Infertile land and no access to roads created deep poverty. During the 1940s, tuberculosis epidemics devastated Potawatomi reservations.

In the 1990s, casino construction led to jobs and capital for northern Michigan reservations for the first time. This has allowed Potawatomi bands to repurchase lands that had been illegally taken during the 125-year period of federal neglect and tribal terminations. Among the Hannahville Potawatomi, this income has helped fund language-immersion camps and schools, where students have produced their own language blog, online storybooks, and cultural videos.

In Southern Michigan, the Pokagan Potawatomi have restored their community harvest powwow: Kee-Boom-Mein-Ka, or "We Are Finished Picking Cranberries." In school, young Pokagan linguists are making their own eBooks and participating in inter-tribal internships. The Nottawaseppi Huron–Potawatomi Cultural Preservation Office is archiving ethnobotanical knowledge and repatriating bones and sacred objects from museums while powering their community center with solar panels.

In Wisconsin, the Forest County Potawatomi own several profitable businesses that fuel the local economy while the people remain culturally conservative in terms of language and spirituality. They maintain traditional ceremonies, and the language is widely spoken. As a statement on the tribal website explains: "Our language carries our story, and our story carries our people."

(For information on the Potawatomi of Kansas and Oklahoma as well as on contemporary communities that originated in the Midwest but have since moved, see the chapter titled "Southern Plains.")

MIDWEST INDIGENEITY

Mother Earth needs us to keep our covenant. We will do this in courts, we will do this on our radio station, and we will commit to our descendants to work hard to protect this land and water for them. Whether you have feet, wings, fins, or roots, we are all in it together.

—Winona LaDuke

BIOGRAPHIES

Hopokoekaw, Glory of the Morning (c. 1715–c. 1832)
Ho-Chunk, Leader

Hopokoekaw was a female chief of the Ho-Chunk who lived to be more than one hundred years old. She was the daughter of a chief, a member of the Thunderbird (leadership) clan, and, according to the Wisconsin Historical Society, was the first woman ever described in the written records of the state. She married Sabrevoir De Carrie, a French officer, sometime before 1730. De Carrie resigned his post to live among the Ho-Chunk on Doty Island as a fur trader. They had two sons and a daughter before the marriage ended and De Carrie returned to Quebec. There is no record of whether Hopokoekaw became a chief before or after her marriage.

During a seven-year fur trade war, Hopokoekaw allied with the French against the Fox and the English. Later, she negotiated peace with the Fox but declared war against the Illiniwek Confederacy, and her French-allied, Ho-Chunk soldiers attacked English forts in the east beginning in 1754. When the British were victorious, Hopokoekaw reconciled with them and refused to join the Ottawa chief Pontiac in his war against the British in 1763. In 1776, the British Captain John Carver described the chief as an ancient sachem, or "queen," of the Winnebagos, who sat in council with the men.

Hopokoekaw died soon after a visit from the author Juliette Kinzie, daughter of colonial founders in Connecticut. Kinzie described the chief as a wizened and playful jokester who enjoyed participating in her grandsons' mischief. The chief died peacefully in bed, smiling, as the sound of thunder rocked the village, a rare occurrence during a blizzard. Her descendants, members of the Decorah family, have a long history as chiefs of the Ho-Chunk.

Pontiac (1720–1769)
Odawa, Leader

Pontiac was born near the Maumee River in present-day Ohio. He was not a hereditary chief among the Odawa but became influential because of his oratory skills and bravery in battle. Following the defeat of their French allies by the British near Lake Erie in 1763, Pontiac's people were stymied by unscrupulous traders, alcohol addiction, and invasive settlement. When the British stopped the flow of French guns and supplies to the Odawa, Pontiac began planning a resistance. Calling together a military confederacy of eighteen tribes, Pontiac's forces began laying siege to English forts across the Midwest. Working with the eloquent Delaware Prophet, Pontiac was able to inspire formerly feuding tribes to unite. Among them were the Ojibwe, Lenape, Wyandot, Illini, Kickapoo, Miami, Potawatomi, Seneca, and Shawnee, who managed to kill about two thousand settlers and sack many British forts. King George responded by issuing a Royal Proclamation in October 1763 forbidding British settlement west of the Appalachians. However, the edict was impossible to enforce. When French reinforcements failed to support the attack on Fort Detroit, Pontiac's resistance was crushed. However, his efforts inspired future confederacies to resist colonization. (For more information on Pontiac, see also the Standing Together section in this chapter.)

Little Turtle (1752–1812)
Miami/Mohican, Leader

Michikinikwa, or Little Turtle, was an important chief among the leaders of an Indian confederacy that resisted colonial expansion in the Old Northwest (Ohio). The coalition of Miami, Lenape,

Wyandot, Shawnee, Potawatomi, Ojibwe, and Odawa achieved the greatest Indigenous victory against an American force in U.S. history. On November 4, 1791, Chief Little Turtle's 1,200 soldiers defeated 1,400 troops led by General Arthur St. Clair, killing about nine hundred of them.

Although he came from a matrilineal society in which men normally did not lead, Little Turtle was made a war chief due to his strategic genius. His successful battle tactics included invading a fort by staging a lacrosse game in which the ball was "accidentally" hit into the fort; plotting with the Native girlfriends of soldiers to lure them out of the fort to be killed; and repeatedly drawing U.S. troops into traps.

Because Little Turtle refused to cede Miami lands, in 1794, General "Mad" Anthony Wayne was sent to retaliate at the Battle of Fallen Timbers. Expecting British support that did not arrive, the Indian confederacy was defeated. As a result, the Greenville Treaty of 1795 claimed Indian lands, comprising most of Ohio and Indiana.

In 1802, Little Turtle petitioned the Ohio and Kentucky legislatures to stop traders from bringing whiskey into Native communities, where alcohol abuse was destroying families. He died at home near the St. Joseph River in July 1812.

Black Hawk (1767–1838)
Sauk, Leader

Màkataimeshekiàkiàk, or Big Black Bird Hawk, was a Sauk chief who resisted the expansion of U.S. settlement into his homeland, located near Rock River in present-day Illinois. As a young man, Black Hawk, a member of the Thunder clan, was a renowned fighter against the Osage and Cherokee, and he helped the British siege an American fort during the War of 1812, after which he is known for halting the torture of American prisoners by some Indians' allies. Black Hawk desired to form a confederacy of Indians to protest the 1804 treaty between Governor William Harry Harrison and three Sauk and Fox men, who were made drunk at the time and were not authorized to sign away all of their tribes' northwest Illinois land.

In 1829, when Black Hawk and his followers returned from a hunting trip, they found their main village, Saukenuk, occupied by white squatters, some of whom had even moved into their homes. "The palefaces," as Black Hawk called them, were plowing up Indian graves. The Sauk tried to live with the intruders, but in June 1831, the U.S. Army came to dislodge the Indians. Seeking Ho-Chunk support, about two thousand of Black Hawk's people escaped by crossing to the Mississippi River. On May 14, 1832, the army attacked, and the Sauk defeated them.

For the next few months, Black Hawk and his people traveled north into Wisconsin, eating what they could find and attacking white settlements along the way. On July 21, 1832, a large army organized in Chicago under the command of General Winfield Scott caught up with them. The Indians displayed a white flag of truce and hoped to escape via the Mississippi, but Black Hawk found the path blocked on August 1st by the cannon-laden steamship *Warrior*. Trapped on the riverbank, the Sauk surrendered on August 3rd, but with reinforcements of about 1,300 troops, the U.S. massacred about three hundred Sauk men, women, and children at Black Axe. About one hundred Sauk escaped with Black Hawk into northern Wisconsin.

On August 27, 1832, Black Hawk and about fifty companions were coerced into surrendering. Black Hawk was imprisoned in Fort Marion, Virginia, for a year. In 1833, he was taken to Washington, D.C., where he met with President Jackson. The leader was allowed to return to his people in Iowa but not as a chief. In the ensuing years, Black Hawk became a celebrity. Many authors vied to write his biography, which he dictated in 1833, and Charles Bird King painted his now famous portrait. Crowds in Philadelphia, Baltimore, and New York gathered to cheer him when his carriage arrived in those cities. Since its publication in 1833, *Black Hawk, an Autobiography* has become a classic.

Before his death in 1838, Black Hawk spoke to a Fourth of July crowd: "Rock River is a beautiful country. I liked my towns, my cornfields, and the home of my people. I fought for it. It is now yours. Keep it as we did; it will produce you good crops." In 1989, the Wisconsin Assembly apologized to the Sauk Nation for attacks on civilians and other improper military conduct.

Tecumseh (c. 1768–1813)

Shawnee, Leader

After the American Revolution, thousands of land-hungry American intruders flooded onto tribal lands in the Midwest. The Menominee, Ojibwe, Potawatomi, Ho-Chunk, and other Indian nations joined Shawnee leader Tecumseh's alliance to resist American advances into the region.

Born near present-day Springfield, Ohio, Tecumseh had a difficult early life. He was six years old when white squatters on Shawnee land killed his father. His mentor, Cornstalk, another great Shawnee leader, was also murdered by settlers. When two of his brothers were killed in battles against the U.S. military, Tecumseh vowed to defend the rights of his people.

As a young teenager, Tecumseh fought with the British during the Revolutionary War, hoping to defeat the Americans who had brought destruction to the Shawnee. After the war, Americans continued to take Shawnee land, often by trickery. Although Native people owned their land together and no one person could sell it, some individuals struck deals with Americans without permission from their communities.

Tecumseh traveled far and wide to organize a confederacy of different tribes to protect the Indian way of life. On November 7, 1811, a U.S. force under the command of future President William Henry Harrison wiped out Prophetstown (also called Tippecanoe), which served as Tecumseh's headquarters. This attack put an end to Tecumseh's hope of a broad Indian alliance. He

and more than one thousand of his followers joined the British army in the War of 1812 against the United States. Because of his military skill, Tecumseh served as a brigadier general and helped capture 2,500 American soldiers. He earned a reputation for treating his prisoners with dignity and tolerance. Tecumseh was killed at the Battle of the Thames in 1813. The confederacy he had spent much of his life building dissolved after his death.

Tenskwatawa (1778–1837)

Shawnee, Prophet

Known as the Shawnee Prophet, Tenskwatawa, whose name means "Open Door," was Tecumseh's younger brother. His oratory helped the Shawnee leader to inspire various tribes to unite in a confederacy against U.S. expansion onto their lands. He was born in Piqua, near present-day Springfield, Ohio, to a Shawnee war chief and his Cherokee–Creek wife. As a result of their defeat at the Battle of Fallen Timbers in 1794, Tenskwatawa's community was leaderless and demoralized throughout his childhood. He became an alcoholic and lost the sight in his left eye during a hunting accident.

In 1806, while living in Lenape villages near present-day Munsee, Indiana, Tenskwatawa was influenced by the cultural and spiritual revival created by the Munsee prophetess, who in 1804–1805 revived the Delaware Big House religion. In February 1806, Tenskwatawa had an out-of-body experience and a vision that he died and went to heaven to see the Great Spirit. He came back with a message for Native people: If the Shawnee would return to their traditional customs and refuse to marry whites, he would be able to cure sicknesses and prevent death among them.

With his brother Tecumseh, Tenkswatawa traveled among many tribes from Wisconsin to Florida, spreading the message. His influence grew after Indiana governor William Henry Harrison challenged him to "cause the sun to stand still" and "the moon to change its course." What followed was Tenskwatawa's accurate prediction of a total eclipse of the sun on June 16, 1806. This feat won him thousands of Indian converts.

Tecumseh and Tenkswatawa founded Prophetstown along the confluence of the Wabash River and Tippecanoe Creek, and many Indians came to live there. In November 1811, against Tecumseh's' advice, Tenskwatawa led an attack on Harrison's troops while Tecumseh was away. During the battle, Tenkswatawa hung back to work his magic against the U.S. soldiers. However, he had no power that day, and the Indians were defeated at Tippecanoe. Few people were willing to follow him after that incident.

Rejected by his brother, Tenskwatawa fled to Canada, returning in 1826 to settle in Wyandotte County, Kansas. George Catlin painted the old man in 1830: Tenskwatawa wears a nose ring and a pensive expression as he holds a firestick wand in his right hand and, in the left, a string of sacred beads given to him during his long-ago vision.

Magdalaine Laframboise (1780–1846)
Odawa, Entrepreneur

The fur trader known as Mme. Laframboise was one of the most successful entrepreneurs in an area of the Northwest Territory that would later become the state of Michigan. The youngest of seven children, she was born to a French father and an Odawa mother at Fort St. Joseph and educated in Quebec until her father died and the family moved to Mackinac Island. Speaking four languages, Ottawa, French, English, and Ojibwe, Laframboise was a skillful intermediary in the fur trade. She married a French trader in 1804, and together, they opened the first permanent store in Michigan, followed by many more trading posts in the Grand River Valley.

Laframboise took over her husband's business after he was murdered in 1806 and expanded into the Lower Peninsula. At a time when the most successful traders were men who earned about $1,000.00 a year (which was a fortune at

the time), Laframboise made between $5,000.00 and $10,000.00 annually. The Ada, Michigan, Historical Society described her as "no ordinary woman," especially since she could compete successfully against such rivals as John Jacob Astor. In 1822, she sold her business to Astor's American Fur Company and retired at the age of forty-one to Mackinac Island, where her sister and niece based their own fur company.

Laframboise built an elegant mansion on Mackinac and taught herself how to read and write in English and French. She dedicated herself to the Catholic church and the education of Native children. During the 1830s and 1840s, she hosted a salon for intellectuals such as Alexis de Tocqueville, Sarah Margaret Fuller, and Juliette Augusta Kinsey. In 1984, the state of Michigan inducted Laframboise into its Women's Hall of Fame.

Keokuk (1783–1848)
Sauk, Representative

Keokuk, whose name means "Watchful Fox," was born around 1783 in the village of Saukenuk in present-day Illinois. He obtained some influence by demonstrating bravery against the Sioux although, being half French, he could not be a hereditary chief. By the early 1800s, the official policy of the U.S. government had become one of forced treaties to acquire Indian land. Disagreements between Keokuk and Chief Black Hawk about how best to deal with the government's treaty-violating incursions divided the Sauk and Fox tribes before Black Hawk's resistance.

After the slaughter of most of Black Hawk's people at Black Axe in 1832, President Andrew Jackson selected Keokuk as the official representative of the Sauk. Although Keokuk was not a chief, Jackson considered him to be cooperative with the United States. Stating a desire to keep the peace, Keokuk moved his people to Iowa in 1820. He signed treaties in the early 1830s, giving away Sauk lands in Rock River County. However, the deal included $20,000 in annual cash payments, which Keokuk would administer.

Later in the 1830s, Keokuk redeemed himself somewhat by traveling to Washington, D.C., to successfully defend Sauk land interests against Sioux claims. In 1845, he exchanged the tribe's Iowa lands for a reservation in Kansas. Keokuk died three years later, amid reports that Black Hawk's followers had killed him. Although it is probable that he died of dysentery, the rumors of murder were due to a widespread belief that Keokuk was not loyal to his own people.

Kenekuk (1788–1852)
Kickapoo, Spiritual Leader

"Putting His Foot Down," or Kenekuk, was the religious and political leader of a community of Kickapoo along the Osage River in Illinois. Before the War of 1812, Kenekuk was inspired by the Shawnee Prophet Tenskwatawa, who advocated armed resistance to white expansion. After the war ended badly for their British allies, the Kickapoo and other Great Lakes tribes were in a state of disarray and destitution. In 1819, the Kickapoo ceded half of the present-day state of Illinois to the U.S. and scattered as far as Mexico during the 1820s. Some Potawatomi people from Michigan later joined in the Kenekuk religion in 1833, after sections of both tribes had been removed to Kansas.

Kenekuk's vision for his people became more accommodating toward whites as time wore on. He worked to create a new moral and religious community for his followers, one that drew on elements of Catholic and Protestant faith as well as traditional Kickapoo beliefs. He banned alcohol and urged his people to take up farming and form friendly relations with their white neighbors. Kenekuk died of smallpox in 1852.

Wabokieshek (1794–1841)
Ho-Chunk, Prophet

The Winnebago Prophet Wabokieshek ("White Cloud") was an important supporter of Black Hawk, the Sauk and Fox leader, during the final conflicts for the old Northwest Territory, also known as the Great Lakes region, in the 1830s. He was born in the heart of the historical Indian resistance battleground for the Midwest, in Prophetstown, Indiana.

A visionary, Wabokieshek preached resistance to white encroachment and culture although he advocated peace during the Winnebago uprising of 1827. Five years later, however, he agreed to take up arms in support of Chief Black Hawk's defense of Illinois lands in 1832.

Wabokieshek told Black Hawk of his visions that the Great Spirit would help defeat their enemies and that, by creating certain ceremonies, the Winnebago Prophet would raise an army of spirit warriors to aid in the battle. The prophet's involvement inspired a number of Ho-Chunk warriors to join the Sauk' cause. Wabokieshek remained at Black Hawk's side throughout the conflict and was with the Sauk chief when he finally surrendered at Prairie du Chien, Wisconsin. He was imprisoned with Black Hawk and traveled with him thereafter. He lived out the rest of his years among the Ho-Chunk.

Jane Johnson Schoolcraft (1800–1841)
Ojibwe, Author

Schoolcraft was the first known Indigenous American to write poetry and traditional stories in her own language. She also contributed articles to *The Literary Voyager or Muzzeniegun*, a weekly poetry and prose magazine published by her ethnologist husband, Henry Rowe Schoolcraft, beginning in 1826. The magazine was popular in New York, Detroit, and other cities, garnering Jane Schoolcraft the attention of prominent writers of the time, some of whom visited her at her home in Saulte Ste. Marie, Michigan.

Her given name was Bamewawagezhikaquay, meaning "Woman of the Stars Rushing Through the Skies." She was born in Saulte Ste. Marie to an Ojibwe mother and an Irish father, who was a fur trader. She received a thorough education in the European and Anishinaabe classics from her parents and in 1809 went to Ireland to complete her studies. She married the ethnologist Henry Rowe Schoolcraft in 1823 after a year of helping him with his research on the Ojibwe language and in collecting traditional stories. They continued their literary work until her death from illness.

Hanging Cloud (c. 1835–c. 1919)
Ojibwe, Warrior

Aazhawigiizhigokwe means "Goes Across the Sky Woman" in Ojibwe. The woman known as Hanging Cloud was also called Ashwiyaa, or "Arms Oneself," and according to the Wisconsin Historical Society, she was a warrior. Born into the Bear Clan at Rice Lake, Wisconsin, Hanging Cloud was the daughter of Chief Nenaa'angebi (Beautifying Bird) and his wife Niigi'o. After the La Pointe Treaty of 1854, their band of about two hundred people joined the Lac Courte Oreilles Lake Superior Chippewa community.

Hanging Cloud was a full warrior council member, entitled to join war dances and ceremonies. Known as the fastest runner in her community, she hunted and participated in battles and raids, using weapons and wearing war paint and eagle feathers tied with ribbons that indicated how many enemies she had killed. She was observed by the author Richard Morse at the 1855 annuity payments at La Pointe, who described her as a slim, dark-skinned woman of about twenty years old, wearing broadcloth leggings under a short skirt, as this outfit was practical for riding.

So respected was Hanging Cloud that after she emerged from a ten-day fast telling of a vision she'd had of raiding the Sioux and bringing back a scalp, a party of warriors traveled with her across the Mississippi so she could do just that. She was also respected for shooting a Sioux would-be assassin who had crept into her father's lodge and wounded Beautifying Bird.

Records from 1855 indicate that after her father died that year, Mdewakanton Dakota Sioux attacked their village. Hanging Cloud's Dakota uncle, Chief Shák'pí, led the attack, and during

the battle, Hanging Cloud killed his son, her cousin. Despite this, she was proud to have defended her village. Hanging Cloud was married three times, all to white men, one of whom was James Bracklin, the first mayor of Rice Lake. She had six children in total.

Mountain Wolf Woman (1884–1960)
Ho-Chunk, Writer/Traditionalist

Xehaciwinga, "Little Fifth Daughter," took the name Mountain Wolf Woman as a child when she was cured of a serious illness by a healer named Wolf Woman. Born in East Fork, Wisconsin, Mountain Wolf Woman grew up in the traditions of her people as a member of the Thunder Clan. She attended school for two years in Tomah, Wisconsin, until she was married against her wishes to a man her brother chose. After her second child was born, Mountain Wolf Woman left her first husband and married Bad Soldier. Together, they moved several times to trap, dig roots, hunt, and gather berries. They had eleven children, and she was the first Ho-Chunk woman to own a car.

In 1958, Mountain Wolf Woman flew to Michigan at the age of seventy-four to collaborate on an autobiography with the anthropologist Nancy Lurie. The book, *Mountain Wolf Woman, Sister of Crashing Thunder,* was published in 1966 and is an important testament to a bygone way of life.

George Morrison (1919–2000)
Ojibwe, Painter/Sculptor

"I see the power of the rock, the magic of the water, the religion of the tree, the color of the wind, and the enigma of the horizon." The popular, modernist painter and sculptor George Morrison brought together landscape, spirituality, and abstraction in his drawings, paintings, prints, and sculptures and is considered the founder of Native modernism. He was prolific, and his work evolved through periods such as abstract expressionism mixed with impressionism and cubism married to surrealism in the 1950s and '60s to monumental wood collages and found-wood "totem" sculptures in the 1970s and small, luminous acrylics in the 1980s and '90s.

Born in a Lake Superior fishing village, Morrison was given the name Wahwahtehgonaygabo ("Standing in the Northern Lights"). Morrison spoke Ojibwe exclusively until the age of six, when he began learning English in school. He received a scholarship to study at the Art Students League in New York in 1943. There, he met artists such as Willem DeKooning and Franz Kline and began exhibiting paintings with them in group shows. He also had a dozen one-man shows between 1948 and 1960. After working in France on a Fulbright Fellowship (1952–1953), he taught art at the Rhode Island School of Design until 1970 and the University of Minnesota.

Morrison retired to the Grand Portage Chippewa community in 1983, but he gained popularity among young artists who had recently discovered his work. In 1999, Morrison was named Distinguished Artist in the Eiteljorg Museum Fellowship for Native American Fine Art. Four years after Morrison's death in 2000, his work was celebrated in a two-person show with Allan Houser that helped inaugurate the Smithsonian's new National Museum of the American Indian in Washington, D.C., in September 2004. The Minnesota Museum of Art in St. Paul holds the largest collection of Morrison's work, some of which is printed in the art book *Modern Spirit, the Art of George Morrison* (2000).

Dennis J. Banks (1932–)
Ojibwe, Activist

Dennis J. Banks (Nowacumig)—activist and author—was born on the Leech Lake Reservation in northern Minnesota. In 1968, he was the co-founder of the American Indian Movement (AIM), which was established to protect the traditional ways of Indian peoples and to engage in legal cases protecting treaty rights. Under the leadership of Banks, AIM led a protest in Custer, South Dakota, in 1973 against the judicial process that found a non-Indian innocent of

murdering an Indian. Banks and three hundred protestors were arrested. Refusing to serve time in prison, Banks went underground but later received amnesty from Governor Jerry Brown of California. Between 1976 and 1983, Banks taught at Deganawida Quetzalcoatl University and Stanford University in California. After Brown left office, Banks received sanctuary on the Onondaga Reservation, where he stayed until 1985, when he surrendered to law enforcement in South Dakota and served eighteen months in prison. Since the late 1980s, Banks has been active in repatriation of Indian remains, organizing sacred runs, traveling worldwide to teach and lecture, and playing roles in feature films such as *The Last of the Mohicans* (1992), *Thunderheart* (1992), and *Older Than America* (2008).

Gerald Vizenor (1934–)
Anishinaabe, Educator/Author/Activist

Gerald Vizenor is professor of American Studies at the University of New Mexico and professor emeritus at the University of California, Berkeley. He was born in Minneapolis, Minnesota, and is an enrolled member of the Minnesota Chippewa Tribe, White Earth Reservation.

The author of more than thirty books of nonfiction, fiction, and poetry, Vizenor also directed the American Indian Employment and Guidance Center in Minneapolis and was a reporter for the *Minneapolis Tribune*, where he investigated the actions of American Indian activists.

Vizenor's poetry collections include *The Old Park Sleeper* (1961), *Matsushima: Pine Islands* (1984), *Summer in the Spring: Anishinaabe Lyrics Poems and Stories* (1993), *Cranes Arise* (1999), and *Almost Ashore: Selected Poems* (2006).

A stereotype-defying writer who puts a postmodern spin on traditional Trickster tales, Vizenor wrote a science fiction novel *Bearheart: The Heirship Chronicles* as well as the novel *Griever: An American Monkey King in China* (1990), which won the New York Fiction Collective Prize and the American Book Award from the Before Columbus Foundation. Vizenor's award-winning nonfiction titles include *Interior Landscapes: Autobiographical Myths and Metaphors* (1990), and his anthology *Native American Literature* (1996) won the PEN Oakland–Josephine Miles Award for Excellence in Literature. Among his honors, Vizenor has received a Lifetime Achievement Award from the Native Writers Circle of the Americas and a Distinguished Achievement Award from the Western Literature Association.

Ada Deer (1935–)
Menominee, Leader/Activist

 The social worker, educator, and activist Ada Deer was born and raised on the Menominee Reservation in Wisconsin. Her life has been a series of "firsts": first Menominee to graduate from the University of Wisconsin, Madison; first Native American to earn an MSW at Columbia University in New York; and in regaining recognition for the Menominee after the tribe was terminated, the first tribal lobbyist to reverse federal Indian policy in United States; in 1993, she became the first woman to head the Bureau of Indian Affairs (BIA).

At the BIA, Deer was a strong advocate for tribal self-determination. Within an agency that was notorious for its bureaucratic disorganization and poor relations with tribes, Deer had to deal with budget cuts; conflicts between tribes and localities over land management, water resources, and mineral rights; tribal recognition; education; and religious freedom. Her approach was to enhance Indian tribes' ability to work cooperatively with businesses, organizations, and government offices, with the goal of Native nations' economic self-sufficiency, on their own terms.

Deer has received numerous awards over her lifetime, including Outstanding Young Women of America in 1966, the White Buffalo Council Achievement Award in 1974, honorary doctorates from the University of Wisconsin, Madison and Northland College, the Woman of the Year

Award from Girl Scouts of America (1982), the Wonder Woman Award (1982), the Indian Council Fire Achievement Award (1984), and the National Distinguished Achievement Award from the American Indian Resources Institute (1991).

During Deer's tenure as assistant secretary, she achieved the recognition of over 220 Alaska Native villages and increased the number of self-governance tribes who now administer their own federal service programs. Within the Clinton Administration, she was a member of the President's Inter-Agency Council on Women, which implements the Platform for Action agreed upon at the U.N.'s Fourth Conference on Women. In addition, she has worked closely with the U.N. Human Rights Committee and State Department initiatives connected to the Decade of the World's Indigenous Peoples. She continues to advocate for social justice, health, education, and economic development on the Menominee Reservation.

Clyde Bellecourt (1939–)
Ojibwe, Activist

Born on the White Earth Reservation, Bellecourt was one of the founders of the American Indian Movement (AIM) with Dennis Banks, George Mitchell, Herb Powless, and Eddie Benton Banai in 1968. His brother, Vernon Bellecourt, was also a force in major activist struggles of the 1970s. On February 27, 1973, they and other leaders led an armed occupation of Wounded Knee, South Dakota, in response to a call for help from traditional Lakota people against a corrupt and violent tribal government that was supported by U.S. BIA officials. Dee Brown's book *Bury My Heart at Wounded Knee* (1971) had established the site as a nationally recognized symbol.

Bellecourt helped draft twenty demands that were put before the government during the occupation of a BIA building in 1972. Among other things, the protestors demanded a separate government for Indians, the restoration of Indian lands, the renegotiation of all treaties, and a special agency in Washington, D.C., for the reconstruction of Indian communities. The White House did not meet these demands but established a task force to meet with AIM and made no arrests for the occupation. Today, he is a coordinator of the National Coalition on Racism in Sports and the Media and leads Heart of the Earth, Inc., a cultural interpretive center. He also continues to found and help run AIM Patrol, which provides security for the Minneapolis Native community.

Elaine Fleming
Anishinaabe, Mayor/Activist

Elaine Fleming was the first female mayor of Cass Lake, Minnesota, and the first Native American mayor. She served three terms from 2003 to 2006. Fleming was also the first Green Party mayor in Minnesota and one of the organizers of Rock the Vote—Rez Style.

From the Leech Lake community, as a child, Fleming followed the annual rounds of the Ojibwe with her family: the spring sugarbush, summer berry-picking and gardening, fall wild ricing, and winter storytelling. In addition, the family has always followed the powwow trail and made their own regalia.

Fleming spent ten years in the U.S. Army and attained her master's degree in education in 1998 and a Master of Fine Arts in 2003. She chairs the Arts and Humanities Department at Leech Lake College. Cass Lake is a Superfund site as a result of chemical dumping by the St. Regis Paper Company. Fleming has characterized St. Regis's activities as "environmental racism," which, in turn, she has characterized as "terrorism in our communities."

Ray A. Young Bear (1950–)
Meskwaki, Writer

Raised on the Mesquaki Tribal Settlement near Tama, Iowa, Young Bear's first language was Mesquaki, which he learned from his grandmother. He first composed poetry in his home language and then translated it into English. His work was first published in 1968. His grandmother urged him to "preserve and collect the language of the Meskwaki," and Young Bear considers himself to be his grandmother's messenger. He and his wife are the founders of the Black Eagle Child performance troupe that presents Meskwaki culture to audiences around the world. Young Bear's poems and novels often contain themes about American Indians' search for identity amid the pressures of living in two different cultures. His books of poetry include *Winter of the Salamander* (1980) and *The Rock Island Hiking Club* (2001). His novels, beginning with *Black Eagle Child* (1992), describe his youth through the character of Edgar Bearchild. He has taught creative writing at Iowa State University.

In a 1994 interview with the *Des Moines Register*, Young Bear said, "The Meskwaki people, of which I am an enrolled member, are part of this area historically, and so we have beliefs that are animistic, meaning we have a wide, unbridled respect for all earthly kinds of life, be it a tree, a stone, or a river. We believe implicitly they are very much alive, breathing, feeling, sharing our existence."

Denise Sweet (1952–)
Anishinaabe, Educator/Author

Sweet was educated at the University of Wisconsin, Eau Claire and is a professor of Humanistic Studies and the chair of the American Indian Studies Program at the University of Wisconsin, Green Bay. She has won several awards for poetry, including the Diane Decorah Award, the Posner Award, and the Woman of the Year Award from the Wisconsin Women's Council and the Native Writers' Circle of the Americas First Book Award for Poetry. From 2004 to 2008, she was the poet laureate of Wisconsin. Her books include *Know by Heart* (1992), *Days of Obsidian, Days of Grace* (1994), and *Songs for Discharming* (1997).

Bill Miller (1955–)
Mohican, Musician/Artist

Miller was given the name Fush-Ya Heay Aka, which means "Bird Song." He began playing guitar at age twelve and is an expert Native American flutist; his drawings and paintings also receive high acclaim. He moved to Nashville in 1984 and recorded his CD *Red Road*, which Tori Amos liked so well, she asked him to open for her band on tour. Miller soon began touring with other bands, including Pearl Jam, the Bodeans, Richie Havens, and Arlo Guthrie. Additionally, he wrote songs with Nancy Griffith, Peter Rowan, and Kim Carnes.

In 2001, the National Academy of Recording Arts and Sciences (NARAS) established Best Native American Music Album as a new awards category, and Bill Miller has won three Grammys since 2005, when his *Cedar Dream Songs* won "Best Native American Music Album."

He continues to collaborate with Native musicians such as Robert Mirabal, R. Carlos Nakai, and Joanne Shenandoah as well as to create public art in Wisconsin. In 2008, the La Crosse Symphony Orchestra performed Miller's *Last Stand* about the Battle of Little Bighorn. Photos from the show, which also featured Native American dancers, are in the Smithsonian's permanent collection.

Kimberly Blaeser (1955–)
Anishinaabe, Critic/Essayist/Writer

Blaeser was raised on the White Earth Reservation in Minnesota by parents of Anishinaabe and German descent. She worked as a journalist before earning her Ph.D. at the University of Notre Dame. Her collections of poetry include *Apprenticed to Justice* (2007), *Absentee Indians and Other Poems* (2002), and *Trailing You* (1994), which won the Native Writers' Circle of the Americas First Book Award. Blaeser edited the anthologies *Traces in Blood, Bone, & Stone: Contemporary Ojibwe Poetry* (2006) and *Stories Migrating Home: A Collection of Anishinaabe Prose* (1999). She has served on the editorial boards of Michigan State University's American Indian Studies Series, the University of Nebraska Press's Indian Lives Series, and as the vice president of the Wordcraft Circle of Native Writers and Storytellers.

Janice Marie Johnson (1955–)
Mohican, Musician

Johnson was born in Los Angeles. Her band, A Taste of Honey, had its biggest hit, "Boogie-Oogie-Oogie," in 1978. The two-million-copy-selling song earned the group a Grammy for Best New Artist and was Billboard's number-one R&B pop song for three weeks. Johnson also sang backup on Lionel Ritchie's LP *Can't Slow Down,* which sold ten million copies. The track has been sampled by several rap and hip-hop artists and was reissued by Capitol Records as a remix in 2000. Johnson continues to perform live; her 2015 CD is called *Hiatus of the Heart.*

Keith Secola (1957–)
Anishinaabe, Musician

Folk and blues rocker Secola is an accomplished artist: award-winning musician, guitarist, and Native flute player, singer, songwriter, and producer. His music is familiar to thousands of fans across North America and Europe. Keith's famous song, "NDN KARS," is considered the contemporary Native American anthem and is the most requested song on Native radio in the U.S. and Canada. Keith Secola is Anishinabe (Ojibwe), originally from the Mesabi Iron Range country of northern Minnesota, and now resides in Arizona. Secola is a seven-time Native American Music Awards (NAMMY) winner, receiving numerous NAMMY nominations in various categories. In 2011, Secola was inducted into the NAMMY Hall of Fame.

Ingrid Washinawatok El-Issa (1957–1999)
Menominee, Activist

Born on the Menominee Reservation, Washinawatok was given the name O'Peqtaw-Metamoh ("Flying Eagle" or "Thunderbird") Woman. By age fourteen, Washinawatok was working with her father to reinstate federal recognition of the Menominee Tribe.

Washinawatok was among the founders of the Indigenous Women's Network, a grassroots organization advocating for the revitalization and protection of Indigenous languages, religions, and cultural practices, including environmental protection, which grew out of a gathering of two hundred women in Yelm, Washington, in 1985. As part of her work with the United Nations she served, in 1994, as Chair of the NGO Committee on the United Nations International Decade of the World's Indigenous Peoples. She became executive director for the philanthropic Fund of the Four Directions in 1998.

Along with other activists, Washinawatok was asked by the U'wa People of Arauca Department, Colombia, to start a school to protect their culture and to aid in defending their land from oil exploration. On February 25, 1999, Washinawatok, along with Hawaiian activist Lahe'ena'e Gay and environmental activist Terence Freitas, were kidnapped by Revolutionary Armed Forces of Colombia (FARC) guerrillas, and the three were found murdered a week later in Venezuela. A FARC commander was extradited to the United States in 2003 to face prosecution in the case, but the charges were dismissed. Washinawatok was honored with a warrior's funeral by the Menominee Nation. She is survived by her husband, Palestinian peace activist Ali El-Issa, and a son, Maehkiwkasic ("Red Sky").

Winona LaDuke (1959–)
Anishinaabe, Activist

 When she was just seventeen years old, LaDuke testified at the United Nations conference in Geneva, Switzerland, about Native environmental concerns, the youngest person to do so. The original research she presented was on the problems of uranium mining on the Navajo reservation and the effects of radiation on Native miners.

A member of the White Earth Nation, LaDuke was born in Los Angeles and attended Harvard University, where she earned degrees in Native economic development and rural development. In 1996 and 2000, LaDuke was the Green Party's vice-presidential candidate. Today, she lives at White Earth, where she cofounded the Indigenous Women's Network and was the founder/director of both the White Earth Land Recovery Project and the foundation Honor the Earth. LaDuke has received many awards, such as *Time* magazine's "Fifty Most Promising Leaders Under Forty" (1994), *Ms.* magazine's "Woman of the Year" (1997), and the Reebok Human Rights Award (1998). In 2007, she was inducted into the Women's Hall of Fame.

LaDuke is the author of several books about Native history, cultures, and legal and environmental concerns, including *Last Standing Woman* (1997), *All Our Relations, Native Struggles for Land and Life* (1999), *The Winona LaDuke Reader* (2002), and *Recovering the Sacred, the Power of Naming and Claiming* (2005). She appears in the movie *Skins* (2002) and several documentaries, including *The Main Stream* (2002) and *Homeland* (2005).

(For more information about Winona LaDuke, refer to the introductory story and to the "Twenty-First-Century Native Nations—White Earth Nation of Anishinaabe" section in this chapter.)

Sheila Tousey (1960–)
Menominee/ Stockbridge/Munsee, Actress

Born in Kenesha, Wisconsin, Tousey initially enrolled in the law program at the University of New Mexico, planning to specialize in Indian law, but she began taking theater arts courses and earned her bachelor's degree in English. Tousey then enrolled in the graduate acting program at New York University's Tisch School of the Arts.

Since her first feature film role in *Thunderheart* (1992), Tousey has appeared in more than a dozen films and numerous plays. Her television work includes playing two different regular characters on *Law and Order* as well as roles in the Tony Hillerman mysteries (2002–2004) and the miniseries *Into the West* (2005).

NORTHERN PLAINS

The horse has the six directions that we use in our ceremonies. The two front legs represent the west and the north. The two back legs represent the east and the south. The head points up; the ears point up, representing *wakantanka*, up above. The tail points downward toward Mother Earth. When you put these six directions together, it creates a sacred center to bring *wowakan* in. It's a sacredness that you can only have with these six directions. You can even pray when you're on your horse, and you can think about a lot of things while you're riding your horse. Some people think about what their ancestors went through—and it's the horse leading the way with its healing power.

With that *wowakan* inside those six directions, you place a man or a woman on a horse and you give the seventh direction, which is the center, the *chokata*, of all things. As we say, *mitakuye oyasin*, everything is related. When you put that all together, you move forward, and you're able to create power as you go.

—Mikey Peters (Brule Dakota), Dakota 38 Wokiksuye Memorial Rider (2014)

A BIRD'S EYE VIEW

[The Buffalo Gap is where] the wild animals came in ... for protection from the icy blasts of winter; and the Sioux likewise went there.... Nature seemed to hold us in her arms.

—Luther Standing Bear (Oglala Lakota), 1928

The sky appears immense over the flats, where clouds mount into ominous and fantastical shapes, looming above a wide, unbroken horizon. The great Northern Plains is a place where the winds whip tall grasses into an endless sea that makes humans feel small. Also called the Great American Desert, the Plains can be austere. Seasons are extreme, from blizzardy winters to blastingly hot summers, and the people and animals who have adapted to these conditions know where to seek shelter and how to cultivate hidden bounties.

Before Euro-American settlement, 501,900 miles of prairie, steppes, grasslands, and sloughs (wetlands) flowed in unbroken waves east from the Missouri River and west to the Rocky Mountains. Grasses fed buffalo and antelope and provided habitats for birds and smaller animals, which attracted and sustained human hunters. Along river valleys, such as the Missouri and the Platte, people had farmed in earthlodge villages since time immemorial. Some nations, such as the Pawnee, were both farmers and hunters in what would become the state of Nebraska, following a seasonal round of planting and harvesting in earth lodge villages and packing along teepees to follow the buffalo herds during semiannual hunts. Earth lodges were built of log frames covered with soil, on which the grass would grow, so they resembled natural hills. They were oval shaped with an extended passageway with a door, and some were large enough to hold the whole village during a ceremony.

Artifacts have dated human occupation in this area to around 200 B.C.E., and the materials found here demonstrate these early peoples' connection to the vast trading complex that spread across North America. As far as we know, the original locations and real names of the peoples who lived on the Northern Plains were, in present-day Kansas: the Waghtochtatta (Oto) and Hutanga (Kansa); in Nebraska: the Ponca, Umonhon (Omaha), and Chahiksichahik (Pawnee); in South Dakota: the Nakota and Lakota; in North Dakota: the Nueta (Mandan), Sahnish (Arikara), and Hiraaca (Hidatsa); in eastern Wyoming: the Tsitsisa and Sutai (both Cheyenne); in eastern Colorado: the Hininoeino (Arapaho); in Montana: the Nakoda (Assiniboine), A'aninin (Gros Ventre), Pikuni (Piegan), Siksika (Blackfeet), and Apsaalooke (Crow).

Today's Northern Plains tribal nations are, by state: Kansas: the Kickapoo Tribe and the Prairie Band Potawatomi Nation; Nebraska: the Ioway Tribe of Kansas and Nebraska, Northern Ponca, Omaha, Winnebago, and Isanti (Santee) Sioux tribes; South Dakota: the Yankton Sioux (Isanti and Nakota) and Flandreau Isanti Sioux tribes the Sisseton—Wahpeton Oyate (Dakota), the Oglala Lakota Nation, and the Rosebud, Crow Creek, Lower Brule, Cheyenne River, and Standing Rock Sioux tribes. The Standing Rock Reservation spans into North Dakota as does Sisseton–Wahpeton Oyate. North Dakota is also home to the Spirit Lake Tribe Nation (Dakota), the Turtle Mountain Band of Chippewa Indians, and the Mandan Hidatsa Arikara Nation. Montana contains the Crow Nation, the Northern Cheyenne Nation, the Fort Belknap Indian Community of Gros Ventre and Assiniboine, the Fort Peck Assiniboine and Sioux tribes, the Chippewa–Cree Tribe, and the Blackfeet Nation.

LEGENDARY LANDSCAPES

Jutting up from the vast, semiarid flatlands, hills and buttes attracted attention as extraordinary places, offered water and shelter, and were often the sites of vision quests. During a vision quest, a person travels alone to an isolated power spot to fast and pray for several days in hopes that the spirits of the place will emerge to guide the seeker on his or her path in life or to provide a message for the community back home. According to Peter Nabokov's *Where the Lightning Strikes,* an exploration of sacred sites, one mound near the Platte River was known variously to the Pawnee as *Pa'haku,* to the Sioux as *Paha Wakan,* and to the Omaha as *Pahe Wahube*—all versions of "sacred hill."

One significant site in a storied landscape is the Black Hills area of western South Dakota, which the Sioux call "the heart of everything that is." To the Sioux, Ponca, Omaha, and Arikara, the hills' dark conifers looked black in contrast to the low-lying, pastel sagebrush that surrounded them for miles. The Kiowa name for this place is Black Rock Mountains while the Cheyenne call it the Island Hills, and to the Comanche, this is the Red Fir Place. Black Hills caves and rock are illustrated with hundreds of drawings depicting origin stories, vision scenes, hunting rituals, fertility symbols, and battle tales. Some of these drawings date back 13,000 years. The Cheyenne tribe has an old buffalo robe in its archives, the skin side scraped white and painted with a map of the Island Hills;

The great Northern Plains were home to vast herds of buffalo (bison) before the arrival of European explorers and settlers.

stars superimposed on the map represent the constellations of an ancient sky.

The Mandan "Heart of the World" is the place where the Heart River joins the Missouri. As Mandan Chief Four Bears said, before the white man came, this was the place where "we lived at the center and thought with our hearts." In central and western North Dakota, twelve vision-quest buttes are home to Hidatsa earth-naming spirits; the chief site is Singer Butte in the Kildeer Mountains. The Crow, who journeyed away from their Hidatsa relatives long ago, revere the Big Horn Mountains as much for their vision-enhancing refuges as for the rare ceremonial tobacco that only grows in this area.

Sacred landmarks are not as much religious altars as cultural touchstones, places of origin or arrival. Bear Butte, also called Devil's Tower, rises 867 feet, just north of the Black Hills. It is the place where the Cheyenne hero Sweet Medicine and his wife learned from the animals how to do the

proper ceremonies so that the Cheyenne would always have food. It is the place where Crazy Horse of the Lakota vowed to stop further white invasion, and Bear Butte is the spot where the Kiowa's' ancestors emerged. The Kiowa name for this deeply ridged butte is *T'sou'a'e*: "Aloft on a Rock."

ROCK RINGS

The ancestors of Native people on the Northern Plains are commonly perceived as having lived in remote areas, far apart from each other, and were not known for building monuments. In truth, they were part of an extensive inter-tribal network, as evidenced by trade items, such as abalone and cowrie shells from the Gulf of Mexico and mica from North Carolina, that have been found in Manitoba. Northern copper and obsidian are buried in the ceremonial mounds of ancient Mississippian sites in present-day Ohio. While the early hunters who roamed the Plains in search of buffalo left no temples like those down south, they created about fifty large rings of rock that date from around 1000 C.E. and remain spiritual centers today.

One of the most famous rock wheels, in Bighorn County in the mountains of north-central Wyoming, was declared a National Historic Landmark in 1970. The Medicine Wheel, in the Bighorn National Forest, is just south of the Crow reservation in Montana and was for centuries a site for fasting and vision quests for Plains youth. Paul Moss, an Arapaho oral historian, explained the wheel's significance in *Hinono'einoo3itoono, Arapaho Historical Traditions* in 1993. Moss says the Arapaho name for the site is the Buffalo Wheel, a place for ceremonies related to the Sun Dance and to other stone wheels as far east as the Great Lakes.

At ten thousand feet, on a level spot near the top of Medicine Mountain, the circle, built of flat and rounded melon-sized stones, is twenty-five yards in diameter, with twenty-eight spokes stretching to a center cairn (stone pile) that is ten feet in diameter. A rope fence around the site is bright, with cloth prayer ties contributed by reverent visitors. Seven other smaller cairns are piled on or near the rim of the wheel. During summer solstice, two of the cairns are aligned with the position of the sun during sunrise, and two others echo the sunset point on the horizon. Other paired piles project the directions of rising stars. Because star paths have changed slowly over time, astronomers have determined that the closest matches between the cairns and celestial orientation points would have occurred between 1200 and 1700 C.E.

According to Paul Moss's oral history, the Arapaho moved from central Colorado to Wyoming in the mid-nineteenth century. Solitary fasting and visions quests were common, and when referring to groups of seven vision seekers, Arapaho root words relating the Buffalo Wheel to the Sun Dance translate to "moving around in a circle" and "moving slowly and carefully during a ceremony." Moss says, "In the old days, things weren't gotten just any old way; it took seven days … Indians [had] eagles, animals…. The spirits are around them—each of the ones who fast there has an accompanying spirit—they were powerful … and the spirits watched over the fasters. A thing wasn't just taken and used for no reason."

If the ceremony was done correctly, after seven days, black eagles arrived to soar in circles above the Buffalo Wheel and cried out toward the people. The people, exhausted from fasting, blew whistles loudly to return the eagles' calls. In this way, the eagles knew the people were strong enough to receive whatever they had prayed for.

The Arapaho history also details how the white man made the buffalo disappear and then outlawed Native ceremonies. "Recently here the [U.S.] government passed a law; they stopped the Sun Dance…. It didn't happen anymore. Then more recently, this freedom of worship was recognized, in the White Man way; more recently, the Sun Dance has come back." Moss's account concludes that although non-Indians are now coming to worship at the Medicine Wheel, leaving cloth offerings, and praying, "*Wohei*, in the old days, they didn't do [ceremonies] just any old way. Only when whatever they were doing had been ceremonially blessed. Learning by observing, watching carefully, that was how everything was done."

FROM THE WOODLANDS TO THE PLAINS

If you have one hundred people who live together, and if each one cares for the rest, there is One Mind.

—Shining Arrows (Crow), 1972

Despite a long history of economic and political forces designed to destroy Plains cultures, all contemporary tribal communities north of Oklahoma have remained loyal to their distinct cultural groups and preserved their heritage. The most common images many non-Indians

Medicine Wheel, an Indigenous sacred site and National Historic Landmark in Wyoming.

apply to all Indian people derive from the Plains culture: famous warrior chiefs in long, eagle-feather headdresses, buffalo hunters on horseback, and small bands of people who carried portable teepees for a free-roaming existence, smoked sacred pipes, and underwent sweat lodge purifications, vision quests, and physically challenging Sun Dance ceremonies. Nonetheless, the Plains lifestyle was relatively new for Indians and was an adaptation to the rapid expansion of colonial settlements as well as a foreign government's political influence. Classic Plains culture began in about 1750 and does not characterize the way these Indigenous people lived for centuries as descendants of the farming and mound-building Mississippian communities that thrived from about 800 to 1500 C.E.. The Plains culture that has captured the popular imagination flourished until the late 1800s when war with the United States ended with the Native peoples clustered on small reservations. By that time, white hunters had slaughtered most of the large herds of buffalo. Without this major resource, traditional Plains culture was no longer possible.

Along with other Paleolithic animals, all horses in North America died out about eight to ten thousand years before European contact. The horses that became part of the wild horse, or American mustang, herds had escaped from early Spanish explorer expeditions. Some Indian nations lived on the Plains, where they built small huts and hunted the buffalo on foot. They domesticated wolves and bred them over generations for their helpful qualities as guardians and pack dogs that pulled travois, or buckskin sleds, when people wanted to move.

Most of today's Plains nations began migrating from the east onto the Plains during the colonial period, mainly after 1650, when European expansion forced many Indians westward. In the east, nations such as the Sioux and Blackfeet lived by hunting, growing corn, and gathering wild foods.

During the 1650s and early 1700s, the Iroquois in upstate New York and southeastern Canada expanded their military campaign to control access to lands and furbearing animals necessary for trade to Europeans. The Iroquois expansion pushed many Algonquian-speaking nations, such as the Ojibwe (Chippewa) and Ottawa, farther west into the upper Great Lakes area. The Ojibwe migrated into present-day Minnesota and, armed with guns from their European trade allies, were pushing the Sioux onto the Plains by the latter half of the 1700s. By the early 1800s, many Sioux bands had moved onto the Plains and adopted buffalo hunting. They also began raiding more sedentary farming people, such as the Mandan, Arikara, and Hidatsa, who were living along the Missouri River. The Sioux eventually settled in present-day central North Dakota.

The experience of the Cheyenne, an Algonquian-speaking nation, is common for the peoples who migrated onto the Plains. In the early 1600s, the Cheyenne were located in present-day southern Canada and made their livelihood by hunting, farming, and gathering wild plants. Iroquois expansion after 1650 pushed the Cheyenne farther west, and in the 1700s, early French explorers reported that the Cheyenne people were living in present-day Minnesota. By the late 1700s, the Cheyenne inhabited eastern North Dakota and, while still growing corn, were increasingly using horses and hunting buffalo. The Sheyenne River in eastern North Dakota is named after them. By the mid-1800s, the Cheyenne moved to the western Plains, where they adapted teepee living and buffalo hunting. Their culture revolved around summer renewal ceremonies, such as the Sun Dance. In the winter, the Cheyenne and other Plains nations, like the Sioux, Blackfeet, and Crow, gathered into small bands and settled in for the cold months with their supplies of food, crafting materials, songs, and stories.

TRADITIONAL LIFE

Everything the Kiowas had came from the buffalo. Their teepees were made of buffalo hides; so were their clothes and moccasins. They ate buffalo meat. Their containers were made of hide or of bladders or stomachs. The buffalo were the life of the Kiowas…. The priests used parts of the buffalo to make their prayers when they healed people or when they sang to the powers above.

—Old Lady Horse (Kiowa), 1968

Cultural Expressions

The buffalo was not just an animal or a food source; it was the essence of life itself. The wellbeing of the buffalo was often the basis of ceremonies. The Mandan traveled in saucer-shaped boats of buffalo hide, and the earliest paintings were done on hide using earth pigments. In 1804, William Clark described a Yankton Nakota village near the mouth of the James River in present-day southern South Dakota: "The Scioues Camps are handsom of a Conic form Covered with Buffalow Roabs Painted different colours and all compact & handsomly arranged."

Lakota culture celebrates White Buffalo Calf Woman, and in one of the nation's earliest examples of oral literature, White Buffalo Calf Woman appears to a group of Lakota hunters at Wind Cave, *Washu Niya,* the breathing place. *Washu Niya* is named for the fog that emanates from the mouth of the cave and is considered to be the spot where all animals entered the world. After turning one of the hunters to dust for gazing upon her disrespectfully, White Buffalo Calf Woman imparts a message of respect for women before she gives the men the gift of the sacred pipe, upon which Lakota spirituality is centered: "On you [the men] it depends to be a strong help to the woman in the raising of children. *Wakan Tanka* smiles on the man who has a kind feeling for a woman." Sacred pipe bowls, representing a woman's womb, are shaped from red catlinite

"Indians Hunting the Bison" (1839) by painter Karl Bodmer. While buffalo (bison) were an essential source of food and hides, they were also spiritually important to Native peoples.

stone and often feature carvings of buffalo. The bowl is affixed to a wooden stem, representing the male. To this day, the birth of a rare female white buffalo calf is considered a miraculous omen of positive change and inspires visitors to travel long distances with offerings for the calf.

Drama

Ritual dramatic performances, such as the Pawnee Hako, were keyed to seasonal buffalo hunts, the planting and harvesting of corn, and celestial cycles. The Pawnee had advanced astronomical knowledge, and their earth lodges were built as observatories so that entranceways and smoke holes were aligned with particular constellations, designed so that the first light of the spring equinox would illuminate the altar. The ceremony known as the Hako among the Pawnee was also enacted by the Omaha and Ponca, and the Mandan, too, built their earth lodges according to celestial diagrams.

According to Alice Fletcher, an anthropologist who recorded Hako songs in the early 1900s, the large, round earth lodge represented both a woman's womb and the universe above. Fletcher quotes a Skidi Pawnee man, who said, "The Skidi were organized by the stars; these powers above made them into families and villages and taught them how to live and how to perform their ceremonies. The shrines of the four leading villages were given by the four leading stars and represent those stars which guide and rule the people."

As among the Pawnee, songs and dances were daily aspects of Plains cultures that expressed people's beliefs. For Dakota ceremonial dancing, men painted their faces and bodies with clan or vision symbols, stiffened their hair with bear grease, and sprinkled their heads with red and white feathers or bird down. The Dakota danced with their hands on their hips, striking the soles of their feet on the ground. There continue to be songs for every occasion: there are songs for victory, to honor someone, for the Sun Dance, sweat lodge, vision quest, courting, hunting, and working; there are death songs and songs for horses.

When the Spanish introduced horses to the Plains, Native people could greatly extend their buffalo-hunting range, and horses became signs of status as well as subjects expressed visually, such as painted shields, wooden carvings, and in the vivid regalia made for horses, including masks that expressed the spirit nature of this animal the Lakota called *sunka wakan*, or "sacred dog." Plains people also adorned their clothing, hide bags, and cushions with colorful, geometric designs stitched of dyed porcupine quills. When trade with Europeans made glass beads available, women began creating works of wearable art using this flexible, light-reflecting medium.

After 1880, poverty forced many Plains Indians to seek clothing from mission charities and government distribution centers. Native artisans altered these clothes to suit their own tastes; the ribbon shirt is one example of tribal modification, in which colored ribbons are sewn on a "cowboy" shirt, creating a vibrant article of Indian clothing. Northern Plains women are famous for their quilts, which feature an eight-pointed star design, which many non-Indians buy as art pieces. The quilts help perpetuate the Plains Indian tradition of giveaways at powwows and ceremonies and on occasions such as welcoming babies and honoring the departed at funerals.

Other materials accessible after interaction with whites were colored pencils and the ledger books used to keep military records. Native men who were imprisoned or employed as scouts in forts were given used ledger books. Native men began expanding the drawings they had formerly made on hide as winter count calendars to create elaborate scenes of battles and daily life on ledger paper. In 1926, more than four hundred ledger drawings depicting Oglala Lakota history were discovered. The artist was Amos Bad Heart Bull (born in 1859). He was a former army scout who spent fifty-three years making ledger drawings. Among them was a map of the Black Hills, depicting sacred sites. Today, ledger art is highly prized, and in 2014, a previously unidentified "War Book" of ledger art that was found on the Little Bighorn battlefield after Custer's defeat has been identified by Harvard's Peabody Museum as containing a self-portrait, probably by Crazy Horse. The identifying characteristics and supernatural aura of the figure match another Crazy Horse portrait by Amos Bad Heart Bull. As Crazy Horse did not allow himself to be photographed, this is a valuable find.

In his book, *Black Elk Speaks,* Crazy Horse's cousin Black Elk explained his relative's particular powers: "Crazy Horse dreamed and went into the world where there is nothing but the spirits of things. That is the real world that is behind this one, and everything we see here is something like a shadow from that world.... It was this vision that gave him his great power, for when he went into a fight, he had only to think of that world to be in it again so that he could go through anything and not be hurt."

Literature

As-told-to-Plains-Indian autobiographies, such as *Black Elk Speaks, Lame Deer, Seeker of Visions, Crow Dog: Four Generations of Sioux Medicine Men, Lakota Woman, Fools Crow, Buffalo Bird Woman of the Hidatsa,* and *Pretty Shield, Medicine Woman of the Crows*, have provided some authentic information about traditional Plains societies and eyewitness accounts of historical events, but contemporary Native scholars question whose voice is speaking at various times in these books—the subjects or the white ethnographers? Beverly Hungry Wolf's accounts of Blackfeet life are thorough although the text may have been mediated somewhat by her German husband. True autobiographies, such as works by Charles Eastman (Santee), Luther Standing Bear (Oglala), Joseph Iron Eye Dudley (Yankton), and Ella Cara Deloria (Dakota/Lakota) are considered to be more reliable.

Technology

Tribal technologies included advanced arrow-making techniques. Specific types of wood were chosen depending on the game. Cedar was useful for hunting water fowl because it floats. June berry bush stalks were the most common

The Advisory Council of the 9th District Federal Reserve Bank of Minneapolis visiting the sculpture of Tashunka Witko (Crazy Horse) in 2014. Crazy Horse's descendants asked this monument in the Black Hills of South Dakota, seventeen miles from Mount Rushmore.

arrow materials, and bows were made from ash tree branches, usually four feet in length. The fiber used for the bowstring was made of the stinging nettle plant or from a material found in the neck of a snapping turtle. These materials combined to drive an arrow clean through an animal as large as a buffalo or a moose.

Games and Sports

Among the many games of chance Plains people played, hand games could be played without words and among people who spoke separate languages. The gambling game continues to be played indoors during the winter. Players hide marked and unmarked bones or sticks in their hands. The scoreboard is made of sharpened sticks stuck in the ground. Any number of people can play; they sit facing one another, and the people on the side holding the token sing and sway from side to side. When a team member on the opposite side guesses who has the bone, he or she takes it. Even today in the digital age, as the singing and drumming builds in volume and speed, the hand game can be quite hilarious.

Archery was a typical game of skill on the Plains and could be played with arrows or darts. Simply shooting at a target wasn't challenging enough though many contests did feature targets, such as the grass-stuffed rings the Omaha, Gros Ventres, Crow, and Lakota made. The Oglala would shoot at another flying arrow while the Pawnee and Ponca shot at arrows laying on the ground so they would surpass previous shots or land in a certain pattern. If a Pawnee player hit an arrow lying on the ground at some distance, he could collect all of the arrows. The Kiowa sometimes threw arrows by hand, competing for distance thrown. Among the Assiniboine, an arrow stuck upright in the ground was the target. The Dakota would throw a bunched-grass target up in the air and try to hit it before it fell while Mandan boys competed to see who could have the most arrows flying in the air at once.

Girls and women played shinny, kicking or batting a ball through a goal with a curved stick. The Arapaho name for shinny is *gugahawat,* and the baseball-sized, disk-shaped ball was made of buffalo hair covered with buckskin. Sometimes the ball was fully beaded with red and white designs. *Ohonistas* was the Cheyenne name of the game, and they painted their balls with figures such as turkey and deer. Dakota women of one camp would play *takapsica* against another camp, and Crow women played against the men as a springtime ritual. Gros Ventre, Arikara, Pawnee, Kiowa, and Wichita women also played shinny. The ballgame is featured in Wichita stories, such as the creation of light upon the earth.

COLONIAL HISTORY

Two centuries ago, French, Scottish, English, and Spanish traders moved onto the northern Plains and brought many changes to the Native people. Traders who were looking to receive buffalo hides in exchange for guns, pots and pans, cloth, and other goods led the way for more intensive settlements in the late 1880s. The Mandan people were popularized in the settlers' imagination after Lewis and Clark praised their ap-

pearance in their writings, and portraits of the dignified people and their impressive earth lodges were painted by Karl Bodmer and photographed by George Catlin. Mandan villages became a popular destination for white tourists.

Diseases accompanied the European newcomers and caused deadly epidemics of smallpox, cholera, and whooping cough that were responsible for dramatic declines in Plains Indian populations during the nineteenth and twentieth centuries. The smallpox epidemics began devastating villages in the 1780s, with the worst occurring in 1832, killing ninety percent of the Mandan and hundreds of Hidatsa.

The mass deaths dramatically reduced Mandan, Arikara, and Hidatsa numbers and forced them to combine clans and mix family lines. Ultimately, the three tribes coalesced and moved to a location near present-day Fort Berthold Reservation in North Dakota. Other Indian nations living on the Plains, such as the Sioux and Pawnee, suffered similar catastrophic population losses though their exact numbers are hard to document.

On July 28, 1847, the French trader Francis A. Chardon recorded in his journal the ravaging smallpox epidemic that had killed hundreds of people—seven-eighths of the Mandan and half of the Hidatsa and Arikara—within a few hours on June 14, 1847. By the autumn of that year, 1,800 Mandan were reduced to twenty-three men, forty women, and sixty to seventy young people. Among the dead was the Mandan second chief, whom Chardon described as "the brave and remarkable Four Bears, lifelong friend of the whites … and beloved by all that knew him."

REMOVAL (1830–1880s)

The United States displaced Plains Indian people by officially moving eastern Indian tribes onto their territories. Starting in 1830, U.S. government policy authorized removal of most Indian nations east of the Mississippi River to new homelands west of the river. Most eastern people were moved to present-day Kansas and Oklahoma groups from the Ioway, Kickapoo,

Potawatomi, Chippewa, and Munsee Delaware migrated to Indian Territory in present-day Kansas. After signing treaties with the U.S. government in 1865 and 1874, part of the Winnebago (Ho-Chunk) nation, formerly located in Wisconsin, settled on a reservation in Nebraska.

Frequently, the Indigenous people considered the Indian newcomers as hostile intruders on their lands and hunting territories. Warfare ensued as the eastern Indians tried to recreate their communities in the West, and Plains Indians, like the Pawnee and Ponca of present-day Kansas, tried to defend their hunting territories. In the 1880s and 1890s, the United States relocated the Pawnee and Ponca to Indian Territory in Oklahoma.

Conflicts on the Plains escalated when the U.S. government assigned territorial boundaries for Indian nations via the 1851 Fort Laramie Treaty. Over the next thirty years, the United States decreased the size of reservations, sometimes forcing several tribes to live in the same enclosure. The Shoshone and Arapaho, once enemy nations, now co-exist on the Wind River Reservation in Wyoming. In Montana, a band of Assiniboine and a branch of the Yankton, both Siouan-speaking peoples, are crowded onto the Fort Peck Reservation while other Assiniboine and the Algonquian-speaking Gros Ventre occupy the Fort Belknap Reservation.

PLAINS INDIAN RESISTANCE

It is not my intention or wish to fight the whites. I want to be friendly and peaceable and keep my tribe so. I am not able to fight the whites. I want to live in peace.

—Black Kettle (Cheyenne), 1864

On November 16, 1864, Colonel John Chivington led heavily armed Colorado volunteers in an unprovoked, brutal attack against a Southern Cheyenne and Arapaho camp of about one thousand people at Sand Creek in Colorado Territory. After the Fort Laramie Treaty of 1851,

The site where the 1851 treaty was signed is now the Fort Laramie National Historic Site in Wyoming. The tents in the background mark the spot of the signing.

the Cheyenne leader Black Kettle had moved his people as far as possible from white forts and settlements whenever necessary. During the first years of the Civil War, when local volunteer militia presence increased as young men sought to avoid conscription, Black Kettle visited President Abraham Lincoln, who was giving a speech in Kansas, and received medals and papers certifying that he was a friend of the whites. The tribe was advised to turn in their arms and camp near a military outpost for protection. At that time, Colonel A. B. Greenwood presented the Cheyenne chief with an enormous garrison American flag, displaying white stars for each of the thirty-four states. Greenwood assured Black Kettle that as long as he flew this flag over his teepee, no soldiers would ever shoot at him.

Black Kettle hoisted this flag proudly, and others in his camp were displaying white flags of surrender above their teepees when Chivington attacked at dawn. Chivington claimed retaliation for Indian raids on white settlers, but ironically, at this time, Black Kettle had recently negotiated the return of four white children who had been kidnapped by another tribe, ransoming his own ponies to assure the children's return to their families. Chivington, however, was on record as saying his mission in life was to kill Indians, and his regiment was embarrassed that they had not killed any Indians in Colorado. As the seven hundred cavalry riders advanced, women, children, and elders fell to their knees in surrender, but the soldiers opened fire with carbines and cannons, shooting and bludgeoning at least 150 of them to death, mutilating the corpses, and carrying off body parts as souvenirs.

The episode sparked outrage in Washington. Federal investigators condemned but never punished Chivington for the massacre. In recognition of one of the most horrendous assaults on American Indians, a public law of November 2000 authorized Sand Creek as a National Historic site. The 12,500-acre site opened in 2002, 170 miles southwest of Denver. Since then, as skulls and scalps are repatriated by museums and private collectors, the Cheyenne and Arapaho are interring these remains at Sand Creek with the proper ceremony.

Revenge for the mass murder at Sand Creek was one motivation for Native resistance on the Plains as Cheyenne Dog Soldiers joined with other nations, whose people already resented U.S. restrictions on their freedom to move about as they had always done. The Lakota, Cheyenne, and Blackfeet fought the United States army and tried to keep white settlers and miners from staying permanently in the area.

The War for the Bozeman Trail, or Red Cloud's War (1866–1868), was fought in defense of Cheyenne and Sioux treaty-authorized territories in Wyoming and Montana as settlers and miners increasingly traveled this passageway to the Oregon Trail in the West. As forts multiplied along this route, Plains warriors led by Red Cloud, Crazy Horse, American Horse (all Lakota), and Little Wolf (Cheyenne) occupied and burned them. These leaders were joined by Sitting Bull and Gall (Lakota) and Dull Knife (Cheyenne) in the War for the Black Hills (1876–1877).

> A very great vision is needed, and the man who has it must follow it as the eagle seeks the deepest blue of the sky.
>
> —Crazy Horse (Oglala Lakota)

On the upper Rosebud Creek in present-day southern Montana, in the spring of 1876, General George Crook's army of 1,300 attacked Crazy Horse's force of 1,200. Crook withdrew after heavy losses. Crazy Horse's camp then joined Sitting Bull and Gall on the Bighorn River in Montana. In June of that year, General George Armstrong Custer and Major Marcus Reno planned to capture the Sioux and Cheyenne on the Bighorn and bring them into reservations with the aid of Arikara and Crow wolves (scouts). During the Plains wars, the U.S. Army received assistance from other sedentary riverside nations, including the Pawnee and Otoe, who had long been suffering raids by the Sioux.

There were female warriors among the Crow, whose bravery at the Battle of the Rosebud was observed by Pretty-shield, a Crow medicine woman, in 1876. "I saw the two women, Finds-Them-And-

Kills-Them and The-Other-Magpie, riding and singing with them [the wolves].... " The-Other-Magpie, who wore a stuffed woodpecker on her head and had her forehead painted yellow, "swung a long coup stick, with one breath feather on its small end," as she sang and rode, striking into the Lakota. "See," she called out, "my spit is my arrows." That day, she saved a Crow wolf who had been knocked from his horse and dispatched a Lakota opponent. On the other side, the strong fighter Buffalo Calf Road Woman (Cheyenne) saved her wounded brother while a few days later, Minnie Hollow Wood (Lakota) earned the right to wear a war bonnet after she joined the fight against Custer's men at Little Bighorn.

After the Rosebud, on June 25, Custer attacked with more than two hundred troops and was outfoxed by the Cheyenne and Sioux's decoy and feinting strategies. Then Crazy Horse and his predominantly Cheyenne warriors attacked Custer's men from the north and west. Gall, after routing Major Reno's forces, charged Custer from the south and east. The U.S. troops were surrounded and completely annihilated.

Little Bighorn was the pinnacle of the Indians' power. They had achieved their greatest victory yet, but despite other brilliant campaigns, the Sioux and Cheyenne were starved and battle-weary. In May 1877, Crazy Horse reluctantly surrendered with eight hundred followers at Fort Robinson in northwest Nebraska. After a flight to Canada, Sitting Bull was in similar straits and chose to surrender in Montana. Outraged over the death of Custer, a popular Civil War hero on the eve of the Centennial, the United States demanded and enacted harsh retribution. Both Sitting Bull and Crazy Horse were murdered in captivity. The Black Hills dispute was quickly resolved by redrawing the boundary lines, placing the Black Hills outside the reservation and open to white settlement.

Sometimes the wind blows over the hilltops at Wounded Knee Creek and moans its mournful death song for the heroes of

"The Custer Fight" 1903 is a painting by Charles Marion Russell depicting the Battle of the Little Bighorn.

Big Foot's band resting peacefully in the bosom of Mother Earth. The guns of the soldiers are silent now as are the moans and groans of the Indians who died there. Little children laugh and play on the grass hillside, oblivious to what happened there one cold winter day many years ago. *Ho, mitakoyapi, iyuskinyan nape ciyuzapi yelo* (My grandchildren, I give you my hand of friendship).

—Sidney H. Bird (Dakota), 1999

The Big Foot Band of Lakota was massacred by the Seventh Cavalry, the final chapter in the nineteenth-century Indian Wars and one of the most appalling tragedies in the nation's history. After Sitting Bull's murder on the Standing Rock Reservation, his followers joined Big Foot at the Cheyenne River Reservation in South Dakota. Unaware that Big Foot no longer advocated the Ghost Dance, a religious movement that envisioned Native American cultural restoration and the disappearance of whites (see also the Great Basin and Rocky Mountains chapter), an army detachment captured the combined group as it tried to take refuge at the Pine Ridge Agency in South Dakota, where they turned themselves in. They were the very last of the Lakota to do so.

One day later, at Wounded Knee Creek, on December 29, 1890, five hundred troops of the U.S. Seventh Cavalry surrounded the encampment of Miniconjou and Hunkpapa Lakota that was flying a white flag of truce. The cavalry had orders to escort the Sioux to the railroad for transport to Omaha and intended to use a display of force coupled with firm negotiations to gain compliance from them. A scuffle broke out while disarming the Indians. By some accounts, a Lakota man raised a rifle horizontally over his head and did not heed orders to drop the gun because he was deaf. The man was shot in the back, and the soldiers then fired on the defenseless Lakota men, women, and children with Hotchkiss guns and rifles, slaughtering an estimated three hundred people. Twenty-one soldiers were awarded the Medal of Honor for their actions.

Wagons were driven into the fields among the frozen dead and their bodies dumped into them like so much cordwood. They were taken to a trench dug by the soldiers and their bodies unceremoniously tossed into the mass grave without as much as a prayer. This was the last act of genocide against the American Indians of the United States.

—Tim Giago (Oglala Lakota), 2014

In 1990, on the hundredth anniversary of the massacre, Lakota spiritual leaders organized a ride from Standing Rock to the grave site, where a ceremony known to the Lakota as "wiping away the tears" was held. Since then, the Lakota and other Native Americans have commemorated the tragedy annually by retracing Hehaka Gleska's (Big Foot's) route to Wounded Knee, a National Historic Landmark. The Takini American Indian Holocaust organization is working to help individual and community survivors heal from genocide, postcolonial stress, and other historical trauma (see also the biographies of Maria Yellow Horse Braveheart and Arvol Looking Horse at the end of this chapter).

RESERVATIONS

By 1880, settlement on reservations became the only option available, and the Plains people reluctantly moved to U.S. government-controlled communities. After resisting removal to Oklahoma in the late 1870s, the Northern Cheyenne settled onto the Tongue River Reservation in eastern Montana. In 1916, a group of Plains Chippewa and Cree, both Algonquian-speaking peoples, found refuge on the Rocky Boy reservation in Montana. In the 1890s, the federal government had excluded several bands of Turtle Mountain and Pembina Chippewa, who had traveled temporarily to Montana to hunt buffalo, from tribal membership and land rights in North Dakota. Chippewa leader Little Shell and his followers joined Cree and Métis (French and Indian) people in a non-federally recognized community that survives at Great Falls, Montana.

People often gathered to live near relatives, and these hamlets became present-day reservation communities. Indian agents had near total control over reservations, and between 1887 and 1934, official U.S. policies discouraged traditional Indian governments. Many ceremonies were banned and forced underground, and Indian cultural expression was generally repressed in favor of Christianity and American social lifestyles. As a result, on many Plains reservations, traditional ceremonies like the Sun Dance were not openly conducted until the 1970s.

Schools and mission churches were often constructed near reservation villages, and missionaries, school teachers, and farmers introduced American modes of life. Federal policies to break tribal identities included mandating that Native children attend schools where their languages and traditions were banned. Many Plains Indians continued to challenge U.S. control, however, by hiding children, a few of whom were undetected. In other cases, government agents took the children to distant boarding schools by force or under threat of canceling benefits to the family. In many instances, parents reluctantly consented to let their children go in the hope that the children would receive better nutrition than was available on their impoverished reservations.

EARLY RESERVATION ECONOMIES

The white man knows how to make everything, but he does not know how to distribute it.

—Sitting Bull (Hunkpapa Lakota),
1885

U.S. reservation policy limited trade and restricted business possibilities on reservations. The upper Missouri River Fort Berthold Reservation, where the Mandan, Hidatsa, and Arikara settled, continued their tradition of growing crops. Downstream on the Missouri River, the Winnebago (Ho-Chunk) also applied their agri-

cultural skills although the soil was nowhere as rich as in the tribe's former Great Lakes homeland. In North and South Dakota, the Sioux on the Sisseton–Wahpeton, Fort Totten, and Yankton reservations developed basic survival agriculture but were unable to purchase the equipment needed for large farms because banks wouldn't give Indians loans. On the other hand, in the western Plains reservations in Montana, many Indians attempted to farm, but the land wasn't fertile enough. The shortage of food crops forced many Indian people to subsist on government rations or to sell reservation lands and use the money to purchase cattle.

Limited farming success on the semiarid prairie inspired the Office of Indian Affairs (later the Bureau of Indian Affairs, or BIA) to begin reservation irrigation projects in the 1890s on the Blackfeet, Crow, Fort Belknap, and Fort Peck reservations in Montana. The tribes paid the cost of the irrigation canals that crisscrossed their farmland. Irrigation also hastened the loss of land when the United States encouraged tribes to sell land to repay the cost of those same irrigation projects. Furthermore, tribes that couldn't afford to maintain irrigation systems were required to operate them for non-Indians who purchased their land.

When farming failed, U.S. government agents supported cattle ranching as an alternative. Ranching required less start-up money, and although Indian ranches remained small, by the turn of the century, Blackfeet ranchers registered over four hundred cattle brands. Both the Blackfeet and the Northern Cheyenne produced quality stock, and meat packers from Chicago purchased cows from these reservations.

The Lakota Indians in South Dakota had less success. Unable to stock their ranges with enough cattle, these tribes leased portions of their reservations to cattle companies at the turn of the century. Pine Ridge and Rosebud cattle operations declined further during World War I (1914–1918), when government officials coerced Indian cattlemen to liquidate their small herds to feed the war effort. This forced the Lakota either to lease or to sell land.

"Fort Totten Trail" (c. 1915) by Henry F. Farny depicts one of the Sioux reservations.

Despite obstacles and hardships, many Plains Indians consider the early twentieth-century cattle ranches as the highlight of their economic history because cows provided a reliable supply of meat. Unfortunately, many western Plains communities never recovered from the loss of their ranches, and today, only a small percentage of ranchers make a profit. On the Northern Cheyenne Reservation, for example, only 10 percent of families make a living by cattle ranching.

LAND ALLOTMENT
(1854–1934)

Our land is more valuable than your money. It will last forever. It will not even perish by the flames of fire. As long as the sun shines and the waters flow, this land will be here to give life to men and animals. We cannot sell the lives of men and animals; therefore, we cannot sell this land.

—Northern Blackfeet Chief
(nineteenth century)

Beginning with the 1854 Omaha Treaty, land allotment—dividing tribally owned common lands into small, individual tracts—became a standard part of Plains treaties and agreements. The General Allotment Act of 1887 made land division mandatory and included a citizenship process, which totally stripped people of their "Indianness" (see also Historical Overview—The General Allotment Act).

Allotment failed for many reasons. Ecologically, dividing semiarid lands was unsound. Economically, reservation Indians were refused credit, making it impossible to farm profitably. Politically, citizenship provisions failed because local communities refused to accept reservation Indians as social or political equals.

After allotment, the government sold entire sections of the remaining reservation lands to white homesteaders, whose descendants continue to live in the midst of the reservation. The Office of Indian Affairs sold land when the agency declared an Indian allottee incompetent for reasons that were unclear. Legal guardians, government agents, or lawyers, who were appointed to manage the affairs of "incompetent" Indians, often benefited from these sales. If an Indian's land was found to contain anything of value, impulsive mixed marriages and mysterious Indian deaths were known to occur.

When an allottee died without a will, the United States granted the estate jointly to all heirs. In many cases, when there were many heirs, shares in the deceased's allotted land were very small. Continuing the joint heirship practice beyond the first generation usually rendered the properties too small to be profitable and forced the owners either to sell or to lease the land. As the family grew, lease checks became smaller, and if family members sold, the land was lost. Administering heirship lands remains a common problem on all Plains reservations and makes resource management decisions difficult.

Allotting land on Plains reservations increased the federal government's role in reservation affairs since more staff were employed to handle additional workloads. For example, the Indian Service established a government banking system known as the Individual Indian Moneys (IIM), wherein the reservation superintendent deposited funds gained from the rent and sale of allotted lands. Consequently, Indians had to trust the BIA to properly manage their money. During the course of the twentieth century, many Indian families did not receive a combined amount totaling billions of dollars in lease money when the BIA somehow lost records of these accounts.

THE RESERVATION NEW DEAL (1934)

Allotment reduced the ability of reservation communities to participate in the prairie agricultural markets and made any downturn in the economy particularly difficult for the reservation. After World War I, Plains communities experienced an agricultural depression that drove tenants off the land and deprived many families of income. By 1930, private relief organizations were dispensing assistance to several reservation communities because many were unable to provide for themselves.

Seeking to relieve suffering throughout the nation, Congress authorized a direct work-release program in 1933 known as the Civilian Conservation Corps (CCC) to employ the jobless in conservation projects. Since reservation unemployment was higher than among nontribal populations, Interior officials created the Indian Emergency Conservation Work (IECW), which provided employment for reservation irrigation, forestry, and grazing projects. For many reservation Indians, this was the first time they had ever worked for wages, and the program generated relief income. Collectively, all New Deal reservation programs were crucial to reduce suffering. For example, nearly ninety percent of the Rosebud Reservation's working population found employment in New Deal direct relief programs during the Depression.

Coinciding with reservation work programs, Commissioner of Indian Affairs John Collier advocated forming tribal corporations to manage tribes' own business affairs. Collier's plan became part of the Indian Reorganization Act (IRA) in 1934 (see also the Historical Overview chapter).

Many conservative Plains tribal communities would not support IRA legislation. The Yankton, Standing Rock, Crow, Wind River, and Fort Peck communities rejected the IRA at tribal elections. Other communities, such as Pine Ridge, voted to accept the Act and drafted new constitutions while less frequently, a few others approved corporate charters.

Tribal support for the IRA decreased by 1940 because the Act failed to increase reservation self-rule. One reason for this dwindling support was that the BIA, instead of turning reservation operations over to tribal governments, actually increased the number of government employees on reservations to administer Indian New Deal programs. This trend was especially aggravating to Indians who witnessed funding increases for the BIA. On the other hand, the passage of the Social Security Act of 1935 enabled many reservation Indians to obtain relief assistance.

WORLD WAR II AND AFTERMATH

America's entrance into World War II (1939–1945) ended congressional appropriations for direct work-relief programs. Jobless workers either entered the armed services or found employment in war-related industries. With a diminishing land base and an increasing population, most reservation Indians worked as field hands while others had limited work opportunities in war-related industries, such as urban munitions plants. Some found work closer to home at the ammunition ordinance storage facility at Igloo, South Dakota, near the Pine Ridge Reservation. Since there were few alternatives for employment, military service became an opportunity for young Indian people, and many enlisted in the U.S. armed services. Indian soldiers sent their pay home to relatives.

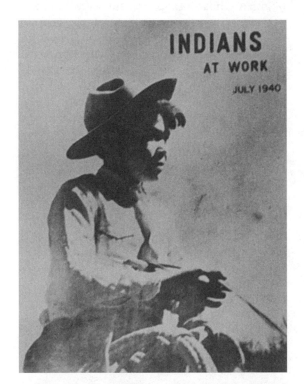

Indians at Work magazine was published by the Office of Indian Affairs (Bureau of Indian Affairs) and was about life on reservations. A benefit was that the publication helped put Indians to work as photographers.

After the war, many returned to their reservations determined to improve their communities' economic, health, and housing conditions. Wartime experiences made the postwar Plains reservation leaders more vocal than their predecessors. These pacesetters wanted greater self-rule to control reservation resources and institutions. Tribal leaders asserted that economic development was their right and planned business projects on reservations. These leaders also insisted upon equal rights with other citizens and demanded that Congress repeal discriminatory legislation, especially the liquor laws restricting the sale of alcohol to Indians. In 1952, the Indian alcohol prohibition was lifted, and today's reservation governments have the right to decide whether or not to allow the sale of alcohol in their communities.

To improve economic conditions, leaders needed to build infrastructure, such as roads, office buildings, and telephone services. However, this was an imposing task because most tribal governments had little capital to pay for such improvements. Plains reservations were distant from markets and possessed neither investment income nor access to credit, which made economic improvement difficult.

Native people wanted to end that pattern of economic dependency and develop their own ranching operations so they could remain in their communities, but their land base was too small. In addition, new farming technology decreased the demand for manual labor, increasing unemployment and sliding people further into poverty.

URBAN RELOCATION (1950s–)

Hills are always more beautiful than stone buildings, you know. Living in a city is an artificial existence. Lots of people hardly ever feel real soil under their feet, see plants grow except in flowerpots, or get far enough beyond the street light to catch the enchantment of a night sky studded with stars. When people live far from scenes of the Great Spirit's making, it's easy for them to forget his laws.

—Tatanka Man/Walking Buffalo
(Assiniboine), 1958

Unable to increase their participation in the local economy, many reservation residents turned to wage work. Ideally, tribal leaders wanted labor-intensive industries to locate either on or near reservations. The benefit to potential employers was that reservations contained a skilled workforce trained during military service or at defense plants. For Indian community members, reservation-based industries would minimize family disruptions and the necessity of leaving home for the oftentimes alien environment of cities.

However, industry leaders were reluctant to establish plants near or on Northern Plains reservations because of the distance from both suppliers and distributors. An alternative was to encourage Indian families to resettle in urban centers, where jobs could be found. In the early 1950s, the U.S. government sponsored programs to assist rural reservation people to migrate to cities and to find jobs. After obtaining employment, often in construction, many lost their jobs during the 1957 recession and returned to their reservations. Others, however, remained in urban areas such as Los Angeles, Chicago, and Minneapolis, where significant urban Indian communities are present today.

Since relocation pulled people away from their communities' social, ceremonial, and family activities, many tribal people preferred to work closer to home. Others worked seasonally in urban areas, usually in the winter, then returned to the reservation during summertime to participate in ceremonies and powwows. As automobiles became more affordable, people could travel greater distances from their homes to work while maintaining contact with their rural tribal communities.

The cities, with their associated pressures and distractions, strained the ability of many Indians to preserve tribal identity because of the need to adjust to the urban environment. Regardless of destination, relocation changed Plains communi-

ties and scattered tribal populations across the country. Although the reservations remain home, these migrations make it more difficult to maintain family relations and ceremonial ties (see also the Urban chapter for more information).

HARDSHIPS AT HOME

The departure for urban environments did not improve conditions for those who remained on the reservation. Throughout the upper Missouri drainage, the U.S. Army Corps of Engineers completed one dam after another in the 1950s and 1960s, forcing several reservation communities to move. Valuable land that provided many reservation residents with food and fuel was lost to flooding. The Fort Berthold, Cheyenne River, Standing Rock, Yankton, Lower Brule, Crow Creek, and Fort Peck reservations lost entire towns and cemeteries to the rising water. The Mandan, Hidatsa, and Arikara were forced to move to New Town, North Dakota, and the Cheyenne River Sioux relocated to Eagle Butte, South Dakota. Damming prairie rivers expanded to tributaries, including the Big Horn River on the Crow Reservation. Dams continued the pattern of Indian nations supplying resources to nontribal consumers while increasing reservation poverty.

Plains reservations did not experience postwar prosperity. Poverty excluded them from the 1950s termination legislation, which was designed to dissolve tribes and turn over their jurisdictions to state governments. Moreover, Plains states refused to assume responsibility over terminated Indian people since the gains in tax revenues would have been far outweighed by the social welfare costs of supporting impoverished Indian communities (see also Historical Overview—Public Law 280).

STEPS TOWARD
SELF-RELIANCE

Let us put our minds together to see what we can make for our children.

—Sitting Bull (Hunkpapa Lakota)

America's War on Poverty, initiated in the early 1960s, provided several Plains nations with hope for economic process. In 1964, Congress extended the Office of Economic Opportunity (OEO) programs to reservations and enabled tribal governments to write and administer Indian Community Action Program (ICAP) development grants. This gave tribal organizations an opportunity to improve the standard of living on reservations by building homes, constructing sanitary systems, and enhancing education. Like previous New Deal direct-relief programs of the late 1930s, the 1960s enterprises provided short-term employment but did not build reservation infrastructure, and government dollars continued to pass from the reservations to non-Indian contractors.

Self-determination—a process enabling tribes to manage their own services—became U.S. policy in 1971 after a speech by President Richard Nixon (U.S. president from 1969–1974). Nevertheless, over the next two decades, the U.S. government maintained control over tribal government budgets and lawmaking through the BIA, making self-determination a hollow victory.

RED POWER

The elders say, "The longest road you're going to have to walk in your life is from here to here, from the heart to the head." But they also say you can't speak to the people as a leader unless you've made the return journey, from the head back to the heart.

—Phil Lane, Sr.
(Yankton Nakota), 1992

Activism on the Plains reservations served as focal points for the American Indian Movement (AIM), a Red Power organization, resulting in a seventy-day siege at Wounded Knee, South Dakota, in early 1973. Wounded Knee evoked strong historical resonance as the site of the Seventh Cavalry massacre of about three hundred unarmed Lakota people in the winter of 1890.

The flag of the American Indian Movement included in the background the colors (left to right) black, yellow, white, and red, with the logo in the middle also being red for the Red Power organization.

Dee Brown's *Bury My Heart at Wounded Knee* shocked a generation of non-Indian activists into adding their voices in support of Native American causes and inspired many people to join Native protest marches across the country, such as the Trail of Broken Treaties.

AIM was only one voice addressing these concerns. Vine Deloria, Jr. (Dakota) raised the consciousness of Indians and non-Indians alike, bringing awareness to the unique character of Native American spirituality in his book *God Is Red*. In other works, such as *Custer Died for Your Sins* and *We Talk, You Listen*, Deloria expressed urgent Indian concerns and criticized Euro-America's failed pluralism, especially the nation's economic system that marginalized the tribes and threatened the remaining land.

SELLING ENERGY

As Indians, we will never have the efficient organization that gains great concessions from society in the marketplace. We will never have a powerful lobby or be a smashing political force, but we will have the intangible unity which has carried us through four centuries of persecution. We are a people unified by our humanity—not a pressure group unified for conquest, and from our greater strength, we shall wear down the white man and finally outlast him. We shall endure.

—Vine Deloria, Jr.
(Standing Rock Sioux), 1969

Neither political activism nor government programs addressed major economic problems when government funds for Indian services declined during the administrations of Presidents Ronald Reagan and George H. W. Bush (1989–1993). In order to generate income, some resource-rich tribes began to investigate selling coal and oil. As fuel prices rose in the 1970s, companies pursued coal and oil contracts with several Plains governments. The international energy crisis became a blessing and a curse to these reservations. Tribal leaders hoped energy leases would provide jobs and increase tribal government budgets.

On the other hand, coal sales were controversial within tribal communities because of the long-range environmental and cultural effects. In the late 1970s, the Northern Cheyenne voted to reject massive coal sales and potentially millions of dollars in royalty income because strip mining threatened to destroy nearly half of their Tongue River land.

Different energy programs characterized each community, but tribes' desire to control their own energy development projects remained a common theme. The Crow entered into coal-mining contracts, the Blackfeet signed oil-exploration deals, and the Fort Peck leadership also opened the reservation to exploration, but oil companies paid Indians lower prices than the general market rate.

Erratic energy markets encouraged tribes to pursue more stable economic projects. The Fort Peck (Montana) and Fort Totten (North Dakota) reservations built manufacturing plants that relied on government defense contracts. The Turtle Mountain community in North Dakota also sought contract work with the U.S. Defense Department for manufacturing trailers to haul heavy military equipment. These were successful tribal

industries, but they employed only a small percentage of the people on the reservation.

Nevertheless, after decades of economic development efforts and despite recent oil and gas booms in some Plains states, Plains reservations are still some of the most impoverished places in United States. Regardless of the standard applied, Plains Indians are among the poorest of the poor. For example, annual per capita income on the Crow Creek (Lower Brule) Reservation was $5,000 in 2014, and unemployment has reached 80 percent among the Northern Cheyenne. High poverty creates low standards of living, poor health, social problems, and early deaths, including some of the highest suicide rates in the world.

CONTEMPORARY CONCERNS

The Black Hills

Since the first land claim filed in 1923, the Sioux have been litigating for the return of the Black Hills. In 1950, the Indian Claims Commission ruled that the 1877 seizure of the territory was a "dishonorable chapter" in Indian affairs and offered monetary compensation. The Sioux have refused cash, including a $105 million settlement offered in 1980, and are holding out for return of the land.

The Cobell Settlement

In 1996, Eloise Cobell, a Blackfeet Indian banker and the treasurer for the Blackfeet tribe, discovered so many errors in the management of funds for lands held in trust by the United States that she filed a lawsuit against the Department of the Interior and the BIA on behalf of more than five hundred thousand landholders across Indian Country. The government's failure to account for or pay out revenue generated from the leasing of tribal lands to non-Indians for more than one hundred years resulted in the largest class-action suit in U.S. history (see also Historical Overview—Cobell Lawsuit).

Paha Sapa, or the Black Hills, of South Dakota, is the spiritual home of the Lakota people, who have been fighting to win back their land since it was illegally taken in 1923.

The Bakken Formation

Deep gas and oil pockets in western North Dakota that have been recently made accessible by new drilling technology comprise one of the largest formations in the lower forty-eight states. The BIA approved more than 1,700 oil and gas leases on or near the Mandan Hidatsa Arikara (MHA) Nation's Fort Berthold Reservation; drilling is underway, and more than one thousand wells are planned to be drilled over the next ten years. Although the BIA stated that "the environmental effects on the reservation will be substantial," the agency has yet to acknowledge the social costs of drilling in the Bakken.

The influx of thousands of out-of-state oil and gas workers, who live in temporary "man camps" near the reservation, has led to hit-and-run deaths on local roads, increased crime, an infestation of gangs selling illegal drugs, and sex trafficking involving Native women, girls, and boys. In December 2014, after six years of oil development, the MHA tribal government was wealthy. While individual tribal members do not receive substantial oil payments, the tribal government does.

In June 2014, an oil field pipeline rupture had leaked contaminated water into Lake Sakakawea, which only as recently as two years ago had begun supplying drinking water to the community of Mandaree after water pipes were installed. The contamination is the result of a mining process called hydrofracturing, which was developed by Halliburton, a company headed by Dick Cheney before he became vice president under George W. Bush. As vice president, Cheney was able to exempt drilling companies from disclosing the chemicals in fracking fluid during passage of the Federal Energy Policy Act of 2001.

Fracking fluid is injected into deep wells under high pressure to enhance production, and two to eight million gallons of water are used to frack one well. The waste water, or produced water, is highly toxic and difficult to dispose of. Attempts to inject produced water into the earth have resulted in earthquakes in some areas. Recent studies conclude the chemicals in the fracking fluids are linked to a multitude of cancers as well as birth defects, infertility, allergies, and autoimmune diseases.

After the spill into the Bear Den ravine leaked into Lake Sakakawea, the vegetation on the nearby shore died, and the water turned a rusty brown. Tribal Chairman Tex Hall declared the reservation water safe to drink but leading tribal members doubted his word. The spill site is a quarter mile from the Mandaree drinking water intake area, according to MHA Environmental Department Director Edmund Baker. A tributary runs from the lake into the Missouri River, which could spread contamination as far as the Mississippi River.

"Our tribal council is so focused on money, money, money," Baker said in August 2014. "And our tribal chairman says: 'Edmund, don't tell me about spills. I'm busy trying to do things for my people.'"

Jolene Birdbear, a former MHA postmaster, stated, "The mentality comes from the state: less regulation, more profit. They're only concerned about the immediate dollars and not about the long-term costs to our land and the future generations of our people."

In December 2014, Tex Hall was voted out due to scandals over his corruption regarding recent murders on the reservation as well as mismanagement of subcontractors and income from his own private oil company. Denounced by many traditionalists and conservationists, Tex

"Last Breath of the Black Snake" was created by Michael Horse (Yaqui/Apache/Zuni) to represent the Cowboy and Indian Alliance's April 2014 resistance to the proposed Canadian Keystone crude oil pipeline.

Hall was replaced by a new chairman, Mark Fox, and other elected officials in whom tribal members have placed their confidence to represent the best interests of the nation.

The Keystone Pipeline

Lakota People, and many other Red Nations people, we have painted our faces. Our allies up north have painted their faces. For sacred water, for *Unci Maka* [Mother Earth], for our generations. As people of the earth, our coming generations have a right to sacred water; no policy, no corporation, no politics should be more important than that.

—Owe Aku ("Bring Back the Way") mission statement (2014)

Owe Aku, led by Debra White Plume (Rosebud Lakota), has been organizing a series of "Moccasins on the ground" nonviolent, direct-action training camps since early 2014 to protest the construction of TransCanada's Keystone North tar sands oil pipeline across the Dakotas. Together with other Native and non-Native activist groups, such as the Cowboy Indian Alliance's Project Reject and Protect, rode to Washington, D.C., on horseback in the spring of 2014 and camped near the White House in teepees for five days to encourage President Obama to reject the pipeline's permit.

On January 9, 2015, when the U.S. House of Representatives approved a bill to force federal approval and the Nebraska Supreme Court sanctioned the route for the pipeline, members of the No KXL Dakota Coalition, Dakota Rural Action, and the Indigenous Environmental Network (IEN), representing similar opponents in that state, filed a motion against the South Dakota Public Utilities Commission to reject TransCanada's request to renew the Keystone permit on January 16th, but the Commission rejected this motion. Despite opposition from farmers, ranchers, tribal nations, nonprofit environmental groups, and individual landowners, on January 21, 2015, TransCanada filed for eminent domain

to run pipelines through Nebraska. Additionally, TransCanada is considering suing the U.S. under NAFTA if the Keystone project is blocked.

In a 2014 report in the British newspaper *The Guardian,* IEN Keystone XL organizer Dallas Goldtooth wrote: "Our resistance to the Keystone XL Pipeline and other tar-sand infrastructure is grounded in our inherent right to self-determination as Indigenous peoples. As the original caretakers, we know what it will take to ensure these lands are available for generations to come. This pipeline will leak; it will contaminate the water. It will encourage greater tar-sand development, which, in turn, will increase carbon emissions.

"As Oceti Sakowin [Great Sioux Nation] people, we cannot stand silent in the face of the potential ecological disaster that the pipeline promises our homelands, along with our brothers and sisters of the Cree and Dene First Nations in Alberta, where this carbon-intensive dirty oil comes from. Our acts of resistance to the Keystone XL Pipeline are a perfect example of us wising up to the ongoing modern colonialist game and a proactive step toward protecting future generations from the worst impacts of climate change."

On the heels of a March 5, 2015, crude oil train derailment near Galena, Illinois, and subsequent conflagration and evacuation of the area, President Obama, who has rejected the pipeline for six years, spoke at Benedict College in Columbia, South Carolina, on March 6th. Responding to a Sierra Club member's question about the XL Keystone Pipeline, the president explained that he vetoed the bill because the pipeline will create few jobs, transport dirty oil from Canada, and only benefit this foreign country. Obama also discussed the catastrophic threats and disruptions posed by climate change.

Personal and Family Safety

Other issues that concern Native Plains people are police brutality and too frequent murders of Native people in places such as Rapid City, South Dakota. Tribal media is bringing awareness to the fact that proportional to their population,

Native Americans are the most likely to be arrested or killed and that Indigenous youth, while comprising 1 percent of the population in a state such as South Dakota, accounts for 70 percent of young people incarcerated in that state.

The high rate of adoption and foster care placement of Native children in non-Indian homes is an ongoing problem, despite the provisions of the Indian Child Welfare Act, which were designed to keep Native children within their communities. In South Dakota alone, about 750 Native children are pushed into the foster care system each year, and there are reports that parents have not received fair hearings, are denied the right to speak in their own defense, present evidence, or see secret petitions against them. They have been denied court-appointed lawyers, and hearings last only a few minutes. It can take months before their children are returned to them, if at all. On March 30, 2015, in a landmark case, a federal judge ruled in favor of three Rosebud and Oglala mothers who had brought a class-action suit against South Dakota's Department of Social Services, which was found to have violated provisions of the Indian Child Welfare Act. This important ruling should keep these violations from happening in the future.

The abduction and killings of hundreds of Native women and girls by sex traffickers and other perpetrators is also an urgent concern. Furthermore, until recently, because of complicated jurisdiction laws, it was almost impossible to prosecute non-Indian men for the rape of Native women on reservations, which leads to a disproportionate number of these crimes. Finally, in March 2015, two years after Congress reauthorized the Violence Against Women Act (VAWA), tribes can claim jurisdiction over non-Native men who commit a violent crime or violate an order of protection against women who live on tribal land.

NORTHERN PLAINS INDIGENEITY

My point in everything is helping my community and the various populations therein to influence the systems that affect them. My goal in life is about mentorship, about figuring out how to instruct others to fulfill their purpose and understand the sense of self-awareness and application of spirituality to everyday life. To understand that we are worthwhile: economically, politically, educationally, and spiritually. We have a lot to offer.

—Gyasi Ross (Blackfeet/Squamish)

The Assiniboine

There are two Assiniboine communities in Montana and others in Saskatchewan and Alberta, Canada. Nakoda is the name the Assiniboine call themselves as they are descendants of the Nakota Sioux who originated from the Lake of the Woods and Lake Winnipeg areas of Canada, where they were on friendly terms with the Cree. Assiniboine means "those who cook with stones" in the Cree language; hence, Assiniboine in Canada are called Stoneys.

The Fort Belknap community is shared with the Gros Ventre (A'aninin), where a combined seven thousand members live on a 675,147-acre reservation, located in north-central Montana, forty miles south of the Canadian border. Although raising cattle and growing alfalfa have been the main occupations, the community has nurtured a six-hundred-head buffalo herd, which will provide meat for a meat packing and smoke house company that will be jointly owned by the Gros Ventre and Assiniboine tribes. Aaniih Community College offers language classes. Elders advise in the creation of educational and cultural programs for KVGA, which has been on the air since 1996 and is the first and only Native radio station in Montana.

The Fort Peck Assiniboine and Sioux Tribe is headquartered in Poplar, Montana, and encompasses 2,093,318 acres although less than half of the reservation is Indian owned. An estimated six thousand of the ten thousand enrolled members reside on or near the reservation in the northeast corner of Montana. Fort Peck is home to two separate Native nations, each composed of various bands: two Assiniboine (Nakoda) divisions are represented, alongside Dakota, Nakota, and Lakota groups of Sisseton–Wahpeton, Yanktonai, and Teton Hunkpapa.

Today, the Fort Peck Tribe is one of the few communities governed by traditional tribal councils. Fisheries are an important source of income as anglers come from all over the country to catch over forty different species in reservation rivers, including enormous walleye, pike, and paddlefish. Fishing tournaments and annual celebrations draw crowds all summer long. With this funding, the Language and Culture Department is developing a tribal immersion school.

Blackfeet Nation

With 15,560 members, the Blackfeet Nation has the largest Native population in Montana. About half of the tribal members live on or near their 1.5-million-acre reservation near Browning. The nation's own name, Niitsitapi, means "the real people." The name Blackfeet was a description of the people's practice of painting or decorating their moccasins with ashes. There are three branches of Blackfeet peoples in Montana and Alberta: the Northern Blackfeet (Siksika), the Blood, and the Piegun (Pikuni).

The main economies on the Blackfeet reservation are ranching and farming of wheat, barley, and hay. Siyeh Development is an umbrella corporation for several businesses, including the Blackfeet Writing Company, which manufactures pencils, pens, and markers. Tribal members may be employed as recreation guides on eight major lakes and 175 miles of fishing streams.

There are two Blackfeet cultural centers in Browning: the Blackfeet Heritage Center and Art Gallery and the Museum of the Plains Indian. Blackfeet Community College is involved in language and cultural preservation, and the Blackfeet Culture Camp offers day tours of the reservation.

Crow Nation

Apsaalooke, "children of the long-beaked bird," is the original name for the Crow people, who live in southern Montana near the sacred Big Horn Mountains. The current two-million-acre reservation boundaries were set by the second Fort Laramie Treaty of 1868. The territory includes high plains and mountains containing oil and coal, and much of the reservation is leased to mining companies although the nation is transitioning to managing their own resources. Currently, one tribally owned coal mine provides employment and royalty payments for members.

The tribal council includes every adult in the 13,394-member Crow Nation, so everyone has a voice in government decisions. Eighty-five percent of the people speak the Crow language, and the nation maintains one of the largest buffalo herds in the U.S. Crow buffalo, or *bishee,* are available to help other tribes start or enlarge their herds.

The Blackfeet Nation reservation is adjacent to Glacier National Park and of comparable size: about 1.5 million acres.

Little Bighorn Battlefield National Monument in Crow Agency memorializes the Sioux and Cheyenne victory over George Armstrong Custer's Seventh Cavalry. Even though the Crow fought on Custer's side, they meet with the

Cheyenne at the site every summer for a friendly re-enactment of the battle.

The Crow Fair is one of the most well-attended powwows in the country, and an astounding array of teepees are pitched by families of dancers, rodeo riders, parade participants, and visitors. Traditionally, the Crow were known as the flashiest dressers on the Plains, who spent days decorating themselves and their horses. The ninety-eighth annual Crow Fair will be held in 2016 and promises to be a splendid display of style and skill.

The Great Sioux Nation (Oceti Sakowin)

In their original eastern woodland environment, the Oceti Sakowin of the Lakota/Dakota/Nakota Nation was a confederacy similar to the Iroquois Six Nations, only with a shared language. The name "Sioux" is a French version of an unflattering Ojibwe description meaning "snakes," but it came to be a label for the Lakota/Dakota/Nakota when spoken of as a whole.

As the Sioux moved onto the Plains in the 1700s, their cultures and dialects became distinct. The Eastern Dakota of the Great Lakes, the Mdewakanton and Wahpekute (both also referred to as the Isanti or Santee), and the Sisseton and Wahpeton bands spoke the "D" dialect of the Siouan language. The Middle Dakota, or the Yankton and Yanktonai, of Minnesota spoke Nakota, or the "N" dialect. (In Montana, the Nakota came to be known as the Assiniboine.) The westernmost Teton, or Lakota, who spoke the "L" dialect, ranged across the Dakota prairies and Black Hills area. The Seven Council Fires of the Lakota Nation include the Oglala ("Scatter Their Own") of the Pine Ridge Reservation, the Sicangu ("Burned Thigh") of the Rosebud Reservation, the Hunkpapa ("Camps at the Entrance") of the Standing Rock Reservation and the Cheyenne River Reservation, the Mnikoju ("Planters by the Water"), the Siha Sapa ("Black Foot"), the Owohe Nupa ("Two Kettle"), and the Itazipa Cola ("Without Bows").

LAKOTA

Lakota communities include five reservations in South Dakota and two, Standing Rock and Sisseton–Wahpeton, that edge into North Dakota. The Black Hills, or Paha Sapa, of western South Dakota is a sacred prayer and ceremonial site for Lakota people. Since the late nineteenth century, when miners discovered gold in Paha Sapa and the U.S. government illegally claimed the hills, Lakota people have been fighting for their return.

Tribal governments, casinos, farms, schools, craft businesses, and buffalo and cattle ranches employ some of the 107,400 tribal members, but unemployment remains high on Lakota reservations, which are some of the poorest areas in the country. Environmental programs are important to the Lakota, who have reintroduced the endangered black-footed ferret on the Cheyenne River Reservation. On Pine Ridge, the Oglala parks department manages wildlife, fisheries, and the buffalo program. Buffalo are crucial to restoring prairie ecosystems that were overgrazed by cattle.

Long-distance running is a favorite sport, and in 1964 Billy Mills from Pine Ridge won an Olympic gold medal in a ten-thousand-meter race. Today, Mills sponsors young runners through his program, Running Strong for America, along with other activities, such as organic gardening. Lakota people also enjoy horseback riding and competing in rodeos.

Cheyenne River Sioux Tribe

Members of four Teton Lakota bands, the Minnecoujou, Two Kettle (Oohenunp), Sans Arc (Itazipo), and Blackfoot (Sihasapa), live on 1.4 million acres at Eagle Butte, South Dakota, in Dewey and Zeibach counties. About 8,100 tribal members reside on the reservation. Unemployment hovers around 88 percent. With less than $7,500 per capita income, these are two of the poorest counties in the U.S. The tribe operates a branch of the Oglala Lakota College, a radio station, and three newspapers. The elementary school is called Takini, which means "survivor," since nearly all of

Billy Mills, a Lakota, is shown here winning the gold in the 10,000-meter race at the 1964 Olympics in Tokyo, Japan.

the students are relatives of those Lakota who were massacred at Wounded Knee.

Lower Brule Kul Wicasa Oyate

About 1,310 members of the Teton Lakota, Sicangu (Brule or Burned Thigh) band live on 132,601 acres near Lower Brule, South Dakota. Median household in 2010 was $21,146, and unemployment was at 52 percent. Situated along Highway 1806 (the Native American Scenic Byway), some attractions at Lower Brule are historic parks, wildlife and cultural tours, buffalo and elk preserves, water sports, and traditional arts and crafts. The Lower Brule Fair and Rodeo is held in August. The Buffalo Interpretive Center, located seven miles east of Fort Pierre, fea-

tures a 330-head herd that grazes a 6,200-acre restored prairie and hosts exhibits on the importance of the buffalo to Plains peoples. The tribe runs the Golden Buffalo Casino, and Brule Farm Corp. is the largest popcorn producer in the U.S.

Oglala Lakota Nation

Of a total enrollment of 46,860 tribal members, there are about 38,000 Oglala Lakota living on Pine Ridge Reservation on 2.1 million acres in Shannon and Jackson counties, South Dakota. Pine Ridge is the eighth-largest reservation in the U.S. The unemployment rate was 89 percent as of 2005. Male life expectancy is age forty-eight. Despite these challenges, Pine Ridge remains a center of Lakota tradition, arts, and activism promoted at

Oglala Lakota College in Kyle, Radio KILI 90.1 FM in Porcupine, and the *Lakota Country Times*.

The Rosebud Sioux Tribe

The over 24,000-member Teton Lakota Sicangu tribe is located near Rosebud, South Dakota. The reservation's original boundaries included 3.2 million acres, of which there are 884,874 acres remaining in trust (the rest is leased). Unemployment is at about 83 percent. Efforts at economic revival include the construction of Spotted Tail Golf Course in Mission and a tribally owned grocery store. The Owl Bonnet Wind Farm is in development. Sinte Gleska University offers more than thirty degree programs and award scholarships in teacher education.

The Rosebud Sioux Tribe teepee spirit camps are maintained by Oyate Wahacanka ("Shield the People") in nonviolent opposition to the Keystone XL tar sands pipeline route. In order to protect treaty rights, clean drinking water, crops, and helpful insects and to avoid increased levels of violence associated with oil worker "man camps" as well as increased cancer rates affecting residents along the pipeline, Lakota leaders issued a statement: "*Unci Maka* is in jeopardy; our Mother Earth is crying. We cannot ignore her. Our strength is each other and our prayer. Our weapons are our minds, our faith, our voices, and most of all, our unity."

Standing Rock Sioux Tribe

The Standing Rock people are members of the Nakota, Dakota, and Lakota (Sioux) nations. The Nakota and Dakota people include the Upper Yanktonai, or Ihanktonwana, "Little End Village," and the Hunkpatina, "End of the Camping Circle." Most of the Lakota are Hunkpapa, "Campers at the Horn," and Sihasapa, or Blackfoot (not to be confused with the Blackfeet of Montana and Canada).

Estimated tribal enrollment is 15,570, with about 8,510 living on the 2.3-million-acre reservation, of which a little less than half is tribally held. Tribal offices are located in Fort Yates, North Dakota, where Sitting Bull College offers

Bachelor of Arts degrees in many subjects. Lakota/Dakota language classes are general education requirements.

In 2007, Standing Rock was one of the first tribes to create a paleontology program to collect and preserve fossils from dinosaur remains, such as Tyrannosaurus, Triceratops, and Ankylosaurus. Also found on the reservation are fossils of prehistoric alligators, crocodiles, birds, mammals, and plants. The SRST Preparatory Fossil Lab has collected more than ten thousand fossils, preserved in sedimentary rock, about half of which are from the dinosaur Edmontosaurus. This is one of the world's largest collections of remains of this large, plant-eating dinosaur from the Cretaceous period. The public can see these fossils at the Tribal Administration Building in Fort Yates, at Prairie Knights Casino, and at Sitting Bull College. Images from the collection are on view online, thanks to a grant from the Institute of Museum and Library Science.

DAKOTA

See also the "Assiniboine" section of this chapter for more on the Dakota.

Crow Creek

There are about two thousand Santee- and Yankton Dakota-enrolled members of the Crow Creek tribe living on a 125,591-acre reservation near Fort Thompson, South Dakota. The main industry is agriculture, and unemployment is at fifty percent. With high school graduation rates below thirty-five percent and the median household income at about $12,000 per year, Crow Creek is one of the most impoverished communities in the United States. Many residents are descended from survivors of the Dakota Conflict of 1862, who were exiled from Minnesota and kept as prisoners of war in South Dakota. As a gesture of postwar healing and reconciliation, the annual Wokiksuya Memorial Ride begins at Crow Creek in December on the anniversary of the mass execution of Dakota men in Mankato, Minnesota (see also the chapter titled "Midwest")

The official flag of the Crow Creek Nation

Flandreau Santee Sioux Tribe (FSST)

The Flandreau Santee Sioux are a people who had once lost everything but over 150 years have rebuilt a community balancing traditional values and faith with the realities of the twenty-first century and continue to broaden our horizons across many disciplines and industries.

—santeesioux.com

The multimillion-dollar Royal River Entertainment Complex at Flandreau is an anomaly in South Dakota as the only destination casino in the state. The Flandreau Santee are nearly fully employed, have the highest per capita income, the highest high school graduation rates, and highest per capita military service of any tribe in the U.S. The casino employs 360 people, has a $6.1 million annual payroll, and engenders $120 million in gross spending in the area.

The 736 members of the Flandreau Santee Sioux are based on 2,356 acres in Moody County, South Dakota. They are descendants of Chief Little Crow's band, who led the fight in 1862 against white squatters on their reservation in Minnesota when the federal government refused to provide rations or payments in exchange for land taken.

The Flandreau Santee maintain a buffalo herd and commercial farm, are developing an industrial park, and have purchased ceremonial land in the Black Hills, near Deadwood, South Dakota. Owner of *The Dakota Journal, The Pueblo Journal,* and other Native media enterprises, the tribe plans to develop a chain of Native American newspapers. The FSST Education Center provides many programs to tribal members and supports a revival of sacred pipe carving, for which tribal members are justly famous.

Sisseton–Wahpeton Oyate (SWO)

The Lake Traverse Reservation, situated mostly in northeastern South Dakota, with a small section in the southeastern corner of North Dakota, is home to about 13,180 members, many of whom work elsewhere in the U.S. or serve in the armed forces. Three casinos provide income, and the tribally owned Sisseton-Wahpeton Oyate Plastics company has been producing film, sheeting, and biodegradable, compostable trash can liners since 2005.

Sisseton–Wahpeton has an extensive fish and wildlife program that surveys and manages waterfowl and game and stocks tribal waters, pond-rearing, and relocating predator fish to larger lakes to maintain diverse fisheries. Tribal communications include the *Sota Iya Ye Yapi* newspaper, and the SWO Language Institute is compiling a dictionary, which was created with help from elders of the tribe.

The community is involved in Idle No More antiracist sports mascot rallies in Minneapolis as well as marches in Rapid City to protest police killings of Native Americans. Additionally, SWO supports the Wokiksuye Memorial Ride, an annual healing event honoring the Dakota people executed after the Dakota Conflict in 1862 (see also the chapter titled "Northern Plains" [section "Crow Creek"]).

Santee Sioux Nation

Tribal enrollment in the Santee Sioux Nation is roughly 2,750, with about 730 living on the

184-square-mile reservation along the Missouri River in northeast Nebraska. Nearly all of the Santee are directly related to the victims of the Dakota Conflict of 1862 (see also the chapter titled "Midwest"). The community is bordered on the north by Lewis and Clark Lake. During construction of the Gavins Point Dam, begun in 1952, flooding that created the lake permanently submerged much of the nation's rich pastureland.

The village of Santee is about a hundred miles from Sioux City, Iowa. Tribal government and Ohiya Casino, the first in Nebraska, are the largest employers; farming and ranching provide some people with a livelihood, but 47 percent of the Santee live below the poverty line.

The Dakota Tiwahe Service Unit (DTSU) offers family programs, such as Fatherhood is Sacred and Teachings of a Horse Nation, which accesses horse skills as therapy for tribal youth. DTSU, which also provides social services, including a domestic violence shelter, is led by Misty Thomas, who, in 2011, was named a "Champion of Change" as part of President Obama's Winning the Future initiative.

Spirit Lake Tribe Nation

The Mni Wakan Oyate of the Sisseton–Wahpeton Dakota (formerly Devils Lake Sioux) reside on the Fort Totten Reservation in north-central North Dakota on the southern shores of Devils Lake. Of 6,700 members, about six thousand live on the 245,120-acre reservation, approximately one-quarter of which is owned by the tribe or by individual members. Flooding from the rising waters of Devils Lake is a challenge; a $70 million FEMA project to reinforce roads acting as dams (RAADS) was begun in 2010.

The Dakota of Spirit Lake are descended from the Wahpeton and the Sisseton. After the Dakota Conflict of 1862, the Sisseton–Wahpeton moved west and settled near Spirit Lake. Some fled to Canada, and Spirit Lake Dakota visit those communities for ceremonies.

Isolated from population centers, unemployment is forty-six percent. Some employment

is available at Sioux Manufacturing Company, which makes Kevlar panels for the U.S. Department of Defense and has been tribally owned for more than thirty years. Some gaming revenue has been invested in Spirit Lake Consulting, founded in 2006 to provide tribal leaders and community members from across the U.S. with courses and workshops in ethical behavior, as traditional Dakotas had strong prohibitions against lying and stealing. Cankdeska Cikana Community College was established in the 1970s to provide employment readiness and to strengthen Dakota culture and language.

The Yankton and Yanktonai Sioux

Oral history has it that in 1804, Meriwether Lewis visited an Ihanktowan Dakota village when he heard that a baby boy had recently been born. Lewis wrapped the baby in an American flag and declared him to be an American. The baby grew up to become the famous chief Struck by the Ree, who worked tirelessly to keep his tribe's land by

Hand-sewn star quilts are popular gift items on the Plains.

traveling to Washington for months in 1857 to negotiate treaties. Despite his efforts, by 1860, the Yankton tribe had ceded all of its land to the U.S. government.

Today, the forty-thousand-acre Yankton Reservation is part of Charles Mix County in southeastern South Dakota, with tribal offices in Wagner. Of approximately 11,600 members, about 3,500 live in the area, speak the Dakota language, and maintain a free-roaming buffalo herd. Fort Randall Casino is the largest employer. Yankton Sioux continue to fight TransCanada's KXL crude oil pipeline. They have been joined by other tribes in this resistance.

Ioway Tribe of Kansas and Nebraska

The Northern Ioway tribe, based in White Cloud, Kansas, is dedicated to the preservation and continuation of cultural knowledge related to the environment, stories, language, songs, and dances. They operate a casino.

Kickapoo Tribe of Kansas

The 19,200-acre Kickapoo Reservation is roughly five miles west of Horton, Kansas. Tribal enrollment was reported at 1,653 as of December 2006. The Kickapoo was the first tribe in northeast Kansas to enter into a compact for gaming, and Golden Eagle Casino is the largest employer in Brown County. In 1981, the Kickapoo Nation School opened, teaching the traditional alphabet and language as part of its K-12 curriculum.

The community's sole source of water is the Delaware River, and people rely on an inadequate 1970s-era water treatment plant. In periods of drought, the river dries to a trickle, and water has to be trucked in. Fire protection and home-building efforts have been hampered (for more information on the Kickapoo, see the Southern Plains chapter).

Mandan, Hidatsa, and Arikara Nation (MHA)

The nation formerly known as the Fort Berthold Three Affiliated Tribes has its headquar-

ters in New Town, North Dakota. New Town was "new" in 1947 after the U.S. Army Corps of Engineers flooded 152,360 acres, 94 percent of MHA homeland, to build Garrison Dam on the Missouri River in north-central North Dakota. The dam created Lake Sakakewea but drowned ancestral villages, graveyards, and prime grazing and farmland forever. The tribe was coerced to accept a $7 million settlement, and despite protests, about 1,700 residents were relocated, some to New Town.

Today's MHA land base is 980,000 acres, less than half of which is in tribal or individually allotted ownership. Estimated enrollment is 10,250, with about 4,050 on the reservation. According to oral history, the Mandan, Hidatsa, and Arikara have always been separate but affiliated Siouan-speaking peoples.

Sacagawea was a Shoshone captive living among the Hidatsa when she was purchased at age thirteen by the Quebecois trapper Toussaint Charbonneau to be his wife. Lewis and Clark engaged the pregnant Sacagawea as a guide and interpreter for their journey west in 1804. On their return through Mandan and Hidatsa villages on the Knife River in 1806, Lewis and Clark left Sacagawea with the Hidatsa (see also the chapter titled "The Great Basin and Rocky Mountains").

Four Bears Casino and Lodge overlooks Lake Sacagawea, and seasonal revenue is generated by activities for visitors, such as golfing, horseback riding, fishing, and yachting. News is provided by radio station KMHA and the *MHA Times*.

Northern Cheyenne Nation

Tsetsehesestahase/so'taahe means "The Beautiful People." The 444,000-acre Northern Cheyenne reservation is located near Busby, in southern Montana. Of the approximately 10,840 tribal members, about 4,940 live on the reservation. Most employment is in tribal schools and offices although there are some jobs in construction, power companies, farming, and ranching.

Chief Dull Knife College is involved in strengthening language and traditions, and the college's John Woodenlegs Library is open to the pub-

Chief Dull Knife College in Lame Deer, Montana, has programs and resources to promote Native tongues and traditions.

lic. Clown dances are held during the Labor Day powwow, and later in September, the college hosts Cheyenne heritage days with crafts, games, races, dancing, and singing, followed by the All Nations Indian Relay Championship, which celebrates the Horse Nation. The Northern Cheyenne Chamber of Commerce in Lame Deer and the Cheyenne Indian Museum at St. Labre Indian School are good places to buy Cheyenne arts and crafts.

Omaha Tribe of Nebraska

The Omaha people, originally from the Ohio Valley, migrated to the upper Missouri area of the Plains by the late seventeenth century. The Omaha are proud to have been the first nation to domesticate wild horses and to have never battled with the United States although tribal members did fight for the Union during the Civil War.

At the center of Omaha spirituality is the Sacred Pole (Umo'ho'ti), considered to be a living being and carved of cottonwood in their original homeland. During pressure to assimilate to white culture in 1888, the Omaha anthropologist Francis La Flesche arranged for the Sacred Pole to be sent to Harvard University's Peabody Museum for safekeeping. The La Flesches are a prominent Omaha family whose members include Susan La Flesche, the first Native American woman doctor to practice modern medicine in the early 1900s. One hundred years later, when the museum agreed to return the pole to the Omaha tribe in 1889, tribal members initiated an annual celebration that is held during their August powwow.

All culturally relevant affairs are overseen by the Omaha Tribal Historical Research Project, including the New Moon Moving interpretive center and museum, which is under development. In August 2015, the Omaha will hold their 211th Umonhon Hedawachi Harvest Celebration in Macy, Nebraska. Macy is the tribal center of the 307,474-acre reservation, which about 5,430 Omaha people call home.

The Plains Chippewa

"Chippewa," a mispronunciation of Ojibwe, is the legal name for those who traveled north of Lake Superior in the early 1700s (see also the chapter titled "Midwest") and intermarried with Cree people and French fur trappers. Their descendants, called Métis or Mitchif, have had a difficult time accessing treaty rights both in the U.S. and Canada.

Most of the Chippewa in North Dakota and Montana are descended from the Pembina Chippewa, traders and middlemen on the Red River of the North and its tributaries on the border of North Dakota and Minnesota. The Little Shell Chippewa of Pembina continue to be denied federal acknowledgment as late as June 2013 on the basis that, as Métis, they have not been recognized as a continuous tribe for the past century. One of the reasons for this identity crisis is that the U.S. government was determined to expel "Canadian Indians" in the late nineteenth century. Another is that Chippewa who were hunting buffalo in points west when enrollment lists were drawn up were not considered to be entitled to land. At this time, there were more than five thousand Chippewa in Montana who had no home to return to.

There are many landless Chippewa who were excluded from recognition in retribution for the Riel Rebellion, led by Métis leader Louis Riel (see also his biography below). Most of those groups who were part of the rebellion did not receive land although after much struggle, Chief Stone Child's band was given a reservation near Le Havre in 1910. Rocky Boy's Chippewa–Cree Tribe (Rocky Boy is a mistranslation of Stone Child) is the only Chippewa–Cree reservation in Montana.

Rocky Boy's Chippewa–Cree Tribe

The Chippewa Cree in Box Elder, Montana, call themselves Annishinabe Ne-I-Yah-Wahk, "Those Who Speak the Same Language." Of a total membership of 6,180, about 2,500 people live on the 122,000-acre reservation near the Canadian border in the Bear Paw Mountains. The tribe owns a resort called the Ski Bowl and is working to develop natural resources to provide more employment. Vivid floral Chippewa–Cree beadwork is in high demand and brings income to craftspeople. Stone Child College offers two-year associate's degree programs in the arts and sciences.

Turtle Mountain Band of Chippewa Indians

The Turtle Mountain Chippewa community is located in Belcourt, North Dakota, in the far north-central part of the state, near the International Peace Garden. Estimated tribal enrollment is 30,100, and the trust land base is 79,176 acres. The original reservation encompassed twenty townships and was reduced to two townships in 1884. The overcrowded territory was soon depleted of game, and Chief Little Shell spent the rest of his life during the 1890s trying to restore the land base and bring home those Chippewa who had been excluded while buffalo hunting in Montana.

Traditions remain strong on Turtle Mountain. The tribe operates the Fifth Generation Chemical Dependence Program to help people recover from drug and alcohol addiction. The Turtle Mountain Tribal Arts Association Art Gallery in Belcourt features authentic artwork by tribal members to em-

power them to become successful entrepreneurs. The novelist Louise Erdrich is a tribal member who has written many award-winning books depicting the historical and present-day lives of her Turtle Mountain characters.

Ponca Tribe

The Ponca Tribe's central office is in Niobara, Nebraska, but the tribe does not have a contiguous land base, as their ninety-six-acre reservation (reduced from their original 2.3-million-acre territory) was given to the Sioux in the Fort Laramie Treaty of 1868. The tribe was ordered to move to Indian Territory, but the chiefs did not like what they saw there. When their petition to return north was denied, most Ponca remained in Oklahoma, but a small group led by Chief Standing Bear returned home. There, they were arrested; however, the trial of Standing Bear resulted in the acknowledgment of the tribe's right to remain in Nebraska.

During the 1950s, the Ponca Tribe was terminated and not reinstated until 1990 (see also the chapter titled "Historical Overview" [section "Termination (1950s)"]. Five offices in Nebraska, South Dakota, and Iowa deliver services to about 2,800 scattered tribal members. The Ponca Tribe's goal is to consolidate their landholdings and protect their right of self-government.

Prairie Band Potawatomi Nation

The Potawatomi Nation in Jackson County, Kansas, has nearly five thousand members, with about seven hundred living on the reservation. The tribal council addresses sovereignty as a means of security, maintaining customs, promoting harmony, and educational, cultural, and economic development, with the purpose of respecting all members' views. In 2015, five of the seven tribal council members were women.

The Land Management Development Department oversees 31,633 of the tribe's 77,400 acres. Projects include a farming program rotating corn and bean crops and a two-hundred-head buffalo herd. Selling hay provides income, and controlled burning rejuvenates pastures and creates healthy grasslands.

It is believed that fewer than twenty-five Native speakers of Potawatomi remain. Language preservation efforts now include use of the Phraselator, which digitally converts spoken English words into Potawatomi. In 1997, the Potawatomi partnered with Harrah's Corporation to open the Prairie Band Casino, which is now Jackson County's largest employer. Within ten years, the nation took over operations from Harrah's and has repurchased tribal lands, including 128 acres of original homeland in Illinois, and has contributed to programs on and off the reservation (see also the chapter titled "Midwest").

Winnebago Tribe of Nebraska

The Nebraska Winnebago were part of the Ho-Chunk Nation residing in Wisconsin (see also the chapter titled "Midwest"). After several nineteenth-century removals to unsuitable locations where the local tribes did not welcome the Winnebago, the Omaha offered them half of their reservation in Thurston County, Nebraska. Part of the reservation lies in Iowa. Two-thirds of that land was lost to allotment, and today, many of the 120,000 acres are leased to non-Indians. In 1975, the tribe won a land claim settlement of $4.6 million, sixty-five percent of which was allocated to tribal programs, while thirty-five percent went to individual payments.

Currently, about three thousand tribal members live on the reservation, and this population is expected to double by 2040 due to a high birth rate and a young population. Forty-four percent of the Winnebago live below the poverty level, but volunteering in the tribe's Buffalo Project keeps young people's spirits up and connects them to the Buffalo Clan Feast Society of the past. Traditional culture is also on display at the Angel Decora Memorial Cultural Center and during the Homecoming Powwow in July.

As the community suffers from high unemployment and poor health, especially diabetes, the Buffalo Project was initiated in the mid-1990s to restore grasslands that had been overgrazed by cattle and to provide a traditional food that helps prevent diabetes. The tribe's two casinos fund a college, where students can study traditional language and culture although currently only about ten percent of the tribal members speak Hocak. Most Nebraska Winnebago are Christian or attend Native American Church ceremonies, which blend Christianity with pan-Native spirituality.

TYING IT UP

Modern reservation life on the Northern Plains is the result of change and continuity, reflecting the ability of Plains Indians to accommodate outsiders without surrendering their cultural heritage. As a result, Plains cultures endure because many tribal members work together as communities to improve life for everyone. Since the 1970s, many Plains tribes have revived the traditional Sun Dance or adopted new versions. The peyote religion, or Native American

The emblem of the Native American Church

Church, also attracts many members among Plains communities. Many powwows retain sacred dances as well as more social and public dances. Traditional giveaway ceremonies are carried out at many powwows. The giveaways affirm friendship ties with members of other Native communities. Urban Indians maintain their cultural ties by either returning to the reservations to take part in the annual ceremonies and powwows or by participating in social activities at urban Indian centers. Many sacred ceremonies and significant aspects of the Plains culture remain strong. Yes, there are legitimate struggles in Native communities, but there are also numerous grassroots organizations, many of them led by Native women, that are working hard to find solutions and bring hope. Plains Indian culture is alive and well.

BIOGRAPHIES

Black Kettle (1803–1868)
Southern Cheyenne, Leader

A Cheyenne leader whose band was attacked in the Sand Creek Massacre in 1864, Black Kettle advocated peace with the Americans and had met with President Abraham Lincoln and the governor of Colorado for negotiations before the massacre. In 1867, he signed a treaty at Medicine Lodge accepting a reservation in Oklahoma. In their new location, in 1867, Black Kettle and his followers were ambushed on the Washita River by Major General Philip Sheridan's troops. One year later, Lieutenant Colonel George Armstrong Custer attacked the Cheyenne on their reservation. Back Kettle and his wife rode out in a blinding snowstorm, hoping to parley with the soldiers, but they were shot dead on sight, and their bodies were trampled by the advancing columns. The regimental band played "Garry Owen" as Custer and his men killed another one hundred Cheyenne, mostly women and children.

Struck by the Ree (1804–1888)
Yanktonai Nakota, Leader

In 1862, during the Dakota Conflict in Minnesota, Struck by the Ree's warriors protected white settlers from attacking Indians, yet his people were exiled from Minnesota after the conflict. In 1865, he reported during the Doolittle Commission investigation of Indian agent fraud that agents commonly took Indian monies and supplies for themselves while illegally charging Indians for rations guaranteed by treaty. According to Nabokov's *Native American Testimony*, Struck by the Ree also reported that drunken frontier soldiers desecrated corpses, burned houses and fields, and demanded sex from Native women: "The women, being hungry, will sleep with them in order to get something to eat and will get a bad disease and then the women go to their husbands and give them the bad disease."

Struck by the Ree's living descendants include Dr. Leonard Bruguier, a respected Native American ethnologist and educator, as well as the musical LaRoche family, who are currently members of the award-winning rock opera band Brulé.

Dull Knife (1810–1883; shown at right) and Little Wolf
(c. 1820–1904; shown at left)
Northern Cheyenne, Military Leaders

During the wars for the Plains (1864–1877), Dull Knife and Little Wolf were notoriously skilled fighters who evaded capture. In 1876, Dull Knife survived General George Crook's attack on his camp on the Powder River in Wyoming but was forced to surrender to relocation of his people to Fort Robinson in Indian Territory (Oklahoma). Dull Knife and Little Wolf led an escape of nearly three hundred people, who fled 1,500 miles to their homeland on the Tongue River in Montana, evading some ten thousand soldiers for six weeks. Sick and starving, the Cheyenne were taken again to Fort Robinson in October 1878.

Dull Knife led his followers on another breakout in January 1879, but only he, his wife, and a few young family members survived the trip to Red Cloud's village on the Pine Ridge Reservation in South Dakota. After Dull Knife's death, the Cheyenne were granted a reservation (1884) in their Montana homeland.

Little Wolf partnered with Dull Knife to drive U.S. soldiers from the Bozeman Trail in 1868 and was active in the occupation and burning of Fort Phil Kearny. During the War for the Black Hills, Little Wolf survived seven gunshot wounds at the Battle of Dull Knife in 1877. After the flight from Oklahoma with Dull Knife, Little Wolf eluded capture for a year after his compatriot surrendered. He became an army scout for General Nelson Miles and was able to remain in his native Montana, but in 1880, he killed another Cheyenne and lost his standing as chief. Little Wolf died in voluntary exile.

Red Cloud (Makhpiya-Luta) (1822–1909)
Oglala Lakota, Chief

Red Cloud was a respected warrior and statesman. From 1866–1868, he successfully led the fight to close off the Bozeman Trail, which passed through the Lakota's, Cheyenne's, and Arapaho's prime buffalo-hunting grounds. Revenge for the murders of about 150 unarmed Cheyenne at Sand Creek in 1864 may also have played a role. At Fort Laramie in 1866, Red Cloud refused to sign a nonaggression treaty and declared war on all non-Indians entering the region.

Red Cloud designed guerilla-like attacks against settlers and miners who were traveling the wagon trails west. In 1866, the Sioux decimated Captain William Fetterman's regiment of eighty-one men, and Indian victories at battles including the Wagon Box Fight and the Hayfield Fight led the army to evacuate the region in 1868 and relinquish the Bozeman Trail. The Sioux cel-

ebrated this announcement by burning every abandoned fort along the trail.

In 1870, Red Cloud traveled to Washington, D.C., to meet with President Ulysses S. Grant to mediate peaceful relations. Once settled at Pine Ridge, Red Cloud worked to establish a Jesuit-run school for Indian children. He is buried on a hill overlooking the Red Cloud Indian School, which was named in his honor.

Big Foot (Spotted Elk, Hehaka Gleska) (c. 1820–1890)
Minneconjou Lakota, Leader

Spotted Elk (Hehaka Gleska) was the name the Minneconjou leader was known by before he took the name Big Foot. He was dedicated to diplomacy with the whites as well as peaceful mediation between tribes. A traditionalist, he advocated some assimilation to the dominating culture, including farming, and was the first Lakota farmer to grow corn successfully. Big Foot was killed, along with some 350 of his people, during the Wounded Knee Massacre in 1890. The last of Sitting Bull's band, they had sought protection at Pine Ridge Agency in South Dakota; they had allowed themselves to be disarmed and were flying white flags of surrender when the soldiers opened fire (see also the section titled "The Plains Indian Resistance" in this chapter).

Standing Bear (Mochunozhi) (1830–1908)
Ponca, Chief

A principal chief who resisted relocation from Nebraska to Oklahoma, Standing Bear lost one-third of his tribe, along with two of his own children, to disease and hunger once they arrived. Accompanied by thirty followers, he set out to return his son's body to Ponca homelands for burial. They were spotted by whites and, fearing an uprising, General George Crook issued an arrest order. They were taken to Omaha, where the landmark Trial of Standing Bear took place. Although federal attorneys argued that Indians were not legally persons under the U.S. Constitution and therefore had no rights, federal judge Elmer Dundy ruled against the attorneys. Standing Bear's party was allowed to continue. Sympathy grew for the Ponca, and with Omaha activist Susette La Flesche, Standing Bear went on a lecture tour. She published a book about him in 1894. Congress granted the Ponca land in Nebraska in 1880, and when he died at the age of eighty, Standing Bear was buried within his homeland.

Sitting Bull (Tatanka Iyotanka) (1831–1890)

Hunkpapa Lakota, Leader

 Sitting Bull was a spiritual leader who came of age during wartime in the mid-1880s, so he became a military leader by necessity. At age twenty-two, he led a warrior society known as the Strong Hearts and went on to mastermind victories in the War for the Black Hills, the Battle of the Rosebud, and at Little Bighorn (see also the section titled "Plains Indian Resistance" in this chapter). In 1876, the U.S. government ordered all hunting bands to report to reservation agencies. It was an impossible situation for Sitting Bull, who was forced to prepare for all-out battle with the army.

To resist capture in the Bighorn Valley, in January 1876, Sitting Bull called together 12,000-15,000 Native fighters in the largest concentration of Plains Indians ever assembled in response to U.S. forces. In June 1877, they defeated General George Crook at the Battle of the Rosebud, and eight days later, they wiped out General George A. Custer's regiment.

After the victories, the large, Native encampment dispersed into small bands since there was not enough food and grazing land to sustain them all in one place. The U.S. increased its military presence and forced many Sioux to surrender. Sit-

ting Bull and his followers escaped to Canada, but the Canadian government offered no refuge, and supplies were low. He surrendered on July 19, 1881, at Fort Buford, North Dakota, where he was held prisoner for two years before being allowed to settle on the Standing Rock Reservation. He continued to oppose assimilation into U.S. culture and promoted the Ghost Dance (see also the chapter titled "The Great Basin and Rocky Mountains"). Sitting Bull was killed by government-paid Indian police in October 1990 over a dispute surrounding a Ghost Dance ceremony.

American Horse (1840–1876)

Oglala Lakota, Leader

 In the 1860s and 1870s, American Horse was a leader in Red Cloud's War, which was fought for control of the Bozeman Trail. He was a cousin of Red Cloud and until his death remained an opponent to U.S. settlement of the western Plains.

In 1870, American Horse accompanied Red Cloud to Washington, D.C., for a meeting with government officials, but diplomatic relations were short-lived. In 1874, after gold was discovered in the sacred Black Hills of the Lakota, miners streamed in. American Horse participated in the War for the Black Hills and the Battle of Little Bighorn, both in 1876. He was captured at the Battle of Slim Buttes later that year. Although Sitting Bull and Gall attempted to rescue American Horse, he had been badly wounded and, refusing medical treatment from his captors, died from his injuries.

Gall (Pizi) (1840–1894)

Hunkpapa Lakota, Military Strategist

 An orphan adopted by Sitting Bull, Gall proved his abilities as a warrior early in life. During the skirmishes for control of the Bozeman Trail, he honed the decoy tactics and guerrilla

techniques that would be effective in the War for the Black Hills. As Sitting Bull's chief military strategist in the Battle of Little Bighorn in 1876, Gall's prowess played a major role in the victory.

After the defeats following Little Bighorn and his flight to Canada with Sitting Bull, Gall surrendered at the Poplar Agency in eastern Montana. He was relocated to the Standing Rock Reservation, where he befriended Indian agent James McLaughlin and adopted white ways. He became unpopular with other Lakota people after negotiating treaties that further divided their lands and refusing to join the Ghost Dance. In a gesture of rejection by another veteran of the wars for the Plains, Kicking Bear omitted Gall's portrait from a famous pictographic version of Custer's defeat.

Louis David Riel, Jr. (1844–1885)
Métis, Leader

Leader of the Northwest Rebellions of 1870 and 1885, Riel was born to a French–Ojibwe father, Louis Riel, Sr., a political leader, and a French mother, Juliette Lagimodere, in the Red River settlement in what is now Manitoba. After graduating from a Montreal seminary school, he went on to study law.

After traveling throughout the United States, Riel returned to the Red River in 1868 and participated in the first resistance to drive off federal surveyors, who planned to section Métis lands into townships. Riel's Comité National de Métis peacefully seized Fort Garry in Winnipeg, took numerous prisoners, and declared a provisional government in 1869. His execution of a prisoner turned locals against him, so Riel fled to the U.S. shortly after his government reached an agreement with Canada to create the province of Manitoba.

Riel was elected twice in absentia to the Canadian Parliament, returning once to claim his seat, only to be evicted by a motion of the House of Commons. He suffered a nervous breakdown and was confined to a mental institution for a short time. Upon his release in 1878, Riel moved to Montana, where he became an American citizen, married, and worked as a school teacher. He returned to Canada to help lead Métis resistance to the settlement of Saskatchewan in 1884, seizing a local church and establishing another provisional, all-Indigenous government. Riel was convicted of treason and executed by the Canadian government in 1885. Some Cree, Ojibwe, and Métis descendants of Northwest Rebellion veterans live in northern Montana (see also the section titled "The Plains Chippewa" in this chapter).

Kicking Bear (1853–1904)
Miniconjou/Oglala Lakota, Leader

A cousin of Crazy Horse and nephew of Sitting Bull, Kicking Bear fought alongside his relatives in several of the wars for the Plains, including Little Bighorn in 1876. In 1889, he and other Lakota met the Paiute prophet Wovoka in Nevada, where the visitors observed a Ghost Dance (see also the chapter titled "The Great Basin and Rocky Mountains"). Kicking Bear advocated for the religion, which promised to return deceased relatives as well as the buffalo to the living and that the whites would disappear. He brought the Ghost Dance to the Standing Rock Reservation, where Sitting Bull became a follower. Soldiers and settlers near the reservation felt threatened by the dance; subsequently, Indian Agent James McLaughlin expelled Kicking Bear from the reservation.

Mistakenly suspected of performing the Ghost Dance, Chief Big Foot's band was massacred at Wounded Knee on the Pine Ridge Reservation (see also the section titled "Plains Indian Resistance" in this chapter). Kicking Bear continued the dance at White Clay on Pine Ridge, causing General Nelson A. Miles to invade Kicking Bear's camp and demand residents to disarm. The surrender of about five thousand Sioux on January 15, 1891, officially ended the Indian Wars in the U.S. Kicking Bear went on to join Buffalo Bill Cody's Wild West Show.

Susette La Flesche (1854–1903)
Omaha, Activist/Teacher

Known by her traditional Omaha name, Bright Eyes (Inshata Theumba), La Flesche worked for women's and Native rights. Her father was Chief Joseph Iron Eye La Flesche, and she was a stepsister of Francis La Flesche, the famous Omaha anthropologist. Her sister, Susan La Flesche Picotte, was the first modern female Native doctor in the U.S., and her home on the Omaha reservation is a historical site. As a young school teacher, Susette La Flesche became involved in publicizing the plight of the Poncas in 1877, organizing a speaking tour of the eastern U.S. with Chief Standing Bear to protest the seizure of Ponca land in Nebraska. In 1894, she and her philanthropist husband edited *The Weekly Independent,* a populist newspaper in Lincoln, and that year, with Standing Bear, she authored *Ploughed Under: The Story of an Indian Chief.*

Charles Eastman (Ohiyesa) (1858–1939)
Isanti Dakota, Physician

Dr. Eastman was four years old when his family fled to Canada to escape the violence in Minnesota during the Dakota Conflict of 1862. His father was captured and sentenced to hang but was pardoned by President Abraham Lincoln and sent to prison instead. Eastman wrote two autobiographies, *Indian Boyhood* (1902) and *From the Deep Woods to Civilization* (1916), as well as many books on Dakota culture. In his autobiographies, he chronicles the years before contact with non-Indians at age fifteen up through his education at Boston University and his many professional jobs, including the founding of the Boy Scouts of America and the Campfire Girls, and his career as a medical doctor on reservations. His presence at the Pine Ridge Reservation at the time of the Wounded Knee Massacre (1890) makes his narrative particularly valuable as a historical record. Throughout his life, Eastman worked to further the cause of Native Americans, including more than twenty years spent lobbying to reinstate his people's (the Santee Sioux's) treaty rights, which were taken from them after the Dakota Conflict of 1862.

Nicholas Black Elk (Hchaka Sapa) (1863–1950)
Oglala Lakota, Spiritual Leader

Black Elk Speaks (a collaboration with John Neihardt, published in 1932) is one of the best known as-told-to Native autobiographies and has attracted a large mainstream audience over the years. The spiritual leader Black Elk was an eleven-year-old eyewitness to Custer's invasion of the Black Hills and, as a young man, participated in the Battle of Little Bighorn. Collaborators often impose their narrative structure on Native texts, and scholars question the extent of their editorial intrusion. However, Neihardt was a poet who managed to capture Black Elk's visionary oration in a book that Vine Deloria, Jr., called "a religious classic."

Luther Standing Bear (c. 1868–1939)
Oglala Lakota, Actor/Activist

Inspired by hearing Sitting Bull speak in Philadelphia in 1884, young Carlisle Indian School student Luther Standing Bear was inspired to continue his education and to tour Europe with Buffalo Bill's Wild West Show in 1902. He was determined to glean anything of value from white culture while maintaining the Lakota traditions of his youth. Later in life, Standing Bear began writing, with the editorial help of E. A. Brinstool, acting in movies, lecturing, and participating in Native political causes. He was an eloquent critic of Euro-American society and wrote to President Franklin Roosevelt in 1933, requesting that Native American studies be included in school curricula. Standing Bear published four autobiographical books, including *My Indian Boyhood* (1931) and *Land of the Spotted Eagle* (1933). He died on the set of the film *Union Pacific*.

Angel De Cora Dietz (c. 1871–1919)
Winnebago, Activist/Artist

 Descended from a long line of Winnebago leaders, Dietz was a well-known activist and artist who bore the traditional names Floating Fleecy Cloud (Hinookmahiwi-Kilinaka) and The Word Carrier. A graduate of Smith College, Dietz continued her artistic studies at Drexel Institute and the Boston Museum of Fine Arts School. She was the director of the Leupp Art Department at Carlisle Indian School from 1906 to 1915, where she encouraged traditional Native visual expression in modern media at a time when this was not popular. Allied with the author Gertrude Simmons Bonnin in Native rights causes, she illustrated several of Bonnin's books. As a professional illustrator, Dietz illustrated Francis La Fleishe's *The Middle Five,* Natalie Curtis's *The Indian's Book,* and Elaine Goodall Eastman's *Yellow Star,* among others. She was a member of the Society of American Indians and a frequent lecturer on Native art who also met with President Theodore Roosevelt to bring his attention to the quality of life on reservations.

Gertrude Simmons Bonnin (Zitkala Sa, Red Bird) (1876–1938)
Nakota, Musician/Author

 After attending a Quaker missionary school for Indians in Wabash, Indiana, Gertrude Simmons Bonnin won prizes for her oratorical skills at Earlham College. She then studied at the Boston Conservatory of music and performed as a violin soloist at the Paris Exposition in 1900. During this time, her stories and essays were printed in the *Atlantic Monthly* and *Harper's Monthly.* Her book *Old Indian Legends* was published in 1901.

Bonnin was elected secretary of the Society of American Indians, the first policy reform organization managed exclusively by Indians, and moved to Washington, D.C., permanently. She spent her career liaising with the Office of Indian Affairs, lecturing from coast to coast, and editing *The American Indian Magazine.* She organized the National Council of American Indians in 1929 and, as the council's president, lobbied in Washington of behalf of Indian legislation. Bonnin continued to publish stories and to perform music; one of her final achievements was composing the Indian opera *Sun Dance* with William F. Hanson.

Henry Roe Cloud (Wonah'ilay-Hunka) (1884–1950)
Winnebago, Educator

 Educator Roe Cloud established the first college preparatory school for American Indians and later served as the first Native superintendent of Haskell Institute in Lawrence, Kansas. As a young man, he changed his Winnebago name, meaning "War Chief," to an English name borrowed from the Reverend Walter Roe, an early influence. In 1910, Roe Cloud was the first Native American student to graduate from Yale. The American Indian Institute, founded by Roe Cloud in 1915, was the first alternative to vocational school for young men. For many years, he worked with his wife Elizabeth Bender Roe Cloud (sister of baseball pitcher Charles Bender) at the National Congress of American Indians and the Society of American Indians. In 1926, as the only Native member of the Institute for Governmental Research (later renamed the Brookings Institute), Roe Cloud helped document the Merriam Report, an investigation

into the terrible conditions on Indian reservations, which helped bring about some positive changes. After working with the BIA for several years, Roe Cloud died on the Umatilla Reservation in Oregon, where he was superintendent.

Minnie Evans (Kewahtnoquah Wishkeno) (1888–1971)
Potawatomi, Leader

Evans had an eventful thirty-five-year career as an advocate for the Prairie Band Potawatomi in Kansas. Elected tribal chairwoman in 1946, she applied wisdom and common sense, rather than a formal education, to become a dedicated expert in Indian law. She fought for her tribe's ten complicated treaty claims during the 1940s and successfully resisted Termination in the 1950s, fundraising for trips to Washington, D.C., to negotiate tenaciously at congressional committee and Senate hearings. BIA officials were disgruntled by Evans and nicknamed her the "Potawatomi Agitator," but she persevered. After a thirty-two-year process of filing nineteen claims cases, the Potawatomi were awarded a multimillion-dollar settlement in the early 1960s. Although the payment amounted to about twenty-five cents an acre for land seized in Illinois and Wisconsin in the 1840s, the money was much needed on the isolated reservation, which had been devoid of natural resources and employment opportunities for more than a century.

Ella Cara Deloria (Anpetu Waste Win, Good Woman of the Day) (1889–1971)
Yankton Dakota, Anthropologist/Linguist/Author

The anthropologist, linguist, and author Ella Cara Deloria was born in Wakpala, South Dakota, and given the name Good Woman of the Day. The daughter of a popular Episcopalian minister, Deloria graduated from Columbia University in 1915. As a professor of anthropology at Columbia beginning in 1929, she wrote *Dakota Texts* (1932), a bilingual book in Dakota and English, and

Speaking of Indians (1944), an exploration of precontact life. Deloria collaborated with the anthropologist Franz Boas at Columbia to write two respected books on the Dakota language. Her novel about traditional Dakota girlhood, *Waterlily* (1988), was published after her death.

Ben Reifel (1906–1990)
Brulé Lakota, Politician

A five-term U.S. congressman from South Dakota, Reifel was born on the Rosebud Reservation to a German father and a Lakota mother. When his father barred Reifel from attending high school, as he was needed on the farm, Reifel began reading voraciously and eventually ran away from home to enroll at a high school 250 miles away. After graduating from South Dakota State University in 1932, he served in the U.S. Army during World War II, was appointed BIA superintendent of the Fort Berthold Agency in North Dakota, and received a doctoral degree in public administration from Harvard University. Upon his return to South Dakota, Reifel administered several BIA offices and was eventually appointed area director in Aberdeen. Reifel ran for Congress in 1960 as a Republican and served until his retirement in 1971.

Oscar Howe (1915–1983)
Yanktonai Nakota, Artist

Howe pioneered a new era in Indian art, using modernist techniques to express traditional subjects. He was born on the Crow Creek Reservation, attended BIA boarding school in Pierre, South Dakota, from the age of seven, and graduated from Santa Fe Indian School in 1938. Abandoning the stereotypical "Indian art" Santa Fe aesthetic in the 1950s, Howe's mature work, done mainly in gouache and casein on watercolor paper, features abstraction, bright color, and clean, dynamic lines. Throughout his life, Howe exhibited internationally and received many honors and awards, including the title Artist Laureate of South Dakota in 1954. Howe left behind a legacy of cultural heritage and pride. More than twenty of his original pieces are on display at the Oscar Howe Art Center in Mitchell, South Dakota.

Elizabeth Cook-Lynn (1930–)
Dakota, Author

Originally famous for poetry, Cook-Lynn is now equally lauded for her fiction and essays. Born on the South Dakota Crow Creek Reservation into a family of scholars and politicians, Cook-Lynn is also a traditional dancer on the powwow circuit. Concerned with the invisibility of Native people in mainstream history texts, she taught Native studies at Eastern Washington University for twenty years before becoming a full-time writer. Her first book, *Then Badger Said This* (1977), was a collection of short stories, poems, and songs inspired by Dakota themes. She addressed legal issues in the novel *From the River's Edge* (1991) and conflicts in academia in *Why I Can't Read Wallace Stegner and Other Essays* (1996). Her most recent book is *A Separate Country: Postcoloniality and American Indian Nations* (2011). The cofounder of *Wicazo Sa (Red Pencil) Review,* an international Native American studies journal, Cook-Lynn received the Lifetime Achievement Award from the Native Writers' Circle of the Americas in 2009.

Vine Deloria, Jr. (1933–2005)
Standing Rock Sioux, Author/Educator

One of Native America's most prominent authors, a social critic, and a respected professor of Native studies, Vine Deloria, Jr., published many books debunking myths about Native Americans and contrasting Native cultural and historical experiences and interpretations with ethnocentric, Euro-American tenets. Beginning in the 1960s, Deloria invoked his trademark sardonic humor to articulate messages of self-determination, metaphysics, and traditional ecology, raising the consciousness of an international audience.

Born in Martin, South Dakota, Deloria served in the Marine Corps, then earned degrees in general science, theology, and law. From 1964–1967, he was executive director of the National Congress of American Indians before becoming a professor of history at the University of Colorado in 1990, where he taught until his retirement in 2000. More than twenty books by Vine Deloria, Jr., were published between 1969 and 2006, including *Custer Died for Your Sins* (1969), *Behind the Trail of Broken Treaties* (1974), *Red Earth: White Lies* (1995), and *Evolution, Creationism and Other Modern Myths* (2002).

Virginia Driving Hawk Sneve (1933–)
Sicangu Lakota, Author/Teacher/Counselor

From the Rosebud Reservation, Sneve earned her bachelor's and master's degrees from South Dakota State University (Brookings). The author of over twenty fiction and nonfiction works on South Dakota history, Indian history, and poetry for children, she has won several awards, including the National Humanities Medal in 2000.

As a mother, Sneve realized that Native Americans were underrepresented in contemporary books and set out to do something about it. She is brilliant at composing works that blend and respect cultures. Her own children are half Norwegian, and she wrote *The Trickster and the Troll,* which brings together the Lakota trickster, Iktomi, and a Norwegian troll. *The Christmas Coat: Memories of My Sioux Childhood* was named in *Smithsonian Magazine's* Best Children's Books of 2011.

Tim Giago (Nanwica Kciji) (1934–)
Oglala Lakota, Journalist/Publisher

Born on the Pine Ridge Reservation, Giago, whose Lakota name means "Defender," began his career as a reporter and columnist for the *Rapid City Journal.* He became owner of the *Lakota Times* and expanded into national news with *Indian Country Today* in 1992. By the time he sold the newspaper to the Oneida Nation in New York in 1998, it was read by fifty thousand people each week and grossed $1.9 million in annual advertising sales. In 2005, *Indian Country Today* was the most influential Native newspaper, sold in fifty states and seventeen countries. Now online as *Indian Country Today Media Network,* the news service covers Native American and Canadian First Nations as well as world news.

Giago has authored three books and won prizes for journalism and human rights work, including the H. L. Mencken Award in 1985, which he returned in 1989 after racist statements in Mencken's papers were revealed. Giago founded the *Native Sun News* in 2009 and is also a columnist for the *Huffington Post.*

Billy Mills (1938–)
Oglala Lakota, Olympian

In 1964, Mills won the ten-thousand-meter race at the Olympic Games in Tokyo. He was the first American ever to win that race, and he did it in record time. Mills, orphaned at the age of twelve, was born on the Pine Ridge Indian Reservation, and he began running to maintain a positive attitude. He accepted an athletic scholarship to the University of Kansas, where he won the Big Eight Conference cross-country championship. After graduation, Mills joined the Marine Corps, and as an officer, he began winning interservice races. The Marines sponsored his Olympic trials, and he joined the team; he remains the only American to win a gold medal in the 10K event. To give back to his community, Mills helped found Running Strong for American Indian Youth and travels three hundred days per year to encourage Native youth to run for their health and cultural pride. In 2012, Mills was awarded the Presidential Citizens Medal by President Barack Obama for his work with Running Strong.

James Welch (1940–2003)
Blackfeet and A'aninin, Author

Welch grew up ensconced in his parents' Blackfeet and A'aninin (Gros Ventre) cultures on the Blackfeet Reservation in Montana. He studied writing and taught at the University of Montana. Welch took his place among the Native American Renaissance writers of his generation, such as N. Scott Momaday and Leslie Silko, when his first novel, *Winter in the Blood* (1974), was reviewed on the front page of the *New York Times Book Review,* prompting the republication of his first book of poetry, *Riding the Earthboy 40* (1971; 1976). *Winter in the Blood* deals with conflicts arising from the colonization. Themes of alienation and loss dominate both works as well as his second novel, *The Death of Jim Loney* (1979). His third novel, *Fools Crow* (1986), won several national book prizes. Along with other novels, he also wrote the Emmy-winning screenplay *Last Stand at Little Bighorn.*

In 2000, he received a Chevalier medal from France and was knighted. *Winter in the Blood* was adapted for the screen and released to critical praise as a film starring Chaske Spencer (Lakota/Nez Perce/Cherokee/Creek) in 2014.

Russell Means (1940–2012)
Oglala–Yankton, Activist

Born in Porcupine, South Dakota, on the Pine Ridge Reservation, Means was director of the Cleveland Indian Center, which later changed its name to Cleveland AIM. In February 1972, an Oglala man, Raymond Yellow Thunder, was beaten, publically humiliated, and died after being locked in a car trunk in Gordon, Nebraska. Means led a caravan of two hundred American Indian Movement supporters to Gordon to demand the arrest of the two perpetrators. He and AIM succeeded in the dismissal of the local police chief and opened a dialogue about race in Nebraska.

One year later, the murder of Wesley Bad Heart Bull led to an altercation between AIM and police at the Custer, South Dakota, courthouse, which turned into a riot. When FBI marshals came to Pine Ridge to enforce security and conduct surveillance, Means, along with several hundred people, occupied the town of Wounded Knee and demanded recognition as a sovereign nation on February 28, 1973. AIM held off hundreds of federal agents for seventy-one days. When it was over, two Indians were dead, and a federal marshal was paralyzed. In 1980, Means served one year in state prison in Sioux Falls, South Dakota. Upon his release, he founded Camp Yellow Thunder in the Black Hills and filed claims for eight hundred acres against the U.S. Forest Service in a case that is still pending.

Means had also been involved in international Indigenous causes. Playing the role of Chingatchgook in *The Last of the Mohicans* in 1992 opened the door to parts in other films, including Disney's *Pocahontas*. He published a biography, *Where White Men Fear to Tread,* in 1995. His son, Tatanka Means, is also a successful actor and comedian.

Leonard Peltier (1944–)
Ojibwe, Activist

An activist working for Indian treaty and civil rights, Peltier figured prominently in the American Indian Movement (AIM). He is now serving two consecutive life sentences in prison after a controversial conviction for killing two Federal Bureau of Investigation (FBI) agents. Born in Grand Forks, North Dakota, Peltier first became involved in AIM in 1970 and soon became part of its inner circle and participated in many of its activities, including the takeover of the Bureau of Indian Affairs' Washington, D.C., offices in the early 1970s.

In 1975, Peltier was living on the Pine Ridge Reservation in South Dakota, which at the time was in a state of civil war between residents, their AIM supporters, and Tribal Chairman Dick Wilson's enforcers. Because of Wilson's agenda to eliminate all political opponents, Pine Ridge was the murder capital of the U.S. at the time. On June 26th, FBI agents Jack Coler and Ronald

Williams and Pine Ridge resident Joe Killsright were killed in a shootout at the Jumping Bull home near Oglala. Leonard Peltier was in the group involved in the shooting exchange. In a disputed trial at Fargo, North Dakota, in which 80 percent of the defense testimony was excluded, Peltier was convicted of the murder of the two agents. Sympathizers, including Amnesty International, consider Leonard Peltier to be a political prisoner of the United States.

John Trudell (1947–)
Santee Dakota, Activist/Broadcaster/Actor

Indians of All Tribes occupied Alcatraz Island in San Francisco Bay from November 20, 1969, until June 11, 1971, in an attempt to attract national attention to the U.S. government's failed Indian policies. Trudell became the occupation's voice through Radio Free Alcatraz, a radio station set up on the island, which broadcast from Berkeley, Los Angeles, and New York City, thus garnering a national audience.

Trudell joined AIM in the spring of 1970 and became a national spokesman, airing AIM's initial concerns about jobs, housing, education, and the protection of Indians from police abuse. He participated in the 1972 Trail of Broken Treaties and became cochair of AIM in 1973, helping to organize the armed seizure of Wounded Knee, a small town in the heart of the Pine Ridge Reservation. Twelve hours after he burned an upside-down American flag in protest during a demonstration in support of Leonard Peltier (see also his biography above), Trudell's wife, mother-in-law, and three children were burned to death in a suspicious house fire on the Duck Valley Shoshone Reservation on February 11, 1979. After this horrific tragedy, Trudell found artistic expression to connect him to reality. He appeared in the documentary films *Incident at Oglala* (1992) and *John Trudell* (2005) and had prominent roles in the feature films *Thunderheart* (1992) and *Smoke Signals*

(1998). He has issued eight albums of spoken word poetry, backed by his rock band Bad Dog.

Janine Pease (1949–)
Crow, Educator/Advocate

 Dr. Pease was the first Crow woman to earn a doctorate degree and has been honored with prestigious awards, including the MacArthur Foundation Fellowship "genius" Award and the ACLU Jeanette Rankin Award. She was also selected as the National Indian Educator of the Year (1990) and named one of the "100 Most Influential Montanans of the Century" by *Missoulian Magazine*. She transformed Little Big Horn Tribal College from a tiny Crow tribal college into a fully accredited junior college, which offers classes taught in the Crow language. Pease (who was then Windy Boy) was the lead plaintiff in a voting rights litigation against Big Horn County (*Windy Boy v. Big Horn County*), which resulted in the first successful Voting Rights Act case on behalf of American Indians.

White Eagle (1951–1995)
Oglala Lakota, Opera Singer

Born on the Rosebud Reservation, White Eagle began singing opera at the age of five after hearing a recording of Mario Lanza. A tenor, he honed his voice by singing in his parents' church and later studied music in New York and San Francisco. In the early 1970s, he began touring with the music group Re-Generations and went on to perform professionally as a classical soloist. White Eagle was the first American Indian to sing lead roles in American musical theater and opera. He graduated from the prestigious Merola Opera Program at the San Francisco Opera in 1985 and performed more than four thousand concerts at venues including the Pennsylvania Opera Theater, Florentine Opera, Cleveland Opera, and Carnegie Hall. In 1989, he was diagnosed with Acquired Immune Deficiency Syndrome (AIDS)

and became an inspiration to many people struggling with the virus. As White Eagle said, "An event is only an event. It is neither good nor bad. It's how you respond to that event that matters." He returned home to Mission in 1994, when he developed AIDS-related dementia, and died one year later in Sioux Falls, South Dakota.

Maria Yellow Horse Braveheart (1953–)
Hunkpapa/Oglala Lakota, Psychologist

In the 1980s, Dr. Maria Yellow Horse Braveheart developed the concept of historical trauma as "the collective emotional and psychological injury, both over the lifespan and across generations, resulting from a cataclysmic history of genocide." Takini is an organization associated with the University of New Mexico in Albuquerque that is devoted to collaborating with Native people and communities to apply Dr. Braveheart's historical trauma intervention model to help them heal from postcolonial stress. Because generations of Indigenous people were exposed to the traumas of genocide, imprisonment, forded assimilation, and institutionalized abuses, they often suffer from identity and cultural losses, poverty, substance, abuse, and despair. Unresolved grief may give rise to anger, sadness, guilt, and shame, and may perpetuate abuse. Dr. Braveheart's healing insights, preventions, and interventions are proving to help Native people and communities recover from historical trauma.

Arvol Looking Horse (1954–)
Lakota, Spiritual Leader

Arvol Looking Horse is the nineteenth-generation keeper of the Sacred Pipe of the Great Sioux Nation, which was given to the Lakota by White Buffalo Calf Woman long ago. He received this responsibility at the age of twelve, when he was living with his grandparents on the Cheyenne River Reservation. The essence of Sioux identity and culture, which Black Elk referred to as the sacred hoop, was thought to have been broken after the massacres, land loss, and destruction of the buffalo herds on the Plains. However, proph-esy also maintains that healing and restoration of Native life will begin in the Seventh Generation after these suppressions. Looking Horse believes his people are living in the time of the Seventh Generation and that his caring for the pipe will help mend the sacred hoop. He refers to the revival of Native languages and cultural practices as a sign of this regeneration. Looking Horse is a frequent speaker at universities, government agencies, and the United Nations and has traveled to Iraq, South Africa, and Tibet to pray for peace. The author of *White Buffalo Teachings* and a columnist for *Indian Country Today*, Arvol Looking Horse is one of the cofounders of the annual Big Foot Unity Rides, which honor the people massacred at Wounded Knee in 1890.

Louise Erdrich (1954–)
Turtle Mountain Chippewa, Author

Early in her career, Erdrich achieved what many writers hope for: Her first novel, *Love Medicine* (1984), became a bestseller. The book launched her career as a member of the second wave of the Native American Renaissance. Set mainly on the Turtle Mountain Chippewa Reservation, the novel weaves together a number of first person narratives and perspectives, including the voice of an omniscient narrator. Many of Erdrich's subsequent novels develop the journeys and connections between familiar characters.

The daughter of a German American father and a Chippewa mother, Louise Erdrich was born in Little Falls, Minnesota, in 1954 and raised in Wahpeton, North Dakota. She was among the first group of Native American women to be recruited and accepted to Dartmouth College shortly after it became coeducational. After graduation, Erdrich returned to North Dakota and conducted poetry workshops throughout the state under the auspices of the Poetry in the Schools Program of the North Dakota Arts Council. In 1979, she completed a master's degree in creative writing from Johns Hopkins University. Erdrich is the author of many award-winning volumes of poetry, children's books, and novels. The most recent of her thirteen novels is *The*

Round House (2012), which won a National Book Award. In 2015, Erdrich won a Library of Congress Award, which is given to fiction writers with "unique, enduring voices." She lives in Minneapolis and owns the store and gallery Birchbark Books and Native Arts. The nonprofit publisher, Wigwaas Press, is affiliated with the bookstore.

William S. Yellow Robe, Jr. (1957–)
Assiniboine, Playwright

Yellow Robe, Jr., is a director, poet, actor, and educator who currently teaches at the University of Maine. Originally from the Fort Peck Reservation in northeastern Montana, Yellow Robe is also an affiliate faculty member at the University of Montana in Missoula. Twenty of his forty-three plays have been produced in theaters across the United States. *Where the Pavement Ends* (2001) is a collection of his one-act plays, and with Dr. Margo Lukens, he published *Grandchildren of the Buffalo Soldiers: And Other Untold Stories* (2009). Yellow Robe is a member of the Penumbra Theater Company of St. Paul, Minnesota, Ensemble Studio Theater in New York, and on the board of advisors for Red Eagle Soaring Theater Company (a Native youth theater company) of Seattle, Washington. He is a recipient of the First Nations Book Award for Drama and was the first Native playwright to receive a Princess Grace Foundation Theater Fellowship, a Jerome Fellowship from the Minneapolis Playwright's Center, and a New England Theater Foundation Award for Excellence.

Jodi Archambault Gillette (1970–)
Lakota, Leader

Gillette, a member of the Standing Rock Sioux Tribe in North and South Dakota, was appointed by President Barack Obama as senior advisor for Native American affairs in April 2012. Prior to joining the White House, Gillette was an economic development planner for her tribe and served as executive director of the Native American Training Institute in Bismarck. Gillette conducted intensive efforts on provisions of the 2013 Violence Against Women Act, which finally recognized the inherent right of tribal nations to prosecute non-Indian perpetrators.

She has served in the U.S. Department of the Interior as deputy assistant secretary and as associate director of intergovernmental affairs. In her current position, Gillette plays an important role in the administration's efforts to continue strengthening the government-to-government relationship between the United States and Indian Country.

Gyasi Ross
Blackfeet/Suquamish, Attorney/Writer

From a traditional family on the Blackfeet Reservation, Browning, Montana, Ross graduated from Columbia Law School in New York City. His goals are to be a good parent and help Native people. He practices law representing tribes for Crowell Law Offices—Tribal Advocacy Group and is co-owner and vice president of Red Vinyl Records. Ross is a contributing writer to several news organizations, including *Indian Country Today*, and is the author of *How to Say I Love You in Indian*.

SOUTHERN PLAINS: TEXAS AND OKLAHOMA

"Bad Indians"

i was told by those old ones
that every song has a special time and a place where it's sang
this is our song
and this our time
they used to say the only good indians were dead indians
i must be a no good at being indian
cuz I feel alive and kicking
we are the bastard reject children of manifest destiny
the offspring of fornicating aimsters
raised by our grandparents who told us
not to confuse being warriors with gangsters
the edward curtis groupies get jazzed by anyone fitting the bill
and America gets juiced by every *Bury My Heart at Walmart* film

—Excerpt from "Bad Indians" by Ryan Red Corn (Osage), 2009

Ryan Red Corn is a member of the 1491s, a sketch comedy group as inter-tribally diverse as the state of Oklahoma itself. Core members of the 1491s include filmmaker Sterlin Harjo (Seminole/Creek), Dakota language and environmental activist Dallas Goldtooth (Diné/Mdewakanton Dakota), poet and comedian Bobby Wilson (Sisseton–Wahpeton Dakota), and Hollywood screenwriter Migizi Pensoneau (Ponca/Ojibwe). Red Corn lives in Pawhuska, Oklahoma, where he co-owns Buffalo Nickle Creative, an advertising agency in the heart of the Osage Nation. Harjo also lives in Oklahoma, but he met Red

Corn at an art show in Colorado. Harjo knew Pensoneau through film festivals, and they met the other future members of the 1491s while sitting on a panel about Native film in Minneapolis.

The multitude of short YouTube videos the 1491s have made satirizing contemporary Native life and non-Indian misperceptions has brought the group fame, if not fortune. An appearance on Comedy Central's *The Daily Show* in September 2014 aroused controversy when Redskins fans responded to a dialogue about Indian sports mascots with violent threats. The 1491s' sketches range from the sublimely silly lampooning of Hollywood stereotypes—actors auditioning to play "sexy" Indian Wolfpack members for the *Twilight* series and the adoption of Johnny Depp into the Comanche tribe—to the serious: *Smiling Indians* presents a montage of happily expressive modern Native people to counteract Edward Curtis's early twentieth-century, stone-faced portraits of "a dying race." Most of the videos employ comedy to examine provocative political issues, such as *Blood Quantum Leap,* in which the dark-complexioned Goldtooth panics when he cuts himself shaving, and by "losing blood," he turns into the light-skinned Red Corn. The concept of blood quantum is controversial because the federal government established these categories to determine degrees of "Indianness," employing terms such as "full blood" and "mixed blood," which offend many Native people, while some use these categories to reject other Indians. The 1491s' most popular video, *Slapping Medicine Man,* critiques both mythologized spirituality and unhealthy reservation lifestyles.

In an interview with *Indian Country Today Media Network* on September 2, 2012, Red Corn said, "The group functions because we're all making comedy from the exact same place. When you're way in the back of the bus, you can see all the shenanigans that go on out in front of you, but if you're way in the front, you have no idea what's going on behind you. I feel like we're WAY in the back."

A BIRD'S EYE VIEW

The hardest weather in the world is there. Winter brings blizzards, hot, tornadic winds arise in the spring, and in summer, the prairie is an anvil's edge. The grass turns brittle and brown, and it cracks beneath our feet.

There are greenbelts along the rivers and creeks, linear groves of hickory and pecan, willow and witch hazel. At a distance in July or August, the steaming foliage seems almost to writhe in fire.

Great, green and yellow grasshoppers are everywhere in the tall grass, popping up like corn to sting the flesh, and tortoises crawl about on the red earth, going nowhere in plenty of time. Loneliness is an aspect of the land.

—N. Scott Momaday (Kiowa), *The Way to Rainy Mountain* (1967)

HISTORICAL TRIBES IN TEXAS

The name "Texas" comes from a Caddo Indian word, *taysha,* which means "friend." Before Europeans arrived, Texas was home to peoples such as the Caddo, Tonkawa, Comanche, Kiowa, and Wichita. Traditionally an area where cultures mingled and sometimes clashed, there are a variety of regions within the vast state. The eastern Gulf Coast had a Mississippian cultural flavor and is still home to one of only three federally recognized tribes in the state, the Alabama–Coushatta (see also the chapter titled "Southeast"). Before there was a border, or the concept of Mexico as a separate country, the Coahuilteco and Carrizo tribes inhabited the southern tip of Texas. Today, a branch of the Kickapoo have a reservation in Eagle Pass as well as communities in Mexico and Oklahoma (although the Kickapoo are originally from the Great Lakes region). Western Texas was held by Pueblo peoples such as the Jumano, who, like many smaller Texas tribes, were decimated by disease and warfare during the nineteenth century. Only the Ysleta del Sur, or Tigua, Pueblo people remain, near El Paso. The majority of Native peoples in Texas were removed to Oklahoma in the mid-1800s.

HISTORICAL TRIBES IN OKLAHOMA

Few of Oklahoma's tribes have a long history in the state, and of those, only the Niukonska (Osage) remain among us. Others, such as the Nuumunuu (Comanche) and Ndeh (Apache), may have been following the buffalo herds

Spiro Mound in Oklahoma contained at least two artifacts engraved with the image of winged, horned serpents.

through the area when Spanish explorers Hernando De Soto (1540) and, later, Francisco Coronado visited (1541). Very early ancestors of the Oklahoma Indians, such as Plainview, Clovis, and Folsom Man, as well as more recent ancestors, had disappeared. All that the Spanish left behind were fragments: a piece of a breastplate, a stirrup. French traders came by canoe in the early 1700s, and their legacy is in the names of rivers: Poteau, Illinois, Sans Bois, Salaison. The great ancient Indian civilizations, with their mounds and their monumental art—such as those unearthed at Spiro in the 1930s—were gone when Lewis and Clark visited Oklahoma after the Louisiana Purchase in 1804 (see also the chapter titled "Midwest" [section "Cahokia"]). By that time, Quapaw, Caddo, and Wichita peoples had settled on this land, establishing their villages and farms.

Generalizing about Native peoples' arrival in Oklahoma is not easy. Communities came at different times and for different purposes, and divisions of the same tribe were often split by migration. Even the rigid recognition of formal tribal units was a political concept borrowed from the European legal tradition. Certainly, land ownership was foreign to Indigenous minds. Further-

more, in a society where bands were free to move away from the main body of a tribe, portions of groups might make their homes in several regions as well as in Indian Territory. Still other tribes never settled anywhere, in the traditional European sense, but rather ranged from the Plains of Texas into the Rocky Mountains and beyond.

Many non-Indians imagine war bonnets and buffalo when they think of Indians, but many of Oklahoma's Native people have woodland or coastal heritages. They are the descendants of the Indian soldiers who resisted white settler expansion in the seventeenth, eighteenth, and early nineteenth centuries. Their brave leaders were the Tecumsehs, the Osceolas, and the Little Turtles (see also their biographies in the chapters titled "Midwest" and "Southeast"), the great warriors of the Seneca, the Shawnee, the Miami, the Creek, the Delaware, and the Seminole. These tribes fought the bloody-pitched colonial and national battles of the eastern forests and the upland rivers. They learned early on the lessons of adaptation and acculturation that allowed them to adopt some U.S. cultural forms while retaining their own ways. That these tribes survived is a testimony to their ingenuity. They saw that change was, paradoxically, their only hope of survival as an Indian people. Their lifeways, the summer rituals, and the reunions are no less Indian because they celebrate the fire or the green corn and not the buffalo.

TODAY'S TRIBES IN OKLAHOMA

The land that is now encompassed within the state of Oklahoma appears on nineteenth-century maps as "Indian Territory." Even today, Oklahoma is the home of the largest number of Indian tribes and peoples within the United States. In the twenty-first century, thirty-eight federally recognized Indian nations continue to exercise their sovereign tribal status within Oklahoma.

In the northeast corner of the state, the Peoria, Miami, Modoc, Ottawa, Shawnee, and Wyandotte are settled near the Seneca–Cayuga and the

Quapaw. Osage land spans much of the north-central portion of the state, bordered by Musco-gee (Creek), Pawnee, and Otoe–Missouria lands to the south; small Kaw, Tonkawa, and Ponca communities are rooted just west of the Osage reservation. In central Oklahoma, there are Semi-nole, Chickasaw, another band of Shawnee, Sac and Fox, Ioway, Potawatomi, and Kickapoo com-munities while Plains peoples are located in the west: Comanche, Cheyenne–Arapaho, Wichita, and Affiliated Tribes (Keechi, Waco, and Tawakonie), Caddo, and Kiowa. Also in the west, two Apache reservations border Texas. Large tracts of eastern Oklahoma are divided between two branches of Cherokee and the Choctaw, bor-dered by two communities of Delaware Indians.

Tribal towns include the Alabama–Quassarte (Coushatta), Kialegee, and Thlopthlocco (both Creek). According to historian Donald L. Fixico (Creek/Seminole/Shawnee/Sac and Fox), tribal towns are independent communities within reser-vations. For instance, the town of Thlopthlocco is situated within the Creek Nation, near Tulsa, but is "kind of a renegade group," focused on speaking only the Mvskoke language and holding traditional dances. In contrast, Fixico refers to the Creek Nation itself as a bureaucracy that practices mainstream American business principles in order to manage the nation's enterprises, such as casinos. While Thlopthlocco has a casino, it is small and informal, yet the community has come into conflict with the Creek Nation over compe-tition for customers.

TRADITIONAL LIFE

The Indian artist must be allowed free-dom to absorb influences outside of his own art forms and see the promise of a new lane of expression that should keep the Indian's art the art form termed "Na-tive Indian painting," and I give my stu-dent every opportunity to execute it.... I have always felt that the term abstrac-tion has been a part of the Indian's artis-tic thinking longer than most European

contemporary influences and perhaps in a [truer] form.

—W. Richard West (Cheyenne–Ara-paho), 1955

Before widespread settlement of non-Indians within the state, nineteenth-century ac-counts of travelers, Indian tribal documents, mis-sionary diaries, government negotiations, mili-tary reports, and trader journals clearly establish that there has never been a single, unified Okla-homa Indian culture. It is as rich and diverse as all of Indian America.

The traditional Indian culture of Plains tribes such as the Cheyenne, Arapaho, Kiowa, and Co-manche is familiar to most Americans. Their seemingly free and independent life has come to symbolize Oklahoma's Native peoples. These were hunter cultures, uniquely varied in many respects. Each depended on the existence of open lands that could be freely roamed and an abun-dant supply of wild game (see also the chapter ti-tled "Northern Plains"). It was a life intimately tied to the earth and to the natural cycles of life. The great oneness of Oklahoma Indian tribes is spiritual. Peoples as seemingly diverse as the Cheyenne, the Cherokee, and the Choctaw re-flect Indian attitudes in their perception of the earth, the universe, and the association of man's spirit and the spirits of animals.

For example, the Cheyenne Wolf Soldiers, the last of the seven great Cheyenne soldier soci-eties to be organized, served as a defensive and protective association. The Cheyenne soldier-so-ciety warrior, draped in the skin of a wolf, sought protective power and acquired strength from the animal. Richard West, the Cheyenne–Arapaho artist who was the founding director of the Smithsonian National Museum of the American Indian, has captured this animal warrior as law-man in his paintings and sculptures of the Wolf Soldier. The Cherokee, too, had many customs and legends about the wolf, which included wolf songs and medicine formulas. Aniwaya, or Wolf Clan, has historically held the role of protector and has been the largest Cherokee clan. Even

Indians of all Nations have a strong connection to Earth, the universe, and nature and its animal spirits.

after the Cherokee had adopted their highly acclaimed constitutional government (1828–1907) and established peace officers or light-horsemen modeled after frontier sheriffs, they turned to the animal powers of the spirit world. Choctaw poet Jim Barnes's poem "Four Things Choctaw" is also a homage to the wolf:

Nashoba. This my father taught/me how to sing: Wolf, I look long/for you—you know how to hide your scrawny hide behind the darkest wind.

Like the elusive wolf, Oklahoma Indian cultural diversity makes signature expressive styles tricky to perceive. However, a classical Oklahoman visual style did emerge in 1928, when the First International Art Exhibition in Prague, Czechoslovakia, showcased new Southern Plains Indian art by the Kiowa Five—all from Oklahoma. The flat-style easel paintings of traditional subjects, such as dances and historical events, inspired a renaissance in Plains art. The original Kiowa Five were: Spencer Asah (c. 1908–1954), James Auchiah (c. 1906–1974), Jack Hokeah (c. 1900–1969), Stephen Mopope (1898–1974), and Monroe Tsatoke (1904–1937). Lois Smoky joined the group at the University of Oklahoma in 1927, making it the Kiowa Six.

In terms of performance and athletics, Oklahoma Indians have historically loved to perform, to play and dance for themselves or crowds, to "play Indian," or just play. Modern Indian teams and professional athletes reflect and continue the legacy of the great Indian professional football teams; Oklahoma's long list of Indian athletes include the most famous of all twentieth-century sports figures, Jim Thorpe (see also his biography at the end of this chapter). No competitive sport in the world can be as exciting as a Sunday afternoon stickball game back in the Oklahoma hills. However, if one sees only the outward performance of the dancers and athletes at play, one misses the spirit of the real world of Oklahoma's Native people.

To Oklahoma Indians, the seasonal socials and ceremonials still matter. To a people who are a part of the cycles of life of this planet, who live outside the artificial atmosphere of central heating and cooling and beyond the control of packaged goods and preplanned public entertainment, the seasons are a measure of life. To Native Oklahomans, the summer celebrations bring more than oppressive heat and fresh tomatoes; they bring to life a world of family, tribe, politics, tradition, and ceremony. In its way, this world is as real the world of the ancestors ever could be.

REMOVAL TO INDIAN TERRITORY (1834–1907)

We never had a thought of exchanging our land for any other, as we think we would not find a country that would suit us as well as this we now occupy, it being the land of our forefathers, if we should exchange our lands for any other, fearing the consequences may be similar as transplanting an old tree, which would wither and die away, and we are fearful that we would come to the same.

—Levi Colbert et al., Chickasaw leaders of the Tennessee Valley (1826)

Since before the founding of the nation, Indian tribes had been driven westward by both warfare and treaty negotiations. Indian settlement in Oklahoma resulted from formal negotiations, informal counsel, bribery, threats, and military force. As early as 1803, Thomas Jefferson had spoken of a permanent Indian area or territory beyond the boundaries of U.S. society. More than sixty Indian tribes originally from other states were ultimately removed to and resettled in Oklahoma. Tribes were removed—particularly at the turn of the century for the northern Indians of Ohio, Indiana, Illinois, and New York—with no system or order. Many once powerful tribes—such as the Shawnee, Sac and Fox, and Potawatomi—were fragmented and reduced in numbers before they arrived in Indian Territory.

In the early years of American Indian policy, settlers and local governments pressured tribal communities to give up their large, communal landholdings. In response, the federal government adopted a policy to compel tribes to exchange their historic homelands for new "permanent" lands on unorganized federal domain in the West, where, theoretically, no conflicts would arise with non-Indians. Under treaty guarantees, this new land was to remain forever in the hands of Indian tribes, who were promised that non-Indians would not be allowed to settle in their midst.

Many tribal groups, sensing the futility of resistance to removal, sought a negotiated compromise that avoided the brutality of a forced military march to their new country. Voluntary migrations and inducements by treaty to relocate portions of such tribes as the Seneca, Quapaw, Osage, Shawnee, Choctaw, Creek, and Cherokee in Oklahoma occurred before Andrew Jackson's

Indian Removal Act was fully implemented in the 1830s. Some tribes were moved several times before they reached Oklahoma.

By the early 1830s, there were established tribal governments in Oklahoma of "old settler" or "western" factions of the Choctaw, Creek, and Cherokee as well as separate, political subdivisions of groups like the Osage, whose greatest numbers would not come to Oklahoma until much later. For example, in 1831, the Seneca exchanged land in Ohio's Sandusky Valley for 67,000 acres north of the western Cherokee while a short time later, another group of Seneca and Shawnee received a similar Indian Territory tract. In 1833, a band of Quapaw moved from the Red River to lands north and east of the Cherokee.

During the Jackson Administration (1830-1838), a companion proposal to the removal policy was that the new Indian commonwealth or territory would be governed by a confederation of tribes. The Western Territory Bill of 1834 proposed an "Indian Territory" that was to be composed of Kansas, Oklahoma, parts of Nebraska, Colorado, and Wyoming. None of these proposals of the 1830s was enacted, and the territory set aside for Indians gradually shrank to what is now the state of Oklahoma.

THE TRAIL OF TEARS

The vast majority of Oklahoma Indian tribes were "resettled" in Oklahoma, most involuntarily, under the nineteenth-century federal Indian removal policy. In the late 1820s and throughout the 1830s, the earliest and most dramatic of the Eastern Indian removals to what is now Oklahoma were those of the Five Civilized Tribes (the Choctaw, Chickasaw, Creek, Cherokee, and Seminole). These tribes were called "civilized" because they adopted constitutional governments, some of their people converted to Christianity, and they formed tribal school systems. Driven out of the South on what is known as "The Trail of Tears," tens of thousands of these people perished on forced marches that were often conducted in the dead of winter. As many as one-third of their tribal

"Trail of Tears—Jackson Says Go," by Valjean Hessing (Choctaw), c. 1966. The watercolor painting depicts Choctaw people hearing the order that they must leave their homes in Mississippi and walk to Oklahoma during wintertime on the Trail of Tears.

members, especially the very young and the very old, died before they reached the new Indian Territory. The agony of this experience is etched in the consciousness of the Five Civilized Tribes and of non-Indian Oklahomans as well. In turn, other tribes, particularly northern woodland peoples, endured experiences often as disastrous on the way to Oklahoma (see also the chapter titled "Midwest" [section titled "The Potawatomi of Michigan and Wisconsin"]). Ultimately, at least sixty-five Indian nations came to be listed historically as having been, at one time or another, Oklahoma tribes. These included: Alabama, Anadarko, Apache, Apalachicola, Arapaho, Caddo, Cahokia, Catawba, Cayuga, Cherokee, Cheyenne, Chickasaw, Chippewa, Choctaw, Comanche, Conestoga, Creek, Delaware, Eel River, Erie, Hainai, Hitchiti, Illinois, Ioway, Kaskashia, Kansa, Kichai, Kick-apoo, Kiowa, Kiowa–Apache, Koasati, Lipan, Miami, Michigomea, Modoc, Mohawk, Moingwena, Munsee, Natchez, Nez Perce, Osage, Oto and Missouri, Ottawa, Pawnee, Peoria, Piankashaw, Ponca, Potawatomi, Quapaw, Sauk and Fox, Seminole, Seneca, Shawnee, Skidi, Stockbridge, Tamaroa, Tawakoni, Tonkawa, Tuscarora, Tuskegee, Waco, Wea, Wichita, Wyandot, and Yuchi.

THE GOLDEN AGE
(c. 1840–1867)

this same moon that made
light for families on
horseback travois and
hard times journeying into
this buffalo country

Crickets cicadas dance
inside my road-weary
head we watch the
night and grassy plains
I tell my sons who
want to sit on every hill
that every shadow is a
buffalo spirit

—Barney Bush (Shawnee),
"Directions in Our Blood" (1988)

The many Plains, Eastern, and Midwestern tribes who joined the earlier inhabitants brought a diversity of Indian culture not present in any other state. To appreciate these varied cultures and what Oklahoma Indians lost after the coming of white immigrants, one must understand the nature of Indian life in their homelands before the Civil War (1861–1865) and the Treaty of Medicine Lodge (1867). It is the culture of this "golden age" to which Oklahoma's modern Indians look with nostalgia. The time before the American Civil War followed the brutal, nearly genocidal, expulsion from their original homelands. Although Native people opposed coming to Indian Territory, ironi-

cally, they found in Oklahoma a quiet haven. Eventually, they came to love this land, but in the end it, too, was taken from them.

Indian tribes in Oklahoma have continuously operated their own sovereign governments. After the end of the bloody Trail of Tears, the Five Tribes established comprehensive governments in Indian Territory and exercised self-rule relatively free of federal interference. The Five Tribes achieved a level of literacy and economic prosperity that exceeded many of the neighboring states. During the golden age, tribal Indian traditions and the economic richness of this new land merged to produce culturally diverse and prosperous Native civilizations.

The crucible of Oklahoma—the sharing of similar historical experiences—has helped produce this spirit and has contributed to the uniqueness of Oklahoma Indian culture. A great many factors have contributed to the evolution of this modern Oklahoma Indianness. Many Oklahoma Indian tribes adapted themselves and their cultures to their new location. Dating from the first half of the nineteenth century, there is a

"As Long as the Waters Flow," 1989, a bronze statue by Apache artist Alan Houser, welcomes visitors to the Oklahoma State capitol building in Oklahoma City.

history of tribal cooperation and inter-tribal meetings among the Indian groups in Oklahoma. Stimulated in part by the federal government's decisions to treat removed and reservation peoples alike and in part by a sense of common problems, these conferences reduced tribal hostility and stimulated united action.

THE CIVIL WAR (1861–1865)

The American Civil War had a dramatic impact on the Five Tribes. A number of tribal members owned slaves and supported the Confederacy. The Choctaw and Chickasaw Nations, whose lands adjoined Confederate Arkansas and Texas, sided with the Confederacy. The three most northerly tribes (Creek, Cherokee, and Seminole) were politically divided but nonetheless made treaties with the South. Loyalist factions continued to favor the North, and many tribal citizens fought on both sides. The Cherokee, Creek, and Seminole each lost as much as twenty to twenty-five percent of their population.

The close of the Civil War and the 1867 Indian Treaty gathering at Medicine Lodge in Kansas signaled the beginning of the end of the old, free Indian nationhood. New treaties forced upon the Five Civilized Tribes at Fort Smith in 1866 and 1867 contained provisions that ceded western portions of their tribal territories, abolished slavery, granted railroad rights of way, and provided for the settlement of other tribes on their former lands and for the eventual allotment of tribal lands. Treaties also paved the way for the U.S. settler onslaught that followed. The signing of the Treaty of Medicine Lodge with leaders of the Kiowa, the Cheyenne, the Arapaho, and the Comanche foreshadowed the federal government's effort to confine the tribes to reservations and to compel them to follow the "white man's road."

WESTWARD EXPANSION

Oklahoma Indians were caught on the crest of one of those major cycles of westward expansion that occur throughout American history.

Westward expansion was itself an old story. Many of the Indians removed to Oklahoma, including the Shawnee, the Cherokee, the Seneca, and the Creek, had been caught in earlier stages of the cycle, but this expansion was somehow different. It was more determined, better organized, much faster, more efficient, and more difficult to resist. Powered by technological marvels, such as railroads, the steam engine, and the mechanical harvester, the new expansion was also propelled by the "go-getter" spirit that infused the nation after the war. The military energy of the Union victory survived on the frontier. Congress, board rooms, taverns, and churches shared a determination to thrust the nation westward. Landless Americans from the east and newer immigrants who had temporarily settled elsewhere demanded Indian lands. There was no place left to remove the Indian to, and there was little sympathy for the preservation of a way of life that left farmlands unturned, coal unmined, and timber uncut.

By 1889, Oklahoma Indian life was changing. The military balance of power rested with the white man. The Plains Indian Wars were coming to an end, with many Oklahoma tribal leaders held captive in distant jails. The brutal massacre at Washita (1868), in which George Armstrong Custer attacked Black Kettle's Cheyenne village, demonstrated the extermination mindset of U.S. soldiers. The "blue coats" appeared more frequently and grew larger and larger in the drawings Native men did in the old ledger books they received from soldiers at the forts where some Indians were imprisoned or worked as scouts. Even the golden days of intense tribal creativity were ending for the Five Civilized Tribes, who were now left fiercely struggling to preserve whatever steps toward acculturation they had earlier made.

LAND RUSH (1889)

By the time the sun rose over the horizon, the circle of elders had already met and decided it was time to hide the path to their settlement. They feared the madness of the people who were living in the town as if they were the carriers of a contagion. They wanted to make certain that the insanity would not form itself like a turn wind in the air and travel up the next red clay pathway to their own world.

—Linda Hogan (Chickasaw),
Mean Spirit (1990)

After the Civil War, other Indians—including many of the powerful Plains tribes, such as the Comanche, Kiowa, and Cheyenne—were removed to some of the western Indian Territory lands occupied by the Five Tribes and other tribal groups, such as the Apache. Thousands of U.S. settlers illegally moved into Indian Territory, and many lawless and violent drifters made Indian Territory a notorious haven for bandits and killers. In an effort to maintain law and order for non-Indians in Indian Territory, Congress established a special federal court for Indian Territory, over which Isaac C. Parker, known as "the Hanging Judge," presided.

The famous Oklahoma land run opened central Indian Territory to U.S. settlers in 1889. Until that fateful year, Oklahoma Indian tribes were, in a real sense, still sovereign; they were "domestic dependent nations," in the words of former U.S. Supreme Court Chief Justice John Marshall. Although they were subject to many federal regulations, Indians owned all the lands that were to become Oklahoma. Non-Indians within their domain were either government or military officials, who relied on Indian tolerance. Illegal intruders were subject to expulsion under existing treaties. These sovereign Indian nations were the only groups in Oklahoma whose political power and landed estate would diminish with the establishment of territorial government, which had begun in 1889 and culminated in the admission of Oklahoma to statehood in 1907.

The land rush opened Oklahoma's Indian lands, and fifty thousand potential homesteaders vied to stake out claims to the ten thousand farms of 160 acres each. It was an epic, if condensed, enactment of the entire frontier-settlement process. The Oklahoma land rush of April 22, 1889, has been recreated in song and story, in novel and in film, but the Oklahoma Indian experience of that day has been largely ignored.

In 1890, the Oklahoma Organic Act reduced Indian Territory to its eastern portion, the lands of the Five Tribes and the Quapaw Agency Tribes. During this time, an Organic Act created Oklahoma Territory in the western part of Indian Territory and established a U.S. territorial government. The Act expressly preserved tribal authority and federal jurisdiction in both Oklahoma and Indian territories.

Before the land rush, Oklahoma was exclusively Indian country in a legal, political, and social sense. By 1975, the Bureau of Indian Affairs reported that Oklahoma Indian tribal lands encompassed only 65,000 acres and that Indians as private citizens owned only a million acres. The size of tribal acreage grows slowly from year to year but is still a fraction of the once great Indian Territories.

OSAGE OIL

Oil was discovered beneath the Osage Reservation in 1896. The Bureau of Indian Affairs (BIA) gave one drilling company a monopoly on the leasing rights to exploit all of the oil and natural gas on the eastern half of the one-million-acre reservation for the next ten years. The Osage did not receive mineral royalties until the 1920s but were able to leverage their potential wealth to delay division of their lands until 1906 (see also the section titled "Allotment (1887-1914)" below). Osage leaders also negotiated that their mineral income would remain tribally owned. While neighboring Native people grew wealthy from individual oil revenue, most Osage controlled their income as a group and were able to convince the BIA to dissolve the oil company monopoly in the eastern part of the reservation when the western half of the oil fields opened. This led to the Osage being proclaimed "the richest nation in the world" by national newspapers during the 1920s.

Oil prices fell during the Great Depression of the 1930s, and by this time, many oil-rich Native landowners had been deceived out of their

The U.S. government opened up the Oklahoma territory to all takers who could stake a claim on April 22, 1889, spurring a frenzied land rush.

land and fortunes. In the mid-1920s, Gertrude Simmons Bonnin (Zitkala-sa), a Dakota activist and founder of the Society of American Indians (see also her biography in the chapter titled "Northern Plains"), filed a report for the Indian Rights Association investigating corruption against Indians in Oklahoma.

Bonnin described the case of Ledcie Stechi, a seven-year-old Choctaw girl who was living with her grandmother in a shack near Smithville, Oklahoma. When Ledcie inherited her late mother's land, and oil was discovered there in 1921, the county judge dismissed Ledcie's uncle as her guardian and appointed Jordan Whitman, owner of the First National Bank of Idabel. In the fall of 1922, Whitman had the land appraised at $90,000.00. Meanwhile, he provided Ledcie and her grandmother with such a small stipend that by 1923, a medical examination found the child to be malnourished and suffering from malaria. Ledcie was placed in an Indian school, where she began to regain her health. However, Whitman demanded she be returned to his custody, and within a month, Ledcie was dead of apparent poi-

soning. The court then appointed a guardian for the grandmother, as she had inherited the land.

In her report, Bonnin commented, "Greed for the girl's lands and rich oil property actuated the grafters and made them like beasts surrounding their prey.... She too [the grandmother] will go the way of her grandchild, as sheep for slaughter by ravenous wolves, unless the good people of America intervene immediately by remedial Congressional action." These types of deceptions and the high murder rate of Oklahoma Indians during the oil years are also chronicled by Linda Hogan (Chickasaw) in her novel, *Mean Spirit*, which was published in 1990.

ALLOTMENT (1887–1914)

I am in that fix, senators, you will not forget now that when I use the word "I," I mean the whole Cherokee people. I am in that fix. What am I to do? I have a piece of property that doesn't support me, and is not worth a cent to me, under the same inexorable, cruel provisions of the Curtis law that swept away our treaties, our system of nationality, our every existence, and wrested out of our possession our vast territory.

—Dewitt Clinton Duncan (Cherokee),
U.S. Senate Committee
Testimony (1906)

During the 1890s, the lands of many Oklahoma tribes were allotted or divided according to the General Allotment Act of 1887 (see also the chapter titled "Historical Overview" [section titled "The General Allotment Act"]). In 1893, the Dawes Commission was established to divide the lands of the Five Tribes. In 1898, Congress passed the Curtis Act to speed up the allotment process. Shortly thereafter, the Oklahoma Enabling Act provided for the admission of Indian Territory and Oklahoma Territory into the Union as the state of Oklahoma. The long-range result of federal policy was that by the time of statehood in 1907, many Oklahoma Indians lost their land because they could not pay taxes on it, and individual titles soon passed to non-Indians, despite the protests of the vast majority of Indians who wished to retain tribal ownership.

Allotment and the opening of Indian Territory to U.S. settlers came at approximately the same time in Oklahoma history, creating a varied series of clashes and conflicts. The disappearance of large parcels of tribally owned land no doubt created a vastly different Oklahoma Indian community as did the aggressive manner in which the Dawes Commission sold Indian farmlands to white townships. Towns with sizable non-Indian populations therefore existed on reservations almost from the moment of settlement.

TRIBAL ENROLLMENT TROUBLES

They told me that as long as the sun shone and the sky is up yonder, this agreement will be kept. He said as long as the sun rises, it shall last; as long as grass grows, it shall last. That is what he said, and we believed it.

—Chitto Harjo (Muscogee), 1906

Among the Five Civilized Tribes, communal lands were shifted to individual members with remarkable speed. In order to assign individual plots of land, the Dawes Commission had to create lists of tribal members, which were called rolls. The Dawes Commission's preparation of the membership rolls began with the Curtis Act in June 1898 and continued through March 1907, with a few additional names being added in 1914. During this process, enrollment was complicated by the foreign concept of blood quantum percentages. "Blood quantum" was a term used by federal agents that referred to how much "Indian blood" a person had. The agents had strange ways of determining Native people's heritage. One method was to scratch a person's chest and judge his or her amount of Indian blood by the color of the scratched skin. In all, the commission placed 101,526 persons on the final rolls of the Five Civilized Tribes. Of this number, federally designated "full-bloods" constituted 26,794; another 3,534 were enrolled as having three-fourths or more Indian "blood"; 6,859 were listed as one-half to three-fourths Indian; and 40,934 were listed as having less than one-half Indian blood.

Many were enrolled against their will, but others escaped the roving enrollment parties. Thus, Oklahoma's mixed-blood Indians are often federally recognized while many full-bloods and their descendants are treated as non-Indian. Other full-bloods enrolled themselves as quarter-bloods or eighth-bloods so that they would not have restrictions on their lands and the need for guardians. As a result, in tribes such as the Choctaw, Seminole, Cherokee, Creek, and Chickasaw, whose rolls have been closed by act of Congress, enrollees' descendants are denied educational and other Indian benefits to which, by their technical blood quantum, they are entitled.

Republican U.S. Senator Henry L. Dawes wrote the Dawes Act of 1887, which gave power to the president to survey Indian lands and then divide them up among individuals. Indians who accepted the disbursement—rejecting tribal life—would become U.S. citizens.

THE FREEDMEN

When the Dawes Commission rolls were drawn at the turn of the century, many traditionalist people like "Crazy Snake" Chitto Harjo (Muscogee) refused to enroll for allotment because they believed that the United States was violating its treaty promises. Harjo led the Snake Resistance against the Dawes Act from 1898 until 1909, when he was imprisoned. Without an organized resistance, when people enrolled and received individual plots, the Muscogee communal tribal land disappeared, yet in the same 1906 Senate hearing in which Harjo made his famous speech about land promised as long as the grass grows, he added, "The government is cutting up my land and giving it to black people. These black people, who are they? They are negroes that came here as slaves. They have no right to this land. It never was given to them. It was given to me and my people, and we paid for it with our land back in Alabama."

As Harjo noted, the Dawes commission allotted land to Creek Freedmen, black people who were former Creek (Muscogee) slaves, runaway slaves who had been harbored among the Creek, or were descendants of both races. The Commission also prepared a roll of 23,405 blacks known as Cherokee Freedmen. The title of this group refers to the former slaves of the Cherokee Nation (which fought on the side of the Confederacy in the Civil War), who were freed by the U.S. government in 1866, giving them "eternal and everlasting" rights as Cherokee citizens. Disputes over the wording of that treaty and the differences between American and tribal citizenship have been ongoing for 150 years. In 2011, after the Cherokee Nation of Oklahoma revoked the tribal citizenship and voting rights of the Freedmen, Congress voted to withhold $33 million in tribal funding until the Freedmen's citizenship was restored. Recent efforts to unify these long-standing disputes among factions of the Cherokee Nation, as yet unresolved, are currently working their way through the U.S. judicial system.

The Cherokee Nation views federal intervention as an infringement on their sovereign right to determine tribal membership. The Freedmen claim the Cherokee decision is not only based on racial bias but is about unwillingness to share profits from tribal enterprises. A 2015 film directed by Marcus Barberry and Sam Russell, *By Blood,* is a portrayal of the Freedmen's ongoing saga.

OKLAHOMA STATEHOOD (1907)

It broke my heart. I went to bed and cried all night long. It seemed more than I could bear that the Cherokee Nation, my country and my people's country, was no more.

—Mary (Cherokee), 1907

Statehood meant the end of any hope for an inter-tribal, traditionally governed Indian Territory. Since 1907, the status of Indian tribes in

Oklahoma has been similar to that of tribes in other states. The popularly held view that Oklahoma Indians are free of state regulations is incorrect. Although when Congress passed the Indian Reorganization Act of 1934 Oklahoma tribes did not immediately have to organize themselves under elected governments and tribal constitutions, two years later, the Oklahoma Indian Welfare Act accomplished the same goal: Governments led by traditional chiefs and tribal councils were no longer recognized.

However, Indigenous sovereign attitudes were not so easily lost, even in the statehood movement. Like all other Indian tribes, tribes in Oklahoma retain powers of self-government and sovereignty. Oklahoma may be the only state in which Indian laws had a significant and long-lasting impact on the form of state government and on the nature of the constitutional legal system, such as limitations on how much land may be bought by corporations.

Another crucial factor in Native influence on state government was that, following statehood, state representatives tended to advocate for the Indians of Oklahoma, particularly the populous and influential Five Civilized Tribes. Added to this was the presence of a great body of "mixed-blood" Indian leaders, who moved easily into the process of creating state governmental structures, and some who represented the interests of the entire state from positions of national leadership.

SOUTHERN PLAINS INDIGENEITY

Everyone laughed at the impossibility of it, but also the truth. Because who would believe the fantastic and terrible story of all of our survival, those who were never meant to survive?

—Joy Harjo (Creek), "Anchorage" (1988)

The state is truly what Chief Allen Wright's Choctaw name for it, Okla Homma, conveys

in a free translation: "Home of the Red People." In 2014, 471,738 Oklahomans were listed as members of Indian tribes by the Bureau of Indian Affairs (BIA) with about one hundred thousand more people identifying themselves as Indian on the 2010 Census. Oklahoma has more Indians from more varied tribes than any other state in the Union. It has more separate tribal groups historically associated with the state and more currently recognized tribes than any other state. A higher percentage of its population is Native, and that population is more widely distributed among the state's counties than in Arizona, New Mexico, or the Dakotas.

In 2010, Oklahoma City ranked fourth behind New York, Los Angeles, and Phoenix in Indian population within city boundaries. The sixty-five-mile radius of Tulsa includes the highest non-reservation concentration of Indians anywhere in the United States. With urban migration, Indians from at least fifty other non-Oklahoma tribes have recently moved to the state. More and more of Oklahoma's Indians have ancestors from two to four, or more, tribes. An Osage–Cherokee, a Kiowa–Miami, and a Creek–Omaha are not unusual. The current generation is producing children who are such combinations as Choctaw–Ponca–Cheyenne–Delaware or Cherokee–Osage–Omaha–Creek–Apache.

Circumstances have greatly reduced their land base and given Indians the lowest income level and the highest unemployment rate of any group in the state. Nevertheless, more Oklahoma Indians are participating in more Native-sponsored activities than in any period since statehood. Indian tribes are again functioning as political and economic units, electing officials, administering programs, and dispensing justice.

Although in some ways, Indian culture is becoming increasingly pan-Indian in the sense that many tribes share such events as powwows and urban planning seminars, within individual people's lives, there are many distinctly personal values and attitudes that are influenced by an Indian heritage. Among Indians of the same generation and of the same tribe, there is no static view of

Indian culture is becoming more and more shared among tribes who have started to do collective activities together, such as powwows.

Indianness—the Native Oklahoma world is dynamic and varied.

While the notion that contemporary Indians live in two worlds has generated the misperception of a kind of Native American cultural schizophrenia, Oklahoma Indians, like Oklahoma non-Indians, live in a world that balances elements of diverse cultural traditions. Two or more cultural currents may coexist so that people must play many roles, but not at the same time. Healthy individuals function in different capacities in the various circles of their lives.

Oklahoma Indians have scattered throughout the world. Thousands of Oklahoma Indians living outside the state plan their vacations to come home for their tribal celebrations. Oklahoma's Red Earth celebration in June is the premiere festival of Native American art and culture in the United States. Whether Comanche, Cheyenne,

Kiowa, Shawnee, Ponca, Delaware, Quapaw, Creek, or Seminole, there is a time and a place for renewal, a need to call for strength from sacred tribal objects, such as arrows or wampum, and there is also a time that brings together Indians from many tribes for powwows and gourd dances, rodeos and competitions, visits and romances.

The summer dances also bring scholars and cultural tourists. However, much of the Native Oklahoman way is lost to the outsider because the Indigenous world has both a public and a private aspect and may, on occasion, involve both. A legend shared by many Oklahoma tribes says that certain Indians can become transparent, turn into leaves on trees, or become small enough to ride on a bird's wing. Oklahoma Indians have been remarkably successful in doing just that. They have succeeded in hiding many aspects of their culture or camouflaging things Native so that the Indianness is kept from the eye of the tourist or even the scholar. The outsider looking for a buffalo misses the deer, the raven, or the bright summer sun itself, which are all very Native.

Other issues divisive in many non-Oklahoma tribes, such as the role of women, have had little disruptive effect in Oklahoma, perhaps because those issues have few historic roots in this population. Oklahoma Native women, many of whom are from matrilineal groups, exert a major and even dominant influence in many tribes and in most Indian families. Furthermore, the close proximity of different tribal communities reduces inter-tribal biases. Finally, the size of the population that is not physically identifiable as Native but is of Indian descent in proportion to the size of the non-Indian population of the state creates a kind of "Indian culturality" that exists in no other state and, at least in the abstract, defines "being Indian" as socially desirable.

However, the late Pamela Chibitty, a Comanche–Shawnee–Delaware who worked at the Native American Cultural Coalition of Tulsa, noted that for many Indians, adjustment is not easy: "Some withdraw into an all-Indian world, shunning non-Indians and modern society; others 'sell out' and go on to the modern white man's world and forget their backgrounds." The varied lives of real Oklahoma Indians expose the bankruptcy of stereotyped images. The Indian lawyer in a three-piece suit can easily transform himself into a feathered championship fancy dancer. An elected county law-enforcement official returns to his office the morning after attending a peyote meeting. A nurse leaves the hospital and goes to have tobacco "treated." A man of 1/256 Indian blood sits in a French restaurant in Tulsa expounding on tribal genealogy while the dark-skinned descendant of a great chieftain of the same tribe tells her high school history teacher not to tell her classmates that she is Indian. An internationally famous Indian artist tours China and Russia to renew her art. Such is the world of the Oklahoma Indian.

The corn road, the buffalo road, and the peyote road are different from one another, but the spirit with which one follows the road, not the

"Kiowa Aw-Day," by Teri Greeves (Kiowa), beaded sneakers, 2004. Our Lives exhibit, National Museum of the American Indian, Smithsonian Institute, Washington, D.C.

road itself, is the essence of Indianness. This Native spirit, an Indigenous way of seeing and of being, makes a one-quarter Chickasaw or a one-eighth Comanche perceive as a Native person. "I believe that there is such a thing as Indian sensibility," T. C. Cannon, a Caddo–Kiowa artist, once explained. "This has to do with the idea of a collective history. It's reflected in your upbringing and the remarks that you hear every day from birth and the kind of behavior and emotion you see around you."

SELECTED CONTEMPORARY NATIVE NATIONS IN OKLAHOMA APACHE

Apache (N'deh) ancestors originally migrated south from the Subarctic regions of western Canada with the Navajo (Diné), with whom they share the Na-Dene language family. They began arriving in the desert Southwest between the thirteenth and sixteenth centuries and spread from present-day Texas to Arizona and from Colorado to the Sierra Madre in Mexico (see also the chapter titled "Southwest"). After hundreds of years of resistance to Spanish, Mexican, and American forces, Apache prisoners of war were confined to reservations in Arizona, New Mexico, and Oklahoma by 1886.

Apache Tribe of Oklahoma (Naishan Apache)

Tribal headquarters are in Anadarko, in southwest Oklahoma, with an enrollment of 6,501. Historically, the tribe has had a close relationship with the Kiowa, which they maintain to this day. Recently, tribal attorneys won a precedent-setting lawsuit: Robert Soto, a religious leader of the Apache, had his eagle feathers confiscated at a powwow. After nine years of litigation, the U.S. Government returned the feathers to him, a case that potentially widens the protection offered Native Americans under the American Indian Religious Freedom Act of 1978.

Fort Sill Apache Tribe (Chiricahua)

The Chiricahua people were formerly based in southwest New Mexico. In the late 1800s, the 712 descendants of eighty prisoners who fought the U.S. cavalry under Geronimo were sent to Fort Sill, near Apache, Oklahoma. The tribe was authorized in 1996 by then Governor Gary Johnson of New Mexico to return to their ancestral land. The Chiricahua bought a thirty-acre parcel in Akela Flats, but after receiving federal designation of this land as a tribal reservation, they faced strong opposition from the present governor of New Mexico, Susana Martinez, who refused to recognize the tribe's legitimacy. According to tribal chief Jeff Haozous, "The governor who opposes us won't be there forever. Our land will be." In January 2014, the tribe filed a lawsuit against the state, and in April 2014, the New Mexico Supreme Court ruled that the Apache may return to their homeland.

Caddo Nation of Oklahoma

Previously known as the Caddo Tribe of Oklahoma, the Caddo Nation is a confederation of several Southeastern tribes, including the Kadohadacho, Nachitoches, and Hasini, speaking the Caddo language. The Confederacy's former homelands spanned present-day western Louisiana and Arkansas and eastern Texas and Oklahoma. After the state of Louisiana took their land in 1835, the Caddo moved to Oklahoma with the Choctaw and Chickasaw (see also the chapter titled "Southeast").

With an enrollment of 5,500, Caddo's tribal jurisdiction is in Binger, Oklahoma. The community actively keeps their ancestral language and traditions alive, including the Turkey, Drum, and Morning dances. In 2013, a leadership schism resulted in a lockout of one of the factions. It was resolved in 2014 by the Southern Plains Court of Indian Offenses by vacating all elected offices and calling for a special election.

CHEROKEE

Most Cherokee people were forced west to Oklahoma by 1839. Led by John Ross, the nation adopted a new constitution and rebuilt their democratic government, churches, and schools. They returned to printing bilingual books and newspapers and maintained higher rates of literacy and education than their non-Indian neighbors. The Keetoowah Band diverged

"Bull Rider" by Charles Pierce (Choctaw), oil on canvas, 2014. Rodeos and bull riding are popular among Native Oklahomans.

from John Ross's group of Cherokee during the Civil War, as the Keetoowah were antislavery and allied with the Union. To retain traditions and resist adopting white ways, in the 1940s, the United Keetoowah Band formed its own community independent of the Cherokee Nation in Oklahoma. Meanwhile, the Eastern Band of Cherokee managed to remain in North Carolina (see also the chapter titled "Southeast").

Cherokee Nation of Oklahoma

With an enrollment of over three hundred thousand, of which 190,000 live in Oklahoma within a tribal jurisdiction that extends to fourteen counties, this is the largest of the three federally recognized Cherokee tribes (although according to the Bureau of Indian Affairs, it is a "successor in interest" and not the historical Cherokee tribe). With its extensive interests in agriculture, real estate, and other business entities, the large and prosperous Cherokee Nation of Oklahoma ($1.6 billion yearly) is a powerful economic force in the state. It has the economic wherewithal to be a cultural force as well. Its newspaper, *Cherokee Phoenix*, is published in English and Cherokee Syllabary. The popular radio show, "Cherokee Voices," plays music in the Native language and features interviews with elders about Cherokee ways.

The nation is in the forefront of the environmental protection and preservation movement. Their Ethnobiology Program is studying ways to protect twenty-five plants and animals important to the Cherokee Nation. Their Natural Resources Program focuses on hazardous fuel reduction, wild land rehabilitation, and fire management in conjunction with the Forestry Division. The Cherokee Seed Project provides access to Indigenous seeds in existence long before European contact, including varieties that "came with us on the Trail of Tears."

Cherokee service outreach extends to other continents, sending Dana Hayworth, a registered nurse, to treat patients with the Ebola virus in West Africa in 2014. Also in 2014, Keith Harper was appointed U.S. representative to the United Nations Human Rights Council in Geneva. He is the first Native American to ever receive the rank of a U.S. ambassador.

(For information on current issues involving the Cherokee Freedmen, see "The Freedmen" section in this chapter.)

United Keetoowah Band of Cherokee (UKB)

The Keetowah were recognized as an independent band of Cherokee in 1946. Among the Keetowah, 13,000 out of 14,300 enrolled members live in Tahlequa. In 2013, the tribe won a lawsuit against the Cherokee Nation of Oklahoma to acquire a seventy-six-acre parcel of land within the bounds of the Cherokee reservation. It was the latest in a series of favorable decisions that recognized the sovereignty of the UKB. The parcel is their village center, which they consider their ancestral sacred ground. The UKB say that for many years, they have been fighting a David-and-Goliath battle with the Cherokee Nation for self-determination. For example, in 1975, they were evicted from the Cherokee tribal office on the grounds of being a "fraudulent" tribe. The UKB claim to be the "real Cherokee," that their name is the original name of the tribe, and that they migrated to Oklahoma before the forced removal (see also the chapter titled "Southeast").

Cheyenne and Arapaho Tribes of Oklahoma

In western Oklahoma, Southern Cheyenne people gathered on reservation lands designated for them to share with the Arapaho after being relocated from the Northern Plains (see also the chapter titled "Northern Plains"). Among the 12,480-member community, located near Clinton and Canton, recent efforts are a plan to separate the Cheyenne and the Arapaho into two federally recognized tribes and a public service campaign, "Meth, Not on Our Land," to combat a 50 percent increase in use of methamphetamines in the community.

In 2014, the tribes' television station, CATV47, began producing *Native Oklahoma*, an award-winning series, broadcast on Oklahoma Educational TV Authority (OETA), to showcase the history and culture of a number of tribes in the state, "an enriching experience for all of us." Each thirty-minute episode features stories produced by the communities themselves, "giving each tribe an opportunity to tell their own stories in their own words," according to the show's producers. The first episode presented ceremonial dances of the Cheyenne–Arapaho, Osage, Cherokee, Choctaw, Ponca, and Kiowa tribes. The March 2015 episode featured Vietnam veterans.

The Southern Cheyenne are proud to count among their members Suzan Shown Harjo, who is Cheyenne on her mother's side of the family and Muscogee on her father's. Harjo, a poet, radio-show producer, and longtime advocate of Native rights, was awarded the Presidential Medal of Freedom in November 2014, the highest honor for a civilian in the United States (see also her biography at the end of this chapter).

The Chickasaw Nation

The Chickasaw are a Muskogean-speaking people who share some cultural similarities with the Choctaw although they speak a separate dialect. After being removed from western Tennessee and northern Mississippi in 1832, the Chickasaw eventually adjusted to their new home in southern Oklahoma. There were 32,372 enrolled Chickasaw members in 2014 with about ten thousand living near Ada.

The Chickasaw Nation began producing documentary films in 2010. The first release, screened on Oklahoma Educational Television Authority (OETA) channels, was *Pearl,* a 107-minute, critically acclaimed biography of Chickasaw aviatrix Pearl Carter Scott. A second film, *Te Ata,* profiling a Chickasaw entertainer and storyteller who was inducted into both the Oklahoma and Chickasaw Nation halls of fame, completed postproduction in early 2015. Te Ata Thompson was named Oklahoma's first "State Treasure" in 1987 and is played by Q'Orianka Kilcher

A statue honoring actress Te Ata Thompson can be viewed at the University of Science and Arts of Oklahoma campus in Chickasaw, Oklahoma.

(Quechua–Huachipaeri); other cast members include Gil Birmingham (Comanche) and Oscar-nominated actor Graham Greene (Oneida).

First Encounter, the debut film in the new Chickasaw Heritage Series, chronicles the clash between the Chickasaw and Hernando de Soto' in 1540, which put a halt to De Soto's invasion. Chickasaw Nation Governor Bill Anoatubby said, "While our first encounter with De Soto has been told from other points of view, we believe our perspective adds significant context to this historical narrative." *First Encounter* earned Best Shot Documentary at the Trail Dance Film Festival in January 2015 and aired on OETA in March of that year. DVDs and a state-standards-based teacher's guide are available on chickasawoutpost.com.

Other notable accomplishments among the Chickasaw community were the election of Lisa John-Billy as Oklahoma state senator (Republican, 2004–present)—the first Native American to serve in the state legislature—and the appointment of Kevin Washburn as head of the Bureau of Indian Affairs in September 2012. Recent cultural achievements include language teacher Irene Digby's induction to the Chickasaw Hall of Fame in 2014.

Choctaw Nation of Oklahoma

Prior to the 1830 Treaty of Dancing Rabbit Creek, the Choctaw (Chata) lived mainly in Mississippi. About 2,500 of the estimated 19,550 Choctaw people died during their forced relocation to Indian Territory (see also the chapter titled "Southeast").

Roughly 48,000 tribal members live on or near Tuskahoma, on the Choctaw Reservation, which is located in the most unemployed county in Oklahoma. Challenging conditions are exacerbated by drought, population growth, and climate change. The tribes originally controlled water rights, and they wanted to be designated by the state as joint owners. In April 2011, the Choctaw and Chickasaw nations sued to win water rights for Sardis Lake's flow near Tuskahoma. A win could prompt a new push for similar rights across Oklahoma based on the Winters Doctrine, a 103-year-old Supreme Court decision that tribes are at the head of the line for water in times of shortage.

Recent cultural advances include the Modern Language Association (MLA) awarding LeAnne Howe the Edison Distinguished Professor of American Literature in March 2015, the first MLA prize for studies in Native American literature and culture for her book, *Choctalking on Other Realities*. In another victory for language activists, the correct spellings of the names of two famous Choctaw leaders, Piominko, a friend of George Washington, and Tishominko, whose image is on the Choctaw Nation's flag, have been restored ("k" to replace "g") to reflect their stature as leaders through the efforts of the director of the Choctaw Tribe's Language Department.

Also in 2015, the Choctaw Nation hosted the first tribal Promise Zone Summit in areas designated by the Obama Administration as areas of rural economic hardship. Additionally, Choctaw basketball player Kenny Dobbs, 6'3" Slam Dunk Champion of the World, toured high schools to inspire students by example on how he overcame adversity.

The Comanche Nation

The Numunu (Comanche) have always been admired as the extraordinary horseback riders known as the Lords of the Plains. Related to the Shoshone, they hunted buffalo from the Northern Plains to far south of the Rio Grande. In the mid- to late 1800s, they fought determinedly against the U.S. Army, the Texas Rangers, and mercenaries sent to exterminate the buffalo on the Plains.

When finally consigned to Fort Sill, Oklahoma, the leader Quanah Parker continued his role as a powerful advocate for his people and strengthened his people's spirits through the ceremonies of the Native American Church (see also his biography at the end of this chapter).

About 23,000 people are enrolled as Comanche members with tribal offices near Lawton, where they share a reservation with the Kiowa and Apache. LaDonna Harris, a founder of several prominent Indigenous and women's rights organizations since the 1960s, continues the strong leadership tradition among the Comanche. President and founder of Americans for Indian Opportunity (AIO), Harris spoke to Peruvian leaders at a Building Bridges Conference in Lima in December 2014 about climate change, energy resources, and tribal interaction with energy corporations (see also her biography at the end of this chapter).

In an October 2014 interview with *Indian Country Today Media Network*, Juanita Paudopony, Comanche artist and dean emeritus of Comanche Nation College, shared her favorite things about the Comanche Nation: modesty, matriarchal families, respect for warriors and medicine people, social gatherings, Southern Cloth dance regalia, diverse musical traditions, and long-range planning. "Our ancestors reflected on the future and thought of the ones we'd never see."

Delaware Tribe of Indians and the Delaware Nation

Descended from the great Eastern nation of Lenape, who were forced away from the Atlantic coast and the Delaware River in 1700, some Delaware people now live among the Stockbridge–Munsee in Wisconsin, some reside in Kansas with their Ojibwe relatives, and most are in Ontario with the Cayuga. About eight thousand Delaware live in two communities in Oklahoma. The Delaware Tribe established itself after a long struggle to receive recognition separate from the Cherokee in eastern Oklahoma, from whom the Delaware had purchased citizen membership in 1867. In the West, the Delaware lived with the Caddo and then were legally merged with the Wichita in Anadarko in 1859 until they were federally recognized as the Delaware Nation near the end of the twentieth century.

James Rementer, language director of the Delaware tribe at Bartlesville, has coauthored a new Lenape history, *Near the Edge: Language Revival from the Brink of Extinction,* a talking dictionary with stories and songs. Rementer, the only living Native Delaware speaker, holds language classes at the Culture Preservation Committee at Bartlesville.

Ioway Tribe of Oklahoma

Ba-kho-je, or "Grey Snow," was the original name of the Ioway people, which refers to the appearance of their villages in winter when the roofs were covered in smoke-smudged snow. The Ioway homeland is near the red, pipestone quarry in southwest Minnesota. The Ioway language is a version of Chiwere Siouan, but it is rarely spoken today. Mid-1700s migrations took the people to Iowa and Missouri, but by 1836, they were forced to cede those lands and accept reservations in two locations: the Northern Ioway in Nebraska and Kansas and the Southern Ioway in Perkins, Oklahoma, which numbers about eight hundred. Most people are Christian, but some maintain their traditional clan system and are known for their ribbonwork.

The Grey Snow Eagle House in Perkins, Oklahoma, rescues raptors like this golden eagle.

The Ioway Tribe's Grey Snow Eagle House in Perkins is the only eagle rescue and rehabilitation program of its kind in the United States. Run by Victor Roubidoux, tribal elder, its mission is to protect injured eagles for eventual release back into the wild or as a refuge for nonreleasable birds. Feathers from moulting are gathered and made available to tribal members for ceremonies. The program increases awareness of the need to protect wildlife and their cultural importance. The tribe also runs a federally funded wind energy farm, providing a renewable energy source to local communities, selling the excess back to the grid, and collecting data for wind energy researchers to analyze.

Kaw Nation

The Kaw name is Siouan for "south wind." The French called the Kaw people Kanza, and in the mid-eighteenth century, it was the largest tribe in the state that bears its name. Descended from the Dhegila Sioux division of the Hopewell culture in the lower Ohio Valley (see also the chapter titled "Midwest"), the Kaw are related to the Osage, Ponca, Omaha, and Quapaw. After heavy resistance, the tribe's Kansas lands were taken, and the people moved to Kay County, Oklahoma, in 1872.

By 1902, the tribe had legally disappeared after losing all tribal land to allotment. Ironically, the chief architect of allotment policy was one-eighth Kaw Indian: Charles Curtis, a U.S. senator from Kansas who became vice president under Herbert Hoover. He reached the highest office of anyone identifying himself as an American Indian, yet the Curtis Act, which bears his name, disenfranchised his own people (see also his biography at the end of this chapter). The Kaw Nation was federally recognized in 1959, and today, 3,660 members share the benefits of a casino, several retail businesses, and an experimental pecan orchard. The language is in decline, but the Kanza museum is working to preserve the legacy of the original sixteen Kaw clans. A recent tribal project is Southwind Energy, which produces green lighting and mobile solar power systems.

The Kiowa Indian Tribe of Oklahoma

Kiowa is headquartered at Carnegie, Oklahoma, and nearby towns with an enrollment of 12,000. In 1998, the U.S. Supreme Court ruled in favor of the Kiowa, a groundbreaking 6–3 decision, which states that Indians enjoy sovereign immunity in contracts made off the reservation.

This ruling does not resolve a crisis the Kiowa have endured since 1913 when the tribe became involved in a protracted dispute with Stewart Stone, a rock-crushing company that intends to mine limestone on Longhorn Mountain, a sacred site used for 150 years for their ceremonies. This time, however, they have no legal recourse to prevent the mountain from environmental degradation because it is not on tribal land. Instead, the tribe is gathering signatures for a petition to save the mountain. "We don't build churches, but we seek the presence of God in sa-

cred places in nature," explains an elder. For more information, see savelonghornmountain.com on Facebook and "Longhorn Mountain Documentary" on YouTube.

In 2014, the community expressed pride in tribal member Chris Wondolowski, soccer forward for the U.S. team and the first tribally enrolled Native American to play at the World Cup. Two Kiowa sisters were also lauded when they were named Living Treasures for the 2015 Native Treasures Indian Arts Festival, which benefits the Museum of Indian Arts and Culture (MIAC) in Santa Fe, New Mexico. Artists Keri Ataumbi and Teri Greeves are enrolled members of the Kiowa Indian Tribe of Oklahoma. Greeves specializes in beadwork, creating large pictorial pieces on hide, umbrellas, and even high-heeled sneakers. In December 2014, Greeves told *Indian Country Today Media Network*: "My grandmother was a beadworker. She too was compelled to bead/express herself and her experience as a Kiowa living during her time.... I must express myself and my experience as a twenty-first-century Kiowa, and I do it, like all of those unknown artists before me, through beadwork."

Keri Ataumbi creates modern, geometric jewelry of natural materials, which she says "falls into the category of wearable art, as it has a conceptual narrative exploration at its core. This inquiry happens through an exploration of imagery and materials to create a small sculpture complete upon its own as well as worn on the body." Both sisters' work has won numerous awards and can be seen in public collections around the world.

Miami Tribe of Oklahoma

The Miami's, or "Downstream People's," homeland once spread across the southern Great Lakes, but by 1846, after the Colonial Wars, the tribe was forced apart (see also the chapter titled "Midwest"). The people were herded at gunpoint onto Erie Canal boats to the Mississippi and on horseback to Kansas. In 1867, the Miami were forced to Oklahoma, then terminated as a tribe in 1897. In Oklahoma, the Miami banded with their cousins, the Peoria, Wea, and Kaskaskia, to buy land from the Shawnee. Oil revenue in the early twentieth century allowed them to build businesses and begin restoring their longhouse culture, and after one hundred years, they won federal recognition.

With an enrollment of 4,400, this community, based in Miami, Oklahoma, is the only federally registered Miami tribe in the United States. With landholdings in five states, the tribe has been making an effort to bind their scattered community. "The work of reclamation includes reclaiming our own people." Working with Miami University of Ohio, the Miami established a Myaama Language Center that provides "Breath of Life" language workshops as well as archival access to Native American language activists and scholars "to review our sleeping tongues." In 2014, the center received a $167,650 grant from the National Science Foundation and the National Endowment for the Humanities to document their endangered language. Other ongoing reclamation work includes developing reservation land to grow organic crops.

Muscogee (Creek) Nation

One of the largest tribes in the United States and part of the original Creek Confederacy (see also the chapter titled "Southeast"), the Muscogee Nation is based in an eleven-county region south of Tulsa, Oklahoma, with a tribal enrollment of over 77,000, over 55,500 of whom live in the state. The nation has its own community hospital and several clinics; it publishes a bimonthly newspaper and a weekly TV show, *Native News Today*, and owns and operates eleven casinos and the Muscogee Business Enterprise, which provides service to entrepreneurs. Services include the Reintegration Program, which helps hundreds of ex-offenders each year. The college of the Muscogee Nation in Okmulgee enrolls an average of five hundred students annually. In 2015, hosted by Chief George Tiger, the college welcomed four hundred people from around Indian Country for the Inter-Tribal Council of the Five Civilized Tribes.

The Muscogee Nation does nothing on a small scale. In 2011, it bought twenty prime acres

along the Arkansas River to develop Jenks Riverwalk Crossing, a multiple facility for entertainment, dining, and shopping.

Osage Tribe

With an enrollment of 13,307, of which 6,247 are living in Osage County, the Osage is the twenty-fifth-largest tribe in the United States with a land trust of more than 1,800 acres. Participating in the Land Buy-Back Program for Tribal Nations (see also the chapter titled "Northern Plains" [section "The Cobell Settlement"]), the tribal government has offered nearly seven hundred non-Native owners in the county a total of $7.4 million to sell their land, which will be restored in trust to the tribe.

In the twenty-first century, the Osage are one of the wealthiest tribes in the country because of the oil boom that began in the 1920s, and its $4 billion mineral rights estate continues to be a major source of income. In a single year, 2009, four million barrels of oil were produced in Osage County. Lucrative mineral rights have long been the cause of suffering as well as a benefit for the community in the form of crime and corruption by government officials and private individuals (see also the section titled "Osage Oil" in this chapter).

Seal of the Osage Nation

Since 2006, a tribal constitution, ratified by two-thirds of the membership, provided new legal and legislative protections, but controversy over finances continues. The Osage Nation's attorney general has asked for a judicial review of the Osage Minerals Council, which owns the mineral rights for the entire county. The Council insists that it is an independent body and therefore not subject to the new tribal laws, and the issue of the Council's autonomy is a source of contention.

Another concern of the membership is the Bureau of Indian Affairs' lax drilling regulations in the county, which are not as stringent as those of the Environmental Protection Agency and not under its jurisdiction. This has resulted in increasingly high emissions of hydrogen sulfate (also known as swamp gas) and other toxic emissions. A related controversy is the Osage Wind Project, which proposes to develop a ninety-four-turbine wind farm on culturally significant tribal land in the county. Some tribal members are against the wind farm because the turbines may kill bald eagles and other birds. The Osage Minerals Council, concerned about oil profits, is involved in multiple lawsuits against the wind farm that have yet to be resolved.

Pawnee Nation of Oklahoma

For the past seven hundred years of recorded Pawnee history, the tribe lived along the North Platte River in Nebraska. About sixty thousand Pawnee lived among four bands: the Chaui, "Grand," the Kitkehaki, "Republican," the Pitahawirata, "Tappage," and the Skidi, "Wolf." They were elaborate ceremonial dramatists and have an honored military tradition (which carries on to this day), enhancing their commanding presence with a hornlike hairstyle in which buffalo fat was used to slick the scalp lock upward and curve it back. Although many Pawnee were scouts for the United States during the Plains Indian Wars (see also the chapter titled "Northern Plains"), they were removed to Pawnee County, Oklahoma, in 1875. Today, 1,791 of more than 3,240 tribal members live in the area.

Renowned scholars and statesmen have sprung from Pawnee culture, particularly within the Echohawk family (see also their biographies at the end of this chapter). In November 2014, the United States Congress held a special honoring ceremony for the Pawnee Code Talkers, who served during World War II. Their descendants received a Silver Medal of Honor, and the Pawnee Nation was presented with a Golf Medal of Honor for services rendered.

SHAWNEE TRIBE

Ancient artifacts of the Shawnee culture have been found along the Ohio River. In the early 1800s, the Shawnee confederated with the Lenape, Miami, Ottawa, and Creek to hold on to their land and resist colonial expansion (see also Tecumseh's biography in the chapter titled "Midwest"). After the tribes who were allied with the British against the Americans lost the War of 1812, the Shawnee were relocated to Oklahoma. The Shawnee separated from the Cherokee Nation of Oklahoma in 2000 when President Clinton restored the tribe to sovereign nation status. With a combined tribal membership of 2,226, about 1,070 live in Miami County.

Absentee Shawnee

The 4,014 members of the Absentee Shawnee live near Shawnee, Oklahoma, on 112,110 acres, 89.25 of which are tribally held. In 2013, Charles Tripp, attorney for the tribe, sued for the return of Deseray, an infant girl who had been unlawfully adopted and removed to South Carolina in violation of the Indian Child Welfare Act. In September 2013, an Oklahoma county judge ordered the return of the infant, the second child to be illegally removed to South Carolina in recent years. "We have to protect our children," Tripp reported to a local newspaper. "We need to redouble our efforts to give them a safe and steady place to grow up in."

Eastern Shawnee

After years of researching historical documents, the tribe at Seneca, Oklahoma, bought a fifty-acre tract near Indian Lake in Logan County, Ohio, in October 2014. The land had been continuously owned by the tribe since 1810 but had been sold illegally when the original heirs died, and the tribe was forced to relocate. More information on Eastern Shawnee history is available on YouTube, where Glenda Wallace, English teacher, chief, and first woman leader of the Eastern Shawnee Tribe gives an hour-long talk, "Homelands, Shawnee, and Ohio," one of many states where the tribe had lived since 1740 and from which fifty thousand were forcibly removed in 1832.

Wichita and Affiliated Tribes (Wichita, Keechi, Waco, and Tawakonie)

The Wichita Reservation is located in the northern half of Caddo County, Oklahoma, along the Washita River. The people have lived on the Southern Plains for more than eight hundred years. Oral history tells that the first man and woman in creation were called Morning Star and the Moon. They received an ear of corn and a bow and arrow to perpetuate the lives of their people. Sometime around 1350 C.E., the Wichita began building their famous villages of towering, conical grass houses. They gardened and traded glazed pottery and turquoise and shell jewelry extensively with the Pueblo and Caddo peoples. After Spanish horses became available in the sixteenth century, the Wichita began hunting buffalo and trading with the Comanche.

In 1835, the American–Wichita Treaty defined all of the local affiliated tribes as "Wichita." Settlers brought diseases and "days of darkness" to the Wichita, who were under attack from the time the Texas Republic was founded in 1836 until the tribes were removed to western Oklahoma in 1855. Confederate troops drove them to Kansas in 1863, where many people starved and died of smallpox and cholera. Upon their return to Oklahoma, allotment undermined their communal way of life. Despite these losses, the Wichita and Affiliated Tribes of Anadarko have preserved many elements of their culture for the future through elders' storytelling, language classes, and annual ceremonial encampments with the Pawnee.

> When they awoke the next morning, they found beside them a stalk of corn that had already grown. A voice said to them that this was Mother Corn; they should use it again…. It was promised further on that they should have their grass lodge built and would be given plenty of things to use, and there would be corn planted by the lodge which they were to eat.
>
> —Takwakoni Jim,
> *The Mythology of the Wichita* (1904)

TEXAS

At one time, Texas was home to several hundred groups of American Indians, but most were killed or removed before Texas became a state in 1845. Today, only three reservations exist in an area that historically was home to thousands, if not millions, of various peoples: the Alabama–Coushatta Indian Reservation (just east of Houston), Ysleta del Sur Pueblo (El Paso), and the Kickapoo Traditional Tribe of Texas (near Eagle Pass). Because of relocation policies, Texas cities have Native residents as far away as Montana and South Dakota.

The Ysleta del Sur Pueblo

The tribal community known as "Tigua" established Ysleta del Sur in 1682 after they left their homelands due to drought. First they sought refuge at Isleta Pueblo (New Mexico) but were captured by the Spanish during the 1680 Pueblo Revolt and forced to walk south for over four hundred miles near their present-day lands in El Paso, Texas. The Tigua settled and built the Ysleta del Sur Pueblo and the acequia (canal) system that sustained a flourishing, agriculturally based economy. Their early financial success started the region's development.

The Pueblo Tribe owns and operates diverse enterprises that provide employment for its citizens as well as others in the area. They pride themselves on being able to meet the economic needs of their community and still maintain their traditional religion, traditions, and values for its over three thousand citizens. The Tigua Indian Cultural Center, located in El Paso, showcases the history, arts, and contemporary lives of the Ysleta del Sur Pueblo.

The Kickapoo

Scattering has tended to result in greater loss of language and culture, with some exceptions. The Kickapoo of Wisconsin who intentionally fled, first to Texas, then Mexico, maintain a sacred fire in Nacimiento, Mexico, that is central to their beliefs about world preservation. They live in traditional reed mat wickiups, and for 45 percent of the people, Kickapoo is their only language. The rest also speak Spanish, and only 5 percent are fluent in English.

The Kickapoo have endured major challenges to remain intact. Removals from 1795 through 1860 split the tribe into two groups. One section was sent to Kansas, where some of them remain as the Kickapoo Tribe of Kansas. Because of government leases to farmers, they own only 37 percent of their reservation. Threatened with termination as a tribe in 1954, they banded with the Prairie Potawatomi to travel to Washington, D.C., where they successfully defended their right to exist. Although most people in Kansas

A group of Kickapoo construct a traditional winter house in Nacimiento, Mexico.

don't speak Kickapoo, many have adopted the Potawatomi's language and traditions.

Meanwhile, on the way to Oklahoma, another group of Kickapoo refused to accept forced settlement. They escaped to Texas, which was an anarchic place in the mid-1800s, rife with constant fighting between Indians and whites. The Kickapoo killed eighteen settlers at Battle Creek in 1838 but were preyed upon by Comanche and Apache raiders. Running to the other side of the Sierra Madre Mountains provided protection, and in 1838, Mexican President Benito Juarez, himself an Oaxacan Indian, gave the Kickapoo 17,000 acres in the state of Coahuila, twenty-five miles northwest of Muzquiz and 125 miles southwest of Eagle Pass, Texas.

In retaliation for Kickapoo raids in Texas, the U.S. cavalry crossed into Mexico in 1873 and kidnapped forty women and children, whom they held hostage at Fort Gibson, Oklahoma, in an attempt to lure the men to Indian Territory. Some Kickapoo relocated and received a reservation in central Oklahoma, but when they were ordered to divide their communal land into smaller, individual plots, many returned to Mexico. By 1905, there were 255 Kickapoo in Kansas, 247 in Oklahoma, and four hundred in Mexico. People from Oklahoma continued to travel to Nacimiento Rancheria several times a year for seasonal ceremonies.

Hardship came again in the 1940s when a drought and overhunting of deer in Coahuila forced the Kickapoo to seek migrant farm work in the United States. Between trips to work on farms across the United States, the undocumented laborers and their families lived in squalor under a bridge in Eagle Pass, Texas. There, they tried to recreate their village out of cardboard and cane. There was only one water spigot available and no toilets; dirt from the roadway above fell into their food as they ate. Their health deteriorated.

Kickapoo leaders began applying for U.S. citizenship and reservation land in 1979. In 1983, after the Native American Rights Fund (NARF) facilitated negotiations among the Kickapoo, the U.S. State Department, the Department of the Interior, the Mexican government, and the Inter-American Indian Institute, a public law was passed to create the Texas Band of Kickapoo. Of the six hundred tribal members, 145 chose U.S. citizenship.

During the recognition process, the Texas Kickapoo raised $300,000 from charitable donations and bought 125 acres in Maverick County, Texas, along the Rio Grande. There, they began raising white-tailed deer on a game farm, as this animal is essential to their diet and ceremonies. In 2001, they opened a casino and invested $3 million of those profits in additional ranch land, a pecan orchard, and construction and landscaping companies. Another $130 million have built a resort, championship golf course, and airport as well as provided training for employees. The tribe opened a school in 2002, and in 2010, Mexico's National Institute of Anthropology and History collaborated with the tribe to develop a Kickapoo language alphabet. The Texas Kickapoo tribe's seven hundred members are fully employed, and their casino provides four thousand jobs in one of the poorest parts of the state. Meanwhile, in Mexico, the sacred fire still burns.

BIOGRAPHIES

John Ross (1790–1866)
Cherokee, Tribal Leader

John Ross led the Cherokee Nation as principal chief from 1828 to 1866. His father was a Scottish trader, who married a part-Cherokee woman. While a young man, Ross became a successful merchant and plantation slave owner. He strongly advocated agricultural and political change for the Cherokee as a means to preserve the nation from U.S. demands for cessions of land and Cherokee migration west of the Mississippi River.

During the 1820s, the Cherokee adopted a constitutional government and became an agricultural nation. At that time, Ross served as sec-

retary to the Cherokee principal chief, Path Killer, who represented the conservative majority that resisted U.S. pressures to migrate west. In 1828, after Path Killer's death, Ross was elected principal chief, and until 1866, Ross led the Cherokee conservatives, who formed the National Party and worked to preserve Cherokee independence from U.S. encroachments.

Lone Wolf (Guipago) (1820–1879)
Kiowa, Tribal Leader

During the 1860s and 1870s, Lone Wolf became one of his tribe's most respected band chiefs. He was one of the signers of the Medicine Lodge Treaty of 1867, which established the boundaries of the combined Kiowa and Comanche Reservation in present-day Oklahoma, and later fought a series of military campaigns against U.S. forces. During the first part of his life, Lone Wolf came to negotiate with U.S. agents in a spirit of peace and hope for close, friendly ties. In 1863, he visited President Abraham Lincoln as part of a delegation of Southern Plains Indian leaders. In 1866, he became principal chief of the Kiowa. When members of his tribe refused to comply with the Medicine Lodge Treaty, Lone Wolf was taken hostage by U.S. authorities.

Although Lone Wolf traveled to Washington, D.C., in 1872 to negotiate a peace settlement, the death of his son at the hands of federal soldiers in 1873 pushed him into war. For the next two years, he and other tribal leaders of the Southern Plains met federal and state troops in a number of consequential engagements. Lone Wolf participated in the Red River War (1874-1875), fighting alongside Quanah Parker, the Comanche leader. The Kiowa and Comanche waged this war to discourage buffalo hunters from killing the buffalo herds. After the battle at Palo Duro Canyon in September 1874, however, Lone Wolf's supply of horses and teepees was devastated. He was forced to surrender at Fort Sill in the Indian Territory in

1875 and was sent to Fort Marion in Florida. Lone Wolf returned to his homeland in 1878 and died one year later of malaria.

Left Hand (Nawat) (1840–1890s)
Southern Arapaho, Tribal Leader

As one of the principal chiefs of the Southern Arapaho, Left Hand trod the delicate line between advocating peace and defending against U.S. invasion. He also represented his people in negotiations with the federal government in the early 1890s. Left Hand was present with the Southern Cheyenne leader Black Kettle at the Sand Creek Massacre in November 1864, when about two hundred Cheyenne men, women, and children were indiscriminately killed by Colonel John Chivington's troops (see also the chapter titled "Northern Plains"). Left Hand was wounded during the shooting, but he refused to return fire against Chivington's forces. His pacifist stance met with skepticism from some of his people.

Quanah Parker (1845–1911)
Comanche, Tribal Leader

In the decades following the American Civil War, Indian groups who refused to relocate to reservations became outlaws. One of the most fearless and powerful of these "renegade" groups was led by Quanah Parker. Parker was the son of Peta Nocona, chief of the Kwahadi Band in Texas, a subgroup within the Comanche Nation, and Cynthia Parker, a non-Comanche captive. Throughout the 1860s, Parker led numerous attacks against U.S. soldiers. He and his band escaped capture longer than most of the Comanche bands in their final days living freely on the Plains.

In the 1870s, however, new, high-powered rifles and increasing numbers of U.S. hunters were systematically killing buffalo and destroying the way of life for the Plains Indians. In 1875, after years of battle and their buffalo nearly gone, Parker and his warriors turned themselves in.

In a few short years, Parker became a successful cattle rancher in Oklahoma. He counseled his people to adapt to the reservation without surrendering their Comanche customs and heritage. Parker adopted the Peyote religion (see also the chapter titled "Southwest"), which offered many Indians a new form of religious belief that provided moral and spiritual support when they were desperately depressed and disoriented from the early reservation captivity of the 1880s and 1890s.

Parker became an appointed judge and served in the court of Indian affairs from 1886 to 1898. By 1890, he was the chief representative for the Comanche people in the allotment of tribal lands (see also the chapter titled "Historical Overview" [section "The General Allotment Act"]). Parker also negotiated for the release of Geronimo by offering refuge to Apache warriors on the Comanche Reservation (see also the chapter titled "Southwest").

Alexander Posey (1873–1908)
Creek, Poet/Journalist

Alexander Posey was a well-known poet and journalist whose skillful satirizing of U.S. culture provided his people with an important sense of identity and belonging during a time when their lands and culture were being stripped from them. Posey was raised in Creek culture by his mother near Eufaula, Oklahoma. He mastered English as a teenager while going to Bacone Indian University in Tahlequah. At the university, Posey learned to set type and began writing.

Much of Posey's work was printed in the *Indian Journal,* a Native Oklahoma newspaper, in which he especially liked to point out Americans' fondness for material possessions, including Indian land. Posey cleverly mixed pidgin English, puns, and inside jokes with a recurring cast of characters who dealt with attempts to change Indian ways through new names, haircuts, and slogans. His humorous comments helped Indians maintain a feeling of unity. Posey was also active in tribal affairs and was superintendent of public instruction for the Creek Nation. In 1905, he helped draft a revised Creek constitution. Sadly, Posey died at the early age of thirty-four during a swimming accident.

Redbird Smith (1850–1918)
Cherokee, Activist

Redbird Smith was an advocate for the restoration of cultural traditions among his people and led a resistance movement against policies of the U.S. government to redistribute Indian lands. He and a number of colleagues revived the Nighthawk Keetoowah Society to protect Indian sovereignty. By the late 1890s, the U.S. government's land allotment policies were finally reaching Oklahoma. For most Indians, allotment was tantamount to cultural and political extinction (see also the chapter titled "Historical Overview" [section "The General Allotment Act"]). The Nighthawk Keetoowah was reorganized in the late 1850s in order to promote political unity among the Cherokee. Smith led a passive resistance movement that used civil disobedience tactics to disrupt enrollments for distribution of allotted land. In 1902, Smith was arrested by federal marshals and forced to sign the enrollment.

In 1907, the Indian Territory became the state of Oklahoma. Smith was elected principal chief of the Cherokee in 1908. His activism continued, and in 1912, he cofounded the Four Mothers Society, dedicated to preserving and advocating for the political and legal rights of Indian tribes. The Nighthawk Keetoowah Society continues to be active today.

Robert L. Owen (1856–1947)
Cherokee, Politician

Robert Latham Owen was elected in 1907 as one of the first two U.S. senators for the state of Oklahoma. He served three terms in the Senate. A member of the Cherokee Nation, Owen taught orphaned Cherokee children and represented the Five Civilized Tribes as a federal Indian agent before entering politics as a Progressive Democrat. In the Senate, Owen focused on national banking policy. The first chairman of the Senate Committee on Banking and Currency, he cosponsored legislation creating the Federal Reserve System in 1913.

James Francis "Jim" Thorpe (1888–1953)
Sauk and Fox/ Potawatomi/Kickapoo, Athlete

Thorpe's Indian name, Wa-Tho-Huk, translates to "Bright Path," and his path was indeed bright, full of glory that led him far from his birthplace in a one-room cabin near Prague, Oklahoma. Thorpe's mother was descended from the great Sauk leader Black Hawk (see also the chapter titled "Midwest"). He was an all-around athlete and excelled in many different sports. Thorpe won Olympic gold medals in the pentathlon and decathlon in 1912 in Stockholm, Sweden, setting records that would stand for decades. In an unfortunate decision, the Olympic Committee took away his medals because his baseball experience compromised his amateur status.

After the Olympics, Thorpe played professional football, baseball, and basketball and was one of the founders of the American Professional Football League, which evolved into the National Football League (NFL). In 1950, he was named "the greatest athlete of the twentieth century" by the Associated Press. After his death of a heart attack, the *New York Times* ran a front-page story, stating that Thorpe "was a magnificent performer.

He had all the strength and speed and coordination of the best players, plus incredible stamina. The tragedy of the loss of his Stockholm medals because of thoughtless and unimportant professionalism darkened much of his career and should have been rectified long ago. His memory should be kept for what it deserves—that of the greatest all-around athlete of our time." Thorpe's medals were finally returned to his family in 1982, and his achievements were restored to the record books.

William W. Keeler (1908–1987)
Cherokee Nation, Chief

In 1949, William Keeler was appointed principal chief of the Cherokee Nation in Oklahoma until 1971. Keeler's initial appointment was made under laws that abolished the Cherokee government in 1907 in an attempt to dissolve the nation. Until 1971, the Cherokee principal chief was appointed by the U.S. president. In 1971, however, the Cherokee regained the right to elect their own leadership.

Starting at age sixteen as a part-time worker, Keeler pursued a corporate business career with Phillips Petroleum Company. In 1951, he was elected to the board of directors. In 1968, he was elected chairman of the board and vice president of the executive department. Because of his reputation as a strong administrator, government agencies often tapped Keeler for advice on solving problems in the oil and refining industry. Keeler actively contributed his services to many public interest groups, including fraternal, veterans, civic, and business organizations.

During Keeler's administration as principal chief, he gained a reputation as an able administrator and leader and served on major government task forces. He also helped establish the Cherokee Foundation, which endeavors to promote the welfare and culture of the Cherokee Nation and its members.

Mary Ross (1908–2008)
Cherokee, Engineer/Mathematician

Ross was a Native American female engineer and one of forty founding engineers of the Skunk Works. She was known for her work at Lockheed Martin on "preliminary design concepts for interplanetary space travel, manned and unmanned earth-orbiting flights." Ross said, "The best thing about being a research engineer was that you were discovering new things every day. I was working on designing vehicles that had never been dreamed of before—I felt immense satisfaction in this." In 1958, Ross stumped the panel on the TV show *What's My Line?* No one would have guessed that the great-great-granddaughter of Cherokee Chief John Ross was a top-notch engineer for the high-flying Lockheed Corporation. She considered her greatest engineering contributions to be the basic research on orbital and "fly-by" space vehicles she conducted in the 1960s. "These vehicles have brought us new information about the universe, and we now know more about the planets than we ever did before. I feel very proud I helped achieve these discoveries," said Ross.

Allan Houser (1914–1994)
Chiricahua Apache, Artist

Allan Houser was an internationally recognized sculptor and painter whose works have a serene but powerful quality that reflects Chiricahua Apache culture. Born in Apache, Oklahoma, he attended Santa Fe Indian School in New Mexico and later studied art at Utah State University. A mural artist and art instructor during the late 1930s, Houser had to give up his artwork when he lived in the Los Angeles area in the 1940s and supported his family by working at various construction jobs. He began wood carving and got a commission to create a stone monument at Haskell Institute in Lawrence, Kansas. The work, entitled "Comrade in Mourning," was a memorial to the Indian casualties of World War II carved from a half-ton block of marble.

In the following year (1949), Houser was awarded a fellowship from the Guggenheim Foundation, which established his career and opened the door to many solo shows at museums in the

Southwest. He won numerous prizes during his midcareer, including the Palmes Acadamique, awarded by the French government in 1954. In 1962, Houser became a teacher at the Institute of American Indian Arts in Santa Fe, New Mexico, and he remained on the faculty there until retiring as head of the sculpture department.

Maria Tallchief (1925–2013)
Osage, Prima Ballerina/Ballet Company Founder and Director

 Elizabeth Maria "Betty" Tallchief was America's first major prima ballerina as well as the first American Indian to attain the title. Tallchief was world-renowned and one of the premiere American ballerinas of all time. Her sister Marjorie was also an accomplished ballerina. Their grandfather helped negotiate a treaty for Osage mineral rights, and after oil was discovered on Osage land they became the wealthiest tribe in the nation. The Tallchief family had always been extremely attentive to their daughters' education, and their new financial gain made piano and ballet lessons affordable. While the girls were young, the family moved to Beverly Hills, California, so they could study with famous teachers. When she was just fifteen, Tallchief danced a solo performance at the Hollywood Bowl.

Tallchief moved to New York City to join the Ballet Russe de Monte Carlo, a highly acclaimed Russian ballet troupe, and when the world-famous George Balanchine became the troupe's director, he recognized Tallchief's amazing talent. In 1947, she became the first prima ballerina of the newly formed New York City Ballet, directed by Balanchine, and was the star dancer until she retired eighteen years later.

She and Marjorie founded the Chicago City Ballet in 1981; she served as its artistic director until 1987. She had many other firsts during her long and much-praised career: first American to perform with the Paris Opera Ballet; first American to perform in Russia; and the first to dance the Sugarplum Fairy in Balanchine's version of the *Nutcracker Suite*. Tallchief was appointed Woman of the Year (1953) by President Eisenhower, inducted into the National Women's Hall of Fame in 1996, and presented with a National Medal of the Arts by the National Endowment for the Arts in 1999. American dance was considered far inferior to European dance before she arrived on the scene; Maria Tallchief changed that impression forever.

Louis W. Ballard (1931–2007)
Cherokee/Quapaw, Composer/Educator/Author/Artist

Born in northeast Oklahoma, Ballard's Quapaw name was Honganozhe, "Stands With Eagles." He composed numerous orchestral, choral, and chamber works with Native American themes or using texts in Native American languages. He compiled several volumes of Native American songs for classroom use. His best known pieces are "Incident at Wounded Knee" and "Why the Duck Has a Short Tail." His music was celebrated at the National Museum of the American Indian in Washington, D.C., in 2006, and after his death, there was a memorial concert presented there as well. Ballard was a professor at the Institute of American Indian Arts in Santa Fe, New Mexico.

Carter Revard (1931–)
Osage, Poet

Nom-Peh-Wah-The (Carter Revard) is a nationally acclaimed writer whose works combine traditional images of Native American culture with contemporary issues. Born in Pawhuska, Oklahoma, he grew up in Buck Creek on the Osage Reservation. In 1952, he went to Oxford University as a Rhodes Scholar, showing exceptional promise both as an athlete and as a scholar. When he returned to the United States, Revard went to Yale University and earned a Ph.D. in English. Revard spent most of his academic career teaching medieval British literature and linguistics at Washington University in St. Louis, Missouri. He is also a gourd dancer, a traditional dance among the Southern Plains Indians (with origins among the Kiowa) and considered by many Indians to be a sacred part of contemporary powwows. Revard's poetry and other writings have won numerous awards and have been published in several anthologies of Native American writing. His own books include *Cowboys and Indians Christmas Shopping* (1992), *Winning the Dust Bowl* (2001), and *How the Songs Come Down* (2005).

N. Scott Momaday (1934–)
Kiowa, Author

Navarre Scott Momaday is recognized as one of the premier writers in the United States. His writings have always reflected his attachment to land and the beliefs of his Kiowa people. In 1969, his novel *House Made of Dawn* (1968) was awarded the Pulitzer Prize for fiction. Born in Lawton, Oklahoma, to Kiowa and Cherokee parents who themselves were teachers, artists, and authors, he grew up in the Southwest and went to government Indian schools. He later attended the Virginia Military Academy and the University of New Mexico. Momaday began writing poetry while teaching on the Jicarilla Apache Reservation. The poems he wrote during this period led to a Creative Fellowship from Stanford University, where he earned master's and doctorate degrees. He taught at the University of California, Berkeley, where he created an Indian literature program.

The Pulitzer Prize-winning *House Made of Dawn* focuses on the role confusion experienced by a young Indian, recently returned from World War II, who no longer feels "at home" on the reservation but also experiences displacement in U.S. urban society. Momaday's second novel, *The Way to Rainy Mountain* (1969), is a description of the three-hundred-year-old migration of the Kiowa from the headwaters of the Yellowstone to the Black Hills as well as Momaday's own remembrances of his family and culture. *The Ancient Child* (1985) is the story of an Indian artist

who searches for his identity. Though mainstream audiences know Momaday best for his novels, the author himself prefers to write poetry. According to Momaday, Indians express themselves naturally in poetic, artistic terms. *Against the Far Morning* (2011) contains some of Momaday's newest poems.

Momaday's honors include the Golden Plate Award from the American Academy of Achievement, an Academy of American Poets Prize, an award from the National Institute of Arts and Letters, and the Premio Letterario Internationale "Mondello," Italy's highest literary award. He is the recipient of a Guggenheim Fellowship, is a Fellow of the American Academy of Arts and Sciences, and holds twelve honorary degrees from American colleges and universities.

Saginaw Grant (1936–)
Sac and Fox/Otoe–Missouria/Ioway, Actor

The actor Saginaw Grant was born at the Indian hospital in Pawnee, Oklahoma. He was raised traditionally on a farm in Cushing, Oklahoma, under the influence of his grandfathers, who were spiritual leaders. Grant is a veteran of the United States Marine Corps and has appeared in numerous films and television shows, including *The Lone Ranger* (2013), *Breaking Bad* (2013), and *Winter in the Blood* (2013). His awards include Best Supporting Actor from the American Indian Film Festival (2002) and First Americans in the Arts (2002) for his role in *Skinwalkers*. Grant received the 2015 Native American Humanitarian of the Year Award from Four Directions Education—an Orange County, California-based nonprofit focused on aiding Native Americans to enter college.

Carter Camp (1941–2013)
Ponca, Activist

Carter Camp was an American Indian Movement (AIM) leader who was born in Pawnee, Oklahoma, and graduated from Haskell Institute in Kansas in

1959. He served in the U.S. Army, stationed in Berlin, from 1960 to 1963 and became a shop steward active in the electrician's union in Los Angeles. He joined AIM in 1968 and founded the AIM chapters in Kansas and Oklahoma. He helped organize the 1962 Trail of Broken Treaties march that led to the occupation of the Bureau of Indian Affairs (BIA) offices in Washington, D.C., where, with Hank Adams (see also the chapter titled "Northern Plains"), he coauthored the "Twenty Points" document of Native concerns, which they presented to the BIA. In 1973, Camp was among the first group of occupiers to seize the Wounded Knee trading post site at Pine Ridge, South Dakota, beginning the seventy-one-day standoff. As spokesman for AIM, Camp signed the agreement ending the occupation and served three years in prison.

Once free again, Camp helped organize the annual Sun Dances held at the Crow Dog compound in Rosebud, South Dakota, and fought for Indian rights and environmental causes, such as opposition to garbage dumping on reservations and tar sands pipelines (see also the chapter titled "Northern Plains"). In an interview for the PBS program *American Experience* in 2009, Camp said about Wounded Knee, "We were pretty sure that we were going to have to give up our lives."

Wilma P. Mankiller (1945–2010)
Cherokee Nation, Chief

Best known as chief of the Cherokee Nation, Wilma Mankiller was born at the Indian hospital in Tahlequah, Oklahoma. She gained an understanding of rural poverty early in life because she witnessed and experienced it. She spent her childhood in the wooded hills of the rural community of Rocky Mountain, where she eventually returned to live with her husband, Charley Lee Soap, a community developer, who is a traditionalist and a fluent speaker of Cherokee. When she was eleven, her family moved to California as part of the Bureau of Indian Affairs' relocation program. From a family of eleven children and with marginal employment for her father, Mankiller also gained insight into the meaning of urban poverty.

Mankiller became active in Indian causes in San Francisco in the late 1960s and early 1970s and gained skills in community organization and program development. She earned a B.S. degree in social work and in 1979 completed graduate work in Community Planning at the University of Arkansas. In 1983, she was the first woman elected deputy chief of the Cherokee Nation. In the historic 1987 election with fifty-six percent of the vote, Mankiller became the first woman elected Cherokee principal chief. Her service as the elected leader of the Cherokee Nation resulted in international media focus and public attention that enabled her to share the story of the Cherokee Nation with the rest of the world. Her administration founded the Cherokee Nation Community Development Department and served a population of Cherokee Nation citizens that increased from 55,000 to 156,000 during her ten-year administration.

Mankiller is the author of a nationally bestselling autobiography, *Mankiller: A Chief and Her People* (1999), and coauthored *Every Day Is a Good Day: Reflections by Contemporary Indigenous Women* (2004). A 2013 feature film, *The Cherokee Word for Water*, was inspired by the true story of the struggle of a rural Cherokee community to bring running water to families by using the traditional concept of "gadugi"—working together to solve a problem. Led by a young Wilma Mankiller, before she was elected chief, and her future husband, Charlie Soap, volunteers built nearly twenty miles of waterline. In the process, they inspired the community to trust each other and reawakened universal Indigenous values of reciprocity and interconnectedness. The successful completion of the waterline sparked a movement of similar self-help projects across the Cherokee nation and in Indian Country that continues to this day. In the film, Mankiller is portrayed by actress Kimberly Norris Guerrero (Colville/Salish–Kootenai/Cherokee) and Soap by actor Moses Brings Plenty (Oglala Lakota).

Hanay Geiogamah (1945–)
Kiowa/Delaware,
Playwright and Film Producer

Born in Lawton, Oklahoma, the playwright Hanay Geiogamah attended Anadarko High School and received his master's degree in theater from Indiana University. After graduation, he was public affairs liaison for Commissioner of Indian Affairs Louis Bruce at the Bureau of Indian Affairs during the Nixon Administration. In 1971, Geiogamah joined the experimental theater group La Mama on New York City's Lower East Side, where his plays *Body Indian, Coon Cons, Foghorn,* and *49* were performed. He went on to found the first Native theater companies, the American Theater Ensemble (1972) and the American Indian Dance Theater, which began performing internationally in 1987.

In 1983, Geiogamah moved to Los Angeles and began producing historical dramas for the Turner Broadcasting Network (TNT), including *The Native Americans: Behind the Legends, The Broken Chain, Tecumseh,* and *Lakota Woman.* Recent film projects include *The Only Good Indian* (2009), starring Cherokee actor Wes Studi, and *Race in Hollywood: Native American Images on Film* (2010), a Turner Classic Movies series. Geiogamah serves on the National Film Preservation Board and was director of the American Indian Studies Center at the University of California, Los Angeles from 2002–2009. His publications include *New Native American Drama: Three Plays* (1980) and *Ceremony, Spirituality and Ritual in Native American Performance: A Creative Notebook* (2011).

Linda Hogan (1947–)
Chickasaw, Author

Born in Denver, Colorado, Linda Hogan, former writer-in-residence for the Chickasaw Nation and professor emerita from the University of Colorado, is an internationally recognized public speaker and writer of poetry, fiction, and essays. Her recent poetry books include *Dark. Sweet. New and Selected Poems* (2014), *Indios* (2012), and *Rounding the Human Corners* (2008). Her novel *Mean Spirit* (1990) won the Oklahoma Book Award, the Mountains and Plains Book Award, and was a finalist for the Pulitzer Prize; *Solar Storms* (1995) and *Power* (1998) were finalists for the International Impact Award. In addition, she has received a National Endowment for the Arts Fellowship, a Guggenheim Fellowship, and the Lifetime Achievement Award from the Native Writers Circle of the Americas. Hogan's nonfiction includes a respected collection of essays on the environment, *Dwellings, A Spiritual History of the Land* (1995) and *The Woman Who Watches Over the World: A Native Memoir* (2001). Hogan was inducted into the Chickasaw Nation Hall of Fame in 2007 for her writing.

Wes Studi (1947–)
Cherokee, Actor

From small-town Oklahoma to international fame as a celebrated actor, Studi has moved audiences with unforgettable performances in *Dances With Wolves, The Last of the Mohicans, Geronimo,* and *Heat* as well as *Avatar: The New World.* The eldest son of a ranch hand, Studi was born at Nofire Hollow, in northeastern Oklahoma. He spoke only his native Cherokee until he was five, when he attended public school. He later enrolled in Chilocco Indian Boarding School in northern Oklahoma, where he remained through high school graduation, yet he never forgot his language.

After serving a tour in Vietnam, Studi joined the American Indian Movement (AIM) and participated in its major campaigns. Shortly after Wounded Knee, Studis moved to Tahlequah, Oklahoma, where he worked for the Cherokee Nation and helped start the *Cherokee Phoenix,* a bilingual newspaper still in publication today. During that time, Studi put his linguistic skills to work and began teaching the Cherokee language in the community.

Studi first took the professional stage in 1984 with "Black Elk Speaks." He expanded to productions for Nebraska Public Television in the summer of 1985. Not long after, he moved to Los Angeles, landing his first film role in *Powwow Highway*. In 2002, he brought legendary character Lt. Joe Leaphorn to life for a series of PBS movies based on Tony Hillerman's books. Studi's other notable television movies include *Crazy Horse, Comanche Moon,* and *Bury My Heart at Wounded Knee*.

In 2013, he was inducted into the National Cowboy & Western Heritage Museum's Hall of Great Western Performers. Throughout his thirty-year career, he's won numerous awards, including several First Americans in the Arts awards and the 2009 Santa Fe Film Festival Lifetime Achievement Award.

John Bennett Herrington (1958–)
Chickasaw, Aviator/Astronaut

In 2002, Herrington became the first enrolled member of a Native American nation to fly in space. (William R. Pogue was of Choctaw ancestry and was a crewman aboard Skylab 4 in 1973–1974, but he was not an enrolled member.) Born in Wetumka, Oklahoma, Herrington earned a bachelor's degree in applied mathematics from the University of Colorado before receiving his commission in the United States Navy in 1984. In 1985, he was designated a naval aviator and moved on to become a patrol plane commander, mission commander, and patrol plane instructor pilot.

Herrington was selected to attend the United States Naval Test Pilot School at Naval Air Station in Patuxent River, Maryland, in January 1990. After graduation, he served as a project test pilot and was selected as an aeronautical engineering duty officer (AEDO). He earned a Master of Science degree in aeronautical engineering

from the U.S. Naval Postgraduate School and was assigned as a special projects officer to the Bureau of Naval Personnel Sea Duty Component after being selected for the astronaut program. During his military service, he was awarded the Navy Commendation Medal, Navy Meritorious Unit Commendation, Coast Guard Meritorious Unit Commendation, Coast Guard Special Operations Service Ribbon, National Defense Service Medal, Sea Service ribbons, and various other service awards.

After more training, Herrington was assigned to the flight support branch of the Astronaut Office, where he served as a member of the astronaut support personnel team responsible for shuttle launch preparations and postlanding operations. He served as mission specialist for STS-113, the sixteenth space shuttle mission to the International Space Station in 2002. During the mission, Herrington performed three spacewalks, totaling nineteen hours and fifty-five minutes. In July 2004, Herrington served as the commander of the NEEMO 6 mission aboard the Aquarius underwater laboratory, living and working underwater. He retired from the Navy and NASA in 2005. To honor his heritage, Herrington carried the Chickasaw Nation flag on his thirteen-day trip to space.

Dana Tiger (1961–)
Seminole/Muscogee/Cherokee, Artist

Dana Tiger is an award-winning, internationally acclaimed artist. She was born on the Muscogee (Creek) Reservation in Oklahoma. Dana was just five years old when her father, legendary artist Jerome Tiger, passed away. She turned to his art as a way to know him, and lessons from her uncle, renowned painter Johnny Tiger, Jr., exposed Dana both to the richness of her culture and to the bounty of her family's artistic tradition. Best known for her watercolors and acrylic paintings depicting the strength and determination of Native American women, Dana's paintings now hang in galleries, universities, Native American institutions, and state buildings nationwide. In recognition of her accomplishments, Dana was inducted into the Oklahoma Women's Hall of Fame in 2001. Dana and her husband Don Blair manage the Tiger Art Gallery in Muskogee, Oklahoma.

In 2002, Dana and her family founded Legacy Cultural Learning Community, a nonprofit with the mission of nurturing creativity within Native youth via the celebration and sharing of tribal languages and culture through the arts. When, in 1992, Lisa Tiger, Dana's only surviving sibling, was told she tested positive for HIV, the virus that causes AIDS, Dana joined her sister in AIDS activism. Dana is outspoken in her advocacy for the rights of women and minorities, especially Native Americans. She has donated paintings for poster projects to a number of worthwhile campaigns, including the AIDS Coalition for Indian Outreach, the American Cancer Society, and the American Indian College Fund.

Keith M. Harper (1967–)
Cherokee, Ambassador

Keith Harper is the U.S. representative to the United Nations Human Rights Council in Geneva. He is the first Native American from a federally recognized tribe to ever receive the rank of U.S. ambassador. Harper was nominated by President Obama on June 10, 2014, and confirmed by the U.S. Senate one year later. Previously, Harper was a partner at the law firm of Kilpatrick, Townsend, & Stockton, LLP, where he was chair of the Native American Practice Group. From 1995 to 2006, he served as senior staff attorney for the Native American Rights Fund. He was a Supreme Court justice for the Poarch Band of Creek Indians (2007–2008) and an appellate justice on the Mashantucket Pequot Tribal Court (2001–2007).

Harper is best known for his work in *Cobell v. Salazar,* a large, class-action lawsuit brought on behalf of more than five hundred thousand Native American representatives against two departments of the United States government in 1996. The case was resolved in 2009 with the

Obama Administration agreeing to a $3.4 billion settlement (see also the chapter titled "Northern Plains" [section "The Cobell Settlement"]). Since Harper was a major contributor to Obama's 2008 presidential and 2011 re-election campaigns, setting overall record levels of campaign donations from Native Americans, his appointment has been criticized. The decision has also been questioned by Indigenous groups worldwide who feel Harper has not supported their causes in the past.

His awards include recognition by *The National Law Journal* as one of "fifty "most influential minority lawyers in America" (2008); listing as a 2010, 2012, and 2013 Washington, D.C., "super lawyer" in Native American law by *Super Lawyers* magazine; and selection as a Leadership Conference on Civil Rights delegate to the World Conference Against Racism in Durban, South Africa, in 2001.

Kevin K. Washburn (1968–)
Chickasaw, Politician

Kevin Washburn was confirmed by the U.S. Senate as the assistant secretary—Indian affairs for the U.S. Department of the Interior on September 21, 2012, and was sworn into office by Secretary of the Interior Ken Salazar on October 9, 2012. In addition to carrying out the department's trust responsibilities regarding the management of tribal and individual Indian trust lands and assets, the assistant secretary is responsible for promoting the self-determination and economic self-sufficiency of the nation's 566 federally recognized American Indian and Alaska Native tribes and their approximately two million enrolled members.

Washburn was raised in Oklahoma and earned a Bachelor of Arts degree in economics from the University of Oklahoma (1989) and a Juris Doctorate from Yale Law School (1993). He came to the Department of the Interior from the University of New Mexico School of Law, where he served as dean until June 2009. Prior to that, he was the Rosenstiel distinguished professor of law at the University of Arizona (2008–2009) and an associate professor of law at the University of Minnesota (2002–2008). Previously, he served as general counsel for the National Indian Gaming Commission (2000–2002) and as an assistant United States attorney in Albuquerque, New Mexico, from 1997 to 2000. He was a trial attorney in the Indian resource section of the U.S. Department of Justice from 1994 to 1997.

His past awards in federal service include the Environmental Protection Agency's Bronze Medal for Commendable Service (2000) for representing the agency in a successful Clean Air Act litigation and Special Commendations for Outstanding Service from the Justice Department (1997, 1998). Among his other books and articles, he is a coauthor and editor of the leading legal treatise in the field of Indian law, *Cohen's Handbook of Federal Indian Law* (2012 edition).

Kent Smith
Comanche/Chickasaw, Zoologist/Educator

As director of Native Explorers (NE), a nonprofit organization based in Oklahoma City, Oklahoma, Dr. Smith wants to ensure that there is an increase in Native Americans entering science and medicine professions. Throughout his education, he was struck by the absence of other Indians in his field and vowed to do something about it. Dr. Smith is also the associate professor of anatomy and coordinator of clinical gross and developmental anatomy at Oklahoma State University Center for Health Sciences and an affiliated research associate at the Sam Noble Oklahoma Museum of Natural History.

Litefoot (Gary Paul Davis) (1969–)
Cherokee/Chichimeca, Rapper/Actor

Besides being an actor and rapper, Litefoot is the founder of the Red Vinyl record label. He has won six Native American Music Awards as well as Artist of the Year. Some of his well-known compositions are "Tribal Bogey," "Native American Me," and "Redvolution." Litefoot played Nightwolf in the movie *Mortal Kombat Annihilation* (1997).

Paul Lombardi (1974–)
Choctaw, Businessman

The president and CEO of TeraThink Corporation, based in Reston, Virginia, Lombardi grew up in an impoverished meat packing district in an Oklahoma Choctaw community. The life lessons he learned there gave him the diligence to found his IT management consulting firm and succeed in a competitive business. TeraThink earned $15.9 million in 2010 and made *Inc.* magazine's list of the five hundred fastest-growing companies for six years in a row as well as the magazine's top ten list of Native American entrepreneurs in 2011.

Bunky Echo-Hawk (1975–)
Pawnee, Artist

A graduate of the Institute of American Indian Arts, Bunky Echo-Hawk is a fine artist, graphic designer, and a nonprofit professional as well as a traditional singer and dancer of the Pawnee Nation and an enrolled member of the Yakama Nation. Throughout his career, he has merged traditional values with his lifestyle and art. He has exhibited in major exhibitions throughout the United States and internationally.

The first Echo Hawk, born around 1855 in Nebraska, was a vigilant defender of his people against assimilation, refusing to change his surname to "Price" when federal officials insisted. In the Pawnee language, they called him "Kutawakutsu Tuwaku-ah." The hawk is a strong warrior who never sings of his own accomplishments, but as other people spread the word throughout the village, he became known as the hawk whose deeds are echoed, or Echo Hawk. His story is told in the children's book *Call Me Little Echo Hawk* (2005) by Terry Echo Hawk. She is the wife of former Idaho State Attorney General Larry Echo

Hawk, who currently teaches at the J. Reuben Clark Law School at Brigham Young University in Provo, Utah.

The Echo Hawk family members spell their name in different ways, but many carry on the tradition of service or "giving back." There are currently several Echo Hawks who serve as attorneys representing tribal interests throughout the United States. John Echohawk is the executive director of the Native American Rights Fund (NARF) in Boulder, Colorado. A cousin, Walter Echo-Hawk, also works as an attorney at NARF. Larry's two sons, Paul and Mark, also attorneys, currently provide legal counsel to the Shoshone—Bannock Tribe in Idaho.

Bunky Echo-Hawk is known for his live art, in which he begins the performance by creating a dialogue with the audience, where socially relevant and meaningful discussion takes place. He guides the audience through conceptualizing a painting, which he creates on the spot for the host organization while participants continue to contribute their ideas, opinions, and personal testimony. In 2008 at the Denver inaugural, he created a portrait of President Obama in his signature hot-candy-colored, graffiti-influenced style. Other painting series include *Skin Ball*, portraits of Native American athletes, and *Gas Masks as Medicine*, depicting environmental racism and injustice in Indian Country.

In 2006, Bunky cofounded NVision, a nonprofit collective of Native American artists, musicians, community organizers, and nonprofit professionals who focus on Native American youth empowerment through multimedia arts. Nike signed Bunky in 2010 to design Native-themed sneakers for the Nike N7 line. As Bunky states on his website, "It is my goal to truly exemplify the current state of Native America through art."

THE GREAT BASIN AND ROCKY MOUNTAINS

It's that whole 'corn pollen, four directions, Mother Earth, Father Sky' Indian thing where everybody starts speaking slowly, and their vocabulary shrinks down until they sound like Dick and Jane, and it's all about spirituality, and it's all about politics. So I just try to write about everyday Indians, the kind of Indian I am who is just as influenced by *The Brady Bunch* as I am by my tribal traditions, who spends as much time going to the movies as I do going to ceremonies.

—Sherman Alexie (Spokane/Coeur d'Alene), 2001

A BIRD'S EYE VIEW

Numerous American Indian communities continue to live today in their ancestral homes in the Great Basin, which encompasses most of Nevada, western Utah, and southeastern Idaho with small portions along California's southeastern border and in south-central Oregon, and in the Rocky Mountains, largely western Colorado, Wyoming, Montana, and eastern Idaho and Utah. Salmon streams flowed west from the coast into Idaho; trout and sturgeon were plentiful in the eastern part of the region. The mountain and intermountain areas were lush with many varieties of roots, berries, and game. Waterfalls were considered to be sacred places where humans and spirits could meet. The mountain tribes lived on the edge of evergreen forests and high prairies, where they traded dried salmon for buffalo meat with Plains people. Mountain peoples include the Kootenai (Ktunaxa), Kalispel (Q'lispe), and Salish (all formerly—and incorrectly—called Flathead Indians), the Nez Perce (Nimipu), Coeur d'Alene (Schitsu'Umsh), and others, such as the Blackfeet (Pikuni and Siksika) and Gros Venre (A'aninin). (See also the chapter titled "Northern Plains" for more information on the Blackfeet and Gros Ventre.)

The Ute (Nut'zi) were also mountain people in western Colorado, living to the west of the Arapaho (Hinonoeino) and southwest of the Southern Cheyenne (Sutai). (See also the chapters titled "Northern Plains" and "Southern Plains" for more information on the Cheyenne and Arapaho.) The Ute built semiunderground pit houses, domed on top with pole frames and woven cedar bark or reed mat coverings. After they acquired horses from the Spanish in the late 1500s, many Ute began hunting buffalo on the Plains and living in buffalo-hide teepees.

The Great Basin peoples, mainly Paiute (Numa, Newe, and Nuwuvi), Goshute (Kutsipiuti), Bannock (Banakwut), and Shoshone (Tukaduka, Nimi, Pohogue, and Kohogue), lived in the high deserts and intermountain regions. The Bitterroot and Rocky Mountains rise majestically, separating this region from the Plateau (see also the chapter titled "Pacific Northwest: Washington State and Oregon"). Large portions of Montana and Idaho contain high deserts and plateaus, where a host of Native Americans lived by harvesting an abundance of roots and berries as well as by fishing and hunting elk and bighorn sheep. Similarly, the Paiute and Shoshone of the Great Basin lived in small bands that hunted for food and harvested roots and pine nuts. The Eastern and Northern Shoshone and the Eastern Utes, like the Cheyenne and Arapaho, lived in teepees. The Western Shoshone, Ute, and Paiute built temporary summer wickiups, cone-shaped brush shelters, and permanent dugout homes partially carved out of the earth, such as into the side of a hill, and extended in front with wood frames, rammed earth, and reed mats.

GREAT BASIN AND ROCKY MOUNTAIN TRIBES AND NATIONS

- Colorado: Southern Ute Tribe and Mountain Ute Tribe (the Mountain Ute Reservation spans into New Mexico and Utah)

- Idaho: Coeur D'Alene Tribe; Kootenai Tribe; Nez Perce Tribe; and Shoshone–Bannock Tribe

- Montana: Confederated Salish Tribe and Kutenai Tribe

- Nevada: Duckwater Shoshone Tribe; Ely Shoshone Tribe; Fort McDermitt Paiute Shoshone Tribe; Fort Mohave Indian Tribe (also in California and Arizona); Las Vegas Tribe of Paiute Indians; Lovelock Paiute Tribe; Moapa Band of Paiute Indians; Paiute–Shoshone Tribe of the Fallon Reservation; Pyramid Lake Paiute Tribe; Reno-

Sparks Indian Colony (Washoe, Paiute, and Shoshone); Shoshone–Paiute Tribes of the Duck Valley Reservation; Summit Lake Paiute Tribe; Te-Moak Tribe of Western Shoshone Indians; Walker River Paiute; Washoe Tribe (also in California); Washoe Communities and Rancheria of Nevada and California; Winnemucca Indian Colony (Western Shoshone); Yerington Paiute Tribe; and Yomba Shoshone Tribe.

- Utah: Ute Indian Tribe of the Uintah and Ouray Reservation; Northwestern Band of Shoshone Nation (Washakie); Paiute Indian Tribe; Koosharem, Indian Peaks, and Shivwits bands of Paiute; Skull Valley Band of Goshute Indians; and Confederated Tribes of the Goshute Reservation (spans into Nevada)

- Wyoming: Arapaho Tribe and Shoshone Tribe

CULTURAL EXPRESSIONS

Literature

In the mountain regions, the Indian nations shared many similar cultural traditions. Indian elders among the Kootenai, Nez Perce, Kalispel Coeur d'Alene, and others, such as the Blackfeet (Pikuni and Siksika) and Gros Venre (A'aninin) say that the Creator placed them in the mountains at the beginning of time. Moreover, they assert that their history began when the earth was young, when plant and animal people interacted closely with the first humans (see also the chapter titled "Northern Plain" for more information on the Blackfeet and Gros Ventre). All of the tribes enjoy a rich, oral tradition about their origins, and tribal elders consider the stories to be both literature and history. Many stories emerged from that time so long ago, and these stories form the basis of Native American cultural history.

The Native people of the mountains and Great Basin have long been engaged in a struggle for survival against European traders and settlers, who moved into the region and nearly destroyed the original inhabitants. In the nineteenth century, many Indigenous communities suffered a

In Indian folklore, the coyote—often taking on human-like characteristics—appears in many tales, sometimes as trickster and sometimes as hero.

Great Basin women were known for their beautiful porcupine quill embroidery, which decorated elkskin clothing and cradleboards. The Ute were expert tanners who traded hides for Pueblo pottery. Today's Ute culture includes handcrafted beadwork, basket making, hide painting, leather work, and pottery.

Mountain people's containers, such as teepee bags, made of raw hide pounded white and decorated with freehand designs painted in earth pigments, were called *isáaptakay* by the Nez Perce. When glass beads arrived as trade items, the mountain tribes specialized in vividly beaded regalia for horse and rider. It took an entire family several months to envision and create each project. The tradition continues in horse parades at powwows today, with adaptations, such as replacing buckskin leggings ties with Velcro.

The creativity of contemporary Great Basin and Rocky Mountains artists is an expression that honors their ancestors, anchored in traditional designs but conveyed in new media.

near-death experience, but like Coyote, who often resurrects himself in stories, so did Native communities.

Coyote stories are common across both regions, and although Coyote plays many roles, several themes repeat among various tribes. Coyote can be a hero or a trickster. As a hero, he saves the people from monsters, teaches them how to catch game animals and how to fool enemies, or creates landforms that can be seen today. As a trickster, he acts out human flaws, such as clumsiness, gluttony, selfishness, immodesty, or just foolishness as a demonstration of what *not* to do. Elders told stories to children during the winter months. These stories were not only entertainments but also instructions for the right way to live in communal societies.

Visual Expressions

My art, my life experience, and my tribal ties are totally enmeshed. I go from one community with messages to the other, and I try to enlighten people.

—Jaune Quick-To-See Smith
(Salish/Kootenai), 1992

Music and Dance

They didn't go all over the floor. My uncle from Nespelem. He used to tell me that you can just draw a little circle on the floor and be able to move around and make all your moves and look good, do everything representation and copy animals and birds, do all the movements of your feet and your knees and your hips and your shoulders and your head and everything, your arms. All within the circle. A good dancer can do that without having to go all over the floor. That is what he'd say. I used to watch him and I never could; it is hard to believe the movements that he could do, he was kind of like a contortionist. Of course, my young mind at the time, it was hard to walk and chew gum at the same time, but here he was, moving one leg this way, and the other one up the other way, and toe going this way, and arm going here, and his head this way, and he's bopping around his shoulders. Everything was all moving, just like instead of one body, it was like he had three or four bodies in one, just all moving, literally like a plastic man. He was fun to watch. He was very fluid.

—Larry Seth (Nez Perce), 2002

The spring Bear Dance is still celebrated by all Ute bands as a new cycle of life. As the bear awakens and rejuvenates in the spring, so do the people. The Bear Dance is the oldest ceremony among the Ute, who say it was given to them by the bear. It is also a social occasion where young people can meet and their families can plan marriages. On the last day of the Bear Dance, the summer Sun Dance dates are announced.

At contemporary Great Basin and Rocky Mountain powwows, visitors can see dances such as the Prairie Chicken, Women's Traditional, and Owl Dance and hear honor, chief, and flag songs. While singing and dancing are deeply spiritual acts, powwows are just plain fun.

Games and Sports

Great Basin and Mountain people enjoyed placing bets on games of chance, such as dice, hand games, and hidden-ball games, but the four-stick game was unique to the region. As in other hand games, pointed sticks are stuck into the ground to keep score. The cylindrical, wooden game pieces of different sizes are carved, painted, or burned with patterns denoting their value. Players arrange the sticks in any of several specific combinations, then hide them under a blanket or basket. The opponent tries to guess the configuration and wins or loses pieces depending on his or her accuracy. Among some tribes, the sticks symbolized male and female. The player juggled them under a basket and positioned them in a chosen pattern, then sang a song honoring the wolf while shaking the basket rap-

idly against the ground while the opponent tried to guess.

Hoop and pole games required high dexterity and were played from coast to coast although the hoops, or targets, and the darts or poles had a wide variety of shapes and forms among different cultures. Many hoops resembled a spiders' web with different point values for the types of holes within. Ute hoops were braided cord decorated with colored beads while Shoshone hoops had sapling rings wrapped with rawhide. Sizes varied; Paiute hoops had the smallest diameter at less than three inches while others could be twenty-five inches across. Darts could be arrows or jointed poles. Men played this game, most often in pairs, completing to throw the poles through the rolling hoop. Some Arapaho men wore hair ornaments based on a netted gaming hoop design. Among ghost dancers, both their personal game song and the design of the hoop were received in dreams.

Women played shinny, a game like field hockey, or double ball. In double ball, two buckskin balls stuffed with sand are connected by a thong. Shoshone and Paiute women used a curved, four-foot-long, forked stick to pass and throw the ball with the object being to toss it over the opposing team's goal post. The goal stakes were four hundred feet apart; play was fast, and the game required endurance. Teams usually competed for prizes, and spectators bet on the game.

COLONIZATION IN THE MOUNTAINS

The Lewis and Clark Expedition

In the first decade of the 1800s, Indians living in present-day Idaho and Montana met Meriwether Lewis and William Clark, who led a U.S. expedition (1806–1809) to explore the Louisiana Purchase: land west of the Mississippi River bought from France in 1803. Native people from the mountains probably met European traders who were following the Columbia River to the coasts of Oregon and Washington.

When the explorers reached the Great Falls (near present-day Great Falls, Montana) of the Missouri River, they needed horses and information in order to cross the Rocky Mountains. With a small party, Lewis set out on foot to find the Shoshone Indians. After some time, the men met several Shoshone women, to whom they gave gifts. The women belonged to the Lemhi Band of Shoshone people, and their leader was Chief Kameawaite. After much effort, Lewis convinced Kameawaite to supply horses and guides to lead the U.S. exploring party over the Rocky Mountains. When the Shoshone and explorers returned to Great Falls, Kameawaite willingly helped Lewis and Clark because they had returned his long-lost sister, Sacagawea. Sacagawea and her French trader husband, Touissant Charbonneau, served as guides for the Lewis and Clark expedition to Great Falls from a Hidatsa village in present-day central North Dakota. Some years earlier, some Hidatsa people had kidnapped Sacagawea, whom Chabonneau purchased when she was fourteen years old. (For more information on Sacagawea, see her biography at the end of this chapter).

Kameawaite contributed significantly to the safe journey of the famous explorers. The Shoshone chief led the expedition through most of present-day Montana and showed them the way into the country of the Salish Indians, in present-day western Montana. In like fashion, the Salish guided Lewis and Clark westward across the panhandle of present-day Idaho.

In October 1805, the Lewis and Clark expedition entered the lands of the Nez Perce, who provided the explorers with kindness, food, and canoes to take them to the Pacific Ocean. With the aid of Nez Perce scouts, the explorers traveled quickly by canoe to the village of the Palouse, who celebrated the arrival of the Suyapo, "Crowned Heads" or "Crowned Hats," by singing long into the night. A host of other Plateau tribes sent representatives to meet the U.S. explorers. The Indians and explorers traded goods, and Lewis and Clark honored some of the chiefs with special medals bearing the words *Peace* and *Friendship*. Relations between the two peoples were friendly, and the explorers soon continued their trip down the Columbia River, in present-day Oregon State. (For more information about the Plateau peoples, see the sections "Washington" and "Oregon" in the chapter titled "Pacific States.")

The Fur Trade

As a result of Lewis and Clark's explorations, the United States government claimed the entire Northwest—including the plateau and mountains—as part of the U.S. and encouraged white settlers to relocate to the region. Lewis and Clark reported the many wondrous things they had seen, including the vast numbers of fur-bearing animals. By 1810, less than a year after Lewis and Clark's journey, British traders traveled through the Northwest in quest of a river route from the interior of Canada to the Pacific Ocean. Soon, three major fur trading companies, the Northwest Company, the American Fur Company, and the Hudson's Bay Company, set up trading posts or factories in the region.

A mural detail from the lobby of the Montana House of Representatives shows Sacagawea guiding explorers Lewis and Clark.

While the British companies worked with Shoshone, Paiute, and Bannock to procure furs, they depended on intermountain tribes for horses. Fort Nez Perce, among other forts, traded with its namesake tribe, which supplied the Hudson's Bay Company with some furs and many horses. The British company benefited from trade with Indians in the intermountain areas until the 1850s, after it had depleted the number of fur-bearing animals and when the United States took control of the region.

Missionaries

The traders and trappers became the first to occupy Indian lands in the region. A few of them tried to convert the Indians to Christianity in the 1830s. The Presbyterian missionary couples Marcus and Narcissa Whitman and Henry and Eliza Spalding established the first missions in the Rocky Mountains. Catholic missionaries fol-

lowed, establishing missions among the Salish, Kootenai, and others. Some Indians gravitated to Christianity while most preferred their own traditional spirituality. Controversy over whether to adopt Christianity split many mountain Indian communities into pro- and anti-Christians.

Germs and Gold

In 1843, a significant event altered the course of events: Joe Meek, William Craig, and other former fur trappers opened a wagon road, later called the Oregon Trail, from Idaho across the Blue Mountains of Oregon, along the Columbia River, and into the Grande Ronde River Valley of Oregon. Soon, many settlers and travelers used the Oregon Trail to travel to the Pacific Northwest Coast. The newcomers established territorial governments in the area, asserting political power over the Indigenous peoples. Tensions mounted as diseases such as measles, in-

"Cavalcade," Alfred J. Miller, painted between 1858 and 1860. Miller was known as "the artist of the Oregon Trail," and this watercolor painting depicts Shoshone men led by Chief Mawoma, staging a grand entry in honor of Captain Robert Stewart near the Rocky Mountains in what is now Wyoming.

troduced by the newcomers, spread among the Indians, threatening their physical survival.

Of equal importance, after Maidu Indians discovered gold in 1848 along the American River in Northern California, miners invaded California, killing Indians with guns and viruses. The California mining frontier moved northward where gold was soon discovered on the plateau and in the mountains (see also the chapter titled "California"). Native people resisted the invasion of their homelands by miners who had little or no regard for Indians or their rights. The miners extended their diggings east into Idaho and Montana.

The United States soon gave more attention to the area, and in 1853, it created two separate territories there. Oregon Territory included lands in present-day Oregon, Idaho, and Wyoming. Washington Territory included lands in present-day Washington, Idaho, and Montana. With the new government came American Indian policy bent on liquidating Indian title to the land, concentrating Indians onto smaller parcels of land called reservations, and establishing military and civil power over the tribes.

In May 1855, during the Walla Walla Council, Washington Territorial Governor Isaac Stevens made treaties with the mountain tribes, creating the Nez Perce and Kootenai reservations, among others. Over time, the U.S. government took nearly all Indian land in the territory, leaving Native Americans with virtually no land base. As a result of territorial government, the United States and its citizens took control of the mountain Indians, but not without a fight.

Shortly after the Walla Walla Council of 1855, white miners discovered gold north of the Spokane River in Oregon Territory. Miners invaded the inland Northwest, and some stole from and murdered a few Indians, which led to retaliation by the Yakama, who executed several miners. War resulted after two Yakama murdered Indian agent Andrew Jackson Bolon. Between 1855 and 1858, the Indians of the Columbia Plateau fought a series of fights with volunteer and U.S. Army troops. After some initial successes, the

Yakama retreated north. In retaliation, volunteer troops from Oregon and Washington invaded the lands of plateau and mountain people who not had been involved in the Yakama conflict, but the volunteer soldiers sought to punish all Indians. The Yakama War concluded at the Battle of Four Lakes and Spokane Plains when the combined forces of Yakama, Palouse, Spokane, Kootenai, Okanogan, and others suffered a loss at the hands of the U.S. military, led by Colonel George Wright. Several tribes, including the Nez Perce, chose not to enter a war with the United States, but all of them felt the threat of the federal government and the settlers who had taken their land.

INDIGENOUS RESISTANCE IN THE MOUNTAINS AND GREAT BASIN

If we ever owned the land, we own it still, for we never sold it. In the treaty councils, the commissioners have claimed that our country has been sold to the government. Suppose a white man should come to me and say, "Joseph, I like your horses, and I want to buy them." I say to him, "No, my horses suit me. I will not sell them." Then he goes to my neighbor and says to him, "Joseph has some good horses. I want to buy them, but he refuses to sell." My neighbor answers, "Pay me the money, and I will sell you Joseph's horses." The white man returns to me and says, "Joseph, I have bought your horses, and you must let me have them. If we sold our lands to the government, this is how they were bought.

—Chief Joseph (Nez Perce), 1849

Ute Conflicts (1853–1879)

Mormon settlers were constantly encroaching on Ute lands and depleting timber and wildlife. The Ute retaliated with raids on Mormon towns in 1853 in what was called the Walker War. In response, President Abraham

Lincoln ordered the Ute to be confined to the Uintah Reservation. Under starvation conditions on the reservation, the Ute began taking Mormon cattle. A young leader named Black Hawk organized an alliance of Ute, Paiute, and Navajo to raid Mormon ranches, who escaped with hundreds of cows and killed five settlers in what was known as the Black Hawk War (1865–1868). A peace treaty was signed in 1868. The final conflict, the "Meeker Massacre," happened in Colorado in 1879, when Indian agent Nathan Meeker tried to convert the White River Ute to farming by plowing over the tribe's pony race track. This infuriated the Utes, who killed Meeker and his ten agency employees, burned the agency, and held Meeker's family hostage for two weeks. The subsequent military confrontation left twenty-three Ute and fourteen U.S. soldiers dead. The soldiers forced the band to move to the Ouray Reservation in Utah.

The Flight of the Nez Perce (1877)

The Nez Perce of present-day Idaho lived peacefully with the United States until 1860, when "traders" found gold on their lands. Gold miners quickly moved into the Nez Perce country, and the Bureau of Indian Affairs responded by shrinking the Nez Perce Reservation to one-tenth its original size. All the Nez Perce chiefs refused to sign the treaty of 1863, except Chief Lawyer, who had no authority to sell Nez Perce lands. Still, he signed the "Thief Treaty," and the ultimate result was war. In 1876, General Oliver O. Howard demanded that the nontreaty Nez Perce move onto the reservation in present-day eastern Idaho.

When the people had no other choice but to accept peace or go to war, they chose to move to the reservation. Nevertheless, war erupted when three young men killed several settlers. In fear of U.S. retaliation, Chief Looking Glass led the Nez Perce out of Idaho, into Montana, and south toward the Crow Indians. When the Crow refused to help, the Nez Perce turned north toward Canada. U.S. forces, led by Colonel Nelson A.

Nez Perce warriors were backed into a conflict with the United States in 1876.

Miles, intercepted the Nez Perce near the Bear Paw Mountains of Montana and accepted the surrender of Chief Joseph, a central Nez Perce leader (see his biography at the end of this chapter).

Rather than return the Nez Perce to Idaho in accordance with the surrender agreement, U.S. General William Tecumseh Sherman transported the men, women, and children to Fort Leavenworth, Kansas, and to Indian Territory, present-day Oklahoma. The Nez Perce remained in Indian Territory until 1885, when the government permitted them to return to the Northwest. Some Nez Perce returned to Idaho, but others, like Joseph, were forced to live on the Colville Reservation in central Washington.

The Battle of Camp Curry (1878)

The Shoshone, Bannock, and Paiute people also made a stand against the United States. Originally, the United States established the Fort Hall Reservation in present-day eastern Idaho for the Boise–Bruneau Band of Shoshone, but soon, the government forced the Bannock to accept reservation life at Fort Hall. Many Bannock decided to go to the reservation and receive rations. The government, however, did not make good on its promises of food, and many Shoshone and Bannock faced starvation. When the Bannock, Paiute, and Shoshone living on the Fort Hall

Reservation tried to continue their seasonal economic migrations for buffalo hunting and the harvesting of roots and berries, it was only a short time before they began to feel pressure from the Bureau of Indian Affairs (BIA) and Christian missionaries to stop. Discontent spread at Fort Hall, and on May 30, 1878, a few Indians stole some cattle and killed two cowboys, which started a series of battles. By June 1878, it had escalated into a significant military conflict. Numbering only seven hundred people, the Bannock and Paiute joined forces in southeastern Oregon, where they fought the Battle of Camp Curry. After the battle, the Bannock and Paiute moved north toward the Umatilla Reservation in present-day Oregon. U.S. forces intercepted the Shoshone and Bannock and returned them to the Fort Hall Reservation.

The Bannock "War" (1878)

The Bannock conflict began when Bannock, Paiute, and Shoshone people in Idaho were restricted to the Fort Hall Reservation, where they began to starve for lack of game animals. Camas roots, the bulbs of the purple-flowered plant *Camassia quamash*, were a major source of food, but when the people traveled to their traditional harvesting area called Great Camas Prairie, they found that white settlers' hogs had eaten most of the camas bulbs. The people were angry, and Chief Buffalo Horn led them on raids of settlers' farms. The Indians were attacked by General Otis Howard's troops in three battles. The only way any of those Native people survived was by hiding in Owyhee Canyon. Those who were captured were sent to a prisoner of war camp, where they suffered atrocities, such as being force-marched to the camp between two American flagpoles, on which soldiers had skewered Indian babies. When elders fell along the way, the people were not allowed to help and were made to step over them as they froze to death. After five years' imprisonment at Fort Simcoe in Washington Territory, of the seven hundred Bannock, Paiute, and Shoshone, only about 170 people made it out alive.

GHOST DANCING IN THE GREAT BASIN (1870s AND 1890s)

In 1865, we had another trouble with our white brothers. It was early in the spring, and we were then living in Dayton, Nevada, when a company of soldiers came through the place and stopped and spoke to some of my people and said, "You have been stealing cattle from the white people at Harney Lake." They also said that they would kill everything that came in their way, men, women, and children.... After the soldiers had killed all but some little children and babies still tied up in their baskets, the soldiers took them also, set the camp on fire, and threw them into the flames to see them burn alive. I had one baby brother killed there ... yet my people kept peaceful.

—Sarah Winnemucca (Paiute), 1883

Contact with settlers came relatively late for the Great Basin peoples, such as the numerous local bands of Paiute, but in the 1850s, many Great Basin Indians, who primarily lived by hunting animals and harvesting roots and plants, went to work for U.S. ranchers and tanners relatively quickly. Many worked for wages as cowboys driving cattle, and others performed a variety of wage-labor jobs, such as planting, cultivating, harvesting grains, and taking care of livestock. The ranchers and farmers were willing to hire the Indian workers since farm and ranch hands were quite scarce in the Great Basin region.

The rapidly changing political and economic situation of the Great Basin region helped spark two social movements, which are often called the 1870 Ghost Dance and the 1890 Ghost Dance. The 1870 movement was started by the Paiute mystic Wodziwob, whose teachings spread primarily among the northern and western California Indians. The California Indians, at this time, were under great distress from disease, poverty,

In 1880, Chief Ouray and other Utes traveled to Washington. D.C. to negotiate a treaty that would unfortunately result in the removal of the Colorado Utes to present-day Utah. Seated left to right: Chief Ignacio of the Southern Utes, Secretary of the Interior Carl Shurz, Chief Ouray and his wife, Chipeta. Standing are Woretsiz and General Charles Adams.

political subordination (see also the "Southwest" chapter), and aggressive miners, who wanted the Indians out of the mining fields. Many California Indians adopted the Ghost Dance-associated hand game, a gambling game with ritual singing and betting while one team tries to hide bones and the other tries to guess who has the bones.

The second, or 1890, Ghost Dance is more well known and was initiated by Wovoka, the son of a Paiute spiritual leader (see also his biography at the end of this chapter). This Ghost Dance drew upon the early teachings of Wodziwob and emphasized the return of relatives and animals who had died in masses over the past several decades. Many Indians had died of diseases, and game, especially buffalo on the Plains, was noticeably declining due to the U.S. campaign to exterminate them. Many Indian nations in the West were gravely concerned that changing conditions threatened their entire way of life.

The Ghost Dance incorporated many Paiute traditions, such as a Round Dance. Performed to

gain communication with or honor dead ancestors, the Round Dance became a central feature of the Ghost Dance, which, from 1888 to 1890, spread rapidly among many western Indian tribes, especially among the Plains nations. The dance was performed to achieve successful transition to the next world after death, and in some versions, the dance was to help facilitate a great worldly change in which many dead ancestors would return to live on earth and the game would be replenished. These events would restore the Indian nations to their former, more prosperous condition, before the intrusion of U.S. settlers and government.

The Ghost Dance movement declined rapidly after the 1890 massacre of hundreds of Sioux and many women and children at Wounded Knee in South Dakota (see also the Northern Plains chapter). After the Wounded Knee massacre, the U.S. government officially outlawed the Ghost Dance, and because Wovoka's predictions of a cataclysmic worldly reorganization did not come to pass, within a few years, the movement declined to only a few tribes, and occasional

Ghost Dance spiritual leaders were sprinkled among some of the Plains nations.

Wovoka encouraged the Great Basin and other Indian people to keep the moral teachings he received in a vision from the Great Spirit by loving one another and living in peace with every one, teachings that he most likely adapted from Christian thought, with which he was familiar. As late as the 1920s, Wovoka told other Indians—usually avoiding discussions with non-Indians—that he had visited with God and that a new world was coming for the Indians.

ALLOTMENT (1887)

We tried to keep on farming, but the Whites came in and homesteaded our land. We could not keep the little patches where we had fenced and raised our crops. The game kept getting scarcer and scarcer. Nearly twenty years went by. We had no money or supplies from the government.... Pretty soon, maybe in fifteen years, engineers surveyed the reservation. When my father asked why they were doing it, they told him that the government was just making a survey to determine the acreage, but it wasn't long before we were allotted and the Whites moved in.... The White man took over everything.

—Martin Charlot (Salish), late 1890s

During the 1880s, reformers of American Indian policies determined that the trouble with Indians was that they held reservations communally and not individually. In an attempt to help Indians, liberal reformers decided to break up reservations into individual lots so that Indians would have private plots and want to work their own ranch or farm. U.S. policymakers reasoned that this land policy would enable Indians to become "civilized" because they would have a direct stake in their own economic livelihood. Most reformers, however, knew little about Indian cultures or economic practices, such as their methods of hunting, fishing, and harvesting. Few, if any, Indians in the Rocky Mountain or Great Basin regions farmed, and it would take years for them to alter their cultures to accommodate this change. Many Indians refused to give up their traditional lifeways in order to adopt farming. Life on the reservations was hard: The people became dependent on U.S. government rations, and most reservations could not adequately support the small Indian populations that lived on the reservation.

In 1887, Congress passed the General Allotment Act, which called for the division of reservations into individual parcels of 160, eighty, or forty acres. Each Indian received an allotment, and the excess land was sold to non-Indian settlers. After twenty-five years, Indian allotees could sell their individual allotments (see also Historical Overview–The General Allotment Act).

LAND LOSS

Like many Native people, the Coeur d'Alene people of Idaho lost a huge portion of their original domain. On November 8, 1873, the president created the Coeur d'Alene Reservation with 598,500 acres. However, in agreeing to the executive order creating the reservation, the Coeur d'Alene lost 184,960 acres of their homeland in eastern Washington and western Idaho. When the government allotted reservation lands from 1905 to 1909 over the objections of Coeur d'Alene Chief Peter Moctelme, the Coeur d'Alene were left with less than one-twelfth of the land they traditionally had lived on.

A situation similar to that of the Coeur d'Alene occurred on the Flathead Reservation of Montana, where the Kalispel (also known as the Pend d'Oreille), Kootenai, and Salish lived. Originally, these tribes held 1,242,969 acres of land. Between 1904 and 1908, the government allotted eighty acres to individuals interested in farmlands and 160 acres to Indians wishing to ranch. A total of 2,378 Indians received allotments on the Flathead Reservation. At the same time, the U.S. government sold 404,047 acres of former Indian lands to U.S. settlers, and the state of Montana took another 60,843 acres for school use. The United States kept 1,757 acres of the Indian lands for itself, thus assuming control over most of the original lands of the Kalispel, Kootenai, and Salish people. On May 2, 1910, the government opened the remainder of the reservation land for settlement and development by non-Indians.

BOARDING SCHOOLS

Before the Black Robes came, each year, we used to choose a boy and send him to the top of the mountain, and he fasted there and made medicine for the people. Then he came back, and we were well. That was all the studying we had to do then … the valley was our home. If we had not learned to think, we would not have been driven out.

—Chief Moise (Salish), 1913

During the late nineteenth and early twentieth centuries, Native Americans lost more than their territories. They also lost elements of their cultures, languages, and families through the efforts of the Bureau of Indian Affairs (BIA) to "civilize" them. White reformers often wanted Indians to abandon their Native cultures, which the reformers considered backward. U.S. policymakers believed that the best road for Indians to travel was to adopt white culture and that Euro-American-style education was the most effective way to "civilize" Native Americans. Indian schools emerged on several reservations, where U.S. teachers tried to discourage Native students from speaking Indigenous languages or from expressing tribal cultures, traditions, and spirituality. Churches established mission schools on some reservations, but by the late nineteenth century, the BIA controlled most reservation educational institutions through the Indian agents and the superintendents.

Although both boys and girls attended these schools, the administrators and teachers focused their attention primarily on boys, mirroring the gender bias prevalent in U.S. society. Teachers taught Native children to speak, read, and write English, and they punished the children when they spoke Indian languages. Indian students studied the subjects that were taught in most U.S. elementary schools of the time, but the major emphasis was on vocational education. Teachers trained girls to be waitresses, maids, and housekeepers, and Indian boys studied printing, masonry, and carpentry. Many Native boys and girls were sent to work in nearby towns and homes, where they learned during on-the-job training but earned little or no money Most reservations had elementary schools, but the BIA sent older children—Shoshone, Bannock, Nez Perce, Paiute, and others—to Carlisle in Pennsylvania, Haskell in Oklahoma, Sherman in California, or one of the other boarding schools. Some Indian boarding schools continue to function today although their attitudes and curricula are more Native-centered.

TWENTIETH CENTURY TRIBAL GOVERNMENTS AND LAND CLAIMS

During the 1930s, Congress passed the Indian Reorganization Act, which allowed tribes to reassert themselves legally in a new way. Indians who accepted the Indian Reorganization Act could place their allotments in a trust, so the lands could not be sold. The tribes could also elect new governments that would draft new tribal laws and constitutions. Some of the tribes, such as the Confederated Salish and Kootenai Tribes of the Flathead Reservation, accepted the Indian Reorganization Act while others did not. Regardless, all of the mountain tribes, and many of the Great Basin tribes, created tribal governments that helped guide them during the twentieth century. Certainly all of the tribes took advantage of the Indian Claims Commission established in 1946.

Prior to the establishment of the Indian Claims Commission (ICC), the United States forced Indian tribes to take their cases directly to Congress, a branch of government not known for

The Kootenai people of the Flathead Reservation were one tribe who accepted the terms of the Indian Reorganization Act, which allowed them to put lands into a trust that no one could sell.

moving quickly to settle Indian land claims. For years, the tribes had taken their problems involving land, water, and resources to Congress without result. The Claims Commission offered tribes a way to sue the federal government for treaty violations involving a host of issues. In every case settled by the ICC, the tribes received money rather than any land returned. Many Native people objected to this arrangement, as they would rather have the land. In settling claims of the numerous bands of Shoshone and Bannock people, the Claims Commission separated the 1957 Shoshone–Bannock claim into several parts, each of which dealt with the northern, northwestern, and western bands of Shoshone separately. The case took so long that the U.S. Court of Claims made their own determination after the ICC expired in 1978. On October 8, 1982, one section of the Shoshone claim, which dealt with federal mismanagement of timber and grazing re-

sources, was settled in favor of the Shoshone bands, who were awarded $1.6 million.

In July 1951, the Nez Perce tribe of Idaho and the Nez Perce living on the Colville Reservation filed petitions with the Indian Claims Commission regarding compensation for the theft of their original homelands, particularly those in northeastern Oregon and western Idaho. The Claims Commission combined the petitions of the two groups into one claim on February 27, 1953. Finally, in 1971, the Commission awarded the Nez Perce $3.5 million.

SELECTED NATIVE NATIONS

The Confederated Salish and Kootenai Tribes

The name of the Flathead Reservation is founded on a misconception. The Salish and

Kootenai people of the Bitterroot Mountains of present-day northwestern Montana did not flatten their babies' heads, as some Columbia River tribes did, but explorers were confused. The Kalispel, who live to the north, were called Pend d'Oreille for a long time because French trappers admired their earrings.

Original territories spanned more than twenty million acres in what are now western Montana, northern Idaho, and parts of southern Canada. Due to settlement pressure, the tribes negotiated the 1855 Treaty of Hellgate for the Flathead Reservation. Of the reservation's 1.317 million acres, 790,000 acres are jointly owned by the 28,325 tribal members, whose goal is to be completely self-sufficient while protecting and enhancing their natural resources and ecosystems.

Summer Bitterroot Culture Camps are free for Salish and Kootenai middle schoolers, who meet youth of other cultures while they increase their knowledge of the natural land and respect for the earth. After the camp, the students build leadership skills by sharing stories at local schools.

The Confederated Tribes own S&K Technologies, which is one of the most successful tribally owned businesses in the nation. Its divisions include Information Technology, Logistics, Aerospace, Engineering, Communications, Environmental/Construction, Advisory/Assistance, and Security. Over $11 million in dividends are invested in programs for the Salish and Kootenai community, such as the language program and a television station.

The Shoshone

The Shoshone, or Newe ("The People") descended from ancient hunter-harvesters whose territory covered southern Idaho, central Nevada, northwestern Utah, and the Death Valley region of California. The Shoshone and their Bannock relatives were bands whose names for each other depended on their main source of food: Salmon Eaters, Sheep Eaters, Rabbit Eaters, and Seed Eaters, to name a few. Shoshone history establishes that the people are indigenous to this area; there is no record

of them arriving from anywhere else. The Uto-Aztecan Shoshonean language group is spoken across the northwestern and southwestern United States and extends into Canada and Mexico.

Interactions with fur trappers (1827–1846) were shocking, as the Shoshone had never seen people waste and destroy natural resources. Shortly thereafter, gold rush miners began crossing over to California, and many settled on Shoshone lands. Conflicts escalated, and in the winter of 1863, near present-day Preston, Idaho, U.S. Army troops commanded by Colonel Patrick Edward Connor massacred more than four hundred Shoshone. The U.S. government rushed to establish reservations for the Shoshone.

As the twentieth century began, the federal government tried to convince all Great Basin Shoshone to move to the Duck Valley Reservation in northern Nevada (see also The Paiute section in this chapter). Only one-third of the people did move, along with Northern Paiute from Oregon and Nevada. For the other bands in Nevada, the government created "colonies," rather than full-size reservations. The Te-Moak Tribe of Western Shoshone united some of these scattered colonies in 1938 and was federally recognized as a tribe at that time.

Fifty-five million acres of Western Shoshone land in Nevada and across four other Great Basin states was guaranteed by the Treaty of Ruby Valley in 1863. The terms of the treaty were that the Shoshone owned the land and its mineral rights forever, except for gold mining, which was permitted there for U.S. citizens. However, since then, Congress has given most of the land to federal agencies, such as the Bureau of Land Management (BLM) and the Department of Energy (DOE). Since the 1950s, the DOE has used this land for nuclear testing, exploding more than one thousand bombs, subjecting Eureka County, Nevada, to more than one hundred tests, more than anywhere else in the world. During the 1960s and '70s, Shoshone attempts to reclaim their land in courts have only resulted in offers of a $26 million cash settlement, which would void the 1863 treaty. The Shoshone have refused the money. In

Tyler Nez and Jazmyne La Mons (right) take part in some traditional games during a weekend Kaibab Paiute Kids Camp in northern Arizona.

1993, the United Nations delivered a mandate to the U.S. government to cease prosecuting the Shoshone and privatizing their lands and to open a dialogue on land and treaty rights. The Western Shoshone are still waiting (see the biographies of Mary and Carrie Dann at the end of this chapter).

The 1.8-million-acre Fort Hall Reservation in southeastern Idaho was established in 1868 for the Shoshone–Bannock people. It was later reduced to less than half that size. Today, 5,680 members of the Shoshone–Bannock Tribe are often employed in ranching, farming, and small businesses. The tribe owns its own agricultural enterprise as well as a construction business. Most important is the twenty-thousand-acre irrigation project that the tribe operates, bringing water to Indians and non-Indians alike. The tribe enjoys its own health center, adult education program, and youth recreation program. The same is true at the Wind River Reservation in Wyoming, where suicide has plagued young people at a rate much higher than the national aver-

age. The tribe established a scholarship fund for college-age students, a daycare center, and health education programs for young people. The emphasis on education and the encouragement of young people to seek postsecondary education is a common element of reservation life among the Indians of the Great Basin and Rocky Mountains.

The Nez Perce

The Nimíipuu ("The People") also call themselves Iceyéeyenim Mamáy'ac, "Children of the Coyote." Lewis and Clark were mistaken when they thought the tribal members called themselves the "pierced noses" (*nez percé* in French). Although nose piercing was not a common custom, the name stuck. Their land spread from Montana into California. The Shoshone and Bannock called them "people under the tule" as they covered their longhouses and conical lodges with woven tule mats. Tule is a water reed that is perfect for roofs and walls as it swells in winter, insulating the home, and shrinks apart in summer to let breezes through.

Some changes that came with settlers were welcome, such as the horse, in the 1730s. The Nez Perce were skilled horse breeders and developed the Appaloosa, a strong breed with dramatic spots. Other changes, such as exposure to diseases (1780s–1850s), were devastating. Smallpox, measles, scarlet fever, and whooping cough germs spread from the east, carried by buffalo traders, and from white sailors up the Columbia River from the west, wiping out half of the Nez Perce population. With the death of so many elders, much essential traditional knowledge was lost forever.

To escape from violent gold miners, horse thieves, and aggression from the U.S. military, in the winter of 1877, Chief Joseph tried to lead his people to Canada, but the U.S. Army pursued them. It took 115 days of traveling over 1,400 miles of mountainous terrain for the army to capture the Nez Perce (see also his biography at the end of this chapter).

Most of the 3,250 Nez Perce live in Idaho while some reside with the Colville in Washington State. The Nez Perce Young Horseman Program and Registry provides trail rides and horse care lessons for young people. The registry has created a new breed of horse by crossing the Appaloosa with the fast Akhai-Teka from Turkmenistan, which is known for its stamina. The new Nez Perce horse is called the Nimíipuu Sik'em.

The Paiute

Researchers once believed that the Northern Paiute came from the south about one thousand years ago and migrated north through the Great Basin. They based this claim on the lack of pottery in the Great Basin before this time. However, this theory contradicted Paiute oral history, which places their ancestors in Oregon before the Cascade Mountains were formed. As a basket making people, the Paiute were not potters and thus left no ceramic artifacts. Instead they wove tule, willow, hemp, and sagebrush fibers to make sandals, baskets, rope, and fishnets. A rabbit fur blanket and a child's sagebrush sandals found preserved in an Oregon cave were found to be ten thousand years old.

Northern Paiute tribes once lived across present-day Idaho, Oregon, and Nevada but lost most of their territory to white miners and settlers. In the 1860s, officials in the mining town of Boise, Idaho, placed a bounty of one hundred dollars for a male Indian scalp, fifty dollars for a female scalp, and twenty-five dollars for each child's scalp, which led to widespread hunting of Paiute Indians. Chiefs signed treaties with the United States, hoping to preserve some safety, freedom, and rights for their people, who as a result were confined to reservations, often shared with their Bannock and Western Shoshone relatives.

As an example of one Northern Paiute community, farming and ranching are mainstays at Duck Valley in northern Nevada for approximately 2,000 Shoshone–Paiute tribal members, about 1,700 of whom live on the 289,819-acre reservation. Once the tribe entered into self-government through the Self-Determination Act of 1975 and began administering their own programs, more funding became available for employment. The reservation of 460 square miles is now held in common by all tribal members. The tribe is restored its salmon population, which is bringing other species, such as badgers, wolverines, and bears back to feed on them. Tourists also come to the reservation for the fishing opportunities. Native people have lost much; they gave up their homelands and way of life, but tribal sovereignty is something they hang on to for the future.

There are many Southern Paiute communities spread throughout the Great Basin. The ancestors of the Las Vegas Paiute were the Tudinu, or "desert people," of southeastern Nevada and parts of Southern California and Utah. In 1826, trappers and traders began crossing Paiute land on the Old Spanish Trail route to California. A railroad town made one band of Paiute landless, and in 1911, ranch owner Helen J. Stewart deeded ten acres of her property in downtown Las Vegas to the Paiute, establishing the Las Vegas Paiute Community. In 1970, the U.S. gov-

A Paiute woman weaves a traditional cradelboard, which is used to carry babies.

ernment recognized the tribe as a sovereign nation. The tribe's downtown Las Vegas Tribal Smoke Shop is the largest single retailer of cigarettes in the United States and is among the top ten nongaming businesses in Nevada. The Las Vegas Paiute diversified cigarette profits into a golf resort in 1995. Their annual Snow Mountain Powwow is held in May.

The Ute

A large tribe, the Ute once spanned the entire Great Basin area and are the Colorado Rockies' oldest residents. The people speak a Shoshonean dialect of the Uto-Azteca language and are related to the Shoshone, Bannock, Paiute, Goshute, Comanche, and some Southern California tribes. Food is sparse in the basin, and harvesting was time consuming. Hunters and harvesters traveled in small groups and alternated sites to give plant and animal families time to revive. The yucca plant was important for making soap, and pine pitch was useful for waterproofing baskets. In winter, families moved out of the mountains and harvested around the home fires in larger groups.

When Spanish invasion began, both men and women were known to fight bravely to defend their communities. When the Spanish would capture Utes for slave labor in Santa Fe, New Mexico, those who escaped often took Spanish horses with them, which is how the Utes came to embrace a horse culture as early as the 1580s. This increased their hunting range, and they were able to go after buffalo on the Southern Plains. They also began raiding the Apache, Navajo, and Pueblo for captives and supplies. Captives and Spanish trade items, such as metal tools and weapons, were bartered for more horses. In the 1700s, the Ute and Comanche had a fifty-year war until the Comanche traveled to Ignacio, Colorado, to sign the Ute Comanche Peace Treaty.

Treaties with the United States were not as beneficial for the Ute. As American pioneers traveled west, they discovered gold and silver in Ute territory, and miners and settlers began to take over Ute lands. The 1849 Abiquiu Treaty required that the Utes recognize U.S. dominion over them and established boundaries for the Ute Nation. In 1863, the treaty at Conejos extinguished all Ute land and mineral rights in the San Luis Valley. The Utes resisted further land cession treaties until the 1874 Brunot Treaty achieved a major land grab by fraud. Government agents led the Ute to believe the tribe was only permitting gold and silver mining in part of the San Juan Mountains, when in fact, the Ute lost four million acres. Negotiations with the state of Colorado in 2009 restored Ute hunting and fishing rights in the off-reservation Brunot area.

The Northern Ute Uintah and Ouray Reservation is located in northeastern Utah, about 150 miles east of Salt Lake City. At more than 4.5 million acres, it is the second-largest reservation in the United States. Tribal membership stands at about 3,020; over half of the members live on the reservation. The largest businesses on the reservation are cattle ranching and mining for oil and natural gas. The Ute Indian Red Pine Treatment Center provides alcohol and drug addiction recovery programs that are culturally based, such as sweat lodges and other traditional approaches, and offers holistic care in addition to talk therapy and twelve-step support groups.

The Ute Mountain Ute Tribe (Southern Ute) is located in southwest Colorado, southeast Utah, and northern New Mexico. Headquartered in Ignacio, Colorado, the tribal office serves about 1,400 members, who live on a 681,000-acre reservation. The people earn their livelihood through tribal businesses, including farming, ranching, a casino, a construction company, and Ute Mountain Pottery. Maintaining traditions is a priority, and the tribe sponsors annual Bear and Sun dances and incorporates traditional healing into tribal health services. The Ute language is taught at the Southern Ute Tribal Academy for children from six months to sixth grade. The academy opened in 2000.

CONTEMPORARY CONCERNS

Mining

To a traditional Indigenous person, land means life. All those things that you have, they come from the earth. Today, they call those things resources. Resources are taken in the name of economy, in the name of money. Who does that? Multinational corporations. They don't care. They're not going to be here tomorrow. What do they care about the children of these children? They don't care. Because they'll be gone. As soon as they take their resources out, they will be gone.

—Carrie Dann
(Western Shoshone), 2007

Beginning in 1991, the U.S. Bureau of Land Management began confiscating herds of horses and cattle from Crescent Valley, Nevada, on the Western Shoshone Reservation. Claiming

the animals were overgrazing the range, dozens of BLM agents arrived wearing bulletproof vests and carrying automatic pistols to round up more than two hundred heads of horses and two hundred cattle again in 1992 and 2002. In February 2003, they took over four hundred of the people's horses at gunpoint. It was foaling season, when many mares were still pregnant. In the dead of winter, newborn colts died of the cold, and many horses starved in the small impoundment corrals, where there wasn't enough to eat.

Immediately after the roundup, the Cortez mining company announced that they had struck gold in the Crescent Valley. The ranch owned by Carrie and Mary Dann sits on one of the largest gold mines in U.S. history. As Mary Dann said, "Overgrazing is not the issue. The issue is land. They want the resource."

With a grazing range available for ten miles in every direction from the Dann ranch, cows and horses could cause little destruction to the environment. However, the gold companies, in their rush to mine, are poisoning the land and water. To extract microscopic bits of gold from solid rock, miners crush the rocks and leach out the gold using cyanide. As the gold lies beneath the water table, hundreds of thousands of gallons of virgin water per day are pumped out and polluted with cyanide ash. As Carrie Dann says, "Ladies and gentlemen, we are killing the earth." (For more information about the Dann sisters, see their biographies at the end of this chapter.)

Sustainable Energy

About twenty miles northeast of Las Vegas, a coal-burning electric plant, Reid Gardner Power Station, bordering the Moapa Paiute Reservation, has been spewing soot and dumping coal ash for years, causing asthma and premature deaths among the Paiute. In October 2010, the plant was planning to expand. Tribal member Calvin Meyers told *Indian Country Today Media Network* that the expansion would worsen an already intolerable situation. "I cannot practice my religion anymore, I cannot eat my natural foods that we gather, I cannot use the skins anymore of the rab-

An aerial photograph of the Reid Gardner Power Station near Moapa, Nevada. The pollution generated by the station has been a concern for local Indians.

bits that we use for clothing, I cannot use the willows for housing … they're all contaminated," he said. "It's not the will of the Paiutes to stop something. It's our will that we survive."

Fortunately, the Southern Nevada Health Board responded with a ruling that will reduce emissions by four thousand tons a year. In June 2012, the BIA approved the Moapa tribe's solar project to replace electricity provided by dirty coal. In May 2014, the Moapa Paiute of Nevada began building the first-ever utility-scale solar energy plant on tribal lands. The plant will generate power for one hundred thousand homes and fund a preserve for an endangered species, the desert tortoise. Also in May 2014, a second solar project was approved, and the Moapa, along with other tribes, received a shared $700,000.00 sustainable energy grant from the BIA as part of President Barack Obama's Climate Change Action Plan.

Water Issues

Native water rights were established when reservations were created and Indians were expected to farm. As they would need water to do this,

there was an implied understanding that Native water rights supersede those of others in the area. However, to achieve this in actuality has been a hard and costly legal fight into the twenty-first century. The Colorado Ute Indian Water Rights Settlement Act was approved by the federal government in 1988 to provide water to the Utes through the Animas Plata project. However, the promised reservoir wasn't filled until 2009. As of 2015, funding is not available to construct water lines from the Nighthorse Reservoir to the Ute reservations.

Montana is a headwaters state, and the Salish and Kootenai tribes are concerned about protecting their water rights compact to preserve clean water for all Montanans in their region. In April 2015, the Montana House of Representatives threatened to reject this compact. This sort of decision would force individuals to defend their water rights in court against private companies in relation to twenty rivers in the state.

The reclamation of an old copper mine upstream of the Duck Valley Shoshone–Paiute Reservation in Nevada is a major environmental concern of the tribes. The mine leaches acid drainage into the Owyhee River, the major source of water for the reservation. The tribe is in negotiation with the state and mining company to clean up the mine.

Language Preservation

Native Americans of the region consider language retention one of their most important projects. Programs for teaching Indian languages among the Nez Perce and Coeur d'Alene began in the 1970s and continue into the twenty-first century with even greater awareness of the need for language preservation. The Nez Perce Cultural Resource Program is staffed by elders, linguists, archaeologists, and ethnographers dedicated to preserving culture, history, and sacred sites. The program helps coordinate the Nimíipuu Language Program, which provides classes to high school and college students as well as community members. The Nez Perce language contains several sounds that don't exist in English, such as many long or stressed vowel sounds. Tribal elders of the Nez Perce developed the *Nimiipuutimt Alphabet Book* in 1997 as a spelling system that represents all of the different sounds necessary to pronounce words correctly. They introduced new letters while taking care to represent the language in the simplest manner.

On the Flathead Reservation, the Kutenai, Kalispel, and Salish initiated a cultural heritage project to preserve their languages, oral histories, and songs so that the younger generation may carry the culture and help the Salish language survive. The Selis and Qlispé Language Program is a community-based language project whose curriculum is focused on the idea that connections among language, land, and culture are significant. Salishstudios.org offers digital recordings of elders speaking the language so that students can listen on their computers or smartphones.

TYING IT UP

today, nothing has died, nothing

changed beyond recognition

dancers still move in circles

children are bilingual: yes and no

still, Indians have a way of forgiving anything

a little but more and more it's memory lasting longer

and longer like uranium just beginning a half-life

—Sherman Alexie (Spokane/Coeur d'Alene), "Powwow" (1992)

The Indians of the Great Basin and Rocky Mountains are a diverse people. All of them enjoyed a long history of growth and development before the arrival of Lewis and Clark, yet all of them have been forced to contend with the United States as well as the state governments near their homes. They have lost most of their native estates and elements of their rich cultural heritages. They have all fought for their lives, sovereignty, and rights. They have all weathered many storms, and they all continue to exist today. Since the 1960s, the tribes have asserted themselves with greater vigor, offering tribally managed educational, health, and economic development programs. The tribes have attempted to preserve their languages and culture through diverse programs, projects, and institutions. The people of this region have a spirit about them tying their past traditions to life today. This spirit has sustained them since the time of creation, and this spirit will propel them beyond the twenty-first century.

BIOGRAPHIES

Sacagawea (b. 1784)
Shoshone, Guide/Interpreter

In the early 1800s, Sacagawea accompanied Meriwether Lewis and William Clark on their historical expedition from St. Louis, Missouri, to the Pacific Ocean. Sacagawea is responsible in large part for the success of the expedition due to her navigational, diplomatic, and translating skills.

Sacagawea was born among the Lemhi Shoshone, who lived in present-day Idaho. When she was only ten years old, a group of Hidatsa kidnapped her and took her to a village near present-day Mandan, North Dakota. In 1804, she was purchased, or won, by French-Canadian fur trader Toussaint Charbonneau. When Charbonneau was hired by Lewis and Clark in 1805, he insisted that Sacagawea accompany the expedition. Sacagawea herself hoped that she would be reunited with the Shoshone Nation during the trip.

Sacagawea proved to be a valuable liaison for the U.S. explorers since she spoke a number of languages, including Shoshone and Siouan. She translated Shoshone into Hidatsa for her husband, who would then translate again into English for the expedition leaders. When language barriers were insurmountable, Sacagawea communicated with the others by sign language. Along the way, she revealed to Lewis and Clark important passageways through the wilderness, foraged for edible plants, cooked, and cleaned. At one point, she saved the expedition's records when her boat capsized. One of the most amazing incidents during the trip was the unexpected reunion of Sacagawea with her brother Cameahwait in August 1805. They met at the Three Forks of the Missouri River in present-day Montana. Cameahwait was then chief of his band. He gave the expedition horses and provided another Shoshone guide, who helped Lewis and Clark reach the Pacific Ocean later that year.

The strength and endurance of this amazing woman cannot be exaggerated. Just two months before the expedition left Mandan, Sacagawea gave birth to Charbonneau's child. Throughout the trip, the teen carried the infant (known as Little Pomp to the explorers) in a cradleboard strapped to her back without hesitation. Sacagawea continued to travel despite a debilitating illness that struck her midway through the trip.

Walkara (Walker) (1801–1855)
Ute, Tribal Leader

Between 1830 and 1855, Walkara was probably the most powerful and renowned Native leader in the Great Basin area, largely western Nevada. His bravery and wisdom earned him nicknames like Hawk of the Mountains, Iron Twister, and Napoleon. Walkara's sheer prowess, physical strength, and agility allowed him to gain enough influence to eventually surmount tribal feuds among the Ute, Paiute, and Shoshone, and to organize fighters who raided an area from the Mexican border almost to Canada and from California to New Mexico.

Walkara collaborated with Indians, mountain men, and Mormons, a religious sect that settled around Salt Lake in present-day Utah. In the winter of 1839, he and several companions stole more than three thousand horses in a daring night raid on the wealthiest Los Angeles rancheros. This escapade earned him the title "Greatest Horse Thief in History." For over a decade, he and his followers demanded goods and supplies from travelers on the Old Spanish Trail, which passed through much of present-day Nevada.

Accepting of the Mormons at first, Walkara even converted to their religion under the persistence of Brigham Young, an early founding leader of Mormonism. However, he soon became frustrated by their invasion of Ute territories. Overgrazing of land, coupled with a measles epidemic and an Indian–Mormon confrontation at Springville, Utah, led him to fight and lose the bitter Walker War in 1853. His power all but gone and his land now in the possession of the Mormons, Walkara died two years later.

Washakie (Gambler's Gourd) (1804–1900)
Salish/Kootenai/Shoshone, Leader

Known for his helpfulness to travelers along the Oregon Trail, Washakie was probably born in Montana's Bitterroot Mountains and eventually went to live with his mother's Eastern Shoshone family in the Wind River Mountains of Wyoming. During the 1820s and 1830s, Washakie became friends with famous mountain men and trappers, such as Jim Bridger and Christopher "Kit" Carson.

Washakie became the principal head of his band in the 1840s, during which time he befriended Brigham Young and spent time at the Mormon leader's home. The Treaty of Fort Bridger in 1863 guaranteed safe passage for U.S. travelers in exchange for annual payments to Washakie. The same year, he signed another treaty, giving the Union Pacific Railroad Company right of way to lay track. The Shoshone served as U.S. military scouts against the Arapaho, Cheyenne, Sioux, and Ute in 1869. In 1876, Washakie and two hundred fighters joined forces too late to help General Crook against the Sioux at the Battle of the Rosebud in southern Montana.

In his honor, Camp Brown was renamed Fort Washakie in 1878. President Ulysses S. Grant gave Washakie a silver saddle, and five years later, President Chester A. Arthur visited Washakie during a trip to Yellowstone Park. In 1897, Washakie was baptized as an Episcopalian. He was buried with full military honors.

Pocatello (1815–1884)
Shoshone, Tribal Leader

Pocatello became headman of the northwestern band of the Shoshone Indians in 1847. His band was forced to defend Shoshone land along the California Trail, Salt Lake Road, and Oregon Trail, as westward expansion and the California gold rush brought more Americans into the northwestern corner of present-day Utah. Pocatello was captured and imprisoned in 1859 but worked to maintain neutrality among the different Shoshone bands as Mormons, miners, ranchers, and missionaries came into the Idaho region. In 1863, he signed the Treaty of Box Elder. By 1872, Pocatello's band was forced to relocate to the Fort Hall Indian Reservation in Idaho when the Union Pacific and Central Pacific railroads connected and brought more U.S. settlers into the region.

In order to be allowed to live on an off-reservation farm, Pocatello converted to Mormonism,

whose followers had settled at Salt Lake City, Utah. The local Americans requested federal troops to force Pocatello and other Shoshone Indians back to the reservation. Pocatello rejected Mormonism and lived the remainder of his life at Fort Hall. He became known as General Pocatello to distinguish him from other members of his family. The town of Pocatello, Idaho, is named after him.

Ouray (c. 1820–1880)
Ute, Tribal Leader

Ouray was born in what became Taos, New Mexico, and became a leader of the Ute. As a young man, Ouray was honored as a skilled fighter, but his efforts shifted to diplomacy as he came to realize that westward expansion of mining was inevitable, forcing the Ute to cede more of their territory.

In 1863, Ouray helped negotiate a treaty with the federal government at Conejos, Colorado, that ceded all Ute lands east of the Continental Divide. Four years later, Ouray assisted Kit Carson, a U.S. Army officer, in suppressing a Ute uprising. In 1868, he accompanied Carson to Washington, D.C., and acted as spokesman for seven bands of Ute. In the subsequent negotiations, the Ute retained sixteen million acres of land. However, miners continued to trespass on Ute lands. In 1872, Ouray's negotiations in Washington, D.C., had an unfortunate result: the Ute were pressured into ceding four million acres for a yearly payment of $25,000. For his services, Ouray received an additional annual payment of $1,000.

Ouray encouraged his fellow tribesmen to farm in an attempt to protect their claims to land. The Ute did not have a farming tradition, however, and Nathan Meeker, a new Indian agent who tried to force them to farm, was evicted from the reservation. This resulted in a military confrontation that left twenty-three Ute and fourteen U.S. soldiers dead. Ouray traveled to Washington, D.C., again in 1880 and signed the treaty by which the White River Ute were moved to the Unitah Reservation in Utah.

Joseph
(1840–1904)
Nez Perce, Tribal Leader

Joseph was a Nez Perce born in the Wallowa Valley, in present-day Oregon. The Nez Perce's traditional territory was located in the area where the present-day states of Washington, Oregon, and Idaho adjoin. The various tribes in this region signed the Isaac Steven's Treaty in 1855, ceding Indian lands in Washington Territory in exchange for reservation lands, homes, tools, and money. As more settlers and miners arrived into the region, however, the treaty was ignored. Like his father before him, Joseph originally carried out a plan of passive resistance to U.S. encroachment and efforts by the government to relocate his people to the Nez Perce Reservation, in present-day western Idaho.

A fragile peace was shattered in 1877, when U.S. settlers began moving into the Wallowa Valley. The government gave the Nez Perce thirty days to relocate. On June 12th, fighting erupted when three young Nez Perce men killed four settlers who had moved into the Wallowa Valley.

After some initial battles in which Joseph showed remarkable military skill by defeating superior U.S. forces, Joseph and his people attempted to escape into Canada. For roughly the next three months, they eluded both U.S. troops and enemy Indian bands. According to historical accounts, the campaign of the Nez Perce in 1877 was characterized by restraint and relative non-violence on the part of Joseph and the tribe. In late September, the Nez Perce were only a few miles from the Canadian border when they found themselves surrounded and outnumbered by forces augmented with howitzer cannons and Gatlin guns, which were early machine guns. On October 5, 1877, Chief Joseph finally surren-

dered, but not before hundreds of Nez Perce escaped to Canada.

When the long journey was finally over, many of the Nez Perce leaders were dead or hiding in Canada. Upon signing the surrender agreement, Joseph gave an eloquent, often quoted, speech at the surrender. In the minds of the American public, Joseph became permanently identified with the courageous journey taken by the Nez Perce. Sent to Indian Territory in Oklahoma, the Nez Perce were allowed to return to Idaho in 1883. Joseph spent the rest of his life on different Indian reservations but was allowed only a brief return to his homeland in the Wallowa Valley. He died on the Colville Indian Reservation in the state of Washington.

Sarah Winnemucca
(1844–1891)
Northern Paiute, Activist and Educator

Sarah Winnemucca was active as a peacemaker, teacher, and defender of her people's rights. She was born near the Humboldt River in western Nevada, the fourth of nine children. At fourteen, she moved in with the family of a stagecoach agent, Major William Ormsby, where she learned English. Winnemucca was able to study at a convent school for only one month before several non-Indian parents objected to the presence of Paiute girls. Thereafter, she found work as a servant and spent much of her salary on books.

The Paiute War began in 1860 and was led by Winnemucca's cousin, Numaga. She and many Paiute were moved to a reservation near Reno, Nevada. During the Snake War in 1866, at the request of military authorities, Winnemucca became the official interpreter in the army's negotiations with the Paiute and Shoshone. Believing that the soldiers could be trusted more than the Indian agents, she voiced her concerns to U.S. Senator John Jones about the mistreatment of Native people by Indian service employees.

Some Northern Paiute, including Winnemucca, were relocated to the Malheur Reservation in Oregon in 1872. While there, she served as interpreter for the agent and taught school. When a new agent arrived and failed to pay the Paiute for their farm labor, the Bannock War of 1878 ensued. The Paiute were forced to leave the Malheur Reservation and were moved to the Yakama Reservation in present-day Washington State.

Winnemucca went to San Francisco and Sacramento in 1879; in lectures to sympathetic audiences, she discussed the treatment of Native people by Indian service employees. Despite widespread public support for the Paiute's right to return to Malheur, there was no funding available. Winnemucca commenced a lecture tour of the East in 1883–1884 and dressed as an Indian princess to draw crowds. While on tour, she met with many sympathizers with Indian rights and published *Life Among the Paiutes, Their Wrongs and Claims*. Winnemucca returned to Nevada and founded a school for Native children with the money she had saved and from private donations. The school operated for three years until funding ran out and Sarah's health faltered. She died of tuberculosis at the age of forty-seven.

Wovoka (Jack Wilson) (c. 1856–1932)
Paiute, Spiritual Leader

The Ghost Dance religion of 1890 originated with a Paiute visionary and prophet who grew up in the area of Mason Valley, Nevada, near the present-day Walker Lake Reservation. His proper name, Wovoka, means "The Cutter" in Paiute. Upon the death of his father, he was taken into the family of a white farmer named David Wilson and was given the name Jack Wilson, by which he was known among local American settlers.

During the late 1880s, Wovoka became ill with a severe fever at a time that happened to coincide with a solar eclipse. In his feverish state, Wovoka received a vision:

"When the sun died," Wovoka told anthropologist James Mooney, "I went up to heaven and saw God and all the people who had died a long time ago. God told me to come back and tell my people they must be good and love one another and not fight, steal, or lie. He gave me this dance to give to my people."

This vision became the basis of the Ghost Dance religion, which was based upon the belief that there would be a time when all Indian people—the living and those who had died—would be reunited on an earth that was spiritually regenerated and forever free from death, disease, and all the other miseries that had recently been brought by white people. Word of the new religion spread quickly among Indian peoples of the Great Basin and Plains regions, but it is said that Wovoka himself never traveled far from his birthplace. A complex figure, he inspired Native people while the local, white settlers feared him throughout his entire life.

Mildred Bailey (1907–1951)
Coeur d'Alene, Jazz Singer

Known as "Mrs. Swing," Mildred Bailey was one of the first women to break into the jazz world. Bailey was born in Tekoa, on the Washington/Idaho border, and grew up in Spokane. She learned to play piano from her mother and began playing and singing in movie theaters in the early 1920s. A neighbor, Bing Crosby, was a friend of her brother's and claimed Mildred Bailey gave him his start when he followed her to Hollywood in the mid-1920s. Bailey, after an early marriage and divorce, headlined in early jazz clubs in Los Angeles and in 1932 became lead singer for a band called the Rhythm Boys, in which Bing Crosby and Bailey's brother were members. At that time, she recorded her first hit, a cover of Hoagy Carmichael's "Rocking Chair."

Bailey was married to musician Red Norvo during most of the 1930s, and their collaboration resulted in such famous songs as "I've Got My Love to Keep Me Warm." After their divorce, Bailey had a dynamic swing career and was a darling of New York's Café Society but succumbed to complications of diabetes and a heart condition in Poughkeepsie at the age of forty-four.

Corbin Harney (1920–2007)
Western Shoshone (Newe), Spiritual Leader/Environmentalist

A spiritual leader of the Newe Sogobia (Western Shoshone), Harney devoted his life to teaching about the devastation of Native lands caused by nuclear bombing and nuclear waste dumping. The Western Shoshone homeland is considered the "most atom-bombed place in the world." Over a thousand nuclear bombs have been exploded at the "Nevada Test Site" by the United States military. Harney took his message around the world to protect all people and the environment. Harney wanted all children to grow up in a healthy world free from environmental pollutants and also wanted the same for all of the earth's waters, lands, plants, animals, birds, and fish. His activism helped convince the Soviet Union to stop nuclear testing; the Americans followed much later in 1992. He and his supporters founded the Shundahai Network, the Western Shoshone word meaning "Peace and Harmony With All Creation." He was the 2003 Nuclear-Free Future Award Solutions Recipient, recognized for his lifetime of struggling to end the destruction caused by nuclear weapons; Elder Harney succumbed to cancer, probably caused by radiation poisoning. Today, the Shundahai Network carries on his work.

The Dann Sisters: Mary (1923–2005) and Carrie (c. 1932–)
Western Shoshone, Spiritual Leaders and Land Rights Activists

Despite the terms of the 1863 Treaty of Ruby Valley, which granted the Western Shoshone their Nevada reservation land in perpetuity, the U.S. Department of Energy (DOE) has used this land to test more nuclear bombs than have been detonated anywhere else in the world. This situation forced two horse-ranching Shoshone sisters into becoming human rights activists to protect their homeland.

Carrie and Mary Dann grew up in the midst of a large, traditional Shoshone family on the land where Danns have lived for five generations; the sisters spoke Shoshone as their home language, learned how to celebrate sacred foods, such as pine nuts, and how to care for horses from their grandmother.

Since 1973, the Dann sisters have protested the land seizure by continuing to graze their cattle on the contested land and refusing to pay grazing fees to the U.S. Bureau of Land Management (BLM). As the Western Shoshone tribal government has been supporting the sisters, the federal government began retaliating in 1974 by suing Chief Raymond Yowell and the Dann sisters for trespassing and ordering them to remove hundreds of cattle and horses from "public land." The Dann sisters lost their case in the Supreme Court and in 1993 requested intervention from the United Nations (U.N.) on the grounds of racial discrimination. The U.N. delivered a decision to the U.S. government in favor of the Shoshone, but the decision was ignored. Also in 1993, Sweden awarded the Dann sisters with the Right Livelihood Award, which has been called "the alternative Nobel Peace Prize."

Mary Dann died in a car accident on her ranch in 2005. Her sister Carrie has continued to protest land theft, mining, and nuclear testing. Along with thirty-eight other protesters, she was arrested for trespassing on the Nevada Test Site in April 2007. Dann, the Western Shoshone Defense Project, and four other tribal and environmental organizations sued U.S. and Canadian company Barrick Gold Corporation in federal court in 2008, seeking to close the largest open-pit gold mine in the U.S., which is leaking cyanide ash into the land and water around Mount Tenabo, a site sacred to the Shoshone. In January 2015, Barrick Gold ordered about 3,500 wild horses to be taken from the Dann land and destroyed.

Four documentary films have portrayed the Western Shoshone' and particularly the Dann sisters' struggle to obtain their treaty rights and protect their homeland: *Broken Treaty at Battle Mountain* (1974), *To Protect Mother Earth* (1989), Oxfam's *Our Land, Our Life* (2007), and *American Outrage* (2008).

Ben Nighthorse Campbell (1933–)
Northern Cheyenne, Politician

A successful politician, businessman, soldier, and athlete, Ben Nighthorse Campbell was a U.S. congressman and senator from 1987 until 2005. He was born in Auburn, California, and served in the Air Force during the Korean War. He also attended San Jose State College during the 1950s, became a judo champion there, and graduated in 1957. Campbell was a member of the U.S. Olympic judo team in 1964.

Campbell became the second Native American elected to the Colorado legislature, where he served from 1983 to 1986. He was voted one of the Ten Best Legislators of 1986 in a survey conducted by the *Denver Post* and News Center 4. A man of many talents, Campbell founded a business called Nighthorse Jewelry Design and owns a horse ranch in Ignacio, Colorado.

As a member of the Democratic party, Campbell was voted into the U.S. House of Representatives in 1987. From 1992 until 2005, Campbell was a U.S. senator, the first Native American elected to the Senate and to serve on the Indian Affairs Committee. Key achievements were his work to pass legislation protecting wilderness and Indian water rights, to establish the National Museum of the American Indian with the Smithsonian Institution, and to develop programs to prevent fetal alcoholism syndrome. Campbell was known to be liberal regarding social concerns but conservative on economic issues. Still, many voters were surprised when he switched from the Democratic to the Republican party in 1995.

After retiring from political office, Campbell founded his own lobbying firm, Ben Nighthorse Consultants, in 2012. Named in his honor, the two-hundred-thousand-acre Lake Nighthorse Reservoir in southwestern Colorado was completed in 2011. A biography, *Ben Nighthorse Campbell, an American Warrior,* by Herman Viola, was published in 1993. Nighthorse and his wife live in Colorado; they have two children and four grandchildren.

Jaune Quick-To-See Smith (1940–)
Salish/Kootenai, Artist

Born in St. Ignatius, Montana, on the Confederated Salish and Kootenai Reservation, Jaune Quick-To-See Smith is a successful artist who creates large-scale paintings, mixed-media pieces, and prints that address both ancestral traditions and contemporary Native concerns. She went to work at age eight to help her family and grew up in a series of foster homes. Despite enduring years of racial bullying in public school, she graduated and went on to earn a bachelor's degree in art education at Framingham State College (1976) and a master's of fine arts degree from the University of New Mexico (1980). She now holds four honorary doctorates. Over the past forty years, Smith has had more than one hundred solo exhibitions and has been reviewed in every major art criticism publication. She has curated dozens of shows featuring Native artists and lectures internationally. Her award-winning work is in the collections of major museums around the world.

Working with representational as well as abstract images, Smith's iconography includes the outlines of horses and buffalo and painted-over photographs, maps, and pages from textbooks. Often juxtaposing images and text, she uses humor and satire to confront topics such as environmental destruction and the oppression and stereotyping of Indigenous cultures.

Smith's public work on display includes the floor design in the Great Hall of the Denver airport, a permanent sculpture in Yerba Buena State Park, San Francisco, and a mile-long history trail in West Seattle. Smith's son, Neal Ambrose Smith, is a printmaker and sculptor.

Rosa Yearout (1940–)
Nez Perce, Rancher/Horsebreeder/ Cultural Traditionalist

As owner of the M-Y Ranch on the Idaho Nez Perce Reservation, Yearout raises the Nez Perce Appaloosa horse breed and owns the largest herd of the famous horses. She always rides on the annual historic Chief Joseph Trail Ride joined by a few hundred riders, all on Appaloosas, as they retrace the same mountainous route as the Nez Perce rode over a hundred years ago in their storied escape to Canada. She has trained to become a credentialed Nez Perce language teacher and is a storyteller and keeper of Nez Perce heritage. Yearout was an advisor for the American Girl Nez Perce doll, Kaya, as well as the Kaya books. She is also the whipwoman for the Chief Joseph and Warriors Memorial powwow. A whipman or whipwoman keeps the dancers organized and enforces the rules in the dance arena.

Adrian C. Louis (1946–)
Paiute, Author

The Lovelock Paiute author Adrian C. Louis was born and raised in Nevada and graduated from Brown University, where he earned a master's degree in creative writing. He lived on the Pine Ridge Reservation in South Dakota from 1984–1997 while working as editor for the *Lakota Times* and *Indian Country Today* and teaching at Oglala Lakota College. Louis was professor of English at Minnesota State University from 1999 until his retirement in 2014. He has written ten books of poems and two works of fiction: the short story collection *Wild Indians and Other Creatures* and *Skins,* a novel. *Skins* was adapted as a feature film by Chris Eyre (Cheyenne–Arapaho), premiered at the Sundance Film Festival, and was released in theaters in 2002. Themes in his writing are surviving reservation life, particularly alcoholism and recovery, and antiwar messages. Adrian Louis's awards include Pushcart

prizes and National Foundation for the Arts grants. His 2006 poetry collection, *Logorrhea,* was a finalist for the *Los Angeles Times* Book Prize. His most recent collection, *Exorcisms,* was published in 2014.

Janet Campbell Hale (1947–)
Coeur d'Alene/Kootenai, Author

Born in Riverside, California, Janet Campbell Hale grew up moving often between the Yakama Reservation in central Washington and the Coeur d'Alene Reservation in northern Idaho. Writing became her refuge from uprooted friendships and an abusive family. By age twenty-three, Hale was the single mother of a six-year-old boy and the author of her first book of poetry, *The Owl's Song.* Hale received her M.A. in English from UC-Davis in 1984. She was an instructor, visiting professor, and writer-in-residence at various universities throughout the1980s and '90s, winning the Pulitzer Prize Nomination for her novel, *The Jailing of Cecelia Capture* (1985), and the American Book Award for *Bloodlines: Odyssey of a Native Daughter* (1994), a memoir. Both books deal with themes of identity and survival as a Native woman. Hale lives on the Coeur d'Alene Reservation, where she writes and paints.

Hattie Kauffman (c. 1960–)
Nez Perce, News Correspondent and Television Anchorperson

The first Native American to ever report on a national network news broadcast, Hattie Kauffman began her broadcast career on college radio at the University of Minnesota.

She was born on the Nez Perce Reservation in Lapwai, Idaho, where she spent the first three years of her life before moving to Seattle with her mother. Kauffman experienced Nez Perce culture when she would go home to the reservation, where her grandfather taught her how to harvest and prepare native foods such as huckleberries, salmon, and deer meat.

Beginning in 1981, Kauffman won four Emmy awards as a reporter and anchor for KING 5

News in Seattle, Washington. Then, ABC's *Good Morning America* called her to New York City in 1987, where she served as special correspondent and substitute anchor. In 1990, Kauffman took a similar position at CBS News and reported for the network for two decades, during which time she also flew back and forth between New York and Los Angeles, reporting for *48 Hours, Sunday Morning, Street Stories, CBS Radio, CBS Special Reports, the Early Show,* and CBS *Evening News.* In 1998, she became senior correspondent for *CBS News.*

In 2010, she took a break from broadcasting and bought a house in Seattle, where she loves to garden, write, and paint in oils. Kauffman's memoir, *Falling into Place: A Memoir of Overcoming,* was published in 2014.

Sherman Alexie (1966–)
Spokane/Coeur d'Alene, Poet/Novelist/Performer

Quoted as saying, "Don't live up to your stereotypes," " Sherman Alexie is known for his funny/angry writing style. He has also written "Poetry = anger x imagination." Alexie grew up in Wellpinit, Washington, on the Spokane Indian Reservation. He has published twenty-four books—thirteen of them before the age of thirty-three—including poetry: *What I've Stolen, What I've Earned* (2013); short stories: *Blasphemy: New and Selected Stories* (2012); and the young adult novel, *The Absolutely True Diary of a Part-Time Indian* (2007).

Alexie's work has won the PEN/Faulkner Award for Fiction, the PEN/Malamud Award for Short Fiction, a PEN/Hemingway Citation for Best First Fiction, and the National Book Award for Young People's Literature. *Smoke Signals,* the movie he wrote and coproduced, won the Audi-

ence Award and Filmmakers Trophy at the 1998 Sundance Film Festival. The twentieth-anniversary edition of his classic short story collection, *The Lone Ranger and Tonto Fistfight in Heaven,* was issued in 2013. Sherman Alexie lives in Seattle with his family.

Tahnee Robinson (1988–)
Eastern Shoshone/Pawnee/Northern Cheyenne/Sioux, Basketball Player

Born on the Wind River Shoshone Reservation in Wyoming, Tahnee Robinson was the first Native player drafted into the WNBA. She was an all-starter and won McDonald's and Gatorade All-American awards while at Lander Valley High School, taking her class of 2006 to the Class 3A state title. She was offered a basketball scholarship to the University of Wyoming but left after her first month at school to have a baby. When the coach at Sheridan College offered her a chance to return, Robinson's family supported the nineteen-year-old single mother in her ambitions by taking care of her son. Robinson led the nation in scoring in the 2008–2009 season and earned NJCAA (National Junior College Athletic Association) All-American honors. The Sheridan Generals won the Region IX championship game due to Robinson's ability to score anywhere from twenty to forty-nine points per game.

After transferring to the University of Nevada as guard, Robinson led the Wolf Pack to record wins and a trip to the All-Western Athletic Conference, where she was named Newcomer of the Year. After being a finalist for the Sullivan Award, Robinson was drafted by the Phoenix Mercury and then traded to the Connecticut Sun in 2011. During the 2013–2014, season she played for Team Elizabeth-Basket in the Ukraine. She signed a two-year shoe deal with Nike and travels to Native communities to inspire young athletes. Recently, Robinson became the spokesperson for the Big Brothers/Big Sisters youth mentoring organization.

SOUTHWEST

Imagine always believing that men and women are equal.

The female was as important as the male.

Women were the ones who owned everything.

We didn't go to war until the women said, "We go to war."

And when the Europeans came, they had this idea that women were not supposed to be the head of family.

In the 1960s, I could not identify with the women's movement because I could never see myself in second place to a man.

Women are the keepers of the culture.

All my relatives, my family, are there with me in spirit, a thousand voices.

—Trailer, *A Thousand Voices*, Silver Bullet Productions (2015)

A Thousand Voices is a documentary film about Native women in what is now New Mexico. The narrative moves from creation stories to the invasions of the Southwest by Spain, Mexico, and the United States, then demonstrates how invasions changed the role of women in the Southwest, and finally, how Native women are reclaiming their power. Narrated by Irene Bedard (Cree), the film features interviews with women from the Navajo Nation, Mescalero and Jicarilla Apache tribes, the Kiowa Tribe, and the Pueblo of Cochiti, Acoma, Laguna, Jemez, Taos, Nambe, San Idelfonso, Santa Clara, Santo Domingo, and Ohkay Owingen (formerly San Juan Pueblo). Speakers include the poet Luci Tapahonso (Navajo) and former New Mexico legislator Georgene Louis (Acoma). It was produced by Silver Bullet Pro-

ductions, a Santa Fe nonprofit organization that offers filmmaking workshops to youth.

The story of how Native women were disempowered, and their powerful determination to reclaim their strength, parallels Indigenous revitalization as a whole.

A BIRD'S EYE VIEW

The wind had a message, the sun had a message, the sky had a message. All I had to do was listen.

—Jennifer Yazzie (Navajo), high school essay (1977)

Mostly a desert, semiarid, and mountainous region, the Southwest is defined by the

Colorado Plateau, which is ringed by some of the highest mountains and lowest deserts in the United States. The flat-topped buttes and mesas of the plateau give the landscape its dreamlike sculptural appearance, featuring natural rock spires, towers, bridges, and arches that can rise up to eight thousand feet. Canyons twisting below the buttes and mesas include the mile-deep Grand Canyon, carved by the Colorado River in Arizona. In that state, the edge of the plateau is defined by the limestone and sandstone cliffs of the Mogollan Rim, which descends to the Arizona-Sonora Desert. The Rocky Mountains muscle up in northeastern New Mexico and eastern Utah. In southwestern Colorado, the Uintah Mountains rise from east to west, and the San Juan Mountains mark where the Colorado Plateau ends in the southwestern part of the state.

The Four Corners region of New Mexico, Arizona, Utah, and Colorado is notable for extreme weather, including some of the hottest and coldest temperatures in the United States. The land base is fragile. Water is a scarce commodity, and drought can bring hardship to the inhabitants. Still, the landscape is breathtaking and has inspired generations of painters, poets, and filmmakers with its dramatic colors: turquoise lakes set high in bluish-green mountain forests, great, sweeping rock formations of rose, violet, and coral, fluffs of sage brush and golden damianita, reaching cacti, and russet adobe houses that glow against draped, red chilies or bright snow. Like human history makers, rattlesnakes, cottontails, and coyotes leave their trails in the warm, desert sand.

Contemporary Indigenous communities of the Southwest include, in west Texas: the Ysleta del Sur Pueblo (Tigua); in New Mexico: the southeast portion of the Ute Mountain Tribe's land base; the Mescalero Apache Tribe and Jicarilla Apache Nation (Ndeh); the Pueblo of Isleta,

Diana Sue Uqualla (Havasupai) blesses the dedication of a new amphitheater at Mather Point created of native limestone on the Grand Canyon's South Rim in October 2010. The landmark feature honors the Native tribes and nations associated with the Grand Canyon.

Santa Ana (Tamaya Nation), San Felipe (Katishtya), Santo Domingo, Cochiti, Tesuque (Tet-sugeh), Nambé, Pojoaque (Po-Suwae-Geh), San Idelfonso (Po-Who-Geh-Owingeh), Santa Clara (Kha'p'oo Owinge), Picuris, Taos, Ohkay Owingen, Jemez (Walatowa), Zia, Sandia, Acoma (Haak'u), Laguna, and the Zuni Tribe. Small Ramah and Alamo Navajo communities reside in the northwestern part of New Mexico while the main Navajo Nation (Diné) territory edges into south-central to southwest Utah and the northeast corner of Arizona.

Also in Arizona are the Tonto, White Mountain, and San Carlos Apache tribes (N'deh); Pascua Yaqui Tribe; Tohono O'odham Nation; the Pima (Akimel O'odham): Salt River Pima–Maricopa Indian Community, Gila River Indian Community, Camp Verde, and Ak Chin Maricopa Community; the Yavapai Nation: Fort McDowell, Yavapai–Apache, and Yavapai–Prescott; Hualapai Indian Tribe; Havasupai Tribe; the Kaibab Band of Paiute Indians and San Juan Southern Paiute Tribe; and the Hopi Tribe. The Colorado River Indian Tribes: Mohave, Chemeheuve, and Hopi; the Quechan Tribe of Fort Yuma; the Fort Mojave Indian Tribe (Aha Makav); and the Cocopah Indian Tribe (Kwapa) span into western California.

EARLY HISTORY

As I see an old Pima / woman walking across the / freshly watered land, I think / about how beautiful / the land is. / I think of how it once was / long ago. As I drift / into the multicolored past / I am changing. I am changing / into a cactus.

—Jessica Ahmsaty (Pima),
high school poem (1983)

Before European colonization, the area of the world now comprising the U.S. Southwest and northern Mexican states was named Aztlán by the Mexica (formerly called Aztecs), a powerful empire in central Mexico. Historians refer to the "Aztecs" as part of a Triple Alliance of peoples in Mexico's central basin, at the center of which was the city of Teotihuacan (founded around 1 C.E.). The ruins of Teotihuacan span around the third-largest pyramid in the world, which is located an hour from present-day Mexico City. The Mexica were the largest group in the alliance; its priests ruled. Aztlán remained a connected cultural and political region under Spanish domination until 1820 and under independent Mexican rule until 1848 when the United States claimed the northern part of Aztlán after the Mexican–American War (1846–1848).

Akimel O'odham (Pima) ancestors are known as the Hohokam, or "those who have gone." Beginning around 1500 B.C.E., Hohokam farmers were among the first in North America to grow corn, beans, squash, and cotton. Corn kernels dated from 2000 B.C.E. probably came from Mexico, and ruins of giant stone ball courts are similar to those created by the ancient Maya people in the Yucatan. Hohokam engineered extensive irrigation canal systems, similar to those in Mexica cities. Built between 900 and 1450 C.E., it featured more than eight hundred miles of main canals that were eighty feet wide with hundreds of miles of narrower branches, the world's largest irrigation project at that time.

The Southwest saw the gradual development of many other farming communities, which by 900 C.E. consisted of multistory buildings and large ceremonial centers. These buildings resemble the round, underground kiva ceremonial rooms found among the present-day Hopi in northern Arizona and the Pueblo villages in eastern New Mexico. First on the Colorado Plateau at Mesa Verde in present-day Colorado were the Ancestral Puebloans, who lived in multistoried cliff dwellings. Between 850 and 1250 C.E., many major trade and ceremonial towns emerged at places known today as Canyon de Chelly and Chaco Canyon. Some one hundred to two hundred large towns developed and were interconnected by walkways and four hundred miles of wide, straight roads. The large cities of Central America appear to have carried on trade with towns as far north as the U.S. Southwest, and objects such as coastal

The Americas Media Initiative sponsors collaborations between Indigenous videomakers north and south to enable marginalized communities, such as the Zapatista Maya of Chiapas (above) to create their own media and tell their own stories.

shells have been found in the area, indicating that trade also took place with the Indigenous peoples living as far west as the Pacific Coast.

Turquoise was so valuable that it was used as money. Mexica traders obtained turquoise from the Pueblo people in exchange for tropical bird feathers. Feathers and obsidian (black, volcanic glass used to make blades) from what is now Mexico have been found in the ruins of Casa Grande (Arizona), and thousands of Mexica and Mayan ceremonial objects are encrusted with turquoise from the American Southwest.

An extreme drought between 1275 and 1300 caused the Southwestern peoples to abandon their towns and move closer to freshwater sources. The Hopi built new villages along the Colorado River while most others moved to present-day eastern New Mexico along the Rio Grande River and its tributaries. In 1540, on the eve of Spanish exploration of northern Mexico, the village-dwelling farmers numbered around two hundred thousand. Other peoples, including many Hohokam speakers, such as the Tohono O'odham, were previously living by irrigation and farming but were forced to rely on hunting and harvesting in the harsh desert area near today's Mexican border.

ATHAPASCAN ARRIVALS

B esides the Pueblo, the most numerous people in the Southwest are the Athapascan-speaking Navajo and Apache, who migrated south from the Subarctic region around the thirteenth century. The Athapascan traded and intermarried with the village peoples and became involved in conflicts over water use and territory. Navajo and Apache groups allied with one or another of the villages. Both absorbed important aspects of Pueblo culture and worldview. The Navajo creation history of early beings struggling to gain greater moral balance by moving from three dark worlds beneath the earth to the present fourth world parallels those of Hopi and other Pueblo. Some Apache groups adopted the ceremonies and dance regalia of the village farming peoples in the form of kachina dancers, which for the Pueblo were ancestral spirit beings who, if properly honored, granted sufficient rain for growing crops. The Navajo and Apache combined new Pueblo elements with their own cultural themes and created complex and powerful creation histories and pantheons of spirit beings.

CULTURAL EXPRESSIONS

We are the people of long ago. / We are the blue-green water / that runs swiftly in the creek. We are the flowers which blossom / in the spring. We are the rain that comes pouring / down in the canyon. / We are the lightning that streaks in the sky.

—Ingrid Putesoy (Havasupai),
elementary school poem (1985)

In the southwestern regions of Arizona and New Mexico, Hopi, Zuni, and other Pueblo people have been farmers for over fifteen hundred years. Their relationship with a fixed place on the land is reflected in their unique, multistory apartment compounds—some of which have been continuously in use for hundreds of years—allow for a community of people to live together with both privacy and shared space. These housing compounds are made of stone and adobe brick, the interior walls plastered with clay and painted. Adobe is made from clay and straw as are the round, outdoor ovens called hornos.

Clay was also molded into pottery in an unbroken tradition that extends back well over one thousand years. Clothing was traditionally made from cotton fibers and other plant materials. Shell and turquoise jewelry reflected a trading network that, even a thousand years ago, extended for hundreds of miles in every direction. Jewelers learned silversmithing from artisans in Mexico, and craftspeople from various nations created tribally specific styles of pounded, carved, and inlaid designs in silver.

Even objects made for daily life or for sale to outsiders can carry sacred meaning if they are made in the proper way. Objects made for spiritual and ceremonial purposes have significance that may be secret or available only to initiated members of a society. A Zuni altar is a highly sacred construction made up of individual expressive forms: carved and painted figures adorned with feathers, painted pottery bowls for cornmeal, and dry paintings made of sand and crushed minerals. Not only do the individual items have power, but together, they activate a constellation of sacred forms when the proper ceremonies are performed over them. Centuries of custom dictate how the component parts are to be made and used and who may be allowed to see them.

Pottery

Of all the ancient craft traditions in the Southwest, the Mogollon, Hohokam, Ancestral Puebloan, and Mimbres pottery styles are most noticeable. Mimbres painted pottery, in particular, appeals to present-day sensibilities with its charming and humorous black and white images executed in a rather abstract, geometric style. The unique pottery-painting tradition faded out by 1200 C.E. as drought set in and Mimbres villages were abandoned. People migrated, formed new

A Mimbres pot depicting a mythical fish

communities, and explored new decorative traditions. Mimbres pottery was rediscovered when archaeological excavations brought it to light after 1910. Contemporary descendants of Mimbres potters continue to draw creative inspiration from these fine designs, sometimes incorporating snake and feather designs into their painted pots.

Around 1100 C.E., Ancestral Puebloan potters of the Southwest learned how to manufacture pottery that was beautifully painted and skillfully fired in open-air kilns. The potter was not only a master of the elegant vessel form, she painted complex, abstract designs using only simple decorative motifs like straight lines, zig-zags, cross-hatching, and spirals. Ancient Ancestral Puebloan pottery had many regional traditions. Potters learned technical information within their own families but might have drawn inspiration for decorative patterns from other pots that were widely traded within the Southwest.

Pueblo Aesthetics

The Ancestral Puebloan tradition is also significant because it leads directly into the living culture of contemporary Pueblo peoples, who occupy ancient villages in northern New Mexico and Arizona alongside their Navajo neighbors. The Ancestral Puebloan tradition began with the Basketmaker culture dating between 1 and 700 C.E., which was noted for its underground houses which survive into contemporary Pueblo communities in the form of ceremonial, underground kivas. The Basketmaker people also produced baskets with geometric patterns echoed in the visual expressions of numerous Native North Americans well into the 1700s. Pueblo kivas, then as now, were designed in line with spiritual beliefs to be sacred and highly symbolic, their walls decorated with multicolored, painted murals. To encourage kachina spirits to visit from time to time, they were depicted in the form of painted leather masks and four hundred different types of kachina dolls, which were created to instruct young children.

The Pueblo peoples also made ceramic vessels in abundance, which were painted in a variety of geometric and figurative motifs in red, black, and white. Most of these objects that were taken to museums before the mid-twentieth century were collected anonymously or stolen. A visit to many museums gives the false impression that Native American crafts are anonymous. Few labels bear the names of the makers, yet in any community, people were familiar with each other's individual styles and distinctive markings; it was not necessary to put one's name on the carving or basket for others to recognize or appreciate the achievement when all lived closely within a small society.

The famous potter from San Ildefonso Pueblo, Maria Martinez, was urged around 1920 to sign the bottoms of her distinctive blackware pots, for buyers would pay more money for her signed works. Over the next two decades, Martinez signed her name to pots made by others, and she polished and signed pots that other women had formed. To the Western way of thinking, this may seem to be a misrepresentation; within the Pueblo worldview, where community balance and group harmony are valued over individual achievement, this was a way in which other artists could share in the high prices brought by Maria Martinez's fame.

Distinctive Styles

The visual cultures of the American Southwest persist in spite of massive Western cultural influences. Painted pottery, basketry, and silver jewelry made for sale to collectors maintain both historic and ancient traditions dating back some two thousand years. The fame of elder artisans inspires younger men and women.

In the Southwest, one of the earliest schools of Euro-American-influenced painting emerged and persisted between 1910 and 1960. The so-called Southwest Style was associated with the influence of Dorothy Dunn of Santa Fe, a non-Native patron. In these works, historic Southwestern ceremonial dances, hunting scenes, and various domestic activities are depicted in a flat, two-dimensional decorative manner that favored a pale color scheme. This sort of watered-down style is now considered "touristy" but is widely available in galleries, gift shops, and home décor catalogs.

Today, many Southwestern Native artists are graduates of the Institute of American Indian Arts (IAIA) in Santa Fe, New Mexico, the only four-year degree art institution in the U.S. devoted to contemporary Indigenous art and arts education. Graduates from all tribes draw on their education in studio arts, cinematic arts and technology, creative writing, and museum studies to create diverse, authentic work. Popular art fairs and markets include the Gallup Intertribal Ceremonial in August, the Heard Museum Guild Indian Fair and Market in Phoenix (March), and the Santa Fe Indian Market (August).

Music and Dance

Ala ini kun maiso yoleme / so now this is the deer person

hunu kun maiso yoleme / so he is the deer person

ini kun tua maiso yoleme / so he is the real deer person

—Yaqui Deer Dance Song

Native music and dance occur everywhere at specific sacred places, like Canyon de Chelly, Arizona, and at public harvestings, such as pow-wows, fairs, and graduation ceremonies. Many performances have secret and invisible meanings that cannot be categorized by outsiders. Even though some music and dance has always been for entertainment, spirituality and worldview affect most of the performances. Many Native ceremonies are practiced to renew the world or keep it in balance. Others, such as those of the Tewa Pueblo, maintain relationships with spirits, each other, and other communities through music and dance. These activities range from extremely private and sacred harvestings, restricted to the initiated or birth clans, to some that are public and joking in nature and that may be accompanied by carnivals and concession stands.

Dance is still important to Native ways of life. Due to their spiritual origins, and because dances are often tied to seasonal or life-cycle events, they are regionally or tribally specific, the singers usually perform in Native languages, and the ceremonies themselves unfold according to local customs. Rather than expressing individual prowess, dancers usually adhere to established patterns and movements. While many dances have vocal and drum accompaniment, often the dancers themselves, activating the rattles and bells that adorn their ceremonial dress, set their own beat.

Many Pueblo dances require the dancers to move forward into the plaza, dance in lines, then move together to the next dance plaza in a circling of the village. Most ceremonies are seasonal, are organized, directed, and regulated by clans and societies, and feature specific roles for ceremonial leaders, singers, dancers, and supporters. Many are called Feast Days because the members of the Pueblo expect their friends, relatives, and sometimes visitors to drop in and accept their hospitality. Some ceremonies are open to outsiders if they respect the sacred aspects of the events, behave with decorum, and do not take pictures or make recordings without permission. Some of the more famous ceremonies are the Zuni Shalako (a masked winter dance), San Ildefonso Corn Dance (a harvest dance), and the Okeh Owingen Deer Dance (a winter game-hunting dance).

Among the Apache and Navajo, curing rituals and girls' puberty ceremonies are the best known contexts for music and dance. The White Mountain Apache Sunrise Dance (for a girl who is becoming a woman) and the Navajo Enemy Way exemplify these ideals. Each reinforces group beliefs and brings a person into the community or back into the community. Apache and Navajo song style are similar: tense, nasal voices, rhythmic pulsation, and clear articulation of words in alternating verses with vocables, words made up of sounds or letters that do not always mean something and are common in Native American music. Both Apache Crown dancers and Navajo Yeibichei (Night Chant) dancers wear masks and sing partially in falsetto or in voices imitating the spirits.

In the desert area and urban sprawl of southern Arizona (Tucson and Phoenix) and in north-

A young Tohono O'odham girl smiles and shows off a peacock feather at a gathering organized by Tohono O'odham Community Action, which is devoted to creating a healthy, sustainable and culturally vital community for the Nation's 28,000 members.

ern Mexico, the Tohono O'odham, Akimel O'odham (Pima), and the Yaqui continue to carry out traditional ceremonies alongside innovative and hybrid ceremonial forms. An older ceremony, the O'odham Chelkona, serves as entertainment and is often performed as a contest dance for local powwows, rodeos, and other events. It includes gift giving, a hopping or skipping dance, feasting, speeches, and games. The Yaqui Deer Dance (a traditional, sacred ceremony) and the Yaqui Pascua (an Eastertime, Catholic Indian ceremony) exist side by side, reinforcing both the tenacity and the adaptability of these people. Visitors can experience a wide variety of Native music and dancing at powwows such as the Gathering of Nations, held in Albuquerque in April.

Instruments

The handheld gourd, turtle shell, hoof, or wooden rattle and the water drum (an instrument unique to North America) are the most common instruments. The Apache and Navajo water drum is played by only one person. It is made from a small container of wood, pottery, or metal, partially filled with water for tuning, covered with a dampened, soft hide stretched tight, and beaten with a stick. It is also found among members of the Native American Church, a Native peyote religion, widespread in North America (see also the Sacred Traditions section in this chapter).

The bullroarer (a thin, wooden plaque attached to a string and swung in a circle) is still used today for ritual and ceremonial events in the Southwest. The Navajo use it in the Yeibichei and the Apache in the Mountain Spirit or Crown Dance (a masked dance in which humans play the parts of the mountain spirits).

Flutes were reserved primarily for love songs; the courting flute was a male instrument. Its music echoes and embellishes well-known melodies attracting the player's sweetheart. The Apache fiddle (made from a mescal stalk) and musical bows are examples of early string instruments. Similar to Mexican–American Norteño music, employing guitars, concertina, and saxophone, Chicken Scratch fiddle music finds popularity among the Tohono O'odham, Pima, Quechan (Yuma), and Yaqui.

Literature

Until later, Coyote told me this, / and he was b.s.-ing, probably.

—Simon Ortiz (Acoma Pueblo), "The Creation, According to Coyote" (1992)

Oral literature can be defined as that body of literary works that people have shared and preserved for many generations through the spoken word. Creation stories are the center of Southwestern worldviews. These sacred stories describe Emergence, in which humans, animals, and plants who lived in a cave below the world as we know it emerged by climbing a reed, tree, or root into the sun. The Emergence creation story was developed with complexity by the Pueblo, Navajo, and Apache in the Southwest. Living within the earth, the people faced serious troubles. Often, their world lacked light and warmth. Such inhospitable conditions drove the people to travel upward, some animals flying, others carried by tall plants that reached the vault of the heavens. The people (often animal persons as well as humans) sought their proper, balanced place in the cosmic scheme of things. Some animal or insect people were cast out of the lower worlds for their misdeeds, and they had to find a way to the next world in order to survive and attempt to live more morally ordered lives, or the next world might also be destroyed by the cosmic beings.

Other forms of oral literature related to storytelling are tales about the Trickster, which takes the shape of Coyote. Depending on the tribal tradition, stories about such characters may be used to teach proper behavior to children, to instruct and inspire adults, to entertain through humor, to present a culture hero who saves the people or otherwise makes the world better by his brave acts, or to tell of how the universe came to be as we know it.

In the early 1970s, Native writers began producing fiction and poetry as never before and emerged as a writing community. The literary ren-aissance found its first voice in Kiowa author N. Scott Momaday (see also his biography in the Southern Plains: Texas and Oklahoma chapter). Laguna Pueblo author Leslie Marmon Silko's works affirm both cultural continuities and change as do the Acoma poet Simon Ortiz's early works: *Going for the Rain* (1976), *A Good Journey* (1977), and *Howbah Indians* (1978). Both authors come from the Pueblo, and in their works, they evoke the long history Native people have endured with both Spanish and English colonizers in the Southwest. (For recent work and other writers, see the biography section at the end of this chapter.)

SACRED TRADITIONS

Drypainting

Colored sand and crushed minerals are the materials used for temporary paintings sifted onto the ground by Southwestern peoples, including the Navajo, Apache, Pueblo, Pima, and Yaqui. Drypainting, also called sandpainting or sand altars, originated among Indigenous people

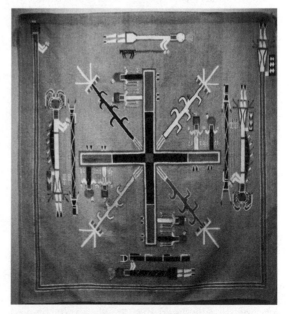

A Navajo rug featuring a drypainting (sand painting) design is displayed at the Gilcrease Museum in Tulsa, Oklahoma. Designs created for public sale are altered so as not to reveal sacred images.

in what is now Guatemala and spread north before Europeans arrived in the Americas.

The Navajo call drypainting *iikáah,* or "The Place Where the Gods Come and Go." These paintings are used in curing and blessing ceremonies, and each type of image has specific songs associated with it. Figures in the paintings represent sacred beings and serve to transmit healing energy from the holy realm to the patient. The paintings are destroyed at the end of the ceremony so that the illness does not remain where other people can contact it. Only trained healers can make drypaintings, and they are not to be sold as "art." Some craftspeople do make small versions for sale, suspending the sand in glue on a wooden support, but they alter and simplify the images so as not to violate the healing tradition.

The Native American Church/Peyotism

Peyote *(Lophophora williamsii)* is a small, turnip-shaped cactus grown in the arid Rio Grande Valley of northern Mexico and Texas. Its substance is not addictive and should not be classified as a narcotic. People eat the bitter, dried top, or "button," to induce heightened perceptions of sound and color. It enhances concentration and highlights spiritual truths with vivid imagery during ceremonies.

Spanish chroniclers observed peyote use in the ceremonies of northern Mexico in the sixteenth century. Its use in these Indigenous community festivals, however, was different than the organized peyote church that later developed. Peyote use was first recorded in the United States among the Mescalero Apache in the 1870s, who then introduced it to the Kiowa, Comanche, and others. As a religion, it spread through Oklahoma (formerly Indian Territory), the Great Plains, the Great Lakes area, and various parts of the Northwest during the same fifty years that Christianity was being advocated by paid, federally backed missionaries. In 1918, several peyote groups incorporated under the state laws of Oklahoma as the Native American Church.

Peyotism took hold in the United States when the Native population had reached its lowest point: Indian peoples, hungry and distressed, were confined to reservations as captured nations; Indigenous political economy was all but destroyed; individualism and the capitalist ethic conflicted with Indian values and traditions; and Native religions were outlawed. Under these extreme conditions, new Native ceremonialism arose, and the peyote church offered its adherents a means of religious expression by which they could maintain a positive identity as Indian people in a hostile, white, soldier-settler environment.

At the same time, peyotism eased the conflicting demands of traditional spirituality and Christianity. The Peyote religion gave the people ways to reassume sacred responsibility: During the peyote ceremony, they confessed their sins, achieved purification, cured sickness, recovered from alcoholism, and created powerful, intertribal bonds. The peyote church, which came to be known as the Native American Church, has not displaced, or replaced, traditional spiritual practices. The traditional ceremonies that were outlawed by the federal government and went underground in the early twentieth century began to re-emerge in increasingly vigorous forms in the 1930s.

In 1954, the peyote religion became international with the incorporation of the Native American Church of Canada, and by the 1970s, there were as many as 250,000 Native members. It is the largest and fastest-growing sacred society in North America. The American Indian Religious Freedom Act (AIRFA) of 1978, which would have seemed to protect such peyote use as a sacrament, did so in name only. In 1990, however, the U.S. Supreme Court struck down federal religious protection for the peyote church in an Oregon case and left it up to the various states to decide whether to criminalize peyote use as violation of narcotics laws by Native Americans. In 1993, President Bill Clinton strengthened protection of Native religious rights when he signed the American Indian Religious Freedom Restoration Act (RFRA), reversing the Supreme Court's ruling. One year later, he signed an amendment to AIRFA legislation explicitly protecting Native American tribal members' use of peyote in traditional ceremonies.

Sports and Games

Southwest peoples ran long distances, not only to keep fit or to deliver messages, but as part of their spiritual beliefs about connecting sacred places by running between them. Some games were sacred and played as part of ceremonies. Others strengthened children physically and taught them life skills. Boys and girls usually played separately; they raced and played competitive archery, stick toss, and foot toss, using stones.

Dating from ancient days, buzz toys were made of two flat disks of wood or bone pierced in the center and threaded with two strings through the holes. Holding a handle in each hand, the strings are twisted until the toy whirls like a yo-yo and makes a buzzing sound. Children tried to stop each other's buzz toys from spinning, and the child whose disk spun the longest was the winner. During the Zuni corncob game, a cob was balanced on a flat stone. Children took turns tossing pebbles toward the cob. The goal was to knock the cob over and have the pebble bounce back to the player.

Pueblo people raced in teams but created an extra challenge by kicking a stick in a soccerlike game. Zuni racers also added this twist, racing in a circle while hitting a ball with a stick toward a goal. Sticks were also painted to resemble dice for a gambling or guessing game that Havasupai men played using corn kernels as counters. A guessing game Pima people played with two teams had each team taking turns lining up facing a goal about fifty yards from the first player in line. The leader of the team walked along the line and placed a pebble or a small object in one player's hand. However, he or she also pretended to give the object to several players. The leader of the opposite team attempted to guess who had the object. Depending on whether the leader was right or wrong, one of the teams' lines of players jumped toward the goal, but first, they had to jump over the upheld leg of the player at the head of the line.

Footraces remain popular in the Southwest. One of the best attended races honors Lewis Tewanima, a Hopi Olympian who was the first American to win a medal in the ten-thousand-meter race (Stockholm, 1912). The race takes place on Labor Day weekend and begins and ends on Second Mesa on Hopi land. The Native organization Wings of America is located in Santa Fe. Rodeo riding, basketball, skateboarding, and golf are other top sports among Southwest peoples. The all-Indian Rodeo Cowboy Association was founded at St. Michaels on the Navajo Reservation in 1957. Navajo people also love basketball: In 1995, Navajo player Ryneldi Bicenti was the first Native American woman to play for a foreign team (the Swiss team). Two films document legendary Navajo girls' basketball teams: *Lady Warrior* (2002) and *Rocks with Wings* (2007). Another film, *4WheelWarPony*, features young skateboarders of the Apache Nation (2008). The first tribally owned championship golf course in the U.S. is also on Apache land: the Mescalero's eighteen-hole course is at a seven-thousand-foot elevation and was opened in 1975. The Santa Ana Pueblo provides golfing for youth at the Notah Begay III Foundation, named after the Navajo/Pueblo pro golfer who is ranked among the top twenty golfers in the world.

COLONIZATION

They would be punished by being driven out of the rich country where they were into the barren desert to the west, where there was no water and the land would not grow corn. They would run and hide, from place to place, and when they met some of their people, they would say: "Where is my wife? Where is my father? Where are my children?"

—Chester Arthur (Navajo), 1930

When Spanish colonization began in the late 1590s, they attacked the Indigenous cities they called pueblos (towns), reducing ninety-eight cities to twenty-one during the next twenty years. By 1628, the missionaries outlawed Native ceremonies and feast days and imposed Catholicism upon the people. The Spanish authorities gave land grants to military officers for past service and also granted the officers the right to enslave Indians. Many Pueblo people were made to work on the ranches and farms of the Spanish officers and upper class. Young Pueblo were forced into the Spanish military, which existed principally to make slave raids into communities near the New Mexico colony. For two centuries, the Navajo, the Apache, and the Ute, who lived in present-day southern Colorado, defended themselves mightily from these raids.

In 1680, the Pueblo spiritual leader, Po'pay, led a rebellion that forced the Spanish and allied Indians, such as the Comanche, to retreat to El Paso (Texas). Their freedom lasted for twelve years until Spanish military forces again regained control of the Pueblo villages in the Rio Grande Valley by 1692.

When the early Franciscan missionaries had physically discouraged Pueblo sacred practices, this forced ceremonies underground. After the Pueblo revolt, when the Spanish returned to the Pueblo, they considered the Indians Catholic but looked away when they practiced their kiva ceremonies. However, from the late 1800s until 1934, the Anglo-Americans suppressed these ceremonies, and again, the Pueblo disguised many of their own practices under a Catholic surface. Thus, today, like many Southwestern Indians, they are both Catholic and traditional.

When the Spanish returned, some Pueblo people left their villages to join the Navajo bands in the north. Many Navajo, Apache, Ute, and Hopi people had helped the Pueblo defeat the Spanish during the Pueblo Revolt. These unconquered peoples would resist Spanish, Mexican (1820–1848), and U.S. colonization for many years. When U.S. military and traders entered the Southwest in full force in 1848 after the Mexi-

The Palace of the Governors in Santa Fe, New Mexico, was targeted by the Pueblo in the 1680 rebellion led by Po'pay. Today it stands as a museum.

can–American War, they met strong opposition from the Native people, particularly the Apache.

THE APACHE

We have come from the earth, and we belong to the earth.

—The White Mountain Apache Tribe

The Apache migrated into the Southwest before the eleventh century. They formed a small part of a large migration of Athapascan peoples from the subarctic north and are closely related to the Navajo. They divided into small bands that spread over a seven-hundred-square-mile territory. Gran Apacheria, as the Spaniards called it, included all of present-day New Mexico and Arizona. According to differences in language or dialect, the Apache formed into two major groups: the Jicarilla, Lipan, and Kiowa (Apache) living on the Southern Plains and the Chiricahua, Mescalero, and Western Apache, who in the 1800s were moving westward into present-day New Mexico and Arizona.

Apache Traditions

The Apache lived by hunting big game, harvesting wild plants, and farming corn, sunflowers, beans, and other foods. They lived in family groups along waterways. Their main shelter was a circular brush lodge with a fire in the center. Each Apachean group was composed of clans: basic social, economic, and political units based on female inherited leadership. From their entrance into the Southwest, the Apache groups were in conflict with the Plains peoples in the east and with the Pima, Tohono O'odham, and Pueblo, then living in what is now eastern New Mexico. Chiricahua history accounts for acquiring goods such as turquoise, corn, and blankets from "enemy people" as a last resort when trade was not possible.

Apache Resistance (1830s–1880s)

During the 1830s, the Apache fought against Mexican attacks, and in 1846, the United States took over New Mexico Territory and became the Apache's enemy, and soldiers and miners flooded into the region. The Apache Wars lasted until the early 1880s, and although the Apache retreated many times into their mountain strongholds, they returned many times to raid soldiers and settlers on both sides of the U.S.—Mexican border. No Apache band was ever conquered militarily although starvation conditions on the run eventually led them to surrender.

In the summer of 1881, a White Mountain Apache brought news of the first Ghost Dance to the Chiricahua Apache by telling them Cochise and spirits of the great chiefs would reappear soon thereafter. That summer, at Cibecue (Arizona) in August, a number of soldiers and the Apache prophet were murdered. When word of this spread, hundreds of U.S. troops poured into Arizona to quell a potential uprising. In retaliation for the soldiers' murder, two Apache scouts were sent to Fort Alcatraz in San Francisco Bay, and three others were later hanged at Camp Grant, near Bonita, Arizona, the site of the 1871 massacre of nearly one hundred Apache men, women, and children. Incidents such as these fed the flames of war.

The Apache might have accepted reservation life in the cooler mountain regions they preferred, if they had been allowed to raise sheep and goats as promised, but when pressured to become farmers, they escaped to the Sierra Madre Mountains in Mexico. Five thousand troops, nearly five hundred Apache scouts, and hundreds of Mexican troops chased the small bands to no avail until General Nelson A. Miles ordered telegraph wires, which could easily be cut down by the Chiricahua, to be replaced by the heliograph, which used the sun to send Morse code messages. With better communications, Miles reduced his forces to a contingent of scouts and sent several of them to contact the Chiricahua leaders Naiche and Geronimo. They agreed to surrender for the final time.

Apache survivors were herded into desolate reservations in present-day Arizona and New Mexico, and some were imprisoned in Florida, where many died of diseases. Geronimo, a Chiricahua Apache spiritual leader, is best known among the Apache leaders who resisted settlement onto reservations. Their resistance assured Apache survival and reservation land bases in Arizona and New Mexico (see also the biographies of Geronimo, Cochise, Natchez, and other Apache leaders at the end of this chapter).

Survival Strategies

There are about 111,800 Apache tribal members living on reservations in the Southwest. Some of the contemporary Apache reservations have been leaders in economic development of reservation resources. The White Mountain Apache in Arizona successfully manage Sunrise Park Ski Resort and Fort Apache Timber Company. The lumber company employs about three hundred Apache residents and grosses about $20 million in annual income. The ski resort is also a major contributor to Fort Apache Reservation economy and is one of the most successful resort ventures in Indian Country.

Other Apache reservations have also invested in tourism by opening cultural centers and annual festivals to the public. In addition, some reservation lands and lakes are open for public fishing and outdoor recreation. Sport fish include the Apache Trout, which the tribe brought back from the brink of extinction. The Apache people

The Apache Trout (*Oncorhynchus gilae*) was on the brink of extinction, but the Apache saved it and it remains a part of their traditions and food resources.

retain strong ties to their culture, language, dances, and other traditions. Powwows are held each year, and often, many Indian people from other reservations attend.

THE NAVAJO NATION

With beauty may I walk.
With beauty before me, may I walk.
With beauty behind me, may I walk.
With beauty above me, may I walk.
With beauty below me, may I walk.
With beauty around me, may I walk.
It is finished in beauty.
It is finished in beauty.

—Navajo Beauty Way Chant

The Navajo Nation, or *Diné Bikéyah,* is the largest Native nation in the United States both in territory and population. With 17 million acres, or 28,803 square miles, the Navajo Reservation in Arizona and New Mexico is larger than ten of the fifty U.S. states. The population is at least 250,000. The present-day Navajo territory is located in the Four Corners region of Arizona, New Mexico, Utah, and Colorado, with land in all but the last.

Traditions

The four sacred mountains of the Navajo are *Sisnaajiní* (Horizontal Black Belt) or Sierra Blanca Peak, *Tsoodzil* (Tongue Mountain) or Mount Taylor, *Dook'o'slííd* (Light Shines From It) or San Francisco Peaks, and *Dibéntsaa* (Big Mountain Sheep) or Mount Hesperus. Each mountain occupies a cardinal four-directions point around the Navajo Nation. The sacred directions and other symbolic designs are represented in the traditional Hogan house, which is octagonal and traditionally made of wooden poles, tree bark, and wood. The doorways faced east to receive the sun's blessings; hogans remain places for ceremonies.

Ceremonies are largely devoted to health and well-being to maintain hózhó: balance, beauty, and harmony. Girls' puberty ceremonies are important;

people trace their descent through their mother's clan. The women are known for their long, silk skirts and velveteen blouses and the men for distinctive, silver concho belts and cowboy hats.

Traditionally hunter-harvesters during the 1700s, many Navajo relied less on hunting and adopted the pastoral life of herding sheep. It became the preferred way of life. A large number of conservative Navajo continue to herd sheep and cattle primarily to feed and clothe their own families while small numbers are sold and traded.

Navajo Textiles

Handwoven sashes, blankets, tapestries, and rugs are magnificent expressions of abstract design and cultural continuity in the Southwest today. Most are still woven, mainly by Navajo women, on the traditional vertical loom. After the Spanish brought sheep to the Southwest, mutton and wool became integral to Navajo culture. During the early twentieth century, reservation traders

An example of a Navajo blanket, woven in 1910, exhibiting typical abstract designs.

dictated which materials and patterns would sell: hand-spun wool yard from churro sheep colored with natural, native plant dyes and woven into large, central patterns in white, gray, and red. Regional patterns, such as Grey Hills designs, popular in the 1920s, featured black, brown, beige, and white. Today, many weavers display their own personal styles, but regional patterns persist, such as the "storm" motif in the western part of the reservation and sandpainting figures from Farmington, Shiprock, and Lukachukai. Wavy stripes have been popular in Crystal since the 1950s while Ganado and Wide Ruins designs in pastel colors emerged in the 1970s.

The motifs on many Navajo wool rugs are not symbolic but simply demonstrate the weaver's powers of creativity and graphic design. Natural plant dyes are now available in eighty-six colors. Styles have expanded to pictorial imagery such as birds and flowers, round rug shapes, and textiles tufted with mohair goat wool. Popular weavers can receive tens of thousands of dollars for their rugs.

Colonialism: The Long Walk

Between 1820 and 1848, Navajo land was claimed by the Mexican Republic although the Navajo never submitted to Mexican authority. The United States annexed Navajo territory under the 1848 Treaty of Guadalupe Hidalgo, which ended the Mexican–American War.

Unlike the Mexican government, the United States used extreme military measures to subdue the Indians and control their land base. The Navajo successfully resisted U.S. control for seventeen years until the U.S. Civil War (1861–1865), when the U.S. Army launched expeditions to search out the Navajo and destroy their livelihood. Cornfields were burned, communities pillaged, fruit trees destroyed, and sheep slaughtered until the Navajo, facing starvation during 1863 and 1864, finally surrendered. The New Mexico trader Kit Carson was commissioned into the army with the rank of colonel and led irregular troops to capture numerous Navajo bands. Carson's troops, with Ute scouts and allies, began

Located on the grounds of Fort Sumner State Monument, the Bosque Redondo Memorial recalls the persecution of Navajo and Mescalero Apache by the U.S. military from 1863 to 1868.

a scorched-earth policy culminating in the Navajo War (1863–1866). Carson's orders were to kill all Navajo men of fighting age and relocate all prisoners to Bosque Redondo (near Fort Sumner in present-day eastern New Mexico).

Eight thousand Navajo were rounded up and forced into a military-administered camp in the barren area, far from their high desert and alpine homeland. While there, a quarter of them died from starvation and exposure. In 1868, a treaty was negotiated with Navajo headmen, and they were allowed to settle on the Navajo Reservation, which has since been greatly reduced in size (see also the biographies of Ganado Mucho, Manuelito, Barboncito, and other Navajo leaders at the end of this chapter).

Oil and Water

From 1868 to 1922, when oil was discovered in Navajo territory, the Navajo were virtually ig-

nored by the federal government. The land had been judged to be worthless, even for Texas longhorn cattle production. The presence of oil, however, led to intense intervention into Navajo affairs. In 1922, the Navajo Business Council was created by the U.S. agent, who needed a centralized authority to grant oil and mineral leases in the name of the entire Navajo Nation. Most Navajo were led by local headmen, who generally did not recognize a central Navajo government and often ignored the Navajo Business Council until its demise in 1936.

The Navajo firmly rejected the Indian Reorganization Act of 1934 (see also the Historical Overview chapter). Instead, the federal government allowed the Navajo to hold a constitutional convention, which proposed a government independent from the bureaucratic power of the Office of Indian Affairs (the Bureau of Indian Affairs, BIA, in the 1940s). The secretary of the interior rejected the Navajo constitution, which was a bold plan for greater Navajo political freedom. Instead, in 1938, the Department of the Interior created a new Navajo Business Council, composed of seventy-four elected Navajo members and a generally elected chairman and vice chairman. This government, known as the "Rules of 1938," provided the basis for the present Navajo Tribal Council.

During the late 1930s and 1940s, the Navajo became embroiled in a political and bureaucratic conflict with the BIA and U.S. government over the issues of grazing sheep and cattle on the Navajo Reservation. Most Navajo made their living from sheep herding—but Navajo herds were generally small and designed mainly for supplying family food although some mutton and wool was traded at local stores for necessary manufactured goods. During the 1930s Dust Bowl period, government officials decided that the Navajo were raising too many sheep for the amount of grasslands and that the overgrazing would lead to ecological ruin of Navajo lands through erosion. Beginning with a massive stock-reduction program, agents of the Agricultural Department slaughtered tens of thousands of Navajo sheep to prevent overgrazing. This conflict soured Navajo and government relations for several decades.

Despite antipathy toward the federal government, Navajo are patriotic about American land itself and have enlisted in the armed forces in great numbers to defend the country during all conflicts. During World War II, the Navajo language was used to create a secret code to baffle the Japanese. The famous Navajo Code Talkers are revered among Native veterans. Major Howard Connor, 5th Marine Division signal officer, said, "Were it not for the Navajo, the Marines would never have taken Iwo Jima."

Although the Navajo Nation possesses water rights sufficient to irrigate and farm five million acres of their land, fewer than one hundred thousand acres are under cultivation. Most of the land is used for grazing five hundred thousand sheep, fifty thousand cattle, and thirty thousand goats. Much of the agricultural production is animal food grain. The agricultural and pastoral economy can potentially be successful, something much desired by Navajo traditionalists struggling to maintain their subsistence economy as well as by some economic experts.

Nevertheless, the Navajo pastoral economy often is rejected by Navajo modernizers, who favor development of Navajo natural resources such as oil, gas, coal, and uranium. Much Navajo land was leased by the federal government during the 1920s and 1930s so that the main income generated from the land is from mineral and mining leases and royalties. The territory is rich in reserve subsurface minerals and resources: one hundred million barrels of oil; 25 billion cubic feet of natural gas; five billion tons of surface coal; and 80 million pounds of uranium. The major companies operating in the Navajo Nation are AMOCO, Exxon, Kerr-McGee, Gulf, and Texaco. Navajo territory includes five hundred thousand acres of commercial forests, which yield millions of dollars in annual stumpage payments. The forest enterprise is controlled by the Navajo government under its Navajo Forest Products Industry.

Survival Strategies

There is a wide gap between the wealth of Navajo territory and the overwhelming poverty of its residents. Unemployment hovers around fifty percent. Most unemployed are unskilled and lacking in formal American education, many speaking little English. Few are familiar with the modern market economy. Even in the twenty-first century, basics such as electricity and running water are unavailable to many rural people. The majority—some seventy-five percent—of employed Navajo work in the public sector, made possible by U.S. government funding amounting to hundreds of millions of dollars annually. The remaining workers on the reservation are employed in commercial agriculture, mining, forestry, wholesale and retail trade, and construction. Around five percent are employed in transportation, communications, and utilities; all are Navajo owned and operated.

About twenty percent of Navajo live off the reservation, and many have migrated to southwestern cities, as well as to San Francisco and Los Angeles, for jobs. Under the federal government's Indian Relocation Program of the 1950s, most Navajo who relocated chose California since a large number were already living there, many having been rail workers for the Santa Fe Railroad since the 1920s. Due mainly to economic necessity, migration to and from the Navajo homeland is constant.

The influx of federal funds has not increased Navajo incomes even to national poverty levels. Federal funds are generally earmarked to relieve symptoms of poverty, not for capital development. The chief beneficiaries are the thousands of Navajo employees running the federal bureaucracy on the reservation; they make up a privileged group with a vested interest in maintaining and enlarging the tribal government bureaucracy.

Unionization

The 1970s saw a rise in industrial activity with the Navajo Nation taking remarkable initiatives. During the construction of the off-reservation Salt River power plant project at Page, Arizona, Navajo workers experienced blatant racial discrimination in pay and duties. They organized and pressed the Navajo Nation to support their

Wings of America National Team High School Runner Daabagoiina Haven (on left), Diné (Navajo), runs with youth at a summer program in Sante Fe, New Mexico in 2015. With the help of Nike's N7 Fund, Wings of America has fostered young Native runners for 25 years.

demands, and newly elected Navajo Chairman Peter MacDonald took up the challenge. Trade unions, until then banned on the reservation, were legalized and supported. The actions taken by Navajo workers and the Navajo Nation awakened workers throughout the Southwest, where the combined Mexican and Indian labor force had long been oppressed by ruling Anglo-Americans. Both New Mexico and Arizona were traditionally antiunion with less than five percent of their workforces organized into trade unions. The Office of Navajo Labor Relations was established to mandate standards for Navajo workers' wages for jobs in or near the reservation. These standards required major construction projects to hire the Navajo on a percentage or quota basis in specific numbers of skilled positions.

Trade unions are now an accepted part of the Navajo social structure but are far more democratic than their typical U.S. counterparts. The Office of Navajo Labor Relations supports local workers' associations within the reservation based in the communities where the workers live. By the late 1970s, practically all Navajo workers in the private sector were members of labor unions.

Some observers have expressed concern at the successful unionization of Navajo workers, who receive nationally mandated union wages. They fear that the high income of Navajo industrial workers will encourage unbridled industrialization as well as an economic elite. However, traditional practices of Navajo family and clan sharing and generosity actually tend to equalize incomes through redistribution by means of gifts of money and goods from the highly paid workers to their less fortunate relatives and neighbors. It also appears that highly paid Navajo workers tend to invest surplus funds in the traditional pastoral economy by purchasing stock, feed, equipment, and trucks.

Education

In 1971, the Navajo Nation supported the formation of Navajo Community College (NCC) at Tsaile, Arizona. The locally controlled Indian community college was the first of its kind, and many Navajo, who did not want to leave the reservation to take college courses, enrolled at NCC. The college was so successful that within a few years, other reservations were starting colleges and having considerable success. Meanwhile, U.S. college institutions were showing extremely poor results retaining and graduating Indian college students. Indian-controlled community colleges have been built on many Indian reservations across the country. The community college movement became one of the most significant events on many reservations during the 1970s and 1980s. It was greatly inspired by the groundbreaking work of the Navajo community and the pioneers who built Navajo Community College, now called Diné College.

Tribal Government

In November 1982, young activist lawyer Peterson Zah won election as Navajo chairman. He was defeated four years later by MacDonald but won again in 1990. In 2015, the Navajo Nation president was Ben Shelly. About 35,000 Navajo vote in the Navajo tribal government elections, and over the years, the government has evolved by borrowing both Western and traditional Navajo institutions. They adopted a court system modeled after the U.S. legal system in 1959 in order to prevent the states of Arizona and New Mexico from extending their courts onto the reservation. The Navajo prefer their own legal system over the U.S. court system.

During the 1970s, the Navajo court system gained power and respect, and many local courts managed disputes in the traditional manner of trying to reconcile contentious parties, according to Navajo cultural views of resolving conflict more so than U.S. legal views. Until the 1950s, the Navajo government suffered from lack of local support, but since then, it has tried to directly incorporate local political communities, often called chapters, into the government and electoral process and in this way gain the support of the communities, which still tend toward local groupings and local leaders. The Navajo government has made considerable strides in attempting to provide a truly representative government, based to some extent on traditional principles, and has developed the largest tribal government organization in Native North America.

THE HOPI

The family, the dwelling house, and the field are inseparable because the woman is the heart of these, and they rest with her. Among us, the family traces its kinship from the mother, hence all its possessions are hers.... A man plants the fields of his wife, and the fields assigned to the children she bears, and informally, he calls them his although in fact, they are not. Even of the field which he inherits from his mother, its harvests, he may dispose of at will, but the field, he may not.

—Petition to the federal government protesting division of tribal lands for individual ownership (Allotment), signed by all of the Hopi chiefs (1894)

The Hopi are descendants of the earliest inhabitants of the Southwest and for centuries occupied a large part of present-day northern Arizona. In their oral history, they recount the arrival of the Paiute and the Ute, the Navajo, the Spanish, then the Americans.

Traditions

The Hopi elders tell of a time long ago, before people were really human beings, when they lived underground; this was the period of the Third World. Before the early beings lived in the Third World, they had to flee two other worlds farther underground because of their immoral behavior and disruption of the social harmony of the First and Second Worlds. For some time, these early people lived in peace with all the animals, and there were no problems, but then, the people began to have disputes. A council was held with animal representatives participating in the discussions. They agreed that the Third World had become morally corrupted and out of balance, and they had to seek peace by migrating from the underworld to a Fourth World above. The Hopi arrived in the Fourth World and encountered a frightening, yet attractive, spirit being, Masau-u, who asked them what they sought. Masau-u told the Hopi they could live on the land of the Fourth World provided that they followed sacred rules. The Hopi would have to perform rituals to provide water for the desert land, and they would have to accept Masau-u's teachings, abiding by his/her social and religious rules. The Hopi agreed and made a covenant to obey Masau-u and serve as caretakers of the land. The Hopi attempt to keep this sacred covenant to this day.

Each Hopi clan retells a variation of the creation, but they all share the same emergence story and consider the land sacred. They believe they must fulfill particular sacred and ceremonial responsibilities. Creating rain for the dry land is essential and is accomplished through prayers and ceremonies held annually in Hopi villages.

The Hopi live in northeastern Arizona, where their reservation is entirely surrounded by the large Navajo Reservation. Hopi society is divided into twelve phratries, or collections of clans, with numerous clans within each phratry. Children always belong to the clan of their mother. Like other Pueblo, Hopi honor kachinas, or rain spirits, and clan ancestors. Clans are extremely important for social and religious relations, and each clan has its own special sacred

Hopi youth work on a springs restoration project, building a water cachement at Castle Springs.

objects and ceremonies. Clan and ceremonial leaders continue to play major roles in Hopi ceremonial and social life. Many Hopi, as well as Pueblo, ceremonies are concerned with creating community harmony and appeasing the kachina spirits to bring rain for the Hopi crops. The Hopi grew several varieties of corn, beans, squash, and other plants. Men hunted animals such as deer and elk, and the women gathered nuts, fruits, and roots.

Hopi Resistance

In the middle and late 1500s, there may have been as many as a dozen Hopi villages along the Colorado River, but they were quickly decimated by early diseases, and by 1600, most Hopi retreated to their present villages in northern Arizona. Starting in 1628, Spanish Catholic missions were established in several Hopi villages. The Hopi helped the Pueblo in the 1680 rebellion, and even after the Spanish reconquest, the Hopi strongly resisted Spanish rule and Catholic religion.

Cultural Continuance

The Hopi occupy about a dozen villages on the reservation. Many still live in multistoried buildings that the Spanish called pueblos. Several Hopi continue to uphold the traditional ways and actively resist U.S. cultural influences in religion, education, and government. During the 1930s, a small number of Hopi voted for adopting a constitutional government under the provisions of the Indian Reorganization Act (IRA) of 1934 (see also the Historical Overview chapter). The Hopi community became divided between those willing to live under the IRA government and those who wanted to retain Hopi political institutions, which incorporated a considerable degree of traditional Hopi customs and religious orientation.

The conservative Hopi have been some of the most active nationalist groups in the United States. Together with the conservative and nationalist Iroquois people of New York and southern Canada, Hopi leaders have appealed to international forums such as the United Nations in order to gain redress for broken treaty agreements and for recognition of Indian national independence. Not all Hopi share the view that the reservation should be recognized as an independent nation within the international community, but the conservative Hopi support strong attachment to tradition, which motivates many to actively seek preservation of Hopi community and religious institutions. About 18,500 people were enrolled in the Hopi Nation in 2015.

THE PUEBLO VILLAGES OF NEW MEXICO

When Europeans arrived, the Maya, Azteca, Inca cultures had already built great cities and vast networks of roads. Ancient prophecies foretold the arrival of Europeans in the Americas. The ancient prophecies also foretold the disappearance of all things European.

—Leslie Marmon Silko (Laguna Pueblo), *Almanac of the Dead* (1991)

Pueblo Traditions

When the Spanish arrived in the 1500s, there were ninety-eight villages, called pueblos by the Spanish, along the northern Rio Grande and its tributaries; within a few decades, there were only nineteen, all of which exist today. The Pueblo homeland once spread into the states of Colorado and Arizona; today, it is contained within eastern New Mexico. Pueblo peoples have similar economic, governmental, and religious structures and speak five distinct languages: Zuni, Keres, Tiwa, Towa, and Tewa, and many more local dialects. The languages remain strong and continue to be taught to children.

Pueblo communities each have their own feast day, named after the community's patron saint. Feast days bring tribal members together to renew their culture, language, and ceremonies. Visitors can experience the dances and songs and participate in activities and family feasts if invited.

Etiquette involves calling the tribal office ahead to confirm dates and access to the reservation (sometimes, private ceremonies limit access), not entering private homes unless invited, acquiring a permit to take photos (some Pueblo do not allow photos at all), and always requesting permission before taking a photo of a person. The Pueblo do not allow alcohol and drugs, and silence is mandatory during dances and ceremonies. Applause is not customary, and there is no walking across the dance area or entering kivas or cemeteries.

Each Pueblo is autonomous and strongly independent; however, all the Pueblo participate in a loose federation, the All Indian Pueblo Council, which traces its origins to the successful 1680 Pueblo Revolt against the Spanish. The leader of the rebellion was Po'pay, a religious leader from San Juan Pueblo (Ohkay Owingen).

The Pueblo Revolt

The revolt started at Taos Pueblo and moved steadily to the southern pueblos, driving the Spanish and some Pueblo allies to El Paso, in present-day Texas. For about a dozen years, the Pueblo enjoyed liberty (see also the biography of Po'pay at the end of this chapter). The Spanish, however, reconquered the Pueblo by 1692 but thereafter refrained from tampering directly with Pueblo internal affairs, particularly religious ceremonies. Many Pueblo, especially those from Jemez Pueblo, did not want to live under Spanish rule and escaped to live among the Navajo and Apache bands, many of which were constantly raiding the Spanish and Pueblo villages for livestock and trade goods. The Pueblo had a profound effect on Navajo and Apache traditions and ceremonies, which were enriched with ideas borrowed from the Pueblo refugees. The remainder of the Pueblo lived under harsh Spanish rule, which demanded Catholic conversion and forced labor on the ranches of Spanish officers and political land grantees.

Land and Water

Under the rule of independent Mexico from 1821 to 1848, only the Pueblo among the

Southwest Indians held full Mexican citizenship. Therefore, when the United States annexed the region, Pueblo people automatically became U.S. citizens, as did the other residents of the area. Not only was citizenship of little use to the Pueblo, but their territories did not fall under the federal government's developing reservation system, which normally put Indian lands under federal protection. Encroachment on Pueblo land, the finest farm land in the Southwest, accelerated rapidly. The Pueblo petitioned and then sued for Indian status, which they finally gained in 1916 through a U.S. Supreme Court decision. Meanwhile, they had lost some of their best lands as well as important religious sites.

A congressional investigation during the 1920s revealed that 12,000 non-Pueblo claimants were living on Pueblo lands. The All Indian Pueblo Council organized delegates from all the Pueblos to regain their lands, which resulted in

U.S. Supreme Court Associate Justice Joseph McKenna delivered the majority opinion in the *Winters v. United States* case that established the Winters Doctrine granting water rights for Indians on reservations.

the 1924 Pueblo Lands Act. Assisting the Pueblo in their fight was John Collier, a young Indian rights activist on the staff of the General Federation of Women's Clubs. President Franklin D. Roosevelt later named Collier the Indian commissioner, a position he held from 1933 to 1945. The Pueblo successfully mounted a campaign among non-Indians and set an important example for other Native peoples across the country.

Pueblo lands are secure, but land in a semi-arid region is of no use without water. The most important contemporary Pueblo Indian struggle is to maintain and to acquire water rights. Water law falls under federal law but has often been under state jurisdiction. Indians fought for and won exemption from state control in the early twentieth century. The Winters Doctrine, arising from a 1909 Supreme Court case, defines Indian water rights and is based on the theory that the federal government reserves power over federal lands, which includes the necessary water supply. The Winters Doctrine implies that Indian treaty rights include the right to adequate supplies of water necessary for agriculture irrigation and to meet their population and economic development needs. However, in a court decision in 1973, the Winters Doctrine was declared to be inapplicable to the Pueblo Indians of New Mexico since the Pueblo were not officially Indians at the time the Winters case was decided.

The Return of Blue Lake

One the most significant events in recent Pueblo history is the return of the sacred Blue Lake and about 55,000 surrounding acres to the Taos Pueblo in 1970. Taos Pueblo had lost the land to the federal government, but after a sixty-five-year court and political struggle, they regained stewardship of Blue Lake, a sacred site in Taos creation history, since it is considered the navel of the universe and the place where the Creator first created people as well as where the spirits of ancestors and the departed live. The Taos hold annual ceremonies at Blue Lake, many of which are crucial to their religious cycle, which, the Taos people believe, ensured the well-being and prosperity of their community. The return of Blue Lake marked one of the few times that the federal government returned a major sacred site and surrounding lands to Indigenous care. It gives hope that in the future, other Indian communities may successfully regain or protect their sacred sites, often unknown to the general public.

Zuni Pueblo

Let's not compliment ourselves too much yet about moving or repatriating or sharing things like this—whether it's an image or physical object—because that's what we should be doing anyway, and also, I think, a song, a prayer, all of these sorts of things are really ancient endowments. They've been composed and sung—a prayer has its place—they are of that place, of that person, and they belong to the people anyway. Whether even if they were said once, the people were blessed with that prayer, or a song was sung, we were blessed by that song, and that's not going to go away. That's the ancient endowment.

—Jim Enote (Hopi/Zuni), executive director of the A:shiwi A:wan Museum and Heritage Center, Zuni, New Mexico (2012)

The nineteen New Mexico pueblos remain strongly traditional communities that continue to practice and perform the major dances and ceremonies of their religions. They have consistently rejected U.S. efforts to significantly alter their religious, social, and cultural orders since they continue to live by many of the religious views and customs of their ancestors.

There are about 62,500 people enrolled in Pueblo communities in New Mexico, of whom about 10,200 identified themselves as Zuni in 2010. Zuni Pueblo is the largest group of Pueblo and is considered to be the most traditional with about eighty percent of the people involved in making art. Zuni, or Halona Idiwan'a ("Middle Place"), is sheltered in a scenic valley between dramatic, red-rock mesas, about 150 miles west of Albuquerque. Tribal landholdings encompass about 450,000 acres.

Self-Determination

During the 1960s and 1970s, Zuni Pueblo became a model for the present-day U.S. government self-determination policy in Indian affairs. Like other Pueblo peoples, the Zuni have a strong tradition of religious community and strong attachments to their social and political freedom. During the 1960s, when federal funds became available through antipoverty programs like the Community Action Programs (CAP), many Indian communities, for the first time, gained access to significant funds and personnel because of direct federal grants to local tribal governments. The Zuni, in the late 1960s, seized this opportunity and, armed with a little-used law that required the Bureau of Indian Affairs (BIA) to contract services to tribal governments, gained control over all BIA programs in the Zuni community. They were able to contract their own courts, police force, school system, and economic base, running these much more effectively and with greater community commitment and participation. The Zuni began to assert their sovereignty and exclude unwanted BIA interference into their government and community affairs.

The A:shiwi A:wan Museum and Heritage Center

The Zuni cultural center was founded in 1992 to be more than a museum where objects are displayed but a place for community members to share knowledge, connect with their heritage, and express themselves artistically. The museum's programs have gained national attention for their dynamic explorations in applying the wisdom of the past to contemporary situations, especially for young people.

CONTEMPORARY CONCERNS

Border Battles

The U.S.–Mexican border in southwest Arizona runs through the Tohono O'odham Reservation. Drug cartels and human smugglers who have been deterred by high-cost security programs elsewhere along the border now cross at the least secure point, the Tohono O'odham Reservation, an area the size of Connecticut. The border fence is low and full of gaps. The reservation police force of only a few dozen officers is responsible for patrolling four thousand square miles of desert. In order to help protect the twenty thousand Tohono O'odham residents, the U.S. border patrol, operating out of a command center in Tucson, has joined in the effort and provided the latest night-vision technology, but most of the police work is still done by tribal officers using traditional tracking techniques called "cutting for sign." Although drug smuggling has declined by forty-six percent along most of the border, according to ABC *Nightline*, nearly five hundred thousand pounds of marijuana were seized on the reservation in 2013, double the amount from the previous year. Native residents, who are often stopped and searched by Border Patrol, feel invaded on their own homeland. Meanwhile, drug and human smugglers are breaking into residents' homes in remote areas, stealing food and cars. As the forces on either side become more aggressive, the Tohono O'odham are caught in the middle.

Mining

Beginning in October 2014, pressure from coal mining companies on Black Mesa on the Navajo Reservation was expressed in the Bureau of Indian Affairs (BIA) impounding of Navajo families' sheep. Claiming that herds of more than twenty-eight sheep per household overgraze the fragile land, helicopters and drones circled overhead as federal SWAT teams with assault rifles set up roadblocks, entered people's land without warning or warrants, and detained residents at gunpoint, mostly impoverished elders.

Among the federal enforcers were Hopi rangers. The so-called Hopi–Navajo Land Dispute involves an area of 1.8 million acres of high desert plateau, where Navajo herders have lived on little-used Hopi land for generations. In 1972, Congress passed Public Law 93-531, which involved the forced removal of more than ten thousand Navajo and the erection of a barbed wire fence 285 miles long. When the Navajo protested during the 1970s, many others joined them, including Hopi traditionalists who believe that the government is mainly interested in clearing the land so that puppet tribal councils can be established and mining companies can gain access to the area's immense deposits of coal, uranium, and oil shale.

By December 2014, the BIA had arrested three people and removed more than three hundred sheep. The residents of Black Mesa believe this latest attack on their livelihood is part of federally funded efforts to restore access to major coal reserves on behalf of corporations such as Peabody Coal, which toxified 103 square miles of Black Mesa during its thirty-year operations, which were shut down in 2005. Residents believe the real threat to the land comes from this residual land, air, and water pollution, not from sheep.

In December 2014, the White Mountain Apache began protesting the U.S. Congress's decision to allow a foreign-owned mining company to appropriate 2,400 acres of Apache sacred land for copper mining. The land grant to the Rio Tinto Mining Company, which is owned by a global corporation with bases in Australia and the United Kingdom, was written into the National Defense Authorization Act of 2015. Despite the international authorization of the United Nations Declaration on the Rights of Indigenous Peoples in 2007, this action demonstrates that Native American nations are not considered fully sovereign but are still treated as wards of the federal government, whose treaty-guaranteed land can be reclassified as national forest and given to foreign corporations.

The Navajo and Pueblo governments are also concerned about the effects of hydrofracturing oil wells on sacred sites such as Chaco Canyon as well as health effects and rising violent crime in neighboring communities as mining toxins and

Sixteen-year-old Naelyn Pike (Chiricahua Apache) at a flashmob protest in Times Square, New York City. The San Carlos Apache are protesting the US government's sale of the sacred Apache Leap and Oak Flat ceremonial sites in southeastern Arizona to a foreign mining company without any environmental impact studies or consultation with the Apache.

oil workers flood the land. Activists are organizing against an oil pipeline, proposed in late 2014, that would run through the Four Corners area. Furthermore, fracking is not viable in desert communities as the process wastes thousands of gallons of water per day, rendering it poisonous due to the chemicals used. (For more information on hydrofracturing mining, see the Northern Plains chapter.)

The Colorado Plateau is an area in which Native communities are under extreme pressure to allow extraction of minerals and fuels from their lands. This unchecked development creates environmental and health problems, damages sacred sites, and wastes water in a drought-prone land. Intertribal Indigenous communities and organizations are working together to address the issue of mining and take back their political sovereignty to protect land, water, and health for the future.

Climate Change

The Southwest is predicted to experience drastic temperature shifts and drought conditions due to climate change. In March 2015, the Colorado Plateau Intertribal Gathering met to share traditional dry farming knowledge in response to the worsening water shortage. The Navajo Nation is already suffering from unprecedented drought and has lost thirty lakes since the water table is not replenishing. Carcasses of livestock and wild animals are piling up where water holes once existed. Having begun to witness changes in temperature, wind, rain, and soil moisture levels and the effects of genetically modified seeds, a coalition of elders and cultural leaders from twelve tribes worked for six years to create the presentation. Traditional dry farming, the protection of heirloom seeds, creation of farmer's markets, and restoration of springs would be hedges against food and water shortages and would support the local farming economy.

TYING IT UP

I like to sleep with piñon smoke
The cold dry air chills my skin, my breath.
Stories descend into the dark,
warm, light circles.

—Luci Tapahonso (Navajo),
"Tsaile April Nights" (1997)

The languages and cultures of the Native peoples of the Southwest endure, and their preservation most likely is ensured. For the Native peoples of the Southwest—the Paiute and the Ute, the Hualapai and the Yavapai, the Mojave and the Tohono O'odham, the Pima and Apache, the Navajo and the Hopi, and the Pueblo of New Mexico—the Southwest is their ancient homeland. Others have come and gone for over three centuries, and those who have stayed have had to learn the lessons of the ancients in order to survive in the vast, harsh land.

SOUTHWEST INDIGENEITY

In the Native American tradition ... a man, if he's a mature adult, nurtures life.

He does rituals that will help things grow, he helps raise the kids, and he protects the people. His entire life is toward balance and cooperativeness. The ideal of manhood is the same as the ideal of womanhood. You are autonomous, self-directing, and responsible for the spiritual, social, and material life of all those with whom you live.

—Paula Gunn Allen

BIOGRAPHIES

Po'pay (d. 1690)
Ohkay Owingeh (San Juan Pueblo), Spiritual Leader

Po'pay was an important spiritual and military leader of the San Juan Pueblo and resisted repeated attempts to convert to Catholicism. He believed in the restoration of traditional lifeways and organized against the Spanish colony's cruel taxation and enslavement of the Indigenous people. He was captured, flogged, and jailed, but the people rallied for his release. In the 1680s, he led a successful resistance against the Spanish in the upper Rio Grande region by uniting several Pueblo villages. Eventually, they even drove out the Spanish from Santa Fe, the seat of the Spanish colony of New Mexico. After the rebellion, for more than a decade, Po'pay was a leader among the temporarily free Pueblo villages.

Mangas Coloradas (1797–1863)
Mimbreno Apache, Tribal Leader

The Mimbreno Apache were closely related to the Chiricahua Apache. Mangas Coloradas was a Mimbreno leader in the early years of the Apache Wars of the 1860s. Coloradas fought two enemies during his lifetime: Mexico and the United States. In the 1830s, the Mexican government paid a bounty for Indian scalps, and in 1837, Mexican miners and trappers, motivated by the bounty, murdered several Mimbreno. Following the massacre, Coloradas united a number of tribes in present-day southern Arizona and New Mexico to rid themselves of the intruders.

The United States Army antagonized Coloradas in 1846 when the government took possession of New Mexico Territory and American miners began pouring into the region. In 1857, a group of miners captured and whipped Coloradas, then released him as a message to other Apache to stay away. Coloradas, who was probably close to sixty years old at the time, survived and stepped up his campaign against the miners.

In the early 1860s, when the U.S. cavalry left the region to fight in the Civil War, the governor of California sent around three thousand troops to the Southwest to protect Anglos. In 1862, Coloradas and his Apache ally, Cochise, attacked the California troops in southern Arizona at a place now known as Apache Pass. Coloradas was wounded but continued to press his attacks. In 1863, he was invited to a peace parley by U.S. military authorities, but the parley was a ruse. Coloradas was murdered at Fort McLane although U.S. authorities reported that he was killed while trying to escape.

Ganado Mucho (1809–1893)
Navajo/Hopi, Tribal Leader

The son of a Navajo mother and a Hopi father, Ganado Mucho grew up to be a successful rancher, band headman, and peacemaker in northeastern Arizona. Mucho was a young man when the Navajo carried out strikes on Mexican troops in the 1830s. From 1846 to 1849, United States troops sent five expeditions in retaliation. Ganado Mucho did not participate in any conflicts, but because of his large herds, he was accused of cattle theft. He successfully denied the charges. In 1858, Mucho became the head of his band.

The ongoing conflicts referred to as the Navajo War of 1863–1866 pitted the Navajo against Kit Carson and his Ute allies. Carson led

U.S. forces through Navajo country on a search-and-destroy operation. Mucho and his followers hid from Carson, all the while encouraging peace. Mucho lost two daughters and a son to raids by Utes and Mexicans. His band surrendered, and he led them on the brutal "Long Walk" from Fort Defiance in Arizona to Fort Sumner at Bosque Redondo in New Mexico.

The Navajo were held as prisoners until Mucho and other leaders signed a peace treaty in 1868. Until his death at age eighty-four, Mucho lived on the Navajo Reservation, rebuilt his ranch, and continued to work for peace between the United States and the Navajo.

Cochise (1812–1874)
Chiricahua Apache, Tribal Leader

From 1863 to 1872, Cochise was the leader of the Apache resistance to U.S. invasion. The Apache Wars began when Cochise, falsely accused of abducting a rancher's child, was imprisoned by an American lieutenant. He escaped, but the ensuing years were a cycle of attack and revenge. From his stronghold in the Dragoon Mountains (southern Arizona), Cochise and his ally, Coloradas, led an effective guerrilla campaign against U.S. and Mexican forces. Although losses and atrocities occurred on both sides and the Apache were forced to return to the mountains, no Apache band was ever conquered militarily. In 1871, Cochise fought efforts to relocate his people to a reservation in New Mexico. A year later, however, the Apache leader agreed to abstain from attacks in exchange for reservation land in eastern Arizona.

Manuelito (1818–1894)
Navajo, Tribal Leader

Born in southeastern Utah, Manuelito rose to prominence for his role in raids against the Mexicans, Hopi, and Zuni. After 1849, both the Navajo and the U.S. Army wanted the pastureland around Fort Defiance, Arizona. Troops destroyed Manuelito's home, crops, and livestock in 1859. Then he and another headman attacked the fort and nearly succeeded in capturing it. Colonel F. R. S. Canby pursued Manuelito and his followers into the Chuska Mountains near the Arizona and New Mexico border. Conflict again erupted in early 1861 after a horse race at the fort in which Navajo spectators claimed that Manuelito had been cheated. Soldiers shot into the crowd of Navajo; ten were killed. After the Navajo War (1863–1866), Colonel Kit Carson forced the Navajo prisoners on the Long Walk to Bosque Redondo, New Mexico. Of all the resistant Navajo bands, Manuelito's held out the longest. However, faced with army pursuit and starvation, he surrendered and joined the captives at Bosque Redondo.

Manuelito and others traveled to Washington, D.C., to petition for the return of the Navajo homelands and signed a peace treaty in 1868. He returned to serve as principal chief and chief of tribal police.

Barboncito (1820–1871)
Navajo, Tribal Leader

In the 1860s, under government orders, the U.S. military tried to resettle or exterminate the Navajo Indians. Barboncito, along with Delgadito (his brother) and Manuelito, led the Navajo resistance from 1863 to 1866. Barboncito was born in Canyon de Chelly in present-day Arizona. He was both a military and religious Navajo leader. In 1860, after soldiers shot a number of Navajo horses, Barboncito and Manuelito led fighters in retaliation at Fort Defiance. After nearly taking the fort, the Indians were pushed back into their mountain strongholds. Stalemated, U.S. military leaders and Indians agreed to a short-lived peace council.

The relocation plans to the barren New Mexico lands pushed Barboncito into open warfare with the United States. Barboncito was captured at Canyon de Chelly in 1864 and taken to Bosque Redondo, where living conditions were barely survivable. One year later, he escaped with about five hundred followers. He later surrendered and, in 1868, signed a treaty that established the Navajo Reservation in present-day New Mexico and Arizona.

Geronimo (Goyathlay) (c. 1825–1909)
Chiricahua Apache, Spiritual Leader

 Originally, Geronimo was a spiritual leader and not a hereditary chief. After Mexicans killed his mother, wife, and children in 1858, Geronimo sought revenge and gained a reputation as a skilled fighter. Apache men would attack Mexican soldiers, then retreat to the Apache Pass Reservation on the American side. When the U.S. closed the reservation after two stagecoach attendants were killed during a clash with the Apache, Geronimo's people joined other Apache bands in the Mexican Sierra Madre Mountains. In April 1877, Indian agent John Clum's men captured Geronimo and took him to the San Carlos Reservation.

In April 1882, Geronimo's fighters killed the reservation chief of police and went to Mexico with some Mimbreno Apache under the leadership of Chief Nana. General George Crook hired Apache scouts from other bands to track the Chircahua and Mimbreno. It took a year of pursuit to force Geronimo to return to the reservation, and in 1885, he again led his people to Mexico in protest after the government forbade the drinking of *tiswin,* an Apache alcoholic beverage. After a series of captures and escapes, Geronimo and his followers finally surrendered to General Nelson A. Miles in July 1886, which ended the Apache Wars in the Southwest.

After imprisonment in Florida and Alabama, Geronimo's people were taken to Fort Sill, Oklahoma, where the Kiowa and Comanche people offered to share their reservation with the Chiricahua. At Fort Sill, Geronimo experimented with farming, baseball, and the Dutch-reformed church. With a collaborator, he wrote his memoirs, *Geronimo's Story of His People*, in 1906.

Lozen (1840–1889)
Chiricahua Apache, War Strategist/Diplomat/Spiritual Leader

The sister of Apache leader Victorio, Lozen was a confidante of Geronimo and one of his trusted messengers. From childhood, she was an excellent shot and horse thief, could outrun boys in races, and was given traditional male responsibilities. She was respected for her ability to sense the presence of enemies through a tingling in her palms. She was also a healer and skilled midwife. Lozen never married as her people needed her to fight Mexican and United States invasion during the Apache Wars (1849–1886). She was a military strategist and spiritual leader. Geronimo sent her to negotiate terms with General Nelson A. Miles, and she accompanied her leader when he finally surrendered. Imprisoned with her people at Mount Vernon Barracks in Alabama in 1887, Lozen succumbed to tuberculosis.

Naiche (Natchez) (1857–1921)
Chiricahua Apache, Tribal Leader

 Naiche was the younger son of the great Chiricahua Apache leader Cochise. When Cochise died, Naiche became leader of the Chiricahua as they were moved north to the San Carlos Reservation in Arizona in 1881. That August, at Cibecue (Arizona), a number of soldiers and an Apache Ghost Dance prophet were murdered; then, hundreds of U.S. troops arrived. Naiche and his followers fled the hot, dusty San Carlos Reservation to avoid further confrontation.

Naiche surrendered after General Crook and his Indian scouts traced them to their Sierra Madre stronghold. In May 1884, the Apache were removed to Turkey Creek in present-day Arizona, where they were instructed to farm. One year later, unhappy with this situation, Naiche, Geronimo, and their followers again fled to Mexico. They raided both sides of the border for the next ten months until General Nelson A. Miles negotiated their final surrender.

By September 8, 1886, Naiche's and Geronimo's people were on a train bound for a Florida prison. Later, they were transferred to Alabama, and finally to Fort Sill in present-day Oklahoma. Naiche welcomed this move because the terrain was similar to Arizona's. His family built a house, and he became a government scout, but an attempt was made to seize even this land from the Chiricahua. They appealed and were finally allotted the Mescalero Reservation east of the Rio Grande in central New Mexico.

Daisy Hooee Nampeyo (c. 1859–1942)
Hopi/Tewa, Potter

Nampeyo was a world-recognized potter who, besides developing her own style, was instrumental in bringing about a revival of ancient ceramic motifs. She was born in Hano Pueblo in Arizona. In the 1890s, her husband, who was working with an archaeologist at the time, helped her to find shards of ancient pottery, on which she based her designs. Nampeyo and her husband often traveled to Chicago to display her work. Her beautiful designs evoked images of an era long past and were quickly embraced by the art world. The Smithsonian Institution purchased her pottery, and soon it was sought after by collectors from around the world. Nampeyo has been credited with bringing about a pottery-making renaissance.

Carlos Montezuma (1867–1923)
Yavapai, Physician/Journalist

Dr. Montezuma was a successful physician who advocated the abolition of the Bureau of Indian Affairs (BIA). In 1915, he wrote the pamphlet "Let My People Go," and in 1916, he founded the magazine *Wassaja: Freedom's Signal for the Indian,* which remained in press from 1916 to 1922. Montezuma was born among the Yavapai Indians in Arizona, but as a boy was captured by Pima Indians who sold him to Carlos Gentile, a white photographer. Gentile named him Carlos Montezuma.

Montezuma graduated from Chicago Medical College and practiced medicine at several reservations until his frustration with conditions led him to take a position at Carlisle Indian School in Pennsylvania. By1896, Montezuma was able to open a successful Chicago private practice. His experiences working in Indian health service made him critical of the BIA and of the reservation system. Presidents Theodore Roosevelt and Woodrow Wilson each asked him to become the commissioner of Indian affairs. Montezuma refused, continuing to advocate for an end to the BIA. For the rest of his life, Montezuma urged citizenship and equal rights for Native people and continually stressed the importance of maintaining "Indianness."

Juan de Jesus Romero (Deer Bird) (1874–1978)
Taos Pueblo, Tribal/Spiritual Leader

If there was one cause in life for which Romero fought, it was the return of the sacred Blue Lake (Maxolo) to the Taos Pueblo. He was hereditary headman of Taos Pueblo as well as its spiritual leader. After 1906, when the Blue Lake area was made part of Carson National Forest, Romero began a personal campaign for the return of the ancestral lands surrounding Blue Lake that the U.S. government had expropriated from the Taos Indians. Romero pressured the government for decades, and after forty-five years, the Taos sued the U.S. for return of the area. In 1965, the Taos rejected a cash settlement in lieu of their original claim.

Romero traveled to Washington, D.C., in 1970 to present his case to President Richard M. Nixon. Finally, the U.S. Senate voted to return Blue Lake to the Taos, along with 48,000 acres of surrounding land. For his lifelong efforts in the fight for Blue Lake, Romero won the prestigious Indian Council Fire Award in 1974.

Carl Nelson Gorman (1907–1998)
Diné (Navajo), Artist

A distinguished artist in several media, Carl Gorman was among the first to employ traditional Navajo motifs in producing contemporary art. Born on the Navajo Reservation in Chinle, Arizona, he came from a distinguished family of cattlemen, traders, weavers, translators, tribal leaders, and silversmiths. During World War II, Gorman served as a Code Talker in the U.S. Marine Corps, and after the war, Gorman studied at Otis Art Institute in Los Angeles, California. He worked as a technical illustrator for Douglas Aircraft, established his own silkscreen design company, and taught Native American art at the University of California, Davis as well as Navajo language courses at D-Q University.

Gorman's works, which include a variety of styles and media, have appeared in numerous solo and group shows and are represented in many public and private collections. In 1973, UC-Davis opened the C. N. Gorman Museum in his honor.

Thomas Banyacya (1909–1999)
Hopi, Spiritual Leader

Banyacya, Hopi elder and traditionalist, spoke out against war and material wealth gained by destroying nature, particularly mining. The Hopi name translates as "peaceful." So faithful was Banyacya regarding the Hopi traditions of peace that he spent seven years in prison rather than be drafted during World War II. Because of Bancycya's stand, by 1953, any Hopi could resist enlistment by becoming a conscientious objector. Banyacya was one of four young men chosen by Hopi elders in 1948 as messengers to share ancient teachings and prophecies with the outside world for the first time. Some prophesies contained warnings, accurately predicting the future

development of the atomic bomb as a "gourdful of ashes." The prophecies also caution that the world will end in a global explosion, or "purification," unless human beings change their destructive ways. Banyacya traveled the world, creating alliances with other Indigenous peoples and frequently speaking at the United Nations for their common causes.

Annie Dodge Wauneka (1910–1997)
Navajo, Health Care Activist

Raised on the Navajo Reservation by her activist father, Chee Dodge, Wauneka led a campaign to improve the health and sanitary conditions of the Navajo. At a time when few women were involved in tribal affairs, she was not only elected to the tribal council but worked tirelessly to educate and ensure that her community receive proper health care services. She penned a Navajo-English medical dictionary so traditional healers and non-Indian doctors could combine both traditional and western medicine for optimum health and build trust within the nation.

Wauneka's husband took on most of the responsibility for their eight children as she fought for health care reform and better care for pregnant women and infants, eye and ear examinations, tuberculosis prevention, and alcoholism treatment. In 1963, she became the first American Indian to receive the Presidential Medal of Freedom. She also served as an advisor to the U.S. Surgeon General and the U.S. Public Health Service. Wauneka not only helped make her people healthier, but she inspired other Navajo to go into the healing practices.

Helen Cordero (1915–1994)
Cochiti, Potter

Cordero began a new tradition when she made her first pottery storyteller doll as a tribute to her grandfather, a great storyteller who was always surrounded by children.

She depicted him with children on his arms, shoulders, and lap. The idea became popular, and today, many potters fashion the Storyteller Doll.

Pablita Velarde (1918–2006)
Tewa (Santa Clara) Pueblo, Painter

Velarde was an acclaimed painter, whose works reflect the culture and heritage of her people. Velarde was born in the Santa Clara Pueblo in New Mexico and educated at the Santa Fe Indian School. Her love for art and talent as an artist has been traced to a childhood eye disease that temporarily restricted her sight. According to one biographer, when Velarde regained her sight, it gave her a new appreciation of visual perception. In 1938, she began creating "memory paintings" in tempera and oil.

One of Velarde's first works is still her most renowned—a series of murals for the Maisle Trading Post in Albuquerque (1938) and at the Bandolier National Monument Visitors' Center (1939) depicting the daily life and culture of the Rio Grande Pueblo. In 1956, Velarde developed an "earth painting" technique using colored rocks that she ground and mixed to create a pliable, textured painting material. In this medium, Velarde's paintings recall ancestral designs and the pictographs from Puye Ruins, near Santa Clara. In 1960, she published an illustrated oral history collection titled *Old Father, the Storyteller.* During her lifetime, Velarde received countless awards for her work.

Charles Loloma (1921–1991)
Hopi, Artist

Loloma's jewelry is among the most distinctive in the world. The originality of his designs stems from the combination of nontraditional materials, like gold and diamonds, with local stones, such as turquoise. Born in Hotevilla, Arizona, he has also received great recognition as a potter. In

1939, he painted murals for the Federal Building on Treasure Island in San Francisco Bay as part of the Golden Gate International Exposition. He was then commissioned by the Indian Arts and Crafts Board to paint murals for the Museum of Modern Art in New York.

After working as a camouflage expert for the U.S. Army in the Aleutian Islands (Alaska), Loloma enrolled in the School for American Craftsmen at Alfred University in New York, a well-known center for ceramic arts. This was unusual since ceramics was traditionally a woman's art among the Hopi. In 1949, he received a Whitney Foundation Fellowship to study the clays of the Hopi area. After that, he and his wife set up a shop in the newly opened Kiva Craft Center in Scottsdale, Arizona. He taught pottery at Arizona State University before heading the Plastic Arts and Sales departments at the Institute of American Indian Arts in Santa Fe, New Mexico. Loloma's jewelry has been exhibited throughout the country and in Europe.

Peterson Zah (1928—)
(Diné) Navajo, Tribal Chairman

From 1982 to 1993, Peterson Zah was first chairman, then president of the Navajo Nation. He attended college on a basketball scholarship and graduated from Arizona State University in 1963. Zah returned to the reservation to teach carpentry, then served as a cultural sensitivity trainer for Volunteers in Service to America (VISTA) in preparation for their service on Indian reservations. In 1967, Zah joined DNA People's Legal Services and later became executive director, a position he held for ten years. Under his direction, DNA lawyers won several landmark Native rights and sovereignty cases at the U.S. Supreme Court.

Zah was elected chairman of the Navajo Tribal Council in 1982 and became chief fundraiser for the Navajo Education and Scholarship Foundation. He founded Native American

Consulting Services, a private firm that developed curricula on Navajo culture and history, and worked with Congress to fund new school construction. When the Navajo Nation Council reorganized and created the new position of president, Zah was elected in 1990, the only Navajo leader to be elected as both chairman and president. Since 1995, he has been special advisor on American Indian affairs to the president of Arizona State University.

R(udolf) C(arl) Gorman (1932–2005)

(Diné) Navajo, Artist

The *New York Times* has called Gorman (son of artist Carl Nelson Gorman) "the Picasso of American Indian art." His parents encouraged him to express himself visually, and he once said in an interview that he could remember making his first drawings when he was three years old by tracing designs with his fingers in the sand and mud of the wash at the base of the Canyon de Chelly Navajo landmark.

Gorman lived in a traditional Navajo home (Hogan) and herded sheep with his grandmother, who shared Navajo knowledge with him. Meanwhile, influenced by the art world of his father, Gorman developed a cosmopolitan style of considerable range and depth. He studied at San Francisco State University and was the first student to receive a grant from the Navajo Tribal Council to study art at Mexico City College. Influenced by Diego Rivera and other Mexican muralists, Gorman's work is characterized by flowing lines and bright colors in paint, clay, and stone lithography prints.

In 1968, Gorman opened the first Native-owned art gallery in Taos. His honors include being the only living artist featured in the show "Masterworks of the Museum of the American Indian," held at the Metropolitan Museum in New York (1973). Over the years, Gorman published several articles about subjects including Mexican art and petroglyphs and wrote illustrated cookbooks, titled *Nudes and Food*.

Fred Begay (1932–2013)

Navajo/Ute, Nuclear Physicist

Born on the Ute Mountain Indian Reservation in Colorado, Dr. Begay was trained to be a farmer by the Bureau of Indian Affairs and never graduated from high school. After serving in the Korean War, he attended the University of New Mexico, earning a bachelor's degree in math and science in 1961, a master's in physics in 1963, and a Ph.D. in physics in 1971. His most notable research was in the use of laser, electron, and ion beams to heat thermonuclear plasmas for use as alternative energy sources. Dr. Begay was featured in the 1979 NOVA documentary, "The Long Walk of Fred Young."

Alfred H. Qöyawayma (1938–)

Hopi, Potter/Bronze Sculptor/ Mechanical Engineer

Qöyawayma is a cofounder of the American Indian Science and Engineering Society, an engineer, and has worked in the development of inertial guidance systems and star trackers.

Paula Gunn Allen (1939–2008)

Laguna Pueblo/Lakota/Lebanese, Novelist/Poet/Essayist

Gunn Allen's voice in contemporary American Indian literature and literary studies is a unique and essential one. She grew up in a multicultural household in Cubrero, New Mexico, where Spanish, German, Laguna, English, and Arabic were all spoken and understood. She began writing poetry in the 1970s and went on to win awards for her work in many forms—as a literary critic (*The Sacred Hoop*, 1986), editor (*Spider Woman's Granddaughters*, 1989, and *Grandmothers of the Light*, 1991), and novelist (*Woman Who Owned the Shadows*, 1983). *Pocahontas: Medicine Woman, Spy, Entrepreneur, Diplomat* was nominated for a Pulitzer Prize in 2004. The last of her six volumes of poetry was *America the Beautiful* (2008).

The mother of four children, Gunn Allen was also a dedicated feminist who stated that her convictions can be traced back to the female-centered structures of traditional Pueblo society. She was the sister of the Laguna Pueblo writer Carol Lee Sanchez and cousin of the novelist Leslie Marmon Silko.

Roger Tsabetsaye (1941–)
Zuni, Artist

Born in Zuni, New Mexico, Tsabetsaye was raised in a traditional community and was in the first class at the Institute of American Indian Arts (IAIA) in Santa Fe, New Mexico, where he studied with Charles Loloma (see also his biography above). At the School for American Craftsmen at the Rochester Institute of Technology, Tsabetsaye majored in silver and metal processing. He is considered an innovator, actively combining a modern abstract art style with traditional subjects.

Tsabetsaye went on to teach art at the IAIA and helped develop the school's curriculum and philosophy. In the late 1960s, he was a Native representative at several conferences in Washington, D.C., to help initiate President Johnson's War on Poverty. He has been a political leader at Zuni Pueblo, focusing on updating the tribe's constitution to reflect community values. Tsabetsaye is also the founder and owner of Tsabetsaye Enterprises in Zuni, a company specializing in jewelry, which he creates with his grandson.

Simon J. Ortiz (1941–)
Acoma Pueblo, Poet/Fiction Writer

Ortiz is one of the most respected and widely read Native American poets. He intends his work to be read aloud, and his writing is characterized by a strong storytelling voice that recalls Acoma oral tradition. He was born in Albuquerque, New Mexico, and raised at Acoma Pueblo; Keres was his first language. The Bureau of Indian Affairs (BIA) schools he attended discouraged his home language, but he maintains that speaking Keres was the foundation of his literary voice. Ortiz's work often deals with alienation and recovery through connection to the land and Indigenous culture.

After a stint in the army and graduation from the University of Iowa with a master's degree in fine arts, Ortiz taught creative writing and Native American literature at various U.S. colleges. In 1969, he received a Discovery Award from the National Endowment for the Arts. In 1982, his volume, *From Sand Creek,* received the Pushcart Prize for poetry.

Ortiz's published poetry includes *Going for the Rain* (1976), *A Good Journey* (1977), and *Woven Stone* (1992). Ortiz also authored two short story collections, *Fightin'* (1983) and *Men on the Moon* (1999). His narrations are featured in the PBS documentary *Surviving Columbus: The Story of the Pueblo People* (1992). Ortiz teaches at Arizona State University.

Michael Chiago (1946–)
Tohono O'odham/Pima–Maricopa, Dancer/Illustrator

Chiago's illustrations and watercolor paintings reflect his experiences as a powwow dancer as well as the ceremonies and daily life of his people. Born in Kohatk Village on the Tohono O'odham Reservation in Arizona, Chiago started dancing and drawing as a boy. After high school, he joined the Marines and served in Vietnam. On returning home, Chiago studied commercial art and magazine layout techniques. He is best known for a style of painting that he developed by himself. He uses watercolor and adds a special coating or glaze to certain parts when the painting is finished, thus producing a surface of unusual depth and brilliance.

Many of Chiago's paintings feature vibrant, dreamlike colors, rather than being strictly representational, and they often depict dramatically attired dancers, drawing on his experiences as a fancy dancer who has toured throughout the United States. The imagery in his paintings derives from the Sonoran Desert cultures of the Tucson Basin and is distinct from other Southwestern cultures, such as the Navajo or the

Pueblo. Chiago's bright murals adorn the Gila River Indian Community's Huukum Cultural Center and the Heard Museum in Phoenix. In 1997, he illustrated a children's book, *Singing Down the Rain*. Chiago was the recipient of Arizona's Living Treasure Award in 2006.

Carol Jean Vigil (1946–2009)
Pueblo, Judge/Attorney

Vigil was the first Native American woman to be elected as a state district judge in the United States and the first female Native American to be elected a state court judge in New Mexico. She was known for fairness and advocating for victims of domestic violence.

R. Carlos Nakai (1946–)
Diné (Navajo)/Ute, Musician

As a composer and musician, Nakai revived the flute tradition by popularizing its haunting sound through his recordings. He was born in Flagstaff, Arizona, and raised on the Navajo Reservation, where his father, Raymond, served as Navajo tribal chairman. A Navy veteran, Nakai earned a bachelor's degree in music and a master's degree in American Indian studies from the University of Arizona; he was later awarded an honorary doctorate.

Nakai originally studied trumpet, but a car accident damaged his mouth in a manner that precluded playing brass horns. The gift of a traditional cedar flute inspired him to learn the instrument. He was signed by Canyon Records in 1982 and recorded his first album, *Changes*, a year later. Since then, he has released forty albums with Canyon, along with appearances on other labels. *Earth Spirit* (1987) was certified a gold record (more than five hundred thousand copies sold) and *Canyon Trilogy* (1989) went platinum in 2014 (selling more than a million copies), the first Native American albums to do so.

Nakai tours worldwide as a soloist, with other musicians, and as part of symphony and chamber orchestras and has contributed to the soundtracks of several feature films. Ever ex-

ploring cross-cultural settings, Nakai founded the jazz ensemble R. Carlos Nakai Quartet and has released collaborations with traditional Japanese, Tibetan, Hawaiian, and Arabic musicians. He has sold more than four million recordings and received Grammy nominations for ten of his albums. In 2005, he was inducted into the Arizona Music and Entertainment Hall of Fame.

Linda Lomahaftewa (1947–)
Hopi/Choctaw, Painter

Linda Lomahaftewa was born in Phoenix, Arizona, and attended high school at the Institute of American Indian Arts (IAIA), where she studied with Lloyd Kiva New and Fritz Scholder. After graduating in 1962, she won a scholarship to the San Francisco Art Institute, graduating with a master's in fine arts in 1971. The connection to her Hopi community on Second Mesa emanates from her abstract acrylic paintings, which feature landscapes, bold geometric shapes, and traditional symbols from petroglyphs and kiva murals in glowing colors. Some of her images echo beadwork, quilting, and appliqué designs.

After teaching in California, Lomahaftewa returned to IAIA in 1976 as a professor of painting and drawing and has held this position for more than thirty years. During the seventies, Lomahaftewa's paintings were shown in more than forty exhibitions across the United States, and she continues to participate in numerous solo and group shows. Lomahaftewa has been frequently listed in *Who's Who in American Indian Arts*. In the 1980s, she began printmaking, incorporating design elements from ancient pottery in bold, abstract patterns.

Leslie Marmon Silko (1948–)
Laguna Pueblo, Poet/Novelist/Essayist

Silko's father was the famed photographer Lee Marmon. Silko studied law before earning a B.A. in

English from the University of New Mexico. Thought Woman, the Pueblo creator, was the inspiration for the storyteller in Leslie Marmon Silko's first novel, *Ceremony* (1977). Silko, who grew up hearing traditional stories from her family at Laguna Pueblo near Albuquerque, wove ancient and modified ceremonial tradition in her novel about a Laguna veteran who returns from World War II in need of healing. The sequence of time in Silko's work also belongs to the Indigenous interweaving of past and present rather than the linear Euro-American narrative. She expanded on this complex time structure in her multivoiced novel *Almanac of the Dead* (1991), which spans four centuries and two continents. Silko had received a National Endowment for the Humanities Discovery Grant for her first short story, "The Man to Send Rain Clouds," in 1969, and in 1981, a MacArthur Foundation Fellowship "genius" Award allowed her to complete *Almanac of the Dead*. Some of Silko's other works include six poetry collections, the essay *Yellow Woman and a Beauty of the Spirit,* the novel *Gardens in the Dunes* (2000), and *The Turquoise Ledge* (2010), a memoir.

Ofelia Zepeda (1952–)
Tohono O'odham, Linguist/Poet

Zepeda was the first Tohono O'odham tribal member to receive a doctorate in linguistics. She has been teaching the Tohono O'odham language at the university level since 1979. Zepeda grew up in Stanfield, close to the Tohono O'odham Reservation, to implement literacy programs in English and the home language. In 1983, she worked with tapes of elderly native speakers to develop the textbook *A Tohono O'odham Grammar.* The tribal language department based its school curricula on Zepeda's work. She was awarded a MacArthur Foundation Fellowship "genius" Award in 1999 and frequently procures grants to fund language and literature programs on the reservation. Her published poetry collections include *Ocean Power: Poems from the Desert* (1995), *Where Clouds Are Formed* (2008), and *Jewed'l-hoi/Earth Movements* (2009). Zepeda has been a professor of linguistics and director of the American Indian Studies Pro-

gram at the University of Arizona as well as director of the American Indian Language Development Institute. She edits *Sun Tracks*, a Native American book series published by the University of Arizona Press.

Luci Tapahonso (1953–)
Diné (Navajo), Poet

Tapahonso was named poet laureate of the Navajo Nation in 2013. Born in Shiprock, New Mexico, Tapahonso's poetry speaks of the Southwestern landscape, her family, and tribal foods. Translated from the Navajo language, her English voice is accented with Navajo breathing rhythms, women's songs, and the energy of *Taahooajii twitaaye:* the total environment of the weather, the land, and the individual in harmony. Tapahonso has said, "I consider Navajo language to be the undercurrent, the matrix which everything in my life filters through."

She studied journalism, then creative writing at the University of New Mexico, earning her master's in 1983. Tapahonso has taught literature at the University of New Mexico and the University of Kansas. She published her first collection of poetry, *One More Shiprock Night,* in 1981. Since then, she has written six books of poetry and three children's stories, including *Saánii Dahataal (The Women Are Singing)* (1993), *blue horses rush in* (1997), and *a radiant curve* (2009), as well as contributed to several anthologies. She has won awards from Native Writers' Circle of the Americas, the Arizona Book Awards, and the American Book Awards. Tapahonso teaches poetry and American Indian literature at the University of Arizona.

Nora Naranjo-Morse (1953–)
Tewa (Santa Clara) Pueblo, Potter

Famously quoted as saying there is no word for "art" in the Tewa language, Naranjo-Morse comes from a large family of potters who live "artful lives, filled with inspiration and fueled by labor and thoughtful approach." By working with clay, she identifies with her sisters, mother, and earlier female ancestors. To express herself, she began making figures, rather than pots or bowls, in about 1976. Her sense of humor comes through in sculptures such as *Pearlene Teaching Her Cousins Poker* (1987), in which she interprets Pueblo ritual clowns (characterized by their striped bodies) as female instead of male and depicts them playing a game of poker, which they are learning from a book. Naranjo-Morse also writes and performs poetry. *Mud Woman: Poems from the Clay* was published in 1993. Her large clay piece, *Always Becoming*, won a contest at the National Museum of the American Indian in 2005 and became the first outdoor sculpture created by a Native American woman in Washington, D.C.

Michael Lacapa (1955–2005)
Apache/Hopi/Tewa, Author/Illustrator/Educator

From Fort Apache Indian Reservation in Fort Apache, Lacapa is best known for his award-winning books. His most famous work was written with his wife and about their own children of mixed heritages, *Less Than Half, More Than Whole*.

Beverly Singer
Tewa/Diné, Filmmaker

Singer is from Santa Clara Pueblo, New Mexico. She has produced more than twenty documentary video projects featuring voices of people with life experience from different Indigenous places in the U.S., Latin America, and North, East, and South Africa. She has been affiliated with several academic institutions, including Columbia University, The New School, Institute of American Indian Arts, and, since 2001, at the University of New Mexico, where she holds tenure in the departments of Anthropology and Native American Studies and directs the Alfonso Ortiz Center for Intercultural Studies. Singer received her Ph.D. in American Studies from the University of New Mexico, an M.A. in Administration from the University of Chicago, and conducted documentary film

study at the Anthropology Film Center in Santa Fe. In 1997, she received a Sundance Institute Award for her film *Hózhó of Native Women*. A founder of the Native American Producers Alliance, she authored *Wiping the Warpaint off the Lens* (2001), a book on Native American independent filmmaking. Singer currently lives in her ancestral home near Santa Clara Pueblo.

Wilfred F. Denetclaw, Jr. (1959–)
Navajo, Zoologist/Educator

Denetclaw grew up in Shiprock, New Mexico, where he helped care for cattle and sheep on his family's farm. He was puzzled why some animals were born healthy while others were ill, often dying of mysterious illnesses. His interest turned into a devoted career in the research of unexplained medical conditions that affect humans. At first, his traditions conflicted with his studies, which required dissection of animals; the Navajo are forbidden to disrespect a corpse. However, Denetclaw conferred with a medicine person to gain understanding and guidance. The traditionalist told him that he was like a modern scout, exploring safe and good places to lead the people—he was exploring a branch of science where few American Indians worked, and his research would certainly result in a healthier and safer life for the community. Denetclaw continued his studies and today is the director of the Cell Molecular Imaging Center (CMIC) at San Francisco State University. Denetclaw studies diseases that have been classified as incurable, searching for the cause for serious conditions like Duchenne muscular dystrophy as well as viral outbreaks and epidemics. He advocates for Native youth to enter the science field and volunteers with the American Indian Science and Engineering Society (AISES) and Society for Advancement of Chicanos and Native Americans in Science (SACNAS).

Debbie Reese
Nambe Pueblo, Educator

Reese grew up on the Nambe Pueblo Reservation; her studies took her to Oklahoma and later to Illinois, where she earned a doctorate in Curriculum and Instruction. At the University of Illinois, she encountered their stereotypical Indian mascot and, along with other Native students and supporters, set out to do something about it. They succeeded in founding the Native American House at the university and began an American Indian Studies program. Eventually, the offensive mascot was retired.

While studying, Reese reviewed books and wrote articles for library and school publications. Her advocacy for fair, accurate, and culturally appropriate American Indian publications for children soon became a lifeline for educators desiring materials that were interesting, historically correct, and did not perpetuate stereotypes and racism. She serves on the Multicultural Advisory Board for Reading is Fundamental and the board for Reach Out and Read's American Indian/Alaska Native Coalition. Sought after for lectures and workshops around the country, she also uses technology to work with libraries, schools, and educators in Canada. One of Reese's most valuable endeavors is her organization and blog American Indians in Children's Literature (AICL). Not only does she provide easily accessible critical perspectives and analyses of Indigenous peoples in children's and young adult books, the school curriculum, popular culture, and society, but she offers alternatives so that even those with limited knowledge about American Indians can find "good" materials without having to troll the aisles of bookstores that often proffer only meager, outdated, and outrageously racist materials. Reese provides choices, viable options that help all children learn the truth and value of theirs and other heritages while ensuring that Native children feel welcomed and included in the classroom and library.

Diane Humetewa (1964–)
Hopi, U.S. District Court Judge for Arizona

In 2013, Humetewa was nominated by President Barack Obama and confirmed by the Senate in May 2014 to become a judge for the U.S. District Court for Arizona, making her the first Native American woman federal judge in U.S. history. She is the third Native American to hold such a position. Humetewa is a citizen of the Hopi Tribe, was a former U.S. attorney for Arizona during the George W. Bush Administration, and was a special counsel and prosecutor for Arizona State University. She received her law degree from the Sandra Day O'Connor College at Arizona State University in 1993. She is considered to be a national expert on Native American issues. Humetewa's appointment brings long-awaited increased Indigenous representation to the federal courts, which play a large role in defining federal Indian law.

Robert Mirabal (1966–)
Tiwa (Taos Pueblo), Musician/Actor/Flute Maker

As a composer, singer, and musician, Mirabal has won many honors, including two-time Native American Music Awards' Artist of the Year, three-time Songwriter of the Year, Grammy awards in 2006 and 2008 for *Sacred Ground* and *Johnny Whitehorse Totemic Flute Chants*. His dozen albums of traditional music, rock and roll, and spoken word are informed by the ceremonial music of his people and world music collaborations. In 2002, PBS broadcast his *Music from a Painted Cave* special. As an actor, Mirabal has appeared in a documentary about Georgia O'Keefe, in guest roles on *Walker Texas Ranger*, and in 2012 on international tour in his own one-man show, *Po'pay Speaks*, about the leader of the Pueblo Revolt (1680). His famous flutes are on display at the Smithsonian Institution's Museum of the American Indian. Mirabal makes flutes the traditional way at his home in Taos Pueblo, where he lives with his family at the foot of the sacred Taos Mountains in northern New Mexico. On his website, Mirabal writes, "What I create comes out of my body and soul in a desire to take care of the spirits of the earth."

Carletta Tilousi (1970–)
Havasupai, Environmental Activist

As a young teenager, Tilousi had earned so much respect from the Havasupai that they chose her to be their speaker on environmental justice issues. The Havasupai have struggled for decades to ban uranium mining from their area. More recently, Tilousi discovered that Havasupai blood samples were being used by researchers at Arizona State University for unapproved research. Tribal members had willingly participated in what was presented as a diabetes study with hopes that the results could shed some light on the soaring rates of diabetes within the tribe, but the blood was used in all kinds of other research that the community felt went against their beliefs and may even be used against them. A court case ensued; the Havasupai won and were able to recover all of the samples.

Notah Begay III (1972–)
Navajo/San Felipe Pueblo/ Isleta Pueblo, Golfer

Notah Begay III won his first of four PGA tournaments in the Reno-Tahoe Open in 1999. He became the third player in the history of professional golf to shoot a fifty-nine on a U.S. pro tour, the Nike Dominion Open, in 1998. Born in Albuquerque, New Mexico, Begay began playing golf at age six. He graduated from the Albuquerque Academy high school and attended Stanford University, where he was a member of the 1994 NCAA Division Men's Golf Championship Team, a three-time All-American, and a teammate of Tiger Woods. He is among the top twenty players listed in the Official World Golf Rankings.

In 2005, with his father, he founded the Notah Begay Foundation, a nonprofit organization headquartered in Santa Ana Pueblo, New Mexico. The foundation supports Native American youth fitness, self-esteem, and opportunities through soccer and golf programs. Begay was named one of *Golf Magazine's* Innovators of the Year in 2009 and works with Native communities to develop golf courses. He is currently an analyst with the Golf Channel.

Lori Ann Piestewa (1979–2003)
Hopi, U.S. Army Quartermaster Corps Specialist

Born in Tuba City, Piestewa was the first Native American woman to die in combat while serving with the U.S. military and the first woman in the U.S. armed forces killed in the 2003 invasion of Iraq. Her death brought the Hopi and Navajo together after many years of discord. Arizona's Piestewa Peak is named in her honor; she was awarded the Purple Heart and Prisoner of War Medal.

PACIFIC NORTHWEST: WASHINGTON STATE AND OREGON

From what you have said, I think you intend to win our country, or how is it to be? In one day, the Americans become as numerous as the grass.... I know that is not right. You have spoken in a roundabout way; speak straight. I have ears to hear you, and here is my heart. Suppose you show me goods; shall I run up and take them? That is the way we are, we Indians, as you know us. Goods and the earth are not equal; goods are for using on the earth. I do not know where they have given land for goods.

—Pee-o-pee-mox-a-mox, at the 1855 Treaty Council

CELILO FALLS

For ten thousand or more years, the village of Celilo Falls ("sea-lie-low") on the Columbia River was the oldest and greatest marketplace on the planet. Like a gigantic, outdoor fish market, vegetable market, flea market, and handicraft market all rolled into one, it was the go-to place in North America. In 1805, Lewis and Clark called Celilo Falls "the Great Mart of all this Country."

At the center of the village was Celilo Falls, the largest waterfall in North America. Its churning, howling, crashing, gyrating waters confused and blinded millions of migrating salmon, making it easy for fishers to catch them. The salmon were so thick that at times, one could almost walk across their backs to reach the other side of the river. Fishers perched themselves on scaffolds suspended over the river, dipping long-handled nets into the waters. An exploring team in the early 1800s documented that as many as five hundred fish were caught in one day by an experienced dip net fisherman. The fish were bigger than toddlers in those days.

Every spring, tribal elders met at Celilo Falls to determine when the fishing season would begin and end. They decided who could fish and who couldn't. No one fished until after the First Salmon ceremony. This sacred ritual celebrated salmon as a vital and delicious food source, blessed on the people by the Creator.

Celilo's famous salmon fishery drew countless people from near and far to fish, but it also attracted families, bands, and clans to trade, gossip, socialize, and play competitive games into the night. Some came to race horses; others came to find a husband or wife.

The annual exchange of regional foods was popular as food festivals are today. Indians from the distant plains traded dried buffalo and deer meat for carefully preserved salmon, a novelty in their diet. People living near the Pacific coast, who had plenty of fish in their region, traded dried clams and wappato roots for dried buffalo meat, a welcome addition.

Dozens of tribal groups also exchanged valuable trade objects. Eastern tribes brought bear grass baskets, buffalo furs, and horses to the trade market. Western groups brought dugout canoes, cedar paddles, and seashells that decorated hide and cloth clothing. Southern groups offered turquoise and obsidian while northern groups traded copper, axes, knives, and tusklike shells.

As the salmon run slowed, signaling the end of another season at Celilo Falls, whether it was two hundred years ago or a thousand years ago, visiting families loaded up travois with bundles of food and trade goods to make the trek home and looked forward to the following year's market.

On March 10, 1957, at 10:00 A.M., an engineer gave the "down gates" signal to twenty-two employees, who then pressed twenty-two buttons. The massive steel and concrete gates of the Dalles Dam choked back the downstream surge of the Columbia River. Six hours later, Celilo Falls, the spectacular natural wonder and ancient salmon fishery, was underwater. Lost. Silenced. The fishing scaffolds from which Indians had caught salmon that fed their families for thousands of years washed away. Nets washed away. The fishermen let them go. Most of the village disappeared in the rising waters. The river that once crashed and boiled through miles of the Long Narrows, miles of basalt chutes, islands, and craggy rock formations, became a placid, twenty-four-mile lake. All that's left is a marker on I-84 denoted as "Ancient Fishing Grounds."

Years before the dam was built, Indians protested, calling on the government to reconsider. The government went ahead and built the dam anyway. Today, if the Dalles Dam were proposed in the same location, it would never be built, according to a federal government official. He said: "It took us so long to learn we could not … destroy history and sacred sites and artifacts."

After the death of the falls, the Bureau of Indian Affairs, with the help of the Army Corps of Engineers, built prefabricated barrack homes for people living in the remains of the village. It neglected to fulfill its promise to build a longhouse so people could conduct their First Salmon ceremony. Years passed, and tribal people finally built a longhouse with a tarp at the top to close it. Money ran out before the top portion could be completed. Finally, in the summer of 2005, the Army Corps of Engineers kept its promise. It built a seven-thousand-square-foot longhouse. In July, the village hosted a celebration and ceremony that attracted national media and five thousand tribal and nontribal people.

The dam did not silence the sacred fish ceremony. Thanks to the perseverance of tribal leaders, the tradition of the annual First Salmon Feast ceremony in mid-April continues in the village of Celilo Falls to this day.

HOW THE CHINOOK BECAME "EXTINCT" (NOT REALLY)

There are a number of Native groups in Washington and Oregon that have been called "extinct," meaning they no longer exist according to the U.S. government. Despite these pronouncements, descendants of these communities have survived, hold on to their heritage, and continue their traditions. The Chinook people, who traditionally lived on the Pacific Coast along the lower and middle Columbia River in present-day Washington and Oregon, are one such group.

Chinook tribes were those encountered by the Lewis and Clark Expedition in 1805 on the lower Columbia River. That may be one of the reasons the Chinook are the most written-about Native group in Washington and Oregon history. The Chinook helped expedition members through the winter, bringing them food and assisting with navigation.

Chinook were also renowned as traders extraordinaire. Because they controlled the waterways into the interior, the Chinook were masters over

A replica of a Chinook plankhouse made of cedar can be seen at the Ridgefield National Wildlife Refuge in Clark County, Washington.

trade north and south along the coast and inland to the Columbia Plateau and beyond. The "Chinook jargon" (consisting of elements of Chinookan, Nootkan, French, and English languages) was the means of communication from Alaska to California. In addition to their prowess as traders, the Chinook also realized the potential of the enormous Columbia River salmon runs. Numbering perhaps 10,500 in the mid-1700s, the Chinook population dwindled to just a few hundred by 1850.

Unfortunately, Lewis and Clark and other explorers left a devastating legacy of diseases in Chinook country. Thousands died from epidemics of smallpox and cholera. By the 1850s, American colonialism had severely disrupted Chinook culture. Besides the decline in population, non-Indian farms and towns sprouted on Chinook land. Bereft of numbers, land, and power, some Chinook moved to neighboring reservations or non-Indian communities; others stayed on their ancestral homelands, gradually adopting new lifestyles in small towns. In 1953, the Chinook Tribe, with no reservation, estab-

lished an organization for political, educational, and social welfare of the tribe. Nevertheless, the Bureau of Indian Affairs, acting alone, terminated its official recognition of the tribe.

The U.S. Department of the Interior again recognized the Chinook Tribe in 2001, then suddenly revoked that status in 2002. The Chinook became one of dozens of tribes which became "unrecognized" as a distinct people in the eyes of the U.S. government. That means that as far as the federal government is concerned, the Chinook people are not entitled to federal dollars to build a tribal center, health programs for seniors, and cultural programs for youngsters. These monies would be some compensation for the lands they lost. Gary Johnson, former chairman of the Chinook Tribe, rejected the claim that they were extinct. "They [the federal government] couldn't be more wrong." That's because some two-thousand-plus Chinook people, descended from ancestors who greeted Lewis and Clark, live across a region from Seattle, Washington, to the Oregon coast and beyond. Indeed, the Chinook still exist.

A BIRD'S EYE VIEW

The Cascade Mountains divide Washington and Oregon into two environmentally different regions: eastern and western. In many almanacs, the Native peoples living in the western coastal parts of Oregon and Washington are lumped with Northwest Coast tribes because the groups share common cultural features: an economic dependence on marine resources, travel by canoe, permanent winter villages, cedar plank architecture, accumulation and control of wealth, and elaborate ceremonial and religious systems. Native peoples in the eastern parts of the two states are usually included with groups in the Columbia Plateau, bordered by the Plains. Their common cultural features include a hunting, salmon-fishing, and root-gathering lifestyle, tule mat-covered pole-frame and semisubterranean architecture, small bands or villages, and a religious system centered around the celebration of First Food. In this chapter, you will read about both halves of Washington and Oregon.

The climate in both halves of the states differ. It rains a lot in western Washington and Oregon, sometimes as much as 150 inches a year in some places. That makes the climate mild, foggy, misty, and damp. East of the Cascade Mountains, the climate is drier, and in some spots almost desertlike.

For Native peoples living in both states, sea and land offered a bountiful environment. The open sea, freshwater rivers, countless lakes, streams, and bays have been home to hundreds of different kinds of fish and sea life. Some western Washington State groups like the Lummi relied more heavily on netting or trapping salmon while the Makah hunted gray and humpback whales. The Coos of coastal Oregon thrived on hunting, fishing, trapping, and gathering plants. Some groups traded extensively; others let traders come to them. An extensive trade between coastal tribes and inland groups, extending across the Cascades, was based on the exchange of dried or smoked salmon for buffalo, antelope, and other meat delicacies.

The coastal part of the region has a mild climate. An ocean current keeps it warm, and westerly winds constantly blow inland. The winds also carry abundant moisture that, blocked by the Cascade Mountains, turns to rainfall. These climatic conditions led to the growth of vast forests of gigantic trees, among the tallest in the world. Colossal evergreen trees of cedar, fir, hemlock, and spruce provided enough wood to make huge longhouses, many kinds of canoes, storage containers, and carved totem poles. The mountainsides are covered with wild plants, shrubs, nuts, and roots, used for making clothing and baskets.

So completely did rivers dominate the western regions, there were practically no trails through the dense forests. People traveled on rivers, and except for those who lived far inland on the slopes of mountains, everyone lived by water and used canoes for transportation. As rivers were so important, peoples kept track of each other according to locations near rivers. The suffix "-amish" indicates "people of" certain river systems: Swinomish, Snohomish, Suquamish, Duwamish.

Early censuses of Native communities are inexact. Population figures gathered by Europeans and others had little knowledge of seasonal rounds that moved whole Native populations within their homelands. Conservative estimates state that tens of thousands of Native people lived in Oregon and Washington in ancient times. Even in the 1850s, following devastating waves of diseases, saltwater coasts and river drainages were home to villages of hundreds, if not thousands.

THE MAKAH

Makah, a Klallam word for "The People," called themselves "Kwe-net-che-chat" or "People of the Point." That's a perfect name for people who live on the northwestern tip of Washington's Olympic Peninsula. The Makah Reservation is the westernmost Indian reservation in the lower forty-eight states. The Makah in present-day Washington State are famous for their skills as whalers and deep-sea navigators.

The Makah understood their environment, using ecological practices to hunt and gather food on land or sea. They used sophisticated navigational, maritime skills and tireless paddling to

A Makah settlement c. 1900. The Makahs' homeland was on the Olympic Peninsula in what is now Washington state.

travel the rough waters of the Pacific Ocean. They carved various types of canoes from western red cedar; each type was created for a particular task. There were war, whaling, halibut, salmon fishing, sealing, and large cargo canoes. There were also small canoes, used for practice by children.

Indirect contact with Europeans in the late 1700s had a devastating effect on the lives of Makah people. Thousands of tribal members died from disease epidemics. According to the tribal website, "[t]he unexplained loss of their family members caused the Makah unfathomable grief, confusion, and fear. Due to this, the transfer of traditional knowledge was disrupted, causing many of the old ways to be lost."

NATIVE LANGUAGES

Washington Native Language Families

Related languages, those that have a common origin, form language families. There are two major language families in Washington State, Salishan and Sahaptian, and numerous dialects.

Oregon Native Language Families

Numerous hands of linguistically diverse tribes resided along the Oregon coast, inland in the Willamette River Valley, and the eastern areas. These groups spoke a number of languages from unrelated linguistic families, such as Athabascan, Sahaptian, Penutian, and Uto-Aztecan.

HOUSING

The typical habitation of Native people in western Washington was the longhouse. The structure was large, capable of sheltering several families. Generally, the families who inhabited a longhouse were related to one another: among the northern matrilineal groups, they were related through the female lineage; among other tribes, the relation was through either the house owner or his spouse.

Inside the longhouse, each family had its own partitioned area. Central fires burned for heat and light, but each family cooked its own meals and ate separately. Families could change houses if they wished, or the house might break up in the summer months while individual families pursued subsistence activities. In the winter, the longhouse served as a ceremonial center; the partitions were taken down to make room for dances and guests. Modern-day architects create similar designs where walls can be moved to accommodate different functions.

Typical dwellings in eastern Washington and Oregon were woven-reed-mat summer houses and semisubterranean, earth-covered winter lodges, which gave way to hide teepees in the eighteenth century.

FOOD RESOURCES

Food Resources of Western Washington and Oregon

Certainly, the most prolific and dependable resource throughout the western areas were the abundant runs of salmon. Five salmon species inhabit the Pacific Coast, spending their adult life in the offshore waters and traveling up freshwater streams to spawn. Native people caught some salmon by trolling in the saltwater, but large numbers of fish taken for preservation were captured in or near the freshwater streams with traps, weirs, and nets. Typically, salmon enter freshwater in the spring; subsequent runs may occur throughout the summer and into the fall.

Because not every stream supported all five species nor successive runs, some groups focused their attention on specific runs of fish and preserved their catch by drying or smoking. Preserved salmon was a staple supplemented with other locally available food resources, such as shellfish, plant foods, marine and land mammals, and waterfowl. Although some salmon fishing took place throughout the year, the bulk of the fish were taken in the spring and fall at specific locations, where the family groups tended to go annually. Probably the most widely employed fishing device at such locations was the weir, a barricade placed across a stream to divert the runs of fish into a trap. While the men worked the traps, the women cut the fish along the hack, removing the bones and internal organs. The filleted fish were then hung on a rack to be preserved by drying winds or in the rafters of the longhouse, where the slow-burning fires would dry them. Some groups preserved as much as five hundred pounds of fish per person through the year. Even to this day, many Native people feel a meal is incomplete without at least a little salmon.

Not all of the summer was spent salmon fishing. For many groups, shellfish—especially clams, mussels, and oysters—provided important food. Shellfish could be taken any time of year although in some areas, the flesh might be poisonous in the summer months. Usually, the "spring tides," when the lowest tides of the year occurred during the daylight hours, were the most important shellfish gathering times. Like salmon, shellfish were dried in abundance, providing not only sustenance but also an important item to trade with groups farther inland.

In late spring, many other types of fish were utilized, depending on local availability. Groups harvested herring (both the fish and the spawn), halibut, rockfish, and other deep-sea fish as well as marine mammals—seals, porpoises, and whales. Whales, especially gray whales, were taken during their migratory pass in the spring. The Makah and Quileute, who were all expert whalers, hunted these large animals from dugout canoes, using hand-thrown spears. Other tribes used a whale that had beached or drifted ashore, but the Makah and Quileute pursued the migrating whales far out at sea. Many miles from shore, for days on end, these whalers would track their quarry in hopes of not only obtaining an important source of food but also the prestige that came with being a successful whaler.

The land mammals most frequently hunted by the coastal peoples were deer, elk, bear, and mountain goat. Either solitary hunters would hunt the animals, or groups would drive them into nets or ambushes. Typically, the inland groups hunted land mammals more. Mountain goats were hunted for their horns, which could be fashioned into implements, usually spoons, and for their wool, which was spun into yarn and then woven into blankets for ceremonial garb and day-to-day use. In addition to mountain goats, some women kept a type of small dog which could be shorn like a sheep; its woolly fur was then spun into yarn.

The time of gathering plant foods began in the spring but was more intensive in the late summer and early fall. Starchy tubers, such as camas and wapato, and broken fern roots were harvested, in some cases from kin-controlled plots. Berries and other fruits were also plentiful and eaten dried and fresh.

Food Resources of Eastern Washington and Oregon

The Columbia Plateau Indians once enjoyed a rich environment oriented toward the region's rivers as fish was their traditional food. They built villages by rivers that boasted a good supply of trout, sturgeon, and salmon, millions of which swam through the waters each year. Much of the salmon was dried for winter use, and some was traded. The fish were split open and cleaned, then hung to dry on large, wooden racks in the sunlight.

Before they acquired horses, the Native groups in eastern Washington and Oregon had more difficulty hunting deer, elk, and bears. After they got horses in the 1700s, they increased their hunting areas by occasionally crossing the Rocky Mountains to hunt for buffalo. Hunting was especially important to groups located far from the Columbia River and its tributaries. Animal meat was a staple in their diets. Smaller game and waterfowl were also available.

Large portions of Washington and Oregon were lush with many varieties of wild fruits and vegetables. Native groups were expert at finding and preparing what grew wild in the valleys, hills, and mountains. Berries, nuts, roots, seeds, and bulbs were all part of their diet. In the springtime, women sharpened willow digging sticks and climbed hills to gather roots. They tugged out bulblike roots called kouse. It was eaten boiled, like cereal, or shaped into cakes to be dried for

This photo of Indians in the Columbia Plateau was taken in 1908.

later. In the summer, women also dug up camas, a wild lily bulb the size of small onions. A major food item, camas was eaten raw or roasted. Bulbs not eaten were steamed, ground into cakes, or made into dough or mush to be used when needed, especially in winter. If dried fish and meat and plant foods ran out and no game could be caught, people had to eat mush made from the inside layers of tree bark.

Along the mountainsides, women and children gathered hawthorn berries, blackberries, strawberries, and huckleberries. Like bulbs, uneaten berries were shaped into cakes and stored. Later, they were used to flavor winter meals of dried fish.

ART TRADITIONS

Artisans in western and eastern regions of Washington and Oregon, such as weavers, basket makers, wood carvers, and stone workers,

spent many hours crafting their handiwork. The art reflected the environments in which they lived. The art of western Washington and Oregon is characterized by cedar bark and mountain goat wool clothing and textiles, carved wooden house posts, and cedar plank houses. The art of the eastern halves of the two states is characterized by buckskin clothing and tule mat architecture. According to Robin K. Wright, an art curator in Seattle, despite the differences of environments and materials, there are "remarkable similarities in artistic traditions [that] exist between east and west, particularly in basketry techniques. Coiled cedar root baskets, decorated with bear grass and cedar bark … in zigzag patterns, are found on both sides of the mountains."

Besides basketry designs, clothing and jewelry in both eastern and western Washington were decorated with tusklike dentalium shells. The shells, harvested off the west coast of Vancouver Island, Canada, were traded extensively

Ceremonial masks are some of the items that might be exchanged during a potlatch, a ceremonial redistribution of wealth.

throughout the coastal and inland regions. After the arrival of Euro-American explorers, traders, and others in the nineteenth century, Native people in both regions of the two states acquired trade goods like metal, glass beads, and trade cloth. These materials were incorporated into the clothing, tools, and art in the east and the west.

In coastal areas, winter months were busy with ceremonial activities such as spirit dances, ceremonial performances, the demonstration of inherited privileges like masked dances, and the most famous ceremony of all, the potlatch. Potlatches, the ceremonial distribution of wealth goods, could take place any time of year to commemorate a naming, wedding, or funeral. Potlatching was a way for an individual to express his social standing in the community and to reinforce that position through the giving away of wealth and feasting with the guests. Numerous other ceremonies also were held, but certainly, the potlatch is the most widely known. Some evidence suggests that potlatching may have increased in the 1800s because of the influx of wealth items through the fur trade and subsequent interactions with Europeans, but that was only one of the dramatic changes to occur during the contact period.

EUROPEAN CONTACT

Many of the earliest explorers of northern North America, such as John Cabot, who sailed from England in 1497, were searching for a direct passage from Europe to China by way of an open sea passage across North America. Such an ocean route would have allowed Europeans an efficient means of carrying on trade with the Near Eastern empires. Considerable European effort was expended before the twentieth century in search of the fabled Northwest Passage.

In their continuing search for wealth and for the Northwest Passage, Europeans eventually reached the Pacific Coast during the latter part of the eighteenth century. In 1778, Captain James Cook sailed past and named Cape Flattery at the northwest tip of Washington State. British, American, and Spanish explorers and fur-trading vessels

worked these waters during the next few years. Initially, the Spanish explored northward from their settlements in Mexico. At first, the Europeans found little to compel them to stay. Some shipboard trade took place, but the North Pacific was not particularly rich in furs. Soon, however, sea otter pelts became marketable in Europe.

In 1789, the Spanish established a post at Nootka Sound on Vancouver Island, and they started the struggle to take control of the trade. Trade eventually included the Russians, Spanish, British, and Americans. The Native people were unconcerned with European political struggles so long as they gained access to manufactured goods. Such items greatly increased Native efficiency and economic well-being. The initial changes brought by the fur trade were primarily in material goods; little change was evident in social or religious life.

In 1795, the Spanish relinquished claim to the area north of the 42 latitude. In 1818, the British and Americans agreed to joint occupation of the area in between. The establishment of land-based trading operations began in 1811 with the building of the American Fur Company's post at the mouth of the Columbia River. Lost during the War of 1812, the post eventually fell into the hands of the Hudson's Bay Company, which came to dominate the fur trade of the North Pacific region until the 1840s, when American settlers began moving into the joint-occupied area. In 1846, the British and Americans negotiated the Treaty of Oregon, establishing the boundary at the 49th parallel between the United States and Canada.

EASTERN OREGON AND WASHINGTON, 1800s–1820s

Even before white intrusion began in earnest, the presence of fur trappers and the removal of beavers initiated dramatic environmental and cultural change. In the first decade of the 1800s, Indians living in present-day eastern Oregon and Washington met Lewis and Clark and their expedition (1804–1806). In October 1805, the expedition entered the lands of the Nez Perce, who

Fort Vancouver (now a national historic site in Washington state) was established in 1824 by the Hudson's Bay Company. Here, the British frequently traded with Indians.

provided the explorers with kindness, food, and canoes to take them to the Pacific Ocean. With the aid of Nez Perce scouts, the explorers traveled quickly by canoe to the homelands of the Palouse Indians, safely reaching the Palouse village of Quosispah. Several residents greeted Lewis and Clark at this village, and they celebrated the arrival of the Suyapo, "Crowned Heads" or "Crowned Hats," by singing long into the night. Palouse, Yakama, Walla Walla, Cayuse, and a host of other tribes sent representatives to meet the visitors. The Indians and explorers traded goods, and Lewis and Clark honored some of the chiefs with special medals bearing the words *Peace* and *Friendship*. Relations between the two peoples were congenial, and the explorers soon continued their trip down the Columbia River in present-day Oregon State.

Lewis and Clark reported the many wondrous things they had seen, including the vast numbers of fur-bearing animals. By 1810, less than a year after their journey, British traders traveled through the Northwest in quest of a river route from the interior of Canada to the Pacific Ocean. Soon, three major fur trading companies, the Northwest Company, the American Fur Company, and the Hudson's Bay Company, set up trading posts or factories in the Northwest.

In 1824, the Hudson's Bay Company opened Fort Vancouver in present-day Washington, and they operated factories or posts. The company worked with tribes to procure furs and depended on them for horses. Fort Nez Perce, Fort Okanogan, Fort Colville, and Fort Spokane, all named after tribes in eastern Washington and Oregon, traded with Indians and supplied the Hudson's Bay Company with some furs and many horses. The British company enjoyed a prosperous Indian trade on the Columbia Plateau area until the 1850s when it had depleted the number of fur-bearing animals and when the United States took control of the region.

TRAILS, TREATIES, AND TUMULT, 1830s–1860s

From the mid-1830s to the 1860s, about four hundred thousand Anglo settlers, married couples, ranchers, farmers, miners, businessmen, and their families traveled the Oregon Trail, a pioneer route to the Pacific Northwest about two thousand miles from Independence, Missouri, to the Willamette-Columbia River region. At first, most of the encounters with Native groups were business transactions. The immigrants offered clothes, rifles, and tobacco in exchange for Native horses or food.

As early as the mid-1840s, however, the white invasion quickly grew, impacting most of the Native peoples of Washington and Oregon. Cultivated fields and livestock pastures replaced the plentiful stands of wild plants, vital Native food sources. Immigrant horses and cattle trampled meadows, where people gathered seeds and camas bulbs. Immigrants' hogs ate the acorns, another important food source. Tensions mounted.

The traders and trappers became the first to occupy Indian lands in the region. A few of them tried to convert the Indians to Christianity, but the major thrust of the mission system in the eastern region began in the 1830s. The Presbyterian missionary couples Marcus and Narcissa Whitman and Henry and Eliza Spalding established the first missions in Washington State among the Cayuse and the Nez Perce. Catholic missionaries followed these early Presbyterian ministers, establishing missions among the Colville, Yakama, Umatilla, and others. Some Indians gravitated to Christianity while others retreated into their own traditional religions. Controversy over whether to adopt Christianity split many Indian communities into pro- and anti-Christians. Between 1836 and 1843, the Whitmans and Spaldings worked diligently among the Indians with mixed results.

The newcomers carried diseases with them, which barely sickened them, but decimated Indian tribes. In 1847, a measles epidemic wiped out many Cayuse. They suspected that Marcus Whitman, a practicing physician as well as a religious leader, was responsible for the deaths of their families. Seeking revenge, Cayuse attacked the Whitman Mission on November 29, 1847. Fourteen Anglo settlers were killed, including both of the Whitmans. Volunteer troops sent to deal with the situation slaughtered a band of Cayuse who had not been involved. This led to the Cayuse War, the first of several Native resistance wars in eastern Washington. It continued for another five years until the Cayuse were finally defeated in 1855 and driven from their Walla Walla homelands. Over the next few years, the Provisional Government of Oregon and later the United States Army battled the Native American peoples east of the Cascades. In Oregon, the Rogue River War erupted in the mid-1850s when Indians rose up against gold hunters and settlers in the coastal regions.

Officials of the Oregon Territory, created by the United States in 1848, pushed for Indian land cession treaties to free up for settlement the fertile coastal valleys by relocating and isolating Native groups onto reservations and establishing military and civil power over them. In 1853, the United States created two separate territories: Oregon Territory included lands in present-day Oregon, Idaho, and Wyoming. The territory of Washington Territory, organized from a portion of the Oregon Territory, included lands in present-day Washington, Idaho, and Montana. With the new governments came American Indian policy bent on extinguishing land title of the coastal Indians.

In 1854, Governor Isaac I. Stevens, who had been appointed as Washington Territory's first governor, made a whirlwind tour of the coastal tribes of Washington Territory, coercing some of them into ceding their lands to the government. He made treaties at Medicine Creek, Point Elliott, and Point No Point. The Indians of Puget Sound secured for only a small portion of their lands and fell victim to the power of the Bureau of Indian Affairs. The treaties, however, recognized traditional fishing and hunting rights on and off the reservation. Next, Stevens turned his attention to the Indians east of the Cascade Mountains.

The Walla Walla Treaty Council of 1855

Governor Isaac Stevens and Oregon Superintendent of Indian Affairs Joel Palmer arranged a meeting on the east side of the Cascades in the Walla Walla Valley between the U.S. and over five thousand Cayuse, Nez Perce, Umatilla, Walla Walla, and Yakama. The so-called Walla Walla Treaty Council in 1855 forever changed the lives of Native peoples living in eastern Oregon and Washington. None requested the council or wanted to surrender their homelands, but representatives of the tribes attended the council to protect their peoples' sovereignty and way of life. Palmer and Stevens pushed their agenda of making three treaties and establishing reserves for the Umatilla, Yakama, and Nez Perce peoples. Palmer warned that white intruders would "steal your horses and cattle" if the Indians didn't agree to boundaries.

The tribes reluctantly made agreements with Palmer and Stevens. In the Walla Walla, Cayuse, and Umatilla Treaty of 1855, the tribes secured a reservation of 510,000 acres and lost over six million acres of land and billions of dollars in resources. The nations reserved the right to hunt, fish, and gather at all usual and accustomed areas on and off the reservation. However, as soon as the treaty negotiations were completed, official announcements were made to the public that lands in eastern Washington were open for settlement. Hoards of Euro-Americans, some ordinary citizens, others land-hungry, gold-hungry land developers, missionaries, and merchants, disregarded property rights of nations and poured into the area, even onto newly created reservation boundaries. Traditional living areas were overtaken immediately as were fishing, hunting, and gathering sites.

The Walla Walla Council of 1855 triggered a major war between many Oregon and Wash-

May. 1855. Walla Walla Council. Governor Stevens with Indians.

An illustration of the 1855 Walla Walla Council showing Governor Isaac Stevens standing at center under the canopy.

ington nations and the government. Between 1855 and 1858, the Indians of the eastern region had a series of fights with volunteer and U.S. Army troops. The Yakama tried to lead a pan-Indian resistance in 1855–1856, which ended inconclusively. They threw themselves into a second resistance effort that drew wide support from the Spokane, Palouse, Coeur d'Alene, and Northern Paiute. It ended with the execution of leaders. Several tribes chose not to enter a war with the United States, but the soldiers sought to punish Indians whether or not they supported the resistance.

ASSIMILATE, ASSIMILATE, 1880s–1950s

From the treaty era to the present, various federal policies were enacted which had a lasting impact on the Native people of Oregon and Washington, beginning with "assimilationist" policy in the late 1800s. Federal policy was designed to convince Indians to abandon their traditional culture, which was considered backward, and assimilate or take on the culture of the dominant forces.

During the 1880s, "reformers" of American Indian policies determined that the trouble with Indians was that they held reservations communally and not individually. In an attempt to "help" Indians, U.S. policymakers reasoned that owning private plots of land would lead Indians to become "civilized" because they would have a direct stake in their own economic livelihood. Most reformers, however, knew little about Indian cultures or economic practice, and many Indians refused to give up their traditional economic practices in order to adopt farming.

General Allotment Act of 1887

Perhaps the most influential policy of the assimilationist period was the General Allotment Act of 1887 (also known as the Dawes Act), which called for the division of reservations into individual parcels of 160, eighty, or forty acres.

Each Indian received an allotment, and the excess land was sold to non-Indian settlers. After twenty-five years, Indian allotees could sell their individual allotments (see also the Historical Overview chapter).

Boarding Schools

Native children from Oregon and Washington were sent to many different boarding schools, but the most common was Chemawa, near Salem, Oregon. Youngsters were also sent to faraway reservation boarding schools, which taught them trades and required them to speak English (see also the Historical Overview chapter).

Yakama Reservation Allotments

The government began allotting the Yakama Reservation in Washington State in the 1890s and continued the process until 1914. Yakama elders and worshippers of the Washani religion— a new religion that taught preservation of Indian land and many traditions—opposed allotment. Some Yakima agreed to take allotments although many felt it contrary to tradition. Because many conservative Yakima resisted taking allotments, 798,000 acres of reservation land was not allotted and remained in tribal hands.

In 1902, Congress passed a resolution directing the secretary of the interior to allot Spokane tribal lands. The Spokane had little choice in the matter: the United States forced 651 members of the tribe to accept allotments totaling 64,750 acres. The government sold the remainder of the Spokane Reservation to non-Indian timber, agricultural, and ranching interests.

Native people adapted the best they could to the changes that Euro-Americans brought. Some farmed their own land both on and off the reservations, and many more worked seasonally on Euro-American-owned farms. Others worked in the timber industry, produced baskets and other crafts for the tourist trade, fished for the salmon canneries, and performed day labor. Many continued to hunt, fish, gather, and trade as their ancestors had for centuries.

Diseases Again

Diseases also impacted the lives of these Indians. While smallpox, measles, and venereal diseases ravaged the tribes in the nineteenth century, tuberculosis, pneumonia, and influenza killed thousands of Indians in the twentieth century. Between 1888 and 1930, among the Indians of the Yakama Nation, more deaths occurred between birth and the age of one than in any other age category. Infant mortality most often resulted from the abovementioned diseases. Each tribe had its traditional Native doctors, men and women who knew the healing herbs, medical techniques, prayers, and songs, but they were too often unable to fight the newly introduced diseases. Some Indians were treated by government doctors, but too many were not. The Native American population in the region suffered severely from infectious disease until the 1930s when the Indian Health Service received more funds to combat them.

Allotment Ends, 1930s

Some of the tribes in Oregon accepted the Indian Reorganization Act while others did not. The Confederated Tribes of the Umatilla Indian Reservation, the Confederated Tribes of the Warm Springs Reservation, and others voted to accept the Indian Reorganization Act. Regardless, all of the eastern plateau tribes created tribal governments that helped guide their peoples during the twentieth century (see also the Historical Overview chapter).

ASSIMILATION RETURNS

The new plans of the federal government during the 1930s were short-lived. After World War II, the United States changed course again. In 1945, Commissioner of Indian Affairs John Collier, who had emphasized cultural pluralism for American Indians, was forced to resign by congressional opponents who sought a return to the policies of assimilation. The new approach was called termination. The idea was to force individual Indians to assimilate into mainstream, English-speaking, Christian American society by getting rid of Indian reservations, by terminating all treaty obligations to Indian nations, and by terminating all government programs intended to aid Indians.

Relocation

Termination policies of the 1950s were enacted in two ways. First, the Bureau of Indian Affairs (BIA) envisioned relocation as a way of emptying the reservations. The relocation policy encouraged reservation residents to move to urban areas where they were to find jobs. However, since the reservation populations were generally not trained to do skilled work, the types of jobs they found were usually low-paying. Making minimum wage, Native people were forced to live in the least desirable parts of cities, and, as a result, urban Indian ghettos were created in cities like Portland and Seattle (see also the Historical Overview chapter).

Termination in Oregon

Three Oregon tribes were terminated: the Klamath of southeast Oregon and the Siletz and Grande Ronde of the Oregon coast. Siletz and Grande Ronde were the reservation homes of the Oregon coastal tribes, and because of their economic success, they were considered likely candidates for termination of their relationship with the federal government. It soon became clear that without their special status as a federally recognized tribe, the Siletz and Grand Ronde had little power to hold their lands together and continue to promote economic well-being. Almost as soon as they were terminated, both tribes sought to be reinstated as federally recognized tribes, an act that was finally granted after nearly thirty years.

The government attempted to terminate the Confederated Tribes of the Colville Reservation in Washington State. Colville tribal members living off the reservation generally favored termination because it would bring them a cash settlement. However, tribal members living on the reservation generally opposed termination because it ended treaty rights and threatened to disperse Indian cul-

The Colville Reservation is located in northeastern Washington. The U.S. government tried to terminate the the treaty with the tribe, but tribal members eventually rejected the effort because it would have dispersed the community.

tures and communities. The leaders of the Confederated Tribes struggled over the issue of termination during the 1950s and 1960s. The most vocal opponent of termination was Lucy Covington, a member of a prominent political family on the reservation. Covington stood nearly single-handedly against proponents of termination, and she never surrendered her position. As a result of her efforts, the tribe never agreed to termination, and it has been solidly opposed to the concept ever since. The threat of termination receded in the 1960s and was finally renounced in 1988 (see also the Historical Overview chapter).

TREATY FISHING RIGHTS OF WASHINGTON AND OREGON, 1850s TO TODAY

Perhaps the most significant issue facing the Indians of Washington and Oregon has been fishing rights. Before the arrival of Euro-Americans, Native peoples had thriving fisheries in Puget Sound and along the Columbia River and its tributaries. The great salmon runs were at the core of the tribal economic, cultural, and ceremonial life.

In legislation creating the Oregon Territory, which opened the area to non-Indian settlement,

Congress promised fair dealings with the tribes. In the series of treaties negotiated between the U.S. government and tribes in the 1850s, the groups gave up much of their land in return for promises of cash payments, other aid, and retention of their fishing rights "at all usual and accustomed grounds and stations." Tribes conceded, however, to share these off-reservation sites with white settlers. Tribes, assured by 1855 treaty negotiations that "this paper (treaty) secures your fish," continued to fish at their usual places.

By the late 1800s, non-Indian trap users, gill-netters, seiners, and trollers encroached on and even blocked access to Native peoples' usual and accustomed fishing grounds. By 1920, sportsmen were competing with commercial fishermen for the salmonlike steelhead trout, declared "a game fish" in 1925. The 1930s and 1940s brought a new threat to Indian fishing rights. Some three hundred dams, big and small, built by the Army Corps of Engineers and private utility companies in the Columbia River basin—which pose environmental threats to salmon by cutting off their spawning migrations—inundated ancient fishing grounds. Logging, farming, and industrial development also took tolls on salmon runs and depleted their numbers.

Despite opposition from state agencies and non-Indian fishers and the demands of more people, more industry, and more recreation, Indians initiated court cases and "fish-ins," fishing in defiance of state law but in accord with Indian treaty rights—to assert their rights. Many Native fishers got arrested. Beginning in 1964, Indian activists turned the arrests into media events, organizing rallies and inviting Marlon Brando, Jane Fonda, and other celebrities to the riverbanks to help sway public opinion.

Several court decisions in the late 1960s and 1970s firmly established in law the tribes' rights to take fish at usual fishing grounds. The Boldt decision of 1974 (*U.S. v. Washington*) acknowledged the right of Indians to fish in common with non-Indians and the right to half of the harvestable fish catch destined to pass through their usual and accustomed fishing grounds. It also established the tribes as comanagers of the salmon resource. The landmark Boldt ruling is now recognized as one of the most important documents of economic and social reform in the history of the Pacific Northwest region. According to University of Washington Fisheries Professor Richard Whitney, Boldt was significant "because of the fact that that a federal judge would look at the law and say, this is what the law requires, and everybody has to live up to it. Not just the tribes and not just the state, but everybody." The decision upheld treaties as being supreme over state law, as stated in the U.S. Constitution.

The decision set off a shock wave of controversy. It cut in half the catch of sport and commercial fishers. Many went out of business. For years after the ruling, enraged non-Indian commercial fishers mounted campaigns against the decision, protesting in courts, in public areas, on rivers, where they fished illegally in defiance of state fishing regulations, and against Federal District Judge George Boldt. The state's resistance to enforcing Boldt led to the Ninth Circuit of Appeals (1975) and the Supreme Court upholding (1979) the Boldt Decision.

In 2014, treaty tribes in western Washington marked the fortieth anniversary of Judge Boldt's ruling with a daylong celebration. Nevertheless, the struggle for treaty fishing rights continues. Since the Boldt decision, there has been a steady decline of salmon in Puget Sound because of environmental policy. The tribes' annual harvest has been lower than in 1974. Salmon habitats that have been damaged need to be restored, which requires the collaboration of tribes, the state, and the federal government.

CONTEMPORARY OREGON AND WASHINGTON INDIAN INDIGENEITY

Tribal Initiatives

Since the 1970s, many tribes have made significant strides in health, education, and economic development. The Colville Tribal Federal Corporation has grown to become one of the largest, most diverse Native American businesses in northeastern Washington. The company currently manages thirteen enterprises that include gaming, recreation and tourism, retail, construction, and wood products.

The Cayuse, Umatilla, and Walla Walla Indians living on the Umatilla Reservation in Oregon have emphasized traditional culture and education. The tribe has established a scholarship fund for college-aged students, a daycare center, language-immersion programs, recreation facilities, and vocational education training.

One of the most active tribes in the region in terms of educational and economic self-determination is the Confederated Tribes of Warm Springs of Oregon, which have established a number of enterprises that contribute to the economy of the reservation. In 1955, the Tribes approved the building of the first powerhouse, the Pelton Dam. Also installed at this time was the Reregulating Dam. In 1964, the Tribes approved the construction of the third dam, the Round Butte Dam. The Warm Springs Power Enterprises manage the Tribes' interest in the largest hydroelectric project within the state of Oregon and oversees the sale of electrical output. The Tribes have carefully logged the western edge of their reservation and since 1967 have owned the Warm Springs Forest Products Industries that harvests its timber on a managed, sustained-yield basis. They also built their own resort and convention center, Kah-Nee-Ta Lodge and Convention Center, which opened in 1972, a museum in 1993, followed by the Kah-Nee-Ta High Desert Resort & Casino in 1995.

The Confederated Tribes and Bands of the Yakama Nation have been successful in promoting their own economic self-determination. The Yakama Forest Products manufactures and sells forest products from the nation's annual timber harvest. Other Yakama Nation projects developed on land of the Yakama Nation Land Enterprise include fruit orchards and farm operations, a forest mill, casino and event center, an RV park resort, sports complex, and industrial park as well

Round Butte Dam, located in Jefferson County, Oregon, created Lake Billy Chinook, as well as a power station, and was approved by the Confederated Tribes of Warm Springs in 1964.

as a regular- and controlled-atmosphere, cold-storage facility. In 1980, the Yakama opened the Nation Cultural Center (YNCC), a unique, multifaceted facility offering a variety of programs that share Yakama Nation's history and culture with all. Beautifully designed, shaped largely like a longhouse, the cultural center contains a library, museum, gift shop, theater, and restaurant.

Programs for teaching Indian languages on Washington's Colville, Spokane, and Yakama and Oregon's Umatilla reservations began in the 1970s and continue with even greater awareness of the need for language preservation. Language preservation and maintenance, curriculum development, and other initiatives also take place at many reservations, including Washington's Makah and Lower Elwha Klallam reservations and Oregon's

Confederated Tribes of Grand Ronde and the Confederated Tribes of Siletz Indians.

While the tribes themselves are responsible for the maintenance of language, university scholars, including Native academicians, have joined hands with some of the tribes to write and teach the language. Native groups in the region consider language retention one of their most important projects.

The prospects for the future are promising. As Native communities in Washington and Oregon continue to assert their sovereignty as a means to develop economically and politically, they will bring about positive change in a culturally sensitive manner. The present era is marked by Indian tribes successfully exerting their legal rights to land and resources and the strengthening of tribal self-governance to promote development. The self-determination policy recognizes tribal interests in regaining greater control over reservation institutions, such as language preservation, education and local administration, and over tribal economic resources such as land, minerals, and hunting and fishing.

Although Natives participate in American society, this does not mean that they have assimilated or any of the other terms that suggest they are no longer Indian. Speaking English, word processing, fishing with modern power boats and synthetic nets, or even carving a dug-out canoe with a chainsaw does not mean that the Natives are any less Indian. Euro-Americans are not expected to cook in the fireplace or support themselves by hitching the horse to the plow. Being a Washington or Oregon Indian today means participating in modem political and economic structures of North American society while maintaining a distinct ethnic identity. It is this identity that will strengthen the efforts toward tribal development—a development that will lead to the persistence of Native identity in the twenty-first century.

Annual Stommish Festival

For thousands of years, the Lummi (Washington State) and other First Peoples of the

Northwest conducted potlatches and celebrated other spiritual observances to create harmony and honor their unique coastal cultures, but as with all other Native religious traditions, the U.S. government outlawed the rituals and gatherings. Lummi veterans of World War I wanted to create a welcoming celebration to commemorate the return of loved ones who fought in World War II.

The Lummi consider the Puget Sound waters their ancestral highways as indeed, the water routes were their main way of travel. The veterans decided to connect the welcome home party to these ancient waterways and traveled the Puget Sound area, even to Canada, to invite other "canoe" nations to join them. They asked everyone to bring their racing canoes, traditional songs and dances, barbecued salmon, and games for children. The people responded, and in 1946, the first-ever Stommish Festival was held on Puget Sound near Bellingham, Washington. Stommish is the Cowichan word for "warrior," and today, returning servicemen and women are honored during the ten-day gathering. Many different nations from all points in the Salish Sea compete in traditional games and the war canoe races. There are several categories for men, women, and children, who race canoes with one, two, four, six, or nine paddlers. Stommish has become the largest annual gathering of canoe tribes, establishing a strong connection among First Nation People of the Pacific Northwest.

March Point

In 2009, Swinomish high school students Nick Clark, Cody Cayou, and Travis Tom considered writing a gangster movie or rap video with their funds from Native Lens, Longhouse Media's film program for Native youth. Instead, they followed their noses to the putrid smell of an oil refinery and chose it as their subject. Their documentary, March Point, illustrates how refineries not only devastate the environment but also destroy the economy of Native people dependent on natural resources for their livelihood.

The teenagers traveled to Washington, D.C., to enlist the help of government officials who could help Washington State reservations. Back home, they interviewed elders, fishermen, and fishing activists and put it all together in a short film, but their work was so impressive, PBS and *National Geographic* gave them more monies to extend the project into an hour-long production. The teens made a real difference as they brought the illegal occupation and destruction of Swinomish lands to national attention. For their stunning film, the three earned internships at the Smithsonian Institution.

BIOGRAPHIES

Seattle (Sealth) (c. 1786–1866)
Suquamish/Duwamish Leader

Seattle, ancestral leader of the Suquamish Tribe, achieved the status of chief of the Suquamish and a confederation of Duwamish bands after planning and executing an attack strategy that saved central Puget Sound people from upriver tribal forces.

Seattle witnessed the transition of his people from ancient lifeways to a new one brought by the arrival of non-Indians and imposed on them by the U.S. government. Missionaries, fur traders, and Euro-American settlers brought new technology, disease, and the concept of private property to Puget Sound.

Throughout the gold rush era of the 1850s, Seattle maintained peace, despite the influx of miners and settlers. He avoided being drawn into the ongoing regional conflicts between non-Indians and Indians that were permeating the Pacific region during this time.

Some tribes, such as the Puyallup and Muckleshoot, who signed the Treaty of Medicine Creek, were angered by the treaty terms and took up arms against the military and settlers, attacking the Elliott Bay settlement. Chief Seattle kept his forces out of the battle and remained at Suquamish. For this action, and because of long friendships with early Seattle residents, the founders of the city of Seattle named the settlement after Chief Seattle in 1852.

By 1855, tensions were mounting, which led to the Yakama War of 1855–1856. Seattle chose not to fight and signed the Point Elliot Treaty, in which he agreed to relocate his people to the Port Madison Indian Reservation, near present-day Bremerton, Washington, and give up the remainder of Suquamish lands. Seattle made trips to the city named after him for inter-tribal meetings.

Chief Seattle is well known around the world for a speech in which he discussed relations between Natives and non-Natives and conveyed Native ideas about life, the afterlife, and natural resources. Initially delivered during the 1850s and first published in a Seattle newspaper in 1887, the speech received very little attention until it resurfaced in non-Native publications during the 1930s. Thereafter, the speech became more widely known, particularly during the late 1960s and early 1970s when it was adopted in numerous guises by environmentalists. However, Chief Seattle never spoke some of the later versions of the speech, and scholars cannot say for sure how much of the initial version was actually his.

Dr. Henry Smith first put the speech into print in the *Seattle Sunday Star* on October 29, 1887. He claimed to have heard the speech around 1853 or 1854 (one scholar states that Seattle delivered it in mid-January 1854. Smith apparently reconstructed the 1887 version from notes in his diary (now lost) he claimed to have taken in the 1850s, but he also said that his 1887 newspaper rendition represented "but a fragment of his speech and lacks all the charm lent by the grace and earnestness of the sable old orator."

Smith's English version of the speech has been quoted and misquoted, resulting in many published versions that range from modern renditions to fictionalized versions that made references to railroads and rotting buffalo. No historical collection contains evidence of anything like the famous speech, so it cannot be precisely attributed to a specific day and year.

Kamiakin (c. 1798–c. 1877)
Yakama, Leader

The main leader of the Yakama during a wave of resistance in the mid-1850s, he inherited a chieftainship from his mother. Kamiakin befriended the first non-Indians to settle in eastern Washington. However, the increased immigration and destruction of Native homelands after the discovery of gold in Washington Territory led him to a war of resistance to the 1855 treaties negotiated by Washington Territorial Governor Isaac Stevens, which his people did not sign. He unified a number of tribes, including the Cayuse, Palouse, and Walla Walla, raising a force of two thousand fighters. Although the fighters won an early battle, defeats followed which ended the war. Kamiakin escaped to British Columbia for a while and then settled with the Palouse people in Idaho.

Leschi (c. 1808–1858)
Nisqually, Leader

Leschi was one of the principal leaders in the Yakama War, the resistance in 1855–1856 to treaties negotiated by Washington Territorial Governor Isaac Stevens. He protested vehemently against the loss of his homeland as well as the reservation appointed for the Nisqually. Commanding a force of one thousand soldiers, Leschi attacked the newly established settlement of Seattle in January 1856. A ship anchored in Puget Sound drove off the attackers and defeated the resistance fighters.

Leschi, who was accused of killing Abram Benton Moses, a non-Indian man in late 1855, was captured and brought to trial in Fort Steilacoom. The first trial failed to convict Leschi. At a second trial, investigators tried to show that Leschi could not have been at the scene of the murder. Nevertheless, he was judged guilty and executed.

In December 2004, a Washington Historical Court of Inquiry and Justice met to discuss the issue of Leschi's innocence. Witnesses gave testimony based on historical evidence in front of a Washington State Supreme Court justice. In the end, Leschi was exonerated for the murder of Moses. Cynthia Iyall, a descendant of Leschi, explained that his exoneration over 140 years after his death was important because "A man who maintained that [Nisqually] people retain their heritage deserves to have the truth be told.... "

Smohalla (1815–1907)
Wanapam, Spiritual Leader

Smohalla lived along the upper Columbia River in present-day eastern Washington State but left this area around 1850 after a dispute with a local chief. Smohalla traveled for several years. Despite being influenced by Catholic missionaries, Smohalla became a warrior. He was wounded and left for dead during an encounter with the Salish. When he returned to his homeland, he claimed to have visited the Spirit World during this near-death ordeal. He brought back a message which, to the Wanapam, had the ring of authenticity due to his death-and-resurrection experience. According to Smohalla, religious truths came to him in dreams, thus the name of his religion: "Dreamer Religion." Among Smohalla's teachings was the repudiation of U.S. culture, including alcohol and agricultural practices.

Smohalla's popularity came at a time when the Indian population of the region was declining due to diseases and land losses to U.S. settlers. He has been credited with the oft-mentioned quotation, "You ask me to plow the ground. Shall I take a knife and tear my mother's bosom? You ask me to cut grass and make hay and sell it and be rich like white men, but dare I cut off my mother's hair?" Smohalla also prophesied that Indians would be resurrected and banish whites from their lands. He taught that Indians would be saved though divine intervention but did not advocate violence. His teachings and sermons were often accompanied by ceremonial music and dance. Smohalla's teachings got him into trouble with U.S. authorities, and he was often jailed. He influenced later prophets who also advocated for resistance and cultural identity.

Mourning Dove (1884–1893)
Colville, Writer

Mourning Dove was the pen name of Christine Quintasket, an Okanogan from the Colville Reservation in eastern Washington State who collected tribal stories among Northern Plateau peoples in the early twentieth century. She described centuries-old traditions with the authority of first-hand knowledge and also wrote a novel based on her experiences. Like her African American contemporary Zora Neale Hurston (1891–1960), Mourning Dove's reputation as a female ethnographer and writer has grown steadily over the past few decades. Her novel, *Cogewea,* is the first known published novel by a Native American woman.

An activist for Indian rights, Mourning Dove wrote that she was grateful to have been born and come of age during the early years of official U.S. Indian policy; she spent her life writing and working to represent Indian culture to a dominant white world. Scholar Janet Finn writes that Mourning Dove "wrote against the dominant grain of Indian image making" and that her work "challenged the capacity of personal ethnographic accounts to 'capture' Native American experience; they countered popular stereotypes of Indian people.... "

John Slocum (d. c. 1897)
Squaxin Band, Coast Salish, Founder of the Indian Shaker Church

Slocum belonged to the Squaxin band of Southern Coast Salish Indians and was the founder of the Indian Shaker Church. He was born near Puget Sound, Washington, but there was nothing particularly remarkable about his life until the fall of 1881, when he became sick and apparently died.

Friends had been summoned and preparations were being made for the funeral when he suddenly revived. He then announced that he had been to visit the judgment place of God and received instructions about certain ways in which Indian people needed to change their lives if they wanted to achieve salvation. This visionary experience became the basis of Tschaddam, or the Indian Shaker Church, as it is known in English. Indian Shakerism has no connection to New England's Protestant Shakerism communities. It does incorporate Christian beliefs concerning God, heaven, hell, and the relationship between sinfulness and damnation, but these ideas are combined with Native concepts, particularly beliefs relating to sickness as a penalty for spiritual offenses.

About a year after his "resurrection," Slocum became gravely ill again. Faced with the impending catastrophe of his death, his wife Mary became hysterical; she approached his prostrate body praying, sobbing, and trembling uncontrollably. When her convulsion had passed, it was observed that Slocum had recovered slightly. This was attributed to her seizure, which was understood as a manifestation of divine power. Thus, curing through "the shake" and laying on of hands became a basic element in Shaker services, which continues to this day.

Lucy Covington
(1910–1982)
Colville, Political Activist

The most vocal opponent of termination in the 1950s, Covington was a member of a prominent political family on the reservation, the granddaughter of Colville chief Chief Moses. She stood nearly single-handedly against proponents of termination, and she never surrendered her position. As a result of her efforts, the tribe never agreed to termination. She utilized unique strategies and her magnetic personality to gain support. Covington helped create a Colville newspaper titled *Our Heritage*, which helped raise awareness for her campaign and also stood as a dedication to Indian culture. Through individual activism and determination, Covington helped keep Colville tribal sovereignty intact, and her persistence halted the liquidation and dismemberment of the Colville reservation.

Violet (Vi) Anderson Hilbert
(1918–2008)
Upper Skagit, Linguist

Hilbert, a tribal elder in Washington State, was a world-renowned language expert dedicated to preserving her Lushootseed language and culture. She cowrote Lushootseed grammars and dictionaries and published books of stories, teachings, and place names related to her Native region, Puget Sound. She began her work in 1967 after she met Dr. Thomas M. Hess, a linguist who encouraged her to learn the writing system he used as he worked on languages of Native people. Hilbert said it became her "responsibility as a great-grandmother to gather, transcribe, and translate" as much as possible of the culture of her people for the benefit of future generations. Hilbert was named a Washington State Living Treasure in 1989 and received a National Heritage Fellowship from the National Endowment of the Arts, presented by President Bill Clinton in 1994.

Fran James
(1923–2013)
Lummi, Basket Weaver

James was a master weaver, creating baskets of all sizes and shapes from natural materials she gathered in western Washington State. Her work included twill-plaited cedar and cherry fiber bags; cedar and bear grass baskets of all shapes and uses; cedar hats; split and braided mats of cattail or cedar; elegant blankets; and robes of handspun, twill-woven mountain goat or sheep wool.

Raised by her grandmother on Washington's Portage Island, James helped care for the older woman's five hundred black sheep. By the time she was nine, James learned from her grandmother how to shear wool from the sheep, spin it, and knit with it. As a little girl, she also learned how to gather traditional materials like cedar bark and roots, bear grass, and wild cherry to make baskets. She peeled the outer bark from trees (after requesting the trees' permission) and turned the strips into baskets. After the bark dried for six months, it had to be soaked in boiling hot water so it would split. Then it had to be thinned down in order to be worked.

James kept Lummi art forms alive by teaching others how to weave and taught at Northwest Indian College. Her works have been shown in major galleries, including the Stonington Gallery in Seattle and Arctic Raven Gallery in the San Juan Islands.

David Sohappy, Sr. (1925–1991)
Yakama/Wenatchi, Fishing Rights Activist

David Sohappy, an elder of the Yakama's Wanapim Band and a traditional healer, is considered a major figure and activist in the Indian fishing rights struggle, an economic issue in the Washington—Oregon region during the 1980s. After he was laid off from a sawmill in the 1960s, David Sohappy, who had been fishing since he was five years old, returned to the traditional Indian way of life, settling in a self-made wooden house on the Columbia River. From there, he undertook a campaign for Indian treaty fishing rights along the rivers in Washington State without regard for limits or season. Sohappy represented the feelings of many northwestern Indians when he argued that his right to fish did not hinge merely on the articles of the Yakama Treaty of 1855. He insisted that the right to use the salmon had first come to the people as a result of Coyote—the trickster, changer—who, according to tradition, broke a dam guarded by monsters at the mouth of the Columbia River and led the salmon into the inland rivers.

For Sohappy, there was no compromising his belief that Indians had the right to fish in "usual and accustomed" places and times. He was arrested numerous times and had 230 fishing nets confiscated over twenty years because of his insistence on fishing out of season. The 1968 case

Sohappy v. Washington State started a series of legal rulings and investigations, which resulted in the 1974 decision by U.S. District Court Judge George Boldt (see also the Treaty "Fishing Rights of Washington and Oregon, 1850s—Today" section in this chapter).

In 1982, Sohappy was caught selling 317 fish in a federal sting operation known as Salmonscam. Convicted of a felony under tough new federal poaching laws, he was sentenced to five years in a minimum-security prison in Spokane and later transferred to a federal jail in California. He served eighteen months before being released in poor health in 1988. Sohappy's imprisonment became a cause célèbre in the Northwest. After his release, he continued to fight for fishing rights.

Billy Frank, Jr. (1931–2014)
Nisqually, Fishing Rights Activist

Frank, Jr., who called himself the "Go-To-Jail Guy," championed Native American sovereignty and was a leader of a civil disobedience movement that insisted on treaty rights (the right to fish in "usual and accustomed grounds and stations") guaranteed to Washington tribes. Between 1945 and 1970, Frank went to jail more than fifty times because he fished at "Frank's Landing," where he and the Nisqually Indian Nation were guaranteed the right to fish forever by a 1854 treaty. The traditions and training passed on to him by his father and grandfather were ingrained. He was determined, like his forebears, to fight for what was rightfully theirs.

To the Washington State Sportsman's Council and the State Department of Fisheries, Frank was demanding special privileges and was illegally poaching. The state, which insisted that it could impose its fishing regulations on tribes despite the treaty, destroyed property and made hundreds of arrests. Despite countless setbacks, Frank was always open to negotiation with other Native nations, state, and federal governments to protect salmon and their habitat so vital to the Nisqually spiritually, nutritionally, and financially.

Frank and others established in 1964 the Survival of American Indians Association to fight state policies. The "fish-ins" and demonstrations that Frank helped organize in the 1960s and 1970s, along with lawsuits, led to the famous *United States v. Washington* (*Boldt*) decision of 1974, named for U.S. District Court Judge George Boldt, a tough law-and-order jurist (see also the Treaty "Fishing Rights of Washington and Oregon, 1850s—Today" section in this chapter).

In 1981, the Northwest Indian Fisheries Commission (NWIFC), which Frank chaired for over thirty years, established working relationships with state agencies and other non-Indian groups to manage fisheries, restore and protect habitat, and protect Indian treaty rights.

Frank was honored with the Albert Schweitzer Prize for Humanitarianism, the 2006 Wallace Stegner Award, the Washington State Environmental Excellence Award, and countless others for his decades-long fight for justice and environmental preservation. Native nations throughout the U.S. followed Frank's lead and held their own "fish-ins" to assert rights promised in treaties but suppressed by states.

Janet McCloud (1934–2003)
Tulalip, Fishing Rights Activist

Janet McCloud (Yet-Si-Blue), a descendant of Chief Seattle's family, was a prominent Indigenous rights activist. Her activism helped lead to the 1974 *Boldt* decision (see also the Treaty 'Fishing Rights of Washington and Oregon, 1850s—Today' section in this chapter).

In 1964, McCloud and her husband, Don, cofounded the activist group Survival of American Indians Association to fight state policies, and McCloud wrote, edited, and published the association's newsletter *Survival News*. In defiance of court orders, in 1965, she and her husband's stepbrother, Nisqually tribal member Billy

Frank, Jr., Puyallup Indian Bob Satiacum, and others organized protests at the Nisqually and Puyallup rivers, into which tribe members cast traditional nets deemed illegal by the state. Invariably, the "fish-ins" led to raids and arrests at the hands of game agents, but the events drew worldwide attention.

McCloud cofounded Women of All Red Nations (WARN), a sister group to the American Indian Movement in 1974. Also in 1974, she helped organize the first Spiritual Unity Gathering of the Iroquoian medicine men, White Roots of Peace, at Snoqualmie Falls. Soon after, she helped organize the Elder's Circle. In that same decade, she founded the Northwest Indian Women's Circle that assisted women in developing leadership skills based on traditional values. The organization focused on issues such as sterilization abuse and problems with the foster care placement and adoption of Indian children.

McCloud's roles of community leader, renowned activist, founder of many Native organizations, mother, grandmother, and great-grandmother prompted Choctaw son-in-law, Jimbo Simmons of the International Treaty Council, and Isadore Tom, Jr., of the Tulalip Tribes to speak to the family about a celebration honoring her achievements and compassion. Her son Mac McCloud said, "[Janet] was the only woman that would make the men try to do right and sit up and pay attention. Not too many people had that kind of respect, and he remembered that." McCloud's eight children stood right beside her as she fought for the fishing rights of Natives. They remember her strength and her generosity. Her fierce love for her people increased as the years went by. She was given the name "Yet-Si-Blue" in a ceremony, meaning "Woman Who Speaks Her Mind."

After her husband died of cancer in 1985, McCloud called their homestead "Sapa Dawn Center," meaning "grandfather dawn," in his honor as he taught young people how to live off the land. She envisioned it as a tranquil retreat for Native children to escape street and reservation life. Soon, hundreds of kids whom she "adopted" flocked there, learning to live in a natural way. In August 1985, hundreds of women from many countries met at Sapa Dawn Center and formed the Indigenous Women's Network, a coalition of Native women from Chile to Canada.

Ramona Bennett (1938–)
Puyallup, Fishing Rights Activist

Ramona Bennett, tribal leader and activist, was born and educated in Seattle and later at Evergreen State College in Olympia, Washington, and the University of Puget Sound, then moved to the Puyallup Indian Reservation in the 1950s, where her mother had grown up. Determined to improve housing, education, health care, and lack of jobs on the reservation, Bennett was elected to the Puyallup Tribal Council in the 1960s. One year, Bennett, who became an effective advocate for the tribe, took more than thirty trips to Washington, D.C. The council could not always afford round-trip plane fare, so she sometimes had to make the three-thousand-mile trip home by hitchhiking.

One of the greatest problems facing the Puyallup in the late 1960s involved their right to fish in the Puyallup River. Because of the high unemployment on the reservation, many Puyallup depended on fishing for their livelihood just as their ancestors had. Non-Indian commercial fishermen, however, were also setting traps in the river. Conservationists became concerned that the fish population was in danger of extinction, largely because of the concerns of commercial overfishing. They persuaded the state of Washington to ban the use of fishing traps in the river's waters, which violated the 1855 Treaty of Point Elliott. The treaty guaranteed local Indians unrestricted use of their reservation resources.

In 1970, non-Indian law-enforcement agents cracked down on Puyallup fishers who ignored the ban. The agents harassed the Indians, confiscated their traps, hauled them off to jail, and even tried to run them over with their powerboats. A group of Puyallup, including Bennett, responded by setting up an armed camp on the riverbank. After a ten-week standoff, agents raided the camp and used tear gas and clubs to subdue the protesters. Bennett was assaulted and, with fifty-nine others, taken to jail and accused of inciting a riot.

The case made international news, and the brutal treatment of the Puyallup was denounced around the world. The U.S. Department of the Interior, which oversaw reservations, examined the Indians' claims to fishing rights on the river. The morning that Bennett's trial was set to begin, the interior secretary stated that the Puyallup owned the land and its resources and that the agents had trespassed on the Indians' territory. The case against Bennett was promptly thrown out of court.

In 1972, Bennett was elected the chairperson of the Puyallup Tribal Council, making her one of the few female tribal leaders in the United States. Although traditionally, women had had leadership roles in many Indian groups, she frequently had to overcome the sexist attitudes of her colleagues. During her eight-year stint as chair of the Puyallup reservation, Bennett made education and health care her highest priorities. She later devoted herself to helping minority children in need. She served as an educational administrator at the Wa-He-Lut Indian School in Olympia and has headed the Rainbow Youth and Family Services, which concentrates on placing homeless minority children in foster and adoptive homes with adults of the same race.

In honor of her work with children and families, the Native Action Network gave Bennett the Enduring Spirit Award in 2003.

Sandra Sunrising Osawa (1941–)
Makah Nation, Filmmaker

Sandra Sunrising Osawa has been an independent producer longer than any other Native American in the country. She was the first Native American independent to produce for commercial television with an information series on Native Americans that aired in 1975 on NBC. She was the recipient of an Outstanding Producer Award for the ten-part series. For decades, Osawa has produced films that accurately portray Indian stories and history from an Indigenous point of view.

Osawa and her husband, Yasu, founded their own production company, Upstream Productions, in Seattle in 1980, which has produced over fifty videos for museums, tribes, and organizations. Some of their most notable films include *Lighting the 7th Fire*, about spearfishing rights in Wisconsin, and *Usual and Accustomed Places*, an in-depth look at treaty issues in the Northwest. In addition, the Osawas present contemporary images of Indian people like portraits of jazz musician Jim Pepper (Kaw) and comedian Charlie Hill (Oneida).

Osawa was raised in Washington State on the Olympic Peninsula. She received a Bachelor of Arts degree from Lewis and Clark College in Portland, Oregon, and was honored with the Distinguished Alumna Award from her alma mater in February 2010. She did graduate work at UCLA's School of Theater, Film and Television and at the Universities of Washington and Oregon.

Hank Adams (1943–)

Assiniboine/Sioux, Fishing Rights Activist

Hank Adams threw himself into the fishing rights struggle in Washington. Born on the Fort Peck Indian Reservation in Montana, Adams grew up on the Quinault Reservation after his mother married a Quinault man. He graduated with honors from Moclips High School and went to the University of Washington but became a self-taught expert of Indian law, serving as lay counsel with such distinction that people assumed he held a law degree.

In 1964, Adams helped organize the march on Olympia in Washington State, which had the purpose of protesting the state attack on Indian treaty fishing rights. Adams became executive director of the Survival of American Indians Association in 1968 and under his administration, Survival led the tribes' public relations and legal strategy. He fought against state fishing regulations on the Nisqually River in Washington, and for his actions, he was arrested often between 1968 and 1971. He was shot in the stomach while he was out protesting on the river but continued in the struggle for Indian fishing rights in Washington until the issue was resolved. Without Adams's contributions, many people feel there would have been no landmark court case, *U.S. v. Washington* (known as the *Boldt* decision).

Adams played a key role in the 1972 Trail of Broken Treaties Caravan, which ended with the siege of the Bureau of Indian Affairs building in Washington, D.C. Adams wrote the trail's Twenty-Point Proposal presented to the White House. The plan called on the federal government to reopen treaty making, among other things. Adams was among those credited with resolving the seventy-one-day siege at Wounded Knee, South Dakota, in 1973. The activist Vine Deloria, Jr., called Adams "the most important Native American in the country," and Adams is the subject of a book of essays and letters compiled by David E. Wilkins (Lumbee) and published in 2011: *The Hank Adams Reader: An Exemplary Native Activist and the Unleashing of Indigenous Sovereignty.*

Richard E. Bartow (1946–)

Yurok/Wiyot, Artist

From Newport, Oregon, Bartow is world renowned for his drawings, paintings, and wood sculptures rooted in Native American transformation tales. Two of his massive totem poles welcome visitors to the National Museum of the American Indian in Washington, D.C.

Gloria Bird (1951–)

Spokane, Poet

Gloria Bird, born in Washington State, is an award-winning poet and writer. She received her bachelor's degree in English from Lewis and Clark College in Portland, Oregon, and her master's degree in literature from the University of Arizona. She is one of the founding members of the Northwest Native American Writers Association and was a contributing editor for *Wicazo Sa Review*. Bird's poetry, prose, literary criticism, and autobiographical essays often center on how the representations of Native peoples, both by themselves and others, can facilitate harmful stereotypes. She has argued, for example, that the portrayal of alcoholism in Indian communities is often exaggerated and that this can contribute to the problem instead of combating it. One of her main goals as a writer, she said, is "to interrogate damaging stereotypes" and to portray her community in a way that is accurate but not exploitative. She has emphasized that her writing records only one woman's experience, not a collective Native identity.

Gloria Bird received a Diane Decorah Memorial Award in 1992 for her book of poetry, *Full Moon on the Reservation*, and an Oregon Writer's Grant from the Oregon Institute of Literary Arts in 1988. Check out Bird's writings in "Autobiography as Spectacle: An Act of Liberation or the Illusion of Liberation?" in *Here First: Autobiographical Essays by Native American Writers*, edited by Arnold Krupat and Brian Swann (New York: Modern Library, 2000) and "Breaking the Silence: Writing as 'Witness'" in *Speaking for the Generations: Native Writers on Writing*, edited by Simon J. Ortiz (Tucson: University of Arizona Press, 1998).

Joe Feddersen (1953–)
Colville, Artist

Joe Feddersen is a sculptor, painter, photographer, and mixed-media artist. He is known for creating artworks strong in geometric patterns reflective of what is seen in the environment, landscape, and his Native heritage. Besides his work as a printmaker and sculptor in glass and fiber mediums, he is a writer, lecturer, and teacher.

Feddersen's work has been presented in solo exhibitions in numerous venues. He received the Eiteljorg Fellowship for Native Fine Art in 2001.

Elizabeth Woody (1959–)
Warm Springs, Poet

Elizabeth Woody, an award-winning poet, studied at the Institute of American Indian Arts

(IAIA) in Santa Fe, New Mexico, and Evergreen State College in Olympia, Washington. In 2012, she received a Master of Public Administration degree through the Executive Leadership Institute of the Mark O. Hatfield School of Government at Portland State University in Portland, Oregon. From 1994 to 1996, Woody was a professor of creative writing at the IAIA. In 1992, she was an invited writer at the Returning the Gift Festival of Native Writers and a featured poet at the Geraldine R. Dodge Poetry Festival. She is a board member of Soapstone, Inc., an organization dedicated to providing a writing retreat for women. Woody has worked in various programs teaching workshops, mentoring, and as a consultant and lectures throughout the country.

Woody received an American Book Award in 1990 for her book *Hand into Stone* from the Before Columbus Foundation. In 1993, she received a Medicine Pathways for the Future Fellowship/Kellogg Fellowship from the American Indian Ambassadors Program of the Americans for Indian Opportunity. She is a recipient of the William Stafford Memorial Award for Poetry from the Pacific Northwest Bookseller's Association and was a finalist in the Oregon Book Awards in poetry for *Luminaries of the Humble* in 1995.

Jewell Praying Wolf James
Lummi, Master Carver

Master carver Jewell Praying Wolf James has been working with wood since childhood when he learned traditional carving from his family. A citizen of the Lummi Nation in northwestern Washington State, James continued totem carving while at the University of Washington.

James prefers to carve totem poles from western red cedar trees that are at least five hundred years old. Western red cedar is a lightweight wood that resists decay and naturally repels insects. Before the ancient trees are cut and taken to his workshop, James makes a prayer ceremony to bless them for allowing him to remove one from the forest. A single totem pole from one of these trees can take up to one thousand hours for James and his assistants to carve and paint using a combination of traditional and modern techniques.

Shortly after the 2001 destruction of the World Trade Center, Jewell Praying Wolf James, from the House of Tears Carvers of the Lummi Nation, began a totem pole project with the intent to help heal people suffering from the experience of 9/11. James and the Lummi Nation, working with several other tribes, created totem poles representing *healing, honoring, liberty,* and *freedom.* The completed Healing Poles Project is comprised of five poles raised at the three attack sites where planes crashed on 9/11: the World Trade Center, the Pentagon, and the flight that crashed in Shanksville, Pennsylvania.

James carved a totem for a journey the Lummi Nation embarked on called "Our Shared Responsibility—the Land, the Waters, the People" to call attention to the proposed shipment of an unprecedented volume of coal and oil from the American heartland to the Pacific Coast. The Lummi Nation has led the opposition to the Gateway Pacific coal export terminal proposed for Cherry Point, Washington. The tribe launched the Totem Pole Journey on August 17, 2014, to unite tribes across the U.S. and Canada and to create greater awareness of the environmental and cultural impacts of coal and oil transportation. For his commitment to building bridges of understanding among Native tribes and federal and state agencies as well as private sector groups seeking ways to protect forest lands, he is the subject of a documentary, *Jewell James: Walking in Two Worlds.*

Shaun Peterson (1975–)
Puyallup, Painter/Carver

Peterson is a painter, print maker, and wood sculptor creating works based on ancient art traditions of Salish-speaking tribal groups (like the Puyallup) that cover the southern regions of western Washington State and southern British Columbia, Canada. Like his ancestors, he sought out guidance of master artisans like Haida artist Bruce Cook III and Makah artist Greg Colfax. Peterson also studied museum collections to learn about Salish art. His early work was related to ceremony in the form of painted drums, rattles, and masks. Later works integrate more nontraditional media into his art, such as glass and metal, while maintaining the features that make the art culturally identifiable.

Peterson's first major public installation came in his first year of training, a thirty-seven-foot story pole for Chief Leschi School in 1996, followed by commissions in Tacoma and Seattle, Washington. Peterson is perhaps best known for his "Welcome Figure," the carved Native Northwest female figure standing twenty feet high above Tollefson Plaza in downtown Tacoma. He has created works for the Elders building and other tribal buildings in his community.

Shoni Schimmel (1992–)
Umatilla Reservation, Basketball Player

Shoni Schimmel is a five-foot-ten professional basketball player who grew up on the Umatilla Indian Reservation. She was an All-American college player at the University of Louisville and a first-round draft pick of the WNBA's Atlanta Dream. Schimmel has said that she has always been obsessed with basketball. By age two, she was allowed to dribble freely around the house. At four, she played in her first tournament. By ten or twelve, she said, she sometimes shot outside until three in the morning. Her parents knew she was safe "because they could hear me dribbling."

Although basketball has long been the most popular sport on Indian reservations, seldom has that esteem translated into great performance in the highest college and professional ranks. An NCAA study indicated that during the 2011–2012 academic year, only twenty-one women and four men identified as American Indian/Alaska Native participated among the 10,151 basketball players at the Division I level.

Schimmel was the subject of Jonathan Hock's film called *Off the Res,* which chronicled her journey to earn an NCAA scholarship. She transferred from Hermiston High School in eastern

Oregon to the larger Franklin High School in Portland, Oregon, to increase her chances of being recruited to a Division school. After her senior year at Franklin, Schimmel was named a first team All-American by *Parade* magazine.

Schimmel was selected to the 2010 Women's Basketball Coaches Association High School Coaches' All-America Team. She participated in the 2010 WBCA High School All-America Game, scoring six points. She chose Louisville for college and became a four-year starter for the Cardinals. As a junior, Schimmel led the team to the championship game of the 2013 tournament. In her senior season, Schimmel averaged 17.1 points per game to lead the team in scoring and was named an All-American by the USWA and Associated Press. She also earned recognition as the 2014 WNBA All-Star Game Most Valuable Player on July 19, 2014, in Phoenix, Arizona.

Schimmel's younger sister, Jude (1993–), a point guard, began shooting hoops with her big sister, Shoni, at age four. She and Shoni remained unstoppable as teammates through high school (their mom was the coach) and also played for University of Louisville with a 3.5 grade point average. As a role model for younger Native Americans, Jude has shared her story in dozens of speaking engagements at reservations in North Dakota, South Dakota, Mississippi, Wisconsin, New Mexico, Arizona, and Oregon. She tells Native American kids about higher education, "I'd like to write a book to show them that whatever I'm doing, and whatever Shoni's doing, it's very, very possible for all of them to do it as well. A lot of people look up to athletes, but when you can see somebody with the student and the athlete part of it, I think it says a lot."

CALIFORNIA

It seemed they had one thing in mind, and that was to get into the gold fields, and they did, and it didn't make any difference how they got in and what was in the road or anything. They just went rushing right through the whole thing, tore [Indian houses] down, tore up villages.

—Axel Roderick Lindgren, Jr. (Yurok elder)

HOW CALIFORNIA INDIAN TRIBES BECAME "EXTINCT" (NOT REALLY)

Despite the declaration by anthropologists, historians, and other writers that several California Indian tribes and cultures are extinct, it is well known among Native peoples that many of these groups are not in fact gone.

In his book, *Abalone Tales: Collaborative Explorations of Sovereignty and Identity in Native California Anthropology*, Professor Les W. Field writes that in addition to suffering the burden of an anthropological extinction sentence, some Native peoples have also suffered from official erasure since they have not been accorded federal or state recognition. Between the work of anthropologists and the machinery of the state, California's unrecognized tribes have endured many decades of collective social and cultural invisibility. In the *Handbook of the Indians of California* (1925), influential American anthropologist Alfred Kroeber declared that certain Native peoples were "extinct."

Among the Native groups Kroeber declared extinct are the Ohlonean-speaking peoples. The tribal entity that represents them today is called the Muwekma Ohlone Tribe. It is comprised of all the known surviving American Indian lineages aboriginal to the San Francisco Bay region who trace their ancestry through three Bay Area missions: Dolores, Santa Clara, and San Jose.

Kroeber also declared the Esselen-speaking people of the Monterey region culturally extinct. On the contrary, according to the Esselen Tribe of Monterey County, there is evidence that some Esselen escaped the missions entirely by retreating to the rugged interior mountains. It now appears that a small group survived into the 1840s before filtering to the ranchos and the outskirts of the growing towns. Their descendants today carry on Esselen traditions.

Kroeber declared that the Fernandeño Indians were "practically extinct." The Fernandeño Tataviam Band of Mission Indians, located in the San Fernando, Santa Clarita, and Antelope Valleys, declares that it has continued as a kinship-based social and political group from the 1700s to the present. It "is one of those Indigenous communities that will persist into the indefinite future whether the United States government recognizes them or not. The Fernandeño Tataviam Band of Mission Indians have demonstrated significant internal recognition, community continuity, and identity for over two centuries and a long and consistent stream of recognized leaders and community-based political process."

Several bands of Gabrielino Tongva, who lived in the Los Angeles Basin for thousands of years, and several bands of Juaneno Indians of Southern California are among other tribes that the federal government doesn't recognize. Besides these groups, other tribes terminated in 1966 are seeking reinstatement or recognition.

ANCIENT TIMES

Academics speculate about where early humans came from, maybe from Asia by boat, maybe across the Bering Strait by land or ice bridge, who then migrated southward. Native peoples of California believe they originated in North America. Native storytellers narrate the story of their origin, and elders even point out actual places that the stories tell about.

At least 15,000 years ago, glaciers covered the mountains and the high valleys of California. Now extinct huge mammals, like the mammoth, saber-toothed cat, and giant buffalo, roamed the chilly and moist landscape. Between 14,000 and ten thousand years ago, the glaciers retreated, and their melting waters raised the sea level. Warmer temperatures dried up immense lakes in low-lying areas and formed deserts. Huge mammals disappeared.

A BIRD'S EYE VIEW

The California of today evolved into a place with many geographic regions in close proximity. (The number of regions differ, depending on the source.) The California climate varies dramatically from north to south. The northern up-

At the time when people migrated into what is now California about 15,000 years ago, animals such as this mammoth lived in the chilly landscape.

lands receive the greatest amount of precipitation, especially in winter, while further south, it is much drier. The coast, a strip of land more than 1,300 miles long, lies between the Pacific Ocean and the Coast Ranges.

Mountain ranges cover much of California. Two major mountain ranges are the Sierra Nevada and the Coast Ranges. The foothills of the Sierra Nevada, located in the eastern part of the state, comprised much of California's Gold Rush trail. The Coast Ranges of California span two-thirds of the state of California and extend 550 to six hundred miles along its coast from the Northern California redwood coast to Santa Barbara.

The northern mountains get lots of rain and snow that feeds streams and rivers. The Central Valley in the center of California is more than four hundred miles long and about fifty miles wide. The Central Valley's rich soil and long growing season make it a good place to raise fruits, vegetables, and grains, but little rain in the summer means people had to build dams, channels, and ditches to bring water. California's deserts lie east of the mountains, which block moisture from the ocean and receive the rain. The Mojave Desert, the state's largest, contains Death Valley, where plants and animals may bake in 115-degree summer heat.

In the varied ecological zones found throughout the state, Native people used the resources in the environment to feed, shelter, and clothe themselves. The land was threaded with many small streams and large rivers, which provided water for drinking, processing wood, cooking, and washing. In many places, large forests provided timber for building and wood for fires.

California regions supplied plenty of food. In the foothills and forests, huge groves of oak trees bore acorns. The coastal waters, tidelands, rivers, and lakes were teeming with salmon trout, clams, oysters, mussels, otters, and sea lions. The valleys and plains offered a year-round menu of seeds, fruits, berries, herbs, and small game. Deer and other game roamed through the woodlands. Even the dessert offered small game and cactus fruit, mesquite beans, and, when watered, cultivated plants.

Food Resource: Acorns

For thousands of years, life revolved around acorns for the majority of California Native peoples, who relied on them for food on a daily basis. The nutritional value of acorns is high, and they are a good source of vitamins A and C and many essential amino acids. Most Native people had little trouble gathering them because some sources say sixteen (other sources eighteen) species of oak, each with its own kind of acorn, grew throughout the state. Californian Native people harvested most acorn species, but they also have their preferences. Many Pomo people have preferred Tan Oak because they feel it has more flavor. The Cahuilla favored Black Oak, Coast Live Oak, and Canyon Oak because the trees produced a lot of acorns and were palatable. Many

Miwuk like Black Oak because it takes less leaching to get rid of tannin acid, a chemical that makes the acorn bitter and unpalatable (and poisonous in large amounts) to humans. Each Native group had its own oak groves within its homelands, and individual families might put ownership marks on several trees. A single large oak tree produces an annual crop of hundreds of pounds a year.

For several weeks during the harvesting season, women and men went into the groves from sunup to sundown, gathering fallen acorns from the ground and knocking them from trees with sticks. Some people climbed the tree and then beat off the nuts with a slender pole. Women gathered the acorns into large burden baskets and transported them to villages for processing. Women made large, squirrel-proof baskets to store quantities of acorns for long periods of time.

Long ago, converting the acorn from an inedible nut high up in an oak tree to soup, mush, or bread required a lengthy process. The acorns needed to be gathered and then dried in their shells, which could take anywhere from a few weeks to a few months. Once dry, the acorns were cracked to remove the nut meat, traditionally done with a stone pestle. The nuts were ground and pounded as fine as possible into flour or meal. The meal was sifted in a basket repeatedly; coarser meal was returned to the mortar for more pounding. Hours of repeated flushing with hot water leached the tannin acid from the acorn flour. Heated stones were used for cooking the leached acorns into a soup, mush, biscuits, or flat bread.

Today, California Indian peoples still consider acorn use important in sustaining their cultural identities, even though it is no longer an everyday food item. Although processing techniques have changed (electric blenders do the processing work of mortar and pestle, buckets replace baskets, and metal pots replace hot stones), acorns persist as a cultural connection between the past and present and a celebration of traditional ways. In a book titled *It Will Live Forever: Traditional Yosemite Indian Acorn Preparation*,

The fishing waters surrounding the Channel Islands off the coast of southern California were a rich source of food for the Indians who first settled in the area.

Coast Miwok/Pomo elder Julia Parker describes why she makes acorns: "I know that lots of times I think, 'Why do I do this? We don't eat it every-day. Why should I do it?' But ... it's a special food. It was life to them in the earlier years, and it is still life to a lot of us who want to learn the ways."

General Food Resources

Northern coastal tribes fished, hunted sea mammals, and collected tidelands resources. Riverine and lakeshore dwelling groups hunted, trapped, and fished. Central Valley, Plains, and foothill tribes hunted and gathered wild food-stuffs. The greatest variety of regional lifeways and economic activities were found in Southern California. The Channel Islands, near present-day Los Angeles, and adjacent coasts were rich in sea-associated resources. Inland groups hunted and col-

lected while tribes living along the Colorado River, and a few neighboring groups, practiced the only agriculture found in Native California.

At the time of the first contact with Europeans (c. 1540), the population of the California Indians was approximately 310,000 to 340,000 people. These astounding numbers made it the most densely populated area in what is now the United States. The mild climate and abundance of wild foods proved more than adequate sustenance for such a population.

SOCIAL ORGANIZATION

Social organization among this population varied. Large tribes like the San Joaquin Valley Yokut and the Yuman along the Colorado River are examples of tribes that have shared a common language and possessed a well-defined territory and a degree of political unity. More common was the organization of populations that were essentially village centered. These groups, too, possessed well-defined territories that ranged in size from one hundred to five hundred persons. Several villages displayed allegiance to one large, central village where the headman or chief resided. Although neither type of social organization permitted chiefs more than limited ceremonial authority, they were most often wise and influential individuals who could galvanize community action if supported by various types of councils made up of lineage elders. While female chiefs were not unknown, the majority were men whose succession to office was hereditary. Other authority figures included a religious practitioner, who was a combination of physician, psychologist, herbalist, and family lineage head. Social and economic stratification existed to a varying degree throughout aboriginal California, but it was most pronounced in northwestern California, which in many ways resembled the hierarchical and ordered societies of the Pacific North area.

LANGUAGES

The Indigenous peoples of California had amazing language diversity before European contact. Native people spoke about three hundred distinct dialects of an estimated one hundred different languages. The languages can be divided into six (some say seven) language family groups. Some California groups, like the Yurok, speak a language of the Algonquian family of eastern North America. Some, like the Hupa, speak a language from the Athabascan family. The Cahuilla, Cupeno, Luiseno, and others speak a language from the Uto-Aztecan family. The Chumash, Pomo, and Yahi speak Hokan languages more commonly found in the Southwest. Speakers of the Penutian languages, the Maidu, Miwok, Wintun, Yokut, and others, have linguistic relatives in British Columbia.

According to Anthropology Professor Les Field, "Even in a state distinguished by extraordinary linguistic diversity, northwestern California is remarkable. Wiyot and Yurok are Algonquian languages. "Tolowa and Hupa are Athabascan; Karuk and Shasta are Hokan, yet these peoples, speaking languages as different as Zulu, Chinese, and Armenian, share many cultural practices, among them a cycle of dance rituals and life cycle ceremonies, with accompanying narratives, that together compose what is often referred to (by both Natives and anthropologists) as the "World Renewal religion."

Linguistic scholars note that the Athabascan language family migrated south from the Pacific North, and the Algonquian language family originated on the Atlantic Coast. The scholars note that the Hokan, Penutian, and Uto-Aztecan language families were truly ancient and Indigenous languages of California.

The Yuki group spoke Yukian, a language family of its own, related to no other. Anthropologists say that Yukian was among six other extremely ancient language families in the world that are related to no other. Scholars say that Yukian no longer has any viable spoken languages left.

CALIFORNIA NATIVE WORLDVIEW

California Native worldview centered typically around seeking a balance between the physical and spiritual well-being of the extended family and tribe. Such balance in both spheres is best understood in terms of reciprocity. For instance, individuals and villages made offerings to the Creator and earth spirits and, in return, expected a favorable relationship between themselves and the natural elements, such as access to game animals, wild foods, favorable winds, sufficient rain, fertility, and the like. Similarly, reciprocity formed the basis for economic relationships among individuals, extended families, and neighboring villages. Each group's territory and its resources were jealously guarded. Trespassing and poaching were serious offenses and were the principal causes of intergroup conflicts that periodically erupted.

EUROPEAN CONTACT

The arrival of Europeans in California illustrates the profoundly different worldviews that clashed as various European empires scrambled to exploit the resources and peoples of the Americas. The story of one of the earliest European encounters illustrates this point well. In 1579, the English explorer Francis Drake anchored somewhere off the Sonoma County coast, in present-day Northern California.

English understandings of that encounter included a number of erroneous assumptions. Records of the Drake expedition refer to the headman of the local Indians as a "king," implying a Europeanlike, highly centralized office of authority that could control both subjects' land and lives. In fact, no such offices of authority existed anywhere in Native California societies. The English also claim this "king" gladly surrendered all of "his" territory and sovereignty to an unknown ruler half a world away. Finally, the English concluded that the Coast Miwok regarded them as "gods." The Coast Miwok, on the other hand, viewed all material objects of the pale strangers who arrived on their shores with fear and refused to accept the newcomers' gifts. At the same time, they offered gifts of baskets, food, and other ritual objects. Following a five-week stay, the newcomers departed, still baffled by the odd reception offered them by the otherwise hospitable people.

SPANISH COLONIZATION: MISSIONS

Permanent colonization created a catastrophe of indescribable proportions for the Indians of California. Spanish colonization began in earnest in 1769, with the establishment of a mission in the Native village of Cosoy, later called San Diego by the newcomers. The Spanish institutions of colonization were the military presidios (or forts) to protect the Franciscan missionaries and later the Hispanic colonists, who established pueblos (civilian towns).

It was the missions, however, that had the greatest impact on the Native population. The Spanish empire's plan was to reduce the numerous free and independent Native villages and societies into a mass of peon laborers. To accomplish this goal, the padres created a six-hundred-mile-long chain of twenty-one missions, with two of them on the Colorado River in the extreme southeastern tip of the state and a string along the coast from San Diego to Sonoma in the north. These institutions were much more than churches. When fully functional, they resembled Caribbean plantations. Under Spanish law, once baptized, the neophytes, as the Indians were called, would be compelled to move from their Native villages into designated areas adjacent to the mission.

Between 1769 and 1836, about eighty thousand California Indians were baptized and subjected to the mission labor and evangelization programs of the Spanish Empire. Once baptized, Indians were not allowed to leave the missions,

Missions like this one in Santa Barbara were established all over what is now California when the Spanish colonized the area in the eighteenth century. The missions worked to convert Indians to Catholicism and to turn them into laborers.

and those who did were rounded up by soldiers and returned. The Indians were forced to shed their languages, dress, religion, food, and marriage customs. Thousands died from exposure to European diseases, to which they had no immunity.

At the missions, the Indians could be more closely controlled. At the age of five or six, the neophyte children were removed from their families and locked in dormlike barracks under the vigilance of padres. This served the dual purpose of indoctrinating the children and ensuring that their parents would not attempt to oppose colonial authority. Indian girls were locked up when not laboring or attending religious services, were freed only after marriage, and, if widowed, were again confined in the female barracks until remarriage or death. Adults were compelled to labor without pay. The soldiers and padres instituted floggings, incarceration, and various labor punishments to compel Native acquiescence to Spanish authority. Neither women nor children were exempt from beatings and other forms of subjugation. One Costanoan Indian neophyte named Lorenzo Asisara reported, "We were always trembling with fear of the lash."

Junípero Serra

Junípero Serra (1713–1784), a Franciscan missionary, was considered the architect of the California missions and founded the first one, San Diego de Alcala, in 1769. Inspector-General Jose Galvez, who had been sent to Mexico to effect administrative reforms, requested that Serra convert Indians of the northern regions (Upper California) to Christianity for the Spanish crown. After founding San Diego de Alcala, Serra founded eight more by 1782, laying the groundwork for the entire chain of missions. Serra prescribed in detail written regulations about the daily routine to be followed at each mission. He condoned lashing Indians who disobeyed.

Efforts to sanctify Junípero Serra began in the mid-1700s, spearheaded by Catholic clergy and laypeople. California Indians and others, including historians, opposed Serra's being declared a saint, arguing that he oversaw the system that uprooted Native peoples, seized their homelands, forced conversions, and worked Indians for no pay. Other historians argue that some of the allegations are untrue or exaggerated. In 1985, Serra was declared venerable. In 1988, he was beatified.

On September 23, 2015, Pope Francis canonized Father Junípero Serra during a mass outside the Basilica of the National Shrine of the Immaculate Conception, the largest Catholic church in North America. Many of the people descended from those who first encountered Serra have a starkly different view of the Spanish friar and protested this action by the pope.

Ron Andrade (Luiseno), executive director of the Los Angeles City/County Native American Indian Commission, said Serra "decimated ninety percent of the Indian population.... Everywhere they put a mission, the majority of Indians are gone, and Serra knew what they were doing: they were taking the land, taking the crops, he knew the soldiers were raping women, and he turned his head." Many tribes, including the Luiseños, Juaneño, and Gabrielino-Tongva, survived the mission era through partial integration with each other and Spanish culture, but others fled inland or lost their culture completely, Andrade said.

"Serra was not the face of evil," says Deborah Miranda, Ohlone Costanoan Esselen Indian, a professor of literature at Washington and Lee Universities, "but there were so many atrocities happening, and he closed his eyes." "I don't think he should be rewarded for that." For Miranda, Serra's complicity outweighs whatever intentions he had. He was driven by ambition, she said, and in his desire to produce results for Spain, he "laid the groundwork to erase our cultures and impose this burden of shame on Indians about being Indian."

Archbishop Salvatore J. Cordileone of San Francisco said he understood why Indians were upset with the Pope's plan to canonize Father Serra. He said that in history, a more powerful civilization "will dominate and seek to transform the weaker one. European powers were going to discover the continent and settle here. Were the Indigenous people better off with the missionar-

Franciscan missionary Junípero Serra founded the first mission in California: San Diego de Alcala, in 1769.

ies or without the missionaries? I would say they were better off with the missionaries."

Professor Steven Hackel of the University of California, Riverside and author of *Junípero Serra: California's Founding Father* said: "It was a very difficult time for California Indians.... Serra didn't believe you could beat Catholicism into an Indian, but he saw them as children, and in the early modern period, good fathers corrected their kids through corporal punishment. I'm not trying to let Serra off the hook, but we need to understand how he understood the world."

Native Resistance to Missions

The missions were only supposed to exist for ten years, a time limit the Spanish Crown deemed sufficient to convert the Indians into a disciplined and subservient labor force for a small elite of Spanish males. Considerable resistance erupted among the "converts" to the harsh meas-

ures of the missions. As Spanish borderlands historian David Weber observed, "Oppressed in body and spirit, many mission Indians sought ways to extricate themselves from the loving embrace of the sons of St. Francis."

Three types of resistance developed to the nightmare that Native groups experienced. The first and most prevalent form of resistance was passive. Many mission Indians either refused to learn Spanish or feigned ignorance of commands given in that language. Slow and poorly performed labor was widely reported and can be seen today in the construction and work of the old missions. Native laborers covertly drew traditional Indian symbols on fired floor tiles and other surfaces throughout the mission's buildings. Both infanticide and abortions were practiced by Native women unwilling to give birth to children conceived through sexual assaults by the soldiers or to supply a new generation of laborers for the colonists. A fascinating aspect of passive resistance was the periodic outbreak of covert Native religious activities to reverse baptisms or offer solace to the terrified masses of neophytes.

Escaping from the Franciscan labor mills seemed to be the best solution once the unsavory and oppressive nature of mission life was evident, but Spanish law and Franciscan practice permitted the soldiers to pursue runaway Indians. The padres kept detailed records of baptized Indians for each village, and squads of soldiers stationed at each mission routinely patrolled the surrounding territories. Furthermore, Native traditions forbade anyone not belonging to a village from demanding refuge there. Non-Christian villages soon learned that if they did offer refuge to runaways, they risked military assaults and hostage taking. Worse still, the fugitives infected non-Christian village populations with the new diseases contracted at the missions. Murderous waves of epidemic diseases and the general poor health of the neophyte population kept many from even attempting the physical rigors of flight. Nevertheless, thousands of Indian neophytes fled. However, only about 10 percent, or about eight thousand, escaped the missions.

Overt resistance to Spanish domination took several forms. A type of guerrilla warfare became prevalent before 1820. Charismatic and talented ex-neophytes like the Coast Miwok Pomponio and the Northern Valley Yokut Estanislao organized stock-raiding attacks against mission, presidio, and civilian herds of cattle, horses, and sheep.

Individuals and groups of mission Indians sometimes poisoned the padres. Four padres were poisoned at Mission San Miguel, and one of them died in 1801. In 1811, a San Diego neophyte killed a padre with poison. The next year, Indians at Mission Santa Cruz smothered and castrated a padre there for making an especially terrifying new torture instrument and being unwise enough to announce he would employ it the next Sunday. In 1836, Southern California Cahuilla Indians kidnapped the padre at Mission San Gabriel and horsewhipped him as so many of their tribesmen had been whipped.

Mission Indian insurrections were spectacular, and several occurred. The earliest revolt occurred at Mission San Diego in October 1775 when one thousand Kumeyaay warriors sacked and burned the mission and killed the padre. In 1781, the Quechan Indians living along the banks of the Colorado River utterly destroyed two missions established in their territory just the previous year. In that rebellion, they killed fifty-five colonists, including four padres, thirty-one soldiers, and twenty civilians. That military action by Quechan Indians prevented access to the only known overland route to California from Mexico for the remainder of the Spanish era.

In 1785, San Gabriel Mission neophytes, organized by a female spiritual leader called Toypurina, were thwarted in their attempt to destroy the mission and kill the padres. At her trial, the defiant holy woman declared, "I hate the padres and all of you for living here on my native soil … for trespassing upon the lands of my forefathers and despoiling our tribal domains."

That sentiment provoked the last large-scale revolt by mission Indians. The Chumash Indians of the Santa Barbara coast had endured nearly three decades of colonization when, in 1824, neo-

The San Gabriel Mission was attacked by spiritual leader Toypurina and her followers in 1785.

phytes from missions Santa Barbara, San Ynez, and La Purisima rose en masse to protect their lives and regain their lost freedom and sovereignty. A pitched battle ensued at Mission Santa Barbara and then the Indians fled. Santa Ynez neophytes also abandoned their mission and joined the others from Santa Barbara at Mission La Purisima, which they took over for longer than a month.

Although most of the rebellious Indians were eventually persuaded to surrender after a siege and full-scale assault by presidio troops using cannons, a significant number of them absolutely refused to return to the missions and instead sought refuge in the interior, where they issued this defiant message to colonial authorities who pleaded with them to return: "We shall maintain ourselves with what God will provide for us in the open country. Moreover, we are soldiers, stonemasons, carpenters, etc., and we will provide for ourselves by our work."

Diseases

It was the foreign diseases that ultimately destroyed the majority of Native peoples. Native Americans had no immunities to even the most common European childhood diseases. A series of murderous epidemics swept through the mission Indian populations from 1777 to 1833. Thousands of Indian men, women, and children succumbed to the previously unknown illnesses. When the missions finally collapsed in 1836, about one hundred thousand Indians had died.

CALIFORNIA UNDER MEXICAN RULE, 1820–1848

After a struggle with Spain, movement created the Mexican Republic (1821), and California became part of Mexico. In Mexico City, there was considerable support to end the mission system and the Catholic control of valuable properties. In 1831–1832, the missions were "secularized" by the Mexican government. Land was distributed to Indians but very quickly taken out of their hands and given to soldiers, settlers,

and others with influence. Many of the former mission churches became parish churches. The Church's landholdings (Alta California) were under the rule of the Mexican Republic until 1846.

The Mexican government forbade the Franciscan padres from demanding labor from the Indians. It allowed Indians to leave the missions, but corrupt officials conspired to prevent a distribution of developed lands to surviving ex-mission Indians. Those tribesmen whose homelands now included missions, presidios, and pueblos were nearly universally deprived of their lands and forced deeply into debt peonage, which resulted in further powerlessness. Many ex-neophytes fled into the interior or to their former tribal homelands, but the landscape had changed profoundly. The horses, mules, sheep, pigs, and goats introduced into the California biosphere ravaged the delicate Native grasses. The animals continued to multiply in alarming numbers. Mission agricultural practices began to systematically squeeze out Native vegetation. The California Indians were not able to live off the land as they were before Spanish colonization.

Some village populations had virtually disappeared from the face of the earth. So many lineages had been destroyed that the previous forms of aboriginal leadership no longer existed. Out of this political vacuum evolved new leaders, who assumed much more authority than had been previously allowed any single individual in aboriginal society. Some assumed the Spanish title of alcalde, or captain, and adapted aboriginal life to include the hunting and capturing of half-wild horses and mules, which provided food and valued trade items. Patterning their tactics on the mission Indian stock raiders of the recent past, a widespread and lucrative stock-raiding complex emerged in postmission California. Among these new leaders was an ex-neophyte Plains Miwok called Yozcolo, who terrorized the Hispanic military and civilian populations around southern San Francisco Bay until he was killed in battle near Los Gatos in 1839.

In Southern California, Cahuilla, Mohave, and Gabrielino peoples joined forces with New

Mexico mountain men in a decade-long series of raids that devastated the livestock of Californios (original Spanish colonists of California or their descendants). One spectacular raid in 1840 involved the theft of more than three thousand horses from ranches as far north as San Luis Obispo to San Juan Capistrano in the south. The Californios pursuing the stolen horses suffered the indignity of having their mounts stolen while resting. Having no choice, they walked across the desert until they were picked up by another group of Californios.

Despite a steady decline in the Native population throughout this period, the constant onslaught of stock raids began to push back interior Mexican outposts. After 1840, numerous interior ranches were abandoned under threat from the now well-mounted and armed groups of "horse thief Indians." By 1845, the Mexican government lost control of the actions of its own citizens. The authority of the Mexican Republic was about to collapse. Meanwhile, both disease and violence had taken a grim toll on Native lives. By 1845, little over one hundred thousand California Indians survived the Mexican Republic's occupation of their territories.

The Bear Flag Revolt and the Mexican War (1846–1848) brought momentous changes for the Native peoples of California. The majority of Indians who were involved in that conflict allied themselves with the Americans. Company H of the California Battalion was made up of Central Valley Miwok and Yokut warriors. In Southern California, loyalties were split. Some, like the Mountain Cahuilla Chief Juan Antonio, fought for the Mexican Republic while others participated on the U.S. side in the Battle for Los Angeles in 1847. However, the new U.S. occupation brought yet more death and labor exploitation to Native groups, whatever their loyalties.

CALIFORNIA GOLD RUSH, 1848–1860

Shortly after the Treaty of Guadalupe Hidalgo ended the Mexican–American War in 1848,

Alta California was annexed by the United States, and gold was discovered in the foothills of Sierra Nevada. A flood of gold miners descended upon California, inundating the state. By the end of 1849, about ninety thousand people had made their way to California, and conflicts between the newcomers and Natives ensured. Most of the Sierra Nevada Indigenous people had been only indirectly affected by Hispanic colonization efforts, which were concentrated along the coast, but now they would bear the brunt of an incredibly violent horde of intruders. Early in the gold rush, a few Indians were employed by miners or mined gold on their own. Soon, Indians found themselves hunted like wild game. According to L. L. Loud in the *Ethnography and Archaeology of the Wiyot Territory* (1918), "In fact, during the early mining days in California, there were gathered together some of the wildest, most reckless, savage, and dangerous men ever collected in a similar area anywhere in the world."

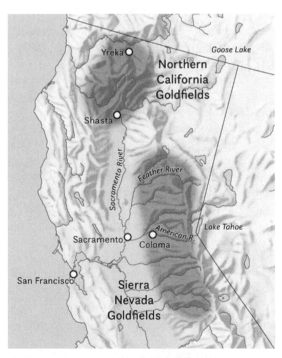

There were two major goldfields in California during the Gold Rush. Indians were often exploited for labor, and Natives were also removed from lands rich in gold in favor of prospectors.

Worse still was a series of California state laws passed in the mid-1850s. An act passed by the California legislature before California became a state on September 9, 1850, facilitated removing California Indians from their traditional lands and separated children and adults from their families, languages, and cultures. The final version of the law provided for "apprenticing" or indenturing of Indian children and adults to whites. The protection of California Indians' traditional practice of gathering acorns was not included in the final version of a law passed in 1850. Other early California state laws limited Native peoples' mobility, prohibited testimony in court against whites, revoked citizenship, and took their lands. As Peter H. Burnett, governor of California, put it in his January 7, 1851, address to the legislature: "That a war of extermination will continue to be waged between the two races until the Indian race becomes extinct must be expected; while we cannot anticipate this result with but painful regret, the inevitable destiny of the race is beyond the power and wisdom of man to avert."

At the same time, the federal government was negotiating treaties with California Indians (1851–1852). These treaties promised the Indians 7.5 million acres of land in exchange for surrendering the remainder of the state. A deluge of protests from non-Indian Californians fearing that the treaty lands might contain gold was sufficient to assure the treaties' defeat in the U.S. Senate, which must ratify all treaties. Afterward, the bewildered and now hunted Indians were subjected to the earliest form of reservation life. The federal government began establishing reservations in the state in 1851. They were located on military reserves where the Native population supposedly would be protected from U.S. citizens by the army. The government reserves in reality served fewer than two thousand Indians at any given time.

The vast majority of California Indians survived the best they could, withdrawing into remote and marginal areas and attempting to avoid contact with U.S. settlers, but violence against them continued by Euro-Americans who casually murdered individuals or formed vigilante groups, financed by local citizens, that hunted down and slaughtered Indians. In *Discovery of the Yosemite*, diary entries from 1851 described militias that actively hunted Indians and burned acorn caches and villages to starve and drive Indians out of the Sierras and foothills. The Hupa Indians of Northern California successfully fought vigilante and militia campaigns of their own until 1864 when they were granted a reservation of their own.

Wiyot Indian Island Massacre: 1860 and 2014

The Wiyot people living in Humboldt Bay (within present-day Eureka) were among the last Native people in California to encounter Euro-Americans. The gold rush era eventually led miners, farmers, ranchers, and loggers to pour onto Wiyot homelands. Relationships between the Natives and outsiders became hostile as intruders tried to eradicate Indians and take over their lands. On the night of February 26, 1860, six white men from the nearby city of Eureka went onto "Indian Island," less than a mile offshore from Eureka, while the World Renewal ceremonies were being held in the ancient village of Tulawat. Armed with hatchets, clubs, and knives, the men brutally murdered elders, women, children, and infants. (The men had left the island to replenish supplies.) That night, people in two other Wiyot villages were also massacred. It was estimated that vigilantes slaughtered almost 250 Wiyot people. The tribe was unable to finish its sacred ceremony.

Francis Bret Harte, a local reporter, wrote in 1860 that "[since] the women and children were unarmed, the murderers mostly saved their ammunition, instead hacking them to death with axes and knives." News about the murders was carried in newspapers across the United States. An investigation failed to identify a single perpetrator, and a grand jury failed to indict anyone. Because of his sympathetic account, Harte was threatened and quit his job. No action was ever taken against the men, locally "known landowners and businessmen," who were never charged. A sympathetic logging mill engineer reported, "We soon found that we had better keep our mouths shut." The attack led to a downward spiral for the

Wiyot. Soldiers rounded up the survivors and put them in the stockyards at Fort Humboldt. Deprived of shelter, nearly half died of exposure to constant rain and starvation. The survivors were removed again to three reservations although they kept escaping and returning to their homeland.

Efforts by Wiyot people to restore the Indian Island site of the massacre were ongoing since 2000. Under the leadership of Cheryl Seidner and her sister Leona Wilkinson, whose great-grandfather survived the massacre, the Wiyot of the late twentieth century conducted a determined campaign to repurchase land on the island, including the massacre site, and heal the psychic trauma caused by near-genocide. The Wiyots purchased and rehabilitated an acre and a half of the island in 2000. In a step toward making amends, the Eureka City Council transferred forty acres on Indian Island back to the Wiyot Tribe in 2004 and 2006, "the only city in California to return a sacred site to Native peoples." In addition, in March 2014, the city of Eureka issued a formal apology to the Wiyot Tribe, noting: "Nothing we can say or do can make up for what occurred on that night of infamy. It will forever be a scar on our history. We can, however, with our present and future actions of support for the Wiyot, work to remove the prejudice and bigotry that still exists in our society today."

One hundred fifty-four years after the massacre on Indian Island, the Wiyot Tribe's World Renewal Ceremony returned to the island the weekend of March 28–30, 2014. Tribal chairwoman Cheryl Seidner explained that during the ceremony, "We're healing the earth, we're healing the ground, we're healing each other, we're healing our families, our communities, our country, and to be so bold as that we're healing the world."

THE MODOC WAR OF 1872–1873

The Modoc Indians were moved from their homeland in northeastern California to share a reservation in Oregon with longtime rivals, the Klamaths. Outnumbered and bullied, the Modoc,

led by Kintpuash (Captain Jack) and Hooker Jim, returned to their homeland in 1870. The Modoc refusal to remain on the reservation ignited a bloody war, the last and largest war against the California Indians, in the treacherous lava beds of Northern California. Under the leadership of Captain Jack, fifty-two Modoc warriors and their families held off an army of over one thousand for nearly a year. In the end, Jack and three others surrendered and were hanged by orders of a paramilitary court. Captain Jack and three other fighters were executed and decapitated following their deaths; their heads were sent to Washington, D.C., and eventually wound up in the Smithsonian Institution. The skulls were collected, in part, to test a popular theory that cranium size was related to intellect and that Indians were inferior to whites. Scientists later rejected the theory—but not before the remains of at least four thousand Indians were stacked in the Army Medical Museum.

In the 1970s, descendants of Captain Jack learned that his skull was at the Smithsonian. In 1984, a determined Modoc woman and distant

An illustration from the May 3, 1873, issue of *Harper's Weekly* depicts Modocs in their stronghold as they fight to retake their ancestral land in California.

cousin of Captain Jack, marched into the Smith-sonian Institution to claim her people's history. The Smithsonian returned the remains to Kint-puash's relatives, along with the skulls of Boston Charley, Black Jim, Schonchin John, and an un-known woman from the Lava Beds.

GHOST DANCE RELIGIOUS MOVEMENT, 1870

By 1870, a new religious movement called the Ghost Dance swept west from Nevada, pre-dicting the end of the world and promising the return of dead relatives and the game animals. Desperate Natives who had experienced first-hand the appalling widespread death, violence, and starvation found the doctrines especially ap-pealing. The movement lasted about two years and revitalized sacred ceremonies among the Pomo, Patwin, and neighboring groups. It also developed a new class of spiritual leaders called dreamer doctors. Finally, the Ghost Dance proph-esy of the end of the world proved true, for the Indian world appeared to be gone.

It is no coincidence that the Ghost Dance swept through California when it did. Just prior to that event, the federal government had inau-gurated a new policy to reform the widespread corruption in the Office of Indian Affairs (re-named the Bureau of Indian Affairs, or BIA, in the late 1940s). Part of President Ulysses S. Grant's Peace Policy of 1869 called for the introduction of educational programs for Indian children. However, that policy once more unleashed hordes of missionaries upon the Indians to "save" them. Native ceremonies were outlawed on many reservations in a misguided effort to make Indi-ans adopt U.S. culture and lifeways.

FEDERAL POLICY, 1870s–1880s

Boarding Schools, 1879

The federal campaign to educate Indian chil-dren was launched aggressively in 1879. Children were sent to off-reservation boarding schools thousands of miles from their homes where they were subjected to military-type disci-pline. Native languages were forbidden, corporal punishment was used freely, and starchy foods dominated their diets. The dormitories echoed with children's homesick and lonely cries. The legacy of these social engineering policies was the creation of several generations of Indians who, ab-ducted from their tribes, returned home as virtual strangers, unable to communicate with their eld-ers and ignorant of the skills and knowledge to continue practicing their culture. Even more sin-ister was the lack of parenting skills in the gener-ations of Indian mothers and fathers. Preventing such practical skills from developing is an effec-tive element in any plan to destroy a people.

Dawes Allotment Act of 1887

The next approach was to divide tribally owned lands on reservations into tiny private parcels. This federal program, called the Dawes Allotment Act of 1887, was intended to introduce the Indians to private ownership of property. If an Indian moved onto his allotment, cut his hair, surrendered his children to the boarding schools, severed his tribal ties, and did exactly as told by the Indian agent for twenty years, he could re-ceive title to his allotment, pay taxes on his land, and become a citizen of the United States. How-ever, like other tribal peoples, California Indians considered this act yet another attack on their re-ligious beliefs about the earth and the tribe's re-lationship to it. In practice, it proved to be a tool to deprive Indians of their remaining lands, and, almost everywhere, Indians opposed the Dawes Act. Nevertheless, the Office of Indian Affairs' missionaries and so-called reformers were unre-lenting in these efforts, and countless others, to make the Indians into what they considered ac-ceptable people.

By 1870, the population of Indians in Cali-fornia was 30,000, and by 1900 it was fewer than 18,000. California Indians survived after 130 years of colonization and foreign domination. This staggering population decline left the Indi-ans dazed, reeling, and deeply demoralized.

Hunger, destitution, homelessness, unemployment, and discrimination were widespread, yet a number of Native leaders worked diligently for their communities.

ACTIVIST ORGANIZATIONS EMERGE, TWENTIETH CENTURY

A group of Southern California citizens organized the Sequoya League. It assisted the Kupa Indians, who had lost a bid in the Supreme Court to keep their ancestral home, now called Warner's Hot Springs in the mountainous interior of San Diego County. Through their efforts, Kupa leaders reluctantly selected a new home nearby at a place called Pala. Similar groups in Northern California helped secure small homesite reservations, called rancherias, for homeless Pomo Indians at Manchester (near Point Arena in Mendocino County) and for Wintun Indians at Chico.

One of the choice ironies of the boarding school experience was the unexpected development of a pan-tribal consciousness that emerged among Indian youth, which gave birth to pan-Indian reform groups. The first reform group to actually include California Indians was the Mission Indian Federation (MIF), founded in 1919. The MIF relentlessly attacked incompetent administrators and policies. Even urban Indians in Los Angeles had an active chapter. The group worked for more autonomy for tribal governments, full civil rights for Indians, protection of Indian water rights, opposition to the Dawes Act, and the elimination of the Bureau of Indian Affairs. In 1921, fifty-seven MIF leaders were arrested for conspiracy against the government for their opposition to allotment. Eventually, all charges were dropped.

The first all-Indian reform group, formed in Northern California by Stephen Knight and other Pomo Indians, was the California Indian Brotherhood. That group sought rancherias for homeless Indians and integration of Indian children into public schools with free lunches and clothing assistance. This farsighted group even sought opportunities for college education for Indian youth.

TWENTIETH-CENTURY STRUGGLES

Broken Treaty Settlements

The problems confronting twentieth-century California Indian survivors had many similarities, with some variation from community to community. One issue united them, however, like no other—the enduring sense of injustice regarding the broken federal treaties of 1851–1852. Since Indians had no voting rights and no way to pressure elected officials, there was little incentive for the treaties to be honored, but Native peoples never forgot those solemn promises and were determined to seek redress. Virtually all reform groups, as well as individual tribes, sought some kind of solution for more than half a century. Eventually, two settlements were reached. The first, in 1944, eventually paid $150 to every California Indian who could prove biological connection to an ancestor alive in 1850. A second effort, through the Indian Claims Commission (a federal entity established on the basis of the pioneering claims of the California Indians), resulted in payment of only $0.47 an acre in compensation for lands outside treaty areas. Despite protests, the government per capita payments to individuals resulted in less than $800 per person paid in 1968. Few desperately poor Indians could turn down even that meager amount. However, a small number of Indians refused to cash those checks in hopes of a different settlement.

Education

Federal off-reservation boarding schools were supplemented by reservation boarding schools and day schools before 1900. These schools allowed families to remain in contact, but chronic illness and lack of clothing, food, and even shoes caused considerable absenteeism, which eventually closed many of them. By 1917, the public schools began to experience increased enrollment of Indian children. When Congress gave U.S. citizenship to all Indians in 1924, a gradual transfer of Indian students to public schools followed, but academic success did not. Racial and cultural prejudices in textbooks and among teachers led to isolation, shame, and feelings of low self-esteem for Indian children and set them up for failure. The classrooms became battlegrounds where Indian children had to endure negative experiences or fight back. The latter course ensured a perpetual cycle of academic failure, condemning generations of Indian children to economic failure and unemployment.

Health

One important focus of reform efforts was health access. While seven Indian hospitals had been established at boarding schools and other sites by 1930, local hospitals often refused to treat the Native population, claiming that was the federal government's responsibility. A growing chorus of criticism prompted the establishment of a separate division of health within the Bureau of Indian Affairs in 1924. Public health nurses were then allowed to provide services to Indians. However, services were still denied to unrecognized and homeless Indians, leaving almost one-third of the Indian population without medical care. A new wave of indignation was forcefully expressed in a federal hearing conducted in 1929, but ironically, these hearings only confirmed a 1912 survey that showed that the health of the Indian population was dismal. Ultimately, the loss of their land base and food resources crippled their ability to rebound.

Land

The Northern California Indians' critical need for land was addressed in a series of congressional acts to provide homesites for landless communities. By 1930, an additional thirty-six parcels of federal trust properties called rancherias (tiny reservations) were established. They had the same status as reservations but were substantially smaller, and they lacked developed water sources.

Indians have been critical of the Bureau of Indian Affairs for failing to protect water rights, a problem that has plagued reservations throughout.

Termination

The policy of "termination," initiated in the 1950s, called for an end to all health, education, and welfare assistance provided by the federal government and envisioned a division of tribal lands to individuals. In reality, it was a resurrection of the discredited Dawes Allotment Act of 1887. California Indians were an early target for termination. After allotment, Indian land would eventually be subject to state property taxation. Until then, immunity from state taxation allowed poverty-stricken Indians to retain their lands. Taxing them would bring about the final dispossession of the land through tax defaults.

In 1953, California came under Public Law 280, an act that furthered termination goals by turning over civil and criminal jurisdiction from federal authorities to state and local authorities. At first, state and local governments were enthusiastic, envisioning an expanded tax base. However, after several years of study, it became apparent that the burden of services it would have to assume far outweighed any tax revenues. Consequently, their enthusiasm began to cool rapidly though not before Congress passed the Rancheria Act of 1958. This act provided for members of reservations and rancherias to decide whether to accept or reject termination. Federal authorities descended upon the isolated and powerless rancheria residents with exaggerated promises of new housing, road and domestic water system improvements, and even college scholarships for Native children. Oblivious to the looming threat of tax defaults, the BIA eventually convinced thirty-six of the most isolated and least politically savvy California Indian groups into committing tribal and cultural suicide by accepting termination. Sure enough, by 1970, five thousand acres of tribal lands were lost to tax defaults and forced sales. The loss of recognition stunned Native communities and cultural and social decay of Indian community institutions accelerated.

CIVIL RIGHTS ERA, 1960s–1990s

The national sweep of the civil rights movement during the 1960s afforded new opportunities for attention to the cause of American Indians. On college campuses, racial minorities and their supporters demanded the hiring of minority faculty and staff, along with aggressive recruiting of minority students. The first college to establish a Native American studies program was San Francisco State University. The program's students were largely made up of non-California Indians relocated to the San Francisco Bay Area from other states under part of a national termination program. Followed shortly by the University of California, Berkeley and the University of California, Los Angeles (UCLA), these programs provided a multidisciplinary approach to the study of American Indians in the past and present.

Most importantly, the new Native studies programs addressed the future of American Indians and tribalism. The idea of actually controlling the future and shaping federal Indian policy made for a kind of self-assurance not witnessed among Native leaders since the Indian Wars of the last century. Furthermore, it produced a new generation of leaders, pressing legal and other avenues toward creating self-sufficient and responsible Native communities, new scholars contributing to the academic study of the American Indians, and numerous public school teachers in classrooms throughout the state. Both UCLA and UC-Berkeley developed important scholarly journals, the *American Indian Quarterly* and the *American Indian Culture and Research Journal*.

More access to health and legal services also emerged during this period. The California Rural Indian Health Board was established in 1968 to

A mural honoring Native Americans can be viewed in the Cesar Chavez Student Center Building on the campus of San Francisco State University. SFSU was the first university to establish a Native American studies program.

fund several demonstration projects in fifteen rural and reservation communities, restoring services that in many cases had been denied to California Indians since 1956. Legal assistance on issues of land, water, and civil rights became available as part of the U.S. government's War on Poverty programs of the 1970s. California Indian Legal Services strengthened tribal ability to oppose BIA policies. They continue to provide important leverage in fighting for the civil rights of Indian individuals and tribes.

This era also gave rise to a succession of land occupations by Native peoples in California, setting a national trend. In fall 1969, nearly one hundred Indian college students from UCLA, UC-Berkeley, and San Francisco State landed on Alcatraz Island to reclaim that abandoned federal prison as Indian land, causing a media sensation around the world. The Native Americans cleverly pointed out that the island was just like the reservations: no water, no electricity, no jobs! They also pointed out that it was isolated from the wealth that surrounded it. At last, Native peoples had discovered a vehicle that would focus attention on the current conditions of America's aboriginal people. Following the Alcatraz occupation, other land occupations occurred, such as the protest attempted by the Pit River Indians at a public utility campground in Shasta County in 1971. The Pomo occupation of an abandoned national defense radio listening station in rural Sonoma County resulted in the establishment of Ya-Ka-Ama (our land), an educational and Native plant center. A similar occupation near the University of California, Davis resulted in the establishment of a fully accredited American Indian junior college called Deganawidah-Quetzalcoatl University.

Unprecedented population growth in California during the 1970s and 1980s resulted in the construction of millions of new homes and businesses, unearthing thousands of California Indian burial and occupation sites. Traditionalists were dismayed that archaeologists intended to add the findings to existing inventories of skeletons and other objects found in Indian burial sites, long neglected and seldom studied, gathering dust in warehouses, archaeology labs, and campus base-

ments. Anthropologists claimed that they were the Indians' best friends and that much valuable information could be gained from the "data," as they euphemistically referred to the remains of Native ancestors. The Indians demanded to know why these human remains were being removed from the ground and why it only happened to Indians.

About this time, it was discovered that the skull of nationally known Modoc War leader Captain Jack was part of the physical anthropology collection of the Smithsonian Institution in Washington, D.C. Outrage over this case and thousands of other lesser-known Indian skeletons and burial goods led to a national program of repatriation of the thousands and thousands of Indian skeletons to their tribes of origin.

In 1978, Governor Edmund G. Brown, Jr., created the Native American Heritage Commission (NAHC), which took on the responsibility of resolving human remains issues associated with construction. The NAHC attempted to compel universities and other state agencies holding human remains to submit plans for the ultimate disposition of the remains and associated burial goods. The NAHC has become an effective clearinghouse for these matters. Federal laws of 1990 mandated that federally funded museums inventory their American Indian human skeleton collections and develop a plan for repatriation to appropriate tribes. While a few archaeologists argued against this policy, most agreed that little new scientific information had been developed from collections that have been in their possession for as long as a century. Native peoples often counter, that, if these human remains indeed possess such valuable data, why, then, are they not being systematically studied? For traditional peoples, it is a simple matter of dignity and the respect all citizens expect of their government and its laws.

CALIFORNIA INDIAN INDIGENEITY

Cultural Renaissance, 1960s–

In retrospect, it seems miraculous that Native cultures in California survived at all, yet they have not only survived but have actually experienced a renaissance.

Malki Museum, the first tribally controlled museum, was established by Cahuilla traditionalists on the Morongo Indian Reservation in 1964. The museum, which has inspired several other Indian museums, is committed to preserving the cultural traditions and history of the Cahuilla Indians and other Southern California Indian tribes. Malki also founded an academic publishing press in 1965, which has printed many high-quality books and materials on Native American culture, including the well-known *Journal of California and Great Basin Anthropology*.

In the 1960s and '70s, the only major venue through which California Indians and scholars of Native California could come together was the intermittent symposia hosted by the American Indian Historical Society, founded in 1964 by Rupert Costo (Cahuilla). These symposia were invitational and largely national in scope. In 1969, the California Indian Education Association received nonprofit status. Its annual conferences focus on curriculum and educational issues affecting American Indians in California.

With its establishment in 1985, the California Indian Conference became the first and only annual conference focused on the Indigenous people of California past to present. The first Algonquian roundtable was supported by the University of California, Berkeley Anthropology Department, Lowie Museum of Anthropology (now Hearst Museum), Linguistics Department, and Native American Studies Program. In the words of Dr. Simmons, the goal of the initial conference was "to provide a regular forum for people working in California Indian studies to share the results of their work." While the conference has grown in size and scope over the years, it remains focused on Native Californians from past to present.

This event brings together scholars, traditionalists, and experts at state and federal levels to share their research and interests in the past, present, and future of California Indians. Usually, it is hosted by a major college. In 2014, the conference was held at California State University at San Bernardino.

In 1987, a unique publication, *News from Native California*, debuted. Ever since, the journal has provided thoughtful stories, essays, and reviews, along with artwork, from across California. The widely read quarterly covers history, ethnography, current events, legislation, the arts, and especially the preservation and revitalization of Native California languages. Malcolm Margolin, the journal's publisher, supported language revitalization efforts in the late 1980s by organizing a language conference that led to the founding of Advocates for Indigenous California Language Survival (AICLS).

AICLS, founded in 1992, is a nonprofit organization devoted to assisting California Indian communities and individuals in keeping their languages alive. The all-Native board, which represents all regions of California, believes that although linguistic documentation of endangered languages is important, its main goal is developing new speakers. Documentation provides the means for language revitalization, especially when there are no speakers left to teach others. It is the dream of the Advocates that California Indian languages will once again be spoken in Native communities.

According to the AICLS website (http://www.aicls.org), there are presently fifty Indigenous languages that still have one or more Native speakers though these numbers are dwindling fast. There are also at least thirty languages with no Native speakers left whose descendants desperately want to regain their languages. Thanks to language revitalization work, Native education centers throughout the state have developed classes in Native languages, culture, and dance.

In 2014, Margolin reported, "Today, when you go to any Indian conference, people often introduce themselves in their Native language. Languages rescued from the jaws of death or in some cases resurrected from the grave…. Finally, somebody is getting up and even just saying in their language, 'My name is _____,' and I'm speaking the Wakchumni language. Welcome to my land!"

Art Traditions

In the late twentieth century, the age-old art of basket weaving, perfected over centuries by California Indians, appeared at risk of dying out. Few younger people were learning to weave, and the mostly older women who continued to weave were finding it increasingly difficult to carry on their work. The demands of family life and the struggle to make a living, together with the destruction of plant habitats, pesticide contamination of gathering areas, and difficulty of obtaining access to gathering sites, were reducing the time and opportunity for plant tending, gathering, and basket weaving.

The need to support weavers and address these problems was confirmed during a statewide gathering of basket weavers in 1991. At the next statewide gathering (in 1992), weavers formed the California Indian Basketweavers Association (CIBA). According to the CIBA website (http://www.ciba.org), the organization helps "basket weavers gain greater exposure and acceptance among the dominant society for their basketry traditions and by providing opportunities for weavers to realize an economic benefit from their basketry skills and knowledge." Producing and selling baskets from harvested materials, as well as working in educational and consultant capacities, gives basket makers opportunities to preserve their culture and heritage and earn an income. Since the formation of CIBA, the number of basket weavers earning a livelihood or supplemental income from selling baskets, teaching, and demonstrating basket weaving at events has grown. CIBA also strengthens and supports the role of California Indian women in overcoming public ignorance and changing public perceptions about California Indian cultures.

While California basket makers have long been acknowledged as the finest in the world, a well-documented decline in the number of practitioners occurred over the last sixty years. Contemporary basket makers like Linda Yamane (Rumsien Ohlone) and Lois Conner (Mono/Chukchansi) have brought back the art of weaving from the brink. They learn from eld-

Photo of baskets made by Yokut Natives of central California that was published in a 1924 issue of *The North American Indian*.

ers as well as ethnographic field notes. They track down and examine baskets in California, elsewhere in the U.S., and European collections, and learn about plant materials required to weave trays, bowls, ceremonial, and winnowing baskets.

Besides the attention given to California basket weavers, California Indian artists, both traditional and contemporary, have established a national reputation in the larger Indian art world. California Indian artists, such as Jean LaMarr, Frank La Pena, Harry Fonseca, L. Frank Manriquez, James Luna, and Kathleen Smith, among others, are considered on the cutting edge of the modern Indian art world.

Sing the Birds (Wikitmallem Tahmuwhae)

Bird Dances and Songs are an age-old tradition among Southern California Native people and for some reason weathered the European onslaught. Maybe Father Serra considered them harmless recreation and no threat to Christianity. The songs are meant to be shared and social in nature, but they are also an oral record of the origins of many nations like the Cahuilla and Kumeyaay and their worldview of how all life came to be. It is amazing that the tradition escaped obliteration. According to oral tradition, they may be 25,000 years old, songs from the earliest ancestors that are still sung today. The Cahuilla peoples have a Bird Singing tradition that is a tribute to each day of the year, with more than 365 songs in their collection.

Usually, the men (and boys) sing while they keep a rhythm by shaking a gourd rattle. Women (and girls) dance along to the music. Traditional California Indian song sets often have dozens of songs and can span over days to celebrate a life event, to honor, to bless, or to mourn. The songs express important concepts that the related cultures share about migrations and life lessons, yet they are all different. They are allegorical and also entertaining when they are not being sung in their entirety. If the songs are being sung during the daytime, for instance, at home, dancing is usually part of it, and it's more for fun. When the entire series is sung, a group gathers and will sing through the night. Dancing may or may not occur during that time. Throughout Southern California, Bird Dancing is popular and part of pow-wows, family get-togethers, or featured at a stand-alone event. A documentary, *We Are Birds*, was made in 2012 and chronicles the tradition.

Chumash Maritime Association

The Chumash Maritime Association was founded in 1996 to reclaim and preserve Chumash traditional maritime heritage. For more than ten thousand years, tomols—flat-bottomed, ocean-going canoes used for fishing and trade—regularly traveled from Humaliwo to Malibu to Point Conception and out across the open water to the

Chumash people paddle a tomol near Santa Cruz Island.

Channel Islands. During the Mission era (1830s), the tomol tradition ended. The first contemporary canoe was built in 1976, using the 1912 plans left by Wisdomkeeper Fernando Librado (see also his biography at the end of this chapter).

In 2008, the Isha Kowoch (Glittering Salmon), a traditional redwood plank tomol built by Matt Ward, arrived in Malibu for the first time in generations. Today, it is permanently housed at the Wishtoyo Foundation's Chumash Discovery Village at Nicholas Beach. In 2001, the tomol 'E-lye'wun (Swordfish), built by the Chumash community under the auspices of the Chumash Maritime Association, made the first crossing in almost two hundred years, from the mainland to Limuw—Santa Cruz Island. There are now eight tomols, and treks to the Channel Islands have become part of Chumash culture again.

The Chumash Maritime Association continues to promote the building, maintaining, and crewing of tomols as well as restore native plants, teach Chumash culture, and sponsor youth camps. Cofounder, president, and attorney Roberta R. Cordero helps build liaisons with other groups and organizations committed to maintaining the maritime environment and culture of traditional Chumash homelands.

CALIFORNIA NATIVE POPULATION 2010

According to the *2013 American Indian Population and Labor Force Report,* published by the U.S. Department of the Interior, an estimated 281,374 American Indians and Alaskan Natives were living on or near reservation lands in California during the 2010 calendar year. These people were eligible to use Bureau of Indian Affairs services.

BIOGRAPHIES

Marin (c. 1781–1839)
Coast Miwok, Activist

According to anthropologist Betty Goerke, who spent thirty years researching Marin and Coast

Miwok culture, Marin was a member, not a chief, of a southern Marin tribe. He managed to live in three worlds: the Miwok world and the worlds of the church and military.

According to General Mariano Vallejo's historical report to the first California State Legislature in 1850, Marin was baptized as a young man at Mission Dolores (in present-day San Francisco) in 1801 and moved to Mission San Rafael Arcangel in Pomo Territory (in present-day San Rafael) after it was founded in 1817.

According to General Vallejo: "In the year 1815 or 1816, a military expedition proceeded to explore the country north of the bay of San Francisco, and upon returning by the Petaluma Valley, an engagement ensued with Marin, in which he was made prisoner and conducted to the station at San Francisco, from which he escaped, and again reaching Petaluma, he united his scattered forces, and thence-forward dedicated his most strenuous efforts to harass the troops in their hostile incursions into that part of the country.... but was again taken captive to San Francisco in 1824; whence being set at liberty, he retired to the mission of San Rafael. He led a delegation to General Vallejo in the 1830s, asking that priests and the military stop whipping their Indian charges. The whipping stopped."

Toypurina (fl. 1780s)
Gabrielino, Leader

Toypurina was a religious and political leader who, in the 1780s, led a short-lived rebellion against the Spanish at the San Gabriel Mission near present-day Los Angeles, California.

Like many Indians of the region in the late 1780s, Toypurina's people were struggling with the institutions of Spanish settlement and rule. In 1785, she planned an uprising against the Mission. She was aided by her apprentice, Nicolas José. Together, they convinced the Indians of six villages to unite against the Spanish. The priests and soldiers in the mission had learned of the uprising, however, and arrested the Indians.

During their trial, Toypurina and José spoke out against the Spanish and the suppression of Indian culture and traditional ceremonies. The accusations fell on unsympathetic ears, and participants in the raid were flogged. Jose was imprisoned in the presidio in San Diego. Toypurina was exiled from her people to the San Carlos Mission in present-day Carmel, California.

Kintpuash (Captain Jack) (c. 1840–1873)
Modoc, Leader

Born somewhere along the Lost River in present-day Modoc County, California, the man whom the U.S. settlers would call Captain Jack was originally given the Modoc name Kintpuash.

He became the leader of his band when his father died in 1846. Captain Jack was drawn into the Modoc Wars through a complex series of events that began in 1864 when the Modoc signed away much of their indigenous territory and were removed to the Klamath Reservation in Oregon. The living conditions on the reservation were miserable; there was much disease and not enough food to support both the Modoc and the Klamath tribe. The Modoc request for their own reservation in California was rejected.

Captain Jack and the Modoc returned to California anyway, but there were many complaints from white settlers, and the federal government ordered troops to the area in 1872. A series of violent incidents ensued; Captain Jack and his followers escaped and worked their way south to a volcanic area with lava formations that offered excellent natural fortifications. Other Modoc joined them so that the rebel group consisted of about two hundred people, eighty of them warriors. They ambushed a wagon train on December 22, obtaining more ammunition, and in January 1873, they successfully repulsed a force of more than three hundred regular soldiers, led by Lieutenant Colonel Frank Wheaton.

Shortly after, General Edward Canby planned to lead another attack and gathered a force of about a thousand men. At the same time, a peace plan was set in motion. The first negotiation on February 28 produced no results, and at the second meeting, Captain Jack produced a hidden revolver and fatally shot General Canby. Modoc warriors Boston Charley and Schonchin John also fired on the peace commissioners that had been sent by President Grant, and the Modoc retreated to another lava formation to the south. Throughout these months, there were scattered conflicts, such as the one that took place on April 26, 1873, when the warrior Scarfaced Charlie attacked a patrol of sixty-three soldiers and killed twenty-five, including all five officers.

Despite their successes, however, the Modoc were badly lacking food and water, and their forces became less unified. General Jefferson C. Davis finally organized a relentless pursuit of the scattered bands that remained, and Captain Jack and other leaders were finally cornered in a cave and captured on June 1, 1873. Captain Jack was executed by hanging on October 3, 1873, and two other Modoc leaders were sentenced to life imprisonment on Alcatraz, a penal facility on an island in San Francisco Bay.

The Modoc War was one of the few Indian wars that ever took place in California since tribes of the California region were not highly organized militarily. Because of this and the relatively late date of the uprising, the Modoc War had a shocking effect on the public, gaining a great deal of national attention.

Bogus Charley (c. 1850–1880)
Modoc, Interpreter

An accomplished speaker of English, Bogus Charley, who took his name from Bogus Creek, regularly acted as an interpreter in negotiations with Euro-Americans. During the Modoc War, he fought against the U.S. Army but laid down his arms when he despaired of any chance to win. He worked as a tracker for the U.S. Army while Kintpuash (Captain Jack) was being sought. After all the Modoc leaders had surrendered, Bogus Charley testified for the prosecution against them during a government trial, resulting in the hanging of Captain Jack and others on October 3, 1873. He was later removed to Indian Territory, where he became principal chief of the Modoc in the latter part of the 1870s.

Fernando Librado (c. 1820–1915)
Chumash, Wisdomkeeper

In 1912, Librado made blueprints of the shape, depth, and design of the tomol (traditional, flat-bottomed, ocean-going canoe), which he shared with ethnographer John P. Harrington. In 1976, the Chumash were able to once again construct the traditional vessel by using Librado's detailed notes of the complex canoe-building process that involved cutting planks from redwood trunks washed up along the California coast, sewing the planks together with twine made from natural fibers, gluing the seams, and sealing the hull of the craft with a mix of natural asphalt and pine sap.

Ishi (c. 1862–1916)
Yahi, Survivor

In 1911, a middle-aged Yahi from Northern California became famous throughout the United States as "the last wild Indian." Ishi was a member of the Yahi (also called Southern Yana) who originally lived along Mill Creek and Deer Creek of the Sacramento River in Northern California.

In August 1911, Ishi wandered out of the brush in Northern California and found himself in the town of Oroville (Butte County). He was the last survivor of a tribe that had gone into seclusion more than forty years before. For much of this time, Ishi had been living in a band that never numbered more than a dozen for most of his adolescent and adult life. His last years before discovery were spent with an old man and woman, probably his parents, and a sister. For the last several months, he had been completely alone, weaponless, pressed by hunger, and his hair still singed from mourning for his relatives.

He gave up a lifetime of hiding and allowed himself to be captured. Apparently, he expected to be killed but was instead placed in jail for a few days and soon afterward was taken to the San Francisco Bay area. Ishi (the Yahi word for "man") was studied by Alfred Kroeber and other anthropologists at the Anthropology Museum of the University of California where he lived until his death in 1916. He had been living a traditional way of life long before California tribes adapted to reservations. He spoke no English and still practiced ancient skills such as flint shaping and bow making, all of which he shared with researchers and others. A number of publications on Yahi language and culture came about because of Ishi's knowledge, but he is probably best known to most Americans because of Theodora Kroeber's book *Ishi in Two Worlds* (1960). For most Americans, Ishi is a romantic symbol of the last unspoiled Native, but to many Native Americans in California, he represents a terrible era of genocide and cultural devastation.

Ramona (c. 1865–1922)
Cahuilla, Celebrity

Ramona was a Cahuilla Indian who lived in present-day San Diego County, California, whose life became the basis of Helen Hunt Jackson's novel *Ramona* (1884). The real-life Ramona was probably born in a cave on the Carey Ranch in Anza, California. She had been married to Juan Diego, who was murdered in dramatic fashion by a local villain named Sam Temple.

The novel, which incorporated a fictionalized romance, became an instant success and spawned a movie in the early 1900s. The real-life Ramona became something of a celebrity, selling finely crafted baskets and photographs of herself to eager tourists at a souvenir stand. Today, the myth of Ramona continues to live in numerous re-enactments and festivals celebrating her life and character. In spite of the attention, Ramona lived a relatively modest life. She was buried at the side of her husband in the old Cahuilla Cemetery of Anza.

The central character in the novel is a romantic figure who bears little resemblance to the real-life Ramona. Jackson came to California in 1881 as an investigative reporter for *Century* magazine. While gathering information, she became entranced with the picturesque lifestyle of the Roman Catholic past of Southern California and wrote a sympathetic portrayal of the context and purposes of Spanish Catholicism and colonization in California. In contrast, *Ramona* was a work of social protest that underscored the oppression of California Indians, often called Mission Indians, who were forced to live and work in the Catholic missions. In her investigative reporting, Jackson recorded the grave population decline of California Mission Indians and the role of the Spanish in this decline. Jackson became determined to write a work that would bring the plight of the Mission Indians to the American public's eye. Ramona was first serialized in 1884 by *Christian Union* magazine.

John Tortes "Chief" Meyers (1880–1971)

Cahuilla, Baseball Player

John Tortes "Chief" Meyers was a Major League Baseball catcher for the New York Giants (1909–1915), Brooklyn Robins (1916–1917), and Boston Braves (1917). Meyers hit over .300 for three straight years as the Giants won three straight National League pennants from 1911 to 1913. Overall, he played in four World Series—the 1911, 1912, and 1913 Series with the Giants as well as the 1916 Series with the Robins.

Meyers was force-fed the nickname "Chief" due to the fact that he was Indian. During that time, the stereotype depicted Indians as stupid, but Chief Meyers was an educated man whose biggest regret was not finishing his college education. While playing baseball in a summer tournament,

Ralph Glaze, former pitcher, noticed Meyers' extreme talent and convinced Dartmouth alumni to provide Meyers with cash, railroad tickets, and a doctored diploma. Meyers hadn't graduated from high school, but the fake diploma got him into Dartmouth. The college discovered the forgery and unenrolled him. Meyers never completed a special program to get reinstated at Dartmouth.

Elsie Allen (1899–1990)

Pomo, Basket Weaver

Elsie Allen is regarded as one of the best known California basket weavers of her generation. From the Cloverdale Rancheria of Pomo Indians of Northern California, Allen broke from tradition and saved Pomo weaving from cultural extinction by teaching traditional basket weaving techniques to non-Indians and Native individuals outside her immediate family. She was important for historically categorizing and teaching California Indian basket patterns and techniques and sustaining traditional Pomo basketry as an art form. She taught at the Mendocino Art Center. Late in her career, Elsie Allen began using commercial materials in her baskets after receiving a vision. One of her last students was her niece, Susan Billy. Allen's book, *Pomo Basketmaking: A Supreme Art for the Weaver*, was published in 1972 and introduced a wide readership to the art of Pomo basket weaving. Allen was also the subject of *Remember Your Relations: Elsie Allen Baskets, Family, And Friends*, 2005 (Dot Brovarney, Susan Billy, and Suzanne Abel-Vidor). Elsie Allen High School in Santa Rosa, California, is named for her.

Frank Day (1902–1976)

Konkow Maidu, Painter

Day, a self-taught painter, played a major role in the 1960s and 1970s revitalization of California's Native American dance and visual arts. Amid presumptions that California Indians were vanishing or had vanished, Day sought to prevent Maidu traditions from being forgotten. He had learned the language, myths, legends, songs, and traditions of his people from his father and other

Maidu elders. During his last two decades of life, Day created more than two hundred paintings. He recorded stories, songs, and memories deriving from his early childhood in the Sierra Nevada foothills of California. In retrieving these cultural traditions from his memory, he employed his imagination in embellishing them for the canvas.

Following the death of his father, Day spent over a decade traveling through Indian Country in the western states. In 1930, he returned to California to work as an agricultural laborer. After a serious injury in 1960, he took up painting as therapy. Day soon began painting Maidu themes, transforming his cultural memory into a visual record by bold color and strong composition.

The importance of Day's vision can be traced through his identity as a Maidu culture bearer, his oral and symbolic interpretation of Maidu heritage, and his seminal role of song-giver to the dance and ceremonial activities of the Maidu Dancers and Traditionalists, a group he was instrumental in founding.

Rupert Costo (1906–1989)
Cahuilla, Journalist/Publisher/ Activist/Leader/Engineer

Rupert Costco and his wife, Jeannette Henry Costo (Cherokee), were prominent leaders in the fight for economic and social rights for American Indians. They turned to journalism and publishing as a way to channel their activism. Born in Hemet, California, Rupert Costo attended Haskell College in Lawrence, Kansas, where he was a star athlete in football. He then attended Whittier College in California, where he played football alongside fellow student Richard M. Nixon under their Indian coach Wallace "Chief" Newman.

During the 1930s to the 1950s, Costo was active in national and tribal politics. In the 1930s, California was a major center of opposition to the Indian Reorganization Act (IRA), a federal law also called the Indian New Deal. Costo, one of the principal leaders of the opposition, believed the IRA was a device to assimilate the American Indian. He called it "the Indian Raw Deal."

In the 1950s, Costo served as tribal chairman of the Cahuilla and was employed as an engineer in California's highway department. After he retired in 1964, Costo and his wife Jeannette founded the American Indian Historical Society in San Francisco. The organization was often in the forefront of Native issues such as the protection of American Indian cemeteries and the correction of history textbooks. He served as president of the society until his death.

The Costos developed and edited publications that accurately reflected the historical role of Native Americans in American society. They published the *Indian Historian*, an academic quarterly journal with articles on Indian history from an Indian perspective. The Indian Historian Press, an American-Indian-controlled, for-profit publishing house, published over fifty books before its doors closed. Between 1973 and 1984, the Costos published *Wassaja*, a monthly newspaper, because they felt the non-Indian press did a bad job covering Indian news. Wassaja's reporters were located on reservations and in big cities with relatively large Native populations. Unlike reservation newspapers, which reported tribal news, *Wassaja* covered national issues such as water and treaty rights. From 1974 until 1983, the Costos also produced the *Weewish Tree*, filled with poetry and artwork submitted by Native children.

At the end of his life, Costo endowed the Rupert Costo Chair in American Indian History at the University of California, Riverside. He and his wife also established the Costo Library of the American Indian, one of the largest collections of research materials dealing with Native life in the United States, especially strong on California Indian cultures, tribal politics, and the rise of Indian sovereignty in the 1970s. The University of California, Riverside renamed the Student Services building as Costo Hall to honor contributions of the Costos to the university.

Mabel McKay (1907–1993)
Pomo, Basket Weaver/Dreamer

A member of the Long Valley Cache Creek Pomo Indians, Mabel McKay was the last Dreamer of the

Pomo people and a basket making prodigy. Never taught to weave a basket, during Dreaming, the Spirit instructed her on each basket she wove. Many people did not understand Mabel's process, but she was successful in explaining that her baskets were living, not just pretty things. McKay was a well-respected scholar. She spoke at universities and served as a cultural consultant for anthropologists. She lectured at the New School in New York City with respected basket maker Essie Parrish (1902–1979) in 1972. As a weaver, her skill and attention to detail brought worldwide recognition to her basketry. Her work is shown in many museum collections in the U.S. and abroad. Weaving for Mabel was a spiritual path, not a craft. In 1994, Greg Sarris (Coast Miwok) published *Mabel McKay: Weaving the Dream* (Berkeley: University of California Press), in which he wove together stories from Mabel McKay's life.

Florence Jones (1909–2003)
Wintu, Religious Healer

Florence Jones was a renowned doctor of ancient healing practices. She was baptized as a Methodist during her childhood but also had traditional religious experiences. At seventeen, she experienced her first trance, after which older Wintu healers cared for her and established her as a healer in her own right. She diagnosed illnesses with the power of spirit helpers acting through her hands during a healing ceremony. She has sucked "pains" from patients, predicted locations of lost objects or lost souls, and administered traditional herbal medicines to patients of her own and neighboring tribes.

In 1987, Jones retired from most of her doctoring duties and confined her practice to doctoring among her people. She oversaw the education of several young Wintun in healing practices. She held public ceremonies at Mount Shasta around Easter and mid-August each year. On August 15, 1995, Florence Jones retired from doctoring during a ceremony that took place on Wintun sacred grounds. Her life was chronicled in a documentary film, *In the Light of Reverence,* which aired nationally on PBS in 2001.

Jane K. Penn (1910–1980)
Cahuilla, Museum Founder

Born on the Morongo Indian Reservation, Jane K. Penn's desire to preserve the traditions, culture, and language of Cahuilla people brought together Katherine Silva Saubel (Cahuilla), Lowell John Bean, and other Native and non-Native friends to found the Malki Museum in 1964, the first nonprofit Indian museum on a California reservation. Penn and Saubel's partnership enabled the dream of a museum and cultural center to become a reality. Penn served as director and treasurer of Malki, keeping it open six days a week without pay. Her careful budgeting made possible a publishing program by Malki Museum Press that has become internationally known: it acquired Ballena Press in 2005 and is known for its excellent educational texts.

The museum's diverse publications emphasize both popular and informative materials which are useful to students, teachers, and the general public. The press also publishes scholarly works aimed at more specific readers and is written by anthropologists, archaeologists, historians, and other researchers. Penn's efforts in Native American affairs brought her statewide attention and an appointment by Governor Jerry Brown to the Native American Heritage Committee. Following in an ancient line of succession in her family, Jane Penn was chosen to be the ceremonial leader of the Wanakik Cahuilla in 1960. She was responsible for all ceremonies at the Big House on the Morongo Reservation, which she performed until her death.

Vivien Hailstone (1913–2000)
Yurok/Karuk/Hupa, Master Weaver/Collector

Vivien Hailstone, a master weaver, was almost single-handedly responsible for the resurgence of weaving among the Karuk, Yurok, and Hupa people in the mid-twentieth century. For more than forty years, Vivien Hailstone ran the I-Ye-Quee Trading Post/Gift Shop in Hoopa, selling sundries, magazines, and gifts to local residents who came by to shop and to visit with the proprietor. The store served as a meeting spot for folks in the community and also provided a venue for basket weavers to sell their work and a way for Hailstone to support and encourage the art of basketry.

During that time, Hailstone developed a large personal collection of artworks by fellow weavers from her area which, when she passed in 2000, was brought together with pieces acquired by her son Albert to form the Hailstone Collection. Eventually, Albert Hailstone donated 219 baskets that belonged to his family to the Clarke Historical Museum, located in Eureka, California. Work by Vivien Hailstone is also included in the Clarke Museum exhibit. A talented weaver in her own right, she specialized in making medallions that were backed with buckskin.

The Hailstone Collection consists primarily of baskets Vivien Hailstone put aside from those she was selling at the gift shop. The collection includes pieces by many well-known Yurok weavers such as Lena McCovey, Queen James, and Ada Charles. Also included are many baskets by Yurok weavers Amy Smoker, Ella Johnson, and Nettie McKinnon. The Hailstone Collection also features a selection of Karuk baskets by the Davis sisters, Madeline and Grace.

Ruby Modesto (1913–1980)
Cahuilla, Religious Practitioner

Ruby Modesto was a renowned religious practitioner who received her dream helper around the time she was ten years old. Born on the Martinez Reservation to a Serrano mother from the Morongo Reservation and a Desert Cahuilla father from the Coachella Valley in California, Ruby Modesto grew up learning the traditional ways of her father's people. She did not speak English or attend school until after she was ten years old. She inherited traditional teachings and traditions through clan relatives, including her father, grandfather, great-grandfather, and uncles, who were all *puls* (religious practitioners). Modesto became a medicine woman later in life, specializing in healing individuals possessed by

demons. Respected for her knowledge of Cahuilla culture, Modesto taught the Native language on the reservation and was a guest speaker at colleges in the area. She also served as an informant to anthropologists, coauthoring a book called *Not for Innocent Ears: Spiritual Traditions of a Cahuilla Medicine Woman* (1980), which includes her autobiography.

Katherine Siva Saubel (1920–2011)
Cahuilla, Cultural Interpreter

Katherine Siva Saubel became "the dominant interpreter of Cahuilla culture and history," according to Professor of Ethnology and Anthropology Lowell John Bean. Despite strong pressures to abandon her language and culture, Saubel, born on the Les Coyotes Reservation in San Diego County, made it her life's work to preserve them, working with prominent linguists and anthropologists, especially Dr. Bean. In 1972, they authored a monumental study of ethnobotanical knowledge of the Cahuilla, much of it based on information from her mother, a Cahuilla medicine woman. Collaborating with other scholars, Saubel wrote a Cahuilla dictionary and grammar book. Her scholarship made her known internationally; her research has appeared in government, academic, and museum publications here and abroad.

In 1964, Saubel and Jane Penn (Cahuilla) cofounded the Malki Museum, California's first museum founded and managed by Native Americans on a reservation. Serving as the museum's president for over forty years, Saubel, who also served as tribal chairwoman for many years, worked tirelessly to preserve sacred and historical sites, prevent hazardous waste disposal on reservation lands, and maintain the sanctity of ancient burial grounds. Besides testifying before the U.S. Senate and California State Assembly, she also served on the governor's California Native American Heritage Commission. The first Native woman inducted into the National Women's Hall of Fame (Seneca Falls, New York) in 1993, Dr. Saubel and ethnolinguist Dr. Eric Elliott collaborated to make a collection of her memories and cultural traditions in a two-volume, bilingual set (English and Cahuilla), published by Malki-Ballena Press Books.

Julia Florence Parker (1928–)
Coast Miwok/Kashaya Pomo, Basket Weaver/Storyteller/Teacher

Julia Florence Parker is one of the pre-eminent basket makers in California. She studied with some of the leading twentieth-century Indigenous California basket weavers. A respected elder of the Federated Indians of Graton Rancheria and longtime resident of Yosemite Valley, Parker is a prolific artist, teacher, and storyteller. With master elders as her teachers, especially her husband's grandmother, Lucy Telles, a famous basket weaver, Parker spent countless hours learning the skills and knowledge required to weave baskets. This involves knowing where land is the healthiest so a weaver can gather materials without destroying the natural balances of the ecosystem.

A National Park Service employee, Parker, the longest-tenured employee at Yosemite National Park, has taught and shared a lifetime of information, especially to younger generations. In 2014, four generations of Parker women were "all learning about baskets and … practicing baskets in their own way," according to Parker. Honored by universities and museums around the world, Parker presented Queen Elizabeth with a basket in 1983 that took a year to make. Parker has been a central figure in the organization and ongoing activities of the California Indian Basketweavers Association. In 2007, the National Endowment for the Arts honored her with a National Heritage Fellowship.

Marigold Linton (1936–)
Cahuilla/Cupeno, Cognitive Psychologist

Marigold Linton, a cognitive psychologist whose research on long-term memory is internationally recognized, was the first Native American woman to become president of the Society for the Advancement of Chicanos and Native Americans in Science in 2004. She also cofounded the National Indian Education Association. Recognized for her lifetime work to increase the representation of Native Americans in scientific endeavors, Dr. Linton was honored with a Presidential Award for Excellence in Science, Mathematics, and Engineering Mentoring at the White House in 2011. Linton's career has established her as a tireless advocate for American Indians to acquire advanced degrees in the sciences.

Linton was the first California reservation Indian to have ever left the reservation to go to a university. She received her B.A. from the University of California, Riverside, did graduate work at the University of Iowa, and received her Ph.D. from the University of California, Los Angeles. All degrees were in experimental psychology.

Frank LaPena (1937–)
Nomtipom Wintu, Artist/Poet/Professor/Cultural Dancer

Born in San Francisco, Frank LaPena is a painter, printmaker, sculptor, poet, retired professor, dancer, and community member of the Nomtipon Wintu. His strong interest and involvement in Wintu culture has influenced his artistic production and his commitment to his community and family. His early adult years were, in part, a rediscovery of his cultural background. LaPena's first exhibition in 1960 at the Arts and Crafts Gallery in Chico, California, dealt with Native American concerns about place and land while being aesthetically informed by the western dialogue of traditional landscape.

In the 1920s, he became interested in the song, dance, and ceremonial traditions of his tribe. He worked with the elders of the Nomtipom Wintu, the Nomlaki Wintun of Northern California, and elders of neighboring tribes, which had a profound influence in shaping work rather than the formal education he received. LaPena was a founding member of the Maidu Dancers and Traditionalists, dedicated to the revival and preservation of these Native arts.

Since 1960, LaPena's art has been exhibited in over twenty one-man exhibits (such as *Frank LaPena: The World is a Gift*), Wheelwright Museum of the American Indian (1989), and numerous group shows across the United States, Europe, Central and South America, Cuba, Australia, and New Zealand. Besides consulting with museums across the country, he maintains a ceremonial life as a singer and dance leader.

Kathleen Rose Smith (1939–)
Miwok/Pomo, Artist/Storyteller/ Food Specialist

Kathleen Rose Smith has been an artist who has shared her culture through stories, art, and food recipes. A member of the Federated Indians of Graton Rancheria, she grew up in the 1940s and 1950s in the Healdsburg area. An artist from early childhood, she graduated from the San Francisco Art Institute in 1977. Over the years, she has held such diverse jobs as park naturalist, art instructor, archaeology field technician, and food columnist for the magazine *News from Native California*. In 2014, Heyday Books published *Enough for All: Foods of My Dry Creek Pomo and Bodega Miwok People*. Smith reveals the practices handed down through generations of her Bodega Miwok and Pomo ancestors and shares how these traditions have evolved into the contemporary ways her family enjoys wild foods. Her knowledge and personal reflections are expressed through recipes, stories, and artwork, recording not only the technical aspects of food gathering but also the social and spiritual—inextricable elements of traditional California Indian food preparation.

James Luna (1950–)
Luiseno, Performance Artist

A performance artist and multimedia-installation artist, Luna lives on the LaJolla Indian Reservation, San Diego County, California. He initially began his art career as a painter, but he branched out into performances and installations, which he has explored for over three decades. His own body has been a major component in his work. For instance, in the 1987 *Artifact Piece* at the San Diego Museum of Man, Luna lay in a display case filled with sand and artifacts, such as Luna's favorite music and books as well as legal papers and ceremonial objects. Nearing the case, many viewers were surprised to find a living being watching them, reversing the voyeuristic experience of museum going. Luna also calls attention to the tendency of museums to present Native American cultures as dead and extinct rather than carrying the history through to modern-day representations.

Luna, who has also been an academic counselor at Palomar College and taught art at the University of California, San Diego, has said that installation/performance art "offers an opportunity like no other for Native people to express themselves without compromise in the Indian traditional art form of ceremony, dance, oral tradition, and contemporary thought, without compromise."

During his career, Luna has received innumerable awards, including Best Live Short Performance at the American Indian Film Festival and the Bessie Award from Dance Theater Workshop in New York. In 2007, he was awarded the Eiteljorg Fellowship for Native American Fine Art.

L. Frank (1952–)
Tongva–Acjachemen, Artist/Cartoonist

L. Frank, the *nom d'arte* of L. Frank Manriquez, is an artist, writer, tribal scholar, cartoonist, and Indigenous language activist. She lives and works in Santa Rosa, California.

Susan Masten (1952–)
Yurok, Political Activist/Tribal Leader

Susan Masten is a political activist involved with many tribal and women's issues. Her life of public service began when she was elected one of the original presidents of the Native American Student Association at Oregon State University. After graduation, she returned home to the reservation and found herself on the front lines of the Salmon Wars, a battle to protect her people's natural resources, cultural identity, tradition, and fishing rights. Masten was instrumental in securing the Yurok's rights to the Klamath River basin, which were reaffirmed in her uncles' U.S. Supreme Court case *Mattz v. Arnet.*

Masten was elected president of the National Congress of American Indians (NCAI) in October 1999 and served for one term. NCAI is the country's oldest and largest tribal membership-based organization representing and advocating for tribal governments and the rights of Native people. She served as the Yurok tribal chairperson from 1997 to 2004.

Masten has testified before Congress, given hundreds of speeches, led workshops at both college and professional events, including topics such as Tribal Sovereignty, Trust Fund Management, Consultation, Resource Management, Co-Management, and Environmental Justice. She cofounded and became copresident of Women Empowering Women for Indian Nations (WEWIN) in 2004.

At home, Masten is active in traditional Yurok practices, including fishing on the Klamath River and caring for her family's basket collection and dance regalia.

Caleen A. Sisk (1952–)
Winnemem Wintu, Leader

Caleen A. Sisk is a spiritual leader and tribal chief of the Winnemem Wintu Tribe, which practices its traditional culture and ceremonies in its territory along the McCloud River watershed in Northern California. For more than thirty years, Caleen was mentored and taught in traditional healing and Winnemem culture by her late great aunt, Florence Jones, who was the tribe's spiritual leader for sixty-eight years. Her traditional teachings and training come from an unbroken line of leadership of the Winnemem Wintu Tribe.

Since assuming leadership responsibilities in 2000, Sisk has focused on maintaining the cultural and religious traditions of the tribe as well as advo-

cating for California salmon restoration, the human right to water, and the protection of Indigenous sacred sites. She has also led her tribe's efforts to work with Maori and federal fish biologists to return Chinook salmon to the McCloud River.

Sisk is also a leading voice in raising awareness of the poor human rights conditions suffered by federally unrecognized tribes and unrepresented Indigenous peoples around the world. She is a regular speaker at the United Nations Permanent Forum on Indigenous Issues in New York where she has campaigned for the U.N. to study the plight of federally unrecognized tribes in the United States.

Sisk was one of five Indigenous leaders from North America chosen to present at the United Nations' 85th Session of the Committee on the Elimination of Racial Discrimination (CERD), which was held August 2014 in Geneva, Switzerland.

Chuck Billy (1962–)
Pomo, Vocalist/Musician

Billy is best known as the vocalist for the thrash metal band Testament although he has provided vocals and guitar for other American and European bands. In 2010, he was part of the Smithsonian National Museum of the American Indian exhibit *Up Where We Belong: Native Musicians in Popular Culture.* In 2013, California State Assemblyman Jim Frazier honored Billy on the State Assembly floor for his positive influence on the Native American community.

Naomi Lang (1978–)
Karuk, Ice Dancer

Lang, a champion ice dancer, was the first Native American female athlete to compete in the Winter Olympics. With skating partner Peter Tchernyshev, she is a two-time (2000

and 2002) Four Continents champion, a five-time (1999–2003) U.S. national champion, and competed at the 2002 Olympic Winter Games.

Born in Arcata, California, Lang studied ballet from the age of three to fifteen and performed with the Grand Rapids (Michigan) Ballet Co. She studied at the Interlochen Arts Academy and at age twelve received an award for "Outstanding Achievement in Ballet." Her skating career began when she was eight, and soon after, she began competitive skating, winning the 1995 U.S. Novice title and the 1996 U.S. Junior silver medal. Professional Russian skater Peter Tchernyshev noticed Lang and invited her to audition with him for ice dancing. Theirs was a successful partnership; both drew on their ballet backgrounds to create beautiful lines and movement. They retired from competition in 2004 but continued to tour with ice shows in the U.S. and Europe. Lang started ice dancing at the age of twelve.

ALASKA

We're not just Eskimos anymore. That's what my grandmother told me. At first, I didn't know what she meant, but now I do. She meant what she said! She said that in the family, we have Alaska's last and its first Eskimos.... I learned in school from the teachers how planes fly. They told us! I told my grandmother and my mother. They laughed. They said that's for me to know. I've never seen a whale.

—Anonymous, Eskimo (1978)

A sealskin ball, about the circumference of a softball, dangles above a stadium floor at heights known to reach eight feet. Male or female contestants sit on the floor, with one hand grabbing their opposite foot. With the other hand remaining on the floor, they spring up and kick the suspended seal ball with the free foot, landing on that same foot before any other part of the body touches the floor. In 2014, Casey Ferguson from Chevak won the gold with a ninety-four-inch High Kick, one of the most popular games at the World Eskimo-Indian Olympics (WEIO) and one of the greatest tests of athletic skill.

To better appreciate the background of the WEIO, picture yourself in a small community village hut three hundred years ago, with the temperature outside at sixty degrees below zero. Everybody inside is celebrating a successful seal hunt. In addition, the villagers are watching games developed by village elders that condition young men for the subzero environment of the Arctic and for hunts that lasted many days. To keep tough, elders developed contests that left no part of the body untested. Games pro-

vided training needed for young hunters to jump across ice floes in the event the sea ice on which they traveled broke away from the shorefast ice. Young hunters needed strength to haul game, ice, and wood over long distances and to pull slippery fish from nets. Hundreds of years ago, a high kick, without the ball as a target, might have functioned as a signal. The shape of a body above the flat tundra was used by hunters to send a message to a village spotter, posted miles away, about the killing of a whale, walrus, or caribou.

The young men demonstrate their athletic prowess and strength while whaling captains watch them with great interest. They are looking for young men with great balance, strength, and endurance to incorporate into their whaling and hunting crews. This community gathering also included feasts and dancing.

Fast forward to 1961, when the world-famous World Eskimo-Indian Olympics were founded. Ever since, the WEIO is held each July in Fairbanks,

Alaska. The four days of games test athletic skill, strength, endurance, concentration, and agility in sports, passed down from one generation of Natives to another over the centuries. In addition to the games, there are dance, art, and cultural displays as well as sewing competitions, Yup'ik, Inupiat, and Indian dance team competitions, and contests for fish cutting, seal skinning, and muktuk (an Eskimo food treat) eating. The Native Baby contest, for children between the ages of six and twenty-four months, grabs everyone's attention. The babies are judged by the traditional clothing they wear. The games come complete with an Olympic flame and the lighting of seal oil lamps. According to the WEIO website, "The logo for the World Eskimo-Indian Olympics is six interwoven rings representing the six major tribes in Alaska—Aleut, Athabascan, Inupiaq, Yup'ik, Haida, Tlingit, and Tsimpsian."

Besides the popular Alaskan High Kick, other games you might see are the Knuckle Hop, Four-Man Carry, Ear Weight, Ear Pull, One-Foot High Kick, One-Hand Reach, Kneel Jump, Eskimo Stick Pull, Indian Stick Pull, Toe Kick, Arm Pull, and Blanket Toss.

ALASKA'S ELEVEN CULTURAL GROUPS

According to the Alaska Native Heritage Center in Anchorage, Alaska, there are eleven cultural groups in Alaska. Each cultural group has occupied a different territory, spoken a distinctive language, and built a unique heritage.

Athabascan

The Athabascan people traditionally lived in interior Alaska, an expansive region that begins south of the Brooks Mountain Range and continues down to the Kenai Peninsula. Athabascan

Among the many rich and beautiful regions where the Athabascan peoples have lived is the Copper River delta in south-central Alaska.

people have traditionally lived along five major riverways: the Yukon, the Tanana, the Susitna, the Kuskokwim, and the Copper River drainages.

There are eleven linguistic groups of Athabascan in Alaska. Within each of the eleven Athabascan language groups there are local dialects, and in the past, each dialect corresponded with a social and geographical unit called a "regional band," made up of from thirty to one hundred nuclear families. (A nuclear family is a unit consisting of parents and their still dependent children.) The eleven language groups themselves were not political units.

Included in this region were six Athabascan subgroups: the Ingalik, the Koyukon, the Tanana, the Tanaina, the Ahtna, and the Upper Tanana. While each group lacked a formal tribal system, each occupied exclusive territory. Within each territory were smaller bands composed of people related by blood and marriage, who followed the seasonal migration of game, and families, who would, for part of the year, live separately in order to fish, hunt, and trap. Bands were responsible for subsistence activities, territorial boundaries, and the settlement of disputes between families.

The Athabascan practiced what is termed "strategic hunting," in which fish were directed into weirs, caribou were corralled, and waterfowl were taken in their breeding grounds.

Resources were always shared because food was sometimes scarce.

The Unangan (Aleut) and Alutiiq (Sugpiaq)

The Unangan (Aleut) and Alutiiq (Sugpiaq) peoples traditionally lived in south and southwest Alaska. Knowledge of the resources in creeks and rivers near villages and the waters of the North Pacific and Bering Sea was imperative. Also essential to the Unangan and Alutiiq were the skills required to harvest the resources.

The Unangan occupy the 1,400-mile-long Aleutian Chain, part of the Alaska Peninsula and the Pribilof Islands in the Bering Sea. An area rich in resources, it supported the densest aboriginal population in Alaska. At the time of the first Russian voyages in the seventeenth century, there were approximately 16,000 Aleut, most residing in the eastern region. The rich marine environment provided the Aleut with a wide variety of sea life, including sea urchins, clams, octopi, fish, sea otters, seals, and whales, which were used for food, clothing, and homes. Birds and their eggs, berries, wild rice and celery, and plant stalks were also part of their diet. The men were skilled open-sea hunters and relied on two-person skin boats (haidarka) for hunting seals and whales.

Aleutian villages were situated along the coast, allowing easy access to the sea. They were small, usually supporting one hundred to two hundred inhabitants. Two to five families lived in semisubterranean houses called barabaras. A person's lineage followed the mother's line, and children were disciplined and trained by the mother's family. Men were responsible for hunting and the care of implements and boats. Women cared for the home and gathered food along the beaches and shallow intertidal zones. Traditional society was divided between a small group of nobles, commoners, and slaves captured in wars with other villages. Aleut chiefs were the most respected hunters, with long experience and exceptional abilities. Chiefs had little power, and decisions required common agreement. Internal conflict was reduced by making war on others for retribution, the taking of slaves, or trading through intermediaries. The family served as the basis of village organization, economic exchange, warfare, and occasionally political authority.

Alutiiq (Sugpiaq)

The Alutiiq have inhabited the coastal environments of south-central Alaska for over 7,500 years. Their traditional homelands include coastal communities such as Prince William Sound, the outer Kenai Peninsula, the Kodiak Archipelago, and the Alaska Peninsula. In the early 1800s, there were more than sixty Alutiiq villages in the Kodiak archipelago, with an estimated population of 13,000 people. In 2014, more than four thousand Alutiiq people lived in rural villages and each of Alaska's major cities.

According to the Alutiiq Museum in Kodiak, Alaska, the Alutiiq share many cultural practices with the other coastal peoples, especially the Unangan/Aleut of the Aleutian Chain and the Yup'ik of the Bering Sea coast. At the time of European colonization, there were distinct regional groups of Alutiiq people, each speaking a different dialect of the Alutiiq language.

The Aleut and Alutiiq cultures were heavily influenced by the Russians, beginning in the eighteenth century. The Orthodox Church is prominent in every village, Russian dishes are made using local subsistence food, and Russian words are part of common vocabulary in Unangax and Sugcestun, Indigenous languages.

Yup'ik and Cup'ik

Yup'ik and Cup'ik peoples traditionally lived in southwest Alaska from Bristol Bay along the Bering Sea coast to Norton Sound. The people are named after the two main dialects of the Yup'ik language. The word Yup'ik represents not only the language but also the name for the people themselves (*yuk*, meaning "person," plus *pik*, which means "real").

The availability of fish, game, and plants determined the location of seasonal camps and villages. Yup'ik and Cup'ik are hunters of moose, caribou, whale, walrus, seal, and sea lions and harvest salmon and other fish from the Yukon, Kuskokwim, and Nushagak rivers. Bird eggs, berries, and roots help sustain people throughout the region.

Traditionally, Yup'ik societies were geared toward the continual search for food. They spent part of the year on the move and some time at a settlement, or "central base." From a dozen to fifty people would travel together. Extended families composed of three to four generations were basic to an individual's life. Families were relatively equal and autonomous; they would often share with others, intermarry, and hunt together. Within each family, people were divided by age and gender. Leaders were usually those who dis-

played exceptional skill or courage and those who were able to anticipate future problems. Spiritual leaders were also influential because of their familiarity with the spiritual world, their curative powers, and their prescience.

Yup'ik families spent the spring and summer at fish camp, then joined with others at village sites for the winter. Many families still harvest the traditional subsistence resources, especially salmon and seal. The men's communal house, the qasgiq, was the community center for ceremonies and festivals which included singing, dancing, and storytelling. The qasgiq was used mainly in the winter months because people would travel in family groups following food sources throughout the spring, summer, and fall months. Aside from ceremonies and festivals, it was also where the men taught the young boys survival and hunting skills as well as other life lessons. The young boys were also taught how to make tools and kayaks during the winter months in the qasgiq.

A Yup'ik man wears a headdress with a wooden bird head in this 1929 photograph.

The women's house, the ena, was traditionally right next door, and in some areas, they were connected by a tunnel. Women taught the young girls how to sew, cook, and weave. Boys would live with their mothers until they were about five years old, then they would live in the qasgiq. Each winter, for a few weeks, the young boys and young girls would switch, with the men teaching the girls survival and hunting skills and tool making and the women teaching the boys how to sew and cook.

The Inupiat and St. Lawrence Island Yup'ik

The Inupiaq and St. Lawrence Island Yup'ik peoples, who call themselves the "Real People," live in north and northwest Alaska. They continue to subsist on the land and sea. Their lives revolve around the whale, walrus, seal, polar bear, caribou, and fish. They gather berries in season. They also hunt birds and fish when conditions are right. These two groups of Native people have been put in the same category because of their similar subsistence patterns, the way they constructed their homes, and their tools. St. Lawrence Island Yup'ik speak Siberian Yup'ik, which is different from the languages spoken by other Yup'ik groups.

Eyak

Eyak people occupied the lands in the southeastern corner of south-central Alaska. Each local group of Eyak had at least one permanent winter village with various seasonal camps close to food resources. There, they harvested the rich salmon fishing grounds of the Copper River to the Pacific coast. The Native village of Eyak is located on the southeastern shores of Prince William Sound in the North Gulf Coast of Alaska. The territory is the traditional meeting place of four peoples, the Eyak, Aleut, Tlingit, and Athabascan. Prince William Sound, Copper River Delta, and the North Gulf Coast were shared among them. The arrival of the Russians, and subsequently Americans, greatly impacted their way of life and culture.

Tlingit, Haida, and Tsimshian

Three major groups occupied southeastern Alaska: the Tlingit, the Haida, and the Tsimshian. Geographically, the area is distinct. It is isolated, with high mountains and dense forest to the east and the Pacific Ocean to the west; it is interlaced by fjords and valleys on the mainland and a string of islands off the coast. It is a bountiful environment, which nurtured a formal and complex social system.

Traditional Tlingit territory in Alaska includes the Southeast panhandle between Icy Bay on the north side to the Dixon Entrance on the south side. Tlingit people have also occupied the area to the east inside the Canadian border. This group is known as the "Inland Tlingit." The Tlingit fished salmon in kin-owned areas and also depended upon other resources of the sea, especially halibut and seal. Clinging to the mountainous shores and rugged offshore islands, Tlingit villages were usually large in comparison to similar groups in Canada. The total Tlingit population at the time of European contact is estimated to have been 15,000.

The original homeland of the Haida people is the Queen Charlotte Islands in British Columbia, Canada. Prior to contact with Europeans, a group migrated north to the Prince of Wales Island area within Alaska. This group is known as the "Kaigani" or Alaska Haida. Today, the Kaigani Haida live mainly in two villages, Kasaan and Hydaburg. Several bands of Haida probably numbered about 14,000 when Russians first had contact with them in the late 1700s.

The original homeland of the Tsimshian is between the Nass and Skeena rivers in British Columbia, Canada. Presently in Alaska, the Tsimshian live mainly on Annette Island, in (New) Metlakatla, Alaska, in addition to settlements in Canada. They numbered approximately 14,500 at the time of first contact.

Food Resources

Water supplied the main food for the Tlingit, Haida, and Tsimshian. One of the most important

The rivers of Alaska have long been an excellent food source, including of the delectable salmon like chinook, coho, pink, dog salmon, and sockeye.

fish was salmon. There are five species: King (chinook), silver (coho), red (sockeye), chum (dog salmon), and pink (humpback or humpy). Steelhead, herring, herring eggs, and ooligans (eulachon) were also caught and eaten. Southeast waters produce an abundance of foods, including a variety of sea mammals and deepwater fish. Some sea plants include seaweed (black, red), beach asparagus, and goose tongue. Other food resources were derived from plants (berries and shoots), and from land mammals (moose, mountain goat, and deer).

Social Organizations of Alaska Natives

Neither primitive nor simple, traditional Native communities in Alaska were extremely well adapted to the physical environment in which they lived, from the Arctic regions of Northern Alaska to the rain forests of the southeast to the cool and windy climates of the Aleutian Chain.

The Alaska Natives were bound by an intricate kinship system that usually specified who could marry and where the couple would live as well as ownership of fishing and hunting places and leadership. These kinship relations also defined the performance of social and religious obligations, like potlatch exchanges, and other ritual reciprocities, such as performing funeral services for in-laws, as among the Tlingit.

There was a precarious balance between the physical environment and the subsistence needs of each community. Natural disasters, population growth, or outside intrusion could easily upset the balance of human and natural environmental relations.

Haida, Tlingit, and Tsimshian Social Organization

Society was divided between two major moieties (divisions), the Eagle and the Raven, which had their own rules and corporate functions. Within each moiety were numerous clans. The clan was the fundamental political unit; each had its own territory, history, and particular traits. The clan was responsible for settling feuds, property, and subsistence activities. The most basic unit was the house, which was run by a "master of the house," a maternal or great-uncle. Houses had their own plots, names, and crests, which displayed major cultural figures in the history of the clan and house. Clans and houses had rights to specific areas for fishing, berry picking, and hunting. In practice, any person could use the sites provided he asked for permission.

Rank and status, built on the accumulation of wealth, underlay the system of clans and houses. Possession of material goods, including slaves, crests, blankets, totems, a generous disposition, oratorical skill, and past accomplishments, determined the position of individuals, clans, and houses. The potlatch was an integral part of Alaskan cultures. It involved a feast, performances, and the distribution of valuable goods. Potlatches were given to honor an individual, and they served to strengthen kin relations, to display one's generosity, and to honor the memory of those who had passed away.

ALASKA NATIVE LANGUAGES

Alaska is home to at least twenty distinct Indigenous languages, according to the Alaska Native Language Center (ALNC), located at the University of Alaska, Fairbanks. These languages reflect the diverse cultural heritage of Native peoples. The center strives to raise public awareness of the gravity of language loss worldwide. Of the state's twenty Native languages, only two (Siberian Yup'ik in two villages on St. Lawrence Island and Central Yup'ik in seventeen villages in southwestern Alaska) are spoken by children as the first language of the home. Like every language in the world, each of those twenty is of inestimable human value and is worthy of preservation. ANLC continues to document, cultivate, and promote those languages as much as possible and thus contribute to their future and to the heritage of all Alaskans.

In 2012, Alaska Governor Sean Parnell established the Alaska Language Preservation and Advisory Council, which published its first report with policy recommendations in July 2014. These include conducting a comprehensive update of speaker numbers and a public awareness campaign about the importance of Native language learning, sponsoring a statewide language summit, requiring Alaska Native schools to comply with the law mandating Native language curricula, and establishing an annual state holiday, Alaska Native Language Day, that symbolically elevates Alaska Native languages to official languages alongside English.

In October 2014, Governor Sean Parnell designated twenty Native languages as official languages of the state by signing House Bill 216. He said "It's a recognition of the languages that compose a rich cultural landscape of this great state. It gives dignity and honor to those languages that exist, and they should have had that honor so much sooner."

CHANGE IN ALASKA NATIVES

According to Paul C. Ongtooguk (Inupiaq), University of Alaska professor of secondary education, and Claudia S. Dybdahl, University of Alaska professor of elementary education, "The hundreds of centuries that Alaska's First Peoples inhabited the land before the arrival of Europeans—more than 99 percent of its history—were filled with change. Generation after generation created new knowledge and responded to transforming natural and social worlds. Climate and animal migration patterns shifted, new technologies arose and spread, religious and spiritual concepts flowered, and wars and alliances emerged from intertribal relations."

THE INVENTION OF SEA KAYAKS

The Unangan people (Aleut) are the inventors of one of the most sophisticated, highly developed inventions ever created: the skin-on-frame sea kayaks, or *iqyax*, pronounced *ik'yah*. The Russian name, *baidarka*, is commonly used in the islands today.

Kayaks used to hunt marine animals were built for survival on the stormy seas of the Aleutian Chain. Russian-era journal accounts from the 1700s and 1800s described them in detail, praising their sophisticated design, speed, beauty, and skill of construction. In 1802, Martin Sauer, British secretary of the Billings expedition, wrote: "If perfect symmetry, smoothness, and proportion constitute beauty, they are beautiful; to me, they appeared so beyond anything that I ever beheld. I have seen some of them as transparent as oiled paper, through which you could trace every formation of the inside." The kayaks varied in length from about thirteen to twenty-one feet, depending on whether they were made for one, two, or three paddlers. Europeans wrote about the superhuman strength and agility of the hunters who paddled them in the stormy Bering Sea and North Pacific.

Within a short period, the knowledge of how to build these vessels would all but disappear,

An Alaskan native floats in a kayak while fishing off the Aleutian islands in this 1897 illustration.

forced out of the collective memory by the disrupting impact of the invading cultures of Russia and, later, the United States. The passing of the technology from one generation to the next, which had gone on for thousands of years, stopped. In the late 1980s, the Unangan community began looking for the way back to the lost *iqyax* technology. They searched out the details from the early Russian-era journal accounts and by studying the vessels themselves, now stored in museums around the world. Marc Daniels, a non-Unangan who mastered the art of making *iqyax*, began apprenticeship programs for Unangan communities. The traditional skin boat renaissance has come a long way since the community began to relearn the technology in the early 1990s. These days, it's possible to see a paddler in a traditional *iqyax* out on the Bering Sea during fair weather!

DISEASES

For some Alaska Native peoples, the first real encounters with the West took the form of lethal new diseases that swept through their communities. They included smallpox, the deadliest of all, as well as diphtheria, scarlet fever, malaria, measles, influenza, whooping cough, typhoid fever, typhus, pneumonia, and tuberculosis. Estimates are that from one-half to three-fourths of Alaska Natives died from these diseases. The loss of life had enormous consequences, fundamentally altering Indigenous cultures and beliefs.

RUSSIAN COLONIALISM (1740s–1867)

With the advent of European expansion in the eighteenth century, circumstances in Native Alaska began to change dramatically. The Russians came first. Russian merchant companies, in search of valuable furs, came armed with weapons and seagoing capabilities that allowed them to conquer the Aleutian Islands, the Kodiak archipelago, and the southern mainland coast by the 1780s. The voyages of Alexei Chirikof and Vitus Bering in 1741 led to awareness of potential profit from sea otter and seal skins. Russian or Siberian fur hunters, the *promishleniki,* came to exploit Alaska's fur resources.

An imperial decree was issued in 1766, claiming Russian dominion over the Aleutians, but there was little government regulation of

Alexander Andreyevich Baranov was the first Russian governor of Alaska and also was involved in the Russian–American Company, which was established by the czar to found settlements in North America.

Russian traders and hunters. In response to this anarchy and the competition with other Europeans, the Russian–American Company was organized in 1799 to establish some kind of control by the Czarist government. The company had absolute domination over all aspects of Russian America. For fifty years, it was brutal in overcoming resistance, asserting control, and maximizing profits. Its practices in the early years included forced labor of the Aleut and possibly some of the Pacific Eskimo people, kidnapping, torturing, and murdering them. The brutal fur traders demanded the service of the Aleut, who were excellent hunters of the valuable sea otter. When the Aleut resisted enslavement, the Russians killed whole groups of them to induce the remaining people to submit. During this time, the populations of fur-bearing animals were plundered.

UNANGAN RESISTANCE

The Unangan of the Aleutian Islands encountered Russian sea otter traders in the 1740s and were rapidly "swept up in a tsunami of dis-

ease, destruction, and warfare, out of which 10 percent survived," according to Paul C. Ongtooguk and Claudia S. Dybdahl. Russian dominance was far less complete in southeast Alaska, in part because the Tlingit and Haida residents of that region had armed themselves with muskets and even cannons acquired from rival British and American trading vessels. The Tlingit burned early Russian outposts in Sitka (1802) and Yakutat (1804), resisted Russian control, and eventually settled into a standoff that allowed mutual trade.

The Russian fur trade did not extend very far inland. In 1847, after Britain's Hudson's Bay Company founded Fort Yukon near the Alaska–Canada border, a few Athabascan communities interacted directly with Westerners.

The Russian–American Company's charter anticipated the conversion of Natives to Christianity and claimed that the "Islanders" (Aleut) would be treated amicably. However, the relationship between the Russians and the Aleut was anything but amicable. Although the exact numbers are not known, it is estimated that 90 percent of the Indigenous population was lost to disease or murder. In this period of rapid change and indescribable disruption, the individual family, community lifestyles, and many aspects of traditional Aleut culture were literally obliterated. The Russian conquerors required changes in dress, dwellings, weapons, tools, religion, and day-to-day routines of Aleut village existence.

At one time, there were fewer than eight hundred to one thousand Russians in all of Alaska. Apart from Kodiak and Sitka, permanent Russian settlements were small, often having only a dozen inhabitants. Most locations were trading posts that were manned by one or two Russians. Over time, Russian profits declined steadily. The adverse economic situation, disastrous effects of the Crimean War (1853–1856), caused Russia to try to interest the United States in purchasing Alaska in 1859. The United States declined the offer until after the Civil War. A Treaty of Cession was signed on March 30, 1867, ratified by the Senate on April 9 and signed by President Andrew Johnson on May 28. A formal transfer of territory was made during a ceremony in Sitka on October 18, 1867. The purchase price was an incredibly low $7.2 million. By the time the United States acquired control of the territory, Russia ruled only a small portion of it.

Prior to payment for Alaska, Americans began moving in to take control of the Russian–American Company. These included forts, schools, foundries, coal mines, farms, and livestock. U.S. expansion into Alaska was also propelled by an interest in fur and, more importantly, gold.

AMERICAN COLONIALISM (1867–1884)

Native people were not consulted in any way regarding the change in "ownership" of their land and resources or their overnight change in nationality. The 1867 land cession treaty with Russia did not clearly define the legal status, basic rights, and matters of land ownership relevant to Alaska Natives. Article III of the treaty did mention Alaska Natives:

"The Uncivilized tribes will be subject to such laws and regulations as the United States may, from time to time, adopt in regard to aboriginal tribes in that country." Congress recognized this obligation in 1884 when it passed the first Organic Act, which extended the civil and criminal laws of Oregon to Alaska: "Indians or other persons in said district shall not be disturbed in the possession of any lands actually in their use or occupation or now claimed by them but the terms under which such persons may acquire title to such lands is reserved for future legislation by Congress."

In the beginning years of U.S. control of Alaska, the area was viewed as being useless and was referred to as "Seward's Folly." Secretary of State William Seward had championed the land purchase. For seventeen years, the government largely stayed out of the everyday lives of Natives and non-Natives, with some exceptions. Scattered incidents of armed conflicts in southeast Alaska were met with aggressive responses from the U.S. Army and Navy, including bombardment of Tlingit villages in 1869 and 1882.

In 1884, Congress passed an Alaska "Organic Act," establishing a civilian government for the area. The "general laws of the state of Oregon" and the mining laws of the United States were to be applied. A gold discovery near Juneau prompted the legislative action. The act's purpose was legal control of mining activity and adjudication of disputes over land. General U.S. land laws were not applied to Alaska, and Native land claims were deferred by the Act: "The Indians or other persons in said district shall not be disturbed in the possession of any lands actually in their use or occupation or now claimed by them, but the terms under which said persons may acquire title to such lands is reserved for future legislation by Congress."

Despite this disclaimer in the Organic Act, land was usually available for the U.S. economic interests who needed it. The first fish canneries

U.S. Secretary of State William Seward orchestrated the purchase of Alaska from the Russians in 1867. Americans at the time thought the land was useless and called it "Seward's Folly."

were built in 1878, and within six years, they were spread along the entire southern coast of Alaska. In 1878, the first gold mining camp was constructed. Gold prospecting and disputes between miners resulted in the territory's first civil government. Legislation in 1891, 1898, and 1900 permitted trade and manufacturing sites, townsites, homesteading, rights of way for a railroad, and the harvesting of timber. Many of the best traditional fishing and hunting sites were taken by non-Natives. Food became scarce as the fish and game populations decreased. Living conditions deteriorated.

By 1910, the large influx of non-Natives and diseases like influenza and tuberculosis greatly disrupted the Native population. When the Russians arrived in Alaska in the mid-1770s, it is estimated that the Alaska Native population stood at about 74,000. When the U.S. took possession of Alaska in 1867, the Native population had fallen to an official count of 28,254. In 1880, at the beginning of three decades of economic development, there were 32,996 Natives in Alaska. By the end of the gold rush era, in 1910, the Native population had fallen 23 percent from the 1880 level to 25,331.

THE STRUGGLE FOR CITIZENSHIP AND LAND RIGHTS

Tanana Chiefs Protest

In interior Alaska in 1915, the Tanana Athabascan chiefs protested against the appropriation of their traditional lands with neither their consent nor compensation for construction of the Alaska railroad. The federal government ignored these protests. The confrontation led to the formation of the Tanana Chiefs Conference to promote the social, civic, and educational advancement of Alaska Natives.

In 1912, eleven Alaska Native men and one Alaska Native woman formed the Alaska Native Brotherhood (ANB). The ANB focused its energies on promoting Native solidarity, achieving

U.S. citizenship, abolishing racial prejudice, and securing economic equality through the recognition of Indian land title and mineral rights as well as the preservation of salmon stocks. Local ANB chapters, called "camps," were located in various Native communities, guided by a central organizational and communications hub known as the Grand Camp that kept ANB delegates in regular contact and informed of political occurrences. Despite its nonsectarian approach, the ANB officers maintained a close relationship with the Presbyterian Sheldon Jackson school.

During this period, the U.S. government considered Native people to be wards of the state. This prompted ANB leaders to fight for citizenship. As the ANB grew in popularity, its leaders became increasingly convinced of the organization's influence over Alaskan politics. In 1921, ANB representative William Paul, Tlingit, attempted to convince officials in Washington to prohibit fish traps from narrow bays and channels in Alaska. Although Paul's request was ignored, his appearance informed federal officials that the ANB was the political voice for Native Alaskans.

The ANB (as well as others in the lower forty-eight states) continued lobbying federal officials to grant Alaska Natives full citizenship status, and, in 1924, the U.S. government acquiesced, passing the Indian Citizenship Act. Following the ANB's attainment of Alaska Native enfranchisement, the Brotherhood attempted to extend its influence by subsequently working with both Native and non-Native labor leaders, eventually establishing itself as an influential labor union and bargaining agent into the 1940s.

Toward the end of the 1920s, ANB leaders denounced as discriminatory a recent announcement by the federal government that a single school system would be established for Native Americans. In 1929, William Paul successfully argued in court that Native parents had the right to send their children to schools of their choice. The attempt to reject separate Indian schools and to compel the federal government to recognize Native people as citizens was an ANB strategy designed to wrest from government control the direction of their lives.

The ANB and its partner organization, the Alaska Native Sisterhood, initiated the struggle for land rights. They announced their intention in 1929 to recover Tlingit and Haida lands by joining forces to pursue a land claim settlement against the U.S. government for millions of acres of land it took to create the Tongass National Forest and Glacier Bay National Park. The U.S. government eventually gave in and passed the Tlingit and Haida Jurisdictional Act of June 15, 1935, enabling the Tlingit and Haida to initiate their land claim against the government in the U.S. Court of Claims. The complex case suffered many reversals and wound on until 1968, when financial compensation was awarded to the Central Council of Tlingit and Haida. No land was regained, disappointing many.

In 1936, the federal government extended to Alaska the Indian Reorganization Act (IRA) of 1934, which provided Native people with increased opportunities for land retention, self-government, and economic development. It enabled the formation of tribal governments at the village level. The ANB supported the IRA, a popular move that further strengthened its political resolve.

WORLD WAR II AND THE ALEUTIAN PEOPLE

On June 3, 1942, the Japanese dropped bombs on Fort Mears at Dutch Harbor in the Aleutian Chain. The raids led to the evacuation of 886 Aleut civilians to Southeast Alaska where they were placed in deplorable conditions by the federal government until the war ended.

On June 16, 1942, the populations of St. George and St. Paul of the Pribilof Islands were evacuated within twenty-four hours for military reasons after the Japanese landed on Kiska and Attu. The Navy relocated the St. Paul Aleut to an abandoned cannery at Funter Bay on Admiralty Island and the St. George Aleut to an old mine site across the bay from the cannery. In many cases, the people had two hours to gather up belongings and were limited to one suitcase each. Many people died in the unsanitary conditions of the camps.

In May 1943, the U.S. Seventh Infantry Division landed 11,000 infantry on Attu Island. After nineteen days of fighting, the Japanese were defeated. In April 1945, after the Aleut returned to Unalaska in the Aleutian Chain, they found their villages vandalized by occupying American forces.

In August 1988, President Ronald Reagan signed the Civil Liberties Act, a law making restitution through payments to Unangan residents of the Pribilof and Aleutian Islands for loss of personal and community property and village lands during the U.S. military occupation of the islands during World War II. The act also apologized for the evacuation, relocation, and internment of Japanese during World War II.

ALASKA, THE FORTY-NINTH STATE, AND HAWAII, THE FIFTIETH STATE

During World War II, national leaders became more aware of the strategic importance of Alaska. This realization, coupled with the influx of money and people, produced a viable effort to achieve admittance into the Union. In his State of the Union message in 1946, Presi-

U.S. Marines defend Fort Mears during the Japanese attack on June 3, 1942.

dent Harry Truman recommended statehood. Owing to partisan opposition and doubts about the financial capability of the territory, recognition was delayed. Finally, a compromise was reached, and Alaska and Hawaii were admitted simultaneously. On January 3, 1959, President Dwight Eisenhower proclaimed Alaska the forty-ninth state. On August 21, 1959, Hawaii became the fiftieth state.

More than thirty years before Alaska was granted statehood, the Alaska Department of the American Legion sponsored a flag design contest for Alaskan children in grades seven through twelve. The creation of Aleut teenager John Ben "Benny" Benson, Jr. (1913–1972) was chosen from over seven hundred entries; he was awarded one thousand dollars and a trip to Washington, D.C. Until then, Alaskans had only flown the U.S. flag over the Alaska Territory, but Benny's flag was used to represent the Territory and later the state of Alaska. Young Benny and his brother had lived in an orphanage for most of their lives, and each night, he looked to the sky to see the constellations—he put the familiar stars into his flag. Benny sent in this description along with his artwork: "The blue field is for the Alaska sky and the forget-me-not, an Alaskan flower. The North Star is for the future state of Alaska, the most northerly in the union. The Dipper is for the Great Bear—symbolizing strength."

ALASKA NATIVE LAND CLAIMS MOVEMENT

The early 1960s was a period of great activism among Alaska Natives. Land rights were a main issue for all Alaska Natives. The Alaska Statehood Act granted the state 104 million acres of land. As public officials began selecting land, imposing rules, and applying laws, Native opposition arose. For example, the Bureau of Land Management, the agency in the Department of the Interior responsible for federal lands, issued a license to the Atomic Energy Commission (AEC), which regulates the use of nuclear materials in the United States, to use sixteen hundred square miles

around Point Hope, an Inupiat village on the northwestern coast of Alaska, for an experimental nuclear explosion to create a deep water port. However, no one consulted the residents of nearby villages. After successfully preventing the use of atomic explosives at Point Hope, the Alaska Natives were confronted with a series of other issues, such as protecting their rights to hunt game and the prevention of the Rampart Dam, which threatened to flood large areas of Athabascan hunting land in central Alaska.

Another issue was the enforcement of the Migratory Bird Treaty Act between Canada and the United States. The treaty prohibits the hunting of migratory birds between March 10 and September 1. In 1961, the Inupiat staged a "duck-in" to protest the restrictions. Many were arrested.

During the 1961–1965 period, Alaska Natives mobilized to protect their land. In March 1961, the president of the Point Hope Village Council wrote to the Association of American Indian Affairs (AAIA), founded in 1923 to provide legal and technical assistance to Indian tribes, and asked for help. The AAIA and the Indian Rights Association, established in 1882 to protect the rights of American Indians, provided funds for intervillage meetings, at which experiences were shared, rights explained, and common solutions proposed. Within six years, twelve regional associations were formed to pursue their respective land claims. Early in 1965, regional leaders formed the Alaska Federation of Natives (AFN), a statewide Native organization that represented the land, political, and social welfare issues of Alaska Natives, to secure their rights, inform the public about their position, preserve their cultural values, and gain an equitable settlement.

The first major bill to settle the claims of Alaska Natives was introduced in June 1967. The key to a congressional decision was oil. In the late 1960s, large quantities of oil were discovered in Prudhoe Bay on the north coast of Alaska. Several large oil companies worked to extract and transport the crude oil to refineries and markets in the lower forty-eight states. The need to construct an eight-hundred-mile pipeline from the production

The Trans-Alaska Pipeline was built during the Jimmy Carter administration to make oil exploration in Prudhoe Bay economically viable.

fields in the North to a shipping terminal in Prince William Sound made it essential to resolve conflicting tribal, state, and federal land claims.

Native villages, in particular Stevens Village, an Athabascan village in the interior, claimed land over the pipeline route and gained a court injunction against construction until Indian title to the land was clarified. Thereafter, the oil companies actively lobbied Congress and President Richard Nixon in order to gain a quick settlement to Native land claims issues in Alaska. By late 1971, an unusual coalition comprised of oil companies, the Alaska Federation of Natives (AFN), a lobbying organization, the state of Alaska, and the federal government moved to settle Alaska Native claims through congressional legislation. President Nixon and the U.S. Senate wanted a domestic source of oil that would counter the increase in prices in 1970 and the shortage of fuel and heating oil. The state of Alaska needed the revenue that private development would generate. The oil industry and the House of Representatives wanted

a permit to build the Alaska pipeline. Conservationists wanted more park and wilderness area, and Alaska Natives wanted their land. The Alaska Native Claims Settlement Act (ANCSA) was signed into law on December 18, 1971.

ALASKA NATIVE CLAIMS SETTLEMENT ACT, 1971

Under terms of the settlement, Alaska Natives were enrolled in twelve state-chartered regional corporations and over two hundred village corporations. The 13th Regional Corporation, representing Alaska Natives living outside the state who were eligible to share in the settlement, received funds but no land. It was created under ANCSA and incorporated in Alaska on December 31, 1975. Headquartered in Seattle, Washington, the for-profit company had approximately 5,500 Alaska Native shareholders. Its original enrollment was composed of Alaska Natives who were no longer residents in the state. Unlike the other twelve Alaska Native regional corporations, the 13th Regional Corporation and its shareholders received only monetary compensation, with no land conveyance, in settlement of aboriginal land claims. The 13th Regional Corporation was involuntarily dissolved by the Division of Corporations, Business and Professional Licensing of the Alaska Department of Commerce, Community and Economic Development on December 31, 2013.

The other corporations were granted clear title to approximately forty-four million acres and received a financial settlement of $962.5 million. In return, all other Native land claims were dissolved. ANCSA cleared the path for the construction of the Alaska pipeline; it also led to the withdrawal of millions of acres of public lands for national parks and forests, scenic rivers, and wilderness areas. State officials were also permitted to select the remainder of their land under provisions of the Statehood Act. In the end, ten percent of Alaska's original land base became privately owned by Alaska Natives, divided among the village and regional corporations.

The native regional corporations include:

- Arctic Slope Regional Corporation
- AHTNA, Inc.
- The Aleut Corporation
- Bering Straits Native Corporation
- Bristol Bay Native Corporation
- Calista Corporation
- Chugach Alaska Corporation
- Cook Inlet Region, Inc.
- Doyon Limited
- Koniag, Inc.
- NANA Regional Corporation
- Sealaska Corporation

When Congress passed ANCSA, it recognized that the economic potential of the lands selected by Native corporations would not be uniformly distributed. As a result, ANCSA contains a natural resource revenue-sharing provision [Section 7(i)]. This section is intended to achieve a rough equality in assets among all Alaska Natives. The section ensures that all of the Alaska Natives will benefit in roughly equal proportions from these assets. Under 7(i), seventy percent of all revenues received by each Regional Corporation from timber and subsurface estate resources must be divided among all twelve Regional Corporations in proportion to the number of Alaska Natives enrolled in each region. At least fifty percent of the revenues received must be redistributed among the village corporations.

Alaska's Native corporations (ANCs) are a major component of Alaska's economy and will become an even bigger force in the future. They

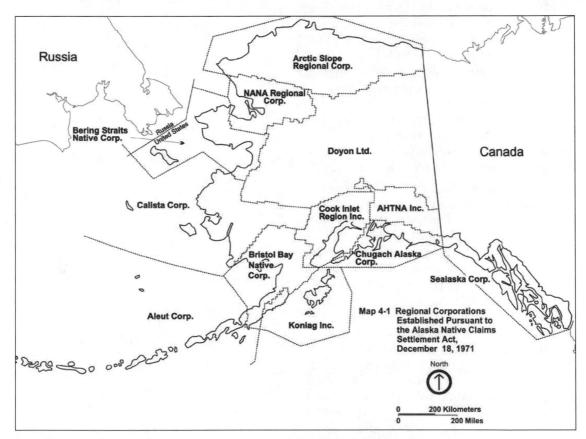

Map of Regional Corporations established by the Alaska Native Claims Settlement Act.

are important to each region they represent and the state as a whole. From Southeast Alaska and the Aleutians to Interior Alaska and the North Slope, these corporations are among Alaska's largest enterprises and employers. According to testimony provided to the U.S. Senate Committee on Indian Affairs in October 2014, the twelve regional ANCs and village corporations employ 58,000 people worldwide, with about 16,000 of those jobs in Alaska. Many of the Native corporations are engaged in the development of Alaska's natural resources but are also diversifying their operations into other business ventures both inside and outside the state.

Some regional corporations are fulfilling ANCSA's economic goals. The Arctic Slope Regional Corporation and the Sealaska Corporation have made the Fortune 500 list of the most successful companies in the United States. Some regional corporations have almost gone bankrupt. The village corporations have had diverse histories as well. Several were threatened with dissolution because they were inactive or failed to file corporate reports required by the state of Alaska. Other villages have been successful revenue-wise, matching the larger regional corporations. According to Rosita Worl, Tlingit, anthropologist and president of the Sealaska Heritage Institute, "Overall, Alaska Native corporations make an extraordinary contribution to the economy of the state."

An important issue that ANCSA legislation did not address was shareholder status for children born after 1971. A major concern has been the dilution and fragmentation of shares as the original 1971 shareholders give or will their shares to children and grandchildren. Some corporations issue special classes of shares to children born after 1971. Some corporations have taken steps to allow younger people to acquire shares. Some descendants receive shares, given or willed, in small blocks. Some shares come with strings. There are voting restrictions for some, and in other cases, special shares can't be inherited. Shareholders with just one or two shares have less of a stake and are often less interested and engaged in the corporation's affairs or its founding goals, mainly the protection of land.

TRADITIONAL SUBSISTENCE WAY OF LIFE, PAST AND STILL PRESENT

Traditional subsistence economies in Alaska were small, self-sufficient, and practical household economies. People used what they produced. Alliances for trade existed. Coastal communities would exchange seal oil for caribou skins, for example, but trading relationships were limited. Food and clothing were locally produced and shared among kin and within local camps. The sharing of resources was common. People were united through blood and marriage. Kinship was a way of organizing labor, establishing rights, forming groups, and distributing wealth.

Aboriginal life was cyclic and inseparable from the patterns and turns of nature. Inuit whalers, for example, hunted caribou in the summer for clothing and bedding and snared small animals for food. In the fall, they returned to the coast for trade and the gathering of food on the beaches. Later, men hunted seals on the open sea until the ice returned. In midwinter, seals, fish, and bears were hunted on the ice. By April, when the ice melted enough, boat crews were in pursuit of bowhead whales. Near the end of June, when the whales had migrated south, birds and seals were the primary sources of food.

The subsistence economy remains central to the lives of most Alaska Natives in the state's two hundred predominantly rural communities located in remote areas. More than 50 percent of rural food comes from subsistence activities. These resources are used for clothing, transportation (fish are given to dog teams), heating, housing, and arts and crafts. Traditional values of sharing, cooperation, and reciprocity also continue. Large extended families still live together. Customary rules guide distribution and consumption of subsistence resources. Many Natives consider themselves first and foremost hunters and fishermen. There is evidence, too, that subsistence economies are not only resilient but growing in certain villages.

Although Native corporations compose a major sector of Alaska's economy, they have not eliminated poverty in the state's two hundred predominantly Native rural communities. Many lack infrastructure and energy sources to attract year-round economic investment. The villages nevertheless survive because people are strongly attached to the land and the subsistence way of life.

Communities in rural Alaska must be able to participate in subsistence hunting and fishing to sustain their lives and cultures. In 1980, the federal government's Alaska National Interest Lands Conservation Act affirmed the right of Alaska's rural residents to continue their customary and traditional practices. However, the state of Alaska held that its constitution does not allow for a distinction between urban and rural residents and that regulations concerning fish and game and hunting and gathering must be the same for all Alaskans. Failure to reconcile the federal and state positions led the federal government to take control of the management of fish and game on federal lands and waters in 1990. Alaska has two sets of fish and game regulations: one for state lands and waters and another for federal lands and waters.

ALASKA INDIGENEITY

Because my roots are from Alaska. I'm the heartbeat of Alaska. I breathe, I walk, I eat what it offers from the land and the sea. I guess I want people in general to respect all the tribes of Alaska Natives. Because we are the very roots of Alaska.

—Mary Ann Immamak

Alaska Tribal Sovereignty Today

The passage of ANCSA left questions about the status of tribes in Alaska and the extent of their jurisdiction. Alaska tribes proceeded to assert their existence and jurisdiction by various governmental activities, including hearing a wide variety of cases in their tribal courts. As they did so, the state of Alaska challenged the existence of tribes and the activity of the tribal courts. The tribes also challenged Alaska to accept their assertions and court decisions. These challenges

were made through both state and federal courts, and the court decisions help to outline the extent of tribal jurisdiction in Alaska. There are still many issues surrounding Alaska tribal jurisdiction that are unclear, but some generalizations can be made.

Over 230 tribes in Alaska exist, which have some level of jurisdiction based on their status as tribes. They can determine their own membership and determine their own form of government, justice system, and internal affairs. Tribal jurisdiction in Alaska tends to be "member based" rather than based on a territory such as a reservation. In other words, tribal courts can hear cases involving tribal members even if they are not officially "Indian Country," defined as a territorial area over which a tribe has jurisdiction. Tribal jurisdiction in Alaska tends to be concurrent with the state of Alaska. Both the state and tribes share jurisdiction, and whichever court hears a case first assumes jurisdiction over the case. Alaska tribes generally have concurrent jurisdiction over domestic relations involving tribal members including adoptions, child protection, domestic violence, marriages, divorces, and probate.

ART TRADITIONS

Alaska Native peoples have been recognized as among the finest artists in the Americas. Native cultures developed and changed partly according to their own dynamics and partly because of contact with other cultures, peoples, and events around them. They created distinctive cultural and regional styles and expressed their religions and social beliefs in a multitude of artistic forms.

In the harsh Arctic region of Alaska, where the only plant materials are tiny flowers and lichen blooming for a brief growing season in the summer, life as well as art traditionally depended on the bountiful animal world: caribou, polar bear, salmon, walrus, whale, and seal. Men carved walrus tusks, caribou antlers, and whale bones into fishing and hunting implements, such as harpoon heads, knives, buttons, and toggles that were both practical and beautiful. Women sewed animal skins into fine and warm garments to protect the wearer and to please the spirits of the animals who had sacrificed their lives so that humans could eat and stay warm.

The Inupiat were renowned for their skill in ivory carving. Tools and personal ornaments were decorated with carvings of Arctic species like polar bears, seals, and whales. Overall, the Inupiat emphasized decorative art. The Inupiat also developed two-dimensional scenes of hunting and camp life depicted on engraved ivory filled with charcoal.

The Yup'ik art was more diverse, abstract, and symbolic. People created religious objects, beautifully decorated hunting gear, delicately carved ornaments, tools, utensils, and baskets of grass. Artisans made exceptional engraved and painted art in ivory and wood, imaginative masks, and finely tailored fur clothing.

The Unangan (Aleut) artists were renowned for their traditional artifacts. Their kayaks were the fastest and most technologically advanced of any in the Arctic world. Their gutskin waterproof clothing was elegant, their tightly woven rye or beach grass baskets the finest, and ritual hunting headgear the marvel of all who viewed them. The

wooden hunting hats and visors were highly abstracted with multicolor scrolls, rosettes, spirals, and pictographs. Their paper-thin bentwood hats were decorated with beaded sea lion whiskers, walrus ivory carvings, and painted designs.

Athabascan art was primarily expressed in clothing design and decoration. Hunters and fishermen, without permanent winter villages, moved by dogsled or foot and found little need to accumulate possessions. They invested their creative energies into doing outstanding skinwork using dyed porcupine quill and moosehair embroidery. Later, they used glass beads, dentalium shell, and other trade goods.

The Tlingit, Haida, and Tsimshian people have used the wood of the cedar trees in their arts for over a thousand years. The thick trunks have been carved into imposing totem poles. The straight-grained wood of the trunk splits long and true, enabling the architect to fashion planks as long as forty feet to make the great carved and painted houses so characteristic of southeast Alaska. Cedar is also easily carved to make the masks, dance rattles, great storage boxes, and feasting bowls that were used in extraordinary numbers by these Native peoples. Cedar bark, thin branches, and roots can be pounced to make soft, flexible weaving material for capes, hats, bags, baskets, and mats. The rich coastal environment not only provided plenty of cedars but also an abundance of foodstuffs. This abundance allowed people more leisure time to devote themselves to art and other expressive aspects of culture.

TYING IT UP

In 2011, the Alaska Department of Labor and Workforce Development estimated that 141,737 American Indian or Alaska Native people lived in Alaska. The two largest Alaska Native alone-or-in-any-combination tribal grouping populations were Yup'ik (34,000) and Inupiat (33,000). The third-largest tribal grouping was Tlingit–Haida (26,080), followed by the Alaska Athabascan tribal grouping (22,484) and the Aleut (19,282). The Tsimshians (4,000) had the

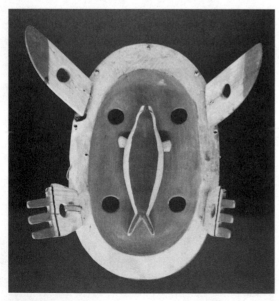

A Yup'ik mask

smallest alone-or-in-any-combination tribal grouping population size. Nearly four in ten (39.2 percent) of the estimated Alaska Native population was under the age of twenty.

BIOGRAPHIES

Katlian (fl. 1800s)
Tlingit, Leader

Born in Sitka, Alaska, war hero Katlian led the Tlingit resistance against Russians who had expanded into Tlingit ancestral homelands to take control of the Northwest Coast fur trade. He led a raid in 1799, capturing the first Russian fort in America, reclaiming pelts hunted on Tlingit lands. Katlian and his fighters held the post for two years until Aleksandr Baranov returned with an armada of ships and a force of 120 Russians and nearly one thousand Unangan (Aleut). The Tlingit retreated but did not surrender. They moved against the fort at Yakutat (a Tlingit–Eyak settlement) in 1805. Because of the Tlingit raids, the Russian traders appealed to the Russian navy for protection. Tlingit militancy was a factor in Russia's decision to sell Alaska to the United States in 1867.

Maniilaq (fl. 1800s)
Inupiaq, Healer/Visionary

Maniilaq was a figure of Inupiat legend and history. He is said to have lived as a hunter and healer in the nineteenth century before European colonists arrived in the Kobuk River basin of northwest Alaska. He was a powerful leader and an interpreter of the tumultuous times precipitated by contact between Alaska Native and European societies. Various stories about him say he heard voices predicting that white people would come to Alaska, that he had prophetic visions of huge boats propelled by fire or that others would fly in the air, and that he heard voices from a higher power.

Maniilaq traveled long-established routes from northwest Inupiaq country to Yup'ik villages in Norton Sound. He was aware of Russian forts, Russian-American goods, and influences as well as villages in his region devastated by a smallpox epidemic. He challenged the healing powers of shamans whose powers were proving useless against the new diseases and said that the Russian Orthodox Church offered an alternative spiritual path to relieve suffering. He also said that traditional values of sharing and balance should be preserved.

In 1978, elders of the Northwest Arctic met to preserve their oral histories by sharing stories about their greatest prophet, Maniilaq. Their remembrances have been preserved in *Maniilaq, Prophet From the Edge of Nowhere*. They describe the amazing life of the nineteenth-century Inupiat leader whose vision and influence enlightened his people and prepared them for change before his mysterious disappearance.

William Lewis Paul (1885–1977)
Tlingit, Attorney/Legislator/Political Activist

Born in Tongass Village in Southeast Alaska, Paul (whose Tlingit name was Shgúndi) was a member of the Raven moiety and Teeyhittaan clan. He became an attorney, legislator, and political activist and was widely known as a leader in the Alaska Native Brotherhood. He and his brothers all attended the Carlisle Indian Industrial School in Carlisle, Pennsylvania.

William and his brother Louis Paul (1887–1956) were founding members of the Alaska Native Brotherhood (ANB), which in the 1920s extended its presence to every Native village in Southeast Alaska. ANB pressed for voting rights, desegregation, and social services as well as advancing the first Tlingit and Haida land claims in Alaska. William Paul served several times as the ANB's grand president and grand secretary.

Paul was the first Alaska Native to become an attorney, the first to be elected to Alaska Territorial House of Representatives, and the first to serve as an officer in the federal Bureau of Indian Affairs. He helped draft the legislation to adopt Alaska's flag in 1927 and played a major role in the Alaska Native Claims Settlement Act (ANCSA) of 1971.

Paul's first run for the House in 1922—1923 was challenged legally and became an ultimately successful test case on citizenship rights of Indians to vote and hold office in 1924.

In the 1950s, Paul brought an important land claims test case, *Tee-Hit-Ton Indians vs. U.S.* (1955), on behalf of his own Tlingit clan. The Supreme Court ruled that it found "nothing to indicate any intention by Congress to grant to the Indians any permanent rights in the lands of Alaska occupied by them by permission of Congress." The land claims case was unsuccessful, but it laid the groundwork for the later ANCSA of 1971.

Ethel Washington (1889–1967)
Inupiaq, Doll Maker

Washington, who has been referred to as "the mother of modern Alaska doll makers," was from Kotzebue. She began making dolls as early as the 1930s, but following the death of her husband in 1951, she created finely crafted doll families in order to support her family. Each set she made was dressed in fur parkas and carried a variety of tools, utensils, or hunting equipment. The faces, whittled with a Boy Scout knife out of wood collected on the Kobuk River, were often carved to resemble someone in the community. Washington became the first doll maker known to non-Native customers. Her success inspired other Kotzebue women to make dolls, including Lena Sours, Rose Francis, Emma Black Lincoln, and Dolly Spencer, the first doll maker to achieve international acclaim.

Ray Mala (1906–1952)
Inupiaq, Actor

Mala, born Ray Wise in the small village of Candle, Alaska Territory, to a Russian Jewish immigrant father and an Alaska Native mother, became a famous actor. In 1921,

an explorer named Captain Frank Kleinschmidt went to Alaska on an expedition to film a picture called *Primitive Love*, in which Mala made his film debut at age fourteen. Mala acted in front of the camera and also served as a cameraman for the picture. This led to young Mala becoming an official cameraman. From 1921 to 1924, he accompanied Knud Rasmussen, the Danish Arctic explorer and writer, on his trip, called *The Great Sled Journey*, to collect and describe Inuit songs and legends.

In 1925, Mala went to Hollywood, where he worked for almost thirty years. He was a cameraman with Fox Film Corporation, before the creation of 20th Century Fox. Not long after, Mala landed his first lead role in the silent film *Igloo*. It's success led to his role as the lead in MGM's *Eskimo/Mala the Magnificent*, filmed with an all-Native Alaskan cast. *Eskimo* was billed as "the biggest picture ever made" by MGM and won the first Oscar for Best Film Editing at the Academy Awards.

Mala gained international stardom, and MGM cast him as the lead in the box-office hit *Last of the Pagans* (1935), filmed entirely on location in Tahiti. His next big role came in *The Jungle Princess* (1936), which, according to the book *The Paramount Story*, "was a huge success and was a whopping money-maker for the studio." He also starred in *Robinson Crusoe of Clipper Island* (1936), one of the first serials the studio had ever made. Mala costarred in Republic Picture's *Hawk of the Wilderness* (1938), which many consider one of the top ten best serials. He also was a cinematographer and worked with Academy Award winner Joseph LaShelle on many pictures, including the Oscar-winning *Laura* (1944), *Les Miserables* (1952), and many other films.

Elizabeth Peratrovich (1911–1958)
Tlingit, Civil Rights Activist

Elizabeth Peratrovich was an important civil rights activist; she worked on behalf of equality for Alaska Natives. In the 1940s, she was credited with advocacy that gained the passage of

Alaska Territory's Anti-Discrimination Act of 1945, the first anti-discrimination law in the United States.

Elizabeth Peratrovich was born in Petersburg, Alaska. She was adopted when very young by Andrew and Mary Wanamaker, a Tlingit couple, who named her Elizabeth Wanamaker. She attended Sheldon Jackson College in Sitka and the Western College of Education in Bellingham, Washington, now part of Western Washington University. On December 15, 1931, she married Roy Peratrovich (1908–1989), also a Tlingit, who worked in a cannery. They lived in Klawaock, where he was elected to four terms as mayor.

Looking for greater opportunities for work and their children, they moved to Juneau. In 1941, while living in Juneau, the Peratroviches encountered extensive social and racial discrimination against Alaska Natives. They petitioned the territorial governor to ban the "No Natives Allowed" signs common at public accommodations in that city and elsewhere. An anti-discrimination act was defeated by the territorial legislature in 1943. As leaders of the Alaska Native Brotherhood and Alaska Native Sisterhood, the Peratroviches lobbied the territory's legislators and represented their organizations in their testimony.

Elizabeth Peratrovich was the last to testify before the territorial Senate who voted on the bill in 1945, and her impassioned testimony was considered decisive. She talked about herself, her friends, her children, and the cruel treatment that consigned Alaska Natives to a second-class existence. She described to the Senate what it meant to be unable to buy a house in a decent neighborhood because Natives were not allowed to live there. She described how children feel when they are refused entrance into movie theaters or see signs in shop windows that read "No dogs or Natives allowed."

The Senate voted 11 to 5 for House Resolution 14, providing "full and equal accommodations, facilities, and privileges to all citizens in places of public accommodations within the jurisdiction of the Territory of Alaska; to provide penalties for violation." The bill was signed into law by Governor Ernest Gruening, nearly twenty years before the U.S. Congress passed the Civil Rights Act of 1964. Acts of the territorial legislature required final approval from the U.S. Congress, which affirmed the resolution.

On February 6, 1988, the Alaska Legislature established February 16th (the day in 1945 on which the Anti-Discrimination Act was signed) as "Elizabeth Peratrovich Day" in order to honor her contributions: " … for her courageous, unceasing efforts to eliminate discrimination and bring about equal rights in Alaska. In 2009, a documentary about Peratrovich's groundbreaking civil rights advocacy premiered on October 22 at the Alaska Federation of Natives convention in Anchorage. Entitled *For the Rights of All: Ending Jim Crow in Alaska*, the film was aired on PBS in November 2009.

Howard Rock (1911–1976)
Inupiaq, Journalist/Activist

Howard Rock, the first editor of the *Tundra Times*, the first Alaska Native newspaper, was also the first Native owner of a newspaper among the Native peoples of Alaska. The paper was the first paper to focus exclusively on Alaska Natives issues and concerns.

Born in the Inupiat village of Point Hope in northeastern Alaska, Rock attended Bureau of Indian Affairs boarding schools, often traveling long distances from home. In the mid-1930s, he attended the University of Washington, Seattle. During the 1940s and 1950s, he worked as an artist, producing work with Inuit cultural themes, and much of his work was bought by tourists. Rock was not happy with his life or work as an artist. In the early 1960s, he returned to Point Hope in search of some direction to his life within traditional Inuit culture.

In the late 1950s and early 1960s, the U.S. government was planning to use an atomic bomb to create a harbor near Point Hope. This project was billed as a peacetime use of atomic energy. The Inupiat people in the area, however, hunted sea mammals like whales and seals, which would be exposed to serious radiation from an exploding atomic device. Since Rock had some writing skills, the village elders of Point Hope commandeered him to join in the protest movement called Inupiat Paitot, or "The People's Heritage." In order to publicize the issue and to gather Native Alaskan and other supporters, the Inupiat Paitot created a newsletter, and Rock became the editor. This newsletter became the means of publicizing Inuit and other Native issues, and, in 1962, it became the Native newspaper the *Tundra Times*. At first, the *Tundra Times* was published in Fairbanks, Alaska, but it soon moved to Anchorage, the largest urban center in Alaska.

Rock became the paper's first editor, serving from 1962 until his death in 1976. Through the *Tundra Times*, he wrote editorials, printed articles, actively brought Native issues to the press, and helped Native villages and regional organizations form protests. In 1965, he helped organize the first Alaska Federation of Natives (AFN) meeting in Anchorage. From 1965 to 1971, the AFN lobbied Congress for a solution to Native land issues in Alaska. In 1971, it helped gain passage of the Alaska Native Claims Settlement Act (ANCSA).

Rock also published articles on Native Arctic culture, history, Native land claims, and social and welfare issues and wrote many commentaries about the events leading up to passage of the ANCSA. The *Tundra Times* became revered as a representative of the Alaska Native communities, and Rock was honored throughout Alaska for his tireless and selfless contributions toward solving Native issues.

John Hoover (1919–2011)
Unangan/Aleut, Sculptor

John Hoover was an American artist known for his creation of contemporary art pieces in wood, bronze, and stone based on Alaska Native and Northwest Coast traditions. He was born in Cordova to a Dutch father and an Aleut-Russian mother. He worked as a ski instructor and commercial fisherman before taking up a career in art

after designing and building a fishing boat in his backyard, which he considered to be a sculpture.

Hoover attended a fine arts school in Seattle from 1957 to 1960. Although known for his sculptures, Hoover began his career as a painter. Paintings from the late 1950s and early 1960s included scenes from his life in Alaska as well as landscapes, seascapes, and images of his life in Washington State. In the 1970s, Hoover received a National Endowment for the Arts grant that supported him while he worked as an artist-in-residence at the Institute of American Indian Arts in Santa Fe, where he studied with Allan Houser, Apache.

Hoover's early oil-painted wood sculptures were inspired by traditional Coast Salish spirit boards on display at the Washington State Museum in Tacoma. He liked the easily carved cedar because of its significance to Northwest Coast people. Hoover transitioned from single-paneled spirit boards to hinged triptychs reminiscent of Russian Orthodox icons (which folded up to protect the image inside during travel) and Northwest Coast transformation masks. In the 1970s, he began to experiment using different shapes with his folding diptychs and triptychs, creating sculptures that when closed resemble one form and transform into another when opened.

As an artist, he sought out his cultural identity and spent a lifetime actively interpreting the shaman stories from written and oral sources about the people of the Northwest Coast and representing these stories in his art. Birds are a recurrent subject in Hoover's work, especially the loon. The loon is a prominent figure in oral traditions of the Inuit, Aleut, and Northwest Coast people because it travels among three worlds: the middle world (land), where humans reside; the upper (air) world; and the under (water) world, both locales inhabited by spirits. Hoover's work gives us insight into the supernatural world of the Northwest Coast.

Hoover's work was exhibited internationally, and his artworks feature prominently in several Anchorage buildings such as the Alaska Native Medical Center and the Alaska Native Heritage

Center. The roster of galleries and museums that have displayed and purchased Hoover's pieces is extensive.

Poldine Demoski Carlo (1920–)
Koyukon Athabaskan, Author

Born in Nulato, Territory of Alaska, Carlo is a founding member of the Fairbanks Native Association (FNA) and has also served for the Alaska Bicentennial Commission Board and as consultant to the Tanana Chiefs Conference. She is the author of *Nulato: An Indian Life on the Yukon,* which was dedicated in memory of her son, Stewart, who died in 1975 in an auto accident. The book has been praised for depicting how a community lives with ancient traditions that are also intertwined with contemporary influences of gold mining, fur trading, and missionaries.

Eben Hopson (1922–1980)
Inupiaq, Leader/Legislator/Activist

Eben Hopson was the first executive director of the Arctic Slope Native Association, which launched the Alaska Native land claims movement in 1965. After 1968, he became president of the Alaska Federation of Natives (AFN), which became a well-financed federation of Native regional associations in Alaska. After AFN, Eben became a special assistant for Native affairs to Alaska Governor William Egan in 1970–1971. He helped shape a new state policy toward Native land claims.

In 1975, Hopson was re-elected borough mayor of the North Slope Borough. That same year, he was invited by Congressman John Melcher (D-Montana), Chairman of the House Interior Subcommittee on Public Lands, to send a planning team to Washington to work with the Committee staff to draft legislation that resulted in the transfer of the Naval Petroleum Reserve #4 to the control of the Department of the Interior. In

1976, Hopson won the party's congressional nomination. He used his congressional campaign to draw national attention to the need for both a national and international Arctic policy to facilitate environmentally safe Arctic energy development.

In 1976, Hopson called upon the Inuit leaders of Greenland, Canada, the U.S., and the U.S.S.R. to form an international organization, called the Inuit Circumpolar Conference (ICC), in order to pursue these goals. The first meeting of the ICC was hosted by Hopson in 1977 in Barrow. Hopson's influence on the international level was greatly enhanced when the International Whaling Commission (IWC) attempted to ban the Inupiat subsistence hunting of the bowhead whale in 1977. Eben traveled to Tokyo and London to plead the Inupiat case that the IWC was not authorized to regulate subsistence whaling. In federal courts in Washington, D.C., Anchorage, and San Francisco, Hopson asserted that the U.S. was not authorized to submit the dietary habits of U.S. citizens to the arbitration of the IWC.

Nora Marks Dauenhauer (1927–)
Tlingit, Poet/Short-Story Writer/Linguist

Nora Marks Dauenhauer is an American poet, short-story writer, and a scholar of the language and traditions of the Tlingit nation in Alaska, of which she is a member.

Dauenhauer was born in Juneau, Alaska and raised in Juneau and Hoonah as well as on her family's fishing boat and in seasonal subsistence sites around Alaska's Icy Straits, Glacier Bay, and Cape Spencer. She graduated in 1976 with a Bachelor of Arts in anthropology from Alaska Methodist University, precursor to Alaska Pacific University.

In 2005, Dauenhauer won a 2005 Community Spirit Award from the First Peoples Fund, a Native American organization that supports the arts. She was one of five recipients of the award, which included a five-thousand-dollar stipend. James Ruppert, professor of Alaska Native studies at University of Alaska in Fairbanks said that Dauenhauer's poems reflect her dedication to traditional culture as well as her broad education and wide-ranging travels. He wrote that she is "informed by the Tlingit worldview; her poems often celebrate the spirit of the land and the people, traditional and contemporary, living and departed." In 2008, she won an American Book Award for *Russians in Tlingit America: The Battles of Sitka, 1802 and 1804*.

In 2011, Dauenhauer was an Ecotrust Indigenous Leadership Award finalist for her decades of work as an internationally recognized linguist, responsible for significant fieldwork, transcription, translation, and explication of Tlingit oral literature, collecting stories from elders. Her writings, fiction, memoir, essays, poetry, and drama have been published, performed, anthologized, and honored. In 2011, Dauenhauer was also inducted in the Alaska State Hall of Fame.

Dolly Spencer (1930–2005)
Inupiaq, Artist/Doll Maker

Dolly Spencer was a well-known maker of exquisite, detailed, traditional-style Eskimo dolls that brought her international fame. Originally from Kotzebue, she became a resident of Homer, Alaska. Her family lived in temporary camps, moving from one to another gathering food such as berries and greens, fishing, and hunting seals or foxes. They collected as much as they could in preparation for winter. In these temporary camps, the family lived in a tent with dozens of dogs. The dogs were more than pets. The family depended on the dogs to transport them by dogsled, even in the summer, and to pull their boat from the shore.

When Spencer was eight years of age, her mother taught her to sew. Her first project was making caribou mittens. Her mother examined her work, and if it was not done well, she would rip out the stitches and make her redo them until they were done to her satisfaction. This attention to detail in sewing was the first of many lessons her mother taught her. As a child, she learned

how to prepare sealskin for sewing by scraping the underside of the pelt and removing the hair.

Spencer left school when she was in the seventh grade when her mother took her to Nome. There, she worked as a dishwasher for a time before becoming a camp cook. After two years as a cook, she worked in a bakery, then in a restaurant. During this time, Spencer married and had children, for whom she made parkas and *mukluks* (soft boots made of reindeer hide or sealskin). Using scraps from these projects, she started work on a doll's dress at the request of a friend, then started making dolls for herself. She used dental floss to sew but switched to sinew at the urging of her husband.

Over the years, Spencer refined her skills in the making of dolls, carefully carving each doll's head and then sewing custom clothing. She used all traditional materials—carved beechwood heads, skin bodies stuffed with caribou hair, and fur and skin garments sewn with sinew. In her dolls, she reproduced traditional dress and customs, hoping that each creation preserved her memories of Inupiat life and served to educate the general public. Besides her 1996 NEA National Heritage Fellowship, Spencer's dolls are in several museums as well as private collections.

Rosita Worl (1932–)
Tlingit, Anthropologist

Dr. Rosita Kaahani Worl has made many contributions to increase awareness about Alaska Native cultures and subsistence economies. She has authored numerous publications on Alaska Native issues and cultural practices, including subsistence lifestyles, Alaska Native women's issues, Indian law and policy, and southeast Alaska Native culture and history.

Born in a cabin, Worl [of the Ch'áak' Eagle moiety of the Shangukeidi (Thunderbird) Clan from the Kawdi-yaayi Hít ("House Lowered From the Sun") of Klukwan and a child of the Sockeye Clan] was raised in southeast Alaska by her grandmother, aunt, and mother and commercially fished with her uncle in Kake. At age six,

Worl was taken to the Haines House to learn English and to be "civilized" and "Christianized." She was there for three years before her mother was able to take her home to live with her twelve brothers and sisters. After high school, Worl ran a program that recruited Alaska Natives for higher education, and in essence, she said, "I recruited myself."

Worl received her bachelor's degree from Alaska Methodist University and her master's and doctorate's degrees in anthropology from Harvard University. In academia, she has served as the social scientific researcher at the University of Alaska Arctic Environmental Information and Data Center. An anthropologist, she was for many years assistant professor of anthropology at the University of Alaska Southeast.

Worl has done extensive research throughout Alaska and the circumpolar Arctic. She conducted the first social scientific study projecting sociocultural impacts of offshore oil development on the Inupiat, and she has studied traditional aboriginal whaling, which gave her the privilege of being one of the first women allowed to go whaling. Worl also served as a scientific advisor to the U.S. Whaling Commission and has conducted research on seal hunting in Canada for the Royal Commission on Sealing. She served on the National Scientific Advisory Committee and the National Science Foundation Polar Programs Committee. Worl also served as special advisor to the Honorable Thomas Berger of the Alaska Native Review Commission and studied the impacts of the Alaska Native Claims Settlement Act (ANCSA).

Worl has been the president of the Sealaska Heritage Institute, which is dedicated to preserving and maintaining the Tlingit, Haida, and Tsimshian cultures and languages, and a board member of Sealaska Corporation. Worl also serves on the Alaska Native Brotherhood Subsistence Committee and the Central Council of Tlingit and Haida Indians Economic Development Commission.

On a state and national level, Worl has served on the board of directors of the Alaska Federation of Natives and chairs the Subsistence

Cultural Survival Committees, the National Museum of American Indians, and the Native American Graves Protection and Repatriation Act National Committee. She was special staff assistant for Native Affairs to Alaska Governor Steve Cowper and served as a member of President Bill Clinton's Northwest Sustainability Commission. Worl was appointed to the National Census Board focusing on American Indian issues and is a founding member of the Smithsonian's National Museum of the American Indian. She also served as a member of the Smithsonian's National Museum of Natural History Arctic Committee.

In addition to her academic and professional accomplishments, Worl is the recipient of numerous honors, including a Ford Foundation Fellowship (1972–1977), International Women's Year Conference (1977), the Gloria Steinem Award for Empowerment (1989), Women of Hope (one of twelve Native women activists in a national poster campaign) (1997), Outstanding Contribution, Alaska Native Heritage Center (2000), Human Rights Award, Cultural Survival (2002), Women of Courage Award, NWPC (2003), Native People Award Enhancing the Native Alaskan Community, Wells Fargo (2004), National Museum of the Indian Smithsonian Institution Honor (2006), University of Alaska Southeast Commencement Speaker (2006), Distinguished Service to the Humanities Award (2008), Governor's Award for the Arts & Humanities, Solon T. Kimball Award for Public and Applied Anthropology, American Anthropological Association (2008), Lifetime Achievement Award, Central Council of the Tlingit and Haida Indian Tribes of Alaska (2011), and the Alaska Federation of Natives Citizen of the Year Award (2011).

Alfred Ketzler (c. 1934–)
Athabascan, Leader/Political Activist

Alfred Ketzler, an Athabascan Indian from Nenana, was chairman of Dena Nena Henash ("Our Land Speaks"), an association which had been organized earlier in 1962 to deal with land rights and other problems. Ketzler was among the first to propose congressional action to preserve land rights instead of court action. He said: "We need a legal title to our land if we are to hold it. Our right to inherit land from our fathers cannot be settled in court. It is specifically stated in early laws that Congress is to do this by defining the way which we can acquire title. We must ask Congress to do this."

Ketzler helped organize a meeting of villages in Tanana, Alaska, in 1962 that became the foundation for the Tanana Chiefs Conference (TCC), the traditional tribal consortium of forty-two villages of interior Alaska, based on a belief in tribal self-determination and the need for regional Native unity. In 1963, Ketzler flew to Washington, D.C., to present a petition asking Secretary of the Interior Steward Udall to freeze state land selections until the Native land claims were settled. As an Alaska field representative for the Association on American Indian Affairs, he was one of five people authorized to negotiate terms of the land claims. Ketzler was elected the first president of TCC in 1969, became the deputy director of the Alaskan Federation of Natives in 1970, and was appointed acting executive director in 1971. Ketzler retired from the TCC in 2002. He also helped organize the first Alaska Native publication, the *Tundra Times*.

Rita Pitka Blumenstein (1936–)
Yup'ik, Traditional Healer/Artist/Storyteller

Rita Pitka Blumenstein was the first certified traditional doctor in Alaska. She is also an artist, teacher, speaker, and storyteller. Rita's teachings have been recorded and published, and she has traveled the world to teach song, dance, basket weaving, and cultural issues. She donates her earnings to Native American colleges.

Born to a widowed mother who lived in the village of Tununak, Nelson Island, Blumenstein arrived while her mother was in a fishing boat. She felt angry not having her father around when she was a girl because he died a month before she was born.

Blumenstein was married to a Jewish man from New York City for forty-three years. They had six children, five of whom died. Blumenstein's own health has not always been good and in 1995, she found that she had cancer. Blumenstein saw that being diagnosed with cancer made her realize that she needed to heal herself at a "deeper" level—concluding that the cancer was due to being angry that her father had not been present in her early years. She is teaching her granddaughter to follow in her footsteps and to be a healer and carry on Yup'ik traditions.

Blumenstein was asked to be a member of the International Council of 13 Indigenous Grandmothers, a group of spiritual elders, medicine women, and wisdomkeepers, since its founding in 2004. The Council has been active in protecting Indigenous rights and medicines and traditional teachings on wisdom. In 2009, Blumenstein was one of fifty women inducted into the inaugural class of the Alaska Women's Hall of Fame.

Nathan Jackson (1938–)
Tlingit, Master Carver

Nathan Jackson, an important Alaskan artist best known for his totem poles, also works in a variety of media creating canoes, carved doors, wood-panel clan crests, carved wooden masks, and engraved gold and silver pieces formed into jewelry.

Jackson belongs to the Sockeye Clan on the Raven side of the Chilkoot Tlingit. As a young adult, he served in the military and then became involved in commercial fishing. While ill with pneumonia and unable to fish, he began to carve miniature totem poles. His interest in art was piqued, and he enrolled in the Institute of American Indian Arts in Santa Fe, New Mexico. Jackson has worked to pass on traditional Tlingit carving skills to younger artists and has offered many demonstrations and workshops in wood carving and design in Alaska and the Pacific Northwest.

Jackson has created more than fifty totem poles, some of which are on display in the National Museum of the American Indian, the Field Museum in Chicago, Harvard University's Peabody Museum, and other museums in the United States, Europe, and Japan. Other totem poles stand outside Juneau-Douglas High School, Juneau's Centennial Hall, in Juneaues Sealaska Building, in Totem Bight State Historical Park, at the Alaska Native Heritage Center, at Saxman Totem Park, and at the Totem Heritage Center in Ketchican, where he has lived. He is a recipient of a National Endowment for the Arts National Heritage Fellowship (1995), a Rasmuson Foundation Distinguished Artist Award (2009), and an honorary doctorate in humanities from the University of Alaska Southeast. Jackson's wife and son are also artists.

William L. Iġġiagruk Hensley (1941–)
Inupiaq, Legislator/Politician/Activist

William L. Iġġiagruk Hensley was active in land claims implementation and rural economic development since the late 1990s when he served as chair of the Alaska State Rural Affairs Commission (1968–1972) and also directed the Land Claims Task Force (1968). He was involved in the formation of the Alaska Federation of Natives (AFN) and served as executive director, president, and cochairman. AFN, a statewide organization, lobbied in Washington for resolution of Native land claims in Alaska during the 1960s. He played an active part in the passage of the Alaska Native Claims Settlement Act of 1971, which granted Alaska Natives $962 million and 44 million acres of land.

Born in Kotzebue, Hensley attended the University of Alaska in 1960 and 1961, then studied at George Washington University in Washington, D.C., and received his bachelor's degree from that school in 1966. He later studied law at the University of Alaska (1966), the University of New Mexico (1967), and the University of California, Los Angeles (1968). Hensley became an Alaska state senator, whose district covered more than 150,000 square miles and had a population of nearly twenty thousand people, 90 percent of whom were Inupiat like himself.

Hensley was a former member of Alaska House of Representatives and Alaska Senate, was the Democratic Party's nominee for U.S. Representative from Alaska (in 1974), lieutenant governor of Alaska in 1990, and was a former Democratic National Committeeman from Alaska.

He has been active in many Native organizations over the years. He founded the Northwest Alaska Native Association (now Maniilaq Association); was the founding president of Alaska Village Electric Cooperative from 1967–1971; was a director of NANA Regional Corporation for twenty years, serving as president and secretary as well as president of NANA Development Corporation; and was a former commissioner of commerce for the state of Alaska. He retired from Alyeska Pipeline Service Company, which he represented in Washington, D.C., for nine years.

Hensley authored *Fifty Miles from Tomorrow: A Memoir of Alaska and the Real People* (2008), a coming-of-age story. According to a *New York Times* review, "Mr. Hensley's account of what it's like to grow up in the far north, fifty miles from the International Date Line, is rarely less than gripping."

Hensley became visiting distinguished professor at the University of Alaska Anchorage College of Business and Public Policy in 2011. His primary focus was to design new curricula centered on Alaska Native business and corporation management and to develop cases that address Native business law and policy. He also taught "Alaska Policy Frontiers," an exploration of Alaska's history, economics, colonization, Indigenous impacts, and modern-day issues. As chair of the First Alaskans Institute board of trustees, Hensley has worked with the trustees and staff to further the organizational vision "progress for the next ten thousand years."

Georgianna Lincoln (1943–)
Athabascan, Legislator

Georgianna Lincoln became, in 1993, the first Native woman to be elected to the Alaska State Senate, where she has championed issues of women and children as well as natural resource management. She was born in Rampart, Alaska, and moved to Fairbanks as a young woman. She once was considered a radical because she spoke out as a woman. Her introduction to Native politics came in the 1960s on behalf of aboriginal land claims, a movement that led, finally, to the Alaska Native Claims Settlement Act of 1971. She developed health and education programs in her region in the 1980s and shaped Alaska public policy in the Alaska State Senate in the 1990s. In 2010, she led Doyon Corporation and its subsidiaries as chair of the board, a board on which she had served for thirty-three years.

In 1996, she was the first Native woman to be a candidate for the U.S. Congress from Alaska, and she has served as a mentor for women across the state within and outside of the Native community. Georgianna also worked as the executive director of the Fairbanks Native Association and as a director at the Tanana Chiefs Conference. She believes that her most significant achievement has been to raise two self-actualized children, who are nurturing her eight curious and joyful grandchildren in Alaska.

Bryon Mallott (1943–)
Tlingit, Politician

 Originally from Yakutat, Bryon Mallott became the lieutenant governor of Alaska in 2014. Byron Mallott's history of public service began in his ancestral home of Yakutat, Alaska, when he was elected mayor at the age of twenty-two. He later went on to serve as mayor of Juneau. Byron's early start in public leadership has grown into a deep, unique knowledge of all aspects of Alaskan life, including commercial fishing, aviation, timber, communications, banking, Alaska Native Corporations, and investments. He has served as the president of the Alaska Federation of Natives, executive director of the Alaska Permanent Fund Corporation, cochair of the Commission on Rural Governance and Empowerment, chair of the Nature Conservancy of Alaska, and president and CEO of First Alaskans Institute and Sealaska Corporation.

Mallott was the Democratic nominee for governor of Alaska in 2014 until he agreed to merge his campaign with that of Independent candidate Bill Walker and become Walker's running mate. Walker and Mallott won the election and took their oaths of office in December 2014.

Sarah James
Gwich'in Athabascan, Environmentalist

Sarah James, along with the late Jonathon Solomon, Sr., and Norma Kassi, both Athabascan, jointly won the Goldman Environmental Prize for "grassroots environmentalists" in 2002. James was raised in a traditional Gwich'in lifestyle and did not begin speaking English until she was thirteen years old. Living in the small community of Arctic Village, she has traveled widely, from Washington, D.C., to foreign countries, speaking out for the rights of Indigenous peoples through grassroots activism. In recognition of her leadership, she has received many awards. In 1993, James received the Alston Bannerman Fellowship award. In 2001, she received a Ford Foundation "Leadership for a Changing World" grant given to "outstanding but little-known leaders." James also received the 2002 National Conservation Land Trust award. In 2004, she was the recipient of the "Ecotrust Award for Indigenous Leadership," and she also received the 2006 Alaska Conservation Foundation "Celia Hunter Award." In 2009, Sarah was inducted into the Alaska Women's Hall of Fame.

James is very thankful for the support of the Gwich'in Nation, her community, her son, and her family. She credits the hard work of the

Gwich'in and other people throughout the United States and the world as having greatly contributed to her successful efforts. The impetus for her activism and the strength of her convictions may be best summarized in her own words, spoken in 2006: "This is my way of life. We are born with this way of life, and we will die with it. It never occurred to me that something had to wake me up to do this. Nothing magic happened to me. Our life depends on it. It's about survival."

David Boxley (1952–)
Tsimshian, Master Carver

David Boxley is a nationally recognized carver from Metlakatla, Alaska's only federal reservation. Raised by his grandparents, Boxley learned many of his tribe's traditions, including the language. After high school, he attended Seattle Pacific University where he received a Bachelor of Science degree. He taught for ten years in high schools in Alaska and Washington State. In 1986, he made a major career decision to leave the security of teaching and to devote all of his energies toward researching and creating totem poles, drums, masks, bentwood boxes, rattles, and silkscreen prints. Boxley credits Jack Hudson (Tsimshian) and non-Native Duane Posco with helping him develop his carving techniques. By using these skills, he become a nationally recognized artist, holding one-man shows in Washington, D.C., and throughout the Pacific Northwest, Alaska, Hawaii, and Europe.

In 1990, during the Goodwill Games, Boxley carved the crown of a "Talking Stick," a unified American eagle and a Russian bear that became a symbol of peace and harmony between the United States and Soviet Union. It became an important part of the summer's Goodwill Games, in which athletes carried the stick from Spokane through Washington and Oregon to Seattle for the opening ceremonies. In the millennium year 2000, Boxley was commissioned to carve a Talking Stick for the office of the mayor of Seattle.

By 2013, Boxley had raised more than seventy totem poles throughout North America and in Europe. His masks, bentwood boxes, and panels have sold in galleries across the nation. His pieces are in collections around the world and owned by distinguished people, including the king and queen of Sweden, the emperor of Japan, the president of West Germany, and the mayor of Chongging, China. Boxley has been deeply involved in the rebirth of Tsimshian culture through the potlatch. In 1982, he held a potlatch in Metlakatla. During that event, he raised a totem pole to honor his grandparents, the first ever to be raised in Metlakatla. Soon after that, he started to compose new songs and dances of the newly created 4th Generation Dance group in Metlakatla.

During Metlakatla's one-hundredth anniversary potlatch, Boxley helped with organizing, carving masks, and creating song and dance. It was the largest event of its kind held in modern times, with three totem poles raised, dancing, gift giving, and feasts that fed one thousand people each evening. As well, this potlatch gave the four clans in Metlakatla the opportunity to enact traditional commemorations.

Boxley has been directly involved in the formation of four successful dance groups: one in his home village of Metlakatla, Alaska, and others in Seattle, Washington. He led the Tsimshian Haayuuk for six years and another called the Git-Hoan ("People of the Salmon"). With Git-Hoan, Boxley melds dance, masks, and songs into a single art. He has written over forty songs in his Native language and carved many masks, rattles, paddles, and other performance items. He implores Tsimshians to hold on to their language.

In 2011, the Smithsonian's Museum of the American Indian commissioned a totem pole that now permanently stands in the foyer of the Museum. The pole was dedicated and raised in January 2012. Boxley considers this totem pole for the Smithsonian his most important commission professionally, but the totem pole he carved for his grandfather has been by far the most important and meaningful personally.

Katherine Gottlieb (1952–)
Unangan/Aleut, Public Health Leader

Katherine Gottlieb won a McArthur Foundation Fellows ("genius") Award in 2004 for visionary transformation of a medical bureaucracy into a quality-driven, patient-centered health service dedicated to the needs of Alaska Natives.

Born in Old Harbor in rural Kodiak Island, Alaska, Gottlieb began her career as a community health aide in her hometown of Seldovia, Alaska. In 1987, she took a position as a receptionist with the then five-year-old Southcentral Foundation, the medical arm of Cook Inlet Region, Inc. She earned a B.A. (1990) and an M.B.A. (1995) with an emphasis on public health from Alaska Pacific University and rose to the position of president and CEO of Southcentral. Gottlieb has spearheaded the growth of the foundation, developing more than seventy-five medical, behavioral health, and community programs that serve more than forty thousand Alaska Natives and their families.

As head of the nonprofit Southcentral Foundation, Gottlieb has elevated the quality of service to the highest standard of medical care and created programs that extend well beyond primary care. The Dena A. Coy Residential Treatment Center is the first residential facility for pregnant women in the United States, focused on preventing fetal alcohol syndrome. Pathway Home, a transitional living center, addresses the challenges of substance abuse, violence, and suicide among Alaska Native teenagers. With the Family Wellness Warriors Initiative, Gottlieb has worked to revitalize the traditional role of Alaska Native men as protectors and providers, making them less inclined to fall into a pattern of domestic abuse. Under Gottlieb's leadership, the Southcentral Foundation network has demonstrated that high-quality health care and effective preventive services are possible, even in communities facing obstacles of poverty and geographic isolation.

Jeanie Greene (1952–)
Inupiaq, Television Pioneer

Jeanie Greene has been a pioneer in Indigenous television programming known throughout Alaska, Canada, and the Lower Forty-Eight by hosting, reporting, and producing a thirty-minute weekly television program called *Heartbeat Alaska*. Every week, tens of thousands of viewers tuned in to watch her reports. Born in a logging town of Sitka, Alaska, her show has talked about everything from Eskimo dog mushers in the 1,100-mile Iditarod to the lack of jobs in Alaska's tiny villages. She fostered better reporting from rural Alaska villages, allowing the residents who lived there to tell their own stories. In 2013, Coastal Television announced the inclusion of award-winning Greene in its lineup and the addition of *Heartbeat Alaska* as regular programming twice a week.

Greene has focused on Alaska Natives, including topics related to precontact, historic, and contemporary issues of the Tlingit and Haida, Aleut, Inupiat, Yup'ik, Athabascan, and Tsimshian people. She has researched documentaries about precontact technologies in ancestries, transformation and issues, and strategies of adaptation. She created a genre of television never before seen in America: Alaska Natives reporting on Alaska Natives. Topics have included subsistence practices of Alaska Natives, fisheries policies and their impacts on Alaska Natives, and on a variety of topics on contemporary social and cultural dimensions of Alaska Native life. Her broad personal and research experiences have provided her with background for ongoing weekly television news and cultural programs since *Heartbeat Alaska's* inception in September 1990. Greene has won numerous awards from Alaska Press Club and has been featured in *People Magazine*, *Columbia Journalism Review*, and *The Quarterly*, among other national and international magazines and books. She received well over a dozen Alaska Press Club awards, including the prestigious 1994 Public Service Award. In 2010, she was chosen as Citizen of the Year for 2010 by Alaska Federation of Natives board of directors, made up of regional and nonprofit representatives statewide.

Heather Kendall-Miller (1956–)
Athabascan, Attorney

Heather Kendall-Miller, the first Alaska Native to graduate from Harvard Law School, has been a senior staff attorney for the Native American Rights Fund (NARF) in Anchorage. For over twenty years, she has represented Alaska Native communities in legal battles involving subsistence hunting and fishing, tribal sovereignty, basic free speech rights, and authority to tax. In 2001, Kendall-Miller was instrumental in winning the historic *Katie John* case, a series of lawsuits aimed at ensuring Alaska Native traditional practices. Kendall-Miller was considered for a seat on the 9th U.S. Circuit Court of Appeals.

In 2014, the Alaska State Legislature honored Kendall-Miller's professional life and work at NARF. The legislature recognized Kendall-Miller's work on the Venetie case, which she argued in front of the United States Supreme Court, and her tireless efforts on the Katie John litigation, "winning the right for Ms. John and other Alaska Native subsistence users to fish at their traditional locations after decades of regulatory prohibitions." The Katie John litigation continues to have enormous implications for Alaska and its Native populations as Alaska Native people seek to maintain their subsistence way of life in the face of increasing competition and regulatory burdens. The legislature also stated that she "has worked on cases for communities across Alaska, covering such diverse topics as tribal sovereignty and jurisdiction, child welfare protection, language preservation, subsistence hunting and fishing rights, land rights, and the impact of global warming on coastal villages and earning a host of prestigious state and national awards."

Aquilina Debbie Lestenkof (1960–)
Unangan (Aleut), Conservation Activist

As codirector of the Ecosystem Conservation Office of the Tribal Government on Alaska's St. Paul Island, Lestenkof has been recognized for her innovative use of both western and traditional Aleut science to enhance the well-being of the people and surrounding wildlife, with a focus on fur seals. For centuries, thousands of fur seals have called St. Paul Island home, yet their numbers have been diminishing. Born on the Pribilof Islands—an island group located near the Alaskan coast—Lestenkof was raised with a sense of responsibility to her community and environment, especially to the Aleutian youth, on environmental conservation issues.

Lestenkof developed the "Pribilof Islands Stewardship Program" to prompt local youth to be proactive with their environment. The program has trained young people to capture seals and free them of ocean debris, monitor shorelines, aid in alien species control, and work side by side with marine biologists. Annual beach cleanings have resulted in rounding up over ten tons of garbage at one time! She also created the Tribal Ecosystem Conservation Office, which encourages residents of St. Paul to pursue careers in wildlife conservation. She is the core character in *People of the Seal: The Story of Alaska's Pribilof Islands*, a documentary produced by the National Oceanic and Atmospheric Administration. For her activism and innovation, Lestenkof has been nationally recognized and is the recipient of the 2001 World Wildlife Fund Award for Conservation Merit, awarded to those who have made significant contributions to local, grassroots conservation and for conservation achievements over a long period of time.

Susie Silook (1960–)
Siberian Yup'ik/Inupiaq, Carver/Sculptor

Susie Silook, from the village of Gambell on St. Lawrence Island, Alaska, in the Bering Sea, is a carver and sculptor who creates works that reflect her determination to maintain the trace of the past in the future, particularly evident in her portrayals of the female deity Sedna. She is a powerful deity in Inupiat as well as in the worldview of many circumpolar Inuit cultures.

Silook works in traditional ivory and whalebone, inspired by the ancestral dolls of St. Lawrence Island that were originally carved by men. Combining her Inupiat belief systems with her own personal and community histories, Silook has contributed a significant body of work to Native American art that critiques the legacies of colonization in the Arctic. As one of the first female carvers to gain critical acclaim in a male-dominated field, Silook has used her considerable talents to depict themes that confront contemporary Alaska Natives, especially focusing on horrific violence against Native women.

Silook's work has been shown and sold all over Alaska and the United States, and her sculptures can be found in the collections of the de Young Museum, the Eiteljorg Museum, the Anchorage Museum of History and Art, and the Alaskan Native Heritage Centre as well as in many other public and private collections. In 2000, she was awarded the Governor's Award for an Individual Artist, in 2001, she held a prestigious Eiteljorg Fellowship, and in 2007, she was a United States Artists Rasmuson Fellow.

Irene Bedard (1967–)
Yup'ik/Inuit/Cree/Métis, Actress

Bedard was born in Anchorage, Alaska; her first role (nominated for a Golden Globe) was as Mary Crow Dog in the television production *Lakota Woman: Siege at Wounded Knee*, which depicted the 1970s standoff between police and Native Americans on the Pine Ridge Reservation, South Dakota. She is the voice of Pocahontas in the Disney animated film *Pocahontas* and was also the physical model for the character. She continues to earn recognition for her work and has received several honors, including two Western Heritage Awards. In 1995, she was chosen as one of *People* magazine's "50 Most Beautiful People."

Sven Haakanson (1967–)
Alutiiq, Linguist/Anthropologist/Carver

Sven Haakanson received a MacArthur Foundation Fellowship ("genius") Award in 2007 for being "the driving force behind the revitalization of Indigenous language, culture, and customs in an isolated region of North America." The Alutiiq Museum, for which he served as director, is an archaeological archive and anthropological repository of cultural artifacts of the Kodiak archipelago. Under Haakanson's leadership, the museum also has served as a traveling resource, bringing innovative exhibitions, educational programming, and field research to the landlocked villages throughout the island of Kodiak by boat and small plane.

Haakanson earned his doctorate from Harvard University and for over ten years served as the executive director of the Alutiiq Museum in Kodiak, Alaska. He also taught at the Kodiak College campus of the University of Alaska in Anchorage and is the former chair of the Alaska State Council on the Arts. In 2013, Haakanson became the new curator of Native American anthropology at the Burke Museum in Seattle, Washington.

With a Ph.D. in anthropology, Haakanson worked to preserve and give contemporary meaning to Native history and local cultures. The Alutiiq Museum provided Haakanson with a unique opportunity to establish and cultivate collaborative relationships with museums throughout the world, whose holdings include ancient Alutiiq artifacts. Bridging cultures and continents, he has orchestrated the exhibition and acquisition of Alutiiq masks and other artifacts dispersed throughout Russia and France in the eighteenth and nineteenth centuries. He also organized first-time, traveling exhibits of antiquities on loan to museums in Alaska.

As an anthropologist, Haakanson led a large-scale study of a sacred Alutiiq site to identify and archive petroglyphs and stone carvings from the southern coast of Kodiak Island. As a skilled carver and talented photographer, his masks and images of tribes and customs depict a way of life rarely seen outside of the region. Through these and other activities, Haakanson has preserved and revived ancient traditions and heritage, celebrating the rich past of Alutiiq communities and providing the larger world with a valuable window into a little-known culture.

Callan Chythlook-Sifsof (1989–)
Yup'ik/Inupiaq, Snowboarder

 Callan Chythlook-Sifsof is an American snowboarder who has competed in snowboard cross since 2005. In 2010, Chythlook-Sifsof became the first-ever Alaska Native in history to land a spot on the 2010 Winter Olympics team that competed in Vancouver. She failed to advance to the finals.

Chythlook-Sifsof was born and raised in Aleknagik, an Indigenous Yup'ik village north of Dillingham, accessible only by air or by boat. She began snowboarding at the age of seven, using a small hill behind her grandfather's house, and later moved through rougher backcountry trails, with fresh powder. At twelve, she and her mother moved to Alyyeska Ski Resort, outside of Anchorage, where she trained in a more usual setting.

Chythlook-Sifsof, a fourth-generation commercial fisherwoman, has been a licensed crew member since the age of five. At age twelve, she took the SAT, attended United States Space Camp twice while growing up, and graduated high school a full year early in 2006.

Chythlook-Sifsof first joined the U.S. national snowboard cross program in 2006, winning the national title in 2007, and earned a spot on the podium her very first time competing at a snowboard cross World Cup in Furano, Japan, on February 2, 2007, finishing in third place. She claimed silver at the 2008 World Junior Championships. She was also the silver medalist in the Winter X-Games in 2011 in Aspen, Colorado.

Besides snowboarding, Chythlook-Sifsof speaks her mind publicly. She wrote an anti-Pebble Mine op-ed piece for the *New York Times* that was published on June 28, 2013. The area where she grew up is gaining attention as the proposed location of the mine, which she argues will "threaten thousands of acres of pristine watershed and the spawning grounds of the largest sockeye salmon run on the planet."

HAWAII

Hawaii—the word, the vision, the sound in the mind—is the fragrance and feel of soft kindness. Above all, Hawaii is 'she,' the Western image of the Native 'female' in her magical allure, and if luck prevails, some of 'her' will rub off on you, the visitor. Tourists flock to my native land for escape, but they are escaping into a state of mind while participating in the destruction of a host people in a native place."

—Kānaka Maoli

There are more Hawaii vacations than there are islands—so whether you're headed to Kauai, Maui, Kona, or Waikiki, you're sure to find your personal island paradise. We warmly invite you to explore our islands and discover your ideal travel experience.

The Hawaiian travel industry uses these advertisements to lure millions to the South Pacific Islands. Most Americans and other tourists of the world have the impression that Hawaii is a magical vacation land, full of dancing hula girls and midnight feasts (luaus) where Native Hawaiians treat visitors like kings and queens. Most tourists believe that "all is well in paradise," but Hawaii is NOT a paradise for Native Hawaiians, who are themselves descendants of kings, queens, and the Kingdom of Hawaii. A little over a century ago in 1893, the United States invaded and then overthrew the Kingdom of Hawaii. Most Native Hawaiians did not agree to have their homelands annexed by the U.S. They consider Hawaii illegally occupied by a foreign government. Nevertheless, Hawaii became the fiftieth state in 1959.

A BIRD'S EYE VIEW

The Hawaiian Archipelago, or Ka Pae 'Aina O Hawaii Nei in the Hawaiian language, is made up of 132 islands, reefs and shoals, extending 1,523 miles southeast to northwest across the Tropic of Cancer between 154 40' to 178 25' W longitude and 18 54e to 28 15' N latitude. "Hawaii" is probably from the Native Hawaiian word for homeland—Owhyhee. The immense territory has almost 6,500 square miles of land, with eight big islands; seven are inhabited. All the islands are named and also have nicknames: Hawaii—The Big Island; Maui—The Valley Isle; Kaho'olawe—The Target Isle; Lana'i—The Pineapple Isle; Moloka'i—The Friendly Isle; O'ahu—The Gathering Place; Kaua'i—The Garden Isle; Ni'ihau—The Forbidden Isle.

Formed as a result of undersea hotspot volcanic activity, which continued to create new islands over millions of years, all the islands had

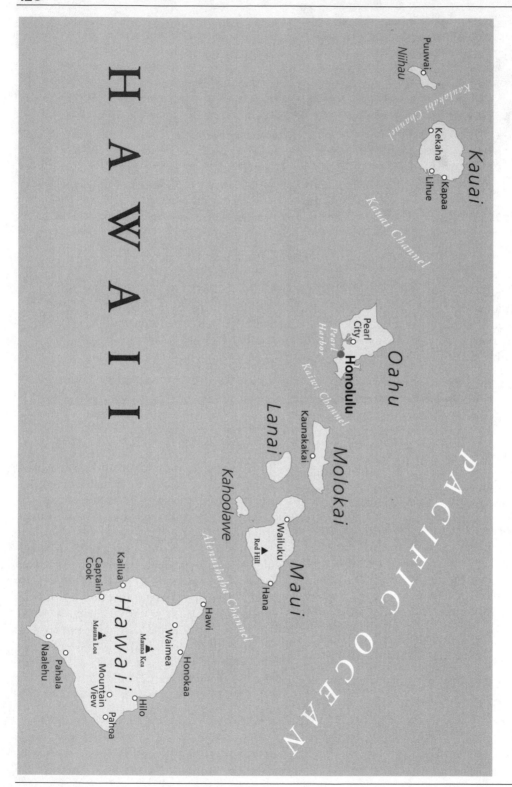

volcanoes at one time, and the scientific evidence of the formation of Ka Pae 'Aina O Hawaii Nei supports the traditional creation accounts. Today, only Hawaii, or the Big Island, has active volcanoes where the land is still growing as a result of land-forming volcanic activity. The Hawaiian Islands sit atop the highest mountain range in the world although the sheer grandeur of the towering slopes is mostly underwater.

Hawaii has a tropical climate with winter lows ranging from the mid-fifties to the high seventies and summer highs in the upper eighties. There are wet and dry seasons, and each island has its particular climate in relation to its mountain ranges. Kauai, the oldest of the islands and the farthest from the hotspot, has the second-highest rainfall on earth. Each island has its own topography: some have mountains that extend to the sea; others have flatter areas divided by mountain ranges. Mauna Kea on Hawaii is 32,808' from top to bottom, making it the tallest mountain in the world; Mount Everest is 29,029' but seems taller as the greater part of Mauna Kea is under the ocean. Hawaii is the widest state measuring from east to west.

Hawaii is the only Native homeland that became an entire state. It is considered the most isolated population center in the world and is 2,390 miles from California; 3,850 miles from Japan; 4,900 miles from China; and 5,280 miles from the Philippines.

IN THE BEGINNING

They came in double canoes, searching northward into an unknown sea. Sailing on strange winds, paddling through doldrum calms, braving high seas and storms, they persisted in their quest for new land.... Their spaceship was the voyaging canoe.... For these were the Children of Tangaroa, Spirit of the Sea, and of Tāne, Tū, Rongo, mighty Spirits of Nature, and the most senior ancestors of the People as well as all other beings in the universe. While other explorers

sailed with the comforting presence of continental coasts off their beam, Polynesians faced the open ocean without fear as their own and only world.

—Herb Kawainui Kāne

Like all civilizations, Hawaii underwent great changes over centuries. It is believed that almost ten thousand years ago, the early ancestors of today's Native Hawaiians set off in their ancient crafts from what is now called Indonesia. Maybe they were pushed out by enemies and needed a safe haven. Maybe they faced famine and had to search for food. Perhaps they just had an adventurous spirit and set off to explore the world. Whatever the reason for their migration, they were a maritime people as comfortable on sea as on land. Without any computers or metal tools, they were master navigators at a time when vessels in other parts of the world rarely traveled out of view of the land. Over centuries, they settled different islands throughout the South Pacific.

These early sailors read the stars, as did most mariners of ancient times, but these travelers had many more methods to navigate unknown waters. They read the patterns of ocean winds, swells, fishing birds, cloud formations, and colors of the sea to find land. Their sailing crafts were self-sufficient islands and carried animals, plants, tools, clothing, and of course, many people. They communicated with the other voyagers through musical instruments, which broadcast across vast expanses of the night ocean.

Most historians believe that the first Polynesians came to Hawaii from the Marquesas; at a later time, the Tahitians invaded and defeated the original settlers. Another school of thought is that there was just one long period of settlement with many changes. Whatever the history, it is certain that the peopling of Hawaii was not just a random act. It would have been impossible to arrive on any of the Hawaiian Islands without a plan. The flora and fauna did not just drift to the lands; they were brought there and from immense distances, and the settlers who brought the animals and plants had done so on other lands of the South Seas for centuries.

Early colonists brought and cultivated *kalo* (taro), *mai'a* (banana), *niu* (coconut), *ko* (sugar cane), and *ulu* (breadfruit). They also brought sweet potato, which is a mystery as it was first cultivated in South America. The Polynesian word for potato is also the Peruvian word *kumara*, changed into the Hawaiian word *uala*. Since the Ancients sailed from one edge of the Pacific Ocean to the other, they probably visited South America, too. Their livestock included *pua'a* (pork) and *moa* (chicken), which supplemented their meals of sea vegetables and fish. They were probably the first aqua-culturists as they created habitats for a variety of fish by modifying streams and inlets. Not only did they build fish ponds, but over the years, they engineered large irrigation projects for kalo cultivation. The people built towns, farms, and *heiau* (temples) in the valleys and along the coasts. Their first *hale* (homes) were on the southern end of the Big Island, but they soon expanded north along the coasts and river valleys, and as the settlements became more populated, they extended further inland. It is estimated that before the Europeans arrived, there were almost a million people in Hawaii, but after European diseases hit the Islanders, their population plummeted. Wherever the voyagers traveled, they kept their traditions and memories of their homelands in the west. They believed that as soon as they died, their spirits would travel to their ancient homelands.

According to some Native Hawaiian historians, the early Polynesians were conquered by the Tahitians from Bora Bora, Huahine, and Ra'iaita. Ra'iaita boasted a major temple and was the religious and scholarly center of its time, comparable to today's Mecca or Vatican City. From across the great Pacific, the *Taputapuatea Marae* ("The Great Temple") drew navigators and priests who exchanged philosophical ideas, knowledge about the universe, and deep-ocean navigation skills. There was even a long-lasting truce negotiated among different factions, which sparked a powerful era of exploration and colonization of Eastern Polynesia, including Hawaii. Chiefs drew

their power from the site, which still exists today. Rocks from the holy temple were carried to different islands to mark new temples.

Hawaii's government was similar to that of Europe and Asia. There were separate kingdoms, rulers, and a caste system: royalty and commoners. The people had a strict code of laws and regulations called *kapu* (tabu or tapu are other Polynesian words for kapu) that determined lifestyle, gender roles, politics, religion, etc. Breaking a kapu law was taboo; in fact, "taboo" itself is an example of Indigenized English from Hawaiian, but kapu meant much more than breaking a forbidden offense; it also meant "sacred," "consecrated," or "holy."

There is a historical account of a great Samoan high priest named Pa'ao, who himself was an adventurer. When he arrived in Hawaii, he was shocked at the dreadful behavior of the high chief. The people were suffering under his administration and appealed to Pa'ao for help. After Pa'ao vanquished the ruler, the people asked him to lead. However, he wanted to retain his role as high priest and felt it prudent to bring a righteous leader to the nation who had the interest and commitment to be chief. This resolution was a turning point in Hawaiian history. Pa'ao convinced Pili, the high chief from Samoa, to take on the job. He arrived in Northern Hawaii with his colossal procession of canoes, and he and Pa'ao together represented both the sacred and the secular branches of Hawaiian government. Pili is the ancestor of King Kamehameha the Great.

KING KAMEHAMEHA

King Kamehameha was not only one of the most gifted and celebrated leaders in Hawaiian history, but his legacy lives on. In spite of many overwhelming challenges, he was able to unite all of the islands into one great nation, the Kingdom of Hawaii, an enormous feat that no one had ever even attempted. Born into a royal family (c. 1753), even his birth is legendary. Kamehameha would be a hereditary chief, but signs indicated that he would become the most powerful chief ever known, and the chiefs' council felt threatened; they ordered him killed at birth.

When Keku'iapoiwa (his mother) went into labor, there was a great storm, and an astounding shooting star (Halley's Comet) lit up the night sky, even more proof of a strong leader. Guards waited in front of the birthing house to kill the baby. Nae'ole, a chief of Hālawa and Keku'iapoiwa's most trusted friend, rescued the child, racing into the stormy night. Nae'ole delivered his precious charge to a young mother's secluded home as planned. Tense moments passed when the pursuing executioners showed up, but the baby stayed quietly hidden in a basket filled with *olonā* fiber. Kamehameha's first days on earth were a dramatic beginning for the courageous leader who was to unite and rule the islands during a time of great cultural change.

A statue of King Kamehameha stands in front of the capital building in Honolulu.

The king-to-be was returned to his parents at the age of five, and after his father's death, Kamehameha was given special training by his uncle, Ali'i Kalani'ōpu'u-a. He learned oral history, religion, warfare, navigation, diplomacy, and skills necessary to excel at sports and games. His education included all that he needed to become an *ali'i'ai moku* (district chief).

Kamehameha accompanied his uncle into many battles, and his military prowess grew; he was considered a warrior of warriors. Kamehameha questioned the bloodshed, thinking it would be better to unite all factions instead of warring with each other. In 1775, he was tested by a high priestess, who ordered him to move *Pōhaku Naha* (Naha Stone), weighing five thousand pounds. Kamehameha not only moved the massive boulder, but he overturned it, earning respect and loyalty. The high priestess had ordained that if he moved the boulder, he would indeed become king of all the islands. When Captain James Cook arrived in Hawaii, Kamehameha was only twenty-five years old, but according to Cook's records, he was already an outstanding warrior and statesman with battle scars and a tall, strong, authoritative, and confident demeanor. Kamehameha turned out to be a wise, pragmatic, and just leader, the most famous of all the Hawaiian monarchs and certainly one of the most notable kings in the world.

Englishman Captain James Cook

Englishman Captain James Cook (1728–1779) was a much decorated explorer, but few know that his voyages were helped by two South Sea Islanders as he searched for the Northwest Passage. In 1769, Tupaia (1725–1770), from Ra'iatea, was taken aboard the British ship *Endeavour* at the insistance of Cook's officers, against his wishes. Tupaia was a brilliant cartographer, but he could navigate without maps to the astonishment of the crew. For the next year, he guided the ship throughout the South Seas and was well received by the Maori in New Zealand. The *Endeavour* stopped to reprovision in Batavia (present-day Jakarta, Indonesia) on its return to England, where Tupaia died of dysentery. The second Polynesian navigator to aid Cook was Omai (c. 1753–1778), from Tahiti, in 1774. He was actually a refugee who had fled from Ra'iatea to Tahiti as a boy. He felt the British could help him free his island from the conquerors and sailed to England to rally support. After living in England for some time, Omai guided Cook back to the Islands and never did see his birthplace again.

By the time Captain Cook found Hawaii in 1778, he had made three voyages to the South Pacific and imagined himself somewhat of an expert in Polynesian cultures, but he was not. His misunderstanding of Hawaiian customs led to his downfall and death.

Makahiki

Makahiki is the season of peace and healing, and it so happened that Cook first came to Hawaii during that time. All warfare is suspended, and the land is put to rest so it can sustain new crops. The worshippers honor Lono, the god associated with fertility, agriculture, rainfall, music, and peace, so he will pass peacefully over their lands. Afterward, Makahiki is celebrated with hula, music, feasting, and the annual Olympic–like games, which featured fierce competitions in boxing, death-defying high-diving, surfing, swimming, wrestling, javelin-throwing, bowling, and sledding. The last part of the season is the *wa'a 'auhau* (tax canoe). The *wa'a 'auhau* was piled high with *ho'okupu* (offerings) for Lono and set adrift far from shore. The festival ended with the chief going out to sea. When his canoe returned and he stepped on land, a group of warriors physically challenged him to prove his worthiness to lead the people. If he was successful at defending himself, he could continue to rule.

Cook's End

Cook first arrived during the Makahiki observance; he and his crew misjudged the Hawaiians by thinking that they were always cheerful and low-key, when in fact, they were enjoying leisure time while waiting for Lono to pass over the land. The English first sighted O'ahu and Kaua'i on January 18, 1778, but conditions made it too hard to dock. The ships followed the same path as the procession honoring Lono, so maybe the Hawaiians thought this a gesture of respect. By this time, the British were joined by thousands of canoes and surfers. Trading began. The British wanted food and water; the Hawaiians were interested in iron objects. The ali'i of Kauai', King Kaumualii, received them warmly when they anchored off his island. Kamehameha accompanied his uncle, King Kalani'ōpu'u-a, to a reception on Cook's ship. After the ships were well stocked, they set out to search for the Northwest Passage.

In January 1779, Cook returned and anchored at Kealakekua Bay, off the Big Island. Kalani'ōpu'u-a invited Cook to a ceremony and gave him lavish presents—it was once again Makahiki, time of peace and generosity. Once more, the British wanted provisions and were a bit greedy according to Hawaiian etiquette. Cook and his men finally left, after wearing out their welcome, but came back a few days later as their ship needed repair.

However, Makahiki had ended, and the Hawaiians were not happy to see the avaricious foreigners. Matters escalated when a British cutter was "borrowed" by one of the Hawaiians. Sharing was customary in Hawaiian culture, and it was not unusual to borrow without asking, but items were always returned. However, Cook considered it a theft.

Cook and his party went ashore to retrieve the boat. His plan was to kidnap Kalani'ōpu'u-a and hold him as ransom for the cutter. Cook's crew had blockaded the harbor so no one could leave; a canoe attempted to pass and was fired upon, killing a chief. After news of the assassination spread, the community gathered in great numbers on the shore, just when Cook showed up with his kidnapping party, King Kalani'ōpu'u-a in tow.

The British began firing, but when they stopped to reload, they were attacked. Cook was fatally stabbed along with four of his men; the rest

A 1776 portrait of Captain James Cook by painter Nathaniel Dance-Holland.

and the prediction of the high priestess concerning the Pōhaku Naha. A twist of fate changed tradition. After Cook's demise, the aged and ill King Kalani'ōpu'u-a divided his kingdom between his son and political heir, Kiwala'o, and his nephew, Kamehameha. Plus, Kamehameha was made the protectorate of the war god, Ku, a great honor. Kamehameha was not as high-ranking as his cousin, but he had possession of the war god, which put him on a more equal footing and spurred his political aspirations.

Kalani'ōpu'u-a's actions not only split the leadership between men of unequal rank but set the stage for civil war among the rulers of the island of Hawaii. Kamehameha began to challenge the authority of his older cousin. He performed rituals that were his cousin's responsibility—it was seen as a terrible insult. After Kalani'ōpu'u-a died in 1782, complications arose over the division of the land, and the battle for power and property began.

Kamehameha's well-trained forces won most of the numerous battles over the next four years. Alliances were made and broken through negotiations and marriages; no one seemed to be the decisive winner or had complete power over Kalani'ōpu'u-a's realm. However, what was decisive was that Kamehameha was a serious contender. Even after his cousin Kiwala'o was killed in battle, the control of the island of Hawaii remained divided.

Kamehameha's Unusual Advisors

In 1785, Kamehameha married Queen Ka'ahumanu (c. 1768–1832), daughter of one of his closest advisors, ali'i Ke'eaumoku Papa'iahiahi, future royal governor of Maui. She was descended from Maui kings and became Kamehameha's favorite wife and confidant. Eventually, she would be prime minister and influence many national decisions. It is said that she and her husband had a turbulent relationship, and they were both possessive and jealous of each other. Ka'ahumanu stood by her husband's ambitions and encouraged him to unite the islands. She proved herself to be a capable and strong ruler.

of the party made it back to the ship, but the incident started a war. Records indicate that Kamehameha conducted himself valiantly during the battle at Kealakekua and attained a bit of notoriety. According to British logs, he carried himself "with an imperiousness that matched and even exceeded his rank as a high chief." The British ships would not leave until Cook's body was returned.

Finally, the captain's remains, wrapped in kapa and covered with a feather cloak, were returned in a funeral procession befitting *ali'i nui* (high chiefs). Cook's crew gave him a naval burial at sea, much to the approval of the Hawaiians. No other Europeans sailed to Hawaii' until 1786. Then, an increasing number of foreign ships began to arrive, including the three expeditions (1792, 1793, 1794) of British Captain George Vancouver.

THE KINGDOM OF HAWAII

Kamehameha was not next in line for his uncle's territory, in spite of the prophecies

Queen Ka'ahumanu, wife of King Kamehameha, would later become prime minister and desired a future Hawaii that was united and independent.

Although the queen would later steer her country away from the traditional religion and embraced Christianity, she vehemently supported Hawaiian sovereignty. It is thought that maybe she viewed the ancient kapa as too oppressive to women and wanted to be as free as her husband to surf, make her own decisions, and even to control her love life. Ka'ahumanu ruled with a firm hand, but she was a brilliant, capable leader who earned everyone's respect.

As well as the queen, two non-Hawaiians were valuable to the king. John Young (British) and Isaac Davis (Welsh) were kidnapped from two different British ships by the Hawaiians. The young Europeans became trusted advisors to Kamehameha, who was extremely pragmatic and opportunistic. The two were language and cultural interpreters. It is thought that the foreigners helped Kamehameha become the supreme king of all the islands by giving his forces the advantage of western weapons, but ultimately, it was traditional Hawaiian war techniques and diplomacy that won the battles.

Unification

In 1791, Kamehameha first united the warring factions of Hawaii Island with all the intrepidness and moxie of any historical empire builder and went on to unify all of the Hawaiian Islands into one royal kingdom in 1810. King Kamehameha had strict immigration policies, but he allowed foreigners to become citizens if they upheld Hawaiian laws and had skills necessary for the health of the regime. He controlled the Honolulu harbor with a brilliantly designed fort constructed of coral bricks, which is still partially standing today. Honolulu was the seat of the government as well as the main urban and trade center in the kingdom.

According to Dr. George Kanahele in his book *Ku Kanaka: Stand Tall: A Search for Hawaiian Values* (University of Hawaii Press, 1986), the values King Kamehameha the Great ruled by included:

- *Mālama* (Caring): A wise king takes care of royalty and commoners alike, "for together, they are the strength of his rule."

- *Ha'aha'a* (Humility): "Looking after the welfare of people arises from an underlying spirit of sensitivity and feeling for others that flows from humbleness rather than from a conviction of superiority."

- *Kåpono* (Integrity): In Hawaiian philosophy, there is a difference in being "honest, upright, good, fair, or worthy."

- *Na'auao* (Intelligence and Wisdom): *Na'auao* combines *na'au*, mind, and *ao*, daylight, to mean "the enlightened mind."

- *Koa* (Courage): "Courage has two sides: the physical and the nonphysical, that is, the emotional, moral, or spiritual. Opposition to a hero comes in many different forms."

Before he became king, Kamehameha had an altercation with some fishermen. He gave chase, but his foot got stuck in a rock crevice. One noticed his predicament and hit him with a paddle so hard that it splintered. As the man prepared to strike Kamehameha again, another fisherman pleaded for Kamehameha's life, and he was spared. The gesture deeply affected Kamehameha, who proclaimed a law to protect the defenseless and to ensure the safety of travelers. A version of the law was incorporated into the Hawaiian state constitution in 1978 and is called *Mamala Hoe* ("Law of the Splintered Paddle").

Throughout his reign, King Kamehameha ascribed to traditional religion in the face of foreign cultural influences. Although he cultivated friendships and alliances with Westerners who could help maintain his status, he tightly controlled Western business and political contacts with Hawaiians. Kamehameha and his government supplied visiting ships with supplies during the fur trade. They traded cargo-holds of sandalwood for Western goods. Kamehameha developed a national army and navy. The military used traditional canoes and uniforms as well as western technology like cannons, muskets, and European ships.

HALE O KAMEHAMEHA (KAMEHAMEHA DYNASTY, 1795–1872)

King Kamehameha died in 1819, leaving a great legacy—a well-functioning government, a large arsenal comprised of tens of thousands of military troops, and many warships as well as a flourishing economy. The House of Kamehameha was the reigning royal family of the Kingdom of Hawaii from 1795 until the death of Kamehameha V in 1872.

King Kamehameha II (Liholiho), 1797–1824

Kamehameha II, also called Liholiho, was Kamehameha's eldest son and became king after his father's death. Kamehameha felt his son lacked focus and leadership ability, and Queen Ka'ahumanu became *Kuhina Nui* (coregent), the

first ever. At Liholiho's lavish coronation, attended by both royalty and commoners, she proclaimed, "Hear me, O Divine one, for I make known to you the will of your father. Behold these chiefs and the men of your father, and these your guns, and this your land, but you and I shall share the realm together."

The dowager queen wielded her power boldly. She even challenged the ancient kapa system by defying taboos, including dining with men. At a state dinner, the queen had prearranged for Liholiho to join the women's table. He did, and that was the beginning of overturning the ancient rules. The erosion of traditional religion may have caused the kingdom's downfall. Indeed, the demolition of the ancient temples under the orders of Liholiho opened Hawaii to the missionaries, whose descendants would later cause the destruction of the kingdom.

King Kamehameha II only ruled for five years. On a much celebrated state visit to England, he and his wife, Queen K. Kamāmalu, were treated with much pageantry. They visited Westminster Abbey, but the king declined to enter because he did not want to desecrate their burial

King Kamehameha II

place. According to Bill Mai'oho, the curator of the Royal Mausoleum of Hawaii, "Liholiho, King Kamehameha II, refused to step in there because he wasn't blood-connected. These were the kings, and he felt he had no right.… He didn't want to desecrate their burial places with his presence or his feet stepping in that area."

Although Liholiho was to meet with King George IV, he and the royal Hawaiian court contracted measles. King Kamehameha II died; his grief-stricken wife passed away as well. Another member of the Hawaiian court did meet with the king of England and was entrusted with royal documents to take back home. Almost a year later, the king and queen's bodies reached Honolulu. Liholiho is remembered best for his opulent lifestyle and party attitude.

King Kamehameha III (Kauikeaouli), 1813–1854

Kauikeaouli was the much younger brother of Liholiho and the longest reigning monarch of Hawaii (1825–1854). As he was only twelve years old when he ascended to the throne, his stepmother, Queen Ka'ahumanu, made most of the decisions and remained *Kuhina Nui* until her death in 1832. He had a difficult time growing up as he was conflicted between his stepmother's fierce adherence to strict Puritan Christian guidelines for the kingdom and the desire to reinstate the original traditions. The queen enacted many changes in Hawaii and opened many schools. She is credited with making Hawaii the most literate nation in the world during that time.

King Kamehameha's elder sister, Kina'u, succeeded Queen Ka'ahumanu' as *Kuhina Nui*, but since the king was of age, she did not exercise the same power. She, like the queen, wanted Hawaii to be a protestant state banning all other religions. The kingdom suffered because of the constant quarrels between the two. Kauikeaouli pushed for freedom of religion. His aim was to keep his nation sovereign while balancing Western ways with Hawaiian traditions.

King Kamehameha III

The king also allowed Americans to experiment with growing Hawaiian sugar cane in 1835. Years before, an entrepreneur from China had opened Hawaii's first sugar mill, which failed, but by 1838, there were twenty mills and foreign-owned plantations firmly entrenched in the islands. King Sugar was taking over Hawaii. There was much jostling among American, French, Russian, and British powers for control of Hawaii's rich agricultural lands. Kauikeaouli had to contend with bickering, invasions, tariffs, and wheeling and dealing among the Anglo interests, plus navigate a successful rule with his own people.

King at a most difficult period in Hawaii's history, Kauikeaouli experienced the influx of scores of foreigners, who brought new problems concerning trade, credit, land titles, and a plethora of new complications. He was the first to break away from traditional rule and share governing. The Declaration of Rights of 1839 recognized three classes having vested rights in the lands; the king was the chief executive, the legislature, and the judiciary. The Legislative Department of the kingdom was composed of the king, the House of Nobles, and the House of Representatives. The king represented the vested right of the Government class, the House of Nobles represented the Chiefly class, and the House of Representatives represented the Tenant class. These rights were not limited to the land but included the right to " ... life, limb, liberty, freedom from oppression; the earnings of his hands and the productions of his mind; not, however, to those who act in violation of the laws." Under Kauikeaouli's reign, Hawaii changed from an absolute monarchy to a Christian constitutional monarchy with the signing of both the 1840 Constitution and 1852 Constitution. The 1840 Constitution gave everyone the right to vote, established the office of *Kuhina Nui*, created an office of royal governors of the various islands, and recognized Christianity as the authoritative religion.

Kauikeaouli developed an international strategy for survival of the kingdom and campaigned for a joint declaration from France and Great Britain honoring Hawaiian sovereignty. The kingdom requested the same from the Americans, who complied by issuing the Tyler Doctrine, which stated that the U.S. desired "no exclusive control over the Hawaiian government but would be content with its independent existence" as long as the Europeans stayed away. In 1843, Hawaiian independence was recognized by twenty-three nations around the world, including the United States. However, the French invaded twice during these times, and the king looked to the U.S. for protection.

Although the king had successfully negotiated agreements with all the powers interested in Hawaii, the European and American quest for expansion was a constant threat. The fate of Hawaii mirrored what was going on in the rest of the world as Indigenous governments and peoples were manipulated and destroyed. "Manifest Destiny" was becoming a popular term in the United States to rationalize its rapid growth as well as the annexation of Texas. The California Gold Rush was in full swing, and California was just a few days' sailing distance from Hawaii. It was now easier for Americans to visit, particularly ad-

venturers who brought along their diseases. Not only were hundreds more Hawaiians wiped out, but the talk of statehood was in the air. When California became a state in 1851, it was a bit worrisome to the Hawaiians.

The Treaty of Friendship, Commerce, and Navigation was signed with the U.S. in 1849. It stated that "each of the two contracting parties engages that the citizens or subjects of the other residing in their respective states shall enjoy their property and personal security in as full and ample a manner as their own citizens or subjects, or the subjects or citizens of the most favored nation, but subject always to the laws and statutes of the two countries, respectively." It also stated that any "citizen or subject of either party infringing the articles of this treaty shall be held responsible for the same, and the harmony and good correspondence between the two governments shall not be interrupted thereby, each party engaging in no way to protect the offender or sanction such violation." Since neither nation ever ended the Treaty, it is still in effect today. However, as was the case with of the rest of Native America, the United States did not honor its word.

A revised constitution was submitted to the legislature and approved by both the House of Nobles and the House of Representatives and signed into law by the king on June 14, 1852. King Kauikeaouli also named his nephew and adopted son, Liholiho, to succeed him. In 1854, His Majesty King Kamehameha III passed away, and Alexander Liholiho ascended to the office of constitutional monarch. From then on, he was known as King Kamehameha IV. The new king spoke about his father's administration: "The age of Kamehameha III was that of progress and of liberty—of schools and of civilization. He gave us a constitution and fixed laws; he secured the people in the title to their lands and removed the last chain of oppression. He gave them a voice in his councils and in the making of the laws by which they are governed. He was a great national benefactor and has left the impress of his mild and amiable disposition on the age for which he was born."

Kamehameha IV (Alexander 'Iolani Liholiho), 1834–1863

The king had traveled extensively with his brother on diplomatic missions while he was still a teenager. In 1850, they arrived in Washington, D.C., from England to meet President Zachary Taylor and Vice President Millard Fillmore and had a successful meeting. Afterward, Liholiho had firsthand experience with American racism when they boarded the train for New York. Having reserved a private compartment, Liholiho was in the car alone awaiting his party. Train personnel almost removed him for being a "nigger." The young prince, although just sixteen, wrote in his journal, "I found he was the conductor and took me for somebody's servant just because I had a darker skin than he had. Confounded fool; the first time that I have ever received such treatment, not in England or France or anywhere else.… In England, an African can pay his fare and sit alongside Queen Victoria. The Americans talk and think a great deal about their liberty, and strangers often find that too many liberties are taken of their comfort just because his hosts are a free people." There were other incidents during the same visit that did not give Liholiho a good impression of Americans, and he was opposed to them having power in his country.

Liholiho married Queen Emma, and they had one child, Albert, whose godmother was Queen Victoria of Great Britain. The royal couple devoted much of their reign to providing quality health care and education for their subjects. Concerned that foreign diseases like leprosy and influenza were destroying the Native Hawaiian population, Liholiho appealed to the legislature (1855) to sponsor a comprehensive health care system that included public hospitals and homes for the elderly. However, the 1852 Constitution had limited the king's authority, and the legislature refused to provide funding. The king and queen did not stop their campaign and appealed to local businessmen, merchants, and the rich to fund the program. The fundraising efforts were successful, and the royal couple built the Queen's Medical Center, one of the most technologically advanced medical centers in the world today. They also developed a leprosy treatment facility on Maui.

The American population was increasing and putting constant economic and political pressure on the kingdom. The children of the missionary immigrants were being educated in the U.S. and returning to Hawaii with American attitudes of white superiority and desiring a life different from their parents, including the right to hold public office and be key players in the country's destiny. The king was concerned that the U.S. would move to annex the kingdom, destroy the monarchy, and brutalize and oppress the people. He removed all Americans from cabinet posts in his government and encouraged Hawaiian trade with other nations. He also felt it would be better to give the Americans what they wanted instead of having it be taken by force. Liholiho unsuccessfully rallied for a reciprocity treaty involving trade and taxes between the United States and Hawaii. To strengthen his nation's economy and lessen its dependence on the United States, Kamehameha IV pushed for agricultural programs that would support Native Hawaiian farming. He founded the Hawaiian Chamber of Com-

King Kamehameha IV

merce and enhanced Hawaii's harbors, hoping to attract more international trade.

Sadly, the royal couple's only child died when he was just four, and the king felt responsible for his death. Overcome with grief and guilt, Kamehameha IV withdrew from public life. A year later, on November 30, 1863, after years of suffering from nerve disorders and asthma, the king died unexpectedly. He was twenty-nine and had only ruled for eight years. He was succeeded by his brother, Lot Kapuāiwa.

Kamehameha V (Lot Kapuāiwa), 1830–1872

The last great traditional chief and the last ruler of the Kamehameha Dynasty, his motto was "Onipa'a": immovable, firm, steadfast, or determined. When Lot came to power, he repealed the laws against "kahunaism." Kahuna practitioners were included on the newly established Board of Medicine and *la'au lapa'au* (Hawaiian traditional medicine) was once again practiced. Kahuna doctors were brought to the capital to record their remedies.

The king refused to sign the constitution and called for a new one. The office of *Kuhina Nui*, whose duties overlapped with those of the minister of interior, was abolished. The bicameral legislative body was also changed from two distinct houses (the House of Nobles and the House of Representatives) to a unicameral house where the " … legislative power of the three estates of this kingdom is vested in the king, and the legislative assembly, which assembly shall consist of the nobles appointed by the king and of the representatives of the people, sitting together."

Under Kamehameha V's administration, several buildings were constructed, including the current Hawaii State Supreme Court; 'Iolani barracks for the royal guards; a new prison; the Royal Mausoleum; schools; warehouses; a mental hospital and quarantine center to process the steady tide of immigrants; and other government projects. The boom burdened the Hawaiian treasury, and the national debt stood at almost $400,000.

King Kamehameha V

Lot never married or had any children, so there was no heir to the kingdom. On his deathbed, he begged his relative and Kamehameha's descendant, Bernice Pauahi Bishop, to ascend him as sovereign. She refused repeatedly. The king died an hour later, as did the Kamehameha Dynasty. The legislature, as per the constitution, elected William Charles Lunalilo as the new king.

WILLIAM CHARLES LUNALILO (1835–1874): FIRST ELECTED KING

Known as the most liberal king, Lunalilo's reign was also the shortest (January 8, 1873, to February 3, 1874). He won the election against David Kalākaua as he was more popular with the people, often referred to as the "People's King." He was the grandnephew of Kamehameha I and the first of two elected monarchs.

Under Lunalilo's leadership, government policy began to change. Whereas his predecessor,

King Lunaililo was actually elected to rule over Hawaii and was called the "People's King."

Kamehameha V, increased the king's powers and sought to restore the absolute monarchy of his grandfather, Kamehameha I, Lunalilo resolved to make the Hawaiian government more democratic. He wanted to undo some changes that Kamehameha V had made to the 1864 Constitution.

Lunalilo felt that Queen Emma, widow of King Kamehameha IV, should be his successor, but she died before he could name her to the office. In his will, Lunalilo set aside lands for the establishment of the Lunalilo Home, the first charitable trust established by a Hawaiian ali'i, to house the poor, destitute, and ill people of Hawaiian descent, with preference given to the elderly. He was succeeded by David Kalākaua.

KALĀKAUA DYNASTY

King David Kalākaua (1836–1891)

Nicknamed "the Merrie Monarch" because of his affinity for the arts, parties, and entertainment, Kalākaua's reign (1874–1891) was filled with as much tragedy and despair as it was with beauty and merriment. He became king during the second age of colonialism, dominated by England and France with the German Empire and the United States close behind toward the end of the nineteenth century. The Pacific was the new frontier, and colonial powers had already carved out big chunks of the landmasses in the world's largest ocean. Not only did the king face domination of his kingdom by outside forces, but he was not even his own people's favorite. Queen Emma ran against Kalākaua for the throne but was defeated by the legislature although she was the people's choice. Her supporters rioted in protest, and the new king called on the Americans and British to quell the rebellion from their ships in the harbor. His reign began on a sour note, and he did not enjoy the lavish celebration afforded other kings.

Kalākaua, fluent in Hawaiian and English, began studying law when he was only sixteen. However, he became involved in government, which interrupted his academics. By the age of twenty, he was already a major on the staff of King Kamehameha IV and had been a leader in the Young Hawaiians, a political group whose motto was "Hawaii for the Hawaiians." Besides his military career, Kalākaua also served in the Department of the Interior and was appointed postmaster general in 1863.

Months after he ascended the throne, Kalākaua sailed to the United States on a diplomatic mission and was received with much fanfare—he was the first king, or any head of state of a foreign nation, to address a joint session of Congress or visit the White House. King Kalākaua and President Ulysses Grant negotiated and then signed the Reciprocity Treaty of 1875, which eliminated the tariff on sugar and other Hawaiian products. Consequently, Hawaii's sugar industry exploded, and the kingdom experienced a period of economic prosperity.

At the same time, Kalākaua pursued a foreign policy that would stress the position of Hawaii as a fully independent nation. He sought to bolster the pride of his own people in their heritage by reviving Hawaiian traditions, including the hula, which he called "the life-blood of his people." To prepare his country for international diplomacy, he sent young royals to be educated and trained in various countries. Kalākaua himself embarked on a world cruise in 1881, the first ruling monarch to ever do so. His charm, manners, and diplomacy impressed every leader he visited. At home, he built 'Iolani Palace as an official residence, and it had electricity, telephones, and indoor plumbing before the White House. The construction cost $350,000, a huge sum at that time, and he was criticized for being a spendthrift. In 1887, Kalākaua's wife, Queen Kapi'olani, and his sister, Crown Princess Lili'uokalani, were honored guests at Queen Victoria's Golden Jubilee in London, the capital of the most powerful nation in the world. He set a course to put Hawaii on the map, and by 1892, the monarchy maintained over ninety consulates, a network which spanned the globe.

King Kalākaua believed in the hereditary right, which was reflected in his government appointments. The "Missionary Party" wanted the Hawaiian government to resemble the United Kingdom's constitutional monarchy where the royals were respected as heads of state but had little power. The party wanted the legislature, not the king, to control the cabinet ministers. This struggle continued throughout Kalākaua's reign. In the same year, the United States began leasing Pearl Harbor and had more of a military presence in the kingdom. Some Anglos wanted the king to abdicate and his sister Lili'uokalani to govern. Other foreigners and descendants of missionaries wanted to destroy the monarchy and annex the islands to the United States. That group formed the "Hawaiian League" and forced Kalākaua' to sign a new constitution, which they had devised, at gunpoint. It became known as the Bayonet Constitution. Americans Sanford Dole and Lorrin Thurston, who was the Hawaiian Minister of the Interior, were part of the conspiracy.

The Bayonet Constitution allowed Americans and Europeans, who were not even naturalized Hawaiians, to vote and run for office and still retain their status as citizens of their respective countries. Asian immigrants were completely banned from voting or acquiring citizenship. Eligible voters must have certain financial means as well. This new constitution benefited only the wealthy, white, foreign plantation owners and allowed the legislature to override any of the king's vetoes. He could not even take any action without the legislature's approval. The worse outcome was that the new "constitution" severely diminished Native Hawaiian voice in government of their own homelands. Their organized resistance resulted in the creation of the Hawaiian Political Party, also known as the Hui Kalai'aina. The Hui Kalai'aina constantly petitioned King David Kalākaua to restore the 1864 constitution as it was the legal constitution of the kingdom.

Kalākaua's distant cousin and veteran of the Italian military, Robert William Wilcox, returned to Hawaii at around the same time as Lili'uokalani returned from attending festivities in England. His student financial support had ended with the new constitution. They plotted to overthrow the king to take back their country, but their plans were discovered. Wilcox was tried for treason, but a jury of his peers refused to execute him. He was exiled, and the incident is called the Wilcox Rebellion. The Missionary Party appealed to the Crown Princess to take over the throne, but she declined as she believed she would become the same powerless figurehead as her brother.

In November 1890, an ill Kalākaua traveled to California for medical treatment. A few months later, he died at a San Francisco hotel (January 20, 1891). His last words were, "Tell my people I tried." His demise signaled what was to come: the eventual destruction of the Kingdom of Hawaii. A great patron of the arts, he composed the Hawaiian national anthem, which is now the state song, "Hawaii Pono'i" ("Our Hawaii").

Queen Lili'uokalani (Lydia Lili'u Loloku Walania Wewehi Kamaka'eha), 1838–1917

In 1891, Queen Lili'uokalani came to power after her brother King Kalākaua's death. She would be the only female monarch as well as the last to rule Hawaii. The kingdom was in turmoil, and the Hawaiian people looked to her to restore their rights and government. She was determined to reinstate the monarchy's power and rid the country of foreign control.

On January 17, 1893, Lili'uokalani, convinced that the U.S. military would intervene if she revised the constitution, waited for the USS *Boston* to leave the harbor. According to the U.S. protectorate policy, at least one military ship must be present in Hawaii at all times. However, the Missionary Party discovered her plan and recalled the ship. The crew assisted the Missionary Party in overthrowing the queen and seizing control of the kingdom, proclaiming a provisional government until Hawaii could become an American territory. Sanford Dole became the president of both the Hawaiian Kingdom and the new provisional government. The queen temporarily relinquished her throne to "the superior military forces of the United States," hoping that the U.S., like Great Britain earlier in Hawaiian history, would restore

Queen Lili'uokalani

Hawaii's sovereignty. She issued a statement to President Grover Cleveland: "I, Lili'uokalani, by the Grace of God and under the constitution of the Hawaiian Kingdom, queen, do hereby solemnly protest against any and all acts done against myself and the constitutional government of the Hawaiian Kingdom by certain persons claiming to have established a provisional government of and for this kingdom, that I yield to the superior force of the United States of America, whose minister plenipotentiary, His Excellency John L. Stevens, has caused United States troops to be landed at Honolulu and declared that he would support the said provisional government. Now, to avoid any collision of armed forces and perhaps loss of life, I do, under this protest, and impelled by said forces, yield my authority until such time as the government of the United States shall, upon the facts being presented to it, undo the action of its representative and reinstate me in the authority which I claim as the constitutional sovereign of the Hawaiian Islands."

President Cleveland stated that the overthrow of the queen was illegal and that U.S. Minister Stevens and American military troops had wrongfully supported the Anglo insurgents. On November 16, 1893, Cleveland, who was an anti-imperialist and against annexation, agreed to restore Lili'uokalani's power if she granted amnesty to the rebels. At first she refused because she wanted them banished. However, she changed her position, and on December 18, 1893, U.S. Minister Albert Willis demanded her reinstatement by the provisional government. It refused. A report by the U.S. Congress on February 26, 1894, found all parties (including Minister Stevens), with the exception of the queen, "not guilty" from any responsibility for the overthrow. The Provisional Government of Hawaii disarmed and disbanded the kingdom's military forces.

Between December 14, 1893, and January 11, 1894, the United States, Japan, and the United Kingdom staged a standoff against the provisional government attempting to force Dole's government to step down. It was known as Black Week. The incident strongly conveyed the message that President Cleveland supported the reinstatement of the kingdom, but the provisional government did not back down and declared the Republic of Hawaii. The kingdom continued to lobby in Washington while the exiled government secretly amassed an army of almost a thousand. A four-day counter-rebellion between January 6 and 9, 1895, began with an attempted coup d'état to restore the monarchy and included battles between Royalists and Republican rebels. Lili'uokalani was arrested when a weapons store was discovered on the palace grounds.

THE REPUBLIC OF HAWAII

The queen was tried by a military tribunal of the Republic, convicted of treason, and sentenced to prison for five years of hard labor. However, her sentence was commuted to permanent house arrest in her own home. She was allowed just one companion and prohibited from any contact with the outside world. For five long years, Queen Lili'uokalani remained imprisoned, but the abuse did not destroy her strong spirit and resolve to save her country.

On January 24, 1895, while still under house arrest, the queen was forced to sign the "Lili'uokalani Dominis," which completely disbanded the Kingdom of Hawaii. She also formally abdicated the throne in exchange for the release (and commutation of death sentences) of kingdom patriots, including Minister Joseph Nawahi, Prince Kawānanakoa, Robert Wilcox, and Prince Jonah Kuhio. Lili'uokalani wrote, "For myself, I would have chosen death rather than to have signed it, but it was represented to me that by my signing this paper, all the persons who had been arrested, all my people now in trouble by reason of their love and loyalty toward me, would be immediately released … the stream of blood ready to flow unless it was stayed by my pen." The Hawaiian Constitution did not provide a legal process for the monarch's abdication and without the approval of the legislature, the document had no legal validity. Still, the kingdom was destroyed, but not the spirits of the *Kānaka Maoli* and *Hawaii Maoli* (Indigenous Hawaiians).

The queen finished her sentence and managed to leave the country, having been able to keep her intentions a secret. Sanford Dole, now president of the Republic of Hawaii, had spies everywhere. Dole even issued her a Republic of Hawaii passport. Once out to sea, Lili'uokalani is reported to have said, "For the first time in years, I drew a long breath of freedom." She and a close circle of advisors had carefully planned this trip to continue their fight against annexation. The colonial government would not have allowed her to leave had they known.

Royalist groups and the Hawaiian-owned press kept resisting annexation. The queen visited Washington more than once to petition first President Cleveland and then President William McKinley to free her land from those in power of the illegal Republic of Hawaii. She hosted receptions for congressmen; some, like South Dakota's Richard Pettigrew, vehemently opposed any imperialist actions on behalf of the U.S. Others pointed out the contradictions in the U.S. wanting to save Cuba from Spanish domination but

After the overthrow of the Hawaiian royal family, Sanford Dole served as president of Hawaii from 1894 to 1900, and then as its governor until 1903.

plotting to dominate Hawaii. Other Americans were opposed as they feared mainland farmers could not compete with the cheap labor available to plantation owners in Hawaii. Americans had strict laws forbidding people of Asian and Near Eastern countries to emigrate to the U.S., and Hawaii had a high population of Japanese workers. This was appalling to the white racists in the States. Hawaii had not only fallen prey to missionaries, entrepreneurs, racists, and the wealthy, but American politicians like Theodore Roosevelt viewed her as a strategic military base to ensure and grow American power.

Back home, Royalist organizations like the Hui Aloha 'Aina and the Hui Kulai'aina organized against the impending annexation of their country. They collected several thousand signatures protesting the Republic. Eventually, the petitions were presented to Congress with the clear message that the rightful owners of the Kingdom of Hawaii wanted the country restored. Scholar Noenoe K. Silva discovered the documents in 1996 while doing research in the National Archives (Washington, D.C.) She reported that nearly every Hawaiian had signed as there were forty thousand signatures. "Everybody's *kupuna* (elder) signed this paper," Silva said, "and they all stood up for their country." The documents were taken to Hawaii for viewing. In January 1999, a ceremony was held when they were returned to the U.S. Senate by the descendants of the four men who originally delivered the documents—former Hawaii Supreme Court Justice William Richardson, Moses Kalauokalani, Edwin Auld, Toni Auld Yardley, and Kaoi Kaimikaua.

The goal of forming a republic was to eventually be annexed by the United States as Anglos believed annexation would ensure a strong economy. Hawaiian exports would be exempt from American tariffs, and the territory would be legally under the protection of the U.S. In spite of the brilliant diplomacy exhibited by the queen and her supporters, the U.S. just bulldozed over them. In 2006, *New York Times* foreign correspondent Stephen Kinzer published *Overthrow: America's Century of Regime Change from Hawaii to Iraq*. He writes, "Why does a strong nation

The flag of the Kingdom of Hawaii

strike against a weaker one? Usually because it seeks to impose its ideology, increase its power, or gain control over valuable resources. America's long 'regime change' century dawned in 1893 with the overthrow of the Hawaiian Monarchy."

The few white elite who controlled the government in a country with a majority of nonwhites began to worry what would happen if they were not annexed by the U.S. Dole was sent to Washington to further lobby for support. The royal delegation was still there and upstaged him by holding a grand reception for their American friends. One newspaper reported of Dole, "He is not the president of the Hawaiians but the representative of the descendants of missionaries, gentlemen who have captured alive the souls which their pious fathers intended to control only after death." But in the end, the white notion of superiority was too ingrained in the hearts and minds of American lawmakers to be fair and govern without prejudice.

THE TERRITORY OF HAWAII

Sugar is king in Hawaii to a far greater extent than cotton was in the Old South. Those rich, warm lands in all the islands are devoted almost exclusively now to the production of sugar cane.

—Ray Stannard Balzer

William McKinley succeeded Cleveland as president in 1897, and in 1898, a formal annexation ceremony was held at 'Iolani Palace.

Hardly any Native Hawaiians attended, and a small number remained outside wearing Royalist *ilima* blossoms on their heads and on their chests; they wore Hawaiian flags with the motto *Kuu Hae Aloha* ("my beloved flag"). Most of the forty thousand Native Hawaiians, including Lili'uokalani and the royal family, protested by staying indoors with closed shutters. The *San Francisco Chronicle* printed a statement from the queen's niece, Crown Princess Ka'iulani, saying, "It was bad enough to lose the throne but infinitely worse to have the flag go down. When the news of annexation came, it was bitterer than death to me."

The Hawaiian flag was lowered for the last time while the Royal Hawaiian Band played the Hawaiian national anthem, "Hawaii Pono'i." Immediately, the American flag was raised to "The Star-Spangled Banner." In a nearby church, women chanted the ancient mourning songs. The Hawaiian people had lost their land, their monarchy, and their independence. The blatant disregard for King Kamehameha's legacy and kingdom was an open wound for the Hawaiian people as they witnessed 'Iolani Palace become headquarters for the rogue Hawaiian government until 1969. A few white people, most of them children of missionaries, were ruling an Indigenous kingdom.

Independent Home Rule Party

Native Hawaiians regrouped, adamant that they would overturn their defeat. Concerned that neither the Democratic Party of Hawaii nor the Hawaii Republican Party could fairly represent them, they created the Hawaiian Independent Party in 1900. Later, it was renamed the Independent Home Rule Party. Robert William Kalanihiapo Wilcox was its first delegate to the United States Congress for the Territory of Hawaii. He addressed the two main Hawaiian organizations Hui Aloha 'Aina and Hui Kalai'āina: "The question of the restoration of the monarchy is gone from us forever. We are now a people, however, who can vote. You all know we have two-thirds of the votes in this country." Wilcox

served one term and was defeated by Prince Jonah Kūhiō Kalaniana'ole of the Republican Party in 1902. The Independent Home Rule Party disbanded in 1912.

Prince Kalaniana'ole

Prince Kalaniana'ole (1871–1922) was the first royal ever elected to Congress. After the tragic death of young Crown Princess Ka'iulani in 1899, Queen Lili'uokalani made Kalaniana'ole and his brother David Kawānanakoa (1868–1908) heirs to the throne. He was a delegate from 1903 until his death, winning a total of ten elections. He developed Hawaii's county system still used today and appointed Native Hawaiians to the civil service positions. The prince combined nineteenth-century politics with the traditional custom of the chiefs delegating authority to competent people. Kalaniana'ole reorganized the Royal Order of Kamehameha I and made Kamehameha Day a national holiday in 1904. He organized the one-hundred-year celebration of the death of Kamehameha I in 1919. In 1920, Kalaniana'ole sent a letter to his fellow senators: "After extensive investigation and survey on the part of various organizations organized for the purpose of rehabilitating the race, it was found that the only method in which to rehabilitate the race was to place them back upon the soil." He was the first to introduce a bill to make Hawaii a state. Several schools and buildings are named in his honor.

Hawaiian Homes Commission Act

While Kalaniana'ole was still in office, the federal government passed the Hawaiian Homes Commission Act (1920). A land trust of approximately two hundred thousand acres was set aside for Native Hawaiians to homestead and maintain traditional ties to the land by raising traditional crops like kalo (taro). Kalaniana'ole did not support the controversial definition of "Native Hawaiians" as "persons with fifty percent or more Hawaiian blood," knowing that many descendants would be excluded. However, he was a nonvoting delegate; the bill passed as proposed. After statehood in 1959, responsibility for the Commission was transferred to Hawaii, but the federal government kept power to enforce the trust and approve land exchanges and legislative amendments affecting the rights of beneficiaries.

Three types of leases are available: residential, agricultural for farming, and pastoral for ranching; one can build a house on an agricultural or farming site. From its inception, there have been many problems. The designated lands are often far from employment, and mortgages for home construction are difficult to obtain. There are more than twenty thousand people on the waiting list, but only around 7,200 leases have been granted in DHHL's ninety-year history.

Military Presence

The sugar barons ruled Hawaii—its economy and its politics. White immigration grew along with bringing workers from other parts of the world to work the plantations of the wealthy. The Native Hawaiians were fast becoming a minority in their own country.

Along with the land appropriation by the plantation owners came the encroachment of the U.S. Navy. The Islands were turned into a military base, and Navy personnel and their wives grabbed available housing. Native Hawaiians were most likely to be homeless of any other group. Thrilled to be in what they called a paradise, sailors were often disrespectful to and violent with the Native population. When incidents between the military personnel and Native Hawaiians involved local police, the police most often took the side of the military. On one such occasion, random Native Hawaiians were rounded up and charged with a fabricated assault on a Navy wife. It made national headlines, and the accused were called the "Ala Moana boys." Even though the innocent young men were tried and exonerated, they were continually harassed

The United States established a huge naval presence at Hawaii's Pearl Harbor, which was then attacked in 1941 by the Japanese. Native Hawaiians had no control over any of these events.

by military personnel. One was killed, another severely beaten, and their lives were all ruined.

The local people and especially the Native Hawaiians had no control over their lives, and when Pearl Harbor was bombed in 1941, Hawaii was placed under martial law. For the duration of the war, the beloved lands were used extensively as bases, bombing practice sites, and rest and recreation spots for military personnel.

STATEHOOD

With the end of World War II came the formation of the United Nations. Countries' leaders gathered in San Francisco in 1945 to endorse a U.N. Charter calling for self-governance of territories under colonial-style conditions. In 1946, the U.N. General Assembly adopted Resolution 66 in which specific U.N. members and the territories they ruled were named. The United States was required to bring self-governance to Alaska, Guam, American Samoa, the Virgin Islands, Panama Canal zone, Puerto Rico, and Hawaii. The U.N. defined self-governance as allowing the people of the territory to make choices of how they would relate to the U.N. member: integration, free association, or independence. The action was intended to sever the bonds of colonization for territories—many African countries were able to free themselves of colonial powers. Countries in the Pacific and Asian regions soon followed.

The U.S. did not meet its obligation to Hawaii. They only offered one of the three choices—integration. Rather than permitting the three choices called for by the U.N., the United States limited the choice to "integration." The choices of free association or independence were never presented to the Hawaiian people. The issue was never raised, not even by the territorial governor. Again, the U.S. defied international laws.

Some Native Hawaiians believed statehood would be an improvement over territory status—their rights would be better served. However, many protested statehood. Several American lawmakers did not think the Native people or any

residents of the territory would be patriotic to the United States and did not want statehood for the territory.

Hawaiian Territorial Senator Alice Kamokila Campbell was one of the dissenting voices regarding statehood. On January 17, 1946, the fifty-third anniversary of the overthrow of the Hawaiian Kingdom and in front of an approving crowd at 'Iolani Palace, she stated: "I do not feel … we should forfeit the traditional rights and privileges of the natives of our islands for a mere thimbleful of votes in Congress, that we, the lovers of Hawaii, from long association with it, should sacrifice our birthright for the greed of alien desires to remain on our shores, that we should satisfy the thirst for power and control of some inflated industrialists and politicians who hide under the guise of friends of Hawaii, yet still keeping an eagle eye on the financial and political pressure button of subjugation over the people in general of these islands."

Campbell opened the Anti-Statehood Clearing House in 1947 and continued to send antistatehood information, reports, and arguments to Congress. She successfully sued to halt the Hawaii Statehood Commission from spending public money to lobby for statehood.

The United States reported to the U.N. General Assembly in 1959 that Hawaii had been extended its right to self-governance and had elected statehood. The U.S. persuaded the U.N. to remove Hawaii from the list of territories subject to self-governance. The action closed the door to Native Hawaiians appealing to the U.N. to support their fundamental right to self-determination.

To qualify to be a voter in Hawaii elections, one only had to reside in Hawaii for one year, including military personnel stationed there. Thousands of immigrants from the U.S., Europe, and Asia resided in the islands, many for employment or other ventures. All who professed to be American citizens could vote. However, those who still considered themselves to be subjects of the Kingdom of Hawaii and refused American citizenship could not vote. The odds were stacked against the kingdom.

In 1959, the Territory of Hawaii was admitted to the Union as the fiftieth state in a proclamation by President Dwight D. Eisenhower. The Native Hawaiians were under their second layer of foreign rule. They had contended with the plantations, military, adventurers, and all sorts of interlopers. Now, the ancient homelands were to become a vast playground, and the exploitation worsened. Hawaii had become the tourist and military satellite of the American Empire.

To make way for the countless hotels that disrupt the skyline, the Hawaiian people's cultural, historical, and religious areas have been devastated since Hawaii became a state. Plus, their land-based resources have been severely compromised. Burial grounds have been bulldozed along with significant archaeological historic sites. Golf courses blanket areas where temples, fishing shrines, homes, ceremonial platforms, and agricultural lands once defined healthy communities.

Hawaiian culture and the ancient sacred sites that remain have been turned into tourist attractions and are defiled in their misuse. Appropriated cultural symbols show up in plastic souvenirs. Tourists attend luaus that have little to do with their real purpose. Gaudy replicas of leis adorn the necks of visitors thrilled by the experience of becoming "Hawaiian," if only for a week. Millions of dollars are pumped into this mockery of Hawaiian culture, and billions more are made by selling it. Ironically, little of this money is used to preserve the culture, recover the language, or contribute to the economy of the Native Hawaiians.

A way of life, once outlawed by ancestors of these very tourists for its "pagan" roots, has been trivialized and morphed into a cash crop. As tourism spreads inland and to beaches, once considered inferior by Anglo tourism standards, Native Hawaiians continue to be displaced. Many people suffer all the consequences of colonialism from poverty to ill health to despair, yet ... they continue. Today, many activists struggle to reclaim both culture and territory; several are committed to restoring the health of their island homeland, which is not the "capital of paradise" as it is billed in the tourist industry. Because of all the overbuilding and pollution, Hawaii bears the unflattering title of "Endangered Species Capital of the World."

Kaho'olawe Island

Kaho'olawe, nicknamed the "smallest island," was a sacred place and a navigational center for the traditional Hawaiians, but the Europeans and then the Americans did not respect its spiritual importance. From 1826–1853, it was a penal colony. Ranchers then transported flocks of sheep and goats, which destroyed all the native plant life. Starting in 1941, the U.S. military used the island for target practice for decades and almost obliterated it. Hawaiians began protesting Kaho'olawe's devastation in 1976, and after the death of two activists, and the jailing of many more, the bombing finally stopped in 1990. In 1994, Congress initiated the return of Kaho'olawe to the state. The Kaho'olawe Island Reserve Commission began the process of restoring the island to its natural habitat and is attempting to save its ancient archaeological sites.

Ni'ihau Island

Nicknamed "the Forbidden Island," Ni'ihau is the smallest inhabited island in the Hawaiian homelands. Believed to be the first Hawaiian home of Pele, the Volcano Goddess, the island is rich with history. Place names honor powerful ali'i and their heroic deeds. Ni'ihau's extremely independent people were the last to be united under King Kamehameha's rule; he sold it to a Euro-New Zealander family for ranch lands. The Sinclair-Robinson-Gay family still owns it and restricts visitations from outsiders, which has preserved Hawaiian culture and values. Ni'ihau has few modern conveniences, no hotels, indoor plumbing, hotels, paved roads, cars, stores, or restaurants. Limited electricity comes from solar power, and there is no medical, police, or fire department. The ranch closed in 1999, and except for a few jobs at the school, there is no longer full-time employment. Because of the shrinking pop-

Ni'ihau Island is the smallest inhabited island in the Hawaiian chain.

ulation, traditional crafts are in decline, too. Families spend more time on other islands nearer to employment. Hawaiian is spoken, and children attend the only solar-powered school in Hawaii.

The little island made big news during World War II just hours after Pearl Harbor was attacked. Islanders knew about tensions between the U.S. and Hawaii but had not heard news of the bombing. A lone Japanese pilot crashed on Ni'ihau, and the residents greeted their guest with traditional Hawaiian hospitality, but they did confiscate his weapons and papers although he protested. Hawila Kaleohano, the resident in charge, asked one of the few non-Hawaiian workers, Harada, to translate. Harada learned of the invasion and chose to help the pilot instead of translating what had happened. Without working boats or radios, the Ni'ihau people were on their own. The pilot, aided by Harada, found weapons and threatened the Hawaiians. Kaleohano and others set out in a rowboat to get aid. After taking hostages, the pilot was killed by Ben Kanahele and his wife Ella. Harada, who had been born and raised in Hawaii, committed suicide.

Kaleohano's party returned to Ni'ihau the next day with military authorities. The December 1942 issue of *Reader's Digest* chronicled the episode, calling those involved "full-blooded descendants of ancient Hawaiian warriors." "They Couldn't Take Ni'ihau, No-How" became America's first World War II victory song. Kaleohano was awarded a Medal of Freedom, and Ben Kanahele received a Medal of Merit and a Purple Heart.

THE HAWAIIAN RENAISSANCE

The Hawaiian Renaissance, built on cultural revivals of the 1960s, gained momentum in the 1970s. Musical innovations based on traditional styles featured a vast array of artists like Gabby Pahinui and the Sons of Hawaii, Keola and Kapono Beamer, and their slack-key compositions, Dennis Pavao, Hui'Ohana, Olomana, and several others. There were intense struggles for lands in areas like Kalama Valley, Kaho'olawe, and Waiāhole/Waikāne. Hawaiians relearned traditional skills of *lo'i kalo* (taro patch) farming and *mālama 'āina* (historical ways of forestry/land healing and restoration).

People began to relearn the Hawaiian language, time-honored Hawaiian crafts, Hawaiian history, and all aspects of Hawaiian culture. Major annual events like the Merrie Monarch Festival, the 'Iolani Luahine Hula Festival, and the Prince Lot Hula Festival rekindled ancient hula practice. The Buddhist temple Honpa Hongwanji Mission of Honolulu, Hawaii, established "The Living Treasures of Hawaii Awards (1976)" "to recognize and honor individuals who have demonstrated excellence in their fields and who have made lifelong and significant contributions toward creating a more humane society without public recognition." Some honorees are: Iolani Luahine (1977), kumu hula, dancer, chanter, and teacher—considered the high priestess of the ancient hula; Rubellite Kawena Johnson (1983), historian and professor emeritus of Hawaiian language; and Morrnah Nalamaku Simeona (1983), kahuna lapa'au (healer).

In 1972, ALOHA (Aboriginal Lands of Hawaiian Ancestry) organized to seek reparations from the U.S. government for crown lands claimed by the Republic of Hawaii and still illegally controlled by the state. In 1974, Native

Hawaiians were included in the Native American Programs Act, which enabled them to be eligible for some Native American assistance programs. The act defined a Native Hawaiian as "an individual any of whose ancestors were natives of the area which consists of the Hawaiian Islands prior to 1778." The Office of Hawaiian Affairs was created (1978) to heal Native Hawaiian problems caused by the kingdom's overthrow, and the Hawaiian language, banned for decades, was restored as the official language of Hawaii (along with English).

Polynesian Voyaging Society

Probably one of the most remarkable achievements of the Renaissance era was the founding of the Polynesian Voyaging Society (PVS) by Herb Kawanui Kāne in 1973. It led to the building and sailing of the *Hōkūle'a* ("Star of Gladness"), a traditional, double-hulled sailing canoe very similar to those of the Hawaiian ancestors. Kāne challenged the Eurocentric assumption that Polynesian exploration and settlement was not planned but rather a result of storm-wrecked vessels set adrift and lucky to find land. Scholars doubted that Polynesian navigators had the ability and transportation to plan and voyage across the vast Pacific. This was all disproved by computer simulations of wind patterns and ocean currents demonstrating that a drifting canoe had no chance of reaching Hawaii, Easter Island, and New Zealand from other parts of Polynesia or Micronesia.

The Hōkūle'a first trip using traditional navigation techniques was more than 2,500 miles from Maui to Tahiti. It took thirty days. Naviga-

The construction of the *Hōkūle'a* proved that a double-hulled canoe could have been constructed deliberately by Polynesians who later settled Hawaii.

tor Nainoa Thompon wrote, "At the arrival into Pape'ete Harbor, over half the island was there, more than 17,000 people." Wherever the Hōkūle'a sailed, she was warmly welcomed by Polynesians and became symbolic of their commonality and pride and a testament to the resourcefulness, inventiveness, and courage of their ancestors. In 2013, the Hōkūle'a and a second canoe, Hikianalia, began a worldwide voyage named *Mālama Honua* ("to care for the earth") to bring attention to responsible stewardship of "island earth." The route takes them to the Atlantic Ocean for the first time. During the four-year trip, they will visit one hundred ports in twenty-seven nations and cover sixty thousand nautical miles; four of the ports are on the U.S. eastern seaboard. Seasoned mariners will be teaching younger crew members to be navigators. Their route can be tracked on http://www.ho kulea.com/worldwide-voyage/.

SPORTS/MUSIC

Native Hawaiians had scores of sports and games like wrestling, swimming, diving, bowling, tobogganing, canoe racing, long-stick fencing, and, of course, surfing. They participated in competitive and dangerous events, which would be considered extreme sports by today's standards. Often, sports events were held as part of a religious observance or to settle a dispute. Sledding was restricted to the chief class and was a dangerous tobogganlike event done on lava bed courses, which were over a mile long and covered in dirt and wet grass to make them slippery. Today, one can see the preserved Keauhou Hōlua Slide in Keauhou on the island of Hawaii.

U'lu maika, a type of bowling, is still played today, and on Molokai, there are the remains of a seven-mile-long course. Stone disks (*u-lu*), carved from lava, coral, limestone, and other materials, were rolled between two stakes about six inches apart. Sometimes the object was to see who could bowl the greatest distance. Another version was a challenge to see who could bowl the *u-lu* between two stakes while a third game

was to test the strength of the *u-lu*'s as they were rolled against an opponent's.

Surfing (*he'enalu*), a centuries-old sport, was introduced to the world by Hawaiians. At one time, it was mainly a pastime for the upper classes, who gained respect through their endurance and skill to ride the waves—they considered it an art rather than a sport. Ancient surfing areas still used today include Kahalu'u Bay and Holualoa Bay.

The performance knowledge of string figures has been revitalized. In traditional times, there were over a hundred string figures, many with their own special songs. The art was used as a memory device to relate ancient accounts.

The iconic hula dancing has six traditional moves with a myriad of interpretations. The smooth, flowing movements were originally part of ceremonial observances. The dance and accompanying vocals recount religious events, similar to reciting the Christmas story or the Haggadah. After Christianity became powerful in Hawaii, hula was banned as it was considered a pagan ritual—missionaries found the sensuous movements vulgar and sinful. The religious performances were forced to go underground. In the 1830s, King Kamehameha III re-established hula when he insisted on religious freedom. The missionaries still did not support the practice, but they compromised by insisting the dancers wear dresses that covered them from top to bottom. These long gowns are known as muumuus.

King David Kalākaua, the last Hawaiian king and a patron of the arts, openly revived the hula and encouraged it to be a theatrical production with new moves, costumes, and songs. The "Merrie Monarch" reinstated it as part of festivals and celebrations. Today, the annual Merrie Monarch Festival in Hilo is held in King Kalākaua's honor and features a weeklong celebration of hula competition, Hawaiian arts fairs, hula shows, and a grand parade through Hilo town.

King Kalākaua is also credited with the popularity of the ukulele (jumping flea), borrowed from the Portuguese laborers imported to work in the sugar plantations in the 1800s. The Native Hawaiians repurposed the European instrument (braguinha), playing it with their own rhythms and compositions. It became the national instrument of Hawaii, so symbolic of Hawaiian music that few know its roots. The Hawaiians also created a fresh guitar sound and are recognized as inventing the "steel guitar" as well as the "slack key" style of playing a guitar.

Like other ancient works, Hawaiian art was often utilitarian, making even the most everyday items beautiful. Kapa, still made today, is a fine fabric created by a very long and laborious process, starting with beating the wood of the *wauke* (paper mulberry) plant. *Hulu manu* (featherwork) was created for beautiful clothing and accessories, especially for capes of high-ranking chiefs.

A different quilting art grew from a blending of traditional Kapa work with the quilt styles of the European missionaries. Designs are drawn from the natural beauty of the islands and the mana of ancestors and often represent a special place, lineage, or historical event as well as contemporary abstract creations or symbolic representations. *Kapa apana* is the Hawaiian quilting method where three layers are sewn together—a decorated top layer, a middle layer of fibers, and

An example of a *Hulu manu* (featherwork) lei.

an undecorated back layer. It is believed that Hawaiian quilts pass along the spirit and blessings of their creators.

TYING IT UP

During the 1980s, Native Hawaiians, bolstered by the Renaissance and integration of traditional language and culture into everyday life and education, strengthened their political and cultural resistance. The decade saw mass organizing, legal suits, occupation and protection of sacred areas, and pride in all things Hawaiian. The government enacted legislation that provided funding for Hawaiian communities and programs.

However, the overdevelopment of the country went unchecked as out-of-state, capital-funded resorts and estatelike homes in the most beautiful areas as well as on conservation lands. Native people continue to resist and protest the foreign building on their lands; many groups demand reparations from the U.S. The "trust" lands are not enough to support the need. In addition, the best properties have been illegally given for either public buildings or private homes of non-Hawaiians. The American military controls over thirty percent of the most populated island of O'ahu and other large plots on the islands of Hawaii, Maui, and Kaua'i that could be used for Native Hawaiian housing. The remaining lands are too remote and often are not buildable properties, and there are no funds to help make the lands livable or accessible. The wealthy corporations continue to have access to the best areas.

In November 1993, U.S. President Bill Clinton signed the Apology Resolution passed by Congress that formally "apologizes to Native Hawaiians on behalf of the people of the United States for the overthrow of the Kingdom of Hawaii." The bill was coauthored by Hawaiian Senators Daniel Inouye and Daniel Akaka. However, many Hawaiians maintain that the Kingdom of Hawaii, although overthrown, still exists. In 2011, Hawaii Governor Neil Abercrombie signed into law Act 195, which officially identifies Native Hawaiians as the Indigenous People of Hawaii.

Hawaiian activists and advocates address economics, health, education, housing, or environmentalism. A revival of ancient religious traditions has offered spiritual support for the dozens of organizations that have sprung up to right the wrongs in Hawaii. The organizations represent many schools of thoughts. Many envision a nation-within-a-nation, similar to that of American Indians and Alaska Natives. However, since the United States has a deplorable record of recognizing the rights of American Indians, there are concerns about that solution. Others clamor for secession from the United States and independent nationhood, and still another faction wants to do away with any Native Hawaiian entitlement programs. There is little agreement concerning the relationship between the United States and Native Hawaiians. A kingdom that once was divided and then united has a rich legacy that may well provide the solution to the future of the Hawaiian people.

BIOGRAPHIES

David Malo or Davida Malo (1793–1853)
Historian

A leading Native Hawaiian historian of the Kingdom of Hawaii, Malo was also a Christian minister and author. He helped form the first Hawaiian Historical Society with another historian, Samuel Kamakau, in 1841 and served as a Maui representative to the first House of Representatives of the Kingdom (1841). He wrote *Moolelo Hawaii*.

Bernice Pauahi Bishop (1831–1884)
Philanthropist/Ali'i

Bishop's estate was the largest private landownership in the Kingdom of Hawaii, made up of about 9 percent of Hawaii's total area. Her concern was for her Hawaiian people, and she left her vast holdings in a trust, which funds the Kamehameha Schools and other charities for Indigenous Hawaiians. She was married to businessman and philanthropist Charles Reed Bishop, who founded the Bernice P. Bishop Museum in 1889 as a memorial to Pauahi.

Emma Aima Nawah (1854–1934)
Journalist/Suffragist/Patriot

Born in Hilo on the Big Island of Hawaii, Nawah was an advisor to Queen Lili'uokalani and Royalist supporter. She and her husband founded the *Ke Aoha Aina* ("The Patriot") newspaper in 1895 and used the press to further their campaign for the return of their country. She also advocated for the Nineteenth Amendment, giving women the right to vote.

Robert William Kalanihiapo Wilcox (1855–1903)
Revolutionary Soldier/Politician

Nicknamed the Iron Duke of Hawaii, Wilcox was a Hawaiian patriot who led the "Wilcox" rebellions. First, he was in the forefront of rebelling against the Kingdom of Hawaii under King Kalākaua and later led an uprising against the Republic of Hawaii. In 1890, he was elected the first delegate to the United States Congress for the Territory of Hawaii.

Joseph Kekuku (1874–1932)
Musician

Kekuku is credited with inventing the steel guitar as a teenager when he was student at the Kamahameha School for Boys. He traveled extensively in Europe and the U.S. teaching, playing, and introducing the world to Hawaiian music. He died in New Jersey having never returned to his homeland.

Victoria Kawēkin Ka'iulani Lunalilo Kalaninuiahilapalapa Cleghorn (1875–1899)

Crown Princess

Heir to the throne of the Kingdom of Hawaii, Crown Princess Ka'iulani became internationally renowned for her wisdom, intelligence, statesmanship, beauty, and determination. She was the daughter of a royal Hawaiian mother and a Scottish father and had grown up hearing the stories of her father's homeland from author Robert Louis Stevenson, her father's friend and countryman. Already an accomplished student, athlete, and equestrian, she sailed to Great Britain to complete her studies and learn her Celtic heritage. A favorite among European royalty, she traveled to different countries raising money for the underprivileged and was pursued by titled young men. Ka'iulani was wise beyond her years and had been raised with all the education and training needed to rule her country. At just seventeen, she sailed from England to the United States on a diplomatic mission to restore the Kingdom of Hawaii. Overnight, she had transformed from a precocious schoolgirl into a diplomat burdened with the future of her country.

The American press had demonized the queen, printing racist images of her, so the public was quite surprised to see the lovely crown princess, who carried herself with grace and confidence. She gave many speeches denouncing the overthrow, met with President Cleveland, and charmed the Americans, who followed her every move. The beautiful Ka'iulani was so impressive that the American press quickly corrected its stereotypical and untrue portrayal of Hawaiian royalty: "She is a tall, beautiful young woman, with a sweet face and slender figure. She has the soft brown eyes and dark complexion that mark the Hawaiian beauty." She had come to the United States, she said, more for the purpose of learning and observing for herself the nature of the people who had been asked to take control of her country than to make a formal petition for

her crown. "That," she said, "is rightfully mine, and if the Americans are the nobleminded people I think they are, they will not be a party to the outrage by which I have lost my birthright."

Ka'iulani died at only twenty-three years old, and both Hawaiians and Anglos mourned. Many believed she was too strong and healthy to become so ill and that the shocking loss of her beloved country killed her.

Helen Kapuailohia Desha Beamer (1882–1952)

Composer/Hula Teacher

Beamer learned the traditional hula from her mother. Since the practice was banned, they did it in secret. She shared her knowledge of ancient ways with her many students, often composing music to go with the dance. She was key in preserving and sharing the ancient customs and was inducted into the Hawaiian Music Hall of Fame in 1995.

Duke Paoa Kahanamoku (1890–1968)

Olympian/Surfer/Actor/Policeman

Called the "Father of Surfing," Kahanamoku introduced the ancient sport to the world. He was a master surfer using a Koa-wood surfboard, much heavier than modern fiberglass boards. He competed in four Olympics swimming and water polo events (1912, 1920, 1924, 1932), winning two gold and two silver medals. He was the first to be inducted into the Swimming Hall of Fame and the Surfing Hall of Fame. An Olympics Hall of Famer, he was named one of the twenty-six all-time sports champions (1967). Considered the greatest freestyle swimmer in the world, Kahanamoku developed the flutter kick, replacing the scissors kick. He rescued a crew of capsized fishermen on his surfboard in Newport Beach, California. Newport's police chief called Duke's efforts "the most superhuman surfboard rescue act the world has ever seen."

Mary Abigail Kawena Wiggin Pukui (1895–1986)

Scholar/Dancer/Composer/Educator

Wiggin Pukui published more than fifty scholarly works and coauthored the definitive *Hawaiian-English Dictionary* (1957, revised 1986), *Place Names of Hawaii* (1974), *The Echo of Our Song* (1974), and *Oʻlelo Noʻeau* (1997). Often credited with crafting the 1970s Hawaiian Renaissance, she was named a "Living Treasure of Hawaii" (1977) and inducted into the Hawaiian Music Hall of Fame (1995).

Isabella Aiona Abbott (1919–2010)

Ethnobotanist/Educator

Dr. Abbott was the world's leading expert on Pacific algae and the first Native Hawaiian woman to receive a doctorate in science.

William S. Richardson (1919–2010)

Justice

Richardson, chief justice of the Supreme Court of Hawaii, was known for making landmark decisions that recognized the state's Indigenous cultural, environmental, and legal history. He limited or prohibited the commercial development of fragile areas, particularly coastlines and beaches. He ruled that the public has the right to access Hawaii's beaches and that land created by lava floes are state, not private, property. Richardson stated, "The western concept of exclusivity is not universally applicable in Hawaii." He cited precedents from the court of the Kingdom of Hawaii and recognized ignored claims of Indigenous Hawaiians.

Claire Kuʻuleilani Hughes

Public Health Nutritionist

Dr. Hughes was the first Native Hawaiian registered dietician and has led groundbreaking dietary and health programs for the Native Hawaiian community in her position as chief of the state Department of Health nutrition branch. In 2011, she was named a "Living Treasure of Hawaii."

Daniel Kahikina Akaka (1924–)

U.S. Senator

Akaka was the first U.S. Native Hawaiian senator (D–1990–2013). He sponsored legislation over a decade known as the Akaka Bill to grant federal recognition to Native Hawaiians—even though they are not an American Indian tribe. The bill never passed. One of his major accomplishments was 1993's Apology Resolution.

Herb Kawanui Kāne (1928–2011)

Artist/Writer/Historian

A key figure in the Hawaiian Renaissance movement, Kāne was a world-renowned artist, historian, sculptor, and writer with over four hundred paintings of the Pacific to his credit. He also founded the Polynesian Voyaging Society and designed seven postage stamps for the U.S. Postal Service. He was the first Native Hawaiian artist to receive international recognition.

Takamiyama Daigorō (1944–)

Sumo Wrestler

Born Jesse James Wailani Kuhaulua, he was the first foreign-born sumo wrestler to win the top division championship (1972). He was also the first foreign-born wrestler to become a manager; his trainees reached high levels in the sport.

Edward Ryon Makuahanai Aikau (1946–1978)

Surfer

As the first lifeguard at Waimea Bay on the island of Oahu, Aikau saved over five hundred people. A champion surfer, he won several awards, including the 1977 Duke Kahanamoku Invitational Surfing Championship. During the second voyage of Hōkūleʻa, the canoe capsized about twelve miles from Molokai. Aikau tried to get help by peddling to land on his surfboard, but disappeared. The crew was later rescued by the U.S. Coast Guard. His disappearance was followed by the largest air-sea search in Hawaiian history. Aikau is remembered for his kindness and bravery.

Haunani-Kay Trask (1949–)
Educator/Activist/Writer

Dr. Trask directs the Hawaiian Studies Program at the University of Hawaii. She opposes the tourism industry and protests the United States military presence in Hawaii. She uses her written works as "weapons against the oppressors." Her works include *Light in the Crevice Never Seen* and *From a Native Daughter: Colonialism and Sovereignty in Hawaii*.

Dr. Trask's sister, Mililani B. Trask (1951), is also an activist and an attorney. Both are active in the organization Ka Lahui Hawaii ("The Hawaiian People").

Charles Nainoa Thompson (1953–)
Traditional Navigator

President of the Polynesian Voyaging Society, Thompson is best known as the first Hawaiian to use traditional Polynesian navigation methods since the fourteenth century. Without western tools, he has navigated two double-hulled canoes (the *Hōkūle'a* and the *Hawaiiloa*) from Hawaii to other island nations in Polynesia.

Noenoe K. Silva (1954–)
Professor/Author

A professor of political science at the University of Hawaii at Manoa, Silva's research uncovered the Kū'e Petitions of 1897 in the National Archives (see also The Republic of Hawaii section in this chapter). She wrote *Aloha Betrayed: Native Hawaiian Resistance*

to American Colonialism (2004) recounting the events of the overthrow of the kingdom.

Israel "Iz" Ka'ano'i Kamakawiwo'ole (1959–1997)
Musician/Sovereignty Activist

The beloved "Iz" became the voice of Hawaii; his medley of "Somewhere Over the Rainbow/What a Wonderful World" was featured in several films and other media. Kamakawiwo'ole died at a young age, but his influence on Hawaiian music is still strong. A talented ukulele player, he artfully incorporated jazz, reggae, and other styles into his songs. Over ten thousand people attended Kamakawiwo'ole's funeral; he was the only nongovernment person to lay in state at the state capitol building.

Kevin James Mawae (1971–)
Professional Football Player

Mawae played in the National Football League (NFL) for sixteen seasons for the Seattle Seahawks, New York Jets, and Tennessee Titans. He was selected for the Pro Bowl six times (1999–2004) and was an eight-time All-Pro. He also served two terms as National Football League Players Association president, which coincided with the 2011 NFL lockout.

Logan Maile Lei Tom (1981–)
Volleyball Player

Tom was the youngest and the first Native Hawaiian to be selected for the Olympic indoor volleyball team and is a silver medalist. She is a four-time Olympian at the outside hitter position and was the best scorer of the Beijing Olympics (2008). Tom has also won gold in other world meets.

Jerome Lee Williams (1981–)
Professional Baseball Pitcher

Williams plays for the Philadelphia Phillies and has been with several MLB teams. On September 20, 2014, he became the first pitcher in MLB history to defeat the same club with three different teams in the same season, defeating the Athletics with the Astros, Rangers, and Phillies.

Natasha Kanani Janine Kai (1983–)
Professional Soccer Player

Kai scored the winning goal for the U.S. Soccer Team in the 2008 Summer Olympics quarterfinal round and is a gold medalist. She played for the Washington Spirit pro team.

Kaui Hart Hemmings
Author

Hemmings' debut novel, *The Descendants* (2007), was adapted into a highly acclaimed film starring George Clooney (2011).

URBAN

Native people have been urban people throughout history; look at Cahokia and Tenochtitlan. We are also free people and have the right to move across this Turtle Island anywhere we want to or need to, and we can keep our connections to our homeland communities or make a new community; cities are still part of this Mother Earth, after all, even if most people forget that fact.

—Gabrielle Tayac (Piscataway)

MINNEAPOLIS, MINNESOTA

The ancient drawings of animals stretch out for yards as if forever frozen in some long-ago march. Above, the traditional designs of flowers and leaves sparkle brightly and colorfully as the day they were made. Flute music winds through the air, inviting and harmonious. The aroma of wild rice stew tantalizes and tempts. A gathering of children and grandparents sit in a circle and speak the local dialect of Ojibwe as they enjoy the outdoors on one of the last warm days of autumn. Crows call to each other from the trees, happy most of their feathered friends have already migrated as there will be more treats for them after the people have left. The day has been calm, serene, pleasant, and warm. Then comes the intrusive sound of the school bus engine starting up and summoning the picnicking children back to the Anishinabe Academy, a public school, where studies focus on Native American culture and language. The field trip and picnic provided an op-

portunity for the children to practice Ojibwe with the elders and enjoy a lunch of wild rice, one of the most popular Ojibwe foods, and another day passes on Franklin Avenue.

Franklin Avenue

Franklin Avenue in South Minneapolis, Minnesota, also called the American Indian Cultural Corridor, is one of the most densely populated Native urban areas in the country. Its sidewalks are embossed with turtles and bears fashioned by Native artists while many buildings display beautiful murals reflecting both the urban and rural roots of the community. The friezes on offices, apartment buildings, and shops replicate Woodlands beadwork and ribbonwork designs. Central to the community is the Minneapolis American Indian Center; its façade boasts a wood collage by the world-renowned Grand Portage Ojibwe artist George Morrison. The multiservice organization offers the community employment training, health and wellness services, cultural preservation activities, an art gallery, and elder and youth programs like Indigenous Lax, a Lacrosse course that trains young people to play the centuries-old game.

Up and down Franklin is proof that this neighborhood is indeed a Native one. The Many Rivers East and West apartment complex, home to many Native people, is also decorated with a Woodlands motif as are community-based organizations, Native-owned businesses, and reservation outreach facilities like Leech Lake Band Urban Office and Mille Lacs Band–Ojibwe Urban Office. Streetlight banners, bike racks, public art, and the designs/decals on bus shelters, benches, and recycling bins all sport Indian themes and images from the heritages of Indigenous peoples in the vicinity. Dull metal electric boxes on corners are decked out in Indigenous designs and slogans, utilitarian objects crafted with the traditional aesthetic that still exists of making everyday items beautiful. Aldi's Market and Dollar Tree share city space with the Ancient Traders Market and the Native American Community Clinic right across the street from the All My Relations Gallery, featuring Native traditional and contemporary art as well as workshops.

American Indian Corridor

The area became the first urban American Indian destination corridor in the U.S. in 2010. It's name, preservation, and revitalization were conceptualized by the Minneapolis-based Native American Community Development Institute (NACDI) over a three-year planning project that included community members, Indian nonprofits, and Indian-owned businesses. Their central idea is to teach an often ignored segment of the urban population how to become an economic and cultural power. Big plans incorporate home and land ownership, housing, entertainment venues, media outlets, and health and wellness resources, which are all known for job growth potential, opportunities for economic stability/ development, and sustainability. NACDI has already bought and renovated buildings for neigh-

borhood businesses, art galleries, and offices and eventually wants to establish an Indian-owned hotel and convention facility. Minneapolis now has the most Natives in major leadership positions and elected officials of any U.S. city. In 2012, Janeé Harteau was appointed the chief of the Minneapolis Police Department, making her the first woman, first gay person, and first Native American to hold the post.

AMERICAN INDIAN MOVEMENT

What we did in the 1960s and early 1970s was raise the consciousness of white America that this government has a responsibility to Indian people. That there are treaties; that textbooks in every school in America have a responsibility to tell the truth … and Americans realized that Native people are still here, that they have a moral standing, a legal standing. From that, our own people began to sense the pride.

—Dennis Banks, AIM cofounder

But it wasn't long ago that the American Indian Cultural Corridor was a dangerous place to live and residents could not have imagined one of their own as a police officer, let alone the highest ranked in the city! Many of the neighborhood planners on the NACDI remember when the area had all the ills of a community in crisis: too little money, too few jobs, too many drugs, too few services, and too little hope. In fact, south Minneapolis is where the American Indian Movement was organized in 1968 to push back against the human rights violations that impoverished, marginalized, and powerless people often endure. Founded by Clyde and Vernon Bellecourt (White Earth Ojibwe), Dennis Banks (Leech Lake Ojibwe), Herb Powless (Oneida), Eddie Benton Banai (Lac Courte Oreilles Ojibwe), and others, AIM first came together to curb the abuse meted out by the largely non-Indian police force. AIM began to "police the po-

Minneapolis, Minnesota, is the home of the American Indian Movement, which was founded there in 1968.

lice" around the Native housing projects, where crimes against Native people often were not investigated or even documented in a police report. The mobilization was successful as false and/or unprosecuted arrests of Indians decreased by more than half in the first year of the organization's existence.

AIM became the major vanguard in the struggles for civil and treaty rights and quickly spread to other cities and communities across the country where Native people were also being brutalized by the police, poverty, and racism. Although Indians had been organizing against and confronting colonialism, both historical and contemporary, for centuries, the American Indian Movement and its call to activism both restrengthened the resolve of Native people to survive on their own terms and brought that determination to the six o'clock news so that all Americans became aware that First Peoples were still here and part of the twentieth century. AIM also gave a formal name to the five hundred years of continuous

struggle against the invasion of Indigenous homelands and all the horrors that resulted.

Education in the Native Community

Anishinabe Academy teachers work to blend the Seven Grandfather Teachings into our lessons. They are foundational to our school culture. These teachings are love, respect, wisdom, bravery, humility, honesty, and truth.

—Anishinabe Academy Handbook (Principal Laura Sullivan, Ho-Chunk)

Although there have been improvements in the Native community and there is quite an impressive plan in place to heal many of the problems, Minneapolis shares the same grim education statistics of other cities with Native populations. The dropout rate for Indian students is the highest of any group. AIM and parents addressed the issue by starting the Heart of the Earth Survival School (HOTESS), a K–12 community-based school with a culturally competent Native curriculum under parental control. The school's success was a model, and soon, survival schools sprang up in different cities. HOTESS operated from 1972 until 2008 (it became a charter school under the city's administration in 1999). Today, the Anishinabe Academy, a Pre-K–8 Minneapolis public magnet school, focuses on high academic achievement through Native American culture and language. The school accepts students from all cultures and was started in 2004. Anishinabe Academy has received high ratings by parents and students.

Urban Troubles

The sex trafficking of Native girls and women is a story 500 years in the making.

—Sarah Deer (Muscogee Creek), professor of law, William Mitchell College of Law in St. Paul, Minnesota

A disturbing problem plaguing Minneapolis and other cities is the disappearance and sex trafficking of Native women and children. Native women are the only group most often sexually victimized by groups other than their own. Two hours away in Duluth, Native women, teens (both boys and girls), and even babies are trafficked and sold for sex on ships in the Duluth harbor. Native prostitutes die from attacks at almost twice the rate of non-Native sex workers, and most have been forced into the industry. The Dog Soldier Mixed Martial Arts organization grew out of the need to stop the rising rates of kidnappings, sex ring incidents, and domestic violence in the Minneapolis metro area. Leader Vaughn J. Lodge (Gros Ventre/Cheyenne/Ojibwe) was approached by several elders to protect the women; he began to teach a self-defense class to train young men and women to step up as warriors and not to become part of the problem. Some theorize that Native women and children

are targets because of the "they no longer exist" attitude of non-Natives that has dehumanized them.

There is a also gang presence in the city, but according to Mike Martin of the Midwest Gangs Investigators Association, Native gangs "are loose-knit groups of 20, 30, 40 individuals," not as organized or intimidating as other American gangs. Some say that Native gangs came about to meet a very real threat from ethnic gangs preying on neighborhood residents while others say gang life attracts young people who have never been allowed to recover from historical trauma and grief. To prevent gangs becoming a bigger threat, former gang members take their motivational program, Real Talk Native, to high school students to teach them about the dangers of joining gangs.

Native Identity

I really think the question about humor is very important. It's one of the most important parts of American Indian life and literature, and one thing that always hits us is just that Indian people really have a great sense of humor, and when it's survival humor, you learn to laugh at things.

—Louise Erdrich (Ojibwe)

Most Native Minneapolis residents are part of families who first came to the city during the federal relocation period of the 1950s and '60s (see the Historical Overview chapter). Franklin Avenue quickly became the heart of this urban neighborhood and remains an integral part of the movement and migrations of Native peoples. It is still the densest concentration of urban American Indian people in the country. It is the place for some major "firsts": the first urban American Indian health clinic, the first American Indian preference housing project, and the birthplace of the American Indian Movement. It has gone through many ups and downs, but community members, organizations, and businesses are helping the district develop a distinct American

Indian identity. Identity is also fortified through the arts and literature. The tranquil, well-appointed Birchbark Book Store near the far end of Franklin Avenue invites patrons to troll through the vast offering of Native books and other materials in both English and Indigenous languages. Owned and operated by award-winning author Louise Erdrich (Turtle Mountain Band of Chippewa), the charming shop nourishes all of the senses and is a haven for scholars, casual readers, and children.

CAHOKIA

A few days' trip downriver or just a day's car drive from the American Indian Corridor in Minneapolis is the port city of St. Louis, Missouri, but near St. Louis is the site of a once great metropolis, Cahokia. Imagine approaching any major twenty-first-century port city. Suddenly, a vast, vertical creature leaps from the horizon, glittering with energy as traffic races around its arterial roads like blood cells invigorating a giant heart. The smoke, dust, and noise emanating from the city streets are a beacon for miles around.

Swap cars for canoes, and this was how a traveler would experience 1000 C.E. Cahokia, the largest city in North America, located on the Mississippi, the longest river in North America. Flourishing farther south were Mayan city-states, the Zapotec complex of Monte Alban, the Toltec's mile-high city, and the multifamily cliff houses (the first vertical apartment buildings) of the American Southwest. Like Mesoamerican cities, Cahokia featured pyramidlike structures, wide plazas, and paved streets. It's possible to imagine sheets of mica and silver designs on the walls reflecting the sun like glass. Cahokia was the epicenter of a network of waterways, both engineered canals and tributaries from the intersections of the Missouri, Illinois, and Mississippi rivers. Trade traffic jostled in and out on flotillas of long canoes laden with copper from the Great Lakes, meteoric iron from Kansas, conch shells and pearls from the Gulf of Mexico, mica from the Carolinas, tortoise shells from Florida,

An illustration (with exaggerated proportions) published in the 1887 William McAdams book *Records of Ancient Races in the Mississippi Valley* that shows the large Monks Mound in what was once the city of Cahokia.

Atlantic sharks' teeth, silver from Ontario, and obsidian from Yellowstone. Exports included carved pipestone religious objects, bows and arrows, elaborate fired pottery, ceremonial tobacco, strongly caffeinated tea leaves, and maize.

This was the urban center of the Midwest (see also the Midwest chapter), founded around 750 C.E. and inhabited until 1350. The population was larger than London and other cities in the world at the same time; 15,000 people traveled its brick streets and lived in its red and white painted wooden houses with slanted, thatched roofs. Almost 125 mounds loomed throughout the city; the largest was a four-level, earthen temple mound taller than the pyramid at Giza in Egypt.

ACOMA PUEBLO, NEW MEXICO

One of the strongest ever seen because the city was built on a high rock. The ascent was so difficult that we repented climbing to the top.

—Spaniard Francisco Vasquez de Coronado

Very different from Cahokia is Acoma Pueblo, also known as Sky City, located an hour away from Albuquerque, New Mexico. Acoma is the name of the people, their pueblo, Spanish for village, and also refers to the famed stone and adobe multistory architecture invented by Southwest Indians. For defense purposes, it was constructed atop a tall, sandstone mesa and is believed to be (along with the Hopi town of Orabi) the oldest continuously inhabited city in the United States. Although many scholars date the founding of the city as 1100 C.E., according to local dialects, "Acoma" itself translates to a "place that is always prepared," and traditional accounts say that the Acoma people have lived on the mesa forever. Acoma, along with other sister villages, covers some seventy acres. Entry to the pueblo was tricky because of the sheer cliffs of the mesa; before current times, it could only be accessed by hand- and toeholds carved into the sandstone. The apartment buildings themselves could only be entered from their tops with ladders. Acoma residents farmed the valleys below their sky city using irrigation canals to bring water. They were also masterful traders and did business with the Aztec and Mayan peoples long distances away.

Spanish Invaders

Acoma residents had their first encounter with Spanish explorers in 1539. Estevan, an enslaved Moroccan and scout for Coronado, was probably the first non-Native to visit the area. The first visit went well, but soon after, the Spanish began demanding grain from community storehouses, which were needed for the Acoma to survive the winter. The Acoma defended their city and drove the Spanish away. They came back seeking revenge and almost devastated the city, killing over eight hundred people and enslaving and torturing survivors. The Acoma population was reduced to less than three hundred. A gesture of peace was offered to the Indians a few decades later by the Spanish; the main goal of the gesture was to Christianize the Indians. Friar Juan Ramirez and Spanish soldiers forced the Acoma to build a mission within their city, which included a church, convent, and cemetery. The Acoma had to hand carry and haul earth, stone, and beams from miles away and up the steep cliffs; it was not their vision for their community.

Acoma Today

The immense church is impressive architecturally and still stands along with the centuries-old buildings that predated the Spanish. Today, most Acoma live full time in nearby Acomita, but some traditionalists still live in the ancient buildings with their glorious mica windows even though there is no indoor plumbing or electricity. Sky City is also used for ceremonies and festivals and is a popular tourist attraction. The Haa'ku Museum and Sky City Cultural Center preserve traditional art forms, language, and history.

TRADITION OF URBAN LIVING

An Ancient Lifestyle

As evidenced by Native record-keeping and oral tradition and supported by archeological and anthropological findings, by the time Europeans arrived, urban living was nothing new for Native peoples. Trade was nothing new for Native peoples; neither was building a sustainable economy or venturing out of one's homeland just to see what was across the river or on the other side of the mountain. Curiosity, artistic expression, inventiveness, religious observance, government, multifamily housing, and community beautification were all experienced by these early city folk. They had known how to live in multiuse homes and apartment-style buildings (longhouses, pueblos, tipis, etc.) and close-knit communities for eons and already had the tools for successful urban living: minding one's own business, sharing resources, community collaboration, waste management, and respect for personal space and belongings.

Spanning what is now the U.S., there are bones of ancient cities—once thriving and vibrant, uninhabited for ages, and part of our storied past. Some likely explanations for the demise of these ancient places could be that the population died from disease, were forced out by climate or topographical changes, were conquered by adversaries, or the citizens or the citizens fled from enemies. However, some traditional accounts say that sometimes the people were concerned about unhealthy living caused by urban sprawl and as a community decided to leave. Just leave and begin again or regain the balance they felt was missing. Whatever the reasons for the deserted towns, and there are many, Native country has always had a variety of municipality types, and cities were certainly one of them.

A Change in Towns

When Europeans came, they usually built their villages on the very grounds of Native towns or close by as the first inhabitants settled in strategic places near key natural resources. However, few European and, later, American townspeople wanted the local people to live among them and aggressively rid the areas of Native peoples, usually forcing them onto reservation lands that were devoid of materials a community needs to thrive. The myth is that Native people are basically rural and like to keep to themselves. However, across America, most Native people would have preferred remaining on their homelands and keeping their original territories, even if it meant sharing them with Europeans.

Indian people are connected to the lands of their ancestors; most ceremonies need to be done in the same place they have been observed since the beginning. Other religions can celebrate Easter, Ramadan, or Passover in any part of the world, but Indigenous rituals are tied to ancestral homelands. Euro-Americans have built their towns right over sacred sites and bulldozed over burial grounds. Today, many non-Native city folks are surprised to see Indians in "their" city, but the very grounds these places were built upon are part of the original lands of millions of people.

A Changing Urbanscape

The growth of Native peoples in urban areas has grown since 1900. Jobs, adventure, displace-

ment, intermarriage, relocation, and a variety of other reasons have given rise to the increase in the numbers of Native city dwellers. Census records (which usually undercount Native populations) show that the percentage of Native people living in metropolitan areas has been steadily increasing for over a century. These figures rarely include Indigenous peoples from Meso and South America, who are usually categorized as Hispanic, although groups are lobbying to change that.

Percentage of Native Population in Cities

Decade	Percent Native Population
1900	0.4
1910	4.5
1920	6.1
1930	9.9
1940	9.2
1950	13.4
1960	27.9
1970	44.5
1980	49.0
1990	51.0
2000	66.0
2010	78.0

U.S. Cities with the Largest Native American Populations

City	Population
New York, NY	111,749
Los Angeles, CA	54,236
Phoenix, AZ	43,724
Oklahoma City, OK	36,572
Anchorage, AK	36,062
Tulsa, OK	35,990
Minneapolis/St. Paul, MN	35,000
Albuquerque, NM	32,571
Chicago, IL	26,933
Houston, TX	25,521
San Antonio, TX	20,137
Tucson, AZ	19,903
San Diego, CA	17,865
Philadelphia, PA	17,495
San Francisco, CA	10,000
Seattle, WA	8,000

Urban Indian Centers

Much of the experience of being an "urban Indian" has been similar to the experiences of immigrants from other countries, who find each other in the midst of a foreign place and sustain and help each other. Sometimes, the circle of friends has been an extension of family from back home; other times, new friendships are forged with Indians from diverse nations who have different customs but share similar values, and of course, there has usually been an intact group that has always lived in the metro area. One interesting phenomenon is that members of tribes that historically did not always have positive relationships with each other learn to negotiate urban space collaboratively. Centers near reservations may have a preponderance of members from those communities, so the city becomes just an extension of the hometown.

Native Americans have created Indian centers in urban areas to provide social, economic, educational, and cultural services where there are substantial Indian populations. Most are multipurpose and may offer housing help, mental health counseling, health clinics, daycare, after-school care, and elder programs. The majority connect Native people to their heritages and host cultural events and activities like powwows, art galleries, gift shops, and traditional instruction in regalia construction, beadwork, dancing, etc. In addition, they often have employment opportunities/training, twelve-step programs, poetry nights, writing circles, fitness classes, and social functions.

Across the country, Indian centers are frequently in the business of advocating for clients and helping them navigate the system. Indian centers also try to effect policy and ensure their members get the same consideration as other urban residents. Something as simple as a birth certificate can take on gigantic proportions for Native city dwellers. In New York City, for instance, one family celebrated the birth of their child by giving him a name in the Cherokee Syllabary (written language with different symbols), but the Department of Vital Statistics refused to record a name that could not be typed. Handwritten data on the birth

The Duwamish Tribe's Longhouse and Cultural Center in Seattle, Washington, is near their historical community. Built in a traditional Puget Salish cedar post and beam style, it was designed by Blackfeet architect Byron Barnes.

certificate form is illegal. Although a Cherokee language font is available, New York City did not care to comply and made it impossible for the child to have his name recorded in the Cherokee Syllabary; the parents were threatened with legal action. Other families have been penalized for taking their children out of school for traditional religious observances, yet Indian students must comply with the Christian and Jewish holidays.

Probably one of the most positive results of urban centers has been the reinforcement of Native heritage. Some urban dwellers claim that moving to areas which were so segregated along cultural and racial lines made them appreciate Native traditions more and gave them a greater sense of identity, and attending urban Native events helps vitalize Indian cultures. As one mother commented at a New York City Native family event, "It's so nice to just breathe the same air as other Native people, even if it's just two times a month." Often, the Indian center is the first contact a city "newbie" will have. Also, sometimes Native professionals have moved to the city to become part of the Indian center staff.

Besides the Indian centers listed here, there are several more resources about and for Native

Americans listed in the appendix in the back of this book.

Education of Urban Indians

Urban Indian children suffer the same dismal dropout rates as reservation students. In 1972 through the federal Indian Education Act, funding became available to urban school districts that enroll at least ten Native children for culturally appropriate educational programs. Each grantee had (has) to ensure that there would be a committee of Indian parents to partner in creating programs and overseeing the budget. Many of the programs were successful and continue to be a good partnership with the Native community and the local educational association (LEA). Buffalo, New York, designed a Native American Magnet School, using federal funding and other monies, that teaches Native languages along with math and science. Some LEA's misspent the money on non-Indian programs.

Cities near reservations have had an easier time signing children up for the Native education programs than large cities with a myriad of Native groups represented. To receive what is a formula grant, the LEA must have a form documenting each eligible student's tribal affiliation. Sometimes, children have been "talked out of being Indian" because teachers are not attuned to Native culture and do not expect to have Indians in their classrooms. In fact, it has often been left up to the teacher to decide each student's ethnicity. Native parents fought for years for the right to determine their own race in completing school forms. By not having these documents on file, the funding is lowered. In New York City, there are one thousand schools, and Native people are spread across all five boroughs—outreach to Indian pupils is a colossal task. The now defunct Native American Education Program (1975 through 1998), once part of the NYC Department of Education, provided cultural instruction, advocacy, and educational guidance for an entire generation of Native New York public school students. Today, the NYC Department of Education, despite community demands, has declined to reapply to the federal government for Indian education funding entitled by law to urban Indian students.

Cities in Indian Country

Technically, all cities are in Indian country, but there are a few U.S. cities located on Native lands. Native nations are the landlords, and although almost eight out of every ten Native people live in urban areas, there are also non-Indians residing and working in cities and towns located on Indian-controlled lands.

In upstate New York, the city of Salamanca, nicknamed the "Gateway to Allegheny State Park" (New York State's largest park), is the only city located almost entirely on an Indian reservation. The Allegheny Seneca are the landlords of this community, which was once a major railroad town and is still a center for the timber industry and forestry in the Northeast. Non-Senecas cannot own land but have long-term leases with the tribe. The Nation operates a casino with a luxury hotel.

Agua Caliente Band of Cahuilla Indians is the largest landowners in Palm Springs, California, with 32,000 acres of reservation lands that spread across Palm Springs, Cathedral City, Rancho Mirage, and into the Santa Rosa and San Jacinto mountains. Tribal businesses include two eighteen-hole championship golf courses, the Spa Resort Casino in downtown Palm Springs, and the Agua Caliente Casino Resort Spa in Rancho Mirage.

The Reno-Sparks Indian Colony (RSIC) is composed of three Great Basin Tribes—the Paiute, the Shoshone, and the Washo. Located in Reno, and Hungry Valley, Nevada, the Colony holds almost two thousand acres, twenty-eight of which are in the central-west part of the city. A main source of revenue for the RSIC is their commercial retail properties. Their tenants include Mercedes Benz, Acura, Infinity, Wal-Mart, smoke shops, and many other locally owned and operated businesses. Earnings from the real estate projects provide funds for the Colony's government, which provides essential services to its members, residents, and other urban Indians.

The Agua Caliente Band of Cahuilla Indians owns the Agua Caliente Resort Casino which is Palm Springs, California. Their reservation spreads across 32,000 acres.

Barrow, Alaska, three hundred miles north of the Arctic Circle, is the northernmost town in the United States and the seat of North Slope Borough—the largest municipality in the world, roughly the size of Minnesota. It is a modern community, but subsistence hunting, fishing, and whaling are still very important to the local economy. Barrow's traditional name is Ukpeaġvik, "Place Where Snowy Owls Are Hunted"; it was incorporated as a first-class city in 1959. The public sector employs almost twenty percent of residents; others work at the numerous businesses that provide services to oil field operations and state and federal agencies. Located on the Chukchi Sea coast, Barrow boasts the largest elementary school in Alaska, where the children have learned to sing "Happy Birthday" in eleven languages. Although Barrow's population is over sixty percent Inupiat, it is also home to people with roots in Macedonia, Korea, Mexico, and others from around the world and the" "lower forty-eight." Travel into Barrow is by plane or boat—there are no roads connecting the city with the rest of Alaska.

Indigenized United States

Not only do Native people live in cities, but many communities have Indigenous names, which were usually geographically descriptive so that the place would be recognized by a visitor. Some of the meanings may be lost while others are named for a specific group of Native people or a particular Indian person. Still others are poor translations or mispronunciations of the original word. From Alabama's Tuskegee (Koasati for "warriors") to Minnesota's Bemidji (Ojibwe for "traversing lake") to Washington's Tacoma (Lushootseed for "snow-covered mountain"), each state has at least one town with an Indigenous name, and most states have many.

NEW YORK, NEW YORK

Lady Liberty

Nonetheless, when many American Indian people see Liberty or Freedom depicted, as in the Statue of Liberty, they view her as an Indian woman, the Mother Protector of America. Far from a patriotic irony that distances Indians from America, she reclaims America as Native and female, a healing mother who rejoins our separated histories....

—Dr. Rayna Green, Cherokee (Curator Emerita, National Museum of American History) comments about exhibit, "An Artistic Perspective: Lady Liberty as a Native American Icon," curated by Nadema Agard (Lakota/Cherokee/Powhatan), New York, New York, 2006

Lady Liberty, the most iconic representation of New York City, has a bird's eye view of the city's five boroughs from her tiny island in the Shatemuc, Lenape for "the river that flows both ways," known today as the Hudson River. She can see the famous Yankee Stadium in the Bronx and cheers for Yankee center fielder Jacoby McCabe Ellsbury, the first Navajo to play major league baseball. Some statistics say that most of the city's Indians live in the Bronx, which the U.S. Census considers to be the most diverse area in the country. There is an 89.7 percent chance that any two residents, chosen at random, would be of different race or ethnicity and that Native people from different areas of the country and hemisphere are part of the diversity of Bronx residents.

Lady Liberty zeroes in on the North Gowanus section of Brooklyn, named after Gouwane, sachem of the Canarsee, who lived and farmed on the shorelines. Today, the once pristine canal, which kept the Canarsee gardens so well watered, is a superfund site. The area is also known as "Little Caughnawaga," named for the Kahnawake Mohawks of Quebec, Canada, skilled iron workers who have lived there with their families for over eighty years building the great city from the Empire State Building to the World Trade Center to many bridges leading in and out of the great metropolis. They are also called Skywalkers.

Already wearing the required shawl to participate in the dancing, Lady Liberty could join the annual American Indian Thunderbird Powwow at Queens Farm, in the borough of Queens. It's New York City's oldest and largest powwow and features three days of inter-tribal Native American dance competitions. The American Indian Thunderbird Dancers, who host the event, are the oldest urban dance group in the country. For several years, Lady Liberty has been hearing a different language spoken in the borough of Staten Island. It is coming from a newer Indian group to move to the "Big Apple." The Mixteco, Indigenous people from Mexico, have maintained their traditional language and speak very little Spanish or English.

Lady Liberty snaps her fingers to the tunes from Broadway hit musical *Jersey Boys*, which has starred Shaun Taylor-Corbett (Blackfeet), who was also in the Tony-winning musical *In the Heights*. Broadway itself is the city's largest thoroughfare, and before there were any theaters on the famed avenue, it was the primary trading route of the Lenape. They called it the Wickquasgeck Trail, and it ran fifteen miles through swampland and thick forest. The colossal statue could almost touch the National Museum of the American Indian, where accounts of the Lenape and other Native people of the Western Hemisphere regale and educate the public. The famous Broadway and the NMAI are both in New York City's smallest borough, Manhattan, taken from the Munsee (Northern Lenape) Manahatta, which is probably their term for the "place where we get bows," because of the hickory trees on the south end of the island.

Lenapehoking

The Lenape were the first people in the area and were part of the large classification of tribes who speak Algonquian-related languages. Their homes were the first apartment buildings on Manahatta, long, dome-shaped, one-story buildings covered with bark. They became incredible agronomists, and there is evidence of their large gardens of corn, beans, and squash. Because they had numerous land routes and waterways available (many have long since been filled in), trad-

Mannahatta/Manhattan, before and after.

ing and moving goods was part of their economy. At different stages of history, business was booming as they dealt with both local and distant nations like the Haudenosaunee, Shinnecock, and Mohican. Inventory was comprised of food, pottery, pelts, weapons, tools, and wampum. To preserve the land from being depleted by overplanting, Lenape villagers had different locations and often moved with the seasons. At the time of European contact, Southern Manhattan and East River islands were the territory of the Canarsie; the northern part of the islands belonged to the Weekquaeskeek.

The Rockaway and Matinecock were another two of the different bands of Lenape in the New York City area, and although most were displaced at different times over the centuries, there are still descendants of the original people. In 2009, filmmaker Eric Paul MaryEa (Matinecock) made a documentary, *The Lost Spirits*, which follows the lives of Queens-based Matinecock and Montaukett families, who have been largely ignored by government officials over their long history.

In 1984, Oklahoma elder Nora Dean Thompson (Touching Leaves Woman) visited both New York City Native people and government officials. A traditionalist, she was one of the few remaining people who had knowledge of the Lenape Big House religion. She was moved to tears seeing the ocean for the first time as references to the great body of water were part of many rituals and she had never seen it. She named the area "Lenapehoking" (*l'nape haki-nk*), meaning "in the land of the Lenape."

Dutch and English Invasion

The Dutch were the first Europeans to arrive, and at first, relations were cordial between the two groups. The Lenape were delighted to trade, and the Dutch were happy to be accepted and treated so well. The camaraderie did not last, however, as in everywhere else in the country, the Europeans became aggressive, and the Native people defended their homelands. Contemporary Abenaki author Joe Bruchac's play, "River of Tides," performed at NMAI, chronicles the journey of Henry Hudson's 1609 voyage up the Shatemuc River, which today bears his name.

In 1624, the newly established Dutch colony began intruding on Lenape homelands and ended up appropriating the entire island (see also the Historical Overview chapter). Wall Street was the financial sector of the Dutch community, and it remains the money center of the country, but it was exactly that—a walled street erected to keep both Lenape locals and English settlers off Dutch territory. The British eventually became owners of the former Dutch colony and renamed it New York. They began to destroy and evict all Lenape from the city, or so they thought. At the lower end of Manhattan stands the Alexander Hamilton Customs House that has been repurposed into the Smithsonian National Museum of the American Indian (NMAI). The site is the exact location of the famous meeting that ended with the Lenape endorsing a document that secured the swindle of Manhattan.

Centuries later at the same site in Southern Manhattan, descendants of both Dutch settlers and the Lenape met again to sign documents. The event, sponsored by Intersections International and named "Healing Turtle Island," was hosted by the Collegiate Church, the "company church" of the Dutch West Indies Company that made New Amsterdam a "company town." Representatives of the church acknowledged publicly the role it had historically played in the cultural marginalization and physical dispersion of the First Peoples, "slowly degrading them (in European eyes) from a people with their own culture and civilization to merely another resource." Lenape representatives from across the Diaspora participated in the historic meeting observed on November 27, 2009, on the first national Native American Heritage Day (as designated by President Obama in June 2009), and in 2014, the Collegiate Church hosted the opera *Purchase of Manhattan* as a way to promote "healing and wholeness between our peoples." An all-Indian cast performed the opera, composed by Brent Michael Davids (Mohican) and author Joseph Bruchac (Abenaki).

Shorakapok (Inwood Park)

Cherokees don't have much show around here, so I am lucky to have this place. I come from Oklahoma, and my tribe used to live in Georgia, where they learned to speak English. Well, I always wanted to come to New York, but my son.... told me I couldn't stand an ordinary house, with steam heat, so he put in an application to get me the post of caretaker here.

—Princess Naomi
(Naomie Kennedy), 1935

The first oyster bar in New York was operated by Lenape in the Inwood Park area centuries ago. They sold the shellfish to both Native and Anglo customers. The original name of the Inwood area in northern Manhattan is Shorakapok, the Lenape term for "the edge of the river."

In the twentieth century, historian Reginald Pelham Bolton (1856–1942) envisioned building an Indian life reservation in Inwood Park as a way of preserving Indian culture and also as a teaching center on American Indians. His plans included hiring Delaware tribal members to construct a replica of an ancient village and be the docents and cultural interpreters. They would live next to the village in more modern housing and be its caretakers as well. In 1926, his plan went into action, and Cherokee Marie Noemi Boulerease Constantine Kennedy, better known as Princess Naomi, was hired for the job. She and her son lived in the caretaker's cottage beneath the famous tulip tree, which was almost seventeen stories tall, a survivor of the once dense forest. Descendants of the original Native people lived in the Inwood area well into the 1930s.

Princess Naomi, who was also vice president of Brooklyn's United Indians of America, kept a museum in her tiny house and sold Native-made items. She was advertised as a New York City subway destination, and children and adults alike recounted their adventures of being in the park with the princess. Known as quite a character, she always dressed in regalia except on Sundays, when "she walked around 207th Street with high heels and everything," according to a local resident. Another Native man lived and worked on the property, and he, too, was not Lenape. Emilio Diaz, of the Chibcha from Columbia, South America, constructed a traditional Lenape house but in cement. He also made trash cans that looked like tree trunks. It is said that the princess and Diaz, along with six hundred other Indians, tried to reclaim Inwood Park as real Indian reservation land but were all evicted by Parks Commissioner Robert Moses in his redevelopment of the area in the late 1930s.

Sherman Coolidge (1862–1932), Arapaho, was an Episcopalian priest and a founder of the Society of American Indians (1911–1923), forerunner of the National Congress of American Indians. On September 28, 1915, he issued a proclamation designating the second Saturday of each May as American Indian Day (AID) and urged Indians to observe the day as a memorial to their "race." Over the years, Native New Yorkers turned the annual serious event into a celebra-

Rev. Sherman Coolidge founded the Society of American Indians, the forerunner of the National Congress of American Indians.

tion in Inwood Park near the great tulip tree, which had become iconic of Indian New York. Thousands attended the event, which, except for occasional interruptions, still exists today. Although the famous tulip tree was felled by a hurricane in 1938, there is still an annual Native celebration, "Drums along the Hudson," in the storied Shorakapok.

Skywalkers

A lot of people think Mohawks aren't afraid of heights; that's not true. We have as much fear as the next guy. The difference is that we deal with it better. We also have the experience of the old timers to follow and the responsibility to lead the younger guys. There's pride in "walking iron."

—Kyle Karonhiaktatie Beauvais
(Mohawk, Kahnawá:ke)

The majority of the famed Mohawk high steel iron workers, Skywalkers, are from the Kahnawá:ke reservation near Montreal, Canada. In the 1880s, tribal members were hired as unskilled laborers on the St. Lawrence bridge project, and it didn't take long for them to excel in high steel construction. They soon earned an international reputation as being the best in the business.

New York City construction companies took notice, and Mohawk specialists were hired to change the city's skyline from horizontal to vertical. The "skywalkers" contracts were usually lower than the non-Native workers and they had limited union membership, but during the century of the building boom, Mohawks comprised over fifteen percent of the high steel tradesmen. They built the Empire State Building, all of the city's bridges, the Time Warner building, Rockefeller Center, the Chrysler Building, the World Trade Center, and most of the other skyscrapers as well. After the Twin Towers were destroyed in 2001, they helped clean it up and are part of the crew rebuilding the World Trade Center that their elders erected.

During the 1940s and 1950s, as many as seven hundred Mohawk families settled in the same Brooklyn neighborhoods and brought their culture with them. Organizations like the Indian League of the Americas (ILOTA) popped up to provide a social and cultural outlet for families. For years, ILOTA sponsored the Barryville, New York, Powwow, one of the biggest in the metro area. On Friday afternoons, a large number would head home to Kahnawá:ke for the weekend, traveling by car up the Great Northway to Canada. Women worked too, often paying the bills during construction down times. The ten-block Gowanus neighborhood was a close-knit community where people helped each other and looked after each other's children. Although there are still many Mohawks in New York today, the neighborhood has shrunk. Many ironworkers rent rooms in the same apartment buildings while their families stay in Canada. Today, many Mohawk as well as other members of the Haudensaunee (Iroquois) live in all five boroughs and work in a variety of fields from education to finance in buildings that their relatives may have built. Building respect for Indigenous cultures is a goal of Kemala Cesar (Mohawk), a master Bharata Natyarn dancer and founder/director of Lotus Music and Dance. Lotus has become a New York institution, where master artists from India, Korea, Burma, China, the South Pacific, the Middle East, the Mohawk Nation, West Africa, and Spain teach and perform. Cesar herself is a master Bharata Natyam dancer. Under her direction, Lotus presents "Drums Along the Hudson." Every spring, Indigenous people gather from around the city and the world in Inwood Park to celebrate Native New York.

Indigenous People from Mexico

People in Mexico City feel ashamed speaking a language other than Spanish. Here (New York City) you have Chinese, Cantonese, Thai, Polish, so they are comfortable speaking their own languages.

—Joel Magallan, 2008

Although Indigenous peoples from Mexico have been living in New York City for generations, the greatest numbers began to migrate in the 1990s; their nickname for New York is "Manhatitlán." Today, there are an estimated five hundred thousand Mexicans in the metro area, primarily from the Mexican states of Puebla, Oaxaca, Guerrero, Morelos, el Estado de Mexico, Veracruz, and El Districto Federal (Mexico City); most identify as Indian. One U.S. Census report has labeled them the fourth largest tribe in the country. Their Indigenous roots are mostly Mixteco, Nahua, Chinanteco, Tlapaneco, and Otom, and at home, many speak the Indigenous languages and newly learned English—few speak fluent Spanish. Most New York institutions and service staff assume that this population speaks Spanish because of their Spanish surnames; the error has caused many problems, particularly in health care and education. For instance, when one family was informed in Spanish that their newborn son had Down Syndrome, all they un-

derstood was the nurse's phrase, "it is God's way." Luckily, they were participants in an Indian family support program, Nitchen, Inc., that advocated for the disabled child.

Indigenous Mexicans have gained a reputation for having an extraordinary work ethic. Because so many are in New York illegally, they may have to take any job, often work for half the minimum wage, do not complain about working conditions, and never refuse to work extra although they are often not even paid for overtime. They are frequently given the most arduous and difficult tasks and work more than one job. Those who have come to the city without their families may endure loneliness for years but send home as much money as they can. They work in the city's restaurants, construction trades, and the flower industry—several are street flower vendors. Still, there are many intact families, where both parents work and may share an apartment with other families trying to make ends meet. Their issues are similar to those of U.S. Indians forced into urban relocation programs and separated from their homelands due to economic and social repressions.

The newest Native people in the "Big Apple" have added their particular cultural heritages to the multicultural mix. On December 12, the feast day of La Virgin de Guadalupe Tonantzín, Poblanos (people from Puebla) celebrate the spiritual tradition of running. At sunrise on the sacred day that honors the Indigenous Virgin Mary, also a symbol of the Tonantzín (Nahuátl language for Earth Mother), spiritual runners from all five boroughs begin running at sunrise toward Manhattan's Church of Our Lady of Guadalupe. They carry torches and unite the communities through a celebration of mass. Also, they run in hopes that this special time may one day become a city holiday and to call attention to their vital contribution to the city's workforce.

Most New Yorkers have been introduced to Dia de los Muertos, or Day of the Dead. The first observance started as a small event hosted by the American Indian Community House (AICH) and has grown over the years. Now the festivities that honor those who have died begins with a pro-

Day of the Dead Celebration hosted by Mano a Mano, an organization promoting Mexican Indigenous culture and arts in New York City.

cession of devotees, faces painted like skeletons, and led through the city streets by Danzantes Mexicas. They pass a cemetery and end up back at the AICH, where a large altar scented with xempaxuchitl (marigolds) is the backdrop for sharing songs, stories, poetry, also known as "flor y canto," flowers, and song.

Mayans from Mesoamerica

It was very difficult in the beginning, but today, the community has grown accustomed to life here.

—Juan Yax (Mayan)

Guatemala has the largest concentration of Indigenous people in Central America, mostly descended from Mayan Indians. Within the Mayan population, there are twenty-one ethnic subgroups, each with its own language. It is estimated that over 93,000 Guatemalans live in New York City; most are Indigenous, and most live in Brooklyn. Collectively, they are called Amerindians as well as Mestizo Guatemalans, who have mixed Indigenous and Spanish ancestry. They suffered horribly during Guatemala's long civil war (1960–1996), where they, as well as middle-class activists, were at the mercy of the government and wealthy landowners. There were over four hundred massacres of Amerindians with tens of thousands murdered and hundreds of their villages destroyed. Because of the war, 75 percent of Amerindians are impoverished; thousands left Guatemala to find a better life. The United States has not recognized Guatemalans as political refugees. Regardless of the reasons Amerindians have fled from their Guatemalan homelands, the most recent immigrants are considered economic migrants, and only one or two percent of Guatemalan requests for political asylum are granted. Many sources feel that because the U.S. has friendly relations with the Guatemalan government and it is not a communist country, the war victims are less likely to be given asylum.

They've carved out a niche among Mexican, Italian, and Russian neighborhoods in Brooklyn; like other immigrant groups, they share resources. The ancient Mayan dialects are spoken on street corners, where hard-working laborers wait, hoping to be picked up for a day's worth of employment painting, cleaning, demolition, yard work, or any other tasks.

In 2012, the Mayan Elders of the K'iche' visited New York City to deliver their ancestors' message to the United Nations. The group was led by Don Tomás Calvo, the highest authority of the Maya, who was called the Mayan Pope. During that year, the Mayan calendar was a hot topic as the ancient prophecies had been misinterpreted as foretelling the end of the world. The Mayan Elders led ceremonies that were open to the public and put a special focus on the Guatemalan community in New York. Their message was clear: this was not the end of the world but a new cycle of a "monumental transition and an opportunity to realign priorities based on the feminine principles of love, gratitude, care, and respect for both humanity and our environment."

The Taino Resurgence

We have always known from childhood that we were Indian people; we were told this by our parents, but it was kept within the family. To be called Indian meant to be a nobody, a dog, or a savage.

—Rene Marcano,
Taino Cacique from Manhattan

A most effective ploy of colonialism is to stomp out Indigenous groups and then label them terminated or extinct. In spite of centuries of removing an Indigenous presence in the Western Hemisphere, the people have survived. One of the best examples of cultural revitalization is of the Native peoples from the Caribbean, the Taino, and New York City is home to many reasserting their Native identity, which according to the people was never lost.

In recent years, scholars like Dr. José Barreiro and Jorge Estevez (both at the National Museum of the American Indian) have been steadily presenting research that not only proves that the Taino still exist, but so does much of the traditional culture. There are several events and organizations in the Metro area that celebrate Taino heritage and strengthen the community.

Founded in 1995, Wanakán ("our center" in Tainey) works in collaboration with the Taino Nation of the Antilles to promote and preserve Taino culture. They offer cultural instruction and help organize the Taino diaspora living in the Metro area. Wanakán has also published the longest-running Taino publication, the *Boletín Informativo*, and advocates for the voices of Taino New Yorkers to be heard.

The United Federation of Taino People promotes and protects the "human rights, cultural heritage, and spiritual traditions of Taíno and other Caribbean Indigenous Peoples for the present and future generations." Its president, Roberto Múkaro Borrero, leads the organization in forging alliances with other Native Nations and hosting cultural events. Thanks to the work of these and other Taino activists, the United States Census now recognizes the Taino people.

Luis Ramos (Bayamanakoel) and his volunteers spend weekends taking the Taino story to the streets. He sets up the Mobile Indigenous Library and Culture Center, stocked with materials about Indigenous cultures, particularly on the Taino, throughout New York City neighborhoods. A hospice social worker, Ramos is also the chairperson of Nitchen, Inc., an intertribal organization supporting Native families. He and other Taino are active with Shorakapok Earth Keepers, a group committed to honoring the history and presence of Indigenous culture in New York City parks.

Indigenous Andeans

I decided to look for people to form an Andean music group, musicians not only from Peru but from the other countries (Ecuador, Bolivia, Chile, Argentina, and Colombia) that once formed the Inca Empire known as Tahuantinsuyo, the Inca word meaning the "four parts of the world": Contisuyo, Antisuyo, Collasuyo, and Chinchaisuyo.

—Guillermo Guerrero (Quechua)

Runasimita Rimankichu? Do you speak Quechua? Throughout the New York City metro area, the dialects of the thousand-year-old language of Quechua, also called *runa simi* ("people's language"), is spoken by Indigenous New Yorkers with roots in the Andes of South America. The New York Quechua Initiative was founded by longtime New York City resident Peruvian American Elva Ambía to preserve both the Indigenous language and cultures from the famous mountains of Peru, Bolivia, Ecuador, Argentina, Brazil, Chile, and Colombia.

The Inkarayku ("because of the Inkas"), led by founder Andres Jimenez, promotes and preserves Andean arts and culture through the performance and education of Indigenous music forms that have evolved into the contemporary mestizo music heard today.

Tahuantinsuyo was founded and is directed by Guillermo Guerrero, a consulting mechanical engineer and folk musician who came from the northern Peruvian Andes in 1973. The Queens-based group researches and performs the traditional music of Andean countries that once formed the "Inca Empire."

Garifuna from Coastal South America

When the Indigenous peoples movement extended itself from North America to the rest of the Americas in the 1980s, not only did the Garifuna join it, they also went a step further and spearheaded the Indigenous peoples movement in the English-speaking Caribbean.

—Joseph O. Palacio, Sr. (Garifuna)
from *Indivisible*, p 96

A unique blending of Caribbean Indigenous groups and enslaved Africans, the Garifuna are a distinct ethnic group, with their own language, beliefs, and practices. Garifuna, which is still spoken in their city homes, is an Arawakan dialect with loanwords from Carib and different European languages. Because of the centuries of being pushed around the Caribbean by colonial powers, they have often kept a low profile; many sought a safe haven in New York beginning in the 1940s. Frequently, they blend in as Latinos or African Americans in the workforce or school, but once at home, they shake their public persona and practice their own culture.

The Garifuna Coalition operates the Bronx-based Garifuna Advocacy Center to provide social, educational, and cultural services to the Garifuna community, who emigrated from the countries of Belize, Guatemala, Nicaragua, Honduras, St. Vincent, and the Grenadines. First-generation New Yorkers most often work in health care and construction and live mainly in the Bronx and Brooklyn. The Garifuna in the United States have joined with other Indigenous nations seeking rights and cultural preservation, and

Garifuna women perform at the 2011 Smithsonian Folklife Festival.

Garifuna groups have sprung up in New York as well and other U.S. cities.

The Budari Dance Company teaches Garifuna cultural heritage. Performers present traditional Garifuna dances and songs such as the Punta, Culio, Parranda, Chumba, Sambay, and Wanaragua in brightly colored regalia. At the Casa Yurumein center in the Bronx, Garifuna language classes are offered and served up with the traditional dish, hoodootoo, a mashed plantains and fish soup. Ancestral photographs and artifacts decorate the walls, and the organization sponsors a Miss Garifuna Pageant. Like other "beauty" pageants in Indian Country, contestants are judged based on their knowledge of their heritage and are expected to be cultural ambassadors.

"Aloha Spirit" in New York City

Today's celebration of *Ka Lā Ku'oko'a* asserts Hawaii is still an independent nation, even under prolonged illegal occupation.

—Na Oiwi NYC (Native Hawaiian advocacy organization in New York City)

According to the U.S. Census, Native Hawaiians have been steadily moving to New York City over the past decade, and today, there are over eight thousand living in the area. Most have come for jobs or school. Both New York University and Columbia University have Native Hawaiian clubs, and every spring, there is a huge picnic in Central Park where the Native Hawaiian community gets together for a day of Hawaiian-style potluck with ono food, kanikapila Hawaiian music, and hula.

Native Hawaiians have found a place in the New York City art scene. Not only can New Yorkers enjoy the beautiful music and dancing, but there are Hawaiian practitioners throughout the city who teach the spiritual and healing benefits of hula. Hawaiians have added their cuisine to New York's "foodie" heritage, and restaurants offering

makana (gift or reward) platters have cropped up in city neighborhoods. In Brooklyn, Native Hawaiians gather at the Onomea Restaurant for tasty treats based on family recipes of Crystalyn Costa, from the Big Island of Hawaii. Poke is on the menu along with spam, Hawaii's favorite snack.

Onomea has hosted Ka Lā Ku'oko' ("Restoration Day"), an annual commemoration asserting that Hawaii is still an independent nation, even under' "prolonged illegal occupation." In 2014, Leon Siu, the minister of foreign affairs of the "Hawaiian Kingdom," came to New York City to address both Native Hawaiians and supporters. "We have the right and the obligation to restore our independence for our children," Siu said. "We can manage our own country."

Red Hook Peacemakers

If you think about when non-Native people came to this land, there were no police, no courts, no jails, and no psychiatric facilities. We only had peacemaking. To see those values being restored even in a small way is amazing.

—Wendy Hill (Haudenosaunee), peacemaker consultant

Peacemaking is a traditional Native American approach to justice and varies from tribe to tribe, where it is used in the tribal court system. It usually consists of one or more peacemakers—often community elders—who bring together all those involved in an offense or conflict, particularly among family members. The peacemakers employ a few basic rules: listen respectfully to all speakers, stay until the end of the session, speak the truth, and no shaming or blaming. It is a restorative practice rather than a punitive one, and it is being employed in the Red Hook section of Brooklyn under the mentorship of Native practitioners and with mostly non-Natives.

Prayers and meals are shared and then the issue is talked out until a resolution can be reached. Peacemaking is mainly used in minor cases involving family and/or community members and prevents the events from escalating and going to court. The goal is to create a more peaceful community. It is hoped that the practice will spread to other communities and will get Americans more interested in using Indigenous knowledge in other areas to resolve contemporary problems.

The United Nations Permanent Forum on Indigenous Issues (UNPFII)

Indigenous peoples all [speak many] different languages, but in our meetings, we are speaking one language. Our relationship to Mother Earth is identical.

—Tonya Gonnella Frichner
(Onondaga)

The United Nations Permanent Forum on Indigenous Issues (UNPFII), based in New York City, advises the United Nations on Indigenous issues related to economic and social development, culture, the environment, education, health, and human rights. Representatives of Indigenous peoples from the United States join with First Peoples from around the world to bring attention to concerns that not only affect them but the health of the entire world. New York attorney Tonya Gonnella Frichner has worked with the U.N. for most of her career and served as the U.S. North American Regional Representative. Every year, the UNPFII convenes in the spring and opens its floor to Indigenous peoples.

Corn Soup

New York City, the country's largest metropolis, is not a melting pot for Indigenous people. It is more like the ultimate bowl of corn soup with corn, beans, squash, meat, and onions all floating around in the same broth. Each ingredient is distinct from the others but together taste delicious. Native people come to New York City,

The official logo of the United Nations Permanent Forum on Indigenous Issues

and other U.S. cities, too, from the Arctic Circle to Tierra del Fuego, for a variety of reasons. Some are descendants of people who always lived there, but in spite of being ignored, dismissed, or discriminated against, they have negotiated the skills to live in two, sometimes three, worlds.

Businesses

Some of the more prominent Native-operated businesses in the United States include the following.

- The First Nations Development Institute, headquartered in Longmont, Colorado, provides assistance to Native Americans to improve economic conditions and develop sustainable businesses.

- The Fry Bread House, owned by Chef Cecilia Miller (Tohono O'odham), serves up fry bread with a wide array of toppings in Phoenix, Arizona. It is a James Beard American Classic award-winning restaurant.

- Hotel Santa Fe in New Mexico is the only Native-owned hotel in Santa Fe.

- The Native American Bank, headquartered in Denver, Colorado, provides banking and financial services to Native American and Alaskan Native individuals, enterprises, and governments.

- The Native American Chamber of Commerce unites Native-owned business and professional firms and is dedicated to culture, commerce, and community. Founded and directed by Carroll Griffin (Cocchia/Blackfoot), it is based in Houston, Texas.

- The Native American Development Corporation, located in Billings, Montana, is a liaison between American Indian businesses in Montana, Wyoming, North Dakota, and South Dakota and state, regional, national, and international economic development organizations and agencies.

- The Residence Inn in Washington, D.C., is owned collaboratively by four different tribes, the first of its kind.

- The Sioux Chef in Minneapolis, Minnesota, is an Indigenous gourmet foods catering company owned by Chef Sean Sherman, Oglala Lakota.

- CRL Health & Fitness, LLC specializes in reducing health and life disparities of Native Americans. CEO and founder Lita Pepion (Blackfeet) is also an activist and a commissioner for the City of Billings Human Relations Commission and works toward social, racial, and economic justice in Montana.

- Tapestries, Etc. is a New York City-based corporation owned and operated by Marsha Vander Heyden (Mohawk/Metis) featuring tapestries from around the globe.

- Tocabe, owned by Ben Jacobs (Osage) and Matt Chandra, is the only American Indian restaurant in the Denver, Colorado, area.

- Wahpepah's Kitchen in Oakland, owned by Chef Crystal Wahpepah (Kickapoo), is the first Native American woman-owned catering business in California.

- First Nations Development Institute headquartered in Longmont, Colorado, provides assistance to Native Americans to improve

Chef Crystal Wahpepah owns Wahpepah's Kitchen in Oakland, California.

economic conditions and develop sustainable businesses.

Work/Law/Education Organizations

The American Indian Science and Engineering Society (AISES), located in Albuquerque, New Mexico, aims to increase the representation of American Indians and Alaskan Natives in science, technology, engineering, and math (STEM) studies and careers.

The Association of American Indian Physicians, in Oklahoma City, Oklahoma, works to improve the health of American Indian and Alaska Natives.

The National Council of Urban Indian Health, based in Washington, D.C., helps develop quality, accessible, and culturally competent health care programs for American Indians and Alaska Natives living in urban communities.

The Society of Indian Psychologists, headquartered in Pittsburgh, Pennsylvania, is a professional society of psychologists, medical professionals, social workers, drug and alcohol counselors, marriage and family therapists, and community counselors who work in areas related to American Indian psychology.

Games/Sports Events

It is no surprise that professional sports teams have attracted Indigenous athletes, and many have played on the nation's hockey, lacrosse, football, and baseball teams. In some cities, there are amateur Native leagues for a variety of sports from bowling to softball to basketball. Cites where there are large populations of Indigenous peoples from South and Mesoamerica feature soccer teams. Some Native sports events feature both contemporary sports and traditional games.

- The Lakota Games on Ice, held in Mitchell, South Dakota (Rosebud Lakota Sioux) is an annual event where participants learn traditional Lakota winter games like Pteheste, a contest to see who can slide a buffalo horn the farthest across the ice. The event is directed by Mike Marshall, an artist and cultural presenter, who crafts all the game objects.

- Striking Eagle Basketball Invitational and Education Fair, Albuquerque, New Mexico, is an annual event for teams from schools that have a Native population of at least twenty percent.

- The annual Indian National Finals Rodeo in Las Vegas, Nevada, draws competitors in rodeo events from eleven regions and from eight years of age to eighty. It is one of the few sporting events where children can compete with their parents and grandparents. INFR also has a Hall of Fame for Native rodeo champions.

- The Ak-Chin Indian Community, Fort McDowell Yavapai Nation, and Salt River Pima-Maricopa Indian Community host the Native American Basketball Invitational (NABI) in Phoenix, Arizona. The largest all-Native basketball tournament in North America, over sixty teams compete. Young

athletes get a chance to showcase their talents for college recruiters.

- The annual Lakota Nation Invitational (LNI), held in Rapid City, South Dakota, started as a small basketball tournament almost forty years ago and is hosted by the Oglala Sioux Tribe. Today, the tournament features almost forty basketball teams, bringing 2,500 students (Indian and non-Indian) and their families to Rapid City for that one sport alone. Competitions include more than basketball: powwow, cheerleading, wrestling, a fashion show, knowledge challenges, art shows, archery, and traditional Lakota-style hand games.

- Wings of America in Santa Fe, New Mexico, selects and trains both a men and women's team of Junior student-athletes (ages 14–19) from the nation's best American Indian runners. The team competes in regional and national running events across the country.

- World Eskimo Indian Olympics is held annually in Fairbanks, Alaska, and draws Native athletes from around the state, who compete in traditional games.

BIOGRAPHIES

Performing Arts

Myra Yvonne Chouteau (1929–)
Cherokee/Shawnee, Ballerina

Chouteau was one of the "Five Moons," or Native prima ballerinas of Oklahoma. In 1962, she and her husband, fellow dancer Miguel Terekhov (1928–2012), founded the Oklahoma City Civic Ballet (now Oklahoma City Ballet) and established the first fully accredited dance department in the United States at the University of Oklahoma at Norman, Oklahoma.

Hortensia and Elvira Colorado
Chichimec/Otomi,
Actors/Storytellers/Writers

The Colorado sisters are the founders of New York's Coatlicue Theatre Company and have both had successful careers as independent artists. Based on traditional accounts and current events, their innovative works present the story of reclaiming stolen histories and of surviving in the face of continued colonization. Born and raised in a small town near Chicago, Elvira and Hortensia have been collaborating for most of their lives and were pioneers in the Indigenous community theater movement. Their celebrated plays include, *Blood Speaks, Coyolxauhquli: Women without Borders*, and *Frida y Diego.*

Brent Michael Davids (1959–)
Stockbridge Mohican,
Composer/Flautist

Born in Madison, Wisconsin, Davids has composed for Zeitgeist, the Kronos Quartet, the Joffrey Ballet, the National Symphony Orchestra, and Chanticleer. In addition to concert music, he writes music for films and composed the score for the 2002 film *The Business of Fancydancing.* Davids lives in St. Paul, Minnesota, and is an active participant with the First Nations Composer Initiative and has served as Composer-in-Residence with the Native American Composers Apprenticeship Project.

Graham Greene (1950–)
Oneida, Actor

Born in Canada, Greene is well known to audiences in the States. He has been nominated for and earned many awards, including an Oscar for *Dances with Wolves.* A favorite of young and adult audiences alike, he has starred in such diverse productions as *The Adventures of Dudley the Dragon, The Twilight Saga: New Moon*, and *Longmire.*

Joy Harjo (1951–)
Mvskoke, Author/Musician

Joy Harjo was born in Tulsa, Oklahoma. She graduated in 1968 from the Institute of American Indian Arts (1968), from the University of New Mexico (1976), and received a Master of Fine Arts degree in creative writing from the University of Iowa (1978). Her seven books of poetry, which include *How We Became Human—New and Selected Poems, The Woman Who Fell From the Sky,* and *She Had Some Horses*, have garnered many awards. These include the New Mexico Governor's Award for Excellence in the Arts, the Lifetime Achievement Award from the Native Writers Circle of the Americas, and the William Carlos Williams Award from the Poetry Society of America. *For A Girl Becoming*, a young adult/coming of age book, was published in 2009 and is Harjo's most recent publication.

She has released five award-winning CDs of original music and in 2009 won a Native American Music Award (NAMMY) for Best Female Artist of the Year for *Winding Through the Milky Way.* Her most recent CD release is a traditional flute album: *Red Dreams, A Trail Beyond Tears.* She performs nationally and internationally with her band, the Arrow Dynamics. Harjo also writes a column, "Comings and Goings," for her tribal newspaper, *The Muscogee Nation News.*

Rosalie M. Jones (1941–)
Little Shell Chippewa, Performer/Teacher

Born on the Blackfeet Reservation in Montana, Jones has studied and taught several dance traditions, including mine, modern, Korean, Hawaiian, East Indian, Conchero, Flamenco, Northwest Coast, Plains, and Woodland. She revitalized performing arts at the Institute of American Indian Arts in Santa Fe, New Mexico, when she served as chair of the department. Jones is the founder and artistic director of DAYSTAR Dance Company, the first Native modern dance company in the U.S. featuring all-Native performers and specializing in the portrayal of the personal and tribal stories of Indian America. The Company has toured throughout the United States and Canada, Europe, and Turkey. She lives in Rochester, New York.

Jana Maria Mashonee (1980–)
Lumbee, Singer/Actress/Author

Jana has been nominated twice for a Grammy and has won nine NAMMY's. Besides being recognized for her beautiful music, she has received national awards for her philanthropy for Native youth through her charity, Jana's Kids Foundation (http://www.janaskids.org), which helps Native youth get an education by granting scholarships. Mashonee is a strong supporter of education and was the first Native woman to graduate from Davidson College, where she earned a bachelor's degree in psychology. The coauthor, with Stephan Galfas, of *American Indian Story: The Adventures of Sha'kona* (2010), she lives in New York City and describes herself as an urban Indian.

Irka Mateo
Taino, Musician/Folklorist

Mateo performs songs and stories based on ancient Taino culture. Mateo performs songs and stories based on ancient Taino culture and lives in New York City. Her music explores the roots and the boundaries of Dominican and Latin American music; she has done extensive research on Indigenous music styles of the Caribbean Islands. Albums like *Vamo a Gozá* include a wealth of Taino vocabulary and rhythms. She teaches and performs internationally and is also a familiar and much-loved act in local Native venues.

Big Chief Russell Moore (1912–1983)
Pima, Jazz Trombonist

Moore played with Lionel Hampton, Louis Armstrong, Lester Lanin, and many other jazz greats. He lived in the New York City metro area and was memorialized in St. Peters, known as the jazz church. Moore had many many adventures in the jazz world. One time he traveled to Alaska with the Louis Armstrong orchestra, and as they deplaned a high school marching band serenaded their arrival. However, the tribute was not for the famous Louis Armstrong, but for Big Chief Russell Moore! The young musicians were all Alaskan Natives and thrilled that a Native professional musician was visiting Alaska.

Mary Kathryn Nagle
Cherokee, Playwright

Playwriting is Nagle's second career; she is also an attorney. She has written and produced several plays in many different venues, including the United Nations. *Manahatta* is an account of the "theft" of New York City, where she lived for a few years. Currently, Nagle is a law partner for Washington, D.C.-based Pipestem, a firm dedicated to protecting and enhancing the sovereign rights of tribal governments and improving the lives of Native people. Her highly acclaimed plays also include *Miss Lead, Fairly Traceable*, and *Sliver of a Full Moon*.

Tanis Parenteau
Métis/Cree, Actress

Parenteau has been featured in several plays, as well as on the big and little screens. She was the lead in *Miss Lead* and costarred as Tammy with Kevin Spacey in *House of*

Cards. Growing up, she was an athlete and competed in figure skating all over Alberta until she was eighteen. She also competed in basketball, volleyball, and track (100m, 200m, 4 × 100m relay, and triple jump), so it was no surprise that Parenteau pursued a degree in physical education with a specialty in athletic therapy. However, right before her college graduation, she was bitten by the acting bug and changed her career path. She lives in New York City.

Oscar Pettiford (1922–1960)
Choctaw/Cherokee/
African American, Jazz Musician

The most recorded jazz bassist in history, Pettiford also gained acclaim for, of all things, playing the cello as a jazz instrument, which he pioneered for the genre. He played with Dizzy Gillespie, Art Farmer, Horace Silver, Coleman Hawkins, Earl Garner, Miles Davis, and many others. Born in Oklahoma, he grew up in Minneapolis and played with his parents and nine siblings in a popular family band. He first gained wider attention in 1942, when he joined the Charlie Barnet band and when he led a bop group in 1943 with Dizzie Gillespie. In the late 1940s, he played with renowned jazz greats Duke Ellington and Woody Herman. It was while he was working with clarinetist Herman that he broke his arm and couldn't play the bass. As a joke, he walked out on stage with a cello, which he had been practicing during his rehabilitation, and it turned out to be a hit. From then on, he played both double bass and cello. In 1958 he moved to Copenhagen, Denmark, recording for European labels until his death in 1960.

Ryan Victor (Little Eagle) Pierce
Nanticoke Lenni–Lenape,
Actor/Singer/Director

Pierce (New York City) is founder of the Eagle Project, which explores American Indian identity as well as multicultural America through the per-

forming arts. His one-man piece *Survivor* was presented at the United Nations in 2014. Under Pierce's leadership, Eagle Project has produced various plays by Native writers, including *Wood Bones, Hunka,* and *Mangled Beams.* In 2015, his one-man play *This Play Is Native Made* debuted in response to the state of New Jersey's continued mistreatment of its indigenous people.

Martha Redbone
Cherokee/Choctaw, Musician

Redbone is an award-winning blues and soul singer based in New York City. Her music is a rich blend of styles inspired by her roots: Native American, Appalachian folk, Piedmont blues, and Brooklyn's "mean streets." From Nashville to London, England, Redbone is a sought-after performer and collaborator.

Madeline Sayet
Mohegan, Director/Writer/Performer

Best known for her directing, Sayet (New York City) is the recipient of The White House Champion of Change Award for Native America. She has directed, *Miss Lead* by Mary Kathryn Nagle (Cherokee) and *Powwow Highway* by William S. Yellow Robe, Jr. (Assiniboine and Sioux Tribes of the Fort Peck Indian Reservation) among many other productions.

Twice As Good
Elem Indian Colony Pomo Tribe, Musicians

The father-son duo of Richard Steward (1951–) and Paul Steward (1984–) has received national acclaim for their unique blues style. Based in Santa Rosa, California, Twice As Good has performed coast to coast at Blues and Native music festivals, plus the duo has a following at Indian casinos. Their fiery, soulful vocals, screaming guitar licks, and driving rhythm earned them the 2010 Bay Area Blues Society at the "Best New Blues Band of 2010," the first Native Americans to receive the award.

Jock Soto (1965–)
Navajo (Dine), Ballet Dancer and Teacher

Once the youngest principal dancer in the history of the New York City Ballet, Soto earned a reputation for being the best ballet partner in the world. He danced feature roles in over forty ballets, thirty-five of which were created just for him. Born in Gallup, New Mexico, and raised in Phoenix, Arizona, he was accepted at the prestigious School of American Ballet (SAB) in New York City when he was a teenager. After a stellar, twenty-four-year performing career, he retired from dancing in 2005 and became a faculty member of SAB. In 2002, SAB presented him with the Mae L. Wein Award for Distinguished Service. Soto's storied life is chronicled in the documentary *Water Flowing Together.*

Literary Arts

Marilou Awiakta (1936–)
Eastern Cherokee, Author

Cofounder of the Far Away Cherokee Association (now the Native American Intertribal Association), Awiakta is an award-winning author and lives in Memphis, Tennessee. A community activist as well as an author, she worked in the Arts-in-Schools program in Memphis and formed poetry workshops in the women's prison there. Awiakta's publications, which often interweave history and poetry, include *Abiding Appalachia: Where Mountain and Atom Meet*, *Rising Fawn and the Fire Mystery: A Child's Christmas in Memphis, 1833*, and *Selu: Seeking the Corn-Mother's Wisdom.*

Ignatia Broker (1919–1987)
Ojibwe, Author/Activist

A real-life heroine, Broker received the Wonder Woman Award (1984) in recognition of her dedication to make the world a better place. She spent many years in Minneapolis, advocating for

the rights of Native people, and helped found the Minnesota Historical Society. Broker's book *Night Flying Woman* recounts the story of her great-great-grandmother and her family's life before and after contact with white explorers

Chrystos (1946–)
Menominee/Lithuanian/French, Poet/Artist/Activist

Chrystos' work raises awareness of urban Indians as well as issues of the disenfranchised Indians, abused children, homeless, African Americans, substance abusers, and two-spirited people. Some of her publications are *Not Vanishing*, *In Her I Am*, and *Fire Power.* She lives on Bainbridge Island, Washington.

James Morales
Mississippi Choctaw, Publisher

Based in Albuquerque, New Mexico, James Morales is the founder and CEO of Native Hoop, a web-based organization that publishes two magazines: *Native Hoop* and *Natives in Ink* (NINK). Since its inception in 2009, *Native Hoop* has offered positive and culturally responsible articles on a wide array of topics written by Native journalists and with an international audience. NINK promotes Native tattoo artwork and artists.

Cynthia Leitich Smith (1967–)
Creek, Author/Educator

 Leitich Smith is a *New York Times* bestselling author of children and young adult fiction. Her stories reflect the lives of contemporary Indian people, often urban residents. *Rain Is Not My Indian Name* (2001) and *Jingle Dancer* (2000) are two of her best-known children's books. She also writes award-winning gothic fantasy for young adults: *Tantalize* (2007), *Eternal: Zachary's Story* (2013), *Feral Curse* (2014), and *Feral Pride* (2015) are

considered some of best in the genre. She hosts a website (www.cynthialeitichsmith.com) that introduces readers to children's and young adult literature resources. Smith also teaches writing and facilitates many workshops for writers. She lives in Austin, Texas.

Christine Stark
Anishinabe/Cherokee
Educator/Journalist/Novelist

In 2012, Stark was named a "Changemaker" by the Minnesota Women's Press for her first-ever study of prostitution and trafficking of Indigenous women, titled *Garden of Truth: The Prostitution and Trafficking of Native Women in Minnesota.* She also published the novel *Nickels: A Tale of Dissociation* and is an advocate for Native women and children who have been victims of sex abuse and trafficking. Stark is based in Minneapolis, but travels nationally to speak on social justice issues and exhibit her artwork. She is an award-winning author and visual artist.

Mary TallMountain (1918–1994)
Koyukon/Athabaska, Writer

TallMountain's stories and poems capture her childhood along the Yukon River and being taken away from her village to mainstream American culture, where she felt like an angry outsider. She also wrote about San Francisco, where she lived and died. For many years she wrote a column called "Meditations for Wayfarers" in the Franciscan publication *The Way.* The Rasmussen Library at the University of Alaska in Fairbanks houses a collection of TallMountain's published and unpublished works. Included in several anthologies, her book *The Light on the Tent Wall* was published posthumously.

Roberta Hill Whiteman (1947–)
Wisconsin Oneida, Poet/Educator

Whiteman is a renowned poet and an Associate Professor of English and American Studies at the University of Wisconsin–Madison. Her most popular works are *Star Quilt* (1984) and *Philadelphia Flowers* (1996). She is recipient of the Wisconsin Idea Foundation's Excellence Award.

Visual Arts

Nadema Agard
Cherokee/Lakota/Powhatan,
Artist/Illustrator/Curator/Educator/Writer

Agard was born and brought up in New York City and is an award-winning artist and repatriation expert. "Lady Liberty as a Native American Icon," "Contact 1609," and "Manahatta Today," which she also curated, are just a few examples of her group art shows. Her publications include *Southeastern Native Arts Directory* and *Selu and Kana' Ti: Cherokee Corn Mother and Lucky Hunter,* as well as several articles and websites. Active in several community organizations, Agard has also worked for the National Museum of the American Indian and the American Museum of Natural History.

Larry Beck (1938–1994)
Yup'ik, Sculptor

Born and raised in Seattle, Washington, Beck was an internationally acclaimed sculptor who often used found industrial and manufactured materials to create stunning pieces that in later years reflected Yup'ik heritage. He received many awards and honors for his Art in Public Places commissions in Golden Gardens Park, Highline Community College and the King County International Airport. Beck used the word "Inua" ("spirit" in his language) in the titles of his masks. He hoped his masks had enough Inua to satisfy the spirit debt he felt was owed to his Yup'ik heritage.

Walter Tutsi Wai Bigbee (1958–)
Comanche,
Professional Photographer

Known internationally for his prized photography, Bigbee's images have appeared in countless publications, including *Time-Life Books* and *Native Peoples* magazine. He has been featured at the National Museum of the American Indian and the Heard Museum. His native name, Tutsi Wai, means "always searching," and he spent part of his youth in Africa, exploring the world and continues to travel the glove. Bigbee credits these experiences to his open-minded view of Creation, but he feels his Numunuu (Comanche) heritage, and his concerns for the natural world, influenced his work the most. An admirer of traditional arts such as bow and drum making, fans, beadwork, tanning, and regalia, he is also a wrangler of wild mustangs.

Tlisza Jaurique
Mexica/Yaqui/
Basque/Xicana, Artist

Jaurique combines traditional Mesoamerican motifs, local fauna, and nationalist colors and sparkles it all with a most unlikely embellishment—glitter. Born in Phoenix, Arizona, Jaurique is heavily influenced by her Mexican Indigenous roots in the Nahua and Yaqui traditions. Traditional Mexican celebrations, like the Day of the Dead and the Feast Day of the Virgin of Guadalupe, are prominent themes, illustrated in a vibrant blend of topography, painting, and sculpture. Some of Jaurique's most well regarded works are "Desatame" and "Mayahuel."

Virgil Ortiz
Cochiti Pueblo, Potter/Designer

Descended from a family of acclaimed traditional potters, Ortiz produces superb clay works that are on display worldwide, but he has contemporized the ancient art by combining it with fashion and décor. He lives both in Los Angeles, California, and Cochiti, New Mexico.

Chris Pappan
Osage/Kaw/Cheyenne River Sioux, Artist

Pappan lives in Chicago, Illinois, and is an internationally recognized painter. His art reflects the dominant culture's distorted perceptions of Native peoples while proclaiming that "we are still here!" He has been awarded several honors, including the Heard Museum Best of Class.

Kay WalkingStick (1935–)
Cherokee, Artist/Educator

Distinguished and celebrated for her unique style of telling Indian stories through art, WalkingStick is a professor emerita of Cornell University. She is featured in an exhibit at the National Museum of the American Indian, "Kay WalkingStick: An American Artist," and lives in Easton, Pennsylvania.

G. Peter Jemison (1945–)
Seneca, Artist/Repatriation
Specialist/Historian

Jemison is the manager of the Ganondagan State Historic Site in Victor, New York, the location of a seventeenth-century Seneca town and a National Historic Landmark. He is also a respected curator, editor, historian, educator, writer, and the representative for the Seneca Nation of Indians on the Native American Graves Protection and Repatriation Act (NAGPRA). Highly regarded for his paintings, videos, and mixed media works on parasols and brown paper bags, Jemison's creations reflect his traditional Seneca belief "that every living thing and every part of creation contains a spiritual force." His art is part of collections in prestigious museums throughout the country and world. Jemison has been the recipient of many awards, including the 2012 Jennifer Easton Community Spirit Award fellowship from the First Peoples Fund in Rapid City, South Dakota. He lives in Victor, New York, and was a founder of the American Indian Community House in New York City.

Dwayne Wilcox (1957–)
Oglala Lakota, Painter

Wilcox is an award-winning artist and is world renowned for his "ledger art," which puts a comic spin on grim subjects. In the 1800s used ledger books were given to Plains people, who created a new style of art, chronicling events and history on top of the pages already filled with numbers and words. It became iconic, and Wilcox continues the tradition. Whether depicting a "cigar store white guy" or Custer in a line-up, his works often make the viewer chuckle and then examine the serious side of his themes.

Activists

Ella Pierre Aquino (1902–1988)
Lummi/Yakima, Activist

A founder of the Seattle Indian Center and the American Indian Women's Service League, Aquino was also a leading voice in the protection of Native children in the foster care system as well as tribal fishing rights. Her activism earned her the title "Give 'em hell Ella" as she was photographed scaling a barbed wire fence in the struggle to take back Fort Lawton.

Audrey Cooper
Cherokee/Sand Hill, Activist/Advocate

Cooper is the director of the Multicultural Resource Center in Ithaca, New York, and has received many awards and commendations for her community service work on issues involving justice, race, and inclusion. Cooper's program, Talking Circles, has received national acclaim for confronting and healing racism. She organizes the annual First Peoples Festival.

Jim Fraser
Cherokee/Edisto, Activist

A long-term federal employee, Fraser served as director of the Office of Special Programs, ETA, US DOL, Region 1, and negotiated grants and contracts for New England Tribes and urban Indian programs, which was recognized as the best run sector. He helped create the Massachusetts Commission for Indian Affairs. He is best known for his leadership in establishing the first National Day of Mourning held in 1970 in Plymouth, Massachusetts. Over five hundred Native Americans attended the inaugural event, which still exists today as a day of protest. He lives in Lexington, Massachusetts.

Suzan Shown Harjo (1945–)
Cheyenne/Hodulgee
Muscogee, Advocate

Harjo lives in Washington, D.C., where she founded Morning Star Institute, which promotes sacred land claims and protection for traditional cultural rights. As an advocate for American Indian rights, she has helped Native peoples recover more than one million acres of tribal lands. In 2014, she was granted the Presidential Medal of Freedom.

LaDonna Vita Tabbytite Harris (1931–)
Comanche, Activist

Founder and president of Americans for Indian Opportunity, Harris has been an advocate for American Indian rights as well as a supporter of civil rights, environmental protection, the women's movement, and world peace. She was a founding member of Common Cause, National Urban Coalition, and National Women's Political Caucus and is a respected leader in the movement to eradicate poverty and social injustice. A proponent of Indian self-determination, she helped the Taos Pueblo regain their sacred Taos Pueblo and the Menominee regain their federal recognition after termination. She lives in Albuquerque, New Mexico.

Bernie Whitebear
(1937–2000)
Colville Confederated Tribes, Activist

Whitebear struggled for the rights of urban Indian people and led a campaign for Native rights to an abandoned fort in Seattle. He led efforts to establish the United Indians of All Tribes Foundation, which provides services for Seattle's Native Americans. He helped put the struggles of urban Indians on the news and over his many years of sacrifice accomplished so much in every area. Although he was a formidable adversary for many government officials, they grew to respect him. Whitebear was bestowed many honors, including the Washington Citizen of the Decade (1997). In 2011, Seattle named a street for him.

Business

Dave Anderson
Choctaw/Ojibwe, Restaurant Founder

Anderson is the founder and owner of the restaurant chain Famous Dave's, which has won over seven hundred awards. Proceeds from his best-selling book, *Famous Dave's Rib-O'Licious!*, benefit Native youth.

Mary "Smoki" Fraser
Rappahannock,
Human Resources Administrator

Fraser, an expert in human resources, was the HRA for a large publishing firm in Massachusetts over her long career. She lives in Lexington, Massachusetts, where she is active in the community and serves on the diversity committee of the New England Deaconess Association.

Carroll Griffin
Cocchia/Blackfoot, Business Owner

Griffin is founder and director of the Native American Chamber of Commerce, which unites Native-owned business and professional firms and is dedicated to culture, commerce, and community. Her projects also include the Native American Achievement Center, which offers education and employment skills, and Hope and Harmony for Humanity, which partners celebrities with major corporations in providing housing, employment, and economic opportunities on rural reservations. Griffin is based in Houston, Texas.

Cecilia Miller
Tohono Oodham, Chef/Restauranteur

Miller owns and operates The Fry Bread House, which serves up fry bread that has become a new tradition since the introduction of wheat flour to the Native diet. Miller's menu offers both sweet and savory frybread with a wide array of toppings, ranging from chile to hominy to chocolate. The Phoenix, Arizona, eatery is a James Beard American Classic award-wining restaurant.

Lita Pepion
Blackfeet, Business owner

Pepion is the CEO and founder of the CRL Health & Fitness, LLC, which specializes in reducing health and life disparities of Native Americans. She is also an activist and a commissioner for the City of Billings Human Relations Commission and works toward social, racial, and economic justice in Montana.

Gelvin Stevenson
Western Cherokee, Environmental Economist

 Stevenson organizes the Greentech Investors Forum and works with AgriPower, a biomass co-gen company, and Organic Energy Corp., which have developed systems that recycle ninety-five percent of municipal solid waste into useable products. He lives in New York City.

Science/Medicine/Social Work/Law/Education

Lori Alvord
Diné (Navajo) Surgeon

Dr. Alvord is the first Navajo woman to become a surgeon and is a dean and director of special projects at the University of Arizona College of Medicine in Tucson. Dr. Alvord combines high-tech surgical skills with the traditional Navajo world view called *hozhoni*, or "walking in beauty." *Hozhoni* is the belief that when the mind, body, and spirit are in harmony, people will have good health. Dr. Alvord grew up on the Navajo reservation in New Mexico and served as a dean at Dartmouth Medical School in New Hampshire; she is also on the National Advisory Council for Alternative and Complimentary Medicine.

Samuel Beeler (1950–)
Cherokee/Sand Hill, Historian/Nurse

Born and raised in Paterson, New Jersey, Dr. Beeler has been a champion for Native rights, particularly Eastern nations who have been marginalized and ignored. He has worked in health care and is active with Native American veterans.

Lisa T. Brooks
Abenaki, Educator/Author

Brooks is a professor of Native American studies at Amherst College in Amherst, Massachusetts, and has written award-winning scholarly books on Native issues. She is active in her Native community, as well as nationally. One of her publications, *The Common Pot: The Recovery of Native Space in the Northeast* (University of Minnesota Press, 2008), examines the historical and literary legacy of the American Indian northeast and illuminates how early Native activists like Occom, Brant, and Apess, among others, used writing as a tool of resistance. Brooks shows that "writing was not a foreign technology but rather a crucial weapon in the Native Americans' arsenal as they resisted—and today continue to oppose—colonial domination."

"Dede" Yazzie Devine
Navajo, Director

For over thirty years, Devine has been the president of Native American Connections, an Albuquerque, New Mexico, company that provides comprehensive behavioral health services (including traditional healing), affordable housing, and community based economic development opportunities in Albuquerque, New Mexico. She serves on local, state, and national boards and committees like the Native Home Capital and People of Color Network, St. Joseph's Hospital and Medical Center, and the Robert Wood Johnson National Mentor for Developing Leadership. Devine has received many citations for her activism: Arizona's Centennial Legacy Project—Arizona's 48 Most Intriguing Women (2012); the Phoenix Business Journal's 25 Most Admired CEOs (2012), and YWCA's Tribute to Women—Business Leader Award (2008).

Joseph P. Gone
Gros Ventre, Psychologist/Professor

Gone examines cultural influences on mental health, as well as the intersection of evidence-based practice and cultural competence in mental health services. A fellow within seven different American Psychological Association divisions, he has been honored as a Noted Scholar at the University of British Columbia, and a Distinguished Visitor at the University of Alberta; he has served on editorial boards of several scientific journals, including *Psychological Clinical Science*, the *American Journal of Community Psychology*, and *Cultural Diversity & Ethnic Minority Psychology*. At press time, Dr. Gone is on the faculty at the University of Michigan, Ann Arbor

Jacque Gray
Cherokee/Choctaw, Psychologist

Dr. Gray is the Associate Director of Indigenous Programs at the Center for Rural Health, University of North Dakota, Grand Forks. She is a noted researcher in several health areas, including suicide prevention, American Indian behavioral health, rural veterans' health concerns, and the role of spirituality in health. Her many projects include the National Indigenous Elder Justice Initiative, National Institute of Mental Health Outreach Partnership, and the Seven Generations Center of Excellence in Native Behavioral Health.

Robyn Hannigan
Narragansett, Geochemist

Hannigan is the founding dean of the School for the Environment at the University of Massachusetts in Boston. She also heads the Hannigan Research Group. Projects comprise Ocean Acidification and Biomineralogy, Geochemical Fingerprinting and Population Ecology, and Paleoclimate Change. Her team's goal is to use geochemistry to study the past and future of the Earth, while learning how to protect the planet's unique systems.

Joseph Kabance
Prairie Band Potawatomi
An Affirmative Action

Administrator and compliance specialist for New York State agencies for almost twenty-five years, Ka-

bance has an in-depth knowledge of federal and state nondiscrimination laws and regulations. Over his long career in public service, he investigated and resolved a myriad of discrimination complaints in all areas. An active jogger and hiker, he is also a leader and member of different New York City Native organizations, including co-chairm of Nitchen, Inc. He is known for his Native-themed, round oil paintings and is the subject of a Tapwe documentary.

Carol Kalafatic
Quechua, Educator

Kalafatic is an activist and educator in the area of Indigenous peoples' sustainable community development, food and agriculture policy, and local-global governance. She is the past director of the American Indian Program, Cornell University, Ithaca, New York. Her research also includes food sovereignty and the role of biocultural diversity in food security and resilience to climate change.

Robin Kimmerer
Citizen Band Potawatomi,
Environmentalist/Author

Kimmerer is State University of New York (SUNY) Distinguished Teaching Professor at the SUNY College of Environmental Science and Forestry in Syracuse, New York. Besides being an environmental professor, she is the founding director of the Center for Native Peoples and the Environment, an organization that blends Indigenous wisdom with scientific knowledge to create teaching programs on sustainability. Kimmerer also educates the scientific community on the benefits of traditional ecological knowledge. In her highly acclaimed book, *Braiding Sweetgrass* (2103), she marries her profession as a botanist with her Potawatomi heritage.

Robert Lilligren
White Earth Band of Ojibwe,
Politician/Director

Lilligren is the first American Indian tribal member to serve on the Minneapolis City Council (2001–2013) and is now the CEO of the Little Earth of United Tribes Housing Corporation, the country's first public housing project for Native Americans. He is known for his role in increasing employment for women and minorities on government-funded projects and for sponsoring the Memorandum of Understanding between Minneapolis and the American Indian Community. Lilligren heads up the nation's only urban housing project, which was founded in 1973 and is home to a thousand Indian people.

Jennie Luna
Quiahuicoatl Meztli, Educator/Dancer

Professor of Chicana/o Studies and Native American Studies at California State University, Channel Islands (CI), Dr. Luna's research focuses on the contemporary history of Danza Mexica/Azteca tradition and its impact on Xicana Indígena identity formation. She was a founder of Danza Mexica while a student at Columbia University in New York City and lives in Camarillo, California.

Robert Eugene Megginson
Oglala Sioux, Mathematician

Megginson is a professor and mathematician at the University of Michigan in Ann Arbor, Michigan. He is one of about a dozen Native people with a doctorate in mathematics and has spent decades encouraging Native students to choose a math career. In 1997, he received the U.S. Presidential Award for Excellence in Science, Mathematics, and Engineering Mentoring. Megginson was honored with an American Indian Science and Engineering Society Ely S. Parker Lifetime Achievement Award (1999) and was named to the Native American Science and Engineering Wall of Fame (2001). His specialty is multi-dimensional (Banach) spaces.

Paulette Fairbanks Molin
Minnesota Chippewa Tribe, Author/Educator

Author of several books, including *The Extraordinary Book of Native American Lists* (with Arlene Hirschfelder), Molin served as assistant dean of the graduate college and director of the American Indian Educational Opportunity Program at Hampton University. She also has been the curator for several key exhibitions recounting the history of education of Native students like "Enduring Legacy: Native Peoples, Native Arts at Hampton" and "To Lead and To Serve: American Indian Education at Hampton Institute, 1878–1923." Dr. Molin lives in Hampton, Virginia.

Kenneth Ridgway
Lenape, Geologist

Ridgway is a professor at Purdue University in West Lafayette, Indiana. His research focuses on tectonics and the structures and changes of the earth's crust. He has led research teams to explore southern Alaska, and his team has investigated other parts of the world, too. He credits his curiosity about how the earth works with his Native heritage and examines the relationship between Western science and Indigenous communities. At Purdue, Ridgway mentors Native students to take their knowledge to Indian "country," and prepares their home communities to become knowledgeable about how their land is used by third parties for mining and drilling. He is active with the American Indian Science and Engineering Society, and in 2012 Ridgway received the National Geographic Bromery Award for his scholarly achievements and mentoring and support for all minorities.

Nicole Stern
Mescalero Apache, Internist

Stern is a physician for the University of California, Santa Barbara, Department of Intercollegiate Athletics. During her career, she has served as Assistant Director of the Indians into Medicine Program at the University of Arizona and as a team physician for various high schools and universities, as well as for the Oklahoma City Blazers professional ice hockey team and the Oklahoma City Redhawks professional baseball team. For several years, she worked in campus health at the University of Arizona.

Gabrielle Tayac
Piscataway, Historian

An activist, author, educator, and curator, Tayac lives in the metro D.C. area and is an historian at the Smithsonian National Museum of the American Indian. Her many projects include the traveling exhibition and book "IndiVisible: African-Native American Lives in the Americas." She grew up in New York City.

Anton Treuer (1969–)
Ojibwe, Educator/Author

Truer is professor of the Ojibwe language and executive director of the American Indian Resource Center at Bemidji State University, Minnesota. Recognized as one of the youngest teachers of Ojibwe language and culture, he has received many awards, including the Ken Hale Prize, Society for Study of Indigenous Languages of the Americas (2012); Sally Ordway Irvine Award for Distinguished Service in Education (2011); and the Outstanding Service Award, MeritCare Health System Board of Trustees (2009).

Mariana Vergara
Mapuche/Aymera, Educator/Activist

Vergara works with Indigenous groups in New York City and Ecuador. She developed Mindfulness into Action, techniques that help individuals build skills to transform their communities based on the application of Indigenous traditional practices. She lives in Dover, New Jersey.

Ponka-We Victors (1981–)
Ponca/Tohono O'odham, Kansas State Representative

Born and raised in Wichita, Kansas, Victors is a community support worker and has been a Democratic member of the Kansas House of Representatives, representing District 103, since 2011. She is the only Native American in the Kansas legislature. In 2013, she became known across the country for confronting a bill that, if passed, would deny in-state tuition to Kansas high school graduates who were undocumented immigrants. Victors spoke to Kansas Secretary of State Kris Kobach and other advocates of the bill: "I think it's funny, Mr. Kobach, because when you mention illegal immigrant, I think of all of you."

Jerry Yakel
Luiseño, Neuroscientist

Yakel is chief of the Neurobiology Laboratory and principal investigator for the National Institute of Environmental Health Sciences, Research Triangle Park, New York. His team studies the debilitating effect of environmental exposures on particular processes in the central and peripheral nervous system that influence many neurodegenerative, neurological, and psychiatric disorders. Yakel has been a principal investigator at the National Institute of Environmental Health Science

Sports/Games

Lane Weston Adams (1989–)
Choctaw, Baseball Player

Adams plays outfielder for the Kansas City Royals MLB team. Although he is a professional baseball player, he also played basketball in his Oklahoma high school. Adams scored 3,251 points, making him the fifth-highest scorer in Oklahoma high school basketball history.

Justin Louis "Joba" Chamberlain (1985–)
Winnebago, Baseball Player

 Chamberlain is a pitcher for the Kansas City Royals and made his baseball debut with the New York Yankees. He was traded to the Detroit Tigers and eventually became a Royal. Joba throws a four-seam fastball that has topped out at 101 mph. His curveball also zips along at 78 to 81 mph.

Norman Maktima

San Felipe/Laguna/Hopi, Professional Fisherman

Maktima is a competition-winning member of the U.S. National Fly Fishing Team and competes in championships here and abroad. His passion for fishing started at just seven years old, and in 1998 he won an individual gold medal and a team silver in 1998 during the Junior World Fly Fishing Championships held in Wales. Maktima is a high desert angler, guide, and instructor. He lives in Santa Fe, New Mexico.

Marcus Ardel Taulauniu Mariota (1993–)

Polynesian/Hawaiian, American Football Quarterback

From Honolulu, Hawaii, Mariota has won many trophies and awards, including the Heisman (2014) and the Rose Bowl MVP (2015). He was the second player drafted (Tennessee Titans) in the 2014 NFL draft; some felt he should have been first. Mariota is the first Samoan to win the Heisman Trophy but he was not comfortable with being singled out. At his acceptance speech, he said that talking about himself "doesn't really fit in" with Polynesian culture. Mariota is seen as a leader who leads by example.

Ted Nolan (1958–)

Ojibwe, Hockey Coach

Nolan was the head coach of the Buffalo Sabres hockey team in Buffalo, New York, until 2015.

During his career, he was a left winger for various teams, including the Detroit Red Wings and the Pittsburgh Penguins, He also coached the New York Islanders and the Latvia men's national ice hockey team. Nolan is active with his foundation, which encourages Aboriginal youth to pursue academic growth for a better future. The Rose Nolan scholarship, which is named for his mother, helps First Nations Women attain their educational and training goals, while being active in their communities.

John Clayton Rice (1938–)

Prairie Band Potawatomi, Surfer

Rice is a champion surfer and surfboard designer from Santa Cruz, California. Santa Cruz is thought to be the first place standup board surfing was done on the U.S. mainland. In 1885, three Hawaiian princes, who were also students in the area, mesmerized crowds by surfing the cold and shark-filled waves. Decades later, Rice, who was an excellent body surfer, spotted surfers on the same site first surfed by the Hawaiian princes, and he embraced the sport so expertly and passionately that he is recognized as a grandfather of Santa Cruz surf culture. Rice was inducted into the International Surfboard Builders Hall of Fame in 2010.

Kelvin Matthew Sampson (1955–)

Lumbee, Basketball Coach

Sampson is head coach of the Houston Cougars, University of Houston, Texas. He grew up in Robeson County, North Carolina, a heavily populated Lumbee area; his father was one of the Lumbee who drove out the Ku Klux Klan. After graduating from Pembroke State College in North Carolina and earning a master's degree in coaching and administration at Michigan State University, Sampson coached at Montana Tech and Washington State University. He went on to become head coach of University of Oklahoma and then Indiana University before his current position. Sampson also coached the 2004 Under-21 USA national team to a gold medal in the Under-21 Tournament of the Americas in Halifax, Nova Scotia. Sampson also coached the U.S. Junior National Team for the Junior World Games in Athens, Greece (1995), the Goodwill Games in Russia (1994), and the West team at the U.S. Olympic Festival in San Antonio, Texas (1993); his team won the silver medal. Sampson was assistant coach for the Canadian national men's basketball team (2012).

Shoni Schimmel (1992–)
Confederated Tribes of the Umatilla Indian Reservation, Basketball Player

 Schimmel, a 5'9" shooting guard, first received national attention as a high school player in Oregon and was named a first team All-American by *Parade Magazine*. Born and raised on the Confederated Tribes of the Umatilla Indian Reservation in Mission, Oregon, her family moved off the reservation to Portland so she would have more basketball opportunities. Her journey is the subject of the documentary *Off the Rez*. Schimmel was chosen for the 2010 Women's Basketball Coaches Association High School Coaches' All-America Team and went on to become a star player for University of Louisville, finishing second on the school's career scoring list. She led her team to a 2013 championship, averaging 17.1 points per game, and was named an All-American by the USBWA and Associated Press. Schimmel was a member of the USA team in the 2013 World University Games held in Kazan, Russia. They won Gold. In 2014, Schimmel was selected in the first round of the 2014 WNBA draft (eighth pick overall) by the Atlanta Dream and was named the WNBA All-Star Game Most Valuable Player (2014).

Miles Thompson (1995–)
Onondaga, Lacrosse Player

Thompson was a champion lacrosse player in college (University at Albany). He and his brother and teammate, Lyle, shared the Tewaaraton Award given to the best NCAA Division I college lacrosse player. During his college career, Thompson played in 61 games and scored 189 goals and 104 assists for 293 points. After college, he was recruited by the Rochester Rattlers, scoring 12 goals with seven assists. Thompson scored 5 goals with one assist during the last game which earned him Cascade Rookie of the Week. At the time of publication of this book, he plays for the Florida Launch.

Christopher Wondolowski (1983–)
Kiowa, Soccer Player

Wondolowski is a top striker in Major League Soccer and plays for the San Jose Earthquakes. He played on the U.S. team in the 2014 FIFA World Cup as a forward or as a midfielder. Wondolowski was MLS's top goal scorer in the 2010 and 2012 seasons and was named the Most Valuable Player of the 2012. His traditional name is Bau Daigh (Bowe Dye), which is Kiowa for "warrior coming over the hill." In 2013, Wondo was chosen for the Division II 40th Anniversary Tribute Team, honoring his time spent at Chico State.

APPENDIX A: CANADA

Spanning from the Northern Atlantic to the Pacific Ocean, Canada covers 3,855,103 square miles (9,984,671 square kilometers) and includes an assortment of geo-climatic regions. It has the world's longest coastline, features vast boreal forests, and a northern polar area. The Rocky Mountains are as tall as the prairies are flat. The country is organized into ten provinces: Alberta, British Columbia, Manitoba, New Brunswick, Newfoundland and Labrador, Nova Scotia, Ontario, Prince Edward Island, Quebec, and Saskatchewan and three territories: Northwest Territories, Nunavut, and Yukon. The Canadian Shield, an ice-scoured area, starts in the center of the country and extends to the east, stretches from the Great Lakes to the Arctic Ocean, surrounds Hudson Bay and covers half the country. The maritime area east of the Shield is separated from the rest of country by low mountain ranges sliced by plains, river valleys, and shared by the Newfoundland and Prince Edward Island. South and southeast of the Shield are the Great Lakes–St. Lawrence fertile lowlands (the most populated area), bordered by the St. Lawrence River, Lake Ontario, and Georgian Bay. Farmlands and ranches dot the great central plains west of the Shield. To the north is the Mackenzie lowland, marked by many lakes and rivers. Canada's westernmost region from western Alberta to the Pacific Ocean, includes the Rocky Mountains, a plateau region, the coastal mountain range, and an inner sea channel which runs between the outer islands and the fjord-lined coast. The Arctic islands, which differ greatly in size and topography, extend north of the mainland to the North Pole.

When Europeans first reached the east coast of the vast lands which make up present-day Canada, diverse Indigenous societies were well established in their respective territories. Although European colonizers may have stereotyped all Natives as hunters without permanent homes, at the time of contact there were people living in established villages in coastal British Columbia, southern Ontario, and western Quebec. Communities in the central area had thriving agricultural traditions. The Europeans "discovered" well-organized governments, societies living in delineated territories. It was most probably the catastrophic population decline resulting from new foreign diseases in the 1500s that made European settlement of the continent possible.

The different cultures encountered by the Europeans shared similarities according to the regions they occupied and the languages they spoke. On the Atlantic coast were the Beothuk, Micmac, and Malecite, whose economy centered on tidal and river fishing. Around the Great Lakes were farming communities—including the Huron and Haudenosaunee—whose towns featured a variety of crops such as corn and tobacco. The prairie peoples—the Assiniboine, Plains Cree, Blackfoot, Sarcee, Saulteaux, and Gros Ventre—had a culture based on the migration of the buffalo. In the coastal mountains, seashore and islands of British Columbia, salmon was the main source of food. Stretching across the country throughout the northern forests were the Montagnais, Naskapi, Abenaki, Ottawa, Algonquin, Ojibwa, and Cree, who had strong fishing and hunting traditions. North of the tree line were the seafaring Inuit. Some of the regions were home to linguistically consistent cultures; in others, such as British Columbia, a wide variety of languages were spoken within a small geographic area. (See "A Closer Look" section.)

THE FIVE NATIONAL GROUPS
THAT REPRESENT ABORIGINAL PEOPLE OF CANADA

1. First Nations are represented by the Assembly of First Nations (AFN), formerly the National Indian Brotherhood. Twentieth-century Indian political activity in Canada began at the local and regional level as national organizing was forbidden by the 1927 Indian Act. Regional influences and differences are apparent in the operation of the AFN. Composed of the 634 (as of 2016) band chiefs from across the country, the assembly is a national advocacy organization representing First Nation citizens in Canada, which includes more than 900,000 people living in 634 First Nation communities and in cities and towns across the country. The group facilitates national and regional discussions, advocacy efforts and campaigns, legal and policy analysis, relationships with various levels of government, including among First Nations and the Crown, as well as public and private sectors and general public. The AFN represents a variety of political viewpoints from militancy to traditional to more conservative and accommodating.

2. As increasing numbers of First Peoples settle in cities and move off reserves, there is a need for a national organization to represent them. The Congress of Aboriginal People (CAP) advocates for all off-reserve status and non-status Indians, Métis and Southern Inuit Aboriginal Peoples, and serves as the national voice for its provincial and territorial affiliate organizations. CAP also holds consultative status with the United Nations Economic and Social Council (ECOSOC), which facilitates its participation on international issues of importance to Indigenous Peoples.

3. Since 1983, the Métis National Council (MNC) has represented the Métis Nation nationally and internationally. It is directed by the democratically elected leadership of the Métis Nation's governments from Ontario westward. Their mandate is to ensure the well-being and rights of the Métis Nation within the Canadian federation.

4. The Inuit Tapiriit Kanatami (ITK), formerly Inuit Tapirisat of Canada, is the national voice of 55,000 Inuit living in 53 communities across the Inuvialuit Settlement Region (Northwest Territories), Nunavut, Nunavik (Northern Quebec), and Nunatsiavut (Northern Labrador), land claims regions, a vast area the Inuit call Nunangat. Founded in 1971 ITK represents the Inuit, both locally and nationally in many areas: environmental; social; cultural; and political. Its governing board is composed of a President and elected heads of the four regional Inuit land claims organizations.

5. The Native Women's Association of Canada (NWAC) works to advance the well-being of Aboriginal women and girls, as well as their families and communities through activism, policy analysis and advocacy. Founded in 1974, the NWAC addresses both gender and racial discrimination in many areas. The Board of Directors that includes the President of NWAC, the President or designate of each of the Provincial/Territorial Member Associations (PTMAs) as well as four Elders and four youth to represent the four directions. Currently, NWAC is tackling these key issues: educa-

tion, employment and labor, environment, health, human rights and international affairs and violence with a special focus on missing and murdered Aboriginal women and girls.

TERMS RELATED TO ABORIGINAL PEOPLES OF CANADA

Aboriginal people—Diverse groups living across the country. The Constitution Act of 1982 uses the term to refer to all Indigenous Canadians including Indians, Métis people, and Inuit people.

Band—a governing unit of the First Nations instituted by the Indian Act, 1876 which defines a body of Indians "for whose use and benefit in common, lands, the legal title to which is vested in Her Majesty, have been set apart; has funds held for it by the federal government, and is declared a band by the Governor-in-Council." There are 634 Bands.

Enfranchised Indians—Aboriginal people who have lost their Indian status, band membership and have the same rights as any Canadian citizen. Indians who served in the military during the world wars, for example, usually became enfranchised, losing their status as Indians.

First Nations people—term for Aboriginal people of a First Nation, a self-determined political and organizational unit (band/reserve) of the Aboriginal community.

Indian—an historical government term referring to the original inhabitants of North and South America and still used to define some Aboriginal peoples under the Indian Act. "Indian" has generally been replaced by "Aboriginal peoples," as defined in the Constitution Act of 1982.

Indian reserve—a tract of land granted to Native people for their use by the Crown and owned by the Crown; they cannot sell it or give it to anyone except the federal government. It is called a "usufructuary right. "

Inuit—The Inuit are those Aboriginal people who inhabit Canada's northernmost regions, including the Mackenzie Delta, the Northwest Territories, the northern coasts of Hudson Bay, the Arctic Islands, Labrador, and parts of northern Quebec. The Inuit were classified with registered Indians for program and jurisdictional purposes in 1939, by a decision of the Supreme Court of Canada. They are the smallest group of Canadian Aboriginal people.

Métis—Those who have ancestral connections to the Métis Nation, a group of Aboriginals with mixed ancestry. They are a distinct group registered with the Métis Nation and represented by the Métis National Council. The contemporary Métis are descendants of the Métis community that developed on the prairies in the 1800s, and of individuals who received land grants and/or scrip under the Manitoba Act, 1870, or the Dominion Lands Act, 1879. Statistics Canada now includes in the category of Métis all people living in any part of Canada who claim mixed Indian and non-Indian ancestry. Métis spokesmen themselves dispute the census figure and suggest the combined population of Métis and non-status Indians is close to one million. Approximately two-thirds of the Métis live in the provinces of Manitoba, Saskatchewan, and Alberta and in the Northwest Territories; the remainder are scattered throughout the rest of the country.

Native Peoples—a term established in the 1970s by the Canadian government as a more appropriate name for Aboriginal peoples.

Non-status Indian—Non-status Indians do not have a distinct constitutional standing but are grouped with the Métis for jurisdictional and public policy purposes. They are descendants of an Aboriginal people but do not meet the requirements of the Indian Act. People can meet the criteria and still not be registered as a Status Indian. The most common reason for loss of status was marriage of a registered Indian woman to a non-Indian. Loss of status has also occurred in other ways, such as voluntary renunciation, compulsory enfranchisement to non-Indian status, and failure of government officials to include some Indian families in the registry. The situation for many non-status Indians changed in 1985, when the federal government amended the Indian Act with Bill C-31 to restore registered Indian status to those women and their children who had lost it through marriage. Aboriginal women's groups welcomed this change.

Off-reserve Indians—people who do not live on their reserves, but may (or may not) be entitled to benefits of programs for other Canadian citizens.

On-reserve Indians—Residents of reserves; the Canadian government has jurisdiction over the reserves.

Status Indian—term for an Aboriginal person who is registered according to the rule of the Indian Act. Also called Registered Indian. To be registered, a Status Indian must have at least one parent registered as a Status Indian or is a member of a band that has signed a treaty. The Canadian government determines status and registration.

Treaty Indian—person who is a descendant of Indians who signed treaties with the colonial government.

TIMELINE OF A FEW SIGNIFICANT EVENTS OF ABORIGINAL PEOPLES OF CANADA

Year	Event
30,000–	Dated to this time, mammoth bones believed to be chipped by humans, 20,000 B.C.E. were discovered in the Yukon's Bluefish Caves in the 1970's. Other evidence of ancient peoples were found in different parts of Alberta.
11,000 B.C.E.	Archaeological sites dating to this time show that early traders created routes to market Batza Tena obsidian, prized for its beauty and sharp cutting edges.
10,500–	Weapons dating to this time have been found far away from the sources of 7,750 B.C.E. their raw material.
c. 1000 C.E.–1500 C.E.	Millions of artifacts and Huron and Iroquois villages dating to this time have been found beginning in the late 1800s.
1497	Giovanni Caboto (John Cabot) claims Cape Breton Island for England. Although he took evidence of Indigenous people back to England, he claims to have had no encounters with any people.
1576	Englishman Martin Frobisher sailed into a bay in present-day Nunavut (named after him), believing he found the route to China.
1606	Frenchman Marc Lescarbot's writes the earliest detailed records of Mi'kmaw life.
1607	Fur trade competition between the Mi'kmaq and Abenaki results in the eight -year Tarrateen War.
1608	The French abandon most of their posts in Acadia and Maine as they seek more lucrative opportunities in Québec.
1610	The Mi'kmaq created the Concordat Wampum Belt with the Vatican, asserting the right to choose either the Catholic or Mi'kmaq religion, or both. Mi'kmaq leader Kjikeptin Pesamoet spends a year in France and determines that accepting the Catholic religion would improve relations with French settlers. He is thought to be the first Indigenous North American to be baptized as a sign of alliance and friendship. At 100 years old, he changed his name to Henri Membertou.

Year	Event
1611	On his deathbed, Kjisaqmaw Maupeltuk rejects the Christian heaven as he wants to be with the rest of his deceased relatives.
1669	Pierre-Esprit Radisson, who worked for the English, sailed along the coast from the Rupert River to the Nelson River both in Hudson Bay. He is credited with laying the foundation for the Hudson Bay Company. He had been adopted by the Mohawk and spoke the language.
1673	Charles Bayly of the Hudson's Bay Company founded a fur-trading post originally called Moose Fort at what is now Moose Factory, Ontario.
1676	Maritime Indigenous Mi'kmaq, Maliseet, Passamaquoddy, Penobscot, and Abenaki Nations re-organized into the Waponahkiyik (Wabanaki Confederacy).
1749	The lowest point in Mi'kmaq-British relations was the scalp bounty the the British placed on Mi'kmaq "rebels."
1763	Royal Proclamation signed that explicitly recognizes Aboriginal title; Aboriginal land ownership and authority by the Crown as remaining intact under British sovereignty. Only the Crown could obtain lands from First Nations and only by treaty.
1778	Captain Cook explores the coast of present day British Columbia and claims it for Britain.
1793	Nuxálk and Carrier guides led Scottish explorer Alexander MacKenzie along the Nuxalk-Carrier Grease Trail, a 6,000-year-old road connecting present-day Montreal, Ontario with the Pacific. It was called the Grease Trails as First Peoples used it to trade oolichan (a Chinook word), a type of oily fish from the Pacific. Over the years, the grease dripped from their packs and gave the road its name. The historic route is part of the cultural legacy of First Peoples.
1799	Makenunatane "Swan Chief," a Dunne-za or Beaver Nation leader, warned his people of the coming changes. Their territory was in the area of present-day Alberta and British Columbia. To survive, he counseled them to live individually instead of communally and initiated fur trade with the Europeans.
1812 of 1812)	When the war ended, Native traditional life eroded rapidly as colonial society (War strengthened.
1821	Hudson's Bay Company established a northern branch in present-day Manitoba called York Factory and traded with the Swampy Cree (Maškēkowak / nēhinawak).
1839	Upper Canada enacts a law to protect Indian reserves, including Indian territory in with Crown lands.
1849	The first British Colony is established on Vancouver Island. The Crown gave trading rights to the Hudson's Bay Company. Head of the British fort, James Douglas began to purchase First Nations land and between 1850 an 1854, signing 14 treaties, until the colony ran out of treaty funds. Small reserves were created as protection from aggressive European settlers. Under Douglas, First Nations were able to buy land like Europeans, but after he retired First Nations people were not permitted to acquire "Crown land." Colonial officials maintained that First Nations title had never been established and therefore compensation was not necessary.

Year	Event
1858	A colony is established on the mainland of British Columbia because of the Fraser River Gold rush. Europeans and Americans argued that the land was empty, free to any immigrants.
1862	One third of the First Nations peoples of British Columbia perished in one of the worst small pox epidemics. It was the beginning of waves of epidemics that decimated First Nations populations.
1867	The British North America Act created Canada comprised of the British colonies of Canada, Nova Scotia, and New Brunswick, all federally united into one Dominion of Canada, also called a Confederation.
1870s	The first residential schools open; repercussions of their brutality are still felt today.
1871	British Columbia joins Dominion of Canada, although the predominately Native population was not included in the decision.
1871–1875	The first five of what are called Numbered Treaties (or Post-Confederation Treaties), are passed. They dealt with Native lands in northwestern Ontario, today's southern Manitoba, southern Saskatchewan and southern Alberta. Altogether, there were eleven treaties signed between the Aboriginal peoples and the reigning monarchs of Canada (Victoria, Edward VII or George V) from 1871 to 1921.
1876	The Indian Act is passed (and revised in 1951 and 1985), which controls the lives of First Nations people from birth to death. The Indian Act gives the federal government power to deny women status; initiate residential schools; create reserves; replace people's Aboriginal names with European names; forbid First Nations individuals to leave reserves without permission from Indian Agents; enforce enfranchisement of any First Nation person admitted to a university; confiscate reserve lands for roads, railways, and other public works, as well as relocate an entire reserve away from a town; lease out uncultivated reserve lands to non-First Nations for farming or grazing lands; make it illegal for First Nations to form political organizations; prohibit anyone, First Nation or non-First Nation, from soliciting funds for First Nation legal claims (this 1927 amendment granted the government control over First Nations to pursue land claims); ban the sale of alcohol and ammunitions to First Nations; prohibit pool hall owners from allowing First Nations people to enter; impose the "band council" system; forbid First Nations from speaking Native languages or practicing traditional religions; to declare potlatch and other cultural ceremonies illegal; forbid western First Nations from appearing in any public dance, show, exhibition, event or pageant wearing traditional clothing; deny First Nations the right to vote; create a permit system to control First Nations selling of agricultural products. It is a piece of legislation created under the British rule for the purpose of subjugating the Aboriginal people.
1879	The Blackfoot Confederacy (*Niitsitapi*) marks this year as *Itsistsitsis/awenimiopi*, meaning "when first/no more buffalo."
1880	Department of Indian Affairs established to oversee implementation of Indian Act.
1883	Secretary of State, Sir Hector-Louis Langevin, was an outspoken advocate of the Canadian Indian residential school system. He pushed hard to close day schools as he believed them inefficient in assimilating Aboriginal children. He argued: "The fact is that if you wish to educate the children you must separate them from their parents during

Year	Event
	the time they are being taught. If you leave them in the family they may know how to read and write, but they will remain savages, whereas by separating them in the way proposed, they acquire the habits and tastes … of civilized people."
1884	The federal government forbade potlatch ceremonies and gave the major responsibility for educating Native children to church operated residential schools. The people resisted these aggressive policies maintaining their hereditary titles still existed. Also, the Great Marpole Midden, an ancient Musqueam village and burial site was uncovered in Vancouver, British Columbia. In 1933, it was designated as a National Historic Site of Canada.
1885	Métis freedom fighter Louis Riel, leads the Métis people of Saskatchewan in an unsuccessful uprising called the Northwest Rebellion. Cree people were involved as well.
1887	A delegation of chiefs from the Tsimshian of Port Simpson and the Nisga'a on the Naas River traveled to Victoria, British Columbia, to petition the provincial government for the return of their territory as well as a formal treaty protecting their rights to remain on their ancestors' lands forever.
1888	*St. Catherines Milling v. The Queen* was a lawsuit that became the leading case on Aboriginal title in Canada for more than 80 years and concerned Ojibway lands in Ontario, the province, a lumber company and the federal government.
1889	First Nations peoples across Canada were forbidden to conduct or participate in any Indigenous ceremonies or practice traditional religions.
1893	Duncan Campbell Scott is appointed Deputy Superintendent General of the Department of Indian Affairs, which he oversees until 1932. He supported a policy of assimilation.
1894	Provisions to the Indian Act provided for compulsory school attendance of First Nations children and Industrial schools, which ran from 1883 to 1923. After 1923 these schools became known as residential schools. The federal government assimilation policy used schools to eliminate First Nations cultural beliefs and practices. Native parents were fined or jailed if they did not send their children to residential schools.
1899	At a protest blockade near Fort St. John, British Columbia, First Nations demanded a treaty and halted the rush of Klondike Gold rush miners. As a result, Treaty 8 was negotiated.
1900	The Beaver peoples suffering from disease and starvation, were the last band to sign Treaty 8.
1907	The Indian residential school (1907–1963) in Moose Factory, Ontario had the highest number of deaths among children attending residential schools, mostly from tuberculosis.
1909–1910	First Nations make application to King Edward VII to have the Privy Council determine Aboriginal title. The Privy Council Office is the secretariat of the federal cabinet that provides non-partisan counsel to the Prime Minister, leadership, departments and agencies of the government. The request was denied.

Year	Event
1910	British Prime Minister Wilfred Laurier visits British Columbia and supports recognition of Aboriginal rights. The provincial governments and federal governor are deeply divided.
1912–1916	New Anglo settlers in British Columbia pressure the government for Indian lands. The McKenna-McBride Royal Commission is appointed to study every First Nations group in British Columbia; in some places, additional lands were reserved while in others reserves were reduced in size.
1915	Allied Tribes of British Columbia was formed to lobby for treaty and title recognition.
1922	Kwakwaka'wakw Chief Dan Cranmer and his guests are arrested for attending his potlatch in Alert Bay, British Columbia. Sacred items and clothing were illegally confiscated and still have not been repatriated. Forty-five people were convicted; 17 imprisoned.
	In 1907, Peter Henderson Bryce, an Ontario Health Department official, documented the horrible conditions and high death rate of Aboriginal children in church-run residential schools. He was fired, but he self-published his report, *The Story of a National Crime: an Appeal for Justice* in 1922. His efforts were ignored by the government.
1927	The Indian Act is amended outlawing First Nations to raise money or retain a lawyer to press forward with land claims. Court actions are effectively blocked.
1931	The Native Brotherhood of British Columbia is established at Port Simpson, with delegates from Masset, Hartley Bay, Kitkatla, Port Essington and Metlakatla.
1942	The U.S. Army Forces selected Iqaluit's (Nunavut) current location as the site of a major air base.
1942–1952	Nutrition experiments were conducted on residential school children, as well as on children living on remote reserves. Dental care was withheld and some children were given vitamin supplements; others were given denatured food. All suffered from malnutrition; research was funded by the Canadian government as well as corporations. First Nations, already suffering from a loss of traditional food sources, were withheld staples like wheat flour on which they had come to rely. Inuit hunters were severely affected; many had to eat their sled dogs.
1949	First Nations people in British Columbia are permitted to vote at the provincial level. The Hudson Bay Company moved its trading post from Ward Inlet to Apex, Nunavut. Historically Apex was the place where most Inuit lived when Iqaluit was a military site.
1951	Parliament repeals some Indian Act provisions, including the banning of dances and ceremonies and the prohibition on land claims against the government. First Nations peoples were allowed to hire lawyers.
1955	Frobisher Bay, Nunavut became the center for U.S.–Canada DEW Line construction operations.
1960	First Nations people are allowed to vote in federal elections. The term, Sixties Scoop was coined by Patrick Johnston in his 1983 report "Native Children and the Child Welfare System." It refers to the Canadian practice, beginning in the 1960s and

Year	Event
	continuing until the late 1980s, of removing high numbers of children of Aboriginal peoples in Canada and fostering or adopting them out, usually into white families.
1960s	Quebec begins exploiting natural resources in Cree territory—James Bay Cree communities are uprooted many times.
1961	National Indian Council was created to represent Indigenous people of Canada, except for the Inuit.
1963	The federal government hired University of British Columbia anthropologist Harry B. Hawthorn to investigate the social conditions of Aboriginal. The Hawthorn Reports of 1966 and 1967 state that "Aboriginal peoples were Canada's most disadvantaged and marginalized population. They were "citizens minus." Hawthorn blamed this on years of failed government policy and the residential school system, which did not prepare students for the work force.
	The U.S. military moved out of Iqaluit.
1965	The Supreme Court upheld the treaty hunting rights of Vancouver Island Aboriginal peoples against provincial hunting regulations.
1968	Nunavut Arctic College was the first agency of government established in anticipation of the creation of Nunavut. In April 1999, it became Nunavut Arctic College when the territory of Nunavut was officially created. Community Learning Centers located in 25 communities of Nunavut bring programs to people throughout the territory.
1969	Prime Minister Trudeau and Minister of Indian Affairs Jean Chrétien, released *the White Paper*, promoting assimilation of First Nations people and dissolve any legal relationship between Aboriginal peoples and the state of Canada in favor of "equality." First Nations counter.
	Union of British Columbia Indian Chiefs formed.
1970s	Indigenous women go missing; the trend continues as many are found murdered. However, the RCMP puts little effort into resolving crimes against Native women. Aboriginal communities appeal for criminal investigations for over 30 years and their pleas go unanswered until 2015.
1970	Frobisher Bay was officially recognized as a Settlement, a village in 1974, and a town in 1980.
1972	The National Indian Brotherhood issues the Indian Control of Indian Education policy that rallies for parental responsibility and local control over education. The federal government accepts in 1973.
1973	In the *Calder* case, the Supreme Court rules that the Nisga'a did hold title to their traditional lands before B.C. was created. The Court splits evenly on whether Nisga'a still have title and the deciding judge dismissed the case on a technicality. The federal government adopts a comprehensive land claims policy. B.C. refuses to uphold the law.
1974	The Grand Council of the Crees, representing nine Northern Quebec Cree communities, is created in to protect Cree rights during hydro-development negotiations between the *Eeyouch* (Cree) and the Quebec and Canadian governments.
1975	After years of protesting the construction of hydroelectric projects on Native land by Native peoples, Quebec and Cree and Inuit communities sign the James Bay Agreement,

Year	Event
	opening the way for new hydro projects. The James Bay Project, initiated in 1971, was designed to produce electricity for Canada as well as for export to the United States. The design consisted of three phases, creating nine dams, thirty-seven generating stations, and thousands of miles of transmission lines. Canada is the world's leading producer of hydroelectric power, most has been the result of flooding and destruction of Indigenous territories. Opponents raise the issue of the negative impact on the thousands of Cree who live in the area, plus the long-term environmental effects of the altering the land on such a massive scale. Both points have been ignored.
1970s and 1980s	First Nations increase their efforts for Native rights and better political organization. Some provinces will still not recognize Aboriginal title nor negotiate treaties.
1982	Canada's Constitutional Act, Section 35, recognizes and affirms existing Aboriginal and treaty rights.
	The government of Canada agreed in principle to the creation of Nunavut.
1983	In a report by Patrick Johnston, he coins the term "Sixties Scoop" to describe the Canadian Native Children and the Child Welfare System practice (1960s to 1980s) of taking (scooping up) Aboriginal children from their families and placing them in foster homes or adopting them out to white families. Lawsuits against the government arose claiming that the practice resulted in a lost generation of children and destruction of culture.
1984	The Inuvialuit Claims Settlement Act gives control of the western Arctic resources to the Inuit.
1985	Changes to the Indian Act extend formal Indian status to the Métis, all enfranchised Aboriginals living off reserve land and Aboriginal women who had previously lost their status by marrying a non-Aboriginal man.
1986	The Supreme Court of British Columbia rules in favor of the Musqueam Band supporting their allegation that the government rented out their lands at a rate far beneath the market rate and gave them no say. Aboriginal groups gained a bit of hopefulness that the courts may be more willing to provide judicial sanction for what Indian peoples have always considered a cornerstone of their relationship with the Canadian state.
	The Quebec government announces plans for the Great Whale Project, which would dam and divert five rivers that flow into Hudson Bay and flood more than 2,000 square miles (5,180 square kilometers) of Cree and Inuit treaty land along the Great Whale River. Most of the power generated will be exported to the United States. James Bay Cree and environmental groups launch a campaign to stop the project.
1987	Frobisher Bay officially becomes Iqaluit, reverting to its original Inuktitut name, meaning "Place of Many Fish."
1989	The Premier's Council on Native Affairs is formed to meet with First Nations to draw up recommendations to the government in many areas. The Ministry of Aboriginal Affair is formed, with Jack Weisgerber as minister.
1990	Elijah Harper (1949–2013) a Chief of his Red Sucker Lake (Cree), Manitoba, held an eagle feather as he refused to accept the Meech Lake Accord because it did not deal

Year	Event
	with any First Nations concerns. Chief Harper was the first "Treaty Indian" in Manitoba to be elected to the Legislative Assembly of Manitoba.
	Mohawk activists engage in an armed stand-off with the Quebec police and Canadian army over the land at Oka. This crisis receives national attention First Nations across the country rally in support of Native rights and the Mohawks Aboriginal title and rights.
	In British Columbia, the *Sparrow v. Supreme Court* decision rules in favor of the Musqueam people's Aboriginal right to fish for food and ceremonial purposes. British Columbia also agreed to participate in First Nations and Canada treaty negotiations. First Nations, B.C. and Canada form a task force to develop a process for land claim negotiations in B.C.
1991	Chief Justice Allan McEachern refuses to hear the Gitxsan-Wet'suwet'en Chiefs' claim in the case of *Delgamuukw v. Her Majesty the Queen*.
	The Royal Commission on Aboriginal Peoples is established to address Aboriginal status issues illuminated by the Oka Crisis and the Meech Lake Accord.
	Cree Grand Chief Matthew Coon Come directs the Cree in a highly publicized protest against the Great Whale project. They take out a full-page advertisement in the *New York Times* and canoe from Hudson Bay to New York City to alert people from the United States of the dangers to the Cree and the environment.
1992–1994	At the First Nations Summit, Canada and B.C. establish the Treaty Commission. Negotiations take place.
1993	The Nunavut Land Claims Agreement was signed in Iqaluit.
1994	The Quebec government abandons the Great Whale Project, partly because of public concern over the harm it would cause to the environment and Cree and Inuit communities.
1995	In British Columbia the Gustafson Lake standoff was said to be the country's most expensive RCMP operation as the police confronted Indigenous activists and their supporters in a month long dispute. The Native people believed the area to be a sacred Shuswap territory. One of the occupiers convicted was James Pitawanakwat, sentenced to three years in jail. He fled to the United States and successfully fought extradition to Canada to finish his sentence, becoming the onlyCanadian Native person ever granted political asylum in the United States. According to Janice Stewart, a magistrate justice of the U.S. District Court in Oregon, "The Gustafsen Lake incident involved an organized group of native people rising up in their homeland against an occupation by the government of Canada of their sacred and unceded tribal land. The Canadian government engaged in a smear and disinformation campaign to prevent the media from learning and publicizing the true extent and political nature of these events." The incident drew support from around the world as a major military operation was directed at a small group of protesters.
	Nunavut residents selected Iqaluit as the capital of the new territory.
1996	The Nisga'a, British Columbia, and Canada sign an Agreement-in-Principle.

Year	Event
	Supreme Court of Canada sets out the test for proof of Aboriginal rights, which focuses on looking at practices, customs and traditions integral to maintaining First Nations cultures.
1998	Supreme Court hands down its unanimous decision on the *Delgamuukw Case*. The court ruled that Aboriginal title to the land had never been extinguished.
1999	The Territory of Nunavut created in the western Arctic—lands, including natural resources, will be controlled by the Inuit.
2000	The federal government approves the Nisaga'a Treaty, and agrees to pay $196 million over 15 years plus ensure communal self-government and control of natural resources in parts of northwestern British Columbia.
2001	Iqaluit received its order of official status as a city.
2002	Iqaluit, along with Nuuk, Greenland, co-hosted the first jointly hosted Arctic Winter Games. The Arctic Winter Games Arena was constructed in Iqaluit for the event.
	The Cree sign the landmark agreement (Paix des Braves) with Government of Quebec, which is an economic deal negotiated as a "nation to nation" agreement. Paix des Braves allows for continued hydroelectric development in exchange for Cree employment in the hydroelectric industry and $3.5 billion in financing over 50 years. The transaction will expand Cree infrastructure, including housing, community centers, health services and educational opportunities.
2005	The Kelowna Accord advocated for $5 billion to improve Native education, health care and living conditions, but the minority Liberal government falls before it can be implemented.
	Supreme Court of Canada rejects the Mi'kmaq claimed treaty right to harvest trees.
2008	Prime Minister Stephen Harper offers official apology to the former students of Indian residential schools, on behalf of the Government of Canada, June 11, 2008. Yet in 2009 at a press conference in the U.S., he states, "We [Canada] also have no history of colonialism."
	Truth and Reconciliation Commission of Canada (TRC) is organized as part of the Indian Residential Schools agreement to investigate and report on the charges of abuse and other ill effects for First Nations children that resulted from the Indian residential school legacy.
2010	Bill C-3 restores status under the Indian Act to grandchildren of Aboriginal women who lost their status through marriage to non-Aboriginal men.
	Canada signs the United Nations Declaration on the Rights of Indigenous Peoples.
2011	Churches apologize (1986 and 1994) for their part in the residential school system. However, the Canadian Conference of Catholic Bishops has never issued a formal apology.
2012	On International Human Rights Day (December 11, 2012), northern Ontario Attawapiskat Chief Theresa Spence started a hunger strike as a public call to Canadian Prime Minister Stephen Harper and the Governor General David Johnston to "initiate immediate discussions and the development of action plans to address treaty issues with First Nations across Canada." Her calm demeanor and peaceful resistance, which

Year	Event
	stressed the importance of dialogue, was televised across the country and the United States as she camped in her teepee in frigid conditions across from Parliament in Ottawa. I just could not take it anymore. I am in this resistance because the pain became too heavy." Chief Spence shared her feelings of alienation and pain she attributes to her residential school experiences. "It was a closed chapter, until one day you realize this generation is facing the same pain we felt at resident school. We want a life of freedom and not a life of pain and fear for the generation." At the same time, four Saskatchewan women, three Native and one non-Native (Jessica Gordon, Sylvia McAdam, Nina Wilson, and Sheelah McLean), had been using the internet to discuss the Canadian Bill C-45, the government's omnibus budget implementation bill that would severely alter control of Native lands and threaten environmental protections for hundreds of waterways. A movement, named Idle No More, was born through the communications among the four. It urged Native communities to continue their centuries of resistance to colonialism by standing up for their lands, sovereignty, cultures and rights. What started as a protest against a particular piece of legislation grew astronomically; the actions not only gained national attention, but spread to the United States and around the world. The movement was fueled by social media. Teach-Ins and Flash Round Dance events in malls, parks and other public places sprung up in tiny towns and large cities. Idle No More is inspired and nurtured by the ongoing incidents of Indigenous opposition to colonization, environmental destruction and by the strength of Indigenous traditional knowledge, cultures, and spirituality of the earth's original peoples. It is one of the largest mass movements in the history of Canada and because of the strong organizing efforts in its early formation, thousands of people can be rallied in a few hours.
	The interim report of the TRC reveals a lack of cooperation on the part of federal government and its failure to provide full access to documents requested by the commission.
2012	Harper holds a summit meeting with First Nations chiefs.
2015	Under the newly elected administration of Prime Minister Justin Trudeau, the Canadian government will begin its long-sought-for inquiry into missing and murdered Indigenous women and girls. In addition, British Columbia will beef up its safety measures on a highway north of Vancouver, nicknamed Highway of Tears as so many Native women disappear or are found murdered along that stretch of road.
	Prime Minister Trudeau appoints two Indigenous Ministers to his cabinet: Hunter Tootoo (Inuit) as Minister of Fisheries and Oceans and the Canadian Coast Guard; Jody Wilson-Raybould (We Wai Kai Nation) as Minister for Justice and Attorney General.
	Iqaluit, Nunavat, started construction on its first mosque for its Muslim population. It is the northernmost mosque in North America.

SOME KEY ISSUES TODAY

First Nations fought long and hard to convince the Canadian government to recognize its rights; no positive legislations or constitutional improvements came about because of the generosity of the federal system. While constitutional recognition signified a landmark achievement for Canadian Indians,

Inuit, and Métis, it did not eliminate the difficulties people struggle with on a daily basis to control their lands, economic stability, cultural preservation and future. The legacies of past government policies have left Aboriginal peoples as the most disadvantaged group in Canadian society. Poor health, high unemployment, substandard housing and incarceration rates are all higher than non-native Canadians. Aboriginal leaders see self-government for their peoples as the only way to improve conditions in their communities. More than 20 years after the passing of the Canadian Constitution Act, major concerns plague Aboriginal communities. Some of the key issues:

• Severe Funding Cuts to Child Welfare Programs—Indigenous-run, culturally appropriate projects designed to augment programs for Aboriginal families are severely underfunded. These projects include family court help programs, community gardens to eliminate child hunger, culturally sensitive training for social workers, etc. The break-down of these life-changing community assistance programs usually can be blamed on government administration far above the community level.

• Staggering Number of Unresolved Cases of Missing Aboriginal Women—Over 1,200 Aboriginal women have been missing and/or murdered since 1990. Yet less than half of the cases have been investigated by Canadian police and of those, less than a quarter have been solved. Activist organizations like Idle No More, Amnesty International, the Inter-American Commission on Human Rights, and Sing Our Rivers Red have been clamoring for a national inquiry. A documentary, *Highway of Tears*, brings attention to a 450-mile (724-kilometer) stretch of highway in northern Alberta, site of several of the disappearances and murders. In December 2015, newly elected Prime Minister Justin Trudeau agreed to go forward with an investigation.

• Poor Health Care—A 2009 UNICEF report has shown that Aboriginal children are twice as likely to be hospitalized for preventative diseases, stemming from substandard primary medical services. Although the country's universal health care system has been internationally praised for having excellent practices, Aboriginal peoples do not receive the same quality care. Part of the problem is that there are government loopholes as to who is responsible for funding.

• Environmental Health and Predatory Mining Companies—Across Canada, mining projects threaten not only Aboriginal homelands, but also the health of the planet. Indigenous communities have been promised royalties, but activists maintain the pittance the people would receive would not be worth the permanent ecological destruction. For instance, in northeastern Alberta, the epicenter of the Athabasca Tar Sands operation is marked by polluted air and toxic ponds chemically laced with arsenic, mercury and carcinogenic hydrocarbons—almost 2,000 ducks died after landing in one of these tailings ponds in 2008. Tailings are a wastewater residue caused by a byproduct of tar sands processing. The ponds are draining into the Athabasca River, which flows into the Mackenzie—the largest river system in Canada—and finally ending up in the Arctic Ocean. Area communities have experienced an increase in cancer. The Athabasca delta once boasted clean rivers, pristine lakes and a healthy boreal forest. Now it is a devastated ecosystem of deforestation with open pit mines and a watershed filled with tumor laden fish. Caribou herds as well as other species have been reduced to a dangerously low level. The Tar Sands project and its proposed Keystone Pipeline are the world's largest industrial project. In 2015, the safety apparatus malfunctioned and spewed 1.3 million gallons (4.9 million liters) of toxic chemicals into a vast area on and adjacent to the Fort McMurray First Nation lands. "Our biggest concern is the land," said Fort McMurray First Nation band councilor Byron Bates to the Canadian Press. "In 50 or 70 years, the oil companies are going to be gone. We want to be able to use our land again. Our biggest concern is to make sure it's brought back to pristine condition." Canadian First Nations have taken the lead in confronting this major ecological disaster, which has terrible repercussions for the entire world. Communities including the Mikisew Cree First Nation, Athabasca Chipewyan First Nation, Fort McMurray First Nation, Fort McKay Cree Nation, Beaver Lake Cree First Nation Chipewyan Prairie First Nation, and the Métis, have organized resistance; Indigenous peoples throughout North America have taken up the struggle to halt the expansion of the tar sands. The land and water rights of Native communities and the safety laws of the entire country have been ignored by the Harper Conservative administration. With the 2015 election of Liberal Party head Justin Pierre James Trudeau, First Nations peoples and environmentalists hope that the predatory mining companies throughout Canada will be constrained and checked.

- Community Healing from the residential school system atrocities—the Truth and Reconciliation Commission completed a seven year investigation in 2015 bringing to light a century of abuse of Native children and their families. Starting in the mid-1800s and ending in 1996, Aboriginal children were removed from their homes and communities and placed in residential schools, operated by various churches with the sanction of the federal government. Like the U.S, the goal was to "de-Indianize" the children by destroying language, culture, as well as familial and community ties. Children as young as four were ripped from their parents and sent off to these unsafe, unsupervised institutions. Upwards of 4,000 Aboriginal children died due to school fires, physical as well as sexual abuses, and unhealthy living conditions. Of the almost two hundred thousand who survived, they suffered the effects of sexual, mental, and physical abuse, shame, humiliation, and deprivation. This torture inflicted on a century of Native peoples affected the health of their communities. However, many of these survivors organized and got the Indian Residential Schools Settlement Agreement passed. The Truth and Reconciliation Commission was founded to provide a holistic and comprehensive response to the charges and ill effects for First Nations children that resulted from the Indian residential school legacy. The Commission was officially established on June 2, 2008, and it was completed in June 2015. From the final report: " Reconciliation must support Aboriginal peoples as they heal from the destructive legacies of colonization that have wreaked such havoc in their lives. But it must do even more. Reconciliation must inspire Aboriginal and non-Aboriginal peoples to transform Canadian society so that our children and grandchildren can live together in dignity, peace, and prosperity on these lands we now share."

POPULATION

The Aboriginal peoples of Canada are a small segment of the total population, but they have had a major role in the country's history. They are also the largest growing segment of the population as well as the poorest. The 2011 National Household Survey (NHS) counted 1,400,685 people with Aboriginal identity in 2011, 4.3% of the total population. The Aboriginal population increased by 232,385 people, or 20.1% between 2006 and 2011, compared with 5.2% for the other Canadians.

The largest numbers of Aboriginal people reside in Ontario and the western provinces (Manitoba, Saskatchewan, Alberta, and British Columbia). Aboriginal people made up the largest percentage of the population of Nunavut and the Northwest Territories.

Almost 852,000 people identified as First Nations—60.8% of the total Aboriginal population and 2.6% of the total Canadian population. Almost 638,000 were counted as being Registered Indians, 74.9% of all First Nations people, 45.5% of the total Aboriginal population and 1.9% of the total Canadian population. One-quarter of First Nations people (213,900) were not Registered Indians, representing 15.3% of the total Aboriginal population and less than 1% of the total Canadian population. The Cree are the largest group of First Nations, with over 200,000 members and 135 registered bands.

In 2011, 451,795 people identified as Métis, 32.3% of the total Aboriginal population and 1.4% of the total Canadian population. However, Métis spokesmen dispute the census figure and suggest the combined population of Métis and non-status Indians is close to one million. The Métis population was 8.0% of the total population of the Northwest Territories, 6.7% of Manitoba's population, and 5.2% of Saskatchewan's population. In metropolitan areas, Winnipeg had the highest population of Métis, 46,325 people, or 6.5% of its total population, followed by Edmonton with 31,780, Vancouver (18,485) and Calgary (17,040). In addition, 11,520 Métis lived in Saskatoon and 9,980 in Toronto.

There were 59,445 people identified as Inuit in 2011, representing 4.2% of the total Aboriginal population and 0.2% of the total Canadian population. Almost three-quarters of Inuit live in Inuit Nunangat (Inuit for territory), which extends from Labrador to the Northwest Territories and comprises four regions: Nunatsiavut, Nunavik, Nunavut, and the Inuvialuit region.

Although Aboriginal peoples remain widely distributed throughout rural Canada, recent decades have witnessed a growing migration to urban areas. In western urban centers such as Vancouver, Edmonton, Calgary, Regina, Saskatoon, and Winnipeg, Aboriginal peoples comprise a substantial portion of the population. The Department of Indian Affairs and Northern Development (DIAND) estimates that approximately one-third of status Indians now live off their reserves.

A CLOSER LOOK AT THE MÉTIS

Métis culture combines many traditions, mainly Cree, Ojibwa, Saulteaux, French and English. Early European fur traders intermarried with Native women; their children grew up knowing these heritages, and it is said this blending of societies made more successful trading relationships. Native people often pushed the unions of their European trading partners and Native women thinking these marriages would benefit their trade business. The women were cultural interpreters, helped resolve intercultural conflicts, and were able to protect Native interests. The European men were fed, clothed, and guided by their wives. Métis were often valuable employees of both fur trade companies: the North-West Company (NWC) and the Hudson's Bay Company (HBC) as they were skilled voyageurs, buffalo hunters, traders, and interpreters. Many aspects of all cultures were retained by descendants of these marriages. For instance, the Métis have blended spiritual traditions of both Native and Christian religions. Christianity, which was usually forced upon them, was incorporated, but traditional values were not forgotten. The Métis people also developed a unique language called "Michif", which is a mixture of both French and Native words and grammar.

Music is a key element of Métis culture and they are best known for their fiddle traditions. After the French and Scots introduced fiddles, the Métis put a new twist on the instrument and the sounds it produced. Due to their high costs, they even began making the fiddles, which have a distinct sound. The bottom string of the fiddle is tuned up from a G to an A; songs are based on syncopation with extras beats to accompany dancing. Heavy in percussive qualities, tunes feature the fiddle and blend in a variety of other instruments like concertina, harmonica, hand drum, mouth harp, and finger instruments (like bones and spoons) and even stomping. Fiddlers dance too, keeping up the frantic pace and never losing the song or the beat. The Red River Jig is a dance style driven by the fiddle music. More a reel than a jig, dancers often compete to see who has the liveliest, most complicated footwork. A local yarn says that "the way to drive a Métis crazy is to nail his moccasins to the floor and play the Red River Jig Métis melodies."

Renown throughout the world for their floral beadwork, the Métis are sometimes referred to as the 'Flower Beadwork People'. The symmetrical work is usually fashioned on a black or dark blue background and adorns jackets, bags, leggings, moccasins gloves, vests and horse gear. Métis often had to sell their beadwork to status Indians, who then sold it to Europeans as buyers valued art by those they considered to be "real Indians." Another popular Métis art form is the Métis or L'Assomption Sash; the hand woven sashes were the most identifiable piece of Métis dress and became a symbol of their people. The name is derived from the small Québec community of L'Assomption, where the tradition began. During the fur trade, they were used as back supports for the voyageurs in their canoes. They are woven from wool yarn, mainly red and blue; different designs represent different families. In historic times, the decorative fringed ends of the sashes doubled as an emergency sewing kit. The long sashes were wrapped around the body and held belongings close at hand. Historical Métis clothing was usually decorated with elaborate designs and colors, which had specific meanings: Red was for the blood spilled fighting for Métis rights; Blue represented the strength of the Métis spirit; Green stood for the fertility of the Métis Nation; White signified the powerful connection to the earth and the creator; Yellow stood for the hope of the future and Black represented oppression.

A CLOSER LOOK AT FIRST NATIONS

Like the United States, First Nations are grouped together by region, language, culture, geography. The six groups are: Woodland—those nations in eastern Canada, whose homelands are dense boreal forests; Iroquoian—those nations in the most southern part of Canada, whose territory boasts fertile agricultural lands; Plains First Nations, whose Prairie grasslands are located in western Canada in present-day Manitoba, Saskatchewan, and Alberta; Plateau First Nations, located mainly in British Columbia and whose area went from semidesert conditions in the south to high mountains and dense forest in the north; Pacific Coast First Nations, whose historical homelands are in present-day British Columbia along the coast; and the First Nations of the Mackenzie and Yukon River Basins (present-day British Columbia, Alberta, and Saskatchewan), whose severe environment is marked by dark forests, barren lands, and the swampy area known as muskeg.

Within these vastly diverse areas are hundreds of nations with different languages, religions, histories, customs, arts, diets, transportation, and housing. There are far too many to highlight in an appendix; some examples by area:

Woodland

The Mi'kmaq peoples have ancient traditions that are perfectly suited for their rugged sea-swept peninsula in present-day maritime provinces. At the Glooscap Heritage Centre and Mi'kmaq Museum in Millbrook, Nova Scotia, visitors can learn how the traditions of drama, art, music, spirituality, history, and language enriched the area. Mi'kmaq towns were located by rivers and bays and related by alliance and kinship. Leadership, based on prestige rather than power, focused on the efficient operation of the fishing and hunting economy. Painting, music, and oratorical skills were valued. The first European contact was with Portuguese, Basque, English, and French fishermen and some fur trading was established for European made metal axes and knives. In the 1600s the French claimed Nova Scotia as part of Acadia, using trade and Roman Catholic missionaries to build pleasant relations with the Mi'kmaq, who became their allies against the British until the 1760s. The Mi'kmaq nation's first treaty with a European nation was an agreement with the Vatican and the Holy See in 1610; the treaty was recorded on a wampum belt, whose symbols represented the incorporation of Mi'kmaq spirituality within the context of Roman Catholicism.

The Mi'kmaq are known for their fine boat making skills; their traditional canoe is wide-bottomed, raised at both ends and the sides curve upwards in the middle. This design facilitated deep sea navigation as well as ease of travel in shallow streams and fast-moving rapids. Constructed of birch bark formed around a light wooden frame, the small canoe could carry several thousand pounds of cargo, but was light enough for one person to carry. Traditionalist Todd Labrador builds the sailing crafts in the way of his ancestors. He also teaches the famous birch bark basket technique. Mi'kmaq were often nicknamed the "porcupine people" for their intricate art and fine detail using porcupine quills in their elaborately decorated Quill and birch bark baskets. They were highly prized by European and American collectors; their unique patterns and bright colors distinguish their creations from other quill artists.

Iroquoian

The Haudenosaunee, or "People of the Longhouse," are also called the Iroquois or Six Nations (See Northeast chapter). The Haudenosaunee have been staunch resistors of colonial assimilationist policies on both sides of the US/Canadian border. A key example of their fortitude is their insistence in making sure the Jay Treaty of 1794 is honored by both governments. The treaty recognized and upheld the rights of all Aboriginal peoples to cross the Canadian/U.S. border freely as the border divided Native nations and pushed foreign citizenship and governance on them. The Akwesasne Mohawk reserve is located on both sides of the border around Cornwall, Ontario. In 1968, Mohawk Grand Chief Michael Mitchell was arrested for failing to pay duty on items he had taken from the Canadian side of the reserve to the American side. Mohawks formed a blockade of the Seaway International Bridge, which passes through the reserve, forcing Canada to uphold the treaty and recognize the right to duty-free passage. The conflict arose again in 1988 when the event was repeated as Chief Mitchell again transported goods across the border and refused to pay. In 2001, the Supreme Court of Canada ruled that the treaty did not necessarily exempt Aboriginals from paying duty. In 2009, the Canadian Border Services Agency was to issue firearms to its agents to enforce the new policy. However, Akwesasne leadership and supporters determined that they would not allow guns on reserve lands and called for negotiations. Their request was ignored, but the border station was abandoned. Today, the facility is still empty and is a reminder of the contentious practice of enforcing a foreign border that cuts through Aboriginal territory.

It is ironic that over a century ago, the legendary Mohawk ironworkers honed their craft by constructing the Seaway International Bridge across Mohawk lands. They went on to build New York City as well as other cities across the border and around the world; they are recognized as being the best at high steel construction. On Friday nights, Mohawks who work in New York City make the six-and-a-half hour drive home to the Kahnawkae Reserve, near Montreal, along the Great Northway or I-87. Sunday night, they head back for a week of "skywalking."

It is not just these seasoned generations of specialty tradesmen who have garnered attention on both sides of the border. The art of "raised beadwork" in all its splendor and magnificence, has earned Mohawk artists, usually women, international fame. This art form of raised beadwork, developed in the last quarter of the nineteenth century, adds texture and interest to the Mohawk motifs of bold patterned flowers, leaves and birds. Northeastern Indians put their own spin on the European influence of glass bead work and began to appliqué-beaded pictures of curvy flowers on vine tendrils onto black velvet. Borders were stylized and intricate. "Whimsies" were invented for the souvenir market during the Victorian era. Mohawk artists, not only kept up with this whimsical trend, but their colorful and eclectic inventory of whimsies raised the art to another level. At first, beadwork was utilitarian, used to decorate everyday objects like bags and moccasins. But with the birth of whimsies, boot shaped pincushions, strawberries, needle cases, scissor cases, smoking caps, picture frames, jewelry, bird ornaments, horseshoes, canoes, watch holders, whisk brooms, and match holders were brilliantly stitched with tiny glass beads. They capitalized on the Victorian fad of collecting hanging boxes by decorating them with ornate beadwork.

The non-utilitarian whimsies as well as the ornately beaded bags became an important source of income for Iroquois women helping to support their families, especially during the construction off-season. In the late nineteenth and early twentieth centuries, they were also sold at train stations and by Mohawk entertainment groups traveling with Wild West shows. Today, these art pieces are still sold at Niagara Falls tourist shops as well as other sites near Mohawk communities, art galleries and of course, Etsy and Ebay. Modern shapes feature red, hot pink, or turquoise velvet scalloped rectangles, valentines and a wide variety of birds. Artists like Barbara Little Bear Delisle, Kahnawkae resident, not only has a following for her work, but she is passing it on to the next generation.

Plains

The Cree are the largest group of First Nations in Canada, with over 300,000 members and more than 136 registered bands. The official census is probably an undercount. Their combined reserve lands are also the largest of any First Nations group. Eight major groups make up the Cree: Attikamekw, James Bay Cree, Montagnais, Moose Cree, Naskapi, Plains Cree, Swampy Cree, and Woods Cree; they live in the provinces of Alberta, Quebec, Ontario, Manitoba, and Saskatchewan plus major cities. There are different dialects of Cree; most also speak both French and English. The Cree often chose home-lands far away from other groups, but were very open to intertribal marriage. Today, many Cree are employed in oil, forestry, or mining professions.

A 1926 Edward S. Curtis photograph features three Cree birch bark baskets, finely crafted and "picture perfect." The Cree have had a long tradition of creating every imaginable container out of birch bark as trees were the most readily available material. The vessels were an important trade commodity and used for cooking, transporting goods and even for storing the prized "grease." Today, the art continues, although it is no longer a trading mainstay. First Nations' people often give birch bark baskets as gifts for Elders, honored guests or to as a tribute to community members for their good deeds.

An ancient art form is Birch Bark biting, practiced and perfected by the Cree hundreds of years ago. The technique consists of folding birch bark several times until it is a triangular shape. Then the artist bites designs into a triangle. Traditionally this art form was done by just a few skilled artisans; contests would be held among biters for the best creations. In historical times, designs were primarily used as patterns on leather clothing. The process of basket making and birch bark biting is an arduous task. First the artist must find just the right piece of bark from a young, supple tree. Five or six sheets can be obtained from a good piece of bark. Large works are rare as the bark cannot have any flaws or blemishes. Then the bark is separated into layers, which requires time and patience. The folding is next and must be precise; sometimes the artist traces the design on the bark with a fingernail, but the most esteemed artists just see the design in their mind and bite away. By using the eye tooth and changing the pressure of each bite, the artist can create shade, texture and intricate detail. The next step is unfolding the bark to reveal the beautiful and symmetrical pictures of a variety of wildlife themes as well as people. Famous birch bark artists like Cree Elder, Sally Milne from Saskatchewan are internationally renowned for the rare artform, which can be found in museums and private collections around the world.

Plateau

The Secwepemc, also known as Shuswap, are a Nation of 17 bands based in the south-central part of British Columbia. Before European contact in the late eighteenth century, the immense 56,000 square miles of Secwepemc homelands stretched from the Columbia River valley on the east slope of the Rocky Mountains to the Fraser River on the west and from the upper Fraser River in the north to the Arrow Lakes in the south. The Nation was organized into an alliance that monitored resources, land use and provided protection for its citizens. Each band was autonomous, but united by a common language—Secwepemctsin—and a similar culture. The economy was based on fishing, hunting and trading.

In the nineteenth century, the Secwepemc way of life and lands were changed by European fur traders, missionaries, gold miners, and settlers. Anglo disease epidemics devastated the Native population; the largest smallpox outbreak in 1862, wiped out 32 villages of the Shuswap. In addition, the British Crown authority replaced the Hudson Bay Company's fur trade monopoly and established Indian reserves. In 1871, British Columbia became a province; the federal Department of Indian Affairs took control of every detail of Secwepemc life. With the blessings of the federal government, the Catholic Church began to convert large groups of Secwepemc peoples followed by era of boarding schools—both disrupted traditional lifeways.

Like many Native groups, the Secwepemc peoples have taken steps to rebuilding their nation and preserving their traditions. Some of their efforts have been home-grown; others have taken them outside their communities to join with other First Nations in seeking justice. The Secwepemc have been an example in recreating a healthy community and have established a number of organizations, institutions and initiatives. For instance, the Secwepemc Cultural Education Society provides a link to the past, an affirmation of the present and a confirmation that there will be a future. The Society created the Secwepemc Ethnobotanical Gardens in 1999 to encourage the continuance and preservation of Secwepemc language, culture and use of native plants. The Secwepemc people were masters of plant medicines and regaining that skill can certainly help the community and heal many contemporary health challenges.

Pacific Coast

The Gitxsan (people of the Skeena River) had an economy that was based on the salmon trade along with other products derived from the vast abundance of natural resources in their territory. They were part of the "grease" trade route established for the bartering of oolichan (candle fish) grease. They are historically allied with their neighbors, Wet'suwet'en with whom they waged a court battle for land rights against British Columbia known as *Delgamuukw v. the Queen*.

The foundation of Gitxsan traditional government is the Wilp and clan system, the key units of society well organized through kinship lines. There are 45 to 65 Wilps, groups comprised of maternally related kin of 20 to 250 members. Each person also belongs to one of four clans. The Wilp and clan determine most aspects of life including property ownership, economic endeavors, residences, education, marriage, inheritance, political activity, and social relationships. The origin of each clan begins with an ancient account that has been handed down through the centuries. Clan members share common ancestors, family crests, properties and privileges; crests are worn on regalia such as dresses, aprons, headpieces, and button blankets used as robes.

The Gitxsan distinctive and spectacular ceremonial robes have been acclaimed the world over for their intricate patterns of Abalone shell buttons. One can determine the wearer's family clan and historical status by the central design on the robe, which can be of three different lengths. The blankets were originally trade items from the Hudson's Bay Company during the mid-nineteenth century, but the Gitxsan and other coastal groups made them their own with decorations of red flannel appliqué and abalone or dentalium shells. Traditionally, they were part of an outfit worn during dance ceremonies; as the wearer danced around the longhouse, the beautiful and intricate patterns were displayed in a grand way. The iconic ceremonial robes became a new tradition and are still made today. The dancer or speaker who wears them for ceremony exudes spiritual power, prestige and respect. Today at the Youth Helping Youth Mentorship Program in Hazelton, British Columbia, young people can learn button blanket construction along with many other traditional arts. The organization is an artistic hub fostering a new generation of artists through mentorship, demonstrations, workshops, tutorials, and traditional learning resources.

MACKENZIE AND YUKON RIVER BASINS

Tłicho (Dogrib)

Tłicho, also known as Dogrib, are a group of Dene and part of the Athapaskan language family. Their name for themselves is Doné, meaning "the People." To differentiate themselves from their Dene neighbors—Denesuline, Slavey, Sahtu Got'ine and K'asho Got'ine—they call themselves Tłicho, meaning "dog's rib." Their territory is east of the Mackenzie River between Great Slave Lake and Great Bear Lake in the Northwest Territory. Their close-knit extended families make it easy to move from one band to another. From a decimated mid-nineteenth century population of around 800, they have at least tripled their numbers.

From ancient times to the present, the Tłicho have depended on the caribou herds; hunting them in the boreal forest during winter and following them to the edge of the barrens in spring and fall. Moose, rabbits, waterfowl and fish have also been a part of their of their diet. The first trading post established on Tłicho lands at the beginning of the nineteenth century, involved them in the fur trade. They survived an attack by the another Dene group and eventually established a lasting peace with the Yellowknife band. Roman Catholic missionaries came into their territory around 1859. Schools weren't established in their towns until the late 1950s. Behchoko (formerly Rae-Edzo) has transformed into a year-round settlement for hundreds of Tłicho. Other, smaller settlements include Detah, near the city of Yellowknife, and hamlets at Whati (formerly Lac la Martre), Gameti (formerly Rae Lakes), and Wekweeti (formerly Snare Lake). In the isolated hamlets, the traditional dependence on hunting, fishing and fur trapping remains crucial. Fur trapping has been declining steadily since the late 1980s; probably as a consequence of the animal-rights movements. With the recent development of four diamond mines within traditional Tłicho lands, many men and women are employed by the mines or the mining support industries.

In 1921 the Tłicho, with other Dene groups of Great Slave Lake, signed Treaty 11. With increasing development pressure in the Mackenzie River valley during the 1960s and 1970s, and with many provisions of the treaty that were never fulfilled, the Dene lobbied the federal government to secure their political, land, and other rights in the NWT. Starting in 1981, the Tłicho united under the Dene nation to negotiate a wide-ranging land claim. Final negotiations failed in 1990; in 1995, the Tłicho began negotiating a separate land claim with the federal government. The outcome provided the Tłicho with ownership of a 15,058 square mile block of land, shared management rights over Crown Land within the claim area, $152 million in compensation paid out over 14 years and a share of federal mineral royalties from the Mackenzie Valley. The Tłicho also gained law-making authority over citizens their lands including education, adoption, child and family services, training, income support, social housing, and Tłicho language and culture.

The Tłicho government is spending much of their funds on the education of Tłicho youth. In 1991, the Tłicho school board devised the educational policy, "strong like two people," building on traditional Tłicho culture and values, infusing them into standard curriculum. Lessons extend far beyond the classroom as students take part in summer canoe trips or winter hunting camps where cultural practices are stressed and children learn from Tłicho traditionalists. By providing their children with this "combined" education, elders believe the children will grow to be "strong like two people."

Inuit

A new territorial flag rose on April 1, 1999 in the Arctic as Nunavut (meaning "our land" in the Inuktitut language), was created. Fireworks and festivals filled the day that Canada's Inuit people finally had a political voice, local autonomy and could govern themselves. The arduous work of negotiations to create the new territory began in 1976, when the Inuit Tapirisat of Canada (now called Inuit Tapiriit Kanatami) and the federal government of Canada discussed dividing the Northwest Territories (NT) to provide a separate territory for the Inuit. In 1982, a plebiscite on division was held throughout the NT and a majority of the residents voted in favor. The land claims agreement was completed in 1992 and ratified by 85 percent of the voters. In 1993, the Canadian Parliament passed the Nunavut Land Claims Agreement Act and the Nunavut Act, which carved Nunavut out of more than half of the NT.

The new territory of Nunavut, which spans three time zones, now contains 808,190 square miles (2,093,190 square kilometers) of ice and snow (about one fifth of Canada and about the size of Western Europe). Nunavut Tourism calls it "one of the largest unspoiled natural paradises on the planet." The *Lonely Planet* guidebook suggests that readers "Picture a treeless, ice-encrusted wilderness lashed by unrelenting weather with a population density that makes Greenland seem claustrophobic." Inuit people have lived on this land high in the Canadian arctic for more than 4,000 years. In Nunavut, the time when the sun disappears and day becomes night is known as "the great darkness." The sun doesn't appear for seven weeks. It skirts below the horizon, offering a few hours of dim light.

As of 2011, the total population of Nunavut was estimated to be around 33,330 people, the vast majority (84 percent) of whom are Inuit. The Inuktitut word for "Inuit" means "human beings" or "the people." The name also refers to the Indigenous people of Nunavut as well as those living in the Northwest Territories, Greenland, and northern part of Alaska. Nearly three quarters of all the Inuit living in Nunavut are less than forty years old.

Some Europeans and Americans still refer to the Inuit as Eskimos, but the Inuit people consider that term to be pejorative. According to Nunavut Tourism, "European colonists and explorers adopted this old Alqonquin name for the Inuit, but the correct Inuktitut term is "Inuit"—the name they call themselves, the plural word for all the Inuit people. The proper singular Inuktitut term for an individual Inuit person is "Inuk."

According to the government of Nunavut, there are 26 communities spread across the territory. A visitor cannot drive to Nunavut and its communities because they are not linked together by highways. Traveling between Nunavut communities is usually done by aircraft or cruise ship. In some cases, it's possible to reach another community by snowmobile, dogsled expedition, or powerboat.

The traditional lifestyle of the Inuit is remarkably adapted to extreme aortic conditions. Their skills for survival have always been hunting (the core of Inuit culture), fishing, and trapping. Agriculture has not been possible in the enormous tundra landscapes and icy coasts stretching across the top of the world from Siberia to Greenland.

There are four official languages in Nunavut: Inuktitut, English, French, and Inuinnaqtun, a variant of the Inuit language spoken in westernmost communities. Inuktitut is the language of 70 percent of Nunavut; English is the first language of 27 percent of the population, French and Inuinnaqtun about 1.5 percent each.

Iqaluit

It's a three-and-half-hour flight to Iqaluit (pronounced *ee-ka-loo-eet*), Nunavut, located on the south coast of Baffin Island at the head of Frobisher Bay (Iqaluit's former name, after Martin Frobisher, who "discovered the bay in 1576). Its name means "place of many fish." It is the only city in Nunavut and also was chosen to become the capital, administrative center, and the political, business, journalism, and transportation hub of this huge territory in a Nunavut-wide plebiscite in 1995. It's now home to many Inuit artists, filmmakers, and musicians. Iqaluit are called *Iqalummiut* (singular *Iqalummiuq*).

Iqaluit has a typical Arctic climate. The city has cold winters and brief summers too cool to permit the growth of trees. Perhaps that's why shrubs are classified as trees. According to a tourist who visited Iqaluit during August, it is "still steeped in traditional ways. Women strolled down Iqaluit's main drag in the 'summer version' of Inuit dress-long embroidered parkas made of cotton or wool, rather than sealskin, their babies tucked into the oversized hoods that hand down their backs." They also carry disposable diapers.

Thousands of years ago Iqaluit was uncharted land, where ancient explorers hunted and camped, drawn by the lands and waters that were prime hunting and fishing rounds. In the eighteenth and nineteenth centuries, other explorers, whalers, and missionaries from Europe and North America arrived. Iqaluit later evolved into a strategic military location during World War II, when, in 1942, it became an American airbase. The base was intended to provide a stopover and refueling site for short range aircraft ferried across the Atlantic to support the war effort in Europe. (At the end of World War II, the American airbase was turned over to the Royal Canadian Air Force). During this time, many Inuit from surrounding camps were recruited to help construct the airstrip, aircraft hangers, and other buildings. In 1950, the Hudson's Bay Company trading post moved to Iqaliut, followed by the arrival of supplies and workers to construct the eastern section of the DEW Line (Distant Early Warning) radar system. Hundreds of construction workers, military personnel, and administrative staff moved into the community. The American military left Iqaluit in 1963.The Canadian government urged hundreds of Inuit people to settle permanently in Iqaluit and other communities with doctors, schools, and social services. Today it's a transportation hub to other Baffin Island communities, as well as to Greenland. On January 1, 1987, the name of the municipality officially changed from "Frobisher Bay" to "Iqaluit," the name Inuit people had always used. In April 2001, Iqaluit was officially redesignated as a city.

You can walk from the center of town, with its impressive modern legislative building (the legislators seats are lined with caribou fur) and governmental offices, to the treeless tundra in about twenty minutes. One might even pass an *inuksuk*, legendary stone markers that Inuit traditionally built as landmarks on many parts of the tundra. Some inuksuit were built to look like humans, to help hunters lead caribou into lakes where they could be more easily killed from a kayak. Like many Nunavut communities, Iqaluit is only accessible by aircraft, dogsled, snowmobile, and some boats. There are no roads leading from Iqaluit to anywhere.

Igloolik

Igloolik (spelled "Iglulik" in Inuktitut) is a vibrant artistic community situated on a small island north of the Arctic Circle between the Canadian mainland and Baffin Island. It is considered to be a cultural epicenter for the Inuit people. Igloolik is also home to Artcirq, the only Inuit circus troupe in the world, and each summer the hamlet hosts the Rockin' Walrus Arts Festival. Igloolik, which was inhabited 4,000 years ago, offers visitors an opportunity to experience the Inuit way of life and enjoy the Northern Lights.

"In traditional times, the day the sun emerged was once the most important day of the year for Inuit people in Igloolik. The first person who saw the sun return, signaling the end of the dark season, would rush back to the sod houses or igloos to tell everyone," 96-year-old Rose Iqalliyuq said through an interpreter. The return of the sun was good news for hunters who could then see far away. People built a great igloo and soapstone lamps, filled with lumps of pink seal blubber which provided illumination during the long nights, were extinguished in a ceremony. Today, the sun festivities take place in school gyms where people welcome back the sun, chant over ceremonial drums, and finish up with a western style square dance. The festival has become a good way to pass on traditional knowledge to youngsters.

The award-winning movie *Atanarjuat* (*The Fast Runner*), 2001, was produced and filmed in Igloolik. Directed by Zacharias Kunuk (Inuk), the nearly three-hour film, based on an ancient Arctic story about a shamanic curse put on the people of Igloolik, became the first feature film made in the centuries-old Inuktitut language (with English subtitles) by an almost entirely Inuit cast and crew. The film won the Camera d'Or for Best First Feature film at the 2001 Cannes International Film Festival and five Genie awards (Canadian Oscars), including best picture, best director, and best screenplay.

According to Kunuk, *Atanarjuat* is about "identity and showing people where they came from, but it's also about survival." The film examines how an ancient tiny Inuit community deals with evil (jealousy, sibling rivalry, infidelity, rape, and murder) in its midst. *Atanarjuat* also functions as a how-to film showing viewers how to build an igloo (shelter) out of ice in a storm.

Contemporary Aboriginal People by Province/Territory

Nova Scotia
Chapel Island First Nation (Micmac)
Eskasoni First Nation (Micmac)
Membertou First Nation (Micmac)
Millbrook First Nation (Micmac)

New Brunswick
Big Cove First Nation (Micmac)
Bouctouche First Nation (Micmac)
Buctouche Reserve, New Brunswick (Micmac)
Fort Folly First Nation (Micmac)
Red Bank First Nation (Micmac)
St. Mary's First Nation (Maliseet)
Woodstock First Nation (Maliseet)

Prince Edward Island
Abegweit First Nation (Mi'kmaq)
Lennox Island First Nation (Mi'kmaq)

Newfoundland and Labrador
The Labrador Metis Nation
Miawpukek First Nation (Mi'kmaq)
Mushuau Innu First Nation
Nunatsiavut Government (Inuit)
Sheshatshiu Innu First Nation

Quebec

Odanak First Nation (Abenaki)
Wolinak First Nation (Abenaki)
Abitibiwinni First Nation (Algonquin)
Eagle Village First Nation (Algonquin)
Kitigan Zibi First Nation (Algonquin)
Atikamekw Nation
Waswanipi First Nation (Cree)
Mistissini First Nation (Cree)
Ouje-Bougoumou First Nation (Cree)
Wemindji First Nation (Cree)
Huron-Wendat First Nation
Malécite First Nation
Listuguj First Nation (Micmac)
Gaspe First Nation (Micmac)
Gesgapegiag First Nation (Micmac)
Kahnawake First Nation (Mohawk)
Mamit Innuat (Montagnais/Naskapi)

Ontario

Akwesasne Mohawk Nation
Alderville First Nation (Ojibwe)
Algonquins of Golden Lake/Pikwàkanagàn
Beausoleil First Nation (Ojibwe)
Chapleau Cree First Nation
Curve Lake First Nation (Ojibwe)
Ketegaunseebee Garden River First Nation (Ojibwe)
Michipicoten First Nation (Ojibwe)
Moose Cree First Nation
New Credit First Nation (Ojibwe)
Pic River First Nation (Ojibwe)
Six Nations of the Grand River Territory (Mohawk, Oneida, Cayuga, Seneca, Onondaga, Tuscarora)
Tyendinaga Mohawk Nation/Bay of Quinte Mohawks
Walpole Island/Bkejwanong First Nation (Ojibwe, Ottawa, and Potawatomi)
Wikwemikong First Nation (Ojibwe and Ottawa)
Metis Nation of Ontario

Manitoba

Birdtail Sioux First Nation
Brokenhead Ojibway Band
Buffalo Point First Nation (Ojibway)
Canupawakpa First Nation (Dakota)
Cross Lake First Nation (Cree)
Dakota Plains First Nation
Dauphin River First Nation (Ojibway)

Fox Lake First Nation (Cree)
Gambler First Nation (Cree)
Keeseekoowenin First Nation (Ojibway)
Kinonjeoshtegon First Nation (Ojibway)
Lake Manitoba First Nation (Ojibway)
Lake St. Martin First Nation (Ojibway)
Little Saskatchewan First Nation (Ojibway)
Long Plain First Nation (Ojibway)
Norway House Cree Nation
Northlands Dene First Nation
Opaskwayak Cree Nation
Peguis First Nation (Cree)
Rolling River First Nation
Roseau River Anishinabe First Nation
Sagkeeng First Nation (Ojibway)
Sayisi Dene First Nation
Split Lake First Nation (Cree)
York Factory First Nation (Cree)
Manitoba Metis Federation

Nunavut
Inuit

Northwest Territories
Acho Dene Koe
Aklavik First Nation
Behdzi Ahda First Nation (Dene)
Dechi Laot'i First Nations (Dogrib)
Deh Gah Gotie Dene Council
Deline Dene Band
Dene Cultural Institute
Dene Nation
Deninu K'ue First Nation (Dene)
Dog Rib Rae
Fort Good Hope (Dene)
Gameti First Nation (Dogrib)
Gwichya Gwich'in
Inuvik Native
Jean Marie River First Nation (Slavey)
K'atlodeeche First Nation (Dene)
Ka'a'gee Tu First Nation (Dene)
Liidlii Kue First Nation (Slavey)
Lutsel K'e Dene
Metis Association of the Northwest Territories
Nahanni Butte Dene Band

NWT Metis-Dene Development Fund (NWTMDDF)
Tulita Dene Nation
West Point First Nation (Dene)
Wha Ti First Nation (Dogrib)
Yellowknives Dene First Nation

Yukon

Carcross/Tagish First Nation
Champagne and Aishihik First Nations (Tutchone)
Kaska Tribal Council
Kluane First Nation (Tutchone and Tlingit)
Burwash Landing, Yukon Y0B 1V0
Kwanlin Dun First Nation (Tagish)
Liard First Nation (Kaska)
Little Salmon/Carmacks First Nation (Tutchone)
First Nation of Na-cho Nyak Dun (Tutchone)
Ross River Dena First Nation (Kaska and Slavey)
Selkirk First Nation (Tutchone)
Ta'an Kwach'an First Nation (Tutchone)
Teslin Tlingit Council
Tr'ondëk Hwëch'in First Nation (Han)
Vuntut Gwitch'in First Nation
White River First Nation (Tanana)

Saskatchewan

Big River First Nation (Cree)
Buffalo River Dene Nation
Clearwater River Dene First Nation
Cumberland House Cree Nation
Flying Dust First Nation (Cree)
Keeseekoose First Nation (Ojibway)
Lucky Man Cree Nation
Muskeg Lake First Nation (Cree)
Onion Lake First Nation (Cree)
Red Pheasant First Nation (Cree)
Sakimay First Nation (Cree)
Saulteaux First Nation (Ojibway)
Shoal Lake of the Cree Nation
Wahpeton Dakota Nation
Metis Nation of Saskatchewan

Alberta

Alexander First Nation (Cree)
Athabasca Chipewyan First Nation
Beaver First Nation
Beaver Lake Cree Nation
Bigstone Cree Nation

Blood First Nation (Blackfoot)
Chipewyan Prairie First Nation
Cold Lake First Nations (Cree)
Dene Tha' First Nation (Slavey)
Driftpile First Nation (Cree)
Duncan's First Nation (Cree)
Enoch Cree Nation
Ermineskin Cree Nation
Fort McKay First Nation (Cree)
Ft. McMurray First Nation (Cree)
Frog Lake First Nation (Cree)
Heart Lake First Nation (Cree)
Horse Lake First Nation (Beaver)
Kapawe'no First Nation (Cree)
Kehewin Cree Nation
Little Red River Cree Nation
Loon River First Nation (Cree)
Lubicon Lake First Nation (Cree)
Mikisew Cree First Nation
Louis Bull Tribe (Cree)
Montana First Nation (Cree)
O'Chiese First Nation (Saulteaux)
Paul First Nation (Cree/Nakoda)
Peerless Trout First Nation (Cree)
Peigan Reserve (Blackfoot)
Saddle Lake Cree Nation
Samson Cree Nation
Sawridge First Nation (Cree)
Siksika First Nation (Blackfoot)
Stoney First Nation
Sturgeon Lake First Nation (Cree)
Sucker Creek First Nation (Cree)
Sunchild First Nation (Cree)
Swan River First Nation (Cree)
Tallcree First Nation (Cree)
Tsuu T'ina First Nation (Sarcee)
Whitefish Lake First Nation (Cree)
Woodland Cree First Nation
Alberta Metis Nation

British Columbia

Adams Lake First Nation (Secwepemc)
Ahousaht First Nation
Anderson Lake First Nation (N'quatqua)
Ashcroft First Nation (Nlaka'pamux)
Bonaparte First Nation (Secwepemc)

Boothroyd First Nation (Nlaka'pamux)
Boston Bar First Nation (Nlaka'pamux)
Bridge River First Nation (St'at'imc or Lillooet)
Broman Lake First Nation (Wet'suwet'en)
Canim Lake First Nation (Secwepemc)
Canoe Creek First Nation (Secwepemc)
Cayoose Creek First Nation (St'at'imc or Lillooet)
Chemainus First Nation (Coast Salish)
Cold Water First Nation (Nlaka'pamux)
Columbia Lake First Nation (Kutenai)
Cook's Ferry First Nation (Nlaka'pamux)
Cowichan First Nation
Cowichan Lake First Nation
Dease River First Nation (Kaska Dena)
Douglas First Nation (St'at'imc or Lillooet)
Ehattesaht First Nation (Nuu-Chah-Nulth)
Fort Ware First Nation (Kwadacha)
Gitanmaax First Nation
Gitlakdamix Band Council
Gitwangak First Nation
Gitwinksihlkw First Nation
Glen Vowell First Nation (Gitxsan)
Halalt First Nation (Cowichan)
Hesquiaht First Nation
High Bar First Nation (Secwepemc)
Hupacasath First Nation (Muh-uulth-aht, Kleh-koot-aht and Cuu-ma-as-aht)
Huu-ay-aht First Nation
Kamloops First Nation (Secwepemc)
Kanaka Bar First Nation (Nlaka'pamux)
Kincolith First Nation (Nisga'a)
Kispiox First Nation (Gitxsan)
Kluskus First Nation (Lhoosk'uz Dakelh)
K'ómoks First Nation
Kwa-Wa-Aineuk First Nation ('Nakwaxda'xw)
Kwiakah First Nation
Kwicksutaineuk-Ah-Kwaw-Ah-Mish
Kyuquot First Nation (Nuu-Chah-Nulth)
Lakalzap First Nation (Nisga'a)
Liard First Nation (Kaska Dena)
Lillooet First Nation
Lower Kootenay First Nation
Lower Nicola First Nation (Nlaka'pamux)
Lower Similkameen First Nation
Lyackson First Nation
Mamaleleqala-Qwe-Qwa-Sot-Enox

Mowachaht First Nation
Mount Currie First Nation (Lil'wat)
Musqueam Indian Band (Coast Salish and only reserve within the city of Vancouver)
Nadleh Whut'en (Dakelh)
Nak'azdli (Dakelh)
Neskonlith First Nation (Secwepemc)
Nicomen First Nation (Nlaka'pamux)
Nooaitch First Nation (Nlaka'pamux)
North Thompson First Nation (Simpcw)
Nuchatlaht First Nation
Nuxalk Nation (Bella Coola)
Okanagan First Nation
Oregon Jack Creek First Nation (Nlaka'pamux)
Osoyoos First Nation (Okanagan)
Pauquachin First Nation (Salish)
Penelakut First Nation
Penticton Indian Board (Okanagan)
Red Bluff First Nation (Dakelh)
Saik'uz First Nation (Dakelh)
Samahquam First Nation (St'at'imc or Lillooet)
Seton Lake First Nation (St'at'imc or Lillooet)
Shackan First Nation (Nlaka'pamux)
Shuswap First Nation (Secwepemc)
Siska First Nation (Nlaka'pamux)
Skawahlook First Nation (Stó)
Skeetchestn First Nation (Secwepemc)
Skookumchuk First Nation
Skowkale First Nation (Stó:l)
Skuppah First Nation (Nlaka'pamux)
Skway First Nation (Nlaka'pamux)
Soda Creek First Nation (Secwepemc)
Spuzzum First Nation (Nlaka'pamux)
Stellat'en First Nation (Dakelh)
Takla Lake First Nation (Witsuwit'en)
Tla-o-qui-aht First Nation (Nuu-Chah-Nulth)
Tl'azt'en Nation (Dakelh)
Toquaht First Nation (Nuu-Chah-Nulth)
Toosey First Nation (Tsilhqot'in and Dakelh)
Tsawataineuk First Nation
Tsawout First Nation (Saanich)
Tseshaht First Nation (Nuu-Chah-Nulth)
Tseycum First Nation (Saanich)
Ts'il Kaz Koh First Nation (Dakelh)
Ts'kw'aylaxw First Nation (Dakelh)
Uchucklesaht First Nation

Ucluelet First Nation (Nuu-Chah-Nulth)
Ulkatcho First Nation (Dakelh)
Upper Nicola First Nation (Okanagan)
Upper Similkameen First Nation
We Wai Kai First Nation (Southern Kwakiutl)
Whispering Pines First Nation (Secwepemc)
Williams Lake First Nation (Secwepemc)
Metis Provincial Council of British Columbia

NOTABLE ABORIGINAL PEOPLE OF CANADA

Eva Aariak (1955–), Inuit

Elected the second premier of Nunavut and the first female to serve as premier (2008), Aariak has been instrumental in promoting Native languages in the territory.

Edward Ahenakew (1885–1961), Plains Cree

Ahenakew was one of the first people to collect and transcribe Cree legends. Born at Sandy Lake in Saskatchewan, Canada, was an author teacher and minister. Because of the devastating epidemics and poor health among his people, he resolved to go to medical school, but had to drop out due to funding and illness. He set out to collect and transcribe Cree legends and stories, which were published in 1925 as Cree Trickster Tales. Ahenakew also helped to publish a Cree-English dictionary and edited a monthly journal in Cree syllabics.

Paul Apak Angilirq (1954–1998), Inuit

A film producer and screenwriter, Angilirq was cofounder and vice president of Isuma, Canada's first Inuit media production firm. He wrote and produced the company's first feature film *Atanarjuat: The Fast Runner* (2001).

Jean-Baptiste (John) Arcand (1942–), Métis

From Debden, Saskatchewan, Arcand is a fiddler and has been writing, performing and recording since childhood. He learned the traditional Red River Métis tunes from his father and has composed over 250 tunes and received many awards and honors, including the Molson Prize (2014), National Aboriginal Achievement Award for Arts and Culture (2003) and the Canadian Grand Masters Fiddling Championship Lifetime Achievement Award (2003). He is recognized by the Métis community for ensuring that this important tradition survives and has been a teacher and mentor to many over his long career. The John Arcand Fiddle Fest, held each August near Saskatoon, attracts fans from around the globe.

Big Bear Mistahimaskwa (c. 1825–1888), Cree

Mistahimaskwa was a powerful head man and chief of sixty five Cree lodges. He is best known his involvement in Treaty 6, as he was one of the few chief leaders refused to sign fearing that it would provide his people with sufficient compensation and protection against further settlement. Big Bear constantly spoke out against the relocation of First Nations onto reserves and the turn toward agriculture. He maintained this view until the buffalo were gone and starvation took hold in his community. He strove to to unite the Northern Cree people, and he once succeeded in attracting more than two thousand Indians to join him in his thirst dance at the Poundmaker Reserve near Battleford, Saskatchewan.

Big Bear was tried for treason-felony found guilty, and imprisoned for three years in Stony Mountain Penitentiary. Due to illness, he was released after serving two years and died shortly after.

Ethel Blondin-Andrew (1951–), Dene

Blondin-Andrew was the first Aboriginal woman to be elected to Parliament representing the Western Arctic district in the Northwest Territories; the first time in1988 and the second in 2004. Under Prime Ministers Chrétien and Martin, she served as Secretary of State then Minister of State, respectively, for Children and Youth.

Matthew Coon Come (1956–), Cree

Matthew Coon Come has been the Grand Chief of the Grand Council of the Cree (Eeyou Istchee) since 1987 and also serves as Chairperson of the Cree Regional Authority. He is known internationally for defending the rights of Indigenous peoples, particularly in his campaign against the Quebec government's James Bay hydroelectric project. He served as the National Chief of the Assembly of First Nations from 2000 to 2003.

Nellie Comoyea (1940–), Inuvialuit

Cornoyea is the chairperson and CEO of the Inuvialuit Regional Corporation. In 1979, she was elected to the Northwest Territories Legislative Assembly and was a founding member of the Committee for Original People's Entitlement (COPE), an organization devoted to the rights of the Inuvialuit of the western Arctic. She was also a land claims officer for the Inuit Tapirisat of Canada.

Georges Erasmus (1948–), Dehcho (Dene)

Erasmus has been a central figure in Aboriginal politics since the 1970s and is the former national chief of the Assembly of First Nations, co-chair of the Royal Commission on Aboriginal Peoples, and president of the Dene Nation (1976). While president, he successfully led efforts to stop the construction of the Mackensie Valley Pipeline, a proposed natural gas pipeline running south from Alaska through the Northwest Territories and British Columbia. In 1985, he was successful in persuading Greenpeace, an international environmental organization, to halt a proposed anti-fur campaign, arguing that it threatened his people's traditional ways of life. The chief negotiator for the First Nations in the Northwest Territories, Erasmus led the region's land claim and self government negotiations for over 12 years.

Peter Irniq (1947–), Inuit

An Inuit cultural teacher and assistant director of the Nunavut, Heritage/Culture, Department of Education, Culture and Employment for the Government of N.W.T., Irniq developed culture and heritage programs and services to meet the needs of the new territory of Nunavut, 1997–1998. He became deputy minister of Culture, Language, Elders and Youth, 1998–1999. His mandate was to be the guardian of traditional Inuit culture and language; he served as the second Commissioner of Nunavut.

Doreen Jensen (1933–2009), Gitxsan

Doreen Jensen, an author, historian and traditionalist, was from Kispoix, British Columbia. She was known for promoting and preserving Aboriginal artwork, teaching Gitxsan language classes, and helping to revitalize traditional practices. She was a respected cultural leader and in 1983, she curated an exhibit at Museum of Anthropology entitled "Robes of Power," which emphasized the importance of regalia to First Nation ceremonies and the key role that women played in producing button blanket/robes. She received the Golden Eagle Feather from the Professional Native Women's Association (2008).

Emily Pauline Johnson (1861–1913), Mohawk

Johnson was from the Six Nations Reserve in Ontario and was an author and performer popular in the late-nineteenth century. Her work celebrated her Aboriginal heritage; her father was a hereditary Mohawk chief. There has been a renewed interest in her work, and in 2002 a complete collection of her poetry was published.

Todd Labrador (1960–), Mi'kmaq

Raised on the Wildcat reservation in Nova Scotia, Labrador's great grandfather was birch bark artist (canoes, baskets, etc.), who taught the craft to Labrador's father, who in turn taught it to him. Labrador was always drawn to the traditional Mi'kmaq culture and wanted to revive birch bark canoe building. After much research and several attempts, he completed his fist full-size canoe in 2004 and has since built canoes in France as well as constructing an ocean canoe for the Canadian Museum of History in Gatineau, Québec. Labrador also teaches and demonstrates different styles of birch bark arts.

George Manuel (1921–1989), Shuswap

Manuel was from the British Columbia Shuswap village of Neskainlith and became chief in the late 1940s. He began to organize the Interior Salish people and in 1958 launched an organization called the Aboriginal Native Rights Committee of the Interior Tribes of British Columbia, which reconstituted itself as the North American Indian Brotherhood in 1960. Manuel was elected president and took his people's land claims to Ottawa. He was active in the formation of the Union of British Columbia Indian Chiefs in 1969, a province-wide organization devoted to the advancement of Aboriginal claims and, in 1970, was elected president of the National Indian Brotherhood, a national organization of Indian groups. Manuel was also a major figure in the World Council of Indigenous Peoples, an international organization of Indigenous peoples.

Daniel N. Paul (1938–), Mi'kmaq

Dr. Paul was born on the Shubenacadie Indian Reserve in Nova Scotia and lives in Halifax. An activist, author, journalist, consultant and volunteer, he has been determined champion of First Nations communities across Nova Scotia for over 30 years. Dr. Paul has been an outspoken advocate against racial discrimination and inequality—his intrepidness has earned him several honors including the Province of Nova Scotia's Grand Chief Donald Marshall Sr. Memorial Senior Award (2007) and the 2006–2007 MECNS Award, Multicultural Education Council of Nova Scotia. Author of over six books and countless articles, his best-known and award-winning publication is *We Were Not the Savages: First Nations History—Collision between European and Native American Civilizations.*

Aqpik Peter, Inuit

A Nunavut speed skater and Olympian, he was the role model/poster boy for the 2010 Winter Olympics.

Susan Point (1952–), Coast Salish (Musqueam)

Point is a contemporary artist from British Columbia, whose distinct style has sparked a revitalization in Coast Salish art. Known for her sculpture, her work is prominent in public spaces like the Vancouver International Airport, and Stanley Park. Point is an Officer of the Order of Canada and has been presented with the Queen Elizabeth II Diamond Jubilee Medal for her contributions to the country. Her "Beaver and the Mink" lithograph was chosen as the gift from the Canadian government to the Smithsonian Institution's National Museum of the American Indian in Washington, D.C.

Buffy Sainte-Marie (1941–), Plains Cree

The first Native person to win an Academy Award (1983 for the song "Up Where We Belong"), Sainte-Marie is also a singer, musician, visual artist, composer, educator, pacifist, and social activist. Her focus in all these areas has been on Indigenous rights. In 1997, she established the Cradleboard Teaching Project, an educational curriculum that teaches the truth about Native Americans.

Ralph Steinhauer (1905–), Ojibway

Steinhauer was the first Native person to serve as lieutenant-governor of a Canadian province (Alberta) and was also a respected chief of the Saddle Lake Reserve. He was a founder of the Indian Association of Alberta, a province-wide organization devoted to the advancement of Aboriginal rights. In 1974, Steinhauer was sworn in as the lieutenant governor of Alberta, a position he held until 1979.

Richard Van Camp (1971–), Tłicho

An author of both adult and children's literature and from Fort Smith, Northwest Territories., Van Camp got his start as a writer on the television series "North of 60." His 1996 novel, *The Lesser Blessed*, was adapted into a film (2012). His children's fiction includes *Nighty Night* (2011) and *Little You* (2013).

Sheila Watt-Cloutier, Inuit

Environmental activist and political representative for Inuit at the regional, national, and international levels, including International Chair for the Inuit Circumpolar Council (formerly the Inuit Circumpolar Conference), Watt-Cloutier has earned countless honors. She was nominee for the 2007 Nobel Peace Prize and received the Right Livelihood Award (often referred to as "The Alternative Nobel Prize") in 2015.

Ashley Callingbull (1998–), Enoch Cree

In 2015, Ashley Callingbull was chosen Mrs. Universe, becoming the first Canadian and the first Aboriginal woman to wear the crown. The beauty queen from Alberta shocked the world when she make it clear she would use the media spotlight to bring attention to issues affecting First Nations like the missing Aboriginal women. She urged Indigenous people to get out and vote in federal elections to get Harper and his conservative administration out of office. When criticized for using her position to advocate for First Nations, Callingbull responded, "Really? People think I'm too political for my first day as Mrs. Universe. Did you really think I was going to just sit there and look pretty? Definitely not. I have a title, a platform and a voice to make change and bring awareness to First Nations issues here in Canada. I'm getting all this media attention and I'm going to use it to the best of my ability. I'm not your typical beauty queen. Look out.… I have a voice for change and I'm going to use it!"

APPENDIX B: MEXICO

From its central towering mountains and deep canyons to its northern expansive deserts to its southern and eastern dense rain forests, Mexico is a land of extremes. Small mountain ranges on the Central Plateau are bordered in the east by the Sierra Madre Oriental mountain range and the Sierra Madre Occidental range in the west. At the southeastern tip of the country, the Yucatán Peninsula, dotted with ancient Mayan structures, extends into the Gulf of Mexico. Few other countries are home to the same vast variety of flora and fauna. Its perfect location between the Equator and the Arctic Circle makes it a "Club Med" for animals fleeing freezing cold in the north and blazing heat in the south. The northern deserts support countless plant and animal species that have adapted to the harsh environment. The northernmost and westernmost of the Mexico's 31 states is Baja California, breeding grounds for gray whales that swim thousands of miles from Alaska every year. Eastern Mexico's coastal wetlands and rain forests are home to thousands of tropical plant species and elusive animals like jaguars and quetzal birds.

Scholars, school curriculum, and popular culture all focus on the ancient and great civilizations of what is now called Mexico. Indeed, the area was the cradle of many great civilizations, including the Mokaya, Olmec (sometimes called the "Mother Culture of Mesoamerica"), Maya, Toltec, Zapotec, Aztec Mexica, and Mixtec. Centuries before the Europeans arrived, these societies flourished in diverse areas such as architecture, mathematics, science, agronomy, engineering, literature, fine arts, social order, and medicine. Today, tourists flock to the ancient cities of Teotihuacán, Chichen Itza, and Calixtlahuaca and are stunned by the brilliance of the people who built these masterpieces a few millennium before computers were invented. However, these same tourists disregard the waiters, maids, tour guides, bus drivers, hotel managers, and shop owners, who are themselves descendents of these incredible civilizations; the inheritors of the world's most studied and glorious contributions to our contemporary societies.

Like the vast diversity of flora and fauna, Mexico also has the largest and most diverse Native population on the North America continent; Peru in South America is the only other country with a comparable population. More than one in ten Mexicans speaks one of 89 Indigenous languages comprising dozens of distinct dialects—there is no official language of Mexico.

The Mexican government defines Indigenous in two ways: a narrow definition that only includes those who speak an Indigenous language; and a broader inclusion of all people who identify as Indigenous or have an Indigenous background even if they do not speak a Native language. Because of these two interpretations, the numbers of Indigenous peoples varies according to who is doing the count. Cultural activists often see the first definition of Indigenous as "statistical genocide." According to the latest census (2010) completed by the National Institute of Statistics and Geography, there were 5,694,928 Indigenous people in Mexico, of many different ethnic groups and making up 21.5% of Mexico's population. That is probably an undercount, but much improved over earlier reports due to the Indigenous organizations pressuring the government to be more inclusive as 84% of those who were counted as Indian also spoke Spanish. Data show that a small fraction of Indigenous peoples remains monolingual.

The Indigenous people of Mexico suffer the same blatant disregard and prejudice, plus a similar history of colonization and genocide, as the rest of Indigenous North America. Most of the early Europeans in Mexico were men, who were not looking for homes as in the United States. They didn't bring their families or colonize in the same way. Centuries of intermarriage created a large Mestizo population, so most Mexicans do have Native ancestry. The Indigenous peoples became workers on large estates and as time went on, the people were often abandoned and neglected. There were no reserved lands set aside for them. It was only in the revised 1992 Constitution that the nation declared itself to be a multicultural country. Before that, the existence and contributions of Indians were relegated to the early history of the country. The majority of Indigenous people live in the southern and south-central region of Mexico. Almost 80% of Native language speakers live in eight of Mexico's 31 states—Oaxaca, Yucatan, Chiapas, Quintana Roo, Guerrero, Hidalgo, Campeche, Puebla, San Luis Potosí, and Mexico City. The five predominant languages spoken are: Náhuatl, Maya, Zapotec, Mixtec, and Otomí.

For the past century each government administration has upheld a policy of assimilation and integration. In 1946, the independent Department of Native Affairs, under the aegis of the Ministry of Education, began teaching Spanish to Indigenous children. However, along with teaching the language, assimilation was promoted, which devalues Indigenous languages, cultures, and self-government/autonomy. Legally, Mexico's Native communities are protected by human rights legislation through the government Department of the National Commission for the Development of Indigenous Peoples (NCDIP). Its mission is to "guide, coordinate, promote, support, foster, monitor, and assess programmes, projects, strategies, and public actions to attain integral and sustainable development and full enjoyment of the rights of Indigenous peoples and communities in accordance with Article 2 of the Political Constitution of the United Mexican States." Until 2003, the department responsible for Indigenous affairs was the National Indigenous Institute (NII). On paper, NII was committed to cultural diversity and maintained that it had an open dialogue with Indigenous communities in its offices throughout the country. But there was criticism that the NII was patronizing and nothing but a token attempt to meet government obligations. NII staff who defended Indigenous communities were persecuted as a result. The National Commission for the Development of Indigenous Peoples does not seem to be resolving issues either. According to a 2014 National Statistics Institute (INEGI) report, around 72% of Indigenous peoples are considered impoverished. Land ownership, natural resources and education are some of the problems still facing communities.

Although the Indigenous communities of Mexico are some of the poorest in North America, the Mexican government prides itself on its ancient Maya and Aztec monuments, and its Indigenous dances, crafts and markets, which add considerably to the country's sightseeing economy. It is ironic that the same Indigenous cultures that are so prized for their tourism appeal face disdain and a government policy of assimilation. Indigenous organizations from small community-based groups to national bodies, struggle for better living conditions. They have rallied for justice and rights in education, health services, potable water, fair wages, political representation, consultation, environmental concerns, and official recognition of their languages and traditional healing modalities. Some groups collaborate with United Nations sanctioned non-governmental organizations (NGOs); others have partnered with local governments.

NATIONAL ZAPATISTA LIBERATION ARMY (EZLN)

The condition of Mexico's Indigenous communities hit the headlines in January 1, 1994. Indigenous peasants from many different ethnic groups, staged an armed rebellion on the day that the North American Free Trade Agreement (NAFTA) went into effect. They took the name National Zapatista Liberation Army (EZLN), from the name of Emiliano Zapata, a popular hero executed by the military in 1919 and a leader of the Zapatistas (see Notable People below). The EZLN took a stand in four towns in Chiapas, the state where Native people had suffered greatly, to call attention to the indignities Indigenous peoples and others had endured. They clamored for better conditions, protection of communal land and an end to government corruption and human rights abuses.

NAFTA was seen as a real threat to Native peoples in many areas and the EZLN had to take action because:

- Native peoples stood to lose jobs, land rights and legal status under the new North American Free Trade Agreement (NAFTA), which eliminated trade barriers among the U.S., Canada and Mexico. All had large Indigenous populations as did Chile and Mesoamerica, which were to be added to the Free Trade Zone.

- NAFTA would not protect the basic rights for Indigenous groups granted by participating national governments. NAFTA did not recognize the unique legal status of Indigenous tribes or tribal governments or reservations.

- NAFTA was a serious threat to Native land rights, especially in Mexico, where most Indigenous peoples do not have reservations, but instead reside in their traditional communal lands recognized for centuries by colonial and then Mexican law. With the lack of protection, these homelands can be sold to outsiders.

- Under NAFTA, U.S. investors can purchase the best lands. Many Native people, not used to the capitalist system, were likely to be cheated out of their ancient land rights. The fear was that millions would become economic refugees in the urban centers of Mexico, U.S., and Canada. With the very prospect of NAFTA's approval in the air, Chiapas Mayan were already being forced off traditional lands by non-Native speculators who were grabbing up potentially valuable areas in anticipation of a big payoff.

- NAFTA had no provisions to protect those Native groups straddling the borders like the Canadian/U.S. nations of Mohawk, Salish-Kooteni, Colville-Okanagan, and Abenaki, or the Mexican/U.S. nations of Cocopah, Kamia, O'odhama, and Kickapoo. NAFTA should have included an agreement that recognized these Native groups split apart by the U.S.–Mexican and U.S.–Canadian borders and included provision for free movement, unification, and Indigenous local government.

- NAFTA had a devastating impact upon all U.S. workers who are working in minimum wage jobs or sectors vulnerable to Mexican low-wage competition, such as manufacturing, trucking, agriculture, and heavy industry. Industry located on or near reservations were especially likely to move to Mexico, where laborers were forced to work for 80 cents an hour without benefits.

- NAFTA did not include protection for Native arts or craftspeople.

After centuries of constant attacks on their lands, people and cultures, Indigenous peoples were not willing to tolerate the new threat of NAFTA; it was the spark that lit the powder keg. The government declared a ceasefire after the initial fighting, agreeing to address the "rebel" concerns and release prisoners captured during the conflict. Negotiations broke down as the government denied most of the demands. At the height of the rebellion, the government forces executed eight suspected members of the EZLN. Also, mandated observers reported that dozens of critics of the regime had (have) been killed or have "disappeared," reportedly at the hands of death squads organized by government forces colluding with private interests. Indigenous women of Chiapas have been brutalized by rape and torture, yet their assailants are rarely charged with any crime.

In the elections of August 1994, Eduardo Robledo Rincón "officially" won the governorship of Chiapas, but the EZLN and opposition leaders were adamant that progressive candidate Amado Avendado was the rightful victor. The EZLN again took action. They created their own government, seized government offices, appropriated radio stations and set up roadblocks. Eventually, the EZLN controlled 38 towns in the state. The new government (called a parallel authority) allowed peasants to confiscate large estates, shut down existing state structures, and instituted new laws favoring Indigenous people and the poor. Across the country people rallied in large demonstrations to support the actions.

The Mexican government began to lose face in the international business community. The value of the peso was cut in half and investors began to look elsewhere to exploit lands. The new administration of President Ernesto Zedillo implemented austere measures to control government spending and inflation. And in February 1995, he ordered a military offensive against the EZLN strongholds, forcing them to retreat into the mountains.

The EZLN and Indigenous organizations represented by the National Plural Indigenous Assembly for Autonomy had been demanding constitutional reforms so that pluri-ethnic independent regions in areas of significant Indigenous population could be established. This would have created a fourth level of government at a regional level that would coexist with municipal, state, and federal government authorities. Regional autonomy would also have permitted Indigenous peoples greater control over their land and resources in accordance with International Labour Organization Convention No. 169. In 1996 the EZLN and Mexican government officials settled by signing the San Andres Accords, which guarantee land rights, regional autonomy, and cultural rights for Indigenous peoples, but the Mexican government did not implement these agreements.

A CLOSER LOOK AT THREE COMMUNITIES

Tarahumara (Rarámuri)

The Rarámuri (Tarahumara) people of Northern Mexico's rugged Sierra Madre mountains are world renown for being some of the most skilled long-distance runners in the world. Their ancestors, originally from what is now the state of Chihuahua, sought refuge in the high sierras and canyons such as the Copper Canyon during the sixteenth century as they fled slave raids by Spanish conquistadors. Safely isolated for hundreds of years, they developed a complex network of trails connecting them to other small communities that raised corn, potatoes, and beans. The main way of transmitting information among the "Rancherias" was by messengers, who ran the trails connecting the communities. The incredible running style of the Rarámuri also enabled them to be expert hunters, chasing down deer and other animals.

The Rarámuri survived the Aztecs, the Spanish, the French, and the Americans, but today they defend their lands from being appropriated by the Mexican army, drug lords or corporations that want to exploit their mineral resources. Massive deforestation to accommodate the mining and logging industries has devastated the Sierra Madre; the Rarámuri face the constant threat of the destruction and theft of their lands that jeopardizes their subsistence economy and future. In 2000, the Mexican Commission of Solidarity and Defense of Human Rights produced a report stating that "the government fails in studying the effects of lumber production on the ecosystem." More than any other place on earth, this is the most biologically diverse ecosystem in North America and supports hundreds of medicinal plants, oak types and pine species. However, it is on the brink of extinction. To worsen matters, the North American Free Trade Agreement (NAFTA) increased foreign investment resulting in the privatization of communal land, which is contrary to Rarámuri culture. The mining of gold and silver has poisoned the land and water. Drug lords also clear-cut vast areas of trees to grow marijuana and opium; forcing and torturing the Rarámuri to cultivate the drugs, while their own crops are neglected and famine increases. Herbicides also pollute and destroy the natural environment on which the Rarámuri depend.

The Rarámuri have tried to help their situation by promoting tourism. Travelers arrive expecting to see a stereotypic image of the "Noble Savage," and a culture unspoiled and unpolluted. Often, out of desperation, the Rarámuri present the expected image—their lifeways have changed more in the past 20 years than in all the centuries they have lived in the Sierra Madres. The communities have also been affected by some of the worst drought in history, caused by the extreme changes in their climate. Due to the lack of water needed for farming, famine is spreading. Oxfam Mexico (a global organization working to right the wrongs of poverty, hunger, and injustice) suggests that the community needs sustainable agriculture which can survive the crises due to climate change.

And still the Rarámuri run. Long-distance running is also done for rituals and competition. Races last from a few hours to a couple of days without a break. Often, men kick wooden balls as they run in "foot throwing," rarajipari, competitions; women use a stick and hoop. Their minimal use of footwear called, huaraches, has been extolled by scholars for protecting the foot while not encumbering the muscles or bones—a natural way to connect with the ground. However, today, the Rarámuri have had many times when they could not complete the races. Because of famine, they don't have the calories for the energy needed for running hundreds of miles. In response to the drought crisis, organizations like Barefoot Seeds, a nonprofit Tarahumara native seed bank in Urique, are trying to help. The Rarámuri diet is explored In the award winning documentary *GOSHEN* (2015). The film examines their low incidence of diseases, thought to be a result of their traditional plant-based diet, while exploring their worsening health in areas where processed foods have replaced their traditional staples.

Wixáritari (Huichol)

The real treasure of the Sierra Madre is the rich cultural heritage of the Wixáritari ("the people"), commonly called the Huichol. The Wixáritari live primarily in the Sierra Madre Occidental range in the states of Nayarit, Jalisco, Zacatecas, and Durango. According to Huichol oral history, when they arrived in their current homelands from the south, the Tepecano were living there. Tepecano history confirms it, but there are no stories of conflict or conquest between them; it seems as if the two groups were compatible. There is historical evidence of a rebellion mounted jointly against Spanish invaders by the two ethnic groups in El Teúl (1592) and in Nostic (1702). Through these and other conflicts the Wixáritari were able to stave off both the Spanish Armies and the Catholic missionaries. For centuries, they maintained their traditional way of life, secluded by the mountains' natural barrier. In the 1970s, the Mexican government, on a mission to enforce its assimilationist policies, opened schools, clinics and agricultural stations to introduce new ways to the Wixáritari. Air strips for small planes were constructed in the most remote areas of the Sierras bringing in tourists and government officials. Ranchers desired the Wixáritari high, grassy plateaus; religious fanatics wanted to convert these isolated people to Christianity. The Wixáritari were not moved and most still observe their original religion.

However, there have been significant changes to the Wixáritari environment, all of it negative. Traditionally, the Wixáritari plant corn, chili, beans, squash and amaranth during the rainy season—the custom is part of their ancient and efficient cycle of life. But the Mexican government endorses exactly the opposite. It promotes mono-cultural planting and supplies hybrid seeds that need dangerous pesticides and artificial fertilizers, replacing the mixed seeds that were traditionally used by Indigenous agricultural peoples. Monoculture, herbicides and pesticides not only destroy communal agriculture practices, but they threaten the physical health of the planters and cause malnutrition within the families.

With the limited output of their customary crops, almost half of all Wixáritari families are forced to leave their communities in the dry season to find poorly paid and dangerous work in the tobacco fields of the Nayarit coast. The Wixáritari prefer tobacco employment over other agricultural work because the stringing of tobacco is done late afternoon or morning, when the temperature is a bit lower and the branches provide shade. It may be cooler, but the damp tobacco leaves drip moisture onto the people; wet skin absorbs pesticides more easily. The nicotine from the tobacco not only causes skin irritations and hives (Green Tobacco Sickness), but the children who work in the fields are even more at risk as they become covered with the sticky resin and absorb the toxic pesticides. From the oldest to the youngest, workers sleep and live under the drying tobacco. They toil without potable water, toilet facilities; they even cook their food beneath the toxic branches. As most cannot read the English labels, they use the empty pesticide cans for drinking, often taking them home as useful souvenirs. Not only are the chemicals harming the people, but also the environment. Even their journey to the coastal tobacco fields is a major undertaking. Wixáritari vulnerable elders, women—many pregnant or malnourished or suffering from tuberculosis, and children arrive in a weakened state—hungry and thirsty. Even the strong men are not in good shape. Few workers are granted food after their long trek; most have to gather their water from the irrigation channels flowing from the Santiago River, one of the most contaminated in Mexico. All the water sources are filled with poisons, yet the Wixáritari still come to work and not just because they so desperately need the pittance they earn to survive. As part of their religious observance, they must visit the ocean. However, even in their villages, DDT has been used to kill malarial mosquitoes. The Wixáritari call the DDT sprayers *matagatos* (cat killers). The effects of most of these chemicals are cumulative over time. The Wixáritari have strict beliefs about their accountability to the balance of the universe. They take the depletion of their homelands very seriously. In 1988, they were awarded the National Ecology Prize of Mexico for their efforts to repopulate the Sierra Madre forests with white-tailed deer.

In the past 30 years, some four thousand Wixáritari have migrated to the cities of Nayarit, Guadalajara and Mexico City. These new urbanites have taken their art with them and introduced it to the world in an updated way. In traditional Wixáritari communities, an important religious object is the nieli'ka: a small square or round tablet with a hole in the center covered on one or both sides with a mixture of beeswax and pine resin into which threads of yarn are pressed. Nieli'kas can be found in sacred places such as house shrines (xiriki), temples, springs, and caves. The yarn paintings are the continuation of thousands of years of religious art practiced by the Wixáritari. The symbolic patterns of plants and animal decorate their cross-stitch embroidery, *xukuri* beaded gourd votive bowls, and a variety of prayer items. Urban Wixáritari began making intricate and elaborate yarn paintings (probably to preserve their traditions), modernizing the nieli'ka. At first, the bright iconic "paintings," were sold to tourist shops as a source of much needed income. Then traditionalists began to use the paintings to share Wixáritari stories and history. The centuries old symbols have their roots in ancient culture. The yarn used today is woven much tighter, is thinner, and has a greater variety of colors, allowing far more detail than the older versions. A relatively new art form is beaded art. Wooden bowls, figurines, or masks are covered in beeswax; then beads of glass or metal are pressed into it making three-dimensional spectacular pieces. Like all Wixáritari art, the bead work features their religious patterns and symbols. Wixáritari art is valued in the international market; the pieces of José Benítez Sánchez and Ramon Medina Silva are well known among collectors.

Efforts are being made to help the Wixáritari preserve and maintain their traditional culture. Apart from the Mexican government's programs, which have often hindered rather than helped, the Cousteau Society founded the Punta Mita project in the state of Nayarit to develop the state's ecotourism in a way that will protect the glorious biodiversity of the Pacific coast and the interior homeland of the Wixáritari. Some 50 major businesses in Mexico, backed by Westin Hotels, have joined forces to develop ecotourism in a way that will protect the glorious biodiversity of the Pacific coast and the interior homeland of the Wixáritari. These business not only educate by selling books about the Sierra Madre flora and fauna, but they also sell Indigenous arts supporting traditional communities.

Maya

The story of the great Mayan civilization is a complex one, woven through different eras and across great spans of time, like that of ancient Egypt. Many aspects of the brilliant history of the Maya are shrouded in mystery. However, we would know much more about them if the Spaniards hadn't destroyed their books and libraries in an attempt to subjugate them and convert them to Catholicism. The Maya were not easy to conquer. Jacinto Canek, a convent-educated Mayan, led an Indigenous rebellion against the colonial government in 1761. Thousands of Natives died and Canek was executed. These and other uprisings during the colonial period gave the Yucatán Maya the reputation of being difficult to defeat.

Although most of their codices and other writings disappeared at the hands of the Europeans, the Maya did not. Like most dynamic societies, Mayan culture changed, but Maya and many of the old customs still remain in Mesoamerica. In Mexico, the Maya primarily live in the states of the Campeche, Quintana Roo, Tabasco, Chiapas, and the Yucatán. After Mexico gained its independence from Spain in February in 1821, Yucatán became part of the Independent Mexican Empire but remained a remote province until 1824, when it was divided into three states: Campeche, Quintana Roo, and Yucatán. Yucatán at one point, seceded from Mexico.

During the Mexican–American War (1846–1848), Yucatán, which considered itself an independent nation, remained neutral. However, in 1847 a major revolt by the Mayan people against the Hispanic population, who had political and economic control of the region, broke out. Named the Caste War (Guerra de Castas), the Maya evicted all of the non-Natives in under a year, except those within the walled cities of Mérida and Campeche. Out of desperation, Governor Santiago Méndez appealed for help to Britain, Spain, and the United States, offering sovereignty over Yucatán to whichever nation could stop the Mayans. The matter was seriously debated in Congress, but the only action taken by the United States was to warn European powers not to interfere. With the Mexican War ended, the non-Native Yucatecans reunited with the Mexican government asking for assistance in suppressing the revolt. Fighting continued between the forces of the Yucatecan government and the independent Mayans through 1901 when the Mexican army occupied the Maya capital of Chán Santa Cruz. The Caste War was probably the most successful modern Native American revolt. Even after it ended, some Mayan communities in Quintana Roo refused to acknowledge Ladino (Jews of Spanish origin) or Mexican sovereignty for another decade. Some say the war was never over and today, almost every town and village show signs of the rebellion. Some buildings have been left unrepaired for over a century; statues of armed Maya freedom fighters stand in town squares; the graves of fallen heroes are tended carefully; and public murals of ancient Maya are overshadowed by murals depicting the Maya during the time of rebellion and conflict. All serve as reminders. Although the Yucatan Maya people revere their distant past, they are focused on recent history and the contemporary struggle to regain power and self-government. It appears that the ancient Maya are celebrated more for the tourism and economic opportunities than what the modern Maya bring to the region.

For hundreds of years, gubernatorial elections were based primarily on the purity of the candidates' Hispanic ancestry, which further oppressed the Maya majority. The first governor of Yucatán born of pure Mayan descent, Francisco Luna Kan (1925–), was elected in 1976. His victory was a symbol of hope for Indigenous people. The Yucatán peninsula, still home to one of the largest Indigenous populations in Mexico, also has the country's largest tourist economy. Yucatán's culture is unique from that of other Mexican states.

Due to their geographic isolation, the Yucatecans have been able to preserve ancient traditions more than many other Indigenous groups in the country. Most still live in traditional housing (na), wear traditional dresses (huipiles), farm (the occupation of their ancestors), speak the Maya language, and observe their original religion, including celebrations to honor rites of passage and benefactor spirits. Maya women are famous for the same back-strap weaving of their ancestors, often using locally handspun yarn and natural vegetable dyes. They create striped and plain white cloth for shawls, shirts, and children's clothes, some with designs that are over 1,200 years old. Tourists covet the colorful hammocks woven from fine cotton string. The Maya also create superb pottery and items woven from palm, straw, reeds, and sisal. Centuries-old dances, both ceremonial and social, are preserved and performed by religious men's fraternities called *cofradias*. And in the center of this bastion of the Maya, tourists flock to the idyllic eastern coastline of Yucatán which juts into the clear blue/green colors of the Caribbean and boasts the world's fifth longest barrier reef. It would be good to investigate the contemporary issues of these storied people, who are still here.

Pueblos Indigenas of Mexico

Aguacateco (Awakateko)	Akateko	Amuzgo (Tzañcue)
Ayapaneco	Chatino (Cha'cña)	Chichimeca Jonaz (Uza)
Chinantec (Tsa jujmí)	Chocho (Runixa ngiigua)	Chocholteco
Ch'ol (Winik)	Chontal	Chontal Maya
Chuj	Cochimi (Laymón, mti'pá)	Cocopah (Es péi)
Cora (Nayeeri)	Cucapá	Cuicatec (Nduudu yu)
Cuicateco	Guarijío	Huarijio (Makurawe)
Huastec (Téenek)	Huasteco	Huave (Ikoods)
Huave	Huichol (Wixárika)	Ixcateco
Ixil	Jacaltec (Abxubal)	K'iche'
Kanjobal (K'anjobal)	Kaqchikel (K'akchikel)	Kekchí (K'ekchí)
Kickapoo	Kikapú (Kikapooa)	Kiliwa (Ko'lew)
Kiliwa	Kumiai (Ti'pai)	Lacandon (Hach t'an)
Lacandón	Mam	Mame (Qyool)

Matlatzinca	Mayo (Yoreme)	Mayo
Mazahua (Hñatho)	Mazateco (Ha shuta enima)	Mazateco
Mexicanero (Mexikatlajtolli)	Mixe (Ayüükjä'äy)	Mixtec (Tu'un savi)
Mixteco	Motocintleco (Qatok)	Nahuatl (N huatl cah)
Ocuiltec (Tlahuica)	Oluteco	Otomi (Hñähñü)
Paipai (Akwa'ala)	Pame (Xigüe)	Pápago
Pima	Pima Bajo	Popoluca (Tuncápxe)
Purépecha (P'urhépecha)	Q'anjob'al	Q'eqchi'
Qato'k	Sayulteco	Seri (Comcáac)
Tacuate	Tarahumara (Rarámuri)	Tarasco
Teko	Tepehua (Hamasipini)	Tepehuan (O'dam, Audam, and Ódami)
Tepehuano	Texistepequeño	Tlahuica
Tlapanec (Me'phaa)	Tlapaneco	Tohono O'odham (Papago)
Tojolabal (Tojolwinik)	Tojolabal	Totonac (Tachiwin)
Totonaco	Triqui (Tinujéi)	Triqui
Tseltal	Tsotsil	Tzeltal (K'op o winik atel)
Tzotzil (Batzil k'op)	Yaqui (Yoeme)	Zapotec (Binizaa)
Zoque (O'de püt)	Zoque	

NOTABLE PEOPLE

Historical

Lady Xoc (C.E. 681–?), Maya

A queen and wife of a great ruler of Yaxchilan, Lady Xoc is considered one of the most powerful and prominent women in Maya history. It is thought that it her influence helped her husband, Itzamnaaj B'alam, become a leader.

Nezahualcoyotl (1402–1472), Acolhua

A philosopher, warrior, architect, poet and ruler of the city-state of Texcoco, Nezahualcoyotl is credited with spearheading Texcoco's Golden Age, which brought the rule of law, scholarship and artistry to the city and set high standards that influenced surrounding cultures. He founded a music academy and invited scholars/musicians from all over Mesoamerica to attend. Under his administration, Texcoco thrived as an intellectual center and boasted an extensive library, which the Spanish destroyed along with most of the ancient texts throughout Mexico.

Cuauhtémoc (c. 1497–1525), Mixtec

Cuauhtémoc was the last Aztec Emperor, ruling from 1520 to 1521. When Hernán Cortés attacked the city of Tenochtitlán, Cuauhtémoc defended the capital during the four month siege. Finally captured by the Spanish, he was tortured to reveal the location of gold, but refused to speak and never revealed any secrets. Cortés was stunned by the young ruler's bravery and fortitude. The conquistador feared him and was afraid to leave him on his own. He took the emperor with him on his conquest of Honduras and ordered him hanged on route. Cuauhtémoc a, symbol of "Indigenist" nationalism, is regaled throughout Mexico. Today, his life is celebrated in popular culture and his face has even decorated currency. Cuauhtémoc is still one of the few non-Spanish boys' names.

Saint Juan Diego Cuauhtlatoatzin, also known as Juan Diegotzil (1474–1548), Chichimeca

Saint Juan Diego Cuauhtlatoatzin is the first Indigenous Roman Catholic saint from the Americas. He and his wife, María Lucía, were among the first to be baptized after the arrival of the Franciscan missionaries in 1524. He had seen at least four apparitions of the Virgin Mary, who each time instructed him to do something helpful in her name.

Benito Juarez (1806 –1872), Zapotec

National hero Benito Juarez served as president of Mexico for five terms (1861–72). He fought against French occupation (1864–67), sought constitutional reforms to create a democratic federal republic, and struggled to transform his liberal ideas into a practical governance and to overcome the bias against his Indian background. His domestic reforms are credited with spurring Mexico to modernize in the last quarter of the nineteenth century and squelch some of the most-blatant remnants of colonialism.

Ignacio Manuel Altamirano Basilio (1834–1893), Nahua

A Mexican writer, journalist, teacher and politician, Basilio is credited with writing the first modern Mexican novel, *Clemencia* (1869). He founded several newspapers and magazines including *El Correo de México* (The Mexico Post), *El Renacimiento* (The Renaissance), and *El Federalista* (The Federalist). His many books and articles chronicled contemporary Mexican society.

Contemporary

Jacobo and Maria Ángeles, Zapotec

Celebrated wood-carving artists from the village of Martín Tilcajete in Oaxaca, the couple's rich artistic tradition is a family business like many other in the area. They create colorful, expressive figurines called *tonas* (animals from the Zapotec calendar) and *nahuales* (animals fused with a human being), known worldwide as *alebrijes*. They and members of their workshop are praised for their imaginative creativity. The Oaxaca state is dotted with artists workshops (most family enterprises) who are potters, weavers, paper artists and metal workers.

Edwin Bustillos (1964—2003), Rarámuri

An agricultural engineer from the Sierra Madre, Bustillos founded the Consejo Asesor Sierra Madre (1992), an organization that aims to conserve and protect the Rarámuri way of life and the environment. He spoke out against the drug traffickers using the area and was awarded the Goldman Environmental Prize in 1996.

José María Bonifacio Leiva Peres and Cajemé / Kahe'eme (1835–1887), Yaqui

Cajemé was a Yaqui military leader from the state of Sonora and helped to expel the French from the area. His service was so exemplary that in Sonora Governor Ignacio Pesqueira appointed him "Alcalde Mayor" of the Yaqui (1872), thinking that Cajemé could pacify the Yaqui people. Instead, he united the eight Yaqui towns into a small, independent republic, announcing that they would not recognize the Mexican government unless the Yaqui were allowed self government. Cajemé restored the traditional Yaqui society creating greater autonomy and self-sufficiency, helped secure economic security for the community, plus built a defense system to protect the Yaqui nation against those that would take away their traditional territory. He became a real source of irritation for the Mexican government, which conspired to capture and execute him; they did this with the help of some Yaqui traitors. For many years following Cajemé's death the Mexican government tried to kill or remove all the Yaqui from the state of Sonora; many were sent as slaves to the Yucatán Peninsula, and thousands died. Many were killed by firing squad or hanged. A sizable group escaped to southern Arizona, the traditional Northernmost region of their territory, where their descendants live today.

Daniel Ponce de León (1980–), Rarámuri

A professional boxer, Ponce de Leon is a former WBC featherweight champion, a former WBO super bantamweight champion, a bronze medalist in the 1999 Pan American Games in the flyweight division, and a member of the 2000 Mexican Olympic team in the featherweight division.

Margarita Gutierrez Romero, Nha-ñhu

From the state of Hidalgo, Romero began her long years of activism defending Indigenous rights through community radio and went on to study journalism at UNAM. Since the uprising in 1992, she has struggled for the rights of Indigenous people in Mexico and throughout the world. She cofounded the Continental Network of Indigenous Women of Abya Yala, the National Plural Indigenous Assembly for Autonomy (ANIPA), the National Indigenous Council (CNI), and is the National Coordinator of Mexico's Indigenous Women (CONAMI) of Mexico. She is currently the President of the State Coordinator of Indigenous Women Organizations of Chiapas.

Emiliano Zapata Salazar (1879–1919), Zapotec/Mestizo

A hero from the state of Morelos, Zapata fought for land and liberty (Tierra y libertad) during the Mexican Revolution. He became a general of the Ejército Libertador del Sur (Liberation Army of the South), commonly known as Zapatistas. The Zapatistas were mainly poor peasants, who had to take time from their soldiering duties to work their land. Before he organized the Zapatistas into an army, Zapata was involved in many land struggles against the wealthy landowners, who constantly stole the peasants' lands and therefore their livelihood. Almost a century later, Indigenous people struggling for justice reorganized the Zapatistas as a symbol of unity and protest.

Rufino Tamayo (1899–1991), Zapotec

Born in Oaxaca de Juárez, Tamayo was a painter active in the mid-twentieth century both in Mexico and New York City, where he relocated after being criticized for his views of the Mexican revolution. He is credited with developing a technique he named, "Mixografia," a unique fine art printing process that allows prints with to be produced in a three-dimensional texture. One of his murals, "Nacimiento de la Nacionalidad" (1952), adorns the Palacio Nacional de Bellas Artes opera house in Mexico City.

Dr. Francisco Epigmenio Luna Kan (1925–), Maya

Dr. Francisco Luna Kan, a medical doctor, was the first Maya person to be elected governor of of the state of Yucatán (1976–1982). His first political office was administrator of the state's rural medical system. Soon after he was elected governor, he headed by train to a government conference in the capital, Mexico City. He was thrown off the train as the railroad personnel did not believe that "this short man of obvious Native American features" was telling the truth about being a governor. He remains active in the government.

Teodora Blanco Núñez (1928–1980), Mixtec

An artist from Oaxaca, Núñez developed a style of ceramics that still influences the potters of the region. The traditional ceramics of Atzompa have a green glaze, but Blanco Núñez kept her pieces the natural beige and/or a reddish color of the clay. She created female and fantasy figures, generously decorated with finely shaped bits of clay placed on the main body. Today her family carries on her pottery tradition in their family compound and each family member has added his or her own flair to Teodora Blanco Núñez' decorative style called *pastillaje*.

Modesta Lavana Pérez (1929–2010), Nahua

An artist, healer, and activist from the state of Morelos, Modesta Lavana Pérez was also an ethnobotanist and nurse. Known for advocating for Indigenous and women's rights, she was also a legal translator of the Nahuatl language for the state of Morelos. Her traditional backstrap loom weavings won many prizes. Before the area had an official clinic, she treated patients in her home.

Comandanta Ramona (1959–2006), Tzotzil Maya

An officer of the Zapatista Army of National Liberation (EZLN), an Indigenous movement based in the state of Chiapas, Commandanta Romona was one of seven female commanders in charge of directing an army that consisted of one-third women. A member of the Zapatista leading council, the CCRI (Clandestine Revolutionary Indigenous Committee), she was a symbol of equality and dignity for impoverished Indigenous women. Frustrated by seeing her community suffer, she joined the EZLN and became the voice of the many women who had been marginalized by the Mexican government as being too insignificant to care about. But after 100,000 people protested in Mexico City, the government realized this "small and unimportant" part of the population was indeed big and no longer willing to obey laws that hurt them. Ramona took control of the Chiapas city of San Cristóbal de las Casas, during the 1994 Zapatista uprising. Despite battling cancer and having a kidney transplant in 1995, she helped found the National Indigenous Congress. She was the first rebel permitted to travel outside of Chiapas by the federal government. Ramona's calm demeanor and perseverance in her struggle for her people's rights made her an symbol of equality and strength.

Ana Lila Downs Sánchez (1968–), Mixtec

A singer-songwriter and actress, Downs performs her own compositions as well as Indigenous Mexican music. She has recorded songs in as Mixtec, Zapotec, Mayan, Nahuatl, and Purépecha and advocates for the preservation of Native languages. A Grammy winner, her music chronicles the history and struggles of the Indigenous people.

APPENDIX C: THE CARIBBEAN

The Caribbean is one of the most diverse and beautiful regions on the planet. An assortment of 7,000 islands, islets, reefs and cays, the Caribbean islands are sprinkled throughout the sea, with North America and South America forming its western borders. Anguilla, Barbados, British Virgin Islands, Antigua and Barbuda, Cayman Islands, Cuba, Guadeloupe, Grenada, Haiti, Dominican Republic, Trinidad, Jamaica and Puerto Rico are some of the better known islands of the Caribbean archipelago. The rich landscape of this equatorial area ranges from volcanic mountains, lakes and limestone cliffs to verdant green hills, mangrove swamps, white sandy beaches and immense tracts of tropical woods. Some islands feature vast and fast-running rivers, steep mountains and dense rainforests. The Caribbean boasts fertile soil, rich natural resources and unique plants and animals. Hundreds of species of birds call the area home and are as colorful as the bright bursts of plants: poinsettia, orchids and passionflowers. In historical times, this great beauty was homelands to diverse cultures, most of whom were as comfortable on water as on land.

Indigenous peoples of the Caribbean were the first to endure the devastating horrors, savagery and inhumanity of the invading Europeans. But centuries before Columbus and his three ships first landed in the Bahamas, First Islanders were farming, building, crafting, and inventing a multitude of words, towns, roads, foods and items still used today.

History books insist that no Indians in the Caribbean area survived the brutality of the Spaniards and later the French and English. However, they did and throughout the islands there are individuals and communities that have always identified as Indigenous. Science affirms their claims with recent DNA testing linking them to the original Caribbean populations.

Today, even as there are various groups and organizations who assert their Indigenous heritage, the Kalinago community in Dominica is the only official reservation (or any lands exclusively for Indians) in the Caribbean. Each colonial power had/has its own relationship with First Peoples and with the theft and subsequent buying and selling of Native lands, governing countries changed. Today the Caribbean islands are considered a sub region of North America and are organized into 30 territories including sovereign countries, overseas departments, and dependencies. Historians believe that the Caribbean was home to different groups at different times with their origins in Meso and South America. A few of the more well-known groups are the Caquetio, Taíno, Carib (Kal) and Ingeri.

CAQUETIO

The Caquetio lived in present-day Aruba, Curaçao and Bonaire and were originally from Northwest Venezuela. Although they moved to Aruba's inland area to escape the Spaniards, it is believed that most of them were slain.

Taíno

Taíno people across the islands and in the Diaspora recognize themselves, each other, and are being increasingly recognized by other Indigenous Peoples. DNA science simply affirms what our elders have been saying all along—we are the descendants of the original inhabitants of the Caribbean islands and we are still here.

—Roberto "Mukaro" Borrero

The Taíno, an Arawak people, were the largest group in the Caribbean. Historians divide them into three main groups: the Western Taíno; the Classic Taíno; and the Eastern Taíno, with other sub groups within the islands.

The Classic Taíno homelands encompassed eastern Cuba, Hispaniola and present-day Puerto Rico. They had a thriving agricultural tradition and an extremely organized government. Hispaniola was divided into five large territories comprised of 45 smaller states, or chiefdoms. Puerto Rico—called "Boriken" by the Taíno—had twenty autonomous Indigenous territories, the most politically influential was Guainia in the southwest of the island led by Cacique (Chief) Agüeibaná.

The Ciboney or Siboney are a Western Taíno people and traditionally lived in the central part of Cuba during the fifteenth and sixteenth centuries. Circa 1450, some residents of Hispaniola established communities in eastern Cuba. Linguistically and culturally, they differed greatly from the Western Taíno and these mixed communities instituted a less-structured political structure unlike the other territories of the Classic Taíno. Jamaica is also considered a western Taíno Arawak homeland. The culinary style of Jamaican Jerk cooking is said to have originate with the Indigenous Peoples of the island. Eastern Taíno homelands included the Leeward Islands of the Lesser Antilles, from the Virgin Islands to Montserrat.

Taíno society was thought to be formed by two classes: Commoners (*naboria*) and nobles (*nitaíno*). Although chiefs or *cacique*, were male, kinship was matrilineal. A few female leaders such as Anacaona and Higuamama were documented by the Spaniards. The cacique was responsible for the welfare of the people and oversaw community work projects and governed with a fair and gentle hand. As in many other Native cultures, the children were more connected to their mothers' families than their fathers. Priests (*Bohique*) advised the leaders and were an integral part of the community.

Taíno towns (*yucayeques*) were built around a central plaza used for public meetings, ceremonies, recreation, and festivals. Round apartment houses (*bohios*), were often large and home to a dozen or more families. The cacique and his family lived in rectangular homes (*caney*) with wooden porches. Taíno words are part of everyday English and Spanish: *barbacoa* (barbecue), *hamaca* (hammock), *kanoa* (canoe), *tabaco* (tobacco), *yuca, batata* (sweet potato), and *huracán* (hurricane) are but a few examples.

The Taíno had a sustainable agricultural system, which required minimal tending. They built large mounds, *conuco*, to plant their crops of yuca or cassava, corn, beans, squash, yams, peanuts, peppers, and tobacco. The conuco was covered with leaves, which prevented soil erosion and created proper drainage. Like today's Islanders, the people also had a fish-based diet.

An early form of baseball/volleyball was first played by the Taíno. Called *Batu*, the game was mainly ceremonial and sometimes played with bats and a hard rubber ball. Each team had 10 to upwards of

30 men, and women sometimes played, too. Played on a rectangular court similar to today's ball fields called *Batey*. The game was often used to resolve conflicts between communities in the way that stickball (lacrosse) was used by mainland Native societies. Since many believe batu is the forerunner of modern baseball, It is not surprising that many of today's best players were born in the Caribbean.

Columbus the Depraved

Contrary to popular belief, Europeans did not think the world was flat, so Christopher Columbus did not have to convince them it was round—most just did not believe you could sail around the world in a lifetime. Queen Isabella did not sell her jewels to finance his voyage; she offered, but at the last minute wealthy investors coughed up the money. Spain was almost bankrupt because it had emptied its coffers fighting the Moors. Columbus was not the first of his crew to see the "new world"; a crewman was, but Columbus paid him off because being the first to "discover" land had some financial reward. Nearly every island in the Bahamas has laid claim to being the first place to be seen by Europeans, but no one is really certain exactly where Columbus' ships landed. What is certain is that Columbus and his intrepid crew landed somewhere in the Bahamas and started a 500-year reign of oppression, genocide, theft of lands/natural resources, enslavement, and terrorism against First Peoples.

Columbus had only been in Taíno territory for a few seconds when he formulated his impressions of them, which he later recorded in his log: "They … brought us parrots and balls of cotton and spears and many other things, which they exchanged for the glass beads and hawks' bells. They willingly traded everything they owned.… They were well-built, with good bodies and handsome features.… They do not bear arms, and do not know them, for I showed them a sword, they took it by the edge and cut themselves out of ignorance. They have no iron. Their spears are made of cane.… They would make fine servants.… With fifty men we could subjugate them all and make them do whatever we want … they are so naive and so free with their possessions that no one who has not witnessed them would believe it. When you ask for something they have, they never say no. To the contrary, they offer to share with anyone.…" At the end of his report, he requested funding from the Spanish king and queen for another voyage to the islands, and in return he would repay them with "as much gold as they need … and as many slaves as they ask."

As there were no census takers in the fifteenth century, it is hard to estimate the Native population. However, it was sizable, and some early Spanish records document three to four million people on Hispaniola alone. Whatever the number, within a few decades the Indigenous population was decimated, and by 1507, the Spanish counted just 60,000; two decades later, just 600 remained. That number seems an undercount because in 1533 the Spanish documented a successful resistance effort by a Taíno chief Enriquillo in which several thousand Indians participated.

At first, it was European diseases that killed thousands of people, but on Columbus's return, he enforced a tribute law, and Taíno were enslaved to work in the fields and mines. The Spaniards' lust for gold was satisfied by forcing adults (ages fourteen and up) to yield a certain amount. This was difficult, since there were no vast fields of gold like the Spaniards envisioned. There were only bits of gold dust in streams, and it was back-breaking, impossible work to gather it up. If they failed, they either fled and were eaten alive by attack dogs or were beaten into supplying cotton and becoming part of a personal slave force to the Spanish. Children were captured and sold as sex slaves—the Spanish had a perverse appetite for nine-year-old girls. The people, who had once lived in healthy and thriving communities with effective and compassionate leadership, became broken. Many suicides and infanticides resulted.

The Taíno are often portrayed by their European conquerors as a docile and compliant people, easily outwitted and overcome. Although the Taíno had more regard for all life and operated by a different moral compass than the Spanish invaders, they were not docile by any means. There are many accounts of their resistance. Columbus had left sailors behind on the Northwest Coast of Aiti, but the group roamed the island in gangs, stealing, raping, and capturing women and children for sex and labor slaves. The Taíno killed them all, which Columbus discovered upon his return. Word spread from community to community, and the Taíno protected their homelands the best they could. But disease, guns, and attack dogs proved to be a force that could not be defeated.

But the Taíno kept trying. Cacique Hatüey (see biographies below), led his army against the Spanish in Cuba in 1511. Enriquillo (Guarocuya), a Cacique from what is now the Dominican Republic, revolted against the Spanish from 1519 to 1533 in a long rebellion. When he was a child, his father and eighty other leaders were assassinated by the Spanish during so-called peace talks. He is considered a Dominican hero. After his father was slain, Enriquillo was raised in a monastery in Santo Domingo; one of his mentors was Bartolomé de Las Casas, a young Spanish priest, who is credited with becoming somewhat of a champion of the Taíno.

Surprisingly, much of this cruelty was chronicled by Bartolome de Las Casas, who had participated in the conquest of Cuba. He was himself a plantation and slave owner, but became vehemently opposed to the Spanish reign of terror and gave up his position as landowner. "Endless testimonies ... prove the mild and pacific temperament of the natives.... But our work was to exasperate, ravage, kill, mangle and destroy; small wonder, then, if they tried to kill one of us now and then.... The admiral, it is true, was blind as those who came after him, and he was so anxious to please the King that he committed irreparable crimes against the Indians...." In further describing the Spanairds, La Casas recounts that "they grew more conceited every day" and after a while refused to walk any distance. They "rode the backs of Indians if they were in a hurry" or were carried on hammocks by Indians running in relays. "In this case they also had Indians carry large leaves to shade them from the sun and others to fan them with goose wings."

The Spaniards "thought nothing of knifing Indians by tens and twenties and of cutting slices off them to test the sharpness of their blades." Las Casas journaled how "two of these so-called Christians met two Indian boys one day, each carrying a parrot; they took the parrots and for fun beheaded the boys." Las Casas shared how the men and women were separated and both given bone breaking work. When they were able to get together after several months, they were hardly able to procreate. The few babies that were born often could not survive as their mothers suffered from malnutrition and exhaustion.

According to Spanish records, some three million people, an estimated 85% of the Taíno people had disappeared by the early 1500s. And along with them the traditional old religion, the government structure, the language, and the ball fields were all gone, too. There was no eighteenth century Bureau of Indian Affairs or seventeenth century treaty negotiations or nineteenth century forced marches like in the rest of the Americas. In fact, "everyone" agreed that the Taíno had ceased to exist. Yet five centuries after the Indians' first and brutal encounter with Columbus, there is proof that the original people did in fact, endure and are still here.

I want to eliminate the myth once and for all that the Indians were extinguished in Cuba.

—Dr. Alejandro Hartmann, Historian and curator
of the Municipal Museum of Baracoa, Cuba

Contemporary Taíno scholars like Alejandro Hartmann, José Barreiro, Roberto Mukaro Borrero, Dr. Juan Martinez Cruzado, Jorge Estevez, Bobby Gonzalez, and others have documented their existence countless times. In a 2002 report, the Smithsonian Institute's National Museum of the America confirmed that Taíno culture was still very much alive in the mountainous regions of Puerto Rico and other Caribbean countries. Spiritual practices, food preparation, agricultural styles (planting in four lunar stages), arts like weaving and canoe constructio,n and music featuring historical instruments like the maraca and guiro are all part of everyday life for these communities that have preserved and perpetuated Taíno heritage through the centuries. University of Puerto Rico geneticist Dr. Juan Martinez Cruzado designed an island-wide DNA study in 2001. The findings determined that 61% of all Puerto Ricans have Amerindian mitochondrial DNA, more than their African or Caucasian ancestry. Dr. Martinez Cruzado repeated the tests in different Caribbean locations with the same results. As mentioned in the Urban chapter in this book, there has been a resurgence and reclaiming of Taíno culture. Throughout the original Taíno lands, there are organizations and museums focusing on the Taíno.

IGNERI

Igneri, thought to be the original Arawak residents of the Windward Islands, were probably absorbed by the Island Caribs arriving from South America. Some believe that the Carib culture had some vestiges of Igneri customs and language.

Kalinago (Carib)

When you ask me what does it mean to be Kalinago, for me it means being an ambassador of my tribe. To promote awareness and what it means to be part of that tribe and portray the accomplishments of it. This is how I want to give back to my community.

—Rainstar Luke (Kalinago), commercial pilot
and subject of documentary, "Celebration of Flight"

Homelands of the Island Carib included the Windward Islands of the Lesser Antilles, from Dominica to the south. They had a kinship with the Kalina or Carib people of South America. They may have absorbed the Igneri, the original Awarakan speaking inhabitants, into their communities as their language was more Arawakan than Carib. By the seventeenth century, the Kalinago also spoke a Cariban-based pidgin language. The Island Caribs are the ancestors of the present-day Kalinago, who maintain that Carib is a pejorative and colonial term, meaning "cannibal." However, various Caribbean governments and Native groups still use the name today. Carib is also the root work of the Caribbean.

The Kalinago Territory is a 3,700 acre reservation on Dominica's east coast and was established in 1903. Today, there are about 3,000 residents, who elect a chief every four years. Their ancestors had come from South America having sailed up the Orinoco River to the Caribbean Sea. They chose to settle on islands that featured rugged terrain as a natural defense against enemies. According to carbon-dating of Kalinago artifacts, it is estimated that they emigrated to the islands around 1200 C.E.

Known for their military prowess, the Caribs were also great artisans and produced many silver products, which they traded with the Eastern Taíno. In their early culture, the women were highly respected and enjoyed considerable political and social power. They were responsible for the children, food production, and clothing as well as rearing the children. They and their children lived apart from the men, whose tasks were hunting and protecting the community. It is thought that Carib structure was more egalitarian than Taíno society. The local government division was probably comprised of longhouses run by one or more chiefs who reported to a central council. Unlike the Taíno, there was no aristocracy although there were village chiefs and war leaders.

The Caribs knew how to farm, but did not rely on agriculture for their main diet, which was high in protein. They were stellar fishermen and comfortable on long voyages. Like many other religions, they had taboos about eating pork as well as turtles and crabs at certain times.

In 1493, Christopher Columbus arrived in Dominica, searching for gold and other riches. Much to his disappointment, he found a beautiful landscape with clear rivers, fertile volcanic soil, towering mountains, and the Kalinago, but no gold. Like others in the Caribbean, the Kalinago treated the visitors with generosity and hospitality, but Columbus enslaved them and almost worked the entire population to death. For the next two centuries, the Kalinago fiercely resisted colonial forces and managed to survive. Their original choice of geography served them well as no matter how many times the island changed hands among the European powers, the rugged terrain and inaccessible shoreline proved to be a perfect defense for the Kalinago. In 1748, under the treaty of Aix-La-Chapelle, Britain and France accepted the Kalinago control of the island, but the truce did not last long. The British renewed its attacks, and although the Kalinago fought back and survived, England finally controlled the island by 1763. The Kalinago were left just 232 acres. It was the island's most mountainous and rocky coastline, too—probably the worst terrain on the island. In 1903, the homelands were expanded to 3,700 acres and named the Carib Reserve. For the first time since the land theft, a Carib chief was officially recognized.

The territory was not very connected to the rest of Dominica and was pretty much self-sustaining. In 1930, the colonial administrator ordered armed policemen onto the reservation to stop the illegal trade with neighboring French-controlled islands, seize smuggled goods, and arrest smuggler suspects. It did not go well. Residents threw stones and bottles when the police tried to confiscate contraband. The officers fired into the crowd, which resulted in the deaths of two Kalinago and beating of the officers, who escaped without prisoners and contraband. The administrator ordered the marines into the area, more shots were fired and the incident came to be called "The Carib War." As a result, the position of chief was eliminated until 1952, in spite of Carib petitions. Also that year, the Carib Council was formed as a department in Dominica 's government. In 1978, Dominica gained its independence from Britain and the Carib Reserve Act was passed, which reinforced the territory's borders and allowed common ownership of land within the Reserve. The Kalinago were the last residents to receive roads (1970) and electricity (1990s).

Today Kalinago Territory is comprised of eight villages, home to 3,000 residents. They elect a chief every four years as well as a representative to the Dominica House of Assembly. Reportedly some of the best herbal doctors, with a pharmacy of 300 different plants, still practice. Traditions are passed down by elders, but few people are fluent in the language.

Farming

In recent years, the Territory has included tourism as part of its economy. Tourists can visit Kalinago Barana Autê, which is a recreation of a traditional Kalinago town. Artisans demonstrate canoe building, cassava bread baking, basket making, and other Kalinago crafts. Their finely constructed hammocks are sold world-wide. Traditional dances and story-telling are performed by their dance group, Karifuna. The Kalinago Home Stay enterprise provides guests the opportunity to live in the community and participate in village life. Additionally, visitors can enjoy the pristine waterfalls and hiking trails. In spite of their resilience and preservation of traditions, they are the poorest group in Dominica, one of the poorest countries in the Caribbean.

In 1987, the Caribbean Organization of Indigenous Peoples (C.O.I.P) was cofounded by Kalinago Chief Irvince Auguiste to unite and advocate for the rights of Native groups in the Caribbean. Member countries include Belize, Dominica, Guyana, Puerto Rico, Saint Vincent, Suriname, and Trinidad and Tobago. Every three years, the chairmanship rotates to a different country. C.O.I.P. participates in the Indigenous Peoples Forum at the United Nations.

Garifuna

According to both oral and written accounts, in 1675 the Carib rescued Ibibio survivors from Nigeria after the slave ship they were imprisoned on crashed near present-day Bequia, a small island. The Indians took the Ibibio refugees to what is now Saint Vincent; eventually, they wed Carib women. Carib society dictated that men must be married and the Africans became integrated into the community. The culture became blended and absorbed other people from different African and Native groups. Over the centuries, they developed a unique Garifuna language that is still spoken today.

By this time, the Carib had resisted European domination and had been pushed to different islands including Saint Vincent and Martinique. Starting in the late-seventeenth century, both Britain and France laid claim to Saint Vincent. The French squatted and began farming on the island in the early 1710s. In 1719 the governor of Martinique sent a force to occupy it, but the Carib drove them away. In 1723 British invaders were also repelled. Finally, in 1748, Britain and France agreed to designate Saint Vincent a neutral island and abandon their attempts to colonize it, although the French settlement continued to grow. Refugees from Africa were still given sanctuary by the Caribs.

The British gained control through the 1763 Treaty of Paris following its victory over France in the Seven Years' War. But French settlers supported the Carib in their resistance to Britain. The revolt was called the Carib Wars. After the death of Carib leader Satuye (Joseph Chatoyer), the Carib surrendered to the British in 1796, having survived European domination longer than any other Native Caribbeans. St. Vincent was the last of the Windward Islands to be conquered.

The British exiled the Garifuna to Roatán, an island off the coast of Honduras—the more African featured Caribs were deported while the more Amerindian looking people were allowed to remain. Racism and divisiveness had long been a European ploy. Of the five thousand Garifuna that were exiled, only half survived the journey as they were starved and weakened. Roatán was too small and had scarce arable lands that could support a community. The Garifuna petitioned Spanish authorities to be allowed to settle in the Spanish colonies. They were hired by the Spanish and fanned out along the coastal regions of Central America.

Music and dance are an integral part of Garifuna culture. The distinctive songs are known for using many percussion instruments; drums are constructed of hollowed-out hardwoods of Central American trees like mahogany or mayflower. Punta, a traditional music that has changed greatly over the years, is the best-known Garifuna style. Lyrics are usually written by women and the accompanying dances are energetic and competitive. Garifuna traditional foods are a delicious blend of Meso-American crops and African staples, including fish, chicken, plantains, bananas, and cassava. Cassava is so important to the culture that other people called Caribs, "Karifuna," which means cassava clan. *Dharasa* is a popular type of tamale made from green bananas. The Garífuna speak an Arawak based language, which has incorporated many Carib words and phrases. Surprisingly, there are very few African loan words—Linguists claim that they can only identify around five. In 2001, UNESCO declared Garifuna language, dance and music to be a "Masterpiece of the Oral and Intangible Heritage of Humanity."

NOTABLE PEOPLE

Anacaona (1474–1503)

Born in Yaguana (present-day Léogane, Haiti), she and her brother Bohechío were equal negotiators when Columbus visited their chiefdom of Xaragua in late 1496. Anacaona and her people at first developed a cordial relationship with the Spaniards and even sailed about their ship. After her brother's death, she became chief of Xaragua; her husband was captured by the Spanish and died on a slave ship. In spite of Anacaona's tolerance of the Europeans, they tried to burn her and eighty-four other Taíno leaders as the group met to honor her. Cacica (feminine form of chief) Anacaona and her Taíno fellow leaders were arrested, charged with resisting occupation and executed. She was offered clemency if she would become a concubine of a Spaniard. However, Anacaona stood with her countrymen, rebellious and independent, until her violent end.

Agüeybaná II (c. 1470–1511)

One of the strongest and most legendary Taíno caciques in "Borikén" (present-day Puerto Rico), Agüeybaná II ("The Great Sun") led his army against the Spanish in the Battle of Yagüecas, also known as the "Taíno rebellion of 1511." Heading the Conquistadors was Juan Ponce de León. Agüeybaná II proved to his people that the Spaniards were men, not Gods, by drowning one of them in a river. The incident empowered the community and Agüeybaná II commanded an army of 11,000 to eradicate the intruders from their homelands. It is thought that he was the first killed in the battle, which caused his troops to withdraw. However, they conducted guerrilla warfare for the next decade. Today, the Cacique is considered a great hero in Puerto Rico; many places are named for him.

Hatüey (?–1512), Taíno Cacique

Considered to be the first freedom fighter in Cuba, Hatüey was a leader on Haiti (Taíno for high mountains), the island now called Hispaniola and present-day countries of the Dominican Republic and Haiti. In 1511, he and his army of 400 arrived by canoe on the neighboring island of Caobana (present-day Cuba) to warn residents what to expect from the invading Spanish, who were close behind him with plans to conquer the island. Hatüey showed fellow Taínos a basket filled with gold and jewels, explaining that this was what the Spaniards worshipped. "For these they fight and kill; for these they persecute us and that is why we have to throw them into the sea.… They tell us, these tyrants, that they adore a God of peace and equality, and yet they usurp our land and make us their slaves. They speak to us of an immortal soul and of their eternal rewards and punishments, and yet they rob our belongings, seduce our women, violate our daughters. Incapable of matching us in valor, these cowards cover themselves with iron that our weapons cannot break."

The people of Caobana did not believe Hatüey's morbid and violent account and few joined him in battle against the Spaniards once they made landfall. Although he did not have the military support he envisioned, he did not hesitate to wage war on the invaders. Using guerilla tactics, he and his men confined the Spaniards to their fort at Baracoa. The enemy caught Hatüey, eventually, and on February 2, 1512, he was bound to a stake and burned alive at Yara. Before his death, one of the accompanying Spanish priests asked him if he would accept Jesus and go to heaven. The Spanish priest Bartolomé de Las Casas, who considered himself a champion of the Indians, documented the incident: "[T]hinking a little, Hatüey asked the religious man if Spaniards went to heaven. The religious man answered yes.… The chief then said without further thought that he did not want to go there but to hell so as not to be where they were and where he would not see such cruel people. This is the name and honor that God and our faith have earned." For his resistance against colonialism, Hatüey is revered as "Cuba's First National Hero."

Excellent Sir Alexander Clarke Bustamante (1884–1977)

Born William Alexander Clarke in the Jamaican parish of Westmorland, Bustamante changed his last name to that of his Iberian sea captain friend. His travel adventures took him around the Caribbean and New York City; he had many jobs in various countries from policemen to soldier to dietitian. He went back to Jamaica in 1932 to became a leader in the struggle against the British Colonial Government. In 1943, he organized the Bustamante Industrial Trade Union and the Jamaica Labor Party, was elected Jamaica's first premier in 1944 serving until 1954.

Pedro Albizu Campos (1891–1965)

Albizo Campos was an attorney and activist and a leading figure in the Puerto Rican independence movement. He graduated at the top of his Harvard Law School class, earning the privilege of valedictorian and giving the graduation speech. However, his bigoted professors delayed his final exams so he could not graduate on time. While at Harvard, Albizu Campos was active in the Irish independence movement. He also was fluent in eight languages.

In 1924, Pedro Albizu Campos joined the Puerto Rican Nationalist Party and was elected vice president. In 1930, he became president and for the rest of his life fought for freedom from economic imperialism for the Puerto Rican people. The United States considered him a dangerous enemy because he organized working-class people, as well as intellectuals, around issues of dominance and exploitation of American corporations. He was imprisoned many times and for many years, but continued the struggle against oppression. Many consider Pedro Albizu Campos to be the father of the Puerto Rican Independence Movement.

Fidel Castro Ruz (1926–)

President of Cuba from 1959 to 2008 and a legend in his own time, President Castro claims Taíno and Spanish ancestry and is the second Caribbean head of state after Jamaica's Alexander Bustamante to celebrate his Indigenous connections.

Michael Auld (1943–), Yamaye Taíno

An artist and educator, Auld is also a writer and folklorist. He teaches illustration, graphic design, sculpture and art history based on Indigenous Caribbean themes. He is active with the United Confederation of Taíno People (UCTP).

Jose Barreiro, Ph.D. (1948–), Guajiro

Born in Camaguay, Cuba, Barreiro is an educator and scholar of Taíno culture as well as an advocate for Native rights. He is the director of the Office for Latin America, at the Smithsonian National Museum of the American Indian. Barreiro's publications include, *The Indian Chronicles* and *Taíno: A Novel*.

Irvince Auguiste (1962–), Kalinago

In 1984 Irvince Auguiste became the youngest Kalinago Chief ever elected in Kalinago history and served until 1994 and still serves on the Kalinago Tribal Council. Under his administration, he resolved border discrepancies with the British and was key in forming the Caribbean Organization of Indigenous Peoples. Auguiste ensured that Kalinago athletes were able to compete in the Caribbean Community and Common Market (CARICOM) Inter-Tribal Games.

APPENDIX D: GREENLAND

One of my dreams is to help revitalize the use of the kayak in Greenland, and I hope to see more races, perhaps even at the level as the famous Iditarod Race.

—Maligiaq Padilla, considered the world's best kayaker.

Greenland hovers at the very top of North America between the Arctic and North Atlantic Oceans; 2,000 miles (3,219 kilometers) east of Canada and 750 miles (1,207 kilometers) west of Iceland. It is the world's largest island (834,000 square miles, or 1,342,193 square kilometers) and the world's only country that has most of its land mass above the Arctic Circle. The Polar ice cap covers 81% of the nation—an area the size of Libya and is said to contain 10% of the world's fresh water reserves. It is also the world's least densely populated country (although it is the fifteenth largest in area), and 88% of its 57,000 residents are Inuit. Most Greenlanders live on the small strips of coastal lands—no roads connect villages. Greenland is an autonomous nation of Denmark. The remote community of Qaanaaq is home to the "Inughuit" (Great People), the most Northern Indigenous group in the world. The sun sets each October and doesn't appear again until the following February; the sun also doesn't set for four months in the summer.

The Arctic is really the canary in the coal mine in terms of climate change.

—Karla Jessen Williamson, Arctic Institute of North America (2003)

Environmental studies of the effects of global warming on Greenland's ice cover are quite shocking and many believe a warning to the rest of the world. As the ice melts increasingly fast, sea levels will rise to dangerously high levels and the natural rhythm of ocean currents will be interrupted. Because of the melting ice, Greenland's mineral resources are becoming more easily accessible and future mining may pose a threat to Inuit communities as well as the environment. Some speculators feel that with the decline of the fishing industry, mining could provide the territory with a promising source of income. There is already conflict among Inuit about the pros and cons of this kind of development.

LANGUAGE

The Native Greenlandic language is spoken by 90% of the people. There are four dialects of the Indigenous language: South Greenlandic, West Greenlandic, East Greenlandic, and Thule. West Greenlandic or *Kalaallisut* is the official language which all children learn in addition to Danish (also official) and English. Greenlandic has few loan words as very descriptive terms are put together to create new words. For instance, *Garasaasiaq* (artificial brain) is the word for "computer;" *naatsiiat* (something for which one waits for a long time to grow up) means "potato" in Greenlandic.

CUSTOMS/HERITAGE

Traditional Inuit culture forms the foundation of contemporary Greenlander life. In the capital city of Nuuk and some other towns, Greenlanders live similarly to the descendants of Danish immigrants. However, across the country community ownership of land and common resources and the practice of interdependence is common as people need to band together in the harsh environment. Although most the majority Greenlanders are connected to the Lutheran Church, the Inuit religion is the main spiritual practice in more remote communities.

Greenland has a strong tradition of oral storytelling and song, preserving ancient accounts and using them to set standards for correct behavior. Artists are world renown carving small wood or bone sculptures called *tupilait,* which depict mystical creatures or arctic animals. The Greenlandic word for art is *Eqqumiitsuliorneq*, meaning "to create things that look strange." Greenlanders still design colorful and complex beaded yokes and capes, that often extend almost to the waist. They crochet part of their accessories, too, creating new/old fashions. They quickly developed a beading art after gaining glass beads from traders in the 1800s.

Until the missionaries banned their use, Greenlanders played on a drum (*qilaat*) carved from an oval wooden frame and covered with the bladder of a polar bear. The qilaat differed from other drums as it was played by hitting the frame with a stick, not the skin. Drum dances are still performed today—they are danced by one man at a time and he is judged by how long he can dance. The *katajjaq* tradition is a singing game played by two women, who face each other using throat singing and animal sounds. The game rarely has a victor as both women start laughing and cannot finish. Rasmus Ole Lyberth, a Greenlandic singer, songwriter and actor, combines traditional elements in his contemporary m music. The internationally popular pop/rock band Nanook, sings only in Greenlandic; their music is featured on the series, "Flying Wild Alaska." Today, Greenlanders have a vibrant music scene and play a variety of styles from jazz to hip hop.

ECONOMY

Fishing is the basis of the Greenlandic economy. Shrimps, halibut and cod are the primary catch. It is estimated that there are an assortment of 850 larger fishing vessels and about 5,000 smaller boats, most owned by Inuit. These smaller operations have been severely impacted by climate changes. At first glance, the northwest coast fishing village of Uummannaq in the Qaanaaq district is a pretty place. Gumdrop colored houses decorate a rocky landscape with a majestic heart shaped mountain in the background. For years, residents have used dog sleds to travel across the winter sea ice to fishing grounds and in the summer after the ice has melted, they fish by boat. However, the winter ice has become too thin to support the sleds—it is melting earlier and becoming less stable. The boats are not built to withstand the large waves caused by the melting ice and are not strong enough to penetrate the ice. Fishermen are becoming less able to go to work and many sink into despair as their impaired livelihood makes them unable to take care of their families.

Sea mammal hunting is becoming increasingly difficult for hunters as the U.S. and EEC's have government bans on import of seal skins. Seals are the main animals hunted throughout the year. Walrus are caught mainly during the spring and autumn when they migrate along the coast. Polar bears are normally hunted in February March, around Smith Sound and Melville Bay. During the brief Arctic summer, the Inughuit hunt Narwhals and white whales.

Tourism has increased in the last two decades and both ships and planes bring people to Greenland to have an "exotic" experience dog sledding, viewing the Northern Lights and vacationing at the home of an Inuit family. Since the 1990s, the annual number of tourists has spiked from 3,500 to 35,000. Greenlanders face the challenge of attracting more tourism while preserving their environment. The Inuit are hoping that an appreciation of their way of life and their region's natural beauty will spark a greater awareness of environment and sustainability.

Katuaq (Greenland Cultural Centre) is located in the nation's capital, Nuuk, in the southwest. Events draw international visitors to its art and performance venue as well as a sports arena (Inussivik), which has hosted the Arctic Winter Games (AWG), an international biennial celebration of circumpolar sports and culture. "The AWG enhance self esteem and promote growth in personal outlooks, promote socialization and cultural awareness, promote positive experiences and personal benefits, provide health and social opportunities, and promote a sense of belonging and strengthens community ties." Athletes compete in games original to the Arctic like "Finger Pull," "One Foot High Kick," "Hand Game," and "Dog Mushing." They also challenge in other in such diverse events as Badminton, Volleyball and Indoor soccer. All together there are twenty different sports categories with age and gender divisions.

TIMELINE

Year	Event
2500–1000 B.C.E.	People referred to by historians as 'Independence I" from Canada settled in north Greenland.
2500–800 B.C.E.	Saqqaq people from Siberia settled in southeast and west Greenland.
700–80 B.C.E.	Independence II people (called the Early Dorset) move to north and northeast, near Independence Fjord.
500 B.C.E.–1500 C.E.	The Tuniit (Dorset) people from Canada settle in the northwest.
982	Norseman Eric the Red, is exiled to Greeland from Iceland.
986	Eric founds Norse colonies in southern Greenland.
1200	Ancestors of the present day Inuit called the Thule Inuit arrive from Canada and settle throughout the island.
1261	Greenland's representatives of Norse Parliament in vote for rule by Norwegian king.
1408	A marriage recorded at the Hvalsey Church in the East Settlement was the last record of the Norse in Greenland.
1500	Norse settlement had all been abandoned.

Year	Event
1700	Another group of people from Canada, called the Copper Inuit, settle in the Thule region.
1721	Believing their subjects still survived despite no contact with the Norse Greenlanders for centuries, Norway-Denmark claimed sovereignty over the territory. A Danish missionary expedition arrives to Greenland to "save the souls" of any of their countrymen who may have reverted to paganism. Instead, they "baptized" Inuit people and set up trading colonies along the coast, imposing a trade monopoly and other colonial rule.
1789–1790	Mathias Fersløv Dalager (Kalaaleq, c. 1769–1843) from Ritenbenk, became the first Greenlandic Inuit to complete a European education. He studied at the Royal Danish Academy of Fine Arts in Copenhagen.
1840s	Israil Nichodimus Gormansen (Kalaaleq, 1804–1857) paints scenes of daily life with India ink and watercolors.
1818–1819	Hans Zakæus (Kalaaleq, 1795–1819) accompanies the John Ross expedition to northern Greenland and documents first European contact with the Inughuit Inuit through lithographic prints.
1850	Kalaaleq hunter Aron of Kangeq (1822–1869), bedridden with tuberculosis, begins painting watercolors that document daily life and oral history.
1860	Survey of Greenlandic printmaking, Kaladlit Ássilialiait (Greenlandic Woodcuts) is published, featuring works by Rasmus Berthelsen, Aron of Kangeq, Jens Kreutzmann, and others.
1857	Rasmus Berthelsen (1827–1901) illustrates Pok, the first book published in Greenland, with woodblock prints.
1861	*Atuagagdliutit*, the first Inuit newspaper founded by Danish geologist, inspector Hinrich Johannes Rink, to preserve Inuit cultural identity. Lars Møller (Inuit, 1842–1926) was illustrator and newspaper was published in Kalaallisut language. Supposedly the first ever color newspaper illustration in the world was published in the *Atuagagdliutit*—a woodcut of American navy visiting Nuuk, Greenland's capital.
1880	The Greenland Dog was recognized by the International Kennel Club. One of the oldest breeds in the world, it was first brought to Greenland by the Sarqaq people 5,000 years ago. Because of climate changes and the decline of sledding, their numbers have declined, too.
1891–1892	American Robert Peary explores north Greenland.
1895–1905	Isak of Igdlorpait (Kalaaleq) paints watercolors, published posthumously in 1969.
1897	Explorer Robert Peary takes six Inughuit Inuit to New York, to be exhibited as living specimens at the American Museum of Natural History. Five die of disease, except for Minik Wallace.
	Late-nineteenth century Greenlandic women begin a new arts tradition of beaded collars.
1902	Knud Johan Victor Rasmussen, born and raised in Greenland by his Inuit mother, returned to Greenland from Denmark for the first of several expeditions exploring the lands and culture of his homelands. He wrote *The People of the Polar North* and although he is referenced as a European, his spoke Inuit and was accepted for his Inuit heritage.

Year	Event
1905	After centuries of disuse, Mitsivarniannga of Ammassalik (Tunumiit), an angakoq (spiritual leader), carves a wooden tupilait (an effigy figure that can cause destruction) with no negative consequences. Others begin to carve them and create a tupilati art form attracting international collectors.
1924	Denmark officially claims Greenland.
1925	Jakob Danielsen (Kalaaleq) depicts hunting scenes in his paintings.
1925–1929	Sculptors in Kangaamiut begin carving soapstone and sperm whale ivory figures.
1940	Nazi Germany begin occupation of Greenland in World War II.
1941	The U.S. military occupies Greenland to deter the Nazis.
1951–1953	Denmark displaces the Inughuit Inuit residents of Pituffik village for the United States' Thule Air Base. Danish authorities also began a social experiment. They removed Inuit children from their parents and culture, relocated them to Denmark for adoption the plan to "transform them into small Danes." Half of the children died.
1953	Greenland gains representation in Danish parliament.
1968	Denmark's parliament and Greenland's national council closed the mining town of Qullissat and in 1972 the mine closed. The remaining population was forcibly relocated to other towns, which caused serious problems for these families. The town became a symbol of the colonialism's destructive power; many well-known politicians have their roots in Qullissat.
1971	Greenland Football Association (GBU) was formed. Today, over 10% of the population play football (soccer), Greenland's national sport, yet there is not one grass pitch in the country. Their coach is from Eritrea; their dream is to become a member of FIFA.
1972	A workshop opens in Nuuk featuring lithography, woodcutting, and etching; it becomes the School of Art in 1981.
1975	Tuukaq Theater becomes a space for acting and dance and spearheads the revival of Uaajeerneq, the masked dance of East Greenland.
1977	The Inuit Circumpolar Council is established with Indigenous representatives from Canada, Greenland, Russia, and the United States.
1979	Greenland gains home rule. Denmark controls foreign affairs and defense.
1982	National Museum in Denmark repatriates thousands of artworks to the Home Rule authorities in Greenland, including 204 watercolors by Aron of Kangeq and Jens Kreutzmann.
1984–1985	Greenland votes to leave the European Union to try to halt unsustainable overfishing by German companies sanctioned by the European Union.
1985	Inuit teacher, artist and politician. Thue Christiansen designs Greenland's flag. Christiansen served as the Greelandic Minister of Culture and Education from 1979 to 1983.
1987	Nordic Institute in Greenland (NAPA) opens.
1993	Aka Høegh, with eighteen Scandinavian artists, creates the Stone and Man sculpture garden in Qaqortoq, becoming the first large-scale international public art project in Greenland.

Year	Event
1993–1997	*The Flying Kayak*, an offering of contemporary Greenlandic art is exhibited in Denmark, Norway, Sweden, Finland, Poland, Spain, and Greenland.
1994	Nuuk Snow Festival (*Nuuk Snefestival*) begins and soon becomes an international snow sculpture competition, using traditional tools.
1995	KIMIK, the Association of Artists in Greenland, is founded.
1997	Katuaq Culture Center opens in Nuuk.
1999	Ice sheets in lower elevations begin melting at a rate of three feet per year.
2004	Science reports the acceleration of the melting Greenland's ice sheet. The Ilulissat Icefjord was inscribed as a World Heritage Site because of its unique glaciological characteristics and its scenic beauty.
2005	Nuuk Art Museum opens.
2006	*Rethinking Nordic Colonialism: A Postcolonial Exhibition Project in Five Acts* shows at the Greenland National Museum and Archives.
2007–2008	International Polar Year conference, sponsored by the Greenland Nation Museum and Archive—main topic is cultural repatriation.
2007	Anersaarta, a group comprised of Indigenous artists and cultural activists, marches in the capital of Nuuk for restoration of Inuit culture. The organization gains sympathy with Parliament who develops funding for cultural events.
2008	Greenland votes for self rule and gains more control over their energy resources. Greenlanders gain the right to self-determination and to define the status of their country on traditions of Inuit life. Kalaallisut becomes the official language.
2008	Taseralik Cultural Center is founded in Sisimiut.
2009	Greenland gained the right to negotiate foreign policy.
2010	*Kuuk*, a fourteen-artist exhibit, explores Greenlandic identity.
2010	Science reports increases in acceleration of ice melt and rising sea levels.
2012	Air Greenland begins commercial flights from Nuuk to Iqualiut, Nunavut.
2012	*Possible Greenland*, an exhibit of Greenlandic and Danish artists and architects, is featured in the Danish Pavilion at Venice Biennale.
2014	Greenland's parliament voted 15 to 14 to overturn a long-standing ban on uranium mining triggering a heated debate.
2015	Under the administration of Prime Minister Kim Kielsen, Greenland plans to have eighteen mines in place by 2018. The government sees the mining industry as a way to become financially independent from Denmark.

NOTABLE GREENLANDERS

Kristian Olsen Aaju is an award-winning writer and artist with several novels, including the thriller, *Kakiorneqaqatigiit* ("The Tattooed Message"). He is the recipient of the 2007 the Greenland Parliament Home Rule silver medal.

Maliina Abelsen, General Manager for Arctic Winter Games 2016, is the Minister for Finance in the Government of Greenland (Greenlandic: Naalakkersuisut). Abelsen has also served as the Minister for Social Affairs (2009–2011).

Jørgen Brønlund (1877–1907) was a Greenlandic polar explorer and educator. He was a childhood friend of Knud Rasmussen and joined him on his first two expeditions to Greenland. An expert interpreter, he kept the travel diary for the company and also drove the dogs. Brønlund died while returning to camp.

Nukaaka Coster-Waldau, a.k.a. Nukâka, is a Greenlandic singer, actress, and a former Miss Greenland.

Aleqa Hammond was Greenland's first female Prime Minister (2013–2014).

Bolatta Silis Høegh uses her art to call attention to social and environmental issues. Daughter of renown artist Aka Høegh, her most famous installation is *Haveforeningen Sisimiut 2068*, a musing of the future state of Greenland and the effects of global warming. Bikinis and anoraks are shown hanging on a clothes line.

Inuk Silis-Høegh is a Greenlandic artist and filmmaker and has been credited with debunking stereotypes about Inuit people. His documentary, *Sumé: Sound of a Revolution*, is about the groundbreaking Greenlandic rock band Sumé (2014).

Theodora Høegh, from Narsaq in South Greenland, is the proprietor and creator of Inuit Young, a natural Greenlandic herbal soap business.

Mimi Karlsen is the Minister for Culture, Education, Research and Church Affairs.

Sara Olsvig is leader of the Inuit *Ataqatigiit* political party and holds one of Greenland's two seats in the Danish Folketing (Parliament).

Sofie Petersen is the Lutheran bishop of Greenland and a respected and outspoken advocate for climate justice.

Karla Jessen Williamson, is the Executive Director of the Arctic Institute of North America (AINA), the first woman and first Greenlander to hold the position.

APPENDIX E:
INDIGENOUS NATIONS/GROUPS
IN NATIVE AMERICAN ALMANAC

UNITED STATES

Major Cultural Groups in Alaska

Aleut (Unangan)
Alutiiq (Sugpiag)
Athabascan
Cup'ik
Eyak
Haida
Inupiat
St Lawrence Island Yup'ik
Tlingit
Tsimshian
Yup'ik

Major California Native Nations

Cahto
Cahuilla
Chemehuevi
Chilula
Chumash
Cupeno
Hupa
Karuk
Kawaiisu

Kitanemuk
Kumeyaay (Diegueno)
Luiseno
Maidu
Mattole
Miwok
Mojave
Mono (Western)
Paiute
Pomo
Serrano
Shasta
Shoshone
Tolowa
Tubatulabel
Wailaki
Wappo
Washoe
Whilkut
Wintun
Wiyot
Yana
Yokuts
Yuki
Yurok

Great Basin and Rocky Mountain Tribes and Nations

Coeur D'Alene

Confederated Salish and Kutenai

Confederated Tribes of the Goshute Reservation

Duckwater Shoshone Tribe

Ely Shoshone Tribe

Fort McDermitt Paiute and Shoshone

Fort Mohave Indian Tribe (also in California and Arizona);

Koosharem, Indian Peaks, and Shivwits bands of Paiute

Kootenai Nez Perce Tribe

Las Vegas Tribe of Paiute Indians

Lovelock Paiute Tribe

Moapa Band of Paiute Indians

Mountain Ute

Northwestern Band of Shoshone Nation (Washakie)

Paiute Indian Tribe

Paiute-Shoshone Tribe of the Fallon Reservation

Pyramid Lake Paiute Tribe

Reno-Sparks Indian Colony (Washoe, Paiute, and Shoshone)

Shoshone

Shoshone-Bannock Tribes Arapaho

Shoshone-Paiute Tribes of the Duck Valley Reservation

Skull Valley Band of Goshute Indians

Southern Ute Tribe

Summit Lake Paiute Tribe

Te-Moak Tribe of Western Shoshone Indians

Ute Indian Tribe of the Uintah and Ouray Reservation

Walker River Paiute

Washoe Communities and Rancheria of Nevada and California

Washoe Tribe (also in California)

Winnemucca Indian Colony (Western Shoshone)

Yerington Paiute Tribe

Yomba Shoshone Tribe

Midwest

Anishinaabe (Ojibwe/Chippewa)

Asakiwaki (Sauk)

Atchatchakangouen

Bodewadmik (Potawatomi)

Cahinnio

Coiacoentanon

Dakota (Sioux)

Ho-Chunk (Winnebago)

Ioway people

Kaskaskaham

Kaskinampo

Kilatlka

Kiwigapawa (Kickapoo)

Mamaceqtaw (Menominee)

Mascouten

Mengakonkia

Meskwaki (Fox)

Mishigamaw

Missouria(Neutache)

Moingwena

Mosopelea

Noquet

Odawa

Peewaarewa

Pepicokia

Piankeshaw

Shawanwa (Shawnee)

Tapouaro

Twightwee (Miami)

Ugakpa (Quapaw)

United Remnant Band of Shawnee

Waayaahtanwa

Wendat (Huron)

Northeast

Abenaki (Eastern and Western)

Cayuga

Huron

Mahican

Maliseet

Micmac

Mohawk

Mohegan

Montauk

Nanticoke

Narragansett

Nipmuc-Hassanamisco

Oneida

Onondaga

Passamaquoddy

Paugussett

Penobscot

Pequot (Eastern and Western)

Piscataway Conoy

Powhatan Renape

Ramapough

Sand Hill Band of Lenape and Cherokee Indians

Schaghticoke

Seneca

Shinnecock

Tuscarora

Unkechaga (Poospatuk)

Wampanoag (Aquinnah, Assonet, Herring Pond, Mashpee, Namasket, Pocassett)

Northern Plains

Blackfeet Nation

Chippewa-Cree Tribe

Crow Nation

Flandreau Isanti Sioux

Fort Belknap Indian Community of Gros Ventre and Assiniboine

Fort Peck Assiniboine and Sioux Tribes

Iowa Tribe of Kansas and Nebraska

Isanti (Santee) Sioux tribes

Kickapoo Tribe

Mandan Hidatsa Arikara Nation

Northern Cheyenne Nation

Northern Ponca

Oglala Lakota Nation

Omaha

Prairie Band Potawatomi Nation

Rosebud, Crow Creek, Lower Brule, Cheyenne River, and Standing Rock Sioux tribes

Sisseton-Wahpeton Oyate (Dakota)

Spirit Lake Tribe Nation (Dakota)

Turtle Mountain Band of Chippewa Indians

Yankton Sioux (Isanti and Nakota)

Southeast

Accohanoc

Accomac

Acolapissa

Adai

Adais Caddo Biloxi-Chitimacha Confederation of Muskogee

Alabama

Apalachee

Arrohattoc

Atakapa

Avoyel

Bayogoula

Bayou LaFourche Band

Beaver Creek

Bidai

Biloxi

Caddo

Calusa

Catawba

Chatot

Chawasha

Cheraw

Cherokee

Chesapeake

Chickahominy

Chickasaw

Chiskiac

Chitimacha

Choctaw

Chowanoc

Coharie

Coree or Coranine

Coushatta

Cuttatawomen

Doustioni

Edisto Natchez-Kusso

Eno

Grand Caillou/Dulac Band

Hatteras

Houma

Isle de Jean Charles Band

Kadohadacho

Kecoughtan

Keyauwee

Koasati or Coushatta

Koroa

Lumbee

Machapunga

Manahoac

Mattaponi

Meherrin

Miccosukee

Monacan

Moneton

Moratok

Moraughtacund

Mugulasha

Mummapacune

Muskogee

Muskogee Creek

Nahyssan

Nansemond

Nantaughtacund

Natchez

Natchitoches Confederacy

Neusiok

Nottaway

Occaneechi

Ofo

Ofogoula

Okelousa

Onawmanient

Opelousa

Ouachita

Pamlico

Pamunkey

Pascagoula

Paspahegh

Pataunck

Pee Dee

Piankatank

Pissasec

Pointe-au-Chien

Potomac

Powhatan

Quapaw

Quinipissa

Rappahannock

Saponi

Sara

Secacawoni

Seminole

Shakori

Shawnee

Sissipahaw

Souchitioni

Sugeree

Taensa

Tangipahoa

Tauxenent

Tawasa

Timucua

Tunica

Tunica-Biloxi

Tuscarora

Tutelo

Waccamaw

Warrasqueoc

Washa

Wateree

Southern Plains

Alabama-Coushatta Coahuilteco

Caddo

Carrizo

Comanche

Jumano

Kickapoo

Kiowa

Ndeh (Apache)

Niukonska (Osage)

Tonkawa

Wichita

Ysleta del Sur (Tigua)

Southwest

Cocopah Indian Tribe (Kwapa)

Colorado River Indian Tribes: Mohave, Cheme-heuve, and Hopi

Fort Mojave Indian Tribe (Aha Makav)

Gila River Indian Community, Camp Verde and Ak Chin Maricopa Community

Havasupai Tribe

Hopi

Hualapai Indian Tribe

Jicarilla Apache Nation (Ndeh)

Pueblos of Isleta, Santa Ana (Tamaya Nation), San Felipe (Katishtya), Santo Domingo, Cochiti, Tesuque (Tet-sugeh), Nambé, Po-joaque (Po-Suwae-Geh), San Idelfonso (Po-Who-Geh-Owingeh), Santa Clara (Kha'p'oo Owinge), Picuris, Taos, Ohkay Owingen, Jemez (Walatowa), Zia, Sandia, Acoma (Haak'u), Laguna; and the Zuni Tribe

Kaibab Band of Paiute Indians

Mescalero Apache Tribe

Navajo Nation (Diné)

Pascua Yaqui Tribe

Pima (Akimel O'odham)

Quechan Tribe of Fort Yuma

Salt River Pima-Maricopa Indian Community,

San Juan Southern Paiute Tribe

Small Ramah and Alamo Navajo communities

Tohono O'odham Nation

Tonto

Ute Mountain

White Mountain, and San Carlos Apache tribes (N'deh)

Yavapai Nation: Fort McDowell, Yavapai-Apache, and Yavapai-Prescott

Ysleta del Sur Pueblo (Tigua)

Urban

Garifuna

Mayan

Mixteco, Nahua, Chinanteco, Tlapaneco, and Otom

Quechua

Taino

Washington/Oregon

Burns Paiute

Chehalis

Colville: Coleville, Wenatche, Entiate, Chelan, Methow, Okanogan, Nespelem, San Poil, Lakes, Moses Columbia, Palus, and Nez Perce

Confederated Tribes of Coos, Lower Umpqua, and Siuslaw Indians

Coquille

Cow Creek Umpqua

Cowlitz (Upper and Lower)

Grand Ronde: Kalapuya, Rogue River, Shasta (Tillamook)

Hoh

Jamestown S'Klallam

Kalispel

Klamath

Lower Elwha

Lummi

Makah

Muckleshoot

Nisqually

Port Gamble S'Klallam

Port Madison Suquamish

Puyallup

Quileute

Quinault

Samish

Sauk-Suiattle

Siletz

Skokomish

Snoqualmie

Spokane

Squaxin Island

Stillaguamish

Swinomish

Tulalip

Umatilla

Upper Skagit

Walla Walla

Warm Springs: Ichishkiin, Wasco, and Numu (Northern Paiute)

Yakama

CANADA

Nova Scotia

Big Cove First Nation (Micmac)

Bouctouche First Nation (Micmac)

Buctouche Reserve, New Brunswick (Micmac)

Chapel Island First Nation (Micmac)

Eskasoni First Nation (Micmac)

Fort Folly First Nation (Micmac)

Membertou First Nation (Micmac)

Millbrook First Nation (Micmac)

New Brunswick

Red Bank First Nation (Micmac)

St Mary's First Nation (Maliseet)

Woodstock First Nation (Maliseet)

Prince Edward Island

Abegweit First Nation (Mi'kmaq)

Lennox Island First Nation (Mi'kmaq)

Newfoundland and Labrador

The Labrador Metis Nation

Miawpukek First Nation (Mi'kmaq)

Mushuau Innu First Nation

Nunatsiavut Government (Inuit)

Sheshatshiu Innu First Nation

Quebec

Abitibiwinni First Nation (Algonquin)

Atikamekw Nation

Eagle Village First Nation (Algonquin)

Gaspe First Nation (Micmac)

Gesgapegiag First Nation (Micmac)

Huron-Wendat First Nation

Kahnawake First Nation (Mohawk)

Kitigan Zibi First Nation (Algonquin)

Listuguj First Nation (Micmac)

Malécite First Nation

Mamit Innuat (Montagnais/Naskapi)

Mistissini First Nation (Cree)

Odanak First Nation (Abenaki)

Ouje-Bougoumou First Nation (Cree)

Waswanipi First Nation (Cree)

Wemindji First Nation (Cree)

Wolinak First Nation (Abenaki)

Ontario

Akwesasne Mohawk Nation

Alderville First Nation (Ojibwe)

Algonquins of Golden Lake/Pikw kanag n

Beausoleil First Nation (Ojibwe)

Chapleau Cree First Nation

Curve Lake First Nation (Ojibwe)

Ketegaunseebee Garden River First Nation (Ojibwe)

Metis Nation of Ontario

Michipicoten First Nation (Ojibwe)

Moose Cree First Nation

New Credit First Nation (Ojibwe)

Pic River First Nation (Ojibwe)

Six Nations of the Grand River Territory (Iroquois)

Tyendinaga Mohawk Nation/Bay of Quinte Mohawks

Walpole Island/Bkejwanong First Nation (Ojibwe, Ottawa, and Potawatomi)

Wikwemikong First Nation (Ojibwe and Ottawa)

Manitoba

Birdtail Sioux First Nation

Brokenhead Ojibway Band

Buffalo Point First Nation (Ojibway)

Canupawakpa First Nation (Dakota)

Cross Lake First Nation (Cree)

Dakota Plains First Nation

Dauphin River First Nation (Ojibway)

Fox Lake First Nation (Cree)

Gambler First Nation (Cree)

Keeseekoowenin First Nation (Ojibway)

Kinonjeoshtegon First Nation (Ojibway)

Lake Manitoba First Nation (Ojibway)

Lake St Martin First Nation (Ojibway)

Little Saskatchewan First Nation (Ojibway)

Long Plain First Nation (Ojibway)

Manitoba Metis Federation

Norway House Cree Nation

Northlands Dene First Nation

Opaskwayak Cree Nation

Peguis First Nation (Cree)

Rolling River First Nation

Roseau River Anishinabe First Nation

Sagkeeng First Nation (Ojibway)

Sayisi Dene First Nation

Split Lake First Nation (Cree)

York Factory First Nation (Cree)

Nunavut

Inuit

Northwest Territories

Acho Dene Koe

Aklavik First Nation

Behdzi Ahda First Nation (Dene)

Dechi Laot'i First Nations (Dogrib)

Deh Gah Gotie Dene Council

Deline Dene Band

Dene Cultural Institute

Dene Nation

Deninu K'ue First Nation (Dene)

Dog Rib Rae

Fort Good Hope (Dene)

Gameti First Nation (Dogrib)

Gwichya Gwich'in

Inuvik Native

Jean Marie River First Nation (Slavey)

Ka'a'gee Tu First Nation (Dene)

K'atlodeeche First Nation (Dene)

Liidlii Kue First Nation (Slavey)

Lutsel K'e Dene

Metis Association of the Northwest Territories

Nahanni Butte Dene Band

NWT Metis-Dene Development Fund (NWT-MDDF)

Tulita Dene Nation

West Point First Nation (Dene)

Wha Ti First Nation (Dogrib)

Yellowknives Dene First Nation

Yukon

Burwash Landing, Yukon Y0B 1V0

Carcross/Tagish First Nation

Champagne and Aishihik First Nations (Tutchone)

First Nation of Na-cho Nyak Dun (Tutchone)

Kaska Tribal Council

Kluane First Nation (Tutchone and Tlingit)

Kwanlin Dun First Nation (Tagish)

Liard First Nation (Kaska)

Little Salmon/Carmacks First Nation (Tutchone)

Ross River Dena First Nation (Kaska and Slavey)

Selkirk First Nation (Tutchone)

Ta'an Kwach'an First Nation (Tutchone)

Teslin Tlingit Council

Tr'ondëk Hwëch'in First Nation (Han)

Vuntut Gwitch'in First Nation

White River First Nation (Tanana)

Saskatchewan

Big River First Nation (Cree)

Buffalo River Dene Nation

Clearwater River Dene First Nation

Cumberland House Cree Nation

Flying Dust First Nation (Cree)

Keeseekoose First Nation (Ojibway)

Lucky Man Cree Nation

Muskeg Lake First Nation (Cree)

Onion Lake First Nation (Cree)

Red Pheasant First Nation (Cree)

Sakimay First Nation (Cree)

Saulteaux First Nation (Ojibway)

Shoal Lake of the Cree Nation

Wahpeton Dakota Nation

Metis Nation of Saskatchewan

Alberta

Alberta Metis Nation

Alexander First Nation (Cree)

Athabasca Chipewyan First Nation

Beaver First Nation

Beaver Lake Cree Nation

Bigstone Cree Nation

Blood First Nation (Blackfoot)

Chipewyan Prairie First Nation

Cold Lake First Nations (Cree)

Dene Tha' First Nation (Slavey)

Driftpile First Nation (Cree)

Duncan's First Nation (Cree)

Enoch Cree Nation

Ermineskin Cree Nation

Fort McKay First Nation (Cree)

Fort McMurray First Nation (Cree)

Frog Lake First Nation (Cree)

Heart Lake First Nation (Cree)

Horse Lake First Nation (Beaver)

Kapawe'no First Nation (Cree)

Kehewin Cree Nation

Little Red River Cree Nation

Loon River First Nation (Cree)

Louis Bull Tribe (Cree)

Lubicon Lake First Nation (Cree)

Mikisew Cree First Nation

Montana First Nation (Cree)

O'Chiese First Nation (Saulteaux)

Paul First Nation (Cree/Nakoda)

Peerless Trout First Nation (Cree)

Peigan Reserve (Blackfoot)

Saddle Lake Cree Nation

Samson Cree Nation

Sawridge First Nation (Cree)

Siksika First Nation (Blackfoot)

Stoney First Nation

Sturgeon Lake First Nation (Cree)

Sucker Creek First Nation (Cree)

Sunchild First Nation (Cree)

Swan River First Nation (Cree)

Tallcree First Nation (Cree)

Tsuu T'ina First Nation (Sarcee)

Whitefish Lake First Nation (Cree)

Woodland Cree First Nation

British Columbia

Adams Lake First Nation (Secwepemc)

Ahousaht First Nation

Anderson Lake First Nation (N'quatqua)

Ashcroft First Nation (Nlaka'pamux)

Bonaparte First Nation (Secwepemc)

Boothroyd First Nation (Nlaka'pamux)

Boston Bar First Nation (Nlaka'pamux)

Bridge River First Nation (St'at'imc or Lillooet)

Broman Lake First Nation (Wet'suwet'en)

Canim Lake First Nation (Secwepemc)

Canoe Creek First Nation (Secwepemc)

Cayoose Creek First Nation (St'at'imc or Lillooet)

Chemainus First Nation (Coast Salish)

Cold Water First Nation (Nlaka'pamux)

Columbia Lake First Nation (Kutenai)

Cook's Ferry First Nation (Nlaka'pamux)

Cowichan First Nation

Cowichan Lake First Nation

Dease River First Nation (Kaska Dena)

Douglas First Nation (St'at'imc or Lillooet)

Ehattesaht First Nation (Nuu-Chah-Nulth)

Fort Ware First Nation (Kwadacha)

Gitanmaax First Nation

Gitlakdamix Band Council

Gitwangak First Nation

Gitwinksihlkw First Nation

Glen Vowell First Nation (Gitxsan)

Halalt First Nation (Cowichan)

Hesquiaht First Nation

High Bar First Nation

Hupacasath First Nation (Muh-uulth-aht, Kleh-koot-aht and Cuu-ma-as-aht)

Huu-ay-aht First Nation

Kamloops First Nation (Secwepemc)

Kanaka Bar First Nation (Nlaka'pamux)

Kincolith First Nation (Nisga'a)

Kispiox First Nation (Gitxsan)

Kluskus First Nation (Lhoosk'uz Dakelh)

K'ómoks First Nation

Kwa-Wa-Aineuk First Nation ('Nakwaxda'xw)

Kwiakah First Nation

Kwicksutaineuk-Ah-Kwaw-Ah-Mish

Kyuquot First Nation (Nuu-Chah-Nulth)

Lakalzap First Nation (Nisga'a)

Liard First Nation (Kaska Dena)

Lillooet First Nation

Lower Kootenay First Nation

Lower Nicola First Nation (Nlaka'pamux)

Lower Similkameen First Nation

Lyackson First Nation

Mamaleleqala-Qwe-Qwa-Sot-Enox

Metis Provincial Council of British Columbia

Mount Currie First Nation (Lil'wat)

Mowachaht First Nation

Musqueam Indian Band (Coast Salish and only reserve within the city of Vancouver)

Nadleh Whut'en (Dakelh)

Nak'azdli (Dakelh)

Neskonlith First Nation (Secwepemc)

Nicomen First Nation (Nlaka'pamux)

Nooaitch First Nation (Nlaka'pamux)

North Thompson First Nation (Simpcw)

Nuchatlaht First Nation

Nuxalk Nation (Bella Coola)

Okanagan First Nation

Oregon Jack Creek First Nation (Nlaka'pamux)

Osoyoos First Nation (Okanagan)

Pauquachin First Nation (Salish)

Penelakut First Nation

Penticton Indian Board (Okanagan)

Red Bluff First Nation (Dakelh)

Saik'uz First Nation (Dakelh)

Samahquam First Nation (St'at'imc or Lillooet)

Seton Lake First Nation (St'at'imc or Lillooet)

Shackan First Nation (Nlaka'pamux)

Shuswap First Nation (Secwepemc)

Siska First Nation (Nlaka'pamux)

Skawahlook First Nation (Stól)

Skeetchestn First Nation (Secwepemc)

Skookumchuk First Nation

Skowkale First Nation (Stól)

Skuppah First Nation (Nlaka'pamux)

Skway First Nation (Nlaka'pamux)

Soda Creek First Nation (Secwepemc)

Spuzzum First Nation (Nlaka'pamux)

Stellat'en First Nation (Dakelh)

Takla Lake First Nation (Witsuwit'en)

Tla-o-qui-aht First Nation (Nuu-Chah-Nulth)

Tl'azt'en Nation (Dakelh)

Toosey First Nation (Tsilhqot'in and Dakelh)

Toquaht First Nation (Nuu-Chah-Nulth)

Tsawataineuk First Nation

Tsawout First Nation (Saanich)

Tseshaht First Nation (Nuu-Chah-Nulth)

Tseycum First Nation (Saanich)

Ts'il Kaz Koh First Nation (Dakelh)

Ts'kw'aylaxw First Nation (Dakelh)

Uchucklesaht First Nation

Ucluelet First Nation (Nuu-Chah-Nulth)

Ulkatcho First Nation (Dakelh)

Upper Nicola First Nation (Okanagan)

Upper Similkameen First Nation

We Wai Kai First Nation (Southern Kwakiutl)

Whispering Pines First Nation (Secwepemc)

Williams Lake First Nation (Secwepemc)

CARIBBEAN
Puerto Rico/Dominican Republic

Jatibonicu Taino Tribal Nation

Taino Turabo Aymaco Tribe of Puerto Rico

The United Confederation Of Taino People (UCTP)

St Vincent

Carib

Garifuna

Dominica

Kalinago

Cuba

Taino-Arawak

MEXICO

Aguacateco (Awakateko)

Akateko

Amuzgo (Tzañcue)

Ayapaneco

Chatino (Cha'cña)

Chichimeca Jonaz (Uza)

Chinantec (Tsa jujmí)

Chocho (Runixa ngiigua)

Chocholteco

Ch'ol (Winik)

Chontal

Chontal Maya

Chuj

Cochimi (Laymón, mti'pá)

Cocopah (Es péi)

Cora (Nayeeri)

Cucapá

Cuicatec (Nduudu yu)

Cuicateco

Guarijío

Huarijio (Makurawe)

Huastec (Téenek)

Huasteco

Huave

Huave (Ikoods)

Huichol (Wixárika)

Ixcateco

Ixil

Jacaltec (Abxubal)

Kanjobal (K'anjobal)

Kaqchikel (K'akchikel)

Kekchí (K'ekchí)

K'iche'

Kickapoo

Kikapú (Kikapooa)

Kiliwa

Kiliwa (Ko'lew)

Kumiai (Ti'pai)

Lacandon (Hach t'an)

Lacandón

Mam

Mame (Qyool)

Matlatzinca

Mayo

Mayo (Yoreme)

Mazahua (Hñatho)

Mazateco

Mazateco (Ha shuta enima)

Mexicanero (Mexikatlajtolli)

Mixe (Ayüükjä'äy)

Mixtec (Tu'un savi)

Mixteco

Motocintleco (Qatok)

Nahuatl (Nāhuatlācah)

Ocuiltec (Tlahuica)

Oluteco

Otomi (Hñähñü)

Paipai (Akwa'ala)

Pame (Xigüe)

Pápago

Pima

Pima Bajo

Popoluca (Tuncápxe)

Purépecha (P'urhépecha)

Q'anjob'al

Qato'k

Q'eqchi'

Sayulteco

Seri (Comcáac)

Tacuate

Tarahumara (Rarámuri)

Tarasco

Teko

Tepehua (Hamasipini)

Tepehuan (O'dam, Audam, and Ódami)

Tepehuano

Texistepequeño

Tlahuica

Tlapanec (Me'phaa)

Tlapaneco

Tohono O'odham (Papago)

Tojolabal

Tojolabal (Tojolwinik)

Totonac (Tachiwin)

Totonaco

Triqui

Triqui (Tinujéi)

Tseltal

Tsotsil

Tzeltal (K'op o winik atel)

Tzotzil (Batzil k'op)

Yaqui (Yoeme)

Zapotec (Binizaa)

Zoque (O'de püt)

Zoque

APPENDIX F:
INDIAN LANDS: DEFINITIONS
AND EXPLANATIONS

There is no legal basis for withholding general services from Indians, with the sole exception of specific termination acts. There is no legitimate foundation for denying Indian identification to any tribe or community. The BIA has no authority to refuse services to any member of the Indian population.

Final report of the American Indian Policy Review Commission, 1976

Federal Recognition of Indian Nations

Federal recognition is the U.S. government's acknowledgment of a tribe as a sovereign nation. Such acknowledgment leads to a tribe's eligibility to receive federal funding and services provided to federally recognized Indian tribes from the Bureau of Indian Affairs (BIA).

Before 1978, requests from Indian groups for federal acknowledgement as tribes were determined on an *ad hoc* basis. Some tribes were acknowledged by Congress, others by executive branch decisions, and some through cases brought in the courts.

After 1978, regulations governing the process for federal acknowledgment required a review of tribal petitions conducted by the Office of Federal Acknowledgment (OFA) in the Bureau of Indian Affairs (BIA). This demanding and time-consuming process has become the dominant means of securing federal recognition, rather than by legislative or judicial means.

OFA's process requires the petitioning tribe to satisfy seven mandatory criteria, including historical and continuous American Indian identity in a distinct community. The vast majority of petitioners do not meet these strict standards. Far more petitions have been denied than accepted.

It took the Shinnecock Nation of Long Island, New York, thirty-two years to be federally recognized. It took the Mashpee Wampanoags of Massachusetts thirty-five years to become federally recognized. Attempts to obtain federal recognition by the Lumbee Tribe in North Carolina began in 1888. Since that time, there have been numerous bills introduced in Congress to recognize the group, but none has passed into law.

According to the Association on American Indian Affairs, which has begun a project aimed at reforming the federal recognition process, the documentary requirements are massive, delays in processing petitions "Dickensian," and the decisions made often indefensible…. The U.S. Congress, the Department of the Interior, Indian tribes, and others all agree that the administrative process for federal acknowledgement is broken.

State Recognition of Indian Nations

State recognition means a tribe has been officially recognized in its respective state, but not by the federal government. For example, Alabama recognizes the MOWA Band of Choctaw Indians that has a reservation north of Mobile. Massachusetts recognizes the Nipmuc Nation that has a reservation in Grafton.

State recognition does not permit gaming or other significant non-gaming benefits. Benefits and rights vary from state to state. One right conferred on members of state-recognized tribes is the right to exhibit as Native American artists under U.S. federal law, the Indian Arts and Crafts Law of 1990.

Types of Native Lands

Allotments—Lands held in trust by the U.S. government for individual tribal members.

Ceded Territory—Lands within a reservation or other legal Native area that have been sold by a tribe or seized by the U.S. government, but Native nations still have certain rights like hunting and fishing.

Checkerboard Lands—Areas that are a combination of non-tribal-owned lands and Native lands, resulting in a checkerboard pattern. As Indian lands were sold off during the General Allotment Act of 1887 (also called the Dawes Act), Indian communities became splintered and cut off from each other. Some non-Natives felt it would hasten assimilation and keep Indians from organizing. Checkerboarding seriously impedes Native farms, ranches, and other economic ventures that need large contiguous sections of land. It also affects the use of land for traditional purposes.

Dependent Indian Community—Any area validly set apart for the use of the Indians under the superintendence of the Government.

Native Hawaiian Homelands—Congress passed the 1921 Hawaiian Homes Commission Act (HHCA), setting aside about 203,000 acres of "ceded" lands for a homesteading program to provide residences, farms, and pastoral lots for those with at least 50% Native Hawaiian ancestry. Today, only 9,748 Native Hawaiians have homestead awards, but 25,937 eligible people are on the waiting list.

Fee Lands—Parcels owned by non-Natives, but within reservation boundaries.

Pueblos—Many reservations in the present day states of Arizona and New Mexico are called pueblos.

Rancherias—There are few, if any, differences between Rancherias and Reservations, but Rancherias are only in California.

Reservations—Designated lands for particular nations; most are under the aegis of the federal Bureau of Indian Affairs and some are under the administration of a state.

Trust Lands—Lands held in trust by the U.S. government for Native nations and sometimes individual Native people.

How Does One Get to Be an Indian?

For most people, being born into a particular group determines ethnicity. In the United States, people who have one drop of African ancestry are considered African American. Yet it has often been just the opposite for Native peoples, who have endured centuries of genocidal policies of one kind or another; and having a non-Native parent, in some cases, can cancel out one's Indianess.

The Bureau of Indian Affairs (BIA) not only determines tribes, but it also decides who is a "real" Indian. To be an official Indian, a person must meet the criteria below, although individual tribes may have different requirements:

- Be at least 1/4 Native (called blood quantum)
- Belong to a federally recognized tribe
- Be granted recognition from the BIA
- Document his/her ancestry for at least three generation back

Each Nation decides its own membership, and this can be complicated. Even if a child is born to two Indian parents—but they are from two different tribes with two different membership criteria—the child may not be enrolled. For instance, one tribe may only enroll children through the mother's line, another through the father's, and if the particular equation does not work out the child will not be considered a tribal member by either group.

Those from "terminated" tribes or tribes not recognized by any government body do not have legal status as Indians. With all of the displacement, wars, and settler colonial tactics, the issue of "Indianess" has been a heated one that often pits Native people against each other. No other group needs to prove how Anglo, African, or Asian they are to apply for loans, education benefits, or other government and private programs. Yet, in some ways, being an "official Indian" provides protection for what little benefits that are earmarked just for Native people. During the allotment era, there were stories of Indian identity being purchased by Anglos in order to acquire Native lands.

Many in the dominant culture share the mistaken belief that life is a "free ride" for Native peoples, but the opposite is true. There is only one pot of money for all Native people, and there are rarely, if ever, increases in it. Usually, there are cuts. Any benefits Indians receive is not welfare; it is a mere pittance compared to the theft of lands, resources, and cultures.

It is offensive to ask a Native person "how much Indian" he or she is. Many people do not like being asked anything about their background; others are happy to speak about it. It is important to remember that no other group in the United States has a whole government department managing its every movement, and no other group has the particular relationship with federal and state governments. It is vital to be informed about First Peoples if one lives in Indian Country, and all of the United States is Indian Country!

APPENDIX G: INDIGENIZED ENGLISH

Abalone, from Costanoan *aulon*.

Acorn squash, from Narragansett *askutasuash*.

Adirondack, possibly from Mohawk *batirontaks,* for "they eat trees."

Aloha, Hawaiian for "hello, goodbye, love."

Alpaca, from Aymara *allpaka*.

Anorak, from the Greenlandic Inuit *annoraq*.

Avocado, from Nahuatl *aguacate*.

Assapan, Virginia Algonquian for "flying squirrel."

Barbecue, from Taino word *barbacu*.

Batata, Carib, for sweet potato.

Bayou, from the Choctaw *bayuk* for "creek, sluggish stream."

Bogue, from Choctaw *bok* for "river or waterway."

Camas, from Chinook Jargon *kamass* for "edible plant of the lily family."

Canoe, from Arawak/Carib *canaoua*.

Caribou, from Micmaq.

Cashew, from Tupí *acaîu*.

Catalpa, from Creek for *Ka* (head) and *talpa* (wing), named for the shape of the flower.

Chicago, Algonquian for "garlic field."

Chili, Nahuatl.

Chinook, Salish for "warm moist wind of the Pacific coast."

Chipmunk, from the Ojibwa *ajidamoon* for "red squirrel."

Cockarouse, Virginia Algonquian for a "person of importance among American colonists."

Cocoa, from Nahuatl *cacahuatl.*

Coho, Salish, for "silver salmon."

Cohosh, from Eastern Abenaki for "several of medicinal plants."

Comanchero, from Ute *kimanci,* "a trader with Indians."

Condor, from Quecha *kuntur.*

Corn pone, from Virginia Algonquian *poan.*

Cougar, Guaraní.

Coyote, from Nahuatl *coyōtl.*

Guacamole, from Nahuatl *aquacate*, and *mōlli*, "sauce."

Geechee from Muskogee named Ogeechee River in Georgia; dialect of African descendants living by river (also called Gullah).

Haole, Hawaiian, for "foreigner or outsider."

Heishi, Navajo, for "shell."

Hickory, from the Virginia Algonquian *pocohiquara.*

Hohokam, from Pima *huhukam* for "ancient one."

Hominy, from Virginia Algonquian *uskatahomen.*

Honk, perhaps from Wampanoag or Narragansett *honck* for "grey goose."

Honu, Hawaiian, for "giant sea turtle."

Hooch, from Tlingit word *hoochino* for "cheap or bootleg liquor."

Hurricane, from Taino *juracín.*

Husky, from Montagnais word *ayashkimew* for "dog that pulls sleds."

Igloo, from the Canadian Inuit *iglu* for "permanent house made of sod, wood, or stone or of temporary shelter made of blocks of snow or ice."

Kahuna, Hawaiian traditional priest.

Kayak, from Alaskan Yupik *qayaq.*

Kayak, from Inuit *qajaq.*

Kinnikinnick, from Unami for "item for mixing in."

Kodiak, Inuit for "island."

Lānai, Hawaiian veranda or patio.

Logan, from Algonquian *pokelogan* for "unusually stagnant or marshy place."

Mackinaw, from Ojibwa *michilmachinak* for "island of the large turtle."

Mahala, Yokuts for "woman."

Mahi-mahi, Hawaiian word for "very strong," name of Dolphin fish.

Malibu, from Chumash word, *Humamaliwoo* for " sound of the waves."

Mana, Hawaiian, for "spiritual power."

Manatee, from Taino *manatí*.

Milwaukee, from Algonquian for "a good place."

Mississippi, from Anishinaabe, *Misi-ziibi* for "Great River."

Moccasin, from Virginia Algonquian.

Mole, from Nahuatl, *mōlli /'mo:l:i,* "sauce."

Moose, from the Eastern Abenaki *mos*.

Muckamuck, from Chinook Jargon *hayo makamak* for "plenty to eat."

Muigwump, from Massachusett *mugguomp* for "an important or independent person, especially in politics."

Mukluk, Yupik, for "boot made of reindeer hide or sealskin."

Muʻumuʻu, Hawaiian, for "loose gown."

Muskeg, Cree, for "swamp formed by accumulated moss or leaves."

Muskrat, from Algonquian word, *mussacus*.

Niagara, Iroquoian, for "overwhelming flood."

Ocelot, from Nahuatl, *ocēlōtl*.

Papaya, from Taino.

Parka, from Inuit, Aleut, or Yupik.

Pecan, from the Illinois *pakani*.

Pele's tears, solidified pieces of lava named after Pele, a Hawaiian deity.

Pemmican, from Cree *pimihkaam* for "trail food."

Persimmon, from Algonquian *pasiminaaaan* for "dried fruit."

Poi, mainstay of traditional Hawaiian diet—paste made from Taro root.

Pokeweed, from Virginia Algonquian *puccon*.

Possum, from Virginia Algonquian *apossum*.

Powwow, from Narragansett *powwaw* for a "council or meeting."

Puka, Hawaiian, for "hole or perforation." *Puka* shells are round with center holes, strung into necklaces.

Punk, from Virginia Algonquian *punnough* for "decayed dried wood for tinder."

Pupu, Hawaiian, for "snacks or appetizers."

Quahog, from the Narragansett *poquauhock*.

Quinoa, from Quecha *kinwa*.

Quonset hut, Algonquian, for "long place."

Raccoon, from Virginia Algonquian, *arougbcun*.

Saratoga, Mohawk, for "springs from the hillside."

Sasquatch, from Salish *seʼsxac* for "wild men."

Sauguaro, Piman, for large cactus.

Seapoose, from Unquachog *seépus* for "dangerous undertow near shore."

Sebago, Abenaki, for "big lake."

Shenango, Onondaga, for "bull thistle."

Shack, possibly from Nahualt *xahcalli*, "grass hut."

Skunk, from Massachusett *squnck*.

Sockeye, from Salish *suk-kegh*.

Squash, from the Narragansett *askutasquash*.

Stogie, perhaps from drivers of *Conestoga* wagons, who smoked cheap cigars.

Succotash, from the Narragansett *msickquatash*, for "boiled corn."

Taboo, from Hawaiian *kapu*, "the forbidding of various things that go against religious customs."

Taconic, Algonquian, for "flint like rock."

Tamale, from Nahualt, *tamalli*.

Tammany, Delaware, for "the affable" and a seventeenth-century chief. Supposedly he showed great friendship to William Penn and later white men formed patriotic organizations called Tammany Clubs that operated on what they imagined Delaware culture to be.

Tapioca, Tupinambí, for "juice squeezed out."

Tipi, Lakota.

Terrapin, from Virginia Algonquian *torope*.

Tobacco, from Taino *tabacu*.

Toboggan, from the Micmac *topaghan*.

Tomahawk, from Virginia Algonquian *tamahaac*.

Tomato, from Nahuatl, *tomatl*.

Tonawanda, Iroquoian, for "swift water."

Tupelo, from Creek *topilwa* + *opilwa* for "tree + swamp."

Tuxedo, Algonquian, for "round-foot-he-has."

Ukulele, Hawaiian word for "jumping flea," describing motion of playing the instrument.

Ulu, Inuit knife.

Umiak, Inuit large boat made of stretched skins.

Vicuña, from Quecha *wik'uña*.

Wampum, from Algonquian (probably Narragansett) *wanpanpiak* for string of white shell beads.

Wapiti, from Shawnee *wapiti*.

Wigwam, from the Eastern Abenaki *wik'wom*.

Wiki, Hawaiian, for "fast," name of airport shuttle and Wikipedia.

Woodchuck, from Narragansett word *ackqutchaum*.

APPENDIX H:
INDIGENEITY FROM SEA TO SEA

Selected Protected/Endangered Sacred and Historical Sites, Heritage Areas, Native-created Monuments, and Public Art/Architecture

"Native American faith is inextricably bound to the use of land. The site-specific nature of Indian religious practice derives from the Native American perception that land is itself a sacred, living being...."

William Joseph Brennan Jr., U.S. Supreme Court Justice

Alabama

- Horseshoe Bend National Park was where the Upper Creek Indian Confederacy valiantly fought Andrew Jackson's forces, March 27, 1814, at the Battle of Horseshoe Bend on the Tallapoosa River. Their defeat weakened their great power and opened large parts of Alabama and Georgia for white settlement.

- Russell Cave National Monument is thought to be the site of one of the earliest Southeast Indigenous communities.

Alaska

- The Gwich'in people and the Porcupine caribou herd live above the Arctic Circle where oil drilling in the Alaska Arctic National Wildlife Refuge threatens caribou calving areas and migration routes, polar bears and other wildlife, and even the very lifeways of the Gwich'in

- Mt. McKinley (Denali) is sacred to the Koyukon Athabaskan.

- Mt. St. Elias is sacred to the Yakutat Tlingit.

- Sitka National Historical Park preserves totemic art and is the site of the last major conflict (1804) between Europeans and Alaska Natives (Tlingit). It is also a sacred site.

Alberta, Canada

• Although it is located in Canada, the Athabascan River Delta's Tar Sands is the largest industrial site in the world. The Alberta Tar Sands, threatens the Athabasca River and vast areas of boreal forest that are home to the Cree, Chipewyan Dene, Dunne-za and Métis peoples. Through the proposed Keystone XL pipeline, the Tar Sands catastrophe threatens sites many hundreds of miles away, including the Ogallala aquifer, which provides 82% of the drinking water and 30% of crop irrigation water for eight states in the Great Plains.

Arkansas

• University of Arkansas Epley Center for Health Professions (Fayetteville) by Childers Architect

Arizona

• Agua Fria National Monument features 450 distinct Native American pueblos; some containing over 100 rooms

• Canyon de Chelly National Monument is located within the Navajo Nation and is one of the longest continuously inhabited landscapes.

• Casa Grande Ruins National Monument preserves Ancient Pueblo Peoples Hohokam structures.

"Devine Legacy on Central" (Phoenix), an affordable Multi-family housing / social services / retail by 7 Directions Architects/Planners (Native owned architectural firm).

• Dzil ncha si an (Mount Graham) is a sacred site of the San Carlos Apache and White Mountain Apache as Dzil ncha si and the location of the Mt.Graham International Observatory. In order to pray on the mountain, Apaches must request permission in writing 48 hours in advance.

• Ironwood Forest National Monument contains more than 200 Hohokam archaeological sites.

• "Kaibeto Creek Independent Living Community" (Kaibeto) by Indigenous Design Studio + Architecture.

• "Navajo Code Talkers Memorial" (Phoenix) by Oreland Joe (Navajo).

• "The Southeast Ambulatory Care Center" (Chandler) by Johnson Smitthipong & Rosamond Associates, Inc.

• Tonto National Monument preserves cliff homes of the Salado culture built during the thirteenth, fourteenth, and early fifteenth centuries.

Arkansas

• Hot Springs National Park is sacred to the Caddo, Quapaw, and others. It is said that it was a place of great peace; all visitors set aside their weapons when they entered.

California

• Boyum Patuk, now known as Mt. Shasta, is sacred to the Winnemem Wintu and endangered by the Shasta Dam. Nearby Medicine Lake Highlands is the spiritual heart of the Pit River Tribe and tops somewhere between twenty and forty million acre-feet of pristine aquifer water, which some say may be California's most important safeguard against prolonged drought. The area is threatened by fracking.

- Lava Beds National Monument includes Petroglyph Point, one of the largest panels of ancient rock art.

- Quechan Indian Tribe's Kw'st'an Sacred Sites at Indian Pass, one of America's 11 Most Endangered Historic Places. Polluted by open-pit mining and cyanide-leaching operations.

- Yosemite National Park was home to Miwok, Pauite and others. Discovery of discovery of gold in California's foothills brought the first non-native settlers to Yosemite Valley around 1850.

Colorado

- Canyons of the Ancients National Monument is preserves the largest concentration of archaeological sites in the United States, primarily Ancestral Puebloan ruins.

- Chimney Rock National Monument includes an archaeological site and Pueblo structures and surrounds the Southern Ute Indian Reservation.

- "Colorado State Services Building" (Grand Junction) by Intermountain Architecture Ltd.

- "Davita World Headquarters" (Denver) by Moa Architecture.

- Denver Art Museum: "Wheel" by Edgar Heap of Birds (Cheyenne/Arapaho).

- Hovenweep National Monument (also located in Utah) is known for the six village groups of the Ancestral Puebloans.

- Mesa Verde National Park preserves over 4,000 known ancient Pueblo archeological sites, including 600 cliff dwellings. These sites are some of the most notable and best preserved in the country.

Florida

- Crystal River Archaeological State Park features mounds and steles. It is said that it is the oldest continuously occupied site in Florida and was a sort of spiritual retreat for many different Native cultures.

- Tampa: "The cenotaph, and Ceremonial Space" by Bob Haozous (Chiricahua Apache).

Georgia

- Etowah Indian Mounds Historic Site is the most intact Mississippian Culture site in the Southeast.

- Ocmulgee National Monument preserves ancient Southeastern Native American culture, including major earthworks built more than a thousand years ago by the South Appalachian Mississippian culture.

Hawaii

- Kaho'lawe Island is home to over six hundred archaeological and cultural sites essential to Native Hawaiians. However, the U.S. Navy turned Kaho'lawe into a bombing range until 1990. Cleanup will take many years.

- Kukaniloko Royal Birthing Stones on Oahu.

- Mt. Kilauea on the Big Island is the birthplace of Pele (goddess of volcanoes).

Idaho

- Nez Perce National Historical Park commemorates twenty-four historic Nez Perce sites including "Heart of the Monster," the most sacred site of the Nez Perce, from where the Creator helped them emerge and defeat evil. Threatened by possibility of an industrial corridor being built along the banks of the Clearwater River for large equipment destined for the Athabascan tar sands.

Illinois

- Chicago Portage Park: "Portage" by Ted Sitting Crow Garner (Standing Rock Sioux).

Iowa

- Effigy Mounds National Monument preserves more than two hundred ancient mounds; many shaped like animals.

Indiana

- Indianapolis Art Center (Indianapolis): "Restful Place" by Truman Lowe (Ho-Chunk).

Kansas

- Haskell-Baker Wetlands: During the horrific Boarding School Era of the nineteenth and twentieth centuries, children forcibly removed and sent to the Haskell Indian Industrial Training School often found comfort in the wetlands. They often went to the area to perform ceremonies (which had been banned). Sometimes runaway students died of exposure in the wetlands and were secretly buried there by their fellow students. Because of these graves, the history of the wetlands, and the experiences that these native children experienced as possessions of the U.S. government, many tribes consider this land sacred. Indian people continue to use the area for prayer, and in 1992, Haskell students constructed a Medicine Wheel. Many believe that the "historical and cultural significance also makes this land worthy of protecting as a National Historic Site."

- Wichita: "The Keeper of the Plains," by Blackbear Bosin (Kiowa-Comanche).

Louisiana

- Poverty Point National Monument is also a World Heritage Site and comprises several earthworks and mounds built between 1650 and 700 B.C.E.

Maine

- Mount Katahdin is a sacred site for the Penobscot and other Wabanki nations in Maine. Every year, they participate in the Katahdin Spiritual Run, a hundred-mile trek by canoe, bike, and foot the top of the mountain.

Michigan

- Migi zii wa sin (Eagle Rock) is sacred to the Keweenaw Bay Indian Community (KBIC), along with other bands. Endangered by sulfide mining.

Minnesota

- Grand Portage National Monument preserves a vital center of Anishinaabeg Ojibwe heritage.

- Grand Casino (Hinckley) by DSGW Architects.

- Pipestone National Monument contains sacred pipestone (catlinite) quarries used to make ceremonial pipes.

Montana

- Bighorn Medicine Wheel and Medicine Mountain, sacred to many Plains tribes, are endangered by logging practices.

- Glacier National Park borders, the Blackfeet and Flathead Indian Reservations. The Blackfeet consider these mountains to be the "Backbone of the World."

- "Indian Memorial" at Little Bighorn Battle National Park by Colleen Cutschall (Oglala-Sicangu Lakota).

- Little Bighorn Battlefield National Monument, located within the Crow Indian Reservation, is the site of the Battle of the Little Big Horn fought between the 7th U.S. Cavalry and the Lakota and Cheyenne Nations, June 25–26, 1876.

- Pompeys Pillar National Monument is a rock formation features several petroglyphs, as well as the signature of William Clark, the only remaining physical evidence found along the Lewis and Clark expedition route. They named it for Sacagawea's son Pomp.

Nebraska

- "Hill Elementary School "(Lincoln) by Encompass Architects, PC.

New Mexico

- Aztec Ruins National Monument—Pueblo structures.

- Bandelier National Monument—Pueblo ancestral homes and territory.

- El Malpais National Monument is the site of an ancient Pueblo trade route and rock art. It was also used to test atomic bombs.

- St. Francis Basilica (Santa Fe): "Blessed Kateri" by Estella Loretto (Jemez Pueblo).

- Museum of Indian Arts & Culture (Santa Fe): "Dancing with the Heartbeat of My Ancestors" by Kathy Whitman-Elk Woman (Mandan/Hidatsa/Arikara).

- Indian Pueblo Culture Center (Albuquerque): " Popé " by Cliff Fragua (Walatowa).

New York

- United States Mission to the United Nations (New York City): "Offering of the Sacred Pipe" by Alan Houser (Chiricahua Apache).

North Dakota

- Knife River Indian Villages National Historic Site features historic, cultural, archeological, and agricultural remnants Northern Plains Indians. More than fifty archeological sites suggest a possible eight thousand year span of habitation, ending with five centuries of Hidatsa earthlodge villages.

Ohio

- Hopewell Culture National Historic Park is comprised of monumental earthen mounds and embankments forming huge geometric enclosures two thousand years ago by Hopewellian era peoples.

Oklahoma

- Arts and Humanities Council of Tulsa Hardesty Arts Center (Tulsa) by Selser Schaefer Architects.
- Gilcrease Museum (Tulsa): "Sacred Rain Arrow" by Alan Houser (Chiricahua Apache).
- Medicine Bluffs, near Lawton is on the National Register of Historical Places, but this most sacred site of the Comanche is still at risk from Fort Sill Army Base, that has used is as a firing range. There are threats of the base expanding.
- Oklahoma City State Capitol Building: "The Guardian" by Enoch Kelly Haney (Seminole).

Oregon

- Cascade–Siskiyou National Monument features nearly one hundred dwelling and root-gathering sites belonging to the Modoc, Klamath, and Shasta.

South Dakota

- Crazy Horse Memorial, a goliath size image, is carved into a mountain located in the Black Hills (Paha Sapa).
- Paha Sapa (Black Hills) is a sacred are for the Lakota, Cheyenne, Omaha and fourteen other nations. Different sites like Bear Butte (Mato Paha) are being threatened by tourism interests, the world's largest motorcycle rally, plus oil and gas interests are eyeing the area for hydraulic fracking.

Texas

- Alibates Flint Quarries National Monument—Historical source of rainbow-hued flint.

Utah

- Nine Mile Canyon's more than ten thousand documented petroglyphs, pictoglyphs, and archaeological sites of the Ute people are endangered by gas exploration and drilling.

Washington

- Olympic National Park, an internationally-recognized Biosphere Reserve and World Heritage Site, contains natural and cultural resources that are a vital part of the heritage of the eight treaty Indian tribes of the Olympic Peninsula.
- Seattle (32nd Avenue and Yesler Way): "Dreamcatcher" by Lawney Reyes (Sinixt).

Washington, DC

- National Museum of the American Indian Gardens: "Always Becoming" by Nora Naranjo-Morse (Santa Clara Pueblo): "We Were Always Here," by Rick Bartow (Wiyot/Mad River Band).

- Smithsonian American Art Museum: "The Death of Cleopatra," by Edmonia Lewis (Ojibwe).

Wisconsin

- Mashkiki Ziibi, heart of the Bad River Ojibwe reservation sits at the base of a watershed which emerges from the Penokee Range, location of the largest iron ore deposit in North America. The Anishinaabe oppose the opening of a new mine that will cause more devestation.

Wyoming

- Devil's Tower National Monument has historical ties with the Arapaho, Cheyenne, Crow, Kiowa and Lakota, and others. In several native languages, it is known as "Bear's Lodge."

- Bighorn Medicine Wheel and Medicine Mountain, sacred to many Plains tribes, remains threatened by logging interests.

APPENDIX I:
SELECTED INDIGENEITY FIRSTS:
PEOPLE, PLACES, AND THINGS

PEOPLE

1765: Christian minister Samson Occum, Mohegan, was the first American Indian to preach to a white congregation in Europe.

1775: Sally Anise, Oneida, started a trading enterprise and became the first successful Native businesswoman.

1815: Jane Johnston Schoolcraft, Ojibwe, is thought to be the first Native woman literary writer, poet, and the first to write poetry in an Indigenous language.

1822: Army Major David Moniac, Creek, was the first Native American to graduate from the U.S. Military Academy.

1829: William Apess, Pequot, wrote the first full-length American Indian biography.

1853: George Crum, Mohawk, created the potato chip.

1854: John Rollin/Ridge Yellow Bird, Cherokee, was the first Native person to publish a novel, *The Life and Adventures of Joaquin Murieta*.

1855: James Bouchard, Delaware, became the first American Indian Roman Catholic priest.

1857: John Rollin/Ridge Yellow Bird, Cherokee, was also the first to edit a non-Native newspaper (*Sacramento Daily*).

1869: Ely Samuel Parker, Seneca, was the first Native American appointed Commissioner of Indian Affairs.

1869: Co-Rux-Te-Chod-Ish, Pawnee, was the first Native person to earn a Medal of Honor.

1884: Kateri Tekakwiha, Mohawk, was the first Native American venerated by the Roman Catholic Church.

1889: Carlos Montezuma, Yavapai, and Susan LaFleshe Picotte, Omaha, were the first two American Indians to become medical doctors.

1898: Lakota Catholic nuns Susan Bordeaux, Ella Clark, Anna B. Pleets, and Josephine Two Bears were the first U.S. Army nurses and served in Cuba during the Spanish–American War.

1891: Sophia Alice Callahan, Creek, published the first novel by a Native woman, *Wynema; A Child of the Forest*.

1900: Robert William Wilcox, Hawaiian, was the first Hawaiian to serve in the U.S. Congress.

1904: William Jones, Fox, is thought to be the first Native American anthropologist earning his Ph.D. from Columbia University as a student of Franz Boas.

1907: Thomas Longboat, Onondaga, was the first American Indian to win the Boston Marathon.

1908: Ikua Purdy was first Hawaiian cowboy winner of the World's Steer Roping championship (1908), and he was the first Hawaiian inducted into the Rodeo Hall of Fame (1999).

1912: Duke Paoa Kahinu Mokoe Hulikohola Kahanamoku was the first Native Hawaiian Olympian to win a gold medal in the 100-meter freestyle and a silver medal in swimming, and medaled three more times in subsequent Olympics. Also, Louis Tewanima, Hopi, was the first American to win an Olympic Medal in the 10,000 meter race that year.

1913: Joseph J. Clark, Cherokee, was the first Native American midshipman to graduate from the United States Naval Academy and the first Native American to become a full admiral (1953).

1913: Zitala-Sa, Yankton Sioux, was the first Native American to create an opera (*The Sun Dance*).

1913: Walter Harper, Athabascan, was the first person to reach the summit of Denali (Mt. McKinley), highest peak in North America.

1916: Jackson Sundown, Nez Perce, was the first Native American to win the World Saddle Bronc Championship (1916), and was first to be inducted into the Rodeo Hall of Fame (1976).

1924: William L. Paul, Tlingit, was first Alaska Native elected to the Territorial Legislature.

1924: Cora Belle Reynolds Anderson, Ojibwe, was elected to the Michigan State House of Representatives, the first Native American woman in a state legislature.

1926: Jessie Elizabeth Randolph Moore, Chickasaw, was the first Native women to be elected to a state office (Oklahoma Supreme Court Clerk. Her statewide emergency relief program was implemented nationally (1933).

1926: Norma Smallwood, Cherokee, was the First Native American "Miss America."

1928: Charles Curtis, Kaw, was the first Native American vice president of the United States.

1933: Dolly Smith Akers, Assiniboine, was the first Native woman elected to the Montana State Legislature.

1939: Ellison Myers Brown, Narragansett, was the second and the only Native to win the Boston Marathon twice (1936, 1939).

1939: Chester L. Ellis, Seneca was the first American Indian to win boxing championships at both national and international levels (Golden Gloves).

1941: James C. Ottipoby, Comanche, was the first Native American in the American Chaplain Corps.

1942: Major General Clarence L. Tinker, Osage was the first Native American to achieve that rank in the U.S. Air Force; Tinker Air Force Base is named for him.

1945: Civil Rights Leader Elizabeth Peratrovich, Tlingit, championed the passing of the first anti-discrimination law in the United States (Alaska).

1948: Alan Houser. Chiricahua Apache) was the first Native American to create a public monument ("Comrade in Mourning").

1949: Maria Tallchief, Osage, was the United States' first prima ballerina.

1950: Isabella Aiona Abbott was the first Native Hawaiian woman to receive a Ph.D. in science.

1950: Bernard Anthony Hoehner, Standing Rock Sioux, was the first known Native veterinarian.

1951: Lloyd Kiva New, Cherokee, was the first Native American to show a collection at an international fashion show (1951). In 1962, he cofounded the Institute of American Indian Arts (Santa Fe).

1952: Herbert Kaili Pililaau, Hawaiian, was the first Native Hawaiian to receive the Medal of Honor.

1953: Arlene Wesley, Yakima, was the first "Miss Indian America" competition winner.

1956: George Blue Spruce Jr., Laguna/Ohkay Owingeh Pueblo, became the first American Indian dentist.

1957: Joseph R. Garry, Coeur d'Alene, was the first American Indian elected to the Idaho state legislature.

1961: Charles Kekumano was the first Native Hawaiian to be the honorary chaplain of the papal household.

1963: Annie Wauneka, Navajo, was the first Native American to receive the Presidential Medal of Freedom.

1964: James Atcitty and Monroe Jymm, both Navajo, were the first Native people elected to the New Mexico House of Representatives.

1964: Billy Mills, Oglala Lakota, was the first and only American to win Olympic Gold in the 10,000 meter race (Tokyo).

1966: Lloyd Lynn House, Navajo/Oneida, was the first American Indian to serve in the Arizona House of Representatives.

1966: William R. Pogue, Choctaw descent, was the first Native American astronaut;.

1969: Dr. Benjamin B.C. Young became the first Native Hawaiian psychiatrist and the first to graduate from Harvard Medical School (1969).

1969: N. Scott Momaday, Kiowa, won the Pulitzer Prize for Fiction for his novel *House Made of Dawn*, the first time for a Native writer.

1970s: Marcia Ann Biddleman, Seneca, was the highest-ranking woman Marine as well as the only woman to serve as weather forecaster.

1971: Arthur Raymond, Lakota, was the first Sioux to be elected to the North Dakota State Legislature.

1972: Elary Gromoff, Aleut, was the first Alaska Native graduate of West Point Military Academy.

1972: Fred Begay was the first Navajo to earn a Ph.D. in physics).

1973: Frank Dukepoo, Hopi, was the first Native American geneticist, and he established the National Native American Honor Society (1982).

1976: Frank Fools Crow, Oglala Lakota, was the first leader of a Native religion to offer the invocation that convened the U.S. Senate—it was in the Lakota language.

1976: Dr. Ted Mala, Inupiaq, was the first Alaska Native Health and Social Services Commissioner (Alaska).

1976: Daniel Kahikina Akaka was the first Native Hawaiian to be elected to the House of Representatives, and she was also the first elected to the U.S. Senate (1990).

1981: Leslie Marmon Silko, Laguna Pueblo, was the first Native recipient of a MacArthur "Genius" Foundation Award.

1981: Jock Soto, Navajo, became the youngest ever soloist dancer with the American Ballet Theater (1981), a position he held until his retirement in 2005.

1982: Dolores K. Smith, Cherokee, was the first Native woman to graduate from the U.S. Naval Academy.

1982: Buffy Saint-Marie, Cree, is thought to be the first Native person to win an Oscar. She co-wrote the song, "Up Where We Belong".

1982: Benjamin Nighthorse Campbell, Northern Cheyenne, was the first American Indian elected to the Colorado House of Representatives.

1983: Arlinda F. Locklear, Lumbee, was the first Native American woman to argue a case successfully before the U.S. Supreme Court.

1984: Jeanne Givens, Coeur d'Alene, was the first Native woman elected to the Idaho House of Representatives.

1984: Brigitte T. Wahwassuck, Potawatomi, was the first American Indian woman graduate of the U.S. Military Academy.

1986: Donald E. Pelotte, Abenaki, was ordained the first Native American Catholic bishop.

1986: John David Waihe'e III became the first Native Hawaiian and the first Indigenous person to be elected governor of any state (Hawaii).

1990: Jason Stevens, Navajo, was the first Native person to win the World Chess Open.

1990: Larry EchoHawk, Pawnee, was the first Native person elected as a state attorney general (Idaho).

1992: Sculptor Alan Houser, Chiricahua Apache, was the first Native artist to receive the National Medal of Arts.

1993: Georgianna Lincoln, Athabascan, was the first Alaska Native women elected to Alaska State Senate.

1994: Robert D. Ecoffey, Oglala Lakota, was the first Native American U.S. Marshall in the Justice Department.

1995: Glenn Godfrey, Alutiliq, was appointed Public Safety Commissioner, the first Alaska Native to hold Alaska's highest law enforcement post.

1996: Lynda Morgan Lovejoy, Navajo, was the first Native woman to serve in the New Mexico House of Representatives.

1996: John Herrington, Chickasaw, was the first tribally enrolled astronaut.

1997: Charles J. Chaput, Prairie Band Potawatomi, became the first American Indian Catholic archbishop.

1997: Dr. Linda Burhansstipanov, Cherokee, was the first American Indian recipient of the American Public Health Association's Award for Excellence.

1997: Sally Ann Gonzales, Yaqui, and Debora Norris, Navajo/Blackfeet, were the first Native women to be elected to the Arizona House of Representatives.

1997: Brook Mahealani Lee, Hawaiian, became the first Native Hawaiian and the first Native person from the United States to win the Miss Universe Pageant.

1998: Carol Vigil (Tesuque Pueblo) was the first woman elected as a U.S. state district Judge and the first Native to win a state judgeship in New Mexico.

2002: Sarah James, Norma Kassi, and Jonathon Solomon (all Gwich'in) received the Grassroots Environmentalism Goldman Prize for their protection of the Aortic National Wildlife Refuge (Alaska).

2002: Susie Walking Bear Yellowtail, Crow, was the first American Indian inducted into the American Nursing Association's Hall of Fame.

2003: Lori Piestewa, Hopi, was the first military woman to be killed in Operation Iraqi Freedom and probably the first Native American woman killed in combat during a foreign war.

2006: Chris Eyre, Cheyenne/Arapaho, was the first Native director to win the Directors Guild of America award for Outstanding Directorial Achievement in Children's Programs (*Edge of America*).

2006: Stan Atcitty, Navajo, became the first American Indian male to earn a Ph.D. in electrical and computer engineering. In 2012, President Obama honored him with the Presidential Early Career Award for Scientist and Engineers, the country's highest tribute for outstanding scientists and engineers.

2007: Jacqueline Left Hand Bull-Delahunt, Rosebud Sioux, became the first Native chairperson of the Baha'i National Spiritual Assembly of America.

2007: Barbara McIlvaine Smith, Sac and Fox Nation of Oklahoma, was the first Native American elected to the Pennsylvania House of Representatives.

2008: Denise Juneau (Three Affiliated Tribes) was elected Montana's Superintendent of Public Instruction, the first Native American woman elected to any statewide executive office in the U.S.

2009: Dr. Yvette Roubideaux, Rosebud Sioux, became the first woman to head the Indian Health Service.

2010: Karlene Hunter, Oglala Lakota, CEO of Native American Natural Foods (Tanka Bar) was the first Native to receive the "Heart in Business" Award, the natural foods industry top honor.

2010: Ponka-We Victors, Ponca/Tohono O'odham) was the first Native woman to serve in the Kansas House of Representatives.

2011: John Baker (Inupiaq) was the first Eskimo to win the Iditarod Trail Sled Dog Race (Alaska).

2011: Tahnee Robinson, Northern Cheyenne, was the first Native woman to be drafted into the WNBA (Phoenix Mercury).

2013: Patricia Michaels, Taos, is the first Native designer to be cast on Project Runway. Native Hawaiian, Kina Zamora was the second (2014). Both made it to the finals; Michaels was the first Native American Designer to show a collection at Lincoln Center for Mercedes-Benz Fashion Week in NYC.

2014: Diane Humetewa, Hopi, became the first Native American woman to be appointed a federal judge—and only the third Native American ever to hold the post (Arizona).

2015: Pope Francis officially declares that Indigenous Peoples should be the principals in any dialogues concerning climate change and the environment, the first time a pope has considered Native voice.

PLACES

- Ancient Andeans like the Chimu and the Moche lived in very dry environments, yet were able to build thriving vast cities because they turned arid areas into prosperous farms. They created extensive aqueducts to transport water to their fields, which were even used by later civilizations.

- Native people were the first to develop "environmental art" that can be only be seen from space. The Nazca created giant artworks that spanned several miles across in width and breadth in what is now Peru

- The official residence of the Hawaiian Monarchy, 'Iolanki Palace, was built in 1882. The only palace in the U.S., it had electricity years before the White House.

- Hawaii was the first and only state to declare a Native Language (Hawaiian) as an official one alongside English (1978).

- The Confederated Salish and Kootenai Tribes in Montana were the first tribal nation to establish a wilderness area (Mission Mountain Wilderness Area—1970).

- The Oklahoma Tribal Flag Plaza in Oklahoma's capital, Oklahoma City, was dedicated in 1996; each of the state's thirty-six tribal governments displays its flag.

- The Inter Tribal Sinkyone Wilderness Council composed of ten Northern California tribal nations bought almost 4,000 acres of redwood forest to establish the first intertribal wilderness area in the U.S. (1997).

- The Zuni Pueblo in New Mexico established the first eagle sanctuary owned and run by American Indians (1999).

- The first National Day of Prayer to Protect Native American Sacred Places was observed at sacred sites across the country by both Native and non-Native supporters (2003).

- The Iowa Tribe of Oklahoma became the first tribe permitted to rehabilitate injured eagles (2006).

- Maine was first state to declare an annual Native American Veterans Day (2009).

- The Embassy of Tribal Nations was opened in Washington, D.C., as a permanent home for the National Congress of American Indians (2009).

- Inupiat Eskimo Village, Noorvik, Alaska, was the first place in the US to be counted in the 2010 census and launched it with a Potlatch Festival.

- The Navajo Nation community of Kayenta Township became the first tribal community to adopt the International Green Construction Code to lessen construction project environmental impact (Arizona 2011).

- The Salt River Pima-Maricopa Indian Community built the first Major League Baseball spring training stadium on Indian lands; Arizona Diamondbacks and the Colorado Rockies train there (Arizona—2011).

THINGS

- Native agronomists developed farming methods that created a majority of the foods consumed in the world today: several varieties of corn, beans and squash, tomatoes, avocados, cassava, manioc, vanilla, honey, maple syrup, peanuts, pine nuts, cashews, brazil nuts, hickory nuts, cranberries, strawberries, blueberries, blackberries, raspberries, chokecherries, persimmons, pineapples, wild rice, quinoa, amaranth, sunflowers, peppers, tomatillo, cassava, etc. Many of the historic farming techniques are being used today to restore arable lands. They also developed non-food crops like bottle gourds, cotton, tobacco, and rubber.

- The historic art of Indigenous peoples throughout the Western hemisphere was often abstract with an emphasis on form rather than subject matter and not limited by representation. It inspired the modern abstract art movement (1930s and 1940s).

- The pre-Inca culture of what is now Peru understood the science of acoustics and designed complicated instruments that amaze today's scientists.

- Mesoamerican people developed the *nepohualtzitzin*, an abacus- like device made from maize kernels (C.E. 900–1000).

- Annealing is the process of heating metal until it is extremely hot and then cooling it slowly so it is soft and pliable. Many groups developed it thousands of years ago to created tools of copper and silver. (c. 5000–4000 B.C.E.).

- The Taino people of the Caribbean are credited with inventing the barbecue and the word is from their language (c. C.E. 1100).

- Aquaculture was perfected by Native Hawaiians, South American, Caribbean and Mesoamerican farmers as early as 1500 B.C.E.

- Anatomical knowledge (c. C.E. 1100), including the skeletal and organ systems, was highly developed by Mesoamerican medical practitioners in comparison with their European contemporaries. Spanish conquistadores chose Aztec physicians over the barber-surgeons they brought with them. Both Aztec and Moche surgeons excised cataracts, performed other delicate eye operations, plastic surgery and even skin-grafting. "The Nahuatl-speaking doctors developed an extensive vocabulary that identified virtually all of the organs that the science of anatomy recognizes today," according to anthropologist Jack Weatherford.

- The Aztecs are credited with founding the first hospital in the western hemisphere (C.E. 1100), which provided a variety of services and were staffed by doctors, surgeons, nurses and midwives along with an extensive pharmacy.

- Hydraulic engineering began in Mesoamerica around 300 B.C.E.

- Most Native peoples practiced daily bathing; many used deodorant. Disposable biodegradable diapers were used.

- Modern day barbershops are similar to those of the ancient Aztec, whose cities had many of them (c. C.E. 1100).

- Mesoamericans invented a mathematical system using a base-20 system and also the zero (30 B.C.E.).

- Sewing needles (10000 B.C.E.); Copper sewing needles (C.E. 800).

- Asphalt was used by both (8000 B.C.E.) California, Mississippian, and Northeast cultures as early as 8000 B.C.E. for waterproofing.

- Native people were the first to extract oil from the ground (1300's).

- Multi-use conservation was employed by almost all Native communities so natural resources were never squandered.

- Native cultures across the hemisphere had the science of astronomy. Unlike astronomical observers elsewhere, Indian astronomers focused on events that happened at the horizon, including the rising and setting of stellar constellations, the sun, the moon, and Venus. They created extensive calendar systems, as well (c. 1500 B.C.E.). Natives were the first to discover that the sun is the center of the universe.

- The Aztecs built complex canals for transporting food, cargo, and people to the *chinampas* (floating gardens used for growing food) in their great metropolis of Tenochtitlan. They also built causeways and sewer systems (C.E. 1300).

- Many nations invented a variety of canoes over thousands of years, including the kayak.

- Chewing gum was invented by New England Indians, who made it from spruce tea sap.

- The Aztec Triple Alliance, in power from 1428 to 1521, is considered to be the first state in the world to implement a system of universal compulsory education.

- Dog breeds bred by Native Americans are the xochiocoyotl (coyote), xoloitzcuintli (known as xolo or Mexican hairless), chihuahua, the Carolina dog, the Alaskan malamute and the today's American Indian dog. Horse breeds Appaloosa and Pinto were developed by Native people after the arrival of Europeans, who brought horses.

- Turkey and llamas were domesticated by Native peoples.

- Native people of the Great Lakes region are considered to be the first metal workers in the world and produced the first copper tubing (5,000 B.C.E.). Electroplating technique was developed during C.E. 500 by the ancient Moche, a thousand years before Europeans invented the same process. The Moche used electricity derived from chemicals to gild copper with a thin outer layer of gold. They also invented gold plating. Metallurgical techniques spread to other parts of the western hemisphere, where local artists and metallurgists developed even more unique methods using a wide range of material, including alloys of copper-silver, copper-arsenic, copper-tin, and copper-arsenic-tin.

- Electricity was invented by Andean cultures (c. 200 B.C.E. to C.E. 600), who produced it through chemical means, but they only used it for electroplating

- Various psychotherapy techniques like "free association" and "talk therapy" were utilized by different groups, such as the Haudenosaunee, Huron, and Aztec, hundreds of years before Sigmund Freud. As a result, there were few incidents of post traumatic stress syndrome. Contemporary mental health practitioners like Dr. David Levine employ these age-old methods.

- Different groups from the Inca to the Inuit were the first in the world to practice freeze drying. The Spanish conquistadors used the Andean technique to transport tons of dehydrated potatoes across the Atlantic Ocean to feed hungry Europeans. Clarence Birdseye learned the method from the Inuit and made freeze drying a commercial success.

- The Inca built extensive granaries throughout their lands to stored surplus crops, including freeze-dried potatoes.

- The Inuit developed the harpoon.

- The ancient Andeans built and the later Incans improved, one of the most extensive road systems in the ancient world, which spanned over 20,000 miles and crisscrossed mountains, rivers, deserts, rainforests, and plains. They I constructed elaborate complex suspension bridges.

- The Inuit were the first to make snow goggles.

- The Inuit designed the world's first parkas.

- The log cabin was an adaptation of the Indian log or longhouse.

- Native people developed the wheel independently of other places in the world.

- Disabled persons were protected by law among Andean nations. They were part of the community and received supplements for what they could not earn or make themselves—thousands of years before the American Disability Act.

- Basketball was first played by Mesoamerican and Southwest cultures about 3,000 years ago. It is believed to be the forerunner of contemporary games that use a bouncing ball.

- Bolas (c. 13,000 B.C.E.) used for hunting and weapons were used in different places of the hemisphere over 15,000 years ago.

- Around C.E. 660, Mesoamerican cultures developed the book, long before Europeans did so. The Spaniards destroyed them as an attempt to eradicate the culture.

- Medical instruments like forceps were invented by the Inca to grasp for surgeries before European colonization.

- Many medicines used today are based upon American Indian pharmacology. Native people were the first to use syringes, anesthesia, oral contraception, and baby bottles. North American Indians have medicinal uses for thousands of plant species..

- Bunkbeds, hammocks, hackysack, Lacrosse, toboggans, surfing, snowshoes, rubber balloons, chewing gum, apartments, and adobe are all Native inventions.

- The Maya were the first to use almanacs (3500 B.C.E.).

- The Haudenosaunee (Iroquois) developed the first confederacy in the world (1500s). It's constitution had three main principles: peace, justice or equity, and "the power of good minds." The successful government greatly influenced the founders of the United States. Ben Franklin stated before the Albany Congress (1754): "It would be a strange thing, if six nations of ignorant savages should be capable of forming such a union, and yet it has subsisted for ages and appears indissolvable, and yet a like union should be impractical for ten or a dozen English colonies."

- Hockey had its roots in Irish hurling, but the game popular today was first played by the Mic Mac Indians in the late 1600's. It was called ricket; a frozen apple was used for the puck. It was based on the widely played Native game, shinny.

- Lahainaluma School for Native Hawaiians, run by Protestant missionaries, was the first American school west of the Rocky Mountains (1831).

- Newspapers *Ka Lama Hawaii* and *Ke Kumu Hawaii* were the first Hawaiian language publications (1834).

- The Native American Church was founded in Reno, Oklahoma (1918).

- The National Indian Education Association (NIEA) is the oldest and largest Indian education organization and is headquartered in Washington, D.C. (1969).

- The Red Lake Band of Chippewa Indians, Minnesota, became the first tribal nation to issue its own license plates (1974).

- The William S. Richardson School of Law, Hawaii's only law school was named after chief justice of the Supreme Court of Hawai'i, Native Hawaiian William S. Richardson. It was the first and only law school to be named for an indigenous person (1968).

- The Native American Rights Fund (NARF) was formed to tackle Native American legal issues (1970).

- The American Indian Press Association was founded (1970).

- The first Native-owned-owned and operated radio station (KYUK) in the U.S. broadcast its first show (Alaska—1971).

- The first Native Youth Olympics was held (Alaska—1971).

- The first American Indian Bank opened in Washington, D.C. (1973).

- The first Inuit Circumpolar Conference was held in Barrow, Alaska (1977).

- The American Indian Science and Engineering Society (AISES) was founded to increase the representation of native peoples in the sciences (1977).

- First Nations Development Institute was founded as an American Indian economic rights organization (1980).

- The Intertribal Agriculture Council was founded to pursue, promote, conserve, and develop agricultural resources for the benefit of Indian people (1987). In 1998, they started American Indian Foods (AIF) a program with the USDA Foreign Agricultural Service that promotes American Indian food businesses internationally.

- The Navajo Nation was the first Native nation to have its flag taken to space (1995).

- *Naturally Native* was the first film written, directed, produced by, and starring Native women and was also funded by the Mashantucket Pequot Tribal Nation of Connecticut, the first time for any Indian Nation (1997).

- The Yakama Nation of Washington State became the first Indian nation to own a professional men's basketball team (Yakama Sun Kings—2005).

- The Choctaw Nation of Oklahoma was the first native nation to receive the Secretary of Defense Employer Support Freedom Award (2008).

- The Cherokee Nation in Oklahoma collaborated with Apple, Inc. to develop Cherokee language software for Apple devices—the first to do so (2010).

- The first national symposium on tribal law was held in Albuquerque, New Mexico (2010).

- Signal 99, a heavy metal band composed of Navajo musicians, was the first Native group to win the Rockstar Energy Drink Uproar Festival (Albuquerque—2011).

- The Mohegan Nation purchased its second professional sport team (New England Black Wolves Lacrosse team, 2014) and became the first Native nation to own a professional team when they purchased a WNBA franchise (Connecticut Sun, 2003).

- The Choctaw Central High School (Mississippi) won the Hunt-Winston Solar Car race with their car named the *Tushka Hashii III* (sun warrior) and won several other awards as well for their engineering and team skills (2010).

- The Confederated Salish and Kootenai Tribes, Montana, was the first tribal nation to own a hydroelectric facility (Kerr Dam—2015). Also, reservation highways feature the most wildlife crossings in the country, which earned the nation the National Wildlife Federation prestigious "Connie" award as the "Outstanding Conservation Organization" in the country (2012).

- Indigenous Food & Agriculture Initiative, University of Arkansas School of Law, Intertribal Agriculture Council, and others host the first annual Summer Leadership Summit for Native Youth in Food & Agriculture at the University of Arkansas School of Law (2014).

- The Rohnerville Rancheria in northern California became the first California Native community to install a renewable energy microgrid system (2015).

- The Miccosukee Indian Tribe of Florida's education system became the first Native school to be granted a waiver from the No Child Left Behind Act. The tribe will be permitted to set its own definition of AYP (adequate yearly progress) and to infuse curriculum with Native American culture (2015).

APPENDIX J:
NATIVE OWNED
AND OPERATED MUSEUMS

Abenaki Tribal Museum and Cultural Center
100 Grand Ave., Swanton, VT 05488

Accohannock Museum and Village
Accohannock Indian Tribe, Inc.
28380 Crisfield Marion Rd., Marion Station, MD 21838
http://www.indianwatertrails.com/village.html

Agua Caliente Cultural Museum
219 South Palm Canyon Dr., Palm Springs, CA 92262
www.accmuseum.org

Ah-Tah-Thi-Ki Museum
34725 West Boundary Rd., Big Cypress Seminole Indian Reservation, Clewiston, FL 33440
http://www.ahtahthiki.com

Ak-Chin Him-Dak Eco Museum & Archives
47685 North Eco-Museum Rd., Maricopa, AZ 85239
http://www.azcama.com/museums/akchin

Akwesasne Museum
321 State Route 37, Hogansburg, NY 13655-3114
www.akwesasneculturalcenter.org

Alutiiq Museum & Archaeological Repository
215 Mission Rd #101, Kodiak, AK 99615
alutiiqmuseum.org

Angel Decora Memorial Museum/Research Center
Winnebago Tribe of Nebraska
100 Bluff St., Winnebago, NE 68071
http://www.winnebagotribe.com/cultural_center.html

Aquinnah Cultural Center
35 Aquinnah Circle, Aquinnah, MA 02535
http://wampanoagtribe.net/Pages/Wampanoag_ACC/index

Arvid E. Miller Memorial Library Museum
N8510 Moh-He-Con-Nuck Rd, Bowler, WI 54416
http://mohican-nsn.gov/Departments/Library-Museum

A:shiwi A:wan Museum & Heritage Center
Pueblo of Zuni
02 E. Ojo Caliente Rd., Zuni, NM 87327
http://ggsc.wnmu.edu/mcf/museums/ashiwi.html

Ataloa Lodge Museum/Bacone College
2299 Old Bacone Rd., Muskogee, OK 74403
http://ataloa.bacone.edu

Barona Cultural Center and Museum
1095 Barona Rd, Lakeside, CA
www.baronamuseum.org

Bernice Pauahi Bishop Museum
1525 Bernice St.
Honolulu, HI 96817
http://www.bishopmuseum.org

Bois Forte Heritage Center
1500 Bois Forte Rd., Tower, MN 55790
www.boisforte.com/divisions/heritage_center.htm

Cabazon Cultural Museum
84245 Indio Springs Parkway, Indio, CA 92203
http://www.fantasyspringsresort.com/prod/cbmi

Catawba Cultural Preservation Project
1536 Tom Stevens Rd., Rock Hill, SC 29730
www.ccppcrafts.com

Cherokee Heritage Center
21192 S. Keeler Dr., Park Hill, OK 74451
http://www.cherokeeheritage.org/

Cheyenne Cultural Center, Inc.
22724 Route 66 N, Clinton, OK 73601

Cheyenne Indian Museum
1000 Tongue River Rd., Ashland, MT 59003
http://www.stlabre.org/

The Chickasaw Cultural Center
867 Cooper Memorial Dr., Sulphur, OK 73086
http://chickasawculturalcenter.com/

Chitimacha Museum
155 Chitimacha Loop, Charenton, LA 70523
www.chitimacha.gov

Chugach Museum & Institute of History & Art
560 East 34th Ave., Anchorage, AK 99503-4196
www.chugachmuseum.org

The Citizen Potawatomi Nation Cultural Heritage Center
1899 South Gordon Cooper Dr., Shawnee, OK 74801
http://www.potawatomi.org/culture/cultural-heritage-center

Colville Tribal Museum
512 Mead Way. Coulee Dam, WA 99116
http://www.colvilletribes.com/colville_tribal_museum.php

Comanche National Museum and Cultural Center
701 NW Ferris Ave., Lawton, OK 73507
http://www.comanchemuseum.com

Fond du Lac Cultural Center & Museum
1720 Big Lake Rd., Cloquet, MN 55720
http://www.fdlrez.com/%5C/Museum/index.htm

Fort Belknap Museum
269 Blackfeet Ave., Harlem, MT 59526

Garifuna Museum
1523 W. 48th St., Los Angeles, CA 90062
http://www.garifunamuseum.com/index.php

George W. Brown, Jr. Ojibwe Museum & Cultural Center
603 Peace Pipe Rd, Lac Du Flambeau, WI 54538
www.ldfmuseum.com

George W. Ogden Cultural Museum
Iowa Tribe of Kansas & Nebraska
3345 B Thrasher Rd., White Cloud, KS 66094

Hana Cultural Center & Museum
4974 Uakea Rd., Hana, HI 96713
http://hanaculturalcenter.org

Harry V. Johnston, Jr. Lakota Cultural Center
Cheyenne River Sioux Tribe
2001 Main St., Eagle Butte, SD 57625
www.sioux.org

Hoo-hoogam Ki Museum
10005 E. Osborn Rd., Scottsdale, AZ 85256
http://www.srpmic-nsn.gov/history_culture/kimuseum.htm

Hoopa Valley Tribal Museum
CA-96, Hoopa, CA 95546
http://online.sfsu.edu/cals/hupa/Hoopa.HTM

Hopi Museum (Hopi Cultural Center, Inc.)
AZ-264, Second Mesa, AZ 86043
http://www.hopiculturalcenter.com/

Huhugam Heritage Center
4759 N. Maricopa Rd, Chandler, AZ 85226
http://www.huhugam.com

Huna Heritage Foundation
9301 Glacier Highway, Juneau, AK 99801-9306
http://www.hunaheritage.org

The Indian Pueblo Cultural Center, Inc.
2401 12th St NW, Albuquerque, NM
www.indianpueblo.org

Ioloni Palace
364 S King St, Honolulu, HI 96813
http://www.iolanipalace.org/

Inupiat Heritage Center
5421 North Star St., Barrow, AK 99723
http://inupiat.areaparks.com

Kanza Museum
698 Grandview Dr., Kaw City, OK 74641
http://kawnation.com/?page_id=4188

Lenape Nation of Pennsylvania Cultural Center
342 Northampton St., Easton, PA 18042
http://www.lenapenation.org/culturealcenter.html

Lummi Records & Archives Center & Museum
2665 Kwina Rd., Bellingham, WA 98226
http://www.lummi-nsn.org/website/dept_pages/culture/archives.shtml

The Makah Cultural & Research Center
Neah Bay, WA 98357
www.makah.com/mcrchome.htm

Mashantucket Pequot Museum & Research Center
110 Pequot Trail, Mashantucket, CT 06338-3180
http://www.pequotmuseum.org/MuseumInfo.aspx

Mashpee Wampanoag Indian Museum
414 Main St., Mashpee, MA 02649
http://www.mashpeewampanoagtribe.com/museum

Mille Lacs Indian Museum & Trading Post
43411 Oodena Dr., Onamia, MN 56359
www.mnhs.og/places/sites/mlim

Monacan Ancestral Museum
2009 Kenmore Rd., Amherst, VA 24521
http://www.monacannation.com/museum.shtml

The Museum at Warm Springs
Native Paths Cultural Heritage Museum
3300 Beloved Path, Pensacola, FL 32507
http://www.perdidobaytribe.org/about/native-paths-heritage-museum-jones-swamp

Museum of Contemporary Native Arts
108 Cathedral Pl., Santa Fe, NM 87508
http://www.iaia.edu/museum

The Museum of the Cherokee Indian
589 Tsali Blvd., Cherokee, NC 28719
https://www.cherokeemuseum.org

Museum of the Plains Indian
124 2nd Ave. N.W., Browning, MT 59417
www.browningmontana.com/museum.html

Navajo Nation Museum
Highway 264 and Loop Rd., Window Rock, AZ 86515
http://www.navajonationmuseum.org

Nohwike' Bagowa-White Mountain Apache Cultural Center & Museum
Fort Apache, AZ 85926
http://www.wmat.nsn.us/wmaculture.html

Nottoway Indian Tribe of Virginia Community House & Interpretive Center
23186 Main St., Capron, VA
http://nottowayindians.org/interpretivecenter.html

Oneida Nation Museum
County Rd. E., Oneida, WI 54155
https://oneida-nsn.gov/Culture

Osage Tribal Museum
819 Grandview Ave., Pawhuska, OK 74056
http://www.osagetribalmuseum.com

Pamunkey Indian Tribe Museum
175 Lay Landing Rd., King William, VA 23086
http://www.pamunkey.net/museum.html

Penobscot Indian Nation
12 DownSt. St., Indian Island, ME 04468
www.penobscotnation.org/museum/Index.htm

The People's Center
53253 Highway 93 W., Pablo, MT 59855
www.peoplescenter.org

Poeh Museum and Cultural Center
78 Cities of Gold Rd., Santa Fe, NM 87506
poehcenter.org

Ponca Tribal Museum
2548 Park Ave., Niobrara, NE 68760
http://www.poncatribe-ne.org/Museum

Potawatomi Cultural Center and Museum
1899 S Gordon Cooper Dr., Shawnee, OK 74801
https://www.fcpotawatomi.com/culture-and-history

Pueblo of Acoma Historic Preservation Office
Sky City Cultural Center
1-40, Exit 102, Acoma, NM 87034
www.skycity.com/index.aspx?nav=1&level=2&pk=58&fk=

QuechanTribal Museum
350 Picacho Rd., Winterhaven, CA 92283

Sac & Fox Nation of Missouri Tribal Museum
305 North Main St., Reserve, KS 66434
www.sacandfoxcasino.com/tribal-museum.html

San Carlos Apache Cultural Center
US-70 @ Milepost 272, Peridot, AZ 85542
www.sancarlosapache.com/San_Carlos_Culture_Center.htm

Seneca-Iroquois National Museum
814 BRd. St., Salamanca, NY 14779
https://www.senecamuseum.org/Default.aspx

Shakes Island
Wrangell Cooperative Association
104 Lynch St., Wrangell, AK, 99929
http://www.shakesisland.com

Sheet'ka Kwaan Naa Kahidi Tribal Community House
456 Katlian St., Sitka, AK 99835
http://www.sitkatours.com

Shinnecock Nation Cultural Center & Museum
100 Montauk Hwy, Southampton, NY 11968
www.shinnecockmuseum.com

Shoshone Cultural Center
90 Ethete Rd., Fort Washakie, WY 82514
https://www.wyomingtourism.org/things-to-do/detail/Shoshone-Tribal-Cultural-Center/8475

Shoshone-Bannock Tribal Museum
I-15 Exit 80, Simplot Rd., Fort Hall ID, 83203

Sierra Mono Museum
33103 Rd. 228, North Fork, CA 93643
www.sierramonomuseum.org

Simon Paneak Memorial Museum
Anaktuvuk Pass, AK 99721
http://www.north-slope.org/departments/inupiat-history-language-and-culture/simon-paneak-memo
rial-museum/our-museum

Six Nations Indian Museum
1462 County Route 60, Onchiota, NY 12989
www.sixnationsindianmuseum.com

Skokomish Indian Tribe
80 N Tribal Center Rd., Skokomish, WA 98584
http://www.skokomish.org/culture-and-history/

Southeast Alaska Indian Cultural Center, Inc.
8800 Heritage Center Dr., Anchorage, AK 99504
www.alaskanative.net/

Southern Ute Museum Cultural Center
77 Co. Rd. 517, Ignacio, CO 81137
www.succm.org

Suquamish Museum
6861 NE South St, Suquamish, WA 98392
www.suquamishmuseum.org

Tamástslikt Cultural Institute
47106 Wildhorse Blvd., Pendleton, OR 97801
http://www.tamastslikt.org

Tantaquidgeon Museum
1819 Norwich New London Tpke., Uncasville, CT
http://www.mohegan.nsn.us

Three Affiliated Tribes Museum, Inc.
404 Frontage Rd., New Town, ND 58763
http://www.mhanation.com

Tigua Indian Cultural Center
305 Yaya Lane, El Paso, Texas 79907
http://www.ysletadelsurpueblo.org/html_pages.sstg?id=120&sub1=125

The Upper Missouri Dakota & Nakoda Cultural Lifeway Center and Museum
Fort Peck Assiniboine & Sioux Indian Reservation, Poplar, MT 59255
http://www.fortpecktribes.org/crd/museum.htm

Ute Indian Museum
17253 Chipeta Dr., Montrose, CO 81401
http://www.coloradohistory.org/hist_sites/UteIndian/Ute_indian.htm

Walatowa Cultural and Visitor Center
7413 NM-4, Jemez Pueblo, NM 87024
www.jemezpueblo.com/

Waponahki Museum & Resource Center
59 Passamaquoddy Rd., Sipayik / Pleasant Point, MN 04667
http://www.wabanaki.com/museum.htm

Yakama Nation Museum
100 Spiel-yi Loop, Toppenish, WA 98948
www.yakamamuseum.com

Yupiit Piciryarait Cultural Center
420 Chief Eddie Hoffman Highway, Bethel, AK 99559
http://bethelculturalcenter.com

Ziibiwing Center of Anishinabe Culture & Lifeways
6650 E. BRd.way, Mt. Pleasant, MI 48858
http://www.sagchip.org/ziibiwing

APPENDIX K:
THE INDIGENEITY OF THE POWWOW

The Powwow is a "new old" custom merging ancient, tribally specific traditions, intertribal contributions, Euro-American influences, and contemporary pan-Indianism. The word "powwow" is from the Narragansett *pau wau*, which probably means "gathering of spiritual leaders." Some believe that the Ponca were the first to hold an event (1804) that was just for dancing, and it spread quickly across the Southern Plains. Another version is that the Grass Dance (not to be confused with the modern Grass Dance) Societies of the Omaha started dances over four hundred years old. The dancers were also warriors and recounted their brave deeds through dances performed for the community. Since the Ghost Dance was outlawed later, perhaps the dance occasions became a secret way of communicating. Authorities, enthralled by the entertainment quality of the powwow, may not have understood its cultural importance. In the late 1890s, the Lakota popularized the powwow on different reservations. Even the Catholic Church became involved scheduling powwows around various Christian holy days.

After Indigenous peoples were forced onto reservations, they were also forced to perform dances for public amusement. Before each performance, they were paraded through town. These obligatory events, according to some, were the beginning of the structure of the modern powwow. Wild West shows presented various dances, reducing sacred dance traditions to secular festivities, as well. The mingling of many different heritages in boarding schools fanned creativity, often out of desperation and homesickness. Dance styles and outfits were shared and designed, providing an innovative outlet for youth who had been ripped away from their families. White America seemed to more readily accept "carnivalized" Indigenous cultures. Dances have always been an integral part of Native life, so although ceremonial dances were forbidden, powwow dances thrived. In a sense, the dance tradition became "anglicized" in order to preserve it. All of these factors contributed to the success of this unique contemporary phenomenon, which continues to change and grow. Over the years, dance styles and content may have changed, but their meaning and significance have not.

Today's powwows have evolved into a contemporary mix of dance, reconnection of family and friends, supermarket of Native goods and arts, and festival. Often families on the "powwow circuit" make their living by selling their handmade products (jewelry, food, and clothing) or winning dance competition prize money. Not only do powwows boost the economy of Indigenous America and provide a setting to connect to other Native people, but for many they provide a vital link to heritage, cultural reassertion, and constancy of traditions. Powwows are famous for their fanfare of colorful cloth-ing, exhilarating drumming/singing, and dance moves, which have all been modified into a dazzling and exciting event enjoyed by both Native Americans and visitors. Held year round across America, from meadows to armories to convention centers, powwows draw people from as far as thousands of miles away. Today's venues often include performances from Indigenous people around the Western hemisphere. The powwow is a major cultural activity that not only helps preserve a rich legacy but also illustrates the tenacity and strength of Native cultures that are living and dynamic.

Each powwow begins with the Grand Entry in which participants enter the sacred dance circle (arbor), dancing their particular styles to a song by the drummers and singers. Leaders of the Grand Entry are the flag bearers, carrying the American Flag, POW Flag, Eagle Staff (Native Flag), and the flags of participating Native nations. The flags are usually carried by Native veterans, who in spite of the horrible treatment by the U.S. government still honor the American flag.

Led by elders, the male dancers usually enter in the same order: men's traditional dancers in their double-feather bustles and performing their high-step moves; men's grass dancers in stunning outfits, sporting long and flowing fringes, their movements similar to wind-blown tall grasses; and men's fancy dancers decked out in a vast array of colors. Elder women then lead in the women dancers: women's traditional dancers who move elegantly and slowly as one in their beautiful intricate regalia; jingle dress dancers with their cloth dresses adorned with handmade tin cones, which jingle to their rhythmic buoy-ant steps; and fancy shawl dancers, twirling and stepping rapidly as their graceful fringed shawls twirl along with them. Next are the teen boys, followed by teen girls, younger children, and tiny tots. The emcee announces each category as they enter. Visitors are asked to stand for the Grand Entry. When all are in the arena, the powwow grounds are blessed with a prayer and the veterans are honored in song.

Although most powwows are intertribal, many feature culturally specific activities like games, foods, special dances, performances, and music. Powwows may be public festivals, but they are Indian indeed with a certain code of ethics that spectators must respect:

- Dress modestly and refrain from wearing tee shirts with profanity or lewd graphics. For some dances, the public is invited to participate—women are usually required to cover their shoulders with shawls—best to take one along.

- Listen and follow the instructions of the emcee.

- Stand for Grand Entry and any honorings or prayers.

- Do not call any Indian clothing "costumes"; the preferred word is "regalia." And never touch anyone's regalia without asking permission.

- Seating next to the arena is reserved for drummers, singers and dancers, visitors may bring their own chairs and sit in the designated area.

- Ask permission before taking pictures or recordings and never photograph prayers or other cere-monies.

- The powwow circle has been blessed; it is sacred and needs to be revered in the same way as any religious gathering place.

- No drugs, alcohol, or weapons allowed.

- Refrain from making disruptive noise.

- Spectators should enjoy themselves, but remember that for many participants, the powwow is a way of earning money. It is also a serious time when participants, who may be marginalized from their own cultures in their daily lives, have the opportunity to connect with their friends, family and heritage. Respect.

A Powwow for every month across America and hundreds more:

January
Sarasota Native American Indian Festival (Sarasota, FL)
https://sarasotanativeamericanindianfestival.wordpress.com/

February
Annual Wildhorse Powwow (Lawndale, CA)
http://www.wildhorsesingers.com/wildhorse-pow-wow/

March
Annual Denver March Powwow (Denver, CO)
http://www.denvermarchpowwow.org/

April
Gathering of Nations (Albuquerque, NM)
http://www.gatheringofnations.com/

May
Annual Monacan Indian Nation Powwow (Elon, VA)
http://www.monacannation.com/powwow.shtml

June
Annual American Indian Center—Chicago Powwow (Elk Grove Village, IL)
http://aic-chicago.org/

July
Annual Thunderbird Grand Mid-Summer Powwow (Floral Park, NY)
https://thunderbirdamericanindiandancers.wordpress.com/events/

August
Annual Crow Fair Powwow (Crow Agency, MT)
http://www.crow-nsn.gov/crow-fair-2015.html

September
Annual Cherokee National Holiday (Tahlequah, OK)
http://www.cherokee.org/AboutTheNation/NationalHoliday.aspx

October
Honolulu Intertribal Powwow (Honolulu, HI)
http://www.honoluluintertribalpowwow.com/

November
Austin Powwow (Austin, TX)
http://www.austinpowwow.net/

December
Tulalip Tribes & Marysville School District Christmas Powwow (Marysville, WA) http://www.tulalip
    tribes-nsn.gov/

APPENDIX L:
INDIGENOUS ANCESTRY AFFILIATION OF SOME NOTABLE PEOPLE

(Only those with tribal affiliation included; not all are substantiated)

Jack Aker, Potowatomie (Professional Baseball Player)

Susan Allen, Sicangu Oyate, Lakota (first Native American woman elected to Minnesota legislature)

William Apess, Pequot (Minister/Writer)

Henry Armstrong, Iroquois (Professional Boxer)

Ebenezer Don Carlos Bassett, Pequot (Considered first African American to be appointed diplomat to a foreign country — Haiti 1869)

Adam Beach, Saulteaux (Actor)

Joey Belladonna, Iroquois (Musician — Anthrax)

Johnny Bench, Choctaw (Professional Baseball Player)

Jessica Biel, Choctaw (Actress)

Chuck Billy, Pomo (Singer — Testament)

Traci Bingham, Wampanoag (Actress)

Jimmy Carl Black, Cherokee, Yaqui, Apache, and Shoshone (Musician — Mothers of Invention)

George Bonga, Ojibwe (Fur Trader)

Sam Bradford, Cherokee (Professional Football Player)

Benjamin Bratt, Quechua (Actor)

James Brown, Apache (Singer)

Jesse L. Brown, Chicksaw/Choctaw (Credited with being the First African American Naval aviator)

Travis Kuualiialoha Browne, Hawaiian (Mixed Martial Artist Fighter)

Olivia Ward Bush, Montaukett (Author/Tribal Historian)

Tonantzin Carmelo, Tongva/Kumeyaay (Actress)

Tia Carrere, Hawaiian (Actress/Singer)

Johnny Cash, Cherokee, (Musician)

Randy Castillo (Musician — Motley Crue)

Kristin Chenoweth, Cherokee (Actress)

Don Cherry, Choctaw (Musician)

Eagle Eye Cherry, Choctaw (Musicians)

Joseph Louis Cook, Abenaki (Continental Army Colonel during Revolutionary War)

Pat Cooper, Choctaw (Professional Baseball Player)

Charlie Cozart, Cherokee (Professional Baseball Player)

Rickey Dale Crain, Choctaw (World Powerlifting Champion)

Art Daney, Choctaw (Professional Baseball Player)

Ronald Maurice Darling, Jr., Hawaiian (Professional Baseball Player)

Jesse Ed Davis, Kiowa (Rock Musician)

Milt Davis, Muscogee (Professional Football Player/History Professor)

Jack Dempsey, Choctaw/Cherokee (Professional Boxer)

Willy Deville, Pequot (Musician - Mink Deville)

Ramona Douglass, Oglala Lakota (Leading Advocate for Mixed Heritage People)

Nathaniel Dunigan, Navajo (International advocate for Ugandan orphans)

Vallie Eaves, Cherokee (Professional Baseball Player)

Shannon Elizabeth, Cherokee (Actress)

Faith Evans, Hawaiian (First Woman to Serve as U.S. Marshall — 1982)

Brett Favre, Choctaw (Professional Football Player)

Theoren Fleury, Metís/Cree (Professional Hockey Player)

Redd Foxx, Seminole (Actor)

Yovani Gallardo, Purepecha (Professional Baseball Player)

James Garner, Cherokee (Actor)

Jim Gladd, Cherokee (Professional Baseball Player)

Meagan Good, Cherokee/Taino (Actress)

Kiowa Joseph Gordon, Hualapai (Actor)

Lance Hahn, Hawaiian (vocalist for Band, J Church)

Rebecca Hall, Sioux (Actress)

Ben Harper, Cherokee (Musician)

Douglas Farthing Hatlelid (Chip Douglas), Hawaiian (musician/producer of the Monkees)

Kaui Hart Hemmings, Hawaiian (Writer)

Dorris Henderson, Blackfoot (Folk Singer)

Jimi Hendrix, Cherokee (Musician)

Don Ho, Hawaiian (Entertainer/Singer)

Hōkū Christian Ho, Hawaiian (Singer/Actress/Composer)

Chief Hogsett, Cherokee (Professional Baseball Player)

Dan Hornbuckle, Eastern Cherokee (DEEP Welterweight Champion)

Debora Iyall, Cowlitz (Singer - Romeo Void)

Shar Jackson, Taino/Arwak (Actress)

Mickie James, Powhatan (Professional Wrestler)

Maren Kawehilani Jensen, Hawaiian (Actress)

Bob Johnson, Cherokee (Professional Baseball Player)

Roy Johnson, Cherokee (Professional Baseball Player)

Angelina Jolie, Huron (Actress)

James Earl Jones, Cherokee/Choctaw (Actor)

Julia Jones, Choctaw/ Chickasaw (Actress)

Paulette Jordan, Coeur d'Alene (Member — Idaho House of Representatives)

Gilbert Francis Lani Damian Kauhi, Hawaiian (Actor/Comedian)

Lonnie Kauk, Ahwahnechee (Professional snowboarder)

Mary Kaye, Hawaiian ("First Lady of Rock and Roll" and a founder of the Las Vegas "lounge" phenomenon)

Eartha Kitt, Cherokee (Actress)

Stepfanie Kramer, Eastern Band Cherokee (Actress)

Denny Lambert, Ojibwe (Professional Hockey Player)

Jason Scott Lee, Hawaiian (Actor)

Ananda Lewis, Creek (Television Personality)

Edmonia Lewis, Mississauga Ojibwe (Artist)

Mance Lipscomb, Choctaw (Blues Musician)

Amber Littlejohn, Cherokee (Professional Figure Competitor)

Gene Locklear, Lumbee (Professional Baseball Player and Artist)

Heather Locklear, Lumbee (Actress)

Kyle Lohse, Nomlaki Wintun (Professional Baseball Player)

Dwight Lowry, Lumbee (Professional Baseball Player)

Agnes Nalani Lum, Hawaiian (Actress/Model)

Greg Maddux, Choctaw (Professional Baseball Player)

Bobby Madritsch, Lakota (Professional Baseball Player)

Randolph Mantooth, Seminole (Actor)

Pepper Martin, Osage (Professional Baseball Player)

Sera-Lys McArthur, Nakota (Actress)

Sandy McCarthy, Mic Mac (Professional Hockey Player)

Rue McClanahan, Choctaw (Actress)

Cal McLish, Choctaw (Professional Baseball Player)

Rickey Medlocke, Blackfoot (Musician — Blackfoot)

Patricia Michaels, Taos (Fashion Designer — Project Runway)

Elaine Miles, Cayuse/Nez Perce (Actress)

Bill Miller, Stockbridge-Munsee (Singer)

Leona Mitchell, Chickasaw (Operatic Soprano)

Jason Momoa, Hawaiian (Actor)

Euel Moore, Chickasaw (Professional Baseball Player)

Bob Neighbors, Cherokee (Professional Baseball Player)

Jordan Nolan, Ojibwe (Professional Hockey Player)

Gino Odjick, Algonquin (Professional Hockey Player)

Rosa Parks, Creek (Civil Rights Activist)

Charlie Patton, Cherokee (Founder of the Blues in the Mississippi Delta)

Jess Pike, Creek (Professional Baseball Player)

Jim Plunkett, Mexican Indian (Professional Football Player)

Daniel Ponce de Leon, Tarahumara (WBC Featherweight Champion)

Elvis Presley, Cherokee (Singer)

Kelly Preston, Hawaiian (Actress)

Phylicia Rashād, Cherokee (Actress)

Della Reese, Cherokee (Actress)

Keanu Reeves, Hawaiian (Actor)

Allie Reynolds, Muscogee (Professional Baseball Player)

Burt Reynolds, Cherokee (Actor)

Branscombe Richmond, Aleut (Actor)

Robbie Robertson, Mohawk (Musician — The Band)

David Laughing Horse Robinson, Kawaiisu (Candidate for Governor of California, 2003)

Ned Romero, Chitimacha (Opera Singer/Actor)

Felipe Rose, Lakota Sioux/Taino (Musician — The Village People)

Nicole Scherzinger, Hawaiian (Singer/Actress)

Marguerite Scypion, Natchez (an African-Natchez whose family successfully sued for their freedom from slavery — Missouri 1836)

Larry Sellers, Osage/Cherokee/Lakota (Actor/Stuntman)

Martin Sensmeier, Athabascan/Tlingit (Actor)

Wini Shaw, Hawaiian (Actress in Warner Bros. Musicals — best known for first singing "Lullaby of Broadway" in Gold Diggers)

Chris Simon, Ojibwe (Professional Hockey Player)

Sonny Sixkiller, Cherokee (Professional Football Player)

Barbara Smith, Sac and Fox, (Member—Pennsylvania House of Representatives)

Keely Smith, Cherokee (Singer)

Shannon Marie Kohololani Sossamon, Hawaiian (Actress)

Sheldon Sharik Souray, Metis (Professional Hockey Player)

Chaske Spencer, Sioux/Nez Perce/Cherokee/Muscogee Creek (Actor)

Woody Strode, Blackfoot/Muscogee (Actor/Athlete)

Donna Summer, Cherokee (Singer)

Taboo, Shoshone (Musician — Black Eyed Peas)

Quentin Tarantino, Cherokee (Film Director)

Toni Tenille, Cherokee (Singer)

Sheila Tousey, Menominee/Stockbridge-Munsee (Actress)

Bryan Trottier, Cree/Chippewa (Professional Hockey Player)

France Winddance Twine, Muscogee (Sociologist/Author)

Carrie Underwood, Muscogee Creek (Singer)

Brendon Boyd Urie, Hawaiian (Musician)

Ritchie Valens, Yaqui (Musician)

Max Wolf Valerio, Blackfoot (Author on transgendered topics)

Eddie Van Halen, Hawaiian (Musician)

Kateri Walker, Chippewa (Actress)

Tim Welch, Assiniboine Sioux (MMA welterweight)

Kitty Wells, Cherokee (Country Singer)

Pete Wentz, Native Hawaiian (Musician — Fall Out Boy)

Amil "Amil" Whitehead, Cherokee (Rapper)

Hank Williams, Muskogee Creek/Cherokee (Country Singer)

Mykelti Williamson, Blackfeet (Actor)

Oprah Winfrey, Chickasaw (Actress)

Link Wray, Shawnee (Rock Musician)

Keke Wyatt, Cherokee (Singer)

Rudy York, Cherokee (Professional Baseball Player)

Maimouna Youssef, Choctaw/ Cherokee/Creek (Musician)

Michael Zinzun, Apache (former Black Panther)

FURTHER READING

General

Anderson, Terry, and Kirke Kickingbird. *An Historical Perspective on the Issue of Federal Recognition and Non-Recognition.* Washington, DC: Institute for the Development of Indian Law, 1978.

Armstrong, Virginia Irving, comp. *I Have Spoken: American History through the Voices of the Indians.* Chicago: The Swallow Press, 1971.

Beitsch, Rebecca. "Wooing Native Americans for the 2010 Census." *Bismarck Tribune.* http://bismarck tribune.com/news/local/govt-and-politics/wooing-native-americans-for-the-census/article_428871c 8-22e8-11df-8a78-001cc4c03286.html (accessed February 26, 2010).

Bruchac, Joseph, ed. *Returning the Gift: Poetry and Prose from the First North American Native Writers' Festival.* Tucson: University of Arizona, 1994.

Bumsted, John M. "American Indian Heritage Month: Commemoration vs. Exploitation: Bering Strait Theory. *ABC-CLIO Schools.* http://www.historyandtheheadlines.abc-clio.com/ContentPages/Content Page.aspx?entryId=1171655 (Accessed January 3, 2016).

Capriccioso, Rob. "Warrior Woman Walks On." *This Week from Indian Country Today.* http://Indian CountryTodayMediaNetwork.com (accessed November 2, 2011).

Centers for Disease Control and Prevention. "American Indian & Alaska Native Populations." http://www.cdc.gov/minorityhealth/populations/REMP/aian.html (accessed January 4, 2016).

Chavers, Dean. "Alcatraz Was Not an Island." *This Week from Indian Country Today.* http://Indian CountryTodayMediaNetwork.com (accessed November 16, 2011).

Cook-Lynn, Elizabeth. *Anti-Indianism in Modern America. A Voice from Tatekeya's Earth.* Chicago: University of Illinois Press, 2001.

———. *New Indians, Old Wars.* Chicago: University of Illinois Press, 2007.

———. *A Separate Country: Postcoloniality and American Indian Nations.* Lubbock, TX: Texas Tech University Press, 2011.

Davis, Mary, ed. *Native America in the Twentieth Century: An Encyclopedia.* New York: Garland, 1996.

Deloria, Philip J., and Neal Salsbury, eds. *A Companion to American Indian History*. Malden, MA: Blackwell Publishing, 2004.

D'Errico, Peter. "UNDRIP: What's in a Name?" *This Week from Indian Country Today*. http://Indian CountryTodayMediaNetwork.com (accessed May 9, 2012).

Dunbar-Ortiz, Roxanne. *An Indigenous People's History of the United States*. Boston: Beacon Press, 2014.

Echo-Hawk, Walter, R. *In the Light of Justice: The Rise of Human Rights in Native America and the UN Declaration on the Rights of Indigenous Peoples*. Golden, CO: Fulcrum Publishing, 2013.

Ewen, Alexander, and Maravic, Ivana. "The Measure of Indians." *American Indian*. Summer/Fall, 2014, pp. 54–55.

"Federal and State Recognized Tribes." *National Conference of State Legislatures, Federal and State Recognized Tribes*. http://www.ncsl.org/research/state-tribal-institute/list-of-federal-and-state-recogni zed-tribes.aspx (accessed February 18, 2016).

Fixico, Donald L. *American Indians in a Modern World*. Lanham, MD: AltaMira Press/Rowman & Littlefield, 2006.

Fleming, Walter C. *The Complete Idiot's Guide to Native American History*. New York: Alpha Books, 2003.

Goodyear, Al. "New Evidence Puts Man in North America 50,000 Years Ago." *Science Daily*. http://www .sciencedaily.com/releases/2004/11/041118104010.htm (accessed November 18, 2004).

The Harvard Project on American Indian Economic Development. *The State of the Native Nations*. New York: Oxford University Press, 2008.

Hirschfelder, Arlene, and Martha Kreipe de Montano. *The Native American Almanac: A Portrait of Native America Today*. New York: Prentice Hall General Reference, 1993.

———, and Paulette F Molin. *The Extraordinary Book of Native American Lists*.

Lanham, MD: The Scarecrow Press, 2012.

———, and Beverly R. Singer. *Rising Voices: Writings of Young Native Americans*. New York: Ballantine Books, 1993.

Hodges, Glenn. "The First Americans." *National Geographic*, Vol. 227, no.1 (January 2015): 124–137.

Horse Capture, George, Duane Champagne, and Chandler C. Jackson, *American Indian Nations: Yesterday, Today, and Tomorrow*. Lanham, MD: Altamira Press, 2007.

Jacobs, Don Trent. *Unlearning the Language of Conquest: Scholars Expose Anti-Indianism in America.* Austin : University of Texas Press, 2006.

Johansen, Bruce E. *The Praeger Handbook on Contemporary Issues in North America*. Vol. 1: *Linguistic, Ethnic, and Economic Revival*. Westport, CT: Praeger, 2007.

———, and Donald A. Grinde, Jr. *The Encyclopedia of Native American Biography: Six Hundred Life Stories of Important People, from Powhatan to Wilma Mankiller*. New York: Da Capo Press, 1998.

Johnson, Troy. *Red Power: The American Indians Fight for Freedom*. Lincoln: University of Nebraska Press, 1999.

Jorgensen, Miriam, ed. *Rebuilding Native Nations: Strategies for Governance and Development*. Tucson: University of Arizona, 2007.

Juettner, Bonnie. *100 Native Americans Who Shaped American History*. San Mateo, CA: Bluebook Books, 2003.

King, Thomas. *The Inconvenient Indian: A Curious Account of Native People in North America*. Minneapolis: University of Minnesota Press, 2012.

———. *The Truth about Stories: A Native Narrative*. Toronto, ON: House of Anansi Press, 2003.

LaDuke, Winona. *Recovering the Sacred: The Power of Naming and Claiming*. Cambridge, MA: South End Press, 2005.

Leahy, Todd, and Raymond Wilson. *Historical Dictionary of Native American Movements*. Lanham, MD: The Scarecrow Press, 2008.

Lee, Tanya H. "Schooled on School: The Major Challenges Facing Native Students." *This Week from Indian Country Today*. http://IndianCountryTodayMediaNetwork.com (accessed August 27, 2014).

Lowawaima, K. Tsianina. *To Remain an Indian: Lessons in Democracy from a Century of Native American Education*. New York: Teachers College, 2006.

MacIsaac, Tara. "3 Distinguished Linguists Examine Mysterious Origin of Native Americans." *Epoch Times*. http://www.theepochtimes.com/n3/1211586-3-distinguished-linguists-look-at-mysterious-origin-of-native-americans (accessed January 21, 2015).

Mann, Charles C. *1491: New Revelations of the Americas before Columbus*. New York: Alfred A. Knopf, 2005.

———. *1493: Uncovering the New World Columbus Created*. New York: Knopf, 2011.

Marks, Paula Mitchell. *In a Barren Land: American Indian Dispossession and Survival*. New York: William Morrow, 1998.

McLuhan, T.C., comp. *Touch the Earth: A Self-Portrait of Indian Existence*. New York, Pocket Books, 1971.

Mason, Dale. *Indian Gaming: Tribal Sovereignty and American Politics*. Norman: University of Oklahoma Press, 2000

Maurer, Evan M. *The Native American Heritage: A Survey of North American Indian Art*. Chicago: Art Institute of Chicago, 1977.

McMaster, Gerald, and Clifford E. Trafzer. *Native Universe: Voices of Indian America*. Washington, DC: NMAI and National Geographic, 2008.

———. *New Tribe: New York /The Urban Vision Quest*. Washington, DC: NMAI, 2005.

Miller, Lee, ed. *From the Heart: Voices of the American Indian*. New York: Vintage Books, 1995.

Moss, Margaret R. "Native Health Disparities: Where is the Outrage?" *This Week from Indian Country Today*. http://IndianCountryTodayMediaNetwork.com (accessed October 26, 2011).

Moya-Smith, Simon. "Harvard Professor Confirms Bering Strait Theory Is Not Fact." *This Week from Indian Country*. http://IndianCountryTodayMediaNetwork.com (accessed July 31, 2012).

Nabokov, Peter, ed. *Native American Testimony: A Chronicle of Indian-White Relations from Prophecy to the Present*. New York: Penguin Books, 1991.

Nathan Associates. *Indian Gaming Industry Report*. http://www.nathaninc.com/resources/indian-gaming-industry-report (accessed January 5, 2016).

Native Village Language Library. http://www.nativevillage.org/Libraries/Language%20Libraries.htm (accessed February 15, 2016).

Newcomb, Steve. "Five Hundred Years of Injustice: The Legacy of Fifteenth Century Religious Prejudice." *Shaman's Drum*. Fall 1992, pp. 18–20.

————. "The Theft of 90 Million Acres of Indian Land." *This Week from Indian Country Today,* http://IndianCountryTodayMediaNetwork.com (accessed February 22, 2012).

Pevar, Stephen. *The Rights of Indians and Tribes: The Authoritative ACLU Guide to Indian and Tribal Rights.* New York: New York University Press, 2004.

Pritzker, Barry M. *A Native American Encyclopedia: History, Culture, and Peoples.* New York: Oxford University Press, 2000.

Ramirez, Marc. "Census Bureau Tackles Undercount of Native Americans." *Seattle Times,* http://www.seattletimes.com/seattle-news/census-bureau-tackles-undercount-of-native-americans/ (accessed May 26, 2010).

Senier, Siobhan, ed. *Dawnland Voices: An Anthology of Indigenous Writing from New England.* Lincoln: University of Nebraska Press, 2014.

Smith, Andrea. *Conquest: Sexual Violence and American Indian Genocide.* Boulder, CO: South End Press, 2005.

Tayac, Gabrielle, ed. *IndiVisible: African-Native American Lives in the Americas.* Washington, DC: Smithsonian Press, 2009.

Tiller, Veronica E. Velarde. *Tiller's Guide to Indian Country: Economic Profiles of American Indian Reservations.* Albuquerque, NM: BowArrow Publishing Company, 2005.

Toensing, Gale Courey. "A Hard and Cruel Act to Follow: The Dawes Act of 1997 Started the U.S. Wholesale Land-Grab of Native Territory." *This Week from Indian Country Today.* http://Indian CountryTodayMediaNetwork.com (accessed February 22, 2012).

Toensing, Gale Courey. "States Trump Peoples." (UN World Conference on Indigenous Peoples). *This Week from Indian Country Today.* http://IndianCountryTodayMediaNetwork.com (accessed October 1, 2014).

Trafzer, Clifford. *Native Universe: Voices of Indian America.* New York: National Geographic, 2004.

Treuer, Anton. *Atlas of Indian Nations.* Washington, DC: National Geographic, 2013.

————. *Indian Nations of North America.* Washington, DC: National Geographic, 2010.

Treuer, David. *Rez Life: An Indian's Journey through Reservation Life.* New York: Grove Press, 2012.

Two-Hawks, John. "Mistakes, Lies & Misconceptions about American Indian Peoples: The B.S. Bering Strait) Myth. *Native Circle.* http://www.nativecircle.com/mlmBSmyth.html (accessed February 4, 2016).

U.S. Census Bureau, *The American Indian and Alaska Native Population, 2010.* January 2012. http://www.census.gov/prod/cen2010/briefs/c2010br-10.pdf.

U.S. Department of the Interior, Office of the Assistant Secretary-Indian Affairs. *2013 American Indian Population and Labor Force Report, January 16, 2014.* http://www.bia.gov/cs/groups/public/documents/text/idc1-024782.pdf.

Waldman, Carl. *Atlas of the North American Indian, Third Edition.* New York: Checkmark Books, 2009.

————.*Who Was Who in Native American History: Indians and Non-Indians from Early Contacts through 1900.* New York: Facts on File, 1990.

Wilkinson, Charles. *Blood Struggle: The Rise of Modern Indian Nations.* New York: W.W. Norton, 2005.

Wilson, James. *The Earth Shall Weep: A History of Native America.* New York: Atlantic Monthly Press, 1998.

Wittstock Waterman, Laura, and Dick Bancroft. *We Are Still Here: A Photographic History of the American Indian Movement*. St. Paul, MN: Borealis Books, 2013.

Alaska

Alaska Native Language Center. "Languages." http://www.uaf.edu/anlc/languages (accessed January 15, 2016).

Aqukkasuk. "Alaska Indigenous. Summary: First Report of the Alaska Native Language Preservation and Advisory Council." https://alaskaindigenous.wordpress.com/category/author-aqukkasuk (accessed July 6, 2014).

Chythlook-Sifsof, Callan J. "Native Alaska, Under Threat." *New York Times*, June 28, 2013.

Crowell, Aron L, Rosita Worl, Paul C. Ongtooguk, and Dawn D. Biddison. *Living Our Cultures, Sharing Our Heritage: The First Peoples of Alaska*. Washington, DC: Smithsonian Books, 2010.

Dauenhauer, Richard, Nora Marks, and Anóoshi Lingít Aaní Ká. *Russians in Tlingit America. The Battles of Sitka 1802 and 1804*. Seattle: Washington University Press, 2008.

Fienup-Riordan, Ann. *Eskimo Essays: Yup'ik Lives and How We See Them*. New Brunswick, NJ: Rutgers University Press, 1990.

Fitzhugh, William W., and Aron Crowell. *Crossroads of Continents: Cultures of Siberia and Alaska*. Washington, DC: Smithsonian Institution Press, 1988.

ICTMN Staff, "20 Alaska Native Languages Become Official State Languages." *This Week from Indian Country Today*. October 15, 2014.

Lee, Molly C., ed. *Not Just a Pretty Face: Dolls and Human Figurines in Alaska Native Cultures*, 2nd ed. Fairbanks: University of Alaska Press, 2006.

McClanahan, Alexandra J., ed. *Growing Up Native in Alaska*. Anchorage: The CIRI Foundation, 2000.

———, ed. *A Reference in Time: Alaska Native History Day by Day*. Anchorage: The CIRI Foundation, 2001.

Metcalfe, Kimberly L., ed. *In Sisterhood: The History of Camp 2 of the Alaska Native Sisterhood*. Juneau, AK: Hazy Island Books, 2008.

Native American Rights Fund. "The Right to Vote for Alaska Natives." *NARF Legal Review*, Vol. 39, no. 2 (Summer 2014): 1–4.

Resource Development Council for Alaska, Inc. "Alaska's Native Corporations." http://www.akrdc.org/issues/nativecorporations/overview.html (accessed January 14, 2016).

Roderick, Libby, ed. *Alaska Native Cultures and Issues: Responses to Frequently Asked Questions*. Fairbanks: University of Alaska Press, 2010.

Schaefer, Carol. "Grandmother Rita Pikta Blumenstein." From *Grandmothers Council the World: Women Elders Offer Their Vision for Our Planet*. Boston: Trumpeter, 2006.

Utter, Jack. "Section M: Alaska." In *American Indians: Answers to Today's Questions*. 2nd edition. Norman: University of Oklahoma Press, 2001.

Wilson, Kenneth F., and Jeff Richardson, eds. *The Aleutian Islands of Alaska: Living on the Edge*. Fairbanks: University of Alaska Press, 2009.

Great Basin, Rocky Mountains, Plateau

Alexie, Sherman. *Blasphemy, New and Selected Stories*. New York: Grove/Atlantic, 2012.

Canfield, Gae Whitney. *Sarah Winnemucca of the Northern Paiutes*. Norman: University of Oklahoma Press, 1983.

Dennis, Yvonne Wakim, and Arlene Hirschfelder. *A Kid's Guide to Native American History*. Chicago: Chicago Review Press, 2010.

Forbes, Jack D. *Native Americans of California and Nevada*. Healdsburg, CA: Naturegraph Publishers, 1969.

Harney, Corbin. *The Way It Is: One Water, One Air, One Mother Earth*. Grass, CA: Blue Dolphin Publishing, 2009.

———. *The Nature Way*. Reno: University of Nevada Press, 2009.

Hittman, Michael. *Great Basin Indians: An Encyclopedic History*. Reno: University of Nevada Press, 2013.

Hunsaker, Joyce Badgley. *Sacagawea Speaks: Beyond the Shining Mountains with Lewis & Clark*. Guilford, CT : Two Dot Books, 2001.

Kauffman, Hattie. *Falling into Place: A Memoir of Overcoming*. Ada, MI: Baker Publishing Group, 2014.

Quick-to-See Smith, Jaune. *She Paints the Horse*. Casper, WY: Nicolayson Art Museum, 2005.

HAWAII

Abbott, Isabella Aiona. *Marine Red Algae of the Hawaiian Islands*. Honolulu: Bishop Museum Press, 1999.

Ah Nee-Benham, Maenette K. P. *Indigenous Educational Models for Contemporary Practice: In Our Mother's Voice. Sociocultural, Political, and Historical Studies in Education*. Mahwah, NJ: L. Erlbaum Associates, 2000.

Aikau, Hokulani K., Karla A. Erickson, and Jennifer Pierce, eds. *Feminist Waves, Feminist Generations: Life Stories from the Academy*. Minneapolis: University of Minnesota Press, 2007.

Balaz, Joseph P. *Domino Buzz*. Hawaii: Iron Bench Press, 2006.

Bowman, Sally-Jo Keala-o-Ānuenue. *The Heart of Being Hawaiian*. Honolulu: Watermark Pub, 2008.

Coffman, Tom. *Nation Within: The History of the American Occupation of Hawai'i*. Kiehi, HI: Koa Books, 2009.

Goodyear-Ka'ʻopua, Noelani, Ikaika Hussey, and Erin Kahunawaika'ala Wright. *A Nation Rising*. Durham, NC: Duke University Press, 2014.

Halualani, Rona Tamiko. *In the Name of Hawaiians: Native Identities and Cultural Politics*. Minneapolis: University of Minnesota Press, 2002.

Harden, M. J. *Voices of Wisdom: Hawaiian Elders Speak*. Kula, HI: Aka Press, 1999.

Holt, John Dominis. *On Being Hawaiian*. Honolulu, HI: Ku Pa'a, 1995.

Kamakau, Samuel Manaiakalani. *Ruling Chiefs of Hawa'i*. Honolulu: Kamehameha Schools Press, 1964.

———. *Ka Po'e Kahiko*. Honolulu: Bishop Museum Press, 1964.

———. *Tale and Traditions of the People of Old: Na Mo'Olelo a Ka Po'E Kahiko*. Honolulu: Bishop Museum Press, 1993.

Kanae, Lisa Linn. *Islands Linked by Ocean: Stories*. Honolulu: Bamboo Ridge Press, 2009.

Kanahele, Elama, Kimo Armitage, and Keao NeSmith. *Aloha Niihau*. Waipahu, HI: Island Heritage Publishing, 2007.

Kanahele, George He'eu Sanford. *Kū Kanaka: Stand Tall*. Honolulu: Bishop Museum Press, 1986.

Kane, Herb Kawainui. *Ancient Hawaii*. Captain Cook, HI: Kawainui Press, 1998.

Kauanui, J. Kēhaulani. *Hawaiian Blood: Colonialism and the Politics of Sovereignty and Indigeneity*. Durham, NC: Duke University Press, 2008.

Liliuokalani. *Hawaii's Story by Hawaii's Queen*. Honolulu: University of Hawaii Press, 2014.

Low, Sam. *Hawaiki Rising*. Waipahu, HI: Island Heritage Publishing, 2013.

Mander, Jerry, and Koohan Paik. *The Superferry Chronicles: Hawaii's Uprising against Militarism, Commercialism, and the Desecration of the Earth*. Kiehi, HI: Koa Books, 2009.

McGregor, Davianna. *Nā Kua'āina: Living Hawaiian Culture*. Honolulu: University of Hawaii Press, 2007.

Silva, Noenoe. *Aloha Betrayed: Native Hawaiian Resistance to American Colonialism*. Durham, NC: Duke University Press, 2004.

Trask, Haunani-Kay. "The Struggle for Hawaiian Sovereignty." *Cultural Survival*, Spring 2000.

Ulrike, Wiethaus. *Foundations of First Peoples' Sovereignty*. New York: Peter Lang Publishing, 2008.

Midwest

Black Hawk. *Black Hawk, An Autobiography*. Lincoln, NE: University of Illinois Press, 1990.

Blaeser, Kimberly. "Dreams of Water Bodies." *Wisconsin Academy of Sciences, Arts and Letters*, Issue 107, 2011.

Chavez, Will. "National Park Service Uses Artist's Paintings." *Cherokee Phoenix*. http://www.cherokeephoenix.org/Article/Index/5790 (accessed December 20, 2011).

Crowley, Matthew. "A Lobbyist in Full." *New York Times Magazine*, May 1, 2005.

Honor the Earth. The Triple Crown of Pipeline Rides (video), 2013. https://www.youtube.com/watch?v=1v6_1DLth9U (accessed January 5, 2016).

Kimmerer, Robin Wall. *Braiding Sweetgrass: Indigenous Wisdom, Scientific Knowledge and the Teachings of Plants*. Minneapolis: Milkweed Editions, 2013.

Mann, Charles. *1491: New Revelations of the Americas before Columbus*. New York: Random House, 2005.

Newell Peacock, Leslie. "The Quapaw Return to Arkansas." *The Arkansas Times*. November 20, 2014.

Peroff, Nicholas C. *Menominee Drums: Tribal Termination and Restoration, 1954–1974*. Norman: University of Oklahoma Press, 1982. p. 202.

Sweet, Denise. "Homing Song: Two Stanzas." *Songs for Discharming: Poems*. Greenfield Center, NY: Greenfield Review Press, 1997. p. 17.

Vizenor, Gerald, ed. *Survivance: Narratives of Native Presence*. Lincoln: University of Nebraska Press, 2008.

———. *Native Liberty: Natural Reason and Cultural Survivance*. Lincoln: University of Nebraska Press, 2009.

Wub-e-ke-niew. *We Have the Right to Exist*. Newfane, VT: Black Thistle Press, 2013.

Zielinski, John M. *Mesquakie and Proud of It*. New York: Photo-Art Gallery, 1976.

Northeast

Adams, Dan. "In the Steps of Long-Lost Kin." *Boston Globe*. http://www.bostonglobe.com/metro/2013/07/06/bermuda-dancers-connect-with-long-lost-relatives-mashpee-wampanoags-pow-wow/4gBCMYSFQfvsukqiAKwtCP/story.html (accessed July 6, 2013.)

Aquinnah Cultural Center. *Wampanoag "People of the First Light: Introduction to Aquinnah Arts History and Culture*. Aquinnah, MA: Aquinnah Cultural Center, 2009.

The Associated Press. "Sacred Artifacts Being Returned to NY's Onondaga Indians by Syracuse-Area Historical Group." *The New Republic*, June 6, 2012.

Blancke, Brian, and Wulff. "'Whose Land Is It Anyway?' The Third Side's Response to Indian Land Claim Conflicts in Upstate New York." http://www.thirdside.org/India.pdf (accessed May 23, 1999).

Boesch, Eugene J. "Native Americans of Putnam County." *Mahopac Public Library*. http://www.mahopaclibrary.org/mplex/addendum.htm (accessed January 15, 2016).

Caruso, Donna Laurent. "Wakening Wopanaak." *This Week from Indian Country Today*. http://IndianCountryTodayMediaNetwork.com (accessed April 27, 2011).

Farris, Phoebe. "Indigenous Arts: Homecoming for the Indians of Bermuda, Home Is Where the Art Is." *Cultural Survival Quarterly*. Vol. 32, no. 3 (Fall 2008).

Fletcher, Matthew L. M., Kathryn E. Fort, and Nicholas Reo. "Tribal Disruption and Indian Claims." *Michigan Law Review First Impressions*. Vol. 112 (January 2014).

Landry, Alysa. "Native History: It's Memorial Day—In 1637, the Pequot Massacre Happened." *This Week from Indian Country*. May 26, 2014.

Lepore, Jill. *The Name of War: King Philip's War and the Origins of American Identity*. New York: Knopf, 1998.

Maine Indians Basketmakers Alliance (MIBA). https://maineindianbaskets.org/annual-basket-markets.

Mann, Charles C. "Squanto and the Pilgrims: Native Intelligence." *Smithsonian Magazine* (December 2005): 95–108.

Mashpee Tribe Traditional Leaders: http://www.mashpeewampanoagtribe.com/traditionalleaders.

Montaukett Indian Nation. "History Overview: Early European Contact Years." http://montaukett.org/?page_id=22 (accessed February 2, 2016).

Mystic Voices LLC, Cast and Crew. "The Story of the Pequot War." http://www.pequotwar.com/history.html (accessed January 14, 2016).

Neuman, Lisa K. "Basketry as Economic Enterprise and Cultural Revitalization: The Case of the Wabanaki Tribes of Maine." *Wicazo Review*. Vol. 25, no. 2 (Fall 2010): 89–106.

Olan, Kay. "Kanatsiohareke, Language and Survival." *This Week from Indian Country Today*, http://IndianCountryTodayMediaNetwork.com (accessed August 3, 2011).

Rogers, Mark. "Long Island's Thriving Native Communities." *This Week from Indian Country*. http://IndianCountryTodayMediaNetwork.com (accessed November 19, 2014).

Rose, Christina. "Cheeseburgers & Wood Pellets in Paradise." *This Week from Indian Country*. http://IndianCountryTodayMediaNetwork.com (accessed September 15, 2014).

Schlossberg, Tatiana. "An Indian Tribe Faces Its Eroding Fortunes." *New York Times*, December 1, 1014: A22.

Stewart, Mark. *New York Native Peoples*. Chicago: Heinemann Library, 2009.

Sultzman, Lee. "First Nations History: Wampanoag History." http://www.tolatsga.org/wampa.html (accessed February 4, 2016).

Whitefield-Madrano. "The Cloth That Binds." *This Week from Indian Country Today*. http://Indian CountryTodayMediaNetwork.com (accessed July 20, 2011).

California

Advocates for Indigenous California Language Survival. "Linguistics and Language Revitalization." http://www.aicls.org/pages/slide1.html (accessed January 4, 2016).

Anthropology Museum. "Past and Present: Acorn Use in Native California." *eGuide for Acorn Use in Native California, a Mobile Classroom Outreach Trunk*. Sacramento: California State University. http://www.csus.edu/anth/museum/pdfs/Past%20and%20Present%20Acorn%20Use%20in%20 Native%20California.pdf (accessed February 23, 2016).

Bancroft, Kim. *They Heyday of Malcolm Margolin: The DAMN GOOD Times of a Fiercely Independent Publisher*. Berkeley: Heyday Books, 2014.

Carrico, Richard L. *Strangers in a Stolen Land: American Indians in San Diego, 1850–1880*. Sacramento, CA: Sierra Oaks Publishing, 1987.

Chacon, Albert. "We Are Birds: A California Indian Story." http://www.wearebirdsdocumentary.com/ home.html (accessed January 22, 2016).

Cook, Roy, ed. "Traditional Origins of Southern CA Bird Songs." *SAIL Studies in American Indian Literatures*, Series 2, Volume 1, Nos. 3 & 4 (Winter 1989).

Eargle, Dolan H., Jr. *California Indian Country: The Land and the People*. San Francisco: Trees Company Press, 1992.

Field, Les W. *Abalone Tales: Collaborative Explorations of Sovereignty and Identity in Native California*. Durham, NC: Duke University, 2008.

Hawkins, Chelsea. *Forgotten But Not Gone*. Santa Cruz, CA: UCSC Press/City on a Hill Press, 2011.

Heizer, Robert F. *The Destruction of California Indians*. Lincoln: University of Nebraska Press, 1993.

Hinton, Leanne. *Flutes of Fire: Essays on California Indian Languages*. Berkeley: Heyday Books, 1994.

Lindsay, Brendan. *Murder State: California's Native American Genocide, 1846–1873*. Lincoln: University of Nebraska Press, 2011.

Lowell, John Bean. "Memorial to Jane K. Penn (1910–1980)." https://escholarship.org/uc/item/7ck8992 m#page-1 (accessed February 2, 2016).

"Many Californians Working to Revitalize Native Languages." *This Week from Indian Country Today*, August 29, 2012.

Margolin, Malcolm. *They Heyday of Malcolm Margolin*. Berkeley: Heyday Books, 2014.

———. *The Ohlone Way: Indian Life in the San Francisco-Monterey Bay Area*. Berkeley, CA: Heyday Books, 1978.

———, ed. *The Way We Lived: The California Stories, Songs & Reminiscences*. Berkeley, CA: Heyday Books, 1993.

———, and Montijo, Yolanda. *Native Ways: California Indian Stories and Memories*. Berkeley, CA: Heyday Books, 1995.

Massey, Skippy. "Wiyot World Renewal Ceremony." *Humboldt Sentinel*, March 18, 2014.

Native American Netroots. "Indians 101: Acorns." http://nativeamericannetroots.net/diary/1055 (accessed September 7, 2011).

Newcomb, Steven. "The California Genocide." *This Week from Indian Country Today*, October 3, 2012.

Pogash, Carol. "To Some in California, Founder of Church Missions Is Far from Saint." *New York Times*, January 22, 2015, p. A12.

Sims, Hank. "Wiyot Tribe: Respectfully, the World Renewal Ceremony is Not a Party." *Lost Coast Outpost,* March 12, 2014.

Trafzer, Clifford. *California's Indians and the Gold Rush.* Sacramento, CA: Sierra Oaks Publishing, 1989.

Walters, Heidi. "Fumbled Apology: Was It Necessary to Water Down Mayor Jager's Letter to the Wiyot?" *Northcoast Journal,* March 27, 2014.

Woo, Elaine. "Katherine Siva Saubel, Preserver of Cahuilla Culture, Dies at 91." *Los Angeles Times,* November 6, 2011.

Yuhas, Alan. "Junipero Serra's Road to Sainthood Is Controversial for Native Americans." *The Guardian.* January 25, 2015.

Oregon/Washington

Anderson, Ross. "What's Wrong with This Picture? Two Centuries after Lewis and Clark, the Chinooks Fight for a Future Denied." *Seattle Times.* July 6, 2003.

Barber, Katrine. *Death of Celilo Falls.* Seattle: University of Washington Press, 2005.

Erikson, Patricia Pierce. *Leschi.* Tacoma: Washington State History Museum, 2006.

International Council of Thirteen Indigenous Grandmothers. *Grandmother's Projects: "Salmon Ceremony."* http://www.grandmotherscouncil.org/salmon-ceremony (accessed January 28, 2016).

McNeel, Jack. "Watershed Heroes: Colville Confederated Tribes Win Sierra Club Award." *This Week from Indian Country Today,* April 3, 2013.

Northwest Indian Fisheries Commission. "Voices at Boldt40." http://blogs.nwifc.org/boldt40 (accessed February 21, 2016).

Oregon Historical Society. "Reservation Life in Oregon." http://www.ohs.org/education/focus/reservation_life_Oregon.cfm (accessed February 17, 2016).

————. "Walla Walla Treaty Council, 1855." *The Oregon Encyclopedia.* http://www.oregonencyclopedia.org/articles/walla_walla_treaty_council_1855 (accessed January 18, 2016).

Oregon Native American Tribes. http://culturalorgon.com/970.

"Remembrances of Billy Frank, Jr." http://billyfrankjr.org/wp/wp-content/uploads/2014/05/Billy-media-coverage-and-condolences.pdf.

Ruby, Robert H., and John A. Brown. *A Guide to the Indian Tribes of the Pacific Northwest.* Norman: University of Oklahoma Press, 1986.

Suquamish Tribe. "History & Culture." http://suquamish.nsn.us/HistoryCulture.aspx (accessed February 27, 2016).

Tirado, Michelle. "In His Own Words: Book Showcases What Fuels the Activism of Hank Adams." *This Week from Indian Country Today.* May 20, 2012.

Umpqua Basin Explorer. "History of Native Americans in the Umpqua Region." http://oregon explorer.info/umpqua/NativeAmericans (accessed January 28, 2016).

Walker, Richard. "40 Years Later: Boldt Decision Celebrations with Some Caution." *This Week from Indian Country Today*, February 12, 2014.

Watt, Lisa J. *Oregon Is Indian Country: The Nine Federally Recognized Tribes of Oregon Student Magazine*. Portland: Oregon Historical Society, 2009.

Wright, Robin K., ed. *A Time of Gathering: Native Heritage in Washington State*. Seattle: University of Washington Press, 1991.

Northern Plains

Brown, Dee. *Bury My Heart at Wounded Knee: An Indian History of the American West*. New York: Macmillan, 1971.

Deloria, Ella Cara. *Waterlily*. Lincoln: University of Nebraska Press, 1988.

Deloria, Vine, Jr. *Custer Died for Your Sins*. New York: Macmillan, 1969.

———.*God Is Red: A Native View of Religion*. Golden, CO: Fulcrum,1973.

———.*Behind the Trail of Broken Treaties*. Austin, TX: University of Texas Press, 1974.

———. *Red Earth, White Lies: Native Americans and the Myth of Scientific Fact*. Golden, CO: Fulcrum, 1995.

———. *Evolution, Creationism and Other Modern Myths*. Golden, CO: Fulcrum, 2002.

Dudley, Joseph Iron Eye. *Choteau Creek, A Sioux Reminiscence*. Lincoln: University of Nebraska Press, 1992.

Eastman, Charles (Ohiyesa). *Indian Boyhood*. Mineola, New York: Dover, 1902.

———.*From the Deep Woods to Civilization: Chapters in the Autobiography of an Indian*. Mineola, NY: Dover Publications, 1916.

Erdrich, Louise. *Love Medicine*. New York: Harper Perennial, 1984.

———.*Tracks*. New York: Henry Holt & Co., 1998.

———. *Four Souls*. New York: Harper Collins, 2005.

———.*The Plague of Doves*. New York: Harper Perennial, 2008.

———. *Shadow Tag*. New York: HarperCollins, 2010.

———.*The Round House*. New York: Harper, 2010.

Howe, Craig, and Kim Tall Bear. eds. *This Stretch of the River: Lakota, Dakota, & Nakota Responses to the Lewis & Clark Expedition and Bicentennial*. Rapid City, SD: Oak Lake Writers' Society, 2006.

Standing Bear, Luther. *Land of the Spotted Eagle*. Lincoln: University of Nebraska Press, 1993.

Waggoner, Josephine. *Witness: A Hú?kpapha Historian's Strong-Heart Song of the Lakotas*. Edited by Emily Levine. Lincoln: University of Nebraska Press, 2013.

Waziyatawin, Angela Wilson, and Carolyn Schommer Wahpetunwin. *Remember This! Dakota Decolonization and the Eli Taylor Narratives*. Lincoln: University of Nebraska Press, 2005.

Welch, James. *Winter in the Blood*. New York: Harper and Row, 1974.

Wilkins, David E. *The Hank Adams Reader: An Exemplary Native Activist and the Unleashing of Indigenous Sovereignty*. Golden, CO: Fulcrum, 2011.

Yellowrobe, William S. *Where the Pavement Ends*. Norman: University of Oklahoma Press, 2000.

Southern Plains

Geiogamah, Hanay. *New Native American Drama: Three Plays*. Norman: University of Oklahoma Press, 1980.

Hogan, Linda. *Mean Spirit*. New York: Simon & Schuster, 1990.

Howe, LeAnne. *Choctalking on Other Realities*. Chicago: University of Illinois, 2013.

Mankiller, Wilma. *Mankiller: A Chief and Her People*. New York: St. Martin's Press, 1999.

———. *Every Day is a Good Day*. Golden, CO: Fulcrum Publishing, 2004.

Momaday, N. Scott. *House Made of Dawn*. New York: Harper & Row, 1968.

———. *The Way to Rainy Mountain*. Albuquerque: University of New Mexico Press, 1969.

———.*Against the Far Morning*. Albuquerque: University of New Mexico Press, 2011.

Rementer, James. "Near the Edge: Language Revival from the Brink of Extinction. The Delaware Tribe of Indians." http://delawaretribe.org/wp-content/uploads/NEAR_THE_EDGE.pdf (accessed June 1, 2013).

Southeast

Barbour, Jeannie, Amanda Cobb, and Linda Hogan. *Chickasaw: Unconquered and Unconquerable*. Photographs by David Fitzgerald. Ada, OK: Chickasaw Press, 2006.

Bird, Traveller. *Tell Them They Lie: The Sequoyah Myth*. Los Angeles: Westernlore, 1971.

Blumer, T. J. *The Catawba Indian Nation of the Carolinas*. Mt. Pleasant, SC: Arcadia, 2004.

———. *Catawba Indian Nation: Treasures in History*. Mt. Pleasant, SC: Arcadia, 2007.

Cherian, Shalom, and Kelsey Jackson. "Henry Berry Lowry." *Lumbee History*. UNC's "Native American Tribal Studies" Course. http://lumbee.web.unc.edu/online-exhibits-2/henry-berry-lowry/ (accessed January 19, 2016).

Conley, Robert. *The Cherokee Nation: A History*. Albuquerque: University of New Mexico Press, 2008.

———.*The Real People Series: The Way of the Priests*. Albuquerque: University of New Mexico Press, 1992.

———. *The Dark Way*. Albuquerque: University of New Mexico Press, 1993.

———. *The White Path*. Albuquerque: University of New Mexico Press, 1993.

———. *The Way South*. Albuquerque: University of New Mexico Press, 1993.

———. *The Long Way Home*. Albuquerque: University of New Mexico Press, 1994.

———. *The Dark Island*. Albuquerque: University of New Mexico Press, 1995.

———. *The War Trail North*. Albuquerque: University of New Mexico Press, 1995.

Custalow, Linwood "Little Bear," and Angela L. Daniel "Silver Star." *The True Story of Pocahontas: The Other Side of History*. Golden, CO: 2007.

De la Vega el Inca, Garcilaso. *History of the Conquest of Florida*. http://mith.umd.edu/eada/html/display.php?docs=garcilaso_florida.xml (accessed February 11, 2016).

Dial, Adolph, and David K. Eliades. *The Only Land I Know: A History of the Lumbee Indians*. Syracuse, NY: Syracuse University Press, 1996.

Doming, Michael. "The Tale of the Tunica Treasure." *The Harvard Crimson*, October 13,1983.

Fiske, Warren. "The Black-and-White World of Walter Ashby Plecker." *The Virginia Pilot On-Line*, August 18, 2004.

Fundaburk, Emma Lila. *Sun Circles and Human Hands: The Southeastern Indians Art and Industry.* Tuscaloosa, AL: University of Alabama Press, 2001.

Gunn Allen, Paula. *Pocahontas: Medicine Woman, Spy, Entrepreneur, Diplomat.* New York: HarperCollins, 2004.

Hollrah, Patrice. "Decolonizing the Choctaws: Teaching LeAnne Howe's *Shell Shaker*." *American Indian Quarterly* Vol. 28, nos. 1–2 (2004): 73–85.

Holmes, Baxter. "Choctaw Stickball: A Fierce, Ancient Game Deep in Mississippi." *Los Angeles Times*, October 18, 2011.

Hudson, Charles. *Southeastern Indians.* Knoxville, TN: University of Tennessee Press, 1976.

Jones, Edwina. *Return to Riverside.* Sylva, NC: Catch the Spirit of Appalachia, 2009.

Jumper, Betty Mae. *A Seminole Legend: the Life of Betty Mae Tiger Jumper.* Gainesville: University Press of Florida, 2001.

Justice, Daniel Heath. *Our Fire Survives the Storm.* Minneapolis: University of Minnesota Press, 2006.

Lee, Dayna Bowker. "Louisiana Indians in the 21st Century." *Louisiana Folklife Program*, 2013.

Lerner, Kira, and Alice Ollstein. "These Native American Tribes Are Fighting to Stop Their Land from Literally Disappearing." *Climate Progress,* January 22, 2015.

Lowery, Malinda Maynor. *Lumbee Indians in the Jim Crow South: Race, Identity, and the Making of a Nation.* Chapel Hill: University of North Carolina Press, 2010.

MacDowell, Marsha L. *To Honor and Comfort: Native Quilting Traditions.* Albuquerque: Museum of New Mexico Press, 2003. P 103-110.

McAdams, Janet, Geary Hobson, Kathryn Walkiewicz, eds. *The People Who Stayed: Southeastern Indian Writing after Removal.* Norman: University of Oklahoma Press, 2010.

McKinney, Karen J. "'There's Always a Story to Tell': Creating Tradition on Qualla Boundary." *North Carolina Literary Review* 13 (2004): 25–40.

Oakley, Christopher Arris. *Keeping the Circle: American Indian Identity in Eastern North Carolina, 1885–2004.* Lincoln: University of Nebraska Press, 2005

Pettus, L. *Leasing Away a Nation: The Legacy of Catawba Indian Land Leases.* Glendale, SC: Palmetto Conservation Foundation, 2005.

"Queen Ann of the Pamunkey." *History of American Women*, July 12, 2009.

Rountree, Helen C. *Pocahontas's People: The Powhatan Indians Of Virginia.* Norman, OK: University of Oklahoma Press,1996.

Sullivan, John, ed. *Through Indian Eyes: The Untold Stories of Native American Peoples.* Pleasantville, NY: Readers Digest, 1996.

Sultzman, Lee. "The Houma." http://www.dickshovel.com/hou.html (accessed January 13, 2016).

"Virginia's First Peoples: Past and Present." *Prince William Network.* Virginia Department of Education, 2014. http://virginiaindians.pwnet.org/ (accessed January 10, 2016).

Watson, Ian. "State Catawba Indian Genealogy." *The Geneseo Foundation.* http://www.ianwatson.org/catawba_indian_genealogy_2004.pdf (accessed February 2, 2016).

Weaver, Jace, *The Red Atlantic: American Indigenes and the Making of the Modern World, 1000–1927.* Chapel Hill: University of North Carolina Press, 2014.

Wells, Mary Ann. *Native Land.* Jackson, MS: University Press of Mississippi, 1993.

World Heritage Committee (UNESCO). http://whc.unesco.org/en/list/1435 (accessed February 18, 2016).

Southwest

Austin, Raymond D. *Navajo Courts and Navajo Common Law: A Tradition of Tribal Self-Governance.* Minneapolis: University of Minnesota Press, 2009.

Denetdale, Jennifer Nez. *Reclaiming Diné History: The Legacies of Navajo Chief Manuelito and Juanita.* Tucson: University of Arizona Press, 2007.

Gorman, R.C. *Nudes and Food.* Santa Fe, New Mexico: Clear Light Books, 1994.

Griffin-Pierce, Trudy. *The Columbia Guide to American Indians of the Southwest.* New York: Columbia University Press, 2015.

Ortiz, Simon. *Woven Stone.* Tucson: University of Arizona Press, 1992.

Rose, Wendy. *Itch Like Crazy.* Tucson: University of Arizona Press, 2002.

Sando, Joe S., and Herman Agoyo, eds. *Po'pay: Leader of the First American Revolution.* Santa Fe, NM: Clear Light Publishers, 2005.

Silko, Leslie Marmon. *The Turquoise Ledge: A Memoir.* New York: Viking, 2010.

Singer, Beverly R. *Wiping the Warpaint Off the Lens.* Minneapolis: University of Minnesota Press, 2001.

Tapahonso, Luci. *a radiant curve.* Tucson: University of Arizona Press, University of Arizona Press, 2009.

Zepeda, Ofelia. *Jewed'l-hoi/Earth Movements.* Tucson: University of Arizona Press, 2009.

Urban

Anderson, Mark. *Black and Indigenous.* Minneapolis: University of Minnesota Press, 2009.

Bahr, Diana Meyers. *Viola Martinez, California Paiute: Living in Two Worlds.* Tulsa: University of Oklahoma Press, 2012.

Blue Spruce, Duane, ed. *Mother Earth, Father Skyline: A Souvenir Book of Native New York.* Washington, DC: NMAI, 2006.

Carpio, Myla Vincent. *Indigenous Albuquerque.* Lubbock, TX: Texas Tech University Press, 2011.

Cengel, Katya. "The Other Mexicans: Indigenous People Come from a World Apart from Spanish-speaking Mexicans." *National Geographic,* June 25, 2013.

Decker, Geoffrey. "Hispanics Identifying Themselves as Indians." *New York Times,* July 3, 2011.

Dekeyser, Juliette. "Native Hawaiians Keep Their 'Aloha Spirit' in NYC." *Voices of New York,* November 7, 2013.

Doxtator, Antonio J., and Renee J. Zakhar. *The American Indians of Milwaukee.* Mt. Pleasant, SC: Acadia Publishing, 2011.

Fixico, Donald L. *Termination and Relocation: Federal Indian Policy, 1945–1960.* Albuquerque: University of New Mexico Press, 1986.

————.*The Urban Indian Experience in America.* Albuquerque: University of New Mexico Press, 2000.

Garfuna Coalition, USA. http://www.garifunacoalition.org/ (accessed February 18, 2016).

Grumet, Robert S. *First Manhattans: A History of the Indians of Greater New York.* Norman: University of Oklahoma Press, 2011.

Harjo, Joy, and Jack D. Forbes, *American Indians and the Urban Experience (Contemporary Native American Communities).* Lanham, MD: Rowman & Littlefield, 2001.

Halawai in NYC. http://www.halawai.org/ (accessed February 18, 2016).

Heilman, Dan. "American Indian Cultural Corridor: New Art, New Enterprise on Franklin Avenue." *The Line Media.* January 19, 2011.

Hiller, Patrick T., J. P. Linstroth, and Paloma Ayala Vela. "'I Am Maya, Not Guatemalan, Nor Hispanic'— the Belongingness of Mayas in Southern Florida." *Forum: Qualitative Social Research,* Vol, 10, no. 3 (September 2009).

Hogan, Gwynne. "Preserving the Language of the Andes in NY." *Voices of NY,* March 10, 2014.

Inseminger, William. *Cahokia Mounds: America's First City.* Charleston, SC: The History Press, 2010.

Jackson, Deborah Davis. *Our Elders Lived It: American Indian Identity in the City.* DeKalb, IL: Northern Illinois University Press, 2001.

Johnson, Troy R. *The American Indian Occupation of Alcatraz Island: Red Power and Self Determination.* Lincoln: University of Nebraska Press, 2008.

Kingsley, Thomas G., Kathryn Pettit, Jennifer Biess, and others. "Continuity and Change: Demographic, Socioeconomic, and Housing Conditions of American Indians and Alaska Natives." U.S. Department of Housing and Urban Development, 2014. Retrieved from http://www.huduser.org/portal/publications/commdevl/housing_conditions.html.

Krouse, Susan Applegate, and Heather A. Howard, eds. *Keeping the Campfires Going: Native Women's Activism in Urban Communities.* Lincoln: University of Nebraska Press, 2009.

LaGrand, James B. *Indian Metropolis: Native Americans in Chicago, 1945–1975.* Urbana: University of Illinois Press, 2005.

"Linguistic Isolation in NYC: Not All Latin American Immigrants Speak Spanish." *Indian Country Today Media Network*, July 15, 2014.

Lobo, Susan, ed. *Urban Voices: The Bay Area American Indian Community, Community History Project, Intertribal Friendship House, Oakland, California.* Tucson: University of Arizona Press, 2002.

Mano a Mano. http://www.manoamano.us/en/mixtecos-in-new-york.html (accessed February 18, 2016).

Miles, Tiya, and Sharon P. Holland, eds. *Crossing Waters, Crossing Worlds: The African Diaspora in Indian Country.* Durham, NC: Duke University Press, 2006.

National Urban Indian Family Coalition. "The Status of American Indian & Alaska Native Children & Families Today." (2008). Retrieved from http://www.aecf.org/m/resourcedoc/AECF-Urban IndianAmerica-2008-Full.pdf.

Native American Community Development Institute. http://www.nacdi.org/default/index.cfm (accessed February 18, 2016).

Regan, Sheila. "Neighborhood Funders Group Visits the American Indian Cultural Corridor." *NACDI Indigenous Times Newsletter.* (Fall 2010). Retrieved from http://www.nacdi.org/default/index

.cfm/community-stories/neighborhood-funders-group-visits-the-american-indian-cultural-corridor/.

Reyes, Lawney L. *Bernie Whitebear: An Urban Indian's Quest for Justice*. Tucson: University of Arizona Press, 2008.

Rodriguez, Roberto. "'Not Counting Mexicans or Indians': The Many Tentacles of State Violence against Black-Brown-Indigenous Communities." *Truth-Out*, February 4, 2015.

Rosenthal, Nicolas G. *Reimagining Indian Country: Native American Migration and Identity in Twentieth-Century Los Angeles* (First Peoples: New Directions in Indigenous Studies). Chapel Hill: University of North Carolina Press, 2014.

Schwartzkopf, Sara. "Top 5 Cities with the Most Native Americans." *Indian Country Today Media Network,* July 29, 2013.

Thompson, Cole. "Inwood's Indian Life Reservation." *My Inwood*. April, 2014.

Turner Trice, Dawn. "Urban Native Americans Feel They Have a Foot in Two Worlds." *Chicago Tribune,* March 28, 2011.

"Video Spotlight: Past, Present and Future of Native Americans in Minneapolis." *Indian Country Today Media Network,* September 7, 2009. Retrieved from http://indiancountrytodaymedianetwork.com/2012/09/07/video-spotlight-past-present-and-future-native-americans-minneapolis-133058.

Weitzman, David. *Skywalkers: Mohawk Ironworkers Build the City*. New York: McMillan, 2010.

Williams, Timothy, "Quietly, Indians Reshape Cities and Reservations." *New York Times*, April 13, 2013.

Canada

Abel, Jordan. *Un/Inhabited*. Vancouver: Talonbooks, 2015.

Aboriginal Tourism BC. https://www.Aboriginalbc.com/.

Assembly of First Nations, http://www.afn.ca/Assembly_of_First_Nations.htm.

Cradleboard Teaching Project. http://www.cradleboard.org/.

Craft, Aimée. *Breathing Life into the Stone Fort Treaty: An Anishnabe Understanding of Treaty One*. Saskatoon, SK: Purich, 2013.

Cree Cultural Institute, http://exhibit.creeculturalinstitute.ca/.

Daschuk, James. *Clearing the Plains: Disease, Politics of Starvation, and the Loss of Aboriginal Life*. Regina, SK: University of Regina Press, 2014.

First Peoples' Cultural Council, http://www.fpcc.ca/.

First Peoples Worldwide, http://firstpeoples.org/.

First Voices, http://www.firstvoices.com/.

Four Directions Teaching, http://www.fourdirectionsteachings.com/.

Gehl, Lynn. *The Truth that Wampum Tells: Canada's Constitutional History through Wampum Diplomacy*. Black Point, NS: Fernwood Publishing, 2014.

Helin, Calvin. *Dances with Dependency: Out of Poverty through Self-Reliance*. Canada: Cubbie Blue Publishing, 2008.

Hill, Gord. *500 Years of Indigenous Resistance*. Vancouver: Arsenal Pulp Press, 2010.

Idle No More, http://www.idlenomore.ca/.

Indigenous and Northern Affairs (Government of Canada), https://www.aadnc-aandc.gc.ca/eng/110010 0010002/1100100010021.

Indigenous Nation, http://www.indigenousnationhood.com/.

Maracle, Lee. *Memory Serves and Other Essays (Writer as Critic)*. Edmonton, AB: NuWest Press, 2015.

Palmater, Pamela D. *Beyond Blood: Rethinking Indigenous Identity*. Saskatoon, SK: Purich, 2011.

Paul, Daniel N. *We Were Not the Savages: First Nations History—Collision between European and Native American Civilizations*. Black Point, NS: Fernwood Publishing, 2007.

The Secwepemc Cultural Education Society (SCES), http://www.secwepemc.org/.

Sellars, Bev. *They Called Me Number One: Secrets and Survival at an Indian Residential School*. Vancouver, BC: Talon Books, 2012.

Tootoo, Jordin John Kudluk. *All the Way: My Life on Ice*. Toronto: Penguin Canada, 2015.

Top Ten First Nations Websites, http://www.rcsd.ca/uploads/Top%2010%20November%20Aboriginal%20Websites.pdf.

Watt-Cloutier, Sheila. *The Right to Be Cold*. Toronto: Penguin Canada, 2015.

Woodland Cultural Centre, http://www.woodland-centre.on.ca/index.php.

Caribbean

Altos de Chavon Regional Museum of Archaeology, http://altosdechavon.museum/eng/index.php/museo.

Caribbean Organization Of Indigenous Peoples (COIP), http://coipnews.blogspot.com/.

"CARICOM Inter-Tribal Games Were Founded in 2012 by Damon Gerard Corrie, a Member of the Lokono-Arawak Tribe of Guyana." http://www.pantribalconfederacy.com/confederacy/News/pdf/games.pdf (accessed February 18, 2016).

Cultural Survival, https://www.culturalsurvival.org/.

Hudepohl, Kathryn A. "Kalinago Ethnicity and Ancestral Knowledge." *Southern Anthropologist*. Vol 33, nos. 1–2 (Spring/Fall 2008).

Kalinago Territory: http://kalinagoterritory.com/.

Manso. "Puerto Rico, Dominica and Cuba Embrace Their Taíno Indian Heritage." *Cuba Headlines*, May 16, 2011.

Poole, Robert M. "What Became of the Taíno?" *Smithsonian Magazine*. October, 2011.

United Federation of Taíno People, http://mukaro.wix.com/taino.

Greenland

Arctic Games, http://www.arcticwintergames.org/.

Dahl, Jenns. *Saqqaq: An Inuit Hunting Community in the Modern World*. Toronto: University of Toronto Press, 2000.

Greenland Culture Center: http://www.katuaq.gl/en/.

Greenland National Museum, http://www.natmus.gl/.

Greenland Today, http://greenlandtoday.com/.

Inuit Circumpolar Conference Greenland, http://www.inuit.org/.

Kitaamiut: West Greenland, http://www.firstnationsseeker.ca/WestGreenland.html.

Mexico

Bessi, Renata. "Mexico: Electoral Reform Threatens the Self-Determination of Indigenous Peoples." *Truthout*, August 4, 2014.

Chiapas Media Project, http://www.chiapasmediaproject.org/.

Continental Network of Indigenous Women of Abya Yala, http://vcontinentalsummitabyayala.blog spot.com/.

Indian Country Today, http://indiancountrytodaymedianetwork.com/.

Indigenous Languages of Mexico, http://www.mexico.sil.org/es/publicaciones/e-lingpub.

McDougall, Christopher. *Born to Run: A Hidden Tribe, Superathletes, and the Greatest Race the World Has Never Seen.* New York: Vintage, 2011.

Pavón, Juan Carlos Pérez Velasco. "Economic Behavior of Indigenous Peoples: The Mexican Case." *Latin American Economic Review*, August 20, 2014.

Restall, Matthew, ed. *Mesoamerican Voices: Native Language Writings from Colonial Mexico, Yucatan, and Guatemala.* New York: Cambridge University Press, 2005.

Tohono O'odham, http://america.aljazeera.com/articles/2014/5/25/us-mexico-borderwreakshavocwith livesofanindigenousdesertpeople.html.

Yucatan Today, http://www.yucatantoday.com/.

INDEX

Note: (ill.) indicates photos and illustrations.